THE OXFORD HANDBOOK OF

INTERNATIONAL LAW IN ASIA AND THE PACIFIC

THE OXFORD HANDBOOK OF

INTERNATIONAL LAW IN ASIA AND THE PACIFIC

Edited by

SIMON CHESTERMAN,

HISASHI OWADA,

and

BEN SAUL

OXFORD
UNIVERSITY PRESS

OXFORD
UNIVERSITY PRESS

Great Clarendon Street, Oxford, OX2 6DP,
United Kingdom

Oxford University Press is a department of the University of Oxford.
It furthers the University's objective of excellence in research, scholarship,
and education by publishing worldwide. Oxford is a registered trade mark of
Oxford University Press in the UK and in certain other countries

First Edition published in 2019
Impression: 1

Published in the United States of America by Oxford University Press
198 Madison Avenue, New York, NY 10016, United States of America

British Library Cataloguing in Publication Data
Data available

Library of Congress Control Number: 2019947979

ISBN 978–0–19–879385–4

Printed and bound by
CPI Group (UK) Ltd, Croydon, CR0 4YY

Acknowledgements

A book like this is only possible with the assistance of a great many people.

We are especially grateful to the contributors who agreed to share their ideas and their time. Such a volume stands or falls on the quality of its chapters and we believe that this will be a reference work for many years to come. Thank you also to those who did not write themselves, but helped us to identify scholars and practitioners that we might otherwise have missed.

At Oxford University Press, Merel Alstein, John Louth, and their colleagues immediately saw the value of broadening the international law discourse—in which OUP plays such a significant role—to include more voices from Asia and the Pacific. Jack McNichol and Brad Rosenkrantz at OUP, and S Lakshmanan at SPi Global, ensured a smooth and timely production process. Their professionalism and their dedication to quality are, we hope, satisfied in this finished product. We also thank the anonymous reviewers for their comments, including in challenging us to reflect on our—and others'—conceptions of 'Asia' and the 'Pacific'.

Simon Chesterman thanks colleagues at the National University of Singapore Faculty of Law for support and advice, especially the outstanding research assistance of Jesslyn Zeng and the administrative support of Jenny Thian.

Hisashi Owada wishes to acknowledge the valuable help and advice he received from his research assistants at the International Court of Justice, in particular Yukiko Takashiba, Kei Nakajima, and Samuel H Chang.

Ben Saul benefited from the assistance of many volunteer student editors at Sydney Law School at the University of Sydney in preparing the final manuscript. Special thanks are due to Oscar Alcock, Sulithi Dewendra, and Matthew Del Gigante; and thanks also to Steven Adler, Denea Bascombe, Rasa Bergin, Nicholas Betts, Sanya Bhatnagar, Avalon Carnall, Rhys Carvosso, Novea Chan, Kailin Chen, Elsie Cheung, Sarah Condie, Mischa Davenport, Kaley DellaSala, Robert Deppeler, Jessica Duan, Rashmi Fernando, Madeline Fisher, Anna FitzGerald, Peijun Gao, Anna Gemmell-Smith, Eirinn Hayes, Claire Ho, Yiwei Huang, Isabelle James, Alex Jeffares, Mindy Kan, Shivank Kaushik, Alison Lee, Nina Li, Chuling Liu, Kate Lumsdaine, Shani Macisaac, Annie McLean, Lucy Nason, Sophia Nasser, Samantha Neayem, Rowan O'Donnell, Amelia Pash, Aleks Pasternacki, Dadar Ahmadi Pirshahid, Miranda Ramjattan, Georgia Reid, Andrew Robertson, Rebecca Salisbury, Dineth Samarasinghe, Fathima Nashwa Samy, Johnny Sorras, Madeleine Stevens, Yang Xiang, Fifi Xu, Jessica Xu, Yilin Xu, Zekun Yang, Gisselle Yaw Brito, and Soo Young Cho.

Insofar as the book has merit, appreciation should be shared with all these people; deficiencies and omissions are attributable to the editors alone.

CONTENTS

PART III INTERNATIONAL LAW IN ASIAN AND PACIFIC STATES

East Asia

Southeast Asia

Table of Cases

International Cases

International Centre for Settlement of Investment Disputes (ICSID)

International Court of Justice (ICJ)

International Tribunal for the Law of the Sea (ITLOS)

Permanent Court of Arbitration (PCA)

United Nations – Office of the High Commissioner for Human Rights (OHCHR)

Committee Against Torture (CAT)

Human Rights Committee

World Trade Organization (WTO)

Jurisdiction

Australia

Bangladesh

Cambodia

Extraordinary Chambers in the Court of Cambodia

Canada

Commonwealth of Independent States (CIS)

Economic Court of the Commonwealth of Independent States

Cook Islands

European Union

Fiji

Samoa

India

Indonesia

Kiribati

Malaysia

Myanmar

Nepal

New Zealand

Pakistan

Papua New Guinea

Philippines

Republic of Kazakhstan

Singapore

Solomon Islands

Sri Lanka

Thailand

Tonga

Tuvalu

United Kingdom

United States of America

Vanuatu

TABLE OF LEGISLATION

Treaties and Conventions

United Nations Resolutions

UN General Assembly

UN Human Rights Council

UN Security Council

Legislation

Afghanistan

Australia

Bangladesh

Cambodia

China

Cook Islands

East Timor

European Union

Fiji

Hawaii

India

Indonesia

Kazakhstan

Kiribati

Kyrgyz Republic

Malaysia

Myanmar

Nauru

Nepal

New Zealand

Niue

Pakistan

Papua New Guinea

Philippines

Samoa

Singapore

Solomon Islands

South Korea

Sri Lanka

Tajikistan

Thailand

Tokelau

Tonga

Turkmenistan

Tuvalu

United Kingdom

United States of America

Uzbekistan

Vanuatu

Vietnam

List of Contributors

Antony Anghie is Professor at the National University of Singapore Faculty of Law and the SJ Quinney School of Law, University of Utah, United States

Romel Regalado Bagares is Professorial Lecturer at Lyceum Philippines University College of Law and General Counsel for KMBI, Philippines

Robert Beckman is Associate Professor at the National University of Singapore Faculty of Law and Head of the Ocean Law and Policy Programme of the Centre for International Law, Singapore

Sharif Bhuiyan is an Advocate of the Supreme Court of Bangladesh, and a Partner and Deputy Head of the law firm, Dr Kamal Hossain and Associates, Bangladesh

Ben Boer is Distinguished Professor, Research Institute of Environmental Law, Wuhan University, China, and Emeritus Professor, University of Sydney, Australia

Samuel H Chang is an Associate at Cleary Gottlieb Steen & Hamilton LLP, United States, and a former Judicial Fellow at the International Court of Justice

Simon Chesterman is Provost's Chair and Dean of the National University of Singapore Faculty of Law, Singapore

BS Chimni is Professor of International Law at the School of International Studies, Jawaharlal Nehru University, New Delhi, India

Jennifer Corrin is Director of Comparative Law and Professor at the TC Beirne School of Law, The University of Queensland, Australia

Marina Girshovich is PhD candidate at the Graduate School of International Studies, Seoul National University, Republic of Korea

Abdul Ghafur Hamid @ Khin Maung Sein is Professor at Ahmad Ibrahim Kulliyyah of Laws, International Islamic University Malaysia, Selangor, Malaysia

Hurst Hannum is Professor of International Law at the Fletcher School of Law and Diplomacy, Tufts University, United States

Kamal Hossain is Head of Firm and Senior Partner of Dr Kamal Hossain and Associates, Bangladesh, and a Senior Advocate of the Supreme Court of Bangladesh

Anbar Jayadi was Assistant Lecturer in the International Law Department at the Faculty of Law, University of Indonesia, Jakarta, Indonesia

Hikmahanto Juwana is Professor of International Law at the Faculty of Law, University of Indonesia, Jakarta, Indonesia

Kenneth Keith is Professor Emeritus at Victoria University of Wellington, New Zealand and a former Judge of the International Court of Justice (2006–15)

Hee Eun Lee is Associate Dean and Professor of Law at Handong International Law School, Republic of Korea

Seokwoo Lee is Professor of International Law, Inha University Law School, Republic of Korea

Li Zhaojie is a Professor of International Law at Tsinghua University School of Law, Beijing, China

Suzannah Linton is Distinguished Professor in the International Law Department of the Law School, Zhejiang Gongshang University, China

Mogami Toshiki is Professor at the School of Political Science, Waseda University, Tokyo, Japan

Mahdev Mohan is Of Counsel at Providence Law Asia, Singapore, and a former Assistant Professor of Law at Singapore Management University

Vitit Muntarbhorn is Professor Emeritus at the Faculty of Law, Chulalongkorn University, Bangkok, Thailand

Hisashi Owada is a former Judge and former President of the International Court of Justice (2011–18) and Japan's former Ambassador to the United Nations in New York (1994–98)

Amrith Rohan Perera is Permanent Representative of Sri Lanka to the United Nations in New York

Catherine Renshaw is Deputy Dean and Associate Professor at the Thomas More Law School, Australian Catholic University, Sydney, Australia

Ben Saul is Challis Chair of International Law at Sydney Law School, The University of Sydney, Australia, and Chair of Australian Studies, Harvard University, United States

Waheguru Pal Singh Sidhu is Associate Professor at the Center for Global Affairs, School of Professional Studies, New York University

Ahmer Bilal Soofi is Senior Managing Partner of Ahmer Bilal Soofi & Co (Advocates and Corporate Counsels), Lahore, Pakistan, and Advocate of the Supreme Court of Pakistan

Surya P Subedi QC is Professor of International Law at the University of Leeds, United Kingdom

Kevin YL Tan is Professor at the S Rajaratnam School of International Studies, Nanyang Technological University, and Adjunct Professor at the Faculty of Law, National University of Singapore, Singapore

Tan Hsien-Li is Assistant Professor at the National University of Singapore Faculty of Law, Singapore

Veronica L Taylor is Professor of Law and Regulation at the School of Regulation and Global Governance (RegNet), Australian National University, Australia

Li-ann Thio is Provost's Chair Professor at the National University of Singapore Faculty of Law, Singapore

Trinh Hai Yen is Vice Dean of the Faculty of International Law, Diplomatic Academy of Viet Nam, Viet Nam

Pratyush Nath Upreti is a lawyer admitted to the Nepal Bar Council and currently a Doctoral Researcher at Sciences Po Law School, Paris, France, and a Transatlantic Technology Law Forum (TTLF) fellow at Stanford Law School

Wang Jiangyu is Associate Professor at the Faculty of Law, National University of Singapore, Singapore

PART I

THEMES, INSTITUTIONS, AND HISTORY

CHAPTER 1

INTRODUCTION

SIMON CHESTERMAN, HISASHI OWADA, AND BEN SAUL

THE growing economic and political significance of the Asia-Pacific region has exposed a tension in the modern international legal order. On the one hand, the Asia-Pacific is home to around 60 per cent of the world's population (4.5 billion people), possesses the largest regional share of the world's economy (one third, by GDP), covers almost a third of the world's land area, and spans vast maritime areas across the Pacific and Indian Oceans. On the other hand, despite their size and increasing power, Asian and Pacific states played a minimal role in creating the international legal norms and institutions that define the current order. Historically, the states of the Asia-Pacific have generally been 'rule takers', since the first colonial encounters in the sixteenth century, rather than 'rule makers'—even if they sometimes challenged the rules, from positions of relative weakness, during successive periods of colonization and decolonization. Still today, Asian states have been seen as less forthcoming, compared with other regions of the world, in joining international agreements, being represented in international organizations, or submitting themselves to binding international dispute settlement.

Much of this is changing. Today there is widespread interest in international law in the Asia-Pacific region among states, practitioners, and scholars. Change has been driven by threats as well as opportunities. On the threat side are transnational challenges such as climate change, environmental harms (atmospheric, maritime, and terrestrial), forced displacement, persistent poverty, human rights violations and international crimes, terrorism, arms proliferation, and simmering flashpoints such as the Korean peninsula and the South and East China Seas. In terms of opportunities, economic integration (including trade and investment), human development, and the proliferation of specialized branches of law, dispute settlement mechanisms, and institutions have encouraged greater domestic implementation of international law across Asia and the Pacific.

Despite these developments, no book has so far attempted to survey in depth the whole field of international law across Asia and the Pacific. Of the existing scholarship, most focuses either on a specific state's experience or a particular specialized branch of international law. Thus, some works explore international law through the limited lens of a small number of national jurisdictions[1] or sub-regions.[2] Many more works are restricted to international law in one national jurisdiction, particularly the larger, powerful states of India,[3] China,[4] and Japan,[5] among a few others.[6] Knowledge about many other jurisdictions, particularly smaller and less developed states, is much sparser, and sometimes defined by unduly narrow, external frames of reference—such as the Khmer Rouge regime and its aftermath in Cambodia, the Vietnam War and its legacy, or foreign interventions in Afghanistan. To the extent that 'Asian' perspectives are articulated, the influence of these major powers tends to belie the diversity of the region.

There are also many works focusing on the application of a particular specialized branch of international law in the region (or a sub-region). These include the law of the sea;[7]

[1] See e.g. RP Anand, *Studies in International Law and History: An Asian Perspective* (Brill 2004) (dealing with India, Japan, Tibet, South Asia, and the themes of dispute settlement, common heritage of mankind, and law of the sea).

[2] CH Alexandrowicz, *An Introduction to the History of the Law of Nations in the East Indies (16th, 17th and 18th Centuries)* (Clarendon Press 1967); Shaun Narine, *Explaining ASEAN: Regionalism in Southeast Asia* (Lynne Rienner Publishers 2002); Mark Beeson and Richard Stubbs (eds), *Routledge Handbook of Asian Regionalism* (Routledge 2012); Seokwoo Lee and Hee Eun Lee (eds), *Northeast Asian Perspectives on International Law* (Brill 2013); Simon Chesterman, *From Community to Compliance? The Evolution of Monitoring Obligations in ASEAN* (CUP 2015).

[3] CH Alexandrowicz (writing as Alexander), 'International Law in India' (1952) 1 ICLQ 289; DN Verma, *India and the League of Nations* (Bharati Bhawan 1968); RP Anand, *The Development of Modern International Law and India* (Indian Society of International Law and Nomos Verlagsgesellschaft 2005 and 2006); RP Anand, 'The Formation of International Organizations and India: A Historical Study' (2010) 23 Leiden J Intl L 5; VG Heide, 'Indian Courts and International Law' (2010) 23 Leiden J Intl L 53; Bimal Patel, 'India' in Bardo Fassbender and Anne Peters (eds), *The Oxford Handbook of the History of International Law* (OUP 2012) 500.

[4] Ann Kent, *Beyond Compliance: China, International Organizations, and Global Security* (Stanford University Press 2007); Xue Hanqin, *Chinese Contemporary Perspectives on International Law: History, Culture and International Law* (Hague Academy of International Law and Martinus Nijhoff 2012); Shin Kawashima, 'China' in Fassbender and Peters (n 3) 451; Phil CW Chan, *China, State Sovereignty, and International Legal Order* (Brill 2015).

[5] Shigeru Oda and Hisashi Owada, *The Practice of Japan in International Law* (University of Tokyo Press 1982); Nisuke Ando (ed), *Japan and International Law: Past, Present and Future* (Kluwer 1999); Louis Perez, *Japan Comes of Age: Mutsu Munemitsu and the Revision of the Unequal Treaties* (Associated University Presses 1999); Thomas Burkman, *Japan and the League of Nations: Empire and World Order* (University of Hawaii Press 2008); Masaharu Yanaghira, 'Japan' in Fassbender and Peters (n 3) 475.

[6] Kenneth Keith, 'New Zealand and International Law: 1963–2013' (2013) 25 New Zealand Universities Law Review 718; Simon Butt, 'The Position of International Law within the Indonesian Legal System' (2014) 28 Emory Intl L Rev 1; Donald Rothwell and Emily Crawford (eds), *International Law in Australia* (3rd edn Thomson Reuters 2017).

[7] James Crawford (ed), *The Law of the Sea in the Asian Pacific Region: Developments and Prospects* (Kluwer 1995); Park Hee Kwon, *The Law of the Sea and Northeast Asia: A Challenge for Cooperation* (Kluwer 2000); Jin-Hyun Paik, Seok-Woo Lee, and Kevin Tan (eds), *Asian Approaches to International Law and the Legacy of Colonialism: The Law of the Sea, Territorial Disputes and International Dispute Settlement* (Routledge 2012); Robert Beckman and Ashley Roach (eds) *Piracy and International Maritime Crimes in ASEAN: Prospects for Cooperation* (Edward Elgar Publishing 2012); Shicun Wu and

international environment law;[8] human rights and refugee law;[9] international criminal law;[10] international economic law;[11] and international dispute settlement,[12] among others.[13] There is also a tradition of theoretical scholarship in the region

Keyuan Zou (eds), *Securing the Safety of Navigation in East Asia: Legal and Political Dimensions* (Chandos 2013).

[8] Ben Boer, Ross Ramsay and Donald Rothwell, *International Environmental Law in the Asia Pacific* (Kluwer 1998); Roda Mushkat, *International Environmental Law and Asian Values: Legal Norms and Cultural Influences* (UBC Press 2004); Koh Kheng-Lian (ed), *ASEAN Environmental Law, Policy and Governance: Selected Documents*, vols I and II (World Scientific 2013); Simon Marsden and Elizabeth Brandon, *Transboundary Environmental Governance in Asia: Practice and Prospects with the UNECE Agreements* (Edward Elgar 2015).

[9] Yash Ghai, 'Asian Perspectives on Human Rights' (1993) 23 Hong Kong LJ 342; Onuma Yasuaki, 'In Quest of Intercivilizational Human Rights: "Universal" vs "Relative"—Human Rights Viewed from an Asian Perspective' (2000) 1 Asia-Pacific J on Human Rights & L 53; Hidetoshi Hashemoto, *The Prospects for a Regional Human Rights Mechanism in East Asia* (Routledge 2003); Sienho Yee, 'The Role of Law in the Formation of Regional Perspectives in Human Rights and Regional Systems for the Protection of Human Rights: The European and Asian Models as Illustrations' (2004) 8 Singapore YB Intl L 157 (2004); Joshua Castellino and Elvira Dominguez Redondo, *Minority Rights in Asia: A Comparative Legal Analysis* (OUP 2006); Randall Peerenboom, Carole Petersen, and Albert Chen (eds), *Human Rights in Asia* (Routledge 2006); Tan Hsien-Li, *The ASEAN Intergovernmental Commission on Human Rights: Institutionalising Human Rights in Southeast Asia* (CUP 2011); Sara Davies, *Legitimizing Rejection: International Refugee Law in Southeast Asia* (Martinus Nijhoff 2008); Tai-Ung Baik, *Emerging Regional Human Rights Systems in Asia* (CUP 2012); Hitoshi Nasu and Ben Saul (eds), *Human Rights in the Asia Pacific Region: Towards Institution Building* (Routledge 2013).

[10] Timothy MacCormack, Michael Tilbury, and Gillian Triggs (eds), *A Century of War and Peace: Asia-Pacific Perspectives on the Centenary of the 1899 Hague Peace Conference* (Martinus Nijhoff 2001); Neil Boister and Robert Cryer, *The Tokyo International Military Tribunal: A Reappraisal* (OUP 2008); Yuma Totani, *The Tokyo War Crimes Trials: The Pursuit of Justice in the Wake of World War II* (Harvard University Press 2008); Simon Chesterman, 'International Criminal Law with Asian Characteristics?' (2014) 27 Columbia J Asian L 129; Barak Kushner, *Men to Devils, Devils to Men: Japanese War Crimes and Chinese Justice* (Harvard University Press 2015); Georgina Fitzpatrick, Tim McCormack and Narrelle Morris (eds), *Australia's War Crimes Trials 1945–51* (Brill 2016); Liu Daqun and Zhang Binxin (eds), *Historical War Crimes Trials in Asia* (Torkel Opsahl Academic EPublisher 2016).

[11] Deborah Cass, Brett Williams, and George Barker (eds), *China and the World Trading System: Entering the New Millennium* (CUP 2003); Christoph Antons and Reto Hilty (eds), *Intellectual Property and Free Trade Agreements in the Asia-Pacific Region* (Springer 2005); Muthucumaraswamy Sornarajah and Jiangyu Wang (eds), *China, India and the International Economic Order* (CUP 2010); Simon Greenberg, Christopher Kee, and Romesh Weeramantry (eds), *International Commercial Arbitration: An Asia-Pacific Perspective* (CUP 2011); Jiaxiang Hu and Matthias Vanhullebusch (eds), *Regional Cooperation and Free Trade Agreements in Asia* (Brill 2014); Wenhua Shan and Jinyuan Su (eds), *China and International Investment Law: Twenty Years of ICSID Membership* (Brill 2015); Abhijit Das and James Nedumpara (eds) *WTO Dispute Settlement at Twenty: Insiders' Reflections on India's Participation* (Springer 2016); Julien Chaisse, Tomoko Ishikawa, and Sufian Jusoh (eds), *Asia's Changing International Investment Regime* (Springer 2017).

[12] Hisashi Owada, 'The Experience of Asia with International Adjudication' (2005) 9 SYBIL 9; Tommy Koh, 'International Law and the Peaceful Resolution of Disputes: Asian Perspectives, Contributions and Challenges' (2011) 1 Asian J Intl L 57; Shahla Ali, *Resolving Disputes in the Asia-Pacific Region: International Arbitration and Mediation in East Asia and the West* (Routledge 2011); Simon Chesterman, 'The International Court of Justice in Asia: Interpreting the *Temple of Preah Vihear* Case' (2015) 5 Asian J Intl L 1.

[13] Ko Swan Sik, *Nationality and International Law in Asian Perspective* (TMC Asser Instituut 1990).

(albeit not confining its arguments to Asia), especially in South Asia, with significant contributions on post-colonialism, Third World Approaches to International Law, law and development, and the history of international law.[14]

A number of specialist journals also periodically publish developments in international law and practice in the region or particular jurisdictions, including the Asian Yearbook of International Law (1991–), the Asian Journal of Comparative Law (2006–), the Asian Journal of International Law (2011–), and various nationally-based yearbooks (YBIL) or journals of international law (JIL): Japanese YBIL (1958–), Indian JIL (1960–), Australian YBIL (1965–), Taiwanese YBIL (1981–), Chinese YBIL (1982–), Chinese JIL (2002–), Indonesian JIL (2003–), Korean YBIL (2013–), Singaporean YBIL (1997–2011[15]), and New Zealand YBIL (2004–). Societies of international law, with which many year books or journals are affiliated, have also been sites for the professional and scholarly circulation of knowledge, including in Japan (1920–), Australia-New Zealand (1935–), South Korea (1953–), Taiwan (1958–), India (1959–), China (1980–), and Singapore (early 1990s–). In addition, the Asian Society of International Law was founded in 2006.

There is, however, no major book covering how Asian and Pacific states (a) as a whole participate in each of the main specialized branches of international law; (b) individually contribute to the making and application of international law on the international plane; and (c) individually implement international law in their national legal systems. This *Oxford Handbook on International Law in Asia and the Pacific* aims to fill these significant gaps in professional and scholarly knowledge. By bringing together pre-eminent and emerging specialists, it offers breadth and depth in the analysis of international law in the region. It looks beyond the few, much-studied regional powers to shed new light on how diverse states from across the region engage with international law domestically and internationally.

1.1 The Scope of 'Asia and the Pacific'

A preliminary question is how and why this *Handbook* defines certain states as falling within 'Asia and the Pacific' (and, indeed, omits others). Much more so than in other

[14] Balakrishnan Rajagopal, *International Law from Below: Development, Social Movements and Third World Resistance* (CUP 2003); Antony Anghie, Bhupinder Chimni, Karin Mickelson, and Obiora Okafor (eds), *The Third World and International Order: Law Politics and Globalization* (Brill 2003); Antony Anghie, *Imperialism, Sovereignty and the Making of International Law* (CUP 2004); Upendra Baxi, 'What May the Third World Expect from International Law?' in Richard Falk, Balakrishnan Rajagopal, and Jacqueline Stevens (eds), *International Law and the Third World: Reshaping Justice* (Routledge 2008) 9; Prabhakar Singh, 'Indian International Law: From a Colonized Apologist to a Subaltern Protagonist' (2010) 23 Leiden J Intl L 79; BS Chimni, 'International Law Scholarship in Post-colonial India: Coping with Dualism' (2010) 23 Leiden J Intl L 23. See also RJ Dupuy (ed), *The Future of International Law in a Multicultural World* (Martinus Nijhoff 1984); Jean D'Aspremont, 'International Law in Asia: The Limits to the Western Constitutionalist and Liberal Doctrines' [2008] Asian YB Intl L 89.

[15] Succeeded by the Asian Journal of International Law.

regions, there have been lively—and insoluble—debates about how to define 'Asia'. Some regions offer neat solutions to their definition, based on geographical contiguity: for example, Africa, North America, and South (or Latin) America are discrete and clearly delineated continents. Other regions are a little more ambiguous but nonetheless settled categories, again by geography: Europe (except for whether it stretches across the Bosphorus to Turkey and includes the island of Britain—even before 'Brexit'—and the huge flanking state of Russia); and the Middle East (centred on the Arabian Peninsula, north to Syria, and complicated mainly by crossing into North Africa to include Egypt). In contrast, Asia sprawls in an ungainly fashion across vast and not obviously inter-connected areas, from Afghanistan and Kazakhstan in the west to Japan in the east, and from Indonesia in the south to Mongolia in the north.

Of course, geography is not the only indicator of regions. No region is 'natural'. Europe, after all, is connected by land through Russia to China and on to Southeast Asia; Europe also connects to Africa via the Middle East. North and South America are linked by the land-bridge of Central America. Only Australia stands alone as a continent—and, being a single state, it can hardly constitute its own 'region'. Regions are necessarily 'socially constructed and hence politically constructed'[16]—perhaps 'imagined communities' on a larger scale, to transpose to the regional level Benedict Anderson's well-known analysis of the rise of the modern nation state.[17] Regions can serve as an intermediate identity between the national and international communities—an identity weaker than the former, but stronger than the latter.

Of course, the reasons why certain regions are imagined as communities can vary. They may be deliberately constructed as instrumental economic or political projects, creating supranational political institutions or cooperative economic unions—or both, as in the case of the European Union (EU). A region may be defined partly by sectoral concerns, such as the creation of regional human rights courts (as in Europe, the Americas, and Africa) or security communities (as in the case of NATO). It can be rooted in underlying grievances, such as the quest for decolonization that shaped the African Union, or a desire to avoid Cold War allegiances that moulded the Non-Aligned Movement. Common identity can also be a driving force (as in the case of the Organization of Islamic Cooperation). A region can also provide a 'practicable'[18] level of organization, cooperation, or coordination greater than that possible at the national level, without going as far as the global level that may be lofty and abstract.

Regions may also be functionally defined for certain purposes, as in the voting blocs allocated by the United Nations system or in datasets created by the World Bank. There are, indeed, different 'Europes' for different purposes, from the twenty-eight EU

[16] Fredrik Söderbaum, 'Theories of Regionalism' in Beeson and Stubbs (n 2) 11, 14.

[17] Benedict Anderson, *Imagined Communities: Reflections on the Origin and Spread of Nationalism* (Verso 1983).

[18] Hélène Ruiz Fabri, 'Reflections on the Necessity of Regional Approaches to International Law through the Prism of the European Example: Neither Yes nor No, Neither Black nor White' (2011) 1 Asian J Intl L 83, 83.

member states (devoted to broad integration) to the forty-seven member states of the Council of Europe (more narrowly focused on human rights). Regional nomenclature can also be externally imposed rather than self-created; descriptors such as the 'Near East' and 'Far East', for example, were hegemonic constructs of colonial powers, naming the peripheries—and have unsurprisingly gone out of fashion.

This *Handbook* does not attempt to settle debate as to the parameters of 'Asia and the Pacific'; indeed, some of the contributors vigorously weigh in on different sides of that debate. For organizational purposes, however, the book modestly nominates forty-three states as falling within these regions: twenty-eight states across the sub-regions of Asia and fifteen states in the Pacific (including the two Australasian states that straddle the Pacific and Asia) (Table 1.1).

Reasonable minds may differ as to where the boundaries should be drawn. The starting point for this volume is the United Nation's 'Asia-Pacific Group' of fifty-five states,[19] from

Table 1.1 States of Asia and the Pacific

East Asia (5 states)	Southeast Asia (10)	South Asia (8)	Central Asia (5)	The Pacific (15)
China[20]	Brunei Darussalam	Afghanistan	Kazakhstan	Australia
Japan	Cambodia	Bangladesh	Kyrgyzstan	Fiji
Democratic People's Republic of [North] Korea	Indonesia	Bhutan	Tajikistan	Kiribati
Republic of [South] Korea	Laos	India	Turkmenistan	Marshall Islands
Mongolia	Malaysia	Maldives	Uzbekistan	Micronesia
	Myanmar	Nepal		Nauru
	Philippines	Pakistan		New Zealand[21]
	Singapore	Sri Lanka		Palau
	Thailand			Papua New Guinea
	Vietnam			Samoa
				Solomon Islands
				Timor-Leste
				Tonga
				Tuvalu
				Vanuatu

[19] UN Department for General Assembly and Conference Management, 'United Nations Regional Groups of Member States' <http://www.un.org/depts/DGACM/RegionalGroups.shtml> accessed 11 January 2019. Note that Turkey fully participates in both the Asia Pacific and Western European and Others Group (WEOG), but for electoral purposes is considered a member of WEOG only. Kiribati is listed by the UN as part of the Asia-Pacific group, like other states in the geographic area of Oceania, but is not formally a member of any regional group because it has never delegated a permanent representative to the UN.

[20] Including the Special Administrative Regions of Hong Kong and Macao. Consistent with practice at the United Nations, Taiwan is formally considered to be a province of China.

[21] Including Tokelau, the Cook Islands, and Niue.

which the Middle East is then excluded (14 states)[22] and the Australasian states of Australia and New Zealand are added (moved over from the UN's 'Western European and Others Group'). Asia is thus understood to span the sub-regions of South Asia, East Asia (sometimes referred to as Northeast Asia), Southeast Asia, and Central Asia. Many of these self-identify as sub-regions through their own institutions, notably the South Asia Association for Regional Cooperation (SAARC) and the Association of Southeast Asian Nations (ASEAN).

The Middle East (uncommonly also known as 'West Asia') is excluded because it is usually viewed as its own distinct region, possesses its own regional institution (the League of Arab States), and has a shared heritage in Islam (minorities notwithstanding). It is also not counted as part of Asia in the practice of certain other international bodies, such as the Asian Development Bank (ADB) and the UN Food and Agriculture Organization (FAO).[23] The present work does not include the Caucasus, either—unlike, for example, the ADB.[24]

1.2 The Pacific

The combination of Asia and the Pacific in this book also requires some justification. The UN groups them as the 'Asia-Pacific' and this terminology is widely used in other settings (such as, for instance, in Asia-Pacific Economic Cooperation (APEC) and the FAO). The title of this book separates them slightly by referring to 'Asia and the Pacific' (as the ADB does), rather than using the more integrated term 'Asia-Pacific', to acknowledge that they are both distinctive regions of their own while also being closely linked by geography, economics, and politics.

The Pacific also identifies itself as its own region, for instance through the Pacific Islands Forum (PIF, eighteen members, including Australia and New Zealand). As for much of Asia, there are significant gaps in the scholarship on international law in the Pacific Island states. This book counts fifteen Pacific Island states in total, although certain other territories are addressed in the chapters on New Zealand (such as Tokelau, the Cook Islands, and Niue) and the Pacific Island states. The book does not extend to the much wider and looser category of twenty-one or so 'Pacific Rim' countries, which would embrace states as disparate and far afield as Russia, the United States, Canada, Mexico, Central America, and parts of South America.

There are, of course, other ways to classify these areas. For example, the World Bank dices things differently by separately grouping 'South Asia', 'East Asia and the Pacific',

[22] Bahrain, Cyprus (also an EU member), Iran, Iraq, Jordan, Kuwait, Lebanon, Oman, Qatar, Saudi Arabia, Syria, Turkey, United Arab Emirates, and Yemen.

[23] The FAO counts 28 Asian member states plus 18 Pacific states (including Australia, France, New Zealand, and the US), totalling 46 states <http://www.fao.org/asiapacific/countries/en> accessed 9 January 2019.

[24] Which includes Georgia, Armenia, and Azerbaijan as part of Asia.

and 'Europe and Central Asia'. Another example is the term 'Oceania', which is sometimes used to link Australasia with the south-east Pacific sub-regions of Melanesia, Micronesia, and Polynesia. Shifting geopolitical currents can also render existing terms unfashionable. Since 2011, certain powers have begun to use the term 'Indo-Pacific' (such as Japan and Australia) or 'Indo-Asia-Pacific' (US) in place of 'Asia-Pacific', reflecting their changing economic and security outlooks. The term 'Indo-Pacific' is not new, however, being first used in Germany as early as the 1920s (*Indopazifischen Raum*), before its more recent resurrection. Whether the new label will come to supplant the old may depend on the power of its sponsors to reshape the discourse. Functional alliances can also reshape terminology, as through membership of free trade blocs like the Trans-Pacific Partnership of 2018 (comprising eleven states from Asia, the Pacific, and South America) or the Asia-oriented Pacific Alliance of 2011 (of four South American states).

The inclusion of Australia and New Zealand in 'Asia and the Pacific' requires explanation. At first sight, these states may seem anomalous in this book, being recent 'white settler societies' in a region of long-settled Asian and Pacific Islander populations, technically belonging to the UN's 'Western Europe and Others Group'.[25] Historically, Australia and New Zealand's political, economic, security, and cultural ties have been much closer to the United Kingdom and, since the Second World War, the United States, than to Asia or the Pacific. Australia also had a history of anti-Asian sentiment until the 1970s, which raised suspicion and scepticism in the region about whether it belonged to it. Still today, many people in Asia—and Australia too—would not think of Australia as naturally part of Asia.

In recent decades, however, Australia and New Zealand have profoundly reoriented themselves towards Asia and the Pacific. Economically, 73 per cent of Australia's trade is with APEC; four of its top five export markets are Asian (China, Japan, South Korea, and India); and eight of its ten Free Trade Agreements in force are with regional states.[26] New Zealand has a similar economic dependency on Asia, with around 71 per cent of its trade with APEC. Australia is also the largest foreign-aid donor in the Pacific, with New Zealand third (very being recently overtaken by China, now in second place).

Demographically, 40 per cent of Australia's overseas born population comes from Asia (and the overseas born population as a whole constitutes over a quarter of Australia's total population); 56 per cent of its annual immigration is from Asia; and China has the third largest migrant community in Australia (after the UK and New Zealand), India the fourth, and Vietnam the fifth. In New Zealand, over a third of the population is Māori (the first inhabitants, descended from Polynesian settlers from the Pacific over 700 years ago), Pacific Islander, or Asian. The top three countries for annual immigration to New Zealand are India, China, and the Philippines.

Institutionally, Australia and New Zealand are well accepted as members of APEC, the ASEAN Regional Forum, the East Asia Summit, the PIF, the ADB, and the Asian

[25] Australia and New Zealand constitute the 'others' in this category, alongside Canada, Israel, and the US.

[26] ASEAN, Singapore, Thailand, South Korea, Japan, China, and New Zealand.

Infrastructure Investment Bank. Australia has strong defence and security ties with many regional states (particularly Indonesia, Japan, and South Korea); and has contributed significantly to regional security (for example, in Afghanistan, Timor-Leste, Solomon Islands, and Bougainville). The 'Realm of New Zealand' has strong cultural and political ties to the south Pacific through its dependent territory, Tokelau, and two freely associated territories, the Cook Islands and Niue. In official discourse, since the early 1990s some Australian leaders have emphasized Australia's 'destiny as a nation in Asia and the Pacific',[27] markedly shifting sociopolitical perceptions of its place in the world. For organizational purposes, this volume groups these two states as part of the Pacific, though they (like certain Pacific-facing Asian states) are also arguably part of Asia.

A final point of explanation is that the book is organized around the state (and its participation in regional institutions) as the dominant international legal person. This necessarily restricts the manner in which certain territorial entities, and other non-state subjects (such as transnational civil society networks, corporations, organized criminal groups, or terrorist groups), can be presented in the book. There are, for example, no separate chapters on Taiwan, Hong Kong, or Macao, despite, for instance, the former two territories having separate membership from China in the ADB. Nor is there a chapter on the six remaining non-self-governing territories in the Pacific—American Samoa and Guam (administered by the US), French Polynesia and New Caledonia (France), Pitcairn (UK), and Tokelau (NZ). As noted earlier, however, some of these Pacific territories are discussed in the chapters on New Zealand and Pacific Island states. Also excluded from separate treatment are territories that are contested or controversial on the basis of self-determination or minority rights claims (such as Tibet in China, Kashmir in India, or West Papua in Indonesia). Limitations of space prevent the book from slicing international law in the region in too many different ways, so the state remains the organizational focus also for reasons of economy.

1.3 The Structure of the Book

The book is organized in three parts that address thematic issues, practice in specialized areas of international law, and the experience and practice of specific states or groups of states.

1.3.1 Themes, Institutions, and Histories

Part I considers cross-cutting issues, focusing on themes, institutions, and history. Chapter 2, by Simon Chesterman, charts the broad history of Asia's engagement with

[27] Australian Prime Minister Paul Keating, 'Australia and Asia: Knowing Who We Are', Speech, 7 April 1992.

international law, in particular through the experiences of India, China, and Japan. He discusses the reasons for Asia's under-participation and under-representation in international law and institutions, arguing that Asian states' ongoing ambivalence towards international law and institutions can also be attributed to the diversity of the region, power disparities among states, and the absence of 'push' factors driving greater integration—even if things are now beginning to change.

In chapter 3, Tan Hsien-Li examines more closely the relationship between Asian regional and sub-regional organizations and international law. Her survey includes ASEAN, SAARC, APEC, and PIF, all mentioned earlier, as well as the Shanghai Cooperation Organization, the Melanesian Spearhead Group, and others. It is commonly said that Asia-Pacific states prefer less formalized institutions than other regions and ones which tend to avoid binding commitments. Conventional reasons for this include their history of colonialism, less legalistic and formalized cultures, and a preference for stricter conceptions of sovereignty. Her chapter argues, however, that the effectiveness of Asia-Pacific regional institutions should not be judged by the criteria applied to other regions—for example, whether or not they are legalized and institutionalized—unless these are explicitly enunciated as part of the organization's aims. Further, she contends that the assumption that more laws and institutions make better regional organizations is flawed. There should be a broader understanding that Asia-Pacific states consciously use and participate in their regional organizations differently than in other regions, and they may prefer less institutionalized models as these serve their purposes better and can still be successful.

Chapter 4, by Antony Anghie, examines debates about Asia in scholarship on the history and theory of international law. He traces the evolution of concepts of sovereignty in the context of Asia's colonial history, and more recent preoccupations with development. What counts as the 'history and theory' of international law is itself continuously changing and he argues that scholars must engage with new materials and issues. These include deeper research on Asian traditions and concepts of rule and governance, justice, and order (including in the region's great religious and philosophical systems); and understanding the history and theory of international law in Asia in global rather than regional terms (for example, through Asian participation in developing a 'Third World Cosmopolitanism'). These also include a turn to other disciplines, such as social/cultural anthropology, to offer new insights into the questions of governance and territory, and the powerful imaginaries of nationhood, sovereignty, and empire, that animate the peoples of Asia, and that have not been entirely displaced by modern concepts of sovereignty and globalization.

1.3.2 Specialized Branches of International Law

Part II then systematically devotes chapters to how each of the main specialized branches of international law have developed in Asia and the Pacific. Chapters 5 to 11 thus respectively address: regional peace and security (by Waheguru Pal Singh Sidhu); human rights (by Hurst Hannum); international humanitarian law and international criminal law (by Suzannah Linton); international environmental law (by Ben Boer); the law of the sea (by Robert Beckman); international economic law (by Wang Jiangyu); and dispute settlement (by Hisashi Owada and Samuel Chang). Each chapter does not claim to provide encyclopaedic coverage, but rather seeks to highlight some of the key developments and trends in the region, whether through treaties, custom, regional institutions, individual state practice, or specific disputes. The purpose of this Part is not to suggest that Asian and Pacific states exhibit unique or even distinctive behaviours or practices in each of these branches (though they may in some areas), but rather to provide, in a single volume, a methodical, contemporary account of what kinds of behaviour may be observed across all thematic areas. Admittedly, Asian and Pacific participation in other specialized areas could have been included (from polar to space law to intellectual property), but for reasons of space the line was drawn at the more prominent branches.

1.3.3 National Practice and Domestic Implementation

Part III focuses on the most neglected dimension in the literature: international law in individual national jurisdictions in Asia and the Pacific. Each chapter reflects on two key issues. First, on the international plane, the authors consider how the state in question has contributed over time (constructively or otherwise) to the making (or unmaking) and application (or violation) of international law. This first section of each chapter sheds light on areas and issues in international law that have been regarded as particularly significant in the context of prevailing national conditions, foreign policy priorities, and historical circumstances. The section also illustrates how some governments have reacted to adverse influences or pressures brought to bear by certain uses of international law.

Secondly, at the domestic level, the chapters in Part III address how the state has implemented or resisted the incorporation of international norms into its own legal order. This section of each chapter typically addresses issues such as monism/dualism, transformation/incorporation, constitutional provisions concerning the position of international law in domestic law, treaty making powers and procedures under domestic law, and the respective roles of the executive, legislature, and judiciary in the domestic legal reception of international law. In addition to the two sections addressed by chapters in Part III, some chapters highlight selected critical themes and scholarship emerging from national practice at the domestic or international levels.

The chapters broadly follow the organization of the table earlier in this introduction. Chapters 12 to 14 cover East Asia, with contributions on China (by Li Zhaojie), Japan (by Mogami Toshiki), and South Korea (by Seokwoo Lee and Hee Eun Lee). Southeast Asia is considered in chapters 15 to 22, including essays on Thailand (by Vitit Muntabhorn), Indonesia (by Hikmahanto Juwana), the Philippines (by Romel Regalado Bagares), Singapore (by Li-ann Thio and Kevin Tan), Malaysia (by Abdul Ghafur Hamid), Vietnam (by Trinh Hai Yen), Cambodia (by Mahdev Mohan), and Myanmar (by Catherine Renshaw). Chapters 23 to 29 turn to South Asia, comprising works on India (by BS Chimni), Pakistan (by Ahmer Bilal Soofi), Bangladesh (by Kamal Hossein and Sharif Bhuiyan), Nepal (by Pratyush Nath Upreti and Surya Subedi), Sri Lanka (by Rohan Perera), Afghanistan (by Veronica Taylor), and Central Asia (by Marina Girshovich). The final set of chapters cover the Pacific (including Oceania/Australasia), namely the Pacific Island states (chapter 30 by Jennifer Corrin), Australia (chapter 31 by Ben Saul), and New Zealand (chapter 32 by Kenneth Keith).

For reasons of space, each chapter does not exhaustively cover all national developments, but provides a sophisticated survey and analysis of some of the most significant developments. Each chapter is also to an extent impressionistic, reflecting the concerns and perspectives of each author. The book is intended to be a survey that stimulates discussion, rather than an encyclopaedia that ends it. Not all forty-three states in Asia and the Pacific are accorded separate chapters, again for reasons of space. The five Central Asian states are treated in one consolidated chapter. The fifteen Pacific Island states are likewise dealt with (albeit without detailed consideration of Timor-Leste, the Marshall Islands, or Micronesia; there are also separate chapters on the larger jurisdictions of Australia and New Zealand). Regrettably, it was not possible to cover adequately six other states: Bhutan, Brunei Darussalam, North Korea, Laos, Maldives, and Mongolia.[28] Some of the omitted states are mentioned in other national chapters—for example, North Korea in the chapter on South Korea, or Timor-Leste in the chapters on Australia and Indonesia—but we hope that our shortcomings will provoke other scholars to fill such gaps with their own accounts.

As we hope is evident, this book is not designed to suggest that there is—or that there should be—a pan-Asian or pan-Pacific approach to international law. Opening the first volume of the Asian Journal of International Law, published less than a decade ago, the editors noted that '[t]here is, of course, no monolithic Asian understanding of international law'.[29] Nevertheless, there are certainly diverse perspectives *from* Asia. As BS Chimni wrote in that inaugural issue '[r]egional or national cultures'—being 'sources of the self'—can 'play an important role in how different civilizations approach international law and international institutions'.[30]

[28] On Laos, see e.g. Bijan Tavakoli, 'Laos', Max Planck Encyclopedia of International Law (article last updated April 2011).

[29] The editors, 'An Asian Journal of International Law' (2011) 1 Asian J Intl L 1, 2. Cf. the inaugural European Journal of International Law, in which the editors similarly sought to avoid suggestions that its publication indicated that there was or should be a 'European approach' to international law: 'Editorial' (1990) 1 European J Intl L 1, 3.

[30] BS Chimni, 'Asian Civilizations and International Law: Some Reflections' (2011) 1 Asian J Intl L 39, 40.

This volume seeks to broaden the discourse of international law in search of a richer understanding of perspectives *from* the region, *about* the region, and including authors *of* the region. As the states of Asia and the Pacific continue to grow in economic and political significance, the breadth or narrowness of that discourse will determine the form and the content of international law—as well as the extent to which its norms and institutions can address the challenges that no state or region can solve on its own.

Singapore, Sydney, Tokyo
July 2019

CHAPTER 2

ASIA'S AMBIVALENCE ABOUT INTERNATIONAL LAW

SIMON CHESTERMAN*

1 Introduction

It is a paradox of the current international order that Asia—the most populous and economically dynamic region on the planet—arguably benefits most from the security and economic dividends provided by international law and institutions and, yet, is the wariest about embracing those rules and structures. Asian states are the least likely of any regional grouping to be party to most international obligations or to have representation reflecting their number and size in international organizations. There is no regional framework comparable to the African Union (AU), the Organization of American States (OAS), or the European Union (EU); in the United Nations (UN), the Asia-Pacific Group of fifty-three states rarely adopts common positions on issues and discusses only candidacies for international posts. Such sub-regional groupings that exist within Asia have tended to coalesce around narrowly shared national interests rather than a shared identity or aspirations.

In part, this is due to the diversity of the continent. Indeed, the very concept of 'Asia' derives from a term used in Ancient Greece rather than any indigenous political or

* This chapter draws heavily upon work first published as Simon Chesterman, 'Asia's Ambivalence About International Law and Institutions: Past, Present and Futures' (2016) 27 European Journal of International Law 945. Many thanks to Antony Anghie, Ayelet Berman, Christine Chinkin, Lynette Chua, Sumi Dhanarajan, Jarrod Hepburn, David Malone, Susan Marks, Diego Germán Mejía-Lemos, Di Otto, James Penner, Vincent-Joël Proulx, Wojciech Sadurski, Ben Saul, Muthucumaraswamy Sornarajah, Katherine Southwick, Tan Hsien-Li, Simon Tay, Thio Li-ann, and Wang Jiangyu for comments on earlier versions of this text. Errors, omissions, and orientalisms remain the author's alone.

historic roots.[1] Regional cohesion is further complicated by the need to accommodate the great power interests of China, India, and Japan. However, the limited nature of regional bodies is also consistent with a general wariness of delegating sovereignty. Asian countries, for example, have by far the lowest rate of acceptance of the compulsory jurisdiction of the International Court of Justice (ICJ) and of membership of the International Criminal Court (ICC); they are also least likely to have signed conventions such as the International Covenant on Civil and Political Rights (ICCPR) or the International Covenant on Economic, Social and Cultural Rights (ICESCR) or to have joined the World Trade Organization (WTO). The proportion of Asian states that are contracting parties to the International Centre for Settlement of Investment Disputes (ICSID) is also the lowest of any region—though on that they are tied with Latin America.

This chapter explores the reasons for Asia's under-participation and under-representation in international law and institutions. Section 2 traces the history of Asia's engagement with international law. The focus will be on three aspects that continue to have resonance today. First and foremost is the experience of colonialism by India and many other countries across the continent; for centuries, international law helped justify foreign rule, later establishing arbitrary standards of 'civilization' that were required in order to gain meaningful independence. Secondly, and more specific to China, the unequal treaties of the nineteenth century and the failure to recognize the People's Republic of China for much of the twentieth century encouraged a perception that international law was primarily an instrument of political power. Thirdly, and of particular relevance to Japan, the trials that followed World War II left a legacy of suspicion that international law deals only selectively with alleged misconduct, leaving unresolved many of the larger political challenges of that conflict with ongoing ramifications today.

The third section assesses Asia's current engagement with international law and institutions, examining whether its under-participation and under-representation are in fact significant. As will be shown, Asia's history offers at best a partial explanation of the current situation. Section 4 discusses how Asia's ongoing ambivalence towards international law and institutions can also be attributed to the diversity of the continent, the power disparities among its member states, and the absence of 'push' factors driving greater integration or organization—though there is some evidence that these views are beginning to change.

2 Asian Experiences

2.1 India and the Legacy of Colonialism

International law in the colonial period was routinely invoked to justify or defend empire and the economic ends that it served. Indeed, as Antony Anghie has argued,

[1] For the purposes of this chapter, the 53 members of the Asia-Pacific Group at the United Nations (UN) will be used unless otherwise indicated.

the imperial project was not merely a foil for international lawyers; it also played a central role in the construction of modern international law as we now understand the discipline.[2] The exclusion of non-European states from full participation in international law was justified variously by reference to culture, religion, and biology. Much of this history can be explained by racism or realpolitik. But even among *bien pensants* international lawyers, the standard of 'civilization' was invoked to exclude the peoples of Africa, Asia, the Americas, and the Pacific from the sovereignty enjoyed by their European counterparts—and then to incorporate them into a system and a market that had been designed by and for European interests.[3] Indeed, the very name of that system—Westphalian—speaks to the origins of modern international law in the settlement of a seventeenth-century dispute in Europe.

There were, to be sure, exceptions. As a nineteenth-century writer wryly noted, the standard of 'civilization' was applied inconsistently by his contemporaries.[4] One contemporary seemed to confine it to 'nations which study Latin', another to those countries with 'fire-arms and the printing press', while a third suggested a quantitative approach based on 'miles of electric telegraph and the largest quantity of daily newspapers'. Nevertheless, the dominant discourse was a European project of excluding the 'other', followed by a 'civilizing mission' intended to make the 'other' more like the 'self'.[5]

Within Asia, this attitude exacerbated tensions between Japan and China as the former successfully sought to be admitted into the company of the 'civilized' in the course of the nineteenth century—arguably at the expense of the latter.[6] Suzuki Shogo goes further to suggest that Japan's imperialist behaviour towards its neighbours can be understood partly because it 'saw the adoption of coercive policies towards "uncivilized" states as an inherent part of a "civilized" state's identity'.[7] That goes too far, but Japan's acceptance by the West was clearly linked to its military prowess. As one Japanese diplomat was said to have observed in the early twentieth century to a European counterpart: 'We show ourselves at least your equals in scientific butchery, and at once we are admitted to your council tables as civilized men.'[8]

[2] Antony Anghie, *Imperialism, Sovereignty, and the Making of International Law* (Cambridge University Press 2005).

[3] Ibid 310–18. See generally Gerrit Gong, *The Standard of 'Civilization' in International Society* (Clarendon Press 1984).

[4] Hon Henry Stanley, *The East and the West: Our Dealings with Neighbours* (Hatchard & Co 1865) 117.

[5] Cf. Edward Said, *Orientalism* (Routledge 1978).

[6] See Junnan Lai, 'Sovereignty and "Civilization": International Law and East Asia in the Nineteenth Century' (2014) 40(3) Modern China 282; Eric Yong-Joong Lee, 'Early Development of Modern International Law in East Asia—With Special Reference to China, Japan, and Korea' (2002) 4 Journal of the History of International Law 42.

[7] Shogo Suzuki, 'Japan's Socialization into Janus-Faced European International Society' (2005) 11 European Journal of International Relations 137, 139. But cf. Hisashi Owada, 'Asia and International Law' (2011) 1 Asian Journal of International Law 3, 8–9 (describing the 'spiritual agony' Japan faced in this period).

[8] Bernard Röling, *International Law in an Expanded World* (Djambatan 1960) 27, quoting H Roos, *Japan in den grooten Oceaan* (HJ Paris 1928) 33.

In the course of the twentieth century, the civilizing mission adopted a more progressivist narrative. The mandates system of the League of Nations sought explicitly to take up the 'sacred trust' of governing those who were 'not yet able to stand by themselves under the strenuous conditions of the modern world'; 'tutelage' of such peoples was to be 'entrusted to advanced nations who by reason of their resources, their experience or their geographical position can best undertake this responsibility'.[9] It bears noting, of course, that the trajectory towards independence was confined to the more 'advanced' colonies—and only to those advanced colonies of powers that happened to be defeated in World War I.[10]

The UN, for its part, ultimately became a vehicle for decolonization on a global scale after 1945. Yet it is clear from the UN Charter that its rhetorical embrace of self-determination was not intended to amount to a right of independence for the one-third of humanity that did not govern themselves when the document was signed.[11] As British Prime Minister Winston Churchill declared in a speech to Parliament during the negotiations over the Charter, 'I have not become the King's First Minister in order to preside over the liquidation of the British Empire'.[12] The compromise that was reached is reflected in distinct chapters of the Charter: the colonies of the defeated powers and the existing League of Nations mandates were placed under the new Trusteeship Council in Chapter XII, while other non-self-governing territories were to be subjected to a more vague system of obligations in Chapter XI. Almost half the territories now listed by the UN as trust or non-self-governing territories were in Africa, but almost one-third were in Asia.[13]

This brief sketch of the colonial experience suggests two ways in which it continues to affect attitudes towards international law in Asia in particular. First, the vast majority of Asian states literally did not participate in the negotiation of most of the agreements that define the modern international order. At the Hague Peace Conferences of 1899 and 1907, for example, there were only four Asian countries[14] present out of twenty-six and forty-three participants respectively. When the Covenant of the League of Nations was signed in 1919, only four of the twenty-seven original members were from Asia.[15] At the Bretton Woods Conference in 1944, which established the World Bank and the International Monetary Fund (IMF), only five of the forty-four

[9] Covenant of the League of Nations 1920, art. 22.

[10] See generally Simon Chesterman, *You, The People: The United Nations, Transitional Administration, and State-Building* (Oxford University Press 2004) 13–18.

[11] UN Charter 1945 arts 1(2) and 55.

[12] Martin Gilbert, *Winston S Churchill, Volume 7: Road to Victory, 1941–1945* (Houghton Mifflin 1986) 254.

[13] See United Nations and Decolonization, 'Trust and Non-Self-Governing Territories (1945–1999)' (United Nations) <http://www.un.org/en/decolonization/nonselfgov.shtml> accessed 30 October 2018, listing 45 African territories, 29 in Asia, 24 in the Americas, and 2 in Europe. Note, of course, that various countries such as Thailand were never colonized.

[14] China, Iran, Japan, and Siam [Thailand].

[15] China, Hedjaz [Saudi Arabia], Japan, and Siam [Thailand].

signatories were from Asia.[16] As for the UN itself, only eight of the fifty-one original members were from Asia.[17] Secondly, when they became independent, Asian states were expected to embrace not only the various treaty obligations but also the structures and forms of international law.[18] Although Christian Tomuschat is correct to note that colonialism is now largely a relic of the past, it is surely an overstatement to conclude, therefore, that colonialism is essentially irrelevant to the contemporary international order.[19]

These observations are not unique to Asia, of course. Indeed, one could make a compelling case that the disenfranchisement of African states during these formative periods of international law was far greater. There were no African representatives at all at the Hague Peace Conferences, only South Africa and Liberia signed the Covenant of the League of Nations, and only four African states were involved in the Bretton Woods Conference and the drafting of the UN Charter. Yet, the situation of Asia is unique in that the states of the region have a majority of the world's population, have the largest share of its landmass, and are projected to overtake Europe and North America in economic output in the coming decades. For such a region to be predominantly a 'rule taker' is a problem that scholars have been trying to explain for some time. In particular, there does not appear to be a comparable example of a great power (or multiple powers) rising within a normative framework not of its own making, where that normative framework has not undergone substantial change or revolution as a result of the new power's values and interests. In addition, the current situation is unusual in that China is better understood not as a 'new', but, rather, as a 'returning' great power.[20]

To such structural considerations, two further historical antecedents need to be highlighted as they loom large (if often unspoken) in considerations of international law: the unequal treaties that were imposed on China in the nineteenth century and the experience of war crimes trials in post-war Japan.

2.2 Unequal Treaties and China

Although China's pre-modern embrace of a form of international law was idiosyncratic, in that it was premised on the superiority of Chinese culture, it placed China at the heart of what was arguably the world's largest trading system of its time.[21] Tensions with

[16] China, India, Iran, Iraq, and the Philippine Commonwealth.

[17] China, India, Iran, Iraq, Lebanon, Philippine Commonwealth, Saudi Arabia, and Syria.

[18] Ko Swan Sik, 'Wang Tieya and International Law in Asia' (2002) 4 Journal of the History of International Law 159.

[19] Christian Tomuschat, 'Asia and International Law—Common Ground and Regional Diversity' (2011) 1 Asian Journal of International Law 217, 221.

[20] See Phil Chan, *China, State Sovereignty, and International Legal Order* (Brill 2015) 1.

[21] Kenneth Pomeranz, *The Great Divergence: China, Europe, and the Making of the Modern World Economy* (Princeton University Press 2000); Yasuaki Onuma, *A Transcivilizational Perspective on International Law* (Martinus Nijhoff 2010) 305–14.

European counterparts rose in the early nineteenth century when China expressed disinterest in purchasing European goods and insisted on diplomatic protocols that were standard in East Asia but alien to the Europeans. China's defeat in the First Opium War (1839–1842) shattered what had arguably been one of the more durable regional regimes, referred to by some as the 'Chinese world order'.[22] The Treaty of Nanking (1842) ceded Hong Kong to Britain and agreed to open five ports for trade. The Second Opium War (1856–1860) was fought to further open the Chinese market, concluding with the burning down of the Summer Palace and the opening of permanent diplomatic representation in the Chinese capital under the Treaty of Tientsin (1858).

These and other treaties are referred to as 'unequal treaties', though that term only came to be used in the 1920s.[23] The perceived injustice of the treaties, which today might have been void for coercion, was both a rallying cry for nationalist sentiment within China and a leitmotif in China's slow embrace of public international law in the early twentieth century.[24] International law in the Qing dynasty came to be seen as a tool to protect and advance Chinese interests rather than a normative framework that governed international affairs as such, though arguably that was also the same position taken by Western powers.[25]

This view of international law as a tool was reinforced in the republican period that followed the fall of the Qing dynasty in 1912. China variously sought to invoke international law provisions to assert its control of Manchuria, Tibet, and Xinjiang as well as to resist ongoing demands by Western powers for extraterritorial jurisdiction within its territory.[26] It also began to challenge the 'unequal treaties' imposed during the Qing period.

In the following two decades, most of the unequal treaties were indeed renegotiated or terminated by agreement, although this was due more to the exigencies of World War II than any perception that the past agreements had been unjustly imposed on China.[27] Such a perception of international law as one instrument of foreign policy among others was reinforced in the communist period of the People's Republic of China, both as an article of ideology and due to the fact that, from 1949 to 1971, it was nominally represented in the UN by what it viewed as the renegade province of Taiwan.[28] Writing in 1966, a professor at National Taiwan University wrote that it was 'beyond doubt' that Communist China recognized the existence of international

[22] John King Fairbank (ed), *The Chinese World Order: Traditional China's Foreign Relations* (Harvard University Press 1968).

[23] Dong Wong, *China's Unequal Treaties: Narrating National History* (Lexington 2005) 1.

[24] Ibid 118–24; Gong (n 3) 144.

[25] Phil Chan, 'China's Approaches to International Law Since the Opium War' (2014) 27 Leiden Journal of International Law 859, 868.

[26] Ibid 871–5.

[27] William Callahan, 'Nationalizing International Theory: Race, Class and the English School' (2004) 18 Global Society 305, 321.

[28] Chan (n 25) 875–82.

law but that its conception was consistent with the socialist vision of law as an instrument of the state rather than as a check on it[29]—an aspect that continues to shape Chinese views of international law today, as discussed below.

2.3 Post-war Japan

Japan was more successful than China at integrating into the international system in the nineteenth century. This was consistent with the Japanese project of incorporating international law into its foreign policy following the Meiji Restoration.[30] Yet the limits of Japan's acceptance by the community of nations were made apparent when its efforts to include reference to racial equality in the preamble to the Covenant of the League of Nations were rejected at the 1919 Paris Peace Conference.[31] As Martti Koskenniemi observes, this made it clear that the non-European world could never be regarded as European, something 'Turkey had always known and Japan was to find out to its bitter disappointment'.[32]

Japan's experience in the aftermath of World War II echoed and reinforced perceptions of its different status in international law.[33] The International Military Tribunal for the Far East (the Tokyo Trial) was the most prominent of these proceedings and has been judged more harshly by history than its counterpart in Nuremberg.[34] Much of what has been written since the Tokyo Trial is highly critical of the 'victor's justice' that tainted the proceedings.[35] Procedural flaws in Tokyo were also the subject of scathing criticism by Justices Radhabinod Pal and Bert Röling, including inequality of arms, lack of time, inadequate translation services, and limitations on defence witnesses, among others.[36]

More relevant for present purposes, however, was the extent to which colonialism and race played a role in Tokyo in a way that they did not in Nuremberg. Although

[29] Hungdah Chiu, 'Communist China's Attitude Toward International Law' (1966) 60 American Journal of International Law 245, 246–9.

[30] Masaharu Yanagihara, 'Japan' in Bardo Fassbender and Anne Peters (eds), *The Oxford Handbook of the History of International Law* (Oxford University Press 2012) 475.

[31] See e.g. Naoko Shimazu, 'The Japanese Attempt to Secure Racial Equality in 1919' (1989) 1 Japan Forum 93.

[32] Martti Koskenniemi, *The Gentle Civilizer of Nations: The Rise and Fall of International Law 1870–1960* (Cambridge University Press 2001) 135.

[33] This section draws upon material discussed in greater depth in Simon Chesterman, 'International Criminal Law With Asian Characteristics?' (2014) 27 Columbia Journal of Asian Law 129.

[34] See e.g. 'War Crimes: Road Show' *Time* (New York, 20 May 1946) 24.

[35] See e.g. Paul Schroeder, *The Axis Alliance and Japanese-American Relations* (Cornell University Press 1958) 228; Richard Minear, *Victors' Justice: The Tokyo War Crimes Trial* (Princeton University Press 1971). More recent accounts have suggested that its legacy might be more nuanced. See in particular Neil Boister and Robert Cryer, *The Tokyo International Military Tribunal: A Reappraisal* (Oxford University Press, 2008).

[36] Bernhard Röling and Antonio Cassese, *The Tokyo Trial and Beyond: Reflections of a Peacemonger* (Polity Press 1993) 50–60.

three Asian judges were appointed (from China, India, and the Philippines), the majority of the tribunal came from the United States (US) and its Western allies. Given the national independence movements then underway in various colonies of Britain, France, the Netherlands, and the US, it is not surprising that Japanese responsibility towards Asia was framed in a manner that emphasized atrocities rather than colonialism.[37]

Race also featured directly and indirectly. The Allied powers claimed the right to speak for 'civilization' in the Tokyo Trial. Although few would question that the crimes being prosecuted would have been condemned by any civilization, the clear understanding was that 'civilization' in this context meant modern *European* civilization.[38] Writing soon after the trials, two American authors criticized Soviet efforts to use them for political purposes, stating—without apparent irony—that this was 'incompatible with the Christian-Judaic absolutes of good and evil which were the foundation of the Tokyo and Nuernberg trials'.[39] Other scholars have discussed the role of race in specific trials, notably that of General Tomoyiki Yamashita.[40]

The political context of the Tokyo Trial also differed from Nuremberg. The decision to protect Emperor Hirohito and keep him on the throne, for example, was intended to facilitate the occupation of Japan. To this end, he was presented as having been manipulated by Japan's military leaders; indeed, General Douglas MacArthur cultivated his image as a 'peace monarch',[41] who voluntarily led his country in the formulation of its new constitution that renounced military force. Though the short-term aim of encouraging cooperation with the occupying powers was achieved, the longer-term consequence was that the Japanese people were absolved—or viewed themselves as being absolved—from the need to reflect on the colonization and oppressive rule of Taiwan and Korea, and the atrocities perpetrated there, in China, and in other Asian states.[42] The effects of this decision continue to be felt today, with periodic calls from China and other states for Japan to apologize repeatedly for its wartime activities, while nationalist sentiments within Japan manifest in the ritual of visiting the Yasukuni shrine to Japan's war dead, including fourteen Class A war criminals.[43]

The significance of the Tokyo Trial to Japan's modern approach to international law should not be overstated. Nevertheless, as Barak Kushner and others have argued, it is not difficult to see how it encouraged a view that international law was a tool for

[37] Yuki Tanaka, Timothy McCormack, and Gerry Simpson, 'Editors' Preface' in Yuki Tanaka, Timothy McCormack, and Gerry Simpson (eds), *Beyond Victor's Justice? The Tokyo War Crimes Trial Revisited* (Martinus Nijhoff 2011) xxviii.

[38] Yasuaki Onuma, 'Beyond Victor's Justice' (1984) 11 Japan Echo 63.

[39] Joseph B Keenan and Brendan F Brown, *Crimes Against International Law* (Public Affairs 1950) vii.

[40] See, e.g., Anne-Marie Prevost, 'Race and War Crimes: The 1945 War Crimes Trial of General Tomoyuki Yamashita' (1992) 14 Hum. Rts. Q 303.

[41] Tanaka et al, 'Editors' Preface' (n 37) xxix.

[42] Yorkio Otomo, 'The Decision Not to Prosecute the Emperor' in Tanaka et al (eds) (n 37) 63.

[43] Madoka Futamura, 'Japanese Societal Attitude Towards the Tokyo Trial: From a Contemporary Perspective' in Tanaka et al (eds) (n 37) 35.

selective engagement with domestic political processes, pursuing some ends, such as the stabilization of post-conflict Japan, while effacing others, such as the ongoing liberation struggles in much of the region.[44]

2.4 History and Law

This section has provided a brief survey of the historical experience of international law in certain parts of Asia. Clearly, a thorough treatment would require vastly more breadth and depth. For present purposes, the intention is not to encompass this experience in its entirety but, rather, to provide a snapshot of three aspects that help to explain the ongoing suspicion of international law in the region. First, international law was perceived to, and did in fact, legitimize the colonial project. Indeed, as Charles Alexandrowicz has argued, one can make the case that much of Asia enjoyed a 'full legal status' that was systematically undermined by the European states, leading to the situation in which Asian states were reduced to the position of supplicants seeking membership in the European order.[45] Secondly, China's experience of international law in general, and the unequal treaties in particular, encouraged a view of international law as being instrumentalist that continues to have an impact today. And, thirdly, Japan's post-war trials and those across the region reinforced the view that international law was a political tool that can and should be used selectively, when it is in one's interest (and capacity) to do so.

That being said, it is important to emphasize that the experience of international law in Asia was far from uniformly negative and that Asian states were not simply passive subjects in this history. Of particular note are the Five Principles of Peaceful Coexistence, adopted in 1954 by China and India and which still figure in the foreign policies of both countries. These principles are broad and hardly controversial, emphasizing (i) mutual respect for each other's territorial integrity and sovereignty; (ii) mutual non-aggression; (iii) mutual non-interference in each other's internal affairs; (iv) equality and mutual benefit; and (v) peaceful coexistence. At the Bandung Conference of African and Asian leaders, which took place the following year, the principles were incorporated in the ten-point Declaration on the Promotion of World Peace and Co-operation, and these in turn formed the normative core of the Non-Aligned Movement. The principles are also enshrined in the embryonic subregional organizations that have emerged across the continent, most notably the South Asian Association for Regional Cooperation (SAARC), the Shanghai Cooperation Organization (SCO) and the Association of Southeast Asian Nations (ASEAN).

[44] Cf. Barak Kushner, 'Ghosts of the Japanese Imperial Army: The "White Group" (*Baituan*) and Early Post-war Sino-Japanese Relations' (2013) 218 (Supplement 8) Past and Present 117, 119.

[45] Charles Alexandrowicz, *An Introduction to the History of the Law of Nations in the East Indies* (Clarendon Press 1967) 10.

Such principles, of course, also served the interests of the nationalist post-colonial leaders by protecting them from external criticism for authoritarian practices as well as limiting interference in controlling state resources.

In substantive terms, Asian states did contribute to the development of international law in the late twentieth century, notably the law of self-determination and the law of the sea. Individual Asian jurists have also held leadership positions in the major courts and international organizations, including two UN secretaries-general. Yet the purpose of this section has been to show why it is not surprising that there is ongoing wariness about international law. It seems plausible that this has had an influence on the low acceptance of, and participation in, international law and institutions highlighted at the start of the chapter. In addition, however, such concerns have fed into substantive disagreements that touch on non-interference, in particular, such as the 'Asian values' debates of the 1990s (concerning human rights relativism and distinctive approaches to governance/democracy and economic development) and the more recent opposition to the 'humanitarian intervention-lite' doctrine of the responsibility to protect (R2P).

3 Asian Engagement

As indicated in the introduction, Asia today is under-represented in various international regimes. To what extent is this significant or a cause for concern? Building on the preceding historical survey, this section will explore the different measures of Asia's participation and representation before considering how these generally low rates may be explained.

The percentage of states that sign treaties is a crude measure of attitudes towards international law. States around the world are known to sign treaties with little intention of complying with their obligations—or to refrain from signing out of excessive caution over the legal and political consequences that might follow. It does appear to be significant, however, that Asian states have consistently been the slowest to form regional institutions, the most reticent about acceding to major international treaties, the least likely to have a voice in proportion to their relative size and power, and the wariest about availing themselves of international dispute settlement procedures.

3.1 Regional Institutions

As mentioned in the introduction, and discussed more fully in chapter 3, there is no Asia-wide regional framework comparable to the AU, the OAS, or the EU. Those few sub-regional organizations that have been created are generally intended for limited functions or exist primarily as a structured series of meetings rather than an independent entity as such.[46] The SCO, for example, created in 1996, is notionally a collective security organization, but it has very few concrete obligations or activities. It is perhaps better understood as a platform for cooperation and confidence building.[47] The same could be said of SAARC, which was launched in 1985. Despite periods of 'turbulent non-growth', it has failed to take on a more significant regional role, largely due to the wariness that any expansion would primarily benefit India.[48] The overlapping organization known as the Bay of Bengal Initiative for Multi-Sectoral Technical and Economic Cooperation (BIMSTEC) also exists primarily to facilitate cooperation.

Most of the other multilateral structures linking Asian countries (sometimes with external partners) are similar forums or frameworks that have minimal functions beyond the convening of a periodic conference. At the continental level, the Asia Cooperation Dialogue has thirty-three members, including all of the ASEAN and Gulf Cooperation Council member states; as the name suggests, its primary function is an annual meeting of ministers. The various economic forums include the Asia-Pacific Economic Cooperation; the Economic Cooperation Organization; the Forum on Regional Cooperation among Bangladesh, China, India and Myanmar; the Indian Ocean Rim Association; the Mekong-Ganga Cooperation; the Pacific Islands Forum; and various other less formal arrangements. The Eurasian Economic Union links Russia and four former Soviet states and was established on 1 January 2015.

The lack of a security forum led a think-tank, the International Institute for Strategic Studies, to launch the Shangri-La Dialogue in 2002, now an annual semi-official meeting of defence ministers in Singapore. This supplements prior intergovernmental structures such as the ASEAN Regional Forum (ARF), launched in 1994, and the subsequent launch of the East Asia Summit (EAS), which first met in 2005. Both the ARF and the EAS were outgrowths of the region's most developed international organization: ASEAN, created in 1967 and growing from five original member states to the present ten members.

For most of its history, ASEAN was broadly consistent with the other Asian entities discussed above. Its foundational document, the Bangkok Declaration, essentially stated a few shared goals and announce an annual meeting of foreign ministers. In the past decade, however, ASEAN has undergone a transformation from a periodic meeting of ministers to setting ambitious goals and launching an 'ASEAN Community' in 2015. Building on the adoption of a Charter that entered into force in 2008—and which

[46] It is also telling that Asia was the last region to have any meaningful network of international law scholars until the Asian Society of International Law was established in 2007. See Owada (n 7); Yasuaki Onuma, 'The Asian Society of International Law: Its Birth and Significance' (2011) 1 Asian Journal of International Law 71.

[47] Stephen Blank, 'Making Sense of the Shanghai Cooperation Organization' (2013) 14 Georgetown Journal of International Affairs 39.

[48] Kishore Dash, 'Dynamics of South Asian Regionalism' in Mark Beeson and Richard Stubbs (eds), *Routledge Handbook of Asian Regionalism* (Routledge 2012) 406.

asserts the organization's legal personality[49]—it is the most important Asian international organization. A central tension in this transformation has been the question of whether the 'ASEAN way', which is defined by consultation and consensus rather than enforceable obligations, is consistent with the establishment of a community governed by law.[50]

In addition to a certain hesitation concerning international obligations generally, a further limiting factor in the case of ASEAN and the other organizations is resources. ASEAN long ago adopted the principle that each member would contribute the same funds to the budget, regardless of the size of its population or economy.[51] This necessarily keeps its annual budget low. In 2012, each member contributed US$1.58 million, for a total budget of US$15.8 million. To put this in perspective, ASEAN's member states contributed US$30.9 million to the UN in the same year, ranging from US$25,852 for Laos to US$8.6 million for Singapore. Even so, ASEAN is probably the best-funded Asian regional organization.

A further aspect of these various organizations that appears to reflect a wariness of granting political independence is that secretariats—if such an entity exists at all—are extremely limited not merely in resources but also in independence. Appointment processes often reflect the view that the nominal secretary-general is more akin to the chair of an ongoing meeting. Much as the presidency of the UN Security Council rotates alphabetically by state, the same principle applies to the secretaries-general of ASEAN and BIMSTEC and is the practice of SAARC and the SCO.

A term frequently heard in relation to Asian regional organizations is 'variable geometry', which indicates flexibility in the participation of different states in specific integration projects.[52] Such an approach is hardly unique to Asia, but it is telling that even ASEAN has included in its Charter an 'ASEAN Minus X formula', allowing member states to opt out of economic commitments.[53] More telling still is the fact that in a series of areas, ASEAN agreements are weaker than their international equivalents. There has been much discussion of the weakness of the ASEAN Human Rights Declaration (discussed in chapter 6), but this is also true in respect of international economic law: ASEAN member states have agreed to stricter obligations in their WTO or bilateral investment treaties (BITs) than they have within the context of the nascent ASEAN economic community.[54]

49 Simon Chesterman, 'Does ASEAN Exist? The Association of Southeast Asian Nations as an International Legal Person' (2008) XII Singapore Year Book of International Law 199.

50 See Simon Chesterman, *From Community to Compliance? The Evolution of Monitoring Obligations in ASEAN* (Cambridge University Press 2015).

51 ASEAN Charter, art. 30(2).

52 See e.g. Philomena Murray, 'Should Asia Emulate Europe?' in Woosik Moon and Bernadette Andreosso-O'Callaghan (eds), *Regional Integration: Europe and Asia* Compared (Routledge 2005) 208.

53 ASEAN Charter, art. 21(2).

54 Lay Hong Tan, 'Will ASEAN Economic Integration Progress Beyond a Free Trade Area?' (2004) 53 International and Comparative Law Quarterly 935, 967.

3.2 Major International Treaties

In addition to the treaties highlighted earlier, Asian states are the least likely to have signed many other human rights, international humanitarian law, and international criminal law treaties. Asian states have the lowest take-up of the ICCPR and ICESCR as well as of the conventions against racism, torture, and discrimination against persons with disabilities. Although all have signed the Geneva Conventions, less than three-quarters have signed the First Additional Protocol, and only two-thirds have signed the Second Additional Protocol (for other regions, the figures are 86 per cent or higher for both).

In the area of international economic law, the picture is slightly different. Although Asian states are least likely to have joined the WTO or to be contracting parties to ICSID, there is evidence that Asian states are using these regimes. India, Japan, and China are the fifth, seventh, and ninth most frequent to appear in WTO cases as applicant states; China and India are the second and third most frequent respondents. Japan is the most frequent participant as a third party; China and India are third and fourth.[55] Nevertheless, a study of the WTO dispute settlement system has concluded that Asian states overall initiate fewer disputes relative to their share of global trade, when compared with the US, the EU, Brazil, and Mexico.[56] One area in which Asia is becoming a leader is BITs. Although as a region it is the only one in which less than 80 per cent of states have at least one BIT in force, China is now party to the second largest number of BITs overall, with Korea and India in the top fourteen.[57]

In environmental law, the absence of US leadership and the economic impact of China and India has meant that Asian voices now play an increasingly significant role, a point considered in more detail in chapter 8.

3.3 Voice

Perhaps the most talked about aspect of international participation, at least by Japan and India, is Asian representation on the UN Security Council. On any measure, however, Asian states are under-represented in the leadership positions of global governance. Asian states constitute more than 25 per cent of the world's countries, occupy 30 per cent of its land mass, generate almost 50 per cent of global gross domestic product (GDP), and encompass 60 per cent of global population. Nevertheless, on key

[55] Data compiled from World Trade Organization, 'Dispute Settlement: Disputes by Country/Territory' (World Trade Organization 2018) <http://www.wto.org/english/tratop_e/dispu_e/dispu_by_country_e.htm> accessed 30 October 2018.

[56] Michael Ewing-Chow, Alex Goh, and Akshay Kolse Patil, 'Are Asian WTO Members Using the WTO DSU "Effectively"?' (2013) 16 Journal of International Economic Law 669.

[57] Data compiled from United Nations Conference on Trade and Development, 'International Investments Agreements Navigator' (UNCTAD Division on Investment and Enterprise 2013) <http://investmentpolicyhub.unctad.org/IIA/IiasByCountry> accessed 30 October 2018.

bodies such as the UN Security Council and the Bretton Woods institutions, Asia remains under-represented. The continent has only one-fifth of the seats on the UN Security Council, including one permanent seat. (The Western Europe and Others Group (WEOG) has one-third of the seats—three permanent and two rotating.) The president of the World Bank, in practice, is appointed by the White House, while the managing director of the IMF has until now been chosen by its European members. Even where Asian states have appropriate representation, however, such as the UN General Assembly, they do not operate as a regional bloc. Unlike the African and Latin American states, for example, the Asia-Pacific Group at the UN never seeks to achieve common positions on policy matters and discussion is generally limited to candidacies for international posts.

Partly as a result of this lack of regional coherence, Asian states tend to have less of a voice in international affairs than their number, size, and power might otherwise warrant. Individual states, notably China, are exercising growing influence, but it is hard to identify areas in which Asian states have had an impact as a group. Building on the Five Principles and the Bandung Conference discussed earlier,[58] the New International Economic Order was perhaps the largest project that Asian states participated in after decolonization. Yet its impact remains the subject of academic debate.[59] There has been some modest success with disarmament and human security, which Japan, in particular, has championed. Nevertheless, as one Korean commentator has observed, human security runs at odds with the dominant discourse of robust sovereignty advocated by most Asian states.[60]

3.4 International Dispute Settlement

A fourth area of representation and participation worthy of note is the fact that Asian states tend to be the wariest of international dispute settlement procedures. Only eight Asian states have accepted compulsory jurisdiction of the ICJ—Cambodia, Cyprus,[61] India, Japan, the Marshall Islands, Pakistan, the Philippines, and Timor-Leste—which amounts to 15 per cent of the Asia-Pacific Group within the UN. By contrast, 30 per cent of Eastern European states, 39 per cent of Latin America and Caribbean states, 41 per cent of African states, and 69 per cent of Western European and Other Group states have signed optional declarations. Unsurprisingly, Asian states are also less likely to have used the ICJ. Only fifteen of the fifty-three Asia-Pacific states have ever appeared before the ICJ, which equates to 28 per cent. The corresponding figures for

[58] See (nn 41–4) and accompanying text.

[59] See Antony Anghie, 'Legal Aspects of the New International Economic Order' (2015) 6 Humanity 145. See also the NIEO entry in the online Max Planck Encyclopedia of Public International Law.

[60] Sung Won Kim, 'Human Security with an Asian Face?' (2010) 17 Indiana Journal of Global Legal Studies 83, 102.

[61] Cyprus is a member of the Asia-Pacific Group at the UN, despite also being a member of the European Union.

other regions are 48 per cent of Latin American states, 50 per cent of African states, 57 per cent of Eastern European states and 79 per cent of WEOG. Of those fifteen Asian states, six first appeared before the ICJ in 2001 or later.

It is interesting to note that there have been only three territorial delimitation cases brought by Asian states to the ICJ: *Temple of Preah Vihear (Cambodia v Thailand)*, *Pulau Ligitan and Pulau Sipadan (Indonesia/Malaysia)* and *Pedra Branca (Malaysia/Singapore)*.[62] In each case, only one aspect of a larger dispute was submitted to the ICJ—the temple in the first case and specific islands in the other two. Whereas the land border between Cambodia and Thailand and the maritime boundary in the other cases might be the subject of ongoing negotiation, these aspects were not susceptible to division or negotiation, apparently encouraging the parties to submit them to third-party adjudication.

Other disputes that have been submitted to international adjudication include the railway lands arbitration between Malaysia and Singapore at the Permanent Court of Arbitration and the Bangladesh–Myanmar maritime delimitation case at the International Tribunal for the Law of the Sea.[63] The majority of Asian territorial disputes, however, remain bilateral or multilateral disputes with little sign of a resolution through third-party adjudication. Prominent examples include Jammu and Kashmir (between India and Pakistan), the border between India and China, the Senkaku/Diaoyu Islands (between Japan and China), the Liancourt Rocks (Dokdo/Takeshima) (between Japan and South Korea), the Kuril Islands (between Russia and Japan), and the disputed islands and waters of the South China Sea (variously involving Brunei, China, Taiwan, Malaysia, Indonesia, the Philippines, and Vietnam).

The South China Sea especially has been the subject of intense diplomatic and legal manoeuvring. Some of China's early claims appeared to suggest a rejection of norms that have been codified in the UN Convention on the Law of the Sea (UNCLOS), to which China is a party. After publishing its famous 'nine-dash line' map in 2009, it was initially unclear whether China was asserting that the entire body of water so indicated was part of its territorial sea or if it was merely claiming islands within the line and the associated territorial seas.[64] In 2013, the Philippines initiated compulsory arbitration under Annex VII of UNCLOS and China refused to participate. The following year, China commenced land reclamation projects in the area, referred to by some in the US military as the 'great wall of sand'.

[62] *Temple of Preah Vihear (Cambodia v Thailand)* (Judgment) [1962] ICJ Rep 6; *Sovereignty over Pulau Ligitan and Pulau Sipadan (Indonesia/Malaysia)* (Judgment) [2002] ICJ Rep 625; *Sovereignty over Pedra Branca/Pulau Batu Puteh, Middle Rocks and South Ledge (Malaysia/Singapore)* (Judgment) [2008] ICJ Rep 12.

[63] *Railway Land Arbitration (Malaysia v Singapore)* (Final Award) 30 October 2014, PCA Case No. 2012-01; ITLOS, *Dispute Concerning Delimitation of the Maritime Boundary between Bangladesh and Myanmar in the Bay of Bengal (Bangladesh/Myanmar)* (Judgment) 14 March 2012, ITLOS Case No. 16.

[64] See Robert Beckman, 'The UN Convention on the Law of the Sea and the Maritime Disputes in the South China Sea' (2013) 107 American Journal of International Law 142.

Such a series of events might have constituted outright rejection of UNCLOS and the tribunal, as well as literally changing the landscape. However, China subsequently softened its position. On the territorial claims, it began to adopt a more nuanced position that backed away from the assertion that the nine-dash line marked its territorial waters. On the arbitration, it refused to take part but published a 'position paper' that the tribunal used as a proxy for its legal position.[65] And on the land reclamation projects, it has not suggested that any artificial islands so created will attract more than the limited rights accorded to such features in UNCLOS.

4 Explaining Ambivalence

Explaining the impressionistic data in the previous section runs the risk of gross generalizations. As emphasized earlier, states choose whether to participate in particular international regimes for a wide variety of reasons and entire books (and other chapters of this book) have been written on the attitudes of specific Asian countries to international law. A preliminary consideration, then, is whether national political structures and rule of law institutions are the dominant factor. It may be hypothesized, for example, that authoritarian states are less likely to submit themselves to external scrutiny or binding international obligations than liberal states.[66] Such countries, it might be argued, are less likely to cede power to international institutions in the same way that they are wary of delegating it to powerful national ones. A preliminary study suggests that this may be a factor but cannot fully explain the particular reluctance of Asian states to accept international obligations.[67]

Using the World Justice Project's (WJP) Rule of Law Index as a proxy for respect for the rule of law, for example, African states rate on average far lower than Asian states in terms of rule of law, with an average weighted score of 0.19. (Asian states average 0.25, Latin American states average 0.29, Eastern European states 0.43, and WEOG states 0.50.)[68] Yet, as we have seen, African states are far more likely to accept many international obligations and participate in international organizations. Similarly,

[65] Ministry of Foreign Affairs of the People's Republic of China, 'Position Paper of the Government of the People's Republic of China on the Matter of Jurisdiction in the South China Sea Arbitration Initiated by the Republic of the Philippines' (Ministry of Foreign Affairs of the People's Republic of China, 7 December 2014) <http://www.fmprc.gov.cn/mfa_eng/zxxx_662805/t1217147.shtml> accessed 30 October 2018.

[66] See e.g. Ann Kent, *Beyond Compliance: China, International Organizations, and Global Security* (Stanford University Press 2007) 2.

[67] A more cynical interpretation might be that Asian states' participation may be driven by a desire for the appearance of compliance but without any good-faith intention to follow through on obligations. As discussed in section 3 above, however, this is an accusation that might be levelled at many regimes.

[68] Data compiled from World Justice Project, *World Justice Project Rule of Law Index 2017–2018* (Washington DC 2018) <https://worldjusticeproject.org/sites/default/files/documents/WJP-ROLI-2018-June-Online-Edition_0.pdf> accessed 30 October 2018.

Freedom House's 'Freedom Rating' suggests that African states are less 'free' than Asian states, and yet this does not appear to have affected the acceptance of international obligations.[69]

Within Asia, there is some interesting variation. Of the twenty-five countries evaluated by the WJP, thirteen score 0.51 and above.[70] Using the examples of international treaties cited earlier, the percentage of those states accepting jurisdiction of the ICJ (3) or the ICC (5), or signing onto the ICCPR (10) or the ICESCR (10), is still lower than the percentage of any of the other regional groupings as a whole. A slightly higher percentage of states graded by the WJP at 0.50 and below have signed the ICESCR (11 of 12). In the realm of international economic law, there does seem to be a correlation between rule of law and membership of the WTO and ICSID. Of the Asian states that scored 0.51 and above, all are members of the WTO and eleven of the thirteen states (85 per cent) are members of ICSID. The proportion of those states that scored 0.50 and below or that were not evaluated is below 67 per cent (see Table 2.1).[71]

Using Freedom House's crude ranking of 'free', 'partly free', and 'not free', it might again be hypothesized that 'free' countries are more likely to accept international obligations, in particular civil and political rights restrictions. This appears to be the case with respect to the global acceptance of the jurisdiction of the ICJ and ICC, in particular, with 49 per cent of states listed as 'free' accepting the ICJ compared with 33 per cent of 'partly free' and 20 per cent of 'not free' states. For the ICC, 85 per cent of

Table 2.1 Percentage of States Participating in Certain International Institutions by UN Regional Groupings (December 2014)

	ICJ (%)	ICC (%)	ICCPR (%)	ICESCR (%)	WTO (%)	ICSID (%)
Asia-Pacific	15	32	66	66	70	68
WJP rule of law > 0.50	*23*	*38*	*77*	*77*	*100*	*85*
WJP rule of law ≤ 0.50	*17*	*25*	*83*	*92*	*58*	*67*
WJP not scored	*11*	*32*	*54*	*50*	*61*	*61*
Africa	41	63	94	89	78	83
Eastern Europe	30	78	100	100	83	91
Latin America and Caribbean states	39	82	88	85	97	67
Western Europe and others	72	86	100	93	90	90

[69] Data compiled from Freedom House, 'Freedom in the World' (Washington DC 2015) <https://freedomhouse.org/report/freedom-world/freedom-world-2015> accessed 30 October 2018.

[70] Singapore, South Korea, Japan, United Arab Emirates, Malaysia, Jordan, Mongolia, Nepal, Philippines, Indonesia, Thailand, Sri Lanka, and India.

[71] Data compiled from World Justice Project (n 68).

Table 2.2 Percentage of States Rated as 'Free' by Freedom House Participating in Certain International Institutions by UN Regional Groupings (December 2014)

'Free' states	ICJ (%)	ICC (%)	ICCPR (%)	ICESCR (%)	WTO (%)	ICSID (%)
Asia-Pacific (13)	31	62	54	38	62	54
Africa (11)	36	91	91	73	91	82
Eastern Europe (13)	46	100	100	100	92	92
Latin America and Caribbean states (22)	36	86	86	82	95	73
Western Europe and others (28)	75	89	100	93	89	89
Global (88)[72]	49	85	88	80	86	78

'free' states are parties to the Rome Statute compared with 61 per cent of 'partly free' and 25 per cent of 'not free' states.[73] Yet when one considers the various 'free' countries, Asian states remain outliers in their unwillingness to sign on to international obligations (see Table 2.2).

Further evaluation of political structures and acceptance of international obligations may yield richer conclusions, but these preliminary data seem to suggest that respect for rule of law nationally does not provide a robust explanation for acceptance of the rule of law internationally. The data fail to explain Asian states' attitudes towards international law. Instead, four themes stand out that, even if they are not unique to Asia, help in understanding current attitudes towards international law and institutions.

The first theme, as discussed earlier, is Asian states' historical experience of international law. Colonialism, the unequal treaties, and the post-war experience encouraged the perception that international law is of questionable legitimacy, can be used for instrumental purposes, and is necessarily selective in its application. As indicated earlier, this might also be applied to other regions. Indeed, it is broadly consistent with a realist critique of international law. However, the invocation of these themes by Asian leaders is more than mere opportunism.

A second factor, which is more specific to Asia, is diversity. Its identification as a continent was exogenously determined; even today, as discussed in the introduction to this book, its precise boundaries remain culturally or politically, rather than geographically, determined. This has contributed to a lack of self-identification on the part of Asian states, relative to their African, European, and Latin American counterparts. Regional coherence, in turn, can have normative consequences—not only obvious in the case of the expanding EU but also evident in the attitudes towards intervention in the AU and the elaborate human rights framework that has been developed under the

[72] The total of 88 includes Kiribati, which is not a member of a UN regional group.

[73] Rome Statute on the International Criminal Court (adopted 17 July 1998, entered into force 1 July 2002, 2187 UNTS 3).

auspices of the Inter-American Court of Human Rights.[74] Although sub-regional division is possible, east, south, central, and west Asia do not display significantly more cohesion; the standout is perhaps ASEAN in the south-east, though even that remains 'thin' compared to other regional organizations.

A third consideration is the power disparities across the continent, in particular the need to balance the great power interests of rising China and India and of a declining Japan. At the regional level, this appears to reduce the attractiveness to other Asian states of organizations or norm formation in which those powers would have dominant voice.[75] This can be seen, for example, in the unenthusiastic response to then Australian Prime Minister Kevin Rudd's attempt to launch an 'Asia Pacific Community' in 2008.[76] Smaller members prefer ASEAN-style arrangements in which sovereign equality is taken more literally (with regard to financial contributions, for example) and in which obligations are comparatively light.

A fourth explanatory factor is that the current regime broadly serves the interests of many Asian states. Lacking the normative pull of the expanding EU, the regional self-identification of Latin America, and the donor pressures confronting many African states, there are few carrots or sticks to incentivize regional organization or the accession to treaties for reasons other than explicit self-interest. An exception to this may be the steps towards economic integration in ASEAN, as well as the more recent moves to create an Asian Infrastructure Investment Bank (AIIB). Other areas in which greater coordination is gaining traction include cross-border environmental harm (such as the Southeast Asian haze problem), human trafficking, and transnational crime (including piracy).

5 Conclusion

Asia participates less, and is less represented, in the international system, and yet it has arguably benefited more from the stability and predictability of that system than any other region. This was described in the introduction to this chapter as a paradox, though it could also be a rational response on the part of many Asian states to take the benefits of the network of institutions and obligations without submitting themselves to its forms and procedures. There are increasing signs, however, that the current situation is unsustainable. In the security sphere, it is premised on security guarantees that Western states—in particular, the US—cannot or will not continue to underwrite. Economically,

[74] On the impact of regions on norm cascades, see Martha Finnemore and Kathryn Sikking, 'International Norm Dynamics and Political Change' (1998) 52 International Organization 887, 902–3.

[75] It is possible, of course, that membership of such organizations might actually serve to constrain great powers in the manner that the UN (arguably) tempers the actions of its larger members through structured processes and socialization to norms.

[76] See Sheryn Lee and Anthony Milner, 'Practical vs Identity Regionalism: Australia's APC Initiative, a Case Study' (2014) 20 Contemporary Politics 209.

the need for a greater Asian voice is not just recognized within Asia but also globally. And, politically, there is evidence that China is unwilling to continue to be a 'rule taker'.

What might such change look like? One possibility is that Asia might offer a genuine alternative to the Westphalian model of international order premised on state sovereignty and international law. The term 'Eastphalia' is sometimes invoked for its contrast with the Western-dominated legal order named after the region in the German state of North Rhine-Westphalia.[77] The precise content of an 'Eastphalian' order can be hard to pin down, however. It typically involves references to Confucianism and communitarianism, as well as more general challenges to the universalism of 'Western' norms—notably human rights—or to the contingency of those norms based on stages of economic development. As Tom Ginsburg and others have observed, however, there is little positive evidence of a new model of regionalism arising in Asia, where most states emphasize a very *West*phalian model of sovereignty in their international affairs.[78]

A second possibility is that Asian states might set up parallel regimes existing alongside their mainstream counterparts, exemplified by the creation of the AIIB in 2015 and moves to establish a new 'Silk Road'. Interestingly, 'Asia' is defined for the purposes of the AIIB as encompassing the UN's 'Asia' and 'Oceania' groupings, the key implication of which is that it includes Australia and New Zealand (which are typically treated as appendages of Western Europe).[79] It is possible that the creation of the AIIB signals a shift in the international order, but this appears to be more of a political and economic shift than a legal one. The AIIB itself is structured in a manner comparable to other institutions, notably the Asian Development Bank. Critics have warned that the AIIB may be less rigorous in its application of environmental and labour standards, but it is not clear that this would amount to an 'Asian values'-style challenge to the legitimacy of these standards as such.

Another prominent possible example that might have represented a genuine effort to opt out of the international order and establish a parallel regime is China's behaviour in the South China Sea. Ultimately, China bluntly rejected the decision of the arbitral tribunal released in July 2016—but its strongly worded statements noticeably did not make reference to the nine-dash line. Nor does China seem likely to withdraw from UNCLOS, given the ongoing benefits it enjoys from the deep seabed regime.[80] In this way, China continues to demonstrate a tolerance and even a preference for legal ambiguity with regard to what, precisely, it is claiming in the South China Sea. This is broadly consistent with its position, for example, on the idiosyncratic status of

[77] Tom Ginsburg, 'Eastphalia and Asian Regionalism' (2011) 44 University of California at Davis Law Review 859, citing Sung Won Kim, 'Eastphalia Rising: An Enquiry into the Emergence of Asian Perspective on International Law and Global Governance' (DPhil thesis, Indiana University 2009).

[78] Ginsburg, ibid.

[79] Asian Infrastructure Investment Bank, 'Articles of Agreement' (Asian Infrastructure Investment Bank, Beijing, 20 June 2015) art. 1(2) <http://www.aiib.org/en/about-aiib/basic-documents/_download/articles-of-agreement/basic_document_english-bank_articles_of_agreement.pdf> accessed 30 October 2018.

[80] *Philippines v China* (Award) 12 July 2016, PCA Case No. 2013–19.

Taiwan. In general, then, suggestions that China is seeking to radically undermine the international order seem overstated.

A third possible scenario, then, is that there will be some kind of convergence of Western and Asian interests in the international order, maintaining the basic structural foundations of sovereign equality of states but with Asian states gradually taking a more prominent role. In 2010 at the second summit of Brazil, Russia, India, and China (the 'BRIC' countries), for example, the leaders articulated a common vision that 'the world is undergoing major and swift changes that highlight the need for corresponding transformations in global governance in all relevant areas'. Nevertheless, they went on to stress that these changes should take place within the existing framework of laws and institutions.[81]

In the much-heralded Asian century, many have argued that Asian states deserve greater representation in the institutions of global governance. That wish is clearly going to be fulfilled. Assumptions that the status quo can continue indefinitely are overly optimistic. Yet suggestions that Asian states will abandon the structures of international order are also overblown. More likely is a larger convergence, an adaptation of existing structures and norms to the new reality—evolution rather than revolution.

Not all of this will be positive. Though the likelihood of a radically different approach to global governance seems low, the traditional view of sovereignty espoused by many Asian states may slow the expansion of human rights and other norms, although it does not look set to reverse them completely. Nor will any change necessarily be coherent. As this chapter has been at pains to stress—and as this volume amply demonstrates—there is no one 'Asian' view of the world. Greater involvement of Asian states will primarily increase pluralism in the international order. And so the category remains a useful one, as the various countries experiment with stronger regionalism, as seen in ASEAN and its various extensions, and in taking a leadership role, most prominently in the case of China. But it would be misleading in the extreme to assume that 'Asia', when it is properly represented in the institutions of global governance, will have anything specific to say.

[81] Second BRIC Summit of Heads of State and Government, 'Joint Statement' (Brasilia, 15 April 2010) <http://www.brics.utoronto.ca/docs/100415-leaders.html> accessed 30 October 2018.

CHAPTER 3

REGIONAL ORGANIZATIONS

TAN HSIEN-LI

1 Introduction

SINCE the establishment of the United Nations at the close of the Second World War, the international order has become increasingly legalized and institutionalized, not only across diverse fields ranging from human rights to trade and investment but across the various regions and sub-regions of the world. The growth of specialist and regional regimes, especially after the Cold War, has been of such a degree that it has raised concerns about the fragmentation of international law.[1] The progress of the international legal order has naturally had an effect upon the Asia-Pacific—there has been an increase in participation by these states on the global plane and in the development of multilateral regimes in the region.

Despite such developments, the Asia-Pacific still engages less with international law as compared to other regions. For instance, the type of organization that Asia-Pacific states prefer to operate among themselves is distinct from other regional organizations and other issue-specific multilateral institutions, in that they are comparatively less formalized and develop less international law of their own.[2] Perhaps because of this preference, and because of their sovereignty-centric outlooks, it is also notable that Asia-Pacific states do not often have their regional organizations represent their collective voice at global intergovernmental forums, such as at the UN. They prefer to form other associations or caucuses or to act as unitary states in the global arena.[3]

[1] Martti Koskenniemi and Paivi Leino, 'Fragmentation of International Law? Postmodern Anxieties' (2002) 15 Leiden JIL 533; Gerhard Hafner, 'Pros and Cons Ensuing from Fragmentation of International Law' (2004) 25 MJIL 849.

[2] See e.g. Peter Katzenstein, 'Regionalism and Asia' (2000) 5 NPE 353; Mark Beeson, 'Rethinking Regionalism: Europe and East Asia in Comparative Historical Perspective' (2005) 12 JEPP 969.

[3] See e.g. Jurgen Ruland and Paruedee Nguitragool, *ASEAN as an Actor in International Fora: Reality, Potential and Constraints* (CUP 2016).

The reasons for Asia-Pacific states' cautious embrace of international law have been traced to, *inter alia*, historical reasons, anti-colonialism, a less legalistic and formalized culture, or a preference to exercise strict sovereignty and autonomy.[4] All this is largely indisputable. Yet, this only clarifies part of the puzzle regarding the weak legalization and institutionalization in Asia-Pacific regional organizations (APROs). Important questions remain:

(1) Why is there an implicit expectation that APROs should be legalized and institutionalized in the first place? Is such an expectation reasonable?
(2) Even as Asia-Pacific states engage more frequently in the international legal order, why do they persist in keeping their regional organizations less formalized? Apart from historical and cultural preferences, what are the practical benefits?
(3) Conversely, some APROs have been recast as legal and institutional entities. What are the critical push and pull factors which compel the member states to take this radical step?

This investigation of APROs is important because data on these organizations are fairly limited. APROs generally conduct fewer assessments of their work and, even if these reports existed, they would be inaccessible due to the organizations' lack of transparency and limited capacity for information technology and public outreach.[5] As a result, there is a dearth of in-depth critical scholarly analysis on APROs. In particular, a blind spot exists within the literature which fosters inaccurate interpretation. There is a certain disconnect in the global 'ideal' and the Asia-Pacific reality of regional organizations, which leads to a somewhat unfair perception of APROs in two main ways.

The first observation is that there is little region-wide analysis. Asian regionalism studies have often been conducted along sub-regional lines such as East, South, and Southeast Asia, where the organizations demonstrate more institutional heft and global recognition, while Pacific regionalism has largely been ignored.[6] Based on the data pool

[4] See generally Simon Chesterman, 'Asia's Ambivalence about International Law and Institutions: Past, Present and Futures' (2016) 27 EJIL 945; Hisashi Owada, 'The Experience of Asia with International Adjudication' (2005) 9 SYBIL 9; Tan Hsien-Li, *The ASEAN Intergovernmental Commission on Human Rights: Institutionalising Human Rights in Southeast Asia* (CUP 2011) 24–71 (pertaining to international human rights law); Miles Kahler, 'Legalization as Strategy: The Asia-Pacific Case' (2000) 54 IO 549.

[5] This is readily evidenced by the skimpily curated homepages of Asia-Pacific regional organizations. See e.g. Shanghai Cooperation Organisation, 'SCO' <http://www.infoshos.ru/en/> accessed 28 December 2017 (the SCO website hosted by the Russian government); Association of Southeast Asian Nations, 'ASEAN' <http://www.ASEAN.org> accessed 28 December 2017; Pacific Islands Forum Secretariat <http://www.forumsec.org> accessed 28 December 2017.

[6] This becomes apparent when surveying the literature on Asia-Pacific regional organizations. See e.g. Louise Fawcett and Andrew Hurrell (eds), *Regionalism in World Politics: Regional Organization and International Order* (OUP 1995); Mark Beeson and Richard Stubbs, *Routledge Handbook of Asian Regionalism* (Routledge 2013).

alone, it is inaccurate to study APROs according to sub-regions or to focus on the more 'prominent' ones in the international order (which tend to have standing relationships with Western powers and thus have more readily-available information) and then assume that those findings are broadly representative of the entire realm of APROs.

The second observation, and arguably the more important one, is that APROs that are less legalized and institutionalized are consequently deemed somewhat less 'competent' than the more robust and formalized regional organizations and arrangements which exist in other parts of the world, with the European and Latin American experiences commonly used as comparators.[7] These formalized European and Latin American regional institutions actively use and develop their own international law, which in turn contributes to how the international community understands regional rules and regimes. In contrast, APROs demonstrate a less frequent usage of and participation in the workings of international law, and thus make fewer contributions to the discourse. APROs have been derided as 'talk-shops' or generators of rhetoric.[8] More tellingly, the regional instruments adopted in APROs have very limited, if any, effect in the domestic orders of the member states—a clear sign as to as their respect for the international law that they make for themselves. It is inevitable that APROs consequently appear underwhelming and less effective.

Careful differentiation of APROs is important to overcome these two misperceptions. In response to these issues and given the limited information available, this chapter studies the seven main regional organizations (and, where relevant, their corollary groupings or institutions) *collectively* across the entire Asia-Pacific. That is, every sub-region of the Asia-Pacific which possesses a significant regional organization is represented. (There exist other, more limited types of regional arrangements that conduct cooperation activities of a sectoral or technical nature such as the Mekong River Commission but these that are omitted do not possess the comprehensive nature of a classical regional organization.) The seven organizations are: the Association of Southeast Asian Nations (ASEAN), the Eurasian Economic Union (EAEU), the Shanghai Cooperation Organization (SCO), South Asian Association for Regional Cooperation (SAARC), the Asia-Pacific Economic Cooperation (APEC), the Pacific Islands Forum (PIF), and the Melanesian Spearhead Group (MSG). (See Figure 3.1.)

[7] See e.g. Francesco Duina, *The Social Construction of Free Trade: The European Union, NAFTA, and MERCOSUR* (Princeton University Press 2006); Jens-Uwe Wunderlich, *Regionalism, Globalization and International Order: Europe and Southeast Asia* (Ashgate 2007); Miles Kahler and Andrew MacIntyre, *Integrating Regions: Asia in Comparative Context* (Stanford University Press 2013); Amitav Acharya and Alastair Iain Johnston (eds), *Crafting Cooperation: Regional International Institutions in Comparative Perspective* (Cambridge University Press 2007); Carlos Closa and Lorenzo Casini, *Comparative Regional Integration: Governance and Legal Models* (Cambridge University Press 2016).

[8] See e.g. Sheldon Simon, 'The ASEAN Regional Forum: Beyond the Talk Shop?' (*NBR Analysis*, July 2013) <https://www.nbr.org/publication/the-asean-regional-forum-beyond-the-talk-shop/> accessed 7 December 2018; N Hasib, 'Analysts Deride SAARC as a "Talking Shop" in Absence of Deals' (*BDNews24.com*, 26 November 2014) <https://bdnews24.com/bangladesh/2014/11/26/analysts-deride-saarc-as-a-talking-shop-in-absence-of-deals> accessed 28 December 2017.

FIGURE 3.1 Regional organizations of the Asia-Pacific

Source: https://www.cia.gov/library/publications/the-world-factbook/attachments/images/large/southeast_asia-political.jpg?1547145654

A very elementary comparative methodology employed in this chapter has uncovered certain traits of how these APROs interact with international law. The reasons why they take on the form and functions they do are due to a complex mix of member states' desires for certain practical gains in light of the internal and external circumstances. This chapter posits that all APROs begin as political organizations and tend to share similar patterns of development which are dependent on variables such as whether and what type of hegemonic actors exist, as well as the political and economic ambitions of the organization collectively or individually as members. It must be highlighted that the adoption of many regional agreements often does not change their status as political organizations. Over time, however, depending on internal and external factors, some APROs may *consciously take firm steps* to become rules- and institutions-based. This deliberate choice to formalize the APRO and its subsequent legalization and institutionalization trajectory are really what distinguishes it from being a political organization.

More importantly, the choice of whether to remain a political organization or transform into a law- and institutions-based one should not be unduly judged. The yardstick by which to measure the 'effectiveness' of APROs should not be whether or not they are legalized, institutionalized, and achieving their aspirations *unless* all these are explicitly enunciated as part of the organizational aims rather than mere expressions of rhetoric. Without descending into the apologetics of Asia-Pacific modalities, it is incongruous to judge APROs based on measures and targets that the member states themselves did not *intend* to adhere to. The assumption that more laws and institutions make better regional organizations is somewhat flawed. There must be a broader understanding that Asia-Pacific states use and participate in their regional organizations somewhat differently than the more legalized structures seen in Europe or Latin America, for example. It should also be recognized that no matter the type of regional organization, soft cooperation modalities continue to be constructed and used on more sensitive issues that impact upon security and foreign policy, and this is seen to some extent even in the world's most formalized regional organization, the European Union.

Accordingly, it cannot be overlooked that Asia-Pacific states may *prefer* less robust models as these serve their purposes better. A political organization with little reliance on law and institutions can be successful. The basic test is whether the APRO has a clear vision and serves the purposes of the member states. The effectiveness of APROs in turn depends on the political dynamic of the region, the external factors, the capacity of the organization, and the collective determination to achieve the common objectives. Ultimately, it will be seen that while the levels of efficacy are variable among the APROs—and the reality is that there will always be APROs that do not appear to achieve any of their stated goals—these APROs do not get dissolved but continue to exist and hold regular meetings. The value of an APRO to member states might be even more basic than substantive cooperation. APROs could exist to fulfil the members' need to have a regional forum to reduce suspicions, foster relationships, share information, and build mutual confidence.[9]

Within this context, this chapter first maps out a conceptual trajectory of how APROs are established and develop thereafter. It then delineates a matrix of the seven APROs into two categories: (1) those that have taken on more legal and institutional characteristics and (2) those which remain steadfastly political and diplomatic in modality. It will elaborate on the particular characteristics of each APRO. This will entail a certain degree of descriptive-analytical writing to adequately explain the aims

[9] Andrew Hurrell, 'Explaining the Resurgence of Regionalism in World Politics' (1995) 21 RIS 331, 334–7 and 341–3.

and motives of each organization, their evolution patterns, their interaction with and usage of international law, and a measure of their effectiveness and benefits to the member states.

2 The Evolution of APROs—A Common Conceptual Narrative of Regional Stability, Economic Development, Sovereignty, and Intergovernmentalism

A survey of the seven major APROs in the region reveals some core features in their establishment and evolution patterns and the behaviour of the member states. No matter when in the period since the late 1960s each organization was established, all of them emerged amid periods of regional instability and mistrust. Yet the intraregional conditions were sufficiently conducive (and external conditions so coercive) such that the member states could set aside differences to come together to build a regional platform at which they could discuss and tackle common issues. Therefore, APROs were not conceived of as defence or military arrangements within the UN Charter sense of security arrangements such as the North Atlantic Treaty Organization. Instead, they were primarily geared towards the resolution of security and economic concerns which included diffusing regional tensions and rivalries, the furthering of economic development, the balancing and managing of powers (especially the hegemons within the groupings), and confidence-building and the enhancement of diplomatic relations among the member states. Each country saw the benefits of cooperation predominantly in light of national gains. Issues that were considered sensitive and an imposition on national policy and sovereignty or could hamper economic development—such as environmental protection and human rights—were not factored into the mandates of these organizations at the time of establishment.

The development of each APRO was hence a somewhat neorealist institutionalist set-up whereby self-interested states constructed and participated in regional regimes not for the common or collective interest but rather for individual benefit. As a result, they were reluctant to bind themselves to rules and institutions as the cost was high. This was not only in terms of the effort necessary to carry out obligations (especially since many Asia-Pacific states continue to have developing status with limited resources and technical capacity) but that the law-abiding state could often be at the losing end if the other member states defaulted or generally had a low respect for regional laws and institutions. Legalization and institutionalization were in some cases eschewed to the extent that even the founding instrument was merely soft law rather than a legally binding treaty. Nonetheless, the status of the founding instrument was little indication of the form and function of the organization. APROs were invariably all set up as intergovernmental political organizations with a strong executive voice by the member states and there was little development of laws and institutions. There was also the prioritization of flexible diplomatic modalities which permitted them to secure the utmost advantage from cooperation but with the lowest penalty incurred.

Due to the strengthening of mutual ties and a reliance on the pledge to refrain from any use of force, the initial phase following the organizations' establishment tended to be one where the states underwent a period of national development, since they were now able to concentrate on domestic matters rather than the threat of external forces. Regular regional meetings fostered positive relations and built the right foundations towards active cooperation. Once national stability and regional relations had progressed to a comfortable degree, and the need to look more outwardly beckoned, these states emphasized cooperation so that they could all prosper together. Nonetheless, the aversion to legal and institutional modalities extended into the collaborative projects. Whether or not these commitments were expressed in hard or soft legal instruments, the overall tenor of cooperation was one that was politically flexible.

Furthermore, supranationalism was largely eschewed. Regional institutions were often not empowered meaningfully in terms of mandate and resources to carry out their rightful tasks. An arguably mistaken understanding of sovereignty vis-à-vis the rule of law and the competence of regional institutions has led to a lack of delegation of powers to regional bureaucracies—even in instances where this did not undermine sovereignty. This fear of regional institutions overstepping their boundaries is unwarranted as there is no way regional secretariats can override national sovereignty and make executive supranational decisions. Regional secretariats are simply not constructed this way. They are instead bureaucracies that carry out the member states' express decisions, and therefore are an extension and facilitation of the sovereign will. This phenomenon was observed even with 'quasi-supranational' institutions (such as those in the EAEU) that supposedly had more autonomy to carry out the tasks of regional cooperation as member states overrode such mechanisms and used intergovernmentalism as their main modality. There was little censure for default or non-compliance. There was the tacit common understanding that the basis and benefits of regional cooperation went deeper and further than mere legal and institutional obedience and the carrying out of regional pledges. Ultimately, all the APROs acted to some degree as loosely-bound, flexible political arrangements aimed at maximizing benefits to the member states.

This developmental trajectory can be seen in varying degrees and different permutations across the seven APROs. The reliance on flexible, diplomatic action continues unhampered until geopolitical pressures compel the member states to take measures for a legal and institutional metamorphosis. That said, the level of cooperation and intraregional trust among the member states needs to be quite high before they are confident that they can take this step together. If the regional relations have not yet built up sufficiently, it would be unlikely that external pressures could make the states willingly bind themselves to one another. These breakaway patterns are a relatively recent phenomenon, occurring only with ASEAN (since 2007) and the EAEU (since 2015), and the results cannot yet be fully ascertained. Nonetheless an interim assessment of the achievements and direction of growth will be made. For the remaining five APROs, there is the continuation of the status quo either out of preference, path dependency, circumstances, or a lack of ambition. Table 3.1 sets out a typology of the seven APROs (inclusive of their membership, objectives, and constitutive laws and institutions) which lie on a spectrum from the more legalized and institutionalized to the more free-form entities.

3 APROs that have Chosen to Integrate: The Prioritization of Laws and Institutions

This section deals with ASEAN and the EAEU, arguably two of the most advanced entities out of the seven APROs. Not only are ASEAN and the EAEU fairly clear in what they want to achieve, the cooperation among the member states in these two organizations has evolved to the extent that legally binding obligations are beginning to be applied to intraregional relations. Moreover, more strongly integrative projects that require synchronization and harmonization, such as the formation of a free trade area, are being taken. One thing to note about these two APROs is that as their legalization and institutionalization take place, they are developing formalization characteristics particular to the Asia-Pacific, which may be unlike what has been seen in other regional organizations.

3.1 The Association of Southeast Asian Nations

Out of the seven APROs, the most developed one in terms of substantive ambition, structure, and achievement is ostensibly ASEAN. This Southeast Asian regional organization comprises ten members—Brunei, Cambodia, Indonesia, Laos, Malaysia, Myanmar, Philippines, Singapore, Thailand, and Vietnam. Presently in its sixth decade, ASEAN has achieved several milestones as an organization and secured the desired benefits for its members since its five founding states—Indonesia, Malaysia, Philippines, Singapore, and Thailand—adopted the non-binding ASEAN Declaration in 1967.[10]

[10] ASEAN, 'ASEAN Declaration (*Bangkok Declaration*, 1967)' <http://asean.org/the-asean-declaration-bangkok-declaration-bangkok-8-august-1967/> accessed 29 December 2017.

Table 3.1 A Typology of the Seven APROs

Classification	Legal and Institutional		Political and Diplomatic				
Organization	Association of Southeast Asian Nations (ASEAN)	Eurasian Economic Union (EAEU)	Shanghai Cooperation Organization (SCO)	South Asian Association for Regional Cooperation (SAARC)	Pacific Islands Forum (PIF)	Melanesian Spearhead Group (MSG)	Asia-Pacific Economic Cooperation (APEC)
Members	Brunei, Cambodia, Indonesia, Laos, Malaysia, Myanmar, Philippines, Singapore, Thailand, and Vietnam	Armenia, Belarus, Kazakhstan, the Kyrgyz Republic, and Russia	Kazakhstan, the Kyrgyz Republic, People's Republic of China, Russia, Tajikistan, and Uzbekistan	Afghanistan, Bangladesh, Bhutan, India, the Maldives, Nepal, Pakistan, and Sri Lanka	Australia, the Cook Islands, the Federated States of Micronesia, Fiji, Kiribati, Nauru, New Zealand, Niue, Palau, Papua New Guinea, Republic of Marshall Islands, Samoa, Solomon Islands, Tonga, Tuvalu, and Vanuatu	Fiji, Papua New Guinea, Solomon Islands, Vanuatu, and the Front de Libération Nationale Kanak et Socialiste (FLNKS)	Australia, Brunei Darussalam, Canada, Chile, China, Chinese Taipei, Hong Kong, SAR, Indonesia, Japan, Korea, Malaysia, Mexico, New Zealand, Papua New Guinea, Peru, the Philippines, Russia, Singapore, Thailand, the United States, and Vietnam
Constituent Instrument(s)	Declaration of the ASEAN 1967 [Bangkok Declaration] Charter of the ASEAN 2007	Treaty of the EAEU 2014	Charter of the SCO 2001	Charter of the SAARC 1985	Agreement Establishing the PIF Secretariat 2000Agreement Establishing the PIF 2005	Agreed Principles of Co-operation among Independent States of Melanesia 1988 Agreement Establishing the MSG 2007	N/A (founded as an informal ministerial-level dialogue group) First political instrument: APEC Leaders' Bogor Declaration 1994

(continued)

Table 3.1 Continued

Classification	Legal and Institutional		Political and Diplomatic				
Objectives	Political-security, economic, sociocultural cooperation and integration	Economic integration	Generally political and security cooperation; scope for broader cooperation	Economic and security cooperation	Economic and security cooperation	Economic development priorities	Economic cooperation
Key features	Intergovernmental structure, consensus decision-making, governing bodies comprising ministers of member states, possesses dispute settlement mechanisms	Customs union, intergovernmental structure, consensus decision-making, governing bodies comprising ministers of member states, possesses dispute settlement mechanisms	Intergovernmental structure, consensus decision-making, governing bodies comprising ministers of member states, specific counterterrorism body	Intergovernmental structure, consensus decision-making, governing bodies comprising ministers of member states	Intergovernmental structure, consensus decision-making, governing bodies comprising ministers of member states	Intergovernmental structure, consensus decision-making, governing bodies comprising ministers of member states	Intergovernmental dialogue group, consensus decision-making

The first breakthrough was the formation of ASEAN as a political organization to counter regional insecurities. This was a landmark step towards normalizing regional relations in an openly hostile post-colonial environment that faced communist pressures both domestically and externally. Concurrently, territorial tensions threatened to erupt into armed conflict—the Philippines had asserted sovereignty over North Borneo, Singapore had been expelled from the newly formed Malaysian Federation to be an independent state, and Indonesia's acts of aggression against Malaysia and Singapore all punctuated the 1960s. Considering that the Association of Southeast Asia set up in 1961 and the Malayan, Philippine, and Indonesian tripartite (Maphilindo) of 1963 had dissolved due to intraregional hostility, the resolve of these states to mend ties was noteworthy.[11]

Given the geopolitical instabilities and 'third world' statuses of the member states, achieving peace and security in order to carry out nation-building was the topmost priority of ASEAN states. ASEAN was therefore a confidence-building security forum in the guise of economic and sociocultural cooperation.[12] By not confronting head-on and thereby escalating mutually sensitive issues, friendly relations eventually developed. The ensuing regional stability allowed the states to focus on their domestic agendas. Political flexibility was so prized that law and institutions were only initiated in ASEAN in 1976 during the groundbreaking inaugural ASEAN Summit.

By the time of the Summit, member states had built up sufficient trust over the first decade to adopt ASEAN's first legally binding instrument, the Treaty of Amity and Cooperation, which emphasized the obligation of the non-use of force, the peaceful settlement of disputes, and the non-interference in one another's domestic matters.[13] They adopted another treaty to formalize and institutionalize regional relations by establishing the ASEAN Secretariat in Jakarta, although the Secretary-General and the Secretariat were to act according to the member states' dictates and had merely administrative rather than executive functions.[14] The ASEAN states also enlarged the economic cooperation framework and its developing institutional capacities to achieve such outcomes.[15]

In all this, power remained firmly vested in the ASEAN states—intergovernmental executive action dominated and did not shift substantively to the institutions that were established. Despite the numerous declarations adopted thereafter, few of the economic

[11] Alastair Taylor, 'Malaysia, Indonesia–and Maphilindo' (1964) 19 IJ 155; Vincent Pollard, 'ASA and ASEAN, 1961–1967: Southeast Asian Regionalism' (1970) 10 AS 244.

[12] Rodolfo Severino, *ASEAN* (ISEAS 2008) 11.

[13] Treaty of Amity and Cooperation in Southeast Asia (signed and entered into force 24 February 1976) art. 2.

[14] Agreement on the Establishment of the ASEAN Secretariat (entered into force 24 February 1976) preamble para 3 <http://asean.org/?static_post=asean-secretariat-basic-documents-agreement-on-the-establishment-of-the-asean-secretariat-bali-24-february-1976-2> accessed 29 December 2017.

[15] Declaration of ASEAN Concord (Bali Concord I) (entered into force 24 February 1976) para B.1–B.4 <http://asean.org/?static_post=declaration-of-asean-concord-indonesia-24-february-1976> accessed 29 December 2017.

partnerships materialized or delivered results.[16] What the ASEAN grouping had procured for its members was, rather, a greater international profile, more trustworthy intraregional bonds, and a regional stability that enabled the ASEAN members to attain middle developing statuses.[17]

True regional cooperation was catalyzed into action only after Cambodia, Laos, Myanmar, and Vietnam joined in the 1990s (Brunei had joined in the 1980s), where these fledgling economies had hoped ASEAN membership would facilitate their national development, as it had done for the original members.[18] Regional crises in the late 1990s and early 2000s—namely, the 1997 Asian financial meltdown and influenza pandemics—further intensified cooperation as ASEAN states realized that the only way for their economies to be resilient and flourish was to integrate more closely. Increasing formalization, through hard and soft laws and institutional bodies, was intended to manage the expanding agendas on security, the economy, and socio-cultural development. There were general instruments encompassing these three broad groups like the Hanoi Plan of Action (1998), Bali Concord II (2003), and Vientiane Action Programme (2003).[19] There were also specific economic instruments such as the Agreement on the Common Effective Preferential Tariff Scheme for the ASEAN Free Trade Area (1992) and the Framework Agreement on the ASEAN Investment Area (1998).[20] For security, there was the ASEAN Regional Forum and the ASEAN Defence Ministers' Meeting, which considered military and comprehensive security issues such as human trafficking and disaster management.[21]

In terms of external relations, ASEAN was also relatively successful in the Asia-Pacific in promoting closer ties with dialogue partners through the ASEAN Regional

[16] Shaun Narine, *Explaining ASEAN: Regionalism in Southeast Asia* (Lynne Rienner Publishers 2002) 28–9.

[17] Elin Bjarnegard, 'Reluctant Tigers: Economic Growth, Erratic Democratization Processes and Continuing Political Gender Inequality in Southeast Asia' in Terence Chong (ed), *Globalization and Its Counter-forces in Southeast Asia* (ISEAS 2008) 284.

[18] Niklas Aschoff, 'Joining the Neighbours: The Accessions to ASEAN in the 1990s' in Tanja Börzel, Lukas Goltermann, Mathis Lohaus, and Kai Striebinger (eds), *Roads to Regionalism: Genesis, Design and Effects of Regional Organizations* (Ashgate 2012).

[19] ASEAN, 'Hanoi Plan of Action' (1998) <http://asean.org/?static_post=hanoi-plan-of-action> accessed 29 December 2017; ASEAN, 'Declaration of ASEAN Concord' (Bali Concord II, 2003) <http://asean.org/?static_post=declaration-of-asean-concord-ii-bali-concord-ii> accessed 29 December 2017; ASEAN, 'Vientiane Action Programme' (2003) <http://www.asean.org/storage/images/archive/VAP-10th%20ASEAN%20Summit.pdf> accessed 29 December 2017.

[20] ASEAN, 'Common Effective Preferential Tariff Scheme for the ASEAN Free Trade Area' (1992) <http://www.asean.org/storage/images/2012/Economic/AFTA/Common_Effective_Preferential_Tariff/Agreement%20on%20the%20Common%20Effective%20Preferential%20Tariff%20Scheme%20for%20the%20ASEAN%20Free%20Trade%20Area.pdf> 7 December 2018; ASEAN, 'Framework Agreement on the ASEAN Investment Area' (1998) <http://www.asean.org/wp-content/uploads/images/2012/Economic/AIA/Agreement/Framework%20Agreement%20on%20the%20ASEAN%20Investment%20Area%20(AIA)%201998.pdf> accessed 29 December 2017.

[21] ASEAN, 'ASEAN Regional Forum' (ARF) <http://aseanregionalforum.asean.org> accessed 7 December 2018; ASEAN, 'ASEAN Defence Ministers' Meeting' (ADMM) <https://admm.asean.org> accessed 29 December 2017.

Forum for regional security, the East Asia Summit for economic development, and the ASEAN Plus forums, in order to engage with the most important dialogue partners such as the United States, China, Australia, India, Korea, and Japan.[22] All these platforms are significant as they brought together Asia-Pacific powers that did not belong to any regional organization of their own (for example, Japan and Korea), or would otherwise not be able to sit round a common table due to longstanding grievances (such as China, Japan, and Korea).

Prior to 2007, ASEAN agreements were estimated to have only a compliance rate of 30 per cent and this was insufficient to reap the envisioned benefits of their cooperation.[23] The lack of compliance also meant that it was quite impossible for the region to transform into a free trade area attractive to businesses and investors.[24] Genuine legalization and institutionalization only came about in ASEAN's fortieth year upon the adoption of the ASEAN Charter (2007). Through this restructuring, ASEAN states have sought a more active and effective engagement with, and in, the international legal order.

Imbued with legal personality, member states thus undertook to build the ASEAN Community founded on the political-security, economic, and sociocultural pillars.[25] The ASEAN Charter also enshrined human rights and democracy as binding obligations upon the member states for the first time in the organization's history, as well as providing for dispute settlement and monitoring mechanisms to improve compliance.[26] To complement ASEAN's very first constituent treaty that was designated as the legal and institutional framework of a rules-based organization, member states adopted a slew of soft legal instruments, such as the ASEAN Community Blueprints, as well as hard laws like the ASEAN Trade in Goods Agreement (2009) and the ASEAN Comprehensive Investment Agreement (2009) (to bring about the single market and production base).[27]

To ensure the execution of these laws, the organizational structure of ASEAN was revised according to thematic and intergovernmental priorities. Therefore, most of the bodies within ASEAN continued to be helmed by state representatives who possessed executive powers of governance in their own countries on matters

[22] See generally ASEAN, 'ASEAN External Relations' <http://asean.org/asean/external-relations> accessed 29 December 2017.

[23] Tommy Koh, Walter Woon, Andrew Tan, and Chan Sze-Wei, 'Charter Makes ASEAN Stronger, More United and effective' *Straits Times* (Singapore, 8 August 2007) A6.

[24] ASEAN, 'Report of the Eminent Persons Group of the ASEAN Charter' (2007) <http://www.asean.org/storage/images/archive/19247.pdf> accessed 29 December 2017.

[25] ASEAN Charter (adopted 20 November 2007, entered into force 15 December 2008) preamble.

[26] Ibid., preamble and arts 1, 2, and 14.

[27] ASEAN, 'Roadmap for an ASEAN Community' ('Blueprints', 2009–2015) <http://www.asean.org/storage/images/ASEAN_RTK_2014/2_Roadmap_for_ASEAN_Community_20092015.pdf> accessed 29 December 2017; ASEAN, 'ASEAN Trade in Goods Agreement' (2009) <http://fta.miti.gov.my/miti-fta/resources/2.ASEAN_Trade_in_Goods_Agreement_.pdf> accessed 29 December 2017; ASEAN, 'ASEAN Comprehensive Investment Agreement' (2009) <http://www.asean.org/storage/images/2013/economic/aia/ACIA_Final_Text_26%20Feb%202009.pdf> accessed 29 December 2017.

of foreign policy, economics and trade, security, human development, and the like. To elaborate, the heads of state or government constitute the grouping's highest decision-making body, the ASEAN Summit; the ASEAN Coordinating Council, which manages and decides on most matters of regional cooperation, comprises all the foreign ministers; and the ministers responsible for specific portfolios or thematic issues in the multi-focus executive governance bodies comprise the ASEAN Community Councils and ASEAN Sectoral Ministerial Bodies.[28] In addition, all levels of ASEAN decision-making have to be by consensus. This is understandably difficult to achieve on sensitive issues, hence it is often critiqued that a minimalist decision based on the 'lowest common denominator' is often taken to suit the comfort level of all the member states.[29] In economic cooperation, however, the ASEAN Minus X modality can be employed, meaning that members which are ready to move ahead on certain decisions or agreements can do so, while the remaining 'X' members will do so at a later date.[30]

The ASEAN Secretary-General, who possesses *de jure* ministerial rank and is present and to be consulted at ASEAN ministerial-level meetings, does not have comparable powers of executive governance, agenda-setting, and decision-making.[31] Instead, there is the Committee of Permanent Representatives, which is housed within the ASEAN Secretariat, to project and protect member states' interests.[32] It is somewhat ironic that these permanent representatives, who are only national ambassadors to ASEAN and *not* of ministerial rank, have the de facto competence to exert their influence in the execution of integration activities.

Although ASEAN members proclaimed the establishment of the ASEAN Community on 31 December 2015, comprising the ASEAN Political-Security, Economic, and Socio-Cultural Communities, it is widely acknowledged that the transformative process is still gradually unfolding.[33] The first decade of state practice under the ASEAN Charter's legalization and institutionalization framework has been patchy as member states face up to the costs of integration. Furthermore, none of the ASEAN dispute settlement mechanisms has been activated. Nonetheless, while there are constant temptations to slide back to the flexible modalities, ASEAN states do realize that transforming into a rules-based organization is the only way forward. Any regression back to diplomatic flexibilities would compromise the substantive achievement of goals both intraregionally and in the wider region. Any failure to comply with agreements with external partners would cause ASEAN to lose the external credibility it so dearly seeks.

[28] ASEAN Charter (n 25) arts 7–10.

[29] Marise Cremona, David Kleimann, Joris Larik, Rena Lee, and Pascal Vennesson, *ASEAN's External Agreements: Law, Practice and the Quest for Collective Action* (CUP 2016) 179. See also Shaun Narine, *Explaining ASEAN: Regionalism in Southeast Asia* (Lynne Rienner Publishers 2002) 33.

[30] ASEAN Charter (n 25) art. 21(2). [31] Ibid. art 11. [32] Ibid. art 12.

[33] ASEAN, 'Chairman's Statement at the 30th ASEAN Summit, Manila' (29 April 2017) <http://asean.org/storage/2017/04/Chairs-Statement-of-30th-ASEAN-Summit_FINAL.pdf> accessed 29 December 2017.

Moreover, there is no way for the ASEAN region to thrive in the contemporary geopolitical and economic environment without law and institutions. The member states appear to recognize that legalization and institutionalization remain the most stable and predictable means of dealing with strategic exigencies in the long term. This is in spite of the examples of the Cambodian and Philippine 'unilateral alignments' with external powers such as China on investment and territorial issues like the South China Sea.[34] Therefore, to succeed the ASEAN Community-building Roadmap that expired in 2015 upon the establishment of the Community, the regional leaders adopted the 'ASEAN 2025: Forging Ahead Together' package of instruments, which articulated ASEAN's next phase of growth from 2016 to 2025.[35] This Roadmap emphatically reiterated the organization's commitment to cooperation through legalization and institutionalization.[36] As a result, the ASEAN grouping remains a forerunner in the Asia-Pacific where the development of and participation in international law is concerned, carving out its own *sui generis* path of intraregional integration.

3.2 The Eurasian Economic Union

The Eurasian Economic Union (EAEU) is one of the newest regional organizations in the Asia-Pacific, only formally established on 1 January 2015 after the adoption of the Treaty of the Eurasian Economic Union by Belarus, Kazakhstan, and Russia in 2014.[37] Two other members, Armenia and the Kyrgyz Republic, joined in 2015.[38] Perhaps because its emergence is at a time where the international order is fairly legalized, or because of its proximity to Europe or the urgency to integrate seriously in the contemporary economic climate, the EAEU is the only other APRO apart from ASEAN which has expressly taken on more legal and institutional dimensions. In fact, it goes further than ASEAN, explicitly modelling itself on the European Union, and it even includes the formation of a customs union and supranational institutions

[34] See e.g. Zhang Haizhou, 'Making Group Investment Viable' *China Daily* (25 December 2016) <http://www.chinadaily.com.cn/business/2016-12/26/content_27771168.htm> accessed 29 December 2017; Ralph Jennings, 'Philippines Takes Strides toward Alliance with China' *Voice of America* (23 December 2016) <http://www.voanews.com/a/philippines-takes-strides-toward-alliance-with-china/3647995.html> accessed 29 December 2017.

[35] ASEAN, 'ASEAN 2025: Forging Ahead Together (2016–2025)' ('*ASEAN 2025*', 2015) <http://www.asean.org/storage/2015/12/ASEAN-2025-Forging-Ahead-Together-final.pdf> accessed 29 December 2017.

[36] Ibid.

[37] Treaty of the Eurasian Economic Union (adopted 23 December 2014, entered into force 1 January 2015) <http://www.un.org/en/ga/sixth/70/docs/treaty_on_eeu.pdf> accessed 29 December 2017.

[38] Treaty on Accession of the Republic of Armenia to the Eurasian Economic Union Treaty (signed 10 October 2014, entered into force 2 January 2015) <https://docs.eaeunion.org/docs/en-us/0017354/itia_11102014_doc.pdf> accessed 29 December 2017; Treaty on Accession of the Kyrgyz Republic to the Eurasian Economic Union Treaty (signed on 23 December 2014, entered into force 12 August 2015) <http://www.eurasiancommission.org/en/nae/news/Pages/12-08-2015-1.aspx> accessed 29 December 2017.

like a commission and permanent court. However, unlike ASEAN and the EU, this Central Asian entity is presently focused solely on economic development rather than security and sociocultural issues, although there is latent potential for such expansion in the future.[39]

At first glance, although the EAEU structure appears geared towards supranational institutional authority, the attitudes and actions exhibited in regional cooperation indicate a less legalized and institutionalized modality. This is because the geopolitical outlooks of the five member states—either individually or regionally—have not quite overcome the need to assert a state-centric type of sovereignty that is common throughout the Asia-Pacific. There remains some reluctance in adhering to the laws and institutions they have constructed for their regionalism efforts to reap results.[40] Nonetheless, the EAEU states seem to view regional cooperation as imperative to national prosperity and have professed to support regionalism to the extent that law and institutions will advance that objective.[41] In this respect, therefore, the EAEU members behave much like the ASEAN states in their transition to a more rules-based and institutions-led mode of operations.

Although the EAEU is a young organization, cooperation activities have been carried out among the member states for some time. The EAEU is a culmination of the regional cooperation efforts in the years prior.[42] The disintegration of the Soviet Union brought about much economic uncertainty and the newly independent post-Soviet states were unsure of how they would transform into market economies, even though some of them had banded together in the loose association of the Commonwealth of Independent States. Consequently, the 'rouble-zone' collapse caused a deep transitional recession in the 1990s that made the affected states inward-looking, focusing on stabilizing the domestic polity and economy.[43] This experience (much like that in the ASEAN region during the Asian Financial Crisis of 1997–8) led the Central Asian states to prioritize economic development and resilience. One way of doing so was through multilateral cooperation, whereupon Belarus, Russia, Kazakhstan, the Kyrgyz Republic, and Tajikistan adopted the Treaty on the

[39] Sean Roberts and Arkady Moshes, 'The Eurasian Economic Union: A Case of Reproductive Integration?' (2016) 32 PSA 542, 544.

[40] Rilka Dragneva and Kataryna Wolczuk, 'Eurasian Economic Integration: Institutions, Promises and Faultlines' in David Cadier (ed), *LSE IDEAS Reports: The Geopolitics of Eurasian Economic* Integration *(LSE Ideas,* 19 June 2014) 10–12 <http://www.lse.ac.uk/ideas/Assets/Documents/reports/LSE-IDEAS-Geopolitics-of-Eurasian-Economic-Intergration.pdf> accessed 7 December 2018.

[41] Roberts and Moshes (n 39) 544. See also Eurasian Economic Commission, *Eurasian Economic Integration: Facts and Figures* (EEC Doc 1H2016) 56–69.

[42] For a chronology of the events culminating in the formation of the EAEU, see Eurasian Economic Union, 'Eurasian Economic Union' <http://mfa.gov.by/en/organizations/membership/list/aa16658947a49c28.html> accessed 29 December 2017 (hosted by the Foreign Ministry of Belarus).

[43] E Vinokurov and A Libman, 'Regional Integration and Economic Convergence in the Post-Soviet Space: Experience of the Decade of Growth' (2012) 50 JCMS 112, 113.

Establishment of the Eurasian Economic Community (EurAsEC 2000);[44] while Uzbekistan's participation was short-lived (2006–8).[45]

The objective of the EurAsEC was straightforward—the formation of a customs union and Single Economic Space.[46] As the regional economies expanded and stabilized during the energy boom of the 2000s, the EurAsEC achieved its major milestone when the three members which shared the closest economic relations—Belarus, Kazakhstan, and Russia—launched a customs union on 6 October 2007.[47] The remaining members were expected to join when they were ready.[48]

Apart from the customs union which actively promoted regional integration, two more significant factors built up the credibility of the EurAsEC as a regional organization relying on law and institutions rather than capricious political diplomacy. The first was its incorporation as an international legal body.[49] The second, and more importantly, was the powers of and active recourse to the EurAsEC Community Court to settle disputes arising from the decisions of EurAsEC bodies or from the provisions of international treaties in force within the EurAsEC.[50] Decisions of the EurAsEC Court were binding on the parties to the dispute.[51] The Court began operating on 1 January 2012, and by 2014 it had considered eight cases which had reached final decision and six cases were pending.[52] Although the number of cases before the Court has been small, the determined usage of the Court—coupled with the launch of the customs union—signals that there has been a certain degree of legal and institutional commitment in the Eurasian economic integration project.

In 2014, on the basis that the efforts of the EurAsEC had been reasonably successful, it was deemed time to progress to the next stage of integration. The EurAsEC was dissolved and the EAEU was formed. In line with the goals of the free movement of goods, services, capital, and labour within the EAEU, the member states agreed to pursue harmonized policies as determined by the EAEU Treaty and applicable

[44] Agreement on the Foundation of the Eurasian Economic Community (EurAsEC Agreement) (signed 10 October 2000, entered into force 30 May 2001) <https://wits.worldbank.org/GPTAD/PDF/archive/EAEC.pdf> accessed 29 December 2017.

[45] EurAsEC, 'About the Eurasian Economic Community' <http://www.evrazes.com/en/about/> accessed 29 December 2017.

[46] EurAsEC Agreement (n 44) art. 2.

[47] EurAsEC Integration Committee Secretariat, 'EurAsEC Today' (Moscow, 2011) 32 <http://www.evrazes.com/i/other/EurAsEC-today_eng.pdf> accessed 29 December 2017.

[48] Ibid. [49] EurAsEC Agreement (n 44) art. 11.

[50] The Statute of the Court of the Eurasian Economic Community (5 July 2010) regulates the operating procedure of the Court, its competence, and legal proceedings: see <http://sudevrazes.org/en/main.aspxqueguideq1681.html> accessed 29 December 2017.

[51] Aliaksandr Danilevich, 'The Court of the Eurasian Economic Community is Tackling Challenges of the Eurasian Integration' (*CIS Arbitration Forum*, 20 August 2014) <http://www.cisarbitration.com/2014/08/20/the-court-of-the-eurasian-economic-community-is-tackling-challenges-of-the-eurasian-integration/> accessed 29 December 2017.

[52] Ibid.

international agreements.[53] Additionally, key EAEU institutions were to manage the economic integration outlined by this legal framework.[54] Broadly speaking, the EAEU works on a hybridized intergovernmental and supranational basis. The highest authority is the Supreme Eurasian Economic Council (SEEC), comprising the presidents of the EAEU states.[55] This is followed by the Eurasian Intergovernmental Council (EIC), composed of prime ministers.[56] At the third level is the Council of the Eurasian Economic Commission (CEEC) that consists of the deputy prime ministers and presides over the Board of the Eurasian Economic Commission (BEEC), which has ministerial-level officials in charge of specific areas such as trade, customs cooperation, energy, and agriculture.[57] The SEEC, EIC, and CEEC make decisions by consensus, while the BEEC does this by two-thirds qualified majority on regular issues and by consensus on sensitive topics ('sensitive' being determined by the SEEC).[58]

Administratively, the Eurasian Economic Commission (EEC) is the permanent supranational regulatory body of the EAEU. Its members are appointed by the CEEC and the BEEC. It acts as the central secretariat that manages the regional integration projects. The core tasks of the EEC are to support the operation and development of the EAEU and to draft proposals on economic integration within the Union.[59] Decisions of the EEC are part of the Union law and are directly binding upon all member states.[60] These competences include: customs tariff and non-tariff regulation; customs administration; technical regulation; sanitary and phytosanitary measures; trade regimes for third parties; macroeconomic, competition, and energy policy; industrial and agricultural subsidies; natural monopolies; state and/or municipal procurement; services, trade, and investments; transport; currency policy; intellectual property; labour migration; and financial markets.[61]

The Court of the EAEU ensures the uniform application of the EAEU Treaty and other relevant treaties by the member states and bodies.[62] According to the Statute of the Court, the right of access to the Court, *inter alia*, belongs to a juridical person registered under the legislation of a member state or a third state, or a natural person registered as an individual entrepreneur in accordance with the legislation of a member state or a third state.[63] Producers and investors of a third state have the right to apply to the Court to protect their interests if actions (or omissions) of the EEC violated the

[53] EEC (n 41) 7–8, 23–5.

[54] Treaty of the Eurasian Economic Union (n 37) arts 3–6.

[55] Ibid. art. 10.

[56] Ibid. art. 14.

[57] EEC (n 41) 34–7.

[58] Treaty of the Eurasian Economic Union (n 37) arts 16–18.

[59] Eurasian Economic Commission, 'Eurasian Economic Integration: Facts and Figures' (EEC Doc 1H2015) 7 <http://www.eurasiancommission.org/en/Documents/broshura26_ENGL_2014.pdf> accessed 29 December 2017.

[60] Treaty of the Eurasian Economic Union (n 37) Annex 1: Regulation on the Eurasian Economic Commission, art. 13. See also Ekatarina Diyachenko and Kirill Entin, 'The Court of the Eurasian Economic Union: Challenges and Perspectives' (2017) 5 RLJ 2.

[61] Treaty of the Eurasian Economic Union (n 37) Annex 1: Regulation on the Eurasian Economic Commission, art. 2(4)(i)–(xx).

[62] Treaty of the Eurasian Economic Union (n 37) art. 19.

[63] Ibid. arts 39–41.

rights and legitimate interests of the economic entity envisaged by the Treaty and/or international treaties within the Union.[64]

While the formation of the customs union is indubitably a marker of integrative success, the lack of statistical data and scholarly scrutiny makes it extremely difficult to assess in greater detail the extent to which the integration of the Eurasian States is occurring. Questions as to whether intraregional and external trade has increased, the specific sectors in which greater or less integration has taken place, and the reasons why remain unanswered. In addition, pertinent policy and political issues continue to be obscure. Annual brochures published by the EEC proclaim ever-growing integration and trade. Conversely, scholarly or policy/think-tank commentaries highlight the problems of strong executive action and Russian hegemony.[65] In relation to these political motivations, although the EAEU is clearly a regional economic project, the contradictions in the integration modalities and the power imbalances among the members highlight the potential of the EAEU being (or becoming) part of the Russian strategic and economic agenda within the region and vis-à-vis external powers such as China or the EU.[66]

At the general institutional level, it is uncertain what the political and substantive motivations for the EurAsEC's transition to the EAEU were, besides the mimicking of the European experience from that of a community to a union. There appears to be little difference between the objectives of the EAEU and those of the EurAsEC, since the organizational goals and framework remain relatively similar. The only clearly visible variations between the organizations seems to be the slight difference in the membership and institutional structure, while the organizational functions do not demonstrate substantive changes.

The Eurasian integration process indubitably sets in place supranational modes of competence. However, observers have noted that this modality is incongruent with the state-centric outlooks which the member states possess, and that policy coordination across the Union is underdeveloped and the institutions of the EAEU remain fairly weak.[67] It is unlikely that these post-Soviet states, particularly Russia, are keen to have the EEC direct their actions. It is more likely that intergovernmental modes of decision-making would be applied in the EAEU. If compared to ASEAN, arguably the only other APRO which is pursuing regional economic integration, the EAEU might be seen as being more committed to regional integration endeavours by virtue of its legal and institutional strictures. However, in terms of adherence to the regional laws and

[64] Belarus Ministry of Foreign Affairs, 'Eurasian Economic Union (EAEU): 40 Frequently Asked Questions' (2015) 5 <http://mfa.gov.by/upload/EAEU-eng-broshura.doc> accessed 18 April 2019.

[65] See e.g. Çaǿla Gül Yesevi, 'New Regionalism in Post-Soviet Territory: Evolution from Eurasian Economic Community to Eurasian Economic Union' (2014) 5 MJSS 1986, 1989; Ksenia Kirkham, The Formation of the Eurasian Economic Union: How Successful is the Russian Regional Hegemony?' (2016) 7 JES 111; Ivaylo Gatev and Glenn Diesen, 'Eurasian Encounters: The Eurasian Economic Union and the Shanghai Cooperation Organization' (2016) 17 EPS 133.

[66] Gatev and Diesen, ibid.

[67] Roberts and Moshes (n 39) 548–9.

institutions in the integration process, it could be that ASEAN and the EAEU are quite similar in practice in that they strongly prefer intergovernmental action and executive dominance in policy-making. Thus, there is a tension between the rule of law and institutions on the one hand and the entrenchment of political decision-making on the other.

4 APROs in the Status Quo: Flexible Cooperation as Political and Diplomatic Entities

From the above, ASEAN and the EAEU are demonstrably more developed in terms of ambition, outlook, and strategy among the seven APROs this chapter examines. The member states of both organizations have consolidated their cooperation efforts and taken steps to formalize their standing as organizations with legal personality in the international order and in their relations among themselves and with external parties. They have done this in order to secure the gains of deeper economic integration, the complex processes of which require the stability and predictability that legalization and institutionalization can provide to an organizational system.

This does not mean that the remaining five APROs, discussed below, are 'inferior' or less useful because the member states have not chosen to integrate more closely or to increase the level of law and institutions in their regional framework. The SCO, SAARC, PIF, MSG, and APEC, which are often criticized for lacking meaning and effectiveness, are organizations that are more fluid in their agenda and outlook and have remained as political and diplomatic entities because such a status arguably better protects their interests. Political flexibility is more attractive to these five APROs due to strategic factors such as the presence of competing powers within the organization or in the wider region. It also impinges less on the member states, be it capacity constraints or compromises on sovereignty. In certain cases, the flexibility and informality pave the way to a wider ambit of potential cooperation.

That said, the expansive flexibility and scope of cooperation can render these regional organizations less effective than they could be. This is especially so if the member states are overly ambitious, such that their collective vision lacks clarity and is often revised, there is a lack of capacity and disorganization in the organization, and there is insufficient political will to ensure substantive cooperation is carried out. In the following, therefore, the SCO, SAARC, PIF, and MSG will be examined for their degree of cooperation and usefulness to members. Such an exercise is admittedly subjective but is arguably authentic on analysis of the existing data. Moreover, the paucity of information, skimpy body of soft laws and political documents emanating from these organizations themselves, and the few scholarly studies produced could indicate the lack of genuine cooperation, in terms of either closer relations or substantive projects.

APEC will be analyzed separately as it can be considered an outlier of sorts, being more a diplomatic forum than a regional organization.

4.1 Shanghai Cooperation Organization

The SCO is an intergovernmental organization established through the Charter of the Shanghai Cooperation Organization (2001) by the six member states of the People's Republic of China, Kazakhstan, the Kyrgyz Republic, Russia, Tajikistan, and Uzbekistan.[68] The SCO succeeded the Shanghai Five, an informal grouping initiated by China in 1996 and which comprised all six SCO members save Uzbekistan. In 2016, India and Pakistan signed the Memoranda of Understanding to formally join the SCO, and became full members at the Tashkent Summit meeting of the SCO heads of state in 2017.[69]

The SCO Charter has an expansive list of aims that includes strengthening regional relations among its members; promoting cooperation on politics, economics and trade, energy, transportation, tourism, science and technology, sociocultural issues, the environment, and education; safeguarding regional peace, security, and stability; and fostering a democratic and equitable international political and economic order. While this does not clearly show what the SCO's *raison d'être* is, two priority areas of cooperation have emerged. The first is confidence-building and the strengthening of regional relations in a challenging environment. The second is security cooperation.[70] The priority of regional security is emphasized in the SCO Charter where, in addition to reducing regional tensions, the member states share a common task of countering the 'three evils' of terrorism, separatism, and religious extremism within their own jurisdictions.[71] In particular, Russia and China were (and continue to be) trying to keep the dissension from the Chechens and Uighurs respectively under control.[72] One prominent success of the grouping has been the de-escalation of border tensions

[68] Charter of the Shanghai Cooperation Organization (adopted 7 June 2002, entered into force 19 September 2003) <http://eng.sectsco.org/load/203013/> accessed 18 April 2019.

[69] André Hantke, 'Will India and Pakistan Cripple the SCO?' *The Diplomat* (9 November 2016) <http://thediplomat.com/2016/11/will-india-and-pakistan-cripple-the-sco> accessed 29 December 2017; Kallol Bhattacherjee, 'India, Pakistan become full members of SCO' *The Hindu* (9 June 2017) <https://www.thehindu.com/news/national/india-pakistan-become-full-members-of-shanghai-cooperation-organisation-sco/article18912600.ece> accessed 18 April 2019.

[70] Peter Korzun, 'SCO: Story of Success and Expansion' *Strategic Culture Online* (29 January 2016) <http://www.strategic-culture.org/pview/2016/06/29/shanghai-cooperation-organization-story-success-expansion.html> accessed 29 December 2017.

[71] 'SCO to Further Contain "Three Evil Forces": Official' *Xinhua* (Beijing, 11 September 2014) <http://www.chinadaily.com.cn/world/2014xisco/2014-09/11/content_18584401.htm> accessed 18 April 2019.

[72] Chung Chien-peng, 'The Shanghai Cooperation Organization: China's Changing Influence in Central Asia' (2004) 180 China Quarterly 889, 998. See also Jyotsna Bakshi, 'Shanghai Cooperation Organization (SCO) Before and After September 11' (2002) 26 Strategic Analysis 265, 269.

through the development of a demilitarized zone along China's northern and north-western borders, the settlement of territorial disputes along the former Soviet–Chinese border, and the non-use of force among the member states.[73] Moreover, a specific counterterrorism body was set up alongside the other executive bodies within the SCO governance structure.[74]

In terms of operations, the governing bodies of the SCO comprise the Council of Heads of State; the Council of Heads of Government (i.e., the prime ministers); the Council of Ministers of Foreign Affairs; the Meetings of Heads of Ministries and/or Agencies; the Council of National Coordinators (national-based departments dealing with SCO regional cooperation); and the Regional Antiterrorist Structure (based in Tashkent, Uzbekistan).[75] All these governing bodies make decisions by consensus, in line with the firm intergovernmental stance of the SCO.[76] The SCO Secretariat, headquartered in Beijing, is headed by the Executive Secretary who is appointed by the Council of Heads of State (as advised by the Council of Ministers of Foreign Affairs).[77] The Secretariat has little decision-making power and is only to provide organizational and technical support to the regional activities and prepare budget proposals.

Apart from the management of tensions, the lack of a firm identity and the indeterminate data on member states' compliance with the weak laws and institutions of the SCO make it difficult to assess whether the wide-ranging organizational objectives have been met or are actively pursued. It is even more difficult to determine if the SCO has underlying strategic agendas such as maintaining the Sino-Russo balance of power,[78] fostering a Sino-Russo partnership,[79] or acting as a counterfoil to the United States' influence in the region.[80] What is apparent, however, is that the SCO operates more as a strategic and security grouping geared towards reducing regional suspicions and building confidence among the members. There is a type of detachment observed among the SCO states. They do not seek to deepen interaction among or with the international community through this regional platform. Besides the fact that there are no notable hard or soft laws promulgated in the SCO, and regional instruments are mainly communiqués and rhetorical or perfunctory declarations, the clear preference among the member states is to use ad hoc, non-institutionalized measures in regional relations.[81]

[73] Flemming Splidsboel Hansen, 'The Shanghai Cooperation Organization' (2008) 39 AA 217, 217–18.

[74] Charter of the Shanghai Cooperation Organization (n 68) preamble.

[75] Ibid. arts 4–11. See also SCO, 'Structure of the Shanghai Cooperation Organization' at <http://eng.sectsco.org/structure> accessed 29 December 2017.

[76] Charter of the Shanghai Cooperation Organization (n 68) art. 16.

[77] SCO, 'Structure' (n 75). [78] Bakshi (n 72) 266.

[79] Eleanor Albert, 'The Shanghai Cooperation Organization' (*Council on Foreign Relations*, 14 October 2015) <https://www.cfr.org/backgrounder/shanghai-cooperation-organization> accessed 29 December 2017.

[80] Hansen (n 73) 218–19 ('the explicit declaration that the SCO is not directed at any "third party"'). Cf. Chung (n 72) 998.

[81] Hansen (n 73) 220–6.

While this could pose problems for the SCO's development, especially if member states seek substantive cooperation in the future, the current model is deemed valuable.[82] The SCO continues to hold regular meetings and the membership of India and Pakistan after many years of being observers are proof of this.[83] Moreover, member states are taking advantage of the improving relations to initiate their own multilateral projects outside the auspices of the organization. For example, China is pushing its ambitious Silk Road Economic Belt project, which operates outside of the SCO framework but entails the support of the Central Asian states.[84] The SCO is hence envisioned to remain a political grouping for the foreseeable future and member states will loosely cooperate where feasible, but otherwise all other international relations are to be conducted by the individual state. This phenomenon—similar to ASEAN's experience in its early years—could be said to reflect the priorities of developing countries in an unpredictable geopolitical environment.

4.2 The South Asian Association for Regional Cooperation

SAARC is the regional intergovernmental organization that comprises the eight member states of Afghanistan, Bangladesh, Bhutan, India, Nepal, the Maldives, Pakistan, and Sri Lanka. It was established in 1985 through the adoption of the SAARC Charter to promote economic and security cooperation in a region which had recurring tensions and mutual suspicions.[85] Apart from these primary objectives, the SAARC Charter also enunciated wide-ranging objectives that encompassed sociocultural development, collaboration and mutual assistance in technical and scientific fields, and cooperation in global forums on issues of common interest.[86] To carry out the tasks of regional cooperation, the SAARC members have put in place an intergovernmental structure of governance. Decision-making is dominated by the executive actors of the member states, operating by consensus. The SAARC governing bodies comprise, at the topmost level, the meetings of the heads of state or government.[87] This is followed by the Council of Ministers, consisting of the foreign ministers of the member states, which deals with the decision-making of regional cooperation;[88] and the Standing Committee, comprising the foreign secretaries, which has competence over the implementation and

[82] King-dong Yuan, 'China's Role in Establishing and Building the Shanghai Cooperation Organization (SCO)' (2010) 19 JCC 855, 867.

[83] Gleb Fodorov, 'Will the Entry of India and Pakistan Paralyze the SCO?' *Russia Beyond* (18 November 2016) <https://www.rbth.com/international/2016/11/16/will-the-entry-of-india-and-pakistan-paralyze-the-sco_648239> accessed 18 April 2019.

[84] Sun Zhuangzhi, 'New and Old Regionalism: The Shanghai Cooperation Organization and Sino-Central Asian Relations' (2004) 3 RIA 600, 608–9. See also Korzun (n 70).

[85] Kanal Mukherjee, 'The South Asian Association for Regional Cooperation: Problems and Prospects' (2014) 14 PDS 373, 374–5. See also SAARC Charter (adopted 8 December 1985, in force (date unknown)) art. 1.

[86] SAARC Charter, Ibid. art. 1. [87] Ibid. art. 3. [88] Ibid. art. 4.

monitoring of the regional projects.[89] There are also Technical and Action Committees which assist the Standing Committee.[90] Lastly, there is a Secretariat which is to assist the governing bodies in the task of regional cooperation.[91]

Much like the other APROs, economic cooperation has been a priority as the organization grows. In 1995, the SAARC members had a bold vision of economic integration for their region. They set in place the steps for the grouping to develop into a free trade area, customs union, common market, and eventually an economic union.[92] However, the South Asian Free Trade Area Agreement was only signed about a decade later in 2004 and entered into force in 2006. Despite the ambition to transform into a trade bloc, which necessitates legalization and institutionalization, SAARC has remained a relatively loose political grouping. Regional cooperation has progressed very slowly and SAARC has not become the envisaged organization with the high level of integration that such an economic union requires.[93]

To date, SAARC has adopted several economic agreements, including the Framework Agreement for Energy Cooperation (Electricity) (2014),[94] the Limited Multilateral Agreement on Avoidance of Double Taxation and Mutual Administrative Assistance in Tax Matters (2005),[95] and broader socio-developmental treaties such as the Charter of the SAARC Development Fund (2008), the Agreement on Establishing the SAARC Food Bank (2009),[96] and the SAARC Convention on Preventing and Combating Trafficking in Women and Children for Prostitution (2002).[97] However, it is unclear the extent to which these measures have been implemented and are effective.

The obstacles that SAARC faces as an organization are deep-seated, running into the interplay of complex factors such as the overt state-centric structure of regional governance and a lack of commitment to regional cooperation. There are of course problems of hegemony and members of differing sizes and capacities, as well as issues of weak governments and the pressure of domestic politics.[98] Beyond the common

[89] Ibid. art. 5. [90] Ibid. arts 6 and 7. [91] Ibid. art. 8.

[92] SAARC, 'Economic and Financial Cooperation' <http://saarc-sec.org/areas_of_cooperation/area_detail/economic-trade-and-finance/click-for-details_7> accessed 18 April 2019.

[93] Sangeeta Thapliyal, 'Potential for Cooperation in South Asia: The Need for a Sub-regional Approach' (1999) 6 SAS 51, 53–4.

[94] SAARC Framework Agreement for Energy Cooperation (Electricity) (2014) <https://powermin.nic.in/en/content/saarc-framework-agreement-energy-cooperation-electricity> accessed 18 April 2019.

[95] SAARC Limited Multilateral Agreement on Avoidance of Double Taxation and Mutual Administrative Assistance in Tax Matters (2005) <http://www.fbr.gov.pk/Downloads/Document/3217/1> accessed 18 April 2019.

[96] Charter of the SAARC Development Fund (2008) <http://www.sdfsec.org/sites/default/files/SDF-Charter%28new%29_6.pdf> accessed 7 December 2018; Agreement on Establishing the SAARC Food Bank (2009) <http://www.ifrc.org/Docs/idrl/N646EN.pdf> accessed 18 April 2019.

[97] SAARC Convention on Preventing and Combating Trafficking in Women and Children for Prostitution (adopted 5 January 2002, entered into force 15 November 2005) <http://saarc-sec.org/digital_library/detail_menu/saarc-convention-on-preventing-and-combating-trafficking-in-women-and-children-for-prostitution> accessed 18 April 2019.

[98] Kishore Dash, 'Domestic Support, Weak Governments, and Regional Cooperation: A Study of South Asia' (1997) 6 CSA 57; Thapliyal (n 93) 56.

substantive objectives as enunciated in the Charter and other treaties, it is further indeterminable whether SAARC achieves the basic aim of regional organizations in facilitating a stable environment in which to promote better relations among the member states. Despite annual meetings, the SAARC grouping has not been able to successfully moderate intraregional suspicions and border tensions continue to flare up into incidents where force is used.

One of the more serious indications of the precarious standing of SAARC was seen in 2016 when the then chair of SAARC, Nepal, had to cancel the summit that year in Islamabad due to a boycott by half of the member states. Following the terror attack on Indian security forces near the Pakistani border, Afghanistan, Bangladesh, and Bhutan followed India's lead in boycotting the meeting.[99] More conspicuously, the membership of the SCO by India and Pakistan, the two largest members of SAARC, signals a preference to work with China and Russia rather than the South Asian states, thereby weakening the organizational integrity of SAARC. In light of all these developments and a consistent pattern of South Asian 'un-cooperation', the utility of SAARC as a political organization is highly debatable.

4.3 The Pacific Islands Forum

Regional cooperation among the Pacific Islands, also discussed in chapter 32, was borne out of shared colonial and post-colonial experiences. In 1971, Australia, the Cook Islands, Fiji, Nauru, New Zealand, Samoa, and Tonga established the South Pacific Forum to work together on issues of common concern as well as to present their collective perspectives in the international community. The grouping changed its name to the Pacific Islands Forum (PIF) in 2000, with the adoption of the Agreement Establishing the Pacific Islands Forum Secretariat, so that the organization could more fully represent its members, which come from both the north and south Pacific.[100] The PIF is described as 'a political grouping of sixteen independent and self-governing states' and currently comprises Australia, the Cook Islands, the Federated States of Micronesia, Fiji, Kiribati, Nauru, New Zealand, Niue, Palau, Papua New Guinea, Republic of Marshall Islands, Samoa, Solomon Islands, Tonga, Tuvalu, and Vanuatu.[101] The 2000 Agreement was superseded by the Agreement Establishing

[99] Ankit Panda, 'SAARC Summit Cancellation Will Sting Pakistan, But Won't Prevent the Next Uri or Pathankot' *The Diplomat* (29 September 2016) <http://thediplomat.com/2016/09/saarc-summit-cancellation-will-sting-pakistan-but-wont-prevent-the-next-uri-or-pathankot/> accessed 29 December 2017.

[100] Pacific Islands Forum Secretariat, 'Agreement Establishing the Pacific Islands Forum Secretariat' (signed 30 October 2000, entered into force date unknown) <http://www.forumsec.org/wp-content/uploads/2018/02/Agreement-Establishing-the-Pacific-Islands-Forum-Secretariat-2000.pdf accessed 18 April 2019.

[101] Australian Department of Foreign Affairs and Trade, 'Pacific Islands Forum is Coming to Cairns' (DFAT Focus, June–September 2009) <https://dfat.gov.au/about-us/publications/Documents/02.pdf> accessed 29 December 2017.

the Pacific Islands Forum (2005) which expressed that the purpose of the Forum was to strengthen regional cooperation and pool regional resources of governance to achieve economic development and security and to address climate change.[102]

The PIF has a simple structure in that its 'preeminent decision-making body' is the Forum Leaders' Meeting.[103] The preferred mode of decision-making is through consensus, although majority voting is acceptable when necessary.[104] At the next level is the Pacific Islands Forum Officials' Committee, which is the executive governing body that guides the Secretariat in policy implementation and advises and assists the Forum Leaders.[105] The Secretary-General and the Secretariat are tasked with implementing the decisions of the Forum leaders as well as providing secretariat support to them and other ministers during meetings. It is notable that the Secretariat's mandate is primarily derived from the annual Leaders' Communiqués and high level ministerial meeting decisions rather than regional laws.[106] In addition, the bulk of the work of the Secretariat is to manage funding assistance schemes to promote the economy, trade, and social development in the member states.

Despite relying on predominantly diplomatic and political modalities for regional cooperation, the PIF members sought to establish a free trade area to facilitate opportunities for sustainable economic growth. The Pacific Island Countries Trade Agreement (PICTA) (2001) is meant to establish a free trade area (only for goods) among all of the PIF countries designated as 'least developed countries' or 'small island states'—therefore excluding Australia and New Zealand—to improve consumer welfare and create jobs.[107] By May 2015, the PICTA had been signed by twelve out of the fourteen Forum Island Countries (FICs) but only seven members have signalled a readiness to trade, thus making the implementation of the treaty extremely challenging. To move things along, the PIF Secretariat is supporting FICs in their domestic markets to facilitate their capacity to trade under the agreement.[108]

Like its other Asia-Pacific counterparts, it is difficult to assess what the PIF has achieved for its member states in the international legal order. The Secretariat has been a central point from which regional aid and development projects can be directed. While this is undoubtedly useful and necessary, these projects run on a country-by-country basis and are generally funded externally or by the richer member states like Australia and New Zealand. There appears to be weak evidence of collective regional action. Apart from being a forum to meet and facilitating a coalition of the small island states, the PIF does not seem to have been able to grow closer relations in order to project the common front that members so desire on the global plane.

[102] Agreement Establishing the Pacific Islands Forum (adopted 30 October 2005, entered into force date unknown) art. 2 <https://gsd.spc.int/sopac/docs/RIF/PIFS_Agreement%20Establishing%20the%20Forum.pdf> accessed 29 December 2017.

[103] Ibid. art. 3. [104] Ibid. art. 5(7). [105] Ibid. art. 5. [106] Ibid. arts 7 and 8.

[107] World Bank, 'Pacific Island Countries Trade Agreement (PICTA)' (2001) <http://wits.worldbank.org/GPTAD/PDF/archive/picta.pdf> accessed 29 December 2017.

[108] PIF Secretariat, 'Post-Cotonou Negotiations' <https://www.forumsec.org/post-cotonou-negotiations/> accessed 18 April 2019.

Furthermore, there exists an undercurrent of tension between the larger and richer members (Australia and New Zealand) and the much smaller and less developed island states by virtue of the power imbalances. The most prominent tensions arise from the strained relations between Fiji on the one hand and Australia and New Zealand on the other. Apart from the temporary ouster of Fiji in 2009 after the military coup of 2006 being one example, Fijian Prime Minister Frank Bainimarama has regularly called for the removal of Australia and New Zealand from the PIF and the inclusion of China as a new regional member.[109] More realistically, the relations within the PIF grouping are perhaps better described as realist and a balancing of powers, with very little consideration for the international legal framework. In this respect, the PIF is somewhat similar to SAARC in terms of achievements and effectiveness.

4.4 The Melanesian Spearhead Group

A counterpart (or competitor) to the PIF is the MSG, comprising the four states of Fiji, Papua New Guinea, the Solomon Islands, and Vanuatu, and the pro-independence movement from New Caledonia—Front de Libération Nationale Kanak et Socialiste (FLNKS). The MSG was established in 2007 through the Agreement Establishing the Melanesian Spearhead Group.[110] It succeeded the Melanesian grouping set up in 1988 for the express purposes of working by consensus to strengthen trade, cultural traditions, and values, and to foster economic and technical cooperation for common development and security. These objectives were enunciated in the Agreed Principles of Co-operation among Independent States of Melanesia (1988).

Interestingly, while there is considerable overlap with the objectives and membership of the PIF, the governance structure of the MSG is very similar to ASEAN's structure in its first three decades. The MSG governing bodies comprise a Summit of the heads of government and the authorized representative of FLNKS, a Foreign Ministers' Meeting, a Senior Officials' Meeting (top-level officers of the foreign ministries), and a Trade and Economic Officials' Meeting.[111] All decisions in the MSG are to be taken in the 'spirit of dialogue, mediation, and consensus'.[112]

The primary impetus of MSG cooperation and operations has been trade and economic development. Of particular note has been the MSG Trade Agreement (MSGTA) that came into effect in 1993, with the original three members (Fiji, Vanuatu, and Solomon Islands) establishing a free trade area in goods. Fiji joined the MSGTA in

[109] Rowan Callick, 'Fiji Wants Australia Out of Pacific Islands Forum' *The Australian* (Sydney, 6 April 2016) <https://www.theaustralian.com.au/nation/foreign-affairs/fiji-wants-australia-out-of-pacific-islands-forum/news-story/5f1551ee2361b0bce27c2c997502d286> accessed 29 December 2017; Marc Lanteigne, 'Choppy Waters: The "Return" of Fiji to Pacific Affairs after the 2014 Vote' (2016) 1 TWT 46, 42–3.

[110] Agreement Establishing the Melanesian Spearhead Group (March 2007) <http://www.msgsec.info/index.php/publication/reports?download=3%3Amsg-agreement> accessed 29 December 2017.

[111] Ibid. arts 9–12. [112] Ibid. art. 4.

1998, thereby cementing its standing within the grouping. In 2005, the four MSGTA signatories adopted a negative-list approach, instead of the previous mode of trading on a positive list. By only specifying the certain types of goods excluded, the trade of a larger swathe of goods were thereby enabled. Discussions are underway to broaden the MSGTA to an MSG Plus agreement, which will include trade in services and labour mobility and will be open to other Pacific Island states.

Two decades after the establishment of the MSG, the organization took on formal international legal status in 2007 and set up a Secretariat in Port Vila, Vanuatu, in 2008. The MSG Secretariat reflects the grouping's priorities and comprises the Office of the Director-General and the three subdivisions on Trade, Investment, and Economic Development, Governance and Sustainable Development, and Operations. According to the MSG, most of the efforts so far have been focused on developing the administrative and legal framework to support all operations.[113]

Apart from the MSGTA obligations, MSG members are carrying out various regional development projects. These range from skills training and labour mobility to regional security. Like the other APROs, the implementation, success, and efficacy of these schemes are often unreported. In terms of diplomatic relations, it is notable that the MSG Secretariat has taken over some of the PIF Secretariat's tasks.[114] In terms of external relations, the MSG seems to hold a certain attraction for aspiring members to gain better economic and political relations with the incumbent MSG members. Indonesia was granted observer status at the MSG in 2011, while in 2013 the West Papua National Council for Liberation applied for membership but has yet to be granted admittance. These signs of increasing effectiveness have led MSG members to proclaim that their organization is the most successful and active of the Pacific groupings and that the MSGTA has played a pioneering role in the regional integration in the Pacific. This has understandably led to some competitive friction with the PIF. However, MSG members have stressed that the organization is not undermining the much larger PIF. Nonetheless, given the PIF's inertia, it remains to be seen whether the MSG will supersede the larger grouping.

4.5 The Asia-Pacific Economic Cooperation

APEC was an initiative mooted by the former Australian Prime Minister Bob Hawke as an organization for fostering economic integration in the region. Established in 1989 as an informal dialogue group without a founding instrument, APEC now has twenty-one

[113] Government of Vanuatu, 'MSG Secretariat Undergoes Strategic Reforms' (*MSG Secretariat*, 3 April 2017) <https://www.gov.vu/en/public-information/144-msg-secretariat-undergoes-strategic-reforms> accessed 18 April 2019.

[114] See e.g. Sandra Tarte, 'Regionalism and Changing Regional Order in the Pacific Islands' (2014) 1 APPS 312; Lawson Samuel, 'MSG: A Uniting Force' (Pacific Institute of Public Policy, 14 May 2013) <http://pacificpolicy.org/2013/05/the-melanesian-spearhead-group-a-uniting-force> accessed 29 December 2017; Iati Iati, 'Pacific Regionalism and the Polynesian Leaders Group' (2017) 106 CJIA 175.

member economies: Australia, Brunei Darussalam, Canada, Chile, China, Chinese Taipei (Taiwan), Hong Kong Special Administrative Region, Indonesia, Japan, Korea, Malaysia, Mexico, New Zealand, Papua New Guinea, Peru, the Philippines, Russia, Singapore, Thailand, the United States, and Vietnam. The term 'member economies' rather than 'member states' is used because of the participation of Hong Kong and Chinese Taipei. While it can technically be classified as a regional organization, APEC operates more like a broad regional forum where member economies come together to discuss issues of common interest. Members participate on the basis of sovereign equality, open dialogue, and respect for the views of all participants. Decision-making is reached by consensus and there are no binding commitments or treaty obligations.

Generally, APEC's structure is based on both a 'bottom-up' and 'top-down' approach. Four core committees on trade and investment, economic and technical cooperation, economy, and budget and management, with their respective working groups, provide strategic policy recommendations to APEC leaders and ministers for the annual agenda-setting. The working groups are then tasked with implementing these initiatives through a variety of APEC-funded projects. Members also take individual and collective action to carry out APEC initiatives in their individual economies under the auspices of APEC capacity-building projects. There is a small APEC Secretariat based in Singapore to provide coordination, technical and advisory support, and public outreach services. The APEC Policy Support Unit, housed within the Secretariat, provides research, analysis, and policy support to APEC initiatives. Additionally, APEC facilitates dialogue between the public and private sectors. The APEC Business Advisory Council, established in 1995, comprises about three members from each of the member economies, with business representatives appointed by APEC leaders. The annual APEC Chief Executive Officer Summit and Industry Dialogues are further instances where regional business leaders confer with senior officials on issues affecting business in the region.[115]

Initially criticized for being ineffectual, APEC has found firm footing as a diplomatic forum. Operating as an informal senior official- and ministerial-level dialogue in its initial years (1989–92), it was not until 1993 when the then US President Bill Clinton initiated having an annual APEC Economic Leaders' Meeting and discussing more substantive cooperation.[116] While there has been some institutional growth, APEC has remained, and is likely to remain, a loose political grouping. This is because its informality has encouraged members to openly share their opinions on region-wide initiatives without censure, and the transparency has, in turn, been helpful to members when deciding whether to participate in regional ventures. For example, the 'APEC

[115] APEC, 'APEC Business Advisory Council' <https://www.apec.org/Groups/Other-Groups/APEC-Business-Advisory-Council> accessed 18 April 2019; APEC, 'US National Center of Business for APEC' <http://www.ncapec.org/ceosummit/index.html> accessed 29 December 2017.

[116] APEC, 'History of APEC' <http://www.apec.org/About-Us/About-APEC/History> accessed 29 December 2017.

Single Window' discussions might have influenced the launch of the ASEAN Single Window mechanism to facilitate free trade in the ASEAN region.[117] Moreover, the flexibility of the forum adapts to allow members to deal with critical geopolitical and economic challenges such as disaster resilience, planning for pandemics, and terrorism.

It is becoming increasingly clear that one of the most valuable characteristics of APEC is that it supports its members in participating in external multilateral legal and quasi-legal endeavours to further free trade and economic growth. This has been seen in, for example, World Trade Organization negotiations,[118] the G-20 Framework for Strong, Sustainable and Balanced Growth in the Asia-Pacific Region and, most recently, the Trans-Pacific Partnership (TPP).[119] Such expansive regional free trade ambitions have generally come under the comprehensive vision for the Free Trade Area of the Asia-Pacific (FTAAP) that APEC leaders mooted in 2006. Further steps were taken in 2010 when APEC leaders mapped out the 'Pathways to FTAAP' which included building on ongoing regional undertakings such as ASEAN+3, ASEAN+6, the TPP, and the Regional Comprehensive Economic Partnership.

As the future of the TPP is uncertain after the US' withdrawal, APEC's position as a forum to discuss ways to enable freer trade in the Asia-Pacific has become even more important. Over the years, APEC has conducted studies to realize the FTAAP, addressed generational trade and investment obstacles, and undertaken sectoral initiatives. These include capacity-building programmes to assist economies in engaging in FTA negotiations on certain topics as well as information exchanges on the status of FTA and regional trade agreement negotiations in the region during the Senior Officials Meetings.

5 Conclusion

From the analysis of these seven regional organizations which span the Asia-Pacific, further differentiation can be made out beyond the bifurcation between 'legal and institutional' and 'political and diplomatic'. The basic factor that separates the two categories is the extent to which member states want to pursue economic integration. The greater degree to which economic development is to be achieved through regional cooperation, the greater the reliance on binding obligations and governance through bureaucratic structures. This is not a unique Asia-Pacific phenomenon but rather a

[117] APEC, 'APEC Leaders' Declarations 2014' <http://www.apec.org/meeting-papers/leaders-declarations/2014/2014_aelm/2014_aelm_annexa.aspx> accessed 29 December 2017.

[118] APEC, 'Supporting the Multilateral Trading System and the 9th Ministerial Conference of the World Trade Organization' (APEC, 7 October 2013) <http://www.apec.org/Meeting-Papers/Leaders-Declarations/2013/2013_aelm/2013_aelm_mts> accessed 13 December 2018. A package of measures to enhance regional connectivity was endorsed, including an APEC Multi-Year Plan on Infrastructure Development and Investment prioritizing public–private partnership projects: See 'History of APEC' (n 116).

[119] 'APEC Leaders Commit to Fighting All Forms of Protectionism, Call for Support for TPP' *Straits Times* (21 November 2016) <http://www.straitstimes.com/world/americas/apec-leaders-commit-to-fighting-all-forms-of-protectionism-urge-support-for-tpp> accessed 29 December 2017.

'natural progression' of regionalism that has also been seen elsewhere in the world. By and large, the general framework for an APRO (especially in the initial stages) is one that employs political-diplomatic cooperation rather than a legal and institutional structure. When the conditions are favourable and more tangible economic gains are desired, Asia-Pacific states will take steps towards formalizing their relations, as seen in ASEAN and the EAEU. While such transformation is inevitably slow due to path dependencies and capacity constraints, the member states are nonetheless willing to bear the integration costs in view of the substantive outcomes.

In the political-diplomatic category of APROs, similar legalization and institutionalization movements may be observed but these are limited to regional economic cooperation. This has been exemplified by the MSG in relation to its trade in goods efforts and also by the earlier phases of ASEAN and the EAEU. That said, while economic development is a priority for such APROs, the constant danger to legalization and institutionalization efforts lies in the entrenched state-centric outlooks of Asia-Pacific states and their reluctance to relinquish flexibility to adhere to rules and institutions, even when this does not undermine their sovereignty.

Where the strategic interest is not predominantly economic but rather more diffuse and wide-ranging, the APROs retain staunchly informal structures where decision-making relies much on intergovernmental consultation and consensus. For instance, if the APRO's objective is more about confidence-building, information exchange, security, and the balancing of internal and external powers, then it would make sense to retain a political organizational identity. Political-security issues are highly sensitive and states are reluctant to tie themselves to legal and institutional rules on such matters. Conversely, the flexible relations accorded by being part of a political organization could, over the longer term, bring about greater trust and better relations.

That said, the usefulness of such organizations to the member states varies. On one hand, there are the important ones like the SCO, pre-Charter ASEAN, and APEC, where members can glean information and build mutual confidence on strategic political and security issues and pan-Asia-Pacific economic ventures. On the other hand, there are also organizations like the PIF and SAARC which are stymied by intraregional tensions, unclear aspirations, and disorganization; so much so that they are either deadlocked or slowly ceding competences to neighbouring regional organizations.

Of course, the sensitive question of whether an APRO serves the purpose of its members is subject to the aspirations and intentions of each member. Nonetheless, for the betterment of the institutional design of APROs in future, regional states should bear in mind that the utility of an APRO, and the advantage it affords any member, is not solely dependent on its legal or political characteristics, but whether the organization is properly set up to do what it proclaims to want to achieve. This is true not only for the exacting demands of legalization and institutionalization but for any type of regional project. Ambitions that are not commensurate with the political resolve and resources to bring the projects into being will inevitably let the member states down. Repeated experiences of this kind may then lead to the decline of the organization.

CHAPTER 4

ASIA IN THE HISTORY AND THEORY OF INTERNATIONAL LAW

ANTONY ANGHIE

1 Introduction

The last few decades have witnessed a growing interest in the history and theory of international law, a trend that inevitably influences the understanding and treatment of the history and theory of international law in Asia. My basic endeavour in this chapter is to sketch out a broad 'history' of Asia and its engagement with international law, while also pointing to some of the enduring theoretical and historiographical issues provoked by that history. The terms 'Asia' and 'international law' are, of course, problematic and must be contextualized.[1]

Each era interprets history according to its own concerns. I have attempted here to suggest how the 'turn to history', which is now such an important aspect of international legal scholarship, has been motivated by varying concerns over time.[2] Three phases might be distinguished in general terms, each of which is characterized by a particular constellation of questions and issues. In relation to the first phase, up to and including the European colonial period, Asian scholars and writers attempted to

[1] The concept of 'Asia' in particular is highly contestable, arguably encompassing a territory extending from the Mediterranean to the Pacific. On the problem of identifying and analyzing 'regions' in international law, see Antony Anghie, 'Identifying Regions in the History of International Law' in Bardo Fassbender, Anne Peters, and Daniel Högger (eds), *The Oxford Handbook of the History of International Law* (OUP 2012). Australia's relationship/inclusion within the Asian region for instance is marked by ambivalence and, inevitably, by some measure of inconsistency.

[2] See Matthew Craven, 'Theorizing the Turn to History in International Law' in Anne Orford, Florian Hoffmann, and Martin Clark (eds), *The Oxford Handbook of the Theory of International Law* (OUP 2016) 21.

understand the trauma of colonization and the role of international law in this process; they sought to develop appropriate responses to protect their own countries and to ensure that they could become members of the 'civilized world'. In the second phase, that of decolonization, Asian jurists revisited their own history in order to argue that they had contributed to the making of international law, and were capable of assuming a responsible position amongst the family of nations. In the third and current phase, the emergence of China and India as global powers has raised new questions about Asian civilizations and Asian approaches to international law.

Some constant themes run through these phases. The first is the theme of sovereignty and the evolution of a particularly Asian approach to it that might be understood in the context of Asia's colonial history. The second, more recent theme has to do with development, and the preoccupation of Asian states with enhancing the economic well-being of their own peoples.

More theoretically, Asia's approach to international law demonstrates what scholars have referred to as an ongoing 'duality' in the words of BS Chimni,[3] or 'ambivalence' in the words of Simon Chesterman.[4] Having surveyed these developments in the history and theory of international law in Asia, I attempt to identify themes that may be of interest to future scholars in the field. Here, my argument is that what counts as the 'history and theory' of international law is itself continuously changing, and that a novel and expansive understanding of this topic would compel engagement with new materials and issues. I make three principal proposals. First, that research should continue and deepen on Asian traditions and concepts of rule and governance, justice, and order. The great religious and philosophical systems of the Middle East, of Buddhism and Hinduism, Islam and Confucianism, and the teachings of old texts such as the *Arthashatra,* have profoundly shaped the history of Asia, and continue in various complex ways to affect Asian polities.[5]

Second, that the history and theory of international law in Asia should be understood in global rather than, as is often currently the case, in regional terms. This is especially so because independent Asian states, from the very outset, attempted to create what might be termed a 'Third World Cosmopolitanism'. Third, a turn to disciplines such as anthropology might offer new insights into ongoing questions regarding governance and territory, and the powerful imaginaries, regarding nationhood and sovereignty and empire, that animate the peoples of Asia, and that have not been entirely displaced by modern concepts of sovereignty and globalization. It is this

[3] BS Chimni, 'International Law Scholarship in Post-colonial India: Coping With Dualism' (2010) 23 Leiden JIL 23.

[4] Simon Chesterman, 'Asia's Ambivalence about International Law and Institutions: Past, Present and Futures' (2016) 27 EJIL 945.

[5] This is to continue a line of inquiry that was urged by scholars such as Nagendra Singh in Nagendra Singh, 'History of the Law of Nations regional Developments' in *Max Planck Encyclopedia of Public International Law*, vol II (2nd edn 1995) 127. Recent developments in the historiography of international law suggest the importance of returning to these materials with new analytic and methodological frameworks.

tension, or synthesis, between the old and the new that gives rise to some of the most compelling and unique features of international law in Asia. In a curious paradox, it appears to be precisely the success and emergence of many Asian states as wealthy and powerful entities in the current global order that have engendered new forms of nationalism that seek in some cases to return to what is nostalgically perceived as a purer past.

2 The Colonial Period

2.1 The Early History

Commonly regarded as the world's most ancient treaty, The Treaty of Kadesh, which sought to establish peace between the Empires of the Egyptians and the Hittites, involved both African and Asian parties. The political communities that existed in Africa and Asia at that time had developed principles that regulated interaction amongst them. The question of how to understand ancient state systems and their operations continues to be a subject of scholarly debate. The prominent Indian scholar, MK Nawaz for example, argued that ancient societies 'lived in isolation from each other, separated by geographical factors and racial considerations. Besides, common international interests of the modern type did not exist in the past to unify them'.[6]

In his detailed account of the scholarly problems involved in trying to explore how those histories should be understood, David Bederman argues that a version of a 'state system'—that is, a system of relatively distinctive and independent political entities—did exist in the ancient world, and this justifies an examination of the principles that operated in such a system and that regulated, for instance, relations amongst Sumerian city-states in Mesopotamia in the period between 2600 and 2350 BC.[7] These states 'concluded treaties [which] had rules concerning diplomatic immunities, and maybe also norms on the conduct of war'.[8] Bederman's important book gives a powerful account of what might be termed the 'International Law of the Ancient World'.[9] This work deals with issues that are of ongoing concern to international law: the sources of law, treaties, and war and peace, the nature of governance, and the status of ambassadors.[10] Interaction between Europe and Western Asia had, of course, occurred for millennia. The conflict between the Greek states and Persian Empire is, after all, a defining event in global history.

[6] See MK Nawaz, 'The Law of Nations in the Ancient World' (1957) 6 Indian Year Book of International Affairs 172, cited in David Bederman, *International Law in Antiquity* (CUP 2001) 18.

[7] See Bederman, ibid. [8] Ibid. 23. [9] See generally, Bederman, ibid.

[10] For other detailed studies of this era, see for instance Amnon Altman, 'The Role of the "Historical Prologue" in the Hittite Vassal Treaties' (2004) 6 Journal of the History of International Law 43 (a fascinating study of early efforts at treaty enforcement through punishment via a curse).

Accounts of the early history of governance in Asian civilizations focus on the political systems that are constructed on the basis of ancient texts and religious teachings. In the case of India, for instance, polities were deeply influenced by the teachings of the *Dharmashastras* and the *Arthashastra*. Thus Patel argues that:

> The Shrutis, the Smritis, the Dharmashastras, and the Puranas establish that the States of ancient India had inter-state, or international relations, among themselves. These relations were carried out according to well-established customs, usages and principles of life based on the Advaita system of philosophy. These sources of international law continued to guide the relations of princely States.[11]

The idea of *dharma* is central to any understanding of Indian society, as it is 'laced with a huge hermeneutic investment of philosophical cultural capital, and political contestation'.[12] It deals with a system of righteousness and duty that applies to individuals and rulers. It is 'eternal law . . . governing the cosmos and as such impervious to human reason and will'.[13] Wide ranging discussions have taken place about the different elements of *dharma*, the sources of *dharma*, its teachings on justifications for violence, and also its application to relations amongst the states of the time. Many comparable issues are raised by the traditional Chinese world order in which three main zones existed—the Sinic Zone, the Inner Asian Zone, and the Outer Zone. At the centre of this system ruled the 'Son of Heaven' to whom all other peoples were expected to pay tribute.[14] Further, a cursory study of the great Indian manual of statecraft, the *Arthashastra*, suggests the sophistication of ancient Indian thinking about governance. Chapters in that volume discuss, in detail and at length, topics such as 'The State and its Constituent Elements', 'Departments of the Government', 'Law and Justice', 'Foreign Policy', and 'Defence and War'.[15] In Foreign Policy, for instance, Kautilya establishes a complex set of rules dealing with relations amongst states based on a series of basic propositions such as the blunt assertion that 'Any king, whose kingdom shares a common border with that of the conqueror is an antagonist'.[16]

It is hardly necessary to say that from at least the early twentieth century, international law scholars have taken an interest in how the Western discipline of international law and its ideas of law, sovereignty, and governance have compared with these Asian traditions and world views. Upendra Baxi is surely right in claiming that any close study of the encounter between these different legal systems, ancient and modern, will generate new understandings of the histories of international law, and that this task has only recently begun.

[11] See Bimal Patel, 'India' in Fassbender et al (eds) (n 1) 500. There are extensive studies of the relationship between Hinduism and international law: see e.g. Surya Subedi, 'The Concept in Hinduism of "Just War"' (2003) 8 Journal of Conflict and Security Law 339; Nagendra Singh, *Juristic Concepts of Ancient Indian Polity* (Vision Books 1980). On Buddhism and International Law, see KN Jayatilleke, 'The Principles of International Law in Buddhist Doctrine' (1967) 120 RCADI 441.

[12] See Upendra Baxi, 'India-Europe' in Fassbender et al (eds) (n 1) 744.

[13] Ibid. 758.

[14] Chi-Hua Tang, 'China-Europe' in Fassbender et al (eds) (n 1) 701.

[15] Kautilya (LN Rangarajan (ed, trs)), *The Arthashastra* (Penguin Books 1992).

[16] Ibid. 529.

2.2 Asia and the Modern Beginnings of International Law

The arrival of maritime European powers in the Far East, following the voyage of Vasco da Gama, signalled a profound change in the political, economic, and legal relations between Europe and the Asian states. What this should not obscure is the still unexplored issue, at least amongst international law historians, as to how complex trading systems were established among the merchants in the Indian Ocean and beyond. Arab traders furthered their reach and influence to Southeast Asia, creating a trading empire of enormous wealth and power that extended from the Mediterranean on one hand to the eastern parts of the Indian Ocean on the other, an empire that transformed the kingdoms of Indonesia from Hindu[17] to Muslim, and this without military conquest. What were the legal techniques by which risk was managed and contracts made and enforced? What were the legal structures developed by merchants from Hrdaman to enable them to trade with the local peoples, and how did they conceptualize such trade? A glimpse of these issues is offered in KN Chaudhuri's magisterial account of trading relations in the Indian Ocean. As he points out, 'There were certainly well-established conventions in commercial contracts in all the trading cities of the Mediterranean and the Indian Ocean. The legal corpus protected merchants when the contracts were concluded between inter-communal members, and the reputation of a port of trade turned on the fairness of its legal traditions'.[18] The types of legal instruments, treaties, and otherwise that would support such a complex regime have not yet been extensively studied, at least by international legal scholars.

Relations between Asian states and the European maritime powers that were gradually consolidating their presence in the region were initially characterized by equality. And it was Asia that then became the arena of a conflict that had long endured in Europe and the Middle East, between Christian and Islamic nations. This occasioned a study of 'Islamic' international law and its version of 'just war' based on *jihad*, including the different variations on the understanding of the term '*jihad*'. The Islamic tradition of international law has a long history.[19] Thus European jurists examined complex issues regarding, for instance, the question of whether Christian nations could

[17] As to the Indianization of South East Asia, see the classic work by George Coedes, *The Indianized States of South-East Asia* (University of Hawaii Press 1968).

[18] KN Chaudhuri, *Trade and Civilization in the Indian Ocean: An Economic History from the Rise of Islam to 1750* (OUP 1985) 12. See also RJ Barendse, *Arabian Seas, 1700–1763*,vol III (Brill 2009). For a detailed study of how the English East Indian Company sought to marginalize Muslim traders, see Nurfadzilah Yahaya, 'Legal Pluralism and the English East India Company in the Straits of Malacca during the Early Nineteenth Century' (2015) 33 Law and History Review 945.

[19] This is associated with the work of Muhammed al-Shaybani. See Mashood Baderin, 'Muhammad-Al-Shaybani' in Fassbender et al (eds) (n 1) 1081–5; Majid Khadduri (ed), *The Islamic Law of Nations: Shaybani's Siyar* (Johns Hopkins University Press 1966); Mohammad Fadel, 'International Law, Regional Development: Islam' in Ruediger Wolfrum (ed), *Max Planck Encyclopedia of Public International Law* (2005); Said Mahmoudi, 'Islamic Approaches to International Law' in *Max Planck Encyclopedia of Public International Law*, (2005).

enter into treaties with Muslim nations. Scholars such as Gentili commented on what they perceived as the Islamic law of war in his treatise *De Jure Belli Libri Tres*,[20] published at the end of the sixteenth century. Illuminating comparisons could be made between the Christian and Islamic law of nations, but to Alexandrowicz it appeared that 'Both [are] considered as the two principal media of expansion, conquest and treaty making'.[21] Both the Islamic and Christian worlds were themselves subjected to violent religious schisms which led to the Thirty Years War as well as the divisions between the Shi'i and Sunni Muslims. The Moghul Empire developed its own treaty practice, refusing to enter into treaties with European traders except in the form of Moghul *firmans*: 'The Moghuls allowed the English and French Companies to rise to the status of grand officers or vassals of the Empire and ultimately negotiated with them within its constitutional framework'.[22] Nevertheless, trade tended to exercise a secularizing influence and, certainly in the East Indies, Western traders were initially regarded with tolerance, especially as the Dutch and the English gradually overtook the Portuguese in power.[23]

It is this period that is the basis of Alexandrowicz's highly influential argument that Western and Asian states dealt with each other as equals, and this encounter generated important international law norms as evident in the treaties entered into by the parties. In this way, Asian states too contributed to the emergence of modern international law before the advent of positivism and the emphatic assertion of a 'standard of civilization' that effectively excluded non-European states. Even at this stage, however, European powers were beset by difficulties in classifying the different entities they encountered, as they ranged from empires to minor sovereigns or vassal states. Of course, Europe itself confronted this problem as Westphalian sovereignty was easier to conceptualize than apply to the complex political formations of seventeenth-century Europe.

Nevertheless, as European states expanded their powers, the character of the treaties they entered into changed correspondingly. Crucially, European states promised to protect Asian states from other European rivals. Thus the Dutch entered into a Treaty with the King of Kandy, Rajasinha II, by which they undertook to rid Sri Lanka of the Portuguese in return for a monopoly of the spice trade in Sri Lanka; a contentious term of the treaty had to do with reimbursement of the costs of the Dutch campaign. The Dutch inevitably claimed that they were not properly paid and that they were therefore entitled to retain the crucial ports they had captured from the Portuguese—ports that

[20] See CH Alexandrowicz, *An Introduction to the History of the Law of Nations in the East Indies (16th, 17th and 18th Centuries)* (Clarendon Press 1967) 91. For a superb recently edited volume of Alexandrowicz's works, together with illuminating introductory essays, see CH Alexandrowicz (David Armitage and Jennifer Pitts (eds)), *The Law of Nations in Global History* (OUP 2017).

[21] Alexandrowicz, *An Introduction to the History of the Law of Nations in the East Indies*, ibid., 91.

[22] Ibid. 94, 18. After the conquest of Bengal by Clive, the company was granted the status of 'diwanee'.

[23] Ibid. 94.

gave them access to the most valuable cinnamon lands of the country.[24] This process of gradual conquest occurred throughout Asia, as European states expanded their power through a combination of military and legal technologies, a trend that was to culminate in the Treaty of Nanking of 1842. For Alexandrowicz, however, even such treaties of protection—in which Asian states promised to deal exclusively with the contracting European party which presented itself as a 'protector' against the depredations of other European states—did not undermine the underlying equality of states.[25] While impressive authority for this view could be cited, the argument is not without its problems.

The European-Asian encounter, of course, had a significant impact on international law for another reason, the significance of which is only now being appreciated in Western international legal scholarship. In 1603, a Portuguese vessel, the *Santa Caterina*, containing a treasure of goods from China worth almost the total English revenues for that year, was captured by a Dutch vessel belonging to the nascent Dutch East India Company, the VOC. This event led to a complex legal dispute and the VOC, seeking to justify its position legally, sought the advice of a brilliant, precocious, and ambitious young scholar, Hugo Grotius. Grotius wrote *Mare Liberum* in defence of the VOC's position. The longer work of which *Mare Liberum* was a part of, *The Law of Prize and Booty*, was discovered only in the nineteenth century.

In defending the actions of the VOC, Grotius, drawing on the works of predecessors such as Vitoria, elaborated on natural rights, trade and sovereignty, property, and war and peace. For Grotius, the right of trade is so fundamental that lawyers 'deny any commonwealth or prince to be able wholly to forbid others to come unto their subjects and trade with them'.[26] The Portuguese had violated this basic principle by claiming a monopoly on trading with the East Indies. Grotius systematically examined all the titles that the Portuguese may have asserted to exclude the Dutch. These included the argument that the Portuguese had acquired title over the East Indies, and that they owned the route to the Indies having been the first to navigate their way to these areas. It is in examining the claim that the Portuguese owned the sea itself—even if they had no title to the territories of the Indies—that Grotius develops his theory of property and sovereignty: 'For now dominion properly signifieth that which so appertaineth unto one that after the same manner it cannot be another's but we call that common whose propriety is conferred among many with a certain fellowship and agreement excluding the rest'.[27]

[24] KM de Silva, *A History of Sri Lanka* (2nd edn Vijitha Yapa Publications 2008) 120. The Sri Lankan government granted China extensive rights to the port of Hambantotat on a 99 year lease in 2017; the basic situation of indebtedness leading to the transfer of control of important ports is depressingly similar.

[25] Alexandrowicz, *An Introduction to the History of the Law of Nations in the East Indies* (n 20) 153–154.

[26] Hugo Grotius (Richard Hakluyt (trs) David Armitage (ed)), *The Free Sea* (Liberty Fund 1609) ch 1.

[27] Ibid. ch 5.

Scholars focused on Asia and its relation with the West have long been studying the Grotius of the East Indies. RP Anand, for instance, argued that the basic principles of the Law of the Sea regime corresponded with Grotius's writing in *the Free Sea* which in turn was heavily influenced by Asian customs and practices which conformed with the idea of what Grotius proclaimed to be 'the free sea'.[28] It is relatively recently that the significance of this work is being appreciated in terms of its broader theoretical implications. Scholars such as Richard Tuck,[29] Edward Keene,[30] Martine van Ittersum,[31] Ileana Porras, and Eric Wilson[32] have all prompted a re-evaluation of Grotius's work, pointing to his long association with the VOC, his efforts to simultaneously defend the VOC and advance the cause of the emerging Dutch Republic, and his conceptualization of the Indies as being beyond the pale, hence, there being an area that was in effect a state of nature. *Mare Liberum* first sketched out themes that were developed in far more detail in his recognized masterpiece—the Old Testament surely of international law—*De iure belli ac pacis.*

If this is the case, then it can surely be argued that international law began, not with the Treaty of Westphalia of 1648, but with an incident off the coast of Singapore in 1603.[33] One could further argue that international law was developed to defend, not the rights of a state, but the rights of a corporation—this at a time when the issue of legal personality and the relationship amongst empires, states, corporations, and individuals was still being theorized and far from clear.[34] The implications are far-reaching in terms of understanding the role of corporations in the colonial enterprise as it played out in Asia.[35] Grotius was roughly the contemporary of another great thinker on the

[28] RP Anand, *Origin and Development of the Law of the Sea: The History of International Law Revisited* (Brill 1983) 88–9.

[29] Richard Tuck, *The Rights of War and Peace* (OUP 2001).

[30] Edward Keene, *Beyond the Anarchical Society: Grotius, Colonialism and Order in World Politics* (CUP 2002).

[31] Martine van Ittersum, *Profit and Principle: Hugo Grotius, Natural Rights Theories and the Rise of Dutch Power in the East Indies, 1595–1615* (Brill 2006).

[32] Ileana Porras, 'Constructing International Law in the East Indian Seas: Property, Sovereignty, Commerce and War in Hugo Grotius' *De Iure Praedae*—the Law of Prize and Booty, or "How to Distinguish Merchants from Pirates"' (2006) 31 Brooklyn Journal of International Law; Eric Wilson, *The Savage Republic: De Indis of Hugo Grotius, Republicanism and Dutch Hegemony within the Early Modern World-system C.1600–1619* (Martinus Nijhoff 2008).

[33] For a superb account of Grotius and the East Indies, see Peter Borschberg, *Hugo Grotius, The Portuguese and Free Trade in the East Indies* (National University of Singapore Press 2011) 47. We are also indebted to Borschberg for his translations of various treaties entered into by the Dutch. See for instance 'Treaty between Admiral Cornelis Matelieff de Jonge and Kong of Kohor, May 17, 1606' in Peter Borschberg (trs, ed), *Journals, Memorials and Letter of Cornelis Matelieff de Jonge: Security, Diplomacy and Commerce in 17th Century Southeast Asia* (National University of Singapore Press 2015) 219; the basic purpose of the agreement was to unite to expel the Portuguese from Malacca. If successful, the Dutch were to be given complete control over the fort of Malacca.

[34] See Koen Stapelbroek, 'Trade, Chartered Companies, and Mercantile Associations' in Fassbender et al (eds) (n 1) 338.

[35] Jose Manuel Barreto, 'Cerberus: Rethinking Grotius and the Westphalian System' in Martti Koskenniemi, Walter Rech, and Manuel Jimenez Fonseca (eds), *International Law and Empire:*

character of the sovereign state, Thomas Hobbes. But whereas Hobbes' masterpiece was preoccupied with the issue of constructing sovereign rule in the midst of civil war, Grotius's vision of sovereignty is concerned with economics; and self-preservation, the most fundamental of natural rights, is elaborated principally in terms of economic survival and the system of trade and property that would enable it. For Grotius, of course, this was a very real issue as the survival of the emerging Dutch Republic depended on the VOC and its trading campaigns.

More particularly, in the context of the Indies, Borschberg notes that the basic thinking of Grotius was to inform all the treaties entered into by the Dutch at this time. Initially, Asian and Western states dealt with each other as equals; indeed, Grotius, in his argument in *Mare Liberum*, was vehement in asserting the sovereignty of Asian states. As he argued, referring to Java, Tabrobana, and the Moluccas:

> These islands we speak of have, and always had, their kings, their commonwealth, their laws and their liberties. Trading is granted to Portugal as to other nations; therefore, when they both pay tribute and obtain liberty of trade of the princes, they testify sufficiently that they are not lords but arrive there as foreigners, for they do not so much dwell there as but by entreaty.[36]

The rulers of Southeast Asia that the Dutch engaged with at this time developed their own ideas of statecraft. One such treatise on the subject, Taj-al Salatin ('The Crown of All Kings') was written by Bukhari al-Jauhari in 1603 in Aceh, north Sumatra,[37] and circulated widely in the region. The initial treaties between European powers and Asian states reflected the relative strength of the Asian rulers, with the trading entities seeking their permission to establish factories. This was in many ways the golden age of intercourse between these societies that scholars such as Alexandrowicz focus on. As Alexandrowicz further explains, Asian states entered into treaties which, as a matter of generosity and courtesy, allowed the foreign traders to establish themselves and even exercise civil and criminal law jurisdiction over their own subjects.[38] Further, Alexandrowicz argues, this suggested a long-standing Asian responsiveness to foreign communities and their established practices of welcoming and safeguarding 'their activities as merchants'.[39]

Later however, as European power grew, merchants sought to increase their rights through 'capitulations', in time obtained by force or the threat of it. These treaties often included provisions by which European states undertook to defend Asian states from other European powers and, in return, sought exclusive trading rights, monetary

Historical Explanations (OUP 2017); Philip Stern, *The Company State: Corporate Sovereignty and the Early Modern Foundations of the British Empire in India* (OUP 2011).

36 Grotius (n 26) ch 2.

37 See Arthur Weststeijn, 'Provincializing Grotius' in Koskenniemi et al (eds) (n 35) 21. The text was written in Malay in Arabic Script.

38 Alexandrowicz, *An Introduction to the History of the Law of Nations in the East Indies* (n 20) 103.

39 Ibid. 97. Thus the Portuguese were allowed to exercise jurisdiction over their own subjects in Macau; but this was with the authority of the Chinese Emperor.

compensation, and, finally, sovereignty over the areas they controlled. Thus in the case of Sri Lanka, by 1766, the last remaining indigenous ruler (the King of Kandy) entered into a treaty which recognized the sovereignty of 'the mighty States General of the free United Netherlands and the mighty Dutch Company over all the maritime provinces of the Island'.[40] In their efforts to protect themselves from one European power, Asian states lapsed into the clutches of other European rivals, who often adroitly exploited divisions amongst the native rulers and dissatisfaction amongst their subjects.

2.3 The Nineteenth Century and the Standard of Civilization

As Asian states fell increasingly into European control—signified, in the case of India for instance, by the battle of Plassey—international jurisprudence had shifted from the broad naturalism espoused by Grotius to the positivism that came to mark the nineteenth century. One of the most prominent features of this jurisprudence was the division it made between 'civilized' and 'uncivilized' states.[41] Broadly and implacably, an international law that was now emphatically based on European norms, rather than some 'universal' natural law, decreed that civilized states were sovereign and that uncivilized states were not. The difficulty remained, however, that states were also regarded as being 'quasi civilized', that is capable of entering into certain limited legal arrangements based on their degree of civilization which earned them some measure of legal personality.

Confusion and uncertainty followed. The content of this standard varied widely. For the nineteenth-century jurist, Whewell Professor of International Law, John Westlake, the test of civilization was 'government', that is, the capacity of the Asian state to establish a form of government essentially European in character that allowed Europeans 'to carry on the complex life to which they have become accustomed to in their home'.[42] Westlake acknowledged, however, that Asian empires had complex lives of their own and ensured law and order, even if (in relation to certain matters such as family and criminal law issues) Western norms were of a different character such that Europeans had to establish a separate system for themselves.[43] It was hard to deny the existence of highly 'civilized' societies in Asia; thus the classic Western writers such as Hall and Oppenheim suggested that these were 'quasi sovereign' states that were nevertheless excluded from complete membership of the family of nations on account of their different standards.

[40] See 'Treaties, Engagements and Sunnuds Relating to Ceylon' in Clive Parry (trs), *Consolidated Treaty Series with Index 1648–1919* (OUP 1969) 502, specifically, the 'Translation of a Treaty between the King of Kandia and the Government of Colombo—24th February 1766'.

[41] See Liliana Obregon, 'The Civilized and the Uncivilized' in Fassbender et al (eds) (n 1) 917.

[42] See John Westlake, *Chapters on the Principles of International Law* (CUP 1894) 141.

[43] Ibid. 142.

Gerrit Gong, in his authoritative examination of the standard of civilization, listed five broad factors including: (i) guarantees for the basic rights of liberty, dignity, property, freedom of travel, commerce, and religion; (ii) an organized and efficient political bureaucracy; (iii) adherence to international law; (iv) adequate and permanent diplomatic exchange and communication; and (v) adherence to cultural norms and practices of 'civilized' international society.[44] Asian states, even if not completely excluded from the realm of civilization, experienced their dealings with European powers at this stage as profound humiliations.[45] Japan and China, which had themselves been imperial powers earlier, felt this inferiority especially keenly. Virtually every Asian state in this phase of relations could identify the notorious treaty that affirmed their subordination. In the case of Sri Lanka, it was the Kandyan Convention of 1815; for Thailand, the Bowring Treaty of 1855; for Japan, the forced opening up of its harbours following the arrival of Admiral Perry; and for China, the Treaty of Nanking of 1842 following the First Opium War. Each of these treaties, despite their deeply unequal character, were invariably termed treaties of 'Friendship and Commerce' desiring to establish 'peace and friendship'.[46]

On the whole, the nineteenth century for Asian states was a time of bewilderment and disorientation caused by ruthless European expansion and their inability to resist it. A crucial feature of this expansion was that international law became emphatically unilateral and Eurocentric, and provided Asian states with very few meaningful rights—whatever the pretensions of reciprocity and professions of friendship and good will. International law enabled Western states to consolidate and present what had been accomplished through war and coercion in the guise of proper and sacrosanct legal relations. This is evident from the Treaty of Nanking, which required the Emperor of China to pay the cost of the military campaign against himself. The right to trade was asserted against the Emperor who had attempted to protect his citizens from the opium sold by the British.

International law had been used by China in defending its sovereignty; Chinese officers had sought the translation by a medical missionary in Canton of Vattel's *Le Droit de Gens* and used that text to support China's positions.[47] This was all to no avail, and it was not until after the Second Opium War that China made a concerted effort to understand and engage with the Western international law on a sustained and systematic basis. Henry Wheaton's classic, *Elements of International Law*, was translated into

[44] Gerrit Gong, *The Standard of Civilization in International Society* (Clarendon Press 1984) 3.

[45] For a broad-ranging survey of international law in East Asia see Shotaro Hamamoto, 'International Law, Regional Developments: East Asia' in *Max Planck Encyclopedia of International Law* (2013).

[46] See generally Saliha Belmessous, *Empire by Treaty: Negotiating European Expansion, 1600–1900* (OUP 2015).

[47] See Chi-Hua Tang (n 14). It is notable that Vattel lavishes praise on China on account, in particular, of its productive use of land for agricultural purposes. Vattel also asserted, unlike Grotius, that states were entitled to restrict trade for the benefit of their citizens.

Chinese in 1864.[48] In Japan, major texts by European authors such as Hall and Heffter were translated in the 1870s.[49] China set on the task of establishing itself as one among the law of nations within the Western system of international relations, thus in effect relinquishing—or appearing to relinquish at any rate—its historical perception of itself as the ruler of the Middle Kingdom.[50] The Kingdom of Thailand employed a number of prominent Western international lawyers to protect their interests during this period, and acted on their advice to seek a place for themselves amongst the family of nations. Participation in international conferences, such as the Hague Conferences of 1899 and 1907, thus took on an additional significance for these Asian states as they wanted to take their place amongst the great gatherings of nations.

The urgent project for Asian states towards the end of the nineteenth century, then, was to qualify as sovereign, 'civilized' nations once more. In Japan, a massive campaign was undertaken to completely transform the legal systems of the country and develop all the institutions and resources of a modern state, such as an industrialized economy and a formidably equipped and trained military. Legal reform was a crucial aspect of these efforts. Japan sent its scholars to all the major Western countries in the world to study the different legal systems in operation and it was especially quick to adapt to the demands of this new situation; a Japanese Red Cross Society was formed in 1877.[51]

In almost every case, the Western system was a stark contrast to the cosmologies that shaped governance and identity in Asian societies and that were often based on highly unequal tributary systems. While the European-Asian encounter might be described in these broad terms, a less studied theme has to do with the manner in which Asian states—all of them striving to adapt to a Western system of international relations from a fundamentally disadvantaged position—deployed that system amongst themselves. They often did this in an effort to consolidate and expand their own power within the region while seeking to prove themselves as proper civilized nations by using Western international law. Japanese expansion, at the expense of a weakened China and its neighbour, Korea, suggests these themes.

While the Treaty of Nanking is a classic 'unequal treaty',[52] many of its elements were reproduced in the treaty between Japan and Korea 1905, by which Korea became a Japanese protectorate, and the Treaty of Shimonseki of 1895 between Japan and China, by which China ceded various territories to Japan after the Sino-Japanese war of 1894. The language of this treaty is impeccably imperial in content as well as in rhetoric—the preliminary language speaks of friendship, and the need to restore peace. Under the

[48] Ibid. 705. See also Li Chen, *Chinese Law Under Imperial Eyes: Sovereignty, Justice and Transcultural Politics* (CUP 2015).

[49] See Kinji Akashi, 'Japan–Europe' in Fassbender et al (eds) (n 1) 732.

[50] See Teemu Ruskola, *Legal Orientalism: China, the United States and Modern Law*, (Harvard University Press 2013) 200.

[51] Akashi (n 49) 737.

[52] For a classic study of unequal treaties and their significance for China, see Wang Tieya, 'International Law in China: Historical and Contemporary Perspectives' (1990) 221 Academie du Droit International, Receuil De Cours, 195 (Brill Nijoff 1990).

treaty, China was required to cede territory, pay war indemnification (as was the case with Nanking), and open certain cities, ports, and towns to trade. Further, Japan meticulously monitored its military operations, claiming to abide strictly according to the laws of war in its infliction of violence in its various wars including the Russo-Japanese war. The American Journal of International Law noted the advances Japan had made in adhering to Western concepts of the conduct of war.[53] The most dramatic event in Japan's swift progress towards becoming a 'member of the Family of Nations' was, of course, the famous naval Japanese victory over Russia in the naval battle of Tsushima in 1905. The Japanese admiral on that occasion had no illusion of what it took to be admitted into the family of civilized nations, declaring that 'Once we defeat you in war we become civilized'.

During this period, as Asian states committed all their efforts and resources to meeting the standard of civilization, a few notable Asian voices were raised in dissent: for Mahatma Gandhi, modern civilization 'is a civilization only in name. Under it the nations of Europe are being degraded and ruined day by day'.[54] For Gandhi, colonialism exercised its power over India, not through military might or the force of law, but through its transformation of the Indian into a consumer: 'the English entered India for the purposes of trade. They remain in it for the same purpose and we help them to do so'.[55]

The drive towards entry into the civilized world took on an entirely new dimension following the First World War. Western claims to embodying 'civilization' completely collapsed as the carnage in Europe unfolded. And, of course, the reverberations of that event were felt throughout the colonized world. A 'New World Order' was inaugurated by the League of Nations and, at Paris in 1919, several Asian states sought to assert themselves. India, having contributed financially and provided manpower support to the British Empire in the Great War, became a founding member of the League of Nations, even though it was not self-governing (unlike Dominion powers such as Australia and New Zealand). This anomaly suggested in many ways—like the Mandate System of the League—the complex issues of sovereignty at the time of transition from colony to statehood.[56] India was one of the eight countries to have a seat in the Governing Body of the League of Nations and used its position to argue against International Labour Organization initiatives regarding working hours, on the basis of the 'backward conditions of India'.[57]

[53] See the review by Crammond Kennedy of two books detailing Japan's international legal practice in (1907) 1 AJIL 4, 1044–52. The books were by FE Smith (later Lord Birkenhead) and Amos S Hershey respectively. It also refers to works by Japanese authors detailing Japan's conduct in the war on China.

[54] Mahatma Gandhi, *Hind Swaraj*, cited in Mahatma Gandhi (Judith Brown (ed)), *The Essential Writings* (OUP 2008) 137.

[55] Ibid. 139.

[56] See Stephen Legg, 'An International Anomaly? Sovereignty, the League of Nations and India's Princely Geographies', (2014) 43 Journal of Historical Geography 96, 98. Legg also offers a useful catalogue of the ways in which sovereignty can be manifested and studied.

[57] Ibid. 99.

Japan, a major beneficiary of the war, assumed its position amongst the great powers as suggested by its presence on the League Council. Japanese international lawyers played important roles in the various committees and institutions created by the League: Yorozu Oda, for instance, was appointed as a judge on the Permanent Court of International Justice.[58] Further, Japan was appointed a mandatory power to the Pacific Territories scattered in the northern Pacific. Nevertheless, the Japanese people felt that this acceptance was only partial. Their efforts to include a clause affirming the equality of all human races in the League Covenant was famously rejected.[59]

More broadly, President Woodrow Wilson's articulation of the principle of self-determination intended to address the problem of nationalism in the Balkans was quickly embraced by colonized peoples everywhere, including Asia. Ho Chi Minh, an obscure cook in Paris at the time, sought to meet Wilson in order to further his country's nationalist campaign against the French. Korea similarly wanted to assert its right of self-determination, but this time against the Japanese who were establishing themselves throughout the League period as a major imperial power through its wars against China.[60] Syngman Rhee's efforts to persuade Wilson to embrace the Korean cause was a failure, and this was all the more personally painful as he had graduated with a doctorate that had been handed to him at Princeton by Wilson himself.[61]

3 Decolonization

The campaign for decolonization that had been growing during the interwar period became unstoppable, and the topic became a major concern of the United Nations itself. The Philippines became independent on 4 July—no coincidence here—1946. However, the birth of India and Pakistan in August 1947 suggested vividly the challenges confronting the 'new states' of Asia. How could modern nation-states be created out of far older polities, whether empires or princely states or tribes, that had been transformed so profoundly by colonial powers? This was to be an enduring problem for many Asian states.

China participated in the second phase of the Dumbarton Oakes Conference in 1943, by which time most of the major decisions had been taken by Russia, the United States, and the United Kingdom. Several Asian states participated in the San Francisco Conference that created the UN. From East Asia, there were India, the Philippines, and China; and from West Asia, Iran, Iraq, Lebanon, and Saudi Arabia. China's delegation included the formidable Wellington Koo, who had been campaigning for the country for many decades, including at the League of Nations. China here argued that every colony had the right to become independent and prevailed in this regard

58 See Akashi (n 49) 740. 59 Ibid. 739.

60 See Erez Manela, *The Wilsonian Moment* (1st edn OUP 2007). 61 Ibid. 200–1.

against the United States, France, and the United Kingdom amongst others.[62] Although India was present at the Conference, its representatives did not take a very active part in the proceedings. Its greatest leaders at the time, including Nehru, had been imprisoned by the British.[63] On the whole, Asian states played only a very minor role in the drafting of the document that continues to operate as the blue print for the international community.

The sense of exclusion animated a number of Asian initiatives shortly afterwards. Nehru organized the Asian Relations Conference held in New Delhi in India in 1947, even as India prepared for independence. Presented initially as a 'cultural conference' its central concern was the role of emerging Asia in a new global dispensation from which it felt excluded. Invitations were issued by the organizing body, the Indian Council of World Affairs (of which Nehru was President), to all Asian countries. Nehru claimed that the natural intercourse that had occurred amongst Asian nations previously had been hindered by colonial rule. Egypt was the sole non-Asian participant. Others present included Palestine and the Soviet Asian Republics, such as Armenia, Kazakhstan, Tajikistan, Georgia, and Uzbekistan, and if these were counted, more than thirty countries were represented at the Conference.[64] The themes taken up by the Conference included National Freedom Movements, Cultural Problems, Women's Problems, Migration and Racial Problems, and Economic Development and Social Services. Most tellingly, economic development became a crucial issue; and it was argued that political freedom was essential for economic freedom, conceived here as a planned economy.[65] It was notable, further, that according to one report, at least for Ceylon, Burma, Indonesia, and Malaya, 'No sooner was Western exploitation denounced than fears emerged of a more stringent Indian and Chinese stranglehold once it had gone'.[66] Questions of Asian regionalism and its effectiveness were also discussed.

Equally, however, it was clear that beyond pleasant generalizations, real differences separated the various states. The Muslim League, for instance, boycotted the Conference. Gandhi attended the last two sessions of the Conference. The conference that was supposed to take place in China two years later never transpired. Instead, it was Sir John Kotelawela of Ceylon who convened the Colombo Conference in 1954. This was attended by Burma, India, Pakistan, and Indonesia, and it was following this event that the idea of a conference in Indonesia gradually formed. In broad terms, Asian states believed that they had an important role to play in international law and relations in the new era following decolonization, but that they were already marginalized from the system.

The Bandung Conference of 1955 was a defining event because firstly, it was attended by both Asian and African countries, and was thus the foundation of the Third World

[62] See *Chi-Hua Tang* (n 14) 720–1.

[63] See RP Anand, 'The Formation of International Organizations and India: A Historical Study' (2010) 23 Leiden JIL 5.

[64] Nicholas Mansergh in (1947) 23(3) *International Affairs* 295–306.

[65] Ibid. 299. [66] Ibid. 300.

movement, the Non-Aligned Movement; and secondly, the Third World outlined their vision of world order in the final communiqué of the Conference.[67] The African countries present at the Conference were Liberia, Libya, Egypt, the Gold Coast, and Ethiopia. Much of Africa was still subject to colonial rule. At the Conference, the Afro-Asian states affirmed their respect for 'fundamental human rights' and recognized 'the equality of all races and of the equality of all nations large and small'. Equally importantly, the Bandung states emphasized the 'sovereignty and territorial integrity of states'[68] and condemned 'intervention or interference in the internal affairs of another country'.[69] For them at least, espousing both these principles created no tensions or contradictions.

Nehru proclaimed that these ideas were based on the concept of '*panchaseel*'—the five principles of peaceful coexistence that are said to have been first articulated in an earlier treaty between China and India. Here, there was a gesture by Asian states towards reviving a distinctively 'Asian' approach to international affairs as part of their contribution to a new system of international relations. Indonesia had earlier articulated Pancasila as its national philosophy. Nehru himself was hazy as to the origins of the idea of *panchaseel*, and commentators have pointed out that many of its principles correspond with the law of the United Nations. Nevertheless, the idea that the 'five principles' are an embodiment of an Asian approach to international relations persists and is continuously highlighted and affirmed, as in 2015 when the anniversary of Bandung was celebrated in China.

Equally important, although less commented on, is the emphasis given at Bandung to economic cooperation in the very first section of the communiqué. The Bandung states 'recognized the urgency of promoting economic development in the Asian-African region'. Significantly, further, they expressed an openness to foreign investment, and stressed the importance of international trade and the creation of agencies within the UN and the World Bank that would be devoted to development issues.[70] The Bandung states, then, were willing to engage with a revised international commercial system. The larger issues raised by Bandung are too complex to be discussed here, and so scholars are welcomed to explore the Bandung legacy in greater depth.[71]

For the purposes of this chapter, we clearly see in the Bandung Conference an attempt to construct a Third World movement, one that transcended Asia and that unified all the colonized peoples of the world. In time, it allied with Latin American countries that had also been arguing for a different global system. Bandung expressed solidarity with the anti-colonial struggles in Algeria and Morocco. The three main

[67] For a major new study of Bandung and its legacies, see Luis Eslava, Michael Fakhri, and Vasuki Nesiah (eds), *Bandung, Global History and International Law: Critical Pasts and Pending Futures* (CUP 2017).

[68] Final Communiqué of the Asian-African conference of Bandung (23 April 1955) art. G(2).

[69] Ibid. art. G(4).

[70] See Antony Anghie, 'Bandung and the Origins of Third World Sovereignty' in Eslava et al (eds) (n 67) 535.

[71] See Eslava et al (eds) (n 67).

themes of this nascent Third World movement then were anti-colonialism; sovereignty; and development. These were elaborated into the major policies of the Non-Aligned Movement too, and are evident in the efforts of that Movement to create a New International Economic Order. This campaign was furthered through various means, including the creation of the United Nations Conference on Trade and Development as well as the formulation of the Charter of Rights and Duties of States as a comprehensive blue print for the international system. The developing states also campaigned for a number of other important resolutions such as the Declaration 1514 against Colonialism. This, then, was a 'Third World Universalism', an idea of universalism that was based, not on some metaphysical theory of 'the human being' or 'natural rights', but on a political programme constructed on the basis of the urgent needs and demands of the vast majority of the world's population which recognized that those needs could not be met without a change in the international system, and that international law was a crucial element of this campaign. What is evident then is that Asian states and scholars, rather than formulating a uniquely 'Asian' approach to international law, sought to deploy and expand on what they saw as the liberating potential of international law to develop a new vision of the discipline, one that was embodied in efforts to create a 'New International Economic Order' (NIEO). For these purposes, Asian states and scholars collaborated with their colleagues from Latin America and Africa. Efforts to identify an 'Asian Approach' to international law should not overlook this dimension of a project that was so extraordinarily ambitious that it is somehow rendered invisible. It is only very recently that international law scholars have begun to reappraise the character and ambition of the NIEO.

The NIEO was in many respects an embodiment of the thinking of major Asian jurists, such as JJG Syatauw,[72] RP Anand, and Wang Tieya, who were trying to formulate the Third World position relating to international law. The principal challenge they faced at this time was to develop a version of international law that would advance the interests of Third World states, a particularly complex task given that international law had been an instrument of conquest and colonization.[73] The broad approach taken by these scholars—and they included not only Asian scholars but others such as Taslim Elias of Nigeria—was to desist from rejecting international law, instead outlining an amended version of it. They believed that the colonial aspects of international law could be excised from the larger body of international law, which could serve the proper purpose of advancing human welfare and well-being. It was precisely at this time that Asian scholars drew on the pioneering work of Alexandrowicz and others who had studied the interaction between Asian and European states.

[72] See the pioneering work, JJG Syatauw, *Some Newly Established States and the Development of International Law* (Martinus Nijhoff 1961).

[73] For a far-reaching analysis of the impact of this dilemma on Indian international law scholarship, see Chimni (n 3). For a pioneering study of China and contemporary international law, see Xue Hanqin, *Chinese Contemporary Perspectives on International Law: History, Culture and International Law* (Martinus Nijhoff 2012).

An interest re-emerged in what was presented as 'Asia's' own history of international law. This was another occasion on which history mattered. In arguing that Asia had its own history of international law, scholars also in effect established that they too were civilized and could participate as equals in the international system.[74]

Further, this view of history supported the argument that a decolonized Asia could enrich international law. This is a sentiment strongly evident, for instance, in the jurisprudence of Judge Christopher Weeramantry.[75] This position was at least in part a response to conservative Western scholars who argued that international law was so fundamentally Western that its rules were entirely foreign to Asian states who would be incapable of complying with them. In addition, the Alexandrowicz view of international law, which focused on that period of equality between Asian and European states, suggested that there was nothing inherently disadvantageous about international law. These were the broad views that are evident in articles such as RP Anand's classic 'Attitude of Asian-African States toward Certain Problems of International Law'. It is notable again that Anand outlines a Third World position on the issue, one that also incorporates the concerns of Latin American states, in which Asian states increasingly shared concern regarding, for instance, the rules of state responsibility. Anand, moreover, was convinced that laws would adapt to change, and that the entrance of the new states that contained the vast majority of the world's population into the system of international relations, and the intensifying interdependence of states, would result in a change to this system.[76]

Enthusiasm and support for international law amongst Asian and developing-country scholars more broadly was at its zenith at this stage. Numerous authors wrote enthusiastically about the law of the sea, the use of force, and international economic law, all in the hope of creating a different and more peaceful world. This campaign largely failed, however, and was followed by the collapse of the NIEO and its replacement by the beginnings of what we now term 'neo-liberalism'. The law of the sea negotiations which had become a fundamental element of the developing states' campaign was also negated by the Western powers. As a result of such developments, Asian states understandably recoiled in disappointment, and Asian scholars adopted a different and far more modest, indeed disillusioned, stance in their writings on international law, and the NIEO and all related initiatives vanished in international law scholarship. The very idea of a 'developing country' perspective on international law seemed impossible, if not embarrassing.

[74] As Chimni puts it, 'The past was recalled and interpreted to service the present' (Chimni (n 3) 28).

[75] *Legality of the Threat or Use of Nuclear Weapons* (Advisory Opinion) [1996] ICJ Rep 226 (Dissenting Opinion of Judge Weeramantry) paras 429–555. Interestingly, he presents the Asian perspective while simultaneously suggesting it is universal. See also *Case Concerning the Gabčíkovo-Nagymaros Project (Hungary/Slovakia)* (Separate Opinion of Judge Weeramantry) [1997] ICJ Rep 7 paras 88–116.

[76] See RP Anand, 'Attitude of the Asian-African States toward Certain Problems of International Law' (1966) 15 ICLQ 55, 63. It is notable that Anand also surveys the experiences of Latin-American countries and suggests the commonalities with Asian and African countries.

Asian states—like the developing countries in general—were by this stage too exhausted to engage significantly in the major transformations that occurred in international law in the time following the fall of the Berlin wall, as the WTO came into existence, investment regimes consolidated and expanded, and major initiatives such as the Responsibility to Protect and the International Criminal Court were enthusiastically advanced, principally by Western international lawyers and institutions. Asian states that had reluctantly followed the programmes on liberalization advocated by international law and institutions were then subjected to the 'Asian Crisis' of 1997 and all the accompanying trauma, including becoming recipients of IMF bail-out programmes with stringent conditions.

Despite this, in the decades that followed, Asian states have made extraordinary progress, as suggested by the accomplishments of China, South Korea, and Singapore, which followed the much earlier example of Japan in increasing their wealth and lifting their populations out of poverty. Each country's accomplishments were distinctive, however, and it is unclear as to what lessons can be generalized from these cases.[77] In each case, however, it is arguable that a strong state was essential for the successful economic transformation, even when, paradoxically, the countries involved were embracing economic globalization.[78] Systematic studies are emerging now about the manner in which international law was used for these purposes and how developing countries adapted to the demands of globalization.[79]

It is notable that China and Singapore, unlike Korea, have liberalized their economies whilst strongly resisting any impingement on their sovereignty through human rights and substantive democracy. A crude duality has emerged here: authoritarianism and the market have operated very effectively in many Asian countries, giving rise to the argument that 'order' and 'stability' are crucial for development. In any event, it was in the arena of human rights that some Asian states asserted themselves most forcefully in the 1990s, by arguing that 'Asian values' were different from putative 'universal human rights'. What is most remarkable, however, is the rapid growth that many Asian states achieved during this period. The dislocation and hardship accompanying globalization were addressed by the social resources of Asian societies that had sustained them for millennia—the community, and more specifically, the family—even while they were subjected to unique pressures. Development and sovereignty, the two major concerns of these societies, interacted in this complex way.

The progress that many Asian states have made, particularly those in East and Southeast Asia, should not obscure the enduring issues they confront, and which

[77] China has succeeded in lifting its people out of poverty on a greater scale than previously witnessed in human history; Korea, which had one of the lowest GDPs in the world in the 1960s, is now a member of the OECD; and Singapore now has among the highest standards of living in the world.

[78] See Ha Joon Chang, *Kicking Away the Ladder: Development Strategy in Historical Perspective* (Anthem World Economics 2002); Alice Amsden, *Escape from Empire* (MIT Press 2009).

[79] See e.g. Gregory Shaffer and Ricardo Melendez-Ortiz (eds), *Dispute Settlement at the WTO: The Developing Country Experience* (CUP 2010); Weitseng Chen (ed), *The Beijing Consensus? How China has Changed Western Ideas of Law and Development* (CUP 2017).

emerged at the very beginning of their creation as sovereign, independent states. The nation-state form that was the prerequisite for sovereignty was foreign to many Asian states, which had developed different ideas of territory and governance.[80] Indeed, nationalism in these new states created an immediate problem by seeming to demand a singularity that did not exist. Whereas in earlier times different ethnicities and cultures had interacted with and accommodated each other in various ways, the edict of the nation-state created a massive insecurity amongst both majority and minority communities in ethnically divided states. It is notable that many Asian countries, shortly after achieving independence, passed nationality laws that left minorities stateless or disadvantaged. The tragic plight of the Rohingya is one product of this phenomenon. The spectre of secession and security have continued to haunt many Asian states. Sri Lanka's particularly bloody war against Tamil separatists, with its ongoing and unresolved issues of accountability and reconciliation, is emblematic in this regard. At the very heart of such conflicts is the meaning of the 'nation-state'.[81]

4 Towards the Present and Beyond

The 'rise' of Asia, occurring at a time when the West is perceived to be in decline, has raised complex and urgent issues about how these developments will affect international law. An odd reversal has occurred: the two major Western states, the United States and the United Kingdom, are turning against the system of globalization which they created. It is now the major Asian states that seek to advance globalization and that are advocates of, for instance, the Trans-Pacific Partnership and Regional Comprehensive Economic Partnership. And it is China, historically the closed, insular empire, that is taking the lead in many of these initiatives. Most particularly, its massive One Belt One Road Initiative simultaneously suggests an alternative past, the Silk Road, and an as yet unknown future for globalization. Looking at this issue more broadly, there appears another instance in which Asia, having mastered the rules of the game of globalization, now finds the rules changed once more. Whereas major Asian states have combined an emphasis on national sovereignty with a gradually opening economy, the United States and the United Kingdom at the time of writing appeared intent on focusing on sovereignty and view economic integration as a threat.

A number of conceptual models have been sketched for understanding these developments. Should they be seen in terms of another reiteration of the realist,

[80] This is evident for instance in the *Temple of Preah Vihear* case and what it suggests about traditional Thai concepts of sovereignty and territory. See *Case Concerning the Temple of Preah Vihear (Cambodia v Thailand)*, (Merits) [1962] ICJ Rep 260; Thongchai Winichakul, *Siam Mapped: A History of a Geo-Body of a Nation* (University of Hawaii Press 1994).

[81] See Itty Abraham, *How India Became Territorial* (Stanford University Press 2014).

'Great Power' story?[82] What does the growing power of China and India presage[83]? Will the rise of Asia result in changes to the liberal, Western-based order that has governed the globe since the nineteenth century? Or will there be the emergence of a truly 'transcivilizational world', with all its promise and perils, as Onuma Yasuaki suggests?[84] This possibility is related to another influential body of scholarship premised on the view that states such as China pursue policies based on more historical ideas of governance and its place in the world, international law being only a malleable instrument for the purposes of advancing this vision. A massive and in many ways neo-Orientalist literature that attempts to understand the inscrutable Other has followed. But it is also surely true that historical ideas of governance and order play a role in the approach of Asian states to international law. Furthermore, in many respects, history plays an ongoing role particularly with regard to inter-Asian disputes.

If Asian states are ambivalent about international law because they view it, surely with justification, as an instrument of power, then it is also an instrument that might be wielded by historical rivals and neighbours. Japan's use of international law in this way in the early nineteenth century left its mark. And history is not simply a scholarly enterprise, but a crucial feature of the most traditional, formal, and positivist arguments made by Asian states in major disputes between Thailand and Cambodia, Singapore and Malaysia, Japan and Korea, China and all other countries involved in the South China Sea dispute. A range of historical issues are generated, first, by the classic law of inter-temporality which means that the rights of the respective countries must be assessed in terms of the law of the time—perhaps the nineteenth century or even earlier, in the case of territorial and maritime boundary disputes. Second, almost all these disputes involve colonial powers, France or Britain, typically, and the treaties they had entered into. In the case of territorial disputes between Japan and its neighbours, crucial questions depend on the 1951 Peace Treaty.[85] Third, there arises the even more radical question of whether historic claims—central to the South China Sea dispute for instance—must be assessed according to Western international law or some other, older, 'regional' system. Similar arguments arise in the disputes between Korea and Japan. The past is indeed not dead; it is not even the past.

Whatever the complexities of the hazardous enterprise of understanding Asia through the lens of 'culture' or 'civilization' it cannot be overlooked that the most prominent feature of contemporary Asian civilization, one that unites countries that are otherwise very diverse, is a preoccupation with growth and development. The legitimacy of many Asian states depends not so much on their adherence to

[82] See Congyan Cai, 'New Great Powers and International Law in the 21st Century' (2013) 24 EJIL 755.

[83] See Muthucumaraswamy Sornarajah and Jiangyu Wang, *China, India and International Economic Order* (CUP 2010).

[84] Onuma Yasuaki, *International Law in a Transcivilizational World* (CUP 2017).

[85] See e.g. Seokwoo Lee and Jon Van Dyke, 'The 1951 San Francisco Peace Treaty and its Relevance to the Sovereignty over Dokdo' (2010) 9 Chinese JIL 741; Sookyeon Huh, 'Title to Territory in the Post-Colonial Era: Original Title and Terra Nullius in the ICJ Judgments on Cases Concerning Ligitan/Sipadan (2002) and Pedra Branca (2008)' (2015) 26 EJIL 709.

applicable constitutional or human rights norms as on their ability to ensure security and deliver development to their people. India and China in particular have now come to expect ongoing prosperity as their destiny and a real affirmation of their ascendance into the ranks of great powers. Growth and development have replaced natural law and religion as the ultimate binding authority on states.

A number of consequences follow if this is indeed the case. First, there is the technocratic issue of how what are now 'middle income' countries can continue to grow and the role of law in this process.[86] Second, and most significantly, there are the environmental consequences of this relentless and inevitable pursuit of more consumption. In Asia, perhaps more than in any other region, we see the contradictions of the global economy unfold. Wealth and well-being is based on economic growth and consumption that have to expand endlessly to ensure both the continuation of the Asian economic model and the satisfaction of the large and growing populations of Asia. Third, whatever the claimed other-worldliness of Asian civilization and religions such as Buddhism, these are all being subjected to massive stress because of the overwhelming civilization of consumption; religious teachings are often distorted into justifications for commodification and excess. Fourth, this emphasis on growth and development has, everywhere, been accompanied by an intensifying inequality which has manifested itself not only in economic but political terms. It is unclear how long the dispossessed, those who have lost even their meagre subsistence existence to the land grabs taking place throughout Asia[87]—this systematic immiseration is as much a feature of the Asian success story as the new cities emerging throughout the continent—will accept their fate in the hope that they too can be a part of the emerging new world.

Fifth, history strongly suggests that states which have immense power almost invariably engage in imperial practices as their increasing populations demand higher standards of living as a confirmation, at a personal and community level, of their growing status and prestige in the world, and that is what matters most for purposes of governance. Unexercised power is pointless. Further, as John Darwin points out, in the course of human history, it is empires that have governed for the longest time. The nation-state is a very recent invention. And Asia contains 'nation-states' that, even when small, have conceived of themselves as empires or empires to be.[88] Indeed, China and India may be viewed as nation-states that conceive of themselves as re-emergent empires and that could in time adopt corresponding policies. Scholarship can tend, consequently, to focus largely on China and India in its accounts of

[86] See Randall Peerenboom and Tom Ginsburg (eds), *Law and Development of Middle-Income Countries: Avoiding the Middle Income Trap* (CUP 2014).

[87] See Andrew Harding and Connie Carter, *Land Grabs in Asia: What Role for the Law?* (Routledge 2015).

[88] A reading of the *Arthashastra* is illuminating because it presents even the smallest states as aspiring to be empires—almost of necessity, as its author conceived of the political universe as compelling expansion—or demise.

'Asian International Law', thus overlooking the issue of smaller, less powerful Asian states and their relationship with international law.

International law scholars trying to understand all these issues are confronted by many challenges. The most traditional approach, and still a very valuable and indeed necessary approach, is to focus on the state. In recent times, however, international law scholarship itself has changed its character. The insights of history, political theory, and sociology—about nationhood and identity,[89] governance,[90] trade, and globalization[91]—are now especially important because all these issues are the subjects again of international law scholarship. Such fields were once present in the writings of Grotius and Vitoria, when the disciplinary boundaries established in the nineteenth century not only did not exist, but would have been incomprehensible. And it is surely important to consider these insights, just as Third World Approaches to International Law scholars have insisted on writing these histories 'from below',[92] without succumbing to sovereign imperatives in the very epistemology adopted. Migrant workers, refugees, indigenous peoples,[93] women,[94] and minorities provide unique, challenging, and necessary perspectives on all these developments, pointing to the violence, exclusions, and discriminations that continue to challenge international law and its operations in Asia. Otherwise the Asian emphasis on the state, evident at least since Bandung,[95] has often also profoundly affected scholarship, demanding implicitly that international lawyers too commit themselves and their work to furthering the project of the state.

Moreover, the 'regional framework' that has inspired this volume and which in itself is a reflection of a turn to 'regional analysis'[96] is also in need of interrogation, even if it is a useful heuristic device and offers valuable insights. What is needed here are global histories that trace the parallels and cross-cutting relationships between developments in Asia, Africa, and Latin America. Arnulf Becker Lorca's work is exemplary

[89] See e.g. Partha Chatterjee, *The Nation and Its Fragments* (Princeton University Press 1993); Ashis Nandy, *Intimate Enemy: Loss and Recovery of Self Under Colonialism* (OUP 1983).

[90] Karuna Mantena, *Alibis of Empire: Henry Maine and the Ends of Liberal Imperialism* (Princeton University Press 2010).

[91] Abdul Sherriff and Engseng Ho (eds), *The Indian Ocean: Oceanic Connections and the Creation of New Societies* (Hurst 2014).

[92] Balakrishnan Rajagopal, *International Law from Below* (CUP 2003); Prabhakar Singh, 'Indian International Law: From a Colonized Apologist to Subaltern Protagonist' (2010) 23 Leiden JIL 79.

[93] Benedict Kingsbury, '"Indigenous Peoples" in International Law: A Constructivist Approach to the Asian Controversy' (1998) 92 AJIL 414.

[94] Cyra Choudhury, '(Mis)Appropriated Liberty: Identity, Gender Justice, and Muslim Personal Law Reform in India' (2008) 17 Columbia Journal of Gender and Law 45; Ratna Kapur, 'Human Rights in the 21st Century: Take a Walk on the Wild Side' (2006) 28 Sydney Law Review 665.

[95] The difficulties of establishing a human rights system in Asia are illuminatingly explored in Hsien-Li Tan, *The ASEAN Intergovernmental Commission of Human Rights: Institutionalizing Human Rights in Southeast Asia* (CUP 2011).

[96] See Anthea Roberts, Paul Stephan, Pierre-Hugues Verdier, and Mila Versteeg (eds), *Comparative International Law* (OUP 2018).

in this regard,[97] as is the recently published collection of essays on Bandung.[98] Such works make the important point that Asia's history should be viewed in relation, not only to the West, but to other regions, Africa, and Latin America. This is especially the case as China, for instance, expands its activities in Africa.[99] BS Chimni's class-based analysis offers another way of understanding Asian international law in a broader perspective.[100] Moreover, as the Bandung Conference and the Non-Aligned Movement suggest, Asian states, at least at that stage, saw themselves as engaged in a common global enterprise on behalf of the poor and powerless.

Whether something of that vision can be reconstructed—whether it is possible to conceive of an alternative cosmopolitanism to contemporary globalization—remains to be seen. But the rich history of Asia suggests that the seeds of such a vision and of different models of human society and behaviour are there to be cultivated and harvested.

[97] See Arnulf Becker Lora, *Mestizo International Law: A Global Intellectual History 1842–1933* (CUP 2014).

[98] See Eslava et al (eds) (n 67).

[99] See e.g. James Gathii, 'Beyond China's Human Rights Exceptionalism in Africa: Leveraging Science, Technology and Engineering for Long Term Growth' (2013) 51 Columbia Journal of Transnational Law 664.

[100] BS Chimni, *International Law and World Order: A Critique of Contemporary Approaches* (2nd edn CUP 2017).

PART II

SPECIALIZED BRANCHES OF INTERNATIONAL LAW IN ASIA AND THE PACIFIC

CHAPTER 5

REGIONAL PEACE AND SECURITY

WAHEGURU PAL SINGH SIDHU

1 Introduction

The attitudes of the key actors in Asia[1]—notably China and India—towards international law in general, and peace and security arrangements in particular, have long been shaped by internal and external factors. Internally, indigenous strategic cultures have evolved over two millennia. Prior to the colonial period, this tended to emphasize the status quo, albeit without well-established norms or the wherewithal to defend them. Post-colonial policies have focused on sovereignty and non-interference, coupled with great power rivalry. The external factors include the debilitating political, economic, and security consequences of colonialism; the experience of the two World Wars; a minimal role in shaping the post-war global architecture; a messy process of decolonization with its disputed borders and contested territories; and the divisive experience of the Cold War.

Since the end of the Cold War and the resurgence of Asian economies, there has been significant movement in the establishment of peace and security institutions. Notable among them are the Association of Southeast Asian Nations (ASEAN) Regional Forum (ARF), the Shanghai Cooperation Organization (SCO), the East Asia Summit (EAS), the Quadrilateral Security Dialogue ('Quad'), and the Indian Ocean Rim Association (IORA). This movement was partly due to regional hegemons seeking a greater role in their neighbourhood and partly due to smaller states seeking to

[1] For this chapter: 'Asia' includes the fifty-five members of the Asia-Pacific group at the United Nations (UN), stretching from Cyprus in the west, to Kiribati in the east, and from Kazakhstan in the north to Tonga in the south, plus Australia, New Zealand, and the United States (ANZUS), and Russia. Though not part of the UN Asia-Pacific group, ANZUS countries and Russia are included by virtue of their geographical location and their peace and security role in the region.

manage the regional hegemons. Simultaneously, China and India also began playing a crucial role in shaping the evolving norms relating to climate change, cyber security, energy security, trade, and outer space.

Today, apart from the unresolved disputes that date back to the creation of the United Nations (UN), Asia is facing a number of new interstate security challenges, including maritime territorial disputes, nuclear proliferation, and geo-economic contests. Moreover, the region has a number of intrastate conflicts, sometimes exploited by external actors in proxy wars. Finally, the region is also confronted with a number of non-traditional transnational threats, including terrorism, international crime, piracy, and pandemics.

What is the normative approach and practice of the states and the region to address these challenges? How will their varied experiences influence their approach to these peace and security issues in the future? Will the region play a more prominent role in the establishment of global norms related to peace and security; will the region become a 'rule shaper'? Is there any distinctive Asian way to deal with peace and security issues?

To address these questions, the chapter will begin with an overview of the historical legacy of Asia towards international law and regional peace and security. It will then consider the impact of the 1945 United Nations Charter, the role of the UN, the prohibition on the use of force, the right of self-defence, and collective security in the region. To what extent did the region adhere to the norms established by the UN Charter? The chapter examines these issues through a series of case studies including the Korean War, Kashmir, Tibet, the India–China War, the Vietnam War, and the liberation of Bangladesh. The following section looks at the post-Cold War behaviour of the region in shaping global and regional peace and security norms through the prism of a couple of case studies on the South China Seas and the North Korean nuclear imbroglio. The final section offers some concluding remarks as to whether there is a distinctively 'Asian way' to approach regional peace and security issues.

2 Early Beginnings

Historically, Asian civilizations from Mesopotamia through to India and China were among the earliest to develop concepts of international law—both written and unwritten. This evolution took place in part due to the expansion of ancient empires, in part due to post-conflict treaties, and in part due to intra-Asian and intercontinental trade and commerce. Some of the earliest international laws on peace and security originated in Mesopotamia in the twenty-fifth to twenty-fourth centuries BCE.[2] The Indian epics of the *Mahabharata* and *Ramayana*, transmitted orally from the eighth or ninth century BCE, reflect antecedents of modern international law. While the *Mahabharata*

[2] Amnon Altman, *Tracing the Earliest Recorded Concepts of International Law: The Ancient Near East (2500–330 BCE)* (Brill 2012).

theorizes the concept of just war (*dharmayuddha*),[3] the *Ramayana* considers the proper and improper use of force.[4] The *Ramayana*'s principles were subsequently transmitted throughout Southeast Asia as later Indian kingdoms extended their reach.

Arthashastra (Statecraft), another Indian treatise written around 300 BCE, is a classic in the later political realist tradition.[5] Compared to Niccolo Machiavelli's *The Prince* (1532), though predating it by some 1,800 years, it has a wide scope covering economic and military policy, and statecraft. The *Arthashastra* elaborates on just war and even discusses the idea of humanitarian intervention.[6] It advocates the need to avoid war as much as possible and to use military force only as a last resort.

India's contribution to international law was further enriched by Ashoka, probably the most famous ruler of the Mauryan dynasty (322–185 BCE), who promoted the concept of *Dhamma* and non-violence or non-use of force in interstate relations.[7] The Ashokan world view, along with Buddhism (which Ashoka embraced and promoted as a state religion), eventually spread peacefully from India all the way to Japan via China and Southeast Asia. It survived colonialism and thrives even today. Many of these traditional ideas and concepts were revived and embraced by India's freedom fighters, such as Mohandas Gandhi—who used non-violence to bring British rule to an end—and today find echoes in the 1950 Constitution of independent India.

China's ideas on international law and peace and security can be traced back to the sixth to fifth centuries BCE and the philosopher K'ung-fu-tzu (Confucius).[8] Scholars examining the writings of Confucius, Mencius, and Xunzi conclude that there is a 'pacifist bias' in Chinese tradition that prohibits war.[9] Adelmann and Shih and other scholars note two aspects of Chinese strategic thought: first, non-violent solutions are preferred to conflict and second, if conflict is unavoidable then defensive warfare is advocated.[10]

Subsequent Chinese thinking on international law and just war is derived from *The Seven Military Classics of Ancient China*,[11] (anthologized around 1080 AD) including

[3] Francis Clooney, 'Pain but Not Harm: Some Classical Resources toward a Hindu Just War Theory' in Paul Robinson (ed), *Just War in Comparative Perspective* (Ashgate 2003) 117.

[4] Raj Balkaran and Walter Dorn, 'Violence in the Vālmıki Rāmāyaṇa: Just War Criteria in an Ancient Indian Epic' (2012) 80 Journal of the American Academy of Religion 659.

[5] Shyam Saran, *How India Sees the World: Kautilya to the 21st Century* (Juggernaut 2017) 9–24.

[6] Manoj Kumar Sinha, 'Hinduism and International Humanitarian Law' (2005) 87 International Review of the Red Cross 285, 289.

[7] *Dhamma* means 'right conduct, duty, religion, law, social justice and responsibility': ibid. 289–90.

[8] Daniel Bell, 'Just War and Confucianism: Implications for the Contemporary World' in Daniel Bell (ed), *Confucian Political Ethics* (Princeton University Press 2007) 226–57.

[9] John Fairbank, 'Introduction: Varieties of the Chinese Military Experience' in Frank Kiermann and John Fairbank (eds), *Chinese Ways in Warfare* (Harvard University Press 1974) 7.

[10] Jonathan R Adelmann and Chih-yu Shih, *Symbolic War: The Chinese Use of Force: 1840–1980* (National Chengchi University 1993) 32 and Nadine Godehardt, 'The Chinese Meaning of Just War and Its Impact on the Foreign Policy of the People's Republic of China' (2008) GIGA Working Papers 88/2008, 10 <http://www.giga-hamburg.de/en/system/files/publications/wp88_godehardt.pdf> accessed 6 October 2018.

[11] Ralph Sawyer (Mei-chün Sawyer (trs)), *The Seven Military Classics of Ancient China* (Westview Press 1993).

Sun-tzu's *Art of War* (dating from the fifth century BCE). While condemning war in general, these writings nonetheless argue in favour of just war. Thus, according to Godehardt,

> the concept of Just War was not only a political instrument for the military strategists but also the foundation for the development of their strategies... War should only be fought when victory is certain. The aim of war is victory or—in a broader sense—peace.[12]

However, as Kane argues, 'none of these schools of thought prescribe detailed laws to regulate war', nor do they 'put much effort into exploring the logical consequences of self-defence either'.[13] This implies, unsurprisingly, that Chinese philosophers tended to be weak strategists. He concludes that Taoism emerges as the 'most useful' Chinese concept on war but also differs most from Western writing in that it relies on intuition rather than the Socratic tradition. As in the case of India, many of these ideas survived the colonial period and were used by leaders such as Mao Zedong in the Long March (1934–35) and in the establishment of the People's Republic of China (in 1949).

These early Asian texts on international law reflect a desire to shape rules in both moral (or idealist) and realist terms, not dissimilar from perspectives developed later in the West. However, the Chinese and Indian texts also reveal some common pan-Asian themes: an abhorrence of war, especially offensive expansionist war; a preference for defensive, just wars with the objective of ensuring peace; a desire to maintain the status quo; and non-intervention by military means in areas beyond their immediate neighbourhood.

These notions were also evident in practice. In the long pre-colonial history there is almost no evidence of civilizational Asian empires seeking to extend their domain beyond their hinterlands.[14] Similarly, with the exception of the Mongol dynasty, there

[12] Godehardt (n 10) 21. See also Alastair Johnston, *Cultural Realism: Strategic Culture and Grand Strategy in Chinese History* (Princeton University Press 1995) and Andrew Scobell, *China's Use of Military Force: Beyond the Great Wall and the Long March* (CUP 2003).

[13] Thomas Kane, 'Inauspicious Tools: Chinese Thought on the Morality of Warfare' in Paul Robinson (ed), *Just War in Comparative Perspective* (Ashgate 2003) 149.

[14] There were, however, two exceptions: first the Kushan empire (1-225 CE), which built extensive trade networks—both overland and overseas—with China during the later Han Period (25–225 CE). At that time, goods from China were primarily transshipped to the West, although some were also consumed domestically. Second, during the middle Chola period (985 to 1044 CE)—which corresponded to the Song period in China—Emperor Rajendra I conducted a naval expedition to Srivijaya (present day Indonesia) around 1025 CE to protect trade with China. Similarly, one of the few times that a Chinese empire launched sea expeditions was under Emperor Ming Yongle of the Ming Dynasty, between 1405 and 1433, when Chinese Admiral Zheng He embarked on seven voyages to Southeast Asia, Sri Lanka, India, the Persian Gulf, and East Africa. However, this sea-borne contact ended because the dynasty became preoccupied with countering the Mongol threat from the north and piracy along China's south coast. See Waheguru Pal Singh Sidhu and Jing-Dong Yuan, *China-India Relations: Cooperation or Conflict?* (Lynne Rienner 2003) 10–11.

is no evidence that Asian powers confronted each other militarily.[15] In fact, both China and India clearly marked the limits of their domain and sought to keep invaders out. For India, the Himalayan ranges served as a natural barrier while China built the Great Wall (from the eighth century BCE).

The primary reason for these pre-colonial Asian powers not seeking imperial extension was that they were satisfied, status-quo powers. According to economic historian Angus Maddison, during the pre-colonial era—from year 1 to about 1500 CE—Asia accounted for over 50 per cent of global GDP, with China and India each having around one quarter of the world's GDP.[16] By and large, Asia was not dependent on global trade or new markets for its prosperity.

However, while Asia had a rich tradition of making international norms and laws, their insular outlook did very little to encourage them to formalize and promote these ideas either regionally or globally: there was no Asian counterpart to the Westphalian state developed in Europe. Moreover, while Asian states were comfortable with the status quo, they were ill-prepared to defend it. The decline and fall of the pre-colonial Asian powers was partly due to their internal inertia and partly to the growing industrial, military, and normative ability of colonial powers who did not accept the status quo and were willing to disregard its rules.

Ironically, it was the colonial experience and the exploitation of sea routes by European powers that provided China and India with a common political history for the first time. These factors forcibly broke Asia's isolation and connected it with the rest of the world. The colonial powers not only defined and created 'Asia' but challenged Asian norms and established new rules and institutions. These would legitimize their control over the process of globalization in general and the world's richest region in particular. They were also willing to enforce these norms militarily, often with volunteers from the very populations that they had colonized.

The colonial experience for China and India was very different. China was never 'colonized' in the classic sense by any single power, though it was nonetheless dominated by a collection of European and, later, Japanese rulers. Conversely, India was first colonized by the East India Company (active in India from the seventeenth century) and then the British monarchy (from 1858 to 1947), who ruled India together for nearly 300 years. During this period, both China and India were exploited and subjugated, and the two civilizations were pitted against each other for the first time. During the Opium Wars (1839–42) it was Indian opium that the British were determined to

[15] The Mongol Yuan Dynasty (1271–1368 CE) at one point occupied the Eurasian continent from Germany in the west to Korea in the east, and from the Arctic Ocean in the north to the Persian Gulf in the south; it treated both China and India as one of its many conquests. Prior to this, only the Kushan Empire (1 to 225 AD) in India shared a common border with the Han Empire (202 BC to 220 AD) in Central Asia—close to the Taklak Makan Desert in Tibet. See Karl Schmidt, *An Atlas and Survey of South Asian History* (ME Sharpe 1995) 22–23; Michael Swaine and Ashley Tellis, *Interpreting China's Grand Strategy: Past, Present, and Future* (RAND Corporation 2000) 31, 37, 48; and BG Verghese, *Reorienting India: The New Geo-Politics of Asia* (Konark 2001).

[16] Angus Maddison, *The World Economy: Historical Statistics* (OECD Development Centre 2004).

forcibly sell in China to pay for China's tea, which was in great demand in England. Under the colonial model of globalization, China and India were inevitably compelled to compete with each other as well as with an increasingly industrialized West—something that Asian civilizations had managed to avoid for over a millennium.

Significantly, Asian powers, especially India, were also complicit in defending the global interests and enforcing the writ of Empire during the colonial period. From the late eighteenth century onwards and until its independence, Indian troops served the colonial cause not only on the Indian subcontinent but in almost every British dominion in Asia and Africa.[17] By the time of the First World War, the British Indian Army had swelled to 1.5 million volunteers, who fought in foreign lands from Baghdad to Ypres, sustaining over 70,000 casualties. While this earned Indians a seat at the Treaty of Versailles negotiations, India had very little influence over the Treaty or any role in the League of Nations. In the Second World War, the British Indian Army fielded a staggering 2.5 million Indians—the largest voluntary army in history—who fought for the Allies in almost every theatre of the global war.[18] The victory of the Allies, particularly in key conflicts in Asia, Africa, the Middle East, and even Europe, was in significant part determined by the role of Indian soldiers.[19] However, despite this, India had only a limited role in determining the post-war international order, and was not given a prominent role in it.

During the Second World War, China and India were compelled by the Allies to cooperate militarily with each other to counter another Asian power, Japan,[20] as they sought to prevent Japan's expansion into their traditional colonial territories. This was exemplified by the construction of the 'Stilwell Burma Road' that linked the two countries through a new overland route, with the express purpose of stopping the

[17] C Raja Mohan, 'India's Military Diplomacy: Legacy of International Peacekeeping' (2014) ISAS Working Paper 190/2014, 3 <https://www.files.ethz.ch/isn/181075/ISAS_Working_Paper_190_-_India%27s_Military_Diplomacy_13062014161354.pdf> accessed 19 April 2019. See also Raghu Karnad, *Farthest Field: An Indian Story of the Second World War* (WW Norton 2015); Yasmin Khan, *India at War: The Subcontinent and the Second World War* (OUP 2015); and Srinath Raghavan, *India's War: The Making of Modern South Asia, 1939–1945* (Allen Lane 2016).

[18] Waheguru Pal Singh Sidhu, 'War, Peace and International Order' *Mint* (New Delhi, 9 November 2014). India provided nearly as many troops as the rest of the British Commonwealth combined.

[19] Some Indians also fought for the Axis powers. Between 1942 and 1945, around 40,000 to 43,000 Indian soldiers, who were part of the short-lived, pro-Axis, Indian National Army (INA or *Azad Hind Fauj*), took part in the Japanese campaign in Burma. The INA was initially conceived by Major Iwaichi Fujiwara of the Japanese Imperial Army to use Indian soldiers against the British. These soldiers—mostly Japanese prisoners of war plus thousands of volunteers from the Indian expatriate populations in Malaya and Burma—were led by Subhash Chandra Bose, a former President of the Indian National Congress, the umbrella movement that was leading India's independence struggle. The INA was not an effective fighting force and collapsed in 1945 following the Japanese rout in Kohima. However, the ill-conceived British decision to try some of the INA officers for treason became a rallying point for India's freedom movement and contributed to the departure of the British. See Office of Strategic Services, 'The Rise and Fall of the Indian National Army' (Current Intelligence Study Number 24, United States of America, 8 June 1945) <http://www.cia.gov/library/readingroom/docs/DOC_0000709795.pdf> accessed 6 October 2018; Robert Havers, 'The Indian National Army, 1942-45' (*HistoryNet*, 18 July 2017) <http://www.historynet.com/indian-national-army1942-45.htm> accessed 6 October 2018.

[20] Sidhu and Yuan (n 14) 11.

Japanese onslaught. This wartime cooperation did not survive, however, nor did it form the basis for a future cooperative regional security arrangement.

Another inevitable consequence of the colonial era was the shift in economic weight from Asia to Europe and the United States. According to the Maddison study, by the end of the Second World War, which also marked the beginning of the end of the colonial era, Asia accounted for a mere 18 per cent of global GDP while Western Europe and the US accounted for over 50 per cent of it.[21] Between 1900 and 1950, the average GDP growth rate for Asian countries was a dismal 1.4 per cent while China and India registered virtually zero per cent GDP growth.

In the wake of colonialism, there were three main Asian schools of thought about the future of the region:

> reactionaries who believed that the continent's long-standing religious traditions would ultimately prevail; moderates who wanted to cherry-pick from the western toolkit while leaving their own societies largely unchanged; and revolutionaries . . . who thought that nothing less than radical secularisation and a new ideology would galvanise their societies to compete in the modern world.[22]

These three schools often coexisted at the same time in the same nations, and the contest between them would determine the approach that Asian countries would take towards the evolving global normative architecture. Even when one of the strands dominated the discourse, as was the case in China, the others lived on in the background.

Notwithstanding these various strands, there were a few common characteristics that almost every Asian nation embraced. These included the concept of state sovereignty, the principle of non-interference by others in their internal affairs, the right to self-defence, and equality among nations. The modern idea of state sovereignty adopted by the Asian powers derived from the Treaty of Westphalia 1648 and was a rejection of the traditional notion based on natural and historic claims, such as those exercised by imperial Chinese kingdoms over their former tributaries. Indeed, this notion of state sovereignty, reiterated in the UN Charter along with the emphasis on self-defence, found wide acceptance throughout Asia, while the concept of collective security did not.

3 The UN Charter and the Cold War

The Second World War formally ended in Asia on 2 September 1945, but not before the first and only use of nuclear weapons against Japan and its humiliating surrender. Prior to the conclusion of the war, the Allies convened the San Francisco conference

[21] Angus Maddison, 'Shares of the Rich and the Rest in the World Economy: Income Divergence Between Nations, 1820–2030' (2008) 3 Asian Economic Policy Review 67, 74.

[22] Ben Shephard, 'From the Ruins of Empire: The Intellectuals Who Remade Asia–Review' *The Guardian* (London, 4 August 2012).

from April to June 1945 to draw up the UN Charter and to establish the post-war world order. Only six of the original fifty-one signatories of the UN Charter were from the Asia-Pacific group.[23] Of these six, two—India and the Philippines—were still colonies and Lebanon was occupied by Allied forces. None of them played a significant role in formulating the UN Charter. Moreover, several key Asian actors did not participate at all, including mainland China (which was in the midst of a violent civil war), Indonesia (whose independence was denied by the Dutch), and Japan (an Axis power still at war).

Of the Asian powers present, India was significant for two reasons. First, even before the San Francisco conference, Jawaharlal Nehru, independent India's prime minister in waiting, was drawn to the idea of 'One World', which had gained currency during the interwar period.[24] Nehru regarded the UN and its central role in ensuring international peace as the Cold War manifestation of the One World concept.[25] In 1948, speaking before India's Constituent Assembly, he argued that the UN, 'in spite of its failings and weaknesses, is something that is good. It should be encouraged and supported... and...allowed to develop into some kind of world government or world order'.[26] Subsequently, article 51 of the Directive Principles of State Policy of India's Constitution, adopted on 26 January 1950, asserted that India would seek to 'promote international peace and security...foster respect for international law and treaty obligations' and 'encourage settlement of international disputes by arbitration'.[27] While the UN is not explicitly mentioned, the world body was clearly the venue to manifest article 51.

Secondly, India, albeit under the British Crown, contributed more men and material to the war effort than any other country in Asia and might have been willing to do the same under the auspices of the UN to maintain international peace and security. However, this contribution was not recognized and India was passed over in consideration of a permanent seat on the Security Council (UNSC), which was given to Taiwan despite its relatively small contribution to the war effort. This oversight stymied the prominent role that the UN could have carved out in Asia.[28]

Aside from the UN Charter, the contours of peace and security arrangements in Asia evolved very differently than in Europe. For instance, in Europe, following the swift and mostly fair Nuremberg trials and the unconditional apology of German leaders, efforts were made to achieve reconciliation and European unity. This was evident in two

[23] These were the Republic of China (Taiwan), India (still under British rule), Iran, Iraq, Lebanon (under Allied occupation), and the Philippines (still under US rule). Additionally, the ANZUS group was also present, with the US leading the proceedings. The Soviet Union, as the other key victorious power, also played a crucial role.

[24] Manu Bhagavan, *The Peacemakers: India and the Quest for One World* (Harper Collins 2012).

[25] Manu Bhagavan, 'India and the United Nations' in David Malone, C Raja Mohan, and Srinath Raghavan (eds), *The Oxford Handbook of Indian Foreign Policy* (OUP 2015) 596–608.

[26] Quoted in Bhagavan (n 24) 121.

[27] Constitution of India 1950 art. 51.

[28] The US and the Soviet Union did raise the possibility of India occupying a permanent Security Council seat in 1955 but Nehru did not take up the offer. See Jawaharlal Nehru (S Gopal (ed)), *Selected Works of Jawaharlal Nehru: Second Series*, vol 29 (Teen Murti House 2001) 231. See also Manu Bhagawan, 'Not just Nehru, even sister Vijaya Lakshmi had strong reasons to decline UNSC permanent seat' *The Print* (New Delhi, 20 March 2019).

regional developments: the creation of the North Atlantic Treaty Organization (NATO) in 1949 with the express objective to 'keep the Soviet Union out, the Americans in, and the Germans down';[29] and the establishment of the six-nation European Coal and Steel Community (ECSC), which, according to Robert Schuman—its principal architect—would 'make war not only unthinkable but materially impossible'[30] and paved the way for the creation of the European Union (EU).

Conversely in Asia, the International Military Tribunal for the Far East (Tokyo Trials) were severely criticized for providing victor's justice, ineffectively addressing Japan's war crimes, and for fundamental procedural flaws.[31] Thus, the Tokyo Trials provided neither justice nor the prospect of reconciliation. Coupled with the absence of any Japanese atonement for its wartime role, efforts at regional peace arrangements among the former combatants were likely to be stillborn. This was evident in the ill-fated deliberations under the UN to conclude the Treaty of Peace with Japan.[32] Neither China, Taiwan, or North and South Korea, the primary victims of Japanese aggression, were invited to participate, while Burma and India stayed away. The Soviet Union and Indonesia, who attended the conference, refused to sign and ratify the Treaty respectively.

Consequently, there was no equivalent of the ECSC or an inclusive peace treaty upon which an Asia-wide community could be built, and efforts to create NATO-like collective defence arrangements did not last. The Southeast Asia Treaty Organization (SEATO) and the Central Treaty Organization (CENTO) were neither effective nor enduring.[33] SEATO was formed in 1954 with the US, France, Britain, New Zealand, Australia, the Philippines, Thailand, and Pakistan as members and was disbanded in 1977 in the wake of the Vietnam War.[34] The 1955 Baghdad Pact with Turkey, Iraq, Great Britain, Pakistan, and Iran (the US never became a full member) was

[29] Attributed to Lord Hastings Lionel Ismay, NATO's first Secretary General. See 'Origins: NATO Leaders' (*NATO*) <http://www.nato.int/cps/su/natohq/declassified_137930.htm> accessed 6 October 2018.

[30] See European Union, 'The Schuman Declaration' (EU 9 May 1950) <https://europa.eu/european-union/about-eu/symbols/europe-day/schuman-declaration_en> accessed 6 October 2018. The six nations included former foes France, West Germany, Italy, Belgium, the Netherlands, and Luxembourg.

[31] Neil Boister and Robert Cryer, *The Tokyo International Military Tribunal: A Reappraisal* (OUP 2008); Kristen Sellars, 'Imperfect Justice at Nuremberg and Tokyo' (2010) 21 European Journal of International Law 1085. Sellars, referencing Boister and Cryer, notes that 'the prosecuting powers at Tokyo violated the principle of legality by creating the new charge of crimes against peace, treated the war crimes charges as almost an afterthought, and breached the undertaking to give the accused a fair trial'.

[32] Treaty of Peace with Japan (adopted on 8 September 1951, entered into force on 28 April 1952, 136 UNTS 1832).

[33] Other short-lived regional groupings included: the Asia Pacific Council, founded by South Korean President Park Chung Hee, as a grouping of anti-communist states in 1966, which disintegrated shortly after in 1972; the Association of Southeast Asia, with Malaya, Philippines and Thailand, founded in 1961, but the Malaya dispute rendered it ineffective; and the Malaysia, Philippines and Indonesia (MAPHILINDO) grouping founded in 1963 but disbanded in 1966, when President Sukarno instituted the policy of *konfrontasi* with Malaysia between 1963 and 1965.

[34] 'Southeast Asia Treaty Organization (SEATO), 1954' (*Office of the Historian, US Department of State*) <https://history.state.gov/milestones/1953-1960/seato> accessed 6 October 2018.

transformed into CENTO following Iraq's withdrawal in 1959. However, 'CENTO never actually provided its members with a means for guaranteeing collective defence' and was disbanded in 1979 following the Islamic revolution in Iran.[35]

Even the 1955 Bandung Conference to showcase Afro-Asian solidarity against colonialism and neo-colonialism did little to ensure peace and security; it was overshadowed by the ideological contest between China and India. Only two regional organizations survived the Cold War. The ASEAN, set up in 1967 by Indonesia, Thailand, Malaysia, Singapore, and the Philippines, sought to reduce tensions and competition amongst themselves, promote socio-economic development, and reduce the regional military influence of external actors. The South Asian Association for Regional Cooperation (SAARC), established in 1985 with Bangladesh, Bhutan, India, Nepal, the Maldives, Pakistan, and Sri Lanka, aimed to promote economic development and regional cooperation.

Although ASEAN is sometimes compared to the EU, it privileges state sovereignty, which is why it functions using the concept of consensus and non-conventional negotiation methods as opposed to legal institutions. ASEAN was also constrained by two factors: first, its unabashed anti-communist stance during the Cold War and second, its inability to include the regional hegemons, notably China, India, or Japan. While this allowed ASEAN's existence, it also limited its scope.[36] The SAARC places an even greater emphasis on state sovereignty and disallows formal deliberations on bilateral disputes as part of its proceedings.[37] Both abjure any form of collective defence arrangement with either other members or organizations.

In the absence of robust regional peace and security institutions or arrangements, it might be expected that the UN would play a greater role in Asia. Indeed, the UN was involved twice early on in the Cold War, in Kashmir and Korea, but these proved to be the exceptions. Partly due to the UN's handling of these two crises, it was side-lined in other Cold War era peace and security issues, including Tibet, the China–India War, Vietnam, and Bangladesh.

3.1 Kashmir: The UN's First Test

Kashmir, along with Korea and the Palestinian question, were among the earliest crises to confront the nascent UN. India first brought the issue of the incursion by tribesmen from Pakistan into Kashmir in October 1947 to the UNSC in December 1947, assuming

[35] 'The Baghdad Pact (1955) and the Central Treaty Organization (CENTO)' (*US Department of State Archive*) <https://2001-2009.state.gov/r/pa/ho/time/lw/98683.htm> accessed 6 October 2018.

[36] See Dace Winther, *Regional Maintenance of Peace and Security under International Law: The Distorted Mirrors* (Routledge 2014) 80–100.

[37] Lawrence Saez, *South Asian Association for Regional Cooperation (SAARC): An Emerging Collaboration Architecture* (Routledge 2011) 17–18.

that the Council would simply brand Pakistan as the aggressor and ask it to withdraw.[38] Instead, the issue was taken up as a dispute between states and became entangled in the broader debates on decolonization, state sovereignty, self-determination, and the Cold War. In all, between 1948 and 1971 the Council passed a total of twenty-three resolutions and set up various commissions to resolve the Kashmir issue. The plan put forth by Australian jurist Sir Owen Dixon, appointed by the Council in 1950, which suggested a partition, came closest to being accepted before it was abandoned. While the Council continued mediation efforts through the 1950s and 1960s, they were to no avail. The last resolution on Kashmir was passed on 21 December 1971, after the 1971 India–Pakistan war, which ended with the emergence of independent Bangladesh.

Following the war, both countries signed the Simla Agreement in July 1972, categorically stating that in respect of Kashmir, 'the two countries are resolved to settle their differences by peaceful means through bilateral negotiations or by any other peaceful means mutually agreed upon between them' and that 'the line of control resulting from the ceasefire of 17 December 1971 shall be respected by both sides without prejudice to the recognized position of either side'.[39] Since then, India has argued that the UN resolutions have been rendered irrelevant and the UN Military Observer Group in India and Pakistan (UNMOGIP) is unnecessary. Despite India's non-cooperation with UNMOGIP, it continues to operate today and has acquired the dubious distinction of being the longest running and perhaps most pointless observer mission in the UN's history.

There are several possible reasons why the UN failed in Kashmir. First, between the late 1940s and the early 1960s, the UN was a new and relatively weak actor on the world stage; its institutions and process were still in formation and, perhaps, it did not have the necessary capacity to address crises of the complexity of Kashmir. Second, despite this limitation, the UN took on a far broader role than it might have. Greater success may have been possible had it only decided on the question of Pakistan's aggression (as it did in the case of North Korea just months later). Third, for India, nothing short of the status quo ante pre-October 1947 would have been acceptable and, with Nehru at the helm until 1964 and his leadership of the Non-Aligned Movement, it would have been difficult for the UN or any group of countries to muscle India into accepting anything less. Similarly, for Pakistan, the pre-October 1947 situation was made untenable by UNSC resolutions and, partly to secure against being branded an aggressor, it joined SEATO and the Baghdad Pact to become closely tied with one of the superpowers, the US, in order to guard against an unfavourable UN outcome.

Kashmir began as a twentieth-century problem born out of messy decolonization. It was nurtured by the concept of self-determination and the Cold War. It has now

[38] This section is drawn from Waheguru Pal Singh Sidhu, 'The International Community and Kashmir: Mission Impossible' in Waheguru Pal Singh Sidhu, Bushra Asif, and Cyrus Samii (eds), *Kashmir: New Voices, New Approaches* (Lynne Rienner 2006) 276–301.

[39] See Government of India, 'Simla Agreement 2 July 1972' (*Jammu & Kashmir*) <http://www.jammu-kashmir.com/documents/simla.html> accessed 6 October 2018.

evolved into a twenty-first-century conflict with characteristics of a regional conflict formation, a distinct and dangerous nuclear dimension, militancy with growing links to global networks, a potentially rising and failing state, and the inability of the key actors to accept the only plausible solution—the present status quo. While the UN brought an end to the 1948 conflict through enforcing a ceasefire, it expanded its mandate and failed to resolve the issue. Ironically, in securing that ceasefire line, the UN might have effectively underwritten the partition of Kashmir for perpetuity.

3.2 Korea: UN's Cold War Baptism by Fire

Following the end of Japanese occupation in 1945, Korea was divided along the 38th parallel, with the North under Soviet control and the South under the other Allied powers. The UN's involvement in Korea began in 1948 with the establishment of the UN Temporary Commission on Korea (UNTCOK).[40] Its mandate was to observe elections after the withdrawal of Soviet and US troops and to report to the UN General Assembly (UNGA). However, contrary to article 32 of the UN Charter, neither North nor South Korea was consulted. Indeed, North Korea never recognized UNTCOK. Simultaneously, Soviet intransigence in allowing UNTCOK access north of the 38th parallel, coupled with the insistence of the US to hold elections only in the South, led to the Commission's failure. UNTCOK was replaced by the UN Commission on Korea (UNCOK), with the even more improbable mandate of unifying North and South Korea. Unsurprisingly, UNCOK collapsed when the North invaded the South on 25 June 1950, marking the beginning of the Korean War.

The US led the UNSC to pass two resolutions establishing a UN-mandated force to 'repel the armed attack' from North Korea,[41] successfully overcoming the first and only attempted boycott of the UNSC by the Soviet Union. The leader of the communist bloc had stayed away from the UNSC to express its disapproval over the refusal to recognize the People's Republic of China as the legitimate representative in the UN instead of Taiwan. However, even after the Soviet Union returned in August 1950, the US engineered the 'Uniting for Peace' resolution, effectively bypassing a deadlocked UNSC and giving the UNGA the power to continue the UN military mission in Korea. The UN forces in Korea were mostly made up of the US and its Cold War allies. Apart from South Korea, only four other Asian nations—Australia, New Zealand, the Philippines, and Thailand—took part in the fighting. To underline its neutrality in the conflict, India chose to provide only humanitarian assistance in the form of an ambulance unit.

The fighting reached a stalemate after the entry of China and the Soviet Union on the side of their ally, North Korea, nuclear threats by the US, and several military advances

[40] See Leon Gordenker, *The United Nations and the Peaceful Unification of Korea: The Politics of Field Operations 1947–1950* (Martinus Nijhoff 1959) 31. India was made chair of UNTCOK 'because of its interest in assuming a leading role in Asian politics' and it was expected to take an 'independent position'.

[41] UNSC resolution 83 (27 June 1950); UNSC resolution 84 (7 July 1950).

and reversals on both sides. The US privately asked India (and the Soviets acquiesced) to take the lead in formulating an armistice.[42] VK Krishna Menon, India's UN representative, drafted the resolution, which was adopted by the UNGA on 1 December 1952. However, the resolution was staunchly opposed by the Soviet Union and China, who suspected India was working at the behest of the US, while South Korea accused India of being 'pro-Communist'.[43] Despite making India a scapegoat, the parties failed to find an alternative solution and eventually accepted India's proposed compromise, reaching an armistice on 27 July 1953.

The UN's mission, which began merely to observe elections, soon evolved into a declaration of North Korea as the aggressor, the launching of military action to repel the attack and, controversially, an attempt to unite the country by force. By the end of the war, the UN had succeeded in preserving the status quo of a divided Korea. However, the UN failed in two fundamental objectives: first, it could not prevent the Cold War from going 'hot' and, second, it was seen to side with one superpower bloc, contrary to its impartiality principle.[44]

3.3 China-India: The Inevitable Contest

The emergence of democratic India and communist China after the Second World War led to expectations that the two ancient civilizations might forge a formidable partnership in the post-colonial world.[45] Instead, serious ideological differences were evident from early on. India was one of the first countries to recognize the People's Republic of China. New Delhi even sent KM Pannikkar, one of its most able and ideologically sympathetic diplomats, as India's Ambassador to Beijing to signal how well-disposed India was to communist China. However, reciprocation on the part of Mao Zedong, China's leader as Chairman of the Communist Party of China, was less than forthcoming. Beijing initially called the Indian Government both a 'puppet' of imperialism and an obstacle to movements of national liberation.[46] It was only when India remained

[42] Chester Bowles, *Ambassador's Report* (V Gollancz 1954) 242. See also 'Foreign Relations of the United States, 1952–1954, Korea, Volume XV, Part 2' (*Office of the Historian, US Department of State*) <https://history.state.gov/historicaldocuments/frus1952-54v15p2/index> accessed 07 October 2018.

[43] Office of Current Intelligence, 'Issues of the Korean Post-Armistice Political Conference' (Central Intelligence Agency Working Draft, 29 July 1953) <https://www.cia.gov/library/readingroom/docs/CIA-RDP91T01172R000300110001-3.pdf> accessed 19 April 2019.

[44] One victim of the UN failure was its first Secretary General, Trygve Lie, who was forced to resign. The other was the desuetude of the UN's collective defence arrangements envisaged under article 43 of the UN Charter.

[45] Sidhu and Yuan (n 14) 10–43.

[46] In October 1949, Mao, in his response to a congratulatory message from BT Randive (Secretary General of the Communist Party of India) on China's successful communist revolution, urged Randive and the Indian communists to overthrow 'the yoke of imperialism and its collaborators' in India. See CV Ranganathan and Vinod C Khanna, *India and China: The Way Ahead After 'Mao's India War'* (Har-Anand Publications 2000) 25.

stolidly neutral in the Korean War, and vociferously advocated for the People's Republic of China to take its place in the UN (despite strong opposition from the US) that Beijing relented and accepted India's anti-imperialist credentials.[47]

In October 1950, the Chinese People's Liberation Army (PLA) marched into Lhasa and brought Tibet under China's control. For China, the annexation of Tibet was the final stage in the unification of the 'five races' in China. For India, a vital buffer zone with China since before the time of the British Indian Empire vanished overnight.[48] Consequently, India might have been expected to defend Tibet's autonomous role to preserve the buffer with China. Indeed, before China's invasion, India supported the autonomy of Tibet as per the 1914 Simla Convention between British India, Tibet, and the Republic of China, and questioned China's sovereignty over Tibet. Similarly, the US, citing the principle of self-determination, argued that 'should developments warrant, consideration could be given to recognition of Tibet as an independent State'. The US State Department asserted that:

> should the Tibetan case be introduced into the United Nations, there would be an ample basis for international concern regarding Chinese Communist intentions toward Tibet, to justify under the United Nations Charter a hearing of Tibet's case in either the UN Security Council or the UN General Assembly.[49]

However, neither India, Britain, nor the US brought the case of Tibet to the UN. When El Salvador brought Tibet's appeal to the UN (since Tibet was not a member), all three states refused to support it. As Hitoshi Nasu notes, Beijing asserted that:

> Tibet was an integral part of China and therefore that the problem of Tibet was entirely a domestic problem of China, to which many states, including the United Kingdom (the former colonial power) and India (the successor of the United Kingdom in the continent), responded with deference.[50]

They argued that the UN should not consider the matter as they were confident that it would be settled peacefully between Tibet and China. Thus, Tibet's case at the UN was 'undercut not by communist countries such as the Soviet Union but by friendly democracies such as Britain and India'.[51]

[47] Surjit Mansingh, 'India and the United States' in BR Nanda (ed), *Indian Foreign Policy: The Nehru Years* (Sangam Books 1990) 162–3.

[48] John Garver, *Protracted Contest: Sino-Indian Rivalry in the Twentieth Century* (University of Washington Press 2001) ch 2.

[49] 'Secret Aide-Mémoir, The Department of State to the British Embassy' (*Office of the Historian, US Department of State*, 30 December 1950) <https://history.state.gov/historicaldocuments/frus1950v06/d376> accessed 07 October 2018.

[50] Hitoshi Nasu, 'Revisiting the Principle of Non-Intervention: A Structural Principle of International Law or a Political Obstacle to Regional Security in Asia?' (2013) 3 Asian Journal of International Law 25, 34–35. See also RP Anand, *Studies in International Law and History: An Asian Perspective* (Martinus Nijhoff 2004) 127–37.

[51] Melvyn Goldstein, *A History of Modern Tibet, Volume 2: The Calm Before the Storm, 1951–1955* (University of California 2007) 82.

Subsequently, the de facto takeover of Tibet became *de jure* when the fifteen-year-old Dalai Lama accepted the seventeen-point agreement with China in May 1951, effectively nullifying any Tibetan claim to an independent status.[52] Several factors might explain why nothing was done to counter China's takeover of Tibet by major powers, either within the UN or outside it. First, the PLA's swift 'liberation' of Tibet coincided with Chinese troops crossing the Yalu River in Korea to confront the US-led forces. Consequently, although the US supported the de facto autonomy of Tibet, its preoccupation with Korea meant that Washington was unwilling to take the lead on the Tibet, leaving the issue to India as it was more directly affected. Second, as early as 1949, India, despite endorsing the 1914 Simla Convention (and the McMahon Line as the border between India and Tibet), was resigned to the fact that 'in no distant future Chinese Communists would take over Tibet' and 'there was little GoI [Government of India] could do'.[53] Instead of fighting a lost cause, New Delhi sought to use the opportunity to improve relations with Beijing and formalize the McMahon Line as the border between the two Asian nations.

To that end, India acknowledged Tibet as an autonomous region of China under the *Panchsheel* Agreement in 1954, although China never accepted the McMahon Line. While *Panchsheel* served as the *leitmotif* of India's non-alignment, in the Sino-Indian context it was as enduring as the 1938 Munich Pact (which failed to prevent the Second World War only a year later). By the late 1950s, serious differences had emerged, particularly over the now demarcated border, and by 1962 the two countries were at war.[54] This war and the unresolved boundary issue continues to affect their relations even today.

In December 1962, Sri Lanka (Ceylon) convened a six-nation Afro-Asian conference in Colombo to bring China and India back to the negotiating table. This conference produced a series of proposals which was more or less acceptable to India.[55] China, worried that the proposed ceasefire line and demilitarized zones might be regarded as

[52] Tsering Shakya, *The Dragon in the Land of Snows: A History of Modern Tibet since 1947* (Pimlico 1999); Ranganathan and Khanna (n 46) 26–27.

[53] 'Telegram, Ambassador in India (Henderson) to the Secretary of State' (*Office of the Historian, US Department of State*, 02 December 1949) <https://history.state.gov/historicaldocuments/frus1949v09/d1044> accessed 7 October 2018.

[54] There are several excellent studies that examine the history and origins of the Sino-Indian border disputes that led up to the 1962 war. See, for instance, WF Van Eekelen, *Indian Foreign Policy and the Border Dispute with China* (Martinus Nijhoff 1964); Alastair Lamb, *The China-India Border: The Origins of the Disputed Boundaries* (Praeger 1964); Dorothy Woodman, *Himalayan Frontiers: A Political View of the British, Chinese, Indian and Russian Rivalries* (Praeger 1969); Neville Maxwell, *India's China War* (Jonathan Cape 1970); Parshotam Mehra, *Negotiating with the Chinese 1846–1987: Problems and Perspectives* (Reliance Publishing House 1989); Steven Hoffmann, *India and the China Crisis* (University of California Press 1990); Gyaneshwar Chaturvedi, *India-China Relations: 1947 to Present* (MG Publishers 1991); and Sahdev Vohra, *The Northern Frontier of India—The Border Dispute with China* (Intellectual Publishing House 1993).

[55] The proposals called for the McMahon Line to be made into the ceasefire line in the eastern sector and for the establishment of a demilitarised zone in the western sector, which would be jointly administered by civilian personnel.

de facto boundaries, rejected them as a basis for negotiations.[56] Subsequently, China and India broke off all bilateral relations, to resume them only two decades later.

Although the Sino-Indian war was primarily a bilateral affair, which Beijing publicly describes as a 'limited border war' and New Delhi as a national humiliation, it is now clear that both the US and the Soviet Union were also involved. Their role (or lack thereof) had a direct impact on the duration and outcome of the conflict. Although the official Soviet policy on the Sino-Indian boundary dispute was to remain neutral, the reality was that Moscow was highly critical of Beijing's handling of the crisis.[57] The US, under the new Kennedy Administration, had developed close ties with India and during the war Washington entered into a formal pact with New Delhi to provide critical logistical support for the war effort.[58] However, as the US became preoccupied with the Cuban missile crisis, this support became tenuous.

After the 1962 conflict, New Delhi moved closer to Moscow (which had broken from Beijing), while China resolved its borders with Pakistan (which included Islamabad ceding territory in the disputed area of Kashmir) and established an enduring security alliance with it. In 1971, during the Bangladesh crisis, the US 'tilted' in favour of Pakistan, which had volunteered to serve as the conduit for the bold Nixon-Kissinger initiative to open direct relations with China. From 1972 until the end of the Cold War, the Soviet-India partnership had to contend with the US-China-Pakistan axis, which went on to cooperate in Afghanistan against the Soviets in the 1980s. The China and India rift, which began in the 1950s and continued to the end of the Cold War, was also complicated by the fact that China was not allowed to join the UN until 1971, when it became a member of the organization overnight and got a permanent seat on the UNSC. Thus, the China-India conflict was another key factor in the inability of the region to establish collective security arrangements. The relationship between the two stilted their approach to working together on international peace and security issues.

3.4 Vietnam War: An Unavoidable Tragedy

The Vietnam War was the direct result of the messy decolonization process of French Indo-China (1887–1954). The desire of France to maintain control of its Southeast Asian colonies, despite the clear rejection of colonial rule by national liberation movements, set the stage for a protracted conflict, especially in Vietnam, that would continue for decades after the French withdrew. Coupled with French intransigence and mismanagement was the US' involvement in the conflict. As the liberation movement in Vietnam was inspired and spearheaded by communist ideology and force, Washington

[56] Ranganathan and Khanna (n 46) 49–51; Xuecheng Liu, *The Sino-Indian Border Dispute and Sino-Indian Relations* (University Press of America 1994) 41–2.

[57] Editorial, 'The Truth about How the Leaders of the CPSU have Allied Themselves with India against China' (1963) 6(45) Peking Review 18, 19.

[58] Mansingh (n 47) 167.

convinced itself—using a newly coined 'domino theory'—that, were the movement to succeed, all of Southeast Asia would become part of the global communist bloc. This made the Vietnam War an unavoidable global tragedy.

At the 1954 Geneva Conference on Indo-China, held outside the UN framework, France proposed setting up international commissions to implement the agreements reached between the parties.[59] However, despite being permanent members of the UNSC, France, Britain, the US, and the Soviet Union deliberately kept the UN from being involved.[60] They argued that since three of the signatories to the agreements—Cambodia, Laos, and Vietnam—(along with China) were not UN members, there was no need for UN involvement. This was in contrast to the leading role the UN was given in Korea and may well have been a consequence of that unsuccessful experience. Instead, a commission comprising India, Poland, and Canada was set up to supervise the execution of the agreements.

However, all the participating countries pledged, to varying degrees, to guarantee the agreements. For instance, the US, which had not signed the accords, unilaterally declared just days later that 'it will refrain from the threat or use of force to disturb them in accordance with article 2(4) of the Charter of the United Nations dealing with the obligation of the members to refrain in their international relations from the threat or use of force'.[61] Yet, barely months later, Washington was building an anti-communist regime in South Vietnam and soon became involved in an open conflict with North Vietnam. It was only in 1965 that the US perfunctorily reported to the UNSC that its military action was justified under article 51 of the Charter.[62] The war continued for another decade and ended only after the North conquered the South in 1975.

The Vietnam War has been described as the 'greatest tragedy that has overtaken the society of nations and the United Nations since the end of the Second World War: neither of these was able to do much to end the conflict'.[63] Opinion varies from those who argue that the war was in clear violation of international law[64] to those who assert that, while the US intervention was legal, the ambiguity of international intervention law is a problem.[65] Even though the war was considered inevitable in Cold War terms, the efforts of the UN to prevent and resolve it were at best 'intermittent

[59] The parties that participated in the conference included Cambodia, China, France, Laos, Soviet Union, UK, US, Viet Minh representing North Korea, and South Vietnam. However, only the participants from Cambodia, France, Laos, and Vietnam signed the agreements on 21 July 1954.

[60] MS Rajan and T Israel, 'The United Nations and the Conflict in Vietnam' in Richard Falk (ed), *The Vietnam War and International Law, Volume 4: The Concluding Phase* (Princeton University Press 1976) 116.

[61] Ibid.

[62] Ibid. 136–7.

[63] Ibid. 114.

[64] Richard Falk, 'What We Should Learn from Vietnam' in Richard Falk (ed), *The Vietnam War and International Law, Volume 3: The Widening Context* (Princeton University Press 1972). Falk is the editor of the epic four-volume *The Vietnam War and International Law.*

[65] Brian Landsberg, 'The United States in Vietnam: A Case Study in the Law of Intervention' (1962) 50 California Law Review 515.

and marginal'.[66] However, it is worth considering whether the involvement of the UN would have led to a peaceful resolution, or whether it would have perpetuated the partition and strife (as is the case in Kashmir and Korea). The absence of UN involvement, ironically, might have contributed to the resolution, albeit at a cost that was much too high.

3.5 Bangladesh: An Inevitable Birth

The partition of British India in 1947 and the creation of Pakistan with two wings, East and West, separated by over 2,000 kilometres of Indian territory, led its founder, Muhammad Ali Jinnah, to bemoan that he was inheriting a 'truncated or mutilated moth-eaten' state.[67] In retrospect, his foresight on the unsustainability of a united Pakistan manifested in the inevitable division of the country in 1971, albeit with the assistance of India.[68]

The birth of Bangladesh can be traced to the first free parliamentary elections in 1970, in which the East Pakistan based Awami League party won the majority, primarily with the promise of a new constitution and greater autonomy for the East. However, the party was blocked from taking office by the Pakistan Army and the Pakistani government, and its leader, Sheikh Mujib-ur-Rahman, was jailed. On 26 March 1971, Bangladesh declared independence, which was accompanied by mass protests throughout the East against the Pakistan Army and their political establishment in the West. The Army brutally suppressed these protests, prompting justified accusations of genocide, and triggered a massive refugee movement into India. In all, India received over 10 million refugees. Guerrilla groups in the East, supported by India, continued to fight the Pakistan Army. On 3 December 1971, West Pakistan, while continuing its crackdown, launched air attacks on India, resulting in open war between the two. India, which was prepared for the war, liberated 'Bangladesh' in a swift military campaign of just 14 days, and the war ended on 16 December 1971.

Significantly, the run up to the war and the war itself involved the world superpowers, with the US and China lined up behind Pakistan and the Soviet Union supporting India. These developments had the potential to escalate the Cold War into a hot one. In 1971, 'the Security Council did not convene or pass any resolutions

[66] Rajan and Israel (n 60) 131.

[67] 'Move to Partition Punjab and Bengal, Text of Mr Jinnah's statement' (*The National Archives [India]*) <http://www.nationalarchives.gov.uk/wp-content/uploads/2014/03/f0371-635331.jpg> accessed 7 October 2018.

[68] The two wings were also distinct in terms of culture, language, economy, and politics. See Richard Sisson and Leo Rose, *War and Secession: Pakistan, India, and the Creation of Bangladesh* (University of California 1991); Archer Blood, *The Cruel Birth of Bangladesh: Memoirs of an American Diplomat* (University Press 2005); Srinath Raghavan, *1971: A Global History of the Creation of Bangladesh* (Harvard University Press 2013); and Gary Bass, *The Blood Telegram: Nixon, Kissinger, and a Forgotten Genocide* (Vintage 2014).

on South Asia from the start of the slaughter in March until the outbreak of the India-Pakistan war in December'.[69] However, once the fighting began, the US and China (as a newly admitted permanent member of the UNSC) accused India of armed aggression and interference in the internal affairs of a sovereign state, and introduced resolutions that called for an immediate ceasefire. While the resolutions were vetoed by the Soviet Union, Moscow pressured India to end the war as soon as possible.

Soon after the war, Thomas Franck and Nigel Rodley argued that the 'use of unilateral force remains and should remain illegal except in instances of self-defence against an actual attack', and,

> the Bangladesh case, although containing important mitigating factors in India's favour, does not constitute the basis for a definable, workable, or desirable new rule of law which, in the future, would make certain kinds of unilateral military interventions permissible.[70]

However, Gary Bass counters this assertion by noting that, although India did act unilaterally, this was not New Delhi's preferred option:

> As its diplomatic record demonstrates, India... would have preferred to act with world support. Far from being a hegemon rewriting the rules of global order or a rogue state unconcerned with world opinion, India was desperate for foreign approval.[71]

The Bangladesh case suggests that the Asian arguments in favour of humanitarian intervention are similar to those of Western democracies, particularly when multilateral institutions are not functioning properly, and that state practice provides a precedent for such action, especially if the outcome is likely to be successful.

4 Post-Cold War: Hope and Despair

During the Cold War, Asia was a site of super power confrontation—both direct (in Korea) and indirect (in Afghanistan, Cambodia, China, India, Laos, Pakistan, and Vietnam). Asia also witnessed a protracted China-India as well as an India-Pakistan confrontation; a short but sharp skirmish between the Soviet Union and China along the Ussuri river in 1969; and the birth of a new nation—Bangladesh. Additionally, in a significant move, China and the US established bilateral relations in 1972. Apart from Korea and Kashmir, the UN was not directly involved in any of these developments. Moreover, there were no region-wide institutions to ensure peace and security. Both

[69] Gary Bass, 'The Indian Way of Humanitarian Intervention' (2015) 40 Yale Journal of International Law 227, 243.

[70] Thomas Franck and Nigel Rodley, 'After Bangladesh: The Law of Humanitarian Intervention by Military Force' (1973) 67 AJIL 276.

[71] Bass (n 69) 276.

ASEAN and SAARC deliberately abjured the peace and security roles played by regional organizations elsewhere. Indeed, apart from ANZUS and the short-lived SEATO and CENTO, there were no regional security arrangements. Instead, there existed a series of hub-and-spoke bilateral security arrangements centred on the US.

The end of the Cold War in Asia, marked by the Soviet withdrawal from Afghanistan in 1989, saw new efforts to normalize relations between countries. Prominent among these were the China-India, India-Pakistan, and India-US rapprochements in the 1990s, as well as the enlargement of ASEAN from five to ten member states, including several communist countries.[72] ASEAN also initiated the ARF in 1994 to promote confidence building and preventive diplomacy, which was followed by the East Asia Summit in 2005 (at which heads of states discussed political issues) and the Regional Comprehensive Economic Partnership (RCEP) in 2012 (to establish a free trade agreement).[73]

The last decade of the twentieth century also witnessed the establishment of the Shanghai Five grouping in 1996 (which evolved into the SCO in 2001); the formation of the Indian Ocean Rim Association for Regional Cooperation in 1997 (which grew into the 21-member IORA); efforts to build a Russia-India-China (RIC) strategic triangle in 1998; and, following the 1996 financial crisis in Asia, the creation of the Group of Twenty (G20) nations in 1999. The RIC was specifically aimed at peace and security in Asia but did not make any headway, primarily on account of the internal divisions.[74] While the G20 focused primarily on economic and financial issues, over time the grouping has also become a venue for managing political and security differences.[75] The turn of the century also saw a surge in UN missions including those in Afghanistan-Pakistan, Cambodia, East Timor, Nepal, Papua New Guinea, and Tajikistan.[76]

[72] The original five ASEAN members—Indonesia, Malaysia, the Philippines, Singapore, and Thailand—were joined by Brunei (1987), Vietnam (1995), Laos and Myanmar (1997), and finally Cambodia (1999).

[73] Today the EAS comprises of the ten ASEAN states and eight other Asian nations, including Australia, China, India, Japan, New Zealand, Russia, South Korea, and the US; while RCEP includes ASEAN plus Australia, China, India, Japan, New Zealand, and South Korea.

[74] See Rajesh Rajagopalan, 'Russia-India-China: The Never-Never Triangle' (11th Berlin Conference on Asian Security, Berlin, September 2017) <https://www.swp-berlin.org/fileadmin/contents/products/arbeitspapiere/BCAS2017_Paper_Rajesh_Rajagopalan.pdf> accessed 20 April 2019; and Xin Zhang, 'High Rhetorical Significance, Low Practical Substance: Do We Need the RIC Format?' (11th Berlin Conference on Asian Security, Berlin, September 2017) <https://www.swp-berlin.org/fileadmin/contents/products/arbeitspapiere/BCAS2017_Paper_Zhang_Xin.pdf> accessed 20 April 2019.

[75] Bruce Jones, 'Onus falls on G20 to manage political tensions' (*East Asia Forum*, 14 July 2014) <http://www.eastasiaforum.org/2014/07/14/onus-falls-on-g20-to-manage-political-tensions> accessed 7 October 2018; Waheguru Pal Singh Sidhu, 'Geopolitics Trumps Geo-economics at Hangzhou' *Mint* (New Delhi, 12 September 2016). This was also evident in the recently concluded 2019 Osaka G20 summit.

[76] These were partly the result of an activist UNSC freed from the Cold War deadlock and partly the result of regional hegemons willing to allow these missions in their backyards. For details of these missions, see 'Political Missions and Offices' (*Repertoire of the Practice of the Security Council*) <http://www.un.org/en/sc/repertoire/subsidiary_organs/special_political_complete.shtml#cat3> accessed 7 October 2018; 'Past Peacekeeping Operation' (*United Nations Peacekeeping*) <https://peacekeeping.un.org/en/past-peacekeeping-operations> accessed 7 October 2018.

The end of the Cold War saw new threats emerge from non-state actors. Notable among them were the rise of the Taliban in Afghanistan-Pakistan and other extremist groups in Bangladesh, Indonesia, and the Philippines. The 11 September 2001 attacks on the US by Al Qaeda led to the establishment of the International Security Assistance Force, mandated by the UN and led by NATO, which continuously operated in Afghanistan from 2003 to 2014, making it the longest running security operation in Asia. Moreover, several countries held joint military exercises to develop cooperative mechanisms. For instance, after the 2004 Indian Ocean tsunami, Australia, India, Japan, and the US led a joint humanitarian assistance and disaster relief mission.

Along with cooperative efforts, in some cases triggered by actions of non-state actors or natural disasters, the post-Cold War period saw a rise in tensions and confrontations among key Asian players. For instance, following the Indian nuclear tests in 1998, and New Delhi naming Beijing's nuclear arsenal as one of the factors behind its decision to go overtly nuclear, China spearheaded UNSC resolution 1172, which condemned the tests and imposed sanctions. While India and the US (which co-sponsored resolution 1172) embarked on a sustained dialogue that led to a bilateral strategic partnership, India's relations with China remained antagonistic, despite the fact that China had emerged as India's biggest trading partner (with bilateral trade worth over US$70 billion).

Two of the most significant peace and security challenges that confront Asia in the post-Cold War era are North Korea's nuclear weapon programme and the imbroglio over the disputes in the South China Sea. These are examined below.

4.1 Nuclear Korea: A Dangerous Gauntlet

North Korea signed the nuclear Non-Proliferation Treaty (NPT) in 1985 but concluded a comprehensive safeguard agreement with the International Atomic Energy Agency (IAEA) in 1992. In 1993, following the IAEA discovery that Pyongyang had underreported its plutonium holdings, the agency asked for special inspections, which North Korea refused.[77] Instead, on 12 March 1993, North Korea gave a three-month mandatory notice of withdrawal from the NPT as per article X of the Treaty (the first such declaration by an NPT member), and notified the UNSC. In response, the Security Council passed resolution 825 (with abstentions from China and Pakistan), which merely asked North Korea to reconsider its withdrawal and encouraged member states to facilitate a solution. On 11 June 1993, one day before its notice of withdrawal would have taken effect, North Korea suspended the withdrawal and agreed to cooperate with the IAEA. This was the result of efforts by the US and China to persuade North Korea to step back.

However, North Korea continued to play a cat-and-mouse game with the IAEA and the Council through 1993, as they refused to cooperate, before (in the face of Council

[77] This section is drawn from Waheguru Pal Singh Sidhu, 'Weapons of Mass Destruction: Managing Proliferation' in Sebastian von Einsiedel, David Malone, and Bruno Stagno Ugarte (eds), *The UN Security Council in the 21st Century* (Lynne Rienner 2015) 323–48.

censure) allowing inspections but provocatively removing fuel from a nuclear reactor before they could take place. North Korea ultimately withdrew from the IAEA on 13 June 1994, by which time US intelligence estimated that it might have built one or two nuclear weapons. Within days, former US president Jimmy Carter visited Pyongyang and paved the way for the so-called Agreed Framework between the US and North Korea. Although negotiated and signed outside the UNSC, the Agreed Framework was endorsed by it.

By the late 1990s, the Agreed Framework began to unravel for a number of reasons, primarily related to the dynamics between Washington and Pyongyang, and the fact that the UNSC was almost entirely out of the loop until 2003. Following US President George W Bush's State of the Union speech in January 2002, where he included North Korea (along with Iraq and Iran) in his 'axis of evil', relations between the states deteriorated even further and the framework collapsed. On 10 January 2003, North Korea announced its withdrawal from the NPT, effective the following day, arguing that it had satisfied the requirement under article X of the NPT. Instead of taking up this issue, the UNSC deferred to the Six-Party Talks process among China, North Korea, Japan, South Korea, Russia, and the US to deal with North Korea's proliferation and its exit from the NPT. Despite five rounds of these talks between 2003 and 2005, Pyongyang neither returned to the NPT fold nor did it stop its nuclear weapon programme.

Instead, in October 2006, North Korea conducted the first of six nuclear tests (the latest one took place in September 2017) and has continued to develop missiles capable of delivering nuclear weapons all over Asia and as far as the US. Since the North Korean nuclear weapon programme first came to light, neither the UNSC, nor the Six-Party Talks, or any other ad hoc arrangement has managed to prevent the proliferation of its nuclear weapons and ballistic missiles, let alone reverse them. According to the March 2018 report of the UN sanctions committee:

> Through the nuclear test and intercontinental ballistic missile tests conducted in 2017, the Democratic People's Republic of Korea appears to have achieved a number of important technical milestones in its weapons of mass destruction capability. There are no indications that such activities will cease, and the stated goals of achieving denuclearization and a peaceful solution to the situation seem increasingly remote.[78]

Coupled with the unresolved conflict on the peninsula—technically the two Koreas are still at war with only an armistice and not a peace treaty—and the absence of regional mechanisms to address the ongoing crisis, the situation remains a dangerous tinderbox for the region and the world. Indeed, following the September 2017 nuclear test along with a series of intercontinental ballistic missile tests by North Korea there was a discernible escalation in tensions between Pyongyang and Washington. US President

[78] UNSC, 'Report of the Panel of Experts Established Pursuant to Resolution 1874 (2009)' (5 March 2018) UN Doc S/2018/171 , 6.

Donald Trump threatened Pyongyang with 'fire and fury' and insulted 'Rocket Man' for being on a 'suicide mission', while North Korea's strongman Kim Jong-un equally churlishly retorted by calling Trump a 'mentally deranged US dotard'.[79]

Yet, the unprecedented and bold decision of the two leaders to meet in Singapore (in June 2018) and again in Hanoi (in February 2019) helped to reduce tensions and carried the prospect of either a promising breakthrough or a spectacular breakdown. The former scenario might be comparable to the 1972 Nixon-Mao summit, which led to normalization of US–China relations. The latter outcome would be akin to the disastrous meeting in 1961 between Soviet dictator Nikita Khrushchev and the neophyte US president John F Kennedy, which partly contributed to the Cuban missile crisis in 1962. In this case, the breakdown of talks at the Hanoi summit (despite the theatrics of the impulsive meeting at Panmunjom on 30 June 2019) indicate that the prospects of failure far exceed the chance of success.

4.2 The South China Sea: Treacherous Waters

By some estimates, the South China Sea is one of the most valuable strategic locations on the planet. It has proven oil reserves of 7 billion barrels and 900 trillion cubic metres of natural gas, and is traversed by half the world's merchant fleet tonnage and a third of all maritime traffic. The value of trade passing through it annually is estimated at over US$3 trillion. This provides a lucrative incentive to littoral states to assert even tenuous claims and, unsurprisingly, there is fierce competition among them to carve out a piece of this prized marine real estate. While the disputes date back to the Second World War, the competition has heated up since the conclusion of the UN Convention on the Law of the Sea (UNCLOS) in 1982 and the creation of Exclusive Economic Zones (EEZs), which give littoral states special rights. China has been particularly assertive in claiming large swathes of the area and taking on the smaller ASEAN nations. However, even the affected ASEAN members—Brunei, Malaysia, the Philippines, and Vietnam—have been unable to resolve their own overlapping claims in the South China Sea. Although ASEAN and China signed a 'Declaration on the Conduct of Parties in the South China Sea' in 2002, little progress has been made in formalizing or enforcing the Code, which is regularly flouted by China and ASEAN states.

In 2013, frustrated with China's growing permanent presence in the disputed area, the Philippines lodged a case with the Permanent Court of Arbitration (PCA) in The Hague under UNCLOS, which marked the first time a legal challenge was brought to the dispute. Although China is a signatory to UNCLOS, its attitude ranged from benign disengagement and denial of the PCA's jurisdiction to intimidation and downright threats. It made little effort to engage with the PCA or to build support for its cause. Had China garnered some modicum of support, its 'optional exception' argument, though legally untenable, might have had some political viability. Instead, as US

[79] Waheguru Pal Singh Sidhu, 'What can be expected from a Trump-Kim Meeting?' *Mint* (New Delhi, 26 March 2018).

Defence Secretary Ashton Carter foretold at the fifteenth annual Shangri-La Dialogue in 2016 (the only Asia-wide security forum, which is run by a London-based think tank), China's actions have built a 'Great Wall of self-isolation'.[80]

In 2016, the PCA ruled that 'there was no legal basis for China to claim historic rights to resources within the sea areas falling within the "nine-dash line"', earning Beijing's wrath, which called the ruling 'ill-founded' and 'naturally, null and void'.[81] Although the ruling is not enforceable, Beijing is unlikely to heed it, and the Philippines is not pushing for implementation in a bid to improve relations with China, it does have some merit. The case shows that instead of resolving the dispute through brute political or military force, there might be a viable legal alternative.

Scholars including Ben Saul have argued (possibly to engage Beijing in international legal processes) that '[f]or China, the flashpoints of Tibet, Taiwan and the South China Sea can all be explained by a proper analysis of China's title to territory under international law'.[82] Other scholars have countered that:

> The hostility for the rule of law during the Cultural Revolution and executive actions indeed shape China's current notion of sovereignty. Article 142 of the PRC's General Principles of the Civil Law provides that if the PRC concludes or accedes to any international treaty that contains provisions differing from the PRC's civil laws, the provisions of the international treaty shall apply, unless the provisions are ones on which the PRC has announced reservations.[83]

Another proposal suggests setting up an international Commission of Inquiry (COI), which would acknowledge, as the UNCLOS arbitration does not, the centrality of the legal issue of territorial sovereignty to the dispute. Such a COI would have two additional advantages. First, the mechanism would help to:

> transition the South China Sea dispute from a dangerously confrontational and emotional political discourse into a technical process of communal inquiry and transnational, professional legal work. Secondly, the COI would be an important step towards giving concrete meaning to aspirations for a more fully institutionalized regional political and economic framework resembling that of the European Union.[84]

Irrespective of the approach followed, resolving the imbroglio through legal, quasi-legal, or diplomatic means based on UNCLOS is imperative not only for the claimant

[80] 'South China Sea: US Warns Beijing against Building "Great Wall of Self-Isolation"' *The Guardian* (London, 3 June 2016).

[81] Tom Phillips, Oliver Holmes, and Owen Bowcott, 'Beijing Rejects Tribunal's Ruling in South China Sea Case' *The Guardian* (London, 12 July 2016).

[82] Ben Saul, 'China, Natural Resources, Sovereignty and International Law' (2013) 37 Asian Studies Review 196, 201.

[83] Prabhakar Singh, 'Sino–Indian Attitudes to International Law: of Nations, States and Colonial Hangovers' (2015) 3 Chinese Journal of Comparative Law 348, 358–9.

[84] Ryan Mitchell, 'An International Commission of Inquiry for the South China Sea? Defining the Law of Sovereignty to Determine the Chance for Peace' (2016) 49 Vanderbilt Journal of Transnational Law 749, 812–13.

countries in the area but also for ensuring global economic well-being and rule of law. The option of a military solution, similar to Japan's ill-conceived efforts to seize oil fields in Southeast Asia on the eve of the Second World War, is fraught with the danger of sparking off another global conflagration.

5 Brave New Developments

Today, Asia is confronted by three types of peace and security challenges: intrastate, interstate, and transnational. Intrastate conflicts range from urban violence to terrorism, the takeover of ungoverned spaces by extremist groups, secessionist movements, and civil wars. These have mostly been conducted with small arms and light weapons, though chemical and biological weapons have also been used.

Second, interstate conflict and proxy wars between regional and global powers, including nuclear-armed states, are also on the rise. These are over territorial, ideological, and normative disputes and are evident in Syria, Yemen, the Korean peninsula, and South Asia; and between Iran and its Arab neighbours, Afghanistan and Pakistan, China and India, the US and North Korea, and the South China Sea littorals. Indeed, the fact that some of these involve nuclear-armed states means that the likelihood of nuclear war cannot be ruled out.

Finally, there is a slew of transnational threats, both human-made and natural, that no single nation can manage on its own. These include pandemics, natural disasters, climate change, regional conflicts, global criminal networks, international extremist organizations, cyber and other forms of attacks, and global proliferation networks.

Against this background, there are renewed efforts to build formal peace and security institutions, but these remain a work in progress. One such noteworthy effort is a report by an independent commission on regional security architecture established by the Asia Society Policy Institute, which included former US national security adviser, Thomas Donilon, former Russian Foreign Minister, Igor Ivanov, former Indian national security adviser, Shivshankar Menon, and former Chinese Foreign Minister, Wang Jisi. Titled 'Preserving the Long Peace in Asia', the report identifies the challenges facing the region and suggests ways to build an effective security arrangement.[85]

The report warns that tensions between the US and China are causing a ripple effect among other Asian nations. While many still look to the US for security, they are increasingly dependent on the Chinese economy. As their economic and security interests diverge, these nations are being compelled to choose between the US and China 'in uncomfortable ways'.[86] The report cautions that while the alphabet soup of

[85] 'Preserving the Long Peace in Asia: The Institutional Building Blocks of Long-Term Regional Security' (Asia Society Policy Institute, September 2017) <https://asiasociety.org/files/uploads/191files/LongPeaceAsia_onlinevers.pdf> accessed 07 October 2018.

[86] Ibid. 12.

regional organizations is 'comforting', it is also 'hazardous'.[87] The multiplicity of organizations in the region allows countries to 'shop for the forum they find most suited to the issue at hand'. This trend 'obviates the necessity of developing a stronger regional consensus around norms and rules of the road'.[88]

In addition, there are at least four other challenges facing Asia's regional architecture: the fast-paced political and economic transitions and the need to manage them flexibly; the growing strategic competition among key actors; the risk of instability or even conflict due to the inability to bridge the trust deficit that permeates key bilateral relationships; and the rapid proliferation of state-of-the-art military and dual-use technologies, which, in combination with the growing mistrust, are 'altering military operations in a manner that further enhances risk' of conflict.[89]

Given this suite of challenges, the report identifies five ambitious functions that regional institutions need to perform, including the need to 'play a binding role', 'mitigate against historical mistrust', 'facilitate better management of crises and disputes', 'rationalize and align the institutions and mechanisms', and have flexibility in setting a forward-looking agenda.[90]

Predictably, none of the existing organizations fulfils all these functions. However, instead of suggesting the establishment of a new organization *ab initio*, the report calls for strengthening the EAS. It suggests retaining the informal nature of the EAS for now but calls for greater institutionalization and an operational role in preventive diplomacy, crisis management, and confidence-building measures in the medium term. In the long term, the EAS should become a 'more formal organization that brings together broader components of security cooperation across the region'. While the report is commendable and the proposals logical, the recommendations are likely to remain on paper unless there is a political impetus to implement them. So far, given the state of relations among the principal actors, the political drive and leadership is missing.[91]

An alternative approach to the more cooperative suggestions made by the Independent Commission on Regional Security Architecture is the Quadrilateral Security Dialogue (or the 'Quad') between Australia, India, Japan, and the US, which was recently revived on the side-lines of the 2017 ASEAN summit. The Quad was originally initiated in 2007 at the prompting of Japanese Prime Minister Shinzō Abe, though its informal origins can be traced to the ad hoc humanitarian assistance and disaster relief mission launched by Australia, India, Japan, and the US in the wake of the devastating Indian Ocean tsunami in 2004.[92] Since then, these four states' navies have worked together on many occasions.

[87] Ibid. 25.

[88] Ibid. 13.

[89] Ibid. 13–14.

[90] Ibid. 14–15.

[91] Waheguru Pal Singh Sidhu, 'Can Insecurity in Asia be Managed?' *Mint* (New Delhi, 8 October 2017).

[92] Waheguru Pal Singh Sidhu, 'The Emerging Indo-Pacific Architecture' *Mint* (New Delhi, 20 November 2017).

There are several factors why the countries chose to revivify the Quad at this juncture. For India, the Doklam border confrontation with China in 2017 and concerns over the latter's so-called Belt Road Initiative (BRI) were crucial considerations. Similarly, following US Secretary of State Rex Tillerson's maiden visit to Asia in 2017, there was a desire to engage Washington more closely in the region. For Australia, and to some extent Japan, the key drivers behind formally reviving the Quad were the concern about the commitment of the Trump administration to the bilateral alliance arrangements, and the quest to buttress them with the Quad commitment. For the US, the Quad offers a way to share its burden of containing China in the newly prioritized Indo-Pacific region.

If successful, the Quad may play a role similar to NATO, with the objective of keeping 'the Chinese out, the Americans in, and the Japanese down'. While managing China and keeping Beijing on the path of status quo, the Quad will also have to ensure the continued engagement and commitment of Washington to the region, which can no longer be taken for granted. Given the disruptive and isolationist tendency of President Trump—evident in his absence from the 2017 EAS—and of possible future US leaders, this is a crucial role that the organization will have to fulfil. Similarly, given Japan's brutal Second World War record that still revebreates in the region, the Quad will also have to reassure other potential future members, including ASEAN member states, that Tokyo's role will remain benign and any revisionist tendencies will be kept in check.

While formal Quad meetings were shelved following strong objections from China in 2007, discussions nonetheless continued. For instance, in 2015 the foreign secretaries of Australia, India, and Japan met ostensibly to firm up the security leg of India's 'Act East' policy. Soon thereafter, the India, Japan, and US trilateral meeting was held in Honolulu. Thus, the Quad continued to function under the garb of two trilateral meetings. Subsequently, since 2015, the India-US Malabar naval exercises have included Japan and are likely to include Australia in the next iteration, thus making the military component of the Quad a reality.

Nonetheless, the Quad's potential is likely to be limited by several internal differences. For instance, while India promotes the principle of 'freedom of navigation', it is reluctant to enforce it through freedom of navigation operations by sailing warships through EEZs, particularly in the South China Seas. Thus, the 2015 Indian Maritime Security Strategy cautions that there may be divergent security perceptions 'with nations that may be traditional friends' (read US). Members of the Quad will have to manage these differences to develop the institution further.

Moreover, while the Quad is a crucial pillar of the peace and security architecture in the Indo-Pacific region, it needs to be buttressed by at least two other pillars. The EAS serves the role of the political pillar, and the Asia Pacific Economic Cooperation (APEC) that of the trade and economic pillar. While all Quad participants are members of EAS, India is still not a member of APEC. This lacuna needs to be remedied if New Delhi is to contribute to all three pillars of the Indo-Pacific architecture. Finally, India will also have to shed its inherent abhorrence for formal military arrangements and cooperation, even though this might bring with it the prospect of being dragged into a war not of its own making. As NATO has shown, sometimes a democratic military alliance is essential to the maintenance of peace.

6 Conclusion

Asia has a rich pre-colonial tradition of international law and managed to preserve peace and enhance prosperity between the key powers in the region. This tradition was brutally replaced by colonial era norms and institutions designed to establish the primacy of non-Asian powers and rules over the original established Asian powers. The end of the colonial era and the advent of the UN did not contribute to restoring either lasting peace in Asia or its primacy in global governance structures. Indeed, even today Asia remains under-represented in the global governance architecture. The post-colonial and post-war roots of insecurity in Asia were driven by the failure to create institutions that could accommodate former enemies, notably Japan and China, and facilitate new security communities.

Japan's inability to apologize for its wartime role and atrocities or to reconcile with its former enemies meant that any regional arrangement, despite the best efforts of the US, was a non-starter. Consequently, Asian nations, along with the US, had to contend with a series of bilateral and sub-regional arrangements. Similarly, the contestation between China and India first evident in the 1950s, following Beijing's annexation of Tibet, meant that efforts to create a cooperative arrangement in Bandung with these two powers also came to naught. Whatever hope there was of a regional institution centred on China and India evaporated following the 1962 war. Indeed, any prospects of pan-Asian solidarity were buried at the Doklam border incident in 2017, which might have become the birthplace of unbridled rivalry between the two most significant Asian powers. While ASEAN did eventually emerge, its role as a regional organization was constrained. Recent efforts to create a web of plurilateral security arrangements, including the ASEAN-led EAS, the China-led BRI, the India-led IORA, and the Japan-led Quad, are still too nascent and unstructured to make an impact.

As Asia in general and China and India in particular continue to grow economically, and are likely to regain the majority share of the global GDP that they last held collectively in 1500, will they also renew their pre-colonial approach to international law? The indications are that while many of the traditional approaches to international law have been reiterated, they suffer from the same limitations: the inability to institutionalize them globally and enforce them collectively.

For instance, India's leaders—from Jawaharlal Nehru to Narendra Modi—have often evoked the phrase *vasudhaiva kutumbakam* (the world is one family), taken from the *Maha Upanishad*, to elucidate the country's global outlook. The term has become part of India's diplomatic lexicon and orthodoxy and is often deployed to defend its position on issues as varied as human rights, climate change, and even reform of the UNSC.

The term has been used to broadly convey India's ideal and liberal concept of global norms, themes of globalization, or global commons. In doing so, it suggests that *vasudhaiva kutumbakam* is an ideal world worth achieving and that it can be created through negotiations alone.[93]

In reality, however, the overly benign and idealist presentation of the concept, which appears to promote values more than interests, has done very little to actually advance India's cause in any of the issues where it has been quoted. India also appears to be reluctant to consider that *vasudhaiva kutumbakam* is not a peaceful construct, but a dysfunctional one with different power centres vying to secure their interests, even at the risk of trampling over common values. Dealing with such a world would require not only the ability to develop common norms to address contentious issues from climate change to cross-border terrorism, but also the political, economic, and military prowess to enforce these agreed-upon norms. India, like many Asian powers, is developing reasonable skills in reinterpreting its pre-colonial norm for the twenty-first century, but is still woefully inadequate in contributing to building, supporting, and enforcing them. As in the pre-colonial era, developing the political, economic, and military wherewithal to implement and enforce these norms will be the real challenge.

93 Waheguru Pal Singh Sidhu, '"Vasudhaiva Kutumbakam" for the 21st century' *Mint* (New Delhi, 21 May 2017).

CHAPTER 6

HUMAN RIGHTS

HURST HANNUM

1 Introduction

Let us begin by acknowledging the impossibility of offering any but the most superficial analysis of human rights law and practice in 'Asia' within the confines of this short chapter. Even if one excludes the fourteen 'West Asian' countries of the Middle East,[1] the variety and complexity of the remaining forty-one states included in the United Nation's regional group of Asia and the Pacific render any meaningful political, economic, or cultural generalizations impossible.[2]

Nonetheless, whether in the context of discussions about 'Asian values' or the economic successes within Asia over the past few decades, Asian states and the rest of the world seem to assume that such a broad geographic and cultural category is useful, at least up to a point. Perhaps 'Asia' is best understood in historical and contemporary contrast to both 'the West' of Europe and North America (with Latin America as a distinct, but closely related, subcategory) and Africa; eliminating these groupings does leave one with a majority of countries that can be described as 'Asian', with Russia having characteristics of both Asia and Europe but historically focused on the latter. With a few exceptions, Asian religious traditions are largely distinct from the Christian influence found in the Americas, Europe, and much of Africa, although Islam

[1] Bahrain, Cyprus, Iran, Iraq, Jordan, Kuwait, Lebanon, Oman, Qatar, Saudi Arabia, Syria, Turkey, United Arab Emirates, and Yemen.

[2] For the purpose of this chapter, 'Asia' is understood as these 41 states, plus Australia and New Zealand. Turkey participates in both the Asian and Pacific and the Western European and Others (WEOG) UN groups and is considered to be a member of WEOG for electoral purposes; it is also a member of the Council of Europe and a party to the European Convention on Human Rights, as is Cyprus. Kiribati is in the Pacific and is considered to be within the Asian and Pacific group, but it has never formally joined a group or designated a permanent representative to the UN. The full listing of regional groups and their membership may be found at United Nations, 'United Nations Groups of Member States' (UN 2018) <http://www.un.org/depts/DGACM/RegionalGroups.shtml> accessed 7 October 2018.

is obviously a heritage found in Africa and the Middle East, as well as in Asia. As Peerenboom writes:

> Asian values are by definition the dominant values that exist in Asia. They form a value cluster with hierarchies and intensities that allow them to be compared to other value clusters. The individual values that make up the cluster do not have to be unique to Asia, provided the cluster of values as a whole, including the relative ranking and weighting of values within the cluster, is distinguishable from the value clusters of other regions.[3]

This chapter will examine human rights in Asia from two perspectives. First, it will examine the engagement (or lack thereof) by Asian states with international institutions concerned with promoting and protecting human rights, legally, rhetorically, and diplomatically. This section will include intra-Asian institutions, such as the Association of Southeast Asian Nations (ASEAN). Secondly, it will attempt to gauge, necessarily in a general way, the domestic status of human rights in a selection of Asian states and the impact, if any, of international norms on domestic behaviour.

2 International Engagement

2.1 Global Institutions

On the level of purely legal commitments, the great majority of Asian and Pacific states have ratified both of the two major UN human rights treaties, the International Covenant on Economic, Social and Cultural Rights (ICESCR) and International Covenant on Civil and Political Rights (ICCPR). Only Brunei, Malaysia, Myanmar, and Singapore have *not* ratified either treaty, while China, Nauru, and Palau have ratified the ICESCR but not the ICCPR. Each covenant has an additional optional protocol, under which states may accept the right of individuals to file complaints against their own country. Only Mongolia has ratified the protocol to the ICESCR (which was opened for ratification only in 2008), while the optional protocol to the ICCPR has been ratified by Australia, Kazakhstan, Kyrgyzstan, Maldives, Mongolia, Nepal, New Zealand, the Philippines, Republic of Korea (hereinafter South Korea), Tajikistan, Turkmenistan, and Uzbekistan.[4]

An additional indicator of a country's formal diplomatic commitment to human rights may be whether any of its nationals serve as expert members of one of the

[3] Randall Peerenboom, 'An Empirical Overview of Rights Performance in Asia, France, and the USA: The Dominance of Wealth in the Interplay of Economics, Culture, Law, and Governance' in Randall Peerenboom, Carole Petersen, and Albert Chen (eds), *Human Rights in Asia* (Routledge 2006) 37.

[4] A full country-by-country list of ratifications of major UN human rights treaties may be found at UN High Commissioner for Human Rights, 'Ratification Status by Country or Treaty' (OHCHR 2018), <http://tbinternet.ohchr.org/_layouts/TreatyBodyExternal/Treaty.aspx?CountryID=5&Lang=EN> accessed 5 October 2018.

UN 'treaty bodies' created by the ICESCR and ICCPR to oversee and review implementation of the obligations undertaken by parties to the treaty. Again, focusing only on the two covenants, as of March 2017 experts from China, India, and South Korea were members of the eighteen-person Committee on Economic, Social, and Cultural Rights (which oversees the ICESCR); only Japan had an expert on the Human Rights Committee (which oversees the ICCPR and also has eighteen members).

The primary UN body concerned with human rights is the Human Rights Council (HRC), state members of which are elected individually for three-year terms by the General Assembly, based on a formula that allots thirteen of the forty-seven seats on the Council to Asia and the Pacific. While there are no permanent seats (countries must leave the Council for at least one year after they have served two consecutive terms), Bangladesh, China, India, Indonesia, Japan, Philippines, and South Korea have been quasi-permanent members of the HRC, elected in every year that they have been eligible.[5] While participation in the HRC is open to observer states also, membership on a regular basis is an indicator of the significance of human rights issues to the country concerned—whether its goal is to advance or impede the UN's work in this area. The fact that larger countries are more likely to be represented is not surprising, given that the HRC meets for at least 10 weeks annually and that active participation requires sufficient diplomatic resources in Geneva, where the Council meets.

The HRC replaced its predecessor, the Commission on Human Rights, in 2006, in part due to dissatisfaction with the alleged politicization and selectivity of the Commission's activities. Unsurprisingly, the Council has turned out to be little different from the Commission, although the election procedure makes it somewhat less likely that a notorious violator of human rights will be elected to the HRC than was the case before its creation. Despite calls in the resolution setting forth the basic operating rules for the HRC for work to be undertaken in an 'objective, transparent, non-selective, constructive, non-confrontational and non-politicized manner', based on 'constructive international dialogue and cooperation', informal voting by ideologically compatible countries is not uncommon.[6]

The creation of new thematic 'special procedures' (experts or working groups that focus on a particular substantive area) in recent years has become even more highly politicized. For example, an Independent Expert on protection against violence and discrimination based on sexual orientation and gender identity in 2016 was adopted by a sharply divided vote of twenty-three in favour, eighteen against, and six abstentions; within the Asian and Pacific group, South Korea and Vietnam voted in favour (along with all of the Western countries), while Bangladesh, China, Indonesia, Kyrgyzstan, and the Maldives voted against; the Philippines abstained.[7] The situation was reversed two years earlier, when a Special Rapporteur on the negative impact of unilateral coercive measures on the enjoyment of human rights was appointed by a vote of 31-14-2, with China, India, Indonesia, Maldives, Pakistan, Philippines, and Vietnam

[5] This list also includes Qatar and Saudi Arabia.

[6] See HRC resolution 5/1 (2006).

[7] HRC resolution 32/2 (2016).

voting in favour; Japan and South Korea, with the West, voted against.[8] South Korea abstained on a resolution on the right to development that was opposed by France and the UK but supported by all other Asian countries.[9] On the other hand, resolutions creating new procedures on the right to privacy[10] and the right of persons with disabilities[11] were adopted without a vote, indicating general consensus among the Council members.

Differences over the substance of human rights do not reflect a categorical rejection of human rights, even by countries such as the Democratic People's Republic of Korea. In 2006, the Council created its only truly new procedure, the Universal Periodic Review (UPR), pursuant to which the human rights record of every UN member state is subject to scrutiny by other states once every four years. The substantive norms for the review are the UN Charter, the Universal Declaration of Human Rights, and any human rights treaties to which the state being reviewed is a party.

The UPR is a system of peer review, and the input of nongovernmental organizations (NGOs) is minimal. The procedure itself offers the opportunity for every state to submit a report on its human rights situation, for other states to make comments and recommendations to the state under review, and for the reviewed state to respond affirmatively or negatively to the recommendations. There is little real dialogue, and the sessions last only a few hours, with equal time being allotted to each state, no matter how large or small or whether its human rights record is generally good or dismal. The Council draws no substantive conclusions on a state's human rights performance, and the outcome is merely a compilation of the interventions and responses of states, not an analysis. Nonetheless, every UN member has participated in this voluntary procedure, which has now completed two rounds of review, thus giving at least symbolic support to the principle that a state's human rights record is a legitimate concern of the international community.

2.2 Regional Institutions

It is not surprising that there is no region-wide human rights mechanism in the Asia-Pacific, given the diversity and geographic spread of the region. However, there are a number of sub-regional institutions that are beginning to address human rights issues in a multilateral context. These institutions tend to be based on 'soft law' declarations rather than legally binding treaties, and they do not provide direct individual access to any form of complaint mechanism. Nonetheless, these institutions are a first step by governments in recognizing the significance of human rights issues in the region, and they may lead to other initiatives in the future.

[8] HRC resolution 27/21 (2014).

[9] HRC resolution 33/14 (2016).

[10] HRC resolution 28/16 (2015).

[11] HRC resolution 26/20 (2014).

2.2.1 *ASEAN*

ASEAN is the most developed of the sub-regional organizations with respect to human rights, although that development has been fairly recent and, to date, relatively minimal. ASEAN was originally formed in 1967 by Indonesia, Malaysia, the Philippines, Singapore, and Thailand, and was later joined by Brunei, Cambodia, Laos, Myanmar, and Vietnam. ASEAN's supreme policy-making body, the ASEAN Summit, takes decisions on key issues pertaining to the realization of the objectives of ASEAN and addresses any emergency affecting ASEAN. The ASEAN Coordinating Council, composed of ASEAN foreign ministers, prepares the meetings of the Summit, coordinates with the various councils to enhance policy coherence and cooperation, and undertakes tasks enumerated in the ASEAN Charter.

Throughout most of its existence, ASEAN has been a relatively informal forum for cooperation among its members, but in the past decade its institutional structure and interest in human rights have expanded. In 2007, the ASEAN states adopted a new Charter, which declares the key principles governing the conduct of ASEAN and its member states, among which are 'respect for fundamental freedoms, the promotion and protection of human rights, and the promotion of social justice. . . . [and] adherence to the rule of law, good governance, the principles of democracy and constitutional government'.[12] Pursuant to article 14 of the Charter, a consultative body, the ASEAN Inter-Governmental Human Rights Commission (AICHR), was created in 2009. Unlike members of other regional human rights bodies, AICHR members are not independent experts; instead, each represents and serves at the pleasure of his or her government. Most Commissioners thus far have been current or former government officials, although academics, the private sector, and NGOs are also represented.

According to its Terms of Reference (TOR),[13] the AICHR acts by consensus and has limited powers, which include the obligation to 'promote and protect human rights and fundamental freedoms of the peoples of ASEAN' and to uphold international standards contained in 'international human rights instruments to which ASEAN Member States are parties'. AICHR's promotional work is to be done 'within the regional context, bearing in mind national and regional particularities and mutual respect for different historical, cultural and religious backgrounds, and taking into account the balance between rights and responsibilities'. The 'promotional' mandate and functions include enhancing public awareness of human rights, promoting capacity-building, encouraging member states 'to consider acceding to and ratifying international human rights instruments', and promoting implementation of 'ASEAN instruments related to human rights'.

Although protection is mentioned, that mandate has not been spelled out through the grant of specific functions and powers. During the AICHR's first formal session, efforts to permit the Commission to receive formal complaints were rejected,

[12] ASEAN Charter (adopted 20 November 2007, entered into force 15 December 2008) <http://hrlibrary.umn.edu/research/Philippines/ASEAN%20Charter.pdf> accessed 4 December 2018.

[13] See AICHR, 'TOR of AICHR' <https://aichr.org/key-documents/> accessed 24 April 2019.

the AICHR being unwilling to imply a power not specifically granted to it under its TOR. The Commission's five-year work plan, adopted in 2015, contains no specific reference to complaints or meaningful oversight, although it does refer to educational activities, capacity-building, and 'coordinat[ing] with relevant ASEAN sectoral bodies to ensure the effective implementation' of the ASEAN Declaration on Human Rights.[14] In addition, the AICHR is to identify the current and potential human rights matters of interest to ASEAN and develop and make recommendations on common ASEAN approaches and positions on these matters.

In 2012, the heads of state adopted the ASEAN Human Rights Declaration, further clarifying the mandate of the AICHR.[15] The Declaration includes civil, political, economic, social, and cultural rights, as well as rights to development and peace. The Declaration is seen by some as a precursor to a formal treaty for the region, as has happened with human rights declarations at the UN and in other regional systems. At the same time, it was criticized by those who disagreed, in particular, with its references to balancing rights and responsibilities (article 6) and respect for different cultural backgrounds (article 7). Then UN High Commissioner for Human Rights Navi Pillay, for example, commented, 'This is not the hallmark of the democratic global governance to which ASEAN aspires, and it will only serve to undermine the respect and ownership that such an important declaration deserves'.[16]

Reflecting the organization's human rights priorities, in 2013 ASEAN adopted declarations on eliminating violence against women and children and on strengthening social protection. It has created a separate Commission on the Promotion and Protection of the Rights of Women and Children[17] and a Committee on the Implementation of the Declaration on the Protection and Promotion of the Rights of Migrant Workers,[18] both intended to implement earlier ASEAN declarations. Like the AICHR, these bodies are composed of governmental representatives.

[14] AICHR, 'Five-Year Work Plan of the ASEAN Intergovernmental Commission on Human Rights (2016–2020)' (adopted 15 June 2015, endorsed at the 48th ASEAN Foreign Ministers Meeting, 3 August 2015) <http://aichr.org/key-documents/> accessed 24 April 2019.

[15] ASEAN, ASEAN Human Rights Declaration (ASEAN 18 November 2013) <http://www.asean.org/wp-content/uploads/images/resources/ASEAN%20Publication/2013%20%287.%20Jul%29%20-%20ASEAN%20Human%20Rights%20Declaration%20%28AHRD%29%20and%20Its%20Translation.pdf> accessed 5 October 2018. On the drafting and contents of the Declaration, see Catherine Renshaw, 'The ASEAN Human Rights Declaration 2012' (2013) 11 Human Rights Law Review 3.

[16] 'UN Rights Chief to Southeast Asian Leaders: Make Your Landmark Human Rights Declaration More Inclusive' (*UN News* 8 November 2012) <http://www.un.org/apps/news/story.asp?NewsID=43446#.WNgUgbjXv20> accessed 5 October 2018. See also American Bar Association (Rule of Law Initiative), *The ASEAN Declaration of Human Rights: A Legal Analysis* (ABA 2014).

[17] See The ASEAN Commission on the Promotion and Protection of the Rights of Women and Children, 'Fact Sheet' (ACWC 2018) <http://humanrightsinasean.info/documents/3> accessed 5 October 2018.

[18] See Human Rights in ASEAN ('HRIA'), 'ASEAN Committee on Migrant Workers' (HRIA 2018) <https://humanrightsinasean.info/asean-committee-migrant-workers/about.html> accessed 5 October 2018.

2.2.2 *South Asian Association for Regional Cooperation (SAARC)*

SAARC was established in 1985 to promote regional cooperation among its member states, but local conflicts have limited its ability to act. The member states of SAARC are Bangladesh, Bhutan, India, Maldives, Nepal, Pakistan, and Sri Lanka. Its charter makes no mention of human rights, and it currently does not have a human rights mechanism. However, in 2002, the organization adopted two treaties linked with specific human rights issues: the SAARC Convention on Preventing and Combating Trafficking in Women and Children for Prostitution and the SAARC Convention on Regional Arrangements for the Promotion of Child Welfare in South Asia. In 2004, the organization adopted the SAARC Social Charter, which concerns many economic, social, and cultural rights. In 2011, SAARC adopted a Charter of Democracy that expresses a 'shared commitment to the rule of law, liberty and equal rights of all citizens' and 'reaffirm[s] faith in fundamental human rights and in the dignity of the human person as enunciated in the Universal Declaration of Human Rights and as enshrined in the respective Constitutions of the SAARC Member States'.[19] No specific mechanisms have been adopted to implement any of these instruments.

2.2.3 *Asia Pacific Forum of National Human Rights Institutions*

The Asia Pacific Forum of National Human Rights Institutions is a twenty-four-member intergovernmental organization whose goal is to promote and support the national human rights institutions (NHRIs) of its members.[20] Members include states from across Asia and the Pacific. Its activities include promoting the establishment of NHRIs and providing education, training, advice, and capacity-building to its members. The Forum's work is not governed by a specific human rights treaty or declaration, but among the thematic issues specifically identified by the Forum as of interest are the rights of women, children, indigenous peoples, older persons, migrants, and persons with disabilities; business and human rights; reproductive rights; respect for sexual and gender orientation; preventing torture; and protecting human rights defenders. The Forum does not have a formal complaint or monitoring mandate, but it makes public statements on current issues in its member states, such as calling for respect for the human rights of a former chairperson of the Philippines NHRI and Secretary of Justice who is a strong critic of President Duterte and who has been accused of drug offences; condemning the killing of protesters in Nepal; and supporting a national enquiry to address human rights violations in Sri Lanka.

[19] SAARC, Charter of Democracy (2011) <http://www.internationaldemocracywatch.org/index.php/saarc-treaties-and-protocols/437-saarc-charter-of-democracy> accessed 4 December 2018. For a commentary written before its adoption, see Surya Deuja, 'Establishing a Robust Regional Human Rights Mechanism in South Asia' (2010) 6 Asian Human Rights Defender 4.

[20] Asia Pacific Forum of National Human Rights Institutions, 'Supporting National Human Rights Institutions' <https://www.asiapacificforum.net/support> accessed 24 April 2019.

2.2.4 *Cross-regional Bodies*

Although not considered to be 'Asia' for the purposes of this chapter, it might be noted that the Arab League adopted an Arab Charter on Human Rights in 1994, which was revised in 2004. In 2014, a new Statute of the Arab Court of Human Rights was adopted.[21] Only a state party 'whose subject claims to be a victim of a human rights violation' may invoke its jurisdiction, although a state may optionally accept that an NGO working in such a state also may have access to the Court. The Court's judgment may be directly enforced within a state that is party to the Statute. It is not known whether any state has yet ratified the Statute, and the International Commission of Jurists has called its adoption 'an empty gesture that will do nothing for the victims of human rights violations in the Middle East and North African region'.[22]

The fifty-seven member states of the Organization of Islamic Cooperation (OIC) are found in Asia, the Middle East, Africa, and Latin America. In 2011, the OIC created a consultative body, the eighteen-member Independent Permanent Human Rights Commission. According to the preamble of the Commission's Statute, the Commission 'shall promote the civil, political, social and economic rights enshrined in the Organization's covenants and declarations and in universally agreed human rights instruments, in conformity with Islamic values'.[23]

3 Domestic Approaches to Human Rights

No region of the world is sufficiently uniform to be analysed purely geographically in terms of its respect for universally or even regionally recognized human rights, and this is obviously true of the Asia and Pacific region. Comparisons may be drawn and categories parsed according to countless criteria, but the only truly meaningful way of attempting to evaluate a country's human rights performance is on an individual country basis.

Given the lack of a sufficiently robust human rights treaty system within Asia, the UN's human rights machinery—treaty bodies, special rapporteurs, the Universal Periodic Review, and statements and resolutions of the Human Rights Council—offer

[21] Unofficial English translations may be found at Arab Centre for International Humanitarian Law and Human Rights Education, 'The Statute of the Arab Court of Human Rights' (ACIHL 2014) <http://www.acihl.org/texts.htm?article_id=44&lang=ar-SA> accessed 7 October 2018; and International Commission of Jurists, *The Arab Court of Human Rights: A Flawed Statute for an Ineffective Court* (ICJ 2015), Annex I.

[22] International Commission of Jurists, *Arab League's Human Rights Court Will Not Bring Justice to Victims of Violations* (ICJ 2014).

[23] The texts of the Commission's Statute and Rules of Procedure may be found at <https://www.oic-iphrc.org/en/oic-human-rights-RI&T> accessed 4 December 2018. For the Commission's history and activities since its creation, see <https://www.oic-iphrc.org/en/home> accessed 24 April 2019.

perhaps the best overview of the status of human rights in a particular country.[24] The United States, United Kingdom, and the European Union produce annual reports on human rights practices around the world; despite the fact that these are governmental or intergovernmental documents, they are generally considered to be reasonably objective in their conclusions (although some countries strongly disagree with the manner in which they may be characterized). China, for example, issues an annual report detailing human rights problems in the United States, following the release of the annual US reports on human rights each spring.[25]

Many national human rights institutions produce regular reports on aspects of human rights within their own countries.[26] Twenty of the states considered in this chapter have created NHRIs; that of Fiji was suspended in 2007 and later withdrew from the Global Alliance of National Human Rights Institutions, which was created in 2006 by NHRIs themselves to coordinate the activities of the NHRI network.[27] Many international and national NGOs are also valuable sources of information about human rights. In addition to well-known NGOs with a global scope, such as Human Rights Watch, Amnesty International, and the Fédération Internationale des Droits de l'Homme, the best-known NGO focusing on Asia is probably the Asian Human Rights Commission, based in Hong Kong.[28]

Attempts to characterize or distinguish different approaches to human rights in Asia frequently include reference to a number of arguments put forward to justify Asian exceptionalism in this field. Perhaps the most widely asserted argument contends that 'Asian values' are different from the Western values that animate today's international human rights norms. Three additional arguments contain elements of the Asian values approach, although not all refer directly to culture. The first perspective emphasizes the overriding importance of national sovereignty and the principle of non-intervention, as a justification for rejecting outsiders' opinions about human rights practices in particular countries. A second argument, related to both Asian values and sovereignty, holds that there is an Asian cultural preference for conciliation over confrontation, making any judicial or quasi-judicial examination of human rights practices inappropriate, whether domestically or internationally. A final argument, not unique to but frequently voiced in Asia, is that economic development should take priority over human rights, particularly

[24] All of these mechanisms may be searched on a country-by-country basis via the website of the Office of the UN High Commissioner for Human Rights (OHCHR) <http://www.ohchr.org/EN/pages/home.aspx> accessed 7 October 2018.

[25] See e.g. State Council Information Office of China, 'Human Rights Record of the United States in 2016' (State Council PRC 2017) <http://english.gov.cn/archive/publications/2017/03/09/content_281475589785800.htm> accessed 7 October 2018.

[26] See generally Office of the High Commissioner for Human Rights, 'OHCHR and NHRIs' <http://www.ohchr.org/EN/Countries/NHRI/Pages/NHRIMain.aspx> accessed 7 October 2018.

[27] Ibid.

[28] A short list of Asian human rights NGOs may be found at Asia Rights, <http://asiapacific.anu.edu.au/blogs/asiarights/new-directory-of-asian-human-rights-organizations/> accessed 7 October 2018.

those civil and political rights that are perceived to be the focus of many non-Asian governments and NGOs.

3.1 Asian Values

Most countries and regions claim that they are 'exceptional' in one respect or another, so the argument by some Asian countries that Asian cultural values are unique should not be surprising. This perspective appears to be strongest in Southeast Asia and has been articulated particularly by Malaysia and Singapore. The best-known statement of this position originated in an Asian regional meeting convened in preparation for the UN's Second World Conference on Human Rights, held in Vienna in 1993. The regional meeting adopted what became known as the Bangkok Declaration,[29] whose language with respect to recognizing the principle of respect for different 'cultural, historical, and religious backgrounds' was essentially reiterated in the 2012 ASEAN Declaration of Human Rights (discussed in section 2.2.1).

A short but useful summary of the 'Asian values' debate identifies the content of Asian values as including: privileging the nation and community over the individual; emphasizing consensus over conflict; calling for social harmony and respect for authority; and prioritizing law, social order, and security over individual civil and political rights.[30] Another analyst describes the 'apparently oxymoronic position' of human rights understanding in Asia as encompassing 'acceptance of universalism in principle, and, on the other hand, the requirement to take into account the cultural specificity of the different peoples living in the continent'.[31] Of course, such assertions are undermined by the diversity of Asian countries themselves, as well as the fact that 'Asian values' have 'often been used by authoritarian regimes for self-serving ends, wherein culture has been called upon to excuse violations of the rights of its citizens, and to shield these violations from international scrutiny'.[32]

While misuse of 'Asian values' arguments does not contradict the notion that there *are* certain values that may be unique or particularly important to Asia (as implied by Peerenboom), the frequent identification of such values with authoritarian regimes does undermine the credibility of the argument.

[29] The text is found in UN, Report of the Regional Meeting for Asia of the World Conference on Human Rights, UN Doc A/CONF.157/ASRM/8, A/CONF.157/PC/59 (1993) 3–7.

[30] See Joshua Castellino and Elvira Dominguez Redondo, *Minority Rights in Asia: A Comparative Legal Analysis* (OUP 2006) 11–22, esp 18–22. A somewhat similar, critical analysis of the 'Asian values' argument is found in Ben Saul, Jacqueline Mowbray, and Irene Baghoomians, 'Resistance to Human Rights Cooperation in the Asia-Pacific: Demythologizing Regional Exceptionalism by Learning from the Americas, Europe and Africa' in Hitoshi Nasu and Ben Saul (eds), *Human Rights in the Asia-Pacific Region* (Routledge 2011) ch 6.

[31] See Frederico Lenzerini, *The Culturalization of Human Rights Law* (OUP 2014) 70.

[32] Castellino and Dominiguez Redondo (n 30). See also Michael Jacobsen and Ole Bruun (eds), *Human Rights and Asian Values: Contesting National Identities and Cultural Representations in Asia* (Hart 2000).

Only three months after adoption of the Bangkok Declaration, the World Conference on Human Rights came to a nuanced, but quite different, conclusion regarding the relationship of regional values to universal human rights. The language that was adopted by consensus after a full discussion of the issue was:

> While the significance of national and regional particularities and various historical, cultural and religious backgrounds must be borne in mind, it is the duty of States, regardless of their political, economic and cultural systems, to promote and protect all human rights and fundamental freedoms.[33]

Although the 1993 conference did not end the political and philosophical debates over whether human rights norms are 'Western' or 'neo-colonial', its statement remains the touchstone for the United Nations and, for all practical purposes, most countries in Asia and the Pacific. Despite continuing assertions that many Asian cultural values are different from, say, European or African values (which may well be true), this has not prevented nearly all Asian and Pacific island countries from ratifying the major human rights treaties (on civil and political rights; economic, social, and cultural rights; and non-discrimination based on race or sex). Palau is the only consistent abstainer, while Bhutan, China, Nauru, and Papua New Guinea are the only countries not to have ratified all four of these treaties. Of course, acceptance of the legal obligations in these treaties may be modified or limited by the reservations filed to certain provisions or even the treaty as a whole, as evidenced by those of Malaysia and Singapore.[34]

3.2 Sovereignty

Early and consistent assertions, particularly by China, that human rights are a matter for domestic law and that consideration of domestic human rights conditions is an inappropriate interference with matters 'which are essentially within the domestic jurisdiction of any state'[35] have largely disappeared in recent years. Every UN member state, including all states from Asia and the Pacific, has now cooperated and participated in two quadrennial Universal Periodic Reviews by the UN Human Rights Council, beginning in 2008. As noted above, this is primarily a peer review process that provides for little dialogue or substantive debate, though countries under review may be presented with scores of recommendations by other states, which can be accepted or rejected without formal consequences. The review is intended to

[33] World Conference on Human Rights, Final Declaration and Programme of Action, UN Doc A/CONF.157/23 (1993) sec I, para 5.

[34] A list of all reservations to the treaties may be found in the UN Treaty Collection, <https://treaties.un.org/pages/Treaties.aspx?id=4&subid=A&lang=en> accessed 7 October 2018. These and similar statistics throughout this chapter are current as of 2017.

[35] The language is taken from article 2(7) of the UN Charter, which states that the UN is not authorized to 'intervene' in such matters.

'[p]romote the universality, interdependence, indivisibility and interrelatedness of all human rights; ... [f]ully integrate a gender perspective; [and] [w]ithout prejudice to the obligations contained in the elements provided for in the basis of review, take into account the level of development and specificities of countries'.[36] The first objective listed is '[t]he improvement of the human rights situation on the ground',[37] which certainly undermines any claim that human rights are not a legitimate concern of the international community or foreign states.

However, the situation is very different when it comes to accepting the right of individuals to submit communications alleging violations of human rights to the bodies that oversee each treaty. For example, among Asian and Pacific countries:

- the right of individual petition with respect to the ICCPR has only been accepted by the four Central Asian countries of Kazakhstan, Kyrgyzstan, Tajikistan, and Turkmenistan, plus Australia, Maldives, Mongolia, Nepal, New Zealand, Philippines, South Korea, and Sri Lanka;
- the comparable right under the Convention on the Elimination of All Forms of Discrimination against Women has only been accepted by the four Central Asian countries, Australia, Cambodia, Cook Islands, Maldives, Mongolia, Nepal, New Zealand, Philippines, South Korea, Solomon Islands, Sri Lanka, Thailand, and Vanuatu;
- the right of petition under the Convention on the Elimination of All Forms of Racial Discrimination has only been accepted by Australia, Kazakhstan, and South Korea; and
- only Mongolia has accepted the right of individual petition under the ICESCR.

Sovereignty does remain a vital concern of countries in the region, but this is more often asserted today in areas such as territorial disputes, including the South China Sea, access to resources, use of force, responsibility for terrorism, the environment, trade, and other traditional concerns of foreign policy. Human rights, at least on the political plane, seems now to be viewed as a legitimate, if rarely welcome, concern of other states, although all countries resent criticism of their domestic human rights practices, even if they may express a rhetorical commitment to them in principle.

3.3 Conciliation versus Confrontation

An early critic, who was then Executive Director of Human Rights Watch, observed that '"consensus-imposing" is a more fitting description of some governments in East and Southeast Asia' than 'consensus-building', which was one of the 'Asian values'

[36] HRC resolution 5/1 (2006) para 3. [37] Ibid. para 4.

defended by a prominent government official of Singapore in the early 1990s.[38] Nonetheless, it does appear to be widely accepted that, for cultural and historical reasons, many Asian societies value communitarian values and stability, in contrast to the more individualistic societies found in the United States and Europe. This is no doubt an oversimplification, perhaps reflecting the shorter history of democracy and participatory politics in many Asian societies, many of which were exposed to individualism and capitalism much later than their contemporaries in the North or West, rather than inherent cultural differences.[39]

In any event, conciliation and true consensus-building are not necessarily antithetical to human rights protection, just as extreme individualism is not always conducive to protecting the human rights of marginalized groups or individuals. For example, indigenous peoples have committed themselves to respect for human rights,[40] despite the fact that they and other groups with more traditional lifestyles are often noted for their consensual approach to decision-making. Electoral systems, such as the proportional representation systems prevalent in Europe, may also be designed to foster compromise, unlike the winner-take-all systems found in the United Kingdom and United States.

In the end, however, consensus cannot always be achieved within society, whether to resolve private disputes or to determine the proper balance to be struck between the rights of the individual and the legitimate needs of the community to promote the general welfare. Thus, the availability of a fair judiciary that is able to deal effectively with complaints about alleged official abuses and miscarriages of justice is essential to any modern society, whether it is culturally more likely to prefer consensus or contestation.

Respect for human rights in Asia and the Pacific does not require adopting the same cultural attitudes as those that are prevalent in other regions, but some Asian governments have been far too quick in using 'consensus' or 'tradition' as an excuse for elitism, discrimination, and authoritarianism. Dispute resolution and consensus-building in ways freely chosen by society are unlikely to violate universal norms of human rights, so long as they are not fabricated by governments whose purpose is to quash dissent rather than to reconcile differences.

3.4 Development

The debate about the relationship between economic development and human rights has continued for decades; it cannot be blithely papered over by invoking the refrain

[38] Arieh Neier, 'Asia's Unacceptable Standard' (1993) 92 Foreign Policy 42, 43, in response to Bilahari Kausikan, 'Asia's Different Standard' (1993) 92 Foreign Policy 24.

[39] Australia and New Zealand are exceptions to this generalization, but that is probably true for much of what has been described in this chapter and Handbook.

[40] See UN Declaration on the Rights of Indigenous Peoples, UNGA resolution 61/295 (2007) paras 34, 44, 46.

that human rights are universal, indivisible, interdependent, and interrelated. The impetus for a discrete 'right to development' came primarily from socialist and developing countries in the context of attempts to create a new international economic order in the 1980s, but few, if any, states now oppose the concept; unlike other human rights, however, the right to development has not been legally set forth in any UN treaty.

The right to development was proclaimed by the UN General Assembly in 1986 as 'an inalienable human right', in the context of which '[t]he human person is the central subject of development and should be the active participant and beneficiary of the right to development'.[41] States 'have the duty to take steps, individually and collectively, to formulate international development policies with a view to facilitating the full realization of the right to development', and 'effective international co-operation is essential in providing ... [developing countries] with appropriate means and facilities to foster their comprehensive development'.[42] When the position of UN High Commissioner for Human Rights was created in 1993, the position was specifically mandated to 'promote and protect the realization of the right to development and to enhance support from relevant bodies of the United Nations system for this purpose'.[43] Amongst the thematic priorities of the High Commissioner's office is '[i]ntegrating human rights in development and in the economic sphere'.[44]

The 1993 Bangkok Declaration, adopted by over forty Asian states and referred to above, also emphasizes that 'the main obstacles to the realization of the right to development lie at the international macroeconomic level, as reflected in the widening gap between the North and the South, the rich and the poor'.[45] It notes further that the creation of uniform human rights norms 'must go hand in hand with endeavours to work towards a just and fair world economic order'.[46]

A long-standing debate within Asia has been whether it is necessary or justifiable to give precedence to economic, social, and cultural rights—in particular, the right to development—as opposed to civil and political rights, given the limited resources available in many developing countries. A recent Chinese government White Paper presents one side of the debate and clearly prioritizes development over most other concerns:

> The rights to subsistence and development are the primary, basic human rights. Poverty is the biggest obstacle to human rights. Without the production and supply of material goods, it is difficult or even impossible to realize any other human right. Development is a means of eliminating poverty. It provides necessary conditions for realizing other human rights, and releases human potential. The right to development is incorporated into other human rights, while the latter create the conditions for people to facilitate development and realize the right to development. *Safeguarding*

[41] UN Declaration on the Right to Development, UNGA resolution 41/128 (1986) annex, paras 1, 2.

[42] Ibid. para 4. [43] UNGA resolution 48/141 (1993) para 4(c).

[44] See OHCHR, 'Integrating Human Rights in Development and in the Economic Sphere' <http://www.ohchr.org/EN/AboutUs/Pages/developmentintheeconomicsphere.aspx> accessed 7 October 2018.

[45] UN, Report of the Regional Meeting for Asia (n 29) preamble. [46] Ibid.

> *the right to development is the precondition for realizing economic, cultural, social and environmental rights, and obtaining civil and political rights.* ...
>
> The people's right to development is realized [in China] through a framework of institutions, strategies, policies and measures that are constructive, practical, efficient, and compulsory....
>
> China continues to enrich and improve a political system suited to its own development by advancing Chinese socialist democracy and rule of law in an all-round way, ensuring effective protection of civil and political rights, and raising the levels of participation in and promotion of the political development process and allowing people to partake in the benefits of political development....
>
> There will always be room for improvement in human rights, and the quest to improve people's right to development is always underway.... Meeting the people's growing material and cultural needs and giving everyone access to sound development are still the primary tasks of the CPC in its governance of the country.[47]

The opposing view, that civil and political rights are essential and a necessary precondition for development and socioeconomic rights, is exemplified by Indian economist and Nobel laureate Amartya Sen:

> Development can be seen, it is argued here, as a process of expanding the real freedoms that people enjoy....
>
> [I]n the context of the narrower views of development in terms of GNP growth or industrialization, it is often asked whether certain political or social freedoms, such as the liberty of political participation and dissent, or opportunities to receive basic education, are or are not 'conducive to development'. In the light of the more foundational view of development as freedom, this way of posing the question tends to miss the important understanding that these substantive freedoms (that is, the liberty of political participation or the opportunity to receive basic education or health care) are among the *constituent components* of development....
>
> Freedoms are not only the primary ends of development, they are also among its principal means. In addition to acknowledging, foundationally, the evaluative importance of freedom, we also have to understand the remarkable empirical connection that links freedoms of different kinds with one another. Political freedoms (in the form of free speech and elections) help to promote economic security. Social opportunities (in the form of education and health facilities) facilitate economic participation. Economic facilities (in the form of opportunities for participation in trade and production) can help to generate personal abundance as well as public resources for social facilities. Freedoms of different kinds can strengthen one another....
>
> Systematic empirical studies give no real support to the claim that there is a general conflict between political freedoms and economic performance.[48]

[47] State Council Information Office of the People's Republic of China, 'The Right to Development: China's Philosophy, Practice and Contribution' (*Xinhua* 1 December 2016) (emphasis added).

[48] Amartya Sen, *Development as Freedom* (Knopf 1999) 3, 5, 10–11, 148, 150, 157 (emphasis in original).

No state, whether developed or developing, claims to be against development, although there is a cacophony of opinions as to how it might best be promoted and who, in both the short- and long-term, should be the primary beneficiaries. Countries that do not respect civil and political rights find that the 'human right' to development offers a convenient alternative that may be used to justify what otherwise might be viewed as human rights violations. Despite the claim in the UN Declaration on the Right to Development that '[t]he human person ... should be the active participant and beneficiary of the right to development', equitable distribution of the benefits of development remains difficult to achieve. Many Asian countries have achieved great progress at the top and sometimes middle of the economic pyramid, while failing to ensure that the poorest are not left behind. Even if the rights to participate in and benefit from development without discrimination are respected, the debate over how to achieve the often nebulous goal of 'development' is not likely to conclude soon, whether couched in terms of human rights or socioeconomic principles.

4 Theory versus Practice

No state respects human rights perfectly, but an issue that lingers behind many criticisms of state violations is whether the violations fall into one of three categories. First, some violations are deliberate, based on a fundamental rejection of at least some universal human rights norms. Secondly, a violation may be deliberate, but based on a different interpretation of human rights rather than a rejection of the right in question per se. Thirdly, violations may be unintentional, insofar as the violations reflect the imperfection of human behaviour and government implementation, rather than a conscious desire to contravene widely accepted international norms.

The arguments based on 'Asian values' and related assumptions discussed above often lead to deliberate violations, based on either the rejection or reinterpretation of existing norms. Authoritarian or one-party rule in Cambodia, China, Laos, Myanmar, and Vietnam is inconsistent with fundamental human rights norms. Sporadic or long-term military rule in Bangladesh, Indonesia, Pakistan, Philippines, and Thailand has similarly undermined basic rights.

Failure to protect human rights may also be unintentional or unavoidable, however, and many rights violations in Asian and Pacific countries stem from the inability of governments to ensure rights that they have formally accepted, through adherence to legally binding treaties or public support for politically significant declarations of rights and principles. The category of 'developing' country is so broad as to be nearly meaningless, but it is the category to which the majority of countries in Asia and the Pacific belongs. Lack of human and economic resources limits a country's ability to ensure the entire gamut of civil, political, economic, social, and cultural rights, and any analysis of the state of human rights in the region must try to distinguish between inability and unwillingness to comply with international human rights norms.

5 Conclusion

> Some people say that Western culture is a motor car culture . . . But motor cars did not exist in the West originally [and only came into existence at a certain point in history]. Having motor cars and not having motors is a distinction between the ancient and the modern, and not a distinction between China and the West.[49]

Continuing this theme, University of Hong Kong law professor, Albert Chen, concludes that:

> [H]uman rights are a modern invention. The rise and globalization of human rights thinking may be interpreted as a sign of humanity's moral progress, a quantum leap in the moral consciousness of humankind. From this perspective, the reception and development in Asia of the theory and practice of human rights is an integral component of the processes of the modernization of Asia.[50]

This conclusion may be too facile, but it is probably true that, if one takes a view over the last two or three decades, there has been a gradual trend towards greater rather than less respect for human rights in Asia and the Pacific. This trend is not linear, and China under President Xi Jinping and the Philippines under President Rodrigo Duterte are stark examples of the difference that a particular leader can make. Nevertheless, the situation of human rights in Indonesia, Laos, Malaysia, Mongolia, Myanmar, Nepal, Singapore, South Korea, Taiwan, and Vietnam has improved since the 1980s. Australia, Japan, and New Zealand have had generally good human rights records for some time, bearing in mind the variations in practice that occur as the result of elections. Despite India's frequent description as 'the world's largest democracy', South Asia remains violent and often unstable, and human rights violations in all states in the sub-region continue. In the Pacific, communal problems continue in Fiji, but the smaller island states are rarely mentioned either positively or negatively. There seems to be an unspoken understanding that it may be appropriate for small, homogeneous states that have retained much of their earlier culture to continue to be governed by traditional systems, so long as core human rights are met—such as protection of physical security, guarantees of civil rights to religion and expression, and good faith efforts to ensure economic and social rights to all on a non-discriminatory basis.

However, even a gradual, if uneven, acceptance of universal human rights as recognized in ratified treaties does not mean that one should expect human rights to be interpreted in exactly the same manner in Asia as in Latin America or Europe, nor that significant differences in respect for human rights within Asian countries will not continue. Universality does not equal uniformity, and most human rights norms are defined in a way that necessarily entails a degree of flexibility in their interpretation and

[49] Fung Yulan in Chen Lai (ed), *Fung Yulan Anthology* (Huaxia 1993) 105, quoted in Albert Chen, 'Conclusion: Comparative Reflections on Human Rights in Asia' in Peerenboom et al (eds) (n 3) 487.

[50] Chen, ibid. 488–9.

implementation. The concept of a state's 'margin of appreciation'—a concept developed under the European Convention on Human Rights—is also relevant to Asia and the Pacific. The necessary balance among competing individual rights, as well as the balance between individual freedoms and the legitimate interests of society and the community (not just the interests of government and its leaders), must be established bearing in mind the particular circumstances of each country.

Human rights criticism of Asian and Pacific governments should not ignore the relevance of societal differences, but the *abuse* of purported cultural norms and the unfounded prioritizing of national security or harmony by authoritarian leaders must be combated. In the end, the consensus reached in 1993 at the UN World Conference on Human Rights, following contentious debates over relativism versus universality, may still offer the best articulation of how human rights should be perceived and implemented in Asia:

> All human rights are universal, indivisible and interdependent and interrelated. The international community must treat human rights globally in a fair and equal manner, on the same footing, and with the same emphasis. While the significance of national and regional particularities and various historical, cultural and religious backgrounds must be borne in mind, it is the duty of States, regardless of their political, economic and cultural systems, to promote and protect all human rights and fundamental freedoms.[51]

This formulation offers little concrete guidance as to which government act or omission might constitute a human rights violation, but it reflects the reality of human rights in the Asia and Pacific region. Most states in the region do adhere formally to international human rights norms, despite widespread unwillingness and/or inability of governments to protect and fulfil these legal obligations. To borrow Jack Donnelly's phrase, a future in which states in Asia and the Pacific respect human rights in a manner that recognizes their 'relative universality' would constitute a significant step forward.[52]

[51] World Conference on Human Rights, Vienna Declaration and Programme of Action, UN Doc A/CONF.57/23 (1993) para 5.

[52] See e.g. Jack Donnelly, 'The Relative Universality of Human Rights' (2007) 29 Human Rights Quarterly 281.

CHAPTER 7

INTERNATIONAL HUMANITARIAN LAW AND INTERNATIONAL CRIMINAL LAW

SUZANNAH LINTON*

1 Introduction

THE notion of the Asia-Pacific is simply a geographic concept that is used here to delineate the area of focus.[1] The countries of the region are—upon even a simplistic consideration of religions, cultures, languages, histories, identities, ideologies, and political systems—so immensely diverse. Absent a common political vision and agreement to act in concert, there is no reason why Japan should behave the same way that Pakistan does in relation to the International Criminal Court (ICC), or why Timor-Leste should have the same attitude to the Convention prohibiting Certain Conventional Weapons 1980 that China has. Further, a distorted impression of the region emerges if one focuses on the great powers (such as China, India, and Japan) or if one insists on hunting down a mythical 'Asian approach' to international law.[2] Diversity

* Thanks to Dean Christopher Gane for welcoming the author as an academic visitor at the Chinese University of Hong Kong's Law School in early 2017 and providing access to the fine research facilities at the Lee Quo Wei Law Library. Thanks also to Judge Kriangsak Kittichaisaree for his insightful comments. This chapter is a shortened version of a more comprehensive draft containing detailed footnotes; the original can be obtained from the author on request at suzannahlinton@gmail.com.

[1] It covers East Asia, Southeast Asia, South Asia, Australia and New Zealand, Polynesia, Melanesia, and Micronesia.

[2] For a sampling of the 'Asian approach' genre, see BS Chimni, 'Is There an Asian Approach to International Law? Questions, Theses and Reflections' (2008) 14 Asian Yearbook of International Law 249; M Sornarajah, 'The Asian Perspective to International Law in the Age of Globalization' (2001) 5

and plurality abound in the region. The fluid that connects these states and binds them to other states is none other than international law. And, as we know, there are many approaches to international law and there is much malleability in its rules.

This chapter takes up the challenge of presenting the approaches of Asia-Pacific states to international humanitarian law (IHL) and international criminal law (ICL), within the context of the international legal framework. Several caveats are essential. The first is the importance of recognizing that the approaches of states can depend on the emphasis that each state places on sovereignty, differences over the substance of particular rules, differences regarding the implementation of particular rules, and other impacting issues such as domestic capacity, self-interest, and historical context. State rhetoric and actions do not, however, always correspond. States will take deliberate decisions on whether to observe their international obligations, and failure to behave in accordance with a rule does not always indicate rejection of it. In sum, understanding how states behave in relation to the law is not really about law.

The second caveat is that necessity obliges the author to be selective and restrained. This is not the place for a meaningful reflection on the Chinese Civil War, World War II, the Korean War, the Vietnam War, the Cambodian War, the wars between India and Pakistan, the liberation struggles in Indonesia, Vietnam, Bangladesh, and East Timor, the complex multi-generational fighting in Afghanistan, or the internal armed conflicts in Sri Lanka, Nepal, the Philippines, India, Indonesia, and Burma,[3] some of which continue to present threats to life and limb as well as to international peace and security.[4] The Stockholm International Peace Research Institute established, in 2016, that 'Asia' has the second highest number of armed conflicts in the world (being either in first or second position consistently since records began in 2006).[5] In 2017, five of the region's countries were engaged in active armed conflicts: Afghanistan, India, Myanmar, Pakistan, and the Philippines.[6]

Singapore Journal of International Law & Comparative Law 284; Frederick Snyder and Surakiart Sathirathai (eds), *Third World Attitudes Toward International Law* (Brill 1987), especially RP Anand, 'Attitude of the Asian-African States Toward Certain Problems of International Law', infra 5.

[3] For a review of eleven countries from a post-conflict perspective, see Suzannah Linton, 'Post Conflict Justice in Asia' in M Cherif Bassiouni (ed), *The Pursuit of International Criminal Justice: A World Study on Conflicts, Victimisation and Post-Conflict Justice* vol 2 (Intersentia 2010) pt III; also Deborah Mayersen and Annie Pohlman (eds), *Genocide and Mass Atrocities in Asia: Legacies and Prevention* (Routledge 2013).

[4] The most pressing are the Korean Peninsula (both internally within the DPRK and in her external relations), Kashmir, Taiwan and China, the South China Sea and her islands and insular features, the East China Sea islands and insular features, and the situation in Burma/Myanmar. Four of the world's nuclear powers are engaged in these volatile situations.

[5] *Stockholm International Peace Research Institute Year Book: Armaments, Disarmament and International Security Summary* (2016) 7 (table showing regional distribution and total number of armed conflicts, 2006–15).

[6] *Stockholm International Peace Research Institute Year Book: Armaments, Disarmament and International Security Summary* (2018) 2.

In the area of ICL, necessity also means that this reflection will focus on those international crimes that are—definitional quibbles aside—now covered in the ICC Statute 1998: aggression, genocide, crimes against humanity, and war crimes. This contribution does not consider how states in the region relate to transnational crimes such as human trafficking and money laundering. It also does not consider extreme human rights violations such as torture, arbitrary killings, and enforced disappearance that do not meet the criteria to be ICC-type crimes. It does not reflect on another area that could be revealing: regional and bilateral cooperation in crime prevention and control. Finally, it is obviously not possible to engage in anything but brief mention of the Asia-Pacific's intimate experience of international crimes, such as the horrors of World War II, Partition-related crimes in India and Pakistan in 1971, Indonesia's 1965 *pogrom*, the devastation of Bangladesh in 1971, the atrocities of the Khmer Rouge in Cambodia in the late 1970s, the crimes in East Timor between 1975 and 1999, the ongoing persecution of the Rohingya in Burma/Myanmar, or the enormous *gulag* that is the Democratic People's Republic of North Korea (DPRK or North Korea).

With the above caveats, the sections that follow offer a succinct overview of how Asia-Pacific states relate to IHL and ICL. Section 2 addresses influential approaches in the region, including how states present themselves in relation to IHL and ICL issues. The third section considers how states engage with the technical issue of responsibility in international law, with an emphasis on IHL and ICL. Sections 4 and 5 examine acceptance of these two bodies of law, arguing that there is no hostility to the basic norms of IHL, but a more unsettled approach to ICL.

2 Influential Approaches

Asia-Pacific states are not passive vassals in the contemporary legal order. Every state in the region, by virtue of its voluntary membership of the United Nations (UN), formally agrees with the principles and purposes of the organization. In addition, twenty-two states from the region are also members of the Non-Aligned Movement (NAM), which has its roots in the 1955 Bandung Conference and whose founding fathers included President Soeharto of Indonesia and Prime Minister Nehru of India.[7] Under the auspices of this strongly anti-colonial movement, the heads of state of the twenty-two Asia-Pacific states have declared their commitment 'to uphold and defend the principles of the United Nations Charter and international law as well as a fuller utilization and means for the peaceful settlement of disputes, as envisaged in the United

[7] See Hennie Strydom, 'The Non-Aligned Movement and the Reform of International Relations' (2007) 11 Max Planck Yearbook of United Nations Law 1. The Asia-Pacific members are Afghanistan; Bangladesh; Bhutan; Brunei Darussalam; Cambodia; Democratic People's Republic of Korea; India; Indonesia; Lao People's Democratic Republic; Malaysia; Mongolia; Myanmar; Nepal; Pakistan; Papua New Guinea; Philippines; Singapore; Sri Lanka; Thailand; Timor-Leste; Vanuatu; and Viet Nam.

Nations Charter'.[8] They also declared themselves, in this context, committed 'to conduct their external affairs based upon the obligations of international law'.

The NAM is strongly Westphalian and the 'Declaration on Principles of International Law Concerning Friendly Relations and Co-operation among States in Accordance with the Charter of the United Nations', adopted on 24 October 1970 by the UN General Assembly, is critical to the movement's approach.[9] The NAM's principles and objectives include:

> the safeguarding of the independence, sovereignty and territorial integrity of States, exercise of self-determination and sovereignty of the non-aligned and other developing countries, achievement of disarmament, especially nuclear disarmament, an end to colonialism and all forms of subjugation, eradication of racism and all forms of racial discrimination, especially apartheid, peaceful co-existence among States, democratization of inter-State relations, peaceful settlement of regional conflicts, attainment of developmental goals by all developing countries and protection of human rights, especially their social and economic dimensions.[10]

The NAM adopts, as a principle, the condemnation of 'genocide, war crimes, crimes against humanity and systematic and gross violations of human rights, in accordance with the UN Charter and international law'.[11] NAM leaders have further declared that:

> all High Contracting Parties have the responsibility to respect and to ensure respect for International Humanitarian Law, to enhance such respect, to ensure that it does not become eroded and that humanitarian principles and respect for human dignity are not diminished.[12]

NAM states do not explicitly support the ICC: at the Kuala Lumpur Summit in 2003, the entry into force of the Rome Statute of the ICC was simply 'noted', although the heads of state or government 'stressed the importance of safeguarding the integrity of the Statute and the need to ensure that the Court remains impartial and fully independent of political organs of the United Nations, which should not direct or hinder the functions of the Court nor assume a parallel or superior role to the Court'.[13] They also noted with concern actions geared at establishing a process to grant immunity to the members of UN-established or authorized peacekeeping operations.

[8] UN General Assembly (UNGA)/UN Security Council (UNSC), '13th Summit Conference of Heads of State or Government of the Non-Aligned Movement: Final Document' (Kuala Lumpur, 2003) UN Doc A/57/759–S/2003/332 (18 March 2003) ('Kuala Lumpur Final Document') Annex I para 120.

[9] Ibid. para 127.

[10] UNGA/UNSC, '10th Summit Conference of Heads of State or Government of the Non-Aligned Movement: Final Document' (Jakarta, September 1992) UN Doc A/47/675–S/24816 (18 November 1992) ch II para 24.

[11] NAM, 'Declaration on the Purposes and Principles and the Role of the Non-Aligned Movement in the Present International Juncture' (14th Summit Conference of Heads of State or Government of the Non-Aligned Movement, Havana, September 2006) para 9(o) ('Havana Declaration').

[12] Statement by the Chair of the NAM at the Conference of High Contracting Parties to the Fourth Geneva Convention (Geneva, 5 December 2001).

[13] Kuala Lumpur Final Document (n 8) para 121.

Heads of state from the NAM have 'expressed concern at the unilateral exercise of extra-territorial criminal and civil jurisdiction of national courts not emanating from international treaties and other obligations arising from international law including international humanitarian law'.[14] Pakistan, India, China, and North Korea comprise four of the world's nine nuclear-armed states. Pakistan and India are both, strangely, members of the NAM, which pursues 'universal and non-discriminatory nuclear disarmament, as well as a general and complete disarmament under strict and effective international control and in this context'.[15] The NAM works towards 'complete elimination of nuclear weapons', whether in terms of their development, production, acquisition, testing, stockpiling, transfer, use, or threat of use.

States in the NAM oppose 'coercive unilateral measures as a means of exerting pressure on Non-Aligned countries and other developing countries', these being 'contrary to international law, international humanitarian law, the United Nations Charter and the norms and principles governing peaceful relations among States'.[16] The support for IHL can be seen in a dedicated section on IHL in the Final Document of the XIII Conference of Heads of State or Government of the Non-Aligned Movement Kuala Lumpur in 2003. This underscored the movement's general concern to ensure respect for IHL and its core principles, and

> urged all parties to conflicts to respect international humanitarian law and human rights instruments, stressed the importance of the promotion and dissemination of these laws and instruments and called upon all parties to take measures to ensure the safety security of international and local humanitarian personnel.[17]

The Final Document went on to reiterate that:

> priority should be given to promoting knowledge of, respect for and observance of obligations assumed under International Humanitarian Law, in particular those of the four Geneva Conventions of 1949 and their 1977 Protocols, and they [the NAM heads of state or government] encouraged States to consider ratifying or acceding to the two 1977 Additional Protocols. In particular, they recognised the obligation of the parties to armed conflicts not of an international character to apply the provisions contained in Article 3, common to the four Conventions. They also emphasised the importance of national implementation of international humanitarian law and urged all States to take such measures as may be necessary to implement their international obligations, including the enactment of legislation and/or regulations.[18]

[14] Ibid. para 124.

[15] Havana Declaration (n 11) para 8(l). For a succinct national position, see the website of the Singapore Foreign Ministry at <https://www.mfa.gov.sg/SINGAPORES-FOREIGN-POLICY/International-Issues/Disarmament> accessed 8 January 2018.

[16] Kuala Lumpur Final Document (n 8) para 126.

[17] Ibid. para 349.

[18] Ibid. para 350. It also appears as para 422 in the Havana Declaration (n 11).

A more formal collective grouping, which reveals a shared vision relevant to our discussion about IHL and ICL, is the Association of Southeast Asian Nations (ASEAN).[19] Of its nine members, only two (Cambodia and the Philippines) are parties to the ICC Statute.[20] All are, of course, party to the Geneva Conventions 1949 (though Vietnam has a reservation, to be discussed later). Just over half are party to the Additional Protocol I 1977: Brunei Darussalam, Cambodia, Laos, the Philippines, and Vietnam (though Philippines has a reservation, to be discussed later). On the other hand, a larger majority remains outside the Additional Protocol II 1977: Singapore, Malaysia, Indonesia, Thailand, Burma/Myanmar, and Vietnam.

The ASEAN Charter's article 2(2) consolidates the principles set out in the organization's foundational Treaty of Amity and Cooperation 1976, which has been influenced by the principles of the NAM (of which all ASEAN states are members).[21] It, *inter alia*, affirms the fundamental importance of 'respect for the independence, sovereignty, equality, territorial integrity and national identity of all ASEAN Member States', 'non-interference in the internal affairs of ASEAN Member States', and 'respect for the right of every Member State to lead its national existence free from external interference'. These are principles that can be found in the UN Charter and the Friendly Relations Declaration 1970, but ASEAN states have prioritized sovereignty. This is the notorious 'ASEAN way', a preoccupation with sovereignty that takes Westphalian statehood to an extreme. The ASEAN Charter also declares that the region is 'a nuclear weapons free-zone' and 'commits to keep it free of other weapons of mass destruction'.[22] It further declares that ASEAN will respond 'effectively, in accordance with the principle of comprehensive security, to all forms of threats, transnational crime and transboundary challenges';[23] respect 'fundamental freedoms, the promotion and protection of human rights, and the promotion of social justice';[24] 'uphold the United Nations Charter and international law, including international humanitarian law, subscribed to by ASEAN Member States'.[25]

3 Acceptance of the Principles of Responsibility

Asia-Pacific states accept the established principles of state responsibility for violations of international law, including ICL and IHL. We can see this in the practice of dispute

[19] The ratification status of ASEAN members can be examined at the ICRC's database: <https://ihl-databases.icrc.org/applic/ihl/ihl.nsf/vwTreatiesByCountry.xsp> accessed 6 December 2018.

[20] For recent analysis, see Lasse Schuldt, 'Southeast Asian Hesitation: ASEAN Countries and the International Criminal Court' (2015) 16 German Law Journal 75.

[21] See also the South Asian Association for Regional Cooperation (SAARC), the Shanghai Cooperation Organization (SCO), and the Pacific Islands Forum (PIF).

[22] ASEAN Secretariat, *ASEAN Charter* (2008) art. 1(3).

[23] Ibid. art. 1(8). [24] Ibid. art. 2(2)(i). [25] Ibid. art. 2(2)(j).

settlement in the region, even if there has been a clear preference for conflict resolution through negotiation and diplomacy. It is to be seen in the approach of states to the International Law Commission's (ILC's) work on state responsibility. Above all, that acceptance is most powerfully to be seen, in the historical context of the region, in article 14(a) of the San Francisco Peace Agreement 1951:

> It is recognized that Japan should pay reparations to the Allied Powers for the damage and suffering caused by it during the war ... Japan will promptly enter into negotiations with Allied Powers so desiring, whose present territories were occupied by Japanese forces and damaged by Japan, with a view to assisting to compensate those countries for the cost of repairing the damage done.[26]

There were also bilateral agreements that affirmed reliance on the fundamentals of the law of state responsibility, for example paragraph 5 of the Joint Communiqué between China and Japan 1972 which provides that: 'The Government of China declares that in the interest of the friendship between the Chinese and Japanese peoples, it renounces its demand for war reparation from Japan'.[27] This acceptance of the fundamentals is not to say that there are no concerns about the more progressive aspects of the ILC's Articles on the Responsibility of States for Internationally Wrongful Acts 2001 (ARSIWA).[28]

Out of the fourteen states that responded to the invitation to comment on the then draft ARSIWA that had been finalized by Professor James Crawford, who currently serves as Australia's judge on the International Court of Justice, China, Japan, and the Republic of Korea (ROK) were the only ones from the region.[29] They were supportive of the draft. China re-emphasized her consistent position that parties to a dispute should

[26] Treaty of Peace with Japan (adopted 8 September 1951, entered into force 28 April 1952, 136 UNTS 45). The Treaty went on to assert that 'the resources of Japan are not presently sufficient, if it is to maintain a viable economy, to make complete reparation for all such damage and suffering and at the same time meet its other obligations' (art. 14(a)), and provided for waivers of that right to reparations (art 14(b)). The 48 signatories included Australia, Cambodia, Indonesia, Laos, New Zealand, Viet-Nam (spelling as per original), and Japan.

[27] This was confirmed in the Treaty of Peace and Friendship between Japan and the People's Republic of China (adopted 12 August 1978, entered into force 23 October 1978, 1225 UNTS 269). Neither the Beijing nor Taipei regimes were invited to the San Francisco talks, due to the impasse over who was the rightful representative of the Chinese people. Both were eventually to enter into separate agreements with Japan, as did Burma, the Philippines, Indonesia, Viet Nam, Malaysia, and the ROK. The agreement with Viet Nam was expressly a 'Reparations Agreement'.

[28] International Law Commission (ILC), Responsibility of States for Internationally Wrongful Acts, UNGA resolution 71/133 (13 December 2016). For Chinese hesitation about the customary status of the *entire* document, see the statement of Duan Jielong, Director-General of Treaty and Law Department of the Foreign Ministry, at the UNGA Sixth Committee (63rd Session) on Item 75, 'Report of the International Law Commission on the Work of its Sixtieth Session, Part Two'; Statement of Ms Xue Hanqin of the Chinese Delegation on Agenda Item 159, Report of the International Law Commission (State Responsibility), 23 October 2000, available at <http://www.china-un.org/eng/zghlhg/flsw/t28552.htm> accessed 8 January 2018.

[29] ILC, 'Comments and Observations Received from Governments' UN Doc A/CN.4/515 and Add.1–3 (March–June 2001).

have the right to freely choose the means that they deem appropriate to settle the dispute peacefully and suggested revision of the articles on dispute settlement. Japan did not see a need for any provisions on this. None of the three states had objections on the general principles in Chapter I, notably the elements of an internationally wrongful act of a state. None had substantial comments on the provisions on Attribution of Responsibility (there was only a mild Japanese comment on article 5 and an even milder one by ROK on article 7).

Further, in their comments on Chapter III on Serious Breaches of Essential Obligations to the International Community, all three states reflected that they had objected to the earlier article 19 and the notion of state crimes and were pleased to see it removed and replaced. The ROK emphasized that 'the obligations erga omnes and the peremptory norms of general international law deserve special treatment in international law, and breaches of these norms should receive treatment more severe than breaches of less serious obligations'.[30] Japan observed that the new provision was 'still haunted by the ghost of "international crime"' and stressed that:

> it cannot be said that there is a consensus about what obligations fall into the category of "serious breaches" and, if such "serious breaches" ever exist, whether some special measures are allowed to be taken, and if so, what the content of the special measures would be.[31]

It is relevant to note here that the Commentary to the ARSIWA reveals a very light trace of state practice from the Asia-Pacific region.[32]

The responsibility of individuals for *some* international crimes was already contained in the domestic law of a number of states before the ICC came into being. Examples of pre-ICC legislation on international crimes of one sort of another can be identified in Australia,[33] China,[34] Cambodia,[35] India,[36] Indonesia,[37] Timor-Leste,[38] Malaysia,[39] and Singapore.[40] Some of these states have conducted domestic criminal justice processes for international crimes, sometimes with international support. Of these accountability

[30] Ibid. 69. [31] Ibid. 67–8.

[32] ILC, 'Responsibility of States for Internationally Wrongful Acts' (2001) II (pt 2) ILC Year Book 31.

[33] War Crimes Act 1945; Genocide Convention Act 1949; Geneva Conventions Act 1957. On Australia's post-World War II trials, see Georgina Fitzpatrick, Tim McCormack, and Narrelle Morris (eds), *Australia's War Crimes Trials 1945–51* (Brill 2016).

[34] See the chapters by Liu Daqun, Wang Xintong, Wang Lijun, Zhang Tianshu, Zhang Binxin, Gao Hong, and Li Dan in Liu Daqun and Zhang Binxin (eds), *Historical War Crimes Trials in Asia* (Torkel Opsahl Academic EPublisher 2016).

[35] Law on the Establishment of the Extraordinary Chambers as amended 2004 (Cambodia).

[36] Geneva Conventions Act 1960 (India).

[37] See generally Suzannah Linton, 'Accounting for Atrocities in Indonesia' (2006) 10 Singapore Year Book of International Law 199.

[38] UN Transitional Administration in East Timor, 'Regulation No 2000/15 on the Establishment of Panels with Jurisdiction over Serious Criminal Offences' (6 June 2000) UN Doc UNTAET/REG/2000/15.

[39] Geneva Conventions Act 1962 (Malaysia).

[40] Geneva Conventions Act 1973 (Singapore).

processes, the most recent have been in Bangladesh, Cambodia, East Timor, and Indonesia.

To illustrate, in the aftermath of a devastating war of independence, Bangladesh adopted national legislation drawing on aspects of the Nuremberg Charter and held a number of trials, before suspending prosecutions for almost four decades.[41] The crimes included genocide, war crimes, and crimes against humanity. Revived in 2000, the accountability process has been divisive domestically and criticized internationally.[42]

Even so, accountability at the individual level has been rare in the scheme of things. Asia-Pacific states are well versed in the language of international justice—an example is the strong NAM statement from the Havana meeting condemning 'genocide, war crimes, crimes against humanity and systematic and gross violations of human rights, in accordance with the UN Charter and international law'.[43] The record of atrocity in the region shows a mismatch between rhetoric and reality. But, this is hardly unique in the world.

However, the situation is not as simplistic as Asia-Pacific states cynically mouthing platitudes, while committing atrocities and standing outside ICL mechanisms. For example, China played a critical role in the investigation of Japanese atrocities for the Far East and Pacific Sub-Commission, hosting it in Chungking, in free China.[44] Asia-Pacific states dispatched personnel to participate in the International Military Tribunal for the Far East (Tokyo Tribunal) process,[45] and at the two ad hoc tribunals for Rwanda and the former Yugoslavia (ICTR and ICTY).[46] In this context, it is important to recall that the ad hoc tribunals would not have existed had China

[41] See Suzannah Linton, 'Completing the Circle: Accountability for the Crimes of the 1971 Bangladesh War of Liberation' (2010) 21 Criminal Law Forum 191.

[42] The Office of the UN High Commission for Human Rights, the US State Department, the European Parliament, the International Commission of Jurists, the International Bar Association, Human Rights Watch, and Amnesty International have expressed grave concerns about the process. See e.g. Abdus Samad, 'The International Crimes Tribunal in Bangladesh and International Law' (2016) 27 Criminal Law Forum 257.

[43] Havana Declaration (n 11) para 9(o).

[44] For more, see Dan Plesch et al, 'UN War Crimes Commission and International Law: Revisiting World War II Precedents and Practice' (2015) The Global Community Yearbook International Law and Jurisprudence 71.

[45] The Tokyo Tribunal had five judges from the region (Australia, New Zealand, China, India, and the Philippines) and other national secondments in the Prosecution. For more, see Yuma Totani, *The Tokyo War Crimes Trials: the Pursuit of Justice in the Wake of World War II* (Harvard University Press 2008); Neil Boister and Robert Cryer, *The Tokyo International Military Tribunal: A Reappraisal* (OUP 2008).

[46] At time of writing, two Asia-Pacific judges are on the Mechanism for International Tribunals: Liu Daqun (China) and Seon Ki Park (ROK). ICTY Permanent judges included Liu Daqun (China, the last Vice-President); Asoka de Zoysa Gunawardana (Sri Lanka), David Anthony Hunt (Australia), Saad Saood Jan (Pakistan), O-Gon Kwon (ROK, former Vice-President), Khalida Khan (Pakistan), Haopei Li (China), Rustam S. Sidhwa (Pakistan), Sir Ninian Stephen (Australia), Wang Tieya (China) and Lal Chand Vohrah (Malaysia). ICTY Ad Litem judges have included Ali Nawaz Chowhan (Pakistan), Amarjeet Singh (Singapore), Ali Nawaz Chowhan (Pakistan), and Chikako Taya (Japan). ICTR Permanent Judges included Jai Ram Reddy (Fiji), Mansoor Ahmed, and Khalida Rachid Khan (both from Pakistan). At the ICC, the ROK's Song Sang-hyun was President from 2009 to 2015; other Asia-Pacific judges have been Judge Kuniko Ozaki (Japan) who was Second Vice-President; Judge Chang-ho Chung (ROK); and Judge Raul Cano Pangalangan (Philippines).

exercised her veto on the Security Council; also, three other Asia-Pacific states serving on the Security Council at the time of the 1993 and 1994 votes (Japan, New Zealand, and Pakistan) voted for their establishment.[47] Furthermore, Asia-Pacific states have made voluntary contributions to the ICTY.[48] Japan has been the largest donor supporting the Extraordinary Chambers in Cambodia in the adjudication of the crimes of the Khmer Rouge.[49] There have also been efforts in international law-making relevant to IHL and ICL taking place within the Sixth Committee of the General Assembly and the ILC, and Asia-Pacific voices are heard there, albeit rather softly.

The most controversial aspect of responsibility, and one deeply entwined with IHL and ICL, is that emerging from the Responsibility to Protect (R2P) doctrine. R2P reframes sovereignty as a responsibility, not a right, of every state and envisages international community intervention in a domestic humanitarian crisis as a last resort. Given the sensitivity about colonial experiences, entrenched regional concerns about sovereignty, and the attendant principle of non-intervention, it is not surprising that many Asia-Pacific states are concerned about this.[50] They do, however, accept that states have an inherent and primary responsibility to provide the first line of protection to their citizens and that states should be supported in this.[51] After all, populations across the Asia-Pacific have in recent memory endured exactly the sorts of abuses—genocide, war crimes, ethnic cleansing, and crimes against humanity—that the doctrine seeks to prevent and contain. What is problematic is intervention, the so-called Third Pillar (whereas the first two pillars respectively concern national protection responsibilities, and international assistance and capacity-building).

The position of states has been evolving and the region seems to have accepted the watered-down consensus version reflected in the 2005 World Summit Outcome Document.[52] Asia-Pacific states contributed to that watering down, particularly with respect to the Third Pillar. The one Asia-Pacific state with the ability to activate the

[47] See generally Xue Hanqin, 'A Point to Meet: Justice and International Criminal Law' (2014) 4 Asian Journal of International Law 35.

[48] The ICTY's website records that voluntary donations and support were given, *inter alia*, by Cambodia, Malaysia, New Zealand, and Pakistan: see <http://www.icty.org/en/content/support-and-donations> accessed 8 January 2018.

[49] Japan's total financial assistance, at time of writing, amounted to US$85 million, which was approximately 32 per cent of the total contribution by donors.

[50] Their objections are succinctly presented by a European Parliament Factsheet on the Responsibility to Protect, <http://www.europarl.europa.eu/meetdocs/2004_2009/documents/dv/factsheet_resptoprotect_6may/factsheet_resptoprotect_6may05.pdf> accessed 8 January 2018: 'There are vocal opponents to these initiatives, particularly within the Non-Aligned Movement and the G-77, who believe that they codify a system of coercion and intervention providing a tool of powerful governments to judge weaker states. Critics have said that these concepts conflict with principles in the UN Charter relating to the use of force, sovereignty, territorial integrity and non-interference in the internal affairs of states'.

[51] See e.g. unofficial transcription of 'Statement delivered on behalf of the Permanent Mission of the People's Republic of China to the United Nations General Assembly informal, interactive dialogue on the "Responsibility to Protect: Timely and Decisive Response"' (5 September 2012) <http://responsibilitytoprotect.org/China%20Statement%20_Transcribed_.pdf> accessed 8 January 2018.

[52] UNGA resolution 60/1 (16 September 2005).

doctrine at the Security Council, China, has not permitted the Council to authorize action in respect of the Syrian conflict that began in 2011. China previously abstained from voting on Security Council resolution 1973 (2011) in respect of the conflict in Libya, thereby permitting what was to become a highly controversial situation involving regime change that was arguably in excess of the mandate.[53] Reviewing the Libyan abstention, it seems that the overriding factors for China were 'the requests of the Arab League and the African Union' not to use her veto; nothing in the Chinese explanation suggests support for the Third Pillar.[54] Reviewing China's explanations of its Syria vetoes, it is also clear that she continues to have concerns about the Third Pillar and its impact on the fundamental principles of sovereignty, independence, and territorial integrity. However, these are not the only factors in her vetoing action in pursuance of the doctrine; of equal significance is her long-standing emphasis on political and diplomatic dialogue to reach solutions.[55] For her part, India is concerned about selectivity in application, potential abuse in the hands of dominant states, erosion of the primacy of state sovereignty, and its own domestic vulnerabilities in the protection of human rights. Such concerns are common across the region, and can be expected to chill the development and application of the principle.

Even so, some observers suggest that there has been a notable evolution in the approach of Southeast Asian states.[56] Even more striking is a 2016 paper from the US

[53] See the Chinese vetoes to draft resolutions S/2014/348 (referring Syria to the ICC), S/2011/612, S/2012/77, and S/2012/538. China and India were among the UNSC members that abstained on UNSC resolution 1973 (17 March 2011) authorizing the use of force in Libya to protect the civilian population.

[54] UN Press Release, 'Security Council Approves "No-Fly Zone" over Libya, Authorizing "All Necessary Measures" to Protect Civilians, by Vote of 10 in Favour with 5 Abstentions' (17 March 2011) SC/10200.

[55] China's veto on 5 December 2016 was exercised to prioritize and preserve the diplomatic initiatives (Liu Jieyi). The veto on 22 May 2014 was exercised because of China's reservations about the Council's referral of situations to the ICC; the need to support the political process; and forcing the issue to a premature vote when states on the Council were not agreed (Wang Min). The veto on 19 July 2012 was exercised because the resolution was flawed and unbalanced, it could be detrimental to the ongoing mediation by ex-Secretary-General Kofi Annan, because of China's commitment to sovereign equality and non-interference, and because the resolution jeopardizes the unity of the Security Council (Li Baodong). The veto on 4 February 2012 was exercised because 'the international community should provide constructive assistance' while fully respecting 'the sovereignty, independence and territorial integrity of Syria', the resolution complicated the situation and was premature given there were other efforts underway and there existed a lack of agreement on the Council (Li Baodong). The 4 October 2011 veto was exercised because the international community should provide constructive assistance while fully respecting 'Syria's sovereignty, independence and territorial integrity'. Also, UNSC actions in Syria:

> should depend upon whether it would facilitate the easing of tension in Syria, help to defuse differences through political dialogue and contribute to the maintenance of peace and stability in the Middle East. Most important, is should depend upon whether it complies with the Charter of the United Nations and the principle of non-interference in the internal affairs of States—which has a bearing upon the security and survival of developing countries, in particular small and medium-sized countries, as well as on world peace and stability. (Mr Li Baodong).

The records of the UNSC debates are at <http://research.un.org/en/docs/sc/quick> accessed 8 January 2018.

[56] Alex Bellamy and Mark Beeson, 'The Responsibility to Protect in Southeast Asia: Can ASEAN Reconcile Humanitarianism and Sovereignty?' (2010) 6 Asian Security 262.

Institute for Peace that claims that China has evolved from being one of the strongest opponents of the doctrine to being supportive of it:

> while China accepts the prudent use of R2P—even permitting the use of force—it does so under two conditions: (1) the principle is invoked strictly within the confines of the 2005 World Summit Outcome language, and (2) applying R2P does not result in significant reforms of the target state's political infrastructure.[57]

4 Acceptance of IHL

States in the Asia-Pacific region today do not demonstrate conceptual or philosophical animosity towards the basic norms of IHL.[58] In fact, going on the basis of submissions made in the course of advisory proceedings before the ICJ concerning the *Legal Consequences of the Construction of a Wall in the Occupied Palestinian Territory* (2004) and the *Legality of the Threat or Use of Nuclear Weapons* (1996), Australia, Bangladesh, North Korea, India, Indonesia, Japan, Malaysia, the Marshall Islands, Nauru, New Zealand, Pakistan, Palau, the Philippines, Samoa, and the Solomon Islands present themselves as humanitarian states and champions of the IHL regime. Like the rest of the world, the Asia-Pacific states are now all parties to the Geneva Conventions 1949, but some of them have maintained substantive reservations or entered declarations or understandings (for example, Australia, Pakistan, Viet Nam, South Korea, and China). Some states have long implemented the Geneva Conventions in domestic law.

There are several reasons why support for IHL *in abstracto* among these states should not be surprising. The first reason is that humanitarianism has indeed 'deep roots in most Asian societies, being the products of complex social and religious systems'.[59] Humanity in warfare in many cultures of the region predates the positive IHL framework that emerged in Europe in the nineteenth century, and even predates the chivalric culture in which scholars often situate the roots of humanitarianism in armed conflict. Humanitarian concerns can be identified in Hinduism,[60] Buddhism,[61]

[57] Courtney Fung, 'China and the Responsibility to Protect: From Opposition to Advocacy' *United States Institute for Peace, Peace Brief 205* (2016) 1; Andrew Garwood-Gowers, 'China's "Responsible Protection" Concept: Re-interpreting the Responsibility to Protect (R2P) and Military Intervention for Humanitarian Purposes' (2016) 6 Asian Journal of International Law 89.

[58] These basic principles, identified in the *Legality of the Threat or Use of Nuclear Weapons Advisory Opinion*, are the principle of distinction, the prohibition of the use of weapons that cause superfluous injury or unnecessary suffering, and the residual principle of humanity contained in the Martens Clause: *Legality of the Threat or Use of Nuclear Weapons Advisory Opinion* [1996] ICJ Rep 266. For more on international humanitarian law in the region, see Suzannah Linton et al (eds), *Asia-Pacific Perspectives on International Humanitarian Law* (CUP forthcoming November 2019).

[59] Pichamon Yeophantong, *Understanding Humanitarian Action in East and Southeast Asia: A Historical Perspective* (Overseas Development Institute 2014).

[60] See e.g. Kaushik Roy, *Hinduism and the Ethics of Warfare in South Asia: From Antiquity to the Present* (CUP 2012).

[61] See e.g. Christopher Weeramantry, 'Buddhism and Humanitarian Law' in VS Mani (ed), *Handbook of International Humanitarian Law* (OUP 2007).

and Sikhism.[62] In Islam, there is some discordance within the faith about how to treat captives but the prevailing view is that which takes up the humanitarian examples and teachings of the Prophet Mohamed.[63] We can also find humanitarianism in ancient martial codes in India[64] and China.[65]

History certainly has a role to play, and the legacy of World War II, played out in enormous swathes of the region, has not been irrelevant to the positive approach to IHL's protective potential. Not only were the world's first atomic weapons used in wartime against the Japanese cities of Hiroshima and Nagasaki, but nuclear weapons came to be tested by the US, the UK, and France in the Pacific and Australia with devastating environmental and human consequences. As a result, the affected and neighbouring nations have long been vocal in their opposition to nuclear weapons and testing. The Pacific Island nations have been instrumental in treaty making processes, notably the Treaty of Rarotonga 1985, the Treaty on the Non-Proliferation of Nuclear Weapons 1968, the Comprehensive Nuclear Test Ban Treaty 1996 (not in force) and the Treaty on the Prohibition of Nuclear Weapons 2017 (not in force). They have also brought in litigation before international bodies, with the most recent attempt being made by the Marshall Islands against India, Pakistan, and the UK, and there were earlier efforts by Australia and New Zealand against France in the early 1970s.[66]

Some of the earliest participants in IHL treaties and arrangements have been from the region. Three of the twenty-six participating nations in the Hague Peace Conference in 1899 were from the Asia-Pacific region: Siam (Thailand), China, and Japan. Siam, one of Southeast Asia's great Buddhist warrior kingdoms, began to engage in IHL treaty participation as long ago as the Hague Convention II on the Laws and Customs of War on Land 1899, Hague Declaration IV(2) concerning Asphyxiating Gases 1899, and Hague Declaration IV(3) concerning Expanding Bullets 1899.[67] That engagement has continued to the present in Thailand: it is already a signatory to the Arms Trade Treaty 2013 and was one of only three states and entities (the others being Guyana and the non-State Holy See) to sign and ratify the Treaty on the Prohibition of Nuclear Weapons on 20 September 2017, the first day it was open for signature.

Another example is Chinese culture, which has an indigenous tradition of humanitarianism that predates the Swiss founder of the Red Cross, Henri Dunant, and medieval European knights, and so IHL is conceptually acceptable in that culture.[68]

[62] See e.g. Gurpreet Singh, 'Sikh Religion and Just War Theory: An Analytical Study', <http://www.sikhinstitute.org/jan_2014/3-gurpreetsingh.html> accessed 8 January 2018.

[63] See e.g. M Cherif Bassiouni, *The Shari'a and Islamic Criminal Justice in Time of War and Peace* (CUP 2015).

[64] See e.g. Mani (ed) (n 63).

[65] See e.g. Ping-Cheung Lo and Sumner Twiss (eds), *Chinese Just War Ethics: Origin, Development, and Dissent* (Routledge 2015).

[66] See e.g. Nic Mclellan, *Prohibiting Nuclear Weapons: A Pacific Islands Priority* (International Campaign to Abolish Nuclear Weapons 2017); *Nuclear Tests Case (Australia v France) (Judgment)* [1974] ICJ Rep 457.

[67] See ratification table (n 19).

[68] Yeophantong (n 61) 9.

The Russo-Japanese War of 1904–05 saw the establishment of the Shanghai International Red Cross Committee (which became the Red Cross Society of China in 1912).[69] 1904 was also the year that China became a party to the Geneva Convention 1864. Of the other early treaties, China is also party to Hague Convention III on Maritime Warfare 1899, Hague Declaration IV(1) prohibiting Projectiles from Balloons 1899, Hague Convention on Hospital Ships 1904, Geneva Convention on Wounded and Sick 1906, and Hague Convention XI on Restrictions of the Right of Capture 1907. Today, China is notably a party to Additional Protocols I and II 1977 to the four Geneva Conventions 1949, and hosts the East Asia Delegation of the International Committee of the Red Cross. Since November 2007, she has had a National Committee on International Humanitarian Law as well as academic institutions dedicated to the study of IHL (at Wuhan and Peking universities, for example).

Japan's inability to reconcile her traditional *Bushido* (samurai warrior) code with the international protection regime for prisoners of wars (POWs) in World War II is notorious, but obscures a more complex picture. Her earliest IHL treaty participation dates back to her accession in 1886 to the Geneva Convention 1864.[70] The Japanese Red Cross Society was founded in 1877 as the *Hakuai-sha* (philanthropic organization) to provide humanitarian assistance during a domestic armed rebellion. It later changed its name to the Japanese Red Cross Society and joined the Red Cross family in 1887. Japan indicated agreement with the principles of IHL by becoming party to Hague Convention II on the Laws and Customs of War on Land 1899, Hague Declaration IV(2) concerning Asphyxiating Gases 1899, Hague Declaration IV(3) concerning Expanding Bullets 1899, Hague Convention IV on War on Land and its Annexed Regulations 1907 (with reservation), Hague Convention on Hospital Ships 1904, and Hague Convention XI on Restrictions of the Right of Capture 1907. Japan was the first Asian country to participate in the International Conference of the International Red Cross and Red Crescent Movement (the fourth, held in Karlsruhe, Germany, in 1887). Today, Japan champions IHL and actively urges states from the region to become parties to Additional Protocols I and II 1977.

There is therefore much to explain why the humanitarian underpinnings of IHL find traction in the region. Of course, given that the basic principles of humanity have been declared to be customary, even *erga omnes*, one would not expect to find intellectual objections to the fundamentals of IHL in this or any other region. In its *Advisory Opinion on the Legality of the Threat or Use of Nuclear Weapons*, the ICJ stated that the 'fundamental rules [of IHL] are to be observed by all states whether or not they have ratified the conventions that contain them, because they constitute intransgressible principles of international customary law'.[71] This enigmatic phrase does not make it

[69] Ibid. 4–6 (analysing Chinese literature on humanitarianism in China).

[70] ICRC Treaty Database, <https://ihl-databases.icrc.org/applic/ihl/ihl.nsf/States.xsp?xp_viewStates=XPages_NORMStatesParties&xp_treatySelected=120> accessed 10 December 2018.

[71] *Legality of the Threat or Use of Nuclear Weapons Advisory Opinion* (n 60) para 79.

clear that they are actually peremptory norms. However, Judge Weeramantry of Sri Lanka was clear that:

> The rules of the humanitarian law of war have clearly acquired the status of jus cogens, for they are fundamental rules of a humanitarian character, from which no derogation is possible without negating the basic considerations of humanity which they are intended to protect.[72]

That being the case, there is opposition to some areas of IHL that are seen to threaten sovereignty and the attendant principle of non-intervention.[73] In a region that was once heavily colonized, it is unsurprising to find resistance to expanding IHL in non-international armed conflict beyond common article 3 of the four Geneva Conventions 1949, and the scope of wars of national liberation beyond the colonial context. Additional Protocol I 1977, ratified globally by 174 states, has not been very popular in a region that has also had its fair share of post-liberation internal conflicts. Even so, the numbers becoming party to it have been rising and the dwindling number remaining outside includes Bhutan, Burma/Myanmar, India, Indonesia, Malaysia, Marshall Islands, Nepal, Singapore, Sri Lanka, Thailand, Pakistan, and Tuvalu. Of those who are party, there are reservations/declarations/understandings from Australia, China, Japan, Mongolia, the Philippines, and South Korea. Additional Protocol II of 1977 is even more warily regarded. There are 168 states parties and a substantial interpretative declaration from New Zealand. Asia-Pacific states comprise almost all of those remaining outside it: Bhutan, Burma/Myanmar, India, Indonesia, Kiribati, Malaysia, Marshall Islands, Nepal, Papua New Guinea, Singapore, Sri Lanka, Thailand, Tuvalu, and Viet Nam.

5 A More Unsettled Approach to ICL

IHL has traditionally been about state responsibility, to ensure that state armed forces behave in accordance with the rules that states themselves create. Individual responsibility under these treaties, which leads into ICL, has until relatively recently been a secondary and rarely used tool for implementation. There are very few treaties that could be described as ICL treaties (the ICC and ad hoc international tribunal statutes are not ICL treaties, but are the constituting documents for criminal justice institutions operating internationally). There is not, for example, a crimes against humanity convention yet, although the ILC's work on the subject has been adopted on first reading as

[72] Dissenting Opinion of Judge Weeramantry in *Legality of the Threat or Use of Nuclear Weapons Advisory Opinion* (n 60) 496.

[73] See e.g. Hisakazu Fujita, 'Application of International Humanitarian Law to Internal Armed Conflicts' in Timothy MacCormack, Michael Tilbury, and Gillian Triggs (eds), *A Century of War and Peace: Asia-Pacific Perspectives on the Centenary of the 1899 Hague Peace Conference* (Martinus Nijhoff 2001) 151–3.

a set of draft conclusions comprising a preamble, fifteen draft articles, and an annex.[74] This has been transmitted to governments for comments (see later discussion).

Asia-Pacific states have not challenged the international criminalization of genocide, crimes against humanity, or war crimes. They do sometimes speak out when such crimes appear to have been committed. After all, these are norms regarded as being so fundamental as to go beyond treaties into custom, and even amount to peremptory norms. This should not detract from the reality that these states are generally reticent to criticize the conduct of other states, have had quibbles on definitional issues, and have had major concerns about the scope and implications of these normative developments. Yet, it is not the principle of responsibility that is challenged. For example, India's objection to the ad hoc tribunals was and continues to be their allegedly 'dubious legality', because India believed that the Council did not have the power to set up courts under the UN Charter.[75] Similarly, her hostility to the ICC does not result from a principled objection to individual responsibility but rather from technical issues with the Rome Statute (see section 5.3).

5.1 War Crimes

The war crimes provisions in the Geneva Conventions 1949 and Additional Protocol I 1977, expressed as 'grave breaches', are tucked away in IHL treaties that are traditional in their structure (that is, only the state may bring a claim for reparation). Regional states, as has been previously noted, display no conceptual objection to IHL and many have adopted implementing legislation. They also do not display hostility to the notion that certain acts are to be criminalized as war crimes in an international armed conflict, although that cannot be said to be the case with internal conflict. The lack of hostility towards the war crimes concept in general could be because of the region's experience of World War II. War crimes trials were held in the aftermath of World War II not only by the returning European colonial powers, but by Australia, the Philippines, and on the Chinese mainland and Taiwan.

One aspect of post-war practice is of interest. The Korean and Vietnam wars saw use of the notion of war crimes against captured enemy fighters. These conflicts saw the use by China, North Korea, and North Vietnam of their reservations to article 85 of the Third Geneva Convention to deny POW status to captured enemy fighters suspected but not convicted of international crimes, the justification being that these fighters had participated in allegedly unlawful acts of war on behalf of their states of nationality.[76]

[74] Sean Murphy, 'Third Report on Crimes Against Humanity' (23 January 2017) UN Doc A/CN.4/704.

[75] UNGA (26th Plenary Meeting) UN Doc A/61/PV.26, 15.

[76] The reservations read as follows: (1) China 'is not bound by Article 85 in respect of the treatment of prisoners of war convicted under the laws of the Detaining Power in accordance with the principles laid down in the trials of war crimes or crimes against humanity by the Nuremberg and the Tokyo International Military Tribunals'; (2) the DPRK 'will not be bound by Article 85, in regard to the treatment of the prisoners of war convicted under the laws of the Detaining Power of prisoners of war for

This controversial interpretation of article 85, which had been the subject of dispute during the Geneva negotiations, led to similar reservations by the other countries of the communist bloc.[77] In the Korean conflict, China viewed all soldiers under UN command as war criminals because they took part in a 'war of invasion by imperialists'.[78] In the Vietnam conflict, North Vietnam refused to apply the POW regime and declared that it 'would regard the pilots who have carried out pirate-raids, destroying the property and massacring the population of the Democratic Republic of Vietnam (North Vietnam) as major criminals caught in flagrante delicto and liable for judgements in accordance with the laws of the Democratic Republic of Vietnam, although captured pilots are well treated'.[79] These reservations still stand, although they have been objected to by a number of states.

5.2 Genocide

The Genocide Convention 1948 has only 149 parties, despite its core prohibition being regarded as a peremptory norm that applies *erga omnes*. Two participating states from the region have reservations that encapsulate domestic sovereignty concerns. The Philippines' reservation insists on preserving 'the existing immunities from judicial processes guaranteed [to] certain public officials by the Constitution of the Philippines' and that:

> nothing contained in said articles shall be construed as depriving Philippine courts of jurisdiction over all cases of genocide committed within Philippine territory save only in those cases where the Philippine Government consents to have the decision of the Philippine courts reviewed by either of the international tribunals referred to in said articles.[80]

As for Burma/Myanmar, she continues to maintain a reservation that her courts and tribunals are not denied jurisdiction and that no foreign courts and tribunals may have jurisdiction over any cases or acts of genocide on her territory.[81]

having committed war crimes or inhumane offences, based on the principles of Nuremberg and the Tokyo Far East International Military Tribunal'; (3) 'The Democratic Republic of Viet Nam declares that prisoners of war tried and convicted of war crimes or crimes against humanity, in accordance with the principles laid down by the Nuremberg Judicial Tribunal, shall not benefit from the provisions of the present Convention as is specified in Article 85'.

[77] See Jean Pictet, *Commentary on the Geneva Convention Relative to the Treatment of Prisoners of War* (ICRC 1960) 413–26; 'The Geneva Convention and the Treatment of Prisoners of War in Vietnam' (1967) 80 Harvard Law Review 851, 862 (author not specified).

[78] Man-ho Heo, 'North Korea's Continued Detention of South Korean POWs since the Korean and Vietnam Wars' (2002) 14 Korean Journal of Defense Analysis 141, 155.

[79] Cited in Howard Levie, 'Maltreatment of Prisoners of War in Vietnam', reprinted in (1998) 70 International Legal Studies 95.

[80] See https://treaties.un.org/Pages/ViewDetails.aspx?src=IND&mtdsg_no=IV-1&chapter=4&clang=_en#EndDec> accessed 6 December 2018.

[81] Ibid.

5.3 Crimes against Humanity

Tabulations of state comments in the Sixth Committee on the work of the ILC on a crimes against humanity convention (68th, 69th, and 70th sessions of the UN General Assembly) reveal that Asia-Pacific states fall in the neutral to positive band, with none being negative, whether about the project or the work being done.[82] A common thread among the Asia-Pacific comments is the concern to ensure that there is consistency with other international instruments. The South Korean delegation 'supports the Commission's formulation of draft article 3, as it is based on the Rome Statute of the International Criminal Court, thus preventing unnecessary conflict with the Rome Statute and according due respect to the ICC as well'.[83] Malaysia has stressed that the study should not undermine the intended universality of the Rome Statute, and that any further work should not overlap with existing regimes, but rather should complement them.[84] As for India, her representative has stressed that 'we consider that it needs in-depth study and thorough discussion in the Commission. The proposed obligations should not conflict with the existing treaty obligations and should not duplicate the existing regimes.'[85] Addressing specifics, Malaysia pointed out that 'the current issues pertaining to impunity of the perpetrators of international crimes, including crimes against humanity, which require urgent attention, are practical issues relating to the investigation and prosecution of such offences, including international cooperation amongst States'.[86] Japan agreed with the tracking of article 7 of the ICC Statute and emphasized the need to avoid conflict with the ICC regime. She also observed that:

> whereas the Rome Statute establishing the International Criminal Court regulates 'vertical relationships' between the Court and its States Parties, it does not prescribe any obligations regarding adoption of national laws of crimes against humanity or inter-state cooperation on these crimes. Japan recognizes that the current work, which will create 'horizontal relationships' among states and regulate inter-state cooperation, will lead to strengthening the effort of the international community for preventing those crimes and punishing its perpetrators.[87]

[82] See <https://www.legal-tools.org/uploads/tx_ltpdb/6th_Committee_Responses_on_CAH_Treaty__Apr_12__2016_.pdf> accessed 6 December 2018.

[83] Rhee Zha Hyoung (South Korea), Statement on the Report of the ILC on the Work of its Sixty-Seventh Session—Cluster-2, UNGA Sixth Committee (70th Session).

[84] Sarah Khalilah Abdul Rahman (Malaysia), Statement on the Report of the ILC on the Work of its Sixty-Fifth Session, UNGA Sixth Committee (68th Session), 30 October 2013, para 3.

[85] Riti Pathak (India), Statement on the Report of the ILC on the Work of its Sixty-Seventh Session—Cluster-2, UNGA Sixth Committee (70th Session), 6 November 2015, 2.

[86] Statement by Edora Ahmad (Malaysia), Statement on the Report of the ILC on the Work of its Sixty-Seventh Session—Cluster-2, UNGA Sixth Committee (70th Session), 6 November 2015, para 10.

[87] Statement by Tomoyuki Hanami (Japan), Statement on the Report of the ILC on the Work of its Sixty-Seventh Session—Cluster-2, UNGA Sixth Committee (70th Session), 6 November 2015, 3.

For Indonesia,

> A convention on crimes against humanity is essential as part of the effort of the international community to fight impunity. . . . the convention should also contain provisions on the obligation to prevent that would clarify the criteria as to how a failure of preventing the acts of crimes against humanity would incur state responsibility.[88]

Singapore expressed some hesitation, reserving her position as the project is still in its early stages: 'the interaction of this topic with existing legal regimes will need to be carefully considered as duplication or conflict with existing regimes could lead to uncertainty'.[89]

China, having been rather passive on this matter, sprang to life in the seventieth Session of the UN General Assembly in 2015. She complained about the draft's over-emphasis on the practice of international judicial organs, the removal of the apparently 'traditional qualifier of "in time of war"', and treating the Rome Statute definition as if it was the universally accepted definition, which China believed it is not (this, China says, 'partly explains why some States are not yet party to the Rome Statute'). Further, China would like 'full consideration' to be given to differences among national legal systems, noting that the list of specific acts which constitute crimes against humanity, including 'enforced disappearance of persons', does not exist in the national legislation of many states. She finally expressed concern with the obligation of states to prevent crimes against humanity as currently drafted, finding it to be too broad.[90] At the seventy-second session, China again reiterated her concerns about the substantive definition. She also expressed concern that 'many provisions of the draft articles lack empirical analysis', queried whether the evidence provided demonstrated that 'the prohibition of crimes against humanity has satisfied the requirement for jus cogens set forth in Article 53 of the Vienna Convention on the Law of Treaties', and called for more discussion on the liability of legal persons.[91]

5.4 Aggression

The crime of aggression is a problematic concept in the region, as it intricately engages with issues of sovereignty, leadership, and global power. Apart from Samoa, the Asia-Pacific's states parties are virtually invisible in published accounts of the Kampala negotiation process that defined the crime for the ICC's jurisdiction and the conditions

[88] Statement by Ferry Adamhar (Indonesia), Statement on the Report of the ILC on the Work of its Sixty-Seventh Session—Cluster-2, UNGA Sixth Committee (70th Session), 9 November 2015 para 5.

[89] Statement by Pang Khang Chau (Singapore), Statement on the Report of the ILC on the Work of its Sixty-Seventh Session—Cluster-2, UNGA Sixth Committee (70th Session), 4 November 2015, para 9.

[90] Statement by Xu Hong (China), Statement on the Report of the ILC on the Work of its Sixty-Seventh Session—Cluster-2, UNGA Sixth Committee (70th Session), 6 November 2015.

[91] Statement by Xu Hong (China), Statement on the Report of the ILC on the Work of its Sixty-Ninth Session, UNGA Sixth Committee (72nd Session), 23 October 2017, 2–4.

of exercise.[92] At the time of writing, Samoa and the State of Palestine are the only states from the Court's 'Asia-Pacific' grouping that have ratified the Kampala amendments; using the present study's conceptualization, it is only Samoa. The position of non-party Security Council member China in this matter is unusual for being vocal. China may have been the second state ever after Poland to prosecute a person for the predecessor offence, the crime against peace, for participation in a 'war of aggression'.[93] At the sixth session of the ICC PrepCom, China stressed:

> that since the precondition for an individual to bear the criminal responsibility is that the state commits an act of aggression, in the absence of a determination by the Security Council on the situation of aggression, the court lacks the basis to prosecute the individual for his criminal liability. Besides, allowing the court to exercise jurisdiction before the Security Council makes the determination was practically bestowing on the court the right of determination on the state act of aggression. This runs counter to the provisions of the Charter. As for the proposal of making the determination by the General Assembly or the International Court, there is no relevant foundation in the Charter. Though the General Assembly could discuss affairs related to international peace and security, on the question of the determination of aggression, the exclusive power the Charter confers on the Security Council is explicit.[94]

From an unofficial Chinese perspective, the Kampala-adopted preconditions for the exercise of jurisdiction over crimes of aggression will harm international peace and security, there being too much discretion given to prosecutors and judges that could potentially lead to abuse and destabilization.[95]

5.5 ICC Participation

In recent times, the shift towards individual responsibility has resulted in an exceptional emphasis being placed on ICL in international relations, accompanied by increasing discussion about extraterritorial exercise of jurisdiction by states, immunities, and intervention in domestic situations by the ICC. This has exacerbated

[92] For example, Stefan Barriga and Leena Grover, 'A Historic Breakthrough on the Crime of Aggression' (2011) 105 AJIL 517; Claus Kreß and Leonie von Holtzendorff, 'The Kampala Compromise on the Crime of Aggression' (2010) 8 Journal of International Criminal Justice 1179.

[93] Roger Clark, 'The Crime of Aggression: From the Trial of Takashi Sakai, August 1946, to the Kampala Review Conference on the ICC in 2010' in Kevin Heller and Gerry Simpson (eds), *The Hidden History of War Crimes Trials* (OUP 2014); also Summary Translation of the 'Judgment of the Military Tribunal, Nanking, regarding Takashi Sakai, 27 August 1946' in File WO 311/563, UK National Archives.

[94] See 'China and the International Court', website of the Permanent Mission of the People's Republic of China to Geneva <http://www.china-un.ch/eng/gjhyfy/hflygz/t85684.htm> accessed 8 January 2018; Zhu Dan, 'China, the Crime of Aggression and the International Criminal Court' (2015) 5 Asian Journal International Law 94.

[95] It is unofficial, but very informed, coming from within the Ministry of Foreign Affairs: Zhou Lulu, 'Brief Analysis of a Few Controversial Issues in Contemporary International Criminal Law' in Morten Bergsmo and Ling Yan (eds), *State Sovereignty and International Criminal Law* (Torkel Opsahl 2012) 29, 31.

concerns about the ICC in the Asia-Pacific region, specifically concerning the *pacta tertiis* rule (under article 34 of the Vienna Convention on the Law of Treaties 1969, a state cannot be bound by a treaty that it is not party to); the notion of universal jurisdiction; and the immunities of state officials.[96] As at January 2019, there are 123 states party to the ICC Statute (counting Burundi's withdrawal), nineteen of whom the Court identifies as being from the Court's 'Asia Pacific' region, which is the most under-represented region in the Court's regime.[97] The nineteen include Jordan, Palestine, the Maldives, and Cyprus, countries that are outside the present study's notion of 'Asia-Pacific'. Australia and New Zealand are included in the Court's 'Western European and Other' grouping. So, for present purposes, there are eighteen states from the region that are parties,[98] and ICC-related international crimes legislation has already been adopted in Australia,[99] New Zealand,[100] Japan,[101] South Korea,[102] Samoa,[103] and the Philippines.[104]

This sobering statistic—a mere eighteen states parties—is surprising given that states from the region had an active role in shaping the ICC Statute.[105] Singapore, South Korea, and the Philippines were in the 'like-minded group' calling for the Court to have an independent Prosecutor, jurisdiction in both international and non-international armed conflicts, independence from the Security Council, and the ability to investigate cases when at least one of several affected states has ratified the Court's statute. Asia-Pacific states with representatives on the Drafting Committee included China, India,

[96] For Chinese perspectives on the ICC's challenges to sovereignty, universal jurisdiction, and immunities, see the chapters by Zhou Lulu, Liu Daqun, Zhu Lijiang, Ma Chengyuan, and Jia Bing Bing in Bergsmo and Ling (eds) ibid.

[97] ICC, Assembly of States Parties, Report of the Bureau on the Plan of Action of the Assembly of States Parties for Achieving Universality and Full Implementation of the Rome Statute of the International Criminal Court, ICC-ASP/16/18 (22 November 2017) para 36. There are 54 States in the Court's conceptualization of the 'Asia-Pacific'.

[98] Afghanistan, 10 February 2003; Australia, 1 July 2002; Bangladesh, 23 March 2010; Cambodia, 11 April 2002; Cook Islands, 18 July 2008; Fiji, 29 November 1999; Japan, 17 July 2007; Marshall Islands, 7 December, 2000; Mongolia, 11 April 2002; Nauru, 12 November 2001; New Zealand, 7 September 2000; Philippines, 30 August 2011; Republic of Korea, 13 November 2002; Samoa, 16 September 2002; Tajikistan, 5 May 2000; Timor-Leste, 6 September 2002; Vanuatu, 2 December 2011.

[99] Australia, International Criminal Court (Consequential Amendments) Act 2002; International Criminal Court Act 2002 (as amended).

[100] New Zealand, International Crimes and International Criminal Court Act 2000; International Crimes and International Criminal Court Amendment Act 2002.

[101] See Kyo Arai et al, 'Accession of Japan to the International Criminal Court: Japan's Accession to the ICC Statute and the ICC Cooperation Law' (2008) 51 Japanese Year Book of International Law 359.

[102] ROK, Act on Punishment of Crimes under Jurisdiction of the International Criminal Court (amended in 2011).

[103] Samoa, International Criminal Court Implementation Act 2007.

[104] Philippines, Act on Crimes against International Humanitarian Law, Genocide, and Other Crimes against Humanity 2009.

[105] See the Official Records of the UN Diplomatic Conference of Plenipotentiaries on the Establishment of an ICC, 1998, vol III. Scrutiny of the Official Records indicates that the most active among the Asia-Pacific States were India, Japan, the ROK, the Philippines, China, New Zealand, Singapore, Samoa, and Australia.

the Philippines, and South Korea.[106] Indonesia, the Philippines, Thailand, and Vietnam made a joint proposal on war crimes,[107] while Bangladesh, India, Nepal, and Sri Lanka made independent and joint proposals on crimes against humanity.[108] An important Singaporean compromise proposal (originally made at the August 1996 Preparatory Commission) was to incorporate article 16 of the Rome Statute[109] (allowing the UN Security Council to defer an ICC investigation or prosecution for a renewable period of twelve months). South Korea's compromise proposal on the difficult matter of jurisdiction was vital for the adopted version of article 12.[110]

Asia-Pacific states also expressed their concerns about the definition of crimes against humanity[111] and about extending war crimes to non-international armed conflict.[112] The Chinese delegation made known her reservations over the preamble, and the crimes against humanity of enslavement, forced sterilization, and coerced disappearance.[113] Concerns from the region (leading China to vote against the Statute and others to abstain) clustered around the dangers of the Court being susceptible to manipulation and lacking independence; interference in domestic affairs; and subjecting non-state parties to jurisdiction which they have not consented to.[114] In the case of

[106] Ibid. 182.

[107] Consideration of the question concerning the finalization and adoption of a convention on the establishment of an international criminal court in accordance with General Assembly resolutions 51/207 of 17 December 1996 and 52/160 of 15 December 1997, UN Doc A/CONF. 183/C.1/L.74 (14 July 1998).

[108] Ibid. and UN Doc A/CONF. 183/C. 1/L.27/Rev. 1 (6 July 1998), UN Doc A/CONF. 183/C. 1/L.35 (July 1998).

[109] Sienho Yee, 'The International Criminal Court and the Security Council: Articles 13(b) and 16' in Roy Lee (ed), *The International Criminal Court, The Making of the Rome Statute, Issues, Negotiations, Results* (Kluwer 1999) 149–52.

[110] Republic of Korea: Proposal regarding articles 6[9], 7[6], and 8[7], A/CONF.183/C.1/L.6; for more, see Sharon Williams, 'The Rome Statute on the International Criminal Court-Universal Jurisdiction or State Consent-To Make or Break the Package Deal' (2000) 75 International Legal Studies 539.

[111] Japan submitted a draft text. China insisted on a nexus to an armed conflict, arguing that crimes against humanity could only be committed in armed conflict. Thailand, Viet Nam, Japan, Australia, and Bangladesh argued that they could also be committed in peacetime. India was later to complain that 'the draft adopted a definition of crimes against humanity with which the representatives of over half of humanity did not agree': see 'Explanation of Vote by Mr Dilip Lahiri, Head of Delegation of India, On the Adoption of the Statute of the International Court' <https://www.legal-tools.org/doc/9f86d4/pdf/> accessed 6 December 2018.

[112] At Rome, states that challenged the notion that war crimes can be committed in non-international armed conflict included China, India, and Pakistan. For more on the negotiations, see Knut Dörmann, 'War Crimes Under the Rome Statute of the International Criminal Court, with a Special Focus on the Negotiations on the Elements of Crimes' (2003) 7 Max Planck Year Book of United Nations Law Online; 'Art 8 War crimes/Crimes de guerre' in William Schabas, *The International Criminal Court: A Commentary on the Rome Statute* (2nd edn OUP 2016).

[113] A report on China and the ICC is at the website of the Chinese Permanent Mission to the UN in Geneva <http://www.china-un.ch/eng/gjhyfy/hflygz/t85684.htm> accessed 6 December 2018.

[114] See 'Explanation of Vote by Mr Dilip Lahiri' (n 113); Bing Bing Jia, 'China and the International Criminal Court: The Current Situation' (2006) 10 Singapore Year Book of International Law 87; Lu Jianping and Wang Zhixiang, 'China's Attitude towards the ICC' (2005) 3 Journal of International Criminal Justice 608.

India, the inadequate addressing of nuclear weapons was a major factor in her abstention.[115] It has been argued that India's ongoing refusal to engage with the ICC and influence its direction (which China is doing) demonstrates 'a lack of flexibility' with regard to the international order that it is trying to reform, and this attitude is an example of her 'traditional unwillingness to trade off even small amounts of sovereignty for cooperative gains'.[116]

Africa's experience with the ICC, involving major issues such as referral by the Security Council of situations in non-party states and the immunities of state officials, has not gone un-noticed in the Asia-Pacific region. For China, she 'has always had reservations concerning the referral by the Security Council of particular country situations to the ICC. This is our principled position.'[117] China has expressed the hope, as if it was not happening, 'that the Court will conduct its work in an objective and impartial way to foster its credibility and win extensive trust and support from the international community, and make contribution to peace and justice'.[118] China has further expressed concern that the Court's handling of some cases 'has aroused worries and concern in the world' about international criminal law.[119] She has expressed disquiet about 'a certain influence to the stability of some regions and the harmony of the countries' relationship, which aroused the universal worries and concerns in the world'.[120] In a nutshell, the Asia-Pacific's only permanent member on the Security Council:

> is of the view that the Court must, first and foremost, observe the guiding principles of the *UN Charter*, ensure that it will not undermine the core value of the Charter in maintaining world peace and security, a basic requirement of the Court, and make itself compatible and complementary with the system established by the Charter to maintain world peace and security.[121]

China has officially expressed hope that the 'court can perform its duty with more cautiousness in the future work'.[122]

[115] See 'Explanation of Vote by Mr Dilip Lahiri' (n 113); Usha Ramanathan, 'India and the ICC' (2005) 3 Journal of International Criminal Justice 627.

[116] Rohan Mukherjee and David Malone, 'Global Responsibilities: India's Approach' (2001) 1 Jindal Journal of International Affairs 182, 187; also Ramanathan, ibid.

[117] UN Press Release, 'Security Council Approves "No-Fly Zone" over Libya, Authorizing "All Necessary Measures" to Protect Civilians, by Vote of 10 in Favour with 5 Abstentions', SC/10200, 17 March 2011.

[118] Statement by Xu Hong (China) at the General Debate of the Eighth Session of the Assembly of States Parties to the Rome Statute of the ICC (20 November 2009).

[119] Statement by Guo Xiaomei (China), on the Report of the ICC to the 65th General Assembly (29 October 2010).

[120] Ibid. [121] Xu Hong (n 120) (emphasis in the original).

[122] Guo Xiaomei (n 121). See also Shang Weiwei and Zhang Yueyao, 'The *Aut Dedere Aut Judicare* Provision in the Proposed Convention on Crimes against Humanity: Assessment from a Chinese Perspective' in Morten Bergsmo and Song Tianying (eds), *On the Proposed Crimes against Humanity Convention* (Torkel Opsahl 2014).

There is active civil society pressure on states in the region to ratify or accede to the Statute, but the states that had concerns at Rome have generally not been persuaded. An example is Indonesia, where in May 2013 the government firmly declared it would not become a party, despite previous regimes having taken preparatory steps as long ago as 2004. There seem to have been two crucial issues: the first a belief in certain quarters that Indonesia's existing legal framework suffices and there is therefore no need to ratify; and the second a fear of the ICC taking 'politicized' interventions in the Indonesian context.[123] China and Indonesia are both illustrative of concerns that were raised in Rome and continue to the present. Observers confirm that the continuing coolness 'reflects the concerns of states within the region as to the potential impact of the ICC on their sovereignty and the possible politicization of the ICC and its investigations'.[124] And there is the puzzling Malaysian example. For decades, the country quibbled about human rights, championed the strain of cultural relativism known as 'Asian Values', and resisted participation in the human rights treaty framework. It therefore came as a great surprise when, in March 2019, Malaysia announced it was acceding to the Rome Statute.[125] A domestic political storm broke out over the sovereignty (immunity) of traditional rulers, the opening up of long-running racial sensitivities, and the exercise of international jurisdiction; the accession was consequently withdrawn one month later.[126]

There are other factors that influence the ratification/accession practice of states. It has been argued that 'countries for whom compliance is likely to be easiest—democracies with little internal violence—are the most likely countries to join the ICC'.[127] By contrast, those with the most to fear tend to avoid ratification.[128] This can of course explain the Northern hemisphere's embrace, but it does not explain why African states were so quick to join. McGreal's study of the Pacific islands suggests that geographically isolated states have a lower incentive to ratify the ICC Statute 'because they are less likely to have to deal with "spillovers" from states in which violations of international criminal law take place'.[129] Such states are also:

[123] Andin Aditya Rahman, 'Ratifying the Rome Statute: Almost There and Back Again', 30 June 2014 <https://pro.hukumonline.com/o/lt53b16e6983a2a/ratifying-the-rome-statute–almost-there-and-back-again> accessed 5 December 2018.

[124] Sarah Williams and Andrew Byrnes, 'Justice for All? Ten Years of the International Criminal Court in the Asia-Pacific Region' (2013) 11 Journal of International Criminal Justice 1023, 1026; Valeriane Toon, 'International Criminal Court: Reservations of Non-State Parties in Southeast Asia' (2004) 26 Contemporary Southeast Asia 218.

[125] Malaysian Foreign Ministry Press Release, 'Malaysia accedes to the Rome Statute of the International Criminal Court' (Putrajaya, 4 March 2019).

[126] Channel News Asia, 'Malaysia U-turns on decision to join war crimes court after political pressure' (Putrajaya, 5 April 2019).

[127] Terrence Chapman and Stephen Chaudoin, 'Ratification Patterns and the International Criminal Court' (2013) 57 International Studies Quarterly 400.

[128] Ibid.

[129] Daragh McGreal, 'A Rationalist View of Rome Statute Ratification in the Pacific Region' (2013) 11 Journal of International Criminal Justice 1091, 1098.

> less likely to face pressure to desist from committing international crimes, less likely to be investigated by the Prosecutor, less likely to be subject to Security Council referral and less likely to find ICC-wanted individuals arriving at their borders.[130]

The study also found that the US' influence in the Pacific islands (through Bilateral Immunity Agreements) is likely to influence ratification behaviour.[131]

6 Conclusion

This overview of the approach of Asia-Pacific states to IHL and ICL, in theory and reality, reveals some warmth. Even so, there is a definite chill in respect of aspects that potentially encroach on independence, sovereignty, and territorial integrity, or that smack of Western neo-colonialism. These are of course subjectively evaluated by each state. In practical terms, this frostiness can be seen in the responses to external threats of accountability against political leaders, the exercise of universal jurisdiction, Security Council referrals to the ICC, Pillar Three of the R2P doctrine, the crime of aggression, and certain formulations of other international crimes (for example, war crimes in non-international armed conflict). However, even within these broad regional trends, there is no uniformity. There is decidedly no collective 'Asia-Pacific approach' that emerges from the present chapter.

In concluding, it is pertinent to consider the possibilities of applying international criminal justice in the region in the future. At the time of writing, two situations on the Korean peninsula—the 26 March 2010 sinking of the South Korean warship *Cheonan* and the 23 November 2010 shelling of the South Korean Yeonpyeong Island—have been considered by the ICC Prosecutor. The Prosecutor declined to investigate further, as 'based on the information available, it currently lacks a reasonable basis to believe that either incident constitutes a crime within the jurisdiction of the Court'.[132]

Further to the 2014 report and recommendations of the UN Commission of Inquiry on Human Rights in North Korea, detailing long-running, systematic, widespread, and gross human rights violations that in many instances appeared to constitute crimes

[130] Ibid. 1109. [131] Ibid. 1096–108.

[132] ICC Prosecutor, Situation in the Republic of Korea, Article 5 Report, June 2014. The investigation found, *inter alia*, in relation to the shelling of the island, that military targets appeared to have been the primary object of the attack. There was no reasonable basis to believe that the DPRK intentionally targeted the civilian population or civilian objects. Also, the information available in response of the shelling of the island was insufficient to provide a reasonable basis to believe that the anticipated civilian impact would have been clearly excessive in relation to the anticipated military advantage of the attack, considering the size and population of the island. In relation to the *Cheonan*, this was a naval vessel and all those on board who drowned in the sinking were military personnel. In general, it is not a war crime to attack military objectives including naval ships or to kill enemy military personnel including sailors on a naval ship. There was insufficient evidence to conclude that the war crime of killing or wounding treacherously under art. 8(2)(b)(xi) had been committed. The investigation can be re-opened if fresh evidence comes to light.

against humanity, the situation in the North Korea itself is one that is ripe for ICC engagement.[133] The UN General Assembly, in furtherance to the UN Commission of Inquiry report, adopted a resolution calling for North Korea to be referred to the ICC, but this has no legal effect.[134] The UN Human Rights Council continues to push the matter and has created a group of experts tasked with finding practical ways to hold rights violators in North Korea to account.[135] The development and testing of nuclear weapons and inter-continental ballistic missiles by North Korea, in violation of UN Security Council resolutions, has escalated tensions with the US, South Korea, and Japan in 2017. Despite some rapprochement over 2017 and 2018, the situation continues to be a threat to international peace and security, with potential ICC issues arising. North Korea is not a party to the Rome Statute and the situation would require Security Council referral, but the barrier is that China has traditionally protected North Korea from international action.

From 2007 to 2017, the ICC maintained a preliminary examination into alleged crimes against humanity and war crimes committed in Afghanistan since 1 May 2003. The Prosecutor's Office found:

> a reasonable basis to believe that, at a minimum, the following crimes within the Court's jurisdiction have occurred:
>
> a. Crimes against humanity and war crimes by the Taliban and their affiliated Haqqani Network;
> b. War crimes of torture and related ill-treatment by Afghan government forces, in particular the intelligence agency (National Directorate for Security), and the Afghan National Police;
> c. War crimes of torture and related ill-treatment by US military forces deployed to Afghanistan and in secret detention facilities operated by the Central Intelligence Agency, principally in the 2003–2004 period, although allegedly continuing in some cases until 2014.[136]

In relation to the role of the US military, the Prosecutor has specific information indicating that at least eighty-eight persons in US custody were allegedly tortured through use of 'enhanced interrogation techniques', and that these 'were not the abuses of a few isolated individuals' but rather 'committed as part of approved interrogation techniques in an attempt to extract "actionable intelligence" from detainees'.[137]

[133] UN Human Rights Council, 'Report of the Detailed Findings of the Commission of Inquiry on Human Rights in the Democratic People's Republic of Korea', UN Doc A/HRC/25/CRP.1 (7 February 2014).

[134] UNGA resolution on the human rights situation in the DPRK adopted by the Third Committee on 15 November 2016, UN Doc A/C.3/71/L.23 (31 October 2016).

[135] UN Human Rights Council resolution 31/18 (23 March 2016): The human rights situation in the DPRK.

[136] ICC Prosecutor, Report on Preliminary Examination Activities 2016 (14 November 2016) para 198.

[137] Ibid. paras 211–13.

The crimes sought to be formally investigated related not just to crimes committed on the territory of Afghanistan, but also in the ICC-state parties of Poland, Romania, and Lithuania (as a result of involvement in US renditions). However, on 12 April 2019, the court's Pre-Trial Chamber II controversially rejected the Prosecutor's request to open an investigation.[138]

Also significant for the region is Pre-Trial Chamber I's 6 September 2018 finding that the ICC has jurisdiction over the alleged deportation of the Rohingya people from Myanmar, a non-state party, to Bangladesh, a state party.[139] Myanmar has seen brutal armed conflicts running for decades, a general state of repression involving serious human rights abuses, and increasing persecution of her Rohingya Muslim minority.[140] This has escalated into a devastating cascade of violence, leading to the extremely serious refugee flow of Rohingya into neighbouring Bangladesh in late 2017. The ongoing situation, now being scrutinized in The Hague, strengthens pre-existing claims of ethnic cleansing, crimes against humanity, and even genocide.[141]

The fourth Asia-Pacific situation that has received the attention of the Prosecutor is that of the Philippines, where President Duterte's 'war' on drugs appears to have involved widespread extrajudicial killings in the name of crime control and prevention. More than 7,000 people have been killed, roughly one-third during formal police operations and the rest by unknown assailants.[142] President Duterte has, in response to the Prosecutor's opening of a preliminary examination, withdrawn the Philippines from the ICC regime.[143] However, this withdrawal does not impact on the inquiry as it was commenced prior to the date on which the withdrawal became effective (17 March 2019).[144] There is of course still potential in the Philippines for the domestic system to demonstrate her ability and willingness to investigate and prosecute. If that

[138] Decision Pursuant to Article 15 of the Rome Statute on the Authorisation of an Investigation into the Situation in the Islamic Republic of Afghanistan, ICC-02/17-33, 12 April 2019.

[139] Decision on the 'Prosecution's Request for a Ruling on Jurisdiction under Article 19(3) of the Statute' and Partially Dissenting Opinion of Judge Marc Perrin de Brichambaut, ICC-RoC46(3)-01/18-37, 6 September 2018.

[140] See e.g. Report of OHCHR Mission to Bangladesh: Interviews with Rohingya Fleeing from Myanmar since 9 October 2016 (3 February 2017); Report of OHCHR: Situation of Human Rights of Rohingya Muslims and other Minorities in Myanmar, UN Doc A/HRC/32/18 (20 June 2016); Human Rights Watch, 'Country Report on Burma' in *World Report 2017*; Human Rights Watch, 'Burma: Massive Destruction in Rohingya Villages' (13 November 2016); 'Thousands of People Have Been "Displaced by Fighting" in Eastern Burma' *Time* (New York, 13 October 2016).

[141] See Marzuki Darusman, Chair, Independent International Fact-Finding Mission on Myanmar, 'Statement to the Special Session of the Human Rights Council on the Situation of Human Rights of the Minority Rohingya Muslim Population and other Minorities in Rakhine State of Myanmar' (5 December 2017); UN Press Release, 'Myanmar: UN Human Rights Chief Calls for International Criminal Investigation of Perpetrators of Violence Against Rohingya' (5 December 2017).

[142] See e.g. Amnesty International, '"If you are poor you are killed": Extrajudicial Executions in the Philippines' "War on Drugs"' ASA 35/5517/2017 (31 January 2017).

[143] ICC Press Release, 'President of the Assembly of States Parties regrets withdrawal from the Rome Statute by the Philippines' (18 March 2019).

[144] Rome Statute of the International Criminal Court (adopted 17 July 1998, entered into force 1 July 2002, 2187 UNTS 90) art. 127.

complementarity requirement is satisfied, there would be no call for the opening of an ICC investigation.

A situation that should certainly be a candidate for the ICC's attention is that of Sri Lanka, where the conflict with the Tamil Tigers (from 1983 to 2009) saw particularly serious violations of IHL and ICL, and the state's response continues to be regarded as inadequate by the international community.[145]

We can therefore see that until the-then Prosecutor of the ICC commenced a preliminary examination into the Korean Yellow Sea incidents in December 2010, the Asia-Pacific was a blank canvass for the court.[146] The Prosecutor now has one matter that is closed but can be re-opened if fresh evidence comes to light (the Korean peninsula incidents), one failed attempt to open an investigation (Afghanistan), one situation undergoing a preliminary examination (the Philippines), and a live investigation (Myanmar/Bangladesh (the Rohingya)).

This looks like a remarkable shift, but it would be wrong to see this as about progressive external forces bringing a new way of thinking into the region. We need to recall how much war crimes adjudication there was in the region after World War II. It would also be a mistake to believe that we are in the midst of a sea change in the attitude to the court, let alone independent supranational judicial activity in the region. The Philippines' withdrawal, the intransigence of the DPRK, Myanmar, and Sri Lanka, the creative lawyering behind the exercise of jurisdiction in the Rohingya situation, and the strange accession-and-withdrawal of Malaysia are salutary reminders that the determination to safeguard independence, sovereignty, and territorial integrity, and to resist what is seen as Western neo-colonialism, is undiminished.

[145] Report of the UN Secretary General's Panel of Experts on Accountability in Sri Lanka (31 March 2011); Report of OHCHR, 'Promoting Reconciliation and Accountability in Sri Lanka', UN Doc A/HRC/25/23 (24 February 2014); UN Human Rights Council resolution 25/1 (9 April 2014): Promoting reconciliation, accountability and human rights in Sri Lanka. See also Kishali Pinto Jayawardene (ed), *A Legacy to Remember: Sri Lanka's Commissions of Inquiry* (The Law and Society Trust 2012).

[146] ICC Press Release, 'ICC Prosecutor: alleged war crimes in the territory of the Republic of Korea under preliminary examination' (6 December 2010).

CHAPTER 8

INTERNATIONAL ENVIRONMENTAL LAW

BEN BOER

1 Introduction

THIS chapter focuses on the development and implementation of the international and regional instruments (also referred to as multilateral environmental agreements, or MEAs) and policies concerning the environment and natural resources across the sub-regions of the Asia-Pacific, in the context of the continuing debate on the need to promote ecological sustainability globally. Many of these instruments and policies began to shape national environmental law responses in the region from the 1970s. Two recent and highly significant instruments are the Paris Agreement on climate change[1] and the Sustainable Development Goals[2] (SDGs) and their associated SDG Targets, both agreed in 2015. The debate on the need for a globally applicable pact on the environment, and the response of the United Nations General Assembly, is also included.

The six sub-regions addressed in the chapter are South Asia, Central Asia, Northeast Asia, Southeast Asia, the Mekong Basin (which overlaps in part with Southeast Asia) and the developing island countries of the Pacific. Australia and New Zealand are dealt with as part of the Pacific sub-region. The chapter examines the functions of the more important regional institutions concerned with environmental management, together with their associated legal frameworks and soft law instruments, for each of the Asia-Pacific sub-regions. Given the vast scope of environmental law, only a small selection of

[1] Paris Agreement (adopted 12 December 2015, entered into force 4 November 2016) adopted under the UN Framework Convention on Climate Change (adopted 4 June 1992, entered into force 21 March 1994) 31 ILM 849. The Climate Convention and the Paris Agreement enjoy universal membership throughout the Asia Pacific.

[2] UNGA resolution 70/1 (25 September 2015): 'Transforming our World: The 2030 Agenda for Sustainable Development and the Sustainable Development Goals'.

the many pressing substantive environmental issues is addressed. These include: the effects of climate change; transboundary air pollution; biodiversity decline, deforestation and land degradation; and oceans and coasts. Another focus of this chapter is the increasing international, regional, and national trend towards recognizing the links between environmental law and human rights, and specifically the promotion of the right to a safe, clean, healthy, and sustainable environment.

This chapter demonstrates that there are major differences between the sub-regions, as well as between countries within the sub-regions, concerning the uptake and implementation of international and regional instruments relating to environmental protection and conservation. An underlying theme is the continuing disparity between 'southern' and 'northern' nations, with the majority of states in the Asia-Pacific falling into the former category. This disparity has influenced the development of environmental policies and laws at both the regional and national levels. A further underlying theme is the transition from a bifurcated and fragmented regime of international and national law to a trifurcated and even more fragmented system of international, regional, and national law.[3]

One of the major contemporary challenges in the region concerns how to address the new sustainable development agenda as expressed in 'Transforming our World: the 2030 Agenda for Sustainable Development' agreed by the UN General Assembly.[4] The Agenda includes seventeen Sustainable Development Goals and associated Targets. Several of the SDGs have direct relevance in terms of the implementation of international and regional environmental law. These include: Goal 12, on ensuring sustainable consumption and production patterns; Goal 13, on combatting climate change and its impacts; Goal 14, on oceans and the marine environment; Goal 15, on the terrestrial environment; and Goal 17, on strengthening the means of implementation. Each of the sub-regions dealt with here has begun to grapple with how to address the SDGs. These efforts are briefly dealt with under the specific sub-regions.

2 The Development of International and Regional Environmental Law

Since the 1970s, there has been an exponential growth of international environmental law around the world, largely as a result of the increasing activity and sophistication of the intergovernmental organizations that have been established since the Stockholm Conference of 1972. The resulting Stockholm Declaration[5] is seen as a progenitor of

[3] For an early analysis of internationalization and regionalization, see Ben Boer, 'The Rise of Environmental Law in the Asian Region' (1999) 32 Richmond Law Review 1503, 1508–11.

[4] UNGA, 'Transforming our World' (n 2);

[5] Stockholm Declaration of the UN Conference on the Human Environment (adopted 16 June 1972) 11 ILM 1416.

modern international environmental law.[6] The involvement and influence of developing countries in the progress of international environmental law has been significant. It stems from the emergence of countries in the south from the grip of colonization[7] and the recognition of their permanent sovereignty over natural resources.[8] The participation of developing countries, including Asian countries, in the further development of international environmental law and policy has continued to the present day.[9]

Equally, in the same period, regional legal regimes have emerged around the world as part of a 'new wave of regionalism', which 'extends regional cooperation to areas such as the environment as well as human rights'.[10] In the Asia-Pacific, it is notable that the Southeast Asian[11] and Pacific Island[12] sub-regions regularly send representatives to many of the major conferences of the parties to MEAs. However, in comparing the Asia-Pacific with, for example, the European Union,[13] these regimes remain at an early stage of development. In terms of the negotiation of regional instruments on environment and natural resources, it is perhaps inevitable that the lowest common denominator of legal provisions, polices, and standards is put forward to achieve consensus, particularly in regions where strong concepts of sovereignty and the

[6] Representative of Canada, 'Report of the Stockholm Conference on the Human Environment' (16 June 1972) A/CONF.48/14/Rev.1, 74: 'the Declaration was more than an inspirational message or an educational tool: it represented the first essential step in developing international environmental law'.

[7] See UNGA resolution 1514(XV) (14 December 1960): 'Declaration on the Granting of Independence to Colonial Countries and Peoples'.

[8] See UNGA resolution 1803(XVII) (14 December 1962): 'Declaration on the Permanent Sovereignty over Natural Resources'.

[9] See Parvez Hassan, 'Role of the South in International Environmental Law' (2017) 1 Chinese Journal of Environmental Law 133; Karin Mickelson, 'The Stockholm Conference and the Creation of the South-North Divide in International Environmental Law and Policy' in Shawkat Alam, Sumudu Atapattu, Carmen Gonzalez, and Jona Razzaque (eds), *International Environmental Law and the Global South* (Cambridge 2015) 109.

[10] Werner Scholtz and Jonathan Verschuuren, *Regional Environmental Law: Transregional Comparative Lessons in Pursuit of Sustainable Development* (Edward Elgar 2015) 3; Louis Kotzé, *Global Environmental Governance: Law and Regulation in the 21st Century* (Edward Elgar 2012) 146–8, who discusses regional governance as an element of global governance; see also Ben Boer, Ross Ramsay, and Donald Rothwell, *International Environmental Law in the Asia Pacific* (Kluwer 1998) ch 3 ('Regional Environmental Issues and Responses') 47ff.

[11] For example, ASEAN, 'ASEAN Joint Statement on Climate Change to the 22nd Conference of the Parties (COP-22) to The UN Framework Convention on Climate Change (UNFCCC)' (6 September 2007) <http://asean.org/asean-joint-statement-on-climate-change-to-the-22nd-conference-of-the-parties-cop-22-to-the-united-nations-framework-convention-on-climate-change-unfccc/> accessed 4 December 2018; ASEAN, 'ASEAN Joint Statement to the Thirteenth Meeting of the Conference of the Parties to the Convention on Biological Diversity (CBD COP 13)' (6 September 2016) <http://asean.org/asean-joint-statement-on-climate-change-to-the-22nd-conference-of-the-parties-cop-22-to-the-united-nations-framework-convention-on-climate-change-unfccc/> accessed 4 December 2018.

[12] For example, SPREP, Pacific Islands prepare for the UN Climate Negotiations, The battle for survival Please adjust to single word space. <https://www.sprep.org/news/pacific-islands-prepare-for-the-un-climate-negotiations-the-battle-for-survival> accessed 28 June 2019.

[13] For example, Suzanne Kingston, Veerle Heyvaert, and Aleksandra Čavoški, *European Environmental Law* (CUP 2017) 1–16.

principle of non-interference in the internal affairs of neighbouring countries continue to be in play.[14]

While the effectiveness of international and regional environmental law regimes must be understood in terms of their implementation globally and regionally, their most direct influence is measured at the national level.[15] There is now broader recognition that environmental governance must be strengthened across the Asia-Pacific, as noted by UN Environment: 'environmental regimes and institutions are still inadequate in many countries of the region, which leads to inadequate policy responses, weak enforcement of laws and regulations, and poor compliance with MEAs.'[16] One hopeful sign with respect to improvement of environmental law and governance is the increased attention paid to the Asia-Pacific by the UN Environment's Division of Environmental Law and Conventions[17] in recent years, which is likely to prove beneficial in addressing legal needs at the regional and national levels across the region.[18]

Although most global environmental conventions have been adhered to by countries in the Asia-Pacific, the achievement of a more consistent, sophisticated, and integrated environmental law regional regime may take some time.[19] While there has been substantial development of regional environmental instruments in the past thirty years, many have consisted of non-binding declarations, resolutions, and accords, with some exceptions. The reasons for this include regional political sensitivities and historical conflicts, economic pressures, lack of scientific consensus, lack of technical expertise, and lack of political will at the national level.[20] However, there are indications at the sub-regional level that more consistency is both desired and beginning to be achieved. In South Asia, Central Asia, and Northeast Asia, after many years of slow progress, the regional intergovernmental organizations are beginning to pick up steam with regard to the scope and depth of their programmes, with more

[14] For ASEAN, see Ben Boer, 'Introduction to ASEAN Regional Environmental Law' in Scholtz and Verschuuren (n 10) 259–67.

[15] Regime effectiveness in Asia is dealt with in some detail by Simon Marsden, *Environmental Regimes in Asian Sub-regions: China and the Third Pole* (Edward Elgar 2017) 12, 14–18.

[16] UN Environment, *GEO-6 Regional Assessment for Asia and the Pacific* (2016) xix <http://web.unep.org/geo/assessments/regional-assessments/regional-assessment-asia-and-pacific> accessed 23 January 2018.

[17] UN Environment, 'Division of Environmental Law and Conventions' <http://web.unep.org/divisions/delc/our-work/environmental-law> accessed 29 June 2019.

[18] Andy Raine and Emeline Pluchon, 'UN Environment—Advancing Environmental Rule of Law in Asia Pacific' (2019) 3 Chinese Journal of Environmental Law 106; Andy Raine and Luan Harford, 'UN Environment and Environmental Law in the Asia Pacific' (2017) 1 Chinese Journal of Environmental Law 2, 257.

[19] See Ed Couzens and Tim Stephens, 'Editorial: The Prospects for a Truly Regional Asia Pacific Environmental Law?' (2017) 20 Asian Pacific Journal of Environmental Law 1, 106.

[20] See Simon Marsden and Elizabeth Brandon, *Transboundary Environmental Governance in Asia: Practice and Prospects with the UNECE Agreements* (Edward Elgar 2015) 228, 230; see also Roda Mushkat, *International Environmental Law and Asian Values: Legal Norms and Cultural Influences* (UBC Press 2004) 127.

regional conventions, agreements, and declarations emerging on various aspects of environmental governance and management, as noted in the sections below.

3 The Regional Institutional Frameworks for Environmental Law

As with other areas of international law, the primary sources of law in the environmental arena remain largely with states.[21] However, the concept of international legal personality has widened in the past few decades and now applies to some international organizations, which have acquired the capacity to contribute to the making of international environmental law.[22] In the Asia-Pacific, such organizations also include several of the regional intergovernmental bodies, as discussed below. Since the 1980s there has been greater emphasis in the region on cooperation over economic integration, free trade, and investment, as demonstrated by the establishment of the Asia Pacific Economic Cooperation forum (APEC)[23] and the drafting of free trade agreements.[24] The emergence of China's Belt and Road Initiative, with its vast investment in infrastructure development around the world, will undoubtedly raise a range of environmental management concerns.[25] This includes the environmental impact assessment standards that should be applied in approving investment decisions and infrastructure projects throughout the Asia-Pacific sub-regions,[26] as well as obligations arising under MEAs, and how such issues will be addressed by environmental law.[27]

Although the trend towards increased cooperation in the implementation of international environmental law has affected the development of regional and some

[21] Thilo Marauhn, 'Changing Role of the State' in Dan Bodansky, Jutta Brunnée, and Ellen Hey (eds), *The Oxford Handbook of International Environmental Law* (Oxford University Press 2007) 733.

[22] Mark Drumbl, 'Actors and Law-Making in International Environmental Law' in Malgosia Fitzmaurice, David Ong, and Panos Merkouris (eds), *Research Handbook of International Environmental Law* (Edward Elgar 2010) 3–4; see also Ben Boer, 'International law-making' in Elisa Morgera and Kati Kulovesi (eds), *Research Handbook on International Law and Natural Resources* (Edward Elgar 2016) 449–72.

[23] Asia Pacific Economic Cooperation, <https://www.apec.org/> accessed 26 August 2017; for an early history of APEC see John Ravenhill, *APEC and the Construction of Pacific Rim Regionalism* (CUP 2001).

[24] Asia Pacific Economic Cooperation, 'Free Trade Agreements and Regional Trading Agreements' <http://www.apec.org/Groups/Other-Groups/FTA_RTA> accessed 26 August 2017.

[25] Brenda Goh and Cate Cadell, 'China's Xi says Belt and Road must be green, sustainable' (Reuters, 25 April 2019) <https://www.reuters.com/article/us-china-silkroad/chinas-xi-says-belt-and-road-must-be-green-sustainable-idUSKCN1S104I> accessed 4 May 2019.

[26] For example, Fernando Ascensão et al, 'Environmental Challenges for the Belt and Road Initiative' (2018) 1 Nature Sustainability, 206–9.

[27] See Flavia Marisi, 'Development Banks as Environmental Governance Actors: the AIIB's Power to Promote Green Growth' in Julien Chaisse and Jędrzej Górski (eds), *The Belt and Road Initiative: Law, Economics, and Politics* (Brill 2019) 505; see also Ben Boer, 'The Green Belt and Road: Challenges for Environmental Law' in *Belt and Road Initiative Legal Forum* (China Law Society 2019) 297.

sub-regional legal regimes in a positive way, the push for increased cooperation in several of the sub-regions has been accompanied by robust assertions of sovereignty, as post-colonial states assert their independence both from former colonial powers and, in the case of several sub-regions, from each other. The Association of Southeast Asian Nations (ASEAN) experience is perhaps the most obvious manifestation of this tendency, especially by the regular, if unfortunate, use of the concept of the 'ASEAN Way' to refer to policies of non-interference and political sovereignty.[28] Although these characteristics are not as manifest in the other sub-regions, some countries in South Asia and Northeast Asia have been, and continue to be, at loggerheads with each other. A consequence is that their political capacity to cooperate on matters such as regional environment governance is affected, and their cooperative institutional structures are thus taking a longer time to mature. On the other hand, in the Pacific sub-region the island countries have emerged from the colonial era and the ravages of sea and land battles of the Second World War to form some of the strongest regional political structures in the whole of the Asia-Pacific.

For the purposes of environmental management, the Asia-Pacific is divided into six sub-regions, each of which has spawned cooperative institutional frameworks with varying levels of effectiveness: South Asia, Central Asia, Northeast Asia, Southeast Asia, the Mekong Basin, and the Pacific.

3.1 South Asian Sub-region

South Asia comprises the eight countries of the South Asian Association for Regional Cooperation (SAARC): Afghanistan, Bangladesh, Bhutan, India, the Maldives, Nepal, Pakistan, and Sri Lanka.[29] The South Asia Cooperative Environment Programme (SACEP), with the same membership as SAARC, was established in 1982 and has a close relationship with SAARC through a memorandum of understanding.[30] SACEP describes itself as the 'intergovernmental environmental organization for the South Asia region'.[31] It is constituted by a set of articles of association.[32] Its functions are to: promote cooperative activities in priority environmental areas of mutual interest; ensure that these activities result in benefit individually or collectively to the member

[28] See Koh Kheng-Lian and Md Saiful Karim, 'The Role of ASEAN in Shaping Regional Environmental Protection' in Philip Hirsch (ed), *Routledge Handbook of the Environment in Southeast Asia* (Routledge 2017) ch 19; Ben Boer, 'Environmental Law in Southeast Asia' in Hirsch (ed) infra ch 8.

[29] South Asian Association for Regional Cooperation About SAARC <http://saarc-sec.org/about-saarc> accessed 28 June 2019.

[30] Memorandum of Understanding on Cooperation in the Field of Environment between the South Asian Association for Regional Cooperation (SAARC) and the South Asia Cooperative Environment Programme (SACEP) (2004).

[31] SACEP, 'What We Do' <http://www.sacep.org/?page_id=781> accessed 1 August 2018.

[32] Articles of Association of the South Asia Cooperative Environment Programme <https://iea.uoregon.edu/treaty-text/1981-southasiacooperativeenvironmentprogrammeentxt> accessed 4 May 2019.

states of the region; extend support as needed through exchange of the knowledge and expertise available among the member countries; provide local resources towards implementation of projects and activities; and encourage maximum constructive and complementary support from interested donor countries and other sources.[33] The environment ministers of each of the countries hold periodic meetings to focus on cooperation concerning the environment, natural disasters, and climate change. SACEP has a broad work programme, including a focus on transboundary environmental issues such as the control and prevention of air pollution and its likely transboundary effects.

SACEP also hosts and coordinates regional arms of international programmes. It serves as the secretariat for the South Asian Seas Programme,[34] a subset of the UN Environment Regional Seas Programme. The South Asian Seas Action Plan[35] includes the five SAARC nations with marine coastlines: Bangladesh, India, the Maldives, Pakistan, and Sri Lanka. The objectives of the Action Plan are to facilitate consultations and technical cooperation; to highlight the economic and social importance of marine and coastal resources; and to establish a regional cooperative network of activities.[36]

SACEP has also sponsored a range of non-binding resolutions and declarations pertaining to the environment and conservation. In 2008, the Jaipur Declaration on South Asia Initiative for Combating Illegal Trade in Wildlife[37] was agreed; it supports the establishment of the South Asia Wildlife Enforcement Network (SAWEN),[38] and reflects the fact that there has been a vast increase in illegal trade in wildlife[39] and its detection[40] in recent years. Importantly, SAWEN's first objective is to take initiatives in bringing harmonization and standardization to the laws and policies in the sub-region concerning conservation of wild fauna and flora.[41]

[33] Ibid. art. 1.

[34] The South Asian Seas Programme was adopted in 1995. SACEP, 'South Asian Seas Programme: An Overview' <http://www.sacep.org/?page_id=2372> accessed 1 August 2018; see also Marsden (n 15) 196–7.

[35] UN Environment, 'South Asian Seas Action Plan' <http://www.unenvironment.org/explore-topics/oceans-seas/what-we-do/working-regional-seas/regional-seas-programmes/south-asian> accessed 1 August 2018.

[36] SACEP, 'South Asia Seas Programme: Objectives' <http://www.sacep.org/?p=2616> accessed 1 August 2018.

[37] SACEP, 'Jaipur Declaration on South Asia Initiative for Combating Illegal Trade in Wildlife' (22 May 2008) Annex XVII GC 11 <http://www.sacep.org/pdf/Declarations/03.Jaipur-Declaration-on-South-Asia-Initiative-for-Combating-Illegal-Trade-in-Wildlife-of-2008.pdf> accessed 1 August 2018.

[38] The South Asia Wildlife Enforcement Network 'provides a platform for its member countries to cooperatively work together in the fight against the burgeoning wildlife crime. It focuses on harmonization of policies and laws; strengthening institutional capacity; sharing of knowledge, experiences and technologies among the member countries; and promoting collaboration with national, regional and international partners to enhance the wildlife law enforcement in the region': SAWEN, 'Welcome to South Asia Wildlife Enforcement Network' <http://www.sawen.org/> accessed 1 August 2018.

[39] See South Asia Wildlife Enforcement Network (SAWEN), 'Retrospective Report 2011–2014' (2014) <http://www.sawen.org/publication/details/sawen-retrospective-report-20112014> accessed 1 August 2018.

[40] SAWEN, 'The SAWEN Bulletin' (2017) Vol 20 <http://www.sawen.org/publication/details/sawen-bulletin-vol-20> accessed 1 August 2018.

[41] SAWEN (n 39) 10.

An important step, from the point of view of progressing the implementation of international environmental law, was the Decision on South Asia's Biodiversity Beyond 2010.[42] This urged South Asian governments and stakeholders to implement decisions of the Conference of the Parties to the Convention on Biological Diversity and to curb the continuing loss of biodiversity, as well as to strengthen the capacity for implementation of the obligations under the Convention, including support for updating national biodiversity strategies and action plans.

In 2010, the SAARC Convention on Cooperation on Environment was agreed. Its objective is 'to promote cooperation among the parties in the field of environment and sustainable development on the basis of equity, reciprocity, and mutual benefit, taking into account the principal policies and legislation in each Member State'.[43] The Governing Council comprises the environment ministers of each member state, and specifies that senior officials meetings will take place every year.[44] The Convention states that it extends 'to exchange of best practices and knowledge, capacity building and transfer of eco-friendly technology' with regard to a wide range of issues, including pollution, climate change, biodiversity, forests, coastal zone management, land degradation and desertification, mountain ecosystems and glaciers, waste management, wildlife conservation, and illegal wildlife trade. While the Convention encourages strong cooperation, it lacks any substantive legal obligations concerning standards for environmental quality or institutional mechanisms for implementation, even though it obliges the Governing Council to 'ensure the full and effective implementation of the Convention by the Parties'.[45]

The only transboundary pollution agreement in the South Asia sub-region is the Malé Declaration on Control and Prevention of Air Pollution.[46] While it is non-binding, it recognizes that transboundary air pollution is likely to increase, and that assessment and analysis of the origin and causes, nature, extent, and effects of local and regional air pollution are required.[47]

In 2014, SACEP produced its South Asia Environment Outlook report, which presented 'concrete evidence that food security, water security and the livelihoods of the people in South Asia are at risk due to climate change, air pollution and other environmental threats'.[48] It also pointed out that a persistent problem was the

[42] Twelfth Meeting of the Governing Council of SACEP, Decision No 11 South Asia's Biodiversity Beyond 2010 <http://www.sacep.org/?page_id=2682> or <http://www.sacep.org/pdf/Declarations/01. Resolution-on-'South-Asia's-Biodiversity-beyond-2010'.pdf> accessed 5 May 2019.

[43] SAARC Convention on Cooperation on Environment (adopted 29 April 2010, entered into force 23 October 2013).

[44] Ibid. art. V(1)–(2).

[45] Ibid. art. II and art. V(4); see further Marsden (n 15) ch 5.

[46] Malé Declaration on Control and Prevention of Air Pollution and its Likely Transboundary Effects for South Asia (adopted 22 April 1998, entered into force 23 October 2013). See further Marsden and Brandon (n 20) 228 and Marsden (n 15) 194.

[47] See section 4.2, below, Regional Air Pollution.

[48] SAARC, UNEP, and Development Alternatives, 'South Asia Environment Outlook 2014' (2014).

ineffective implementation of environmental laws, action plans, and programmes.[49] In addition, in anticipation of the drafting of the UN Sustainable Development Goals,[50] SACEP generated its own Post-2015 South Asia Development Agenda.[51] The South Asia Environment Outlook 2014 and the Post-2015 South Asia Development Agenda amount, in effect, to a 'state of the environment report' for South Asia. The last recorded region-wide State of the Environment Report was in 2001, together with six individual country reports.[52] The Post-2015 South Asia Development Agenda recognizes that 'SAARC countries already have policy and legislative frameworks in place for sustainable development . . . . [T]he weakness lies in the implementation of these policies, monitoring and evaluation of the schemes, governance of development programmes and in the inter-ministerial coordination of sustainable development plans'.[53]

In summary, notwithstanding the various instruments and policy documents that have been generated in recent years, and despite the call by the South Asian Wildlife Network for harmonization and standardization of laws and policies regarding flora and fauna,[54] the South Asian sub-region as a whole cannot yet be said to host an effective environmental management regime.

3.2 Central Asian Sub-region

Central Asia comprises Kazakhstan, Kyrgyzstan, Tajikistan, Turkmenistan, and Uzbekistan. These countries face a range of serious environmental challenges, partly as a result of having been member states of the Soviet Union, which was dissolved in 1989. These challenges include scarcity of water resources through diversions from several major rivers, land and water pollution from mining and other industrial activities, especially concerning the Aral Sea, and the effects of climate change.[55] Unlike the other sub-regions, the Regional Environment Programme for Central Asia, sponsored by the European Union,[56] is still in its formative stages. A basic State of the

[49] Ibid. 155.

[50] UN, 'UN Sustainable Development Goals' <http://www.un.org/sustainabledevelopment/sustainable-development-goals/> accessed 1 August 2018.

[51] SACEP, 'Post 2015 Sustainable Development Agenda' <http://www.sacep.org/pdf/post2015_sada.pdf> accessed 1 August 2018.

[52] SACEP Technical Reports, South Asia State of Environment Report, and individual reports for Bangladesh, Bhutan, India, Nepal, and Sri Lanka in 2001 and for the Maldives in 2002: see <http://www.sacep.org/?page_id=216> accessed 1 August 2018.

[53] SACEP (n 51) 40.

[54] Convention on Biological Diversity (adopted 5 June 1992, entered into force 29 December 1993, 1760 UNTS 79).

[55] Rajat Nag, Johannes Linn, and Harinder Kohli (eds), *Central Asia 2050: Unleashing the Region's Potential* (Sage 2017); see also Uuriintuya Batsaikha and Marek Dabrowski, 'Central Asia: Twenty-five Years after the Breakup of the USSR' (2017) 3 Russian Journal of Economics 296, 298; Marsden (n 15) 81; Central Asian International Environmental Forum Report 2018 <https://www.carececo.org/en/main/ckh/publications/tsamef-2018-otchet/> accessed 28 June 2019.

[56] Known as EURECA <https://ec.europa.eu/europeaid/regions/central-asia/eus-development-cooperation-central-asia-environment_en> accessed 27 November 2017.

Environment Report was produced in 2015.[57] The Regional Environmental Centre for Central Asia, known as CAREC,[58] has established country offices in all five of the member states. A Framework Convention on Environmental Protection for Sustainable Development[59] was opened for signature in 2006 but is not yet in force. The purpose of this comprehensive Convention is 'to ensure the effective protection of the environment for sustainable development in Central Asia'.[60] The Convention's provisions are consistent with modern environmental principles found in other international and regional instruments. It includes a range of general obligations, and covers environmental protection and sustainable development, monitoring and impact assessment, air pollution, conservation and sustainable use of water resources, protection and rational use of land resources, waste management, conservation of mountain ecosystems, and biodiversity.[61]

A Subregional Sustainable Development Strategy for Central Asia was prepared in 2009 in collaboration with UN Environment. It states that it 'is intended to create appropriate conditions for constructive dialogue between CA countries, to provide a connection channel for state agencies and civil society (bodies of local self-government, social organizations and etc.), and engage certain private sector entrepreneurs in the process of decision making concerning problems of balanced development of their economies and improvement of the environmental condition'.[62] Despite the Strategy and its subsequent implementation initiatives, absent the coming into force of the Convention, and with inadequate institutional arrangements, an environmental management regime for Central Asia remains inchoate.

3.3 Southeast Asian Sub-region

Southeast Asia comprises the ten ASEAN countries of: Brunei, Myanmar/Burma, Cambodia, Indonesia, Laos, Malaysia, the Philippines, Singapore, Thailand, and Vietnam. It is intended that Timor-Leste will join ASEAN in due course.[63] ASEAN

[57] FLERMONECA, Regional Environmental Centre for Central Asia, Environmental Agency of Austria, and Zoï Environment Network, 'The State of the Environment in Central Asia: Illustrations of Selected Environmental Themes and Indicators' (2015) <https://issuu.com/zoienvironment/docs/soe-regional-eng> accessed 27 November 2017.

[58] CAREC <https://www.carececo.org/en/> accessed 3 February 2018.

[59] Framework Convention on Environmental Protection for Sustainable Development in Central Asia (adopted 22 November 2006) <https://www.ecolex.org/details/treaty/framework-convention-on-environmental-protection-for-sustainable-development-in-central-asia-tre-143806/> accessed 28 June 2019.

[60] Ibid. art. 3.

[61] Ibid. arts 4–13; see further Marsden and Brandon (n 20) 246–7 and Marsden (n 15) 110.

[62] Subregional Sustainable Development Strategy for Central Asia <http://www.rrcap.ait.asia/Publications/SSDS%20CA.pdf>; note however, that an SDG strategy.

[63] Ganewati Wuryandari, 'East Timor's Membership of ASEAN: Prospects and Challenges' <http://www.aseancenter.org.tw/upload/files/OUTLOOK_003_02.pdf> accessed 4 December 2018; Claire Carter, 'East Timor's Accession to ASEAN' (*ASEAN Today*, 31 August 2017) <http://www.aseantoday.com/2017/08/east-timors-accession-to-asean/> accessed 3 February 2018.

was established in 1967 with six states, by the adoption of the ASEAN Declaration.[64] The ASEAN Secretariat is based in Jakarta.[65] Until 2007, ASEAN was an informal regional grouping.[66] The ASEAN Charter conferred legal personality on the organization, thus giving it more authority both within the sub-region as well as beyond it.[67]

ASEAN hosts an institutional framework for environmental cooperation, the most important element of which is the ASEAN Senior Officials on the Environment, a body of state representatives that meets annually.

ASEAN has generated several regional treaties. In 1985 it concluded a comprehensive environmental instrument entitled the ASEAN Agreement on the Conservation of Nature and Natural Resources.[68] However, it has not yet been able to attract a sufficient number of ratifications for it to come into effect.[69] It has nevertheless played some part in the development of international environmental law, being seen as a forerunner to the Convention on Biological Diversity[70] and, within ASEAN states, national environmental law and policy.[71]

The first binding treaty was the Southeast Asia Nuclear-Weapon Free Zone Treaty 1995,[72] which obliges parties not to: develop, manufacture, or otherwise acquire, possess, or have control over, nuclear weapons; station nuclear weapons; test or use nuclear weapons; or engage in associated activities. The second was the ASEAN Agreement on Transboundary Haze Pollution 2002,[73] which was drafted largely to address the Indonesian forest fires that have played atmospheric havoc on a number of Southeast Asian states since the 1990s. Although the Agreement came into force in 2003, Indonesia did not ratify it until 2014. The objective of the Agreement is 'to prevent and monitor transboundary haze pollution as a result of land and/or forest fires which should be mitigated, through concerted national efforts and intensified regional and international co-operation' (article 2). The Agreement adopted the same principle[74] as that found in Principle 2 of the 1992 Rio Declaration on Environment and Development: 'The Parties have, in accordance with the Charter of the United Nations and the principles of international law, the sovereign right to exploit their own resources

[64] The ASEAN Declaration (8 August 1967) (Bangkok Declaration).

[65] See ASEAN <https://asean.org/asean/asean-secretariat/> accessed 5 May 2019.

[66] See Koh and Karim (n 28) 316.

[67] ASEAN, 'Charter of the Southeast Asian Nations' (2007) art. III.

[68] ASEAN Agreement on the Conservation of Nature and Natural Resources (adopted 9 July 1985, not yet in force).

[69] For reasons for the lack of an adequate number of ratifications, see Koh Kheng-Lian, 'Asian Environmental Protection in Natural Resources and Sustainable Development: Convergence versus Divergence?' (2007) 4 Macquarie Journal of International and Comparative Environmental Law 43; see also Barbara Lausche, *Weaving a Web of Environmental Law* (Schmidt 2008) 191.

[70] Convention on Biological Diversity (n 54).

[71] See Lausche (n 69) 191–2.

[72] Southeast Asia Nuclear-Weapon Free Zone Treaty (adopted 15 December 1995, entered into force 28 March 1997, 1981 UNTS 129).

[73] ASEAN Agreement on Transboundary Haze Pollution (adopted 10 June 2002, entered into force 25 November 2003) (Haze Agreement).

[74] Rio Declaration on Environment and Development (1992) 31 ILM 874, except for the addition of 'and harm to human health'.

pursuant to their own environmental and developmental policies, and the responsibility to ensure that activities within their jurisdiction or control do not cause damage to the environment and harm to human health of other States or of areas beyond the limits of national jurisdiction'.[75] The Agreement emphasises joint emergency assistance,[76] technical cooperation, and scientific research.[77] Despite its formal language, the Agreement is not robust in terms of enforceability: 'Any dispute between Parties as to the interpretation or application of, or compliance with, this Agreement or any protocol thereto, shall be settled amicably by consultation or negotiation'.[78]

A third instrument is the ASEAN Centre for Biodiversity Agreement 2005,[79] ratified by all ASEAN members. It is intended to facilitate cooperation with respect to conservation of biodiversity and the fair and equitable sharing of the benefits of biodiversity in ASEAN states. The Centre is given juridical personality and can sue in its own name,[80] but the Agreement cannot be characterized as a legally binding document in the sense of being enforceable. Consistent with the 'ASEAN Way' and in keeping with the approach of the Haze Agreement, it provides that '[a]ny dispute concerning the interpretation or implementation of the Agreement shall be settled amicably through consultation or negotiation'.[81]

Although ASEAN has not yet established a strong regional environmental law regime, it has nevertheless negotiated a wide range of soft law instruments on environmental and natural resource issues. Despite the fact that they are non-binding, a number have nevertheless played some role in shaping the laws and policies of ASEAN states.[82] In recent years, ASEAN has also contributed more vigorously on the international stage to negotiations on climate change, such as its Joint Statement on Climate Change to COP21 at the Conference of the Parties that generated the Paris Agreement on Climate Change in 2015.[83]

With regard to the implementation of the SDGs, the Declaration on ASEAN Post-2015 Environmental Sustainability and Climate Change Agenda[84] by ASEAN states' Heads of Government recognized the growing need to address global and

[75] Haze Agreement (n 73) art. 3.1. [76] Ibid. arts 12–15.

[77] Ibid. arts 16 and 17. [78] Ibid. art. 27.

[79] Agreement on the Establishment of the ASEAN Centre for Biodiversity (signed April 2005, entered into force 23 July 2009); for analysis see Marsden (n 15) 155–6.

[80] Ibid. art. 9. [81] Ibid. art. 12.

[82] Soft law has become increasingly important in the environmental law realm around the world as 'half-way stages in the law-making process': Patricia Birnie, Alan Boyle, and Catherine Redgwell, *International Law and the Environment* (3rd edn OUP 2012) 34. ASEAN's tendency to produce declarations, charters, and other soft law instruments on environment and natural resources is a well-known example of this process, although too often they remain as 'half-way' without progressing to a more solid legal character. For a comprehensive listing of these instruments; see Koh Kheng-Lian (ed), *ASEAN Environmental Law, Policy and Governance: Selected Documents*, vols I and II (World Scientific 2013).

[83] ASEAN Joint Statement on Climate Change to the 21st Session of the Conference of the Parties to the UN Framework Convention on Climate Change (COP21) (2015).

[84] Concluded 27th ASEAN Summit in Kuala Lumpur, 21 November 2015.

transboundary environmental concerns. It also mentioned ASEAN's obligations to ensure environmental sustainability and achieve sustainable development. It committed ASEAN states to strengthening international cooperation through the 2030 development agenda and through the SDGs. It also obliged them to strike a balance between economic growth, social development, and environmental sustainability, and to strengthen ASEAN's commitments on the 2015 Development Agenda and the Sustainable Development Goals.

In 2017, the ASEAN environment ministers adopted updated Terms of Reference for the ASEAN Senior Officials on the Environment (ASOEN) and its Working Groups, with the intention of facilitating better regional cooperation, consistent with the ASEAN Community Vision 2025. An ASEAN Strategic Plan on Environment (ASPEN) 2016–2025 was also prepared, including action plans to address strategic environmental priorities. This plan is intended as a comprehensive guide for ASEAN cooperation, thereby strengthening the regional environmental framework in an unprecedented fashion.[85] The Ministers also adopted the ASEAN-China Strategy on Environmental Cooperation 2016–2020[86] and the ASEAN-UN Action Plan on Environment and Climate Change.[87]

The fifth ASEAN State of Environment Report, released in 2017, reflects an increasingly sophisticated approach to regional environmental management.[88] It recognized legal weaknesses in various environmental sectors, such as water, illegal fishing, and chemicals, and suggested various regional or national legal frameworks[89] that may assist in operationalizing the new policies and initiatives.

3.4 The Mekong River Basin Sub-region

The Mekong River Basin sub-region is a distinct law and policy arena in Asia which overlaps in part with the ASEAN sub-region. The six riparian countries of the Mekong are Cambodia, China, Laos, Myanmar, Thailand, and Vietnam. Apart from China, all are members of ASEAN. Cambodia, Laos, Thailand, and Vietnam are often referred to as the Lower Mekong countries. Each of the Lower Mekong countries and Myanmar have committed to the SDGs, with local strategies put in place to monitor their

[85] Brunei Darussalam, 'Press Release: 14th ASEAN Ministerial Meeting on the Environment and the 13th Meeting of the Conference of the Parties to the ASEAN Agreement on Transboundary Haze Pollution Environment Division' (ASEAN Cooperation on Environment, 14 September 2017).

[86] See <http://environment.asean.org/wp-content/uploads/2017/02/ASEAN-China-Strategy-on-Environmental-Cooperation-2016-2020.pdf> accessed 4 December 2018.

[87] ASEAN Secretariat, 'An Overview of ASEAN-UN Cooperation' (August 2017) <http://asean.org/storage/2012/05/Overview-of-ASEAN-UN-Cooperation-As-of-1-August-2017-clean.pdf> accessed 5 February 2018.

[88] ASEAN Secretariat, 'Fifth ASEAN State of the Environment Report' (2017) <https://environment.asean.org/soer5/> accessed 23 January 2018.

[89] For example, with respect to biota and ecosystems, see ibid. 227; for coasts and oceans and marine litter, see ibid. 228.

implementation.[90] Cambodia, Laos, Thailand, and Vietnam are members of the Agreement on the Cooperation for the Sustainable Development of the Mekong River Basin 1995,[91] while China and Myanmar are 'Dialogue Partners' and attend the Mekong River Commission's (MRC's) meetings. A Protocol attached to the Agreement established the MRC as the institutional framework through which the Agreement is implemented. However, given its broad focus and unenforceable nature, the Agreement and its Protocol cannot be regarded as an environmental management regime except in the limited sense of facilitating scientific and technical cooperation and providing institutional support for the environmental assessment of major projects such as hydropower development.

The MRC has forged various links with other sub-regions and countries, including a memorandum of understanding (MOU) between the MRC and China, drawn up in 2002 (updated in 2013), which provides for daily river-flow and rainfall data in the Chinese province of Yunnan, to assist with forecasting downstream water levels on the Mekong River during the flood season months.[92] An MOU between the MRC and the ASEAN Secretariat was concluded in 2010,[93] the objective of which is 'to provide a framework for developing and maintaining cooperation between the two secretariats in the field of their common interests and to ensure close coordination, and better utilization of resources so as to achieve effective outcomes on regional cooperation for the sustainable development of the Mekong River Basin'.[94]

The transboundary issues concerning water allocation and use, particularly with respect to hydropower generation and the building of dams, has a long history of both cooperation and conflict in the Mekong Basin.[95] The non-binding procedures[96]

[90] Open Development Mekong, 'Sustainable Development Goals' (*Open Development Mekong*, 27 April 2018) <https://opendevelopmentmekong.net/topics/sustainable-development-goals/> accessed 5 February 2018.

[91] Agreement on the Cooperation for the Sustainable Development of the Mekong River Basin (adopted 5 April 1995, entered into force 5 April 1995) <http://www.ecolex.org/details/treaty/agreement-on-the-cooperation-for-the-sustainable-development-of-the-mekong-river-basin-tre-001223> accessed 29 January 2018.

[92] Mekong River Commission, 'Upstream Partners' <http://www.mrcmekong.org/about-mrc/upstream-partners/> accessed 29 January 2018.

[93] Memorandum of Understanding between the Mekong River Commission Secretariat and the ASEAN Secretariat (adopted 4 March 2010) <http://www.mrcmekong.org/assets/Publications/agreements/MOU-ASEAN.pdf> accessed 27 August 2017.

[94] Ibid. art. 15.

[95] Ben Boer, Philip Hirsch, Fleur Johns, Ben Saul, and Natalia Scurrah, *The Mekong: A Socio-Legal Approach to River Basin Development* (Routledge 2016) ch 3.

[96] Guidelines on Implementation of the Procedures for Notification, Prior Consultation and Agreement (adopted 31 August 2005) <http://www.mrcmekong.org/assets/Publications/policies/Guidelines-on-implementation-of-the-PNPCA.pdf> accessed 29 January 2018. Attempts are being made to revise these guidelines, but the intention is that they will continue to be non-binding: Alessandro Sassoon, 'Mekong River Commission to Revise Dam Guidelines' (*Phnom Penh Post*, 2 February 2018). See also Mekong River Commission, *An Introduction to MRC Procedural Rules for Mekong Water Cooperation* (2018), which includes associated technical guidelines on data sharing, water use monitoring, water use cooperation, flow maintenance, and water quality.

developed by the parties to the Mekong Agreement concerning notification, prior consultation, and agreement for hydropower development in the Mekong Basin have proved largely ineffective with respect to the planning, building, and operation of dams on the mainstream.[97] They also lack any specific public participation requirements.[98]

While the International Court of Justice has recognized that 'it may now be considered a requirement under general international law to undertake an environmental impact assessment where there is a risk that the proposed industrial activity may have a significant adverse impact in a transboundary context, in particular, on a shared resource',[99] this jurisprudence has not yet been given substantive effect in the Mekong.[100] The MRC has, since 2004, made attempts to complete a set of guidelines for transboundary environmental impact assessments, with the 2018 version being the most comprehensive.[101] Tellingly, in terms of the strong sense of sovereignty of the Lower Mekong countries, there is no notion of making these guidelines more robust, or in any sense enforceable, as specifically recorded in its Statement of Intent: 'This Guidance is not an International Treaty and does not contain rights and obligations regulated by International Law.' Given the strength of this statement, it is not surprising that none of the Lower Mekong countries have signed up to the Convention on Environmental Impact Assessment in a Transboundary Context 1991 (Espoo Convention),[102] or its Protocol on Strategic Environmental Assessment 2013.[103] Despite this, a strategic environmental assessment (SEA)[104] with regard to hydropower development was agreed to be conducted 'to bring a more integrated, informed and precautionary approach to mainstream development'. However, the SEA was seen to be only partially successful, with several countries forging ahead with major dams on the mainstream of the Mekong, despite a strong recommendation to postpone such

[97] Philip Hirsch, Kurt Mørck Jensen, Ben Boer, Naomi Carrard, Stephen FitzGerald, and Rosemary Lyster, 'National Interests and Transboundary Water Governance in the Mekong', Australian Mekong Resource Centre Report, May 2006, ch 3.

[98] See Marsden (n 15) 143.

[99] *Pulp Mills on the River Uruguay (Argentina v Uruguay)* (Judgment) [2010] ICJ Reports 14, 73.

[100] See also Earth Rights International, 'Environmental Impact Assessment in the Mekong' (2016) 126–34.

[101] Mekong River Commission, 'Guidelines for Transboundary Environmental Impact Assessment in the Lower Mekong Basin' (Working document) <www.mrcmekong.org/assets/ . . . /TbEIA-Guidelines-Final-version-25-9-2018.pdf> accessed 28 June 2019.

[102] Convention on Environmental Impact Assessment in a Transboundary Context (adopted 25 February 1991, entered into force 10 September 1997, 1989 UNTS 309). Since 2014, any UN member is able to accede to the Convention; see also Marsden and Brandon (n 20) 105.

[103] Protocol on Strategic Environmental Assessment to the Convention on Environmental Impact Assessment in a Transboundary Context (adopted 21 May 2003, entered into force 11 July 2010, 2685 UNTS 140).

[104] International Centre for Environmental Management, 'Strategic Environmental Assessment of Mainstream Dams' (Mekong River Commission, October 2010) <http://www.mrcmekong.org/about-mrc/completion-of-strategic-cycle-2011-2015/initiative-on-sustainable-hydropower/strategic-environmental-assessment-of-mainstream-dams/> accessed 2 August 2018.

decisions for a period of ten years to allow for the 'potentially far-reaching impacts' to be better understood.[105]

While the Lower Mekong countries and Myanmar will continue to be vital members of ASEAN, the Greater Mekong Sub-region (GMS), consisting of China and the five other Mekong countries, may in the future be the basis for further development agreements, as portended by the GMS Programme.[106] As stated in the 2011 country report on China's Participation in Greater Mekong Sub-region Cooperation: 'Environmental cooperation is an important component of GMS cooperation, and China highly values its environmental exchange and cooperation with the other GMS countries'.[107] With the increasing importance of China's Belt and Road Initiative, such cooperation is likely to become closer in the Greater Mekong Sub-region.[108]

3.5 Northeast Asian Sub-region

The North-East Asian Sub-regional Programme for Environmental Cooperation (NEASPEC)[109] includes China, Japan, Mongolia, North Korea, the Russian Federation, and South Korea. In contrast to the South Asian, Southeast Asian, and Pacific sub-regions, a unifying regional political organization has not yet developed. For pragmatic political reasons, NEASPEC was established in 1993 under the auspices of the Sub-regional Office for East and North-East Asia of the UN Economic and Social Commission for Asia and the Pacific based in Bangkok. This Sub-regional Office functions as the NEASPEC Secretariat. In a similar way to the ASEAN Senior Officials on the Environment, NEASPEC has established a senior officials group that meets yearly, and is regarded as the governing body of NEASPEC.

[105] See Jeremy Carew-Reid, 'The Mekong: Environmental Assessment of Mainstream Hydropower Development in an International River Basin' in Hirsch (ed) (n 28) 334; see also Boer et al (n 95) ch 5.

[106] The GMS Programme began in 2002. See Naohiro Kitano, 'The Impact of Economic Cooperation on Asian Countries: Focus on the Mekong Region and Central Asia' in Yasutami Shimomura and Hideo Ohashi (eds), *A Study of China's Foreign Aid: An Asian Perspective* (Palgrave Macmillan 2013) 171.

[107] 'Country Report on China's Participation in Greater Mekong Sub-region Cooperation' (*China Daily*, 16 December 2011) <http://usa.chinadaily.com.cn/china/2011-12/16/content_14279772.htm> accessed 5 May 2019; see also National Development Reform Commission, 'Country Report on China's Participation in Greater Mekong Subregion Cooperation' <http://en.ndrc.gov.cn/newsrelease/200804/t20080430_208063.html> accessed 5 May 2019.

[108] See for example, Wang Yi, Foreign Minister of China at the Sixth Greater Mekong Sub-region Summit: 'The Greater Mekong sub-region, once an important area along the ancient Maritime Silk Road, is now where the Silk Road Economic Belt connects with the 21st Century Maritime Silk Road. This puts the GMS countries in a solid and unique position in the Belt and Road cooperation': Wang Yi, 'Working Together to Write a New Chapter of Sub-regional Cooperation' (Chinese Ministry of Foreign Affairs, 31 March 2018) <http://www.fmprc.gov.cn/mfa_eng/zxxx_662805/t1547074.shtml> accessed 2 August 2018.

[109] See North-East Asian Sub-Regional Programme for Environmental Cooperation (NEASPEC) <http://www.neaspec.org/> accessed 27 August 2017.

After many years of slow progress, NEASPEC has in recent times become more active across the sub-region. It describes itself as 'a comprehensive intergovernmental cooperation framework addressing environmental challenges in North-East Asia'.[110] It promotes a practical approach to sub-regional cooperation based on consensus, capacity-building, information sharing, technology transfer, and collaborative financing. It provides a multilateral-cooperation platform for governments, for national, sub-regional, and international institutions, for the private sector, and for civil society in order to mitigate environmental impacts. It also aims to strengthen technological and managerial capabilities at the national level, and works to identify common policy approaches and objectives of member states. Importantly in the context of this chapter, it also aims to link national strategies with sub-regional and global initiatives.[111] NEASPEC has prepared a Strategic Plan for 2016–2020 that focuses on transboundary air pollution, biodiversity and nature conservation, marine protected areas, low-carbon cities, desertification, and land degradation.[112]

Significantly, the Plan specifically links each of these programme areas to one or more of the SDGs.[113] It also includes monitoring and evaluation of approved activities across the sub-region. Given its schematic nature, the Plan only mentions national legal mechanisms. In contrast to the other sub-regions, there is no contemplation of any sub-region-wide environmental instrument. The reasons for this are no doubt because of the history of conflict and animosity between several of the Northeast Asian states. The only extant transboundary agreement is a limited one focused on the Tumen River, involving China, Russia, and North Korea, and which is only in part concerned with environmental governance.[114] Although Northeast Asia remains the least developed in terms of a sub-regional environmental law regime, it has demonstrated a stronger determination in recent years to promote cooperation across its environmental programmes.

3.6 Pacific Island Sub-region

The Pacific Island sub-region is serviced by several regional organizations that include an environmental focus. The Secretariat of the Pacific Community (SPC),[115]

[110] See NEASPEC, 'About NEASPEC' <http://www.neaspec.org/about-neaspec> accessed 27 August 2017.

[111] NEASPEC, 'Background and Objectives' <http://www.neaspec.org/about-neaspec> accessed 28 August 2017.

[112] UN Economic and Social Commission for Asia and the Pacific, 'Review of the Strategic Plan of NEASPEC: NEASPEC Strategic Plan 2016–2020' (2016) 2 <http://www.neaspec.org/sites/default/files/6.%20SOM20%20NEASPEC%20Strategic%20Plan.pdf> accessed 28 January 2018.

[113] Ibid. 3–4.

[114] Agreement on the Establishment of the Tumen River Area Development Coordination Committee (adopted 30 May 1995) <https://nautilus.org/aprenet/agreement-on-the-establishment-of-the-tumen-river-area-development-coordination-committee-1994/> accessed 4 December 2018; see also Marsden (n 15) 203–12.

[115] The organization changed its name from the South Pacific Commission in 1997 to reflect its Pacific-wide membership.

established in 1947, comprises twenty-two Pacific Island countries and territories[116] and five 'metropolitan' countries.[117] The SPC deals with a wide range of regional issues, including human rights, public health, geoscience, agriculture, forestry, water resources, disaster management, fisheries, education, statistics, transport, energy, gender, youth, and culture, with a view to assisting Pacific Island people to achieve sustainable development.

The most important intergovernmental organization concerning the environment is the Secretariat of the Pacific Regional Environment Programme (SPREP). It is one of the partner agencies of the SPC and has the same membership. SPREP's focus is on the 'protection and sustainable development of the region's environment'.[118] Of all the regional environment programmes in the Asia-Pacific, SPREP is the most active, with extensive terrestrial and marine conservation programmes, and a strong focus on climate change. SPREP having commenced in 1982, the agreement to place it on a legal footing was completed in 1993.[119] The purposes of SPREP are 'to promote co-operation in the Pacific region and to provide assistance in order to protect and improve its environment and to ensure sustainable development for present and future generations'.[120] SPREP's four key priorities areas are biodiversity and ecosystem management, climate change, environmental monitoring and governance, and waste management and pollution.[121]

The Pacific sub-region hosts several binding regional environmental treaties. The primary instrument is the Convention for the Protection of the Natural Resources and Environment of the South Pacific Region 1986 (Noumea Convention).[122] Another instrument that was in effect superseded by the Noumea Convention is the Convention on Conservation of Nature in the South Pacific 1976.[123]

[116] American Samoa (US Territory), Cook Islands (free association with New Zealand), Federated States of Micronesia, Fiji, French Polynesia (an overseas Department of France), Guam (US Territory), Kiribati, Marshall Islands, Nauru, New Caledonia, Niue, North Mariana Islands (US Territory), Papua New Guinea, Palau, Pitcairn Islands (British Overseas Territory), Samoa, Solomon Islands, Tonga, Tokelau, Tuvalu, Vanuatu, and Wallis and Futuna (French Overseas Collectivity).

[117] Australia, France, New Zealand, the United Kingdom, and the United States.

[118] SPREP, 'SPREP Strategic Plan 2017–2026' (2017) 2 <http://www.sprep.org/attachments/Publications/Corporate_Documents/strategic-plan-2017-2026.pdf> accessed 30 January 2018.

[119] Agreement Establishing the South Pacific Regional Environment Programme as an Intergovernmental Organization (adopted 16 June 1993, entered into force 31 August 1995, [1995] Australian Treaty Series 24).

[120] Ibid. art. 2(1).

[121] SPREP, 'SPREP Annual Report 2017' (2018) 3 <https://www.sprep.org/publications/sprep-annual-report-2017> accessed 5 May 2019.

[122] Convention for the Protection of the Natural Resources and Environment of the South Pacific Region (adopted 24 November 1986, entered into force 22 August 1990, (1987) 26 ILM 38) (Noumea Convention). See also Protocol concerning Cooperation on Combatting Pollution Emergencies in the South Pacific Region (adopted 25 November 1986, entered into force 22 August 1990 (1987) 26 ILM 59) and Protocol for the Prevention of Pollution of the South Pacific Region by Dumping (adopted 25 November 1986, entered into force 22 August 1990 (1987) 26 ILM 65).

[123] Convention on Conservation of Nature in the South Pacific (adopted 12 June 1976, entered into force 26 June 1990 [1990] Australian Treaty Series 41, suspended in 2008).

In the 1980s, disputes arose between the United States and some small Pacific Island states over access to highly migratory fish species.[124] These resulted in the Treaty on Fisheries between the Governments of Certain Pacific Island States and the Government of the United States of America 1987.[125] Further multilateral agreements have been negotiated through the Forum Fisheries Agency[126] on the regulation of fish stocks, including the Wellington Convention for the Prohibition of Fishing with Long Driftnets in the South Pacific 1990,[127] the Niue Treaty on Cooperation in Fisheries Surveillance and Law Enforcement in the South Pacific Region,[128] and the Tokelau Arrangement for the Management of the South Pacific Albacore Fishery 2014.[129]

The South Pacific Nuclear Free Zone Treaty 1985,[130] negotiated pursuant to article VII of the Non-Proliferation Treaty 1968,[131] focuses on non-proliferation and keeping 'the region free of environmental pollution by radioactive wastes and other radioactive matter'.[132] Originating from the French atmospheric nuclear tests in the 1970s,[133] this Treaty became directly relevant when France recommenced underground testing at Mururoa and Fangataufa Atolls in the mid 1990s.[134]

The Waigani Convention on Hazardous Wastes 1995 (Waigani Convention)[135] is an agreement developed under article 11 of the Basel Convention.[136] It is administered by the Pacific Regional Centre for the Joint Implementation of the Basel and Waigani Conventions, based within SPREP. The Centre was set up to 'promote the

[124] See Martin Tsamenyi, 'The South Pacific States, the USA and Sovereignty over Highly Migratory Species' (1986) 10 Marine Policy 1, 29–41; Martin Tsamenyi, '*The Jeanette Diana* Dispute' (1986) 16 ODIL 353–67.

[125] Certain Pacific Island States–United States: Treaty on Fisheries (adopted 2 April 1987, entered into force 15 June 1988, (1987) 26 ILM 1048).

[126] The Forum Fisheries Agency was formally established by the South Pacific Forum Fisheries Agency Convention 1979 (adopted 10 July 1979, entered into force 9 August 1979 [1979] Australian Treaty Series 16).

[127] Convention for the Prohibition of Fishing with Long Driftnets in the South Pacific (adopted 29 November 1989, entered into force 17 May 1991 (1990) 29 ILM 1449); for other fishing treaties and agreements in the Pacific see Forum Fisheries Agency, 'Treaties & Agreements' <http://www.ffa.int/treaties_agreements> accessed 5 February 2018.

[128] Niue Treaty on Cooperation in Fisheries Surveillance and Law Enforcement in the South Pacific Region (adopted 9 July 1992, entered into force 20 May 1993, 1974 UNTS 45).

[129] Tokelau Arrangement for the Management of the South Pacific Albacore Fishery (signed 22 October 2014, in force 14 December 2014).

[130] South Pacific Nuclear Free Zone Treaty (adopted 6 August 1985, entered into force 11 December 1986, 1445 UNTS 177).

[131] Treaty on the Non-Proliferation of Nuclear Weapons (adopted 1 July 1968, entered into force 5 March 1970, 7 UNTS 161).

[132] Ibid. 169–71.

[133] *Nuclear Tests (Australia v France)* [1974] ICJ Reports 253.

[134] *Nuclear Tests (New Zealand v France)* [1995] ICJ Reports 288.

[135] Convention to Ban the Importation into Forum Island Countries of Hazardous and Radioactive Wastes and to Control the Transboundary Movement and Management of Hazardous Wastes within the South Pacific (adopted 16 September 1995, entered into force 21 October 2001, 2161 UNTS 91).

[136] Convention on the Control of Transboundary Movements of Hazardous Wastes and their Disposal (adopted 22 March 1989, entered into force 5 May 1992, 1673 UNTS 57).

environmentally sound management of waste in a coordinated manner through better integration of regional strategies and relevant conventions'.[137]

While the Pacific Island sub-region has the lowest population and one of the largest geographical areas of the whole Asia-Pacific region, its environmental law regime can be regarded as the most complete, even though practical implementation of the various international and regional MEAs holds many challenges precisely because of its small population, large area, low level of development, and limited natural resources.

4 Major Environmental Law Challenges in the Asia-Pacific

The Asia-Pacific experiences many of the same environmental problems as most of the world's other geopolitical regions, but some issues are of particular prominence for the region. These include the effects of anthropogenic climate change, air pollution, and depletion of terrestrial and marine biodiversity. These are dealt with below, along with the emerging issue of recognition of environmental rights.

4.1 Climate Change

Across the Asia-Pacific, the effects of climate change have increased vulnerability, with rising sea levels affecting the environment and populations of low-lying coastlines and low-lying island states, while montane regions are increasingly subject to insufficient snowfall, with consequent lack of summer melt and thus inadequate river flows. All aspects of the environment are affected detrimentally by climate change: the atmosphere, with increasingly extreme weather events; water scarcity; flooding; saltwater contamination of freshwater lenses on atoll islands; degraded land and soil; depletion of biodiversity in general and forest ecosystems in particular; and acidification of oceans and shrinking of coastlines through rising sea-levels. Each of these impact on people and communities in myriad ways, especially through forced migration, agricultural challenges, and food and water security. All of these are also linked to various human rights, such as the right to property, shelter, livelihood, food, and water.

According to GEO-6, of all of the world's countries affected by sea-level rise up to 2050, seven of the ten most vulnerable countries are found in the Asia-Pacific region.[138]

[137] SPREP Pacific Regional Centre, 'Pacific Regional Centre for the Joint Implementation of the Basel and Waigani Conventions' <http://www.sprep.org/att/publication/000447_2005_09PRC.pdf> accessed 30 January 2018.

[138] 'Nearly 40 million people in India (1st) will be at risk, more than 25 million in Bangladesh (2nd), more than 20 million in China (3rd) and Indonesia (4th), nearly 15 million in the Philippines (5th), and nearly 10 million in Viet Nam (7th) and Japan (8th). Other Asian countries in the top 20 include Republic of Korea (12th), Myanmar (13th), Malaysia (16th) and Thailand (20th)': UN Environment, *GEO-6 Regional Assessment for Asia and the Pacific* (n 16) 32.

The worst impacts of climate change are projected for the sub-regions of the Pacific, South Asia, and Southeast Asia.

Each Asia-Pacific sub-region has placed a broad focus on the phenomenon of climate change, in terms of both mitigation and adaptation strategies. Some countries have put legislative mechanisms in place to promote clean energy and to implement adaptation strategies.[139] None of the sub-regions has, however, taken specific legal steps at a regional level to promote their strategies. In light of obligations arising both under SDG 12 on climate change and more generally, determined regional and national legal reforms would be desirable to address the effects of climate change.

ASEAN produced its Singapore Declaration on Climate Change, Energy and Environment in 2007.[140] It calls for a wide range of actions to mitigate and adapt to the effects of climate change, including ongoing cooperation on energy efficiency and the use of cleaner energy (such as from renewable and alternative sources). The Pacific sub-region has been the most active with regard to regional climate-change strategies. Climate change is identified by SPREP as its 'principal concern' due to the vulnerability of many Pacific Island states, particularly because of their low-lying topography. In 2009, in response to climate-change threats, SPREP established the Pacific Adaptation to Climate Change programme. This is a partnership between fourteen Pacific Island countries, with the objective of increasing the resilience of island communities to the effects of climate change.[141] One SPREP study has suggested that a protocol focused on climate change issues could be added to the Convention on the Protection of the Natural Resources and Environment of the South Pacific Region (Noumea Convention);[142] such a protocol 'could encourage a much more consistent approach, at a national level across the Pacific, to the effects of climate change, in general, and to ecosystem-based adaptation, in particular'.[143]

139 For South Asia see SACEP, 'Adaptation to Climate Change' <http://www.sacep.org/?p=3111>; for Central Asia see ENVSEC 'Climate Change and Security in Central Asia' <http://www.osce.org/secretariat/355471?download=true> accessed 4 December 2018; for Northeast Asia see NEASPEC, 'Strategic Plan 2016–2020' <http://www.neaspec.org/sites/default/files/NEASPEC%20Strategic%20Plan_after%20SOM20.pdf> accessed 4 December 2018; for ASEAN see 'ASEAN Cooperation on Climate Change' <https://environment.asean.org/asean-working-group-on-climate-change/> accessed 4 December 2018; ASEAN, 'Plan of Action to Implement the Joint Declaration on Comprehensive Partnership between ASEAN and the United Nations (2016–2020)' (2016) <http://asean.org/storage/2012/05/ASEAN-UN-POA-FINAL-AS-OF-5-SEP-2016.pdf> accessed 4 December 2018; for the Pacific see SPREP, 'Pacific Adaptation to Climate Change' <http://www.sprep.org/pacc> accessed 4 December 2018.

140 Singapore Declaration on Climate Change, Energy and Environment (adopted 21 November 2007) <http://asean.org/?static_post=singapore-declaration-on-climate-change-energy-and-the-environment> and ASEAN Joint Statement on Climate Change 2014 <https://environment.asean.org/asean-working-group-on-climate-change/> both accessed 25 June 2019.

141 Pacific Adaptation to Climate Change (n 139).

142 Noumea Convention (n 122).

143 Ben Boer and Pepe Clarke, 'Legal Frameworks for Ecosystem-Based Adaptation to Climate Change in the Pacific Islands' (SPREP/PROE/Australian Aid 2012) 11, see also ibid 45. <http://www.eldis.org/document/A62935> accessed 2 August 2018.

4.2 Regional Air Pollution

A major issue in various parts of the Asia-Pacific has been transboundary air pollution from industrial activities, transport, and the burning of forests and peat lands. Air pollutants are responsible for millions of premature deaths globally each year, with around two-thirds of them across the industrialized Asian sub-regions.[144] Notwithstanding the very significant scale of the problem, the development and implementation of binding instruments on air pollution at the sub-regional level are still in their early stages.

In South Asia, the Malé Declaration on Control and Prevention of Air Pollution and its Likely Transboundary Effects for South Asia was agreed by all member countries of SACEP, and is described as 'the first regional environment agreement in South Asia to tackle transboundary air pollution through regional cooperation'.[145] It recognizes the need for SACEP countries to carry out studies and programmes on air pollution in each country of South Asia. It also promotes improvement of national reporting systems and strengthening scientific and academic efforts in the understanding and tackling of air pollution in the region. The Malé Declaration Reports indicate that monitoring, modelling, and other scientific analysis, training, and meetings are taking place to operationalize the instrument, with the data gathered providing a basis for stimulating regional cooperation further.[146] However, there is no hint as yet that the Declaration will be used as a basis for stimulating legislative action at a national level in the SACEP countries.[147]

In Southeast Asia, transboundary air pollution has been a recurring problem since the 1990s. The main source has been carbon dioxide emissions from the clearing of forests by burning for conversion to palm oil plantations. The draining and burning of peatland is also part of the clearing process, and releases more carbon dioxide than the burning of the forests themselves.[148] This has caused severe problems for human health as well as affecting visibility for aircraft and shipping. Although the matter was

[144] World Health Organization, 'One Third of Global Air Pollution Deaths in Asia Pacific' (WHO, 2 May 2018) <http://www.wpro.who.int/mediacentre/releases/2018/20180502/en/> accessed 2 August 2018.

[145] Regional Resource Centre for Asia and the Pacific, 'Malé Declaration on Control and Prevention of Air Pollution and its Likely Transboundary Effects for South Asia' <https://thimaaveshi.files.wordpress.com/2009/10/male-declaration_98.pdf> accessed 12 February 2018.

[146] See SACEP, Malé Declaration Reports <http://www.sacep.org/?page_id=5586> accessed 4 December 2018. The latest report is SACEP, 'Malé Declaration 1998–2013: A Synthesis–Progress and Opportunities' (September 2013) <http://www.sacep.org/pdf/Male-Declaration-Publications/2013.09-Male-Declaration-Progress-&-Opportunities-Synthesis-Report.pdf> accessed 22 January 2018.

[147] In 2012, it was suggested that legally binding air pollution reduction agreements be put in place under the Malé Declaration; see Parvez Hassan, 'From Pakistan' in Asian Development Bank, 'South Asia Conference on Environmental Justice' (2012) 11 <https://www.adb.org/sites/default/files/publication/30433/south-asia-conference-environmental-justice.pdf> accessed 2 August 2018.

[148] Koh Kheng-Lian, 'A Survey of ASEAN Instruments Relating to Peatlands, Mangroves and Other Wetlands: The REDD+ Context' (2013 Special Edition) International Journal of Rural Law and Policy 1; 'Stop Burning Rain Forests for Palm Oil' (*Scientific American*, 1 December 2012) <http://www.scientificamerican.com/article/stop-burning-rain-forests-for-palm-oil/> accessed 5 May 2018.

tangentially addressed in the ASEAN Agreement on the Conservation of Nature and Natural Resources 1985,[149] the countries of the region directly addressed the issue in the ASEAN Agreement on Transboundary Haze Pollution in 2002.[150] However, Indonesia—the country with the greatest responsibility for air pollution arising from forest clearing and fires—did not ratify the Haze Agreement until 2014.[151] The objective of the Agreement is to prevent and monitor transboundary haze pollution as a result of land and/or forest fires, which are required to be mitigated through concerted national efforts and intensified regional and international cooperation. This should be pursued in the overall context of sustainable development and in accordance with the provisions of this Agreement (article 2). Building on earlier initiatives, the ASEAN Coordinating Centre for Transboundary Haze Pollution Control has been established in Indonesia.[152] The Agreement specifies that signatories should 'ensure that appropriate legislative, administrative and financial measures are taken' (article 11). Indonesia has not begun to comply with the Agreement with any seriousness concerning national legislative provisions.[153] Although a regulation was passed in early 2017 aimed at reducing peat burning,[154] it was quashed by the Supreme Court of Indonesia later in the same year.[155]

In Northeast Asia, the ongoing problems of transboundary air pollution, particularly between Russia, China, and Japan, had not been addressed by NEASPEC until recently. The North-East Asia Clean Air Partnership (NEACAP) was established in 2014 as a voluntary sub-regional framework. Its aim is to address the protection of the environment and human health from air pollution in the sub-region. It is intended to complement the Long-Range Transboundary Air Pollutants in Northeast Asia mechanism and the East Asian Acid Deposition Monitoring Network, as well as focusing on new science-based, policy-oriented cooperation.[156]

[149] ASEAN Agreement on the Conservation of Nature and Natural Resources (n 68).

[150] Haze Agreement (n 73).

[151] See further Koh and Karim (n 28) 323–32; Boer (n 27) 120–1.

[152] ASEAN Secretariat, '14th ASEAN Ministerial Meeting on the Environment and the 13th Meeting of the Conference of the Parties to the ASEAN Agreement on Transboundary Haze Pollution' (ASEAN, 13 September 2017) <http://asean.org/14th-asean-ministerial-meeting-environment-13th-meeting-conference-parties-asean-agreement-transboundary-haze-pollution/> accessed 4 December 2018.

[153] Dio Herdiawan Tobing, 'Indonesia Drags Its Feet on ASEAN Haze Treaty' (*The Conversation*, 8 September 2017) <https://theconversation.com/indonesia-drags-its-feet-on-asean-haze-treaty-81779> accessed 31 January 2018. For further discussion see Roda Mushkat, 'Creating Regional Environmental Governance Regimes: Implications of Southeast Asian Responses to Transboundary Haze Pollution' (2013) 4 Washington and Lee Journal of Energy, Climate and Environment 103, 137ff; see also Marsden (n 15) 157–68.

[154] Minister of Environment and Forestry Republic of Indonesia, Regulation Amending Regulation Number P.12/Menlhk-Ii/2015 concerning Development of Industry Plantation Forests, PermenLHK No 17/2017.

[155] Hans Nicholas Jong and Lusia Arumingtyas, 'Indonesian Supreme Court Strikes Down Regulation on Peat Protection' (*Mongabay*, 2 November 2017) <https://news.mongabay.com/2017/11/indonesian-supreme-court-strikes-down-regulation-on-peat-protection/> accessed 9 July 2018.

[156] NEASPEC, 'Transboundary Air Pollution' <http://www.neaspec.org/our-work/transboundary-air-pollution> accessed 22 January 2018.

NEACAP has initiated a wide range of research and capacity-building work. Its core programmes include exchange of information and data; air pollution monitoring through existing programmes and frameworks; national and regional air pollution transport and deposition modelling; proposing potential technical and policy measures; development of common technical and policy scenarios based on integrated assessment modelling and projections; exchange of information on emerging technologies and potential for technological cooperation on mitigating pollution; sharing of information on good national environmental practices; and proposing potential technical and policy measures.[157] However, it emphasizes flexibility in the promotion of voluntary participation and contributions with regard to establishing a new sub-regional framework, and draws attention to 'its legal and political nature'.[158]

4.3 Biodiversity Conservation

The conservation of biodiversity is of increasing concern globally, with regular reports from official bodies and non-government organisations documenting the decline of species and habitats. The Asia-Pacific region is very rich in terms of its biological diversity, hosting seven of the world's seventeen 'mega-diverse' states.[159] These are Australia, China, India, Indonesia, Malaysia, Papua New Guinea, and the Philippines.

The 2019 global assessment report of the independent Intergovernmental Science-Policy Platform on Biodiversity and Ecosystem Services (IPBES) states that '[n]ature and its vital contributions to people, which together embody biodiversity and ecosystem functions and services, are deteriorating worldwide'.[160] It records that 75 per cent of the terrestrial environment and 66 per cent of marine environments have been 'severely altered' by human actions to date.[161] The reports urges: 'the biodiversity-relevant 2030 Sustainable Development Goals (SDG) and the 2050 Vision for Biodiversity cannot be achieved without transformative change'. An IPBES assessment report prepared specifically for the Asia-Pacific states that while the region 'has achieved rapid economic growth, it is undergoing one of the highest rates of

[157] NEASPEC, 'Transboundary Air Pollution in North-East Asia' (6 March 2017) NEASPEC/SOM (21)/1, 14–16.

[158] Ibid. 6.

[159] The 17 countries represent 'more than two-thirds of all (known) life forms and the majority of tropical rainforests, coral reefs and other priority systems': Department of the Environment and Energy Australia, 'Megadiverse countries' <http://www.environment.gov.au/biodiversity/conservation/hotspots> accessed 22 January 2018; also Russell Mittermeier et al (eds), *Megadiversity: Earth's Biologically Wealthiest Nations* (Cemex 1997).

[160] IPBES, *Summary for Policymakers of the Global Assessment Report on Biodiversity and Ecosystem Services* <https://www.dropbox.com/sh/yd8l2vou4jqptp3/AACpraYjOYWpTxAFv5H-2vrKa/1%20Global%20Assessment%20Summary%20for%20Policymakers?dl=0&preview=Summary+for+Policymakers+IPBES+Global+Assessment.pdf&subfolder_nav_tracking=1> accessed 5 May 2019.

[161] IPBES, Media Release <https://www.ipbes.net/news/Media-Release-Global-Assessment#_Scale_of_Loss>, accessed 6 May 2019.

urbanization and agricultural expansion in the world. This has come at a high environmental cost, causing degradation and loss of biodiversity.'[162]

A central aspect of terrestrial biodiversity conservation is the sustainable management of forests. The Asia-Pacific region's tropical forests, in particular, are important both for maintenance of biodiversity and with respect to global climate.[163] Indeed, the Southeast Asian sub-region 'hosts the world's third largest expanse of tropical forests after the Amazon and Congo basins, and a treasure of terrestrial biodiversity'.[164] Southeast Asia also has the highest rate of endemism in the world for birds and mammals, and the second highest rate of endemism for vascular plant species. However, it also has one of the highest rates of deforestation.[165] The depletion of forested areas throughout the region for conversion to palm oil plantations has been very significant, with over 50 per cent of forest loss in Indonesia and Malaysia associated with this practice. Other affected countries in Southeast Asia are the Philippines and Thailand.[166] The rate of timber extraction exceeds other tropical regions such as those in Africa and Latin America,[167] and much of the land conversion is illegal.[168] In the Pacific Island region, rainforest logging is also a major concern, especially in the high-island countries of Fiji, Papua New Guinea, Solomon Islands, and Vanuatu.[169]

Although the imperatives of anthropogenic climate change have introduced a range of governance strategies to combat deforestation, including REDD+ (reducing emissions from deforestation and forest degradation),[170] attempts to introduce an international instrument to deal with forest conservation have to date been unsuccessful. The current soft law accord is the UN Forest Instrument, renamed in 2016.[171] The Instrument 'articulates a series of agreed policies and measures at the international and national levels to strengthen forest governance, technical and institutional capacity, policy and legal frameworks, forest sector investment and stakeholder participation'.[172]

[162] IPBES, *The Regional Assessment Report on Biodiversity and Ecosystem Services for Asia and the Pacific* (2018) xii <https://www.ipbes.net/assessment-reports/asia-pacific>.

[163] Asia Pacific Forests and Forestry to 2020, 'Forest Policy Brief 01: Forests for a Greener Future' <http://www.fao.org/fileadmin/templates/rap/files/NRE/Forestry_Group/1_Forests_for_a_greener_future.pdf> accessed 4 December 2018; FAO, 'State of the World's Forests 2016: Forests and Agriculture: Land-Use Challenges and Opportunities' (2016) <http://www.fao.org/3/a-i5588e.pdf> accessed 22 January 2018.

[164] Frances Seymour and Peter Kanowski, 'Forests and Biodiversity' in Hirsch (ed) (n 28) 159.

[165] Ibid. 160–2.

[166] Varsha Vijay et al, 'The Impacts of Oil Palm on Recent Deforestation and Biodiversity Loss' (2016) 11(7) PLOS ONE 1, 2.

[167] ASEAN Secretariat, 'Fifth ASEAN State of the Environment Report' (2017) 82.

[168] Ibid. 88.

[169] See for example 'Sustainable Management of Tropical Forests in the Pacific ACP States', July–August 2002 *The Courier ACP-EU* <http://ec.europa.eu/development/body/publications/courier/courier193/en/en_030.pdf> accessed 22 January 2018.

[170] Seymour and Kanowski (n 164) 169–73.

[171] UNGA resolution 70/199 (22 December 2015): 'United Nations Forest Instrument'. Previously this scheme was named the Non-Legally Binding Instrument on All Types of Forests 2007.

[172] Ibid.

However, for the foreseeable future, without a more specific approach, accompanied by legal teeth, the Instrument will remain largely ineffective.

One aspect of the conservation of biological diversity that has not attracted as much attention as other environmental issues at an international level is that of land degradation. However, there is now a much wider understanding that land and its basic element, the soil, are by their nature fundamental aspects of terrestrial biodiversity. With some 33 per cent of the world's arable land being lost to soil erosion or pollution in the last forty years,[173] and with increasing knowledge of the effect that soil erosion and land pollution have on people and the rest of the environment, there is now greater awareness of the need for stronger law and policy relating to land degradation. The links to food and water security and the human right to food are also being realised.[174]

The degradation of land and soil has also become a more important topic because of their relationship to climate change. Soil areas are the second-largest reservoir of carbon after the world's oceans. They have an important function as natural carbon sinks, as well as in terms of the release of carbon to the atmosphere. Because of unsustainable agriculture and grazing practices, land degradation is becoming a significant factor in global[175] and regional climate change policy.[176] Most of the world's regions suffer from land degradation,[177] and land degradation in the Asia-Pacific has also increased in significance in recent decades.

The causes include soil erosion, salinization, desertification, deforestation, forest fires, overcultivation, inefficient irrigation practices, overgrazing, overexploitation of resources, and uncontrolled mining activities.[178]

Most states do not have adequate legislation to address the broad range of processes involved in land degradation. A number of global initiatives have been important in establishing international rules which, when transposed to the national level, can be directed towards the control and prevention of land degradation. The most prominent of the multilateral instruments relating to land degradation control areas is the United Nations Convention to Combat Desertification in Countries Experiencing Serious Drought and/or Desertification, Particularly in Africa.[179] However, the Convention is

[173] D. Cameron, C. Osborne, C. Horton, and M. Sinclair, 'A Sustainable Model for Intensive Agriculture', Grantham Centre Briefing Note (December 2015) 2 <https://www.manitobacooperator.ca/news-opinion/news/developing-a-sustainable-model-for-intensive-agriculture/> accessed 5 May 2019.

[174] See Ben Boer, Harald Ginsky, and Irene L Heuser, 'International Soil Protection Law: History, Concepts, and Latest Developments' in Ginsky et al (eds), *International Yearbook of Soil Law and Policy* (Springer 2017) 49, 57.

[175] Charlotte Streck and Agustina Gay, 'The Role of Soils in International Climate Change Policy' in Harald Ginsky et al (eds), *International Yearbook of Soil Law and Policy 2016* (Springer 2017) 105.

[176] J. Verschuuren, 'Towards an EU Regulatory Framework for Climate-Smart Agriculture: The Example of Soil Carbon Sequestration' (2018) 1 Transnational Environmental Law at doi:10.1017/S2047102517000395.

[177] See generally, Secretariat of the United Nations Convention to Combat Desertification, *Global Land Outlook* (UNCCD 2017).

[178] UN Environment, *GEO-6: Global Environment Outlook: Regional Assessment for Africa* (2016) <https://www.unenvironment.org/resources/report/geo-6-global-environment-outlook-regional-assessment-africa> 45, and UN Environment, GEO-6 Regional Assessment for Asia and the Pacific (n 16) 66–67.

[179] United Nations Convention to Combat Desertification (UNCCD) 33 ILM 1328 (1994).

geographically limited to arid, semi-arid and dry sub-humid regions of the world. The Convention contains regional annexes for Africa, Asia, Latin America and the Caribbean, the northern Mediterranean, and central and eastern Europe. The annexes specify how the Convention is to be implemented for each region and provides for regional and sub-regional action programmes. However, as with many environmental issues, most of the protection and conservation activities must be taken at the national level.[180] Calls for an international instrument addressing land degradation in general, not just for desertification, have been made since the early 2000s. Progress on developing such a regime continues to be slow.[181]

One of the key mechanisms for the conservation of biodiversity *in situ* is the establishment of protected areas at national level. This is directly promoted by article 8(a) of the Convention on Biological Diversity,[182] the listing of wetlands under the Ramsar Convention,[183] and, less directly, by the natural heritage listings under the World Heritage Convention.[184] While there has been a substantial improvement in the number and coverage of terrestrial and marine protected areas in the Asia-Pacific,[185] many problems remain with regard to their sustainable management.[186]

The question of migratory species, as part of the conservation of biological diversity and catered for by the Convention on Migratory Species of Wild Animals (CMS),[187] is also of importance in each of the sub-regions. Countries across the Asia-Pacific are signatories of Memoranda of Understanding (MOUs) under the CMS, depending on whether they are range states of particular animal species. The MOUs reflect an integrated ecosystem approach to species management, regardless of political boundaries. For example, there are MOUs on marine species relevant to states across the Asia-Pacific, including sharks,[188] cetaceans,[189] dugongs,[190] and turtles.[191]

[180] UN, 'The role of regions under the UNCCD' <https://www.unccd.int/convention/regions>.

[181] Ben Boer and Ian Hannam, 'Developing a Global Soil Regime' (2015) *International Journal of Rural Law and Policy*, Special Edition 1 'Soil Governance'; see also Ben Boer and Ian Hannam, 'Land Degradation' in Emma Lees and Jorge E. Viñuales (eds), *The Oxford Handbook of Comparative Environmental Law* (OUP 2019) 438.

[182] Convention on Biological Diversity (n 54).

[183] Convention on Wetlands of International Importance Especially as Waterfowl Habitat (adopted 2 February 1971, entered into force 21 December 1975, 996 UNTS 245).

[184] Convention for the Protection of the World Cultural and Natural Heritage (adopted 16 November 1972, entered into force 17 December 1975, 1037 UNTS 151).

[185] UN Environment (n 16) 124. [186] Ibid. 125.

[187] Convention on Migratory Species of Wild Animals (adopted 23 June 1979, entered into force 1 November 1983, 1651 UNTS 333). The majority of states in the Asia Pacific are not parties to the Convention.

[188] UNEP/CMS Secretariat, 'MOU on the Conservation of Migratory Sharks: Signatories and Range States' <http://www.cms.int/en/legalinstrument/sharks-mou> accessed 1 February 2018.

[189] UNEP/CMS Secretariat, 'MOU for the Conservation of Cetaceans and their Habitats in the Pacific Islands Regions: Signatories and Range States' <http://www.cms.int/en/legalinstrument/pacific-islands-cetaceans> accessed 1 February 2018.

[190] UNEP/CMA Secretariat, 'MOU Dugong Signatories and Range States' <http://cms.int/dugong/en/signatories-range-states> accessed 1 February 2018.

[191] UNEP/CMS Secretariat, 'Convention on Migratory Species Memoranda of Understanding' <http://www.cms.int/en/cms-instruments/mou> accessed 31 January 2018.

The trafficking of wildlife continues to be a major threat to the conservation of biodiversity worldwide, and illicit trade in endangered species of fauna and flora is a particularly serious issue in the Asia-Pacific. There continues to be a market demand for rare animals[192] for the exotic pet trade and for animal parts (primarily for use in 'traditional' medicine)—sourced especially from Indonesia, Malaysia, and Myanmar—which is leading to the depletion of species diversity. The Convention on International Trade in Endangered Species (CITES)[193] is thus of special relevance in the region. While many Asia-Pacific countries are signatories to CITES, GEO-6 identifies 'ineffective control of international demand and illegal trade' as being a continuing and significant threat, and urges that the prevention of habitat loss should be addressed by maintenance of forest cover and preserving protected natural areas.[194] Asian markets for illegally traded animals and animal parts are being investigated and monitored across the region by a number of bodies.[195]

4.4 Marine and Coastal Environment

With regard to the management of the marine environment, the UN Environment's Regional Seas Programme now operates in eighteen of the world's regions. In the Asia-Pacific, the programmes include the East Asian Seas, Pacific, South Asian Seas, and Southeast Pacific Seas.[196] The global programme has a focus on the implementation of the SDGs.[197]

The Asia-Pacific hosts many long coastlines and contains a range of archipelagic states. Its marine and coastal environments are thus of great significance for fishing and aquaculture for the whole of the region. Protecting these marine and coastal areas is

[192] Worldwide Fund for Nature, 'Facts about the Exotic Pet Trade' <http://www.animalplanet.com/tv-shows/fatal-attractions/lists/facts-exotic-pet-trade/> accessed 5 May 2019.

[193] Convention on International Trade in Endangered Species (adopted 3 March 1973, entered into force 1 July 1975, 995 UNTS 243). Most Asian States are members, while more than half of the Pacific Island states are not.

[194] UN Environment (n 16) 125.

[195] For example, UNODC-CITES Asia Wildlife Enforcement and Demand Management Project <https://www.unodc.org/brussels/en/unodc-cites-asia-wildlife-enforcement-and-demand-management-project.html> accessed 5 May 2018.

[196] Only the East Asian Regional Seas Programme is directly administered by UN Environment; the others are administered by their regional organizations: UN Environment, 'Why Does Working with Regional Seas Matter?' <http://www.unenvironment.org/explore-topics/oceans-seas/what-we-do/working-regional-seas/why-does-working-regional-seas-matter> accessed 14 February 2018; see also Marsden (n 15) 215.

[197] UN Environment, 'Moving to Strategy and Action: Regional Seas Outlook for the implementation of the Sustainable Development Goals' (2017) Regional Seas Reports and Studies No 200 <https://www.unenvironment.org/resources/report/moving-strategy-and-action-regional-seas-outlook-implementation-sustainable> accessed 13 February 2018.

central to adequate nutrition and addressing food insecurity.[198] Seafood provides a protein source for a significant proportion of Asia-Pacific peoples.[199] Adequate environmental management of marine and coastal areas is also important for transport connectivity and tourism as a part of promoting economic development and conserving national and local cultural and natural heritage.

Global concern for illegal, unreported, and unregulated fishing is also of relevance to coastal states in the Asia-Pacific region, and has resulted in specific legal and policy responses. Despite the various agreements, a good deal of illegal, unreported, and unregulated (IUU) fishing[200] is carried out in the Asia-Pacific[201] and around the world, with losses estimated at some USD $150 million per year.[202] In the Pacific sub-region,[203] the extensive Exclusive Economic Zones declared under UNCLOS 1982[204] provide income from fishing agreements with distant water fishing nations. This exploitation is managed through fishing agreements controlled under the Pacific Islands Forum Fisheries Agency.[205] For example, in 2005 a specific sub-regional agreement was negotiated for skip jack tuna, along with a sub-regional agreement setting out the terms and conditions for tuna purse-seine fishing licences.[206] As a result of extensive research the very significant extent of IUU fishing is beginning to be understood.[207]

[198] FAO estimates that the number of undernourished people, in terms of dietary energy supply, was 486.1 million in the Asia-Pacific region: FAO, *Asia and the Pacific Regional Overview of Food Security and Nutrition 2018—Accelerating progress towards the SDGs* (Bangkok, 2018).

[199] The percentages of populations that depend on seafood for protein range from 37% in Cambodia to 2% in India: Steve Needham and Simon Funge-Smith, 'The Consumption of Fish and Fish Products in the Asia Pacific Region Based on Household Surveys' (2015) 12 FAO RAP Publication 87ff.

[200] Food and Agriculture Organization, 'Illegal, Unreported and Unregulated Fishing' (2016) <http://www.fao.org/3/a-i6069e.pdf> accessed 9 July 2018.

[201] Perpetrators in South East Asia are alleged to be vessels from China, Thailand, and Vietnam; see Peter Chalk, 'Illegal Fishing in Southeast Asia: A Multibillion-Dollar Trade with Catastrophic Consequences' (*The Strategist*, 17 July 2017) <http://www.aspistrategist.org.au/illegal-fishing-southeast-asia-multibillion-dollar-trade-catastrophic-consequences/> accessed 9 July 2018.

[202] Pacific Islands Forum Fisheries Agency, 'Annual Report 2016–2017' (2017) 4.

[203] For example, the Convention for the Prohibition of Fishing with Long Driftnets in the South Pacific (n 127).

[204] UN Convention on the Law of the Sea (UNCLOS) (adopted 10 December 1982, entered into force 16 November 1994, 1833 UNTS 397) Part V.

[205] The Forum Fisheries Agency is based in Honiara, Solomon Islands: Pacific Islands Forum Fisheries Agency <http://www.ffa.int/> accessed 20 December 2017.

[206] Members are: Federated States of Micronesia, Kiribati, Marshall Islands, Nauru, Palau, Papua New Guinea, Solomon Islands, and Tuvalu. See: A Third Arrangement Implementing the Nauru Agreement setting forth Additional Terms and Conditions of Access to the Fisheries Zones of the Parties (adopted 16 May 2008, entered into force 15 June 2008).

[207] See MRAG Asia Pacific, 'Towards the Quantification of Illegal, Unreported and Unregulated (IUU) Fishing in the Pacific Islands Region' (2016) <http://www.ffa.int/files/FFA%20Quantifying%20IUU%20Report%20-%20Final.pdf> accessed 31 January 2018.

Further, the 1986 moratorium on commercial whaling[208] continues to cause tensions with respect to the concept of so-called 'scientific whaling',[209] especially in the Southern Ocean, resulting in significant adverse findings in the International Court of Justice against Japan concerning the breach of its international obligations under the International Whaling Convention in implementing its whaling program.[210]

Over recent years, the South China Sea dispute has also caused a good deal of angst in the region, particularly concerning environmental damage and interference with fishing activities from land reclamation and airstrip development on ecologically sensitive reefs. This culminated in an arbitral proceeding under UNCLOS[211] brought by the Philippines against China in the Permanent Court of Arbitration.[212] The Arbitral Tribunal found that 'there is no legal basis for any Chinese historic rights, or other sovereign rights and jurisdiction beyond those provided for in the Convention' in the waters of the South China Sea claimed by China, within what it referred to as the 'nine-dash line'.[213]

Marine pollution is also a continuing concern in the Asia-Pacific, with high levels of marine and coastal pollution from both land and vessel sources.[214] Land-based sources of pollution contribute to some 70 per cent of all marine pollution.[215] This is a particularly severe problem in parts of the Asia-Pacific due to: the rapid expansion of many coastal communities as a result of industrial developments; agricultural run-off; the coastal ship-breaking industry in some South Asian and East Asian countries; and new tourism developments.[216] The effect on particularly sensitive marine environments, such as reefs, is severe across the Asia-Pacific.

One of the major contemporary challenges is that of plastics pollution, with an estimated 8 million tonnes of plastic being disposed of globally in the ocean every year.[217] In 2016, the UN Environment Assembly passed a resolution concerning marine

[208] International Whaling Commission, 'Commercial Whaling' <https://iwc.int/commercial> accessed 31 January 2018.

[209] International Convention for the Regulation of Whaling (adopted 2 December 1946, entered into force 10 November 1948, 161 UNTS 361) art. VIII.

[210] *Whaling in the Antarctic (Australia v Japan: New Zealand Intervening)* (Judgment) [2014] ICJ Reports 226.

[211] UNCLOS (n 204).

[212] *Republic of the Philippines v People's Republic of China* (South China Sea Arbitration Award of 12 July 2016) Permanent Court of Arbitration Case No. 2013–19 <https://pca-cpa.org/en/cases/7/> accessed 5 May 2019. For discussion on the environmental and fishing issues see Tim Stephens, 'The Collateral Damage from China's "Great Wall of Sand": The Environmental Dimensions of the South China Sea Case' (2017) 34 Australian Yearbook of International Law 41.

[213] *Republic of the Philippines v People's Republic of China*, ibid. para. 692.

[214] For Southeast Asia see Peter Todd, Xueyuan Ong, and LM Chou, 'Impacts of Pollution on Marine Life in Southeast Asia' (2010) 19 Biodiversity and Conservation 1063; and generally on marine environmental protection, see Donald Rothwell and Tim Stephens, *The International Law of the Sea* (2nd edn Hart 2015) ch 15.

[215] Rothwell and Stephens, ibid. 529; see also UN Conference on Environment and Development, *Agenda 21: Programme of Action for Sustainable Development* (UN 1993) ch 17 para 18.

[216] Gaudioso C. Sosmena, 'Marine Health Hazards in South-East Asia' (1994) 18 Marine Policy 175; GEO-6.

[217] See UN Environment, 'UN Declares War on Ocean Plastic' <http://web.unep.org/unepmap/un-declares-war-ocean-plastic> 4 December 2018.

plastic litter and microplastics. It stressed prevention and minimization strategies and environmentally sound waste-management systems as well as clean-up actions.[218] UN Environment subsequently prepared a report on the phasing-out of single-use plastics.[219] In addition, the Conference of the Parties to the Basel Convention has also focused on marine plastic litter and microplastics in its work programme for 2018–19.[220] A discussion has begun on the need for a new international instrument on plastics pollution, but no definite proposals have been put forward to date.[221]

In the Asia-Pacific, research indicates that over half of the plastic material comes from five countries: China, Indonesia, the Philippines, Thailand, and Vietnam.[222] ASEAN has joined the movement against plastic pollution, with various of the sub-region's countries taking specific legal measures to combat it.[223]

4.5 Regional Human Rights Law and Environmental Concerns

The question of environmental rights has attracted considerable attention around the world in recent years. The research carried out by the UN Special Rapporteur on Human Rights and the Environment, first appointed in 2011,[224] has been central to increasing this focus. In early 2018, the Special Rapporteur released a set of sixteen framework principles focusing on the main human rights obligations of states relating

[218] The UN Environment Assembly recognizes that 'the presence of plastic litter and microplastics in the marine environment is a rapidly increasing serious issue of global concern that needs an urgent global response taking into account a product life-cycle approach, and acknowledging that the levels and sources of marine plastic litter and microplastics, and the resources available to tackle the issue, can vary between regions, and that measures need to be taken and adapted as appropriate to local, national and regional situations': UN Environment Assembly, '2/11 Marine Plastic Litter and Microplastics' (2016) <http://wedocs.unep.org/handle/20.500.11822/11186?show=full> accessed 2 August 2018.

[219] UN Environment, 'Single-Use Plastics: A Roadmap For Sustainability' (2018) <https://www.unenvironment.org/resources/report/single-use-plastics-roadmap-sustainability> accessed 2 August 2018.

[220] See <http://www.basel.int/Implementation/MarinePlasticLitterandMicroplastics/Overview/tabid/6068/Default.aspx> accessed 4 December 2018 (under the Basel Convention on the Control of Transboundary Movements of Hazardous Wastes and Their Disposal (adopted 22 March 1989, entered into force 5 May 1992, 1673 UNTS 57).

[221] Giulia Carlini and Konstantin Kleine, 'Advancing the International Regulation of Plastic Pollution Beyond the United Nations Environment Assembly Resolution on Marine Litter and Microplastics' (2018) 27(3) RECIEL 234–44.

[222] Ocean Conservancy and McKinsey Center for Business and Environment, 'Stemming the Tide: Land-Based Strategies for a Plastic-Free Ocean' (2015) <https://oceanconservancy.org/wp-content/uploads/2017/04/full-report-stemming-the.pdf> accessed 14 October 2018; see also Beatriz Garcia, Mandy Fang and Jolene Lin 'Marine Plastic Pollution in Asia: All Hands on Deck!' Chinese Journal of Environmental Law 3 (2019) 7.

[223] ASEAN Secretariat, 'ASEAN Joins Movement to Beat Plastic Pollution' (ASEAN, 2 July 2018) <http://asean.org/asean-joins-movement-beat-plastic-pollution/> accessed 2 August 2018.

[224] UN Office of the High Commissioner on Human Rights (OHCHR), 'Special Rapporteur on Human Rights and Environment' <http://www.ohchr.org/en/Issues/environment/SRenvironment/Pages/SRenvironmentIndex.aspx> accessed 1 August 2018.

to the enjoyment of a safe, clean, healthy, and sustainable environment.[225] In his final report, he recommended that the human right to a healthy environment be recognised in a global instrument. In March 2018, the UN Human Rights Council resolved to continue the mandate of the Special Rapporteur for another three years.[226] In a separate development, the UN General Assembly agreed, on the basis of an initiative by the French Club des Juristes, to set up a working group to discuss further steps towards the adoption of a 'Global Pact for the Environment'.[227] Part of the deliberations on the proposed pact resulted in a report from the UN Secretary General entitled 'Gaps in International Environmental Law and Environment-Related Instruments: Towards a Global Pact for the Environment'. The report explores gaps in the international regulatory regimes on: protection of the atmosphere; the conservation of biological diversity; the protection of soils, freshwater resources, and oceans and seas; and hazardous substances, wastes and activities. It also discusses gaps in environment-related instruments concerning trade, investment, intellectual property, and human rights.The governance structure, implementation, and effectiveness of international environmental law was also canvassed. The proposed Pact is seen as 'a logical next step in the evolution of global environmental governance. The adoption of an overarching statement of principles is consistent with the practice in many other areas of international law'.[228]

The trend towards recognizing environmental rights has been manifested in a variety of ways across the Asia-Pacific. Many individual nations have included various formulations of environmental rights in their national constitutions.[229] Of the Asia-Pacific

[225] OHCHR, 'Framework Principles on Human Rights and the Environment', UN Doc A/HRC/37/59 (2018) <http://www.ohchr.org/EN/Issues/Environment/SREnvironment/Pages/FrameworkPrinciplesReport.aspx> accessed 14 October 2018.

[226] HRC resolution 37/8, 'Human Rights and the Environment' (22 March 2018) <https://documents-dds-ny.un.org/doc/UNDOC/GEN/G18/099/17/pdf/G1809917.pdf?OpenElement> accessed 5 May 2019; see further John Knox, 'The United Nations Mandate on Human Rights and the Environment' (2018) 2 Chinese Journal of Environmental Law 83.

[227] UNGA resolution 72/277 (10 May 2018): 'Towards a Global Pact for the Environment'. See also IUCN, 'Global Pact for the Environment' <https://www.iucn.org/commissions/world-commission-environmental-law/our-work/global-pact-environment> accessed 1 August 2018.

[228] See further, Yann Aguila and Jorge E Viñuales, 'A Global Pact for the Environment: Conceptual Foundations' (2019) 28 RECIEL 3–12; Christina Voigt, 'How a "Global Pact for the Environment" Could Add Value to International Environmental Law' (2019) 28 RECIEL 13–24; Duncan French and Louis J. Kotzé, 'Towards a Global Pact for the Environment: International Environmental Law's Factual, Technical and (Unmentionable) Normative Gaps' (2019) RECIEL 28:25–32; John H Knox, 'The Global Pact for the Environment: At the Crossroads of Human Rights and the Environment' (2019) 28 RECIEL 40–7; and Ben Boer, 'Environmental Principles and the Right to a Quality Environment' in Ludwig Krämer and Emanuela Orlando (eds), *Principles of Environmental Law* (Edward Elgar 2018) 52–76.

[229] Ben Boer, 'Environmental Law and Human Rights in the Asia Pacific' in Ben Boer (ed), *Environmental Law Dimensions of Human Rights* (Oxford University Press 2015) 166–71. For a global list of national constitutions that include some form of environmental rights, see James May and Erin Daly, *Environmental Constitutionalism* (Cambridge University Press 2016) 281–92; see also Erin Daly et al (eds), *New Frontiers in Environmental Constitutionalism* (UN Environment 2017); David Boyd, *The Environmental Rights Revolution: A Global Study of Constitutions, Human Rights and the Environment* (UBC Press 2012) 164, 299.

sub-regions, Southeast Asia is the only one to have its own human rights instrument, the 2012 ASEAN Human Rights Declaration.[230] While the Declaration conforms for the most part to the international standards laid down by the 1948 Human Rights Declaration[231] and the 1966 Covenants,[232] implementation of the instrument remains at a low level. The chief reason for this is that the Declaration lacks appropriate provisions on implementation and enforcement.[233] Nevertheless, it contains a provision on environment-related rights, as well as a specific environmental right. Article 28(a) to (e) includes rights to an adequate standard of living, adequate and affordable food, freedom from hunger, access to safe and nutritious food, adequate and affordable housing, and safe drinking water and sanitation, and article 28(f) directly recognizes the right to a safe, clean, and sustainable environment. The environmental provision of the Declaration is consistent with the UN's increasing focus on the right to a quality environment,[234] discussed above.

Finally, with regard to environmental rights, the UN Declaration on the Rights of Indigenous Peoples 2007,[235] adopted by a number of Asia-Pacific states,[236] recognizes that 'respect for indigenous knowledge, cultures and traditional practices contributes to sustainable and equitable development and proper management of the environment',[237] and that 'Indigenous peoples have the right to the conservation and protection of the environment and the productive capacity of their lands or territories and resources'.[238]

With the increasing awareness of the links between human rights and environmental degradation, these developments are likely to have various repercussions in the Asia-Pacific sub-regions, adding to the possibility of negotiations taking place for further regional human rights instruments with an environmental component at sub-regional level.[239]

5 Conclusion

The development and implementation of international and regional environmental law in the Asia-Pacific region varies considerably from one sub-region to another, with

230 ASEAN Human Rights Declaration (adopted 18 November 2012); see also Boer (ed), *Environmental Law Dimensions of Human Rights*, ibid. 138.

231 UNGA resolution 3/217 (1948): 'Universal Declaration of Human Rights' para 71.

232 International Covenant on Economic, Social and Cultural Rights (adopted 16 December 1966, entered into force 3 January 1976, 993 UNTS 3); International Covenant on Civil and Political Rights (adopted 16 December 1966, entered in force 23 March 1976, 999 UNTS 171).

233 Catherine Renshaw, 'The ASEAN Human Rights Declaration 2012' (2013) 13 Human Rights Law Review 3, 557.

234 See also Boer 'Environmental principles and the right to a quality environment' (n 228) 60.

235 UNGA resolution 61/295 (2007): 'United Nations Declaration on the Rights of Indigenous Peoples'.

236 With some abstentions. 237 Ibid. preamble. 238 Ibid. art. 29.

239 For example, in the Pacific Island region, where the possibility of a regional human rights instrument has been discussed for some years; see Boer, 'Environmental Law and Human Rights in the Asia Pacific' (n 229) 156.

wide disparities between the sub-regions concerning the implementation of international environmental treaties and, where they exist, the regional environmental instruments. These variations are due to the differing economic circumstances, political histories, cultural attitudes, and lingering colonial influences within each regional grouping. The many differences between sub-regions and within sub-regions reflect the fragmentation of legal and policy approaches, with the result that environmental law and policy regimes across the Asia-Pacific remain largely incomplete. However, there has been a stronger tendency in the past twenty years to develop more integrated and consistent legal frameworks for environmental management at sub-regional levels.

Among the key findings and policy messages of UN Environment's GEO-2016 for the Asia-Pacific is the need to strengthen environmental governance 'for effective policy diffusion at multiple scales'.[240] It argues that the mandates, operational arrangements, and capacity of national institutions 'need to be assessed and revitalized so that they are able to effectively discharge their current responsibilities, and in the future, respond to increased demand from SDGs which call for governments to take strong and decisive environmental actions'.[241] The question is how best to effect such transitions.

One aspect of this question is the increased focus on environmental law education in universities, with some countries having made the study of environmental law compulsory throughout the jurisdiction.[242] In addition, 'training-the-trainer' programmes such as those conducted by IUCN Academy of Environmental Law in conjunction with the Asian Development Bank are a significant indicator of the higher level of importance being placed on environmental education by law schools.[243] Greater attention is also being given to the development of specialist courts[244] and the training of specialist judges in the realm of environmental law in a number of countries.[245] In this context, it is also important to note that courts across the region are incorporating various international environmental law principles within their judgments.[246] Another development is the establishment of the Global Judicial Institute on the Environment,

[240] UN Environment (n 16) xix. [241] Ibid.

[242] For example, China, Indonesia, and India.

[243] Rob Fowler, 'The Role of the IUCN Academy of Environmental Law in Promoting the Teaching of Environmental Law' (2017) 8 IUCN Academy of Environmental Law eJournal 32 <https://www.iucnael.org/en/e-journal/previous-issues/86-journal/issue/640-issue-2017#> accessed 5 May 2019.

[244] For example, specialist courts have been established in China, Thailand, and Malaysia and a system of certification of specialist judges has been introduced in Indonesia; see generally George Pring and Catherine Pring, *Environmental Courts & Tribunals: A Guide for Policy Makers* (UN Environment Programme 2016) 1 <http://wedocs.unep.org/bitstream/handle/20.500.11822/10001/environmental-courts-tribunals.pdf?sequence=1&isAllowed=y>.

[245] See Asian Judges Network on Environment and Asian Development Bank <https://www.ajne.org/about/asian-judges-network-environment> accessed 5 May 2019.

[246] Some brief examples include: India: *Vellore Citizens Welfare Forum v Union of India* AIR1996 SC 2715 (adoption of the precautionary principle as part of national law); Pakistan: *Shehla Zia v WAPDA* PLD 1994 SC 6 (right to a healthy environment, application of precautionary principle); *Maple Leaf Cement Factory Ltd v Environmental Protection Agency* [Lahore High Court] Case No. 115949/2017 (application of the principle 'in dubio pro natura'—if in doubt, decide for nature).

which draws members from around the world, with strong representation from the Asia-Pacific.[247]

There is no doubt that the Asia-Pacific region will continue to be a dynamic one in relation to the further development and implementation of both international and regional environmental law regimes. With increasing attention being given to the enhancement of regional environmental management programmes, the national environmental law regimes should continue to be strengthened. However, across the Asia-Pacific, a great deal more work needs to be done to ensure that the global and regional environmental policy settings, including the SDGs, are adequately implemented, so that the myriad serious environmental problems facing the region are more expeditiously addressed through the medium of environmental law at international, regional, sub-regional, and national levels.

This conclusion is reinforced by the *Asia and the Pacific SDG Progress Report 2019* (ESCAP, Bangkok, 2019), which states 'On its current trajectory, Asia and the Pacific will not achieve any of the 17 SDGs by 2030. To live up to the ambition of the 2030 Agenda, accelerated progress is required on all fronts.[248]

[247] IUCN, 'World Commission on Environmental law: Global Judicial Institute on the Environment' <http://www.iucn.org/commissions/world-commission-environmental-law/our-work/global-judicial-institute-environment> accessed 5 May 2019.

[248] *Asia and the Pacific SDG Progress Report 2019* (ESCAP, Bangkok, 2019). IX (https://www.unescap.org/publications/asia-and-pacific-sdg-progress-report-2019> accessed 1 July 2019.

CHAPTER 9

LAW OF THE SEA AND ASIAN STATES

ROBERT BECKMAN

1 Introduction

The modern law of the sea is set out in the United Nations Convention on the Law of the Sea 1982, as modified by the Agreement relating to the Implementation of the Convention 1994 (UNCLOS).[1] UNCLOS establishes a legal order for all use of the oceans, has been universally accepted, and has been described as a 'constitution' for the oceans. This chapter focuses on how Asian states have contributed to, participated in, and implemented the UNCLOS regime. The term Asian states is used rather loosely, but includes states in South Asia, Southeast Asia, Northeast Asia, and the Western Pacific.

This chapter focuses on Asia's active participation in the law of the sea in four ways. First, it explains the role played by Asian states in the negotiations leading to UNCLOS, and their continued participation in UNCLOS institutions. It also explains that some provisions in UNCLOS are direct responses to concerns of Asian states or to issues raised by the particular geography of Asia. Second, it describes how Asian states have generally accepted UNCLOS and followed its provisions in making claims to maritime zones and in resolving their maritime boundaries. Third, it discusses how Asian states have been involved in developing the dispute settlement regime set out in UNCLOS, both in cases instituted by them and in cases brought against them. Fourth, it briefly examines how Asian states have responded to certain challenges with regard to uses of the oceans, including threats to maritime security, illegal fishing activities, and protection of the marine environment.

[1] For the historical background, status, and text of UNCLOS, see <http://www.un.org/Depts/los/convention_agreements/convention_overview_convention.htm> accessed 4 December 2018.

2 The Law of the Sea before UNCLOS

Like most areas of international law, the law of the sea developed gradually through the practice of states, giving rise to principles of customary international law such as the principle of freedom of navigation on the high seas, the principle that ships on the high seas are subject to the exclusive jurisdiction of the flag state, and the right of innocent passage through the territorial sea.

After its establishment in 1945, the United Nations saw the need to develop a rules-based order for the oceans. As soon as it was established in 1949, the International Law Commission began to examine the topic. It issued a report in 1956, which served as the basis for negotiations at the 1958 United Nations Conference on the Law of the Sea. The 1958 Conference was attended by eighty-six states. It was one of the first conferences at which the number of developing countries was significant. The result of the 1958 Conference was the adoption of the four 1958 Geneva Conventions on the Law of the Sea, as well as an optional protocol on the settlement of disputes.

On 13 December 1957, before the 1958 Conference began, Indonesia declared a territorial sea of 12 nautical miles (nm) and set the stage for its claim to sovereignty over its archipelagic waters, that is, the waters separating the islands within its archipelago. Indonesia was among the states at the Conference who advocated a 12 nm territorial sea. In addition, Indonesia and the Philippines proposed that the Conference recognize that states like theirs which were comprised of archipelagos be permitted to draw straight baselines around their islands and claim sovereignty over the waters inside those baselines.

The naval and maritime powers opposed both the 12 nm territorial sea and the proposal for archipelagic waters because they feared that that the freedom of their navies to navigate through and fly over important sea lanes in Southeast Asia would be impeded.

The 1958 Conference reached agreement on the basic principles governing the high seas, territorial sea, and continental shelf. However, the Conference rejected the proposal to recognize the concept of archipelagic waters. Additionally, the delegations at the 1958 Conference were not able to reach agreement on the breadth of the territorial sea or on the breadth of a fishing zone.

In 1960, a second UN Conference was convened to try to reach agreement on two outstanding issues—the breadth of the territorial sea and the breadth of a fishing zone. The 1960 Conference failed, and the result was uncertainty with respect to the passage of ships through narrow chokepoints in routes used for navigation, as well as uncertainty with respect to the rights of coastal states to the fisheries resources off their coasts. Following the failure to reach agreement on the breadth of the territorial sea in 1958 and 1960, many Asian states, including China, Malaysia, India, and Mauritius, took steps to claim a 12 nm territorial sea.

The impetus for a third UN Conference on the Law of the Sea was a speech in 1967 by Ambassador Arvid Pardo of Malta in which he proposed that the mineral resources of the deep seabed be declared the 'common heritage of mankind'. The United Nations decided to establish a new conference to address not only the issue of access to the mineral resources of the deep seabed, but all uses of the oceans. Their goal was to reach agreement on a universally accepted convention that would govern all uses of the oceans.

2.1 Negotiations Leading to UNCLOS 1982

The modern law of the sea is a result of the nine years of negotiations at the Third United Nations Conference on the Law of the Sea (Third UN Conference) that led to the adoption of UNCLOS on 10 December 1982.

Asian states fully participated in this major law-making effort. Many were developing countries that had been former colonies, and they were keen to play a role in negotiations to establish a new legal regime to govern access to ocean resources and passage rights in maritime zones. Like states from other regions, Asian states did not adopt regional positions on the major issues being considered at the Third UN Conference negotiations. Instead, delegations established informal negotiating groups comprising members with common interests on important issues. Delegations from Asian states were active and influential in several of the informal negotiating groups:[2]

- Coastal States Group: Fiji, India, and Pakistan;
- Landlocked and Geographically Disadvantaged States Group: Bahrain, Iraq, Nepal, Singapore, and United Arab Emirates;
- Straits States Group: Indonesia, Malaysia, and the Philippines; and
- Archipelagic States Group: Fiji, Indonesia, and the Philippines.

In addition, several diplomats and lawyers from Asian states played key roles in negotiating the Convention. The first President of the Third Conference was Ambassador Hamilton Shirley Amerasinghe of Sri Lanka, who served from 1973 until his death in 1980. He was succeeded as president by Ambassador Tommy Koh of Singapore, who had been serving as Chairman of the First Committee, which was dealing with the deep seabed regime. The leaders of the Indonesian delegation, Dr Mochtar Kusumaatmadja and Dr Hasjim Djalal, were instrumental in negotiating the new regimes on archipelagic states and straits used for international navigation.

The individual who arguably had the greatest impact on the drafting of UNCLOS was Ambassador Satya Nandan of Fiji. He served as rapporteur of the Second Committee, which dealt with the traditional law of the sea issues. In this role he was the

[2] Tommy Koh and S Jayakumar, 'Negotiating Process of UNCLOS III' in Myron Nordquist (ed), *United Nations Convention on the Law of the Sea: Commentary*, vol 1 (Brill Nijhoff 2013) 29–134.

draftsman of the Second Committee's Single Negotiating Text of the Convention. He also chaired the informal 'Nandan Group' which proposed compromise texts on some of the most contentious and difficult issues. In addition, in his capacity as Under Secretary-General for Legal Affairs of the United Nations, he chaired the informal consultations that negotiated the changes to Part XI on the deep seabed mining that were adopted in the 1994 Implementation Agreement.

2.2 Ratification of 1982 UNCLOS by Asian States

UNCLOS was opened for signature at Montego Bay, Jamaica on 10 December 1982. Fiji deposited its instrument of ratification on the same day, and became the first state to ratify the Convention. UNCLOS did not enter into force until 16 November 1994, which was one year after the deposit of the sixtieth instrument of ratification or accession. The only other Asian states to ratify UNCLOS prior to 1994 were the Philippines, Indonesia, Micronesia, and the Marshall Islands. Most of the Asian states ratified the Convention between 1994 and 1998, shortly after it entered into force. By the end of 1998 there were 129 parties to the Convention.[3]

As of December 2017, there are 168 parties to the Convention, including the vast majority of the Asian states.[4] All of the coastal states in Asia are parties except Cambodia, DPR Korea, Iran, and Syria. Of the landlocked states in Asia, two—Laos and Nepal—are parties. The following seven are not parties: Afghanistan, Bhutan, Kazakhstan, Kyrgyzstan, Tajikistan, Turkmenistan, and Uzbekistan. Given that all of the major coastal states in Asia are parties, it can be concluded that UNCLOS has been generally accepted in Asia, as it has been in the rest of the world.

2.3 Participation in UNCLOS Institutions

The International Tribunal for the Law of the Sea (ITLOS) was created by the Convention and is located in Hamburg. The first election of twenty-one judges took place in 1996. Judges are elected for a term of nine years. The Convention provides that there shall be no fewer than three members from each major UN regional group. The Asian group has five judges on the Tribunal. China, India, Japan, and Republic of Korea have each had a judge on the Tribunal since it was established in 1996.[5] The fifth

[3] For the text and current status of UNCLOS, including a chronological list of states depositing instruments of ratification or accession, see: <http://www.un.org/Depts/los/convention_agreements/convention_overview_convention.htm> accessed 4 December 2018.

[4] Multilateral Treaties Deposited with the Secretary-General, Chapter XXI <https://treaties.un.org/pages/ParticipationStatus.aspx> accessed 4 December 2018.

[5] From China, Judge Gao Zhiguo (since 2008) succeeded Xu Guangjian (2001–07) and Zhao Lihai (1996–2000). From India, Judge Neeru Chandra (since 2017) succeeded Chandrsekhara Rao (1996–2017).

Asian seat was held by Lebanon until a judge from Thailand was elected in 2017.[6] Three Asian judges have been elected to serve as the President of ITLOS. Judge P Chandrasekhara Rao of India served as president from 1996 to 1999, Judge Shunji Yanai of Japan served as president from 2011 to 2014, and Judge Jin-Hyun Paik from the Republic of Korea will serve as president from 2018 to 2020.[7]

The International Seabed Authority (ISA) was established to regulate the exploration and exploitation of the mineral resources on the deep seabed beyond the limits of national jurisdiction (the Area). Its main decision-making body is the Council, which consists of thirty-six members. In its formula to achieve an equitable geographic distribution, Asia has been allocated nine places on the Council. The composition of the Council from 2015 to 2020 includes the following states from Asia: China, Japan, India, Republic of Korea, Australia, Indonesia, Bangladesh, Fiji, and Tonga.[8]

The Commission on the Limits of the Continental Shelf (CLCS) was established to review claims to states to an extended continental shelf, beyond the 200 nm limit of the Exclusive Economic Zone (EEZ). It consists of twenty-one members who are elected by the states from among the state parties, having due regard to ensure an equitable geographic distribution. The following five states from Asia have members on the CLCS from 2017 to 2020: China, Japan, Republic of Korea, Malaysia, and Oman.[9]

The International Maritime Organization (IMO) was established long before UNCLOS to establish conventions, practices, and procedures to regulate merchant shipping. The IMO plays an important role in the law of the sea because it is the institution that is referred to in numerous provisions of UNCLOS by the phrase 'competent international organization'. Asian states play a major role in the IMO. Kitack Lim of the Republic of Korea began a four year term as the IMO Secretary-General on 1 January 2016. His predecessor was Koji Sekimuzi of Japan. The following ten Asian states are members of the forty-person IMO Council, the executive organ of the IMO, for the 2016–17 biennium: Australia, China, Japan, Republic of Korea, India, Indonesia, Malaysia, Philippines, Singapore, and Thailand.[10]

From Japan, Judge Shunji Yanai (since 2005) succeeded Soji Yamamoto (1996–2005). From Korea, Judge Paik Jin-Hyun (since 2009) succeeded Park Choon-Ho (1996–2008).

[6] In 2017 Judge Kriangsak Kittichaisaree of Thailand was elected to the seat held by Joseph Akl of Lebanon from 1996 to 2017.

[7] For information on ITLOS, see <http://www.itlos.org/en/the-tribunal/> accessed 4 December 2018.

[8] For information on members of the ISA Council, see <https://www.isa.org.jm/files/documents/EN/Council/Council1996-2020.pdf> accessed 12 December 2018.

[9] For information on the CLCS and its members, see <http://www.un.org/Depts/los/clcs_new/clcs_home.htm> accessed 4 December 2018.

[10] For information on the IMO, see <http://www.imo.org/en/About/Pages/Default.aspx> accessed 4 December 2018.

3 Asian States and Claims to Maritime Zones

One of the major achievements of UNCLOS was the establishment of a clear demarcation of rights and jurisdiction in the oceans. Some of the issues most pertinent to Asia are discussed below.

3.1 Historic Waters

A claim that certain waters are 'historic waters' subject to the sovereignty of the coastal state is a claim based on customary international law, not UNCLOS. Generally speaking, a state must demonstrate that it has exercised open, effective, long-term, and continuous authority over the waters, and that other states have acquiesced to that claim. Several states in the Asia-Pacific have claims to historic waters, including Australia, Cambodia, China, India, Sri Lanka, and Thailand. The United States (US) has protested all of the above claims.[11] Vietnam had claimed historic waters in the Gulf of Tonkin, but it no longer seems to make this claim. Its 2012 legislation on the law of the sea makes no reference to historic waters.

India and Sri Lanka have claims to the sea between the mainland of India and the island of Sri Lanka, consisting of Palk Strait, Palk Bay, and the Gulf of Manaar. These waters are known for their beds of pearl oysters and chank (mollusc) fisheries. Both states claim that these waters have been their historic waters since time immemorial. Both states issued official proclamations to that effect in 1977. India and Sri Lanka have delimited their maritime boundary in this area through three separate agreements between 1974 and 1977.[12]

3.2 Baselines

All maritime zones must be measures from baselines drawn along land or insular territory. The normal baseline is the low-water line along the coast. There are two major exceptions in UNCLOS permitting states to employ the use of straight baselines.

The first exception is in article 7 on straight baselines. It permits coastal states with deeply indented coastlines or a fringe of islands along their coast to employ the method of straight baselines, subject to certain conditions. Several Asian states have drawn straight baselines in circumstances that are arguably contrary to the conditions set out

[11] Ashley Roach and Robert Smith, *Excessive Maritime Claims* (3rd edn Martinus Nijhoff Publishers 2012) 35–54.

[12] RB Anand, *Studies in International Law and History: An Asian Perspective* (Springer 2004) 237–8.

in article 7. The US has officially protested the use of straight baselines in a manner that is not consistent with the provisions in UNCLOS. It has challenged the use of straight baselines by the following Asian states: Cambodia, China, Japan, Myanmar, Republic of Korea, Thailand, and Vietnam. The US has also objected to the straight-baseline claims of Taiwan.

The second exception is in article 47 on archipelagic baselines. It permits archipelagic states (states constituted wholly by one or more archipelagos) to draw straight baselines joining the outermost islands and drying reefs of the archipelago, with certain restrictions. States employing the use of archipelagic baselines are required to publicize their baselines by either indicating them on charts or providing to the UN a list of geographic coordinates. The archipelagic states in Asia that employ the use of archipelagic straight baselines include Fiji, Indonesia, Kiribati, the Philippines, the Maldives, Papua New Guinea, Solomon Islands, Tuvalu, and Vanuatu.[13] China has employed the use of straight baselines around the Paracel Islands in the South China Sea as well as around the Senkaku/Diaoyu Islands in the East China Sea,[14] despite the fact that there is no provision in UNCLOS permitting them to do so. The US has protested in both cases.[15]

One paragraph in UNCLOS was drafted to address concerns raised by Bangladesh that the normal baseline rule of a low-water line along the coast could not be applied to the highly unstable coast of Bangladesh. As a result, paragraph 2 of article 7 of UNCLOS was designed specifically to address, at least to some extent, the concerns raised by Bangladesh at the Conference.[16] The uncertainty concerning its baselines made it extremely difficult for Bangladesh to reach agreement through negotiation on its maritime boundary in the Bay of Bengal with either India or Myanmar. Its maritime boundaries were finally resolved many years later after Bangladesh instituted compulsory dispute settlement procedures against both Myanmar and India.

3.3 Territorial Sea Regime

The sovereignty of a coastal state extends to a belt of sea adjacent to the coast known as the territorial sea. The rules governing the territorial sea had been set out in the Convention on the Territorial Sea and the Contiguous Zone 1958.[17] However, no

[13] Kevin Baumert and Brian Melchior, 'The Practice of Archipelagic States: A Study of Studies' (2015) 46 Ocean Development and International Law 60.

[14] MZN 89 2012, LOS of 21 September 2012, available at <http://www.un.org/Depts/los/LEGISLATIONANDTREATIES/STATEFILES/CHN.htm> accessed 4 December 2018.

[15] The most recent US Diplomatic Note on China's claims in the South China Sea is published in the *Digest of United States Practice in International Law* (2016) <http://www.state.gov/documents/organization/272098.pdf> accessed 4 December 2018.

[16] Myron Nordquist (ed), *United Nations Convention on the Law of the Sea 1982: A Commentary*, vol II (Brill Nijhoff 1993) 101.

[17] Convention on the Territorial Sea and the Contiguous Zone (adopted 29 April 1958, entered into force 19 June 1964).

agreement could be reached in 1958 on the breadth of the territorial sea. The maritime and naval powers wanted to limit the breadth to three nautical miles so that there would be a belt of high seas through the chokepoints in major shipping lanes, such as the Straits of Malacca and Singapore. Many coastal states insisted on 12 nm, and some even proposed 200 nm. The result was a stalemate, with no consensus and widely divergent State practice.

The negotiations leading to UNCLOS on the breadth of the territorial sea were linked to the demand of archipelagic states, led by Indonesia, the Philippines, and Fiji, that the international community recognize the sovereignty of archipelagic states over the waters inside their archipelago. This was a challenge to the naval and maritime powers because several major shipping lanes pass through large archipelagic states such as Indonesia.

The negotiations at the Third UN Conference to resolve these issues focused on what passage regimes should govern passage through the Straits of Malacca and Singapore and passage through the Indonesian archipelago. The result of the negotiations was agreement that the maximum breadth of the territorial sea would be 12 nm, and that new passage regimes would be established for straits used for international navigation and archipelagic states, which will be discussed further below.

Almost all Asian states now claim a 12 nm territorial sea. Jordan still claims a territorial sea of 3 nm and Iran claims a territorial sea of 6 nm.[18] Japan and Korea claim a 12 nm territorial sea generally. However, Japan has retained a 3 nm territorial sea in the waters bordering five international straits, and the Republic of Korea has retained a territorial sea of 3 nm in the waters bordering the Korea Strait. This leaves a corridor of sea in the straits that is subject to freedom of navigation rather than to the regime of transit passage through a strait used for international navigation.

The practice of Asian states with regard to passage in the territorial sea has generally been consistent with the provisions in Part II of UNCLOS on the territorial sea.[19] However, there is some divergent practice on the right of innocent passage of warships and ships carrying highly radioactive nuclear materials. The issue with respect to warships is whether coastal states have the right to require notice or authorization for such passage. This issue was the subject of a highly contentious debate at the Third UN Conference.[20] The major naval powers take the position that neither requirement is consistent with UNCLOS. The legislation of India and Vietnam requires such ships to give prior notification for the passage of warships (although the 2012 Law of the Sea of Vietnam seems to have withdrawn that claim[21]). The following Asian states require authorization for the passage of warships: Bangladesh, China, India, Iran, Maldives,

[18] Roach and Smith (n 11) 136–8. The 3 nm territorial sea of Japan borders the following straits: Soya (LaPerouse), Tsugaru, Osumi, and the Eastern and Western Channels of the Tsushima Strait.

[19] Roach and Smith (n 11) 136–48. [20] Ibid. 239–43.

[21] *Digest of United States Practice in International Law 2013* (2014) 371 <http://www.state.gov/s/l/2013/index.htm> accessed 4 December 2018.

Myanmar, Pakistan, Philippines, Sri Lanka, and Syria. The US has made official protests to any State that requires prior notice or authorization.[22]

With respect to the passage of ships carrying highly radioactive nuclear materials, the major powers have maintained that they have a right of innocent passage so long as they carry the documents and meet the requirement of the IMO and International Atomic Energy Agency as provided in article 23 of UNCLOS. Some Asian states have expressed concern about the passage of such vessels in their territorial sea. For example, when it ratified UNCLOS, Malaysia made a unilateral declaration concerning the passage of nuclear-powered vessels or vessels carrying nuclear material.[23] Bangladesh was more specific in its unilateral declaration, and stated that it was of the view that such vessels had to have prior authorization.[24]

3.4 The Regime of Straits Used for International Navigation

The new regime on straits used for international navigation was designed to address the failure at the first and second UN conferences on the law of the sea in 1958 and 1960 to agree on the breadth of the territorial sea. The two superpowers maintained that it should be 3 nm because this would guarantee that in most choke points on international shipping routes there would be a belt of high seas where all states had the freedoms of navigation and overflight. This would enable them to move their aircraft carriers through international straits with air cover above and submarine cover below. Coastal states maintained that the breadth of the territorial sea should be at least 12 nm, which would bring most of the choke points on international shipping lanes under the sovereignty of coastal states, subject to the right of innocent passage.

The compromise at the Third UNCLOS was reached in negotiations between the US and the leading members of the Straits States Group, Indonesia, Malaysia, and Fiji. The straits that were foremost in the minds of the negotiators during the negotiations were the Straits of Malacca and Singapore. Given its dependence on international trade, Singapore's interests were aligned with those of the two superpowers and major maritime states like Japan.

The compromise was to recognize a 12 nm territorial sea, but to create a new regime for straits used for international navigation that struck the balance more in favour of navigation rights than rights of protection of coastal states. The regime of transit passage through straits used for international navigation differs from innocent passage in four ways: (1) it includes overflight as well as navigation; (2) submarines may

[22] Roach and Smith (n 11) 243–51.

[23] Malaysia Declaration of 14 October 1996. The text of all declarations to UNCLOS and all objections to declarations is available on the website of UN Treaty Collection, Multilateral Treaties Deposited with the Secretary-General (n 4). For a summary and the view of the US, see Roach and Smith (n 11) 254–8.

[24] Bangladesh declaration of 14 December 2009 in UN Treaty Collection, Multilateral Treaties Deposited with the Secretary-General (n 4).

navigate submerged; (3) it can never be suspended; and (4) the rights of coastal states to regulate ships exercising transit passage is severely restricted.

The three states bordering the Straits of Malacca and Singapore—Indonesia, Malaysia, and Singapore—have been cooperating since the Third UN Conference in the 1970s to manage navigational safety and ship-source pollution in the Straits of Malacca and Singapore.

There are no straits used for international navigation in South Asia, but if one defines the Asia-Pacific to extend to Iran, then the regime would apply to the Strait of Hormuz at the entrance to the Persian Gulf. The Strait of Hormuz is bordered by Iran and Oman.[25]

The position of the US Government is that the regime of transit passage also applies to two of the Kuril Straits between Japan the Russian Federation. The status of these straits is complicated by the fact that they border islands occupied by the Russian Federation but also claimed by Japan.[26] It is also the position of the US Government that the Torres Strait between the Cape York Peninsula of Australia and Papua New Guinea is a strait used for international navigation subject to the right of transit passage.[27]

3.5 Archipelagic States Regime

Both Indonesia and the Philippines were instrumental in the development of the archipelagic regime set out in Part IV of UNCLOS. The Philippines consists of approximately 7,100 islands dispersed over a large expanse of water with a coastline length of about 18,000 kilometres.[28] Indonesia consists of 18,108 islands which are also scattered over a wide expanse of sea. Both wanted their archipelagos to be treated as a single unit, the territorial sea of which should be drawn between the outermost islands, and the waters inside these baselines as internal waters. Indonesia in particular carried out an intensive diplomatic campaign in the lead-up to the Third UN Conference on the Law of the Sea to garner support for the archipelagic regime. Thus, Part IV provides a definition of an archipelagic state, and allows such states to draw archipelagic (straight) baselines connecting the outermost islands, enclosing the inter-connecting waters in which a special regime of archipelagic waters would apply. The sovereignty of archipelagic states is recognized over their archipelagic waters, but all ships have a right of innocent passage through the archipelago, and all ships and aircraft have a right of 'archipelagic sea lanes passage' on designated sea lanes or on routes normally used for international navigation.

[25] Roach and Smith (n 11) 293–6. [26] Ibid. 296–7. [27] Ibid. 336–42.

[28] Mary Ann Palma, 'The Philippines as an Archipelagic and Maritime Nation: Interests, Challenges and Perspectives' (2009) RSIS Working Paper No 182 <http://www.rsis.edu.sg/wp-content/uploads/rsis-pubs/WP182.pdf> accessed 4 December 2018.

During the negotiations at the Third Conference some states proposed that continental states with offshore archipelagos should also be permitted to draw straight baselines around the islands in their mid-ocean archipelagos. India was one of the states supporting this proposal because it has more than 1,000 islands and islets, including the Andaman and Nicobar archipelagos at the northern entrance of the Malacca Strait. However, the proposal was not accepted; it was decided to limit the regime to archipelagic states.[29]

Indonesia has implemented the archipelagic regime more or less consistently with UNCLOS. It published its archipelagic baselines in 2002, and then amended them in 2008 to bring them into conformity with the provisions on archipelagic baselines in article 47 of UNCLOS.[30]

Indonesia has also taken measures to establish archipelagic sea lanes through its archipelagic waters, as is called for in article 53 of UNCLOS. After entering into informal consultations with interested states such as Australia and the US, Indonesia proposed the adoption of three north–south sea lanes to the IMO as provided in article 53. The IMO Maritime Safety Committee adopted the partial system of archipelagic sea lanes in Indonesian archipelagic waters by resolution MSC 72(69) of 19 May 1998. As a result of the procedure followed in Indonesia's archipelago, in 1999 the Maritime Safety Committee of the IMO approved guidance for ships transiting archipelagic waters of archipelagic states.[31]

The Philippines strongly advocated the concept of archipelagic waters and archipelagic baselines during the negotiations leading to the adoption of UNCLOS, which it ratified in 1984. However, for many years its national laws remained inconsistent with the UNCLOS provisions on archipelagic waters and archipelagic baselines. Finally, in 2009 it passed an Archipelagic Baselines Act and brought its national legislation into conformity with the provisions in Part IV of UNCLOS.[32] The Philippines has not designated any archipelagic sea lanes in its archipelagic waters. However, an Archipelagic Sea Lanes Act was introduced in the Philippine Senate in July 2016.[33] A similar bill

[29] Nordquist (ed) (n 16) 401–3.

[30] The List of Geographical Coordinates of Points of the Indonesian Archipelagic Baselines based on Government Regulation of the Republic of Indonesia No 38 of 2002, as amended by the Government Regulation of the Republic of Indonesia No 37 of 2008, is available from the UN Division for Ocean Affairs and the Law of the Sea (DOALOS) (2009) Law of the Sea Bulletin No 69, 81–104 <http://www.un.org/Depts/los/LEGISLATIONANDTREATIES/PDFFILES/DEPOSIT/idn_mzn67_2009.pdf> accessed 4 December 2018. An illustrative map is available at: <http://www.un.org/Depts/los/LEGISLATIONANDTREATIES/PDFFILES/MAPS/idn_mzn67_2009.jpg> accessed 4 December 2018.

[31] IMO SN/Circ.206 of 8 January 1999 and Corr 1 of 1 March 1999.

[32] Republic Act No 9522, An Act to Define the Archipelagic Baselines of the Philippines, in DOALOS (2009) Law of the Sea Bulletin No 70, 32–5 <http://www.un.org/Depts/los/doalos_publications/LOSBulletins/bulletinpdf/bulletin70e.pdf> accessed 4 December 2018.

[33] Philippines Archipelagic Sea Lanes Act 2016 (PHL) <http://www.senate.gov.ph/lis/bill_res.aspx?congress=17&q=SBN-92> accessed 4 December 2018.

was introduced in the House of Representatives in 2015[34] to authorize the designation of archipelagic sea lanes. Both are currently pending.

The Maldives is the only archipelagic state in the Indian Ocean. The following states in the Pacific have archipelagic claims: Fiji, Kirabati, Marshall Islands, Papua New Guinea, Solomon Islands, Tuvalu, and Vanuatu.[35] A recent study by two lawyers from the US Department of State concluded that although the interpretation and application of the provisions in UNCLOS on archipelagic claims can be challenging for the archipelagic states, there appears to be a consensus that the rules governing the maritime claims of archipelagic states are those set out in UNCLOS. The authors maintained, however, that the baseline systems employed by the Maldives and Papua New Guinea do not meet the criteria established for archipelagic baselines in UNCLOS.[36]

The provisions in UNCLOS on archipelagic states contain one article that was designed to address a particular geographic peculiarity in Southeast Asia. The peculiarity is that the archipelagic waters of Indonesia around the Natuna Islands in the southern part of the South China Sea lie between east and west Malaysia. West of the Natuna Islands is the State of Johor in peninsular Malaysia, and east of the Natuna Islands is the State of Sarawak on the island of Borneo in East Malaysia. Article 47(6) of UNCLOS was drafted to deal with this circumstance, and it reads as follows:

> If a part of the archipelagic waters of an archipelagic State lies between two parts of an immediately adjacent neighbouring State, existing rights and all other legitimate interests which the latter State has traditionally exercised in such waters and all rights stipulated by agreement between those states shall continue and be respected.

Malaysia and Indonesia entered into a bilateral treaty in 1982 to give effect to this provision. The treaty sets out the rights of Malaysia in the territorial sea and archipelagic waters of Indonesia lying between East Malaysia and West Malaysia, as well as in the airspace above the territorial sea, archipelagic waters, and territory of Indonesia.[37]

Although article 47(6) only applied to this specific area when it was drafted, it is now applicable in one other area within the Indonesian archipelago. Timor-Leste became independent in 2002. Its territory consists of the eastern half of the island of Timor, as well as the Oecusse enclave in the western half of the island, which is part of Indonesia. Therefore, since the land territory of Timor-Leste is separated by the archipelagic waters of Indonesia, this provision also applies to Timor-Leste.

[34] Xianne Archangel, 'House Bill Seeks to Establish Archipelagic Sea Lanes' (*GMA News*, 1 April 2015) <http://www.gmanetwork.com/news/news/nation/462998/house-bill-seeks-to-establish-archipelagic-sea-lanes/story/> accessed 4 December 2018.

[35] Baumert and Melchior (n 13). [36] Ibid. 65.

[37] The text of the Treaty is available at UN Office for Ocean Affairs and the Law of the Sea, *The Law of the Sea: Practice of Archipelagic states* (UN 1992) 144–55.

3.6 Contiguous Zone

The contiguous zone is a 12 nm belt of seas between 12 and 24 nm in which the coastal state can exercise the control necessary to its customs, fiscal, immigration, and sanitary legislation. Many Asian states including Indonesia, Malaysia, the Philippines, and Singapore, have not claimed a contiguous zone.

One issue that has arisen is whether it is permissible under UNCLOS for a coastal state to extend its rights in the contiguous zone beyond the four categories listed in article 33. It was proposed at the Third Conference that coastal states be permitted to enforce laws to protect their national security interests in the contiguous zone, but this proposal was rejected. Nevertheless, the following Asian states have legislation providing that they can protect their security interests in their contiguous zone: Bangladesh, Cambodia, China, India, Iran, Pakistan, Sri Lanka, and Syria.[38]

3.7 Exclusive Economic Zone Regime

The EEZ was one of the innovations of UNCLOS. At the Third UN Conference negotiations a consensus was reached by the mid-1970s on giving coastal states expanded rights and jurisdiction in an EEZ extending to 200 nm from its baselines. Most states in the Asia-Pacific claimed an EEZ soon after the consensus was reached in the negotiations; they did not wait until the Convention was adopted in 1982.

The practice of most Asian states with respect to the EEZ has generally been consistent with the provisions in UNCLOS. However, some Asian states have extended other national laws and regulations to place restrictions on activities in their EEZ which may exceed the jurisdiction of coastal states as set out in UNCLOS or which may infringe the rights of other states that are set out in article 58 of UNCLOS. The controversial areas concern regulation of three types of activities by foreign vessels.

First, controversy continues on whether foreign ships and aircraft may carry out certain military activities in the EEZ of other states without giving prior notice or seeking prior authorization. Several Asian states made unilateral declarations when signing or ratifying UNCLOS stating that, in their view, certain military activities may not be conducted in their EEZ without the consent of the coastal state. Most of these declarations are limited to the conduct of military exercises or manoeuvres, especially those involving the use of weapons or explosives. The following Asian states have made unilateral declarations stating that, in their view, military activities involving the live firing of weapons may not be carried out without the consent of the coastal state: Bangladesh, India, Malaysia, and Pakistan. The US and some of its allies have protested these restrictions on the ground that they are contrary to the provisions in UNCLOS.[39]

[38] Roach and Smith (n 11) 154–7.

[39] Roach and Smith (n 11) 383–91. For the text of the declarations to UNCLOS see the website of UN Treaty Collection, Multilateral Treaties Deposited with the Secretary-General (n 4).

Thailand's declaration states that the enjoyment of the freedom of navigation excludes military exercise or other activities which may affect the 'rights or interests' of the coastal state. This declaration is very broad and arguably inconsistent with UNCLOS because it suggests that activities inconsistent with the 'interests' of the coastal state may not be carried out without its consent. Article 58 of UNCLOS provides that when exercising freedoms of the high seas in the EEZ of another State, due regard must be given to the 'rights and duties' of the coastal state.

Second, another controversy is the extent to which coastal states have the right under UNCLOS to regulate the laying and repair of submarine cables. Under articles 58 and 79 of UNCLOS, all states have the right to lay submarine cables and pipelines in the EEZ or on the continental shelf of other states. Coastal states may take measures to prevent pollution from pipelines in their EEZ or on their continental shelf, but not cables. Similarly, the delineation of the course of a pipeline on the continental shelf or in the EEZ of the coastal state is subject to the consent of the coastal state, but not the delineation of the course of a cable. For example, article 22 of Malaysia's Exclusive Economic Zone Act states that the delineation of the course of both pipelines and cables is subject to the consent of the coastal state, and that the Malaysian Government can impose conditions on the laying of both cables and pipelines to prevent pollution of the marine environment.[40]

Third, China has raised a controversy by appearing to claim that its nationals have 'historic rights' to exploit the natural resources anywhere within its nine-dash line in the South China Sea, even in areas that are the EEZ of other states. The Tribunal in the South China Sea Arbitration considered this issue, and made the following decision in 2016:

> DECLARES that, as between the Philippines and China, China's claims to historic rights, or other sovereign rights or jurisdiction, with respect to the maritime areas of the South China Sea encompassed by the relevant part of the 'nine-dash line' are contrary to the Convention and without lawful effect to the extent that they exceed the geographic and substantive limits of China's maritime entitlements under the Convention; and further DECLARES that the Convention superseded any historic rights, or other sovereign rights or jurisdiction, in excess of the limits imposed therein.[41]

3.8 Continental Shelf Regime

The 1946 Truman Proclamation made the US the first state to claim the exclusive right to exploit the non-living resources of the continental shelf adjacent to its coast. Many other coastal states followed and the doctrine was accepted in the 1958 Convention on

[40] Exclusive Economic Zone Act 1984, Act No 311 (Malaysia); Roach and Smith (n 11) 461.

[41] *The South China Sea Arbitration (Republic of Philippines v People's Republic of China)*, PCA Case No. 2013–19, Award of 12 July 2016 para 1203(B)(2).

the Continental Shelf. Most Asia-Pacific states that were able to claim a continental shelf did so by the mid-1970s.[42]

The continental shelf regime existed before UNCLOS, but what was not clear until UNCLOS was the breadth of the continental shelf. UNCLOS clarified the definition by providing that coastal states have sovereign rights to explore and exploit the resources of the continental shelf, to a minimum of 200 nm. In certain cases, dependent on whether they meet certain criteria, states may extend their continental shelf claim beyond 200 nm to the outer edge of the continental margin.

Under UNCLOS states claiming a continental shelf beyond 200 nm were required to submit information to the Commission on the Limits of the Continental Shelf that was established under the Convention. Parties to UNCLOS agreed that states intending to make a submission to the CLCS were required to do so by 13 May 2009. However, states that were not able to submit all of the required information were permitted to make a 'partial submission' or to submit 'preliminary information'.[43]

The first Asian states to make submissions to the CLCS were Australia and New Zealand, the two states in the region that are able to claim the largest extended continental shelf. Individual submissions have also been made by: Bangladesh, China, Cook Islands, Fiji, India, Indonesia, Japan, Kiribati, Maldives, Micronesia, Myanmar, Pakistan, Palau, Philippines, Republic of Korea, Sri Lanka, Tonga, and Vietnam. Also, there have been three cases of Asian states making joint submissions: (1) Federated States of Micronesia, Papua New Guinea, and Solomon Islands; (2) Malaysia and Vietnam in the South China Sea; and (3) Tuvalu, France, and New Zealand.[44]

In addition, the following Asian states have submitted 'preliminary information' to the CLCS indicating that they intend to submit a claim at a later date: Brunei Darussalam, China, Fiji, Mauritius, Federated States of Micronesia, New Zealand, Papua New Guinea, Republic of Korea, Solomon Islands, Togo, and Vanuatu. Finally, preliminary information has been submitted jointly by Fiji and Solomon Islands as well as by Fiji, Solomon Islands, and Vanuatu.[45]

3.9 The Area

'The Area' refers to the seabed and subsoil beyond the limits of national jurisdiction, that is, beyond the outer limit of the continental shelf of coastal states. The International

[42] Robin Churchill and Vaughan Lowe, *The Law of the Sea* (2nd edn Manchester University Press 1988) Appendix 1: Claims to Maritime Zones.

[43] See Issues with Respect to Article 4 of Annex II of the Convention: <http://www.un.org/Depts/los/clcs_new/issues_ten_years.htm> accessed 4 December 2018.

[44] See submissions to the CLCS: <http://www.un.org/Depts/los/clcs_new/commission_submissions.htm> accessed 4 December 2018.

[45] See submissions to the CLCS: <http://www.un.org/Depts/los/clcs_new/commission_preliminary.htm> accessed 4 December 2018.

Seabed Authority in Jamaica administers deep sea mining in the Area under Part XI of UNCLOS and the 1994 Implementation Agreement. The ISA has entered into 15-year contracts with twenty-seven contractors for exploration for polymetallic nodules, polymetallic sulphides, and cobalt-rich ferromanganese crusts in the Area. China, India, Japan, Republic of Korea, and Singapore have entered into contracts either directly or as sponsoring states. In addition, the following smaller Asian states have entered into contracts with the ISA as sponsoring states: Cook Islands, Kiribati, Nauru, and Tonga.[46]

4 Asian States and Maritime Claims from Offshore Features

One of the most challenging issues that Asian states have faced in the implementation of UNCLOS is that of maritime claims based on offshore features. Under UNCLOS the only offshore features that are subject to a sovereignty claim are islands as defined in article 121(1), that is, naturally formed areas of land surrounded by and above water at high tide. Islands are normally entitled to the same maritime zones as other land territory, but article 121(3) contains an exception. It provides that 'rocks which cannot sustain human habitation or economic life of their own shall have no exclusive economic life or continental shelf'. In other words, 'rocks' are a subset of 'islands' that are only entitled to a territorial sea and contiguous zone.

Article 121(3) has been a source of controversy in the South China Sea. In 2007, Malaysia, the Philippines, and Vietnam made submissions to the CLCS claiming an extended continental shelf in the South China Sea beyond the outer limit of their 200 nm EEZ.[47] Their claims to a 200 nm EEZ were measured only from the baselines along their mainland coast or main archipelago. They did not claim an EEZ from any of the islands in the Spratly Islands over which they claim sovereignty. This suggests that their position was that all of the islands in the Spratly Islands were rocks within article 121(3) that were not entitled to an EEZ of their own. This issue was considered in the Arbitral Award in the *South China Sea Arbitration* between the Philippines and China.[48] The unanimous decision of the Tribunal was that none of the islands in the

[46] For information on the contracts entered into by the ISA, see <http://www.isa.org.jm/deep-seabed-minerals-contractors> accessed 4 December 2018.

[47] 'Commission on the Limits of the Continental Shelf (CLCS), Outer Limits of the Continental Shelf beyond 200 Nautical Miles from the Baselines: Submissions to the Commission: Joint submission by Malaysia and the Socialist Republic of Viet Nam' (UN Office of Legal Affairs) <http://www.un.org/Depts/los/clcs_new/submissions_files/submission_mysvnm_33_2009.htm> 4 December 2018.

[48] *The South China Sea Arbitration (Republic of Philippines v People's Republic of China)*, PCA Case No. 2013–19, Award on Jurisdiction and Admissibility, 29 October 2015; *The South China Sea Arbitration (Republic of Philippines v People's Republic of China)*, PCA Case No. 2013–19, Award of 12 July 2016.

Spratly Islands were 'islands' entitled to an EEZ and continental shelf of their own.[49] The Tribunal also ruled that several of the features in the Spratly Islands are low-tide elevations that are not subject to a separate claim of sovereignty.

A controversy over rocks and islands has also arisen in East Asia with regard to a claim by Japan to an EEZ and extended continental shelf from the tiny island of Okinotorishima. Both the Republic of Korea and China have formally objected to Japan's EEZ and continental shelf claims from the island on the ground that the island is a rock that is not entitled to an EEZ or continental shelf of its own.[50]

Another potential legal issue is the fact that one of the island groups in the South China Sea over which China claims sovereignty is Macclesfield Bank.[51] Macclesfield Bank is a completely submerged reef. Therefore, it is part of the seabed, and is not subject to a claim of sovereignty.[52]

5 Asian States and Maritime Boundaries

Prior to agreement at the Third UN Conference to give coastal states the right to establish a 200 nm EEZ, maritime boundary agreements focused on the territorial sea and continental shelf. Once UNCLOS provided for a 200 nm EEZ the negotiation of maritime boundary agreements became important for both fisheries resources and hydrocarbon resources.

Article 15 of UNCLOS on the delimitation of overlapping territorial sea claims was not controversial. However, the provision in paragraph 1 of articles 74 and 83, setting out the rule on how to delimit the maritime boundary in the event of overlapping EEZ or continental shelf claims, was one of the most contentious articles in the negotiations leading to UNCLOS, and it was one of the last to be agreed upon at the Third Conference. Paragraph 3 of these articles anticipates that it will often be difficult for states to reach a final maritime boundary agreement. Therefore, it calls for states in areas of overlapping claims to make every effort to enter into provisional arrangements of a practical nature, pending a final agreement. It further calls upon them during this

[49] PCA Award of 12 July 2016, ibid., para 1203(B)(7).

[50] Reaction of States to the submission made by Japan to the Commission on the Limits of the Continental Shelf, Communication of China dated 6 February 2009, and Communication by the Republic of Korea dated 27 February 2009 <http://www.un.org/Depts/los/clcs_new/submissions_files/submission_jpn.htm> accessed 4 December 2018.

[51] 'Statement of the Government of the People's Republic of China on China's Territorial Sovereignty and Maritime Rights and Interests in the South China Sea' (Ministry of Foreign Affairs of the People's Republic of China, 7 December 2016) <http://www.fmprc.gov.cn/mfa_eng/zxxx_662805/t1379493.shtml> accessed 4 December 2018. Macclesfield Bank is Zhongsha in Chinese.

[52] The US is the only State that has officially protested China's claim of sovereignty over Macclesfield Bank. See US Diplomatic Note 2016 (n 15).

interim period not to take any unilateral actions that would jeopardize or hamper the reaching of a final agreement. Not surprisingly, these provisions have been the subject of litigation under the UNCLOS dispute settlement regime.

States in Northeast Asia have been unable to agree on maritime boundaries because of the complex history of their political relations and the existence of sensitive disputes on sovereignty over offshore islands.[53] There have been provisional arrangements with respect to fisheries zones, including one between Japan and Taiwan.[54] Provisional arrangements on hydrocarbon resources have also been negotiated between Japan and the Republic of Korea, and between Japan and China.[55]

The one major obstacle to delimiting the maritime boundaries in Southeast Asia has been the sovereignty disputes over the islands in the South China Sea, especially the disputes over the Paracel Islands and the Spratly Islands. Nevertheless, states in Southeast Asia have been very active in resolving their maritime boundaries or entering into provisional arrangements. Indonesia has led the way by negotiating maritime boundary agreements with most of its neighbours. Almost all of the states in Southeast Asia are members of the Association of Southeast Asian Nations (ASEAN), and this may have contributed to them developing a sufficient amount of trust to agree on maritime boundaries with their neighbours. States bordering the Gulf of Thailand have entered into joint development arrangements in several situations where they could not agree on their maritime boundaries.[56]

Indonesia's practice has gone against the trend towards a single EEZ boundary for the water column and the seabed. It negotiated continental shelf boundaries with many of its neighbours in the early 1990s when there was an emphasis on the principle of natural prolongation in relation to the continental shelf. Now that most EEZ boundaries are negotiated based on the equidistance principle, Indonesia has insisted on separate boundary agreements for the water column and the seabed.

The south-west Pacific has been described as a 'sea of tranquillity' compared to Northeast Asia and Southeast Asia because it has the fewest sovereignty disputes and the best political climate. In addition, a significant fact is that there are large distances between the islands and, consequently, clear boundaries are not necessary to resolve issues of access to natural resources. Fisheries issues are being addressed at the regional level and the area is not rich in hydrocarbon resources.[57]

[53] Choon-ho Park, 'Central Pacific and East Asian Boundaries' in Jonathan Charney and Lewis Alexander (eds), *International Maritime Boundaries* vol 1 (Martinus Nijoff 1993) 297–8; Ted McDorman, 'Central Pacific, East Asia, Southeast Asia' in Jonathan Charney and Lewis Alexander (eds), *International Maritime Boundaries*, vol 5 (Martinus Nijoff 2005) 3440–2.

[54] Dustin Kuan-hsiung Wang, 'Taiwan-Japan Fisheries Agreement: Light at the End of a Dark Tunnel' (2016) 1 Asia-Pacific Journal of Ocean Law and Policy 127.

[55] Hui-gwon Pak, *The Law of the Sea and Northeast Asia: A Challenge to Cooperation* (Boston Kluwer Law International 2000).

[56] Tara Davenport, 'Southeast Asian Approaches to Maritime Boundaries' (2014) 4 Asian Journal of International Law 309; Choon-Ho Park (n 53) 298–9; McDorman (n 53) 3442–7.

[57] McDorman (n 53) 300–1.

South Asian and West Asian states bordering the Indian Ocean delimited the majority of their maritime boundaries through negotiations. One major exception was the Bay of Bengal. However, in 2011 Bangladesh invoked the compulsory binding dispute settlement procedures in UNCLOS against both India and Myanmar in order to resolve the boundary disputes. As a result, ITLOS determined the boundary between Bangladesh and Myanmar,[58] and an arbitral tribunal established under Annex VII of UNCLOS determined the boundary between Bangladesh and India.[59]

Australia negotiated a series of agreements on its boundaries in the Timor Sea with Indonesia in the 1970s. When the former colony of East Timor became independent in 2002, the new state of Timor-Leste entered into new agreements with Australia on the joint development of hydrocarbon resources in the Timor Sea. However, in 2016, Timor-Leste invoked the compulsory non-binding conciliation procedures in UNCLOS against Australia. Australia challenged the competence of the conciliation commission and lost. The conciliation proceeded and on 1 September 2017 it was announced that Timor-Leste and Australia had reached agreement on the central elements of a maritime boundary delimitation between them in the Timor Sea.[60]

6 Asian States and Settlement of Disputes on Law of the Sea

One of the features that distinguishes UNCLOS from most international treaties is that parties to the Convention are bound by a system of compulsory and binding dispute settlement. States consent to this dispute settlement regime when they become parties to the Convention.

States can declare which of four judicial or arbitral forums they prefer for the resolution of disputes with other parties on the interpretation or application of the provisions of the Convention. Interestingly, the only Asian states that have made a clear choice in advance are Australia and Fiji. Australia declared that it prefers ITLOS or the International Court of Justice (ICJ), without specifying which has precedence over the other. Fiji declared that it prefers ITLOS.

States are also permitted under article 298 to declare that they do not accept the compulsory binding procedures in Section 2 of Part XV for certain categories of

[58] *Dispute concerning Delimitation of the Maritime Boundary between Bangladesh and Myanmar in the Bay of Bengal (Bangladesh/Myanmar)* ITLOS Case No. 16, Judgment of 14 March 2012.

[59] *The Bay of Bengal Maritime Boundary Arbitration (Bangladesh v India)*, PCA Case No. 2010–16, Award of 7 July 2014.

[60] 'Press Release: Conciliation between the Democratic Republic of Timor-Leste and the Commonwealth of Australia' (Permanent Court of Arbitration, 1 September 2017) <https://www.pcacases.com/web/sendAttach/2303> accessed 4 December 2018.

disputes. These include disputes on the interpretation or application of the provisions on maritime boundary delimitation, disputes on historic bays or titles, dispute on military activities, and disputes on certain law-enforcement activities.

China, the Republic of Korea, and Thailand have declared they do not accept any of the procedures in Section 2 of Part XV for any of the categories listed in article 298. Australia, Palau, and Singapore have declared that they do not accept the compulsory binding procedures for disputes on the interpretation or application of the provisions on maritime boundary delimitation.

States are also permitted, under Annex V on Conciliation and Annex VII on Arbitration, to nominate four persons who could serve as conciliators and four persons who could serve as arbitrators. Although most Asian states are parties to UNCLOS, only eight states have nominated persons to serve as arbitrators or conciliators: Australia (4), Indonesia (4), Japan (3), Mongolia (2), Republic of Korea (1), Singapore (4), Sri Lanka (2), and Thailand (1).

Asian states have unilaterally instituted proceedings against other states in accordance with the compulsory binding procedures in Part XV of UNCLOS in several cases:

- In 1999, Australia and New Zealand instituted proceedings against Japan in the *Southern Bluefin Tuna* cases and requested provisional measures from ITLOS. An arbitral tribunal established under Annex VII then heard the case and ruled that it lacked jurisdiction.[61]
- In 2002, Russia instituted proceedings against Australia before ITLOS for prompt release of *The Volga*.[62]
- In 2003, Malaysia instituted proceedings against Singapore in the *Case Concerning Land Reclamation by Singapore in and around the Straits of Johor*, alleging that Singapore's land reclamation activities breached its obligations under UNCLOS to protect and preserve the marine environment. Malaysia's request for provisional measures was heard by ITLOS, pending the constitution of an arbitral tribunal under Annex VII. The two states settled the case as a result of the provisional measures ordered by ITLOS.[63]

[61] *Southern Bluefin Tuna (New Zealand v Japan; Australia v Japan)*, ITLOS Case Nos 3 and 4, Provisional Measures Order of 27 August 1999; *Southern Bluefin Tuna (New Zealand v Japan; Australia v Japan)*, Award on Jurisdiction and Admissibility, 4 August 2000 (2002), XXIII RIAA 1–57.

[62] *The 'Volga' (Russian Federation v Australia)*, ITLOS Case No. 11, Prompt Release Judgment of 23 December 2002.

[63] *Case concerning Land Reclamation by Singapore in and around the Straits of Johor (Malaysia v Singapore)*, ITLOS Case No. 12, Provisional Measures Order, 8 October 2003; *Land Reclamation by Singapore in and around the Straits of Johor (Malaysia v Singapore)*, Decision of 1 September 2005 (2008) XXVII RIAA 133–45.

- In 2007, Japan commenced proceedings against the Russian Federation before ITLOS on the prompt release of its fishing vessels, in the *Tomimaru* and *Hoshinmaru* cases.[64]
- In 2009, Bangladesh instituted proceedings against Myanmar on its maritime boundary dispute in the Bay of Bengal. The case would have been heard by an arbitral tribunal under Annex VII, but after proceedings were instituted the two states agreed to refer the case to ITLOS.[65]
- In 2009, Bangladesh also instituted proceedings against India on its maritime boundary dispute in the Bay of Bengal. The case was decided by an arbitral tribunal established under Annex VII.[66]
- In 2010, Mauritius instituted proceedings against the United Kingdom alleging that the UK had breached its obligations in UNCLOS to protect and preserve the marine environment and with regard to the management of fisheries resources. It was heard by an arbitral tribunal established under Annex VII.[67]
- In 2014, the Philippines instituted compulsory proceedings against China in the *South China Sea Arbitration.* China refused to participate in the case, but it proceeded to be heard by an arbitral tribunal under Annex VII in accordance with the provisions in UNCLOS.[68]

Proceedings have also been instituted against Asian states under the dispute settlement procedures in UNCLOS. In 2015 Italy commenced proceedings against India in a dispute regarding the exercise of criminal jurisdiction by India in the 'Enrica Lexie' incident, in which two Italian marines, who had killed two Indian fishermen, were arrested by India on board an Italian tanker. Italy requested provisional measures from ITLOS pending constitution of an arbitral tribunal under Annex VII.[69]

In 2016 Timor Leste invoked the compulsory non-binding conciliation procedures against Australia in their maritime boundary dispute. Australia's declaration under article 298 precluded Timor-Leste from instituting compulsory binding procedures

[64] *The 'Tomimaru' (Japan v Russian Federation)*, ITLOS Case No. 15, Prompt Release Judgment of 6 August 2007; *The 'Hoshinmaru' (Japan v Russian Federation)*, ITLOS Case No. 14, Prompt Release Judgment of 6 August 2007.

[65] *Dispute concerning Delimitation of the Maritime Boundary between Bangladesh and Myanmar in the Bay of Bengal (Bangladesh/Myanmar)* ITLOS Case No. 16, Judgment of 14 March 2012.

[66] *The Bay of Bengal Maritime Boundary Arbitration (Bangladesh v India)*, PCA Case No. 2010–16, Award of 7 July 2014.

[67] *The Chagos Marine Protected Area Arbitration (Mauritius v United Kingdom)*, PCA Case No. 2011–03, Award of 18 March 2015.

[68] *The South China Sea Arbitration (Republic of Philippines v People's Republic of China)*, PCA Case No. 2013–19, Award on Jurisdiction and Admissibility of 29 October 2015; *The South China Sea Arbitration (Republic of Philippines v People's Republic of China)*, PCA Case No. 2013–19, Award of 12 July 2016, para 20.

[69] *The 'Enrica Lexie' Incident (Italy v India)*, PCA Case No. 2015–28, Provisional Measures Order of 29 April 2016; *The 'Enrica Lexie' Incident (Italy v India)*, ITLOS Case No. 24, Provisional Measures Order of 24 August 2015.

against Australia, but article 298 permitted it to institute compulsory but non-binding conciliation procedures. A conciliation commission was established in accordance with the provisions in Annex V of UNLCOS,[70] resulting in an agreed settlement.

In two instances Asian states have also voluntarily referred disputes concerning sovereignty over disputed islands to the ICJ. The first was a dispute between Indonesia and Malaysia,[71] and the second was a dispute between Malaysia and Singapore.[72] Such disputes are, strictly speaking, not law of the sea disputes because there are no provisions in UNCLOS on how to determine which state has the better claim to sovereignty over a disputed island. Nevertheless, they are examples of states agreeing to resolve peacefully sensitive sovereignty disputes by agreeing to refer them to the ICJ.

Overall, Asian states have been active participants in dispute settlement procedures for law of the sea disputes. Asian states have been no less active than states from other regions in utilizing the dispute settlement procedures in UNCLOS.

7 Challenges Relating to Management of Living Resources

7.1 Illegal, Unregulated, and Unreported Fishing

One of the major problems faced by many developing countries in the Asia-Pacific is combating illegal, unregulated, and unreported (IUU) fishing by foreign vessels in their exclusive economic zone. In the Asia-Pacific region, IUU fishing has been estimated to cost between US$4.5 billion and US$5.8 billion a year. The quantity of fish taken by IUU fishing activities in the region account for about 8 to 16 per cent of the total reported catch per year. It is estimated that Indonesia loses US$4 billion per year in illegal fishing.[73]

Many countries in the Asia-Pacific do not have adequate resources or enforcement capacity to address IUU fishing in their EEZ. Several countries, including Australia, Japan, and the US, have provided technical and financial assistance to coastal states in the Asia-Pacific to enhance the capabilities of their coast guards to combat IUU fishing and other maritime crimes.

One of the measures that would assist in addressing the problem would be for all states in the region to ratify and implement the FAO Agreement on Port State

[70] *Conciliation between the Democratic Republic of Timor-Leste and The Commonwealth of Australia*, PCA Case No. 2016–10.

[71] *Sovereignty over Pulau Ligitan and Pulau Sipadan (Indonesia/Malaysia)* (2002) ICJ Rep 625.

[72] *Sovereignty over Pedra Branca/Pulau Batu Puteh, Middle Rocks and South Ledge (Malaysia/Singapore)* Judgment of 23 May 2008 (2008) ICJ Rep 12.

[73] Mary Ann Palma, Martin Tsamenyi, and William Edeson, *Promoting Sustainable Fisheries: The International Legal and Policy Framework to Combat Illegal, Unreported and Unregulated Fishing* (Brill 2010) 9.

Measures to Prevent, Deter and Eliminate Illegal, Unreported and Unregulated Fishing. As of 18 October 2017, there were fifty-one parties to the Agreement. Parties in the Asia-Pacific include Australia, Indonesia, Japan, Myanmar, New Zealand, Palau, Republic of Korea, Sri Lanka, Thailand, Tonga, and Vanuatu.

Australia has the capability of defending its waters and has been quite aggressive in pursuing vessels illegally fishing in its EEZ. In August 2003, the Australian authorities pursued *Viarsa 1*, a Uruguayan-flagged fishing vessel, for more than twenty-one days over 3,900 nm across the Indian/Southern Ocean until the vessel was final arrested with the help of South African authorities and other members of the Commission for the Conservation of Antarctic Marine Living Resources.[74]

7.2 Regional Cooperation on Fisheries

The legal basis for regional cooperation to manage fisheries resources sustainably is in the 1995 Fish Stocks Agreement.[75] As of November 2017, there are eighty-six parties to this Agreement, including most of the Pacific Island nations and the major fishing nations in Asia, including Japan, Republic of Korea, the Russian Federation, Thailand, and Vietnam. The most important Asian states that are not parties are China and Malaysia. A regional fisheries management organization could be established for the South China Sea if these three states became parties to the Fish Stocks Agreement. If no system to sustainably manage the fisheries is established, the fisheries are likely to collapse.

There are several regional fisheries organizations in the Asia-Pacific. They include the following:

1. Indian Ocean Tuna Commission (IOTC). The IOTC is an intergovernmental organization mandated to manage tuna and tuna-like species in the Indian Ocean and adjacent seas. The objective of the Commission is to promote the conservation and optimal utilization of tuna and tuna-like stocks covered by the IOTC Agreement, and to encourage sustainable development of fisheries.[76]
2. Western and Central Pacific Fisheries Commission (WCPFC). The WCPFC is a treaty-based organization that was established in 2004 to conserve and manage tuna and other highly migratory fish stocks. The secretariat is based in Pohnpei, in the northern Pacific state of the Federated States of Micronesia. All of the major

[74] 'Poachers pursued over 7,000 kilometers' (Australian Antarctic Division, 25 May 2004) <http://www.antarctica.gov.au/magazine/2001-2005/issue-6-autumn-2004/feature/poachers-pursued-over-7-000-kilometers> accessed 4 December 2018.

[75] Agreement for the Implementation of the Provisions of the United Nations Convention on the Law of the Sea of 10 December 1982 relating to the Conservation and Management of Straddling Fish Stocks and High Migratory Fish Stocks (adopted 4 August 1995, entered into force 11 December 2001, 2167 UNTS 3).

[76] See <http://www.iotc.org/> accessed 4 December 2018.

states in the region that are important to the sustainable management of tuna stocks are parties to the WCPFC, including China and Chinese Taipei (Taiwan).[77]

3. Commission for the Conservation of Southern Bluefin Tuna (CCSBT). The CCSBT is headquartered in Canberra. Members now include Australia, European Union, Indonesia, Japan, New Zealand, Republic of Korea, South Africa, and Taiwan (fishing entity).[78]
4. South Pacific Regional Fisheries Management Organisation (SPRFMO). The SPRFMO is an intergovernmental organization that is committed to the long-term conservation and sustainable use of the fishery resources of the south Pacific Ocean and in so doing safeguarding the marine ecosystems in which the resources occur. The SPRFMO Convention applies to the high seas of the south Pacific, covering about a quarter of the Earth's high-seas areas.[79]
5. Asia-Pacific Fishery Commission (APFIC). APFIC was founded in 1948 to promote the full and proper use of living aquatic resources in the region from the Indian Ocean to the Pacific Ocean. APFIC works to improve understanding, awareness, and cooperation concerning fisheries issues in the Asia-Pacific region. Its Secretariat is at the FAO Regional Office for Asia and the Pacific in Bangkok, Thailand. Member countries are Australia, Bangladesh, Cambodia, China, France, India, Indonesia, Japan, Malaysia, Myanmar, Nepal, New Zealand, Pakistan, Philippines, Republic of Korea, Sri Lanka, Timor-Leste, Thailand, UK, USA, and Vietnam.[80]
6. Southeast Asian Fisheries Development Center (SEAFDEC). SEAFDEC is an autonomous intergovernmental body established in 1967. The mission of SEAFDEC considered and adopted by the Special Meeting of the SEAFDEC Council 2017 is 'To promote and facilitate concerted actions among the Member Countries to ensure the sustainability of fisheries and aquaculture in Southeast Asia'. SEAFDEC comprises eleven member countries: Brunei Darussalam, Cambodia, Indonesia, Japan, Lao PDR, Malaysia, Myanmar, Philippines, Singapore, Thailand, and Vietnam. It operates through the Secretariat located in Thailand and has five technical departments.

7.3 Whaling in the Southern Ocean

Japan's policy of whaling in the Antarctic Ocean has been a continued source of controversy, especially in Australia and New Zealand. The International Whaling Commission imposed a ban on commercial whaling effective in 1986. However,

77 See <http://www.wcpfc.int/> accessed 4 December 2018.

78 See <http://www.ccsbt.org/> accessed 4 December 2018.

79 See <http://www.sprfmo.int/> accessed 4 December 2018.

80 See <http://www.fao.org/asiapacific/apfic/en/> accessed 4 December 2018.

Japan continued to hunt a limited number of whales under the exception provided for whaling for purposes of scientific research.

In 2010, Australia and New Zealand instituted proceedings against Japan in the ICJ in the *Whaling in the Antarctic* case.[81] This case was not a dispute on the interpretation or application of UNCLOS, but a dispute on the 1946 Whaling Convention. The basis of jurisdiction in the case was the 'optional clause declarations' made by all three states under article 36(2) of the ICJ Statute. The ICJ determined that it had jurisdiction. In its 2014 ruling the ICJ concluded that the special permits issued by Japan for the killing, taking, and treating of whales were not granted 'for purposes of scientific research' pursuant to the 1946 Whaling Convention. Following the ruling of the ICJ, Japan made adjustments to its whaling policy in order to comply with the decision, but it also announced that it would continue to permit the killing of a limited number of minke whales for scientific purposes. It maintains that its whaling activities are necessary for scientific study and that they are not inconsistent with the sustainable management of whale stocks.

On 6 October 2015, Japan took steps to prevent further cases being instituted against it for its whaling activities. It amended its optional clause declaration (accepting the jurisdiction of the ICJ) in order to exclude 'any dispute arising out of, concerning, or relating to research on, or conservation, management or exploitation of, living resources of the sea'.[82]

In December 2018, Japan announced that it would withdraw from the International Whaling Commission effective 30 June 2019 and that, from July 2019, it would resume commercial whaling in its territorial waters and EEZ. It further stated that it would not conduct any whaling in Antarctic waters or in the southern hemisphere.[83]

8 Maritime Security Challenges in the Asia-Pacific

8.1 Piracy and Armed Robbery against Ships

Piracy and armed robbery against ships is periodically a problem in Southeast Asia, but most attacks are on ships in the territorial sea or archipelagic waters. Therefore, such attacks are not piracy under UNCLOS, but armed robbery against ships, which is governed by the law of the state in whose waters the attack took place.

Cooperation to address the issue is challenging because most Asian states jealously guard their sovereignty in their territorial sea and archipelagic waters. They are

[81] *Whaling in the Antarctic (Australia v Japan; New Zealand intervening) (Judgment)* [2014] ICJ Rep 226.

[82] See <http://www.icj-cij.org/en/declarations/jp> accessed 4 December 2018.

[83] See <https://www.mofa.go.jp/ecm/fsh/page4e_000969.html>.

reluctant to enter into any arrangements that would give foreign vessels the right to patrol their waters or to arrest vessels in waters subject to their sovereignty. Some bilateral and sub-regional cooperation has been established, but they usually provide for coordinated patrols, where each state patrols its own waters, rather than joint patrols, where foreign vessels may patrol their waters.

Notwithstanding these sensitivities, Asian states have entered into regional or sub-regional arrangements to combat threats to maritime security:

1. The ReCAAP Information Sharing Centre was established under the Regional Cooperation Agreement on Combating Piracy and Armed Robbery against Ships in Asia (ReCAAP), a regional government-to-government agreement to promote and enhance cooperation against piracy and armed robbery in Asia. It is based in Singapore.[84]
2. The Malacca Straits Patrol (MSP) is a cooperative arrangement between the navies of Indonesia, Malaysia, Singapore and Thailand to ensure the security of the Straits of Malacca and Singapore. It consists of three elements. First, the Malacca Straits Sea Patrol consists of coordinated sea patrols and information sharing. Second, the 'Eyes-in-the-Sky' combined maritime patrols reinforce the sea patrols with air surveillance. Third, the MSP Intelligence Exchange Group is an information-sharing platform managed by the Information Fusion Centre (IFC).
3. The IFC is a regional maritime security centre hosted by the Republic of Singapore Navy and located at Changi Naval Base in Singapore. It was established in 2009 to provide actionable information to regional maritime enforcement agencies on international maritime crimes and threats to maritime security. Liaison officers from twenty-three countries have been assigned to the IFC.[85]
4. Indonesia-Malaysia-Philippines Cooperation in the Sulu Sea was established in June 2017 by Indonesia, Malaysia, and the Philippines, who agreed to joint maritime patrols to combat terrorism and transnational crimes in the Sulu Sea.

Many of the activities characterized as piracy and armed robbery against ships can be dealt with under the so-called 'counter-terrorism conventions' that are under the purview of the UN Office on Drug Control. Particularly relevant are the Convention for the Suppression of Unlawful Acts against the Safety of Maritime Navigation 1988 (SUA 1988) and the International Convention against the Taking of Hostages 1979. These conventions would be useful tools for combating certain acts if all of the states in a region or sub-region were parties and had implemented their obligations. Unfortunately, these Conventions cannot be utilized to combat such acts in the waters in and

[84] See <http://www.recaap.org> accessed 4 December 2018.

[85] See <https://www.gov.sg/~/sgpcmedia/media_releases/mindef/press_release/P-20160927-1/attachment/Fact%20Sheet%20on%20Information%20Fusion%20Centre.pdf> accessed 4 December 2018.

near the Straits of Malacca and Singapore because Indonesia is not a party to either Convention and Malaysia is not a party to SUA 1988.[86]

8.2 Illegal Immigration and Human Trafficking by Sea

One of the most complex and intractable problems of maritime security that several states in the region have had to face is illegal immigration and human trafficking by sea. The migration of 'boat people' from Vietnam at the end of the Vietnam War was a serious problem for many countries in Southeast Asia. It was only resolved after a Comprehensive Plan of Action was adopted in 1989 by the Indo-China countries, first-asylum countries, and resettlement countries, with assistance from the UN High Commission for Refugees.

Irregular immigration by 'boat people' has become a highly contentious political issue in Australia since 2011 because an increasing number of refugees and displaced persons fleeing conflict in West Asia and the Middle East travel by boat to Australia, sometimes with assistance from criminal syndicates. As a result, Australia amended its visa policy to enable it to detain persons attempting to enter Australia without a valid visa and to hold them in offshore detention centres pending processing.

The most recent crisis of 'boat people' are Rohingya fleeing Myanmar. The problem has become more complex because of allegations that some of the Rohingya are being picked up by criminal syndicates for purposes of human trafficking; some are allegedly forced to work on fishing boats with little or no compensation.

The rules governing these issues are a complex mix of domestic security law and international law. The latter includes UNCLOS, IMO conventions, international human rights law, refugee law, and relevant transnational organized crime conventions. It is a serious problem of security and human rights that cannot be resolved without an unprecedented level of cooperation between interested states and international organizations.

8.3 Proliferation of Weapons of Mass Destruction

Following the attack on the World Trade Center in New York on September 11, 2001, there was increased concern regarding the security of merchant ships and about the transportation by sea of weapons of mass destruction (WMD). As a result, the IMO adopted new measures to increase the security of ships and ports. In addition, the 2005 Protocol to SUA 1988 was adopted to create new offences in light of the threat of

[86] See generally, Robert Beckman and Ashley Roach (eds), *Piracy and International Maritime Crimes in ASEAN: Prospects for Cooperation* (Edward Elgar Publishing 2012).

maritime terrorism.[87] The 2005 SUA Protocol entered into force on 28 July 2010 and, as of April 2018, there are 39 state parties.[88] Interestingly, the only Asia-Pacific states that are parties are Turkey, New Zealand, and six small island developing states in the Pacific.[89]

The US also took the initiative to establish two cooperative mechanisms to address the threat of the proliferation of WMD by sea. The first is the Proliferation Security Initiative (PSI). It is a global initiative intended to stop trafficking in WMD, or their delivery systems, to and from states and non-state actors of proliferation concern. If a state agrees to cooperate with the US under the PSI, they commit to developing procedures to facilitate the exchange of information and to cooperating in the interdiction of shipments of WMD and delivery systems. More than 100 states are participating in the PSI, including many Asia-Pacific countries. Notable exceptions include Bangladesh, China, India, Indonesia, Myanmar, and Pakistan.[90]

The second US-led initiative is the Container Security Initiative (CSI). It was established in 2002 by the US Bureau of Customs and Border Protection, an agency of the Department of Homeland Security. Its purpose is to increase security for container cargo shipped to the US. Under the CSI, teams target and examine high-risk cargo before it is laden on board a vessel bound for the US. CSI operates in fifty-eight ports world-wide, including ports in the Asia-Pacific, screening 80 per cent of the container cargo destined for the US. CSI ports in Asia include major container ports in China, Hong Kong, Japan, Korea, Malaysia, Pakistan, Singapore, Sri Lanka, Taiwan, and Thailand.[91]

8.4 Regional Cooperation on Maritime Security

ASEAN has established various mechanisms to address issues of maritime security both between member states, and between member states and non-member states.

The ASEAN Regional Forum has issued statements on issues such as cooperation against piracy and other threats to maritime security, and it has developed an Action Plan and a Work Plan on Maritime Security.

In 2010 the ASEAN Maritime Forum was established as a mechanism to discuss issues of maritime security, such as maritime security and cooperation in ASEAN,

[87] IMO, 'Maritime Security and Piracy' <http://www.imo.org/en/OurWork/Security/Pages/MaritimeSecurity.aspx> accessed 4 December 2018.

[88] See <http://www.imo.org/en/About/Conventions/StatusOfConventions/Documents/StatusOfTreaties.pdf>.

[89] See <http://www.imo.org/en/About/Conventions/StatusOfConventions/Documents/status-x.xlsx>.

[90] US Department of State, 'Proliferation Security Initiative' <http://www.state.gov/t/isn/c10390.htm> accessed 4 December 2018

[91] US Customs and Border Protection, 'Container Security Initiative in Summary' (May 2011) <https://www.cbp.gov/border-security/ports-entry/cargo-security/csi/csi-brief> accessed 30 June 2019.

maintaining freedom and safety of navigation, addressing piracy, protecting the marine environment, and promoting eco-tourism and fisheries cooperation.

In 2012, the Expanded ASEAN Maritime Forum was established to enhance discussion and dialogue, on issues of maritime security, between ASEAN member states and outside powers with an interest in maritime security in the region. It includes the ten ASEAN countries plus Australia, China, India, Japan, New Zealand, South Korea, Russia, and the US. It was convened in response to the statement of the ASEAN Leaders, as well as the Leaders of the East Asia Summit.

ADMM Plus consists of the Defence Ministers of the ten ASEAN member states and eight dialogue partners. It has a working group on maritime security and has been action-oriented. It has established a communication hotline and has held several exercises, including maritime-security and counterterrorism exercises in the South China Sea.

The Council for Security Cooperation in the Asia Pacific (CSCAP) is a non-governmental process for dialogue on security issues in the Asia Pacific. CSCAP provides an informal mechanism for scholars, officials, and others in their private capacities to discuss political and security issues and challenges facing the region. It also provides policy recommendations to various intergovernmental bodies, convenes regional and international meetings, and establishes links with institutions and organizations in other parts of the world to exchange information, insights, and experiences in the area of regional political-security cooperation. CSCAP activities are guided by a Steering Committee co-chaired by a member from an ASEAN Member Committee and a member from a non-ASEAN Member Committee.

9 Regional Cooperation on the Marine Environment

There are five regional seas programmes in the Asia-Pacific that come under the Regional Seas Programmes of the UN Environment Programme (UNEP):

1. The Secretariat of the Pacific Regional Environment Programme (SPREP) is the primary regional organization in the Pacific that is concerned with environmental management and sustainable development. SPREP is located in Samoa. Members are American Samoa, Australia, Cook Islands, Federated States of Micronesia, Fiji, France, French Polynesia, Guam, Kiribati, Marshall Islands, Nauru, New Caledonia, New Zealand, Niue, Northern Mariana Islands, Palau, Papua New Guinea, Samoa, Solomon Islands, Tokelau, Tonga, Tuvalu, UK, USA, Vanuatu, and Wallis and Futuna.
2. The East Asia Seas Programme is administered by UNEP through the Coordinating Body on the Seas of East Asia (COBSEA), which is based in the United Nations Economic and Social Commission for Asia and the Pacific (ESCAP) offices in

Bangkok, Thailand. Member countries are Cambodia, China, Indonesia, Republic of Korea, Malaysia, Philippines, Singapore, Thailand, and Vietnam.[92]

3. The Northwest Pacific Action Plan (NOWPAP) Regional Coordinating Unit is co-hosted by Japan and the Republic of Korea. Participating countries are China, Japan, Republic of Korea, and the Russian Federation.[93]
4. The South Asia Seas regional seas programme has adopted an action plan (SASAP) that is administered by the South Asia Cooperative Environment Programme (SACEP). Participating countries include Bangladesh, India, Maldives, Pakistan, and Sri Lanka.[94]

SPREP is most active of the regional seas programmes in the Asia-Pacific. The level of cooperation in the other programmes lags behind that of regional seas programmes in other regions.

Two regional programmes in the Asia-Pacific that are not part of the UNEP Seas Programmes have been successful in promoting cooperation to protect the marine environment. They are:

1. *Partnerships in Environmental Management in the Seas of East Asia (PEMSEA)* is an intergovernmental organization operating in East Asia to foster and sustain healthy and resilient oceans, coasts, communities, and economies across the region. It is based in Manila, Philippines.[95] It has been successful in promoting integrated coastal and marine area management.
2. *The Coral Triangle Initiative on Coral Reefs, Fisheries, and Food Security (CTI-CFF)* is a multilateral partnership of six countries working together to sustain extraordinary marine and coastal resources by addressing crucial issues such as food security, climate change, and marine biodiversity. The six countries are Indonesia, Malaysia, Philippines, Papua New Guinea, Solomon Islands, and Timor-Leste.[96]

9.1 South China Sea

The South China Sea has been an area of contention because of competing sovereignty and maritime claims, but it can also be an area for cooperation to protect and preserve the marine environment.

[92] See <http://www.cobsea.org> accessed 4 December 2018.

[93] See <http://www.iotc.org> accessed 4 December 2018.

[94] See <http://www.unenvironment.org/explore-topics/oceans-seas/what-we-do/working-regional-seas/regional-seas-programmes/south-asian> accessed 4 December 2018.

[95] See <http://www.pemsea.org> accessed 4 December 2018.

[96] See <http://www.coraltriangleinitiative.org> accessed 4 December 2018.

The 2002 *China-ASEAN Declaration on the Conduct of Parties in the South China Sea* (DOC) calls for the parties to explore and undertake cooperative activities in specific areas, including marine environmental protection. The ASEAN states and China are now negotiating a Code of Conduct (COC) on the South China Sea. It is hoped that the COC negotiations will result in some concrete measures to cooperate to protect the marine environment in the South China Sea. Such cooperation should be possible if it does not involve activities in areas of overlapping claims.

Article 123 of UNCLOS provides a legal basis for cooperation among the states bordering the South China Sea. It specifically provides that states bordering a semi-enclosed sea should cooperate to coordinate the implementation of their rights and duties with respect to the protection and preservation of the marine environment.

9.2 Straits of Malacca and Singapore

Indonesia, Malaysia, and Singapore have been cooperating in managing the Straits of Malacca and Singapore (SOMS) since the early 1970s. They have established a Tripartite Technical Experts Group (TTEG) that meets regularly to discuss measures to enhance safety and prevent and reduce pollution from ships in the SOMS. The three littoral states have jointly proposed that the IMO adopt various measures on safety and pollution. The measures adopted by the IMO at their request include a traffic separation scheme and other routeing measures, a vessel traffic system, and a mandatory ship reporting system.

In 2005, the three states established a Cooperative Mechanism in the SOMS that enables user states and other stakeholders to cooperate with the three littoral states in enhancing the safety of navigation and in preventing and reducing ship-source pollution in the SOMS. The Cooperative Mechanism makes the SOMS the first strait in the world to implement article 43 of UNCLOS, which provides that user states and states bordering a strait used for international navigation should, by agreement, cooperate on enhancing safety and preventing pollution.[97]

10 Conclusion

There may be areas of international law that were made by the Western powers, without the active participation of Asian states, but the modern law of the sea set out in UNCLOS is not one of them. Many Asian states played a significant role in the

[97] See <http://www.cm-soms.com/> accessed 4 December 2018. See also Leonardo Bernard, 'The Cooperation Mechanism in the Straits of Malacca and Singapore' in Myron Nordquist, John Norton Moore, Robert Beckman, and Ronan Long (eds), *Freedom of Navigation and Globalization* (Brill Nijhoff 2015) 196–218.

negotiations leading to UNCLOS, and Asian states have continued to play a role in its implementation and development.

Most Asian states recognize that UNCLOS establishes a stable and predictable rules-based order for the oceans. Asian states have not only implemented most of the UNCLOS provisions in good faith, but they have played significant roles in developing UNCLOS through the practice of states and the institutions created under it. Asian states have also utilized the dispute settlement mechanisms in the Convention in order to resolve disputes on the interpretation or application of its provisions. In short, they have contributed to the processes that have enabled UNCLOS to become a universally-accepted Convention that has withstood the test of time.

Another issue is whether the UNCLOS regime can be developed and adapted to respond to new challenges resulting from developments in science and technology. Negotiations are currently taking place to negotiate a new implementation agreement to govern biological diversity in areas beyond national jurisdiction. UNCLOS will also have to be adapted or developed to address issues such as sea level rise, ocean acidification, plastic ocean debris, and the employment of unmanned vessels. None of these issues is unique to Asia, but they present serious challenges to Asian states.

CHAPTER 10

INTERNATIONAL ECONOMIC LAW AND ASIA

WANG JIANGYU

1 Introduction

International economic law (IEL), which is based on liberal economic theories,[1] holds a special meaning for Asia because it has been associated with colonization, modernization, and globalization ever since it was first encountered by countries in the region. Asian countries' subscription to IEL is thus a historical journey. The 'Most Favoured Nation' (MFN) principle in world trade law always reminds the Chinese people of their bitter initial engagement with international economic rules, which were violently imposed on them as part of the system of unequal treaties with the Western powers in the nineteenth and early twentieth centuries. Even today, Chinese textbooks of history, international law, and political education describe this MFN approach as 'biased (against China), [a] unilateral MFN' [*pianmian zuihuiguo daiyu*], which only made China suffer from foreign invasion and exploitation.[2]

Japan likewise accepted the same MFN obligation, which was '*unilateral* in obligation, *unlimited* in scope, and *unconditional* in operation', first in the Treaty of Peace and Amity 1854 between the United States (US) and Japan, which 'opened' Japan's door to the outside world.[3] India's encounter with the Western rules of the international economic system started with its colonization by the British Empire. It is important to note that, in those times, peoples of Asia, alongside the natives of Africa, the Americas,

[1] Tomer Broude, 'At the End of the Yellow Brick Road: International Economic Law Research in Times of Uncertainty' in Colin Picker, Isabella Bunn, and Douglas Arner (eds), *International Economic Law: The State and Future of the Discipline* (Hart 2008) 15.

[2] See e.g. Yang Gongsu, *Wanqing Waijiao Shi* [*Diplomatic History of the Late Qing Dynasty*] (Peking University Press 1991) 102–4.

[3] Shinya Murase, 'The Most-Favored-Nation Treatment in Japan's Treaty Practice during the Period 1854-1905' (1976) 70 AJIL 273, 274–5.

and the Pacific, were excluded from enjoying the benefits of international law by the prevailing 'standard of civilization' doctrine.[4]

In more recent times, IEL has played an instrumental role in helping Asian countries to achieve modernization. Generally, Asia's participation in the making of IEL has been rather limited, but a number of Asian countries, including Japan, Korea, China, India, and certain Southeast Asian countries (which are the countries covered in this chapter), have benefited from the Western-dominated international economic order by making use of its rules, though at different times of history.

This chapter considers the state and future of Asian countries' participation, compliance, and contributions with respect to IEL and highlights issues that may prompt future research. These issues are possibly caused by Asia's historical and contemporaneous position in the international economic system. It begins by examining how the selected Asian countries were integrated into the modern world economic system and subjected to the IEL that sustains it. It then looks at Asia's participation and compliance records in IEL, followed by an examination of regional and international economic organizations and rules in Asia, which have largely been developed through regional economic integration. The chapter then turns to several recent IEL-related initiatives in Asia, including the Asian Infrastructure Investment Bank, the New Development Bank, and China's Belt and Road Initiative. It concludes by summarizing the theoretical and practical challenges presented by the rise of Asia in the development of IEL.

2 IEL and Asia's Modernization

As noted, Asia's encounter with IEL started with Western invasion and/or colonization, which featured, *inter alia*, unequal treaties and unilateral MFN treatment. Before that, the Chinese world order dominated East Asia, based on the traditional system of suzerain-vassal relations between the Middle Kingdom and the peripheral countries (including Korea). Japan lived in the shadow of the Chinese world order, but largely maintained its own independence. India was occupied by hundreds of small kingdoms waiting to be united into one colony by the British. Asian countries were, however, gradually brought into the modern international economic order over the past century and a half. Japan was the first major Asian nation accepted by the West into the world of the 'civilized' nations.

In the European-dominated discourse, this integration process embodies the 'civilizing mission' which set China and other Asian countries in the nineteenth and twentieth centuries on a historical course towards a modernized Asia.[5] Thus, for most Asian countries, the agonies they suffered in their journeys to independence—which were

[4] Simon Chesterman, 'Asia's Ambivalence about International Law and Institutions: Past, Present, and Futures' (2016) 27 EJIL 945, 948.

[5] Ibid. 948.

associated with tremendous injustices—were the prices they paid for modernization, especially for its economic and social dimensions. In the end, they were expected to join the liberal international order whose economic dimension relies on IEL to exist and operate. As G John Ikenberry has argued, this system is open to all states and able to integrate outsiders into its framework.[6]

Japan was the pioneering Asian country to be integrated into the liberal economic system. Its progress accelerated after World War II (WWII), when Japan fully surrendered to the US-led international economic order, from which it benefited through (re) industrialization and modernization.[7] Japan quickly recovered from the trauma of the war and became one of the world's most important economic powers and a full member of the Western-dominated world economic system.

India's post-independence development, however, offers a contrasting example. Being a former British colony, independent India initially adopted a three-decade-long socialism-inspired economic model, which featured, to a substantial extent, economic planning, state ownership, and protectionist foreign trade and investment policies.[8] During that period, India was, however, fully embraced by the liberal international system by serving as a full member in almost all of the major international economic organizations, including the General Agreement on Tariffs and Trade 1948 (GATT). India's economic liberalization started in 1991, which was also the turning point in India's relations with the liberal international economic order. In the following decade, a globalizing India embarked on both domestic and foreign economic liberalization. For instance, peak import tariffs on non-agricultural goods were reduced from 150 per cent in 1992 to 15 per cent in 2002–03.[9] The reward for the liberalization was an average annual growth of above 6 per cent in the same period. As remarked by an Indian observer, 'in the case of India, globalization has been a boon. India has made critical use of it . . . to restructure its economy and leverage growth'.[10] India's most dynamic export sector is information technology-enabled services for global companies, which doubtlessly has benefited from the General Agreement on Trade in Services 1994 (GATS).

China, in its modern Reform Era, is usually regarded as one of the biggest beneficiaries of the international economic system. In the late 1970s, long before India's economic liberalization, China began to open its door to international trade and

[6] John Ikenberry, 'The Rise of China and the Future of the West. Can the Liberal System Survive?' (2008) 87 Foreign Affairs 23, 30.

[7] Terutomo Ozawa, *Institutions, Industrial Upgrading, and Economic Performance in Japan* (Edward Elgar 2005) 34 (noting that 'Japan was the very first of Asian countries to exploit the growth stimuli of the Pax Americana, initially by pursuing labour-driven industrialisation and exporting labour-intensive goods to the West').

[8] For instance, India's peak tariff was 350% before 1991, one of the highest in the world. See Omkar Goswami, 'Elephants Can Dance: India's Responses to Globalization and the Challenges She Faces' in David Kelly, Ramkishen Rajan, and Gillian Goh (eds), *Managing Globalization: Lessons from China and India* (World Scientific 2006) 75.

[9] Ibid. 83. [10] Kaushik Basu, 'India Globalizing' in Kelly et al (eds) (n 8) 55.

investment, thus voluntarily subjecting itself to IEL. Nicholas Lardy noted that, even before China's accession to the World Trade Organization (WTO) in 2001, it had already significantly changed and liberalized its original planned economy-based foreign trade regime to allow more trading rights to Chinese enterprises in importing and exporting, to lower import tariffs, to reduce non-tariff barriers, and to enable more flexible exchange rates and capital controls.[11] China's WTO accession was an even greater game changer in reshaping not only China's own trade regulation but also China's position in the international economic system. In addition to general obligations such as the universal, unconditional MFN for all WTO members, and the pledge to administer all its laws in a 'uniform, impartial and reasonable manner' and ensure transparency in its legal system, China committed to open its markets by relaxing or eliminating over 7,000 tariffs and non-tariff barriers. For example, China agreed to bind all of its tariffs (that is, not to increase duties above agreed levels) and accepted an average bound rate of 8.9 per cent for industrial goods, which was lower than that of India, Brazil, and most developing countries. It also agreed to open important services sectors to foreign investors.[12]

3 Asia's Participation in IEL and Institutions

3.1 National Models of Participation in the International Economic System

Participation in IEL means a country's involvement in the making and enforcement of it. Participation takes the forms of negotiating for market access, rule-making in international governmental forums, using international economic dispute resolution mechanisms, being represented at and partaking in international economic organizations, and other IEL-related initiatives. Overall, Asia may have benefited most from the global economic architecture underpinned by IEL, but its under-participation and under-representation in IEL and its institutions are conspicuous. Of course, this is consistent with Asia's general practice in international law.[13] However, several initiatives taken by China may pose some degree of systemic challenge to the international economic order.

There are loosely four models of participation in the post-war international economic system by Asian countries, represented respectively by Japan, India, Singapore,

[11] Nicholas Lardy, *Integrating China into the Global Economy* (Brooking Institution Press 2002) 32. See also Jiangyu Wang, 'The Evolution of China's International Trade Policy: Development through Protection and Liberalization' in YS Lee (ed), *Economic Development through World Trade* (Kluwer International 2007) 191, 196–7.

[12] Lardy, ibid. 79; Wang, ibid. 198–9.

[13] Chesterman (n 4).

and China. Japan embraced the Western-led international economic system ostensibly with its whole heart but developed a differently styled capitalism. India has never been viewed as an outlier of the liberal international order but pursued protectionism in the name of development until recent years. China was a self-proclaimed representative and leader of the developing world, but in practice took up a neo-liberal developmental approach, and may now intend to establish parallel institutions to compete for dominance in the international economic order. Singapore represents some smaller Asian economies in Asia which committedly abide by both the rules and spirit of the liberal international economic order.

3.2 Japan

Japan was excluded from the creation of the Bretton Woods institutions including the GATT, the World Bank, and the International Monetary Fund ('IMF') because it was one of the major enemy states during and for a short while after WWII (in contrast, Nationalist China and India (in the name of British Raj) attended the Bretton Woods Conference in 1944). Japan's economic growth tremendously benefited from the reduction in trade and investment barriers brought about by the Bretton Woods system.[14] By the early 1970s Japan emerged as one of the wealthiest and technologically advanced industrial nations and was an important member in all international economic institutions of the time. Japan joined the World Bank and IMF in 1952, and hosted the Annual Meeting of the World Bank Group and the IMF in 1964, which marked its full return to the Western-dominated international economic community. It became the second-largest member of the World Bank in 1984. Japan has contributed generously to the IMF's lending capacity and technical assistance, and now possesses a quota of 6.15 per cent in the Fund's total votes, which is the second largest after the US.[15]

Japan applied to join the GATT in 1952 but its application was initially opposed by the existing GATT members. It became a provisional GATT member in 1953 and a full member in 1955, with strong support from the US. It subsequently participated in the successive rounds of multilateral trade negotiations (including the 'Tokyo Round' of 1973–9). The sheer size of its economy made Japan a member of the 'Quadrilateral' or 'Quad' meeting, which brought together trade ministers from the US, European Union, Japan, and Canada. These were regarded as the most important trading nations of the time.[16] Japan, however, was not active in using GATT's dispute settlement

[14] Marcus Noland, 'Japan and the International Economic Institutions', Paper at the Centre for Japanese Economic Studies with Biennial Conference 'Can the Japanese Change? Economic Reform in Japan', Macquarie University Sydney, Australia (Peterson Institute for International Economics 2000) <http://www.piie.com> accessed 11 December 2018.

[15] See 'IMF Members' Quotas and Voting Power, and IMF Board of Governors', IMF, 12 January 2019 <https://www.imf.org/external/np/sec/memdir/members.aspx>.

[16] WTO, 'Statement by Renato Ruggiero on the "QUAD" Meeting', WTO 1995 Press Releases, Press/27, 23 October 1995.

mechanism.[17] Even when anti-dumping investigative authorities in the US ruled against Japan in numerous anti-dumping cases, 'neither the Japanese firms nor the Japanese government ever formally protested these rulings by petitioning GATT'.[18]

The establishment of the WTO in 1995, of which Japan is a founding member, marked a turning point in Japan's attempt to proactively defend its trade interests and pursue international trade leadership. Japan believes the WTO offers powerful tools to help it resist discriminatory trade protection measures by its trading partners.[19] Immediately in 1995, Japan requested, pursuant to the WTO's *Understanding on Rules and Procedures Governing the Settlement of Disputes* (DSU), consultations with the US on an automobile dispute, establishing one of the few disputes initiated in the first year of the WTO's dispute settlement body.[20] The US opted to settle the case.[21] At the time of writing, Japan had brought twenty-three cases to the WTO as a complainant and had appeared as a respondent in fifteen cases and as a third party in 173 cases.[22] Still, overall, Japan was habitually believed to 'punch below its weight' for decades, as Japan's influence on the global economic policy architecture was relatively small and disproportionate to the size of its economy, which used to be the second largest in the world.

3.3 India

India presented a different story in the global economic system. India, of course, has never been an outlier of the post-war international order. It is a pluralistic, constitutional democracy and currently an important economic partner with a liberalizing economy.[23] However, in most of the years after its independence in 1947, India did not fully subscribe to the liberal spirit of the international economic order. In global economic institutions, India has focused on the issue of development, in addition to defending its own protectionist trade policies. As early as the Bretton Woods Conference of 1944, the Indian delegation, which represented the then British-run government of India but was largely treated as an independent mission, pushed for special and differential treatment for poor countries because of their developmental needs: 'Countries like India and China with a large population and a comparatively low

[17] Noland (n 14).

[18] Masahiro Okuno-Fujiwara, 'Industrial Policy in Japan: A Political Economy View' in Paul Krugman (ed), *Trade with Japan: Has the Door Opened Wider?* (University of Chicago Press 1991) 271.

[19] Noland (n 14).

[20] WTO, *US—Imposition of Import Duties on Automobiles from Japan under Section 301 and 304 of the Trade Act of 1974—Request for Consultations by Japan* (22 May 1995), WT/DS6/1.

[21] Noland (n 14).

[22] WTO, 'Member Information: Japan and the WTO' (WTO, 2018) <http://www.wto.org/english/thewto_e/countries_e/japan_e.htm> accessed 11 December 2018.

[23] Kanti Prasad Bajpai, 'India in the International Order: Challenger and Stabilizer' in Kelly et al (eds) (n 8) 307.

standard of life should be given special considerations in any international plan'.[24] In line with its development strategy, India adopted an import-substitution based international trade policy, which 'had the direct effect of limiting its participation in world trade' by taking on heavy import tariffs and non-tariff barriers such as quantitative restrictions, although India was one of the twenty-three founding contracting parties of the GATT in 1947.[25]

India took a hardline position towards multilateral liberalization in the Uruguay round of trade negotiations from 1986 to 1994. It consistently demanded special and preferential treatment for developing countries, and was vehemently opposed to the introduction of new issues including, ironically, the inclusion of trade in services under GATT, although it eventually accepted the final agreement.[26] In the WTO, it was also mainly the Indian delegation's relentless effort that led to the emphasis on 'development' in the new round of trade negotiations, which was even named the 'Doha Development Round'.[27] This came after India threatened to boycott the so-called Singapore Issues (including transparency in government procurement, trade facilitation, competition policy, and trade and investment). The WTO's Ministerial Conference in Geneva in July 2008—intended for WTO members 'to settle a range of questions that would shape the final agreement of the Doha Development Agenda'[28]—collapsed because of the lack the agreement between India, whose position was supported by China, and the US on the special safeguard mechanism, which would have allowed developing countries to raise tariffs temporarily in response to import surges and price falls. The US Trade Representative hence accused India and China of having 'thrown the entire Doha round into the gravest jeopardy of its nearly seven-year life' by 'controlling a large group of even poorer nations'.[29]

One may argue that India has made significant contributions to the development of IEL simply because of its agitated promotion of the institutionalization of the special treatment for developing countries in various forums, but mainly in GATT/WTO law.[30] India had already played a prominent role in rule-making in the GATT period, having been a driving force behind the introduction of the development provisions in

[24] Eric Helleiner, 'India and the Neglected Development Dimensions of Bretton Woods' (2015) Economic and Political Weekly 31, 34 (quoting Indian delegate NR Sarkar).

[25] TN Srinivasan and Suresh Tendulkar, *Reintegrating India with the World Economy* (Institute for International Economics 2003) 14.

[26] Suparna Karmakar, 'From Uruguay to Doha: India at the Negotiating Table' in Suparna Karmakar, Rajiv Kumar, and Bibek Debroy (eds), *India's Liberalisation Experience? Hostage to the WTO?* (SAGE Publications 2007) 56, 69. See also Debashis Chakraborty and Amir Ullah Khan, *The WTO Deadlocked: Understanding the Dynamics of International Trade* (SAGE Publications 2008) 5.

[27] Paul Blustein, *Misadventures of the Most Favored Nations* (Public Affairs 2009) 127–30.

[28] WTO, 'The July 2008 Package' (WTO, 2018) <http://www.wto.org/english/tratop_e/dda_e/meet08_e.htm> accessed 11 December 2018.

[29] CL Lim and Jiangyu Wang, 'China and the Doha Development Agenda' (2010) 44 Journal of World Trade 1309, 1310.

[30] Julia Ya Qin, 'China, India and WTO Law' in Muthucumaraswamy Sornarajah and Jiangyu Wang (eds), *China, India and the International Economic Order* (CUP 2010) 167.

GATT in the 1960s and the negotiations of the Generalized System of Preferences (GSP) at the UN Conference on Trade and Development, 'which established the norm that developed countries should provide preferential tariff treatment to developing countries on a generalized, non-reciprocal and non-discriminatory basis'.[31] The GSP was later incorporated into the GATT and became the foundation for the GATT Enabling Clause in 1979, which allows for derogations to MFN treatment under GATT article I. It was also India's resistance to the introduction of new issues in the Uruguay Round that helped to limit the scope of the rules on investment and intellectual property to their trade-related aspects.[32] In short, India has played a leading role in championing the cause of developing countries and in legislating on the development rules in world trade law. The enforceability of the development rules is admittedly rather weak and can hardly be effectively subject to the GATT/WTO's dispute settlement mechanism. However, the codification of the development needs of developing countries in IEL at least marked the Western-dominated world economic community's recognition that developing countries do have to be treated specially and more favourably even in a liberal international economic order.

India became an active participant in trade dispute settlement after the WTO's establishment in 1995. It has to date appeared in twenty-three cases as complainant, twenty-four cases as respondent, and 129 cases as third party. That is, India is directly involved in at least two cases every year, one brought by itself and the other against it. Still, India's approach to dispute resolution in the WTO tends to be 'to settle rather than litigate'.[33] India lodged its first WTO dispute by requesting consultation with Poland concerning Poland's preferential treatment of the European Communities in its scheme on automobiles. The case was quickly settled in 1996 after Poland agreed to a modest import quota favourable to Indian products.[34] As a matter of fact, only a minority of the WTO cases involving India led to the final decision of a panel or the Appellate Body.

However, a number of cases involving India resulted in landmark decisions, representing India's contributions to WTO jurisprudence. For instance, two India-related cases, *US–Wool Shirts and Blouses*[35] and *EC–Tariff Preferences*,[36] have shaped the jurisprudence on burden of proof. In *US–Wool Shirts and Blouses*, the Panel and Appellate Body ruled that India, as the complainant, had to establish a presumption of inconsistency of US safeguard measures with the Agreement on Textiles and Clothing 1994 (ATC) but the US, the respondent, had the obligation to produce

[31] Ibid. 195. [32] Ibid. 195.

[33] Abhijit Das, James Nedumpara, and Shailja Singh, 'Introduction: WTO Dispute Settlement at Twenty: Insiders' Reflections on India's Participation' in Abhijit Das and James Nedumpara (eds) *WTO Dispute Settlement at Twenty: Insiders' Reflections on India's Participation* (Springer 2016) 1.

[34] WTO, *Poland—Import Regime for Automobiles—Notification of Mutually Agreed Solution* (11 September 1996) WT/DS19/2.

[35] WTO, *United States—Measures Affecting Imports of Woven Wool Shirts and Blouses from India* (25 April 1997) WT/DS33/AB/R.

[36] WTO, *European Communities—Conditions for the Granting of Tariff Preferences to Developing Countries* (7 April 2004) WT/DS246/AB/R.

evidence to rebut the presumption.[37] In *EC–Tariff Preferences*, India claimed that the EC's tariff preferences in favour of the ATC countries were inconsistent with the principle of non-discrimination under the Enabling Clause. India argued that, as the complainant, it only needed to make a prima facie case of the EC's violation of GATT article I:1. The Panel agreed with India, but its decision was reversed by the Appellate Body, which ruled that India had the good faith obligation to identify which provisions in the Enabling Clause the EC practice was alleged to have contravened.[38]

These two decisions articulated a clear standard on the burden of proof in WTO settlement. In addition, *EC–Tariff Preferences* was the first case in GATT/WTO history to elaborate on the Enabling Clause.[39] India's effort in the *US–Shrimp* case (along with Thailand, Mexico, and Pakistan) to push back against the adoption of *amicus curiae* submissions was not successful because the Appellate Body ruled that the Panel had the right to accept them.[40] However, in a special meeting of the WTO General Council in 2000, a majority of WTO members that spoke voiced objection to the Appellate Body's acceptance and consideration of *amicus* briefs.[41] To a large extent, this could be viewed as a contribution of India (along with other developing countries) to the rule-making in the WTO's dispute settlement in a negative sense, namely, by blocking the adoption of unfavourable rules. In addition, *US–Shrimp* was also the first case in GATT/WTO history to recognize that environmental protection falls within the objectives of the world trading system.[42]

Apart from its active participation in the WTO, India is not particularly lively in Western-dominated global economic institutions such as the IMF or World Bank. It has been observed that:

> India has been a more important and influential player in the trade institution than in the financial institutions. This was in part an inherent consequence of the fact that in the financial institutions creditor nations have more power than borrowers, while in the WTO power stems from market size; while India has always been a borrower in the Bank and the Fund, it has been a relatively attractive market despite the closed nature of its policies. As a result, India has been more actively involved in issues of a systemic nature in the WTO than in the financial institutions.[43]

India and the IMF will be further examined in section 3.5 on Asia and IMF reform. Suffice to say that, since it embarked on economic liberalization in 1991, India is becoming increasingly open to global economic cooperation and less sensitive on absolute protection of sovereignty in international economic affairs. It may even ease its usual rigid position on trade and development in the future. India's change in

[37] WT/DS33/AB/R (n 35) 14. [38] WT/DS246/AB/R (n 36) para 118.

[39] Qin (n 30) 200.

[40] WTO, *United States—Import Prohibition of Certain Shrimp and Shrimp Products* (12 October 1998) WT/DS58/AB/R, para 109. See also CL Lim, 'The Amicus Brief Issue at the WTO' (2005) 4 Chinese Journal of International Law 85.

[41] WTO General Council, 'Minutes of Meeting held on 22 November 2000', WT/GC/M/60.

[42] Qin (n 30) 200.

[43] Arvind Subramanian, 'India and Global Economic Policy Making' (2007) 3 India in Transition <https://casi.sas.upenn.edu/iit/asubramanian> accessed 25 December 2017.

mindset and practice in the international economic system might have a profound impact on the evolution of IEL, especially with respect to development issues.

3.4 China

Every Asian country is unique in its approach to the international economic system, and China's experience in this regard is incredibly full of twists and turns. The Republic of China was a founding member of all three major international economic institutions, namely, the IMF, World Bank, and GATT. After the People's Republic of China (PRC) was established in 1949, the Nationalist Chinese Government in Taiwan continued to occupy Chinese seats in those institutions for decades and the PRC was not officially involved in the World Bank and the IMF before 1980. It applied to 'resume' its GATT membership in 1986, but had to join the WTO as a new member in 2001.

Accession to global international economic institutions was a result of China's determination to conduct market-oriented economic reform at home and open to foreign trade and investment after the disastrous Cultural Revolution of 1966–76, which brought the Chinese economy to the verge of collapse. It was also a gesture that China was willing to be bound by the rules of IEL and to rise within the liberal international economic system. China's remarkable economic development and growing influence since it began integrating into the world economy prove that it is one of the largest beneficiaries of the US-led international economic order. On the other hand, acceptance of China into global economic institutions shortly after it embarked on its Reform and Opening-up Policy 1979 certainly evidenced the openness of the Western-dominated liberal international economic order.

China's performance in global economic institutions has never been radical or dramatic, but it has been sending mixed signals. In many respects, it is a good global citizen, who has been using international economic organizations 'to gain more goods and information from the international system'[44] so as to push for domestic economic reform. In this process, China has also embedded itself intensively in the global network of institutions. China, however, is far from being a rule-maker in this system, in that it does not possess the 'structural power' to 'influence rules, norms and the "structure" of the relationship patterns' within the existing Western-dominated international system.[45]

Nevertheless, China has been perceived by many as a potential challenger and even a threat to the system, possibly with the intention of overhauling it some day in the future. This impression stems, in part, from China's own economic capabilities. After all, it has become the second-largest economy in the world and is expected to be the largest in a few years. But the impression of China as a potential challenger also comes

[44] Marc Lanteigne, *Chinese Foreign Policy: An Introduction* (Routledge 2009) 57.

[45] Ibid. See also Susan Strange, 'The Persistent Myth of Lost Hegemony' (1987) 41 International Organization 551.

from a general perception that China intends to make changes to the governance structures and rules of international institutions in its own favour, so that it may acquire dominance in those institutions. A closer examination of Chinese practice in the various institutions will help to understand China's evolving attitude towards IEL.

John H Jackson remarked in 2001 that China's accession 'is the most significant activity in the WTO's seven-year life so far'.[46] As mentioned, China paid a huge price by making immense concessions to other WTO members in its fifteen-year negotiations to join the world trade community. But China certainly also understood the tremendous benefits it would reap from WTO membership. In the year of its WTO accession, China was the sixth leading exporter and importer in world merchandise trade.[47] In a decade, it became the world's second-largest economy, the second-largest importer, and the largest exporter.[48] As Chinese President Hu Jintao remarked on the tenth anniversary of China's accession to the WTO,

> China's accession to the WTO is a milestone in China's reform and opening-up, bringing us into a new era to further open up. To join the WTO was a major strategic decision based on our comprehensive analysis of the situation at home and abroad in order to push forward China's reform and opening-up and socialist modernization drive.[49]

China's role in the WTO was initially described as a 'system-maintainer' rather than a 'system reformer', let alone a 'revisionist power',[50] with the only 'exception being its behavior on issues seen to impinge on its sovereignty and dignity'.[51] Another study of the record of China's first decade of membership in the WTO even indicated that China appeared to be a 'stubborn status quo power' that was becoming 'a key player within, and not as a challenger to, the existing multilateral system'.[52] With respect to trade negotiations and rule-making, Chinese performance in the first decade of its WTO membership certainly conforms to the 'low profile' impression. As this author observed elsewhere,

> Although China has been active in the Doha negotiations, it has not become 'a leader of diplomacy, with a potential for coalition-seeking'. It has not sought to

[46] John Jackson, 'The Impact of China's Accession on the WTO' in Deborah Cass, Brett Williams, and George Barker (eds), *China and the World Trading System: Entering the New Millennium* (CUP 2003) 19.

[47] WTO, *International Trade Statistics 2002* (WTO 2002) 24.

[48] WTO, 'China's Trade Profile' <http://stat.wto.org/CountryProfile/WSDBCountryPFView.aspx?Country=CN> accessed 9 January 2019.

[49] Permanent Mission of China to the WTO, 'China in the WTO: Past, Present and Future' (December 2011) <http://www.wto.org/english/thewto_e/acc_e/s7lu_e.pdf> accessed 25 December 2017.

[50] Margaret Pearson, 'China in Geneva: Lessons from China's Early Years in the World Trade Organization' in Alastair Johnston and Robert Ross (eds), *New Directions in the Study of China's Foreign Policy* (Stanford University Press 2006) 242.

[51] Ibid.

[52] James Scott and Rorden Wilkinson, 'China as a System Preserving Power in the WTO' in Dries Lesage and Thijs Van de Graaf (eds), *Rising Powers and Multilateral Institutions* (Palgrave Macmillan 2015) 199.

> 'rewrite some of the rules of the game in the international arena'. Instead, China has been fairly described as 'a constructive member working to pursue its interests which for the most part correspond to the organization's goals of greater multilateral liberalization'.[53]

China's approach of not seeking leadership and not being a trouble-maker changed in the WTO's mini-ministerial conference in 2008, when China firmly sided with India on the special safeguard mechanism at the end of the negotiations and was blamed by the US Trade Representative (USTR) for causing the whole talks to collapse.[54] Indeed, post-2008 the WTO may have seen a more aggressive China, but its contribution to WTO rule-making is still not conspicuous. Admittedly, it has made many submissions to reform WTO rules, opportunistically focusing on those rules unfavourable to China's own interests. For instance, it strongly called for the abolition of the non-market-economy status provisions in the Anti-Dumping Agreement 1994, which, coupled with the corresponding provisions in China's WTO Accession Protocol 2001, had caused Chinese companies to suffer from discrimination in dumping margin calculations. With respect to the procedural rules in WTO dispute settlement, China also appealed to developed countries to 'exercise due restraint' in cases against developing countries.[55]

China's experience in WTO dispute settlement went through an interesting learning curve. In the first few years after its WTO accession, China adopted a rather conciliatory approach in dispute settlement. Between 2001 and 2008, it only initiated three cases against other WTO parties, but was sued in thirteen disputes. In those thirteen cases in which China was the respondent, mutually agreed solutions were reached in six. This 'quietude' began to change in 2009. Seven of the fourteen cases filed in that year involved China, while China alone bought three cases to defend its trading rights. To date, it has brought twenty cases against other WTO members, and has appeared as the respondent in forty-three cases and as a third party in 164 cases.[56] The profound implication of 'China's emergence as a major player in dispute settlement is the most significant change in the identity of the system's top participants since the establishment of the WTO'.[57]

In terms of the contribution China may have made to WTO jurisprudence, one has to distinguish between the cases filed by China and those filed against it. China certainly intends to establish jurisprudence in the WTO concerning the discriminatory treatment of China as a 'non-market economy' (NME) through repeatedly bringing legal actions against developed economies, in particular the US and European Union.

[53] Lim and Wang (n 29) 1309–10. [54] Ibid.

[55] Pasha Hsieh, 'China's Development of International Economic Law and WTO Legal Capacity Building' (2010) 13 Journal of International Economic Law 997, 1027.

[56] WTO, 'China and the WTO' <http://www.wto.org/english/thewto_e/countries_e/china_e.htm> accessed 12 January 2019.

[57] Matthew Kennedy, 'China's Role in WTO Dispute Settlement' (2012) 11 World Trade Review 555, 559.

One of the most significant cases is *US–Anti-Dumping and Countervailing Duties*,[58] in which the Appellate Body found much in China's favour. It systematically clarified the definition of 'public body' in WTO agreements, and ruled that 'double remedies'—namely the application of anti-dumping duties and countervailing duties to the same imported products—were generally invalid under the Agreement on Subsidies and Countervailing Measures 1994.[59] Most recently, China initiated two requests for consultations, which paved the way for it to bring the US and European Union to the WTO's Dispute Settlement Body (DSB), to challenge provisions in their trade laws for determining the normal value of NME countries in anti-dumping proceedings involving products from China.[60]

Nonetheless, it is those cases brought against China which demonstrate the extensive impact IEL can have on China. In *China–Auto Parts*,[61] the Panel and Appellate Body, at the request of the European Communities, the US, and Canada, found that Chinese measures of levying a 25 per cent tariff on auto parts imported for production/assembly in China violated China's obligations under GATT and the Agreement on Trade-Related Aspects of Intellectual Property Rights 1994 as well as China's WTO commitments. This was the first case in which China opted to go through the whole legal process to obtain an Appellate Body report, although the final legal defeat had been expected. China fully implemented the WTO decision by calling a stop to the WTO-inconsistent measures, indicating its willingness to act within the world trading system and comply even with unfavourable rulings. However, the realities of China's compliance depend also on whether the nature of the WTO decision contradicts the core of the Chinese government's governing philosophy.

China also lost to the US in *China–Publications and Audiovisual Products*,[62] in which the Panel and Appellate Body found that Chinese measures restricting the importation and distribution of publications, audiovisual home entertainment products, sound recordings, and films for theatrical release violated China's obligations under its Accession Protocol, GATS, and GATT. Immediately after the ruling, China informed the DSB of its intention to implement the decision and it reached an agreement with the US on the reasonable period of time needed for implementation. China subsequently stated several times at the DSB that it had ensured full implementation of the decision. This was, however, questioned by the US, who refused to

[58] WTO, *US—Definitive Anti-Dumping and Countervailing Duties on Certain Products from China* (11 March 2011) WT/DS379/AB/R.

[59] Ibid.

[60] WTO, *United States—Measures Related to Price Comparison Methodologies* (December 2016) WT/DS515/15; WTO, *European Union—Measures Related to Price Comparison Methodologies* (December 2016) WT/DS516/11.

[61] WTO, *China—Measures Affecting Imports of Automobile Parts* (15 December 2008) WT/DS339/AB/R.

[62] WTO, *China-Publications and Audiovisual Products* (11 May 2012) WT/DS363/19; WTO, *China—Measures Affecting Trading Rights and Distribution Services for Certain Publications and Audiovisual Entertainment Products* (21 December 2009) WT/DS363/AB/R.

acknowledge that China had fully complied with the Appellate Body report's recommendations and rulings.[63]

But, overall, China has appeared to be a responsible player in WTO dispute settlement. It 'has played the role of a system-maintainer under the DSU, not that of a reformer or of a transformer', and has generally complied with the DSB's decisions when its trade measures were found to be WTO-inconsistent.[64] China's compliance record with some DSB recommendations and rulings might be ambivalent, but it has never refused to accept the DSB's jurisdiction, challenged the composition of a panel, raised objections to the procedures, or blocked the DSB agenda. This is in stark contract with the well-known four 'No's, namely 'non-acceptance, non-participation, non-recognition and non-enforcement', that China proffered in the South China Sea Arbitration, concluded under the UN Convention on the Law of the Sea 1982 dispute settlement procedures in 2016.[65] Likewise, China displays less obedience in the IMF, discussed in the next section.

3.5 Asia and the IMF Governance Reform

The IMF, the 'central institution of global financial cooperation',[66] has been facing a crisis of being marginalized in the international economic system and hence is working on reforming itself to improve its legitimacy and efficiency. One of the key issues is IMF governance reform, which requires action in three areas: 'representation on [the] IMF Executive Board, realignment of IMF voting shares, and . . . procedures to choose IMF management'.[67]

The governance structure of the IMF is disconnected from current world economic realities as it does not give adequate weight in its decision-making processes to rising Asian economies, including China and India. Historically, leading industrial economies including the US, European Union, and Japan have held a majority of the total votes, which enables them to pass many decisions by simple majority. In addition, the US always holds more than 15 per cent of the votes so that it can veto major decisions concerning the structure of the IMF, the adoption of which requires an 85 per cent threshold.

Major rising economies in Asia are significantly under-represented in the IMF. Before 2008, China held 2.928 per cent of the total IMF votes, which put it on par with Canada but behind the US (17.023 per cent), Japan (6.108 per cent), Germany

[63] See the WTO's information page on DS363 <http://www.wto.org/english/tratop_e/dispu_e/cases_e/ds363_e.htm> accessed 12 January 2019.

[64] Kennedy (n 57) 588.

[65] See Jiangyu Wang, 'Legitimacy, Jurisdiction and Merits in the South China Sea Arbitration: Chinese Perspectives and International Law' (2017) 22 Journal of Chinese Political Science 185.

[66] Edwin Truman, *A Strategy for IMF Reform* (Petersen Institute for International Economics 2006) 2–3 (quoting IMF Managing Director Rodrigo de Rato).

[67] Ibid. 9.

(5.968 per cent), France (4.929 per cent), United Kingdom (4.929 per cent), Italy (3.242 per cent), and Saudi Arabia (3.210 per cent). The voting shares of India, South Korea, and Singapore were, respectively, 1.916 per cent, 0.760 per cent, and 0.406 per cent. A reform in 2008 increased China's voting share to 3.803 per cent and India's to 2.336 per cent.[68] At that time, however, China's economy was about to overtake Japan as the second largest in the world. On the other hand, European economies were drastically over-represented in the IMF (with about 30 per cent of the total voting rights).

In December 2010, the IMF, mandated by a G20 conference, approved a package of 'landmark' reforms,[69] which called for shifting a 6 per cent quota share to emerging economies and reducing representation of advanced European economies on the IMF Executive Board. This reform package was approved by the US Congress in December 2015. As a result, China's quota share is now 6.41 per cent and voting share is 6.09 per cent, while India's voting share is 2.64 per cent. The US still maintains its veto power by holding 16.52 per cent of the total votes, followed by Japan's 6.15 per cent.[70]

This modest reform certainly still does not reflect the increased economic importance of emerging Asian economies. The Chinese economy is now about two-thirds of the US economy and several times the GDPs of Japan and the major European powers, but its voting share is still lower. In addition, the tradition of leadership selection mandates that the President of the World Bank is always appointed by the US and that the Managing Director of the IMF always comes from Europe (but has to be accepted by the US).

From China's perspective, it seeks, with loud rhetoric, to increase its influence in the IMF but has not been particularly rigorous in pursuing this objective. It takes what is given to it by the IMF, but does not have confidence that it will be fairly treated within it. It was happy about the inclusion of its currency, the Renminbi, in the Special Drawing Rights basket as a fifth currency from 1 October 2016, because this inclusion marked a milestone in Renminbi's long march towards internationalization.[71] However, its disappointment at the modest increase of its quota, as well as the slow approval of the 2010-reform by the US Congress (which hesitated to increase Chinese influence in the IMF), might lead China to establish alternative international financial institutions in which it can play a leadership role, as examined below.

[68] IMF, 'Quota and Voting Shares before and after Implementation of Reforms Agreed in 2008 and 2010', 2011 <http://www.imf.org/external/np/sec/pr/2011/pdfs/quota_tbl.pdf> accessed 12 January 2019.

[69] IMF, 'IMF Survey: G-20 Ministers Agree 'Historic' Reforms in IMF Governance' (IMF Survey Online, 23 October 2010) <http://www.imf.org/en/News/Articles/2015/09/28/04/53/sonew102310a> accessed 25 December 2017.

[70] IMF, 'IMF Members' Quotas and Voting Power, and IMF Board of Governors' <http://www.imf.org/external/np/sec/memdir/members.aspx> accessed 31 December 2017.

[71] IMF, 'IMF Adds Chinese Renminbi to Special Drawing Rights Basket' (IMF News, 30 September 2016) <http://www.imf.org/en/News/Articles/2016/09/29/AM16-NA093016IMF-Adds-Chinese-Renminbi-to-Special-Drawing-Rights-Basket> accessed 11 December 2018.

3.6 The Rise of China-led International Economic Institutions

The single most significant development in IEL in Asia in recent years is China's drive to establish and lead new international economic institutions. The first multilateral institution that China proposed creating (in October 2013) was the Asian Infrastructure Investment Bank (AIIB), which was launched in December 2015 with fifty-seven founding members and which now has eighty members from Asia and Europe. The stated purpose of the AIIB is to provide financing for 'investing in infrastructure and other productive sectors' so as to 'foster sustainable economic development, create wealth and improve infrastructure connectivity in Asia'.[72] As suggested by the 'Asian' in its name, the AIIB is an Asian-based international economic institution, headquartered in Beijing, and is categorised as a multilateral development bank (MDB), or a 'multilateral financial institution' as stated in its Articles of Agreement 2015.

The AIIB can be further characterized as a 'regional' international economic institution. It obviously hopes to be valued as an Asian institution by Asians and, at the same time, regarded as a global institution worldwide. It does so by dividing membership into regional members, which are located in Asia and Oceania, and non-regional members. Its thirty-eight regional members, including Australia, New Zealand, and Russia, now hold 79.0685 per cent of the subscriptions of the AIIB's total capital stock and 77.1190 per cent of the total votes. The twenty non-regional members from Europe and Africa are assigned 22.8810 per cent of the total voting power.[73] According to its Articles of Agreement, AIIB lending can be extended to member countries or entities in member territories, as well as international or regional agencies for development.[74]

The AIIB has been touted as a rival to existing Bretton Woods institutions, such as the US-led World Bank or the Japan-led Asian Development Bank. Putting aside China's motivation for creating the AIIB, it does have the most influential position in the Bank through institutional arrangements. First, China is its largest shareholder, contributing half of the Bank's US$100 billion capital and holding 27.4499 per cent of voting shares. India, the second largest member state, owns 7.9 per cent of the total votes. The disparity in voting power between China and other members is unparalleled in the world of MDBs.[75] With such capital holding, China has veto power in the AIIB.[76] However, in negotiations with European countries China reportedly committed to forgo the veto power by agreeing to lower its shareholding to below 25 per cent in order to invite more new members to join the bank and also proposed

[72] AIIB Articles of Agreement 2015 art. 1:1.

[73] See AIIB's membership information <http://www.aiib.org/en/about-aiib/governance/members-of-bank/index.html> accessed 12 January 2019.

[74] AIIB Articles of Agreement 2015 art. 11:1(a).

[75] Martin Weiss, *Asian Infrastructure Investment Bank (AIIB)*, Congressional Research Service Report R44754 (2017) 9.

[76] AIIB Articles of Agreement 2015, art. 28:2(ii).

that no single country dictate decision-making.[77] Secondly, the AIIB does not have a resident Board of Directors and so its day-to-day management is delegated to its Beijing-based President, officers, and staff. In addition, more decision-making power is given to regional countries and its largest shareholder, China.[78]

Another China-driven multilateral development institution is the New Development Bank (NDB), also known as the BRICS Development Bank. It was an initiative of the BRICS countries (Brazil, Russia, India, China, and South Africa) in 2013 and was formally established in July 2015, a year before the AIIB's inauguration. Headquartered in Shanghai, the NDB is also an MDB, mandated to 'mobilize resources for infrastructure and sustainable development projects in BRICS and other emerging economies and developing countries'.[79] It has an initial authorized capital of US$100 billion and subscribed capital of US$50 billion, which is 'equally distributed amongst the founding members'.[80] Thus, each BRICS country holds 20 per cent of the NDB's total capital stock as well as the same share of the total votes. The founding members' shareholding—together with the voting power—will change with the admission of new members but should not be reduced to below 55 per cent.[81] Clearly, the capital structure and voting system determine that decision-making in the NDB is equally weighted amongst Brazil, Russia, India, China, and South Africa, although China has the largest economy. However, the fact that the NDB is based in Shanghai and that its first President is Indian, demonstrates the relatively large influence of Asia's two emerging economies, especially China's leadership position in the BRICS group. The NDB's location is certainly a geographical signal that development financing is moving east.

3.7 Rising Asia's Impact on IEL and International Economic Order

Taking a holistic view, the following general observations may be made about Asia, IEL, and the international economic order. The first point must be that Asian countries are generally good citizens in the contemporary US-led international economic system and are rule-takers in IEL. They have benefited from the system, prospered within it, and are largely satisfied with the status quo of the international economic order. Asian countries which have conducted market-based liberalization and been integrated into the system seldom challenged the rules of the system explicitly, and, apart from India's notable contribution to the development rules in the WTO, they have not made much visible contribution to agenda-setting, norm-creation, and rule-making in the

[77] Lingling Wei and Bob Davis, 'China Forgoes Veto Power at New Bank to Win Key European Nation's Support', *The Wall Street Journal* (23 March 2015) <http://www.wsj.com/articles/china-forgoes-veto-power-at-new-bank-to-win-key-european-nations-support-1427131055> accessed 12 January 2019.

[78] Weiss (n 75) 8–11.

[79] NDB Articles of Agreement 2014 art. 2.

[80] NDB Articles of Agreement 2014 art. 7.

[81] NDB Articles of Agreement 2014 art. 8.

international economic order. Asian countries are also significantly under-represented in international economic institutions.

Second, notwithstanding the discriminatory 'WTO-plus' obligations applied to China, Vietnam, and possibly other Asian countries, the development models adopted by Asian countries, at least in their initial stages, might not be consistent with the 'spirit' of the liberal international economic order. That is, they might have made use of the 'loopholes' or 'grey areas' of IEL, however contrary to the liberal order's objectives of a market economy and trade liberalization. Japan's development model, characterized as 'classical developmentalism' in the first few decades after WWII, is such an example. It was observed that 'Japan had a government that used industrial policy to protect infant industries and restrict foreign capital's access to the domestic market, while actively cultivating strategic industries for export to foreign markets'.[82] China's economic policy in the Reform Era was arguably termed as 'neo-liberal developmentalism' because it introduced bold market forces to remodel its old planned economy.[83] But China is also known for the extensive use of protectionist tools including industrial policy, subsidies, and non-tariff measures to promote economic development.[84]

Generally, the economic modernization in East Asia has been portrayed as the 'East Asia Model'.[85] This model has several strands of policy choices, and those which are related to international trade and investment include, *inter alia*, flexible exchange rate policies to reinforce export competitiveness, strong state–business connections to coordinate national economic strategy and market competition, and governments' activist policies (which include selective use of tariff measures and export incentives to buttress industrialization and exportation).[86] Arguably, these policies went against the liberal 'spirit' of the post-war international economic system. However, Asian countries, most notably China, are still being accused of using the same or similar industrial policies to charge competition at the expense of the developed markets.[87] In a recent public hearing by the USTR, a USTR Assistant Secretary unequivocally spoke of the need 'to find effective ways to address those Chinese government practices that

[82] Bai Gao, 'Neoliberal and Classical Developmentalism: A Comparative Analysis of the Chinese and Japanese Models for Economic Development' in Xiaoming Huang (ed), *Modern Economic Development in Japan and China* (Palgrave Macmillan 2013) 69.

[83] Ibid. 72.

[84] See e.g. Ling Liu, *China's Industrial Policies and the Global Business Revolution: The Case of the Domestic Appliance Industry* (Routledge 2005) ch 2. See also Dwight Perkins, 'Industrial and Financial Policy in China and Vietnam: A New Model or a Replay of the East Asian Experience?' in Joseph Stiglitz and Shahid Yusuf (eds), *Rethinking the East Asia Miracle* (OUP and World Bank 2001) 247.

[85] See World Bank, *The East Asian Miracle: Economic Growth and Public Policy* (OUP 1993).

[86] Shahid Yusuf, 'The East Asian Miracle at the Millennium', in Stiglitz and Yusuf (eds) (n 84) 1.

[87] David Lawder, 'USTR Lighthizer: Trump challenging China's industrial policies—radio interview' *Reuters* (26 July 2017) <http://www.reuters.com/article/us-usa-trade-china-lighthizer/ustr-lighthizer-trump-challenging-chinas-industrial-policies-radio-interview-idUSKBN1ABoDR> accessed 25 December 2017. See also 'What might a trade war between America and China look like?' *The Economist* (5 February 2017) <http://www.economist.com/the-economist-explains/2017/02/05/what-might-a-trade-war-between-america-and-china-look-like> accessed 12 January 2019.

may violate the spirit of the WTO that nevertheless may not fall squarely within the WTO disciplines'.[88]

These concerns must raise some fundamental questions about belief in the universality of IEL. If WTO law, being one of the most important pillars of IEL today, is not able to govern national trade practices, and major trading nations believe that they must resolve their trade disputes outside of the WTO, the collapse of IEL must be highly probable. On the other hand, if the international economic system (of the WTO or other international or regional arrangements) cannot develop rules to govern the major trade disputes between trading nations, IEL might deserve to have its fate signed and sealed. To some extent, this might be the greatest challenge—coming from Asia—to world trade law in particular and IEL in general.

Third, a fundamental question should be asked about the impact of the rise of China-led, Asia-based international economic institutions on the orientation of global economic governance and the stability of the international economic system. Will these institutions help China to posit itself as a new hegemonic power in a new international economic order (and eventually a new China-led world order) with a different system of rules of law? This kind of concern may be overly-anxious at this stage for a few reasons. One may maintain that an Asian approach in general—and the Chinese approach in particular—tends to conduct reform in a gradual, non-threatening, and cooperative manner, with a view to seeking partnership and mutual benefit. This can be seen in the governance structure of the China-led institutions such as the NDB and AIIB, discussed earlier, in contrast to US dominance in the World Bank and IMF.

On the other hand, the lending policy and practice of these China-led MDBs will have a significant impact on the landscape of infrastructure financing, at least in the developing world. Financing from the traditional Bretton Woods institutions is known for the 'conditionalities' attached to the loans, which had created a situation where 'a succession of economic crises in Russia, Asia and Latin America along with growing disparities in wealth within the developed world led to disillusionment with neo-liberal policies and the engines of globalization which profited from it'.[89] In contrast, the AIIB and NDB articles of agreement do not mention any conditionalities. Indeed, the AIIB has announced the proposal not to attach any conditions to its loans. Developing countries are likely to turn towards these China-led institutions because they believe this approach would help rebalance the international economic order towards economic growth based on partnership and cooperation, not Washington consensus-based liberalization imposed upon them by the traditional lenders and donors. The proliferation of this development philosophy will in turn put pressure on

[88] David Lawder, 'US business groups say WTO unable to curb many Chinese trade practices' *Reuters* (5 October 2017) <http://www.reuters.com/article/us-usa-china-trade/u-s-business-groups-say-wto-unable-to-curb-many-chinese-trade-practices-idUSKBN1C92UL> accessed 25 December 2017.

[89] Muthucumaraswamy Sornarajah and Jiangyu Wang, *China, India and the International Economic Order* (CUP 2010) 3.

the traditional Bretton Woods institutions and may compel them to compromise on conditionalities.

In the long run, more profound changes may happen to the international economic system with the continuing rise of Asia in general, and China and India in particular, in international relations. The new international economic institutions may be used by emerging Asian economies to project their economic power, learn rule-making skills, institutionalize their newly acquired international status, and expand their geopolitical influence. For instance, it had been widely believed that the AIIB was to be used to finance the 'One Belt, One Road' initiative, a Chinese grand strategy of boosting the links between China and dozens of countries along a land route and a sea route, to make China the hub of the Asia-Europe area.[90] However, it is fair to say that these new initiatives are still conducted within the existing IEL framework. Whether the emerging Asian giants, especially China, will rise within the international order or impose a new consensus for international economic relations remains to be seen.

4 Internalizing IEL in Asia: Regionalism and Regional Economic Institutions

Asian countries rarely appear collectively on the world stage. Unlike Europe or even Latin America, Asia does not have extensive networks of regional institutions binding the countries together. Karns and Mingst note that three factors underlie the development of regionalism: identity, internal or external threats, and leadership.[91] In this sense, 'Asian regionalism has been both belated and limited'.[92] Though geographically close to each other, Asian states do not have a shared perception of being part of a definable region with which they can align their national interests. Many Asian countries were former European colonies and gained their independence only after WWII. Even as colonies or semi-colonies, many of them suffered the brutal invasion from the Japanese Empire. These experiences generated strong attachment to state sovereignty and fear of Asia's domination by any single power. In addition, competition among China, the US, Japan, and now India prevents any single power from exercising effective leadership to keep Asian countries together.

Nevertheless, Asian countries have jumped on the third wave of regionalism and appear to be proactive in strengthening regional organizations and pushing for regional integration. It was observed that 'Asian and Asia-Pacific regional institutions tend to be

[90] Weiss (n 75) 2.

[91] Margaret Karns and Karen Mingst, *International Organizations: The Politics and Processes of Global Governance* (Lynne Ripener Publishers 2004) 148–9.

[92] Ibid. 189.

informal with specific rules, no binding commitments, small secretariats, and an emphasis on consensus decision-making'.[93] Asian practice in the recent wave of regionalism still retains the essential characteristics of this 'Asian way' of doing things, but seems also to be open to more legalism embodied in the new generations of free trade agreements (FTAs).

4.1 Asia's Traditional Regional Economic Institutions

There are three major traditional regional economic institutions: the Asian Development Bank (ADB), Asia-Pacific Economic Cooperation (APEC), and Association of Southeast Asian Nations (ASEAN), discussed below. In addition, the eight-member[94] South Asian Association for Regional Cooperation (SAARC), established in 1985, can be more briefly mentioned in an economic context. SAARC members signed a regional Agreement on South Asian Free Trade Area (SAFTA) in 2004 with a view to exchanging tariff concessions through product-by-product or positive-listing approach. The process of trade liberalization through SAFTA has, however, been rather slow, and hamstrung by political disagreements.

4.1.1 *Asian Development Bank*

The ADB is the oldest surviving regional multilateral institution in Asia and the Pacific. Opened in Manila in 1966, originally with thirty-one members, it was tasked to finance development and foster economic growth and cooperation in developing Asia (excluding the socialist countries). It currently has sixty-seven members, with forty-eight of them from the Asia-Pacific. Its Charter mandates that 60 per cent of the decision-making power must be retained by regional members.

The ADB had initially been a Japan-driven institution, building upon a Japanese proposal in 1963. It was mainly staffed by Japanese nationals in its early days, and still has the informal rule of always electing a Japanese president. A close connection between the ADB and Japan's Ministry of Finance since the ADB's earliest days makes it possible to channel 'Japanese regional economic and financial objectives into the Bank's policies'.[95] However, internal power struggles for leadership between Japan and the US increasingly led to the latter also becoming a dominant player in the Bank.[96] Currently the US and Japan tie for first place in the Bank's decision-making system, each holding 15.607 per cent of its total subscribed capital and 12.784 per cent of its voting power. China and India take the third and fourth positions in the Bank, having 5.454 per cent and 5.363 per cent of the voting power respectively.[97]

[93] Ibid. 190.

[94] Afghanistan, Bangladesh, Bhutan, India, Maldives, Nepal, Pakistan, and Sri Lanka.

[95] Michael Wesley, *The Regional Organizations of the Asia-Pacific* (Palgrave Macmillan 2003) 27.

[96] Ibid. 28–9.

[97] Asian Development Bank, *Annual Report 2017*, 60.

The ADB's biggest challenge today is how to compete with the AIIB in Asian development financing. It would not be surprising if many of the ADB's traditional clientele went to the AIIB for support. It also faces another unprecedented challenge: the retreat of US leadership from the ADB, as the Trump Administration has not appointed a US ambassador to the ADB Board of Directors. These may be signs that the ADB has entered a new era which is witnessing the rise of both China and 'America First'.

4.1.2 *Asia-Pacific Economic Cooperation*

APEC was created in 1989 to facilitate trade and discuss economic policies among its now twenty-one state-economy members. Its organizational nature is self-defined as the following:

> APEC operates as a cooperative, multilateral economic and trade forum. Member economies participate on the basis of open dialogue and respect for views of all participants. In APEC, all economies have an equal say and decision-making is reached by consensus. There are no binding commitments or treaty obligations. Commitments are undertaken on a voluntary basis and capacity building projects help members implement APEC initiatives.[98]

Despite the rather cynical criticism about APEC that '[i]t is difficult to think of another institution that has gone from the enthusiasm of creation to the disillusionment of stagnation quite so rapidly',[99] APEC has actually made significant contributions to IEL in at least two areas: regional community building and promotion of trade liberalization—ideas which have led, and will lead, to more significant regional and international free trade initiatives.

On regional community building, the establishment of APEC gave the Asia-Pacific a more concrete identity by creating a forum for leaders and ministers to regularly communicate on economic cooperation and policy coordination. It is distinguishable among international organizations in that it also brings business leaders together to have dialogue with state leaders, through the APEC Business Advisory Council.[100] Further, APEC has the important function of engaging the US, as a Pacific Rim country, in Asia.[101]

APEC's promotion of trade and investment liberalization has achieved mixed results, regarded by some as its 'biggest failure'.[102] I would argue, however, that the liberalization ideas and projects promoted by APEC have already had tremendous impact on both the discourse and practice of transnational economic activities in Asia and globally. APEC included trade and investment facilitation in its agenda

[98] APEC, 'About APEC' <http://www.apec.org/About-Us/About-APEC> accessed 11 December 2018.

[99] Nick Bisley, 'APEC: Asia-Pacific Economic Cooperation' in Mark Beeson and Richard Stubbs (eds), *Routledge Handbook of Asian Regionalism* (Routledge 2012) 350.

[100] Ibid. 359.

[101] Hu Weixing, 'Building Asia-Pacific Regional Institution: The Role of APEC' (2013) 77 Procedia—Social and Behavioural Sciences 65, 67.

[102] Bisley (n 99) 356 (stating 'APEC's biggest failure to date has been its trade liberalization programme').

decades ago, which paved the way for the adoption of the Trade Facilitation Agreement at the WTO's Bali Ministerial Conference in 2013. The concept of 'open regionalism' adopted by APEC, which emphasizes open membership and unilateral liberalization ('concerted unilateralism'), has increasingly become a norm in international economic relations.[103]

The grand idea of a Free Trade Area for the Asia-Pacific (FTAAP) also came from APEC in a study of 2004, since then endorsed by the US, China, and APEC leaders. If realized, the FTAAP would ideally consolidate the piecemeal free trade arrangements into one mega-FTA, thus avoiding the overlap and fragmentation of rules and standards in Asia's existing FTAs.

4.1.3 *Association of Southeast Asian Nations*

The ten-member ASEAN, discussed in chapter 3, is probably the most developed and influential regional organization in Asia. With a combined GDP of US$2.6 trillion, ASEAN is now the sixth largest economy in the world, and the third largest in Asia (after China and Japan). While it started as a limited political association for regional peace and stability, over time it has promoted ASEAN-centred trade agreements (discussed in the next section). ASEAN's weakly institutionalized structure is intended to facilitate the famous 'ASEAN Way', which describes a distinctive ASEAN approach to regional cooperation based on consultations and consensus rather than Western-style legalism and formalism.[104]

4.2 Trade Regionalism: The Proliferation of FTAs in Asia

4.2.1 *The Rise of Regionalism in Asia*

For Asian countries, regional integration makes sense both economically and geostrategically.[105] But major Asian economies, including China, Japan, Korea, and ASEAN countries, were already busy with negotiating and concluding FTAs of their own before regional-level integration achieved some meaningful progress. When national ambitions and regional ideas are intertwined, the regionalization process is inevitably complicated by national interests, nationalist sentiments in historic and contemporary bilateral relations, and power politics.

On the other hand, regional integration is also necessarily a legalization process. Through FTAs, countries establish rules and standards to govern their external economic relations, and agree to bind themselves to legal obligations under IEL. A particular model of bilateral or regional economic arrangements, once codified into regional

[103] See Fred Bergsten, 'Open Regionalism' (1997) 20 The World Economy 545.

[104] Amitav Acharya, 'Ideas, Identity, and Institution-building: From the "ASEAN Way" to the "Asia-Pacific Way"?' (1997) 10 The Pacific Review 319, 329.

[105] Asian Development Bank, *Emerging Asian Regionalism: A Partnership for Shared Prosperity* (Asian Development Bank 2008) 13.

trade agreements or FTAs as part of IEL, will impose constraints on state behaviour. That could explain why none of the major economies in Asia would easily subscribe to the regional integration model proposed by others, given their complicated bilateral relations as well as each country's peculiar relations with the US.

The 'battle of models' leaves great room for power politics, as there is little doubt that 'the prevailing great powers at this historical moment are keen to use legal rules and institutions to advance their interests and institutionalize their power',[106] both regionally and globally. Thus, Asian regionalism is one of the best examples through which one can investigate 'the role of law in shaping international politics' and 'the role of politics in shaping international law',[107] as well as the possibility of using international (economic) law to limit injurious power politics.

4.2.2 *ASEAN-based Trade Liberalization*

Regionalism in East Asia dates back to the formation of the ASEAN Free Trade Area in 1992.[108] However, this could not be taken as the beginning of serious regionalization as its performance was rather 'dismal'[109] and 'had minimal economic impact'.[110] As such, '[b]efore 2000, regionalism in the Asia-Pacific region was distinguished by its absence'.[111] At the end of the 1990s, highly trade-dependent countries in ASEAN, most notably Singapore, began to look at FTAs in response to recent events including the 1997–8 Asian Financial Crisis, the collapse of the WTO's meeting in Seattle in 1999, and China's anticipated accession to the WTO in 2001. The first bilateral FTA, the Japan-Singapore Economic Partnership Agreement, was signed in January 2002, having been considered since late 1999.

The landmark regional integration initiative that kicked off a wave of regionalism in Asia was the ASEAN-China FTA (ACFTA), which, surprisingly, was proposed by the then Chinese Premier Zhu Rongji at the ASEAN-China Summit in November 2000. In November 2002, China and ASEAN countries were able to sign a Framework Agreement for the ACFTA. The ASEAN-China Free Trade Area, which is based on a range of agreements between China and ASEAN on trade in goods, services, investments, and other matters, came into being on 1 January 2010, as the world's biggest regional trade deal measured by population and the third largest by nominal GDP.

[106] Anne-Marie Slaughter, *International Law and International Relations: vol 285 of Recueil des cours* (Hague Academy of International Law and Martinus Nijhoff 2000) 9, 199.

[107] Ibid. 198.

[108] Rahul Sen, '"New Regionalism" in Asia: A Comparative Analysis of Emerging Regional and Bilateral Trading Agreements involving ASEAN, China and India' (2006) 40 Journal of World Trade 553, 554.

[109] Lay Hong Tan and Samtani Anil, 'The Shifting Paradigm in Regional Economic Integration: The ASEAN Perspective' (SSRN 22 August 2002) <http://ssrn.com/abstract=325484> accessed 11 December 2018.

[110] Richard Pomfret, *Regionalism in East Asia: Why Has It Flourished since 2000 and How Far Will It Go?* (World Scientific 2011) 25.

[111] Ibid.

The ACFTA set the framework and precedent for the FTAs that ASEAN signed with Korea in 2007, Japan in 2008, Australia and New Zealand in 2009, and India in 2009.[112] In Asia, China, Japan, and Korea were newcomers to regionalism, but the ASEAN+1 FTAs signed by them show that 'the three major East Asian countries have undergone a strategic policy change from favouring the multilateral approach for global free trade to actively participating in regional grouping in order to regain their growth momentum after the [Asian Financial Crisis]'.[113] In tandem with pursuing the ACFTA, China had entered into ten FTAs by 2010, with economies including Chile, Costa Rica, Hong Kong, Macau, New Zealand, Pakistan, Peru, Singapore, and Taiwan.[114]

4.2.3 *The Battle of Regionalism Models*

From the beginning of this wave of regional economic integration, Asian countries were struggling with identifying its geographical scope, out of mainly geopolitical concerns. Several regional groupings were proposed but favoured by different major powers. China initially indicated its willingness to negotiate a trilateral FTA among China, Japan, and South Korea. The concern about strong domestic opposition within the three north-east countries led them to agree that ASEAN would be an ideal bridge to hold East Asia together, which led to the idea of an ASEAN+3 model of regionalism. The ASEAN+3 FTA was officially proposed by China[115] and favoured by South Korea and ASEAN, at least initially.[116]

The ASEAN+3 model of regional cooperation commenced when China, Japan, and South Korea were invited to the informal ASEAN Leaders' Meeting in December 1997 amid the Asian Financial Crisis.[117] Since then, numerous intergovernmental initiatives have been developed under the umbrella of ASEAN+3, including successful regional financial cooperation through the Chiang Mai Initiative (which is Asia's only regional liquidity support arrangement), a regional economic surveillance process, and an Asian bond market.[118] It was also the model envisaged by the East Asian Vision Group in its

[112] In the case of the ASEAN-Japan FTA, it was noted that, '[p]rompted by the China + ASEAN framework agreement, Tokyo followed suit'. See Khairy Tourk, 'The Political Economy of East Asian Economic Integration' (2004) 15 Journal of Asian Economics 843, 857.

[113] Jong-Wha Lee and Innwon Park, 'Free Trade Areas in East Asia: Discriminatory or Non-discriminatory?' (2005) 28 World Economy 21, 23.

[114] See Jiangyu Wang, 'China and East Asian Regionalism' (2011) 17 European Law Journal 611, 613.

[115] Masahiro Kawai and Ganeshan Wignaraja, 'Multilateralizing Regional Trade Arrangements in Asia' in Richard Baldwin and Patrick Low (eds), *Multilateralizing Reginalism: Challenges for the Global Trading System* (CUP 2009) 501.

[116] Khairy Tourk, 'The Political Economy of East Asian Economic Integration' (2004) 15 Journal of Asian Economics 843, 858.

[117] Masahiro Kawai and Ganeshan Wignaraja, 'ASEAN+3 OR ASEAN+6: Which Way Forward?', ADB Institute Discussion Paper No 77 (Asian Development Bank 2007) 6 <http://www.adb.org/sites/default/files/publication/156716/adbi-dp77.pdf> accessed 25 December 2017.

[118] Ibid.

2001 report which recommended the establishment of an East Asian Free Trade Area (EAFTA) embracing the ASEAN+3 grouping.[119]

China has been a firm supporter of the EAFTA and East Asia's regional integration, on the condition, however, that it is based on the ASEAN+3 model. China's enthusiasm for this model was well received by ASEAN and was written into a Joint Declaration signed by Chinese Premier Wen Jiabao and the heads of the ten ASEAN governments in October 2003. Through it, China and ASEAN agreed to '[m]ake the ASEAN Plus Three mechanism as the main channel to move forward cooperation and regional economic integration in East Asia as a whole so as to promote sustainable development and common prosperity there'.[120]

Japan initially supported the idea of ASEAN+3, but quickly backed down from it.[121] Instead, Japan proposed a bigger regional deal, or the ASEAN+6 grouping, which covers ASEAN+3 plus Australia, New Zealand, and India.[122] The China-Japan rivalry appeared to be more visible in 2004–5. ASEAN leaders, by a suggestion of the East Asian Vision Group, convened the First East Asia Summit (EAS) in Kuala Lumpur on 14 December 2005. Arguments about whom to invite—China or Japan—preceded it: 'China favoured a guest list limited to ASEAN+3. Japan, seeking counterweights to China's influence, argued successfully for Australia, India and New Zealand to be included'.[123] The EAS has since become a pan-Asia forum for the sixteen countries, known as ASEAN+6.

Obviously, Australia, New Zealand, and India were brought into the EAS to check the growing influence of China, despite China's Premier Wen Jiabao's call that East Asian regionalism should be 'led by the East Asian countries'.[124] In that sense, the first EAS 'can be seen as a significant setback for Chinese diplomacy'.[125] On the other hand, China's lack of interest in participating in negotiations for a Comprehensive Economic Partnership in East Asia based on ASEAN+6, proposed by Japan in 2006 as a counter-proposal to China's idea of an ASEAN+3 FTA, was one of the main reasons that the ASEAN+6 regionalism made little progress in 2007–9. The politicization of regionalism turned economic integration in Asia into word games: '[i]t is now understood that the core of East Asian cooperation lies in ASEAN as the "driving force", with

[119] East Asian Vision Group Report 2001, 'Towards an East Asian Community: Region of Peace, Prosperity and Progress' <http://www.mofa.go.jp/region/asia-paci/report2001.pdf> accessed 26 December 2017.

[120] ASEAN and China, 'Joint Declaration of the Heads of State/Government of the Association of Southeast Asian Nations and the People's Republic of China on Strategic Partnership for Peace and Prosperity', Bali, 8 October 2003.

[121] Kawai and Wignaraja (n 115) 501 note concerning the caution that Japan holds about the ASEAN+3 FTA proposed by China, '[Japan's] official view is that, before negotiating an FTA/EPA, China must clearly demonstrate that compliance with all the commitments made in WTO accession negotiations'.

[122] Ibid. [123] Pomfret (n 110) 95.

[124] Philip Bowring, 'Towards an "Asian Union"' *The New York Times* (18 June 2005) <http://www.nytimes.com/2005/06/18/opinion/philip-bowring-toward-an-asian-union.html> accessed 20 May 2017.

[125] Ibid.

ASEAN+3 as the "main vehicle" for the realization of an eventual East Asian economic community, with the EAS as "an integral part of the overall evolving regional architecture"'.[126] In fact, regional economic integration conducted by Asians themselves stalled at that time, thanks to the lack of East Asia's indigenous leadership, which was caused by the China–Japan rivalry.

4.2.4 *The Rise and Demise of the Trans-Pacific Partnership*

When the Trans-Pacific Partnership (TPP) negotiations were concluded by twelve Pacific Rim states in February 2016, it was immediately recognized as the 'largest regional trade accord in history', with its members representing roughly 40 per cent of global GDP and one-third of world trade.[127] It included the Asian states of Singapore (which initiated it in 2003), Brunei, Japan, Malaysia, and Vietnam, plus neighbouring Australia and New Zealand. However comprehensive and significant it may have been, the US-led TPP is now dead (at least in its original form) as a result of US President Trump's executive order to pull the US out of it in January 2017, on the basis that the US prefers to deal bilaterally with other states.[128] The fall of the TPP saw the rise of the negotiations for a Regional Comprehensive Economic Partnership (RCEP), discussed below.

4.2.5 *Regional Comprehensive Economic Partnership*

The RCEP is basically the ASEAN+6 model of Asian regionalism. This is no coincidence: most of the TPP's Asian members are also parties to the RCEP. Contrary to popular media belief that the RCEP is a China-led trade deal to counter-balance the TPP, the RCEP is actually an ASEAN-driven mega-FTA project launched in November 2012, with a view to maintaining 'ASEAN Centrality' in the development of Asian regionalism.[129] With the US' departure from the TPP, the RCEP is those Asian countries' only choice for establishing a Pan-Asian free trade area. This trade deal is strongly supported by China, while the US is not taking part. The sixteen participating countries account for 'almost half of the world population, 31.6% of global output, 28.5% of global trade, and a fifth of the global foreign direct investment inflows in 2016'.[130]

Compared with the TPP, the RCEP is more limited in scope and may lead to a shallower degree of regional economic integration. One of the principles guiding the

[126] Kawai and Wignaraja (n 114) 509.

[127] Kevin Granville, 'The Trans-Pacific Partnership Accord Explained' *The New York Times* (5 October 2015) <http://www.nytimes.com> accessed 26 December 2017. The 12 countries are Australia, Brunei, Canada, Chile, Japan, Malaysia, Mexico, New Zealand, Peru, Singapore, US, and Vietnam.

[128] US President, 'Presidential Memorandum Regarding Withdrawal of the US from the Trans-Pacific Partnership Negotiations and Agreement: Memorandum for the US Trade Representative' (*The White House*, 23 January 2017) <http://www.whitehouse.gov/the-press-office/2017/01/23/presidential-memorandum-regarding-withdrawal-united-states-trans-pacific> accessed 26 December 2017.

[129] See Yoshifumi Fukunaga, 'ASEAN's Leadership in the Regional Comprehensive Economic Partnership' (2015) 2 Asia and the Pacific Policy Studies 103 (stating that '[o]ne of the biggest motivations in proposing the RCEP was ASEAN's desire for its centrality').

[130] 'Joint Leaders' Statement on the Negotiations for the Regional Comprehensive Economic Partnership (RCEP)', 14 November 2017, Manila, Philippines ('Joint Leaders' Statement 2017') paras 3 and 6.

RCEP negotiations is that this FTA will take into consideration 'the different levels of development of the participating countries' and accommodate 'appropriate forms of flexibility including provision for special and differential treatment, plus additional flexibility to the least-developed ASEAN Member States'.[131] The incorporation of the development dimension differentiates the RCEP from almost all other FTAs, which possess the singular objective of promoting market openness.

The conclusion of the RCEP has been repeatedly delayed. The differences and difficulties arising out of the distrust and different levels of economic development of RCEP partners are likely to lead to the conclusion of a low-grade FTA, if an agreement can be reached at all. Still, if completed, the RCEP will be a historic deal in terms of regional integration in Asia. First, it will instil confidence in free trade and globalization. The retreat from the TPP and the resort to economic nationalism of the Trump Administration have undermined such confidence. Secondly, even though the RCEP would become an agreement for shallow integration, it can still 'keep markets open, deepen economic integration and narrow the development gap among the member states'.[132] Importantly, the RCEP model 'may not be equivalent to the "gold standard" that the TPP espoused to be, but it will provide a clear pathway toward that goal'.[133]

Further, the RCEP will provide a platform to consolidate all the ASEAN+1 agreements, thus doing away with the 'noodle-bowl' effect by unifying the different rules of origin and other regulatory formalities. Lastly, and probably most significantly, the RCEP will be the first Pan-Asia FTA to bring together all the major economies in East, South, and Pacific Asia into an integrated market, with profound implications for the building of both a common market and a common Asian identity. In the long run, however, the exclusion of the US and other Asia-Pacific countries is not desirable, for both economic and geopolitical reasons. Asian regionalism should be Asia-Pacific oriented in the long run, eying also countries on the Americas' side of the Pacific. The path to regionalism in this vast area is undoubtedly the FTAAP, an agreement that covers possibly all the Pacific Rim economies.

5 Conclusion

Asia is an interesting and increasingly important player in the international economic system. The relationship between IEL and Asia has entered an unprecedented stage. The following offers a summary of the increasingly complex factors in this relationship.

[131] ASEAN, 'Guiding Principles and Objectives for Negotiating the Regional Comprehensive Economic Partnership', November 2012, Principle 4 <https://asean.org/storage/2012/05/RCEP-Guiding-Principles-public-copy.pdf> accessed 12 January 2019.

[132] Rebecca Fatima Sta Maria, 'RCEP More Relevant than Ever' *The Jakarta Post* (20 February 2017) <http://www.thejakartapost.com/academia/2017/02/20/rcep-more-relevant-now-than-ever.html> accessed 21 May 2017.

[133] Ibid.

First, while Asian countries have different models of development, Asia overall has benefited from the post-war liberal international economic order and the legal system that underpins it. It historically used IEL to foster its economic growth and is now lending support to the universality of IEL in an age of rising populism and anti-globalization sentiment. Complying with IEL provided opportunities for Asian economies to be treated as ostensibly equal participants and so to enjoy market access, non-discrimination, and the rules-based world economic order. Despite their rather depressed initial conditions, most Asian countries have been transformed by IEL into market economies or economies in which the market increasingly plays a decisive role.

Secondly, major Asian economies' participation in international trade dispute settlement has generated important or even landmark decisions in WTO jurisprudence. On the other hand, Asian countries have not yet secured a place on the centre stage of the world economy with respect to rule-making and agenda-setting. They are, in the main, rule-takers in the international economic order. Apart from India's contribution to the development aspect of international trade law, major Asian economies played an insignificant role in norm-creation, rule-making, and agenda-setting in IEL. Even for dispute settlement, they seemed to be mainly objects whose trade polices provided many negative examples of what should not have been done by WTO members. Japan's and India's performance in the international economic system demonstrated that Asia was not able to translate economic might or international influence (among developing countries) into entrepreneurship or rule-making power. It remains to be seen whether the rise of China and India will change the situation.

Thirdly, Asian countries are woefully under-represented in international economic institutions, which substantially limits their roles in global economic governance. Meaningful reforms to reconnect global institutions such as the IMF and World Bank to the realities in the international economic system have proven to be exceed ingly difficult, as this would involve extorting concessions from the adamant vested interests in those institutions. This dilemma is leading to two consequences. One, international economic organizations are gradually losing not only their efficiency in dealing with crises but also their legitimacy. Two, rising powers unhappy with the status quo are moving to build their own global economic organizations in direct competition to the Western-dominated Bretton Woods institutions. In this regard, the rise of the China-led institutions such as the AIIB and NDB postulates profound challenges and it is an open question whether Asia and the West can work together to integrate these alternative competing financial institutions into the liberal international economic order. An even bigger challenge—with tremendous uncertainties—is what a new international economic order will be if the existing liberal order has to be modified markedly to accommodate the geopolitical ambition and different development philosophies of the rising Asian powers, especially China.

Fourthly, Asia has experienced dramatic proliferation of FTAs in the last two decades without, however, momentous regional economic integration even in East Asia, let alone a Pan-Asian free trade area. Successful regionalism requires the pursuit of a common identity and leadership. In the sense that regionalization is also a legalization process, the development of trade regionalism has contributed to the incremental construction of a rules-based economic order in Asia. On the other hand, the lack of political will to cooperate has generated a battle between different integration models led by different powers. Asia's bumpy path to regional economic integration suggests that legalization of regional economic relations is, after all, premised on the development of cooperative international relations.

Finally, the rise of populism, economic nationalism, and anti-globalism in Europe and the US has put Asia in a crucial place to defend free trade and globalization. Factors such as relatively fast economic growth and stable domestic environments help keep Asian economies inclined to maintain the status quo in the international economic system. On the other hand, this new development is also pushing Asia into the spotlight: Asian economic systems and state-led development models, which used to be ignored or merely tolerated by the liberal international economic order, are now become the focus of attention in Western foreign policy debates, including whether they are consistent with IEL.

In the best scenario, the rise of Asia has at least offered an opportunity for Asia and the West to work together to make the international economic system and its underlying IEL more inclusive and possibly more just and efficient. This in turn may provide a legal framework to address the new disputes among trading nations. A rising Asia will be able to provide increasing input to this process.

CHAPTER 11

INTERNATIONAL DISPUTE SETTLEMENT

HISASHI OWADA AND SAMUEL H CHANG

1 Introduction

In the spring of 1899, representatives of twenty-six states convened in the seventeenth century summer residence of Dutch Queen Wilhelmina for the first Hague Peace Conference. Among the six agreements concluded there was the Convention for the Pacific Settlement of International Disputes 1899, recognizing arbitration as the preferred method of settling international disputes of a legal nature and establishing the Permanent Court of Arbitration (PCA). Of the twenty-six participating states, only four were from the Asia Pacific region: China, India, Japan, and then-Siam.

There are today a combined 121 states parties to the Convention 1899 and its 1907 revision. In the intervening century, interstate dispute resolution has materialized from a vague aspiration to a network of standing courts, arbitral bodies, and specialized tribunals. Over the same period, the Asia-Pacific has grown to a region of roughly forty states representing over half of the world's population and nearly half of global economic output, with increasing political weight on the global stage. To be sure, these parallel developments share a post-war order founded on the ideals of the international rule of law and the free flow of capital. But by most popular accounts of Asia, both developments progressed largely independently of one another, as Asian states have long been perceived to eschew international law and litigation while engaging head-on in economic exchange.

This chapter aims to test part of that perception. In recognizing the challenges raised by the breadth and depth of the topic, and in keeping with the practical nature of this handbook, we begin with an empirical synopsis of non-Western states' participation in various dispute settlement mechanisms. For this, we have compiled data at the regional, sub-regional, and state levels for various subject matters, mechanisms, and treaties. Our review of state practice in the section below is not intended to substitute for a systematic empirical study on Asian participation in dispute settlement—a much-needed endeavour for which we hope this chapter might serve as a basic starting point. What this chapter does offer, however, is a snapshot of state practice in Asia vis-à-vis other non-Western regions.[1] And from this snapshot, three thematic characteristics of the region can be gleaned.

1.1 Geographic and Topical Diversity

The first is the diversity of state practice within Asia. As certain commentators have observed, the idea of an Asian or Asia-Pacific 'region' is a somewhat artificial construct that risks shoehorning into a unitary body an expansive geographic area marked by great ethnic, cultural, economic, and historical diversity.[2] Our analysis of state practice supports this view. The figures below will make clear that Central Asian states, Pacific Island states, and the rest of Asia (admittedly a motley grouping in itself, consisting of Australasia and East, South, and Southeast Asia) all have markedly different approaches towards international dispute settlement mechanisms.

Intersecting this sub-regional diversity is the diversity of approaches within any given state towards different areas of concern. Thus, participation in international dispute settlement varies not only according to sub-region, but also according to the area of law. For instance, Asian states are significantly more active in trade and investment disputes than African states. But they have much lower participation in international criminal law than all other non-Western states. Similarly, Central Asian states have been largely absent from the International Court of Justice (ICJ) (and perhaps less surprisingly, law of the sea disputes), whereas they are the most active among Asian states in investment arbitration. These many variables belie any simple summation of a single 'Asian approach' towards international law.

1.2 Facility with Dispute Settlement

The second characteristic is that Asian states on the whole are generally quite willing to substantively engage with international courts. A greater share of Asian states have submitted written statements to ICJ advisory proceedings than African or Latin American states. And after accounting for sub-regional diversity, we see that Northeast, Southeast, and South Asian states (that is, Asian states excluding the Central Asian and

[1] Where not stated otherwise, this chapter follows the volume's geographical grouping of Asian states (used interchangeably with 'Asia-Pacific')—that is, the UN Asia-Pacific Group, with the addition of Australia and New Zealand and the exclusion of Middle Eastern states (based on the UN Food and Agriculture Organization definition), for a total of 42 states.

[2] José Alvarez, 'Institutionalised Legalisation and the Asia-Pacific "Region"' (2007) 4 New Zealand Journal of Public and International Law 15; Hisashi Owada, 'The Rule of Law in a Globalizing World—An Asian Perspective' (2009) 8 Washington University Global Studies Law Review 187, 202.

Pacific Island states) have similar participation rates as Africa and Latin America in contentious proceedings of the ICJ. Part of this, no doubt, is due to the increased use of the Court by Asian states over the last two decades.

In the fields of trade and investment, Asian states have initiated more cases in the World Trade Organization (WTO) than states in Africa and Latin America combined. Asian states have also signed more bilateral investment treaties (BITs) than African or Latin American states and have a higher rate of membership in the International Centre for the Settlement of Investment Disputes (ICSID) than Latin American states. With respect to the law of the sea, Asia is second only to Latin America for cases initiated under the dispute settlement procedures of the UN Convention on the Law of the Sea 1982 (UNCLOS).

1.3 Hesitation towards Institutional Commitments

The above notwithstanding, the third characteristic is that there remains in Asia a cautious hesitation towards open commitments to international dispute-resolution mechanisms. The most glaring omission is that of any pan-Asian dispute settlement body. Whereas Africa, Europe, and Latin America all have regional human rights courts and sub-regional courts of different varieties, only the Central Asian states participate in any standing regional court.

Nor is this hesitation towards formal binding commitments limited to the regional level. Asian states are also reluctant to commit in advance to multilateral dispute settlement procedures. This holds true across all Asian sub-regions and in comparison with other regions of the world. Although Asian states have been active in contributing to the ICJ's advisory proceedings and have increasingly initiated contentious cases, they remain hesitant to make 'compulsory jurisdiction' declarations under article 36 of the ICJ Statute 1945. Asian states are also more likely to opt out of optional treaty provisions that grant compulsory jurisdiction to the ICJ. They have also been hesitant to commit to the compulsory jurisdiction of the International Tribunal on the Law of the Sea (ITLOS) or ICJ in settling law of the sea disputes under UNCLOS or other agreements. With respect to investor-state dispute settlement (ISDS), Asian states in recent years have been moving towards retaining more control over the scope of proceedings.

In sum one can say that Asian states have not been afraid to proactively engage with international law or to utilize existing dispute settlement mechanisms on a case-by-case basis. There remains, however, some hesitation to commit in advance to compulsory jurisdiction or to establish any robust regional dispute settlement mechanism.

We begin with an overview of state practice in international dispute settlement forums, followed by a review of regional adjudication in Asia. We then explore potential historical and structural reasons for the discrepancy between the region's practice and its institutional development. In short, we propose that the immense diversity within Asia, combined with geographic and historical contingencies (particularly in the Cold War era), may have inhibited efforts towards fully embracing regional legal integration in the form of dispute settlement. This is true even if Asian states are quite comfortable with global mechanisms on a case-by-case basis.

2 Interstate Mechanisms

2.1 International Court of Justice

Since 1955, when the ICJ first heard *Right of Passage over Indian Territory (Portugal* v *India)*, the Court has handled twenty-one contentious cases involving an Asian party. In many ways, the practice of Asian states before the ICJ is representative of the three themes discussed above.

2.1.1 *Compulsory Jurisdiction*

Asian states are significantly more hesitant to commit to the compulsory jurisdiction of the ICJ than other regions.[3] With respect to declarations under article 36(2) of the ICJ Statute, seven Asian states, or 17 per cent of the region,[4] have recognized compulsory jurisdiction, compared to 43 per cent of African states and 39 per cent of Latin American states (Figure 11.1):

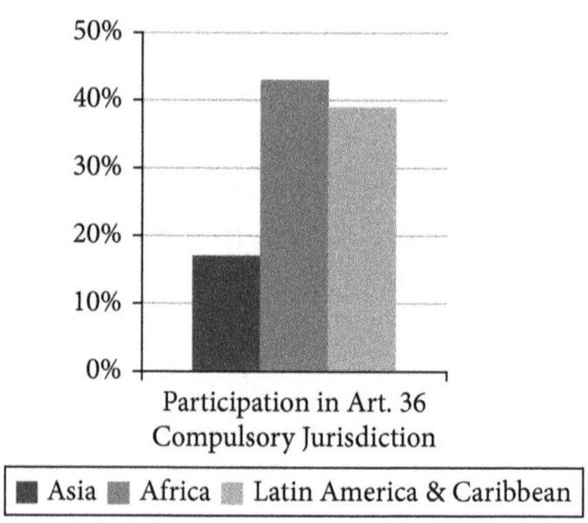

FIGURE 11.1 ICJ Article 36 participation rates

[3] This holds true even when excluding Pacific Island states, small states (states with populations of less than one million), and/or Central Asian states.

[4] The seven Asian states that have made article 26 declarations are: Cambodia, India, Japan, Marshall Islands, Pakistan, Philippines, and Timor-Leste. Nauru and Thailand made declarations for specified periods of time which have since expired.

The same applies to optional compromissory clauses in multilateral and bilateral treaties for the compulsory jurisdiction of the ICJ. Among treaties invoking the compulsory jurisdiction of the Court over the last quarter century (1993–2018),[5] there were 182 instances (4.33 treaties per state) of Asian states agreeing to the jurisdiction of the Court, compared to 376 instances of African states (6.96 treaties per state) and 247 instances of Latin American states (7.48 treaties per state) (Figures 11.2 and 11.3):

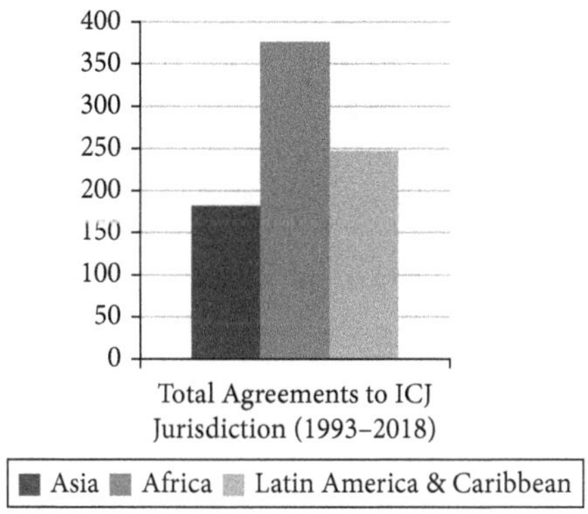

FIGURE 11.2 ICJ jurisdiction, total agreements (1993–2018)

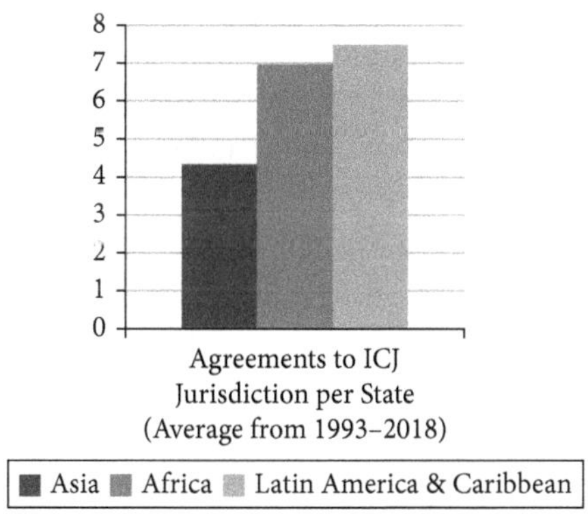

FIGURE 11.3 ICJ jurisdiction, average agreements per State (1993–2018)

[5] These 28 treaties include many with robust participation from the international community—including the International Convention for the Suppression of Terrorist Bombings 1997, International Convention for the Suppression of the Financing of Terrorism 1999, UN Convention against Transnational Organized Crime 2000 ('Palermo Convention'), UN Convention against Corruption 2003, and International Convention for the Suppression of Acts of Nuclear Terrorism 2005.

Moreover, the lower participation of Asian states in the compulsory jurisdiction of the ICJ could not simply be attributed to a passive approach to dispute settlement or a lower participation rate in treaty making generally. Rather, Asian states have taken affirmative steps to opt out of clauses invoking the compulsory jurisdiction of the Court. Even where an Asian state has ratified a treaty, it is more likely to submit a declaration to opt out of the Court's jurisdiction than other non-Western states (Figure 11.4):

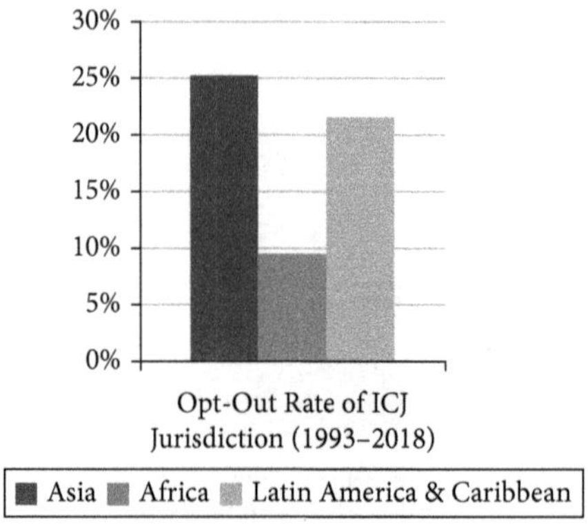

FIGURE 11.4 ICJ jurisdiction, opt-out rates (1993–2018)

Nor should Asian states' hesitation to cede jurisdiction to the Court be attributed to a general unwillingness to participate in the work of the Court or to engage in the shaping of international law. As of 2018, 55 per cent of all Asian states have submitted written statements to advisory proceedings,[6] a higher participation rate than Africa (43 per cent) or Latin America (52 per cent). When excluding Central Asian and Pacific Island states, the participation rate of Asian states in advisory proceedings is even higher, rising to 63 per cent.

2.1.2 *Participation in Contentious Cases*

Nonetheless, Asian states trail other non-Western states in their participation in contentious cases of the ICJ. As of 2018, twenty-one ICJ cases have involved Asian parties. A total of thirteen Asian states, or 31 per cent of the region, have been party to a contentious dispute,[7] compared to 48 per cent of African and Latin American states (Figure 11.5). The rate of applications filed by Asian states—perhaps a better indicator of a region's propensity for international litigation—also lags behind other non-Western regions. Twenty-six per cent of Asian states have initiated a case before the

[6] These 23 states are: Australia, Bangladesh, China, Democratic People's Republic of Korea, India, Indonesia, Japan, Kazakhstan, Malaysia, Maldives, Marshall Islands, Micronesia, Nauru, New Zealand, Pakistan, Palau, Papua New Guinea, Philippines, Samoa, Solomon Islands, Sri Lanka, Thailand, and Vietnam.

[7] These 13 Asian states are: Australia, Cambodia, India, Indonesia, Japan, Malaysia, Marshall Islands, Nauru, New Zealand, Pakistan, Singapore, Thailand, and Timor-Leste.

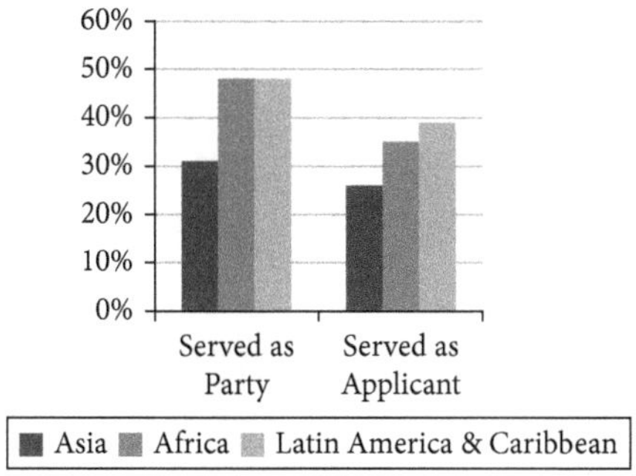

FIGURE 11.5 ICJ dispute participation rates

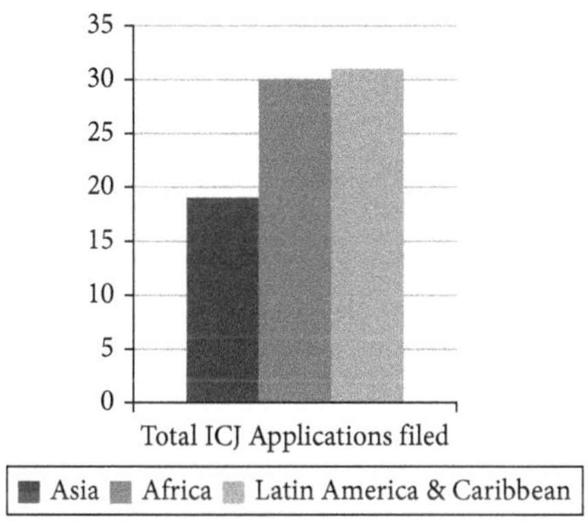

FIGURE 11.6 Total ICJ applications filed

Court (either by application or joint special agreement), compared with 35 per cent of African states and 39 per cent of Latin American states (Figure 11.5). In absolute terms, nineteen contentious cases were initiated by Asian states, compared to thirty from Africa and thirty-one from Latin America (Figure 11.6).

2.1.3 *Sub-Regional Diversity*

In the aggregate, the above findings appear to support the prevailing view that Asian states eschew settling their disputes by state-to-state litigation. There are two caveats to the traditional narrative, however. The first is found in the diversity within Asia itself. Accounting for sub-regional disparities reveals that Asia's low participation rate in ICJ cases is largely attributable to the five Central Asian states and thirteen small Pacific Island states (Figure 11.7). When those states are excluded, the participation rate in ICJ disputes rises to 46 per cent, with 38 per cent of states having filed an application. These rates are nearly identical to those of Africa and Latin America (compare with Figure 11.5).

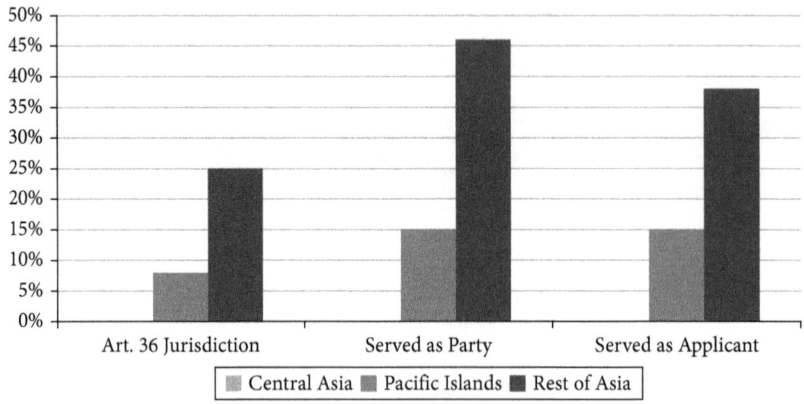

FIGURE 11.7 ICJ participation rates by sub-region

2.1.4 *Increasing Participation*

The second caveat is found in looking at developments over time. Of the twenty-one cases involving Asian states, twelve were initiated during the fifty-two year period from 1947 to 2009. In contrast, nine cases—all of them filed by Asian states—have been initiated since 2010, confirming earlier predictions of 'a general trend towards greater involvement of Asia in the promotion of international law through the development of the jurisprudence of the Court'.[8]

In sum, even though Asian states as a whole remain cautious about committing in advance to the compulsory jurisdiction of the Court, they are quite comfortable engaging with the Court on a case-by-case basis. This is especially true in the last decade, when Asian states have increasingly made use of the Court to settle contentious disputes.

2.2 Trade and Investment

A similar picture also emerges when one looks at the participation of Asian states in the trade and investment context—specifically, the WTO Dispute Settlement Body and ISDS. Each is discussed below.

2.2.1 *WTO Dispute Settlement*

Since the first case was submitted to the WTO Dispute Settlement Body in 1995 (*Singapore v Malaysia*, concerning import prohibitions on polyethylene and polypropylene), Asian states have been quite active in the WTO system. Although Asian states in the aggregate appear less likely to initiate WTO cases than Latin American states,

[8] Hisashi Owada, 'The Experience of Asia with International Adjudication' (2005) 9 Singapore Year Book of International Law 9.

a significant share of WTO cases has been initiated by Asian states. This is explained by the concentration of cases involving the larger Asian economies. In absolute terms, over a quarter of WTO disputes have been initiated by Asian states. As of 2018, Asian and Latin American states have together initiated about half of all 541 WTO disputes, filing a total of 152 and 136 complaints respectively.[9] African states, in contrast, have yet to file a single case (Figure 11.8).

2.2.1.1 SUB-REGIONAL DIVERSITY

As with the ICJ, there is also a wide range of participation rates according to the sub-regions within Asia. Here as well, Central Asian and Pacific Island states tend to participate significantly less (Figure 11.9). When excluding those regions, we see that over 60 per cent of the rest of Asia has filed at least one complaint before the WTO

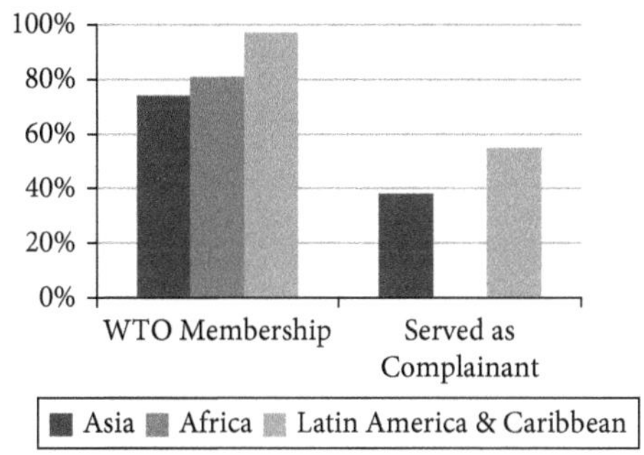

FIGURE 11.8 WTO participation rates

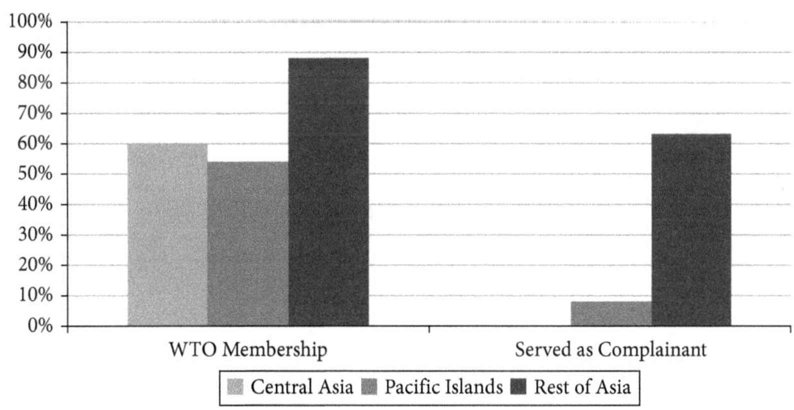

FIGURE 11.9 WTO participation rates by sub-region

[9] The figure for Asian states includes complaints filed by Chinese Taipei and Hong Kong. See Chronological List of Disputes Cases <http://www.wto.org/english/tratop_e/dispu_e/dispu_status_e.htm> accessed 9 January 2019.

Dispute Settlement Body—surpassing the 55 per cent participation rate of the Latin American region (compare Figure 11.9 with Figure 11.8).

One can zoom in even further to the state level. The following tables list (1) the sixteen Asian states that have filed a WTO complaint (Table 11.1); and (2) the ten WTO members worldwide that have filed the most complaints (Table 11.2). As would be expected, the lists roughly correlate with economic size—a reminder that participation in the WTO Dispute Settlement Body is not a perfect measure of litigiousness. Nevertheless, the complaints demonstrate at a minimum a state's willingness and capability to engage in international litigation with respect to trade. As Table 11.2 reveals, four of the ten most active participants in WTO disputes worldwide are Asian states, suggesting that Asia is very much involved in the development of international-trade jurisprudence.

Table 11.1 Most Active WTO Members (Asia)

	Complaints Filed
India	24
Japan	23
South Korea	18
China	17
Thailand	13
Indonesia	11
New Zealand	9
Australia	8
Pakistan, Philippines, Vietnam	5
Samoa	3
Bangladesh, Malaysia, Singapore, Sri Lanka	1

Table 11.2 Most Active WTO Members (Worldwide)

	Complaints Filed
United States	124
European Union	97
Canada	38
Brazil	32
India, Mexico	24
Japan	23
Argentina	21
South Korea	18
China	17

2.2.2 *Investment*

With respect to ISDS, we also see similarities with the approach of Asian states towards the ICJ. Specifically, Asian states have been willing to participate in investment treaties and to shape the development of investment law, but have thus far been less likely to commit to or participate in investor-state arbitrations.

Data from ICSID and the United Nations Conference on Trade and Development (UNCTAD) suggest that Asian states are generally comfortable with participating in and developing international investment law. The region has a similar membership rate in the ICSID Convention as Africa, and a significantly higher rate than Latin America (Figure 11.10). Likewise, as of 2018 Asian states have signed nearly 1,000 BITs compared to 819 by African states and 585 by Latin American states (Figure 11.11).

Although there is currently no centralized public registry for investor-state arbitrations, the available data reveal that Asia has lower participation rates than Latin America both as respondent states and as the home states of claimants. In absolute terms, Latin American states have been parties to nearly twice as many investor-state disputes as Asian states (Figure 11.12). The gap between Asia and the rest of the world

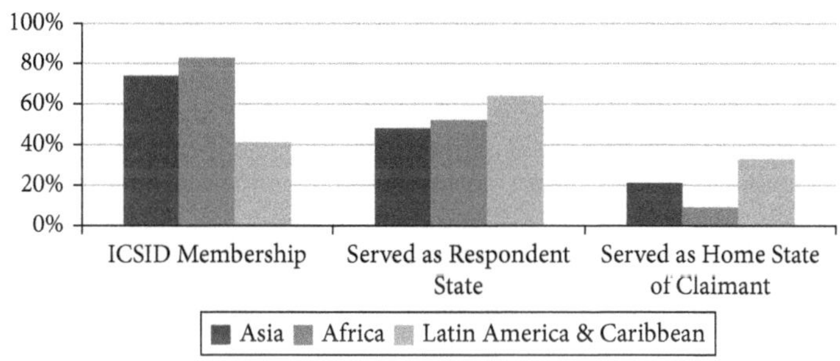

FIGURE 11.10 Investment dispute participation rates

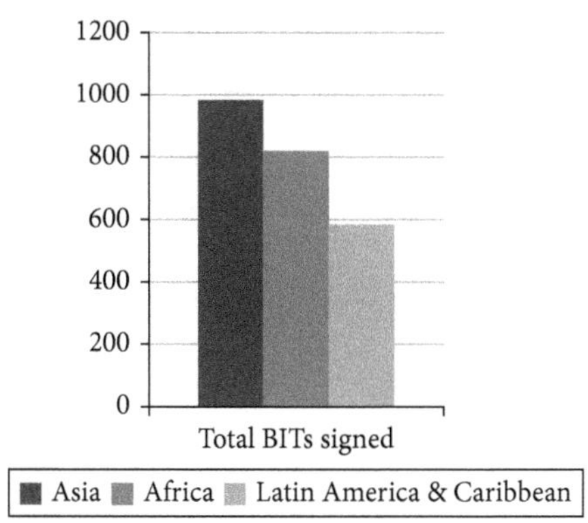

FIGURE 11.11 Total BITs signed

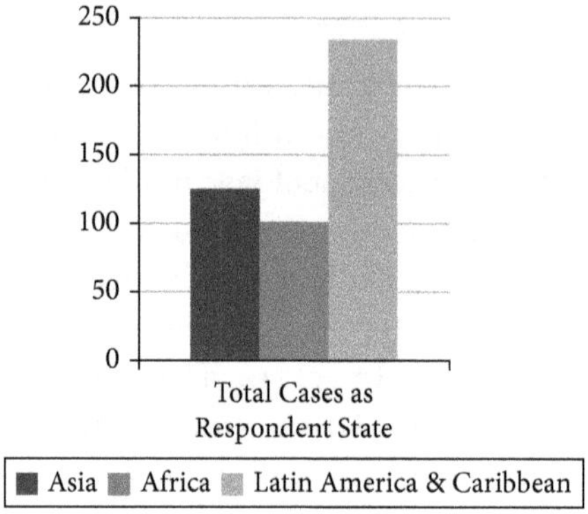

FIGURE 11.12 Total investment dispute cases as Respondent State

appears to have widened from 1994 to 2010, before narrowing from 2011 onward.[10] Moreover, investors from Asia-Pacific states make up roughly only four per cent of ISDS cases, whereas 20 per cent of the global stock of foreign direct investment came from the Asia-Pacific.[11]

2.2.2.1 SUB-REGIONAL DIVERSITY

When one again zooms in on the sub-regional level, however, a more refined picture emerges. Sub-regional diversity is again noticeable. Central Asian states have been particularly active in ISDS, with all five having been a respondent to an investment arbitration, and two of the five (Kazakhstan and Uzbekistan) having been the home state of a claimant (Figure 11.13).

As for the rest of Asia, 63 per cent have served as a respondent and 29 per cent have been the home state of a claimant (Figure 11.13). These participation rates are

FIGURE 11.13 Investment dispute participation rates by sub-region

[10] Luke Nottage and Romesh Weeramantry, 'Investment Arbitration in Asia: Five Perspectives on Law and Practice' (2012) 28 Arbitration International 25; Rahul Donde and Julien Chaisse, 'The Future of Investor-State Arbitration: Revising the Rules?' in Julien Chaisse, Tomoko Ishikawa, and Sufian Jusoh (eds), *Asia's Changing International Investment Regime* (Springer 2017) 215.

[11] Ibid. 231.

comparable to those of Latin America, and significantly higher than those of Africa (compare with Figure 11.10). Pacific Island states are virtually absent.

At the country level, Central Asian states make up four of the most active states in investor-state arbitrations (Table 11.3 below). South and Southeast Asian states are also active, with India, Pakistan, Indonesia, Vietnam, the Philippines, Sri Lanka, and Laos among the most common respondent states in Asia. Perhaps unsurprisingly, the larger and more developed Asian economies have tended to serve more frequently as the home states of claimants (Table 11.4 below).

2.2.2.2 RECENT DEVELOPMENTS

As with other regions of the world in recent years,[12] the Asia-Pacific has experienced renewed resistance against investment arbitration, adding a degree of uncertainty to its future course.[13] In 2011 Australia announced that it would no longer include ISDS provisions in its trade agreements, before a later government subsequently qualified

Table 11.3 Asian Respondents in Investor-State Arbitrations

	Cases as Respondent
India	23
Kazakhstan	17
Kyrgyzstan	13
Turkmenistan	10
Pakistan	9
Uzbekistan	8
Indonesia	7
Vietnam, Philippines	5
Laos, Mongolia, Sri Lanka	4

Table 11.4 Asian Claimants in Investor-State Arbitrations

	Cases as Home of Claimant
China, India, Kazakhstan	5
Australia, South Korea, Singapore	4
Japan, Malaysia	3
Uzbekistan	1

[12] In Latin America, for instance, Bolivia, Ecuador, and Venezuela have terminated certain BITs and withdrawn from ICSID. In Africa, South Africa announced that it would not renew old investment treaties and canceled certain BITs. See Martina Francesca Ferracane, 'Investor-State Dispute Settlement (ISDS) Cases in the Asia-Pacific Region—The Record' in Chaisse et al (eds) (n 10) 237–8.

[13] Donde and Chaisse (n 10) 217.

that it would assess each new agreement on a case-by-case basis.[14] India is reported to have terminated at least fifty-seven BITs since 2013, pursuing a new policy of narrowing ISDS in new agreements and renegotiating existing ones.[15] Sri Lanka has likewise announced an intention to move away from traditional investment agreements, while Indonesia has sought to terminate more than sixty BITs.[16]

At the same time, such developments may not signal a full-scale retreat from ISDS so much as a reorientation. Recent multilateral and bilateral agreements continue to provide for ISDS, while offering states greater control over the scope of their liability. The Association of Southeast Asian Nations (ASEAN) Comprehensive Investment Agreement 2009 (ACIA) entered into force in 2012 and provides for ISDS covering ten Asian states.[17] Article 40(3) of ACIA aims to cede greater control of interpretation to states by providing that joint interpretations by states parties are binding on a tribunal.[18]

The China-Australia Free Trade Agreement (ChAFTA)—signed in 2015—provides for ISDS over a broad definition of direct and indirect investments.[19] ChAFTA, however, goes even further than ACIA in that it grants states parties not only authority over interpretation, but also over application. Thus, where a regulatory measure concerning public welfare is challenged, the respondent state may suspend proceedings for a 90-day consultation period with the other treaty party. If the states agree that the challenged measure is excluded from the agreement, the tribunal is bound by that decision.[20] It remains to be seen how such provisions may evolve in the coming years and how much of a chilling effect they may have on investors. But given continued economic development and the entry into force of new investment agreements, it is not unreasonable to expect Asia to comprise an increasing share of global investment disputes.

2.3 International Criminal Law

Although the Asia-Pacific has been home to two 'third-generation' hybrid criminal courts (the Extraordinary Chambers in the Courts of Cambodia and the Special Panels of the Dili District Court in Timor-Leste), Asian states have been largely hesitant to

[14] Ferracane (n 12) 238.

[15] Donde and Chaisse (n 10) 217 n 68; Rohit Bhat, 'Will India do away with investor state arbitration?' (Kluwer Arbitration Blog, 23 August 2017) <http://arbitrationblog.kluwerarbitration.com/2017/08/23/will-india-away-investor-state-arbitration> accessed 9 January 2019; Kavaljit Singh, 'ISDS is unsuited to meet today's global challenges' (letter to the Editor) *Financial Times* (8 May 2017) <http://www.ft.com/content/ed08cd0c-2fea-11e7-9555-23ef563ecf9a> accessed 9 January 2019.

[16] Donde and Chaisse (n 10) 217 n 66; Sam Luttrell, 'ISDS in the Asia-Pacific: A Regional Snap-Shot' (2016) 19 International Trade and Business Law Review 20, 35.

[17] ASEAN Comprehensive Investment Agreement (signed 26 February 2009, entered into force 24 February 2012).

[18] Donde and Chaisse (n 10) 218–19. [19] Luttrell (n 16).

[20] Donde and Chaisse (n 10) 218–19.

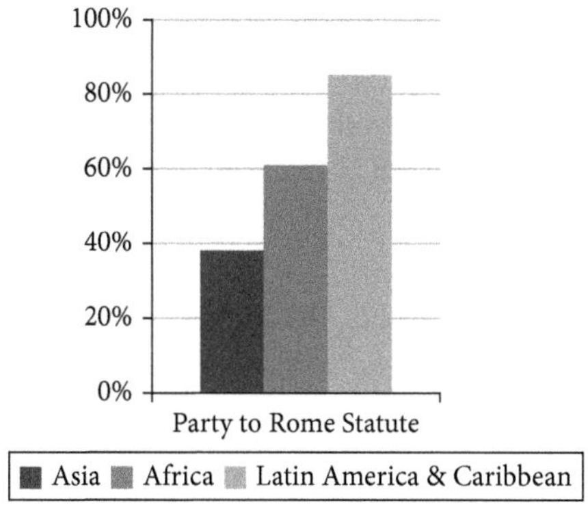

FIGURE 11.14 Rome Statute participation rates

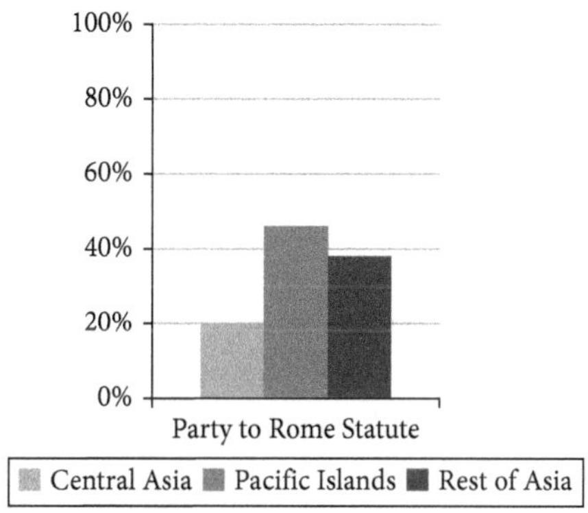

FIGURE 11.15 Rome Statute participation rates by sub-region

embrace the International Criminal Court (ICC) (Figure 11.14).[21] Across every sub-region of Asia, the majority of states have opted not to sign or ratify the Rome Statute of the ICC 1998 (Figure 11.15). Of the eighteen Asian states parties to the Rome Statute as of 2018, only Samoa has signed the Kampala amendments on the crime of aggression. The same pattern holds true with respect to the judicial settlement of disputes concerning multilateral criminal law treaties. For such treaties over the last quarter century, Asian states have granted compulsory jurisdiction to the ICJ around 32 per cent of the time, compared to 62 per cent for African states and 68 per cent for Latin American states.[22]

[21] See e.g. Hanqin Xue, 'A Point to Meet: Justice and International Criminal Law' (2014) 4 Asian Journal of International Law 35.

[22] This consists of the following eight treaties: UN Convention against Transnational Organized Crime 2000 and three Protocols thereto (Protocol against the Smuggling of Migrants by Land, Sea and Air 2000; Protocol to Prevent, Suppress and Punish Trafficking in Persons, especially Women and Children 2000; and Protocol against the Illicit Manufacturing of and Trafficking in Firearms, their Parts

2.4 Law of the Sea

Participation in UNCLOS varies dramatically across the Asian sub-regions—the Convention has been ratified by all Pacific Island states, no Central Asian states, and 88 per cent of the remaining Asian states (Figure 11.16 below). The latter is roughly in line with the participation of African and Latin American states, which have 89 per cent and 88 per cent participation rates in UNCLOS respectively.

2.4.1 *Choice of Procedure under UNCLOS*

By default, all states parties to UNCLOS are subject to binding procedures of an arbitral tribunal constituted in accordance with Annex VII of the Convention.[23] States are free, however, to make declarations selecting ITLOS or the ICJ as potential dispute-resolution mechanisms.[24] Asian and African states have been somewhat reluctant to grant jurisdiction to either body, with only four Asian states and six African states issuing any such declaration. In contrast, ten Latin American states (30 per cent of the region) have issued a declaration selecting either ITLOS, the ICJ, or both.

Among the thirty-four Asian states parties to UNCLOS, only Australia, Fiji, and Timor-Leste have provided declarations under article 287 choosing ITLOS as a means of dispute settlement concerning the interpretation or application of the Convention (in addition, Bangladesh made a declaration selecting ITLOS for two specific disputes). Australia and Timor-Leste are also the only Asian states to have granted jurisdiction to the ICJ. With respect to the optional exceptions in article 298, Australia, Palau and, most recently, Singapore made declarations under article 298(1)(a) excluding binding judicial procedures for disputes over sea boundary delimitations. China, South Korea,

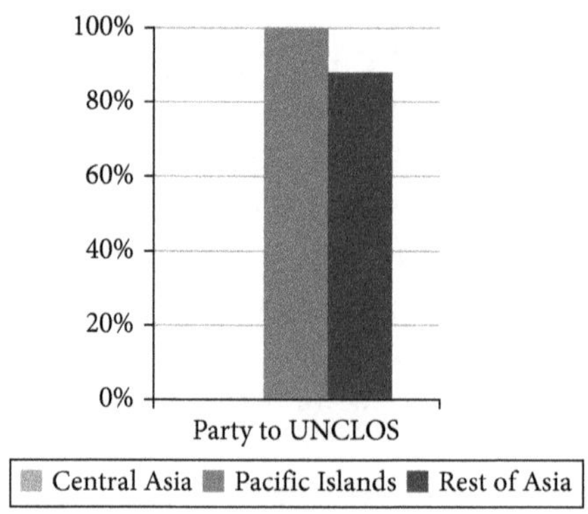

FIGURE 11.16 UNCLOS participation rates

and Components and Ammunition 2000); UN Convention against Corruption 2003; International Convention for the Protection of All Persons from Enforced Disappearance 2006.

[23] UNCLOS art. 287(5). [24] UNCLOS art. 287(1).

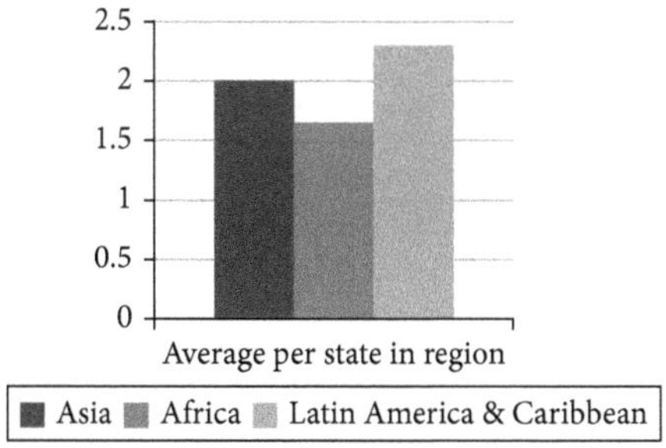

FIGURE 11.17 Agreements granting ITLOS jurisdiction

and Thailand made declarations excluding disputes over sea boundary delimitations (article 298(1)(a)), military activities (article 298(1)(b)), and Security Council functions assigned to it by the UN Charter (article 298(1)(c)).

By comparison, five African states have granted jurisdiction to ITLOS, and another African state has granted jurisdiction to both ITLOS and the ICJ. Among Latin American states, four have granted jurisdiction to ITLOS and another has selected ITLOS for a specific dispute. One state has granted jurisdiction only to the ICJ, and three states have selected both ITLOS and the ICJ. Seven African and seven Latin American states have made declarations under article 298 opting out of specific topics of dispute.

Finally, fifteen multilateral and five bilateral agreements apart from UNCLOS have conferred jurisdiction on ITLOS. Asian states have been parties to these agreements in a total of eighty-four instances, compared to eighty-nine instances for African states and seventy-six instances for Latin American states. As Figure 11.17 shows, Asian states have on average granted jurisdiction to ITLOS at a higher rate than African states, but at a lower rate than Latin American states.

2.4.2 *Contentious Cases*

Since UNCLOS came into force in 1994, a total of thirty-eight contentious cases have been heard either under the auspices of ITLOS or an arbitral tribunal under Annex VII of the Convention.[25] In all, Asian states have been quite active participants in maritime dispute settlement procedures, surpassed only by Latin American states among all world regions (Figure 11.18). Over a third of all ITLOS or Annex VII cases have involved at least one Asian state. And over a quarter of all cases were initiated by an Asian state (Figure 11.19 below). Seven Asian-Pacific states have thus far initiated cases under either mechanism: Australia, Bangladesh, Japan, Malaysia, Myanmar, New Zealand, and the

[25] Seven disputes have involved cases with both ITLOS and the PCA, as article 290(5) of the Convention grants jurisdiction to the ITLOS for provisional measures pending the constitution of an arbitral tribunal.

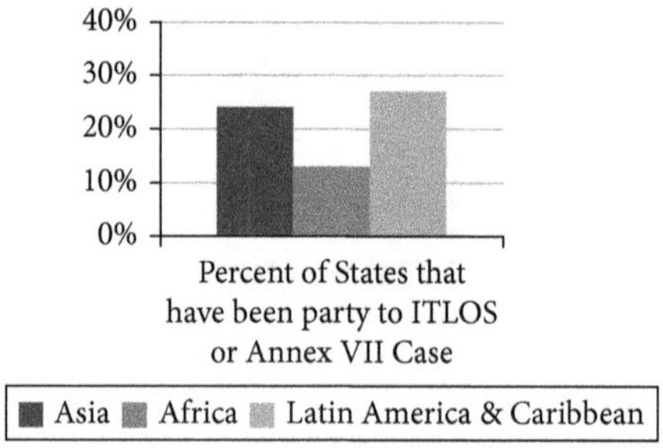

FIGURE 11.18 Maritime dispute settlement participation rates

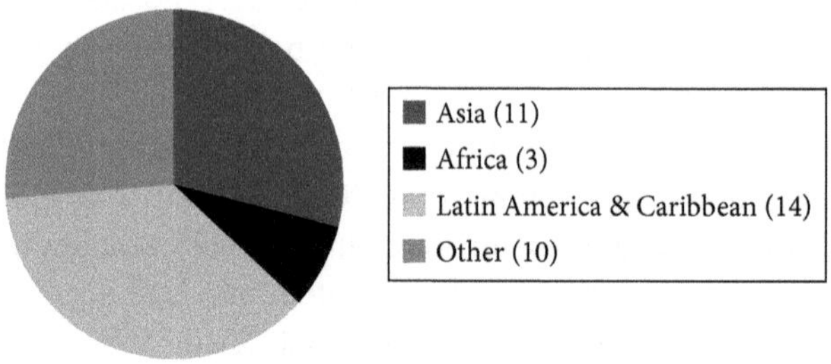

FIGURE 11.19 ITLOS and Annex VII cases initiated

Philippines. By comparison, five African states and seven Latin American states have initiated cases under the same mechanisms.

With respect to ITLOS specifically, eight of the twenty-five contentious cases heard by the Tribunal since 1997 have involved Asian states.[26] Four of the cases were requests for provisional measures pending the initiation of proceedings under Annex VII.[27] Three were brought under article 292 of UNCLOS for the prompt release of detained vessels and crews.[28] And one involved the delimitation of maritime boundaries, the first such case addressed by ITLOS.[29]

[26] By comparison, African states have also been party to eight cases and Latin American states have been party to 11 cases.

[27] *Southern Bluefin Tuna (New Zealand v Japan; Australia v Japan), Provisional Measures* (ITLOS Case Nos 3 and 4) Order of 27 August 1999; *Case concerning Land Reclamation by Singapore in and around the Straits of Johor (Malaysia v Singapore), Provisional Measures* (ITLOS Case No. 12) Order of 8 October 2003; *The 'Enrica Lexie' Incident (Italy v India), Provisional Measures* (ITLOS Case No. 24), Order of 24 August 2015.

[28] *The 'Volga' (Russia v Australia) Prompt Release* (ITLOS Case No. 11) Order of 23 December 2002; *The 'Hoshinmaru' (Japan v Russian Federation), Prompt Release* (ITLOS Case No. 14) Judgment of 6 August 2007; *The 'Tomimaru' (Japan v Russian Federation), Prompt Release* (ITLOS Case No. 15) Judgment of 6 August 2007.

[29] *Dispute concerning Delimitation of the Maritime Boundary between Bangladesh and Myanmar in the Bay of Bengal (Bangladesh/Myanmar)* (ITLOS Case No. 16) Judgment of 14 March 2012.

Thirteen cases have been arbitrated under Annex VII of UNCLOS, the majority being instituted from 2009 or later under the auspices of the PCA. Of the thirteen cases, five involved one or more Asian states as a party.[30] Perhaps the most notable among these cases is the *South China Sea Arbitration* 2016, in which China did not participate. In a more recent government white paper, China has maintained its position that 'for disputes over territories and maritime rights and interests, the sovereign states directly involved should . . . seek a peaceful solution through negotiation and consultation'.[31]

3 Regional Mechanisms

As the above section demonstrates, the participation of Asian states in multilateral dispute-resolution forums escapes any simple encapsulation—different states approach different issues in different ways. The status of regional legal coordination and judicial settlement in the Asia-Pacific, on the other hand, is immediately striking when viewed against the backdrop of other regions. Latin America lays historical claim to the first court of international law and is home to the active Inter-American Court of Human Rights. Africa saw a proliferation of international courts towards the close of the twentieth century. And both the Court of Justice of the European Union and the European Court of Human Rights are deeply integrated with European domestic legal systems. The Asia-Pacific, in contrast, has yet to establish a single pan-regional tribunal.

With this background, even the most ardent defenders of the status of international law in Asia have recognized that the region lacks the same development of regional organizations and judicial bodies as other parts of the world. As Professor Alvarez acknowledged:

> Beneath the welter of impressive names/acronyms . . . are arrangements that are at the low 'non-legal' end of the obligation, precision, and delegation tables as defined by the authors of the Legalization issue. . . . They are anything but centralized, hierarchical institutions capable of rule-making by majority vote or binding judicial decision. . . .
>
> It is true that unlike Europe, the Americas, and Africa, Asia lacks a regional human rights court; or an organization charged with legal harmonization as compared to even the relatively weak [OECD] . . . or a collective security arm as legalistic as the North Atlantic Treaty Oganization . . . or a regional charter for economic integration as legalized as that of the EU or even the NAFTA.[32]

[30] *Southern Bluefin Tuna* (n 27); *Land Reclamation Case* (n 27); *Bay of Bengal Maritime Boundary Arbitration between Bangladesh and India (Bangladesh v India)* PCA Case No. 2010–16, Award of 7 July 2014; *In re Arbitration Between the Republic of the Philippines and the People's Republic of China*, PCA Case No. 2013–19, Award of 12 July 2016; *The 'Enrica Lexie' Incident* (n 27). By comparison, African states and Latin American states were parties in three cases each.

[31] State Council of the People's Republic of China, 'Full Text: China's Policies on Asia-Pacific Security Cooperation', White Paper, Part I, 11 January 2017, <http://english.gov.cn/archive/white_paper/2017/01/11/content_281475539078636.htm> accessed 9 January 2019.

[32] Alvarez (n 2) 22.

Professor Tan Hsien-Li, who provides a helpful review of regional organizations of the Asia-Pacific in chapter 3 of this volume, largely agrees with the above characterization. With respect to dispute settlement specifically, it is still the case that no pan-Asian adjudicatory body exists in any area of international law.

3.1 ASEAN

Interstate dispute-resolution procedures under the ASEAN system can be characterized as a slow evolution from consensus-driven, voluntary procedures of general application towards progressively defined and proscriptive rules in specific areas of law. The Treaty of Amity and Cooperation in Southeast Asia 1976, signed by the founding members of ASEAN, contains a chapter on dispute resolution through a High Council. The chapter provides, however, that the functions or recommendations of the High Council shall apply only if all parties to a dispute agree on their application.[33] Under the ASEAN Charter, the Treaty of Amity continues to apply to any disputes that do not concern ASEAN instruments.[34]

Twenty years after the Treaty of Amity, the Protocol on Dispute Settlement Mechanism 1996 provided for the establishment of ad hoc panels to make findings on facts and agreements related to certain ASEAN economic agreements. However, the Senior Economic Officials Meeting (SEOM), consisting of state representatives, was authorized to not appoint a panel so long as it 'considers it desirable to do so', and was required only to 'consider the report of the panel' before issuing a ruling.[35]

The Protocol 1996 was then replaced by the ASEAN Protocol on Enhanced Dispute Settlement Mechanism 2004 (EDSM), modelled after WTO dispute settlement procedures. Unlike its predecessor, the EDSM requires a consensus decision by the SEOM in order to override a party's request for a panel.[36] Likewise, the findings and recommendations of the panel will be adopted unless a party appeals or the SEOM decides by consensus not to adopt the report.[37] Despite the strengthened provisions, however, member states have resorted instead to the WTO.

In 2010, ASEAN states adopted the Protocol to the ASEAN Charter on Dispute Settlement Mechanisms[38] as part of a conscious move towards refashioning ASEAN as

[33] Treaty of Amity and Cooperation in Southeast Asia (signed and entered into force 24 February 1976) arts 15–16.

[34] ASEAN Charter (adopted 20 November 2007, entered into force 15 December 2008) art. 24(2).

[35] ASEAN Protocol on Dispute Settlement Mechanism (signed 20 November 1996) arts 4(3), 7.

[36] ASEAN Protocol on Enhanced Dispute Settlement Mechanism (signed and entered into force 29 November 2004) art. 5(1).

[37] Ibid. art. 9.1.

[38] Protocol to the ASEAN Charter on Dispute Settlement Mechanisms (adopted 8 April 2010, not yet in force).

a rules-based organization. It provides for settlement of disputes concerning the interpretation or application of the ASEAN Charter and certain other ASEAN instruments (while excluding ASEAN economic integration agreements). It envisages settlement mechanisms ranging from consultation, good offices, mediation, and conciliation to arbitration, but not including judicial settlement. As of 2019 it has still not entered into force because all ten ASEAN states have not ratified it. Future reform is probable in light of the 2015 establishment of the ASEAN Economic Community.

Although the ASEAN Charter provides separately for the creation of a human rights body and dispute settlement mechanisms, a human rights tribunal has yet to be established. Instead, the ASEAN Intergovernmental Commission on Human Rights was formed in 2009 with ten participating member states operating by consensus. In 2012 the ASEAN Human Rights Declaration was adopted as 'a roadmap for the regional human rights development'.[39] Certain provisions have received criticism from the UN High Commissioner for Human Rights and members of civil society, particularly for wording that appears to limit certain fundamental rights beyond what is permitted under international law.[40] Article 6, for example, states that '[t]he enjoyment of human rights and fundamental freedoms must be balanced with the performance of corresponding duties as every person has responsibilities to all other individuals, the community and the society where one lives'. Article 7 requires that rights be considered 'in the regional and national context bearing in mind different political, economic, legal, social, cultural, historical and religious backgrounds'. And article 8 provides that the exercise of fundamental rights could be limited for the purpose of safeguarding public morals.

3.2 SAARC

In November 2005, the seven member states of the South Asian Association for Regional Cooperation (SAARC) signed the Agreement for Establishment of SAARC Arbitration Council (SARCO).[41] Article II of the Agreement sets SARCO's first objective and function as 'provid[ing] a legal framework within the region for fair and efficient settlement through conciliation and arbitration of commercial, investment and such other disputes as may be referred to the Council by agreement'.[42]

The Council is far from a standing court, however, and aspires, in its own words, to be 'the most sought Arbitration Forum in the region'.[43] Apart from its

[39] ASEAN, Press Release of the Fifth ASEAN Intergovernmental Commission on Human Rights, Jakarta, 25–29 April 2011 <http://asean.org/press-release-of-the-fifth-asean-intergovernmental-commission-on-human-rights-jakarta-25-29-april-2011-2> accessed 9 January 2019.

[40] Mong Palatino, 'Human Rights Declaration Falls Short' *The Diplomat* (28 November 2012) <https://thediplomat.com/2012/11/human-rights-declaration-falls-short> accessed 9 January 2019.

[41] Afghanistan was subsequently admitted as the eighth amember state in 2007.

[42] Agreement for Establishment of SAARC Arbitration Council (signed 13 November 2005) art. II(a).

[43] SARCO, 'About Us' <http://sarco.org.pk/about-us> accessed 15 January 2019.

intergovernmental composition, SARCO is thus comparable to other Asian arbitral institutions like the Hong Kong International Arbitration Centre, Chinese International Economic and Trade Arbitration Centre, Japanese Commercial Arbitration Association, Australian Centre for International Commercial Arbitration, Kuala Lumpur Regional Centre for Arbitration, or Indian Council of Arbitration.

3.3 Central Asia

Among all of Asia, only the Central Asian states are party to any operational regional dispute settlement mechanism. Following the collapse of the Soviet Union, twelve former Soviet republics, including the Central Asian states, formed the Commonwealth of Independent States (CIS). Notably, the CIS includes an Economic Court, which is seated in Minsk, Belarus and has jurisdiction over interstate economic disputes. These include disputes concerning implementation of obligations under CIS acts, disputes over the compatibility of domestic legal acts with CIS acts, and interpretation of CIS acts and national legal acts of CIS member states. Among the Central Asian states, Kazakhstan, Kyrgyzstan, Tajikistan, and Uzbekistan are parties to the Court.

From 2000 to 2014, the Eurasian Economic Community (EAEC), along with its Court of the Eurasian Economic Community, existed to facilitate economic integration among Eurasian states. In 2015 the EAEC gave way to the Eurasian Economic Union (EAEU), modelled loosely on the European Union. The EAEU's Court of the Eurasian Economic Union, also located in Minsk, replaced the EAEC Court. It has jurisdiction over member states concerning compatibility of international treaties within the Union, as well as over obligations under the Treaty on Eurasian Union, international agreements within the Union, and decisions of Union bodies (including the Commission of Eurasian Union). Economic entities may also seize the Court to challenge decisions and actions of the Commission.[44] At this time, only Kazakhstan and Kyrgyzstan among the Central Asian states are members of the EAEU. The two states have disagreed on whether the CIS Economic Court should be discontinued in light of the new EAEU Court.[45]

3.4 The Long Road to a Pan-Asian Court

Asia's reported 'ambivalence' towards international law generally is well recognized.[46] But the above review of state practice presents a somewhat different puzzle with respect to international dispute settlement specifically. Far from lagging behind other non-

[44] See chapter 28 in this volume on 'Central Asian States'. [45] Ibid.

[46] Simon Chesterman, 'Asia's Ambivalence about International Law and Institutions: Past, Present and Futures' (2016) 27 European Journal of International Law 945.

Western regions, Asian states appear to have engaged with certain multilateral dispute settlement mechanisms with relative facility and frequency. Why then has regional coordination for the judicial settlement of disputes remained undeveloped? This is all the more remarkable considering that Asia ranks comparably to or higher than other non-Western regions under various economic, rule of law, and peace indices yet, unlike the other locales, it lacks any regional economic or human rights court.[47]

The historic dissonance between practice and institutional development in the Asia-Pacific can be analysed along three basic components shared, to varying degrees, by most regional courts. To the extent that any of these factors have been frustrated by historical, cultural, or political circumstances, one could better assess the feasibility of any future coordination towards establishing a standing Asian tribunal.

3.4.1 *Organizational Considerations*

The first component is the organizational foundation that serves as an institutional and procedural vessel for adjudication. It is no coincidence that some of the most robust regional courts have arisen out of economic unions and international organizations. This does not mean that the organization must serve a distinctly integrative purpose, but it does require at a minimum some recognition of a coherent regional identity and purpose (take, for instance, the Organization of American States).

Any consideration of regional cohesion in the Asia-Pacific, in turn, must begin with the demographic reality that the region is home to over half of the Earth's population, and the geographic reality that the region spans thousands of kilometres, divided by expansive mountain ranges and bodies of water. As one of the authors has previously observed, '[c]ategorizing such a diverse group of states and cultures into a single, coherent "region" risks oversimplification and thus blurs the distinct diversity that exists among them'.[48] A further consequence of the region's geography is that a number of Asian states are largely congruent with ethnic and cultural identities that predate Western colonization, in contrast to the colonial partitioning of much of Africa. Although ossified identities in Asia might help facilitate internal cohesiveness, they lend themselves less readily to pan-continental identity.[49]

The experience of Latin America provides a clear contrast. For all of its internal distinctions, Latin American languages, legal traditions, and cultures share a common history of Iberian colonization. It has thus been fertile ground for appeals of pan-American unity since at least the time of Simón Bolívar in the nineteenth century. This is no less true in the field of international law, where a strong tradition of solidarist thought developed. In the nineteenth century, Argentinian lawyer Juan Bautista Alberdi pushed for a continent-wide federation of Spanish American republics. He

[47] Ibid. [48] Owada (n 2) 202.

[49] As ICJ President Abdulqawi Yusuf has remarked of the African experience, 'Pan-Africanism has its roots in a revolt by Africans and people of African descent against what Aimé Césaire called "the influence of the colonial, semi-colonial or para-colonial situation"'. See Abdulqawi Yusuf, *Pan-Africanism and International Law* (Hague Academy of International Law/Brill 2014) 13–14.

envisioned 'an international peace court' for the continent and eventually a 'union of the nations into a vast social body of so many heads of states, governed by a thought, by an opinion, by a universal and common judge', where '[t]he law will come by itself as the new law of life of this body'.[50] Chilean lawyer Alejandro Alvarez continued this line of thought in the early twentieth century, advocating for a 'distinctively American (i.e., Western Hemisphere) system of international law'.[51]

It is perhaps unsurprising then that Central America was home to the first standing international court in 1907, the Central American Court of Justice. During the interwar period, Mexico and Panama played leading roles in developing mixed-claims commissions adjudicating claims against the defeated powers. These claims, it has been noted, 'produced an avalanche of case law that was far larger in bulk than that of the PCIJ [Permanent Court of International Justice], and more varied as well'.[52]

Latin America was thus positioned to embrace and contribute to the explosion of international and regional bodies and courts following the Second World War. As one eminent historian of international law has observed, post-war international adjudication developed primarily in the regional setting:

> [I]t is not acceptable to say that there was [in post-war development] a continuous elaboration and implementation of international adjudication and jurisdiction and that "in the regional sphere further progress was also achieved". At best, progress occurred, not "also", but "exclusively" in regional contexts.[53]

Yet in Asia, the interwar and post-war periods were marked by civil and interregional conflict. More than Africa or Latin America, Asia was at the heart of the ideological divisions of the Cold War, further complicating any efforts towards pan-Asian unity. To varying degrees, Bangladesh, Burma, Cambodia, China, Indonesia, the Korean peninsula, Laos, Malaysia, Thailand, and Vietnam were all host to violent Cold-War proxy conflicts. Moreover, to the extent that Soviet thought influenced the region's approach to international law, such legal philosophy generally emphasized principles of state sovereignty, non-intervention, and strict equality of states.[54] Such principles do not, in themselves, lean naturally towards regional integration and common binding legal commitments, which leads us to the second component of regional adjudication.

3.4.2 *Substantive Considerations*

Geographical and historical hurdles to regional cohesion help explain why international adjudication in Asia lagged behind other regions during the twentieth century. But they do not fully explain why this situation has remained long after the end of armed conflict, decades of economic growth, and technological leaps in transportation and telecommunication. After all, ASEAN has expanded to include the larger East Asia Community in recent decades. In any event, a new administrative body could always be

[50] Stephen Neff, *Justice Among Nations* (2014) 287–8. [51] Ibid. 291. [52] Ibid. 358.
[53] Wilhelm Grewe, *The Epochs of International Law* (Walter de Gruyter 2000) 667.
[54] Neff (n 50) 383.

established in connection with a self-standing tribunal, as with the Assembly of States Parties of the ICC.

But international adjudication requires more than an organization with states parties. It requires at its core a set of judicially enforceable rules—a substantive legal arrangement underlying the potential range of disputes, such as a regional human rights or trade agreement. Even more than the organizational component, this requires a certain level of shared political commitment to legal convergence. It is here that perhaps the greatest obstacle to an Asian mechanism for international adjudication lies.

As an oft-cited articulation of a so-called 'Asian approach' to international law, the Five Principles of Peaceful Coexistence issued by China and India in 1954 called for '[m]utual non-interference in each other's internal affairs'.[55] The Five Principles were then expanded a year later at the Bandung Conference 1955 into a ten-point declaration, which reaffirmed the importance of '[a]bstention from intervention or interference in the internal affairs of another country'.[56] Where the declaration also called for the pacific settlement of international disputes, including by 'judicial settlement', it reiterated that the means must be 'of the parties' own choice'.[57]

The emphasis on sovereign prerogative may pose few difficulties to legal harmonization where state practices and policies naturally converge. But where differences persist, arriving at an enforceable legal instrument will require states to resort to a combination of compromise or broad principles of agreement, subject to future adjudication. Neither is without potential influence on the internal affairs of a state, which must then be weighed against the perceived benefit of the codification of rights enforceable against the state.

This evaluation may in turn be coloured by certain historical and cultural conceptions of the role of the state. In generalized terms, the rule of law in the Western natural law tradition may be perceived as a transcendental end in itself, holding primacy over the state and thereby serving to limit the government. But as at least one political scientist has remarked, East Asian political development historically began instead with the state, out of which derived the authority of the legal order.[58] Under such an instrumentalist view of law, the limitations brought on by legal obligations may be more readily viewed to outweigh any inherent benefit of codification.

Whatever the merits of the cultural-historical argument, more concrete political obstacles may be at play as well. The process of arriving at common legal commitments across a region as large as the Asia-Pacific will inevitably implicate both domestic stakeholders and the regional balance of powers. This is further complicated by the demographic disparities within Asia and their resulting sensitivities. Whereas smaller

[55] Agreement between the Republic of India and the People's Republic of China on Trade and Intercourse between Tibet Region of China and India (signed and entered into force 29 April 1954, 299 UNTS 4307).

[56] Final Communiqué of the Asian-African conference of Bandung, 24 April 1955.

[57] Ibid.

[58] Francis Fukuyama, *Political Order and Political Decay: From the Industrial Reolution to the Globalization of Democracy* (Farra, Straus, and Giroux 2014) 337.

states must strike a delicate balance between accommodating and checking regional powers, larger states have their own concerns. In a certain sense, one might say that Asia is already home to at least two interregional courts: the Supreme People's Court of China and the Supreme Court of India each have jurisdictions comparable in size to the combined population of the European and African Unions. As might be expected, territories of such scale come with sensitive regional, class, and religious distinctions.[59] This is not to say that international legal convergence is incompatible with internal diversity, only that political considerations may be complicated by internal dynamics in such circumstances.

3.4.3 *Constitutive Considerations*

Lastly, regional courts also consist of a constitutive, human component. Any dispute settlement mechanism ultimately requires human capital to staff, utilize, and develop its body of law. Moreover, long-run sustainability and legitimacy demands domestic representation and buy-in from public officials and local constituencies. To these ends, human capital encompasses not only academic instruction and institutional experience in litigation and international law, but also an adequately developed professional bar to interface with civil society.

Significant progress has been made in recent years. The Asian Society of International Law filled a long-standing gap when it was established in 2007 to serve as a forum for professional development and the promotion of the international rule of law. The Society's flagship publication, the Asian Journal of International Law, has further strengthened the exchange and development of international law scholarship relating to the region since its inaugural issue of 2011.

Locally based institutions have also played a role in the promotion and development of international law. Modelled after the eponymous academy in The Hague and hosted by the Xiamen University Law School in Fujian, China, the Xiamen Academy of International Law has introduced established scholars from around the world to Asian audiences of students and practitioners. More recently, the Asian Business Law Institute, based in the Supreme Court of Singapore, has commissioned research aimed at facilitating the practical convergence of Asian business laws. As of 2018, the institute has initiated projects on foreign judgments, data privacy, and business reorganization. International commercial litigation has also blossomed in recent years, as evidenced by growing caseloads in an ever-expanding list of arbitral institutions and liaison offices across Asia.

[59] See e.g. Henry Kissinger, *On China* (Penguin 2012) 523 ('no issue preoccupies Chinese leaders more than the preservation of national unity'); Xue Hanqin, 'Chinese Contemporary Perspectives on International Law: History, Culture and International Law' (2012) 355 Collected Courses of the Hague Academy of International Law 41 ('In its international relations, China invokes sovereignty often as a defence against external interference in domestic affairs'); Po Jen Yap and Holning Lau, 'Public Interest Litigation in Asia: An Overview' in Po Jen Yap and Holning Lau (eds) *Public Interest Litigation in Asia* (Routledge 2011) 3 ('The Supreme Court of India's fostering of public interest litigation is partly a response to the failures of the Indian government to remedy social ills in Indian society').

To be sure, the growth of human capital in international adjudication is in part endogenous to the availability of international dispute settlement mechanisms. The existence of a meaningful adjudicatory forum facilitates legal proceedings, which in turn breed knowledge and expertise. At the same time, experience cautions against a 'build it and they will come' approach without due regard for the purpose, structure, and transparency of the mechanism. Recall that the Enhanced Dispute Settlement Mechanism of ASEAN has yet to process a single dispute in over a decade of existence. In the absence of any regional adjudicatory body, then, international arbitration may serve for the time being as a key channel to develop the professional infrastructure and human capital necessary for any regional system of international adjudication.

4 Conclusion: The Past and the Future

The findings of this chapter reveal a range of approaches towards international litigation both according to sub-region and legal issue. Perhaps surprisingly, we found a significant portion of the region to have similar participation rates in dispute resolution to other non-Western regions. Many of these states have proactively engaged with international adjudication on a case-by-case and issue-by-issue basis.[60]

Yet, there still remains something to be said about a certain hesitation within the region towards international dispute settlement—a hesitation that cannot be completely explained by subject matter. This is particularly salient in Asian states' reluctance to commit in advance to compulsory settlement of disputes and the absence of any operational regional adjudicatory body. In nearly every subject area of law, for instance, Latin American states have been more active than Asian states in developing and committing to dispute settlement mechanisms. The above findings are significant because while they acknowledge a distinct 'Asian' hestitation towards international litigation, they cut against the common trope that Asian states tend to avoid international litigation because of the influence from a Confucian culture that shuns adversarial conflict.[61]

What then can explain the lingering hesitation towards international dispute settlement? The answer may be something closer to the opposite of conventional wisdom concerning regional insularity and consensus-over-conflict decision-making. Rather, the diversity of history, legal traditions, languages, and cultures in the region—spread across a sprawling and divided geographic area—have stymied the development of a strong common identification with a larger 'Asian community'. And when regional

[60] Owada (n 2) 203 (positing that the situation in Asia 'may be nothing more than the result of strategic calculations guiding the policy decisions of governments in the region not to engage in legalized institutions in certain issue-specific areas').

[61] See e.g. Miles Kahler, 'Legalization as Strategy: The Asia-Pacific Case' (2000) 54 International Organization 549; Jurgen Haacke, 'ASEAN's Diplomatic and Security Culture: A Constructivist Assessment' (2003) 3 International Relations of the Asia-Pacific 57.

courts began to flower in the post-war period in other parts of the world, Cold War proxy conflicts further delayed similar development in Asia. Finally, demographic size disparities and historic conceptions of the role of international law vis-à-vis the state may continue to complicate attempts for the region to arrive at substantive, legally enforceable commitments.

Any attempts at cultivating regional dispute settlement mechanisms or Asian participation in international litigation—leaving for another discussion whether such attempts are necessary or appropriate—would do well to first address the underlying conditions discussed above. Some factors, like geography and demographic disparities, are largely immutable. Others, like differences arising from conceptions of the role of the state and historic conflicts, may require still more time to bridge. And yet matters like frictions between legal systems, international legal training, facility with the dominant languages of international law, and promotion of the international rule of law could be readily addressed with concrete proposals.

In line with the economic development and overall reduction of armed conflict in Asia over the decades following the Cold War, the region has witnessed a steadily growing engagement with international adjudication. Whether this trend will continue in the coming years, and whether it will extend to the formation of a regional mechanism, remains to be seen.

PART III

INTERNATIONAL LAW IN ASIAN AND PACIFIC STATES

EAST ASIA

CHAPTER 12

CHINA

LI ZHAOJIE

1 Introduction

The rise of China is a defining feature of the 21st century. China is now the second largest economy and within a decade is likely to be the single largest economy in the world.[1] It will be the first time since King George III (1760–1820) that a non-Western, non-English-speaking, non-liberal democratic state will occupy that position, as one commentator puts it.[2]

China is already the world's largest trading country. In investment, China is the world's second or third largest source of foreign direct investment and rising.[3] China has also been increasing its efforts in the internationalization of its currency. The *renminbi* (RMB) is used for approximately 15 per cent of total global trade and rising. Moreover, it is one of four currencies that currently make up strategic drawing rights (SDRs) of the International Monetary Fund.[4] With the further liberalization of China's capital account, the RMB is gaining momentum to become a fully-fledged global reserve currency.[5]

Another notable development is China's 'Belt and Road Initiative', due to be completed in 2049. The scheme involves infrastructure investment along the old Silk Road between China and Europe (which was in use from the third century BCE until the early eighteenth century CE). The value of contracts signed under the scheme came within a whisker of US$1 trillion in 2016—not bad for something that only started in

[1] Depending on the measure—purchasing power parity or market exchange rates.

[2] Kevin Rudd, 'US-China 21: The Future of US China Relations under Xi Jinping', Summary Report, (Belfer Center for Science and international Affairs, Harvard Kennedy School, April 2015) 1.

[3] China Power <https://chinapower.csis.org/trade-partner> accessed December 2018.

[4] He Yafei, 'RMB's SDR Inclusion Revs up Globalization' *China.org* (Beijing, 18 March 2016).

[5] 'Chinese Yuan Gaining Momentum to Become Global Currency' *China Daily* (Beijing, 9 November 2015).

2013. Chinese exports to the sixty-odd Belt and Road countries overtook those of China to the United States and the European Union.[6]

According to conventional wisdom, wherever a country's economic power goes, its political influence soon follows. China's extraordinary economic growth has already led to a profound shift in the centre of global geo-economic gravity. With this shift in economic power, there also comes an inevitable shift in political power.

The consequences of this shift manifested themselves first in the Asia-Pacific region, which now contains two thirds of the world population and more than half of the global economy. A bifurcation is underway, as many states already experience or perceive a tension between their historic security ties to the US and their growing economic dependence upon China. New geopolitical, geo-economic, and geostrategic fault-lines are emerging. The shifting balance of economic power is also beginning to take place globally, with China's economic presence in Africa, Latin America, and Europe challenging the long-standing economic primacy of the US.

China's growing economic and political role will begin to reshape the norms, rules, and institutions of the contemporary international order. It will reverberate across geopolitics, global trade, investment, capital flows, reserve currency status, climate change, human rights challenges, and global population movements. And it will exert its influence on the great questions of war and peace in the decades ahead.

These developments are compounded by the fact that, in the last few years, China has become increasingly assertive in its conduct of foreign affairs. In the current Chinese leaders' worldview, 'rich and powerful' China must now start playing a much bigger role in the world. No longer will China need to 'hide its strength, bide its time, and never take the lead'—the foreign policy orthodoxy followed for decades by China and conceived by Deng Xiaoping, China's leader from 1978 to 1989. China must now pursue a proactive foreign policy to maximize China's economic and security interest, as stated by China's leader, Xi Jinping, in November 2013. China will no longer remain silent on the future of the international order, which China argues it had no role in creating. Instead, China is beginning to engage in the long-term reform of that order.[7] To use President Xi's words directly, China will 'struggle for the future international order'. This new and brave approach is known as the 'two-guides' policy, proposed by Xi in February 2017. Under it, China should now 'guide the international community' to jointly 'maintain international security' and 'build a more just and reasonable world order'. On the ninety-fifth anniversary of the founding (in 1921) of the Chinese Communist Party, Xi's celebratory speech asserted that the Chinese people were 'fully confident that they can provide a China solution to humanity's search for better social institutions'.[8]

[6] 'Tortoise v Hare: Is China challenging the United States for Global Leadership?' *The Economist* (London, 1 April 2017).

[7] Rudd (n 2) 11.

[8] Xi Jinping, '习近平在庆祝中国共产党成立95周年大会上的讲话' CPCNews.cn (Beijing, 1 July 2016).

2 Great Power Status

According to Nathan and Scobell, the term 'great power' might be vague, but by any measure China deserves to be regarded as one due to: 'the extent and strategic location of its territory, the size and dynamism of its population, the value and growth rate of its economy, the massive size of its share of global trade, and the strength of its military'.[9] China has become one of a small number of countries that have significant state interests in every part of the planet and that command the attention, whether willingly or grudgingly, of every other country and every international organization. Perhaps more importantly, China is also widely seen as the only country that poses a possible threat to US dominance. China's rise, coupled with its increasingly 'assertive' behaviour on its 'core-interests of state', and on its maritime territorial claims in particular, has led to anxiety, fear, tension, and even distrust—typical features of a power shift in international relations.[10]

For present purposes, the central question is whether these shifts in the regional and global distribution of power as driven by China's rise can occur peacefully, in a manner which preserves the stability of the post-war international system as well as its underlying values and institutional arrangements. In other words, will China's rise take place at the cost of the present international order?

In international law circles, this question has been understood in the following ways: what kind of impact will China's rise precipitate in the contemporary international legal system? Is the rise of China a help or a hindrance to the contemporary rules-based international order? If it is a help, what can China in the course of its rise contribute to that system's operation and its further development? Conversely, what impact has that system had on the rise of China? Can China's rise be accommodated by the contemporary international legal order?

There are certainly not new questions. They have been asked ever since China participated in the Westphalia-based international legal system. What makes them distinct today is the change in the context in which these questions have been framed. A long time ago, China as a victim-minded underdog of the Western world order was seen as a potential rebel against the then prevailing international legal system. Today, with its rise to world great-power status, China is depicted as a stakeholder in the present international system. In the quest for answers to these questions, the following preliminary points are worth noting.

2.1 The China 'Threat'

First, widespread perceptions that China, as a result of its rise, poses a growing security threat to the contemporary international system are misguided. Notwithstanding the

[9] Andrew Nathan and Andrew Scobell, 'How China Sees America' (2015) 91(5) Foreign Affairs 32.

[10] This is particularly the case where China is widely regarded as the only country that can possibly pose a threat to US dominance. Ibid.

fact that China's relative power has grown significantly in recent decades, China's international status as the world's largest developing country has not changed and will long remain in the foreseeable future. If measured in terms of GDP *per capita*, China is a relatively poor country, much lagging behind the developed world and fraught with enormous domestic problems. As such, China has been staying focused on the reforms and policies to deal with the daunting challenges caused by disparities and inadequacies in its domestic economic and social development, and to avoid falling into the 'middle-income trap'. On the other hand, while China will continue its military build-up to 'close the gap', there is no serious prospect of it reaching parity with the US' overwhelming military power before mid century.[11]

The corollary requirement of China's foreign policy and strategy is thus to create a peaceful international environment favourable for addressing these pressing challenges from within. To that end, the tasks of China's foreign policy have been defensive and have not changed since the Cold War era, namely: to blunt destabilizing influences from without, to avoid territorial losses, to reduce its neighbours' suspicions, and to sustain economic growth and social development.[12]

What has changed in the past two decades is that China is now deeply integrated into the global economic system. Its internal and regional priorities have therefore become part of a larger quest: to define a global role that not only serves Chinese interests but also wins acceptance from other powers.[13]

In order to dispel 'China threat' misgivings, the Chinese government decided first to qualify the rise of China as a 'peaceful rise', and then to replace 'peaceful rise' with 'peaceful development', so as to do away with the revanchist character of the term 'rise'. This was followed by the publication of two white papers on the subject in 2005 and 2011, respectively. While mapping out China's peaceful development road, these two official documents, and the latter one in particular, highlight the points: that China's peaceful development policy carries forward the Chinese historical and cultural tradition, which has been framed as a harmonious whole in the traditional Chinese world outlook; that its peaceful development road (or peaceful rise) is determined by China's basic national conditions; and that its peaceful development is a choice that is in conformity with global trends. It emphasizes that China's choice of peaceful development reflects its new outlook of global security based on mutual trust, mutual benefit, equality, and coordination, and its willingness to be a responsible stakeholder in global governance. So, a prosperous and developing China, a 'harmonious and stable' country under the rule of law, will make more contributions to world peace.

A decade ago, *Foreign Affairs* published an article by Princeton's John Ikenberry entitled: 'The Rise of China and the Future of the West: Can the Liberal System Survive?'[14] Ikenberry advised, albeit from a different perspective, that the US should not fear China's rise. He firmly believed that China as a rising power was neither willing

[11] Rudd (n 2). [12] Xi (n 8). [13] Ibid.

[14] John Ikenberry, 'The Rise of China and the Future of the West: Can the Liberal System Survive?' (2008) 87(1) *Foreign Affairs* 23.

nor able to challenge the existing international order. This was because the contemporary order is built around rules and norms of non-discrimination and market openness, creating conditions for rising states to advance their expanding economic and political goals within it. China was one of the beneficiaries of this order, and hence it was unlikely that China would aspire to overthrow it. In addition, China had no capacity to overthrow it because the existing order as designed and led by the US was liberal rather than imperial, unusually accessible, legitimate, and durable. Thus, even if the US declined, the existing order would continue.

Indeed, according to Robert Zoellick, a former US Deputy Secretary of State, China's rise was not a threat because China does not seek to spread radical, anti-American ideologies, does not see itself in a death struggle with capitalism, and does not believe that its future depends on overturning the fundamental order of the international system.[15] Chinese leaders have also vowed to the world community that China's development must be achieved through transcending the traditional ways for great powers to emerge. The Chinese government has reiterated that, in translating its newly accumulated power into great authority in the contemporary international system, China has decided to choose not to follow the path of Germany leading up to World War I or those of Germany and Japan leading up to World War II, when these countries violently plundered resources and pursued hegemony. Neither will China follow the path of the great powers vying for global domination during the Cold War.[16] This should be viewed as China's way of acknowledging the historical problems associated with rising powers and of signalling to the rest of the world that China seeks to manage this process in order to avoid military conflict. It also reflects China's efforts to define its future global position.

The Chinese government also understands that, in an era of global interdependence and integration, one country's development and prosperity remain dependent on that of others. Thus, even after China becomes the world's largest economy, its continued prosperity remains more dependent on the prosperity of others and its global competitors (and vice versa). The richer China becomes, the greater will be its stake in the security of sea-lanes, the stability of world trade and financial regimes, nuclear non-proliferation, the control of global climate change, and cooperation on public health. Therefore, China must continue to 'hold high the banner of peace, development, cooperation, and mutual benefit and adhere to its fundamental foreign policy goal of preserving world peace and promoting common development'.[17]

[15] Robert Zoellick, 'Whither China: From Membership to Responsibility?' (Remarks to National Committee on US-China Relations, New York City, 21 September 2005).

[16] Zheng Bijian, 'China's "Peaceful Rise" to Great-Power Status' (2005) 84 Foreign Affairs 18. According to Henry Kissinger, what Zheng Bijian provided in his article is a 'quasi-official' policy statement of China (see Henry Kissinger, *On China* (Penguin Books 2011) 499).

[17] Report Delivered by Xi Jinping at the 19th National Congress of the Communist Party of China.

2.2 International Law

A second preliminary point is that modern international law owes its origin to the rise of the European family of nations some 400 years ago. It was introduced into China as a by-product of European imperialistic expansion onto the Chinese scene in the middle of the nineteenth century. The Chinese experience with this Western legal learning was by no means an easy one. It took nothing less than a traumatic encounter and lasting memories of the humiliation, domination, and oppression by foreign powers, under the unequal treaties regime. As part of Western civilization, international law, so vital and beneficial to the relations among states of European background, proved more destructive than constructive to the Chinese. It was the challenge of survival in the face of national subjugation and extinction at the hands of Western imperialism that forced the Chinese to accept such international law concepts as sovereignty, nation, state, equality, and independence. The Chinese are history-conscious people. When being urged to adhere to the rules of international law, the visceral reaction by the Chinese has been profoundly influenced by this historical experience.

The impact of foreign imperialism on modern Chinese history can be measured partly by the extent to which it precipitated the breakdown of the age-old Sinocentric world order and reduced China to a semi-colonial society under the unequal treaties regime. It can also be measured by the extent to which the same destructive force awakened China and instilled in its people the determination to revive China in the modern world that had been forcibly thrust upon it by the West. Today, although the teaching, research, and dissemination of international law have become part of China's steady efforts to achieve its aspirations for national rejuvenation, early Chinese experience with international law still remains a key to understanding China's present attitude towards international law. Indeed, the perennial concern with its status, security, and territorial integrity, as shaped by its historical legacies, still overshadows China's legal behaviour in the conduct of its foreign relations.[18]

As advised by one commentator,[19] with China's rise into a great global power, the future of humanity much depends on whether China will behave with the same ruthless cynicism and cause as much misery and mayhem as its predecessors, or whether it will break the pattern and tear asunder the great-power-rising paradigm by rising peacefully. In this regard, we have to admit that there is no precedent, no guidebook one can take off the shelf, and no historical mentor one can turn to.

[18] Li Zhaojie, 'Legacy of Modern Chinese History: Its Relevance to the Chinese Perspective of the Contemporary International Legal Order' (2001) 5 Singapore Journal of International and Comparative Law 314.

[19] Jean-Pierre Lehmann, 'China's historic quest for a peaceful rise' *The Straits Times* (Singapore, 23 July 2015) <http://www.straitstimes.com/opinion/chinas-historic-quest-for-a-peaceful-rise> accessed 23 January 2019.

Whether China ultimately succeeds or fails will of course depend greatly on China, but it will also depend on the attitudes and acts of the existing and erstwhile great powers. Western sermons are not helpful. To build a better and more peaceful world, a collective constructive approach is *sine qua non*. A degree of humility is also warranted on the part of the Western powers (and Japan); they should recognize that they did not rise peacefully and indeed, as they rose, China was abused. This might go some way towards avoiding a Chinese syndrome of revenge. On the other hand, it must be pointed out that China's rise has been achieved by accepting greater interdependence, and its ability to exert influence depends on the responses of other nations.

In a sense, China is often viewed as a 'dissatisfied power' with a lengthy agenda to remould the international legal system. China is asked, and has agreed, to adhere to rules that it did not play a significant part in creating. It expects, and sooner or later will act on this expectation, that the rules-based international system will evolve in a way that offers a level playing field for China to participate in its making. But the Chinese government clearly understands that this happens only in a gradual manner through incremental reforms to international relations and through steadily augmenting its own institutional capacity as well.

It is thus particularly noticeable that, in its foreign policy pronouncements of the early twenty-first century, the Chinese government intentionally removed the previous expression of 'the establishment of a new international political and economic order' and replaced it with '[w]e will continue to take an active part in multilateral affairs, assume our due international obligations, play a constructive role, and work to make the international order fairer and more equitable'.[20] This shift in policy is further reflected by its proposition that all countries should uphold the purposes and principles of the United Nations Charter, observe international law and universally recognized norms of the international community, and promote democracy, harmony, collaboration, and win-win solutions in international relations.[21]

This must be perceived as a significant transformation of China's mind-set with regard to its attitude towards international law, from a victim-minded underdog, sceptical of the values and utilities of international law, to an active status-quo keeper of the present international legal order. Moreover, there are also reasons to believe that, as a nation on the rise, China will actively take its rightful place at the head table of world politics and enjoy its attendant prerogatives in becoming centrally involved in further international law-making. Thus, future decades will see greater increases in China's influence in reshaping the norms and rules of international law and international institutions.

[20] Hu Jintao, 'Uphold High the Great Banner of Socialism with Chinese Characteristics and Strive for New Victories in Building a Moderately Prosperous Society in All Respects' (Speech to the 17th National Congress, 15 October 2007).

[21] Ibid.

2.3 International Institutions

The contemporary international order, while being a more-or-less unified, liberal, and rules-based system, is a dynamic complexity, consisting of many different components and layers. It includes global and regional institutions as well as a dense network of treaties and regimes, together with various rules and norms, ranging from those governing state sovereignty to those protecting human rights. These institutions and regimes are inter-connected but have distinct aims. They also vary widely in their reach and purpose.[22]

As a result, China's participation in this order proves a diverse and complex one. Being a willing partner by and large, its decision to support the prevailing system is not a binary one. China has joined almost all intergovernmental organizations at the global level. China has become party to some 400 multilateral treaties. Meanwhile China rejects some rules, accepts others, and seeks to rewrite yet others, depending on its perception of how these rules, institutions, and regimes affect its state interests. China is a founding party to several of the global institutions at the centre of the present international order, including the UN. China joined the World Trade Organization only in 2001 after a lengthy negotiation. China has long been a party to many regional institutions, including the Asian Development Bank and the East Asia Summit.

As for multilateral treaties and regimes, China has a complex history of participation in them. For instance, the Nuclear Non-proliferation Treaty 1968 made China one of the five nuclear states, but China did not ratify it until 1992. It now participates, to some degree, in all the multilateral regimes governing nuclear, chemical, and biological weapons. In addition, China has helped construct some of the prevailing norms governing post-World War II international relations, and the degree to which China played a role in shaping international standards varies widely as its definition of state interests has evolved.

China has played a more active role in the non-proliferation of nuclear weapons. It supported the P5+1 negotiations with Iran and compliance with the global sanctions regime, which resulted in the Joint Comprehensive Plan of Action of 2013 under UN auspices. Most notably, China has voted for all the UN Security Council resolutions for sanctions against North Korea's nuclear and missile programmes.

China has demonstrated leadership in combating climate change. China used to be regarded as one of the main obstacles to a global climate agreement in 2008, but now its words are the *lingua franca* of climate-related diplomacy. Parts of a deal on carbon emissions between China and the US were incorporated wholesale into the Paris Pact on climate change of 2016. China helped determine how that accord defines what are known as 'common and differentiated responsibilities', namely how much each country should be responsible for cutting emissions. In this matter, China's role is particularly constructive.

[22] Richard Fontaine and Mira Rap-Hooper, 'How China Sees World Order' *The National Interest* (Washington DC, 20 April 2016).

In terms of foreign aid, since 2010 it has steadily moved away from net recipient status to net donor status. In 2014, during the Ebola outbreak in West Africa, China kicked off its largest ever response to an international humanitarian crisis, by offering US$123 million (RMB 750 million) worth of humanitarian aid to the global Ebola control efforts.

In the past, China was a fairly inactive member of the UN Security Council (UNSC), often abstaining from voting or taking a stand only when another member state was also willing to adopt the same position. Such a passive stance is gone. China now takes the UN, and, in particular, its Security Council, as the primary framework for legitimating collective action, and for matters of international peace and security.

China maintains that the UN must remain the bedrock of the present international order and the preferred platform for multilateral responses to common challenges. Moreover, it regards the UN system as a useful asset for its own international influence. It further regards the UN as an indispensable vehicle for developing an international order in which there is not simply one superpower that unilaterally directs world political, economic, social, and security questions, but where these questions are addressed by all states of the world on an equally participatory basis.

China has tripled its contributions to the UN budget and now stands as the third-largest donor after the US and Japan. It deploys thousands of troops on UN peacekeeping missions and is the second-highest financial contributor, after the US, to the UN peacekeeping budget. It edges towards a more active position in the UN, but it is not trying to dominate it. For example, it reacts to, rather than initiates, sanctions policy against North Korea.

In China's view, the purposes and principles of the UN Charter serve as the underlying pillars of the contemporary international legal system in that they promote cooperation among its member states, preserve their sovereignty and territorial integrity, ensure non-interference and non-aggression, and prohibit the use of force unless unanimously consented to by the five permanent members of the UNSC.

Together, these factors suggest that China is not turning its back on the existing international order or challenging the underlying pillars of that order across the board. Instead, an increasingly powerful China wants to maintain most elements of that order and to expand its influence within that order. This is because China sees that order as being able to accommodate its interests and those of other developing countries in their pursuit of peace and development. For that purpose, China is neither a revolutionary power bent on overthrowing things, nor a usurper, intent on grabbing global control.

2.4 The Globalized Economy

China openly acknowledges that it has benefited greatly from today's international system, particularly through facilitating the export-based growth over thirty years that has underpinned China's economic rise. For that reason, China has no intention of rejecting or repudiating the international order. Instead, it sees itself as its defender and builder. Its slogan-styled foreign policy statements, such as 'new type of diplomacy with Chinese characteristics' or 'struggle for future international order', do not imply that China intends to build a 'New Jerusalem'. On the contrary, they should be perceived as China's aspiration to see a future international order formed and developed with its active participation and positive contribution. As declared by Chinese Foreign Minister Wang Yi in September 2015, 'China is a staunch supporter of the current international order'.[23] This is because it has no reason to challenge the international order founded on the victory over fascism, neither has it the motivation to overturn the international system in which China has comprehensively participated.

There are now about 200 sovereign nations, as a result of decolonization beginning seventy years ago, and almost all of them are members of the UN. Such a state of affairs renders the prospects of building global consensus on anything of substance increasingly difficult, if not impossible. It is further exacerbated by the globalization of everything from terrorism, finance, pollution, and pandemics to unauthorized population movements. The uncomfortable truth is that the existing system of global governance is becoming increasingly dysfunctional. This has been demonstrated by its cumbersome response to global challenges and crises. For this reason, no one can assume, *a priori*, that a greater Chinese role in the present rules-based international system is, by definition, a hindrance. That is simply not the case. The question is whether the unfolding dynamics of its rise will result in a rules-based international system that is better than the present one.

In this regard, an exemplary case is the creation of the Asian Infrastructure Investment Bank (AIIB), a new multilateral development institution at the regional level that was initiated by China in 2013. According to the Chinese government, the AIIB as an alternative serves to complement, rather than rival, the existing international financial institutions, such as the World Bank and the Asian Development Bank. AIIB supports regional infrastructure projects, helping fill a multitrillion-dollar gap in financing for railways, roads, power plants, and other infrastructural needs in the world's fastest-growing region. However, the US saw it as a challenge to the existing regional and global development institutions that it helped establish in the decades after World War II. The US not only refused to join the AIIB itself, but also launched a quiet diplomatic campaign to dissuade its allies from doing so.

The US argued that the new banking institution could undermine the existing system by offering investment without imposing anti-corruption and environmental standards. Some also implied that China had a deeper purpose: to construct an alternative set of China-oriented international institutions free from both US dominance and the liberal international system designed and led by the US in the wake of World War II. Actually, this stated uneasiness about standards masked a geopolitical concern that the AIIB in question might be a further step in an effort by China to project its economic influence across Asia.

[23] Wang Yi, '中国是现行国际秩序的坚定维护者' (Mission of the People's Republic of China to the European Union, 16 September 2015).

The US attempt to halt or marginalize the bank failed. Except for Japan, a host of close US allies defied Washington's objection and joined AIIB as founding members in a last-minute stampede. One commentator observed that the AIIB might have its flaws, but opposing the very existence of a source of capital for countries that badly need it is a fool's errand.[24] Indeed, while its creation by China may signal a shift in the contemporary international order, given the fact that the AIIB itself is structured in a manner comparable to other existing institutions, this shift appears to be the case from geopolitical and geo-economic perspectives rather than from a legal one.[25]

A lesson to be taken from the AIIB case may be that new regimes and organizations initiated by China will not automatically lead to the erosion of the rules-based prevailing order. A distinction should be made between attempts to undermine the international rules and a move forward towards wholesale complementarity and improvement. In that regard, a rising China proves to be a more constructive as well as a necessary partner, rather than an underminer, in enhancing the present international order to meet shared international challenges.

2.5 China as a Stakeholder

As a final preliminary point, it must be noted that China resents the US notion that it needs to become a 'responsible' stakeholder in the present international order that was designed—in China's opinion—mainly to suit the interests of the US and the rest of the West. It sees this notion as condescending, with its implication that China is presently an 'irresponsible' stakeholder. Actually, as the above analysis has demonstrated, China has been playing a constructive role in international and regional issues and has made significant contributions to world peace and development. China has been actively participating in the formation of new rules and institutions, including some of the values underpinning it. China will:

> always stand on the side of peace and stability ... commit itself to equity and justice ... always work for world peace [and] contribute to global development. It will likewise firmly uphold the authority of the multilateral architecture ... oppose protectionism in its different forms, become more involved in global governance, and [make economic globalization] more inclusive, mutually beneficial, and equitable.[26]

This officially stated position in its discourse on the future of the international order should by no means be taken as simply empty rhetoric. Rather, it indicates clearly that

[24] Fontaine and Rapp-Hooper (n 22).

[25] Simon Chesterman, 'Asia's Ambivalence about International Law and Institutions: Past, Present and Futures' (2016) 27 EJIL 972.

[26] Li Keqiang (Premier of the State Council of PRC), Report on the Work of the Government, 5th Session of the 12th PRC National People's Congress, 5 March 2017 <https://wenku.baidu.com/view/33013364e3bd960590c69ec3d5bbfd0a7856d567.html> accessed 23 January 2019.

China now possesses not only new-found material power but also a new moral authority of persuasion, enabling it to play a greater role in shaping, guiding, and improving the world.[27] At a time when the world is facing tremendous challenges, the fact that its most populous country pledges to be a responsible stakeholder, committed to building a safer and better world, should be welcomed.

3 China's Aspirations

Against this background, a widely-asked question is whether China is moving forward to challenge the US for global leadership. Diminishing US power and its apparent withdrawal from its commitment to the rules-based international system has made this question more poignant.

Such speculation has been met with blunt denials by the Chinese government and academic commentators. As stated by the Chinese Foreign Minister Wang Yi in February 2017 during his visit to Australia, China does not want to lead or replace anyone. As its national strength is still limited, it must focus on its own development: 'We must remain clear headed about the various comments demanding China to play a "leadership role"'.[28] He later commented that the international community expects China to play a greater role in the stability and development of the world: 'While being willing to positively undertake its international responsibilities, China has never ever intended to lead the world. And in an era of globalization, what the world needs is solidarity-based partnership rather than a single-handed hero'.[29]

Scholars in China also tend to think that the argument for China's global leadership is anything but an unfounded myth.[30] This is because, notwithstanding the splendid achievements China has so far reaped from its economic development, glaring capacity gaps still exist, preventing China from assuming a truly global leadership position. Indeed, being a leader of the liberal international order requires China to commit a huge amount of resources. While China is now a net donor of foreign aid, it is far from achieving the donor status of many OECD countries; China still lacks foreign aid laws and a specialized development assistance agency analogous to the US Agency for International Development to coordinate development assistance.[31]

In addition, China has to address its serious soft power discrepancy in exercising global leadership. While it is indisputable that China's influence is on the rise, that

[27] Huang Zheping, 'Chinese President Xi Jinping Has Vowed to Lead the "New World Order"' *Quartz* (22 February 2017).

[28] Colin Packham, 'China, United States Cannot Afford Conflict: Chinese Foreign Minister' *Reuters* (7 February 2017).

[29] '外交部长王毅：中国从未想过要领导世界' *21Jingji.com* (20 March 2017).

[30] Yanzhong Huang, 'China's Superpower Status not enough to Replace US as Global Leader (Yet)' *Forbes* (29 August 2017).

[31] Ibid.

influence is mainly the result of its wielding of hard power, and less about soft power (such as cultural attractiveness, or appeal of its domestic development model built on the basis of its political, economic, social, and legal systems). Many of the extravagant soft power projects, including the overseas Confucius Institutes, have not worked out well in promoting China's image.[32]

China's domestic political economy is also hindering its efforts to project global leadership. Preoccupied by mounting domestic challenges, from air pollution to a potential middle-income trap, Chinese leaders will have to fight an uphill battle to mobilize the resources and internal support for playing the global leadership role. 'China's poverty line is still less than $1 a day, which still falls below the World Bank's global poverty line standard of $1.90 a day.'[33] As a scholar was quoted as saying, 'How can people expect a country whose poverty line is only about $400 a year to feed up people worldwide?'

More importantly, the present state of China's domestic governance can hardly be an exemplar for the liberal international order. Externally, Chinese leaders argue against 'any attempt to cut off the flow of capital, technologies, products, industries, and people between economies'. Internally, however, the government is doing the opposite by imposing additional controls on the inflow of information and outflow of capital. Although the Chinese government has reasons to do that, it would lead people to question the sincerity of its posited global leadership.[34] Indeed, global leadership starts with strength at home.

With the above paragraphs of observation in mind, the inquiry of China's attitude towards the contemporary international legal system reveals the following findings.

3.1 China's Self-Perception

First, the last two decades have seen a profound transformation of China's mentality from a victim-minded underdog in the old international legal system to an active status-quo keeper of the present international legal order. In the years following its founding in 1949, the People's Republic of China participated in a range of diplomatic and trade relations with states from the communist Warsaw Bloc and the developing world. But that participation was characterized by doubt, mistrust, and reservations that were reflected in the international law writings of Chinese scholars from the 1950s to the 1970s.

The policy of reform and opening to the outside world that began forty years ago, in 1978, precipitated a fundamental shift in this mind-set. With the continuing rapid expansion of China's engagement with the international community and its active involvement in the process of globalization and global governance, international law provides a more useful framework of reference for Chinese decision-makers in their

[32] Ibid. [33] Ibid. [34] Ibid.

assessment of internationally related matters and in the formulation of their policies of action. It plays an increasingly important role in the input, output, and feedback processes of China's domestic and foreign policy system. Today, China feels relatively more confident in, and comfortable with, the international system, although obstacles and resistance still exist. This has been, and continues to be, evidenced by China's phenomenally frequent reference to international law in dealing with its relations with other nations. Today's international legal system, as a whole, is perceived by China as an indispensable legal instrument for promoting China's proactive foreign policy. In 2014, Chinese Foreign Minister Wang Yi delivered a principled message on supporting the rule of law in the international community. He declared that '[u]pholding international rule of law is a momentous choice China has made based on its own experience' and that 'China has consistently upheld international rule of law in its diplomatic practice'.[35]

At the same time, however, China's policy of integrating with and participating in the present international system, particularly the process of reshaping new rules and institutions of the system, still follows a sovereignty-centred and state-empowering paradigm. The logic is simple. China must actively participate in the processes of the international legal system in order to have its own interests and concerns reflected and accommodated in that system, thus enhancing its influencing power for the purpose of realizing its great aspiration of national rejuvenation. At the same time, it also wishes to minimize the trade-off of its sovereignty.

Here, one can discern the relevance of China's historical experience for its international behaviour today. Given the state's pivotal historical role in advancing China's civilizational greatness and in maintaining its territorial integrity, and contrasting this historical glory with a century of humiliation under the unequal treaties regime, the sovereignty-centred and state-empowering Chinese perspective of international law can hardly be surprising. Indeed, since the overthrow of the last dynasty (the *Qing* dynasty) in 1911, the ability to maintain China's sovereignty over its internal and external affairs has become the *raison d'être* of any Chinese government, regardless of its ideological persuasion.

From this standpoint, China still perceives international law through the lens of statism. In its opinion, international law is still essentially 'the law of states, by states and for states'.[36] This sovereignty-centred and state-empowering approach to China's relationship with the international legal order reflects to some extent China's 'big power aspirations'. Thus, national political independence and global economic interdependence have become two means towards a sovereignty-centred end. Such a perception obviously affects the reception of international legal standards by China and ultimately its response to international law-related matters.

[35] Wang Yi, 'China a Staunch Defender and Builder of International Rule of Law' *PRC Ministry of Foreign Affairs* (24 October 2014).

[36] Bin Cheng, 'How Should We Study International Law?' (1994–1995) 13 Chinese Year Book of International Law and Politics 214, 218.

3.2 International Dispute Settlement

Secondly, an exemplary case in this regard is China's approach to international dispute settlement. In general, China considers that sovereign states should be able to choose the means of settling interstate disputes, rather than disputes being subject, without their consent, to compulsory adjudication or arbitration by third-party international tribunals. It believes that bilateral negotiations and conciliation are the most appropriate way to settle disputes between states. Therefore, as observed by a commentator, in most cases, when China enters into a multilateral treaty, it will opt out, through reservations, of any provisions obliging contracting parties to refer their treaty-related disputes to third-party settlement mechanisms.[37]

When the Philippine government initiated an arbitration case against China in accordance with the dispute settlement provisions of the UN Convention on the Law of the Sea 1982 (UNCLOS), concerning a range of issues relevant to the ongoing sovereignty dispute in the South China Sea,[38] China responded with 'fury and fire'. As vehemently argued by the Chinese government, the Philippines, by unilaterally initiating arbitration by a third party (a Permanent Court of Arbitration (PCA)-hosted tribunal), violated its presumably binding commitment to settle disputes only through bilateral negotiation and to exclude any third-party procedure. Such commitments were made through several formal bilateral Sino-Filipino agreements and were originally affirmed by both countries in the 2002 Declaration of Conduct regarding South China Sea disputes. Hence the Filipino submission constituted a 'deliberate act of bad faith and a violation of the international legal norm *pacta sunt servanda*, and the compulsory third-party dispute settlement procedures under the UNCLOS do not apply'.[39]

From the very beginning of that case, China has entirely refused to participate in the arbitration process and has completely rejected the ruling from the Tribunal by regarding that entity as illegitimate and illegal, and the award rendered thereby as null and void and inapplicable to China.[40] Noticeably, China's refusal to participate is consistent with its previous practices. The Qing dynasty government rejected Portugal's request in 1909 to refer Macau-related boundary disputes to the PCA. The Republic of China government refused to appear before the Permanent Court of International Justice in 1926 in relation to a dispute arising from China's denunciation of the Treaty of Amity with Belgium. In the 1960s, the People's Republic of China rejected an Indian proposal to resolve Sino-Indian boundary disputes through an international tribunal.[41]

[37] Harriet Moynihan, 'China's Evolving Approach to International Dispute Settlement' *Chatham House* (London, 29 March 2017).

[38] For the Chinese views on that case, see Michael Swaine, 'Chinese Views on the South China Sea Arbitration Case between the People's Republic of China and the Philippines' (2016) 51 China Leadership Monitor <http://carnegieendowment.org/files/CLM51MS.pdf> accessed 5 December 2018.

[39] Ibid. [40] Ibid. [41] Moynihan (n 37).

All of this reflects the prevailing sentiment in China regarding international dispute settlement, namely that as international tribunals are foreign-made, they are not trusted as being able to offer a level playing field for China. China prefers either direct negotiation or mediation, conciliation, or other forms of settlement that do not require it to surrender control over the outcome of the dispute to a third party from a world community in which it lacks confidence.

China's categorical and complete rejection of the South China Sea arbitration has aroused serious concerns that the Chinese government is seeking to opt out of the rules-based international order. For that point, a commentator suggests that China's approach to the settlement of international maritime disputes needs to be evaluated from a broader perspective rather than simply the South China Sea issue.[42] For instance, China is increasingly ready to accept adjudicative methods of dispute settlement when it considers that the benefit of doing so outweighs the economic and political costs. Since China became a World Trade Organization (WTO) member, it has been a respondent in thirty-nine disputes (the third-highest number of all 164 members) and has initiated fifteen cases itself (putting China in the top ten initiators of cases). China has also been active as a third party by intervening in 136 cases. Where China has lost cases before WTO, it has cooperated at each stage of the proceedings and it generally has a good record of compliance.[43]

The rationales behind these different approaches to international dispute settlement rest on the belief that, in the realm of trade, governments that wish to sustain and promote open markets and free flows of investment have a self-interested incentive to act in a responsible manner. They are prepared to sacrifice some autonomy (sovereignty) for improved collective returns. The WTO has been a major factor in both China's economic growth and its domestic reform. China has had over 3,000 laws revised in order to bring its legal system into compliance with WTO standards. Moreover, the resolution of interstate trade disputes does not directly involve the so-called 'core interests' of sovereignty as politically charged as those implicated in the South China Sea dispute. Indeed, China's stake in the South China Sea arbitration is too big for it to afford to lose.

It is interesting to note that, in the South China Sea arbitration, the Chinese government published a position paper on the question of jurisdiction in an attempt to engage in the debate, albeit outside the formal proceedings. The position paper was treated by the Tribunal as China's de facto pleading, or 'non-participatory participation'. This has been credited within the Chinese government as an 'experiment' and should be seen in the context of its strategic ambition to develop a greater mastery of international law.[44]

Equally noticeable is that some scholars in the Chinese international law community argued that China should participate in the arbitration, at least in the jurisdictional phase, since this would enable China to do full justice to its legal arguments, rather than

[42] Ibid. [43] Ibid. [44] Ibid.

shouting from the sidelines. This argument certainly failed, but it is nonetheless significant in that China's concerns were articulated by reference to UNCLOS norms (concerning jurisdiction, albeit not formally participating in the proceedings themselves) rather than from outside it.[45]

3.3 Human Rights

Thirdly, China's sovereignty-bound thinking is most persistent and resonant in the domain of international human rights. The most recurring theme in the Chinese human rights discourse is the primacy of state sovereignty—no state sovereignty, no human rights. This argument, at least in part, rests on historical and cultural grounds. For the former, a century of humiliation convinced the Chinese that without national independence there would be no guarantee for their basic human rights.

Culturally, the traditional notion drew the meaning of human beings from their social being in an intricate web of social relationships, rather than from their atomized autonomy. Thus, values such as liberty and autonomy were not prized as ends in themselves in the way that they have been in Western nations. This does not suggest that there is no respect for human dignity in the Chinese cultural context, but rather its basis is different. Respect for human dignity, as viewed by the Chinese, lies in the integrity of harmonic and orderly social bonds. It is meant to be exercised for the purpose of fostering collective welfare through moral exhortation internalized in the individual, rather than by means of the legal formality of government power vis-à-vis the individual.[46]

Once China recognized that human rights had become an integral part of global normative politics, it decided to opt into the UN human rights forums. China has now acceded to most of the UN-sponsored multilateral human rights treaties, including the International Covenant on Economic, Social and Cultural Rights 1966, which China ratified in 2001. It signed the International Covenant on Civil and Political Rights 1966 in 1998, but has yet to ratify it.

Concomitant with this development is a gradual move away from the classical notion that how a state treats its own citizens is not a matter of international concern. China has apparently accepted the proposition that a country's human rights performance is inextricably linked to its international image and reputation. This acceptance is manifest in its incremental modification and expansion of the concept of human rights, its greater participation in the activities of the UN human rights framework and, in particular, the phenomenal development in China's domestic governance of 'the socialist rule of law with Chinese characteristics'. Moreover, China is actively involving itself in the UN human rights forums and has participated in the Universal Periodic

45 Ibid.

46 James Hsiung (ed), *Human Rights in an Asian Perspective* (Paragon 1986) 11.

Review (UPR) by the UN Human Rights Council. At its second UPR in 2013, China acknowledged that it had human rights problems and accepted a high number of recommendations from other states.

Actually, compared with thirty years ago, China has made remarkable progress in the protection of human rights. This is the case particularly in its efforts to eradicate poverty. According to the World Bank, the poverty rate in China in 1981 was 63 per cent of the population. This rate declined to 10 per cent in 2004, indicating that about 500 million people had climbed out of poverty during this period. In 2016 alone, 10 million people were lifted above the poverty line.

Along with the 'no sovereignty, no human rights' argument, China views the maintenance of public order and social stability as a paramount obligation of the state, even at the expense of the fundamental rights of dissidents. Indeed, in China there is a shared concern about social stability, but the daunting challenge is how to balance it with human rights requirements.

In any event, China continues to see human rights in stronger aspirational terms, rather than in legal terms. It argues for priority to be placed on socio-economic rights and the right to development. It insists that human rights should be implemented in the light of the given political, social, and economic conditions of a country. Naturally, however, this gives rise to tensions between China and the West.

Noticeably, Western criticism of China's human rights situation often depicts China as an authoritarian one-party state, whose ethos, by its very nature, is a threat to the Western-driven ethos of the international legal order. In other words, there is a profound Western impatience with the dominant existing paradigm of international law—of statism—and a desire to replace it with a paradigm of an international law of humanity, where the priority would be given to individual human rights.

This is a challenge to China that concerns the development of future paradigms of international law. At a deeper level, this is a civilizational question, given that China's stance is not simply a product of its history since 1949. It also concerns the influence of Confucian, Daoist, Buddhist, and other philosophies on the place of the individual in community, the nature of authority, and especially the role of reasoning and logic in relation to feeling and emotion in human relations. What avenues of change are open to China, so that it can participate positively in the evolution of the international community, and develop patterns of the rule of law and accountability which enable it to connect positively with the Western world?

3.4 Selective Adaptation

Fourthly, at the operational level, China's sovereignty-centred approach to international law follows the model of 'selective adaptation'. This means that China's practice in international law today represents a dynamic process of selectively adapting international legal norms to its own needs for 'peaceful development', a code word for the rise of China. For that purpose, international law is still seen as a legal tool or instrument to be used for enhancing China's own state interests, rather than as a normative framework that governs international relations. There is nothing wrong with such a model, given that almost all states in the world see it in the same way. What is troubling, however, is the corollary of the unqualified notion of state interest. It implies that whenever there is conflict between state interests and international law, the former prevails over the latter. History shows that a great many heinous abuses, atrocities, and violations can be perpetrated in the name of state interests.

What comes with this selective adaptation model is a growing concern about how to have the Chinese domestic legal system live up to the requirements of international norms in a complementary manner. From a legal point of view, complementarity as such has at least the following normative strands. From the standpoint of compliance, most international legal norms cannot work without the constant help, cooperation, and support of national legal systems. Thus, to faithfully perform its international legal obligations, China needs to incorporate rules of international law into its domestic legal order by making the latter compatible with the former.

While actively participating in international legal institutions, however, the Chinese government still seems reluctant to make efforts to transform its domestic legal system into an international law-friendly one. To a large extent, this is due to the silence of China's Constitution 1982 on this matter. As a result, in domestic governance, China hardly leads in terms of making blanket constitutional commitments to the operation of international treaties and international customary rules. The inadequacy of China's domestic legal system in this respect also indicates its insufficient institutional capacity, which is in need of urgent attention. A positive development is that this matter has drawn close attention from the Chinese academic community.

Closely related to the question of complementarity is the question of legitimacy. Legitimacy as a legal term is often used to mean the quality of a rule which derives from the perception, on the part of those to whom it is addressed, that it has come into accordance with the right processes. Thus, some rules in themselves seem to exert more pull to compliance than others, simply because they are perceived to be legitimate by the actors themselves. In this respect, legitimacy as a dynamic factor concerns the extent to which members of local communities accept the purposes and consequences of selective adaptation. Therefore, the more legitimate an international legal norm is considered to be, the better chance it has of being accepted and ultimately implemented in a domestic legal order.

4 Conclusion

In the inquiry into China's attitude towards international law, one area which China attempts to draw attention to is the importance of the Five Principles of Peaceful

Co-existence (FPPC). As stated by Xi Jinping in 2014, in commemoration of the sixtieth anniversary of the FPPC:

> The Five Principles of Peaceful Coexistence have become the basic norms governing international relations as well as basic principles of international law .... In the new era today, the spirit of the Five Principles of Peaceful Coexistence, instead of being outdated, remains as relevant as ever; its significance, rather than diminishing, remains as important as ever; and its role, rather than being weakened, has continued to grow.[47]

This has also been echoed by Chinese Foreign Minister Wang Yi, when he delivered his well-known message that China is a staunch defender and builder of the international rule of law.[48] The 2016 Sino-Russian Declaration on the promotion of international law also highlights the principles of state sovereignty,[49] without mentioning such increasingly important international law regimes as human rights, environmental protection, and so on. In a sense, an impression has been made that China appears to be a 'Westphalia fundamentalist' in its approach to international law today.

It is believed that a variety of factors have led to this state of affairs. The most critical one is the mounting anxiety in China about its national security. For China, there is no clear distinction between internal and external security. Internal decay invites external aggression. This is a cold lesson China has learned from its modern history. Beijing's greatest fear these days has been that outsiders will meddle in Chinese affairs if the cohesion of the regime breaks down. Indeed, China has long been preoccupied with the fear of the so-called foreign hostile forces which are seeking to weaken, undermine, and sabotage China from within, and contain China's diplomatic freedom to manoeuvre from without. This growing fear has been particularly exacerbated by the ever deteriorating level of trust between China and the US, which has in turn thrown the two countries into a security dilemma.

Whereas China's chant of the FPPC reflects its serious concern about challenges to its national security, such concern has not affected, and will not affect, its recognition of the necessity and usefulness of international law in governing international relations. Indeed, a state's international legal behaviour tends to be more consistent and stable than its foreign policy behaviour. In this regard, China's practice in international law follows the overall guidelines of its foreign policy, as most countries do. But it never intends to act as it pleases outside the parameters of recognized international legal norms and rules. Furthermore, China sees itself largely benefiting from the continued operation and development of the contemporary international legal system. And to the extent that China has set out to build up institutions such as the AIIB, they supplement

[47] Xi Xinping, Speech on the Anniversary of the 'Five Principles of Peaceful Coexistence' <http://www.china.org.cn/chinese/2014-07/09/content_32902379.htm?W=kijzx> accessed 23 January 2019.

[48] Wang Yi (n 35).

[49] Joint Statement by the People's Republic of China and Russian Federation on the Promotion of International Law <http://www.fmprc.gov.cn/web/zyxw/t1375313.shtml> accessed 23 January 2019.

the existing international system, or at least constitute an institutional bypassing of the present system rather than threatening to supplant it. Meanwhile, China is growing more assertive in global and regional forums. This should be taken as an emerging power's quest for a greater voice or discursive power in global and regional institutions, rather than for their repudiation. China increasingly perceives its participation, and concomitant influence, to be preferable to going a different way.

CHAPTER 13

JAPAN

MOGAMI TOSHIKI

1 Introduction

When a book chapter is titled something like 'Japan and international law' or its reverse, there are two ways to elaborate on the topic. One is to focus on Japan as a state and describe its diplomatic behaviour in relation to international law; the other is to focus on academic works with regard to Japan's international law behaviour. This chapter adopts the first approach, although the undertaking will be qualitatively different from merely collecting state practice and compiling the 'foreign office international law' in a Japanese fashion. Rather, it will argue that a relatively consistent trait runs through Japan's international law behaviour, despite its ostensibly inconsistent and/or haphazard outlook.

The characteristics that this chapter will elaborate on are that, on the plane of international law, Japan has generally been a conformist state maintaining itself in line with the trends set by the dominant powers of each period, with some important aberrations in favour of its national interests. Being an attempt to synoptically grasp the essence of the history of Japan's behaviours, the argument is destined to be overarching, without detailed and corroborative factual descriptions, which often tend to end up in uncritically taking notes of 'foreign office international law'.[1] The objective of this chapter is to demonstrate the distinctive features of Japan's international law behaviour, if any, instead of tracing its state practices without analysing what they may mean to the world as a whole. Also, the author's interest lies in illuminating Japan's position in the historical development of international law—whether good or bad; it seems necessary by now to interpret behaviour from the viewpoint of global history. A new sort of historiography in international law is being desired more than ever,

[1] Inspired by David Bederman, 'Foreign Office International Legal History' in Matthew Craven, Malgosia Fitzmaurice, and Maria Vogiatzi (eds), *Time, History and International Law* (Martinus Nijhoff 2011) 45–6.

which is not confined to a mere chronological accumulation of state practices, or recollecting the explications of some chosen 'distinguished' international lawyers.

The sections that follow begin with Japan's embroilment with international law in the course of its efforts to revise the unequal treaties concluded with about a dozen Occidental (European and American) states, when Japan had been categorized (in the nineteenth century) among the 'barbarian' states in the world. After gradually overcoming this unequal status, it became a late-coming big power around the end of World War I. This big power then plunged into World War II, with the result that it was then branded an aggressor state and was penalized in an international tribunal. After that defeat, it turned into both a serious complier of new (that is, post-World War II) international law and a state deeply obedient to the US. These factors have brought about complex international law behaviour as well as serious constraints in Japan's choice of international law action.

2 Starting as Barbarian

Almost all the non-European states were born into a pre-established legal community of *jus publicum europaeum* as 'barbarians' at best. International law as it is now called was created and developed in Europe[2] with some historical necessity. It was imposed on other states, both ancient and new, who often had little experience of European types of diplomacy and 'international relations', including wars of conquest, occupation, and colonization. As these non-European states were less developed by European standards, the then prevalent laws of European creation were effectively 'imposed' on these less-than-members of the international 'community'.

The chimerical trichotomy of states into 'civilized (people)', 'barbarians', and 'savages' was coined first by an American anthropologist, Lewis Henry Morgan, in 1877.[3] Chimerical as it may have been, this typology was soon accepted by several international law scholars as legally relevant, including James Lorimer, Theodore Woolsey, Henry Bonfils, and Robert Phillimore. Roughly speaking, the typology was predicated on the distinction between 'European Christians and the Rest'. Being accepted by influential international lawyers, it was incorporated into the world of international law, if not as a legal rule then at least as a basic jurisprudential mindset. In particular, Lorimer defined the distinction beautifully as the trilogy of 'civilized men (or states)', 'barbarous or semi-barbarous states', and 'savages'[4]—and played an effective role to impress that

[2] Onuma Yasuaki, 'When Was the Law of International Society Born?' (2000) 2 Journal of the History of International Law 1, 5–7. For a critique of this theorization, see China Miéville, *Between Equal Rights: A Marxist Theory of International Law* (Pluto Press 2006) 165–6.

[3] Lewis Henry Morgan, *Ancient Society* (Holt 1877) 7–18. Morgan's trichotomy is further divided into sub-categories. See ibid. 12–13.

[4] James Lorimer, *The Institute of the Law of Nations*, vol 1 (William Blackwood and Sons 1883) 13, 217.

the distinction was jurisprudentially legitimate. Grewe summarizes this as saying that only 'civilized mankind' was able to entertain international recognition.[5]

It should be noted that with this typology *only* a discriminatory myth was invented and nothing more. On the contrary, it had already worked as a legal principle: the living space of 'savages', as they would be called later, was treated legally as *terra nullius* and the principle of *occupatio* was applied to these no man's lands. The fate of the 'barbarians' was slightly better as their territories were not occupied with legal justification but were *only* imposed upon by the rules of consular jurisdiction and extraterritoriality. The discriminatory distinction survived in international law for a long time—indeed, it lives on in article 38(1)(c) of the Statute of the International Court of Justice, which refers to 'general principles of law recognized by civilized nations'.

Japan, together with China, the Ottoman Empire, Persia, and Siam, had to start its process of modernization on the basis of this distinction (less unfortunately as 'barbarian', rather than 'savage'). It was forced to cease its self-seclusion from the outside world by opening itself around 1857–8. Treaties of friendship and commerce were concluded with sixteen European and American countries, some of which were forcibly concluded 'unequal' treaties.[6] They were concluded by the outgoing Tokugawa Shogunate (a feudal military government from 1600 to 1868), but succeeded to by the 'restored' imperial Meiji Government (1868–1945).

Many of the treaties concluded between 1854 and 1873 contained articles providing for consular jurisdiction, extraterritoriality, and the deprivation of Japan's customs autonomy. The revision of these treaties became an adamant objective of the new government, as they were 'a serious source of public resentment',[7] for they were regarded as 'shame and humiliation'.[8]

Thus, the process of legal modernization began. At the same time, there was the process of the Europeanization of Japan, from its government systems, both military and civil, down to people's lifestyle. An outstanding European model was Preussen (Prussia), with the first Japanese Prime Minister, Ito Tomobumi, being an unfailing admirer of that rising European country.[9] It is important to note that legal modernization was equal to the Europeanization of governmental and social systems, which would later involve the militarization of the country.

[5] Wilhelm Grewe, *The Epochs of International Law* (de Gruyter 2000) 454.

[6] These were: Austro-Hungary, Belgium, Denmark, France, Great Britain, Hawaii, Holland, Italy, North German Confederation, Portugal, Prussia, Russia, Spain, Sweden-Norway, Switzerland, and the US. See, Michael Auslin, *Negotiating with Imperialism: The Unequal Treaties and the Culture of Japanese Diplomacy* (Harvard UP 2004) appendix 1. It should be noted that the degree of inequality differed from treaty to treaty.

[7] Stephen Neff, *Justice among Nations: A History of International Law* (Harvard UP 2014) 317.

[8] Louis Perez, *Japan Comes of Age: Mutsu Munemitsu and the Revision of the Unequal Treaties* (Associated University Presses 1999) 63. See also Louis Perez, 'Revision of the Unequal Treaties and Abolition of Extraterritoriality' in Helen Hardcare and Adam Kern (eds), *New Directions in the Study of Meiji Japan* (Brill 1997) 320.

[9] Jan Roß, 'Als Japan preußisch wurde' *Die Zeit* (No 9/2018, February 2018).

Japan was also very quick at incorporating the prevailing international law, by publishing translations of international law books and dispatching officials to study abroad.[10] It was quicker than the other 'barbarians' to acquire and accumulate the knowledge of European international law,[11] though no such adjective ('European') was added and the term was simply translated into Japanese as 'universal public law'. For the receiving end, being European was being universal in those days.

This modernization *qua* Europeanization process, with the acquisition of international law knowledge, also connoted that Japan quickly accustomed itself to the 'rules of the game' of the imperialistic world, where the acquisition of colonies was commonplace and wars for that purpose were not regulated. Some authors even suggest that the knowledge of the international laws of warfare facilitated Japan waging one war after another after the Meiji Restoration, but it is not to the point. What matters is the truth that each time Japan won a war—against China in 1894–5, against Russia in 1904–5, and in the First World War against Germany in 1914–18—Japan's international status was proportionately elevated. This was especially true at the end of the First World War, when Japan participated in the Paris Peace Conference as one of the 'Big Five' states to lead the conference. It later became one of the permanent members of the Council of the League of Nations (with only three others, due, of course, to the non-participation of the US).

This promotion to big-power status marked Japan's escape from the 'barbarian' group. The original means to achieve this goal—the revision of the unequal treaties—had been attained between 1894 and 1897,[12] and was finally completed in 1911 with the conclusion of the Japan-US Treaty of Commerce and Navigation, which restored Japan's autonomy on tariffs. But promotion up to big-power status was presumably more decisive. Each time Japan resorted to international violence and won it, it was regarded as being more 'civilized'. Quite ironically, the competence to wage superior violence became evidence of a country's degree of civility. Such was the criteria to determine pseudo-legally the uncanny grouping neatly articulated by Lorimer.

It should be added that this process of civilizing entailed another layer of victimization with regard to a 'savage' or 'barbarian' state. Japan extended colonial rule in Korea and finally annexed it in 1910. It also stepped up its intervention in China, which was in a way breaking apart, finally acquiring the interests in Dalian and Lushun in 1905 after competing and/or conniving with the European powers, particularly after the Russo-Japanese War. Thus, Japan was loyally implementing the imperialistic rules of the game, as if colonization and semi-colonization, as well as the use of force therefor, were

[10] Neff (n 7) 314–15; see also Kinji Akashi, 'Japan-Europe' in Bardo Fassbender and Anne Peters (eds), *The Oxford Handbook of the History of International Law* (OUP 2012) 731–5.

[11] Gaurier contrasts in this regard Japan and China and highlights the early appearance of international law authors such as Sakuye Takahashi (1867–1920). See Dominique Gaurier, *Histoire du droit international* (Presses universitaires de Rennes 2014) 568.

[12] For a complete list of the years of entry into force and revision of related treaties, see Perez, *Japan Comes of Age* (n 8) 188 (appendix B).

part of international law among the dominant powers.[13] Though it is questionable and problematic to say that these acts were fully lawful in those days, it was apparent that no clear rule of international law was available to prohibit the acts. Japan as a nascent imperialistic power was simply conforming to the prevalent system of legal rules (or the absence thereof) and, more perfectly, to the political imperialistic rules.

3 Rapid Civilization until the End of the First World War

Japan's participation in the First World War was said to be accidental, as the government was at first reluctant to take part, being only interested in the German-occupied south Pacific territories. It finally accepted the military invitation from the British government and fought battles with Germany, mainly in China. Though accidental, participation bore fruit for Japan: the status of a victor of this Great War and the elevation to a 'civilized' big power comparable to Europeans, as described earlier. In the meantime, Japan's aggressive advancement into China was steadily escalating, with rude acts like the 21 Demands of 1915 to concede more interests to Japan there.[14] The final stage of Japan's collapse was being set unknowingly.

As if to reflect the accidental nature of its victory, Japan's manner of participation in the Paris Peace Conference was not quite enthusiastic, particularly with regard to the establishment of the League of Nations. Only Japan among the Big Five did not prepare a draft for the forthcoming Covenant of the League.[15] It should be said that, despite it being conformist in several ways, Japan was not fully mature enough to catch up with the big tide to restructure the world and the rules of the game, sticking instead to the old nineteenth-century rules and the gains that it had at last won.

Being a conformist does not mean actively pushing for a qualitatively new global order. Japan exemplified this by focusing on the immediate semi-colonial interests of China (Shandong) and the south Pacific islands, and being 'silent partners'[16] in Paris. Without being committed to the elaboration of a constitution of the world (at that time), the Japanese government was rather hostile to the construction of the League, siding with the nationalistic segment of its nation, which even regarded the League's 'pacifism' as an Anglo-American conspiracy.[17]

[13] Friedrich von Martens (Fyodor Fyodorovich Martens), as legal representative for Russia, is quoted as condemning Japan's act as 'a flagrant violation of international law': Stephen Neff, *War and the Law of Nations* (CUP 2005) 182.

[14] For a detailed account of these demands, see Kajima Peace Research Institute (ed), *Nihon Gaikoushi [The Diplomatic History of Japan]* vol 11 (Kajima Peace Research Institute 1971) ch 1.

[15] Thomas Burkman, *Japan and the League of Nations: Empire and World Order* (University of Hawaii Press 2008) 60.

[16] Ibid. 63.

[17] The pronouncements of Konoe Fumimaro, a subsequent Prime Minister: ibid. 56–7.

This episode itself may be nothing more than an immature narrow-mindedness, but it seems to this author more serious than that: it could signify that, in spite of its conformism, Japan was not truly amenable to internationalism, whether great power internationalism or a more equality-oriented internationalism.[18] Reliance on great power internationalism would encourage a power to construct a legal regime that would legitimize its domination and control of the world, where it is important to be *de jure* and not merely de facto. Believing in an equality-oriented internationalism (which had not yet taken shape in those days) would encourage a power to be legally minded, for it would involve mobilizing a new legal imagination. Japan was neither of these, being instead a lopsided conformist.[19]

This insensitivity was not only serious in itself but also somewhat ominously suggestive of Japan's course which would soon be derailing it. Although the League of Nations appeared another embodiment of the great power dominance (which it was, to a considerable extent), something new was being born. In particular, some international legal embryos were in development with regard to the legal evaluation of the use of force, the rules of warfare and war victims, the rules concerning colonialism, the legal notion of human rights, and so on. Japan would soon have to pay for its reluctance in the formation of a new edifice of internationalism and, later, in proportion to this reluctance, in the trend of new international law-making[20] when the legal evaluation of use of force was quietly changing under the cover of imperialism.

4 From Conformism to Conservatism

When one keeps behaving as a conformist without noticing changes that are underway, one tends to fall into a simple conservatism. This largely applied to Japan in its League years.

First, its foreign policy enthusiasm was directed to securing the profits of the League Mandate system which, in Japan's understanding, was almost synonymous with annexation,[21] and was therefore seen as a continuation of colonialism. Although this understanding was legally mistaken, politically it was not. And it was for this reason

[18] The notion of internationalism in this regard remains ambiguous even today. When great powers venture into establishing an international organization ('for peace') at the cost of great wars, it can be both an internationalist enterprise but at the same time a hegemonic one. On the other hand, internationalism can mean a movement for equalization and empowerment of states as well as peoples.

[19] This is about the Japanese government, but not necessarily its citizens. There were a variety of different opinions at this lower level.

[20] It should, however, be noted that the Japanese Society of International Law showed enthusiasm in its own way for the Hague Conference for the Codification of International Law in 1930, with the commitment of the government. For this, see, Kajima Peace Research Institute (ed), *Nihon Gaikoushi [The Diplomatic History of Japan]* vol 14 (Kajima Peace Research Institute 1972) 415–25.

[21] This is what Baron Makino, a Japanese representative at the Paris Peace Conference, reported to the Foreign Ministry: Burkman (n 15) 69–70.

that Japan was supportive of the idea to insert the Monroe Doctrine in the Covenant,[22] article 21 of which read:

> Nothing in this Covenant shall be deemed to affect the validity of international arrangements, such as treaties of arbitration or regional understandings like the Monroe doctrine, for securing the maintenance of peace.

This was a rare case in which Japan was willing to express its strong intention and it reflects what legal rules were necessary for Japan in those days. The article is both a perplexing and a monumental provision in the sense that it guaranteed the notion of the sphere of interest in a sacrosanct (so-to-speak) treaty for *universal* peace, and that it was proposed by a regional hegemon that never became a member of the organization founded on that Covenant. But this weird provision was exactly what Japan needed as a newly installed great power and regional hegemon in Asia. As is often the case, a great power's use of legal rules can be subjective and/or arbitrary—Japan in this era was merely following suit.

Equally well known, or better known, is the fact that Japan insisted on the insertion in the Covenant of an article providing for racial equality between and among nations. Although it was supported in the conference by smaller powers, the proposal was turned down in the League of Nations Committee by the resistance and opposition of a few countries—Australia in particular and ultimately the US[23]—largely due to their domestic race issues. According to some historic documentation, Japan was rewarded with the interests Chinese Shandong (China) in exchange for the withdrawal of the proposition.[24] Though it was a realpolitik solution that is easy to understand, Japan's contribution to the formation of international law would have been drastically different if it had succeeded in inserting such a provision with so much potential to enrich and disrupt the future of international law.

By then, the presumed agreements between this conformist Japan and the *senior* great powers were gradually turning into discordance. It was typically expressed in the military dispatch to Siberia (Russia) during and after the Paris Conference, where Japanese activities were exceptionally salient to the extent that Japan became diplomatically distanced.[25] At the same time, the anti-Anglo-American sentiment was steadily growing on the domestic scene, partly because of the poor result for Japan in the Paris Conference, thereby estranging it from the former models it aimed to catch up with. In addition, political convulsions in China were growing stronger, and the deal over Shandong led to a movement on 4 May 1919, which would later lead to an all-out war of resistance after 1931.

Thus, the catching-up process of Japan, which started in 1868 in the search for equal treaty relations, finally led the country not only to catch up with the predecessors but also to overstep the legal/political rules set by them, and to bring about conflicts with

[22] Ibid. 79. See also Margaret MacMillan, *Paris 1919* (Random House 2001) 96.

[23] Kajima Peace Research Institute (ed), *Nihon Gaikoushi [The Diplomatic History of Japan]* vol 12 (Kajima Peace Research Institute 1971) 172–92.

[24] Burkman (n 15) 85.

[25] A 'diplomatic isolation' according to Burkman, ibid. 22.

them. It is important that those Anglo-European senior imperialists were not simply contented with the old imperialistic rules, but were simultaneously deforming some of them in accordance with their interests and/or repositioning themselves in the direction of a nascent international law system. It is ironic that this new system was being created in the struggle with fascist/totalitarian powers, which Japan was turned into through its own aberrations in the process of modernization. Whatever the aspirations of Japan, the modernized and civilized international law existed, or at least definitively started existing, somewhere else. Japan was becoming a conservative or arguably reactionary state in terms of international law, even among the big powers.

Instead of sensing this normative and systemic change in the direction of a new universalism, Japan was contented with a dreamy idea of regionalism. Assertions like a Pan-Asian Federation or Japan's prominence in Asia were voiced.[26] Unilateralism and regionalism prevailed, which portended the advent of the ostensibly altruistic notion of a Greater Asia Co-Prosperity Sphere, which included a school of a Greater Asia International Law, heavily influenced by Nazi (or fascist) international law.[27] Such was Japan's imagery of *Landnahme* (territory taking), to use Carl Schmitt's word,[28] turning its competing colonialism into regionally monopolizing colonialism or hegemonic regionalism. This was pursued in accordance with the kind of international law rule which was now almost defunct—or else, in accordance with an emerging revolutionary rule, on the basis of Nazi-inspired *Grossraum*.

5 The League Years: A Great Power Turned into an Aggressor

Japan's League years saw a few positive signs alongside the negative ones on the path to further deterioration. Above all, Shidehara Kijuro was Foreign Minister between 1924 and 1927 and from 1929 to 13 December 1931. His policy was said to be basically peace-oriented and multilateralist, which was then labelled 'Shidehara diplomacy'.[29] It should not be overlooked that there were also a few prominent personalities who were called 'internationalists', such as Nitobe Inazo, Adachi Mineichiro, and Sugimura Yotaro,

[26] For an overall description and analysis of this issue, see Eri Hotta, *Pan-Asianism and Japan's War 1931–1945* (Palgrave Macmillan 2007). See also Burkman (n 15) 201–6.

[27] For typical examples of the notion of Greater Asia International Law, see Matsushita Masatoshi, *Daitoua Kokusaihou no Shomondai [Problems of the Greater Asia International Law]* (Nihon Houri Kenkyuukai [Research Group of Jurisprudence of Japan] 1942); Yasui Kaoru, *Oushuu Kouiki Kokusaihou no Kiso Rinen [The Basic Concepts of the European Greater Region International Law]* (Japanese Society of International Law/Yuhikaku 1942). For a groundbreaking account of the fascist origin of this idea, see Madeleine Herren, 'Fascist Internationalism' in Glenda Sluga and Patricia Clavin (eds), *Internationalisms: A Twentieth Century History* (CUP 2016) 109–10.

[28] Carl Schmitt, *Der Nomos der Erde* (first published 1950, Duncker & Humblot 1960) 48–51.

[29] See Klaus Schlichtmann, *Shidehara Kijûrô: Staatsmann und Pazifist* (Deutsch-Japanischen Juristenvereinigung 1997) 302–17.

working in the League Secretariat, Permanent Court of International Justice, International Labour Organization, and so on, but their internationalism was not vigorous enough to work as a bulwark against the government's law-breaking aberrations. The actual record of Shidehara diplomacy itself was mixed, particularly with regard to China. Overall, the international law behaviour of Japan worsened throughout the period. Notably, in September 1931, the invasion into Manchuria in China began, spurring Shidehara's resignation.

The invasion of Manchuria marked the beginning of the final collapse of Japan's pursuit of modernization *qua* Europeanization, now with the violation of international law instead of the rectification of legal inequality. It is not the purpose of this chapter to make a full account of the facts of this use of force without justifiable legal cause. Instead, a bulleted list of a few main events that are legally relevant will suffice:

- 18 September 1931: the Kwantung Army, a branch of the Japanese army, starts military activities near Mukden, and thus invades Manchuria.
- 21 September 1931: the Chinese government appeals to the Council of the League Nations, which requests *both sides* to observe a ceasefire.
- 7 January 1932: the United States issues the Stimson Doctrine, which would refuse to recognize any situation created by the illegal use of force.
- 11 March 1932: the Assembly of the League endorses and legitimizes this Stimson Doctrine, without explicitly mentioning it.
- 24 September 1932: the Report of the Lytton Commission is presented, which negates Japan's allegation of 'self-defence' in Manchuria, and the 'voluntariness' of the establishment of Manchukuo.
- 6 December 1932: the Assembly entrusts the adoption of the conclusion about the incident to a Committee of Nineteen, which finds against Japan.
- 24 February 1933: Foreign Minister Matsuoka Yosuke delivers a speech to the General Assembly justifying his country's acts. The Assembly votes on the report of the Committee of Nineteen, adopts it by a vote of 42-1-1, thereby excluding the legal room for Japan's negative vote to have effect as a veto.
- 27 March 1933: Japan sends notice of its withdrawal from the League.

Matsuoka's speech to the Assembly was symbolic of the nostalgia for the era that Japan had come through during its modernization, the era which was now about to disappear; it was also expressive of the legal anachronism that Japan still believed to be the rule. He kept looking down upon China as a 'lazy and backward' country, filled with anarchy. It was, according to him, not a sovereign state in the *Western* sense of the term, and Japan had been a 'great *civilizing* and stabilizing force' there. Accordingly, he said that the Assembly 'should know the economic and political necessities of Japan in that territory'.[30] Here the

[30] Address by Yosuke Matsuoka, Chief Japanese Delegate, at the 17th Plenary Meeting of the Special Assembly of the League of Nations, 24 February 1933 (1933) League of Nations Official Journal, Special Supplement 112, 16–20.

legal justification, if any, was completely confused with power political opportunism. Moreover, it was based on the chimerical trichotomy of the nineteenth century which Japan had had to fight, while downgrading China further from a 'barbarian' to a 'savage', who was destined to be occupied by a 'civilized' nation.

This is how Japan fell into becoming an aggressor. Although the legal determination as such was rendered only in 1946, the determination would have to be retroactive, without which no *ex post facto* action like punishment would be possible. Therefore Japan became an aggressor judicially in 1946 but legally in 1933 when it was unable to justify itself legally in the world forum of the day. In this sense, despite the more common appellation '15 years' war' (1931–1945), it would be more aptly named '15 years' aggressorhood', in order to reflect the legal evaluation of the outcome of Japan's modernization—which was simultaneously blind conformism.

In sum, Japan started as a 'barbarian' in the European-made world of international law, overcame it in about forty years, became a more 'civilized' big power, and finally fell to the level of aggressor, the worst of all the international legal statuses. In this process, the country gradually went from being a least aggressive country to becoming a leading aggressor together with two European powers (Germany and Italy). It is ironic that throughout the entire period, Japan's self-recognition probably remained the same—conforming to the international rules of the game all the way. It did not recognize, until its total defeat, that the rules were gradually changing, or at least it kept refusing to recognize it.

Of particular relevance is the role that the Stimson Doctrine played in determining the legal status of Japan's behaviour. As noted above, the Assembly in its Resolution of 11 March 1932[31] endorsed this Doctrine by quoting its essential components. On this basis it created a new systemic rule of international law by stating without any ambiguity that states had to respect:

1. the undertaking to preserve as against aggression the territorial integrity and existing political independence of the League of Nations members (by referring to the quotation of article 10 in its Appeal to the Japanese government on 16 February 1932);
2. the obligation to submit all disputes or conflicts to pacific means, in harmony with the Pact of Paris 1928 (the so-called Kellogg-Briand Pact); and
3. the principle not to recognize any situation, treaty, or agreement which may be brought about by means contrary to the Covenant or Pact of Paris (which is the Stimson Doctrine).

This juxtaposition could even be regarded as a precursor of article 2, paragraphs 3 and 4 of the UN Charter 1945. Unfortunately, Japan had not been active in formulating the foundational documents above—the Covenant or the Pact of Paris—and therefore

[31] (1932) League of Nations Official Journal, Special Supplement 101, 87–8.

was not keenly cognizant of the legal change that had been latent but finally surfaced in this Resolution. Although Japan was still a member of the League of Nations on this particular day, it would make no difference whether it was a member or not, as its ensuing behaviour vividly demonstrated. Japan's conformism to international law and the dominant trend in the 'civilized' world thus became outdated and out of focus. It was only conforming to itself, if together with two other fascist outcasts.

6 A Criminal State Turned Client State

Japan's defeat contained, in its final stage, a few international law issues that might have worked in its favour: the invasion by the Soviet Union of territories lost to Japan in the 1904–5 war, based on a secret agreement in Yalta but in violation of the non-aggression agreement; the dropping of nuclear bombs on Hiroshima and Nagasaki in 1945; and attacks against innocent civilians there and in many other cities. However, as is almost always the case with post-war settlements, those potentially off-setting elements were dissipated in the course of the prosecutions before the International Military Tribunal for the Far East (Tokyo Tribunal) and similar national criminal proceedings in several Southeast Asian countries. No more could have been expected for Japan as a criminal state, though the issues did hold weight with some of the judges.[32]

I do not elaborate on this process, which itself deserves thousands of pages. Japan contributed to the formation or codification of international law. The crimes against peace established in the Tokyo Trial, together with those in the Nürnberg Trial, also gave birth to crimes against humanity. There may be legitimate bases to find fault with the confirmation of these crimes at those historic moments, yet the atrocities committed by Japan and Nazi Germany could not have passed with impunity. Even if they were not mature crimes under international law, they were at least illegal acts in light of the laws that had been accumulated of a more or less universal nature.[33]

In this way, Japan started its life of rehabilitation after the Tokyo Trial and under occupation by the allied powers, particularly the US. It regained independence with the

[32] See the dissenting opinions of Justices Bernard (France), Röling (Netherlands), and Pal (India) in Neil Boister and Robert Cryer (eds), *Documents on the Tokyo International Military Tribunal: Charter, Indictments and Judgments* (OUP 2008) 661–1426. See also Neil Boister and Robert Cryer, *The Tokyo International Military Tribunal: A Reappraisal* (OUP 2008) 290 (describing the defence argument for Japan by counsel Ben Blakeney).

[33] It should be noted that the limits of legal positivism became apparent in such a *Grenzsituation* (limit situation) in Karl Jaspers' terminology: both Japan and Germany could have been absolved of legal responsibility according to legal positivism, with its emphasis on states' sovereign consent to duties that will bind them. But the extraordinary atrocities committed by them necessitated the advent of radically new law and provoked a different basis of legal judgment from the former strictly state- and consent-based positivism. Whether one calls it natural law or not depends on the theoretical framework of the author.

conclusion of the Peace Treaty in San Francisco with most of the Allied Powers (1951–2), and was admitted into the United Nations in 1956. Equally important, a new Japanese Constitution was promulgated in 1946 and entered into force in 1947, with a ground-breaking provision that prohibited the state from waging war and abandoned the right to belligerency and armed forces. The conceptual core of this provision resembles that of the Pact of Paris, which had partly condemned Japan as being guilty of crimes against peace. Also, its philosophy of peace marked a qualitative difference from that of the UN Charter, which entered into force in 1946 and had the notion of collective security at its core.[34] In any event, Japan made a fresh start as a peaceful and hopefully law-abiding nation in the post-war world.

Having chosen to be a non-bellicose and civilian (as opposed to militaristic) country, Japan generally remained a quiet and civilized member of the international community for a long period. The ongoing presence of the US military, either as occupier or alliance partner, should, however, be taken into account in interpreting Japan's uncommon status and behaviour. In addition, though it was complex, the 'Peace Constitution' essentially determined the nature of Japan's international law behaviour—though some may assert that the Constitution adversely constrained Japan's freedom of action on the international scene. Either way, post-war Japan has not engaged in war (not to mention aggressions), has eschewed drastic military build-up and nuclearization, and has mostly engaged in trade without serious friction with others. While it has seen fisheries disputes with the Soviet Union (now Russia), South Korea, China, and a few others, none of these has deteriorated into conflict. All in all, it has been a law-abiding, serene, materially developed member of the international community. Mention should also be made of the fact that Japan, as a developed country, has contributed enormously to developing countries with its economic and technical assistance, as well as cultural cooperation and environmental protection.

On the negative side, however, its low-key position on the international scene was characterized by a new sort of conformism: its ties to the US. Whether Japan's military security has been protected by this military alliance is not the subject of this chapter; rather, the concern is several serious problems that this unfailing conformism has caused. First, there are matters of fairness, or those related to human rights, that have been disrespected, if not totally violated, under both domestic and international law. Secondly, conformism has also imposed constraints on Japan's international law behaviour, including perhaps on international law jurisprudence itself.

Of notable importance among other examples of conformism and human rights neglect is the situation in Okinawa, where about 74 per cent of all the US military

[34] For the argument of the author himself, see Mogami Toshiki, *Kokusai Kikouronn Kougi [International Organization]* (Iwanami Shoten Publishers 2016) 85–9, analysing the UN collective security system as the creation of international power with little mechanism to control it. The same work also compares it with the comparable system of the League of Nations, which had in fact started without that particular concept and ended up in failure, although there were several successes in peaceful resolution of conflicts (ibid. 55–9). See also Mogami Toshiki, 'Toward *Jus contra Oligarchiam* – A Note on Critical Constitutionalism' (2012) 55 Japanese Yearbook of International Law 371, 384–5.

installations based in Japan are concentrated, while the small prefecture occupies only 0.6 per cent of the land surface of Japan. It was placed under the administration of the US military until 1972, which was virtually the continuation of wartime occupation. Although sovereignty—conveniently called 'residual sovereignty' based on article 3 of the Peace Treaty with the Allied Powers in 1951—was 'returned' to Japan in that year, the bases and other military installations remained almost the same. Among other things, this brought with it the accidents and wrongful behaviour that military exercises and the presence of such installations incurs, ranging from the crashes of planes or helicopters on the sites of schools to rapes and murders by military personnel.[35]

Most of the perpetrators or those legally responsible are protected by an international agreement: the Japan-US Status of Forces Agreement 1960. In addition to the sweeping range of jurisdiction exercised by the US, the Agreement stipulates that when such crimes are committed or accidents occur and the jurisdiction of both states overlap, the military authorities of the US shall have the primary right to exercise jurisdiction, particularly if the offences arise 'out of any act or omission done in the performance of official duty' (article XVII, 3(a)(ii)). This primary right is rarely conceded to Japan, which in its turn is rarely serious about demanding that it is. Thus, this wide and flexible provision has allowed the perpetrators or those responsible to evade trials in Japanese courts as they were seldom surrendered to the Japanese authorities and were let out of the Japanese (nominally legal) territory from the US bases.[36] However dissatisfied the victims and other citizens of Okinawa may be, the Japanese government is unwilling and unable to do anything, under the cover of an international agreement.

On the other hand, there exists another arm of international law which, instead of shielding crimes from judicial examination, finds that the situation on this small island constitutes a sort of discrimination. For example, the UN Committee on the Elimination of Racial Discrimination (CERD), in its Concluding Observations on Japanese Government's periodic report in 2010, expressed its concern about 'the persistent discrimination suffered by the people of Okinawa'.[37] It reiterated the report of the Special Rapporteur on Contemporary Forms of Racism that the 'disproportionate concentration of military bases' exclusively in that prefecture has a negative impact on the enjoyment of rights by the people. In short, the CERD concluded that there was an element of racial discrimination in this unequal treatment. Some may take issue with the characterization of 'racial', but it is nonetheless some kind of discrimination—for the other parts of Japan are not suffering from the same victimhood, even after

[35] For a documented general survey, see Gavan McCormack and Satoko Oka Norimatsu, *Resistant Islands: Okinawa Confronts Japan and the United States* (Rowman & Littlefield 2012); Aketagawa Tooru, *Okinawa Kichi Mondai no Rekishi: Hibu no Shima, Ikusa no Shima [The History of the Base Issues in Okinawa: Non-war Island, or Warring Island]* (Misuzu Shobou 2008).

[36] See e.g. Shimabukuro Jun and Abe Kohki (eds), *Okinawa ga Tou Nihon no Anzennhoshou [Revisiting Japan's Security from Okinawa]* (Iwanami Shoten Publishers 2015), especially ch 5.

[37] Committee on the Elimination of Racial Discrimination, UN Doc CERD/C/JPN/CO/3-6 (2010) para 21.

disregarding the slight ethnic difference between the Okinawans and the long-time descendants of mainland Japan.[38] Of particular importance is that these people are singled out and subjected to exclusive burdens. A few non-governmental human rights organizations also submitted a report to the UN Human Rights Council in 2015, which condemned the discrimination by quoting the same report of 2006 by the Special Rapporteur on Racial Discrimination.[39]

The Japanese government is only bending to the will of the US military, but in doing so it contravenes more universal norms of international law if the findings in the CERD or the NGOs in the Human Rights Council are correct. Conformism is, after all, the lack of independent judgement. It is necessary for Japan to review, from time to time, whether its conformism is in tune with the norms possessing or gaining universal legitimacy towards the construction of a more egalitarian, peaceful, fair, and symbiotic world, where a sensitive rule of law prevails.

But in reality, this conformism has also involved Japan in several wars, despite its own non-waging of them owing to the Peace Constitution. It supported the US in the Korean War in the 1950s and the Vietnam War in the 1960s, and fully participated in the Cold War, confronting China and the Soviet Union in particular. Taking a position is inevitable in any world of politics, but whether these positions were autonomous is at best dubious. In this period of high politics, the laws of disarmament, arms control, and the regulation of the use of force were stagnating. On the other hand, a new kind of international law arising out of the aspirations of the developing countries was growing irresistibly. There is little evidence that the Japanese government was hostile to these trends in the formation of new international law, but there is equally little evidence that it was positive and playing a leading role in this innovating wave.

A decisive turning point in Japan's conformism was the Gulf War in 1991, where US-led coalition forces mounted a crusade against Saddam Hussein's Iraq after its invasion in Kuwait. It is highlighted here not as a matter of political criticism, but as a telling case for the analysis of the direction in which Japan's conformism steered it.

The US was (or several influential political figures were) keen to embroil Japan in the war being led by the US coalition, notwithstanding Japan's Peace Constitution prohibiting the state from engaging in wars or the threat or use of force.[40] Despite the apparent eagerness of the Japanese government to send troops in defiance of the

[38] The Japanese government on occasion rebuked the Concluding Observations of the CERD, particularly with regard to the 'indigenousness' of the Okinawan people. See e.g. Comments by the Government of Japan regarding the Concluding Observations adopted by the Committee on the Elimination of Racial Discrimination, UN Doc CERD/C/JPN/co/3-6, March 2011 <http://www.mofa.go.jp/policy/human/pdfs/race_rep_concluding_fu1103.pdf> accessed 4 December 2018.

[39] See e.g. the joint written statement by two civic human rights organizations, UN Doc A/HRC/30/NGO/92 (2015).

[40] For the factual record of the political developments on the Japanese and American sides, neither of which was monolithic but varied and nuanced, see Asahi Simbun, *Wangan Sensou to Nihon [The Gulf War and Japan]* (Asahi Shimbunsha 1991). The description in this paragraph is the author's summary from this documentary book.

Constitution, vehement criticism from the public finally dissuaded the government. It gave up actual participation, and instead chose to participate financially by making an enormous contribution of US$13 billion.

By traditional interpretation, this financial participation could arguably be judged a violation of the law of neutrality and therefore as being tantamount to participation in the war as a party,[41] unless the authorization of the use of force by the Security Council resolution 678 is regarded as having the effect of robbing the war of its nature as war between equal parties, thereby redefining it as a kind of the exercise of public power that is superior to war between peers. But it is questionable that such an interpretation was established at that time.

In any case, the war itself became one authorized by the Council resolution and was legal to that extent[42] (it was also claimed to be an exercise of collective self-defence, at the invitation of Kuwait, under article 51 of the UN Charter). If so, and if we forget about the disagreement with its own Constitution, Japan's conformism to the US was now merged with the conformism, once again, with the international law majority of the world. Of course, whether the majority decision at this time will endure and be legally effective in the future remains to be seen. The notion of peace by war is always precarious, even if a one-time victory might look quite effective in one particular case at a special moment. This conventional wisdom was what the philosophy of Japan's Peace Constitution was intended to overcome. But nowadays the Japanese government is able to conform peacefully with the majority of the world in its international law behaviour, although it demonstrated sheer obedience to its master at the outset.

During these times a slogan was voiced by the conservative party and its ideologues, calling on Japan to be an 'ordinary/normal state' by ridding itself of the spell of the Constitution. The connotation of this call was that Japan had been an extraordinary state without the constitutional right to belligerency. Such has been the mindset of normalcy as a state harboured by the conservative, Constitution-revisionist forces in Japan. It is tantamount to saying that an ordinary/normal state is one that is equipped with the right to belligerency and armed forces, and is presumably ready to engage in wars—in today's terminology, the use of force. Admittedly, the majority of states may possess the right to belligerency and armed forces; yet the states that are freely waging wars are never the majority, and moreover, all of them are legally constrained by article 2(4) of the UN Charter. Therefore, the criterion of international legal normalcy is not as self-evident as the Japanese Constitution-revisionists tend to believe.

Indeed, it seems idiosyncratic for Japanese conservatives to believe that being on the side of the numerical majority (particularly if its master is within it) guarantees

[41] Opinions would surely diverge about this point. If the above could be the case, it would only be about the state itself but not its nationals, who may be held free to provide the belligerents with credits and other forms of assistance. See Charles Rousseau, *Le droit des conflits armés* (Pedone 1983) 394–9.

[42] The legality of this authorizing resolution was dubious, to say the least, in view of the fact that there is no provision in the Charter which allows the Security Council to delegate the (UN) use of force to some chosen member states. Yet, with the accumulation of similar resolutions that ensued, it is now possible that this kind of authorization has become legal.

its normalcy, and justifies and legitimizes its international law behaviour. Little consideration is given to the possibility that there can be other means of interpreting and enforcing international legal rules than those held by the majority; and there is little orientation towards Japan being independent in its own judgement for the legal betterment of the world. Of course, no state should ever be free-wheeling in a violent and destructive way to trample and infringe upon the rights of others, as Japan often did until 1945.

7 Alternatives

'Embracing defeat'[43] could have been a better choice for Japan than reverting to the pre-war state by claiming to be 'ordinary/normal'. Japan's contribution to the changing international legal order could have been far greater if it were a civilian/merchant state, not posing military or non-military threats or engaging in any military aggressiveness, but instead contributing to the development of less-developed peoples, to environmental protection, and to the strengthening of human rights protection and humanitarian assistance. If all this were done it would have been an enormous contribution, something that participation in a few uses of force could never match. But Japan has almost escaped this posture of self-restraint.

Despite the innumerable cases in which Japan has contributed to international society in a law-abiding way, there exist a few more international legal problems that Japan has been prevented from solving due to its conformism with its master and its own intention to return to being a classical sovereign nation-state. One is that Japan has been flatly negative in the efforts to abolish nuclear weaponry, in spite of the eschatological sufferings of its people in Hiroshima and Nagasaki. The government has continuously submitted draft resolutions 'towards the total elimination of nuclear weapons' to the UN General Assembly since 1994, but these have been regarded as formal rather than substantive commitments.[44] The government, based on a strong affirmation of nuclear deterrence, was clearly opposed to judging the use of nuclear weapons as illegal when the International Court of Justice (ICJ) was requested to render an advisory opinion on that question.[45] The representative of the government in the

[43] John Dower, *Embracing Defeat: Japan in the Wake of World War II* (WW Norton 1999). What would be embraced is, of course, not the defeat itself but its consequent legacies—that is, peace and democracy. Dower, ibid. 30, says: 'What matters is what the Japanese themselves made of their experience of defeat, then and thereafter; and, for a half century now, most of them have consistently made it the touchstone for affirming a commitment to "peace and democracy". This is the mantra of post-war Japan'. See also ibid. chs 12 and 13.

[44] See e.g. UN Doc A/C.1/73/L.54 (2018). 'Formally' because, first, there is concurrently quite a number of similar resolutions every year and, secondly, Japan's actions are regarded as being half-hearted because it has not committed itself to the Treaty on the Prohibition of Nuclear Weapons 2017, which aims at the total abolition of the weapon.

[45] *Legality of the Threat or Use of Nuclear Weapons* (Advisory Opinion) [1996] ICJ Rep 226.

ICJ even contradicted the testimonies of the mayors of Hiroshima and Nagasaki on the catastrophic results of nuclear attack.[46] There were some international lawyers who, being supportive of the government, criticized the ICJ which, according to them, unduly dared to declare on the (il)legality of the use of that weapon.

Whether one affirms or negates nuclear deterrence may be a political question, but whether the use of nuclear weapons is lawful or not is no longer solely a political question but also a legal question. In the light of current international humanitarian law, it can be found to be illegal, as was most eloquently and persuasively shown in the dissenting opinion of Judge Weeramantry.[47] If the question is already in the realm of legal discourse, and can be determined in the negative, then there is no free choice: one has to abide by the legal dictate whether one likes it or not.

Once again, Japan might have conformed to the US and the nuclear deterrence camp, but it was not conforming to the majority of the international law world. The request for the advisory opinion, though not adopted in the UN General Assembly by a large majority,[48] had been propelled by enormous non-governmental movements and was therefore legitimized by an emergent 'international public policy',[49] which is suspicious of the legality of the weapon. If this can be taken as the *opinio juris* of the international community, then Japan's choice was not in conformity with the majority of the world. We are not certain how Japan will be able to solve this contradiction between its conformism to the master and its nuclearism allies (which include its political enemies), and its non-conformism to the non-nuclear majority on the side of the rule of international humanitarian law, that is awaiting the final reconfirmation by the international community as a whole.

The defiance of the majority in this matter was again clearly expressed by Japan when the Treaty on the Prohibition of Nuclear Weapons 2017 was adopted in the negotiating conference in the UN by 122 states and territories. Japan did not participate in the voting, not even in the treaty negotiation; before the onset of the negotiation Japan had cast a negative vote in the First Committee against the holding of the conference itself. The Japanese government justified these acts by asserting that such a treaty would lack effectiveness because the nuclear weapon states would not accede to it.[50] There may be some truism in this understanding of the matter, yet this negative attitude disappointed the victims of Hiroshima and Nagasaki, as well as those states

[46] Statement by the government representative Kawamura Takekazu, Verbatim records 1995/27 (7 November 1995) 18–22, followed by the testimonies by the Mayors of Hiroshima and Nagasaki, who stressed the inhumanity and illegality of the use of nuclear weapons. After the testimony by the Mayor of Hiroshima, President Bedjaoui thanked the Mayor for his 'moving declaration': ibid. 32.

[47] Dissenting opinion of Judge Weeramantry, *Nuclear Weapons* (n 45) 429.

[48] UNGA resolution 49/75K (15 December 1994) UN Doc A/RES/49/75K (adopted by votes 78-43-38).

[49] Vera Gowlland-Debbas, 'The Right to Life and Genocide: The Court and an International Public Policy' in Laurence Boisson de Chazournes and Philippe Sands (eds), *International Law, the International Court of Justice and Nuclear Weapons* (CUP 1999) 315–37, especially 334–7.

[50] A quotation from the press conference by Ambassador Takamizawa to the Conference on Disarmament: *Mainichi Sinbun*, 28 March 2017.

and peoples sincerely advocating the abolition of this ultimately inhumane weapon. No new aspiring norms[51] can be born out of such negative posture, though it could not be the sole responsibility of Japan, even if it is the sole victim state of that ultimate weapon.[52]

Another thorny problem that resists going away[53] is the so-called 'comfort women' issue with Korea. Many of the women who were forced to be 'sex slaves' (in the UN terminology) for Japanese soldiers are still alive, together with the anger of the Korean people. It should be clarified that the Japanese government and civic organizations have done several things by way of apology: the government made official apologies to the victims[54] and a large-scale civic organization was established in cooperation with the government, which compensated those who came out as former sex slaves.[55] Yet no satisfaction has been attained on the Korean side, and this issue remains a bone of contention. There could be several reasons for this, one of which is that all the facts are not yet ascertained, particularly as to whether forced trafficking of the women was officially organized by the Japanese government or the military. Two reports by Special Rapporteurs were issued in the UN organs, the Coomaraswamy Report to the former Commission of Human Rights of 1996, and the McDougall Report to the Sub-committee of the Human Rights Committee of 1998,[56] both of which were highly critical of Japan. Yet, as several factual errors and analytical imprecisions in both reports were identified by researchers and commentators, they did not become decisively authentic accounts or the basis for mutual recognition.

If we confine our concerns here to what Japan is expected to do, it seems that the government should be (and should have been) more serious about official fact-finding instead of leaving it to the surveys of private parties, sometimes even to rumours and hearsay, which have only caused confusion. The assumption of legal responsibility

[51] Cf. Samuel Kim, *The Quest for a Just World Order* (Westview Press 1984) 207, who uses this term for a 'right to solidarity' in general. See also Mogami Toshiki, 'The Right to Peace' in *Kokusai Rikkenshugi no Jidai [The Age of Global Constitutionalism]* (Iwanami Shoten Publishers 2007) 267–8 (article first appeared in 1989), which emphatically applies the concept to the right to peace.

[52] See e.g. Secretary-General António Guterres, in his speech in Nagasaki 2018, who defined the nuclear weapon survivors of Hiroshima and Nagasaki as 'leaders for peace and disarmament' and criticized the nuclear weapon states: <http://www.un.org/sg/en/content/sg/speeches/2018-08-09/remarks-nagasaki-peace-memorial-ceremony> accessed 4 December 2018.

[53] An expression used by Ernst Nolte in a nation-wide controversy about the war responsibilities of Germany. See Ernst Nolte, 'Die Vergangenheit, die nicht vergehen will' *Frankfurter Allgemeine Zeitung* (6 June 1986) <http://www.staff.uni-giessen.de/~g31130/PDF/Nationalismus/ErnstNolte.pdf> accessed 4 December 2018.

[54] Statement by the Chief Cabinet Secretary Yohei Kono on the result of the study on the issue of 'comfort women', 4 August 1993 <http://www.mofa.go.jp/policy/women/fund/state9308.html> accessed 4 December 2018.

[55] In particular, the Asian Women's Fund which was founded in 1995. For this see Onuma Yasukai et al (eds), *'Ianfu' Mondai to Ajia Josei Kikin ['Comfort Women' & Asian Women's Fund]* (Toshindo Publishing 1998).

[56] Report of the Special Rapporteur on Violence Against Women, Its Causes and Consequences (Coomaraswamy Report), UN Doc E/CN.4/1996/53/Add.1 (4 January 1996); Final Report of the Special Rapporteur on Contemporary Forms of Slavery: Systematic Rape, Sexual Slavery, and Slavery-Like Practices During Armed Conflict (McDougall Report), UN Doc E/CN.4/Sub.2/1998/13 (June 1998).

could become endless without facts established and agreed to as far as possible. Conversely, if there are facts agreed to the maximum extent possible, there can be some durable solutions, as the Bergier Commission achieved for the fulfilment of Swiss responsibility for the damages suffered by Jewish people during the Second World War.[57]

Additionally, this issue could be a good opportunity for Japan to contribute to the theoretical clarification of the question of statutory limitations as applied to crimes against humanity, if the sex-slave issue is categorized as such. It is a question that international law should have solved by now, instead of asserting that acts that were not illegal at the time of commission cannot be held illegal by the present criteria—a lopsided application of the principle of intertemporal law as formulated by Max Huber in the *Palmas* case.[58] International law thinking has recently seen changes in several ways, one of which is about the concept of the effect of time.[59] With some conceptual transformations it might become possible to attribute legal responsibility retrospectively to past acts, if the past acts are traumatically grave.[60] As far as this task is concerned, the comfort women issue is not simply a political issue, but can be turned into a theoretical one about which the Japanese government and academia could make contributions for a breakthrough on the issue of time in international law.

8 The Academic Side

Finally, mention should be made of the role that academia has (and has not) played in the deployment of the state's international law behaviour, from the 'barbarian' days to the present 'client state'[61] days. Of course, the review of each and every scholar's work is beyond the scope of this study, so the description will be limited to a general overview.

First, since the days of the revision of unequal treaties, there has been enough space for academia to be identified with the government. The government was in the process of catching up with the 'advanced' states of the West, and so was the task of

[57] Independent Commission of Experts Switzerland—Second World War, *Reports 2001/2002* <http://www.uek.ch/en/>.

[58] For a good account of the 'misunderstanding' about the Huber award, see Paul Tavernier, 'Relevance of the Intertemporal Law' in James Crawford, Alain Pellet, and Simon Olleson (eds), *The Law of International Responsibility* (OUP 2010) 397–403.

[59] See, above all, Rosalyn Higgins, 'Time and the Law: International Perspectives on an Old Problem' (1997) 46 ICLQ 501–20.

[60] What seems theoretically necessary is to theorize on the possibility of 'rewinding time' as far as ethically unresolved issues are concerned and to pave the way for fulfilling legal responsibilities for past atrocious acts, like the slave trade or colonial domination. It is a matter of 'reparatory justice'. See Hilary McD Beckles, *Britain's Black Debt: Reparations for Caribbean Slavery and Native Genocide* (University of the West Indies Press 2013); Ralph Gonsalves, *The Case for Caribbean Reparatory Justice* (Strategy Forum 2014).

[61] A term used by Gavan McCormack in Gavan McCormack, *Client State: Japan in the American Embrace* (Verso 2007).

academia. It has been aggressive in importing and incorporating the state practices and international law research of the West.

Reflecting this close affinity between the government and academia, there have not been rich incentives for international law scholars to treat international law issues fully independently, not to mention critically, from the position of the government, with a few remarkable exceptions like the determined criticism of the invasion of Manchuria.[62] Studies (or repetitions) of 'foreign office international law' have generally been the mainstream, with their precision—admirable in their own way—and their fundamental concordance with governmental foreign policy. Curiously enough, although this positioning is itself quite political, it has been regarded as apolitical, while views critical of governmental policies tend to be regarded as highly political, usually in the field of international security issues/law or international human rights issues/law. Discussions about sensitive agendas like the territorial disputes with China or South Korea tend to be carefully avoided, particularly from perspectives critical of the official governmental position. The same can be true of domestic issues like Okinawa.

Second, as a result of the general trend above, the mainstream in this field has been either legal positivism, with its emphasis on state practices, or a kind of the pure theory of law, with its emphasis on the exclusion of the (selectively) 'political'. As far as the two can be conceptually merged,[63] Japan's mainstream has been consistent and constant in its state-centrism and legal conservatism on the side of the status quo, which can be equal to conformism. Should the government and/or mainstream academia decide to depart from this conformism, they could collapse.

Third, the general or dominant trend of legal conservatism has usually resulted in the insufficiency of theoretical orientation in international legal studies. Few, if any, new theories have been created; if the demand for new theories is a tall order, the lack of theoretical orientation in the analyses remains a serious problem. Legal positivism was and is there to be accepted, to be made use of *mutatis mutandis*, but it may not work when unprecedented, unpracticed problems challenge international law. But even traditionally, no theory of *dédoublement fonctionnel*[64] ('role splitting') was born, no attempt to revive natural law theory was made, no theory of World Order Models-inspired international law was born, and no theory of critical legal studies was born.

[62] Yokota Kisaburo, then Professor at the Tokyo Imperial University (currently University of Tokyo), clearly criticized the invasion, saying that the Japanese Army's actions were in no way acts of self-defence and that the recommendation of the Council of the League of Nations for the withdrawal of forces was not ultra vires: Yokota Kisaburo, 'Kokusai Renmei: Mushiro Touzen no Kanshou' ['The League of Nations: A Rather Just Intervention'] *Teikoku Daigaku Sinbunn [The Imperial University Times]* (5 October 1931). Apparently this brave article was written after the Resolution of 30 September but before the rejection by Japan of the draft resolution of 24 October. For this articulation, see, 'League of Nations Assembly Report on the Sino-Japanese Dispute' (1933) 27 AJIL Supplement: Official Documents 119–53.

[63] For accounts of this odd but natural merger, see Neff (n 7) 364–71.

[64] For an account of this notion of Georges Scelle, see Martti Koskenniemi, *The Gentle Civilizer of Nations: The Rise and Fall of International Law 1870–1960* (CUP 2001) 327–38.

I would not say that these theories are all worth accepting, but the problem is whether or not academia is ready to address new problems and, if required, to face them from a new theoretical perspective. With only a few exceptions, like the theory of transcivilizational law[65] or critical constitutionalism (or normative multilateralism),[66] such a drive has been mostly lacking. It is time for Japanese academia to try to be more creative, independently from the governmental inertia, and not in the direction of catching up with the West, but for the sake of better contributing to the solution of global problems—including overcoming Euro(-American) centrism.

[65] See Onuma Yasukai, *International Law in a Transcivilizational World* (CUP 2017).

[66] On the convergence of these concepts, see Mogami Toshiki, '*Perpetuum Mobile*: Before and After Global Constitutionalism' in Takao Suami, Anne Peters, Dimitri Vanoverbeke, and Mattias Kumm (eds), *Global Constitutionalism from European and East Asian Perspectives* (CUP 2018) 29–57.

CHAPTER 14

SOUTH KOREA

SEOKWOO LEE AND HEE EUN LEE

1 Introduction

The Republic of Korea (South Korea) came into existence in 1948 with the establishment of the South Korean Constitution. This event was preceded by United States military occupation from 1945 to 1948 and, before that, Japanese colonization from annexation in 1910 until independence at the end of World War II in 1945. The tumultuous experiences of the Korean nation in the twentieth century, within the context of international relations in Northeast Asia, has had a significant impact on South Korea's attitude towards and practice of public international law.

Joseon, as Korea was referred to in the late nineteenth and early twentieth centuries, was confronted with public international law introduced by Western imperial states that challenged the existing 'Sinocentric' normative system. Relations between or among China and the many political entities around it, such as Korea, Japan, and Vietnam among others, were regulated until this point. Eventually, the seismic shift that resulted in the devolution of the Sinocentric order led to the demise of Joseon, despite appeals to state sovereignty under public international law in the face of Japanese imperialism. This inevitably set the stage for the creation of the modern South Korean state. With its roots as a former Japanese colony, and having undergone the forceful division of the Korean peninsula because of the Korean War, South Korea's primary international legal issues have emerged from these past experiences that still require resolution.

South Korea today is an active participant in the international legal system, in large part due to its vibrant export-oriented economy, its status as an Asian middle power, as well as its emergence as a robust democracy. These factors have contributed to the country becoming immersed in international legal issues. This chapter seeks to briefly explain South Korea's historic experience with international law and how that history and legacy continues to play an essential role in shaping the contours of South Korean foreign relations. This chapter also examines how the Korean legal system implements international law domestically and highlights some of the recent developments in its application. Lastly, the chapter identifies different themes that have emerged over time alongside South Korea's interaction with her neighbours and the broader global community.[1]

2 History

Before the establishment of the modern South Korean state and preceding the introduction of Western international law into East Asia, there existed a regional normative system that regulated the relations between or among China and the many political entities around it. This normative regional system, referred to as the 'Sinocentric order', was based on the concept of China as the 'Middle Kingdom'. At its centre, civilized China was ruled by an emperor who received his mandate from heaven. The emperor was referred to as the 'Son of Heaven' and the Chinese dynasties were called 'Celestial Empires'.

In contrast to the principle of sovereign equality, the traditional interstate relations found in Northeast Asia were reflective of a hierarchical tributary system. China was the hegemonic power at the centre while other nations were peripheral, situated at varying degrees of proximity. Political authority was also metaphorically modelled on China's paternalistic familial relations. Given the influence of Confucianism and the Confucian worldview of political authority, the relationship between China and Joseon was one of 'elder brother' and 'younger brother' respectively.[2] Within the context of these 'familial' relations, China was adept at sustaining agreements with 'the appearance and rhetoric, but not the substance, of the tribute system's hierarchy' when it grew weaker at times.[3] The mutual obligations created by the tributary system 'imposed on both parties moral rather than legal obligations'.[4]

Within the context of this relationship, while trade ties were an essential element of the tribute missions, it was not their primary goal. Instead, Joseon's acknowledgement of Chinese suzerainty provided China with a key affirmation of its self-understanding as the centre of the world. At the same time, Chinese acknowledgement and reception of Korean royalty provided them with important certification of their legitimate claims to the throne.

As far as its international relations were concerned, the tributary system provided Korea with a measure of stability. It allowed the small kingdoms of Korea to exist in relative peace and isolation despite their bigger neighbours to the east and west. Even

[1] Portions of this chapter were adapted from Seokwoo Lee and Hee Eun Lee, *The Making of International Law in Korea: From Colony to Asian Power* (Brill Nijhoff 2016).

[2] Ibid. 19–22.

[3] Jacques de Lisle, 'China's Approach to International Law: A Historical Perspective' (2000) 94 American Society of International Law Proceedings 267, 270.

[4] Ibid.

though Korean kingdoms submitted tribute to China, they possessed full autonomy when it came to their domestic and external affairs and were not subject to the political authority of the Chinese emperor.

However, this autonomy began to whittle away as Western forces weakened China's influence in the region. China's position as the 'Middle Kingdom' could not be sustained when Western industrialized states came into contact with East Asia. Because East Asian powers failed to acknowledge these Western states as sovereign equals, given their adherence to the traditional tributary system, equality was forced upon them.

When Joseon initially encountered Western states, there was a difficulty in understanding the precise status of Joseon as a political and legal entity. The question arose as to whether Joseon was a vassal state subject to Chinese rule or an independent sovereign state. For Joseon, there was an advantage for it to be regarded as a vassal state in terms of its avoidance of international responsibility, while at the same time enjoying the benefits of being an independent sovereign state in all other respects. In contrast, China placed an emphasis on the status of Joseon as an independent state, so that China would not carry the burden of the international responsibility for Joseon as a suzerain state, which it was supposed to assume. However, it continued to assert Joseon's dependency on China with the intention of putting Joseon under its political influence. Despite this initial confusion, Western countries treated Joseon as a sovereign state.[5]

For Joseon, the tumult created by the introduction of Western forces in East Asia exposed it to an impending international political change that was well beyond its control and appeared to parallel the flux in Joseon's internal politics. In 1864, the Joseon king died without having named an heir. The Queen dowager unexpectedly named an eleven-year-old son of Prince Hŭngsŏn as heir. The Prince was to control the reins of power until his son came of age. In honour of his new authority, Prince Hŭngsŏn was given the title of Taewŏn'gun, or Grand Prince.

Taewŏn'gun was determined not to negotiate with the foreign powers. However, the most immediate push to open Korea came not from the West, but from within the region. In 1875, two years after Taewŏn'gun had stepped down from power and his son had become king, the Japanese, in a tactic reminiscent of the American strategy to force open Japan, sent a modern warship to Kanghwa Island. In the ensuing battle, Japan demanded that Joseon provide access to its ports as reparations for the damages it claimed from the conflict. Under duress, Joseon signed the Treaty of Amity and Friendship between Japan and Korea of 1876 (also known as the Ganghwa Treaty), which opened three ports to unrestricted trade with Japan and, perhaps more significantly, declared that Korea was 'an autonomous state enjoying the same rights as Japan'.[6] This was the first time that Joseon had engaged in direct negotiations with a foreign power, which resulted in a treaty formulated under the principles of Western

[5] See Lee and Lee (n 1) 19–22.

[6] Treaty of Amity and Friendship between Japan and Korea (February 1876) art. 1.

international law rather than on the more traditional relations established within the Sinocentric order.

Western international law had come to the Korean peninsula. The turbulent events in East Asia saw the upending of the long-standing Sinocentric order by Western imperialism and the eventual rise of Japan. Like many smaller powers and nations around the world at this time, Korea became a protectorate and a colony, and then came under foreign military occupation, before the modern South Korean state was established after the conclusion of World War II. The introduction of Western international law to Korea can be traced alongside the changes that were occurring within the international system due to the political reality of imperialism, the shocks caused by two successive world wars, and the creation of the United Nations system.

3 Implementation

South Korea adopted a civil law system that gives primacy to fixed written laws. The development of South Korea's legal system can best be understood in relation to its historical context, particularly from the last imperial Joseon dynasty through the colonial and the post-colonial contemporary period. While South Korea's legal tradition was mostly influenced by Confucianism during the Joseon dynasty, there were early attempts, though unsuccessful, by foreign legal advisers in the late nineteenth century to modernize Korea's traditional law.

The legal system of Korea underwent drastic changes during the colonial rule by Japan between 1910 and 1945, as the Japanese government tried to apply to Korea its civil law system, which was based on the continental European legal system.[7] Such legal changes imposed under colonial rule created challenges, as Korea was faced with a conflict between its deep-rooted Confucian traditions and the newly incorporated European-oriented legal principles. After South Korea gained its independence in 1945, the issue of reconciling Confucianism and colonialism in South Korean law was additionally intertwined with the novel principles of constitutionalism that came about due to the growing influence of the Anglo-American legal system in Korea.

As a democratic republic, South Korea has three principal branches of government: executive, judicial, and legislative. The South Korean government is a presidential system wherein the President is elected by nationwide direct ballot for a single five-year term and serves as Head of State. The stability of the three branches of government is maintained by a system of checks and balances. As part of the executive branch, the Ministry of Foreign Affairs is tasked with responsibilities that include, but are not limited to, diplomacy, external economic policy, and administration of treaties and international agreements.

[7] Kipyo Kim (ed), *Introduction to Korean Law* (Springer 2012).

Under the South Korean legal system, codified laws are the primary source of law, which include: (1) statutes passed by the National Assembly; (2) decrees issued by the President and various ministries; (3) rules and regulations adopted by government agencies and local governments; and (4) international agreements.

Article 6(1) of the Constitution of the Republic of Korea 1948 ('the Constitution') stipulates that 'treaties duly concluded and promulgated under the Constitution and the generally recognized rules of international law shall have the same effect as the domestic laws of the Republic of Korea'. In accordance with this constitutional mandate, international law has been generally accepted as part of the domestic law of South Korea and incorporated into the domestic legal system. This provision stipulates that treaties, one of the two main sources of international law, have the same effect as the domestic law of South Korea. While there is no specific mention of customary international law, the term 'generally recognized rules of international law' is understood to mean customary international law in general. Therefore, it is apparent that treaties and customary international law can be incorporated into the domestic legal system according to the Constitution.

For instance, in a case decided by the Constitutional Court of Korea, the Court considered the issue of whether the term 'law', found in article 68(2) of the Constitutional Court Act with regard to what law the Court should apply, could be interpreted to include 'treaties'. The Constitutional Court recognized that it had made an earlier judgment that held that the provisions of a treaty can have the same effect as domestic law and thus the treaty's provisions are subject to an evaluation of their constitutional validity.[8] Given that the treaty provision in this case was concluded and approved for ratification by the National Assembly, it was held that it had the effect of domestic law pursuant to article 6(1) of the Constitution and thus had the equivalent effect of domestic legislation.[9]

While the Constitution stipulates that treaties and customary international law have the same effect as the domestic laws of South Korea, it does not explicitly explain the level of effect of international law within the domestic legal system. Due to this vagueness, the level of effect of international law within the domestic legal system has been left to interpretive theories. Article 5 of the Addenda of the Constitution stipulates that 'treaties in force at the time this Constitution enters into force, shall remain valid unless they are contrary to this Constitution'.

In principle, Korean courts may apply treaties signed and ratified by South Korea and customary international law in court proceedings in the same way the courts apply Korean domestic law. In particular, of the two forms of international law that have the same effect as that of the domestic law of South Korea, those in the form of customary international law will be recognized per se as Korean domestic law as they pertain to 'generally recognized rules of international law'. On the other hand, treaties will only

[8] Constitutional Court [97 Heon-ga 14] (29 April 1999).

[9] Constitutional Court [2000 Heon-ba 20] (27 September 2001).

be recognized and become applicable in South Korea upon the completion of the ratification process.

Article 6(1) of the Constitution does not make clear whether South Korea adopts a monist or dualist approach with regard to the relation between international law and domestic law. This ambiguity gives rise to a number of questions, such as whether treaties and general international laws can become part of Korean domestic law without reference to a legislative enactment, and whether domestic law or international law should be given primacy in circumstances when a treaty or customary international law that has become effective in South Korea conflicts with a domestic law. The majority view in South Korea is that both treaty and customary international law generally have the same effect as legislative enactments and that the Constitution has supremacy in relation to international law. In the event that a treaty or customary international law is in conflict with Korean domestic law, their validity is decided based on the principles of *lex posterior derogat legi priori* (a later-in-time rule prevails) and *lex specialis derogat legi generali* (special law prevails over general law).

3.1 Treaties

3.1.1 *Treaty-Making*

Under the Constitution, treaty-making is within the authority of the President (article 73 of the Constitution). However, all technical-level work for treaty-making is carried out by the International Legal Affairs Bureau of the Ministry of Foreign Affairs and a procedure of consultations with various domestic institutions should be followed before the President can conclude and ratify treaties. From a procedural standpoint, there are three types of treaties made in South Korea: treaties requiring consent to ratification by the National Assembly; treaties not requiring consent to ratification by the National Assembly; and so-called 'treaties by notification' made via a simple procedure by the Minister of Foreign Affairs.

The first step of the domestic procedure for treaty-making is an examination by the International Legal Affairs Bureau. It reviews the wording of the text of the treaty, legal conflicts with other treaties or domestic laws, the type of treaty, and whether a treaty requires consent to ratification by the National Assembly. After this step, proposed treaties are sent to the Ministry of Government Legislation for review. It is required under the Law of Government Organizations that the Ministry of Government Legislation must review all proposed legislation, including treaties, before being sent to the State Council for deliberation. This review examines whether the proposed treaty is in conflict with existing domestic law. Additionally, the Ministry examines whether the proposed treaty requires consent to ratification by the National Assembly, as stipulated in article 60(1) of the Constitution, and provides its opinion on the matter.

When this review is completed, a proposed treaty is reviewed by the Council of Vice Ministers, which undertakes a practical discussion regarding the text of the treaty.

Afterwards, the treaty is submitted for deliberation to the State Council under article 89(3) of the Constitution.

When the proposed treaty is reviewed and the State Council decides that the treaty should be concluded, it is sent to the Prime Minister for approval, and then finally to the President. With the completion of this procedure, the President appoints an official with full powers to sign the treaty as approved. However, in exceptional cases, a treaty may be signed first before being sent to the State Council for deliberation.

If the signed treaty requires ratification by the President, it must go through the ratification procedure again. But in reality, a treaty concluded through resolution by the State Council, with subsequent approval of the Prime Minister and the President, will be ratified without the additional ratification procedure by the President.

Article 60(1) of the Constitution stipulates that the National Assembly shall have the right to consent to the conclusion and ratification of treaties. Specifically, consent by the National Assembly is necessary for:

> treaties pertaining to mutual assistance or mutual security; treaties concerning important international organizations; treaties of friendship, trade and navigation; treaties pertaining to any restriction in sovereignty; peace treaties; treaties which will burden the State or people with an important financial obligation; or treaties related to legislative matters.

The executive administration submits to the National Assembly a motion for consent to the ratification as a general item, not as a legislative bill. The National Assembly only decides whether it consents to the ratification of a treaty, which is determined in an Assembly plenary session after the completion of an internal procedure. The resolution passes when more than half of all votes are cast in favour by more than one-half of the National Assembly members who are eligible to vote.

Regardless of whether a treaty is formal or informal and/or whether the consent to the ratification by the National Assembly is required or not, all treaties that become binding in South Korea are promulgated domestically by notice in the Official Gazette, titled under 'treaty'. This is a natural process given that, under the Constitution, a treaty has the same legal effect as domestic law.

In South Korea, there are agreements that are signed and concluded with the full power of the Minister of the Foreign Affairs that do not go through the whole procedure of the deliberation by the State Council, Presidential approval, or consent to ratification by the National Assembly. This type of agreement is referred to as 'Goshiryu Joyak' in Korean, which means 'treaty by notification'. This type of treaty refers to supplementary agreements concluded within the scope authorized by treaty provisions for the implementation or execution of the original treaty, or for minor modifications, or through the organizational resolution of a multilateral treaty provision adopted by an international organization.

A treaty that falls into this category is concluded by the Minister of Foreign Affairs in consultation with the related ministries. Generally, a treaty by notification is posted in Gwanbo as 'Goshi' (meaning 'notification') by the Ministry of Foreign Affairs. There is a legal question as to whether a 'treaty by notification' falls under the category of 'treaty' since those types of agreements are not promulgated as a 'treaty' but noticed as 'Goshi'. However, when viewed from article 2(1)(a) of the Vienna Convention on the Law of Treaties 1969, there is no doubt that a treaty by notification is a treaty under public international law that is legally binding in South Korea.

By the end of 2018, the total number of treaties concluded by South Korea was 3,288.[10] From 2011 to 2018, South Korea concluded 543 bilateral treaties whereas only 66 were concluded in the entire period from 1948 to 1960. While these bilateral treaties generally concerned economic matters such as avoiding double taxation and investment protection, the multilateral treaties South Korea entered into in recent years have, for the most part, dealt with global matters such as trade, human rights, and disarmament.

3.1.2 *Legal Effect of Treaties*

Given that article 60(1) of the Constitution requires that the National Assembly give its consent to the particular kinds of treaties that the article identifies, there is debate within South Korea as to the domestic legal effect of different types of international agreements. Some theories suggest that treaties which are concluded with consent to ratification by the National Assembly have the same effect as acts enacted by the National Assembly; whereas treaties that are not, and are concluded only by the executive branch, have the same effect as decrees which are lower in legal effect than acts.

However, as reflected in judicial decisions, there is no discrimination in terms of legal effect between a treaty that receives consent to its ratification by the National Assembly and a treaty that does not have to obtain such consent. Therefore, because the Constitution mandates that 'treaties duly concluded and promulgated under the Constitution . . . shall have the same effect as the domestic laws of the Republic of Korea', if a provision of either kind of treaty conflicts with a domestic law, then the principles of *lex posterior* and *lex specialis* will apply.

In a case involving the application of the Warsaw Convention as amended at The Hague 1955 ('Amended Warsaw Convention'),[11] the Supreme Court noted that the civil law of South Korea was *lex generalis* and that the Amended Warsaw Convention 'shall have precedence in its application as *lex specialis* in the general body of civil law'.[12]

As to the matter of whether international law can take precedence over constitutional provisions, the Constitution recognizes the priority of its own terms over other

[10] The Ministry of Foreign Affairs at <http://www.mofa.go.kr/eng/wpge/m_5439/contents.do> accessed 22 June 2019.

[11] [Hague] Protocol to Amend the Convention for the Unification of Certain Rules Relating to International Carriage by Air, Signed at Warsaw on 12 October 1929 (adopted 28 September 1955).

[12] Supreme Court [82 Da-ka 1372] (22 July 1986).

domestic legislation. Thus, it is generally understood that when article 6(1) of the Constitution stipulates that 'treaties have the same effect as domestic laws', here the domestic laws do not include the Constitution, which would appear to give supremacy of the Constitution over international law. Nevertheless, the Constitutional Court indicated that:

> the interpretation of individual articles of the Constitution must be done in harmony with international norms set out by the UN, e.g. Universal Declaration of Human Rights, International Human Rights Covenants, ILO Agreement and recommendations, etc. If domestic laws do not comply with these norms, though they may not immediately be declared unconstitutional, the above norms must be utilized as important standards in determining the constitutionality of such laws.[13]

In this case, the Constitutional Court understood that there should be a harmonious interpretation of the Constitution that is not in conflict with international law.

3.2 Customary International Law

Customary international law is treated as 'generally recognized rules of international law' as indicated in article 6(1) of the Constitution. In principle, Korean courts may apply customary international law in judicial proceedings in the same way they apply Korean domestic law.

In a case regarding an employment suit brought by a Korean national against the US government and one of its affiliated organizations, the Supreme Court directly applied customary international law. It noted that a state, under international law and custom, does not submit to the jurisdiction of another state. It provided that:

> According to customary international law, while a sovereign act of a state is not subject to the jurisdiction of another State in principle, one cannot say that it is customary that even the judicial acts of a State are immune to the jurisdiction of another State.[14]

South Korea is not a party to any treaties that provide for limited sovereign immunity and has not enacted domestic legislation that establishes this principle. Therefore, the Court's direct reference to customary international law, noting that the principle of limited sovereign immunity applicable to employment matters within Korea was a part of customary international law, demonstrates its direct applicability within the Korean legal system.[15]

[13] Constitutional Court [2004 Heon-ba 47] (24 April 2008) (Opinion of Judge Song Doo-hwan Regarding Unconstitutionality).

[14] Supreme Court [97 Da 39216] (17 December 1998).

[15] However, the use of customary international law by Korean judges is rare. Academic research and studies on the application of international law by the Korean judiciary have shown that references by

4 Issues

South Korea's experience in international relations is unique. It was a country that was colonized in the early twentieth century, achieved independence, and then rose from the ashes of the Korean War to become an Asian power. The word 'miracle' is often used to describe South Korea's transformation as it emerged from Japanese colonialism and subsequently became a divided nation occupied by communist forces in the north and the US in the south. This division culminated in the Korean War from 1950 to 1953 that ravaged the peninsula, rendering Korea one of the poorest countries in the world. By 2014, South Korea was ranked the eleventh-largest economy in terms of GNP.

Korea's modern history traces the tumultuous events of Northeast Asia as the long-standing Sinocentric order was upended through Western colonialism and Japanese aggression which eventually led to World War II. The post-World War II era for South Korea was marked largely by the Cold War. Since the fall of the Soviet Union, South Korea has been in the midst of a reconfiguration of the balance of power in the region, due in no small part to the economic prowess of both China and Japan, the nuclear ambitions of North Korea, and US national interests. The post-Cold War era in Northeast Asia continues to be marked by power politics, but it has also seen a higher profile of international law in the region due to the forces of globalization and issues of regional concern such as access to ocean resources and trade, and other non-security matters.

Particularly for South Korea, international law has gained greater prominence in recent years as South Korea has entered into free trade agreements with both the European Union (entering into force in 2011) and the US (entering into force in 2012). It is also currently negotiating a potential trade treaty with China and Japan. Moreover, a number of South Koreans have served as judges on the International Criminal Court and the International Tribunal for the Law of the Sea (including as presidents of each court), while former Minister of Foreign Affairs Ban Ki-moon served as UN Secretary-General (2007–2016).

South Korea's ascendance tracks neatly with the advent of globalization and the growing importance of international law in managing the increasing interactions between states themselves and non-state entities such as multinational corporations, non-governmental organizations, and international organizations such as the UN. South Korea's rise has occurred in one of the most dynamic and dangerous parts of the world: Northeast Asia. Encompassing the People's Republic of China, North and South Korea, and Japan, the region has undoubtedly taken on greater global geopolitical and economic significance. It is under these conditions that international law has taken on a greater role in South Korea.

Korean judges to international law in decisions have largely been limited to merely introducing individual agreements and conventions.

As a result, a number of themes have emerged with the development of international law in Korea. Significant legal issues resulted from the Japanese occupation of Korea until the end of World War II. Moreover, the conclusion of World War II catapulted the Korean nation into the Korean War, which resulted in the division of the Korean peninsula into North and South, generating a number of important international legal issues. Additionally, law of the sea matters are of paramount interest to South Korea as a littoral state. South Korea's economy is dependent on seaborne trade as the state is surrounded by water on three sides, with the fourth side, its gateway to the Asian continent, blocked by North Korea.

4.1 The Legacy of Japanese Annexation

Following US Commodore Matthew Perry's entry into Japanese ports and the subsequent treaty that was made between Japan and the US, Japan actively pursued Westernization and rapidly began to conclude treaties. Japan became a signatory of the Geneva Conventions in 1886, signing the Declaration of Paris the following year.[16] This marked the beginning of Japan's entry into the 'Family of Nations', as it was the one and only Asian country to be so included. The ultimate breakthrough occurred in 1894 with the signing of the Anglo-Japanese Treaty of Commerce and Navigation, only sixteen days prior to Japan's declaration of war on China, which recognized the equal freedoms of residence, travel, property, trade, and navigation.[17] Throughout its war with China, Japan appealed to the West through letters and writings of Japanese scholars that testified to its 'scrupulous observance of international law'.[18]

The Sino-Japanese War came to an end on 17 April 1895, with the conclusion of the Shimonoseki Treaty providing for the complete independence of Korea and cession of certain territories.[19] In the same year, Japan established a pro-Japanese cabinet in Joseon, which was soon ousted by Queen Min. Japan retaliated by brutally murdering the Queen, thereby angering not only the Korean people but also the Russians, who went on to deploy units to assist Joseon.[20] Under strong Russian influence, a new Korean Empire was established.[21]

Having lost control in the Korean peninsula, Japan began to ally itself more with the West, signing its first mutual defence treaty with England on 30 January 1902 and another on 12 August 1905. The latter recognized Japan's 'guidance, management and

[16] Sakuye Takahashi, *Cases on International Law during the Chino-Japanese War* (Cambridge 1899) 30.

[17] Jon Van Dyke, 'The Introduction of Western International Law into Japan', Conference Paper, 'When East Meets West: Asian Approaches to International Law', Joint Conference of the Korean, Chinese and Japanese Societies of International Law, Seoul, 27 June 2011.

[18] Yoshiro Matsui, 'Modern Japan, War and International Law' in Nisuke Ando (ed), *Japan and International Law: Past, Present and Future* (Kluwer Law International 2001).

[19] Kenneth Lee, *Korea and East Asia* (Praeger Publishing 1997) 132.

[20] Ibid. 133.

[21] Ibid. 134.

protection' over Joseon.[22] Beginning in 1904, Japan forced the Korean Empire to sign a series of agreements, including the Protectorate Treaty 1905, to consolidate its control.[23] Culminating in formal annexation, the Korean Empire signed the Treaty of Annexation on 29 August 1910, making Korea a part of Japan.[24]

The legacy of the Japanese annexation of Korea is the presence of a number of lingering and unresolved issues detrimental to South Korea–Japan relations. One is the problem of 'comfort women', which encompasses South Korean demands for an apology and appropriate restitution along with compensation for Koreans who were engaged in forced labour. Another is the issue of sovereignty over Dokdo, small islets in the East Sea (Sea of Japan). Each of these issues is discussed below.

4.1.1 *Dokdo*

Dokdo (Takeshima to Japan) are tiny islets in the possession of South Korea, located in the East Sea (Sea of Japan) approximately 216 kilometres from the Korean mainland and roughly 87 kilometres from South Korea's Ulleung Island. Despite their relatively small size, the islets have been a source of great tension between South Korea and Japan. Japan asserts that Dokdo belongs to Japan while South Korea claims that Dokdo is properly under Korean sovereignty.

From South Korea's perspective, the Dokdo issue is not only a matter concerning legal arguments over which country has rights to Dokdo. It is also an issue that must be viewed in light of the historical context of Japanese imperialism broadly and, more specifically, the Japanese colonization of Korea in the first half of the twentieth century. The rhetorical force of South Korea's claim is based on the view that Dokdo was the first Korean territory to be taken at the commencement of Japanese expansionism into Korea and the Asian continent, which culminated in Korea's eventual annexation and colonization and ended with Japan's defeat in World War II by the Allied Powers. From the South Korean point of view, a full appreciation of South Korea's claim to Dokdo requires a measure of empathy for Korea's status as a victim of Japanese aggression.

South Korea's Dokdo claim is thus influenced by this perceived historical injustice. It is from this vantage point of victimization which South Korea's understanding of the Dokdo issue and its arguments can be fully understood. Since 'Korean memory is preoccupied with moral judgment',[25] the tenor and tone of South Korea's narrative regarding Dokdo is primarily based on the perception that Dokdo was historically Korean territory that was stolen by Japan and then returned and repossessed by South Korea.

South Korea's claim over Dokdo starts with the historical connection to and sovereignty over Dokdo due to its geographical proximity to South Korea's Ulleung

[22] Ibid. 136.

[23] Djun Kil Kim, *The History of Korea* (Greenwood Press 2005) 121.

[24] Ibid. 14.

[25] Mikyoung Kim, 'Introduction: Memory and Reconciliation in East Asia' in Mikyoung Kim (ed), *Routledge Handbook of Memory and Reconciliation in East Asia* (Routledge 2017) 5.

Island. On that basis, given Korea's long-standing ownership of Dokdo, Japan's official incorporation of Dokdo in 1905 and subsequent possession until 1945 was illegal, and thus had no bearing on the question of Dokdo's sovereignty. Further, once World War II came to a close, the pronouncements and decisions of the Allied Powers between 1942 and 1952, along with the ratification of the San Francisco Peace Treaty 1951, confirmed and legitimized Korea's eventual repossession in 1948. Finally, South Korea's claim to Dokdo concludes with the declaration of the Peace Line in 1952 and South Korean actions in relation to Dokdo until the present day. In sum, South Korea has cast the Dokdo issue as one that concerns a historical injustice, the illegal taking of Dokdo in 1905 that was remedied when Japan had to return Dokdo to Korea, and South Korea was made whole.

4.1.2 *Comfort Women*

The issue of comfort women has remained a 'psychological thorn' in South Korea–Japan relations, a representative issue of the past that still needs to be dealt with. The issue concerns women who were taken to the battlefield and forced into sexual slavery by the Japanese government and its military from the early 1930s until Japan's defeat in 1945.

Comfort stations were first installed by the Japanese navy as a preventive measure for mass rape that could result in venereal diseases and opposition from local people during the 1932 Shanghai Uprising. The number of comfort women is estimated to be between 80,000 and 100,000 (with some estimations reaching 200,000), 80 per cent of whom were Joseon women, while others came from the Philippines, China, Taiwan, and the Netherlands.

The issue of comfort women was not readily discussed in public due to the nature of the crimes committed. With the launching of the Korean Council for Women Drafted for Military Sexual Slavery by Japan in November 1990, the issue of comfort women was finally raised in earnest. Various activities continued among civic groups, the South Korean government, and international human rights organizations, with weekly Wednesday protests in front of the Japanese Embassy in Seoul urging the resolution of the issue.

The Japanese government, however, at first denied the very existence of comfort women, until documents evidencing the direct involvement of the Japanese government were uncovered, in addition to the testimonies of the victims. On 4 August 1993, together with the second Government Report, the Japanese government acknowledged the involvement of the Japanese military and authorities, as well as forced drafting and fatigue duty. As a result, Japan's Chief Cabinet Secretary, Yohei Kono, released a statement recognizing this grave violation of human rights and expressing his apologies. However, Japan maintained that legal responsibility regarding these comfort women had been settled by the bilateral Claims Agreement 1965 and refused to provide compensation.

On 28 December 2015, South Korea and Japan announced the reaching of an agreement that claimed to resolve the issue 'finally and irreversibly'. Both governments proclaimed that the resolution of the long-standing dispute was expected to renew their relationship. However, in light of the discrepancies between the perspectives of the Korean victims and the content of the 2015 Agreement, there exists doubt, especially in South Korea, as to whether the Agreement was a great leap forward as proclaimed.

4.1.3 *Forced Labour*

During the Japanese occupation of Korea, Japan began to run short of labour in the production of munitions as it fought the Sino-Japanese War and World War II. In 1939, Japan legislated and promulgated the National Mobilization Law and in 1942 legislated and implemented provisions for officially mobilizing Koreans to procure a labour force from all regions of the Korean peninsula. As labour shortages and supplies continued, Japan implemented a de facto conscription of Korean civilians under a National Conscription Order beginning in October 1944.

Those subjected to forced labour were either forcibly sent over to Japan with other conscripts pursuant to a conscription notice, or sent pursuant to employment applications for Japanese munitions companies under deceitful job placements that guaranteed their return after their employment and training. They were placed in companies such as Mitsubishi Heavy Industries and Nippon Steel Corporation and were subjected to horrible conditions, working three eight-hour shifts per day, and with only one to two limited outings per month. Following the completion of their daily tasks, workers ate and slept at the quarters provided by the companies, where the quality and the quantity of food provisions were severely insufficient and sleeping quarters were cramped. Barbed wire fences limiting entry and egress surrounded their sleeping quarters, and strict surveillance by military police during both working hours and holidays diminished the liberty of everyday life. The conscripts were subject to de facto forced labour, as any correspondence with family back in Korea was screened and censored and thus limited in content, those caught escaping were severely beaten, and wages were not properly paid.

After liberation, the issue of compensation for forced labourers became a concern, and the South Korean and Japanese governments discussed the normalization of diplomatic relations and post-war compensation beginning in late 1952. Finally, on 22 June 1965, the Treaty on Basic Relations between the Republic of Korea and Japan for the Normalization of Diplomatic Relations was concluded together with its annexed Agreement between the Republic of Korea and Japan Concerning the Settlement of Problems in Regard to Property and Claims and Economic Cooperation ('Claims Agreement'). Through the Claims Agreement, Japan agreed to provide Korea with US $300 million in grants over ten years and US$200 million in loans while providing that 'the claims rights between [Japan and South Korea] and between their nationals... have been *settled completely and finally*' (emphasis added).

According to the Agreed Minutes drafted during this process, the scope of the 'Outline of the Property and Claims Settlement Agreement between South Korea and Japan (8 items)' included the restitution of claims of South Korean organizations or natural persons against Japan and its people of their government bonds, public bonds,

Japanese bank notes, outstanding receivables of drafted Koreans, and other claims. One view is that the South Korean government included the compensation for the conscripted workers in its negotiation of the Claims Agreement with Japan. The Japanese government has thus insisted that all rights to claims of the victims of forced labour were extinguished pursuant to the Agreement.

Nevertheless, claims were brought in Japan and in South Korea simultaneously for the recovery of payment for outstanding wages, damages, and compensation. Japanese courts from the District Court level to the Supreme Court of Japan dismissed the claims, noting that the Claims Agreement extinguished any rights the South Korean claimants may have had. Lower Korean courts ruled similarly, stating that the claimants' right to compensation for damages and payment of wages was extinguished and additionally, once the Supreme Court of Japan dismissed their case, the principle of res judicata acted as a bar to recovery.

However, the Supreme Court of South Korea reversed the lower court decisions,[26] holding that the purpose of the Claims Agreement 1965 did not address the issue of compensation for harm caused by Japanese colonization but was for the purpose of resolving the financial and civil debt/credit relationship between South Korea and Japan based on article 4 of the San Francisco Peace Treaty 1951. It concluded that the Claims Agreement extinguished neither the individual rights to claim compensation for forced labour nor South Korea's rights to diplomatic protection of its nationals. Further, the Supreme Court held that it was not within the power of the South Korean state to directly extinguish the rights to claims of its nationals without their consent. Moreover, even if it were to be permissible under international law for a state to extinguish the rights of its nationals through treaties, considering that a state and its nationals are different legal persons, the people's rights cannot be deemed to have been extinguished unless specifically provided for in the treaty. The Supreme Court vacated the decision of the High Court and remanded the case for retrial.

4.2 International Legal Issues Arising from a Divided Nation

Though Korea was liberated from Japanese colonialism at the conclusion of World War II, the Korean peninsula faced significant geopolitical instability that eventually led to the division of the country. The immediate post-World War II environment saw the emergence of the Cold War that pitted the Soviet Union and China against the US in Northeast Asia. Following Japan's retreat, the US occupied South Korea from 1945 to 1948, with the objectives of 'imposing their own vision of modernity . . . based on

[26] Case No. 2009 Da 22549, 1st Division Judgment (24 May 2012) Supreme Court of Korea. See English translation and commentary by Seokwoo Lee, '2009 Da 22549, Issued May 24, 2012 (Supreme Court): Supreme Court of Korea, 1st Division Judgment on Japanese Forced Labor re Mitsubishi Heavy Industries' (2014) 2 Korean Journal of International and Comparative Law 216.

democratic principles, promoting South Korean culture and nationalist ideology, and, most important[ly], establishing a South Korean political system compatible with the pursuit of America's international objectives'.[27] Finally, in August 1948, the Republic of Korea was established. Although US troops were originally scheduled to depart in mid 1949, South Korea ended up under US military occupation following the Korean War. The war ended on 27 July 1953, with the signing of the armistice by the military commanders of both sides that sought to 'ensure a complete cessation of hostilities and of all acts of armed force in Korea until a final peaceful settlement is achieved'.

Though there was a cessation of active armed conflict, North and South Korea have engaged in sporadic skirmishes that have resulted in the deaths of civilians and soldiers from both sides in the area of the disputed Northern Limit Line (NLL) in the West Sea (Yellow Sea) and the Demilitarized Zone. Particularly in regards to the West Sea (Yellow Sea), the issue of the legality of the delimitation set forth by the NLL has contributed to the conflict in this area.

4.2.1 *Northern Limit Line*

The UN Command and the North Korean army established a Military Demarcation Line on land at the time they signed the Inter-Korean Armistice Agreement on 27 May 1953, but did not extend it into maritime areas. The seaward extension, the NLL, was drawn by UN Commander General Mark Clarke on 3 August 1958. It is a line that is roughly equidistant between the North Korean coastline and five tiny South Korean islands (Paengnyongdo, Taechongdo, Sochongdo, Yongpyo-Yolto, and Udo, which, taken together, contain five square miles of land) that hug the North Korean coast but are controlled and claimed by South Korea. Its purpose was to prevent a clash between the military vessels and aircraft of both sides, and seems originally to have been designed to prevent South Korean naval vessels and aircraft from going north. It has been challenged by North Korea ever since, because it was declared unilaterally and because North Korea views the NLL as an infringement on its sovereignty and its access to the sea. Because the NLL is not mentioned in the Armistice Agreement itself, its status and that of the waters around it remain contentious.

South Korea acknowledges that the NLL declaration was not officially part of the agreement that marked the end of hostilities between the two countries, but argues that the NLL has become the de facto border for a number of reasons. These include firstly that North Korea did not object to the NLL until October 1973; secondly, that North Korea implicitly recognized the NLL several times; and thirdly, that the Basic Agreement of 1991 stipulates in article 11 that 'the South–North demarcation line and areas for non-aggression shall be identical with areas that have been under the jurisdiction of each side until the present time'. Further in this respect, article 10 of the Protocol on Non-Aggression states that:

[27] Steven Hugh Lee, 'Military Occupation and Empire Building in Cold War Asia: The United States and Korea' in Tsuyoshi Hasegawa (ed), *The Cold War in East Asia 1945–1991* (Stanford 2011) 104.

> the South–North sea non-aggression demarcation line shall continue to be discussed in the future. Until the sea non-aggression demarcation has been settled, the sea non-aggression zones shall be identical with those that have been under the jurisdiction of each side until the present time.

South Korea thus claims that the NLL cannot be subject to unilateral challenge or discussion except by way of a comprehensive agreement to bring permanent peace to the Korean peninsula. South Korean resistance to creating a joint development zone encompassing territory on both sides of the NLL is based partially on the concern that such an agreement would nullify the line and cede territory to North Korea. The US concurs that the Basic Agreement 1992 between North and South Korea stipulates that both Koreas must respect the line until and unless a new agreement can be reached.

North Korea counters that when the NLL was drawn, UN Command did not inform Pyongyang, which neither acknowledged nor accepted it. It argues that the NLL illegally restricts its access to the open sea and should be redrawn further to the south to more closely reflect the land demarcation between the two countries. North Korea asserts that it has challenged the line on many occasions over the past fifty-five years, particularly as the value of the blue crab harvest in the area has become more apparent. It also argues that its vessels have regularly fished in the waters claimed by the South; and that since March 1955, it has claimed under customary international law a 12 nautical mile territorial sea from its coast, which extends well south of the NLL. Because the NLL hugs the North Korean coastline, Pyongyang claims that it unfairly gives too much ocean space to South Korea.

4.2.2 *South Korea and the Law of the Sea*

South Korea is surrounded by water on three sides; towards the west is the West Sea (Yellow Sea), to the south is the Korea Strait, and to the east is the East Sea (Sea of Japan). Given that North Korea is situated to the north and because ground transportation is essentially blocked by the Demilitarized Zone, South Korea relies on the ocean for its economic livelihood and well-being. This includes fisheries and inbound and outbound sea-freight traffic, which has been crucial to South Korea's rapid economic development as an export-oriented economy. As a result, sea-lane safety and the securing of passageways have been necessary for South Korea to sustain its economic growth through foreign trade via shipping and securing sea power for national security. Situated at the centre of the Northeast Asian seas, the waters that surround South Korea are important from an economic, military, and strategic perspective.

More recently, intensified competition over maritime jurisdiction and for marine resources among the Northeast Asian states, along with island sovereignty disputes, have made the issues of maritime order and safety of sea lanes a critical strategic concern directly relevant to state survival, as well as to the peace and safety of the region. South Korea has had to engage with legal matters pertaining to the law of the sea that are of vital importance, especially in relation to maritime delimitation in the zones established by the UN Convention on the Law of the Sea (UNCLOS), which has affected relations with China and Japan.

4.2.3 *Maritime Delimitation between Korea and China in the West Sea (Yellow Sea)*

The West Sea (Yellow Sea) is a semi-enclosed body of water measuring about 520 nautical miles from north to south and roughly 380 nautical miles from east to west. The total area covered by the West Sea (Yellow Sea) is 400,000 square kilometres. There is an unresolved maritime boundary between South Korea and China within the West Sea (Yellow Sea). Both states have ratified UNCLOS. Article 57 of UNCLOS permits each coastal state to declare an exclusive economic zone (EEZ) of 200 nautical miles from the coast or 'from baselines from which the breadth of the territorial sea is measured'. Since the West Sea (Yellow Sea) is less than 400 nautical miles wide, none of the coastal states is able to declare full zones because their EEZ claims would overlap. The extent of the overlap is exacerbated by arguably excessively straight baselines that have been claimed by the countries.

Because the area is rich in natural resources, with the capacity for year-round fishing, it has been difficult for the coastal countries to agree on maritime delimitation. Tension over these resources endangers security in Northeast Asia, and conflicts are likely to continue as long as the region's maritime boundaries remain unresolved.

South Korea has maintained since the 1960s that the most equitable approach to maritime delimitation in the West Sea (Yellow Sea) is to utilize the equidistance principle, whereby the EEZs of South Korea and China would be delimited at the median line. This position is somewhat inconsistent with South Korea's approach towards its boundary dispute with Japan in the East China Sea, where South Korea argues for the natural prolongation approach. South Korea justifies the difference by referring to the goal of delimitation which is to reach an 'equitable' result.

China's approach towards delimitation also has its inconsistencies because it favours the natural prolongation approach in the West Sea (Yellow Sea) dispute with South Korea while maintaining that an equidistant line should divide its boundary with North Korea in the Gulf of Korea and with Vietnam in the Gulf of Tonkin. Perhaps most importantly, the natural prolongation approach does not appear to apply in any significant, geographic way to the West Sea (Yellow Sea) because the sea area has a flat, shallow, and a relatively featureless seafloor throughout. This is unlike the East China Sea, where the seabed drops off sharply at the Okinawa Trough near the small Japanese islands.

4.2.4 *Maritime Delimitation and Territorial Disputes between Korea and Japan in the East Sea (Sea of Japan)*

The delimitation of maritime boundaries between South Korea and Japan in the East Sea (Sea of Japan) and the East China Sea also remains unsettled, except in the southern part of the continental shelf in the East Sea (Sea of Japan). Prompted by the need for the exploitation of oil on the continental shelf, South Korea and Japan agreed to jointly develop the disputed continental shelf south of Jeju Island in 1974, in addition to delimitating the continental shelf in the Korea Strait.

The Dokdo (Takeshima) issue lies at the core of the dispute over maritime boundary delimitation between the two countries. It appears that South Korea is engaging in negotiations with some flexibility in regards to its position; the options it has put forward include the median lines between Ulleung Island and Oki Island and/or between Dokdo and Oki Island. Given the continuing negotiations, South Korea's final stance has not yet been officially confirmed, although more weight has been put on the latter option since 2006. Japan claims a median line between Ulleung Island and Dokdo, arguing that Dokdo belongs to Japan. Both countries' claims enclose Dokdo within their own EEZs.

4.2.5 *Piracy*

In the first case of its kind, the Supreme Court of South Korea upheld the exercise of universal criminal jurisdiction over pirates who were convicted of hijacking a Korean vessel in the Indian Ocean. On 15 January 2011, Somali pirates hijacked the *MV Samho Jewelry*, a South Korean-flagged vessel, on the high seas in the northern Indian Ocean. After securing control of the *Samho Jewelry* and its crew, the pirates took and transferred to their mother ship approximately US$12,000 worth of goods and demanded ransom from the ship's owners. However, a South Korean naval special forces group, the Cheonghae Unit, headed by the destroyer *Choi Young*, was tracking the *Samho Jewelry* and mounted a rescue operation less than one week after the hijacking. The operation led to the deaths of eight pirates (including their leader) and the capture of five others, while the crew was unharmed except for the captain, who had been seriously wounded by the pirates.

After unsuccessful attempts were made to move the pirates to a third country for criminal prosecution, they were transported to South Korea and handed over to the South Korean Coast Guard. On 7 February 2011, the pirates were sent to the Busan District Prosecutor's Office, where they were indicted on 25 February 2011 on eight counts of criminal acts related to piracy: forcibly taking the ship; forcibly taking property on the ship; forcibly operating the ship; demanding ransom to release the hostages; firing at soldiers; inflicting physical assault, threats, and bodily harm on the crew; using the crew as 'human shields'; and firing on the captain. The pirates were also charged with maritime robbery and attempted murder, robbery and attempted murder, obstruction of justice (special operations) and infliction of injury, and violation of the Punishment for Damaging Ships and Sea Structures Act.

At their trial, the pirates argued that their rights to due process had been violated, citing article 12 of the Constitution, as they had been transferred to South Korea without a proper procedural basis under Korean law. They also claimed that they were not arrested pursuant to a warrant and that a warrant was not issued during the transfer period; that they had not received any legal assistance; that due process had not been guaranteed when they were detained by the South Korean military; and that despite physical assaults by the *Samho Jewelry*'s sailors during their arrest, the military made no effort to protect them. Because their presence in Busan was forced on them without due process, they challenged the Court's jurisdiction over the case.

Despite these arguments, all of the defendants were convicted. The Court held that pursuant to the Criminal Procedure Act it possessed territorial jurisdiction over the case given that the defendants were all located in South Korea at the time. Another key issue was determining who was responsible for the shooting of the captain. The Court found that only one defendant, Mahomed Araye, had fired at the captain. However, the question of whether the pirates as a group had colluded to shoot the captain was a secondary issue, with regards to which all the pirates denied any involvement. The Court eventually decided that it was difficult to conclude that the pirates had conspired to kill the captain during the gunfight with the South Korean special forces unit.

Among the issues the Korean court considered, the most important was whether the South Korean special forces unit had the authority to arrest and detain the pirates. The jurisdiction it exercised in subduing the pirates may be grounded in international law under article 105 of UNCLOS and various UN Security Council resolutions, but the basis under Korean law was unclear. The basis for the personal jurisdiction of Korean courts over the pirates was found in both international and domestic law. The international legal basis is provided for in article 105 of UNCLOS, article 6 of the Convention for the Suppression of Unlawful Acts Against the Safety of Maritime Navigation 1988, and article 5 of the International Convention against the Taking of Hostages 1979. South Korea has ratified all three instruments. South Korea's first piracy case led to the proposal of important amendments to Korean law that sought to incorporate and give effect to the principle of universal jurisdiction for the most serious international crimes.

5 Conclusion

The development of international law in South Korea can be traced from the upending of the Sinocentric order in the late nineteenth century to Japanese colonialism from 1910 to 1945 and South Korea's independence in 1948. The modern history of South Korea has demonstrated the instability of international relations for small states. With the advent of globalization and the growing importance of international law in coping with the increasing interactions between states, South Korea's economic and political rise has occurred within the context of the dynamic changes that have occurred in Northeast Asia. South Korea has been and continues to be forced to manage its relations with North Korea and its two powerful neighbours, China and Japan, along with its principal ally, the US. However, as international law has developed, so too has South Korea's use of it. South Korean experiences of international law as a mid-power state, within the geopolitical circumstances of Northeast Asia, proffer the lesson that international law is an indispensable means to sustain order in a volatile region.

SOUTHEAST ASIA

CHAPTER 15

THAILAND

VITIT MUNTARBHORN*

1 Introduction

The relationship between Thailand (previously known as Siam until the middle of the twentieth century) and international law depends largely on how the discussion is framed.[1] Is the point of departure: what is the state's interaction with 'modern' international law, particularly since 1511 when the Portuguese first arrived on Southeast

* The author wishes to thank warmly the following for their kind assistance: Deputy Permanent Secretary (Thai Ministry of Foreign Affairs) Thani Thongphakdi, Ambassador Ittiporn Boonpracong, Director General Chirdchu Raktabutr, Khun Vorapote, Dr Suntariya, Art Paisit Pusittrakul, Nong Boon and Poom, the UN Library Geneva, and the Library of Law Faculty, Chulalongkorn University, Bangkok. All views expressed are personal. Some of the Thai publications cited below are based on Buddhist Era (BE). This is 543 years before Anno Domini (AD). Please note also that Thai authors are generally known by the first name and that a number of court cases in Thailand are not published officially. The first draft of this article was written at the end of 2016 and it was submitted for editing by the beginning of 2017 before the passage of Thailand's new Constitution (2017). Much of the information in the article is thus until the end of 2016. The author has updated some of the information to reflect the constitutional and other changes from 2017 until the beginning of 2018, where relevant.

[1] For background, see: David Wyatt, *Thailand: A Short History* (Yale University Press 2003); Stefan Hell, *Siam and the League of Nations: Modernization, Sovereignty and Multilateral Diplomacy, 1920–1940* (River Books 2010); Sompong Sucharitkul, 'Asian Perspective of the Evolution of International law: Thailand's Experience at the Threshold of the Third Millennium' (2002) 1 Chinese Journal of International Law 527, 535:

> The very first point of contact that the Kingdom of Siam (later Thailand) experienced with a European country took place in the form of an encounter with . . . a naval fleet dispatched by the Vice-Roy of Portugal across the Indian Ocean from Goa. The Portuguese were the first to have reached Asian shores by maritime route. If Marco Polo had succeeded in crossing the frontier line between Europe and Asia by the discovery of the 'Silk Trail' departing from Venezia and heading for China in East Asia, it was Vasco da Gama who performed successfully the circumnavigation of the Continent of Africa via the Cape of Good Hope, setting sail from Lisbon and crossing the Indian Ocean to reach Goa on the Malabar Coast on the Indian sub-continent where the Portuguese gained their first foothold in Asian soil.

Asian shores? Or is there another point of departure, which is more longitudinal: can various roots of international law be identified in the region, even before that time? Conversely, if a less vertical and less state-centric approach is to be taken, what is the nexus between non-state actors in the development of international law and practice, and how is this played out in the lives of people and communities in a more horizontal manner?

This chapter moves between these points of departure; all three questions are borne in mind while analysing Thailand's contribution to international law. In this quest, some initial facts are useful to set the scene. The population of the country today numbers around 68 million people, with a low birthrate and an ageing society. The country has never been colonized; although it was not immune to colonial pressures, especially from the eighteenth to early twentieth centuries. During this period, it suffered from the superimposition of various treaties concerning extraterritoriality which exempted the nationals of colonial powers from local laws. It saw part of its territories chipped away by the colonial presences in the region and wars near its borders, particularly in the nineteenth century and early part of the twentieth century, but it survived, in part due to the resilience of its policies and the fact that it was a geographic buffer between colonial rivals.

Siam was one of the original states from the Asian region that took part in the formation of the international legal system, notably the Hague Conference in 1899, which resulted in various treaties on the law of war, followed by the 1907 Hague Conference that resulted in a host of treaties on rules and regulations concerning the conduct of war—strictures of great consequence still today.[2] Siam took part in the First World War—it declared war, and was on the winning side. It was a member of the League of Nations and contributed to key international developments, such as the evolution of treaties against human trafficking and discussions on narcotic drugs and health care for the population. Bangkok was also a venue for international conferencing.

During the League of Nations era, Siam had to take various positions as part of the emerging international system. When Japan invaded Manchuria, a part of Chinese territory, members of the League were asked to endorse a resolution to condemn the invasion, but Siam declined to do so. Then, Italy invaded Abyssinia (later Ethiopia), and the League passed a resolution to condemn the Italian action. Siam voted for the resolution.

The role of Siam during the Second World War was a challenging one, and the country was on the losing side at the end of the war. There was an alternative Free Thai Movement, operating from abroad, which helped to liberate the country. Siam

See further: Vitit Muntarbhorn, 'One Hundred Years (1914) Retrospect—A Hundred Days (2014) Prospect—A Hundred Years (2114) Prospects: Public International Law' (2016) 1 Thailand Journal of International Law 3, 13.

[2] For Thailand's participation at The Hague conferences see James Brown Scott, *Proceedings of The Hague Conferences* (Oxford University Press 1920).

remained intact after the war, partly due to deft diplomacy and its strategic position as a buffer. In retrospect, depending on which *optique* of history is chosen, the country's record might be described as ambivalent, on the one hand, or astute, on the other.

In the diplomatic juggle to set up the United Nations (UN) after the war, Thailand sought membership, played its hand diplomatically—balancing between the powers which could facilitate entry—and gained admission. It was then affected by the Cold War between the superpowers of the United States and the Soviet Union, manifested in the Southeast Asian region by the decades-long Indochina War and related conflicts. Between the 1960s and 1980s, the Cold War was raging in the region around Thailand, and there was fear of a domino effect whereby the country might be subsumed under the spread of communism from the vicinity. Yet, it survived. It was one of the founders of the Association of Southeast Asian Nations (ASEAN) in 1967, and it was one of the key players that brought peace to Cambodia and the region in the 1990s. Previous enemies became friends, and by the end of the millennium ASEAN had become a ten-member entity in a region of peace.

Thailand is an active member of the UN. It was a member of the UN Security Council, the UN Economic and Social Council, and the UN Human Rights Council at various times in recent decades. It recently lost its bid to again become a member of the Security Council and the Human Rights Council. From a longitudinal perspective, albeit a somewhat subjective one, it can be said that the country enjoys substantial political weight as a developing country, with a sense of moderation in its foreign policy.

Considering it from a more internal perspective, it should not be forgotten that, until 1932, the national system in Thailand was based on an absolute monarchy. Since that time, there have been experiments with democratic rule, but there have been many coups and constitutions. The latest coup took place in 2014, overturning a civilian government, and in 2017, Thailand promulgated a new constitution—its 20th Constitution, referred to in section 3.2, which was approved at referendum in 2016. At the beginning of 2018, the Government was still under military control. The general population were waiting for a date to be fixed for elections, with a potential return to civilian rule. These facts have also had some impact on Thailand's relationship with international law, especially in regard to political space, rights, and freedoms.

While the country has never been colonized, it has not been impervious to outside pressures. European-related influences led to reform of the antiquated governmental and legal system from the nineteenth century onwards, with the Criminal Code and the Civil and Commercial Code introduced at the beginning of the twentieth century. The legal setting is primarily based on the civil law system, with some common law influences. There is a three-tiered court system. Changes in 1997 led to a broader range of courts, and Thailand now also has a constitutional court and a range of administrative courts. These exist side by side with military courts. Islamic family law is also recognized in parts of southern Thailand.

2 Thailand's Contributions to International Law

Three examples can be chosen to illustrate the country's key contributions to and relationship with international law. Two examples can be singled out as Thailand's 'positive' relationship with international law, when viewed from the comfort zone interlinking the national and international systems. By contrast, at times there is definitely a sense of discomfort—the discomfort zone—as will be seen in the third example to follow. Thailand's contribution to international law can thus be described as eclectic.

2.1 Contributions to Specialized Areas of International Law

From the viewpoint of 'modern' international law and history, Thailand's long-standing constructive relationship with the international system stands out in a number of ways. The first interrelationship with the advent of colonial powers from the sixteenth century was in regard to the arrival of religion (Christianity/missionaries) from Europe (thus freedom of religion), trade and commerce (thus freedom to trade), and interchange between emissaries (thus diplomatic privileges and immunities).[3] These would provide the groundwork for reciprocity in international relations and contribute to the development of both treaty-based law and customary international law on these matters. However, the evolution of these elements was superseded by more aggressive policies on the part of colonial powers from the eighteenth to early twentieth centuries. These policies gave rise to negative practices such as the spread of colonization and subjugation of the local population; extraterritoriality and lack of accountability of foreign presences; pressures for cessions of territories; and the effect of 'gunboat' diplomacy affecting many parts of the Asian region. Even though Thailand remained free from colonization, it was affected by these pressures.

2.1.1 *Laws of War*

A concrete positive interplay between the nation state and the international setting was evident in Thailand's participation at the two Hague Conferences and the adoption of various treaties on the laws of war. The country became a party to a range of relevant treaties from 1899 onwards. After the Second World War, the country also ratified the four Geneva Conventions of 1949 as part of the transition from the laws of war to international humanitarian law, which placed more of an emphasis on the protection of victims, particularly civilians, in times of international and domestic armed conflict.

[3] Sucharitkul (n1).

By a welcome coincidence, if a less modernistic approach is to be taken, the roots of the laws of war and international humanitarian law can also be identified in this region as predating the advent of the European powers. Indian influence, particularly on the laws of war and concretization of law as an educational discipline as evolved in South Asia, permeated Southeast Asia many centuries before European influence. In fact, Buddhism arrived from the Indian sub-continent with Emperor Asoka—who was also an advocate of the rules of engagement in war, predating modern international humanitarian law. It was he who issued the Kalinga Edicts, which prohibited the killing of prisoners of war, while advocating for the humane treatment of civilians.[4] Those precepts would become entrenched in the polity of the Southeast Asian region, for example in the Stone Inscription of King Ramkamhaeng from the Middle Ages in the country now known as Thailand, which propounded humane treatment in times of war.[5] On the etymological side, it should not pass unnoticed that most Thais today have names with Indian/Sanskrit roots. Many traditions in contemporary Thailand are a reflection of Hindu and Brahmin rites originating in India. The legal system in Thailand was heavily influenced by Indian laws and traditions before the advent of European-influenced changes, particularly from the nineteenth century.

2.1.2 *Refugees and Humanitarianism*

On a more horizontal front, the many regions and traditions in Thailand and their linkages with non-state actors, especially the local population, should not be overlooked. While the country is majority Buddhist, Thailand has other cultures and religions which interplay with aspects of international law. In southern Thailand, for example, there is a large Muslim population. Islam has also nurtured a humane approach towards the grant of asylum to help those in need, with implications for refugee protection. In the past and at present, the idea of helping the poor by means of Zakat—a levy on the rich to help the poor—continues to be practised in Thailand among the Muslim population. This contributes to the development of anti-poverty actions as well as the quest for a more equitable society, which can also inspire international law and policy.

From the angle of refugee intake and protection, Thailand has been host to more asylum-seekers than any other Southeast Asian country in recent times, even though it is not a party to the Convention Relating to the Status of Refugees 1951.[6] Since the 1970s, millions have arrived at Thailand's borders and/or flowed through its doors. Even today, it is the temporary home to some 100,000 Myanmar asylum-seekers and

[4] Regarding Kalinga Edicts, see Shravasti Dhammika, *The Edicts of King Asoka: an English Rendering* (Buddhist Publication Society 1993).

[5] For Ramkamhaeng's stone inscription, see: *Jaruk Samai Sukothai [Inscriptions of the Sukothai Era]* (Krom Silpakorn [Fine Arts Department], Buddhist Era (BE) 2528); *Suksa Sila Jaruk Kong Por Khun Ramkamhaeng [Study of the Stone Inscription of King Ramkamhaeng]* (Mahidol University BE 2527) (in Thai); Chulalongkorn University (ed), *The Inscription of King Ramkamhaeng the Great* (Chulalongkorn University 1984).

[6] See further Vitit Muntarbhorn, *The Status of Refugees in Asia* (Clarendon Press 1992).

refugees waiting for a permanent solution, as well as asylum-seekers and refugees from the Middle East, South Asia, Central/North Asia, West Asia, and Africa. Interestingly, it has done more than many countries (of any region) which are parties to the 1951 Convention Relating to the Status of Refugees to help shelter refugees; there is the ironic truth that the mere fact that a country is a member of an international treaty (on refugees or other issues) is not necessarily a guarantee of effective implementation. Having said that, the local situation is not perfect and there are grey areas, such as the ongoing issue of shelter for Rohingya refugees and the background conflict in Myanmar, which acts as a push factor for their departure and then influx into Southeast Asian countries, including Thailand.

2.1.3 *Thailand's Leadership within ASEAN*

A third key example of Thailand's contribution to international law is the country's leadership in regionalism and the evolution of ASEAN. Thailand was one of the founders of ASEAN, and the birth document of ASEAN is known as the Bangkok Declaration 1967.[7] The 1960s and 1970s were the time of the Indochina War, which surrounded Thailand. In 1975, the governments of Laos, Cambodia, and Vietnam changed hands, with socialist/communist regimes taking over the reins of power. This was superseded by civil war between different groups in Cambodia.

Throughout the 1980s, the most important development in the ASEAN region was the fact that ASEAN recognized and supported the Cambodian Government in exile. It was comprised of three Cambodian groups resisting the regime in power in Phnom Penh, backed by Vietnam, which controlled Cambodia from 1979 until the Peace Accord over ten years later. A diplomatic battle was fought for a decade in the UN General Assembly concerning which government should be recognized, sit in the seat in the General Assembly, and represent Cambodia. Some ten UN General Assembly resolutions in the 1980s were led by ASEAN, upholding the seat for the Cambodian Government in exile.[8] In relation to international law, this was a distinctly fascinating case where the recognition of the government was anchored on the Government in exile as the legitimate government, backed by these resolutions, rather than on the regime in effective control of the country. In reality, in this situation, legitimacy rather than effectiveness/efficacy prevailed as the rationale for the recognition of the government in international law (contrary to some international thinking).

[7] For ASEAN history and documents, see: Kernial Singh Sandhu, *The ASEAN Reader* (Institute of Southeast Asian Studies (ISEAS) 1992); Sharon Siddique and Sri Kumar (eds), *The Second ASEAN Reader* (ISEAS 2003); Ooi Kee Beng and others (eds), *The Third ASEAN Reader* (ISEAS 2015).

[8] For key UN General Assembly resolutions on the matter from 1979 onwards: UNGA res 34/22 (14 November 1979); UNGA res 35/6 (22 October 1980); UNGA res 36/5 (21 October 1981); UNGA res 37/6 (28 October 1982); UNGA res 38/3 (27 October 1983); UNGA res 39/5 (30 October 1984); UNGA res 40/7 (5 November 1985); UNGA res 41/6 (21 October 1986); UNGA res 42/3 (14 October 1987); UNGA res 43/19 (3 November 1988); UNGA res 44/22 (16 November 1989); UNGA res 45/3 (15 October 1990); UNGA res 46/18 (20 November 1991). The 1991 resolution confirmed the peace process in the country and helped to set up the UN Transitional Authority in Cambodia (UNTAC).

The 1990s witnessed peace in Indochina and previous enemies all became members of ASEAN. Thailand's positive contribution of this era, apart from the peace process in Cambodia and opening the door to other Southeast Asian countries to join ASEAN, was its call for a Free Trade Area in ASEAN. Thus, the ASEAN Free Trade Area was born in 1992, and this led to greater community-building, with 2015 as the target for the realization of three ASEAN Communities: the ASEAN Economic Community, the ASEAN Political Security Community, and the ASEAN Socio-cultural Community.

Regarding human rights in ASEAN, Thailand was also a proponent of the establishment of an ASEAN human rights mechanism and took the broadest approach to the mandate of such a mechanism. It was one of the few ASEAN countries which wanted extensive powers for the ASEAN Intergovernmental Commission on Human Rights, inaugurated in 2009, particularly with the call for protection powers for the Commission to receive complaints of human rights transgressions and to undertake investigations, even though this was rejected by most other ASEAN countries.[9] While the Commission does not yet have these protection powers, the call for more effective human rights protection continues to resonate at the national, regional, and international levels.

2.1.4 *Territorial Dispute Settlement*

In contrast to the two positive contributions to international law discussed above, the discomfort zone par excellence concerning Thailand's relationship with international law relates to international dispute settlement on territorial issues, particularly the International Court of Justice's (ICJ's) momentous judgement on the *Temple* case and its various phases lasting over half a century. The case concerned a dispute between Thailand and Cambodia relating to sovereignty over an ancient temple—the Preah Vihear (or *Khao Phra Viharn*, in Thai)—bordering the two countries. The experience has been more dramatic and traumatic for the country than any other international legal issue, affecting national pride and sentiments. It also explains the country's hesitation towards the ICJ and may have resulted in several reservations entered by Thailand to international treaties, whereby the country does not consent to dispute settlement by the ICJ. The dispute dates back to the ICJ's decision in 1962, with twelve judges voting as follows:

> The Court,
>
> by nine votes to three,
>
> **Finds that the Temple of Preah Vihear is situated in territory under the sovereignty of Cambodia;**
> Finds in consequence,
> by nine votes to three,

[9] See further Vitit Muntarbhorn, *Unity in Connectivity? Evolving Human Rights Mechanisms in the ASEAN Region* (Nijhoff Publishers 2013).

> **that Thailand is under an obligation to withdraw any military or police forces, or other guards or keepers, stationed by her at the Temple, or in its vicinity on Cambodian territory;**
>
> by seven votes to five,
>
> **that Thailand is under an obligation to restore to Cambodia any objects of the kind specified in Cambodia's fifth Submission which may, since the date of occupation of the Temple by Thailand in 1954, have been removed from the Temple or the Temple area by the Thai authorities.**[10] [emphasis added]

Basically, the Court repudiated Thailand's claim over the temple. The Court found that the country was 'estopped' by its own conduct from rejecting a map dating back to colonial times; the Court viewed this map as indicating that the temple belonged to Cambodia. The disputed map (known as Annex I, dated 1907, and linked with a treaty of 1904 between Siam and France) was drawn up at a time when Cambodia was under French colonial rule.

However, matters did not end there as, decades later, Cambodia invoked the Court's power to interpret its 1962 judgement and this led to various provisional measures being ordered by the Court in 2011, followed by a further judgement in 2013. In regard to the 2011 case, even though Thailand asked the Court to dismiss the request for provisional measures, the Court proceeded to order both parties to immediately withdraw military personnel from the disputed area and imposed on them a provisional demilitarized zone.[11] It also underlined in its reasoning that its orders on provisional measures have a binding effect, creating legal obligations. Locally, there was a lull after the Court's order of provisional measures, with a wait-and-see attitude pending the judgement which was to follow in 2013.

In the final phase of the judgement in 2013, the Court found that Cambodia also had sovereignty over the promontory of the temple (in addition to the temple itself).[12] In reality, it offered a compromise. There were two key elements in paragraph 108 of the Court's judgment. First, the Court found unanimously that it had jurisdiction, under article 60 of its ICJ Statute, to interpret its 1962 judgment and that the case was admissible. This responded to the request of Cambodia for the Court to deliberate on the issue. Secondly, it declared unanimously:

> by way of interpretation, that the Judgment of 15 June 1962 decided that Cambodia had sovereignty over the territory of the promontory of Preah Vihear, as defined in

[10] *Case Concerning the Temple of Preah Vihear (Cambodia v Thailand)* (Merits) [1962] ICJ Rep 6.

[11] *Provisional Measures: Request for Interpretation of the Judgement of 15 June 1962 in the Case Concerning the Temple of Preah Vihear (Cambodia v Thailand)* (Order) [2011] ICJ Rep. For comments: Vitit Muntarbhorn, 'Preah Vihear – A Matter of Shared Responsibility' *Bangkok Post* (Bangkok, 2 August 2011) 9; Vitit Muntarbhorn, 'Preah Vihear Temple, A Measure of Shared Destiny' *Bangkok Post* (Bangkok, 3 August 2011) 9.

[12] *Request for Interpretation of the Judgement of 15 June 1962 in the Case concerning The Temple of Preah Vihear (Cambodia v Thailand)* (Judgement) [2013] ICJ Rep. For comments: Vitit Muntarbhorn, 'ICJ sets down Preah Vihear Ground Rules' *Bangkok Post* (Bangkok, 13 November 2013) 11.

> paragraph 98 of the present Judgment, and that, in consequence, Thailand was under an obligation to withdraw from the territory the Thai military or police forces, or other guards or keepers, that were stationed there.[13]

In making this ruling, the Court rejected Cambodia's attempt to claim that the disputed map represented the frontier between the two states. Concurrently, it clarified the issue of territorial sovereignty by highlighting that Cambodia's sovereignty pertained not only to the temple itself but also to the 'promontory of Preah Vihear', and that Thailand was obliged to withdraw from that area. As a consequence, the two countries will, in future, have to sit down peacefully together to identify the geographic extent of that 'promontory' based upon the Court's indications. Thai–Cambodian relations have improved recently, and the more comfortable political climate implies that there is no need to hasten bilateral negotiations pursuant to the Court's judgement. Both countries are awaiting new elections as of late 2018.

3 International Law-*cum*-National Law: Thai Constitutions and Courts

Thailand's legal system emerged in the last half of the nineteenth century during the reign of King Rama V. This was in part due to the various colonial pressures on the country's doorstep, impelling the country to modernize its structure, particularly in relation to its bureaucracy, judiciary, and educational system. The country's first Criminal Code came into existence in 1908, followed by the Civil and Commercial Code a few years later. To a large extent, the system is based on the civil law derived from continental Europe, while there are also some key common law influences (partly due to the fact that during the past century, several notable Thai judges were trained in England). Thailand's shift from absolute monarchy was witnessed by the birth of the first Thai Constitution in 1932. It should not be forgotten, however, that military predominance has been the rule rather than the exception since the end of the Second World War.

3.1 Relationship with Treaty-making: Before 2017

The Thai approach to the relationship between international and domestic law is essentially dualistic, but there are nuances to be borne in mind, including the relationship between international law and the Constitution. Before the 2007 Constitution, there were three situations where ratification of a treaty by the national parliament via

[13] *Temple of Preah Vihear* ibid.

passage of a national law was needed before submission of an instrument of ratification at the international level:

(i) Where the treaty affected the state's territory;
(ii) Where the treaty affected the jurisdiction of the state (including sovereign rights in extraterritorial areas); or
(iii) Where the treaty needed implementing legislation.[14]

These three categories were generally understood to be separate and were not necessarily interlinked.

In 2000, there was a test case before the Constitutional Court of Thailand. It concerned Thailand's potential ratification of the Convention on Biological Diversity 1992 (which Thailand had already signed).[15] The Cabinet was of the opinion that the Convention could be ratified without passage of a national law through the Thai Parliament as there was no need for implementing legislation on the issue (i.e., the third category as above). The Ministry of Foreign Affairs added that the Convention did not affect the territories or jurisdiction of the state, thus also not requiring the passage of a law through parliament. The Council of State, an advisory body, indicated otherwise, suggesting that an implementing law was necessary for the Convention, particularly on the issue of access to genetic resources under the Convention, and this necessitated passage of a law through parliament prior to ratification at the international level.

The Court followed the latter reasoning and found that the Convention was a treaty impacting on the jurisdiction of the state and thus needed approval and implementing legislation by parliament prior to ratification at the international level. Subsequently, the decision was questioned by a commentator as too closely interlinking the second and third categories; the Court's reasoning seemed to suggest that a treaty needing implementing law in the country prior to ratification at the international level should be understood (possibly automatically) as a treaty impacting upon Thailand's jurisdiction.[16] According to the commentator, the two categories are separate; namely, the fact that a treaty needs a local implementing law does not necessarily imply that the treaty affects the jurisdiction of the state (or vice versa).

[14] See e.g. s 224 of the Constitution 1997 which stated: 'A treaty which provides for a change in the Thai territories or the jurisdiction of the State and requires the enactment of an Act for its implementation must be approved by the National Assembly'. See further Vitit Muntarbhorn, *The Core Human Rights Treaties and Thailand* (Nijhoff publishers 2016) 6.

[15] *In Re Convention on Biological Diversity of 1992*, Constitutional Court, 5 October 2000, Judgement No.33/2543. For analysis see 'Thailand' in (2009) 9 *Asian Yearbook of International Law* 276, 279.

[16] Noppanidhi Suriya, 'Sonti Sanya Nai Rattatamanoon' ['Treaties under the Constitution'], *Thammasat Law Journal* 22 (Part 2) 173, 194; 'Korn Ti Ja Maa Pen Matra 224 Kong Rattathammanoon Haeng Raj-Arnajak Thai Be 2540 Lae Panha Ti Tham Maa Lueng Karn Winichai Kong Sarn Rattathammanoon Ti 33/2543' ['Before the Advent of Article 224 of the Thai Constitution BE 2540 and Problems after the Judgement of the Constitutional Court No.33/2543'], *Thammasat Law Journal* 32 (June BE 2545) 2, 289, 317.

This grey area has been overtaken by the following events, to some extent. In 2007, after a coup in 2006, a new Constitution came into effect, imposing more conditions on the executive branch of government to seek parliamentary approval before concluding or ratifying a treaty. The political undertone was that the toppled civilian government was viewed by critics as all too easily concluding agreements concerning free trade areas (particularly bilateral ones) between Thailand and other countries, thereby disadvantaging the interests of the country. Section 190 of the 2007 Constitution limited the powers of the executive branch in negotiating and finalizing the process of becoming a party to international treaties; it involved the National Assembly (parliament) much more in vetting this process. In essence, section 190 imposed the condition that the treaty (-making) must be approved by the National Assembly in a range of situations, namely: where it would result in a change in Thai territory; where it would affect an extraterritorial area over which the country has sovereignty; where implementation by an Act (of parliament) is required; where it would have an extensive impact on national security (economic and social); or where it would bind considerably national trade, investment, or budgets.[17] This has now been adjusted by the latest Constitution as below.

3.2 Relationship with Treaty-making: Since 2017

It should be noted from the outset that, as in past practice, treaty-making is a prerogative of the monarch. In that setting, it is the executive branch (the government/cabinet, with help from the relevant ministry) which negotiates and signs treaties. This is explicitly covered by Part 8 of the 2017 Constitution. In section 178, the 2017 Constitution imposes upon the executive branch the need to consult parliament and the public and to seek approval from parliament prior to ratification of a treaty at the international level, in regard to five categories of treaties:

(i) Where the treaty affects the state's territory;
(ii) Where the treaty affects an extraterritorial area over which Thailand is competent to exercise sovereignty or its jurisdiction;
(iii) Where the treaty requires a national implementing law;
(iv) Where the treaty would extensively impact the national economic or social security of the country; or
(v) Where the treaty would considerably bind the national trade, investment, or budget.[18]

[17] For the English translation of the Constitution 2007: Somdet Phra Paramintharamaha and others, 'Constitution of the Kingdom of Thailand 2007' (*National Human Rights Commission of Thailand*, 18 September 2015) <http://www.nhrc.or.th/getattachment/a763edba-e97a-4dbf-98cc-a95160221069/.aspx> accessed 27 September 2018.

[18] For the English translation of the Constitution 2017: Legal Opinion and Translation Section of the Foreign Law Division Under the Legal Duty of the Office of the Council of State, 'Constitution of the

The second category would affect areas such as Thailand's continental shelf and exclusive economic zone (EEZ), over which the country exercises 'sovereign rights' per the law of the sea. This provision has been replicated to a large extent in recent constitutions and has been retained in this 20th Constitution.

The new Constitution clarifies the types of treaties linked with the fourth and fifth categories above (which are subjected to parliamentary scrutiny and approval and which were not specified in the Constitution 2007) in section 178(4): namely, free trade treaties, customs unions, treaties related to use of natural resources, treaties which lead to the country's loss of natural resources, or other treaties stipulated by law. This is closely linked to current negotiations with various Asia-Pacific countries, such as the emerging Regional Comprehensive Economic Partnership (RCEP), as well as renewal of the free trade agreement with Japan.

Hesitation towards executive acts was seen in a case before Thailand's Constitutional Court in 2008 concerning a Joint Communiqué between Thailand and Cambodia that had been concluded by the civilian administration in 2008.[19] The Communiqué recognized Cambodia's registration of the temple above as a World Heritage site under UNESCO auspices. This document was concluded between the executive branches of Thailand and Cambodia and it was done without passage of a law in the Thai Parliament. Upon deliberation, the Court decided that the Communiqué was a treaty falling under section 190, thus needing parliamentary approval prior to its conclusion. The Court even went so far as to indicate that approval needed to be sought not only in regard to a situation where the country's territory was affected, but also where it *might be* affected by the agreement.

3.3 Interface with Domestic Law

What about situations where a Thai law or practice might be in conflict with an international custom or treaty? The general position is that the courts will do their best to interpret Thai law as being consistent with international custom. Section 4 of the Civil and Commercial Code (1925) also opens the door to enable courts to take into account customs and general principles of law. Moreover, section 34 of the Code states:

> Where any proceeding is to be carried out wholly or in part through the medium of or by request to the authorities in any foreign country, the Court shall, in the absence of any international agreement or provision of law governing the matter, comply with the general principles of international law.

This interrelates with a situation where the courts might recognize customs and principles of law (namely, customary international law) where they have been

Kingdom of Thailand' (*Constitutional Court of the Kingdom of Thailand*) <http://www.constitutional-court.or.th/occ_en/download/article_20170410173022.pdf> accessed 27 September 2018.

[19] Thai Constitutional Court, *Judgment 6–7/2551* (8 July BE 2551).

integrated into the domestic setting by statutory law, as well as where the latter is absent. Case law on the matter is sparse. A key area where local law and practice would abide by international custom is in regard to the privileges and immunities of diplomats, even before Thailand became a party to the Vienna Convention on Diplomatic Relations 1961. Looking back to the country's own practice from the sixteenth century onwards, where emissaries to and from Siam carried out their functions safely, it is ostensible that this was a well-established area of customary international law, irrespective of ratification of a treaty on the subject. Another area where an international custom has been followed by the Thai judiciary is in regard to the right of hot pursuit on the high seas, where a foreign boat has breached Thai fisheries law, even where no Thai law expressly provides for the rule.[20]

With regard to the reception of treaties nationally, what is to happen if there is a conflict between a national law and a treaty? Are local courts bound by a treaty where there is no national implementing law? The general position is that Thai law prevails, and the courts will consider international treaties only to the extent that they have been transformed into Thai national law. In practice, the situation may be more nuanced. Interestingly, in 2012, a local administrative court was petitioned by prisoners who had been shackled (usually leg chains) by the authorities, and their claim before the court was to invalidate the act of the authorities on the basis of international human rights law.[21] It should be noted that at the time, both the Criminal Code and Thai Constitution prohibited torture, although there was no clear definition of the malpractice. The Ministry of Foreign Affairs sent a statement to the court indicating that rights under the Universal Declaration of Human Rights were part of customary law. It added that the International Covenant on Civil and Political Rights 1966 (ICCPR) and the Convention against Torture 1984 (CAT) were binding on Thailand. At the time, the country was a party to those two treaties, but there was no implementing law transforming them into Thai law, although there was an old Prisons Act 1936[22] which gave the authorities discretion on whether or not to use shackles.

The court at first instance found that there was a breach of the ICCPR and that the application of the Prisons Act (which had been invoked to justify the use of shackles for fear that the prisoners might try to escape) was in conflict with it. However, on appeal to the highest administrative court, the decision was overturned. The Court referred directly to the CAT as binding on the country but found that implementation of the

[20] Kriangsak Kitichaiseree, 'Effectuation of International Law in the Municipal Legal Order of Thailand' (1995) 4 Asian Yearbook of International Law 171, 184, 173.

[21] Particularly the Universal Declaration of Human Rights, adopted by UNGA res 217 A(III) (10 December 1948); the UN Standard Minimum Rules on the Treatment of Offenders, adopted by UNGA res 2076 (13 May 1977); International Covenant on Civil and Political Rights (adopted 16 December, entered into force 23 March 1976, 999 UNTS 171); and Convention Against Torture and Other Cruel, Inhuman or Degrading Treatment or Punishment (adopted 10 December 1984, entered into force 26 June 1987, 1456 UNTS 85).

[22] Prisons Act 1936 (as amended in 1977, 1979, 1980, and 2017).

Prisons Act in this case was not in conflict with CAT.[23] On analysis, it is not altogether clear what would have happened if the Court had said that implementation of the Prisons Act was in breach of the CAT—where there was (and still is) no implementing law.

In another case, the Constitutional Court found that judicial regulations prohibiting persons with disabilities from becoming judges were not only in breach of national law but also the Convention on the Rights of Persons with Disabilities 2006 (CRPD).[24] Again, it is not altogether clear what would have happened if there was no law implementing the CRPD at the national level. In this case, however, even prior to Thailand's ratification of the CRPD, the 2007 Constitution had already prohibited discrimination, *inter alia*, in regard to disabilities. The country had also passed a national law on protection of persons with disabilities against discrimination, replicating the provisions of the CRPD to a great extent, to prepare for ratification, which ensued later. Given the dualist approach towards the relationship between Thai domestic law and international law, as seen in the Thai constitutions referred to above, there is no national law which automatically implements the provisions of a treaty. The general practice is that prior to ratification of a treaty, a national law transforming the treaty into a national law is required if the treaty is to be implemented in the Thai legal system.

The knowledge base of local judges on international law may also be relevant. On a salutary note, even under the dualistic approach, if local judges are well trained on international law, this offers opportunities for them to be inspired by international law, which may affect their discretion when interpreting and applying national law.

4 Critical Themes Concerning Thailand and International Law

The interrelationship between Thailand's domestic law and international law can be identified through the following critical themes: peace and security; jurisdiction/territory; human rights and humanitarian law; trade and commerce; and sustainable development and environmental protection.

4.1 Peace and Security

It should not pass unnoticed that Thailand has intermittently been under military rule, with its own emphasis on national security, for many years since the end of the Second

[23] *Sataporn Kochpan et al v Corrections Department*, Khadi Mai Lek Dum [Black Number Case] 862/2552, Khadi Mai Lek Daeng [Red Number Case] 283/2557, Supreme Administrative Court (22 June BE 2557).

[24] Constitutional Court Ruling 15/2555, *Re Sirimit Bunmun*, Royal Gazette, Vol 129 Part 100 Kor (18 October BE 2555).

World War. Particularly from the 1950s until the 1970s, there was much preoccupation with countering the spread of communism in the Southeast Asian region. The situation was all the more complicated because of the Indochina war raging in the region surrounding Thailand. The country was also the seat of an organization known as the Southeast Asia Treaty Organization (formed in 1954), essentially a self-defence pact between a number of countries, primarily targeting communism as its adversary. The organization fell by the wayside in 1977. The governments of Laos, Cambodia, and Vietnam also changed hands in 1975. The Khmer Rouge came to power in 1975 in Cambodia, followed by numerous atrocities. There then ensued another war in Cambodia, for a decade from the end of 1978, involving various Cambodian factions and Vietnam. Thailand was a supporter of the Khmer coalition (which also included the Khmer Rouge) as the Government in exile from Cambodia, which fought against the Vietnam-backed faction in power in Cambodia until the UN-backed peace process came into existence in the early 1990s.

The country abides by the UN Charter and cooperates broadly on issues of peace and security. The most salient aspect of this is Thailand's contribution of peacekeepers to UN peace-keeping forces. For instance, in 1999, the UN hospital in Timor-Leste was run by Thai military doctors and nurses when Thailand was on the cusp of independence. Thai peacekeepers have also worked in Africa, and the current policy is to strengthen contribution on this front, especially as the Thai–UN relationship of today is based on a partnership framework (rather than donor–donee relationship).

In recent years, Thailand has become a party to over a dozen anti-terrorism treaties and cooperates with the UN Security Council in transparency and accountability measures.[25] It has ratified many treaties on disarmament, ranging from the Nuclear Non-Proliferation Treaty 1968 to the Comprehensive Nuclear Test Ban Treaty 1996, the Convention against Biological Weapons 1972, and the Convention against Chemical Weapons 1993. It is the lead country on action against anti-personnel mines, partly as it is a party to the Convention on Anti-Personnel Mines 1997. However, it is not yet a party to some treaties which bridge the gap between disarmament and humanitarian law, such as the Convention on Cluster Munitions 2008.

Thailand is also a party to the UN Convention against Transnational Organized Crime 2000 and its Palermo Protocol to Prevent, Suppress, and Punish Trafficking in Persons, especially Women and Children 2003. It is, moreover, a party to many treaties against drug trafficking as well as to the UN Convention against Corruption 2003. It cooperates internationally, regionally, and bilaterally on many anti-crime activities, including action against drug trafficking and money laundering.

Thailand was a supporter of the UN reform process which led to the World Summit Outcome Document in 2005, including the notion of Responsibility to Protect (R2P) and the establishment of the UN Peace-Building Commission, among several other

[25] See e.g. Thailand's reports to the UN Counterterrorism Committee: <http://www.un.org/sc/ctc/resources/assessments/> accessed 11 December 2018.

new institutions. However, the fervour for R2P has been dampened in recent years, and Thailand has decreased its support for R2P.

At the regional level, the country's membership of ASEAN opens the door to various forms of cooperation on peace and security issues. These include the implementation of the ASEAN Political and Security Community Blueprint 2015. In that context, there is the important commitment to the ASEAN Treaty of Amity and Cooperation 1976, the implementation of the Southeast Asian Nuclear Weapons Free Zone 1995 (also known as the Bangkok Treaty), and the implementation of the ASEAN Declaration on the Conduct of Parties in the South China Sea 2002. There is now a further commitment to 2025 as outlined in the regional plan under the title of 'Forging Ahead Together'.[26]

ASEAN also provides a forum for wider discourse on peace and security issues, involving all five permanent members of the UN Security Council and many other countries beyond ASEAN, in the form of the ASEAN Regional Forum. This has been bolstered by cooperation between defence ministers, confidence-building measures, and preventive diplomacy, including joint training and cooperation against piracy and terrorism. There is also now an ASEAN Convention on Counter-Terrorism 2002 as well as an ASEAN Convention against Trafficking in Persons 2015.

4.2 Jurisdictional/Territorial Spectrum

Thailand has an array of treaties on extradition, prisoner transfers, and mutual legal assistance with other countries. Even without a bilateral treaty, the country's Mutual Legal Cooperation Act 1992 provides a basis for engagement with other countries, with the Attorney General's Office as the central authority for connectivity.

In relation to territorial issues, there remain a number of challenges, varying in sensibility. Thailand has land frontiers with four countries: Cambodia, Laos, Myanmar, and Malaysia. The situation with Cambodia was referred to earlier in relation to the *Temple* case. Although the frontier is now quiet, there were skirmishes prior to the ICJ's provisional orders of 2011 and this influenced the Court's superimposition of the demilitarized zone on the two countries, with a view to protecting a World Heritage site. Parts of the border are not yet demarcated, but there is a Memorandum of Understanding (MOU) of 2000 between Thailand and Cambodia on the survey and demarcation of the land boundary, with a Thai-Cambodia Joint Commission acting as a bridge between the two countries.[27] As both countries are members of ASEAN, there

[26] ASEAN, *ASEAN 2025: Forging Ahead Together* (ASEAN Secretariat 2015).

[27] International Crisis Group, *Waging Peace: The Thai-Cambodia Border Conflict. Asia Report No 215* (International Crisis Group, 6 December 2011) <http://www.crisisgroup.org/asia/south-east-asia/thailand/waging-peace-asean-and-thai-cambodian-border-conflict> accessed 11 December 2018. On maritime delimitation see Captain Somjade Kongrawd, 'Thailand and Cambodia Maritime Disputes' (*Global Security*, 2009) <http://www.globalsecurity.org/military/library/report/2009/thailand-cambodia.pdf> accessed 7 September 2017.

is an institutional platform for peaceful discourse, even though territorial disputes tend to be dealt with bilaterally. Border trade between the two countries is now flourishing and there is an MOU on migrant labour with correlative cross-border flows.

Border delimitation is still an issue on some fronts with both Laos and Myanmar, and there have been some skirmishes in the past. Thailand and Laos share a 500 km border, much of which is not well demarcated. There was fighting between Thailand and Laos in 1987 and 1988 (at Ban Romklao), partly in relation to a disputed map dating back to 1907 when Laos was a French colony.[28] The situation is peaceful today, for a variety of possible reasons. Laos is now a member of ASEAN. There is much cross-border trade between Thailand and Laos, and there is an MOU to regulate the cross-border flow of migrant workers. There is also a Thai-Lao Joint Boundary Commission where discussions can take place to promote peaceful interaction.

With regard to Myanmar, there is a long border of some 2,400 km, part of which is not yet demarcated. The relevant treaty is the Yandabo Treaty of 1826 between Thailand and Britain, which was the colonial power in Myanmar (then Burma). A clash took place in 2001 (at Ban Pang Noon) with further skirmishes in 2002.[29] Myanmar is now a member of ASEAN. There is also thriving cross-border trade and an MOU on migrant workers with Thailand. A Joint Boundary Committee was established in 1993. On the frontier with Malaysia, all is quiet. Interestingly, decades back, a river, which had acted as a legal boundary between the two countries (the river Kolok), changed its course and the two countries are in the process of concluding a new agreement to recognize the new boundary peacefully.[30]

Maritime matters are critically important, especially as Thailand is a maritime zone-locked country surrounded by the various zones of neighbouring countries, including India, Myanmar, Malaysia, Indonesia, Cambodia, and Vietnam. Thailand is a party to the four Law of the Sea Conventions of 1958 and signed the United Nations Law of the Sea Convention (UNCLOS) in 1982. However, it took Thailand three decades to ratify UNCLOS and it did so in May 2011, after parliamentary approval. There is an accompanying declaration which attests to the step-by-step, cautious approach taken, particularly in relation to article 310 of UNCLOS, such as a statement that ratification does not imply recognition or acceptance of any territorial claim made by a state party to the Convention.[31] There were various exclusions in the declaration in regard to

[28] Erik Guyot, 'Sibling Rivalry: The Thai-Lao Border Conflict' (The Institute of Current World Affairs, 2015) <http://www.icwa.org/wp-content/uploads/2015/10/ERG-10.pdf> accessed 7 September 2017.

[29] Tanvi Pate, 'Myanmar-Thailand Border Dispute: Prospects for Demarcation' (New Delhi, Institute of Peace and Conflict Studies, 8 July 2010) <http://www.ipcs.org/comm_select.php?articleNo=3186> accessed 7 September 2017.

[30] Suriya (n16) 183.

[31] Thai UNCLOS Declaration: Ministry of Foreign Affairs, 'Thailand Becomes State Party to the United Nations on the Law of the Sea (UNCLOS) 1982 and the Agreement Relating to the Implementation of the Convention' (Royal Thai Embassy, 17 June 2011) <http://www.thaiembassy.sg/press_media/news-highlights/thailand-becomes-state-party-to-the-united-nations-convention-on-the-law> accessed 27 September 2018.

article 298 of UNCLOS, concerning dispute settlement in relation to disputes about the interpretation of sea boundary delimitations or those involving historic bays or titles. Interestingly, since the country has not yet chosen which mechanism should apply to settle disputes, the implication of UNCLOS is that (by default) arbitration comes into play as the mechanism under the Convention in such a context.[32]

The country has four straight baselines and one historic bay in the Gulf of Thailand. It claims 12 nautical miles (nm) for its Territorial Sea, 24 nm for the contiguous zone, and 200 nm for its EEZ. The country has a number of maritime agreements with its neighbours; while the situation is regulated on several fronts, there remain some grey areas concerning delimitation and overlaps between zones. There are agreements with Malaysia, Indonesia, India, Myanmar, Cambodia, and Vietnam. The most convergent and operational is with Malaysia, where the two countries have had a Joint Development Area (JDA) since 1979, which acts as a temporary measure to jointly explore natural resources in the area, pending final maritime delimitation.[33] Thailand claimed its continental shelf in the Gulf of Thailand in 1973, and this was complemented by the JDA with Malaysia and then a delimitation agreement with Vietnam in 1997. There are overlaps between Cambodia and Vietnam's zones, among others, which have yet to be settled. There is an MOU with Cambodia on Overlapping Maritimes Claims to the Continental Shelf 2011, which opens the door to dialogue. In reality, the atmosphere is now low key, especially since the sensitive land-related issue which was the subject of the recent ICJ case necessitates a period of calm, reflection, and gradual discourse.

4.3 Human Rights and Humanitarian Law

Thailand's record on human rights and its link with international law is commendable on several fronts, but there remain key challenges, particularly in relation to political rights and the quest for democracy. Thailand has done well in economic, social, and cultural issues. There have been reductions in poverty in line with global targets and there is good access to the basics of life, such as education. The country's universal healthcare system has been lauded worldwide, and it has had a humane policy on HIV/AIDS prevention and response for decades. However, there are still wide economic disparities between rural and urban people, which may give rise to insecurity and instability.

The real conundrum is in regard to political rights, partly due to the non-democratic nature of the political power base. There are issues concerning constraints on freedom of expression and peaceful assembly; invocation of executive orders, bypassing an open parliamentary process; and the use of military courts to try civilians. The debate at the

[32] UN Convention on the Law of the Sea (adopted 10 December 1982, entered into force 16 November 1994, 1833 UNTS 3) (UNCLOS) Part XV and Annex VII.

[33] See Joint Development Area: Malaysia-Thailand Joint Authority <http://www.mtja.org/> accessed 27 September 2018.

beginning of 2017 centred around a proposed amendment to the Computer Crimes Act (2007), which would enable authorities to censor information flows more easily. Elections took place in March 2019 but the final results were not known as of April 2019.

In terms of formal commitment to international human rights treaties, the country is now a party to seven of the nine core international human rights treaties.[34] It has signed the Convention against Enforced Disappearance 2006, but has not yet committed to the Convention on the Rights of Migrant Workers and their Families (although it is also a party to several International Labour Organization conventions).[35] While there was an initial tendency to enter many reservations in ratifying a treaty, this has now diminished, and there is an increasing withdrawal of the reservations already entered. The country has been through two cycles of the Universal Periodic Review before the UN Human Rights Council, where most of the difficult areas of the review concerned political rights and related constraints.[36] While it has signed the Statute of the International Criminal Court, there has been reticence towards ratification, partly due to the potential implications of international criminal responsibility in the national setting.

With regard to international humanitarian law, while it is a party to the four Geneva Conventions 1949, it is not a party to any of the Additional Protocols to these treaties. The situation concerning disarmament was discussed earlier. The official government position has underlined that there is no armed conflict on Thai territory, but there is currently violence in southern Thailand where there is a large Muslim population and where there are major human rights issues, such as the impact of maladministration, overuse of emergency laws, violations by the authorities, killings, and other incidents caused by non-state armed groups. This is linked with the call for improved protection of human rights and more space for power-sharing with the local population, as well as broader public participation in a spirit of peace and reconciliation. The difficult situation in the south has been a long-standing problem, particularly affecting the regions of Pattani, Naratiwat, Yala, and parts of Songkla, with the most recent phase of violence commencing in 2004. While there are ongoing negotiations between the Thai

[34] Convention on the Elimination of All Forms of Discrimination against Women (adopted 18 December 1979, entered into force 3 September 1981, 1249 UNTS 13); Convention on the Rights of the Child (adopted 20 November 1989, entered into force 2 September 1990, 1577 UNTS 3); International Convention on the Elimination of All Forms of Racial Discrimination (adopted 7 March 1966, entered into force 12 March 1969, 660 UNTS 195); International Covenant on Civil and Political Rights (adopted 16 December 1966, entered into force 23 March 1976, 999 UNTS 171); International Covenant on Economic, Social, and Cultural Rights (adopted 16 December 1966, entered into force 3 January 1976, 993 UNTS 3); Convention Against Torture (n 21); and the Convention on the Rights of People with Disabilities (adopted 13 December 2006, entered into force 3 May 2008, 2515 UNTS 3). See further Muntarbhorn, *Core Human Rights Treaties* (n 14).

[35] International Convention for the Protection of All Persons from Enforced Disappearance (adopted 20 December 2006, entered into force 23 December 2010, 2716 UNTS 3); International Convention on the Protection of the Rights of All Migrant Workers and Members of Their Families (adopted 18 December 1990, entered into force 1 July 2003, 2220 UNTS 3).

[36] UN Human Rights <http://www.ohchr.org> accessed 27 September 2018.

authorities and various non-state actors from the south to stem the tide of violence, it is a long and winding road, waiting for tangible results.

4.4 Trade and Commerce

The country is a member of the World Trade Organization (WTO) and its predecessor, the General Agreement on Tariffs and Trade. It is a party to the Marrakesh Accords and has been involved in a range of cases before WTO dispute settlement panels. One of the most sensitive has been the *Tobacco* case, where the Philippines lodged a complaint that Thailand was using discriminatory measures against the import of tobacco products from the Philippines, which had been manufactured by a major transnational company. The Court found in favour of the Philippines in 2011.[37] However, the story did not end there, as the Thai authorities then took action to prosecute some of the executives from the company for various alleged wrongdoings in Thailand, as well as further proceedings concerning compliance issues with the WTO.[38] This is a challenging case of trade liberalization versus protectionism, intermixed with the intricacies of political and national interests.

Another critical area concerns intellectual property and access to medicine, especially HIV/AIDS medication. One of the WTO agreements is the Agreement on Trade-Related Aspects of Intellectual Property Rights 1994 (TRIPS), which has a provision permitting the use of compulsory licences to produce and import a patented product, even without the patent holder's permission. In particular, article 31 of the Agreement opens the door to compulsory licences where there is a 'national emergency or other circumstances of extreme urgency or in cases of public non-commercial use'. The TRIPS was later clarified by the Doha Declaration 2001, which recognized the flexibilities for the state party in defining what constitutes a 'national emergency or other circumstances of extreme urgency'.[39]

In 2006, Thailand issued a compulsory licence for an anti-retroviral drug to help treat persons with HIV/AIDS, invoking the TRIPS Agreement and the Doha Declaration.[40] The cost of the medicine has declined markedly and access to healthcare has been much improved as a result. On a connected issue, access to medical care has also been provided to non-nationals and is partly supported by the Global AIDS Fund.

[37] WTO, *Thailand—Customs and Fiscal Measures on Cigarettes from the Philippines* (17 June 2011) WT/DS371/AB/R.

[38] Amy Lefevre and Aukkarapon Niyomyat, 'Thai Prosecutor Charges Philip Morris Thailand in Cigarette Imports Case' *Reuters* (19 January 2016) <http://www.reuters.com/article/us-thailand-tobacco-idUSKCN0UX099> accessed 7 September 2017.

[39] See further: Mingchanok Tejavanija, 'A New Kind of Drug War: Thailand's Taking on the Pharmaceutical Industry to Improve Access to HIV/AIDS Drugs Through the Use of Compulsory Licencing' (2011) 28 Arizona Journal of International and Comparative Law 659, 692, 659–60.

[40] Ibid.

However, in the aftermath of the compulsory licence, the country was put on a priority watch list of a major power, and some companies refused to sell various drugs to it.

In regard to ASEAN, as indicated earlier, Thailand was a major proponent of the ASEAN Free Trade Area, and there is now a much freer flow of goods on many fronts. Liberalization has expanded to services and investment and, to a lesser extent, capital. The current aim of liberalization is to open up more sectors related to services, some of which are linked with the freer flow of skilled workers. Much remains to be done to ensure mutual recognition of qualifications on this front. By contrast, the flow of migrant workers (particularly 'blue collar' or non-executive) is not covered by regional liberalization. This is instead left more to the bilateral level, for example through various MOUs on the cross-border flow of migrant workers between Thailand and neighbouring countries. The current trend is to move towards a broader geography of liberalization. ASEAN already has close cooperation from China, Japan, and South Korea in an ASEAN Plus Three relationship. Thailand is now part of the movement towards the RCEP with other East Asian countries and is considering the possibility of joining the (now modified) Trans Pacific Partnership.[41]

As in many other regions, there remain various impediments to the liberalization of trade and commerce, such as the existence of non-tariff barriers and exceptions which still need to be rolled back more effectively. The human element behind all this should not be forgotten; an increase in a country's trade and commerce does not automatically translate into substantive gains in the shared wealth of the population unless there are also equitable distribution policies, resource allocations, and expanded public space. The flow of goods, services, capital, information, communications, and technology should not neglect the human dimension to be protected in the process, no less the destiny of migrant workers and their families, or measures to prevent and overcome abuses and exploitation, such as human trafficking, smuggling, and clandestine flows.

4.5 Sustainable Development and Environmental Protection

The development-related aspects of international law have gained prominence in Thailand not only through more treaties but also through global policy commitments such as the Millennium Development Goals (MDGs) 2000–15 and now the Sustainable Development Goals (SDGs) 2015–30. Thailand's preoccupation with the development perspective can be traced back to national development plans which were initiated half a century ago. However, these were top down at the outset, although they were later

[41] ASEAN, 'Regional Comprehensive Economic Partnership (RCEP)' (ASEAN, 3 October 2016) <asean.org/?static_post=rcep-regional-comprehensive-economic-partnership> accessed 27 September 2018. See also Office of the US Trade Representative, 'The Trans-Pacific Partnership' (Office of the US Trade Representative) <https://ustr.gov/trade-agreements/free-trade-agreements/trans-pacific-partnership/tpp-full-text> accessed 27 September 2018.

adjusted to become more participatory and bottom up. In 1986, the country voted for the UN Declaration on the Right to Development, which posited a more comprehensive perspective with political, economic, social, and cultural implications; more gender sensitivity towards women's development; and a more people-sensitive approach to democracy and equitable distribution of resources.[42] The call was for both national and international restructuring to nurture broad-based, people-centred development.

The MDGs concretized the constituents of development by enunciating eight major goals from 2000 to 2015, and Thailand attained most of them comfortably. For instance, Goal 1—to reduce poverty by half in all countries—was attained in Thailand long before 2015. The country worked on the basis of MDGs-plus (rather than MDGs), aiming to achieve more than the minimum MDG stipulations. Currently, the drive is to fulfil the SDGs' seventeen goals from 2015 to 2030.[43] The easier targets include access to education and healthcare, while the more difficult targets are the ones linked with political overtones, such as SDG 16, which calls for an inclusive society, rule of law, and respect for rights and freedoms, including compliance with the international agreements thereon.

Environmental protection has come to the fore increasingly in recent decades, with many grassroots groups representing a human rights agenda. In addition to staging key demonstrations advocating for environmental protection (which are currently difficult under the military-controlled system), these groups have also used courts (particularly the administrative court) quite effectively to impugn state action and interlinked business interests, such as the call for transparent environmental and health impact assessments prior to approval of projects which could harm the environment. Like the other ASEAN countries, Thailand has done well in becoming a party to many environment-related treaties.[44] It is a party to the International Framework Convention on Climate Change 1992, the Kyoto Protocol 1997, and the Paris Agreement 2016, which aims to cap global warming at an increase of no more than two degrees Celsius, necessitating national contributions to reduce emissions.[45] However, the promises by Thailand at the international level have to be reflected more effectively at the local level in terms of preventing and attenuating negative impacts on local communities and their livelihoods.

In the relationship between humanity and the environment, the issue of natural disasters has visibly emerged, and Thailand has committed itself to regional and global arrangements, bearing in mind that the annual extensive flooding in Thailand is likely to worsen due to global warming, paralleled by the ominous backdrop that 'Bangkok is sinking'. The various arrangements include the ASEAN Agreement on Disaster

[42] UNGA res 41/128 (4 December 1986): Declaration on the Right to Development.

[43] UN Development Programme, 'Sustainable Goals Development' <http://www.undp.org/content/undp/en/home/sustainable-development-goals.html> accessed 27 September 2018.

[44] ASEAN environmental agreements: Central Intelligence Agency, 'The World Fact Book' <https://research.un.org/en/docs/environment/treaties> accessed 27 September 2018.

[45] Paris Agreement 2015 <http://unfccc.int/files/meetings/paris_nov_2015/application/pdf/paris_agreement_english_.pdf> accessed 27 September 2018.

Management and Emergency Response 2005, which provides for standby arrangements among ASEAN states to help each other, and global policy commitments, such as the Sendai Framework on Disaster Risk Reduction 2015–30, which posits action and cooperation on disaster preparedness, mitigation, and response.[46] These arrangements are also interlinked with the SDGs, which offer forward-looking opportunities for the next decade and beyond.

5 Conclusion

Thailand's relationship with international law elicits a long-term view, inviting retrospection, introspection, and prospective action. As a seasoned member of the international system, Thailand has learned and contributed much in terms of the shared wisdom for survival, progression, and cooperation (in terms of what to do and what not to do), as the global and local dynamics continually change. Ultimately, the synergy between Thailand and international law cannot be ascertained by means of an inter-state or inter-organizational relationship alone. A sense of humanity and the human face of international law must not be overlooked or sidelined. This is all the more poignant as the international law of the future will have to deal with not only human actors (their strengths, foibles, interests, and vested interests), but also non-human actors, already present with drones and robots (including those which are self-automated to kill).

The quandary is almost daring and daunting (if not haunting): will international law (and humanity) successfully provide an animated response to the forthcoming inanimate actors?

[46] For the Sendai Framework see UN Office for Disaster Risk Reduction, 'UN World Conference on Disaster Risk Reduction' <http://www.wcdrr.org/conference/programme> accessed 11 December 2018.

CHAPTER 16

INDONESIA

HIKMAHANTO JUWANA
AND ANBAR JAYADI

1 Introduction

From the beginning of its establishment as a state, alongside the formation of the Indonesian government, Indonesia—as a nation—committed itself to participating on the international stage. Paragraph 4 of the Preamble of the Constitution of the Republic of Indonesia 1945 ('1945 Constitution') shows such commitment. It provides that the Indonesian government will 'participate in the establishment of a world order based on freedom, perpetual peace, and social justice'.[1] Indonesia not only wants to engage in world affairs, but such engagement must serve the purpose of creating 'freedom, perpetual peace, and social justice'. The Preamble is a starting point for those who want to study the development of international law in Indonesia.

Besides the 1945 Constitution, Indonesia's role in the Bandung Conference of 1955 is another pivotal point since Indonesia was not only one of the initiators of the Conference,[2] gathering together countries such as India and Pakistan to discuss a proposal for it,[3] but it also hosted the Conference in the Indonesian city of Bandung. In other words, Indonesia showed leadership in holding a conference of which one aim was to strengthen 'postcolonial solidarity' among Asian-African countries.[4] Further, as the Final Communiqué of the Conference laid out, the Conference worked towards

[1] An unofficial translation of the Constitution of Indonesia 1945 is available at <http://www.unesco.org/education/edurights/media/docs/b1ba8608010ce0c48966911957392ea8cda405d8.pdf> accessed 24 April 2019.

[2] See further Luis Eslava, Michael Fakhri, and Vasuki Nesiah (eds), *Bandung, Global History, and International Law: Critical Pasts and Pending Futures* (Cambridge University Press 2017).

[3] N'Dri Therese Assie-Lumumba, 'Behind and Beyond Bandung: Historical and Forward-looking Reflections on South-south Cooperation' (2015) 2 Bandung: Journal of Global South DOI 10.1186/s40728-014-0011-5.

[4] See Luis Eslava, Michael Fakhri, and Vasuki Nesiah, 'The Spirit of Bandung' in Eslava et al (eds) (n 2) 3.

cooperation among Asian-African countries, for instance, in the fields of economics, culture, human rights, and self-determination.[5] The Conference itself, as Makau Mutua asserts, was the 'symbolic birthplace' of the Third World Approach to International law (TWAIL).[6] The celebration of the sixtieth anniversary of the Bandung Conference was held in Indonesia in 2015,[7] asserting the importance that Indonesia places on this day in maintaining collaboration among Asian-African countries.

Nevertheless, the development of international law in Indonesia is not merely about the 1945 Constitution and the Bandung Conference. It is also about Indonesia advancing her interests at the international level and making her voice count. For example, Indonesia fought for the notion of archipelagic states to be adopted in the United Nations Convention on the Law of the Sea 1982 (UNCLOS). At the regional/Southeast Asia level, Indonesia brings international law matters to the Association of Southeast Asian Nations (ASEAN). On top of that, the relationship between international law and national law is of paramount importance in understanding of the development of international law in the Indonesian legal context.

This chapter will examine three main topics concerning Indonesia and international law. First and foremost, it will discuss Indonesia and the politics of international law-making. As mentioned earlier, Indonesia wants her voice to be heard on the international stage. However, in doing so, according to Hikmahanto Juwana, Indonesia is not free from politics.[8] This view means two things. Indonesia uses international law as a political instrument to pursue her interests; and other (and often developed) countries use international law to advance their interests, for instance economic ones, towards Indonesia.[9]

Secondly, this chapter will discuss the relationship between international law and Indonesian national law. This discussion concludes that to date, there is not yet a consensus, especially among Indonesian scholars, as to what the place of international law is in Indonesia's national legal system. Lastly, this chapter will discuss the relationship between Indonesia and the regional body, ASEAN. We chose this topic because

[5] See 'Final Communiqué of the Asian-African Conference of Bandung', 24 April 1955 <http://franke.uchicago.edu/Final_Communique_Bandung_1955.pdf> accessed 22 March 2018. See also the website of the Asian-African Museum in Bandung <http://asianafricanmuseum.org/perpustakaan-museum-asia-afrika/> accessed 30 October 2018.

[6] Makau Mutua and Antony Anghie, 'What is TWAIL?' (2000) 94 Proceedings of the Annual Meeting of the American Society of International Law 31.

[7] Museum Konperensi Asia-Afrika, 'KTT AA 2015' <http://asianafricanmuseum.org/ktt-aa-2015/> accessed 15 May 2018.

[8] See Hikmahanto Juwana, 'Hukum Internasional Sebagai Instrumen Politik: Beberapa Pengalaman Indonesia sebagai Studi Kasus' ['International Law as Political Instruments: A Case Study of Indonesia's Experiences'] (2012) 5 Arena Hukum 106 <http://arenahukum.ub.ac.id/index.php/arena/article/view/100> accessed 30 October 2018.

[9] See Hikmahanto Juwana, 'Hukum Internasional Dalam Konflik Kepentingan Ekonomi Negara Berkembang dan Negara Maju' ['International Law within the Context of Conflicts of Economic Interests between Developing and Developed Countries'] (2001) 8 Jurnal Hukum 105 <http://journal.uii.ac.id/IUSTUM/article/view/4855/> accessed 30 October 2018.

Indonesia contributes to making international law important in ASEAN. For instance, Indonesia played a significant part in the establishment of a regional human rights commission under the ASEAN Charter.

Nonetheless, it is important to note that this chapter is not meant to represent all discussions about the development of international law in Indonesia or to serve as an encyclopedia of Indonesia and international law. Instead, this chapter aims to point out essential events with the hope of providing readers with a general depiction of Indonesia and international law. Additionally, the term 'Indonesia' in this chapter shall not be interpreted strictly, as in certain events it may refer to the 'Indonesian government', and in other events it may refer to 'Indonesian academics' or 'Indonesian society in general'. As such, the term 'Indonesia' must be interpreted in context.

2 A Short Background to the Indonesian Legal System

As of 2017, Indonesia's population was 242 million people.[10] This places Indonesia in the top ten most populous countries in the world.[11] Indonesia is also regarded as 'the largest economy in Southeast Asia'.[12] The philosophical foundation of Indonesia, as a nation-state, is *Pancasila*. *Pancasila* comprises five core principles. The first principle is 'The Belief in One God'; the second is 'A just and civilized humanism'; the third is 'Unity of Indonesia'; the fourth is 'Democratic citizenship led by wise guidance born of representative consultation'; and the fifth is 'Social justice for all the people of Indonesia'.[13] Indonesia's political and legal system is established under the 1945 Constitution. Indonesia once adopted a centralized governmental system but, in the Reform era, Indonesia moved to a decentralized system, which means there are substantial roles for local governments. For example, there is more authority in budgeting, and power to legislate, at the provincial, city, municipality, and village levels.[14]

Indonesia's domestic legal system bears the influence of the civil law tradition. This is attributed to Dutch colonization,[15] which originated in the commercial activities of the

[10] As of 2011: Statistics Indonesia (Badan Pusat Statistik), *Statistical Yearbook of Indonesia 2017*, 1 <http://www.bps.go.id/website/pdf_publikasi/Statistik-Indonesia-2017.pdf> accessed 23 July 2018.

[11] World Bank, 'Indonesia Overview' <http://www.worldbank.org/en/country/indonesia/overview> accessed 23 July 2018.

[12] Ibid.

[13] Translation of Pancasila is provided in the *Statistical Yearbook of Indonesia 2017* (n 10) 37.

[14] See further Anwar Nasution, 'Government Decentralization Program in Indonesia', Asian Development Bank Institute, Working Paper No 601, October 2016 <http://www.adb.org/sites/default/files/publication/201116/adbi-wp601.pdf> accessed 23 July 2018.

[15] See further Hikmahanto Juwana, 'Courts in Indonesia: A Mix of Western and Local Character' in Jiunn-Rong Yeh and Wen-Chen Chang (eds), *Asian Courts in Context* (Cambridge University Press 2014) 303.

Dutch East India Company in the seventeenth century and was formalized under direct Dutch rule as the Dutch East Indies from 1800 to 1949 (albeit disrupted by Japanese military occupation from 1942 to 1945). The obvious example is Indonesia's Civil Code, which was 'inherited' from the Dutch and is still in force to this day. Nevertheless, Indonesia also received a certain extent of common law influence, especially in term of legislation making.[16] One example is the Law No. 5 of 1999 on Competition that 'adopts numerous concepts from the US's Sherman Antitrust Act and Clayton Antitrust Act'.[17]

Regarding Indonesia's standpoint towards international law, as Damos Dumoli Agusman argues, Indonesia somewhat deviates from the Dutch as her former colonizer.[18] The reason for this is that, at the very beginning of her 'life', Indonesia regarded international law as 'unfriendly' and 'favour[ing] the colonial power'.[19] This stance led Indonesia to later initiate the Bandung Conference in 1955, which was an important step towards the creation of the Non-Aligned Movement.[20]

According to Agusman, the following are three patterns in the way Indonesia has reacted to international law:

(i) 'the hostile' one (1945–1966), by which Indonesia, through her leader President Soekarno, 'induced negative sentiments in Indonesia towards international law';[21]
(ii) the 'no cold shoulder' approach (1966–1998) by which, under the leadership of President Soeharto in the New Order era, there was a welcoming reaction to international law;[22] and
(iii) 'the Reform era' (1998 to the present time),[23] in which the focus is no longer so much on international law (particularly the question of its place in Indonesia's legal system) but instead on 'strengthening the constitutional framework'.[24]

From Agusman's point of view, we can see that Indonesia has a changing—if not inconsistent—stance towards international law.

Furthermore, Indonesia has faced several internal conflicts that received international attention, including the situations in East Timor (now Timor-Leste) from 1975 to 1999,[25] Aceh from 1976 to 2005, and West Papua (which was ceded to Indonesia by The Netherlands in 1963, followed by a referendum in 1969). However, the official stance remains that internal conflicts, for example in West Papua, are matters of national domain in which the participation of foreign parties is frowned upon.[26]

[16] Ibid. 314. [17] Ibid.

[18] Damos Dumoli Agusman, 'The Dynamic Development on Indonesia's Attitude Toward International Law' (2015) 13 Indonesian Journal of International Law 1, 2.

[19] Ibid. 3. [20] The Bandung Conference is discussed in section 3.2.

[21] Agusman (n 18) 10. [22] Ibid. 11. [23] Agusman's article, ibid., was published in 2015.

[24] Ibid. 14. [25] This situation is discussed in section 3.1.

[26] See for example Hikmahanto Juwana, 'Pakar: Insiden Papua Berkaitan dengan Kedaulatan' ['An Expert: West Papua Incident is about Sovereignty'] (*Republika Online*, 30 August 2012) <http://www.

To briefly conclude, Indonesia is a country with a rich history that affects Indonesia's outlook on international law. This chapter will explore further on this theme.

3 Indonesia and the Politics of International Law-Making

In participating and advancing her interests in the international law arena, Indonesia is not free from politics. Nonetheless, before delving further into the discussion, there are three things to be clarified. First and foremost, this section will emphasize the view of 'international law as a political instrument'.[27] Proceeding from this view, we will explain first how Indonesia uses international law as political instruments and secondly how other countries use international law to put pressure on Indonesia. The second point to clarify is that this section is by no means claiming that international law is *always* used as a political instrument, including by states such as Indonesia. Last but not least, this section regards (international) law and (international) politics as two separate notions.[28]

3.1 Political Aspects Surrounding Indonesia's Practices

In the context of Indonesia, Juwana divides the political use of international law into two categories of trends, namely: (i) Indonesia uses international law to bring her interests onto the international stage, and (ii) other countries use international law to put pressure on Indonesia.[29] In regard to the former, the Indonesian government has experienced both success and failure. Regarding the latter, the Indonesian government in some instances succumbed to other countries' interests and in others it resisted international pressures.

As Juwana explains, one success story of Indonesia bringing her interests onto the international stage is the adoption of the notion of 'archipelagic states' in Part IV of UNCLOS 1982.[30] In contrast, a failure came when Indonesia wanted the recognition of the Geo-Stationery Orbit as Indonesia's territory.[31] However, the political aspect is not only confined to what Indonesia wants but also to what Indonesia does not want. One example of the latter is the reluctance of the Indonesian government to accede to the Refugee Convention 1951 and its Protocol 1967 despite the increasing number of asylum

republika.co.id/berita/nasional/hukum/12/08/30/m9k8d5-pakar-insiden-papua-berkaitan-dengan-kedaulatan> accessed 23 July 2018.

27 Juwana (n 8).

28 The division between (international) law and (international) politics might not be that distinctive. Nonetheless, it is not the purpose of this section to go deeply into the debate about the distinction.

29 Juwana (n 8). 30 Ibid. 111. 31 Ibid. 112.

seekers and refugees in Indonesia.[32] Another example is the unwillingness of the Indonesian government to ratify the International Labour Organization (ILO) Convention No. 169 on Indigenous and Tribal Peoples 1989, due to the complexity of the issue of *masyarakat adat* (indigenous peoples) in the President Habibie era (1998–1999) in Indonesia.[33]

Other states and international organizations have used international law to apply pressure to Indonesia.[34] One example is the case of East Timor (now Timor-Leste), of which Indonesia took control from Portugal, the colonial power, in 1975. From that time, there was a push from the international community, especially from the UN Security Council,[35] which produced a number of resolutions regarding East Timor.[36] Despite the Security Council's seemingly constant affirmation of Indonesia's territorial integrity and its government's efforts in East Timor,[37] the pressures were evident in the substance of the Security Council's resolutions and UN intervention in East Timor.

Thus, in Resolution 384 (1975), the Security Council recognized 'the inalienable right of the people of East Timor to self-determination and independence in accordance with the principles of the Charter of the United Nations'. In Resolution 1236 (1999), the Security Council welcomed 'the intention of the Secretary-General to establish as soon as practicable a United Nations presence in East Timor'. The Security Council decided, in Resolution 1246 (1999), 'to establish until 31 August 1999 the United Nations Mission in East Timor'.[38] A referendum was held in East Timor in August 1999, followed by a temporary UN Transitional Administration in East Timor and the independence of East Timor from Indonesia in 2002.

Another push was for the Indonesian government to form a court to prosecute the alleged perpetrators of international crimes in Timor Timur.[39] Indonesia accordingly

[32] See further discussion in Dita Liliansa and Anbar Jayadi, 'Should Indonesia Accede to the 1951 Refugee Convention and Its 1967 Protocol' (2015) 3 Indonesia Law Review 324 <http://ilrev.ui.ac.id/index.php/home/article/viewFile/161/pdf_71> accessed 22 March 2018.

[33] See Umi Nurhayati, 'Aspek Politik dalam Proses Ratifikasi Konvensi No 169 (Indigenous and Tribal People Convention) di Indonesia pada Era Habibie' ['Political Aspects in the Ratification Process of ILO Convention No 169 (Indigenous and Tribal People Convention) in Indonesia in the Habibie Era'], Undergraduate Thesis, University of Jember, Indonesia, January 2002 <http://repository.unej.ac.id/handle/123456789/77590> accessed 22 March 2018.

[34] Juwana (n 8) 111.

[35] Hikmahanto Juwana, 'Special Report Assessing Indonesia's Human Rights Practice in the Post-Soeharto Era: 1998-2003' (2003) 7 Singapore Journal of International & Comparative Law 644, 668 <http://www.asianlii.org/sg/journals/SGJlIntCompLaw/2003/24.pdf> accessed 23 July 2018.

[36] UNSC Resolution 384 (22 December 1975), Resolution 389 (22 April 1976), Resolution 1236 (7 May 1999), Resolution 1246 (11 June 1999), Resolution 1257 (3 August 1999), Resolution 1262 (27 August 1999), Resolution 1264 (15 September 1999), and Resolution 1272 (25 October 1999).

[37] For example, while UNSC Resolution 1264 (1999) repeated the 'successful conduct of the popular consultation of the East Timorese people', it also reaffirmed 'respect for the sovereignty and territorial integrity of Indonesia'. Such affirmation was repeated in UNSC Resolution 1272 (1999).

[38] The mandate of the UN Mission in East Timor (UNAMET) was later extended until 30 September 1999 by UNSC Resolution 1257 (1999), and was again extended until 30 November 1999 by UNSC Resolution 1262 (1999).

[39] Juwana (n 8).

established a Human Rights Court (*Pengadilan HAM*) in 2000.[40] However, this was an ad hoc court which lacked further implementing regulations to make it work.[41]

One more example of putting Indonesia under international pressure concerns Indonesia's participation in the global trade regime, for example, the Agreement on Trade-Related Aspects of Intellectual Property Rights 1995 (TRIPS).[42] This participation might be mutual, though, in the sense that the developed countries need Indonesia as a big market and Indonesia herself needs cooperation for gaining economic benefits. For example, Parikersit and Wairocana argue that the national interest of Indonesia is not always in conflict with the World Trade Organization (WTO) and might even benefit from it.[43] Even so, one might question the impact of Indonesia's participation in the WTO in some areas, for example in poverty reduction.[44]

To sum up, Indonesia's practices concerning international law involves political aspects in which there is an interplay among Indonesian government interests, developed states interests, and the interests of the international community as a whole.

3.2 International Law (from the West): Indonesia's Experience Matters

To date, Indonesia's achievement of having the notion of 'archipelagic state' included in UNCLOS is taught in classroom discussions of international law and the law of the sea. The reason for this is that this achievement is evidence of making Indonesia's experience matter in international law. There has been quite a discussion about the concerns and efforts of Indonesia (and the Philippines) towards the recognition of archipelagic states at the international level.[45] It was at the Third Law of the Sea

[40] Through Law No. 26 of 2000 on the Human Rights Court. See Zainal Abidin, 'Pengadilan HAM di Indonesia' ['Human Rights Court in Indonesia'], ELSAM [Institute for Policy Research and Advocacy], 18 September 2014 <http://referensi.elsam.or.id/2014/09/pengadilan-ham-di-indonesia/> accessed 22 March 2018. See also Hikmahanto Juwana, 'Beberapa Masalah Hukum Internasional dari Dugaan Pelanggaran Hak Asasi manusia di Timor Timur' ['International Law Issues of the Allegation of Human Rights Violation in Timor Timur'] (2000) 11(34) Mimbar Hukum 117 <http://i-lib.ugm.ac.id/jurnal/download.php?dataId=2399> accessed 22 March 2018.

[41] Ibid. [42] Juwana (n 8), 111.

[43] I Gusti Ngurah Parikersit and I Gusti Ngurah Wairocana, 'The Rise of the Spirit of National Interest and the Existence of World Trade Organization Agreement: A Case Study of Indonesia' (2017) 4 Padjajaran Journal of Law 319.

[44] See Anne-Sophie Robilliard and Sherman Robinson, 'The Social Impact of a WTO Agreement in Indonesia' in Thomas W Hertel and L Alan Winters (eds), *Poverty and the WTO: Impacts of the Doha Development Agenda* (Palgrave Macmillan and World Bank 2006) 319.

[45] See among others Charlotte Ku, 'The Archipelagic States Concept and Regional Stability in Southeast Asia' (1991) 23 Case Western Reserve Journal of International Law 463; Hasjim Djalal, 'Regime of Archipelagic States', ASEAN Regional Forum, Manila, March 2011 <http://aseanregionalforum.asean.org/files/Archive/18th/ARF%20Seminar%20on%20UNCLOS,%20Manila,%208-9Mar2011/Annex%20K%20-%20Prof%20Hasjim%20Djalal%20-%20Regime%20of%20Arch%20States.pdf> accessed 5 November 2017; Vivian Louis Forbes, *Indonesia's Delimited Maritime Boundaries* (Springer 2014).

Conference (1973–1982) of UNCLOS 1982 that the concept of archipelagic states was recognized.[46] Hasjim Djalal points out, at least for Indonesia, that the efforts to make the concept of archipelagic states recognized were enormous.[47] After the failure of promoting the concept in the First Law of the Sea Conference (1956–1958), Indonesia started to use the concept at the domestic level through the enactment of Law No. 4 of 1960 in Indonesian Waters. In that law, the Indonesian government's Djuanda Declaration of 1957—a declaration that embodied a concept of *tanah air* (homeland)—was transplanted into the Law on Indonesian Waters. Then, after years of efforts at the national level, finally at the Third Law of the Sea Conference the concept of archipelagic states was recognized in UNCLOS.[48]

At present, the Indonesian government maintains her stance as an archipelagic state. Nonetheless, the government develops policies that address Indonesian sovereignty over her territorial waters. One example is in the field of combatting illegal fishing. The current Minister for Maritime Affairs (at the time of writing in 2018) has a vessel-sinking policy for vessels that undertake illegal fishing in Indonesian waters.[49] As such, through her Ministry of Maritime Affairs, Indonesia takes protection of her territory seriously.[50]

Another milestone in making Indonesia's voice count internationally was the Bandung Conference. The Bandung Conference, or the Asian-African Conference, was initiated by Indonesia, Burma, India, Pakistan, and Ceylon (now Sri Lanka).[51] These countries invited twenty-four other countries to participate, which from Asia included Afghanistan, Cambodia, China, Iran, Iraq, Japan, Laos, Nepal, Philippines, Thailand, North Vietnam, and South Vietnam.[52] The Conference considered 'problems of common interest and concern to countries of Asia and Africa and discussed ways and means by which their people could achieve fuller economic, cultural and political co-operation'.[53] As with Mutua's proposition on TWAIL, the Bandung Conference was a way for Asian and African countries to make their voice heard and recognized on the international stage, by first cooperating with each other.

Notwithstanding this intention, to the present time there remains a question as to whether the Bandung Conference, and hence TWAIL itself, succeeded in deconstructing—if not rebuilding—the international legal order.[54] The recent sixtieth anniversary of the Bandung Conference in 2015 might provide a perspective as to whether the initial intention of the Conference has been achieved in the present day. Such celebration

[46] Ku, ibid. 463. [47] Hasjim Djalal (n 45). [48] Juwana (n 8) 111.

[49] See among others Hikmahanto Juwana, 'Sinking Ships Legitimate to Combat Illegal Fishing' *The Jakarta Post* (6 December 2014) <http://www.thejakartapost.com/news/2014/12/06/sinking-ships-legitimate-combat-illegal-fishing.html> accessed 21 March 2018.

[50] Ibid.

[51] See 'Final Communiqué of the Asian-African Conference of Bandung (24 April 1955)' <http://franke.uchicago.edu/Final_Communique_Bandung_1955.pdf> accessed 22 March 2018.

[52] Ibid. [53] Ibid.

[54] For further discussion see Andrew Phillips, 'Beyond Bandung: The 1955 Asian-African Conference and its Legacies for International Order' (2016) 70 Australian Journal of International Affairs 329.

allows the gathering of Asian-African countries and, as Juwana put it, this gathering still maintains relevance for the current situation of the Asian-African countries, where several of them face, for example, industrialization processes and internal conflicts.[55]

As such, Juwana proposed that Asian-African countries must do more work, especially in facing 'a new form of colonialism' that is 'the economic dependency on the developed states'.[56] In doing so, Juwana suggested that Asian-African countries must do three things: construct universal values in coherence with global dynamics; work towards economic independence from the developed states; and commit to solving their internal conflicts.[57] The sixtieth anniversary Conference itself, at the end, produced three important documents, namely the Bandung Message 2015, New Asian-African Strategic Partnership,[58] and Declaration for Palestine.[59] The common thread among these three documents is a push for the Asian-African countries to work together for stronger cooperation. As for Indonesia, it has been said that Indonesia must be the 'Asia-Africa Centre'.[60]

The examples of UNCLOS and the Bandung Conference show us Indonesia's attempts to make her experience matter on the international stage. Nonetheless, we should contemplate such experiences in terms of their relevance to the present and the future, which was the case with the Bandung Conference and its sixtieth anniversary Conference in Indonesia.

4 Indonesia and the (Unresolved) Relationship between International Law and National Law

This section will explore various examples to show the relationship between international law and Indonesia's national laws. However, before doing so, it will point out

[55] Hikmahanto Juwana, quoted in Ike Agestu, 'Setelah 60 Tahun, Asia-Afrika Hadapi Kolonialisme Model Baru' ['After 60 Years, Asia-Africa Face a New Model of Colonialism'] (CNN Indonesia, 21 April 2014) <https://www.cnnindonesia.com/internasional/20150421121252-106-48094/setelah-60-tahun-asia-afrika-hadapi-kolonialisme-model-baru> accessed 17 May 2018.

[56] Ibid.

[57] Hikmahanto Juwana, quoted in 'KAA ke-60 Sukses, 3 Hal Ini Bisa Bikin Geger Eropa' ['The Success of the 60th Asian-African Conference, These Three Things Can Appall Europe'] *Tempo* (20 April 2015) <https://nasional.tempo.co/read/659013/kaa-ke-60-sukses-3-hal-ini-bisa-bikin-geger-eropa> accessed 17 May 2018.

[58] <http://www.bandungspirit.org/IMG/pdf/naaspcomplete-bandung_of_states_2005.pdf> accessed 17 May 2018.

[59] See the Secretariat of the Cabinet of Indonesia, Outcomes of the 60th Asia Africa Summit, 22–23 April 2015 <http://setkab.go.id/inilah-hasil-hasil-ktt-asia-afrika-ke-60-di-jakarta-22-23-april-2015/> accessed 17 May 2018.

[60] See among others 'Pesan Bandung' ['Bandung Message'] *Investor Daily* (26 April 2015) <http://id.beritasatu.com/home/pesan-bandung/114480> accessed 17 May 2018.

examples of major international legal instruments ratified or adhered to by Indonesia. It will then discuss the place of international legal instruments within Indonesia's national law and before Indonesia's national courts, namely the Supreme Court and the Constitutional Court.

4.1 Ratification of International Legal Instruments

In the field of human rights, Indonesia has acceded to a number of treaties, including the International Covenant on Civil and Political Rights 1966 (ICCPR), International Covenant on Economic, Social and Cultural Rights 1966 (ICESCR), and the International Convention on the Elimination of All Forms of Racial Discrimination 1965 (CERD).[61] The accession instrument of the ICCPR is Law No. 12 of 2005, for the ICESCR it is Law No. 11 of 2005, and for the CERD it is Law No. 29 of 1999.

Nevertheless, the ratification instrument is not always in the form of a Law (*Undang-Undang*) but may be contained instead in a Presidential Regulation (*Peraturan Presiden*). The latter is usually used for a more specific and practical international legal instrument, for example Presidential Regulation No. 23 of 2017 on the Ratification of the Credit Guarantee and Investment Facility Articles of Agreement, in the context of ASEAN+3 (ASEAN, China, Japan, and Korea).[62] For the former, as prescribed in article 10 of Law No. 24 of 2000, the ratification is in the form of Law (*Undang-Undang*) if the international agreement concerns a matter of (i) politics, peace, defence, or state security; (ii) territorial issues; (iii) sovereignty or sovereign rights; (iv) human rights or the environment; (v) the formulation of new norms; or (vi) foreign loans or grants.

It is not always clear whether there are direct implementing regulations of international legal instruments. Nonetheless, the judges of the Constitutional Court of Indonesia often refer to international legal instruments such as the ICCPR and ICESCR.[63] The reference is made in the sense that the judges mostly take note of them as significant human rights instruments for Indonesia.[64] As for national instruments, direct reference to international legal instruments is made in Law No. 39 of 1999 on Human Rights. This Law makes a direct reference to the Universal Declaration of

[61] Other international human rights instruments that are ratified by Indonesia are available at UN Human Rights, Status of Ratification <http://indicators.ohchr.org/> accessed 21 March 2018. For further discussion on human rights in Indonesia see, for example, Anbar Jayadi, 'What Constitutes as Limitation of (Human) Rights in Indonesian Legal Context?' (2017) 3 Hasanuddin Law Review 290 <http://dx.doi.org/10.20956/halrev.v3i3.1203> accessed 30 October 2018.

[62] The Indonesian-language version of this Presidential Regulation is available at <http://sipuu.setkab.go.id/PUUdoc/175173/PERPRES%2023%20TAHUN%202017.pdf> accessed 30 October 2018.

[63] One may browse the Constitutional Court's rulings at <http://www.mahkamahkonstitusi.go.id/> accessed 30 October 2018.

[64] See for example Constitutional Court ruling No. 140/PUU-VII/2009 on the constitutional review of blasphemy law.

Human Rights 1948 in its preamble: 'whereas as a member of the United Nations, the nation of Indonesia has a moral and legal responsibility to respect, execute, and uphold the Universal Declaration on Human Rights promulgated by the United Nations'.[65]

Of course, there are more international human rights instruments that are ratified or acceded to by Indonesia. Those instruments include the Convention against Torture and Other Cruel, Inhuman or Degrading Treatment or Punishment 1985 (UNCAT) on 28 October 1998; Convention on the Elimination of All Forms of Discrimination against Women 1979 (CEDAW) on 13 September 1984; Convention on the Rights of the Child 1989 (CRC) on 5 September 1990; and Convention on the Rights of the Persons with Disabilities 2006 (CRPD) on 30 November 2011. As for an example of enactment (if not transformation or direct implementation) of these instruments into Indonesia's national laws, one can look at Law No. 8 of 2016 on Persons with Disabilities and Law No. 23 of 2002 on Child Protection (later amended by Law No. 35 of 2014). Additionally, Indonesia is in the process of drafting a Law on Elimination of Violence against Women.[66]

For further evidence of Indonesia's fulfilment of her international human rights obligations, one can look at the UN Human Rights Council's Universal Periodic Review (UPR), for which Indonesia submitted her national report in February 2017.[67] The report outlines Indonesia's progress in respecting the promotion and protection of human rights. Nonetheless, in her report, Indonesia emphasizes the importance of 'local context' in applying universal human rights standards in Indonesia.[68]

In the field of environmental law, Indonesia has ratified or acceded to some international legal instruments, including the UN Framework Convention on Climate Change 1992 (UNFCCC) and Convention on the International Trade in Endangered Species of Wild Flora and Fauna 1973 (CITES). On the latter, there was an extensive study in 2015, from the Indonesia Program of the Wildlife Conservation Society (WCS) and the United States Agency for International Development (USAID), that assessed CITES implementation in Indonesia.[69] In general, the study found that implementation of CITES in Indonesia needs improvement and, regarding laws or legislation, such improvements should take into account non-native species under CITES and develop better 'preventative measures' to prevent illegal trade of wildlife.[70]

[65] An English version of Law No. 39 of 1999 is available at <http://www.ilo.org/dyn/natlex/docs/ELECTRONIC/55808/105633/F1716745068/IDN55808%20Eng.pdf> accessed 30 October 2018.

[66] The draft Law on Elimination of Violence against Women is available at <http://www.dpr.go.id/doksileg/proses2/RJ2-20170201-043128-3029.pdf> accessed 17 May 2018.

[67] UN Human Rights Council, National Report submitted in accordance with paragraph 5 of the Annex to Human Rights Council Resolution 16/21: Indonesia, A/HRC/WG.6/27/IDN/1, 20 February 2017.

[68] Ibid. 22. Indonesia's UPR took place in May 2017: UN Human Rights Council, Report of the Working Group on the Universal Periodic Review: Indonesia, A/HRC/36/7, 14 July 2017.

[69] Indonesia Program of the Wildlife Conservation Society for USAID, 'Changes for Justice Project Wildlife Trade, Wildlife Crimes and Species Protection in Indonesia: Policy and Legal Context' (USAID, 6 March 2015) <http://pdf.usaid.gov/pdf_docs/PA00KH4Z.pdf> accessed 21 March 2018.

[70] Ibid. 39.

As for direct implementation of regulations, Law No. 5 of 1990 on Conservation of Living Resources and their Ecosystems is, as the WCS and USAID reported, 'the principal legislation for CITES Implementation'.[71] Besides, there are the Government Regulation No. 7 of 1999 on Preservation of Animal and Plant Species and Government Regulation No. 8 of 1999 on the Utilization of Wild Plant and Animal Species, which more practically implement Law No. 5 of 1990.

For climate change, the First Nationally Determined Contribution in 2016, prepared by the Indonesian government, stipulates that the 'Indonesian Environmental Protection and Management Law of 2009 secure the legal framework to support 2015–2019 strategies and actions, which would serve as enabling conditions for a long-term policy of 2020 and beyond'.[72] From this statement, one can consider that Law No. 32 of 2009 on Environmental Protection and Management is a further elaboration of Indonesia's obligations and commitments on the climate change issue.

In the field of international trade, one can look at the issue of intellectual property rights. Indonesia ratified TRIPS,[73] enacted domestic legislation, namely Law No. 30 of 2000 on Trade Secrets, Law No. 31 of 2000 on Industrial Designs, and amended the Law on Patents, Law on Trademarks, and Law on Copyright. Nevertheless, these changes bring problems for Indonesia. On the one hand, it is quite difficult for Indonesia to adequately enforce these laws as the Indonesian government lacks enforcement capacity. On the other hand, Indonesia herself might not be that compatible with these laws because, as Simon Butt points out, 'many features of Indonesia's economic, social, cultural and legal order appear to contradict fundamental precepts of intellectual property'.[74]

Based on the explanation above, from the ratification or accession to international legal instruments in the three areas of human rights, environmental law, and international trade (particularly intellectual property), it can be seen that there are different trends among those areas. On human rights, Indonesian law is more welcoming of the instruments. Although it is unclear in the implementing regulations, the international human rights instruments such as ICCPR and ICESCR can be traced even into the Constitutional Court of Indonesia. As for environmental law, especially the issues of climate change and wildlife, the implementing regulations and explicit commitments of the Indonesian government are apparent, for example, in Indonesia's First Nationally Determined Contribution in 2016.

Then, on intellectual property rights, the issue is complicated as the existing implementing regulations of TRIPS do not guarantee the welcoming of such regulations in

[71] Ibid. 17.

[72] The document is available at <http://www4.unfccc.int/ndcregistry/PublishedDocuments/Indonesia%20First/First%20NDC%20Indonesia_submitted%20to%20UNFCCC%20Set_November%20%202016.pdf> accessed 21 March 2018.

[73] An overall profile of Indonesia and the World Trade Organization (WTO) can be found at <http://www.wto.org/english/tratop_e/tpr_e/tp378_e.htm> accessed 30 October 2018.

[74] See Simon Butt, 'Intellectual Property in Indonesia: A Problematic Legal Transplant' in Tim Lindsey (ed), *Indonesia: Law and Society* (Federation Press 2008) 620.

Indonesia. The reason for this is twofold. On the one hand, the Indonesian government lacks enforcement mechanisms. On the other hand, the substance of the regulations does not fit in with the Indonesian context. Despite this trend, the fact that the Indonesian government ratifies and/or accedes to the international legal instruments and, at the very least, that the Indonesian government attempts to make such instruments relevant in Indonesia's domestic law, should be considered as part of Indonesia's contribution to the development of international law.

4.2 What is the Place of International Law?

One may start with article 11(2) of the 1945 Constitution in finding out what place international law holds within Indonesia's national legal system. Article 11(2) states:

The President in making other international agreements that will produce an extensive and fundamental impact on the lives of the people which is linked to the state financial burden, and/or that will require an amendment to or the enactment of a law, shall obtain the approval of the House of Representatives.

While the provision empowers the president, alongside the House of Representatives, to bind Indonesia to international legal instruments,[75] there is not yet a consensus on how to interpret this provision, or on what the right interpretation of it should be.[76] Further elaboration of article 11 of the 1945 Constitution is contained in Law No. 24 of 2000 on International Agreements.[77] In general, Law No. 24 of 2000 further regulates the details of the procedures for the Indonesian government when it wants to bind Indonesia to international agreements, for example whether the ratification or accession will be done in the form of Law (*Undang-Undang*) or Presidential Regulation (*Peraturan Presiden*).[78]

The next issue is how to implement the ratified or acceded international legal instruments at the national level. There are at least two mainstream answers. One

[75] Of course, the next question will be 'To what extent does the House of Representative have roles in the ratification or accession process of Indonesia?' Nevertheless, this chapter will not delve into this as literature on constitutional law in Indonesia would be a better setting to discuss that at length. There is a recent (as of March 2018) constitutional review before the Constitutional Court that focuses on the role of the House of Representatives in the process of ratification or accession of Indonesia to international agreements. See Case No. 13/PUU-XVI/2018 <http://www.mahkamahkonstitusi.go.id/index.php?page=web.Berita&id=14363#.WrH385NubsE> accessed 21 March 2018.

[76] The debate on this issue emerged especially during the constitutional review of Law No. 38 of 2008 on the Ratification of the ASEAN Charter. The ruling of the Constitutional Court of Indonesia on this is available at <http://www.mahkamahkonstitusi.go.id/public/content/persidangan/putusan/putusan_sidang_33%20PUU%202011_ASEANcharter_telah_baca_26Feb2013%20final.pdf> accessed 21 March 2018.

[77] The Indonesian-language version of Law No. 24 of 2000 [Undang-Undang Nomor 24 Tahun 2000 tentang Perjanjian Internasional] is available at <https://pih.kemlu.go.id/files/uu0242000.pdf> accessed 24 April 2019.

[78] See Law No. 24 of 2000, arts 10 and 11 (art. 11 still calls it a Presidential Decree [Keputusan Presiden]).

approach is that the instrument must first be transformed into national law and that then, once the transformation is complete, one can start talking about the fulfilment of Indonesia's international obligations. The second answer is that the transformation of the international legal instrument is not required because, at the time the instrument is ratified or acceded to, the obligation on Indonesia to observe the instrument is already there; as such, Indonesia is automatically bound by the obligations. Which approach to take relates to the issue of whether Indonesia is a monist or dualist country. Kusumaatmadja and Agoes argue that Indonesia acknowledges her obligations under international legal instruments without waiting for regulations implementing those instruments.[79] Nevertheless, there is not yet a consensus among Indonesian international law scholars on this matter.[80]

For further research on this issue, one can peruse two significant cases before the Constitutional Court of Indonesia that sparked the debate about the place of international law in Indonesia's legal system. The first is the constitutional review of Law No. 38 of 2008 on the Ratification of the ASEAN Charter. One of the contested issues in this case was the petitioners' argument that the ASEAN Charter, as an attachment to Law No. 38 of 2008, is inseparable from the Law itself and, as such, it is justifiable to review the constitutionality of the ASEAN Charter.[81] However, regarding this argument, the question was then 'is challenging Law No. 38 of 2008 equal to challenging the ASEAN Charter?' The judges of the Constitutional Court did not reach consensus in their attempt to answer this question, as Judge Hamdan Zoelva issued a dissenting opinion. He asserted that the Law is only a model of 'consent to be bound by a treaty'.[82] Therefore, one cannot challenge the constitutionality of the ASEAN Charter through Law No. 38 of 2008.

The second case, Case No. 13/PUU-XVI/2018, is about the role of Indonesia's national House of Representatives in the ratification of international legal instruments.[83] The petitioners' main argument is that Indonesia's national House of Representatives should be more involved in the ratification process of international legal instruments;

[79] Mochtar Kusumaatmadja and Etty R Agoes, *Pengantar Hukum Internasional [Introduction to International Law]* (Center for the Study of the Archipelago, Law and Development and PT Publisher 2003).

[80] Simon Butt succinctly summarizes the various stances on this matter: see Simon Butt, 'The Position of International Law within the Indonesian Legal System' (2014) 28 Emory International Law Review 1. See also Damos Dumoli Agusman, 'Indonesia dan Hukum Internasional: Dinamika Posisi Indonesia terhadap Hukum Internasional' ['Indonesia and International Law: The Dynamics of Indonesia's Position on International Law'] (2014) 15 Jurnal Opinio Juris 8 <http://pustakahpi.kemlu.go.id/app/Indonesia%20dan%20Hukum%20Internasional%20Dinamika%20Posisi%20Indonesia%20terhadap%20Hukum%20Internasional.pdf> accessed 21 March 2018.

[81] The document on this review is available at <http://www.mahkamahkonstitusi.go.id/public/content/persidangan/putusan/putusan_sidang_33%20PUU%202011_ASEANcharter_telah_baca_26Feb2013%20final.pdf> accessed 17 May 2018.

[82] Ibid. 200.

[83] Documents related to the case are available in the Indonesian language at <http://igj.or.id/wp-content/uploads/2018/12/13_PUU-XVI_2018.pdf> accessed 24 January 2019.

'more' in the sense that the House of Representatives should review all international legal instruments before Indonesia's ratification.

In general, the response from the Government of Indonesia has been that the involvement of the House of Representatives in ratification would make the process inefficient, since it would involve a lengthy bureaucratic process in the House of Representatives.[84] In the Court Session on 22 May 2018, Dr Damos Damoli Agusman (from the Ministry of Foreign Affairs of the Republic of Indonesia) asked this practicality-related question of the expert witness from the petitioners' side, Dr Boli Sabon Max (a constitutional law expert from Atma Jaya University, Jakarta): '[i]f Dr Max adopted the view that all agreements must go through the House of Representatives, how to anticipate the practical difficulties? That is, every year the Republic of Indonesia signed 200 documents per year'.[85] The Court finally decided the case in October 2018. In summary, the Court ruled that for certain agreements, the House of Representatives will be involved in the ratification process, namely agreements on political issues, territorial boundaries, sovereignty, human rights, the environment, the formulation of new legal rules, and foreign loans.[86]

To summarize, there is not yet a consensus, especially among Indonesian scholars, as to what the place of international law is in Indonesia's national legal system. The next section will elaborate further on the place of international law in Indonesia's national courts.

4.3 International Law before Indonesia's National Courts

This section will examine the two main national courts in Indonesia, namely the Constitutional Court of Indonesia and the District Court. The objective is to sketch out whether Indonesian courts use international legal instruments. Given the abundant cases in both the Constitutional Court and the District Courts, this section will only highlight specific case(s) on human rights and environmental law, since these themes were also the focus when discussing the ratification or accession practice of Indonesia.

Simon Butt, in 'The Position of International Law within the Indonesian Legal System', uses the *Landside case* of 2003 to explain the status of international law in

[84] Ibid.

[85] See the Court Transcript of 22 May 2018 (in Indonesian language), 15–16 <http://www.mahkamahkonstitusi.go.id/public/content/persidangan/risalah/risalah_sidang_10035_20180626090829_PERKARA%20NOMOR%2013.PUU-XVI.2018%2022%20MEI%202018%20.pdf> accessed 23 July 2018. The expert from the side of the President of the Republic of Indonesia, Hikmahanto Juwana, asserted in the Court Session on 22 June 2018 that there are alternatives for the involvement of Indonesian citizens through, among others: (a) civil society, (b) opinions in the mass media, and (c) focus group discussion sponsored by the relevant ministry. See the Court Transcript of 22 June 2018 (in Indonesian language), 46–7 <http://www.mahkamahkonstitusi.go.id/public/content/persidangan/risalah/risalah_sidang_10074_PERKARA%20NOMOR%2013.PUU-XVI.2018%20tgl%2025%20Juni%202018.pdf> accessed 23 July 2018.

[86] See documents related to the case (n 83), 266.

Indonesia's Supreme Court.[87] Simon Butt argues that the principle in Indonesian law which says that judges cannot reject a case just because there is no law could be a way for judges to apply international law.[88] Despite this possibility, it is common to hear that judges in the Supreme Court are reluctant to refer to international legal instruments simply because such instruments are international in nature and not national laws per se.

Besides the *Landside case*, there was a recent case in the District Court of Samarinda City in 2014.[89] The case involved a suit brought by citizens of Samarinda City, under the name of *Gerakan Samarinda Menggugat*, against the Ministry of Energy and Mineral Resources, Ministry of Environment, Governor of East Kalimantan, Mayor of Samarinda City, and People's Representatives Council of Samarinda City. The citizens complained about the irresponsibility of the national and local governments in failing to make corporations responsible, through laws and policies, for their conduct.[90] One argument was that the governments failed to fulfil their obligations to protect the environment, including those arising from Indonesia's ratification of the UNFCCC and Kyoto Protocol.[91] The judges in the District Court of Samarinda City did not, however, refer to the UNFCCC and Kyoto Protocol but relied on national laws, including Law No. 32 of 2009 on Environmental Protection and Management. Nonetheless, such reference by the petitioners is a vital sign that Indonesian citizens are aware of Indonesia's international obligations and use that awareness in court to push governments to fulfil their environmental protection obligations.

Regarding the issue of international law and the Constitutional Court of Indonesia, it has been fairly well discussed in the literature.[92] Both Simon Butt and Adriaan Bedner point out that the use of human rights instruments in the Constitutional Court is widespread, as the instruments are referred to in order to better explain the rights in the 1945 Constitution of Indonesia.[93] Nonetheless, the direct reference to international human rights instruments such as the ICCPR and ICESCR still matters, in the sense that it shows that international agreements may not need to be transformed formally into Indonesian Law (*Undang-Undang*) to be relevant at the domestic level. This view might sound like a simplification of the matter, as it is still uncertain as to what extent

[87] See Butt (n 80). [88] Ibid.

[89] Case No. 55 / Pdt. G / 2013 / PN.Smda. At the time of writing, the District Court of Samarinda has decided the case at the district level. It is essential to take this case into account as it relates to Indonesia's ratification of the UNFCCC and the obligations arising from it.

[90] The Ruling of the District Court of Samarinda City No. 55/Pdt.G/2013/PN.Smda, 2014. See also further discussion on this case in Yetty Komalasari Dewi and Anbar Jayadi, 'Enhancing Corporate Responsibilities to Fulfill the Right to Clean Environment: A Lesson Learned from Indonesia', International Union for the Conservation of Nature Academy of Environmental Law Conference Paper, Oslo, 24 June 2016.

[91] See the Ruling of the District Court of Samarinda City No. 55/Pdt.G/2013/PN.Smda, 2014, 25.

[92] See Butt (n 80); Adriaan Bedner, 'Indonesian Legal Scholarship and Jurisprudence as Obstacle for Transplanting Legal Institutions' (2013) 5 The Hague Journal on the Rule of Law 253 (Bedner points out the use of international legal instruments in the context of legal transplants).

[93] Butt (n 80); Bedner, ibid.

the courts (the Constitutional Court, the District Court, and Supreme Court) will position international law at the domestic level. Will international law matter more than just as a general reference point in the courts?

5 Indonesia and ASEAN

The Association of Southeast Asian Nations is a regional organization comprised of ten member states, including Indonesia.[94] ASEAN has a motto, 'One Vision, One Identity, One Community'.[95] This part will discuss ASEAN specifically as it pertains to Indonesia.

Indonesia herself played a significant role in establishing and developing ASEAN.[96] Firstly, Indonesia was one of its co-founders.[97] As such, Indonesia is considered one of the leading countries in ASEAN. Secondly, in many regional issues in ASEAN, such as migration and maritime issues, Indonesia is looked upon as 'the natural leader of the ASEAN'[98] to start the cooperation that will hopefully provide solutions for such issues.[99]

Furthermore, in a more specific field, one of Indonesia's roles in ASEAN is strengthening human rights protections.[100] For instance, as pointed out by Heiduk, it was Indonesia who ensured the establishment of a human rights commission under the ASEAN Charter[101]—the ASEAN Intergovernmental Commission on Human Rights (AICHR).[102] Other than drafting the ASEAN Human Rights Declaration, the AICHR also undertakes 'research, trainings, and workshops related to pertinent issues on human rights'.[103] Nevertheless, even though Indonesia contributes to the advancement

[94] The members are, in alphabetical order, Brunei Darussalam, Cambodia, Indonesia, Lao PDR, Malaysia, Myanmar, Philippines, Singapore, Thailand, and Viet Nam: 'ASEAN Member States', <http://asean.org/asean/asean-member-states/> accessed 23 July 2018.

[95] ASEAN, 'ASEAN Motto' <http://asean.org/asean/about-asean/asean-motto/> accessed 23 July 2018.

[96] See further Adijaya Yusuf, *Association of South East Asian Nations (ASEAN)* (Kluwer Law International 2001).

[97] Other co-founders are Malaysia, Philippines, Singapore, and Thailand. See ASEAN, 'About ASEAN' <http://asean.org/asean/about-asean/> accessed 23 July 2018.

[98] See Ralf Emmers, 'Indonesia's Role in ASEAN: A Case of Incomplete and Sectorial Leadership' (2014) 27 The Pacific Review 543.

[99] See for example Hikmahanto Juwana, 'Kewajiban ASEAN Melindungi Myanmar' ['ASEAN Obligations to Protect in Mynamar'] *Kompas* (14 September 2017) <https://kompas.id/baca/opini/2017/09/14/kewajiban-asean-melindungi-myanmar/> accessed 5 November 2017.

[100] See Felix Heiduk, 'Indonesia in ASEAN: Regional Leadership between Ambition and Ambiguity', SWP [German Institute for International and Security Affairs] Research Paper No. 6, April 2016, 12 <http://www.swp-berlin.org/fileadmin/contents/products/research_papers/2016RP06_hdk.pdf> accessed 23 July 2018.

[101] Ibid.

[102] ASEAN Intergovernmental Commission on Human Rights website <http://aichr.org/about/> accessed 29 January 2019.

[103] Ibid.

of human rights at the ASEAN level, ASEAN itself as an intergovernmental body is not always successful in protecting and fulfilling human rights in the ASEAN region. One recent example is the issue of Rohingya people in Myanmar, whom experts called upon ASEAN to protect.[104] The ASEAN Chairman condemned the crisis in Myanmar in a Statement on the Humanitarian Situation in Rakhine State.[105] However, this statement has been criticized for not explicitly addressing the 'Rohingya' and some have expressed disappointment towards ASEAN because of this.

Aside from human rights, Indonesia also plays a part in shaping ASEAN–European Union (EU) trade relations. As addressed in the 16th ASEAN Economic Ministers-EU Trade Commissioner Consultation, Indonesia's Trade Minister stated that Indonesia's desired outcomes include the benefits of a free trade agreement (FTA) for Indonesia's small and medium-sized enterprises (SMEs).[106]

For all Indonesia's roles, Indonesia herself has also benefited from the existence of ASEAN through the opening of opportunities such as food security, environmental protection, and the internationalization of higher education. ASEAN itself and ASEAN-level cooperation contribute to such openness. For instance, Dilip Dutta and Fajar Hirawan identify that Indonesia–ASEAN trade opens the possibility for Indonesia to achieve her own food security.[107] Another example is in the field of the environment, where the ASEAN Agreement on Transboundary Haze 2002 became the push for Indonesia to tackle haze pollution that is not only harmful to Indonesian citizens but also to citizens of neighbouring countries such as Malaysia and Singapore.[108]

Moreover, ASEAN membership is another exciting topic in observing the relationship between Indonesia and ASEAN. One might want to look at the extent to which Indonesia plays a role in decision-making about Timor-Leste's membership of ASEAN. Indonesia's Foreign Minister Retno Marsudi stated at the beginning of 2018 that Indonesia always supports Timor-Leste's application.[109] Another membership issue is about the offer from Indonesian President Jokowi that he welcomes Australia to be a new member of ASEAN.[110] Despite this welcoming remark,

[104] Juwana (n 99).

[105] The ASEAN Chairman's Statement is available at <http://asean.org/storage/2017/09/1.ASEAN-Chairmans-Statement-on-the-Rakhine.pdf> accessed 22 March 2018.

[106] 'Indonesia pins hope on ASEAN-EU FTA to support SMEs, palm oil' *The Jakarta Post* (25 March 2018) <http://www.thejakartapost.com/news/2018/03/25/indonesia-pins-hope-on-asean-eu-fta-to-support-smes-palm-oil.html> accessed 17 May 2018.

[107] Dilip Dutta and Fajar Hirawan, 'The Role of Indonesia-ASEAN Trade in Achieving Food Security in Indonesia', The University of Sydney Economics Working Paper Series 2017–13, November 2017, <http://econ-wpseries.com/2017/201713.pdf> accessed 17 May 2018.

[108] See Kexian Ng, 'Transboundary Haze Pollution in Southeast Asia: The Effectiveness of Three Forms of International Legal Solutions' (2017) 10 Journal of East Asia and International Law 221.

[109] 'Menlu Sebut RI selalu Dukung Timor Leste Jadi Anggota ASEAN' ['Foreign Minister Said Indonesia Always Support Timor Leste to be ASEAN Member'] (CNN Indonesia, 31 January 2018) <http://www.cnnindonesia.com/internasional/20180131132539-106-272896/menlu-sebut-ri-selalu-dukung-timor-leste-jadi-anggota-asean> accessed 17 May 2018.

[110] See for example 'Ajakan Jokowi agar Australia Gabung ASEAN Dinilai Sulit Terwujud' ['Jokowi's invitation for Australia to join ASEAN is considered difficult to materialize'] *Kompas* (19 March 2018)

as Juwana points out, it might not be that easy as the membership needs approval from other ASEAN members.[111]

Concerning the internationalization of higher education, Indonesia benefits from ASEAN in at least in two ways. Firstly, Indonesian students are exposed to chances to study abroad at the ASEAN-level as the ASEAN University Network allows them to do so. Secondly, the discussion about international law in Indonesia includes the development of ASEAN itself, not only as a regional and intergovernmental organization but also in terms of the legal frameworks produced by ASEAN. This way, Indonesian students, particularly those specializing in international law, are enriched with knowledge about ASEAN and its legal frameworks.[112]

To briefly review, Indonesia and ASEAN benefit from each other. Indonesia played roles in both the establishment and development of ASEAN, while it continues to gain some advantages from it.

6 Conclusion

This chapter has discussed three main topics about Indonesia and international law: firstly, Indonesia and the politics of international law-making; secondly, the (unresolved) relationship between international law and Indonesian national law; and thirdly, the relationship between Indonesia and ASEAN. In addition, throughout the chapter, other relevant questions on Indonesia and international law are laid out.

Since her establishment as a state, alongside the formation of the Indonesian government, the nation of Indonesia has committed herself to participate on the international stage, as shown in paragraph 4 of the Preamble of the 1945 Constitution. The cementation of this is that Indonesia has been involved in international law-making in the sense of (i) contributing something to it, such as the notion of archipelagic states and through the Bandung Conference; and (ii) participating in it by means of the ratification of international legal instruments such as the ICCPR and CEDAW.

Despite this, there is an unresolved relationship between international law and Indonesia's national law: to transform or not to transform? However, the practice of taking international legal instruments into account is there, particularly in the Constitutional Court. While the judges in the Supreme Court are somewhat reluctant to refer

<https://nasional.kompas.com/read/2018/03/19/10144871/ajakan-jokowi-agar-australia-gabung-asean-dinilai-sulit-terwujud> accessed 17 May 2018.

[111] Ibid.

[112] See generally on legal education in Indonesia and its changes, Hikmahanto Juwana, 'Legal Education Reform in Indonesia' <http://www.aseanlawassociation.org/Hikmahanto_Juwana.pdf> accessed 23 July 2018.

to international legal instruments, there are examples, such as in Samarinda City, where citizens have used international principles when arguing before the District Court. This is a sign of citizens' awareness about international law.

As for Indonesia and ASEAN, the relationship is likely to be mutual. While Indonesia plays roles in developing ASEAN, ASEAN itself contributes to developments within Indonesia, such as in the fields of food security, trade, and the internationalization of higher education.

CHAPTER 17

THE PHILIPPINES

ROMEL REGALADO BAGARES

1 Introduction

At the international level, Spain acquired dominion over the Philippines on a claim of discovery in the sixteenth century, establishing a permanent settlement in what is now the city of Cebu in 1565.[1] The sinking of the United States battleship *USS Maine* in Havana, Cuba on 15 February 1898 presaged the end of over three hundred years of Spanish colonial reign in the Philippines.[2]

When US Commodore George Dewey's modern armada defeated the antiquated Spanish flotilla in Manila Bay on 1 May 1898, the laws in force over the islands were the Spanish Civil Code of 1889, the *Enjuiciamiento* Civil of 1888, the Penal Code of 1887, the *Ley de Enjuiciamiento Criminal* of 1888, the Code of Commerce of 1888, the Mortgage Law of 1889, and the Law of Waters of 1866, as well as a host of Spanish decrees.[3]

Following its cession by Spain under the terms of the Treaty of Paris 1899 (TOP) to the US, in exchange for US$20 million,[4] the Philippines became an 'unincorporated' US territory,[5] complete with a US-style legal system that combined a Spanish civil law heritage with Anglo-American common law—a 'mestizo'[6] legal system. In 1917, at the height of World War I, an American-controlled Philippine Supreme Court made its first ruling involving a question of international law, citing mostly Anglo-American sources. It held that customary international law did not support 'days of grace' and 'safe-conducts' granted to merchant vessels of an enemy lying in the ports of a belligerent at the commencement of hostilities.[7]

[1] Teodoro Agoncillo, *History of the Filipino People* (Malaya Books 1967) 83.

[2] Pacifico Agabin, *Mestizo: The Story of the Philippine Legal System* (University of the Philippines Law Center [hereafter UP Law Center] 2011) 169–70.

[3] H Lawrence Noble, 'Development of Law and Jurisprudence in the Philippines' (1922) 8 American Bar Association Law Journal 226.

[4] [1899] USS Doc No. 55–63, pt 2, 3–11. Signed on 10 December 1898, it took effect on 11 April 1899.

[5] Agabin (n 2) 172.

[6] Ibid. 169–216.

[7] *Compagnie de Commerce v Hamburg Amerika* [1917] GR No L-10986 [En Banc] 31 March 1917.

In 1920, the Philippine Supreme Court held[8] that the country had by then developed a Philippine common law based almost exclusively on Anglo-American common law, 'except where conflicting with local customs and institutions'.[9] It also affirmed that the islands were an unincorporated territory of the US, thus also confirming the validity of the TOP two decades after its signing.[10]

In 1928, the Philippines was ushered into modern international law by the Swiss arbitrator Max Huber in the *Las Palmas* arbitration, where the US tried to claim Miangas island as part of the title ceded to it by Spain through the TOP. The island—known as Las Palmas to Spain—lay within the boundaries of the TOP, between Southern Philippines and what was then the Dutch East Indies colony (now Indonesia). Ruling that inchoate title must ripen into legal title through effective occupation, Huber ruled for the Netherlands, then Indonesia's colonial master.[11]

US rule over the Philippines was interrupted by the Japanese occupation in World War II (1942–5), a period that also gave birth to landmark jurisprudence on the laws of war and international criminal law.[12] On 4 July 1946, the US formally granted independence to the Philippines. The Philippines—one of the original signatories to the Universal Declaration of Human Rights 1948 (UDHR)[13]—was among the newly decolonized states that pushed the UN to adopt implementation mechanisms for the International Bill of Human Rights.[14]

In 2016, the Philippines won a landmark ruling in its arbitral case before the Permanent Court of Arbitration (PCA) against China over disputed maritime areas in the South China Sea, under the UN Convention on the Law of the Sea 1982 (UNCLOS).[15] Among other important findings, the PCA held that China's Nine Dash Line claim was

[8] *In Re Shoop* [1920] GR No L-15895 [En Banc] 29 November 1920; 41 Phil Rep 213, 29 November 1920.

[9] Ibid. 247; Footnote 1, item 11 of *In Re Shoop* (ibid. 256) cited *Compagnie de Commerce v Hamburg Amerika* (n 7), providing proof of the Philippine embrace of Anglo-American common law.

[10] *In Re Shoop* (n 8) 216–17.

[11] *Island of Palmas* [or *Miangas*] (*United States v Netherlands*) (Award) [1928] II RIAA 829, ICGJ 392 (PCA 1928), 4 April 1928, Permanent Court of Arbitration [PCA].

[12] The Supreme Court handed down at least 30 landmark rulings from war crimes trials involving Japanese officers and their Filipino collaborators during the war. From 1945 to 1947, American-run military courts tried war criminals in over a hundred prosecutions that resulted in a 90 per cent conviction rate and 69 executions, including those of generals Yamashita Tomoyuki and Homma Masaharu. Under a National War Crimes Office (August 1947–December 1949), Filipino courts convicted 138 Japanese soldiers and civilians out of 155 total arraigned accused, sentencing some 79 of them to death. Forty seven executions were carried out in 1948 and over two years later, in January 1951, another 14 were suddenly put to death. See Konrad Lawson, 'Universal Crime, Particular Punishment: Trying the Atrocities of the Japanese Occupation as Treason in the Philippines, 1947–1953' (2013) 23 Zeitschrift für Globalgeschichte und vergleichende Gesellschaftsforschung 57.

[13] Universal Declaration of Human Rights (UDHR), UNGA res 217 A (III) (10 December 1948). The Philippines was one of the original states to adopt it.

[14] Steven Jensen, 'How the Global South Shaped the International Human Rights System' (Universal Rights Group, 16 March 2016) <http://www.universal-rights.org/blog/how-the-global-south-shaped-the-international-human-rights-system> accessed 9 September 2018.

[15] UN Convention on the Law of the Sea (adopted 10 December 1982, entered into force 16 November 1994, 1833 UNTS 397).

superseded, as mere historic claim to title, by China's subsequent obligations under UNCLOS.[16]

Any discussion on contemporary Philippine practice of international law has been largely limited to the contrasting roles played by the 'Incorporation Clause' and the 'Treaty Clause' of the successive constitutions.[17] In this chapter, I expand the discussion to the wider avenue of what I call 'entry points' in the Philippine constitutional and legal firmament. Here I correlate Professor André Nollkaemper's theory of the dual direct effect of international law[18] with the dualist approach identified with Professor Merlin M Magallona, former Dean of the University of the Philippines College of Law and the country's foremost scholar of the Philippine practice of international law.[19]

Section 2 discusses the monist and dualist tendencies exhibited by the Incorporation Clause and the Treaty Clause of the 1987 Charter, which are the primary entry points of international law in Philippine jurisdiction. I take note here of the paradoxical phenomenon of the supposedly dualist device of treaties opening a quasi-monist door to international legal obligations in the form of executive agreements that do not require the concurrence of the Senate but become binding on the Philippines by Executive imprimatur. Moreover, as quasi-monist devices, executive agreements function both as a sword, giving direct effect to international law—especially in the protection of rights—and as a shield, raising barriers to public or international accountability according to political considerations.

Sections 3 to 6 outline four other entry points for international law in Philippine practice: direct effect by the Supreme Court's rule-making powers, constitutionalization, international law in the State of Exception, and statutory application. These entry points are often glossed over in available literature, or are otherwise unrecognized for what they are able to actually do. Yet they exhibit the tensions, conflations, and paradoxes of constitutional adjudication of international legal questions in Philippine courts.

Section 7 concludes the chapter with a discussion on the implications to international law in Philippine practice of the rise to power of President Rodrigo Roa Duterte,

[16] *In re Arbitration Between the Republic of the Philippines and the People's Republic of China*, PCA Case No. 2013–19, Award (12 July 2016). A separate ruling on jurisdictional issues was also handed down by the tribunal ahead of the merits ruling: *In re Arbitration Between the Republic of the Philippines and the People's Republic of China*, PCA Case No. 2013–19, Jurisdiction and Admissibility (29 October 2015).

[17] Merlin Magallona, *The Supreme Court and International Law: Problems and Approaches in Philippine Practice* (UP Law Center 2010); Merlin Magallona, *The Philippine Constitution and International Law* (UP Law Center 2013); Merlin Magallona, *A Primer in International Law in Relation to International Law* (UP Law Center 1997); Aloysius P Llamzon, 'The Generally Accepted Principles of International Law as Philippine Law: Towards A Structurally Consistent Use of Customary International Law in Philippine Courts' (2002) 47 Ateneo Law Journal 249.

[18] André Nollkaemper, 'The Duality of Direct Effect of International Law' (2014) 25 EJIL 105.

[19] A Filipino legal scholar who has, more than any other, written a sustained critique of the Philippine practice of international law, with nearly 40 authored or co-edited books, in an academic career spanning at least half a century.

a populist leader with an undisguised disdain for constitutional and international rules that protect the civil and political rights of citizens.

2 Monist and Dualist Tendencies and Entry Points

The dualist tendency in the Philippine practice of international law is found in section 21, article VII of the 1987 Charter, which encapsulates what has been called the 'Doctrine of Transformation'[20] in Philippine law, which states that: 'No treaty or international agreement shall be valid and effective unless concurred in by at least two-thirds of all the Members of the Senate'.

Thus, international law becomes part of Philippine law by legislative concurrence; in this case, the Senate, which has been charged by the 1987 Charter as the competent organ of the legislature with such a duty. The monist tendency is embodied in section 2, article II of the Charter (in the chapter dealing with its Declaration of Principles and State Policies):

> The Philippines renounces war as an instrument of national policy, adopts the generally accepted principles of international law as part of the law of the land and adheres to the policy of peace, equality, justice, freedom, cooperation, and amity with all nations.[21]

2.1 The Incorporation Clause and the Treaty Clause: The Dual Sword and Shield Functions

Roughly, these two correspond to what Professor Nollkaemper calls the dual 'sword' and 'shield' function, respectively, of the 'doctrine of direct effect of international law'.[22] As Professor Nollkaemper explains regarding this duality of the direct effect of international law:

> Direct effect may function as a powerful sword that courts can use to pierce the boundary of the national legal order and protect individual rights where national law falls short. But more often than not, the conditions of direct effect legitimize the

[20] Magallona, *The Supreme Court* (n 17).

[21] A nearly identical provision is found in the 1935 and 1973 Constitutions. The 1935 Constitution, drawn up during the American Commonwealth era, drew from German, Spanish, and other continental sources for the Incorporation Clause, a marked departure from the overwhelmingly American influence on the document. See Llamzon (n 17) 258–60. The Supreme Court has given conflicting interpretations of this article of the constitution.

[22] Nollkaemper (n 18) 105.

> non-application of international law and shield the national legal order from international law. International law provides support for both functions. But above all, it defers the choice between these functions to national courts. The practice of direct effect of international law exposes how national courts play a critical political function at the intersection of legal orders.[23]

But in writing of tendencies, rather than of antipodes, I diverge in part from the view of Professor Magallona, who has characterized Philippine practice around these two provisions as 'dualist'. Professor Magallona posits a two-step process of the internalization of international law in the domestic sphere via the Incorporation Clause and the Treaty Clause, the first being 'comprised of the power of judicial review by which courts may determine the constitutionality'[24] of such 'generally accepted principles of international law', and the second being that of the clause functioning as a gateway for international law through legislative fiat, principally by Senate concurrence.[25]

Thus, he distinguishes between 'objective international law' in the international sphere, and 'the Philippine practice of international law'[26]—as internalized and made part of national law.

The Incorporation Clause does not make its adopted principles of international law self-executing, because they must be individualized and identified by judicial determination.[27] The task of courts confronting questions of the constitutionality of a treaty is not to sit as an international tribunal confronting before it a case involving objective international law. It is not supposed to subordinate the constitution to treaty obligations, but, rather, tackle the issue as a question of constitutionality, that is, whether the treaty brought before it is consistent with or contravenes the constitution.[28]

I follow Professor Magallona's theory of the court's adjudicative role, but I do not share his view that its exercise makes this feature of the Philippine constitution dualist. Rather, I argue that the Incorporation Clause exhibits monist tendencies, because by its operation through judicial fiat, international law is adopted into Philippine law without an implementing law. In this sense, the principles are self-executing, or, in the words of Professor Nollkaemper, it is here where a court protects an international right '*as such*' and 'without being dependent on prior or subsequent legislation pertaining to that particular right'.[29]

Moreover, to speak of tendencies is also to recognize that the categories are not exclusive. The supposedly dualist Treaty Clause itself has inaugurated a class of international obligations that paradoxically exhibit monist tendencies or features—as in the case of executive agreements. By jurisprudential nuance, such quasi-monist

[23] Ibid. 105–6; further: 'The doctrine was first enunciated in the European context in the *Van Gend en Loos v Nederlandse Administratie der Belastingen* [1963] Case 26/62 [Full Court] 5 February 1963, decided by the European Court of Justice'.

[24] Magallona, *The Philippine Constitution* (n 17) 65. [25] Ibid. [26] Ibid. 22.

[27] Ibid. 22. [28] Ibid. 21. [29] Nollkaemper (n 18) 110.

devices may sometimes also function both as a sword, as they give direct effect to international law, and as a shield, as they raise barriers to exacting public or international accountability, pursuant to certain foreign policy prerogatives. The entry points may open and close, as the court so rules.

I agree with Professor Magallona that the failure of the Supreme Court to properly distinguish between these two spheres of international law—as well as between the function of the Incorporation Clause and the Treaty Clause—has led to a 'crisis' in the law of treaties in jurisprudence, as the Supreme Court has all too often confused (a) the nature of treaty obligations and that arising from generally accepted principles of international law referred to in the Incorporation Clause,[30] and (b) the task of adjudication of a national court and that of an international court or tribunal in relation to international legal questions.

2.2 The Self-Executing Sword of Philippine Precedents for International Humanitarian Law and International Human Rights Law under the Incorporation Clause

Three cases dealing with the application of the Incorporation Clause from the Philippine experience in World War II illustrate the duality of international law as recognized early on in Philippine jurisprudence.

Go Kim Cham v Valdez[31] involved the question of the validity of a judgment in a civil case rendered by a civilian court during the Japanese occupation from 1942 to 1945. Ruling in the affirmative, the Supreme Court said that under the international law on occupation, 'the proceedings of the legislative, executive, and judicial departments of a *de facto* government are good and valid'[32] and those judicial acts and proceedings that are not political in nature, 'remained good and valid' even after liberation, by the principle of *postliminium* in international law,[33] insofar as 'the belligerent occupant has the right and is burdened with the duty to ensure public order and safety during his military occupation'. Thus, it held, citing section III of The Hague Conventions of 1899 and of 1907[34] and 'the principles of international law, as they result from the usages established between civilized nations, the laws of humanity and the requirements of the public of conscience'.[35]

These treaty provisions and principles of international law were incorporated via section 3, article II of the 1935 Constitution, which provides that '[t]he Philippines renounces war as an instrument of national policy, and adopts the generally accepted principles of international law as part of the law of the Nations'.[36] But the judgment

[30] Magallona, *The Supreme Court* (n 17) 5.

[31] [1945] GR No L-5 (En Banc) 17 September 1945; 75 Phil Reports 113 [1945].

[32] Ibid. 130. [33] Ibid. 131. [34] Ibid. 124. [35] Ibid. 136. [36] Ibid.

in *Go Kim Cham*,[37] although it was the first such case to speak of the duality of international law—of treaty law also restating what is customary international law—is not as well known as the next two cases, which addressed the question of legality and involved key figures of the Japanese occupation army in the Philippines.

Yamashita v Styer[38] involved the war crimes trial of Tomoyuki Yamashita, the Commanding General of the Japanese Imperial Army in the Philippines during World War II. The Japanese general had objected to the trial on due process grounds, as he was being tried for crimes alleged to have been committed under a treaty—the Hague Conventions of 1899 and 1907—to which the Philippines was not a party.

The Supreme Court upheld the constitutionality of the Military Commission trying him, under the applicable laws of war as part of the law of nations.[39] The ruling is precedent to the principle that grave breaches of the Hague Conventions incur international individual criminal liability.

But it was the concurring and dissenting opinion of Mr Justice Perfecto that gave greater clarity to the proposition that a treaty may exhibit a dual nature, insofar as such a treaty may also embody customary international law.[40] His decidedly monist opinion may serve as Philippine precedent for the binding nature of international humanitarian law as customary, predating the holding of the International Court of Justice on the dual nature of international legal norms in the *North Sea Continental Shelf Case*[41] by at least twenty-three years. The state, by incorporation of Philippine courts, may simply adopt from other jurisdictions the applicable code of international crimes and penalties to try war crimes.[42]

Kuroda v Jalandoni, over the protestations of another ranking Japanese officer, held that even if the Philippines was not a party to the Hague and Geneva Conventions, it was still bound to their norms by virtue of the Incorporation Clause, under which the provisions of the treaties were considered part of the law of the land as 'generally accepted principles of international law'[43] binding on all states. The 1935 Constitution, 'has been deliberately general and extensive in its scope and is not confined to the recognition of rule and principle of international law as continued in treaties to which our government may have been or shall be a signatory'.[44]

[37] This was also affirmed in a criminal proceeding from the Japanese occupation, the case of *Alcantara v Director of Prisons* [1945] GR No L-6 [En Banc] 29 November 1945. See especially the concurring opinion of Mr Justice Joya: 75 Phil Reports 496–506; Joya at 497–594.

[38] [1945] GR No L-129 [En Banc] 19 December 1945; 75 Phil Reports 563–697 [1945].

[39] Ibid., citing *Ex parte Quirin* [1942] 317 US 1.

[40] *Yamashita* (n 38) 577–96.

[41] *North Sea Continental Shelf (Germany v Denmark)* (Order) [1968] ICJ Rep 9.

[42] *Yamashita* (n 38) 596. Taken on appeal to the US Supreme Court (as at that time the Philippines was still an American colony), the case gave birth to the precedent for the principle of command responsibility: *In Re Yamashita* [1946] 327 US 15–17.

[43] *Kuroda v Jalandoni* [1946] GR No L-2662 [En Banc] 26 March 1949; 83 Phil Reports 171–94 [1946].

[44] Ibid. 178.

2.3 The UDHR, the Incorporation Clause, and Jurisprudential Anomalies

In *Mejoff v Director of Prisons*,[45] the Supreme Court held that the unduly prolonged detention of an alleged Japanese spy of Russian descent—for nearly four years—violated the UDHR, whose provisions it deemed part of Philippine law as generally accepted principles of international law under the Incorporation Clause of the 1935 Constitution, in particular, 'the right to life and liberty and all other fundamental rights applied to all human beings'.[46] This is the very first case in Philippine jurisprudence holding that the UDHR is customary in nature (even as early as 1951) and exacts international legal obligations on the Philippines.[47]

Yet the Supreme Court has been rather heterogeneous in its appreciation of the distinction between these two entry points of international law—the Incorporation Clause and the Treaty Clause—in the constitution.

Agustin v Edu[48] confused the two entry points (and the sources of international law they are supposed to draw from) with each other, by saying that the assailed Vienna Convention on Road Signs and Signals 1968 is part of the generally accepted principles of international law referred to in the Incorporation Clause. Under the principle of *pacta sunt servanda*, it is binding on the Philippines. It would have sufficed to say that we are bound to follow the treaty as a party to it under the same principle. Besides, as Professor Magallona also notes, it has already been transformed as national law through the Treaty Clause, by Senate concurrence.[49]

Mijares v Rañada[50] clarifies what the phrase 'generally accepted principles of international law' as found in the Incorporation Clause means in Philippine law, holding that it embraces both customary norm and general principles of law. However, it also conflated one with the other, as it ruled that the procedure of foreign enforcement of judgments is part of the law of the land since it is customary in nature.[51]

2.4 Treaties in the Form of Executive Agreements: Shield and Sword

Philippine jurisprudence distinguishes between international agreements that are policy-making in nature (treaties) and those that merely carry out policy or pertain

[45] His first petition was denied in the case of the same name: [1949] GR No L-2855 [En Banc] 30 July 1949.

[46] [1951] GR No L-4254 [En Banc] 26 September 1951; 90 Phil Reports 71 [1951].

[47] Since then, a slew of cases has followed *Mejoff's* precedent. Just two days later, the Supreme Court invoked the UDHR in a similar case, *Borovsky v Commissioner* [1951] GR No L-4352 [En Banc] 28 September 1951.

[48] [1979] GR No L-49112 [En Banc] 2 February 1979; 88 SCRA 195 [1979].

[49] Magallona, *The Philippine Constitution* (n 17) 29.

[50] [2005] GR No 139325 [Second Division] 12 April 2005, 455 SCRA 397 [2005].

[51] Ibid. 421.

to details of national policy or matters that are temporary in nature (executive agreements). As the landmark 1961 case of *Commissioner of Customs v Eastern Trading* put it,

> International agreements involving political issues or changes of national policy and those involving international arrangements of a permanent character usually take the form of treaties. But international agreements embodying *adjustments of detail* carrying out well-established national policies and traditions and those involving arrangements of a more or less *temporary* nature usually take the form of executive agreements.[52]

The 1987 Charter follows the rule as it refers to a 'treaty' and an 'international agreement'. Executive Order 459 1997 states in section 2 that an international agreement is 'a contract or understanding, regardless of nomenclature, entered into between the Philippines and another government in written form and governed by international law, whether embodied in a single instrument or in two or more related instruments'. Treaties are international agreements—including compacts like conventions, declarations, covenants, and acts—'entered into by the Philippines [that] require legislative concurrence after executive ratification'.[53] Despite the difference in nomenclature, both are considered binding under Philippine law.

Here, the Treaty Clause, as gate-keeping shield, refuses entry of international law into Philippine law without Senate concurrence; but once a treaty is transformed into national law by concurrence, it can then open the door to a class of international obligations that pierces the national legal order as a sword would, in the form of executive agreements. In other words, the dualist device of the Treaty Clause paradoxically may become a quasi-monist door for other international obligations.

2.5 Treaties, Philippine-US Relations, and the Court's Critical Political Function

The fraught legal history of the Philippines as a former colony of the United States—and the controversial role often played by the Supreme Court in it[54]—is demonstrated in cases arising from its post-1946 continuing military alliance with a former colonizer.

[52] [1961] GR No L-14279 [En Banc] 31 October 1961; 3 SCRA 351, 356–357 [1961].

[53] The order also details the procedure for the entry of force of a treaty or an executive agreement in domestic jurisdiction. See J Eduardo Malaya and Maria Antonina Mendoza-Oblena, 'Philippine Treaty Law and Practice' (2010) 35 Integrated Bar of the Philippines Journal 1.

[54] Professor Magallona has also written a critical legal history of US military bases in the Philippines in his works. Merlin Magallona, *Legal Issues in the RP-US Visiting Forces Agreement* (UP Law Center 1998); Merlin Magallona, *Military Bases and Nuclear Weapons: US Neocolonialism in the Philippines* (UP Law Center 1991); Merlin Magallona, *US Marshall Plan for the Philippines: US Military Bases and Foreign Monopoly Capital* (NHRP 1989); Merlin Magallona, *A Brief Guide to Philippine Views on the US Bases* (Karrel 1986); Merlin Magallona, 'The New Bases Treaty: Political and Legal Issues' in *International Law Issues in Perspective* (UP Law Center 1996) 171–200.

In these cases, the critical political function of courts is evident, though largely used to reject expanded checks on the conduct of foreign relations by the Executive.

About a year after the Philippines was granted independence by the United States, on 14 March 1947 the two countries signed a Military Bases Agreement[55] governing the use by the US armed forces of the Clark Air Force Base and the Subic Naval Base.[56] On 30 August 1951 the two countries signed the Mutual Defense Treaty (MDT), agreeing to come to the aid of each other against any external armed attack on their territory, armed forces, public vessels, and aircraft.[57]

The Philippine Senate, in an historic vote on 16 September 1991, rejected the proposed Treaty of Friendship, Cooperation and Security between the two countries, which was intended to extend the presence of US military bases in the Philippines, pursuant to section 25, article XVIII of the 1987 Charter.[58] That provision states:

> Sec. 25. After the expiration in 1991 of the Agreement between the Republic of the Philippines and the United States of America concerning Military Bases, foreign military bases, troops or facilities shall not be allowed in the Philippines except under a treaty duly concurred in by the Senate and, when the Congress so requires, ratified by a majority of the votes cast by the people in a national referendum held for that purpose, and recognized as a treaty by the other contracting state.

On 10 February 1998, the Philippines and the United States of America signed a new Visiting Forces Agreement (VFA).[59] On 27 May 1999, the Philippine Senate concurred in the VFA.

A year later, the first legal challenge against the VFA was filed with the Supreme Court. In the consolidated case of *Bayan v Zamora*,[60] petitioners questioned its constitutionality, saying that while the VFA was indeed concurred in by the Philippine Senate under the Treaty Clause of the constitution, the United States treated it merely as an executive agreement, as the American side did not submit it to the US Congress in a similar manner.[61] Thus, the VFA failed to comply with section 25, article XVIII of the 1987 Charter.[62] The Philippine Supreme Court, saying that the words in the constitution are to be understood in their ordinary meaning, held that the phrase 'recognized as a treaty' in section 25, article XVIII of the constitution 'means that the other contracting party *accepts or acknowledges* the agreement as a treaty'.[63] It is

[55] Agreement between the Republic of the Philippines and the United States of America Concerning Military Bases (adopted 14 March 1947, entered into force 26 March 1947, 43 UNTS 271).

[56] *Bayan v Zamora* [2000] GR No 13857, GR No 138572, GR No 138587, GR No 138698 [En Banc] 10 October 2000; 342 SCRA 449 [2000].

[57] Ibid. 464; Mutual Defense Treaty between the Republic of the Philippines and the United States of America (adopted 30 August 1951, entered into force 27 August 1951, 177 UNTS 133).

[58] *Bayan v Zamora*, ibid. 464.

[59] Ibid. 465; Agreement Between the Government of the Republic of the Philippines and the Government of the United States of America Regarding the Treatment of United States Armed Forces Visiting the Philippines (adopted 10 February 1998, entered into force 1 June 1999, TIAS 12931).

[60] *Bayan v Zamora*, ibid. 465. [61] Ibid. 465. [62] Ibid. 487–8.

[63] Ibid. 488.

enough that the American side has given assurances that the VFA has the force and effect of a treaty in American law because, anyway, under international law, an executive agreement is as binding as a treaty.[64]

Lim v Executive Secretary[65] answered in the affirmative the question of whether joint 'Balikatan' war exercises between the Philippines and the US were covered by the VFA. Petitioners assailed the terms of reference for the war exercises, which were contained in an exchange of notes. The VFA allows US personnel to engage, for certain periods, in 'activities', which was undefined, and this proved to be the bone of contention for the petitioners.[66] The Supreme Court, noting the 'expression is ambiguous, permitting a wide scope of undertakings subject only to the approval of the Philippine government',[67] applied articles 31 and 32 of the Vienna Convention on the Law of Treaties 1969[68] on the general and supplementary means of interpretation to flesh out the meaning of the term. Applying article 31, the Supreme Court said to interpret a treaty, its text (which is presumed to embody the intention of the parties) and context, as well as other aids, may be examined. As for article 32, the Supreme Court held that supplementary means of interpretation are not intended to be autonomous and divorced from the general rule.[69]

The Supreme Court traced the VFA's roots to the 1951 Philippines-United States Mutual Defense Treaty, adding that the MDT and the VFA, as treaties binding under the principle of *pacta sunt servanda*, must be read with the constitution.[70] The Supreme Court allowed that the word 'activities' was deliberately made ambiguous 'to give both parties a certain leeway in negotiation', such that US forces may visit the Philippines 'for purposes other than military'.[71] However, citing the transitory section of the constitution on the presence of foreign troops in the country, the Supreme Court said 'neither the MDT nor the VFA allow foreign troops to engage in an offensive war on Philippine territory'.[72]

In *Nicholas v Romulo*,[73] the Supreme Court was again confronted by the issue first raised in *Bayan v Zamora*, following a controversial tussle for custody over an American serviceman convicted of the rape of a Filipina that took place while the former was in the country for the Balikatan exercises. The victim, joined by various groups, brought suit before the Supreme Court after her American tormentor—who was detained at a Philippine jail after his conviction and while his case was on appeal—was moved by American authorities in the dead of the night to the US Embassy in Manila without a court order but with the consent of their Philippine counterparts.[74]

The petitioners claimed that the VFA deprives the Supreme Court of its exclusive power under section 5(5), article VIII of the 1987 Charter to adopt rules of procedure for

[64] Ibid. 488–90. [65] [2002] GR No 151445 11 April 2002; 380 SCRA 739 [2002].

[66] Ibid. 752–3. [67] Ibid. 753–4.

[68] Vienna Convention on the Law of Treaties (adopted 13 May 1969, entered into force 27 January 1980, 1155 UNTS 331).

[69] *Lim* (n 65) 754. [70] Ibid. 752. [71] Ibid. 755. [72] Ibid. 759.

[73] [2009] GR No 175888 [En Banc] 11 February 2009; 578 SCRA 438 [2009].

[74] Ibid. 453–4.

all courts in the country. The Supreme Court disagreed, finding that international law grants immunity from local jurisdiction to foreign armed forces entering another state's territory,

> to the extent agreed upon such that the power of the court of [a] host country to adopt rules of procedure is not curtailed; instead 'the laws (including rules of procedure) of one State do not extend or apply except to the extent agreed upon to subjects of another State due to the recognition of extraterritorial immunity given to such bodies as visiting foreign armed forces'.[75]

This principle of immunity, according to *Nicholas,* is part of the law of the land via the Incorporation Clause.[76] *Nicholas* distinguishes between custody during trial and detention after conviction, so that it directed American and Philippine authorities to negotiate for an agreement on detention facilities controlled by the Philippines pursuant to section 10 of thc VFA.[77]

Petitioners argued that under the US Supreme Court's judgment in *Medellin v Texas,*[78] treaties entered into by the United States are not automatically part of American domestic law unless they are self-executing or are the subject of an implementing law. This, they said, is unequal treatment by the Americans, as section 25 of the transitory provisions of article XVIII the 1987 Charter itself requires that the two sides should subject such an agreement to the concurrence of their respective legislatures. The Supreme Court held that reliance on *Medellin* is misplaced, as it does not apply to the VFA; rather, under American jurisprudence[79] and the US *Case-Zablocki Act,*[80] the VFA is considered self-executing.

In *Saguisag v Ochoa,*[81] another executive agreement came into question: the Enhanced Defense Cooperation Agreement (EDCA). The agreement authorizes the US military forces to have access to and conduct activities within certain 'agreed locations' in the country, where prepositioned equipment and supplies may be stored by the Americans.[82]

The Supreme Court upheld the constitutionality of EDCA, ruling that the treaty required in section 15, article XVIII of the 1987 Charter also contemplates an executive agreement on foreign military bases, troops, or facilities, provided, '(a) it is not the instrument that allows the presence of foreign military bases, troops, or facilities; or (b) it merely aims to implement an existing law or treaty'.[83] Thus the EDCA, according to the Supreme Court, is of a piece with the VFA as an implementing tool of the 1951 Philippines-US Mutual Defense Treaty.[84]

[75] Ibid. 463, citing *Weinberger v Rossi* [1982] 456 US 25. [76] Ibid. 464.
[77] Ibid. [78] [2008] 552 US 491. [79] Ibid. 466.
[80] Ibid., citing Case-Zablocki Act, 1 USC 112b(a) (1976 ed Supp IV). Professor Magallona argues that the Supreme Court's treatment of *Medellin* and the Case-Zablocki Act is misleading: Magallona, *The Supreme Court* (n 17) 22–5.
[81] [2016] GR No 212426, GR No 212444 [En Banc] 12 January 2016; 342 SCRA 241 [2016].
[82] Ibid. 317. [83] *Saguisag* (n 81) 346. [84] Ibid. 369–70.

Saguisag provides important finer clarifications on the difference between a treaty and an executive agreement. First, it ruled that executive agreements as such must proceed from an express or implied authorization under the constitution, statutes, or treaties and not create new international obligations, otherwise they are void from the beginning. Second, treaties are superior to executive agreements.[85] In the case of the former, where legislative imprimatur is required, the treaty is given the same status as a statute, so that in case of a conflict, the later law takes precedence over the earlier law, under the principle of *lex posterior derogat priori*. However, both treaty and executive agreement 'are nevertheless subject to the supremacy of the Constitution'.[86]

It is also notable that the Supreme Court has extended the logic of the executive agreement to an exchange of notes as an alternative form. Its use has become a deciding factor in suits before the Supreme Court against foreign-funded projects alleged to have been tainted with corruption[87] and in upholding the constitutionality of a comprehensive Non-Surrender Agreement between the Philippines and the United States shielding a broad class of Americans from the jurisdiction of the International Criminal Court (ICC) when in the Philippines.[88]

Thus in cases involving executive agreements and exchanges of notes, a further paradox is noted: by virtue of an open door maintained by their dualist mother treaties, they enter domestic jurisdiction as international law given direct effect without need of further legislative action to be transformed into Philippine law, thus exhibiting monist tendencies; yet they also perform the dual functions of a sword and a shield. As a sword, they are made part of Philippine law by direct effect. But as a shield, they are used as a device to shield certain foreign interests from public or even international accountability.

2.6 International Law as a Shield: the International Criminal Court and Filipino Comfort Women

In *Pimentel v Executive Secretary*, petitioners asked the Supreme Court through a *mandamus* suit to compel the Executive to transmit the signed papers of the Rome Statute to the Senate to comply with procedures of the Treaty Clause.[89] The argument was that the Rome Statute, being an embodiment of *jus cogens* prohibitions and *erga omnes* obligations, is part of the law of the land as a restatement of generally accepted

[85] Ibid. 370.

[86] The precedent for this may be found in *Gonzales v Hechanova* [1961] GR No L-21897 [En Banc] 22 October 1963; 9 SCRA 230 [1963].

[87] See e.g. *Abaya v Ebdane* [2007] GR No 167919 (First Division) 14 February 2007; 515 SCRA 720 [2007].

[88] *Bayan Muna v Romulo* [2011] GR No 159618 [En Banc] 1 February 2011; 641 SCRA 244 [2011].

[89] [2005] GR No 158088 [En Banc] 6 July 2005; 462 SCRA 622 [2005].

principles of international law, hence it is obligatory on the Philippines to become a state party.

The Supreme Court dismissed the suit, saying the issue falls within the ambit of the 'political question' doctrine, it being a matter of the exercise by the President of his discretion as chief architect of foreign policy.[90] At the same time, it held that 'the power to ratify is vested in the President, subject to the concurrence of the Senate'.[91] It ruled that since the role of the Senate is limited only to giving or withholding its consent, or concurrence, to the ratification, it is 'within the authority of the President to refuse to submit a treaty to the Senate or, having secured its consent for its ratification, refuse to ratify it'.[92]

In recent memory, one of the most egregious examples of the direct effect of international law used as a shield is the case of *Vinuya v Executive Secretary*,[93] a suit filed by seventy survivors of the Japanese Comfort Women system in the Philippines during World II, who belonged to a group called *Malaya Lolas* (Free Grandmothers). The petitioners filed a suit asking the Court to enjoin the Philippine government to exercise diplomatic protection for their benefit and press their claims against Japan for the abuses they suffered as Comfort Women.[94]

Over claims by the petitioners that theirs was a cause founded on *jus cogens* norms and *erga omnes* obligations against impunity,[95] the Supreme Court held that, among other things: (i) the question was political in nature, involving the Chief Executive's exercise of its foreign policy prerogatives, and hence it was outside the power of judicial review; (ii) under the San Francisco Peace Treaty[96] the parties, including the Philippines and Japan, had agreed that the treaty extinguished all private claims; and, most controversial of all, (iii) there was little support in international law for the petitioners' claims that the rape and sexual slavery they suffered under the Japanese Comfort Women system violated *jus cogens* norms and *erga omnes* obligations existing at the time of their commission.

The ruling sparked a public furore after counsel for petitioners brought to the Supreme Court's attention, in a supplementary motion for reconsideration, their charge that many crucial passages of the majority opinion—written by Mr Justice Mariano Del Castillo—not only plagiarized foreign authors[97] (Evan Criddle and Evans Fox-Decent, Christian Tams, and Mark Ellis) word-for-word in many places but even twisted their meaning to suit the ruling's desired conclusion. Lawyers for the petitioners

[90] Ibid. 632. [91] *Pimentel* (n 89) 633.
[92] Ibid. 637. [93] [2010] GR No 162230, 28 April 2010; 619 SCRA 533 [2010].
[94] Ibid. 540. [95] Ibid. 541–2.
[96] Security Treaty Between the United States and Japan of 8 September 1951 (entered into force 28 April 1952) TIAS 2491.
[97] These were Evan Criddle and Evans Fox-Decent, 'A Fiduciary Theory of Jus Cogens' (2009) 34 Yale Journal of International Law 331; Christian Tams, *Enforcing Erga Omnes Obligations in International Law* (CUP 2009); and Mark Ellis, 'Breaking the Silence: Rape as an International Crime' (2007) 38 Case Western Reserve Journal of International Law 225.

charged that the authors in fact supported their argument that rape, torture, and sexual slavery were already prohibited by international law in World War II.[98]

2.7 Constitution versus International Law: UNCLOS

In *Magallona v Ermita*,[99] the Supreme Court held that the Philippines' treaty obligations under UNCLOS do not conflict with the constitution. At the heart of the case are two contending views of Philippine sovereignty over its national territory. On one hand, the nationalists insist on the TOP 1899[100] and associated treaties as the most authoritative documents establishing the precise boundaries of Philippine land and maritime territory. On the other hand, the modernists[101] wish to give up the argument from *uti possedetis juris* embodied in the TOP in favour of fully embracing the 'calibrated but widely accepted maritime zones' of the UNCLOS regime.

The suit challenged the constitutionality of the new Baselines Law, Republic Act 9522 2009, which only shortened one baseline, repositioned some base points and re-classified territories in the Kalayaan Group of Islands (Spratly Islands) and the Scarborough Shoal as regimes of islands generating their own applicable maritime zones.[102] Petitioners claim that the law violates the constitution, which embodies the pre-UNCLOS III demarcation of Philippine territory under the Treaty of Paris and related treaties. Under the 'National Territory Clause' of the 1987 Charter, sovereignty over territorial waters extends hundreds of nautical miles around the Philippine archipelago, embracing the rectangular area delineated in the Treaty of Paris.[103]

But *Magallona* held that there is no conflict between UNCLOS III and the constitution, because the former 'has nothing to do with the acquisition (or loss) of territory',[104] as the new Baselines Law, which amends its predecessor, RA 3046 1961, is only a piece of legislation passed to 'delimit with precision the extent of [the Philippines'] maritime zones and continental shelves'.[105]

The Supreme Court held that the baselines of the Philippines would still have to be drawn in accordance with new Baselines Law, namely from the 'outermost islands and drying reefs of the archipelago', and 'cannot be drawn from the boundaries or other portions of the rectangular area delineated in the Treaty of Paris'.[106] It so held even

[98] *In the Matter of Charges of Plagiarism etc against Associate Justice Mariano C. Del Castillo* [2011] AM No 10-7-17-SC [En Banc] 10 October 2010.

[99] [2011] GR No 187167 [En Banc] 16 August 2011; 665 SCRA 476 [2011].

[100] [1899] USS Doc No. 55–63, pt 2, 3–11.

[101] Raul Pangalangan, 'Recent Developments in Philippine Baselines Law' (East Sea (South China Sea) Studies, 15 February 2012) <http://nghiencuubiendong.vn/en/conferences-and-seminars-/the-third-international-workshop-on-south-china-sea/673-recent-developments-in-the-philippine-baselines-law-by-raul-c-pangalangan> accessed 28 July 2018.

[102] *Magallona v Ermita* (n 99) 484. [103] Ibid. 488–9. [104] Ibid. 489.

[105] Ibid. 490. [106] Ibid.

assuming the petitioners' theory that the Philippine territory embraces the islands and all the waters within the rectangular area delimited in the Treaty of Paris. Brushing aside the argument that the UNCLOS III baselines contradict the constitutional delineation of internal waters, the Supreme Court said regardless of the characterization, 'the Philippines exercises sovereignty over the body of water lying landward of the baselines, including the air space over it and the submarine areas underneath'.[107]

While agreeing with the petitioners that the Philippines is not obliged under article 46 of UNCLOS to declare itself an archipelagic state pursuant to UNCLOS,[108] the Supreme Court deferred to the legislature, which had enacted the law under question for such a purpose.[109] The ruling—as a scholar notes—did not expressly nullify the TOP but only ruled it irrelevant to the case.[110] Thus, 'far from being the triumph of the modernist view, the *Magallona* ruling actually demonstrates the rhetorical and symbolic power of the nationalist position'.[111]

Magallona notwithstanding, the Philippines has not withdrawn the relevant declarations it made when it signed UNCLOS on 4 May 1982, in particular, that its signing does not affect its sovereign rights as successor of the United States of America, under the Treaty of Paris between Spain and the United States of America of 10 December 1898, and the Treaty of Washington between the United States of America and Great Britain of 2 January 1930; and that 'the concept of archipelagic waters is similar to the concept of internal waters under the Constitution of the Philippines, and removes straits connecting these waters with the economic zone or high sea from the rights of foreign vessels to transit passage for international navigation'.[112]

Magallona preceded the Philippines' subsequent resort in 2013 to compulsory dispute mechanism procedures under chapter VII of UNCLOS, before the International Tribunal of the Law of the Sea, vis-à-vis China's 'Nine Dash Line' claim.[113]

3 The Direct Effect of the Supreme Court's Rule-Making Powers

3.1 The Prerogative Writs as Entry Points

A third entry point is the rule-making power granted to the Supreme Court for the protection of constitutional rights. Section 5(5), article VIII of the 1987 Charter states

[107] Ibid. 498. [108] Ibid. 506. [109] Ibid. 491.
[110] Pangalangan (n 101). [111] Ibid.
[112] UN Division on Ocean Affairs and Law of the Sea, Declarations and Statements <http://www.un.org/depts/los/convention_agreements/convention_declarations.htm#Philippines%20Understanding%20made%20upon%20signature%20(10%20December%201982)%20and%20confirmed%20upon%20ratification> accessed 25 July 2018.
[113] See the discussion in the introduction of this chapter.

that the Supreme Court shall have the power to 'promulgate rules concerning the protection and enforcement of constitutional rights'. Cases decided by the Supreme Court involving the new rules have invariably applied international law in the cases brought before it under the same rules, in surprising ways.

Three writs came out of the Supreme Court's exercise of this power: the *Writ of Amparo*,[114] *the Writ of Habeas Data*,[115] and the *Writ of Kalikasan*,[116] in response to the raging issues of the day. Of the three, the proceedings on the *Writs of Amparo* and of *Kalikasan* have proven most productive as generators of international law in Philippine practice.

3.2 The Jurisprudence of the Writ of Amparo

Manalo v Secretary of National Defense, the very first case decided by the Supreme Court under the new *Writ of Amparo* rule, noted that the rule was one of the recommendations of the two-day National Consultative Summit on Extrajudicial Killings and Enforced Disappearances sponsored by the Court on 16–17 July 2007.[117] It then surveyed the UDHR, the International Covenant on Civil and Political Rights (ICCPR),[118] the jurisprudence of the UN Human Rights Committee, the Inter-American Court of Human Rights, and the European Court of Human Rights, to establish 'the right to life, the right to liberty and the right to security of the person'[119] that must be given protection by the Supreme Court under its constitutional mandate. Thus, drawing from UN instruments,[120] the Supreme Court defined extralegal killings and enforced disappearances in this way:

[114] It is a remedy for any person whose right to life, liberty, and security is violated or threatened with violation by an unlawful act or omission of a public official or employee, or of a private individual or entity. It covers extralegal killings (ELKs) and enforced disappearances or threats thereof. See The Rule on the Writ of Amparo, AM No 07-9-12-SC 25 September 2007.

[115] It is a protective remedy available to any person whose right to privacy in life, liberty, or security is violated or threatened by an unlawful act or omission of a public official or employee, or of a private individual or entity engaged in the gathering, collecting, or storing of data or information regarding the person, family, home, and correspondence of the aggrieved party. See The Rule on the Writ of Habeas Data, AM No 08-1-16-SC 22 January 2008.

[116] This remedy consists of an order issued by the court directing or enjoining any person or government agency to perform or desist from performing an act in order to protect, preserve, or rehabilitate the environment. See the Rules of Procedure for Environmental Cases AM No 09-6-8-SC 13 April 2010.

[117] [2008] GR No 180906 [En Banc] 7 October 2008 568 SCRA 1 [2008].

[118] International Covenant on Civil and Political Rights (adopted 16 December 1966, entered into force 23 March 1976, 999 UNTS 171). The Philippines was an original signatory to the treaty but became a party to it only on 23 October 1986, just months after the ouster of the late Filipino dictator Ferdinand E Marcos Jr.

[119] *Manalo* (n 117) 52–61.

[120] Ibid.

> [T]he Amparo Rule was intended to address the intractable problem of 'extralegal killings' and 'enforced disappearances' its coverage, in its present form, is confined to these two instances or to threats thereof. 'Extralegal killings' are 'killings committed without due process of law, i.e., without legal safeguards or judicial proceedings.' On the other hand, 'enforced disappearances' are 'attended by the following characteristics: an arrest, detention or abduction of a person by a government official or organized groups or private individuals acting with the direct or indirect acquiescence of the government; the refusal of the State to disclose the fate or whereabouts of the person concerned or a refusal to acknowledge the deprivation of liberty which places such persons outside the protection of law'.[121]

Razon v Tagitis[122] considers not only established Philippine doctrines on human rights but provides an astonishingly comprehensive discussion of relevant international law jurisprudence and practice, including that of regional and national bodies (including the Organization of American States, the European Court of Human Rights, and the American courts), international instruments and bodies (the UDHR, ICCPR, International Covenant on Economic, Social and Cultural Rights, Rome Statute of the International Criminal Court (ICC), Convention on Enforced Disappearance 2007, and UN Human Rights Committee), and hybrid international tribunals (such as the Sierra Leone Special Court, the Special Panels for Serious Crimes in Timor-Leste, and the Extraordinary Chambers in the Court of Cambodia).[123] Further, the Supreme Court said that while the Philippines at the time was not yet a party to either the Rome Statute or the Convention on Enforced Disappearance,[124] both the definition and prohibition on enforced disappearance are now part of customary international law so that the Philippines is bound to observe them pursuant to the Incorporation Clause.[125]

It held that it is the duty of the government to provide effective remedy to victims of human rights violations, and to conduct 'effective investigations, organization of the government apparatus to extend protection to victims of extralegal killings or enforced disappearances (or threats thereof) and/or their families, and bringing offenders to the bar of justice'.[126] Moreover, it held that 'these rulings effectively serve as the backdrop for the Rule on the Writ of Amparo', and despite the gaps, the sources of law discussed 'provide ample guidance and standards on how, through the medium of the Amparo Rule, the Court can provide remedies and protect the constitutional rights to life, liberty and security that underlie every enforced disappearance'.[127]

Razon v Tagitis expressly holds that the *Writ of Amparo*, issued pursuant to the rule-making powers of the Supreme Court, is founded on relevant international law that had been made part of Philippine law either through the Incorporation Clause or the Treaty

[121] Ibid. 38. [122] [2009] GR No 182498 3 December 2009; 606 SCRA 598 [2009].
[123] Ibid. 679–83. [124] Ibid. 679. [125] Ibid. [126] Ibid. 680–1.
[127] In 2012, the Philippines passed a law against enforced disappearance.

Clause. Thus, the rule-making power of the Supreme Court may serve to amplify international law—especially where it pertains to the protection of rights.

3.3 The Jurisprudence of the Writ of Kalikasan

Arigo v Swift[128] was a *Writ of Kalikasan* case, although eventually rendered moot by the turn of events, which saw the Supreme Court performing its symbolic function when it engaged in a long discussion of articles 30, 31, and 32[129] of UNCLOS on the limits of immunity extended to warships that entered internal waters and caused environmental damage, including warships of states that are not parties to the Convention. In this case, a US minesweeper, *USS Guardian*, ran aground and caused extensive damage in Tubbataha, a Philippine National Marine Park in the Sulu Sea famous for its rich coral reef diving spots.[130] The Supreme Court said in *obiter* that the UNCLOS provisions in question are relevant to the controversy, and although the treaty upholds the immunity of warships from the jurisdiction of coastal states while navigating the latter's territorial sea, it also provides that the flag states shall be required to leave the territorial sea immediately if they flout the laws and regulations of the coastal state, and that they will be liable for damages caused by their warships or any other government vessel operated for non-commercial purposes under article 31.[131] The Supreme Court said the United States, which has undertaken leadership in international affairs, ought to be subject to the obligation of states to cooperate for the protection and preservation of the marine environment under article 197 of UNCLOS.[132]

3.4 Judicial Notice as Tool for Direct Effect

In *Kookoritchkin v Solicitor General,*[133] a 1948 naturalization case involving a former officer of the Russian White Army who fled to the Philippines after the 1917 Bolshevik Revolution, the Supreme Court not only granted citizenship to the petitioner but also impliedly recognized, by judicial notice of political repression in Soviet Russia, his right to *non-refoulement*, on a well-grounded fear of political persecution in his state of origin.

[128] [2014] GR No 206510 16 September 2014; 735 SCRA 102 [2014].
[129] Ibid. 137–40. [130] *Arigo* (n 128) 119–21.
[131] Ibid. 141. [132] Ibid. 140–1.
[133] [1948] GR No L-1812 27 August 1948; 81 Phil Reports 435 [1948].

4 Constitutionalization and Direct Effect

4.1 Constitutionalization and the Commission on Human Rights

A fourth entry point is constitutionalization. Although the Supreme Court has not used the term, the sense that human rights norms have been grafted into various provisions of the constitution is clear in the relevant cases—yet another example of direct effect functioning as a sword.

Simon v Commission on Human Rights[134] is the first Philippine case on the applicability of international human rights norms in Philippine law. *Simon* held that the chief focus of the investigatory powers of the national Commission on Human Rights (CHR) established by the 1987 Charter is limited to violations of self-executing civil and political rights, but economic, social, and cultural rights require implementing legislation.[135]

Discussions of the Constitutional Commission show that the relevant provisions of the UDHR and the ICCPR had been made 'integral parts' of the Bill of Rights of the 1987 Charter.[136] The Supreme Court said that the discussions on the powers of the CHR eventually took form as section 18, article XIII of the 1987 Charter empowering the Commission to 'investigate, on its own or on complaint by any party, all forms of human rights violations involving civil and political rights', with no mention of the other rights.[137]

4.2 Constitutionalization and Indivisibility of Rights

However, in *Oposa v Factoran*,[138] the Supreme Court also ruled that are certain norms that are so basic that they predate even the constitution, notably, the right to a balanced and healthful ecology.[139] This right has been constitutionalized in section 16, article II of the 1987 Charter.[140] Contra *Simon, Oposa* may be a precedent for the indivisibility and interdependence of civil, political, economic, and social rights in the constitution, insofar as the Supreme Court ruled that while the environmental right is found in the *Declaration of Principles and State Polices* and not under the Bill of Rights, 'it does not follow that it is less important than any of the civil and political rights enumerated in the latter'.[141] Such right, said the Supreme Court, 'belongs to a different category of

[134] [2004] GR No 100150 [En Banc] 5 January 1994; 229 SCRA 117 [1994].
[135] Ibid. 132–3. [136] Ibid. 131–2.
[137] Ibid. 132. [138] [1993] GR No 101083 [En Banc] 30 July 1993; 224 SCRA 792 [1993].
[139] Ibid. 804. [140] Ibid. 885. [141] Ibid.

rights altogether' as 'these basic rights need not even be written in the Constitution for they are assumed to exist from the inception of humankind'.[142]

Oposa, which inaugurated the sign of inter-generational rights in environmental law, implies what should logically arise as a legal effect of constitutionalized international law. Constitutional principles are first-order norms, which occupy the top rung, higher than that of statutes. And if set against other norms that are less than constitutional in nature, constitutionalized international law should take precedence. That, at least, is the theory.

5 Direct Effect of International Law in the State of Exception

Perhaps *Republic v Sandiganbayan*[143] is the lone case study in Philippine jurisprudence that defies specific characterization as an entry point, but this may be explained by the circumstance of its birthing, criticisms of the decision notwithstanding.[144]

On 25 February 1986, following the ouster by a civilian-backed military revolt of the dictatorship of the late strongman Ferdinand E. Marcos, who had ruled the Philippines with an iron hand for twenty years, the new government installed in its wake by a 'People Power' movement set aside the constitution the dictator had established in 1973 to legalize his hold on power.[145]

Between that date and the enactment of the Freedom Constitution on 25 March 1986—a span of just one month—the revolutionary government occupied a so-called constitutional *interregnum*, when there was no constitution to speak of. During that brief period, the revolutionary government made a series of issuances that ostensibly violated fundamental due-process rights.[146] The Supreme Court made a direct turn to international law—the UDHR and the ICCPR—as a source for protecting the civil and political rights of Filipino citizens during the interregnum, even without an Incorporation Clause. Both, according to the Court, embodied generally accepted principles of international law that were binding on the revolutionary government of Mrs Corazon Aquino.[147] At the time, the Philippines was not yet a party to the ICCPR, although it was a signatory to it and had voted for the UDHR.

As it was, the UDHR and ICCPR were applied in *Republic* as objective international law directly on Filipinos as direct possessors and subject of rights.[148] Here, we encounter the 'direct effect' of international law where, as Professor Nollkaemper notes, the 'court relies on international law as an exclusive basis for its decision',[149] and allows the

[142] Ibid. [143] [2003] GR No 104768 [En Banc] 21 July 2003; 497 SCRA 10 [2003].
[144] Magallona, *The Supreme Court* (n 17) 73–9.
[145] *Republic v Sandiganbayan* (n 143) 50–1. [146] Ibid. 51. [147] Ibid. 51–2.
[148] See the critique in Magallona, *The Supreme Court* (n 17) 73–9.
[149] Nollkaemper (n 18) 110–11.

exercise of judicial power to apply international law in the national legal order, where this, without direct effect, would not be possible.[150]

6 Direct Effect by Statutory Application

6.1 The Philippine Civil Code and Revised Penal Code

A host of Philippine statutes expressly reference international law. Article 14 of the Civil Code[151] states that:

> Penal laws and those of public security and safety shall be obligatory upon all who live or sojourn in the Philippine territory, *subject to the principles of public international law and to treaty stipulations* [emphasis added].

The first clause of the article actually deals with the principle of territoriality, as held by the Supreme Court in *Del Socorro v Van Wilsem*,[152] correlating it with article 2 of the Revised Penal Code (RPC)—Act No. 3815 1930.[153]

Textually, it may be read as saying that penal laws and those of public security, as they apply to all who live and sojourn in Philippine territory, are subject to—or are to be interpreted and applied according to—applicable principles of public international law and treaty obligations. Or it could mean that the second clause of the provision, when invoked in the appropriate case, needs to be correlated with the Incorporation Clause and the Treaty Clause to be given full effect. 'Applicable principles of public international law' conceivably refers to the former while 'treaty obligations' pertain to the latter.

Arguably, the Court in *Republic v Sandiganbayan*[154] lost an opportunity to expound on its application by failing to use the provision as a device for applying international norms in the domestic sphere, in the absence of the Incorporation Clause. It bears stressing that, during the interregnum, the Civil Code was in effect and had not been cancelled, and given the state of emergency confronting the country at that time, the provision would apply as the problem arose out of a situation involving 'public security'.

Article 2 of the RPC also parallels article 14 of the New Civil Code's emphasis on the territorial application of Philippine criminal law in the Philippine archipelago but allows exceptions 'as provided in the treaties and laws of preferential application', including those that cover persons who 'commit any of the crimes against national

[150] Ibid. [151] Republic Act 386 (1950).
[152] [2014] GR No 193707 [Third Division] 10 December 2014; 516 SCRA 517 [2014].
[153] Ibid. 532. [154] *Republic v Sandiganbayan* (n 143).

security and the law of nations, defined in Title One of Book Two of this Code'. And yet, the said Title of the RPC 1930 referred to only contains provisions on crimes against national security, and none against the law of nations.

However, article 2 of the RPC has been amended by Republic Act 9851, the Philippine Act on Crimes Against International Humanitarian Law, Genocide, and Other Crimes Against Humanity of 2009, which allows the exercise of universal jurisdiction in Philippines courts over crimes that are also cognizable by the Rome Statute, namely, genocide, war crimes, and crimes against humanity.

6.2 New Laws at the Convergence of Human Rights and Humanitarian Law

The aforementioned RA 9851 2009 may be the first and only Philippine legislation that has a full chapter devoted to various sources of international law as aids to the interpretation and application of its provisions, to wit:

> Section 15. Applicability of International Law - In the application and interpretation of this Act, Philippine courts shall be guided by the following sources:
> (a) The 1948 Genocide Convention;
> (b) The 1949 Geneva Conventions I-IV, their 1977 Additional Protocols I and II and their 2005 Additional Protocol III;
> (c) The 1954 Hague Convention for the Protection of Cultural Property in the Event of Armed Conflict, its First Protocol and its 1999 Second Protocol;
> (d) The 1989 Convention on the Rights of the Child and its 2000 Optional Protocol on the Involvement of Children in Armed Conflict;
> (e) The rules and principles of customary international law;
> (f) The judicial decisions of international courts and tribunals;
> (g) Relevant and applicable international human rights instruments;
> (h) Other relevant international treaties and conventions ratified or acceded to by the Republic of the Philippines; and
> (i) Teachings of the most highly qualified publicists and authoritative commentaries on the foregoing sources as subsidiary means for the determination of rules of international law.

Moreover, section 17 amounts to a reverse application of the *aut dedere aut judicare* principle, as it allows Philippine authorities to defer to any investigation or prosecution already being conducted by another court or international tribunal and instead to extradite any accused to the appropriate international court or to another state 'pursuant to the applicable extradition laws and treaties'.

The Republic Act 9745, the Anti-Torture Act of 2009, in its section 2(d), declares that it is the policy of the state:

> (d) To fully adhere to the principles and standards on the absolute condemnation and prohibition of torture as provided for in the 1987 Philippine Constitution; various international instruments to which the Philippines is a State party such as, but not limited to, the International Covenant on Civil and Political Rights (ICCPR), the Convention on the Rights of the Child (CRC), the Convention on the Elimination of All Forms of Discrimination Against Women (CEDAW) and the Convention Against Torture and Other Cruel, Inhuman or Degrading Treatment or Punishment (CAT); and all other relevant international human rights instruments to which the Philippines is a signatory.

The Republic Act 10353, the Anti-Enforced Disappearance Act of 2012, also states in its Declaration of Policy that:

> the State adheres to the principles and standards on the absolute condemnation of human rights violations set by the 1987 Philippine Constitution and various international instruments such as, but not limited to, the International Covenant on Civil and Political Rights (ICCPR), and the Convention Against Torture and Other Cruel, Inhuman or Degrading Treatment or Punishment (CAT), to which the Philippines is a State party.[155]

The RA 9745 2009, RA 9851 2010, and RA 10353 2012 are all laws that advance the protection of rights. With the exception of the Anti-Enforced Disappearance Law, RA 10353 2012, they were passed pursuant to Philippine treaty obligations, but they also point to treaties other than those that they directly draw from in implementing legislation.

The Philippines is not yet a party to the Convention against Enforced Disappearance but it has already passed RA 10353, which embodies its standards. It bears recalling that in *Razon v Tagitis*,[156] the Supreme Court ruled that the prohibition on enforced disappearance as a rule of international law now forms part of Philippine law through the Incorporation Clause.

6.3 'Soft law' Transformed into Law by Extraordinary Powers in the State of Exception

Pharmaceutical and Health Care Association of the Philippines v Duque[157] held that resolutions of the World Health Assembly are 'soft law' or 'non-binding principles and practices that influence state behavior'.[158] However, it also ruled that the International Code of Marketing of Breast Milk Substitutes, a code adopted by the World Health

[155] Republic Act 10353 Declaration of Policy.
[156] [2009] GR No 182498 3 December 2009; 606 SCRA 598 [2009].
[157] [2007] GR No 173034 [En Banc] 9 October 2007; 264 SCRA 265 [2007].
[158] Ibid. 299.

Assembly in 1981, although soft law, became part of the law of the land when it was adopted and turned into the Philippine Milk Code by an executive order issued by then President Corazon Aquino under the Freedom Constitution, under which she held extraordinary legislative powers prior to the ratification of the 1987 Charter.

7 Conclusion: Backsliding from International Law?

The Philippine practice of international law is dynamic, if heterogeneous. With the exception of politically charged issues, when it has frequently used international law as a shield, the Supreme Court has largely given direct effect to international law as a sword for the protection of rights, drawing from a distinguished jurisprudential history, at least, from its experience under World War II.

The traditional monist-dualist debates over the Incorporation Clause and the Treaty Clause of the constitution has now expanded to include other entry points—actual and potential—of international law into Philippine law. Legal theory is only beginning to catch up with these developments.

The year 2016 was a watershed for Philippine contemporary political and legal history, with the election into the Presidency by a wide margin of Mr Rodrigo Roa Duterte. Mr Duterte, a populist politician, has capitalized on widespread discontent with the failed promises of post-1986 liberal democratic governments before him, projecting the image of decisive political will to a huge majority of voters with violent and vulgar rhetoric.[159]

In his first two years in office, he has, among many acts that tend to undermine the rule of law, launched a deadly 'tokhang'[160]drug war that has since claimed thousands of lives;[161] declared Martial Law in Southern Philippines following a sixth-month siege by

[159] See Walden Bello, 'Duterte's Revolt against Liberal Democracy' (2018) Global Dialogue <http://globaldialogue.isa-sociology.org/dutertes-revolt-against-liberal-democracy> accessed 5 May 2018; Bonn Juego, 'The Philippines 2017: Duterte-Led Authoritarian Populism and Its Liberal-Democratic Roots' (2017) 28 The Journal of the Italian Think Tank on Asia 129.

[160] Visayan term for 'knock-and-plead', a bloody method that Mr Duterte reportedly perfected when he was mayor of the city of Davao for two decades.

[161] Over a 10-year period, from 1975 to 1985, the Task Force Detainees of the Philippines (TFDP) recorded 3,257 ELKs attributable to the martial law regime. See Rachel Reyes, '3,257: Fact Checking The Marcos Killings, 1975–1985' *The Manila Times* (12 April 2016) <http://www.manilatimes.net/3257-fact-checking-the-marcos-killings-1975-1985/255735> accessed 18 May 2018. The Martial Law figures pale in comparison to the numbers being counted in the ongoing drug war launched by the President, which official figures place at 4,279 killed in police anti-drug operations, and another 2,668 killed in drug-related incidents. See Rambo Talabong, 'At least 33 Killed Daily in the Philippines since Duterte Assumed Office' (*Rappler,* 15 June 2018) <http://www.rappler.com/newsbreak/in-depth/204949-pnp-number-deaths-daily-duterte-administration> accessed 15 July 2018.

ISIS-inspired Philippine Islamist groups of the city of Marawi;[162] set aside the South China Sea arbitral ruling in favour of rapprochement with China;[163] ousted a hostile Chief Justice of the Supreme Court;[164] and announced the withdrawal[165] of the country's membership from the Rome Statute following a decision by the ICC's Office of the Trial Prosecutor to open a preliminary examination over his drug war.[166]

All told, Mr Duterte's first two years in office represent a simultaneous assault on many fronts against liberal democratic institutions established by the 1987 Charter following the ouster, from his twenty-year-old stranglehold on power, of the late strongman Ferdinand E Marcos Jr.

This chapter is written against this backdrop of uncertainties in the Philippine political and legal landscape. The Supreme Court is now hearing two consolidated petitions against the unilateral withdrawal from the ICC made by President Duterte without Senate concurrence,[167] as well as a landmark *Writ of Amparo* petition challenging the conduct of his drug war.[168] Once again, the question of international law becomes relevant where the Supreme Court, in the language of Professor Nollkaemper's theory of the duality of direct effect of international law, is called to discharge a critical political function.

[162] Affirmed by the Supreme Court in *Lagman v Medialdea* [2017] GR No 231658, GR No 231771, GR No 231774 [En Banc] 4 July 2017. In *Lagman*, the Supreme Court, by characterizing the siege of Marawi by a known terror group as an act of rebellion, provided the President with a constitutional basis for a Martial Law declaration (as well as its eventual perpetual extension) where it previously did not exist. Under the constitution, there are only two valid grounds for such a declaration: invasion and rebellion, under section 18, article VII of the constitution.

[163] Renato de Castro, 'The Duterte Administration's Foreign Policy: Unraveling the Aquino Administration's Balancing Agenda on an Emergent China' (2016) 35 Journal of Current Southeast Asian Affairs 139.

[164] *Republic of the Philippines v Sereno* [2018] GR No 237428 [En Banc] 11 May 2018. The Solicitor General succesfully prosecuted an unprecedented *quo warranto* proceeding against Chief Justice Ma. Lourdes PA Sereno on transparency grounds, amid intense interpersonal friction between her and many of her own colleagues. Instead of closing ranks behind her, her colleagues voted 8–6 to remove her from office. Her colleagues publicly resented what to them were, among other things, her imperious disregard of the rule of collegiality, which she denied.

[165] The Department of Foreign Affairs, 'PH Officially Serves Notice to UN of Decision to Withdraw from the ICC' (16 March 2018) <https://dfa.gov.ph/dfa-news/dfa-releasesupdate/15975-ph-officially-serves-notice-to-un-of-decision-to-withdraw-from-icc> accessed 18 May 2018.

[166] ICC Office of the Trial Prosecutor, 'Statement of the Prosecutor of the International Criminal Court, Mrs Fatou Bensouda, on Opening Preliminary Examinations into the situations in the Philippines and in Venezuela' (8 February 2018) <http://www.icc-cpi.int/Pages/item.aspx?name=180208-otp-stat> accessed 18 May 2018. The withdrawal took effect on 17 March 2019 without the Supreme Court ruling on the two petitions, which are pending to date.

[167] *Senators v Cayetano* GR No 238875, filed on 16 May 2018, and *Philippine Coalition for the International Criminal Court v Executive Secretary* GR No 239483, filed on 8 June 2018. As of this writing, the two cases, now consolidated, are still being heard by the Supreme Court.

[168] *Sr Ma Juanita R Daño v The Philippine National Police*, GR No 234484, filed on 18 October 2017, on behalf of the families of 35 alleged victims of *tokhang* operations in a Manila slum. This is the very first time that the *Writ of Amparo* has been invoked for the protection of a community—and one in a slum at that.

But it must do so—as Professor Magallona would have it—prudentially, not granting superiority *per se* to international law—but performing such a task in the Philippines' postcolonial present with a careful respect for constitutional structures and precedents. It must do so in a way that preserves and protects constitutional rights, and with a nod towards justice as the true foundation of national constitutional prerogatives.[169]

[169] Disclosure: the author was co-counsel for petitioners in several cases reported in this chapter, namely *Pimentel* (n 89), *Vinuya* (n 93), *Magallona* (n 99), and *Saguisag* (n 81); and he serves as lead counsel in *Philippine Coalition for the International Criminal Court* (n 167). He also helped to develop the case and draft the petition filed with the Supreme Court in *Sr Ma Juanita R Daño* (n 168).

CHAPTER 18

SINGAPORE

LI-ANN THIO AND KEVIN YL TAN

1 Introduction

After more than 140 years of British rule, Singapore became an independent state as part of the Federation of Malaysia in 1963. However, Singapore's time in the Federation was brief and it seceded from it on 9 August 1965, becoming independent a second time as the unitary Republic of Singapore.[1] By signing the Separation Agreement of 9 August 1965 and passing the Constitution and Malaysia (Singapore Amendment) Act, Malaysia became the first country to recognize Singapore's independence. Britain, Singapore's former colonial master, followed suit the day after. On independence, Singapore inherited and retained a Westminster-style Constitution, with a ceremonial President as head of state, and actual executive power reposed in the Prime Minister and his Cabinet, who are drawn from the members of Parliament. Due to its small size, Singapore remained a unitary state, with the government being responsible for all national and municipal matters.

On 2 September 1965, Singapore's Foreign Minister S Rajaratnam sent a cable to the United Nations (UN) Security Council, applying for UN membership and requesting the Security Council to process the application at its next meeting.[2] He further cabled to the Security Council a declaration accepting the 'conditions contained in the Charter of the United Nations', along with an undertaking to fulfil them.[3] Two days later, Prime Minister Lee Kuan Yew made a further declaration, which was sent to the UN Secretary-General, echoing the same declaration that Rajaratnam had sent out two

[1] The events leading to this have been recounted and discussed in considerable detail in Kevin YL Tan, *International Law, History and Policy: Singapore in the Early Years* (Monograph No 1, Centre for International Law, National University of Singapore 2011).

[2] UNSC, 'Cable from the Minister of Foreign Affairs of Singapore Addressed to the Secretary-General' (2 September 1965) UN Doc S/6648.

[3] Ibid.

days earlier.[4] On the afternoon of 20 September 1965, Singapore's application was moved at the Security Council by Malaysia and co-sponsored by the Ivory Coast, Jordan, and the United Kingdom.[5] Despite the Singapore delegation's fear that the Soviet Union would veto Singapore's admission, it was 'smooth sailing' because of Malaysia's strong support.[6] Six other delegates spoke up in support of Singapore's application and the resolution to admit Singapore was unanimously adopted.[7]

The General Assembly's 1332nd Plenary Session was held the very next day, on 21 September. The Assembly was presided over by the newly-elected chairman, Amintore Fanfani of Italy, who took the delegates through the resolutions to admit three new states—the Maldives, the Gambia, and Singapore. The draft resolution to admit Singapore as a UN member was adopted by acclamation and the Singaporean delegation—comprising Deputy Prime Minister Toh Chin Chye, Foreign Minister S Rajaratnam, and Permanent Secretary Abu Bakar Pawanchee—was escorted to its place in the General Assembly Hall. Singapore had become the UN's 117th member.[8] Rajaratnam stated:

> Now that Singapore has been received into the fold of the United Nations, I would like to assure this Assembly that my country will join with other nations in their efforts to realize the aims and objects of the United Nations Charter. For us, the essentials of the Charter are the preservation of peace through collective security, promotion of economic development through mutual aid and the safeguarding of the inalienable right of every country to establish forms of government in accordance with the wishes of its own people. My country stands by these three essential principles and will give loyal and unflinching support to the United Nations in its efforts to promote them.[9]

Rajaratnam then assured the Assembly that the British bases on the island were there with Singapore's consent and were to ensure Singapore's security. Under no circumstances would they be used as bases for aggression.[10] Rajaratnam made another important point in his speech—that Singapore had 'chosen the path of non-alignment' in that it had no wish to be 'drawn into alliances dedicated to imposing our way of life on other countries'. This did not, however, mean that Singapore would be indifferent 'to basic issues of right and wrong or that it will evade taking a stand on matters which it considers vital lest it displease some member nations, including those with whom it has close ties'.[11]

[4] 'No 7930. Singapore: Declaration of Acceptance of the Obligations Contained in the Charter of the United Nations' (4 September 1965) 545 UNTS 152. This declaration was presented to the UN Secretary-General on 13 September 1965.

[5] See UNSC Official Records, 20th year, 1243rd Meeting (20 September 1965) S/PV.1243.

[6] Gretchen Liu, *The Singapore Foreign Service: The First 40 Years* (Editions Didier Millet 2005) 29.

[7] UNSC res 213 (20 September 1965).

[8] UNGA res 2010 (XX) (21 September 1965).

[9] UNGA Official Records, 20th Session, 1332nd Plenary Meeting (21 September 1965) A/PV.1332, 12, para 152.

[10] Ibid. para 156.

[11] Ibid. paras 160–1.

Pawanchee was designated Singapore's first representative to the UN. He presented his credentials on 29 September 1965, but he could do little else as he had no staff or facilities with which to conduct operations in New York. It was not until 1967 that Singapore dispatched its first permanent representative to the UN. Wong Lin Ken, a senior lecturer in history at the University of Singapore, was named Singapore's first Ambassador to America and concurrently Singapore's Permanent Representative to the UN. He held these posts for two years (1967–8) before being succeeded in the latter post by Tommy Koh, then a young academic from the Faculty of Law at the University of Singapore, who later became a major Singapore figure in international law and affairs.

The following account starts by first looking at Singapore's role in international and regional organizations like the UN and the Association of Southeast Asian Nations (ASEAN), and particularly at the role played by key Singaporean representatives in these organizations. The chapter then considers how international law is implemented in Singapore by domestic tribunals and by Parliament, and rounds off with a discussion on the implementation of human rights norms in the context of state imperatives concerning human welfare and development.

2 International and Regional Organizations

2.1 Singaporeans in the International Arena

From its earliest days, Singapore committed itself to being an active player in the international community.[12] Its participation in key international and regional organizations is all the more visible due to the many high-calibre personalities representing Singapore at these various organizations. At the UN, its permanent representatives—most notably Tommy Koh (1968–71; 1974–84), S Jayakumar (1971–4),[13] Kishore Mahbubani (1984–9), and Chan Heng Chee (1989–91)—displayed extraordinary diplomatic acumen and capability and were prominent in key meetings and deliberations. Significantly, only Mahbuhani was a career diplomat, while the rest were academics; Koh and Jayakumar were both law professors.

Tommy Koh has been Singapore's most visible and active representative on the international stage. On 13 March 1981, he was elected President of the Third UN Conference on the Law of the Sea in place of the late Hamilton Shirley Amarasinghe

[12] On Singapore's many roles at the UN, see Tommy Koh, Lin Lin Chang, and Joanna Koh (eds), *50 Years of Singapore and The United Nations* (World Scientific 2015).

[13] Jayakumar went on to become, among other things, Singapore's Foreign Minister and Deputy Prime Minister. His recollections of Singapore's efforts in international law and diplomacy are recounted in S Jayakumar, *Diplomacy: A Singapore Experience* (Straits Times Press 2011).

of Sri Lanka. He was lauded for his handling of the Third Conference and the drafting of the UN Convention on the Law of the Sea 1982 (UNCLOS).[14] The Conference concluded in New York on 30 April 1982 and UNCLOS was opened for signature on 10 December 1982. Koh was again in the limelight at the UN when, on 5 March 1990, he was elected Chairman of the Preparatory Committee for the UN Conference on Environment and Development (UNCED). In June 1992, Koh was elected Chairman of the Main Committee of the UNCED (the 'Earth Summit'). In August 1993, Koh was appointed the UN Secretary-General's Special Envoy on a peace mission to Russia, Estonia, Latvia, and Lithuania.

Other prominent personalities who represented Singapore in international organizations and meetings included Chao Hick Tin, who—as Head of the International Affairs Division of the Attorney-General's Chambers—was involved in the drafting of the Vienna Convention on the Law of Treaties 1969[15] and UNCLOS; Amarjeet Singh, who was *ad litem* Judge on the International Criminal Tribunal for the Former Yugoslavia from 2000 to 2003;[16] Halimah Yacob, who served on the International Labour Organization's Governing Body from 1999 to 2011;[17] and Noleen Heyzer, who was the first woman from the global South to head the UN Development Fund for Women (UNIFEM) and also served as UN Under-Secretary-General from 2007 to 2015.

2.2 The United Nations

Despite its diminutive size, Singapore has participated actively in the UN and many of its related organizations, bodies, and commissions, and has even taken up key leadership positions in several instances. For example, Singapore joined the UN Commission on International Trade Law (UNCITRAL) in November 1970 and participated so actively that it supplied three UNCITRAL chairmen over a forty-year period.[18] Singapore was also elected onto the UN Committee on Contribution for the triennium 1989–91 and held a non-permanent seat in the UN Security Council in the 2001–2 term.[19]

[14] See Tommy Koh and S Jayakumar, 'The Negotiating Process of the Third United Nations Conference on the Law of the Sea' in Myron Nordquist (ed), *United National Convention on the Law of the Sea 1982: A Commentary,* vol 1 (Martinus Nijhoff 1985).

[15] See Tommy Koh, 'Singapore and International Law: A 50 Year Review' (Law Society of Singapore Biennial Lecture, 8 October 2015) <https://cil.nus.edu.sg/wp-content/uploads/2015/10/Tommy-Koh-Speech-Singapore-and-International-Law-A-50-Year-Review.pdf> accessed 23 September 2017.

[16] See Amarjeet Singh, 'The World's First Independent War Crimes Court: Reminiscences and Reflections' in Koh, Chang, and Koh (eds) (n 12) 119.

[17] See Halimah Yacob, 'Singapore and the International Labour Organization (ILO)' in Koh, Chang, and Koh (eds) (n 12) 125.

[18] They were Warren Khoo, Goh Phai Cheng, and Jeffrey Chan. See Jeffrey Chan Wah Tuck, 'Singapore and UNCITRAL' in Koh, Chang, and Koh (eds) (n 12) 152.

[19] See Kishore Mahbubani, 'Singapore and the Security Council' in Koh, Chang, and Koh (eds) (n 12) 9.

Other UN specialized bodies in which Singapore has played an active part include the International Civil Aviation Organization (ICAO), the International Maritime Organization (IMO), the World Trade Organization (WTO), and the International Monetary Fund (IMF). Singapore joined both the ICAO and IMO almost as soon as it was admitted to the UN in 1966. Since 2003, it has been a member of its Council. A Singapore expert has, since 2005, also been part of the Air Navigation Commission. Singapore currently participates in over 100 ICAO expert bodies covering all aspects of international aviation.[20] Since October 1993, Singapore has been a member of the IMO Council, the IMO's executive body. In November 2000, Chen Tze Penn, Director-General of the Maritime and Port Authority of Singapore, became the first Singaporean to be elected Chairman of the IMO Council (2001–3).

Singapore became a member of the General Agreement on Tariffs and Trade (GATT)—the precursor of the WTO—on 20 July 1973. When the WTO was inaugurated on 1 January 1995, Singapore's Permanent Representative to the United Nations in Geneva, K Kesavapany, was elected for a one-year term as Chairman of the WTO's General Council, its highest policy-making body. Singapore hosted the first WTO Ministerial Conference from 9 to 13 December 1996, and in February 1998, See Chak Mun, Singapore's Permanent Representative to the WTO, was appointed Chairman of the WTO Committee of Trade and Environment. Singapore hosted the WTO Ministerial Meeting and the World Bank and IMF Annual Meeting in 2006.[21]

On 3 August 1966, Singapore became the 104th member of the IMF and the World Bank. Singapore has received assistance from the IMF since it joined and over the years has also supported the IMF in its various initiatives. In 1998, Singapore established the IMF-Singapore Regional Training Institute. Tharman Shanmugaratnam, the Deputy Prime Minister of Singapore, served as Chairman of the IMF's International Monetary and Financial Committee from 2011 to 2015.[22]

2.3 Other International Organizations

Other than the UN and its specialized agencies and bodies, Singapore is a member of numerous international organizations. The most significant of these are ASEAN, which it helped establish in 1967; the Commonwealth, which it joined upon independence in 1965; and the Non-Aligned Movement, into which it was admitted in 1969.

ASEAN grew out of the Indonesian Confrontation when five Southeast Asian states—including Singapore—decided to establish a regional organization to promote

[20] See Civil Aviation Authority of Singapore, 'Singapore and ICAO' in Koh, Chang, and Koh (eds) (n 12) 113.

[21] See K Kesavapany, 'Singapore and the World Trade Organization (WTO)' in Koh, Chang, and Koh (eds) (n 12) 66.

[22] See Chia Der Jiun, 'Singapore and the International Monetary Fund (IMF)' in Koh, Chang, and Koh (eds) (n 12) 132.

economic growth, social progress, cultural development, peace, and security in the region. Throughout its history, Singapore has been one of ASEAN's strongest advocates and supporters. It hosted the fourth ASEAN Summit in 1992, when negotiations began for the ASEAN Free Trade Area. Singapore also hosted the 13th ASEAN Summit in 2007 and the 32nd and 33rd Summits in 2018. Singapore has thus far provided two Secretaries-General to ASEAN since the establishment of the Secretariat in 1976: Chan Kai Yau (1982–4) and Ong Keng Yong (2003–5).

By dint of its membership in ASEAN, Singapore is also a member of the ASEAN Regional Forum which was established in 1994 to 'foster constructive dialogue and consultation on political and security issues of common interest and concern; and to make significant contributions to efforts towards confidence-building and preventive diplomacy in the Asia-Pacific region'. Singapore is also the home to the Secretariats of the Pacific Economic Cooperation Council and the Asia Pacific Economic Cooperation, which were established in 1990 and 1993 respectively.

Singapore has been a permanent observer of the Arctic Council since 2013; despite being 7,000 km away from the Arctic Circle, its interest relates to fears concerning climate change and global warming as a low-lying coastal nation one-degree north of the equator. The melting of Arctic ice and the opening up of new northern sea routes potentially impacts Singapore as a transshipment hub, such that it shares common interests with the Arctic Council with respect to research or the development of maritime infrastructure to facilitate safe shipping in the region. To contribute to the development of the Arctic region, Singapore has provided full scholarships, under the Singapore-Arctic Permanent Participants Cooperation Package, for students from Arctic indigenous communities to study disciplines such as maritime law and public policy at Singaporean institutions. In 2015, Singapore hosted the first Arctic Circle Singapore Forum to draw attention to Arctic issues in Asia.[23]

3 Impact

Singapore's most visible contribution to the UN system has been in sending some of its best diplomats to represent the Republic in various capacities. One of Singapore's most significant contributions and engagements within the UN system has been its initiative in forming the Forum of Small States (FOSS), an informal grouping of small states with populations of less than 10 million. The idea for the grouping came from Singapore's UN Permanent Representative Chew Tai Soo, who observed that small states were often excluded from the inner sanctums of negotiations; lacked in-depth information on what went on in the UN; and were proportionally under-represented in the UN's

[23] Sam Tan, 'What is the connection between Singapore and the Arctic Region?' *Today* (Singapore, 24 May 2016).

principal organs and specialized agencies.[24] The first meeting of the sixteen 'core members' of FOSS met at the Singapore Mission in New York on 22 March 1992 to establish the Forum. Initially, the Forum acted as a platform for small states to support each other's candidatures in elections to the various UN and UN-related bodies. Later, its scope of activities was broadened to include a programme of talks on international issues by prominent academics or senior diplomats.[25] At the time of writing, the FOSS comprises 107 member states. It has been chaired by Singapore's UN Permanent Representative since its inception.

Singapore is also part of another small-state initiative, the Small-5 or 'S-5', comprising Costa Rica, Jordan, Liechtenstein, Singapore, and Switzerland. Encouraged by the World Summit Outcome recommendations, this group began working together in late 2005 to improve the UN Security Council's operations, to increase the involvement of non-Security Council member states in its work, and to enhance the Council's accountability. In March 2006, the S-5 Group circulated a draft resolution that proposed, among other things, improving the relationship between the General Assembly and the Security Council; better interaction between the Council and troop-contributing member states involved in peace missions; and restrictions on the use of the veto in cases of genocide, crimes against humanity, and serious violations of international humanitarian law.[26] Unfortunately, this draft resolution was withdrawn in 2012, following pressure from the large states and especially from the P5 members of the Security Council.[27]

A third Singapore initiative involving the UN's smaller states was the establishment of the Global Governance Group (also known as the '3G'), established in 2009. The group, comprising thirty small and medium-sized states,[28] was set up to bridge the widening gap between the actions and deliberations of the G20 countries and other states.[29] As the Convenor of 3G since its inception, Singapore has attended and represented the 3G in all G20 Summits since 2010.

Since the late 1980s, Singapore has also taken part in the UN's peace-keeping and peace-building efforts. In December 1990, Singapore accepted an invitation to send a seven-member Singapore Armed Forces team to participate in the UN Iraq-Kuwait Observer Mission. In June the following year, Singapore accepted yet other UN

[24] Chew Tai Soo, 'A History of the Forum of Small States' in Koh, Chang, and Koh (eds) (n 12) 35.

[25] Jayakumar (n 13) 64.

[26] See UNGA, 'Enhancing the Accountability, Transparency and Effectiveness of the Security Council' (15 May 2012) UN Doc A/66/L.42/Rev.2.

[27] See UNGA, 'Switzerland Withdraws Draft Resolution in General Assembly Aimed at Improving Security Council's Working Methods to Avoid "Politically Complex" Wrangling' (16 May 2012) Press Release GA/11234.

[28] Members of 3G are: Bahamas, Bahrain, Barbados, Botswana, Brunei Darussalam, Chile, Costa Rica, Finland, Guatemala, Jamaica, Kuwait, Liechtenstein, Luxembourg, Malaysia, Monaco, Montenegro, New Zealand, Panama, Peru, Philippines, Qatar, Rwanda, San Marino, Senegal, Singapore, Slovenia, Switzerland, United Arab Emirates, Uruguay, and Vietnam.

[29] See Vanu Gopala Menon, 'Singapore and the Global Governance Group (3G)' in Koh, Chang, and Koh (eds) (n 12) 39.

invitations to provide military observers and police officers to the UN Angola Verification Mission II and the UN Mission in Western Sahara. On 31 March 1992, Singapore sent a 75-man contingent as part of the peace-keeping force of the UN Transitional Authority in Cambodia, to demonstrate its commitment in playing a constructive role in the peaceful resolution of the Cambodian conflict. In September 1999, Singapore announced its intention to participate in the UN's Multi-National Force for East Timor. In August 2002, Major General Tan Huck Gim became the first Singaporean to be appointed Force Commander of any UN peace-keeping force when he took command of the UN Mission of Support in East Timor.[30] The Singapore Armed Forces also sent ten medical teams to Timor between 1999 and 2002.

At the WTO, Singapore organized the first Ministerial meeting in 1996 and also lobbied for the reform of the GATT procedure to deal with trade disputes. It was the first WTO member to seek recourse under the WTO's dispute resolution mechanism when, in 1995, it requested consultations with Malaysia under the WTO Understanding on Rules and Procedures Governing the Settlement of Disputes.[31] A number of Singapore diplomats have been requested to serve in WTO dispute cases, either as chairman or panellist, including Tommy Koh, See Chak Mun, Chew Tai Soo, S Tiwari, Elizabeth Chelliah, Minn Naing Oo, and Margaret Liang.[32] Other initiatives include Singapore's agreement with the UN Development Programme (UNDP) in 2012 to establish a Global Centre for Public Service Excellence (GCPSE) in Singapore, and the establishment in 2005 of a World Intellectual Property Organization (WIPO) office in Singapore. The GCPSE, which has been operational since December 2012, brings together officials, leaders, policy-makers, and experts to debate and collaborate in dealing with public challenges of the day by identifying trends, innovations, and public solutions.

At a regional and international level, Singapore and ASEAN's role in protesting the Vietnamese invasion of Kampuchea (Cambodia) in 1978, and the campaign to allow the Khmer Rouge government of Democratic Kampuchea to keep its seat at the UN[33] was significant for two reasons. First, the invasion galvanized and united the then five

[30] See Singapore Armed Forces, 'The SAF and UN Peace Operation' in Koh, Chang, and Koh (eds) (n 12) 237; and Singapore Police Force, 'Policing in a Foreign Land' in Koh, Chang, and Koh (eds) (n 12) 247.

[31] Margaret Liang, 'Singapore's Contribution to the WTO Dispute Mechanism: Reflections of a Singapore Negotiator' in Koh, Chang, and Koh (eds) (n 12) 99.

[32] Ibid. 100–1.

[33] On this conflict, see Muthiah Alagappa, 'Regionalism and the Quest for Security: ASEAN and the Cambodian Conflict' (1993) 47 Australian Journal of International Affairs 189; Kishore Mahbubani, 'The Kampuchean Problem: A Southeast Asian Perception' (1983–84) 62 Foreign Affairs 407; Justus van der Kroef, 'ASEAN, Hanoi, and the Kampuchean Conflict: Between "Kuantan" and a "Third Alternative"' (1981) 21 Asian Survey 515; Shaun Narine, 'ASEAN and the Management of Regional Security' (1998) 71 Pacific Affairs 195; Lee Jones, 'ASEAN Intervention in Cambodia: From Cold War to Conditionality' (2007) 20 Pacific Review 523; and Adulgaffar Peang-Meth, 'The United Nations Peace Plan, the Cambodian Conflict, and the Future of Cambodia' (1992) 14 Contemporary Southeast Asia 33.

ASEAN states 'in a way that no other issue had before'.[34] Second, the ASEAN states collectively argued against the Vietnamese invasion on the basis of international law. Tommy Koh, Singapore's then Permanent Representative to the UN, had the unenviable task of leading the ASEAN delegation to argue that it was the 'lesser of two evils' to allow the representative of the murderous Khmer Rouge regime to keep its seat—and uphold the principle of territorial sovereignty and inviolability—than to condone the Vietnamese invasion and occupation of Cambodia.[35]

Singapore has long supported the work of ASEAN and was instrumental in the final 'legalization' of the organization. Although ASEAN was established in 1967, it was unclear—for the next forty years—what its legal standing was. It was not until the signing of the ASEAN Charter in 2007 that ASEAN was finally established as a legal entity with legal personality. While the idea for the Charter was not Singapore's, it was Singapore Foreign Minister George Yeo who persuaded his counterparts to adopt a 'visionary' approach to drafting the Charter. Yeo favoured a 'top down' approach and envisaged the drafting as a two-stage process: first by establishing an Eminent Persons Group (EPG) to formulate and make key recommendations to the ASEAN leaders; and second to appoint a High-Level Task Force (HLTF) to do the actual drafting.[36] The EPG completed its work in 2006 and submitted its final report to the ASEAN leaders at the twelfth ASEAN Summit in Cebu, Philippines in January 2007, and the HLTF completed the draft that same year.[37]

3.1 Making International Law

Singapore's Constitution does not specifically vest its treaty-making or treaty-ratification power in any specific organ of government. As foreign relations are a function of executive power, it is the Singapore Cabinet that has treaty-making and ratification powers. There is no requirement for the legislative branch to ratify treaties signed by the executive. Decisions on the signing of, or accession to, treaties is made by the Cabinet which—in the British traditional fashion of assuming collective responsibility for government—will then delegate the task of working out the technical details to the Ministry of Foreign Affairs. Unlike the Foreign and Commonwealth Office in Britain, Singapore's Foreign Ministry has no legal division and thus works hand-in-hand with the International Affairs Division (IAD) of the Attorney-General's Chambers. Under article 35(7) of the Constitution, the Attorney-General is the government's legal adviser. During treaty negotiations, it is common to have officers from the IAD present

[34] S Dhabalan, 'Scenes from the Cambodian Drama' in Tommy Koh and Chang Li Lin (eds), *The Little Red Dot: Reflections by Singapore's Diplomats* (World Scientific & Institute of Policy Studies 2005) 41.

[35] Tommy Koh, 'My Adventure with International Law' (2001) 5 Singapore Journal of International and Comparative Law 277, 279.

[36] Jayakumar (n 13) 94–5.

[37] See Walter Woon, *The ASEAN Charter: A Commentary* (NUS Press 2016) 14–27.

alongside the Foreign Ministry officials. Ratification of treaties is also done by the Cabinet and often signed under the hand of the Foreign Minister.

To 'make' international law a state must have significant and notable state practice recognized by other states or take an active part in proposing changes to major multilateral treaties during their negotiations. As a small state, Singapore's state practice is not particularly unique, but it has taken a very active part in the negotiation of numerous treaties. Tommy Koh's chairmanship and stewardship of the Third UN Conference on the Law of the Sea has already been noted, but Singapore's contribution to the Conference and the resultant UNCLOS did not stop there. Singapore has been a key member of a group of 'land-locked and geographically-disadvantaged states' (LGDS), which became a significant negotiating block in the drafting process. The LGDS argued vocally for greater freedom of navigation and overflight—thus creating a regime of transit passage—and for a robust dispute resolution mechanism. The group was also instrumental in pushing article 43 of UNCLOS, which required littoral states to cooperate in the establishment and maintenance of navigational safety and other improvements in aid of international navigation and to prevent, reduce, and control marine pollution. Another treaty which Singapore played a major role in developing was one to simplify the registration of trademarks in WIPO. This treaty, known as the Singapore Treaty on the Law of Trademarks, is the only treaty to be named after Singapore.[38]

3.2 Using International Law

Singapore is 'small and surrounded'[39] by larger neighbouring states. Given these vulnerabilities, Singapore is committed to a global order governed by the international rule of law. Such an order is considered key to preserving state sovereignty, mitigating the asymmetries of interstate power, and dampening the prospect of 'might is right' as the driver of international relations.[40]

A crucial facet to this goal is the pacific settlement of disputes through peaceful negotiations or third party adjudication. In an apparent departure from quiet diplomacy, Singapore has been willing to submit disputes it had with Malaysia to arbitration or to the International Court of Justice, where both sides have accepted the ruling, without letting adverse decisions sour bilateral relations.[41] It advocates that 'that is how international disputes should be settled'.[42]

[38] See Burhan Gafoor, 'Merits of Multilateralism' in Koh, Chang, and Koh (eds) (n 12) 79.

[39] Joe Freeman, 'The Singapore Story is the Israel Story' *Tablet* (Israel, 25 March 2015).

[40] PM Lee Hsien Loong, 'National Day Rally Speech 2016' (ITE College Central, Singapore, 21 August 2016) <http://www.pmo.gov.sg/national-day-rally-2016> accessed June 2017.

[41] CL Lim, 'The Uses of Pacific Settlement Techniques in Malaysia-Singapore Relations' (2005) 6 Melbourne Journal of International Law 313.

[42] PM Lee Hsien Loong (n 40).

For example, Singapore submitted its territorial dispute, dating back to 1979, with Malaysia over Pedra Branca island, to the International Court of Justice, which issued its judgement on 23 May 2008.[43] It submitted to arbitration its dispute with Malaysia over a development charge issue in relation to the Points of Agreement on Railway Land 1990.

Even where Singapore is not a claimant state and does not take sides on competing territorial claims, it earned China's ire by affirming the decision of the Arbitral Tribunal convened under Annex VII of UNCLOS brought by the Philippines against China which rejected China's claims in the South China Sea.[44] In relation to that case, Singapore stated that 'as a small state', it strongly supports 'the peaceful resolution of disputes among claimants in accordance with universally recognized principles of international law, including UNCLOS, without resorting to the threat or use of force'.[45] It urged 'all parties to fully respect legal and diplomatic processes'. China rejected the ruling by the Permanent Court of Arbitration and, in thinly veiled criticisms, asked Singapore to respect its claims and to be objective and fair as the country coordinator of ASEAN–China dialogue relations.[46]

Malaysia made a failed application for provisional measures against Singapore to the International Tribunal for the Law of the Sea (ITLOS) under article 290(5) of UNCLOS, claiming that Singapore's land reclamation activities in the Johor Straits had intruded into Malaysian territory and harmed the marine environment and livelihood of Malaysian fishermen. After rejecting this application at the hearing in Hamburg, the Tribunal in 2003 ordered both governments to convene a group of four independent experts to verify the facts.[47] Ultimately, the expert report, which both governments accepted,[48] largely exonerated Singapore and the dispute was amicably settled, with

[43] *Sovereignty over Pedra Branca/Pulau Batu Puteh, Middle Rocks and South Ledge (Malaysia/Singapore)* [2008] ICJ Rep 2. See S Jayakumar and Tommy Koh, *Pedra Branca: The Road to the World Court* (National University of Singapore Press 2009). In February 2017, Malaysia applied to the ICJ to revise its decision on the basis of new discovered facts, which Singapore will oppose: Danson Cheong, 'Malaysia's Fresh Challenge on Pedra Banca "Without Merit": MFA' *The Straits Times* (Singapore, 2 July 2017).

[44] Jane Chan, 'Singapore and the South China Sea: Being an Effective Coordinator and Honest Broker' (2016) 21 Asia Policy 41.

[45] Ministry of Foreign Affairs, 'MFA Spokesman's Comments on the Ruling of the Arbitral Tribunal in the *Philippines v China* Case under Annex VII to the 1982 United Nations Convention on the Law of the Sea (UNCLOS)' (Singapore, 12 July 2016) <http://www.mfa.gov.sg/content/mfa/media_centre/press_room/pr/2016/201607/press_20160712_2.html> accessed 30 December 2018.

[46] 'China asks Singapore to Respect its Position on South China Sea Tribunal Ruling' *Today* (Singapore, 7 August 2016); Kor Kian Beng, 'Singapore Can be a Better Friend to China if it Builds Web of Friendships with Other Nations' *The Straits Times* (Singapore, 25 August 2016).

[47] ITLOS, 'Case Concerning Land Reclamation by Singapore in and Around the Straits of Johor *(Malaysia v Singapore)*, Provisional Measures' (Order, 8 October 2003) <http://www.itlos.org/fileadmin/itlos/documents/cases/case_no_12/Order.08.10.03.E.pdf> accessed 30 December 2018.

[48] Singapore Government, 'Case Concerning Land Reclamation in and around the Straits of Johor *(Malaysia v Singapore)*, Joint Press Statement' (Press Release, 9 January 2005).

both parties signing a Settlement Agreement in 2006.[49] This order 'compelled the two Parties to return to a co-operative mode'[50] and to settle their differences by reference to an objective report.

Moreover, through invoking GATT and WTO dispute-settlement procedures, Singapore was able to induce Malaysia to rescind protectionist measures relating to import prohibitions on two types of petrochemicals in 1994. As a result, it withdrew its complaint in 1995.[51]

More recently, to promote Singapore's capacity as a hub for resolving Asian disputes, Singapore signed a joint declaration with ITLOS in 2015 undertaking to provide it with a neutral venue and facilities for hearing Asian disputes.[52]

4 Domestic Implementation

4.1 Legislative Transformation

The Singapore Constitution does not provide for the automatic implementation of international law and, following British practice, Singapore adopts a dualist approach to the application of its international legal obligations. All treaty obligations are met by existing legislation or through transformative legislation.

4.2 Singapore Courts

Singapore courts recognize article 38 of the Statute of the International Court of Justice[53] as an authoritative statement of the sources of international law, clearly distinguishing between primary sources and subsidiary methods for determining the existence of universally binding customary international law (CIL).[54] The courts discount arguments based on *lex ferenda* or soft law, like the Beijing Statement of Principles of the Independence of the Judiciary in the LAWASIA Region

[49] Singapore Government, 'Case Concerning Land Reclamation by Singapore in and Around the Straits of Johor: Settlement Agreement, Joint Press Statement' (Press Release, 26 April 2005); see generally Cheong Koon Hean, Tommy Koh, and Lionel Yee, *Malaysia & Singapore: The Land Reclamation Case—From Dispute to Settlement* (Straits Times Press 2013).

[50] Tommy Koh and Jolene Lin, 'The Land Reclamation Case: Thoughts and Reflections' (2006) 10 Singapore Yearbook of International Law 1, 5.

[51] WTO, 'Dispute Settlement 1: Malaysia – Prohibition of Imports of Polyethylene and Polypropylene' <http://www.wto.org/english/tratop_e/dispu_e/cases_e/ds1_e.htm> accessed 30 December 2018.

[52] 'Singapore Becomes Venue in Asia to Settle Disputes Relating to Law of the Sea' *The Straits Times* (Singapore, 31 August 2015).

[53] Statute of the International Court of Justice, annexed to the Charter of the United Nations 1945.

[54] *Yong Vui Kong v Public Prosecutor* [2010] 3 SLR 489 para 98.

(which contains non-specific hortatory statements underscoring the importance of the judicial role in securing rights and criminal sentencing).[55]

Although the Constitution is silent on the issue, Singaporean courts have made clear judicial pronouncements on the reception and status of international law within the domestic legal order.[56] The courts have affirmed a dualist approach, which apprehends international and municipal law as two distinct legal orders. Treaties are not self-executing but must be legislatively incorporated to be given domestic legal effect, following the English position that treaties do not 'create independent rights, obligations, powers or duties'.[57] If treaties were self-executing, this would contravene the separation of powers in enabling the executive to legislate through its treaty-making power.

The courts have recognized that multilateral treaties may embody CIL norms, such as the right of innocent passage through the territorial sea for non-coastal state vessels in article 28 of UNCLOS;[58] the 'moving frontier rule' in relation to state succession embodied under article 29 of the Vienna Convention of the Law of Treaties and article 15 of the Vienna Convention on Succession of States in respect of Treaties;[59] and the right of consular access under article 36(1) of the Vienna Convention on Consular Relations (VCCR).[60] In the latter case, the prosecution's non-protest against invoking article 36(1) of the VCCR, a treaty Singapore was not then party to, is a form of tacit consent treated as evidence of *opinio juris*.

The courts have primarily focused on whether state practice is 'both extensive and virtually uniform'[61] to ascertain whether a putative CIL norm is clearly established. One judgment held that the right to property under article 17 of the Universal Declaration of Human Rights 1948 (UDHR) did not embody CIL given the 'widespread state practice allowing for collective sales [of property] by majority vote'.[62]

Another judgment affirmed that article 5 of the UDHR, which prohibits torture and cruel or inhuman treatment or punishment, constituted CIL, but rejected arguments that the content of the norm prohibited the death penalty generally and hanging as

[55] It was invoked in *Public Prosecutor v Nguyen Tuong Van* [2004] 2 SLR 328 but Kan J found it did not assist defence counsel's argument that mandatory death sentences were illegal: paras 99–100.

[56] Thio Li-ann, 'International Law in the Courts of Singapore: Still a Little Island?' (2013) 19 Asian Yearbook of International Law 1.

[57] *The Sahand* [2011] 2 SLR 1093 para 33 (High Court). In the same way, Singapore's international law obligations under an extradition treaty do not create domestic rights directly as these 'exist on different planes': *Public Prosecutor v Tan Cheng Yew* [2013] 1 SLR 1095 para 56 (High Court).

[58] *The Trade Resolve* [1994] 4 SLR 424 para 23 (High Court). Singapore ratified the UN Convention on the Law of the Sea on 17 November 1994.

[59] *Sanum Investments Ltd v Government of the Lao People's Democratic Republic* [2016] 5 SLR 536 paras 47–9.

[60] Although Singapore was not then party to the VCCR, the High Court, in examining Singapore state practice and the non-objection of the public prosecutor, concluded that article 36(1) applied to Singapore as a matter of customary international law: *PP v Nguyen* (n 55) paras 31–7. Singapore acceded to the treaty on 1 April 2005.

[61] *Yong Vui Kong v PP* (n 54) para 98.

[62] *Chan Kin Foo v City Developments Ltd* [2013] 2 SLR 895 paras 28–32.

a mode of execution specifically.[63] To show the lack of consensus on the issue, the Court in that case took note of a UN Commission on Human Rights report which stated that, as of 1 December 2002, there were seventy-one retentionist and seventy-seven abolitionist countries in relation to the death penalty.[64] It also held that although the majority of states did not impose a mandatory death penalty (MDP) for drug trafficking, there were some thirty-one states which did. This 'significant number' was sufficient to indicate a lack of international consensus to support a CIL rule prohibiting the imposition of the MDP.[65]

4.3 Interpretation

Courts in Singapore are required to adopt a purposive approach to the interpretation of statutes[66] and, as an aid to interpretation, the court is permitted to look at all manner of extra-legislative material, including international treaties and agreements.[67] Although established CIL norms do not have to be legislatively incorporated, they do not automatically apply as part of Singapore law because, without judicial recognition, they are 'merely floating in the air' until 'applied as or definitively declared to be part of domestic law by a domestic court'.[68] CIL rules are received as part of Singapore common law and do not enjoy constitutional rank, such that domestic statutes prevail over CIL norms.[69] Applying dualist logic, the Court of Appeal rejected the view that a *jus cogens* norm automatically acquired the status of constitutional law upon reception, as this would mean that the views of other states could dictate the meaning of the Singapore Constitution 'regardless of what the people of Singapore, expressing their will through their elected representatives, think'.[70] It found no reason why a norm, which enjoyed the highest status under one legal system, should enjoy similar status within another legal system, which supports a positivist view of consent-based international obligation.

Thus CIL norms attaining the status of peremptory norms 'cannot override a domestic statute whose meaning and effect is clear'.[71] In reviewing the summary records of the First Session of the Vienna Convention on the Law of Treaties 1969, the Court of Appeal concluded that *jus cogens* norms, which invalidate inconsistent treaties, applied at the interstate rather than intrastate level.[72] Reflecting a state-centricity

[63] This was in the 2005 decision of *Nguyen Tuong Van v Public Prosecutor* [2005] 1 SLR 103 para 92.

[64] UN Commission on Human Rights, 'Question of the Death Penalty: Report of the Secretary-General Submitted Pursuant to Commission Resolution 2002/77' (30 January 2003) 59th Session UN Doc E/CN.4/2003/106.

[65] *Yong Vui Kong v PP* (n 54) paras 94–9.

[66] Interpretation Act 1965 c 1 s 9A.

[67] Ibid. s 9A(3).

[68] *Yong Vui Kong v PP* (n 54) para 90.

[69] *Nguyen Tuong Van v PP* (n 63) para 44 (citing *Chung Chi Cheung v The King* [1939] AC 160).

[70] *Yong Vui Kong v Public Prosecutor* [2015] 2 SLR 1129, 1148.

[71] Ibid. para 38.

[72] Ibid. para 36.

and nationalist orientation deeply protective of popular sovereignty, the courts will apply national law over *jus cogens* norms, which cannot nullify inconsistent statute or judicial precedent, even if this incurs international responsibility.

Presumably, Singapore courts will, 'as far as possible',[73] interpret domestic law consistently with Singapore's international legal obligations. The courts have, however, noted 'inherent limits'[74] in referring to international human rights law to interpret the Constitution, particularly where the constitutional text or history precludes the incorporation of the international norm in question. For example, the intentional omission of a prohibition against torture from the text of the Constitution precluded the courts from 'legislating' new constitutional rights under the guise of constitutional interpretation—rather, it falls to Parliament to amend the Constitution or enact new laws.[75] Singapore courts have also rejected regional tests, such as that of the proportionality review associated with European Court of Human Rights jurisprudence.[76] Where human rights treaties are judicially referenced, it is usually to reiterate domestic rules such as the joint parental responsibility norm in section 46(1) of the Women's Charter 1961, which is endorsed by article 18 of the Convention on the Rights of the Child (CRC).[77]

Where a statute refers to any treaty or international agreement, section 9A(3) of the Interpretation Act 1965 (Cap 1) permits reference to it to assist in interpreting statutory provisions. For example, the Court examined the meaning of 'import' in the UN Single Convention on Narcotic Drugs 1961 which Singapore became party to in 1973. In doing so, it sustained a broad reading of 'import'—in section 7 of the Misuse of Drugs Act 1973 (Cap 185), which was enacted to give effect to Convention obligations—beyond a mercantilist sense to encompass movement of drugs through Singapore for distribution elsewhere.[78] Parliament, in enacting legislation to give effect to treaties, may include provisions that go beyond treaty terms, which will prevail over the treaty provisions where the statutory wording is clear.[79]

The courts have imposed deterrent sentences for breaches of statutory offences designed to implement treaty obligations. One example is possessing endangered birds without import permits, which 'went against the spirit' of Singapore's obligations to cooperate with other states to 'preserve their endangered species' under the

[73] *Yong Vui Kong v PP* (n 54) para 59. [74] Ibid.

[75] Ibid. para 95. See Thio Li-ann, 'Reading Rights Rightly: The UDHR and its Creeping Influence on the Development of Singapore Public Law' (2008) Singapore Journal of Legal Studies 264.

[76] *Chee Siok Chin v Minister for Home Affairs* [2006] 1 SLR(R) 582 para 87. The Court of Appeal has also noted that the European Convention on Human Rights 1950 applied to Singapore when it was a British colony, but that the Singapore Chapter on Fundamental Liberties is not based on it: *Yong Vui Kong v PP* (n 54) para 61.

[77] *CX v CY (Minor: Custody and Access)* [2005] SGCA 37, [2005] 3 SLR 690, 700 para 26.

[78] *Ng Kwok Chun v Public Prosecutor* [1992] 3 SLR(R) 254 (CA).

[79] *Tan Ah Yeo v Seow Teck Ming* [1989] 1 SLR(R) 134 (High Court).

Convention on International Trade in Endangered Species of Wild Fauna and Flora 1973 (CITES).[80]

In relation to judicial review in cases involving international law and the exercise of executive prerogative powers, the courts have clarified that matters of 'high policy' such as treaty-making and foreign affairs (for example those implicating international boundary disputes) are immune from review. This is because the courts consider such cases to be a matter of the separation of powers, which requires deference to the executive branch. International treaties which have been incorporated into the domestic legal order may, however, be reviewed.[81]

Where the politically sensitive issue of state recognition is concerned, the courts adopt a 'one voice' policy guided by the separation of powers. An example is where a court refused to depart from the executive view that Taiwan was not a state, pursuant to the 'one-China policy', and so Taiwan could not claim sovereign immunity.[82] This follows the stipulation in section 18 of Singapore's State Immunity Act 1979 (Cap 131) that an executive certificate was conclusive evidence of whether any country was a state. The non-issuance of such a certificate was treated as indicating non-recognition,[83] rather than as an ambiguity inviting the courts to independently evaluate and make conclusions on questions of statehood.[84]

The adherence to the 'Westphalian notion of sovereignty',[85] under which states exercised absolute sovereign powers within their territorial boundaries, is reflected in Singapore's treatment of the act of state doctrine. In Singapore, the doctrine is based on international law considerations, rather than the shift towards a constitutional separation of powers extant in US jurisprudence.[86] A court will not adjudicate upon the legality of the acts of a foreign sovereign state which affects property or people within that state's jurisdiction, in deference to foreign state sovereignty, which is the historical basis of the English act of state doctrine that Singapore courts follow. It remains unclear whether Singapore courts will develop exceptions to the doctrine, such as that evident in English public policy, where English courts refuse to accept the validity of foreign state acts where these contravene fundamental international law norms or constitute a

[80] *Public Prosecutor v Kuah Kok Choon* [2000] 3 SLR(R) 752 para 30. CITES, which Singapore acceded to on 30 November 1986, is implemented by the Endangered Species (Import and Export) Act (Cap 92A). On the difficulties faced by national authorities in discharging monitoring obligations under CITES, see the analysis of *Public Prosecutor v Wong Wee Keong* [2015] SGDC 300 in B Ong, LH Lye, and J Chun, 'Regulating International Trade in Endangered Species–Transhipments of CITES-Listed Species via Singapore' (2016) Singapore Journal of Legal Studies 277.

[81] *Lee Hsien Loong v Review Publishing Co Ltd* [2007] 2 SLR(R) 453 paras 95–9.

[82] *Civil Aeronautics Administration v Singapore Airlines Ltd* [2004] 1 SLR 570 paras 12–28. The Court affirmed the declaratory theory of recognition.

[83] Ibid. para 11.

[84] See Olufemi Elias, 'The International Status of Taiwan in the Courts of Canada and Singapore' (2004) 8 Singapore Year Book of International Law 93; CL Lim, 'Non-Recognition of Putative Foreign States (Taiwan) under Singapore's State Immunity Act' (2006) 11 Asian Yearbook of International Law 3.

[85] *Republic of the Philippines v Maler Foundation* [2014] 1 SLR 1389 para 42.

[86] Ibid. para 48.

gross human rights violation.[87] This would have the effect of grounding normative principles of legitimacy which go beyond state consent.[88]

4.4 State Implementation of International Legal Obligations

In implementing treaty obligations, the Singapore government adopts both legislative and non-binding measures. Where trade, commerce, and other economic initiatives are concerned, the object is to align with international standards through facilitative legal harmonization, achieved by way of binding legislation. For example, the International Arbitration Act 1994 (Cap 143A) incorporates the UNCITRAL Model Law on Commercial Arbitration, which buttresses Singapore's position as a significant regional arbitration centre. The Electronic Transaction Act 2010 (Cap 88) was enacted to implement the UN Convention on the Use of Electronic Communications in International Contracts 2005.[89]

In the field of intellectual property (IP) law, a sea change in attitudes occurred in Singapore's shift towards a high-technology, knowledge-based economy in the 1980s, involving, for example, engineering design and computer services. In 1968, the Law Minister, EW Barker, in moving before Parliament what became the Copyright (Gramophone Records and Government Broadcasting) Act 1968, stated that Singapore had 'no intention of becoming signatories to these [IP] conventions' as they 'are for the benefit of the developed countries who refuse to share their knowledge'.[90] Although Singapore had attended many international conferences on the protection of copyright, designs, and patents, the Minister's statement reflects the hostility typical of Third World countries towards IP rights, which were seen to stifle economic growth.

However, by the 1980s, IP rights had become part of the strategy to build the external economy and efforts were made to harmonize Singapore law with international norms. Thus, the Trade Marks Act 1998 (Cap 332) was enacted to give effect to Singapore's obligations under the Agreement on Trade-Related Aspects of Intellectual Property Rights 1994 ('the TRIPS Agreement').[91] Amendments to the Trade Marks Act in 2004

[87] *Oppenheimer v Cattermole* [1976] AC 249; *Kuwait Airways Corp v Iraqi Airways Co* [1995] 1 WLR 1147, [1995] 3 All ER 694.

[88] Li-ann Thio, 'English Public Policy, The Act of State Doctrine and Flagrant Violations of Fundamental International Law: *Kuwait Airways Corp v Iraqi Airways Co* (2002)' (2003) 18 Connecticut Journal of International Law 585.

[89] Other statutes designed to give effect to international treaties relate to transport: Carriage by Air (Montreal Convention, 1999) Act (Cap 32B); environmental law: Endangered Species (Import and Export) Act (Cap 92A); diplomatic relations: Diplomatic and Consular Relations Act (Cap 82A); security and weapons: Chemical Weapons (Prohibition) Act (Cap 37B) and the Sale of Goods (United Nations Convention) Act (Cap 237A).

[90] Second Reading, Copyright (Gramophone Records and Government Broadcasting) Bill 28 Singapore Parliament Reports, col 823 (23 November 1968). This law was intended to protect the livelihood of local musicians and three sound recording companies.

[91] *Novelty Pte Ltd v Amanresorts Ltd* [2009] 3 SLR(R) 216 para 162 (CA).

were adopted to give effect to Singapore's bilateral obligations under the US-Singapore Free Trade Agreement 2003. In particular, that Agreement required Singapore to accede to the standards of the Joint Recommendation concerning Provisions on the Protection of Well-known Trade Marks 1999, which contains standards 'even higher than those contained in the TRIPS Agreement'.[92]

Singapore gave effect, through subsidiary legislation, to various binding Security Council resolutions relating to freezing Iranian assets used to support Iran's nuclear proliferation activities.[93] Under the United Nations Act 2001 (Cap 339), the Law Minister is empowered to make regulations to give effect to article 41 of the UN Charter, which deals with non-forcible measures the Security Council may order UN members to adopt. Singapore generally does not become party to a treaty unless it assesses that its domestic legal framework is able to give effect to the treaty obligations.[94] To accommodate cultural and religious minority rights, Singapore has made reservations to various human rights treaties such as the Convention on the Elimination of All Forms of Discrimination against Women 1979 (CEDAW) and the CRC, acceding to both in 1995. Thus, gender inegalitarian laws in relation to Muslim family and personal law, under the Administration of Muslim Law Act 1966 (Cap 3), are immunized from article 2(f) of the CEDAW (which prohibits discrimination against women). This diminishes the transformative impact treaties might otherwise have on domestic law,[95] although Singapore has subsequently removed reservations to certain human rights treaties.[96]

However, the government prefers to adopt non-binding guidelines or plans in order to implement other types of treaties, particularly those relating to human rights law and

[92] Ibid. para 163. [93] *The Sahand* [2011] 2 SLR 1093 para 26.

[94] The omission of the fair trial clause in article 9 of the Convention on the Prevention and Punishment of Crimes Against Internationally Protected Persons (adopted 14 December 1973, entered into force 20 February 1977, 35 UNTS 167) was explained during the Second Reading of the Internationally Protected Persons Bill as being unnecessary, as anyone prosecuted under the Act would be entitled to due process under Singapore law: Zainul Abidin Rasheed, Singapore Parliamentary Reports (6 March 2008) vol 84. In relation to International Labour Organizations (ILO) conventions, the Manpower Minister has stated that Singapore will ratify an ILO convention 'only when we feel fully comfortable and confident that our legal framework will not in any way clash with the legal framework imposed by the ILO': Lee Boon Yang, Singapore Parliamentary Reports, vol 70. So too in acceding to the CRC, the government considered it was not accepting any rights going beyond those prescribed in the Singapore Constitution as Singapore laws adequately protected the rights of the child: 'Instrument of Accession, Convention on the Rights of the Child' (2 October 1995) para 3.

[95] Li-ann Thio, 'Reception and Resistance: Globalization, International Law and the Singapore Constitution' (2009) 4 National Taiwan University Law Review 335, 353; Li-ann Thio, 'Singapore Human Rights Practice and Legal Policy: Of Pragmatism and Principle, Rights, Rhetoric and Realism' (2009) 21 Singapore Academy of Law Journal 326.

[96] In 2004, Singapore removed its reservation to article 9(2) of CEDAW after equalizing nationality rights by amending article 122 of the Singapore Constitution, to allow Singaporean women married to foreign men to transmit citizenship by descent to their children. This was previously restricted to Singaporean men.

labour law.[97] For example, Singapore acceded to the Convention on the Rights of Persons with Disabilities 2006 (CRPD) in 2013. Singapore seeks to give effect to the CRPD's values and a more inclusive society through promotional 'Enabling Masterplans', which are formulated in consultation with civil society, and inter-Ministerial disability-related policies and activities are coordinated by a Standing Committee on Disabilities.[98]

The decision to approach these issues through policy rather than legal obligation has been consistently criticized by UN committees. The UN committees urge Singapore to adopt a more legalistic approach, such as through incorporating CEDAW as part of national legislation or creating dedicated national mechanisms to deal with the advancement of women[99] and children.[100] An exception may be a modification to the Penal Code in 2007 which gives effect to the Convention on the Prevention and Punishment of the Crime of Genocide 1948, although it has little practical effect.[101] Rather than comprehensive laws incorporating human rights treaties, discrete amendments to existing law are presented as fulfilling treaty obligations. For example, the criminalization of commercial sex with minors was said to be 'in line' with the CRC.[102] Domestically, it mainly falls to Parliament and civil society to ensure compliance with treaty standards through political means, rather than through the courts enforcing justiciable rights.

The government also had occasion in 1979 to denounce International Labour Organization Convention 105 on the Abolition of Forced Labour, in part over disagreement concerning the meaning of 'forced labour' under domestic laws applicable to prisoners.[103]

Where Singapore has come under international pressure *not* to implement a judicial sentence, as it did when US national Michael Fay was sentenced to six strokes of the cane after conviction of an offence under the Vandalism Act 1966 (Cap 341) in 1994, it stood firm on the rule of law and its sovereign right to enforce domestic law and order. It was subject to questionable claims that it had violated human rights through

[97] ILO Convention No. 100 (Equal Remuneration for Men and Women) (adopted 29 June 1951, entered into force 23 May 1953, 165 UNTS 303) is implemented by the non-binding Tripartite Declaration between the Ministry of Manpower, Singapore National Employers Federation, and National Trade Unions Congress.

[98] Committee on the Rights of Persons with Disabilities, 'Initial Report, Singapore, Implementation of the Convention on the Rights of Persons with Disabilities' (30 June 2016) UN Doc CRPD/C/SGP/1.

[99] CEDAW Committee, 'Concluding Observations: Singapore' (10 August 2011) UN Doc CEDAW/C/SGP/CO/4 paras 10, 12, 18.

[100] CRC Committee, 'Concluding Observations: Singapore' (4 May 2011) UN Doc CRC/C/SGP/CO/2-3 paras 9, 15.

[101] Penal Code (Amendment) Act 2007 (No. 51 of 2007) s 28.

[102] Ho Peng Kee, Singapore Parliamentary Reports (22 October 2007) vol 83, col 2175, referenced in *Tan Chye Hin v Public Prosecutor* [2009] 3 SLR 873 para 9.

[103] ILO, 'The Elimination of all Forms of Forced or Compulsory Labour 2002' (compilation of reports sent by various countries to ILO by 2001) 218–19 <http://digitalcommons.ilr.cornell.edu/forcedlabor/11> accessed 30 December 2018; Yogesh Tyagi, 'The Denunciation of Human Rights Treaties' (2008) 79 British Yearbook of International Law 86, 178.

applying corporal punishment, and the US government, to signal its disapproval, reportedly sought to prevent Singapore from hosting the first WTO inter-ministerial committee in 1996. As a matter of comity and pragmatism, the Singapore Cabinet eventually responded to the US President's plea for clemency by reducing the number of Fay's strokes from six to four.[104]

5 Human Rights, Human Welfare, and Development

Singapore is one of several Asian countries associated with advancing the 'Asian values' debate in human rights discourse. This emerged in the 1990s, primarily as a debate between academics and diplomats,[105] framed as a cultural relativist challenge to universal human rights law. Contrary to Western experience, economic liberalization and growth were experienced by various Asian countries without political liberalization, henceforth presenting an alternative law and development model.

The Ministerial statement delivered by Singapore at the 1993 World Conference on Human Rights in Vienna[106] remains the most authoritative articulation of Singapore's official position towards human rights. A few points are highlighted. First, Singapore articulated the 'trade-off thesis', namely that a developing nation in the early stages of nation-building may restrict civil-political liberties to ensure the political stability needed to buttress trade and foreign investment within a rule of law environment, which in turn secures contract and property rights. Liberalization will increase with economic growth.

Second, Singapore accepted that human rights are a civilizing force and a matter of international concern. It distinguishes between 'core' human rights, such as those in the Universal Declaration of Human Rights 1948 (UDHR), and 'contested' political claims which invoke human rights to gain legitimacy. The latter sustain a predilection towards 'human rightism'[107] and 'reckless activism',[108] which ignores the fact that a

[104] Firouzeh Bahrampour, 'The Caning of Michael Fay: Can Singapore's Punishment Withstand the Scrutiny of International Law' (1995) 10 American University International Law Review 1075. See Singapore Ministry of Foreign Affairs, *50 Years of Singapore Foreign Policy* (Ministry of Foreign Affairs 2016) 53. Singapore adopts a strong sovereigntist position when it comes to letting its criminal justice system run its course, even if this involves foreigners (as in the cases of Filipino Flor Contemplacion and Dutchman Johannes van Damme for homicide and drug-trafficking) and foreign outrage.

[105] For example, see Bilahari Kausikan, 'An East Asian Approach to Human Rights' (1995–96) 2 Buffalo Journal of Human Rights 263.

[106] Wong Kan Seng, 'The Real World of Human Rights' (Vienna, 16 June 1993) Singapore Government Press Release No: (20/JUN, 09-1/93/06/16), reproduced in (1993) Singapore Journal of Law Studies 605. See generally Thio Li-ann, 'Pragmatism and Realism Do Not Mean Abdication: A Critical Inquiry into Singapore's Engagement with International Human Rights Law' (2004) 8 Singapore Year Book of International Law 41.

[107] Alain Pellet, 'Human Rightism and International Law' (Gilberto Amado Memorial Lecture, 18 July 2000).

[108] Joseph Raz, 'Human Rights in the Emerging World Order' (2010) 1 Transnational Legal Theory 31.

case has to be made for the duties imposed by rights, and which go beyond merely showing that a putative right is valuable to the right holder. Beyond the UDHR, legitimate particularities should be recognized without allowing these to be a 'shield for dictators',[109] perhaps in terms of a global 'margin of appreciation' (a doctrine developed by the European Court of Human Rights, which accords a degree of latitude to states in the implementation of their human rights obligations). There are conflicting views over how to interpret accepted rights, and over whether a claim is a right. Foreign Minister Wong Kan Seng stated further that Singaporeans, among many others, did not agree that free expression encompassed pornography and maintained that 'the right to marry is confined to those of the opposite gender'. As the human rights idea is 'historically specific', the lack of international consensus in a plural world is to be expected. Singapore recognizes that others dispute its view that the right to development is inalienable because 'poverty is an obscene violation of the most basic of individual rights'.[110]

Third, Singapore is realistic in appreciating that human rights are not a tool for realizing utopia, and that real welfare gains, such as healthy environments, high educational standards, and non-corrupt government, involve compromises. This may be described as a 'human welfare' approach, which focuses on practical success rather than abstract prescriptions or justiciable entitlements. It advocates a 'pragmatic' approach towards human rights, in cooperating where there is consensus and agreeing to disagree if needed, rather than a self-righteous ideological dogmatism more interested in feeling virtuous than effectively doing good.[111] Rather than seeking to impose one pattern of socio-political arrangements, states should focus on promoting 'humane standards of behaviour' and meeting the basic needs of their citizens.[112]

Fourth, human rights are not absolute; each country must find its own equilibrium in balancing rights holistically against competing rights, duties, and goods. Both the courts and government have identified Singapore as being 'communitarian',[113] eschewing the individual autonomy/rights-oriented focus emphasized by liberalism. Singapore treats human rights not as trumps but as important policy items and aspects of good governance.

Critics denounce the 'Asian values' argument as an apology for power, which maximizes state discretion and minimizes accountability to external standards or independent control mechanisms. That said, Singapore became party to three human rights treaties in 1995 (CEDAW, CRC, and the Genocide Convention); it thereby became socialized into the state-reporting process, consulting with civil society and

[109] *Chee Siok Chin v Minister for Home Affairs* [2006] 1 SLR(R) 582 para 132, discussing differing standards of public conduct across countries.

[110] Wong (n 106). [111] Ibid. [112] Ibid.

[113] Singapore Parliament, *Shared Values* (White Paper, CMD No 1, 1991) para 30; *Public Prosecutor v Kwong Kok Hing* [2008] 2 SLR(R) 684 para 17.

engaging with dialogue before the relevant UN committees. It also participates in the Universal Periodic Review (UPR) of the UN Human Rights Council.[114]

For Singapore's second UPR, in 2016, the Inter-Ministerial Committee on Human Rights conducted two rounds of consultations with civil society groups. Matters of concern raised during the review process included preventive detention without trial, corporal punishment, the death penalty, equality-based claims related to the criminalization of homosexual sex, and promotion of the rights of migrant workers and the disabled.[115] In its response, Singapore stated it had carefully reviewed the 236 recommendations it received at the twenty-fourth UPR Working Group and noted that many of the recommendations were already being implemented. Those recommendations it disagreed with were said to be 'predicated on unfounded assertions, inaccurate assumptions or erroneous information', or otherwise 'not appropriate in our national context'. Singapore took note of recommendations to establish a national human rights institution, affirming its commitment to the rule of law and pointing out the many avenues Singaporeans had to articulate grievances before the government.[116]

Treaties like the CEDAW and the CRC have broadened the rights discourse, as they contain socio-economic rights absent from the Singapore Constitution. Singapore acceded to the CRPD in 2013 and signed the International Convention on the Elimination of All Forms of Racial Discrimination 1965 in 2015. It has hosted visits by independent experts or special rapporteurs on the right to development, contemporary forms of racism, and the enjoyment of human rights by older persons.[117] As part of ASEAN, Singapore supports the formulation of human rights in the ASEAN Human Rights Declaration 2012. In addition to civil-political and socio-economic rights, the Declaration contains the third generation rights to development and to peace, which are open-ended and hortatory in nature, lack a clear specification of concrete duties, and are more difficult to monitor or measure.

Singapore submits to the weakest monitoring processes, primarily involving a reporting process and dialogue. It has refused to become party to mechanisms which allow for individual communications, as under the CEDAW Optional Protocol, as this would 'infringe on a nation's sovereignty'. It considers that states bear primary responsibility for human rights protection and regards the need to guard against 'foreign interference' as a 'fundamental principle of governance'. It notes that

[114] Singapore participated in the first cycle of UPR in 2011. Related documents are available at: <https://www.ohchr.org/EN/HRBodies/UPR/Pages/SGIndex.aspx>accessed 30 December 2018.

[115] Human Rights Council, 'Report of the Working Group on the Universal Periodic Review: Singapore' (15 April 2016) UN Doc A/HRC/32/17.

[116] Human Rights Council, 'Addendum: Views on Conclusions and/or Recommendations, Voluntary Commitments and Replies Presented by the State Under Review' (13 June 2016) A/HRC/32/17/Add.1, paras 1–4, 34.

[117] See Singapore's homepage hosted by the UN High Commissioner for Human Rights Office: <http://www.ohchr.org/EN/Countries/AsiaRegion/Pages/SGIndex.aspx> accessed 30 December 2018. See also the compilation of Singapore-related human rights documents: Human Rights Council, 'National Report: Singapore' (2 February 2011) UN Doc A/HRC/WG.6/11/SGP/2.

complaints about gender discrimination could be channelled through domestic institutions like 'the Government Ministries, the courts and ultimately, Parliament'.[118] Singapore has not created a dedicated human rights institution and prefers to mainstream human rights through inter-ministerial coordination. However, as an ASEAN member, it is subject to the weak monitoring of ASEAN bodies like the ASEAN Inter-Government Commission on Human Rights, a consultative body whose primary functions are conducting thematic studies and training workshops; it is not empowered to receive individual communications. These functions do not threaten state sovereignty or the cardinal ASEAN principle of non-interference in the internal affairs of member states.[119]

Singapore clearly voices contrarian views or dissent where it does not regard something as a human right or it disagrees with the interpretation of a right. In 2005, Singapore joined other states to lobby for a statement that the death penalty was a matter of criminal justice, not human rights, and that states had the sovereign right to decide whether to impose capital punishment.[120] In 2016, the Foreign Minister reiterated this stand, underscoring that no major international treaties proscribed capital punishment. Articulating these alternative perspectives is a valuable source of state practice which contributes to human rights discussions, such as asking whether the death penalty, in limited circumstances, has a role to play in protecting the sanctity of life and serving broader social interests.[121] Singapore is unlikely to accede to certain UN human rights treaties 'because of reservations on some specific provisions such as corporal punishment and the death penalty'.[122]

Singapore has participated in joint statements rejecting the universal applicability of conscientious objection to military service. This demonstrates a lack of general acceptance necessary for that norm to attain to the status of universally binding CIL.[123]

Some UN committees have criticized Singapore for adopting a welfare approach rather than a human rights framework involving justiciable entitlements and measurable obligations.[124] On that view, realizing welfare goals depends more on a

[118] Yu-Foo Yee Shoon, Singapore Parliamentary Reports (22 May 2007) (Optional Protocol, CEDAW), vol 83, col 892.

[119] AICHR, *Terms of Reference, Guiding Principles 2.1* (ASEAN Secretariat 2009).

[120] Burhan Gafoor, 'Merits of Multilateralism' in Koh, Chang, and Koh (eds) (n 12) 81.

[121] Ministry of Foreign Affairs, Press Release: Transcript of Minister Vivian Balakrishnan's Intervention at the High-Level Side Event at UNGA—'Moving Away from the Death Penalty: Victims and the Death Penalty' (21 September 2016). The Court of Appeal considers it appropriate in sentencing to weigh the community's 'strong feelings' in deciding whether to impose capital punishment, which reflects society's indignation towards acts that are 'so grievous an affront to humanity' as to warrant it: *Kho Jabing v Public Prosecutor* [2016] SGCA 21 para 90; *Public Prosecutor v Kho Jabing* [2015] 2 SLR 112 para 44.

[122] Singapore Parliamentary Reports (28 February 2008) (Budget: Head N—Ministry of Foreign Affairs) vol 84, col 1206.

[123] Commission on Human Rights, 'Letter, Permanent Representative of Singapore to Chairperson' (24 April 2002) 58th Session UN Doc E/CN.4/2002/188.

[124] CEDAW Committee, 'Summary Record' (7 September 2001) 514th Meeting UN Doc CEDAW/C/SR.514, para 30.

government's good faith and sagacity, and such approach is subject to political rather than legal modes of accountability. Regarding the right to development, as Singapore 'believes that all people have a right to social and economic development',[125] it engages in international cooperation to promote the 'more rapid development of developing countries'.[126] It does so under the Singapore Cooperation Programme by sharing its experience and training foreign officials in public administration, port and water management, and civil aviation.[127] Singapore was actively involved in elaborating the Sustainable Development Goals (SDGs) in relation to the 2030 UN Agenda for Sustainable Development,[128] and is supporting the SDGs by working with the UNDP and UN Habitat to promote sustainable cities and water and sanitation solutions.

In 2013, Singapore tabled its first UN General Assembly resolution, titled 'Sanitation for All'.[129] One hundred and twenty states supported the proposal to mark 19 November as World Toilet Day. It chose to champion what was originally an initiative of the World Toilet Organization, a Singapore-founded non-profit organization, as a human development issue with human rights implications. Advocating clean sanitation for all beneficially supports the human right to health and to water, and contributes to poverty eradication, a key plank of the right to development.

6 Conclusion

International law has been described as 'a sword to advance our aggressive interests, and as a shield to protect our defensive interests'.[130] Singapore clearly appreciates the virtues of a rules-based global order as key to ensuring the sovereignty of all states, regardless of their size. While valuing multilateralism and ASEAN regional integration, Singapore also concludes bilateral free-trade agreements, reflecting its brand of pragmatic realism based on 'practical self-interest' and 'not vague idealism'.[131]

While it highly values territorial sovereignty, Singapore has also adopted extraterritorial legislation allowing it to unilaterally deal with transboundary problems, by attaching civil and criminal liability to agri-business corporations, whether Singapore-linked or otherwise, who use fires outside Singapore and cause haze pollution.[132]

[125] Singapore Ministry of Foreign Affairs (n 104) 112.

[126] UNGA res 41/128 (4 December 1986): Declaration on the Right to Development, art. 4(2).

[127] Singapore Ministry of Foreign Affairs (n 104) 109. See also Tan York Chor, 'Who Owns the UN?' in Koh, Chang, and Koh (eds) (n 12) 72.

[128] UNGA res 70/1 (21 October 2015).

[129] UNGA res A/67/L.75 (17 July 2013).

[130] Walter Sim, 'International Law is "Sword and Shield" to Advance and Protect Singapore's Interests: Tommy Koh' *The Straits Times* (Singapore, 8 October 2015).

[131] S Rajaratnam, 'Statement to the 20th Session of the General Assembly, 21 September 1965' in Koh, Chang, and Koh (eds) (n 12) xx.

[132] Transboundary Haze Pollution Act 2014. See 'Transboundary Haze Pollution Act Not about National Sovereignty, MEWR' *Channel NewsAsia* (Singapore, 15 June 2016).

While Singapore may seek to harmonize its domestic law with international standards in the realms of trade, investment, and IP, there is divergence in the field of public law in relation to human rights and criminal justice.

Singapore sees itself as a 'price-taker and not a price-setter in international affairs'.[133] Even so, its efforts to speak up for its vital interests and to act as an 'honest broker' in helping to mediate disputes among other states—reflecting its brand of realistic rather than radical internationalism—allow Singapore to punch above its weight in seeking to influence international relations. In so doing, Singapore seeks to 'cherish independence without denying the reality of interdependence of nations'.[134]

[133] Chong Zi Liang, 'Singapore's Foreign Policy in a Changing World' *The Straits Times* (Singapore, 16 October 2016).

[134] Rajaratnam (n 131) xxii.

CHAPTER 19

MALAYSIA

ABDUL GHAFUR HAMID @ KHIN MAUNG SEIN

1 Introduction

Any study on Malaysia is to be founded on two essential elements; first, that it is a federal state, and second, that it practises the dual system of Islamic law and civil law. Since it is a federal state, the Federal Constitution of Malaysia 1957 provides for a division of powers between the federal government and the state governments. As a dual legal system, there are two parallel systems of courts: civil courts on one hand and *Shari'ah* courts on the other, with Islamic law under the exclusive jurisdiction of states.

Based on the above postulations, this chapter attempts to answer the following questions. Firstly, on the international plane, how has Malaysia contributed to the making, implementation, and enforcement of international law? Secondly, at the domestic level, how has Malaysia implemented or resisted the incorporation of international law in its domestic legal order? Lastly, the chapter will examine critical themes relating to the application of international law, focusing in particular on Malaysian practice with regard to human rights.

The approach will be doctrinal, relying mainly on primary sources, such as the Federal Constitution of Malaysia 1957, relevant Malaysian statutes, judicial decisions, official documents of the Ministry of Foreign Affairs of Malaysia, and international conventions to which Malaysia is a party. Mainstream scholarly writings, particularly those by Malaysian scholars, are cited as secondary sources.

2 Distinctive Contributions by Malaysia to International Law

In the beginning of the nineteenth century, the Malay Peninsula was an agglomeration of independent states and was not a single political entity.[1] 'The Malays were the

[1] Khoo Kay Kim, 'Nineteenth Century Malay Peninsula' in Zainal Abidin Wahid (ed), *Glimpses of Malaysian History* (Dewan Bahasa & Pustaka 1970) 51.

dominant population and they functioned under a political structure at the apex of which was the hereditary ruler called the Sultan or Yang di-Pertuan.'[2] At that time, these Malay states with hereditary rulers enjoyed the status of independent sovereign states and their rulers enjoyed sovereign immunity under international law.[3]

2.1 The Formation of Malaysia

Colonial rule took root in Malaysia with the British acquisition of the island of Penang in 1776.[4] In 1895, the British formalized its rule by directly controlling the 'Federated Malay States', comprised of Negeri Sembilan, Pahang, Perak, and Selangor, and indirectly controlling the 'Unfederated Malay States' of Johor, Kedah, Kelantan, Perlis, and Terengganu.[5] On 1 February 1948, the Federation of Malaya,[6] a federation of eleven states (two of the British Straits Settlements—Penang and Malacca—and nine Malay states),[7] was formed.[8]

[2] Ibid. See also Ahmad Ibrahim, *Towards a History of Law in Malaysia and Singapore* (Stamford College Press 1970) 1; Chandra Muzaffar, *Protector: An Analysis of the Concept and Practice of Loyalty within Malay Society* (Aliran 1979).

[3] See *Mighell v Sultan of Johore* [1894] 1 QB 149, where the Sultan of Johore came to England in 1885, took the name of Albert Baker, and promised to marry Miss Mighell, who subsequently initiated an action for breach of promise to marry. The English court held that the Sultan was entitled to immunity even though up to the time of suit 'he has perfectly concealed the fact that he is a sovereign, and has acted as a private individual'. In *Duff Development Co Ltd v Govt of Kelantan* [1924] AC 797, the Government of Kelantan by a deed granted mining rights to a company. A dispute arose as to whether Kelantan was subject to the jurisdiction of an arbitrator appointed under the arbitration clause provided in the deed. The House of Lords acknowledged Kelantan as an independent sovereign state and rejected the argument that the Government had waived its immunity by reason of the arbitration clause in the deed. Again, in *Sultan of Johore v Tungku Abubakar* [1952] MLJ 115 (Privy Council, Appeal from Singapore), the Privy Council allowed a stay of proceedings applied by the Sultan on the ground that he was a sovereign ruler, referring to a letter of 1 February 1951, written by the British Secretary of State to the Rulers of the Malay States, categorically asserting that 'His Majesty's Government regard Your Highnesses as independent sovereigns in so far as your relations with His Majesty are concerned'. In this respect, Green is of the view that 'it may be said in the case of the Federation of Malaya in the early fifties that the Federation itself remained a protectorate and was not an independent state, while the statement of the Secretary of State was narrowly confined to relations between the Sultans and His Majesty': LC Green, 'Malaya/Singapore/Malaysia: Comments on State Competence, Succession and Continuity' in Kevin Tan (ed), *Singapore and International Law: The Early Years* (Centre for International Law 2010) 128.

[4] Ibrahim (n 2) 1.

[5] Mohamed Salleh bin Abas, 'Federation in Malaysia: Changes in the First Twenty Years' in Mohamed Salleh bin Abas, *Selected Articles and Speeches on Constitution, Law & Judiciary* (Malaysian Law Publishers 1984) 15.

[6] In Malay—*Persekutuan Tanah Melayu*.

[7] The 11 states in the Federation were: Johor, Kedah, Kelantan, Malacca, Negeri Sembilan, Pahang, Penang, Perak, Perlis, Selangor, and Terengganu.

[8] See the Federation of Malaya Agreement 1948. See also Malik Munip, 'The 1948 Federation of Malaya Agreement: a Precursor and a Template for Merdeka Constitution' *The New Straits Times* (23 August 2014).

The genesis of Malaysia's journey to an independent sovereign state was the establishment of the Reid Commission, whose report was in the form of a draft constitution for the Federation of Malaya.[9] On 5 August 1957, the Federation of Malaya Agreement 1957 was entered into by the Representative of the British Government and the Malay Rulers for the establishment of the Federation of Malaya as an independent sovereign state. A constitution for the proposed Federation of Malaya was annexed as the First Schedule to the Agreement.[10] The Federation of Malaya Constitution came into force on 27 August 1957 but formal independence was only achieved on 31 August 1957.[11]

An interesting issue in this respect is the international legal status of the Malay rulers after independence:

> There is nothing . . . in the Federation of Malaya Independence Act[12] which suggests that the Rulers enjoy any status as such outside Malaya, and there is nothing to indicate that the immunity which they formerly enjoyed before the English courts[13] would still subsist. It is also fairly clear that, with the reduction of the Native states to the position of constituent parts of Federation, the immunity formerly afforded to them could no longer be claimed.[14]

The only exception was that Yang di-Pertuan Agong (the King), as the Supreme Head of the Federation elected for a five-year term by the Conference of Rulers,[15] enjoyed sovereign immunity under international law.[16]

The federation was first established as the 'Federation of Malaya' and it was changed to the present name 'Malaysia' only when three more states were admitted. On 9 July 1963 the Governments of the Federation of Malaya, UK, North Borneo, Sarawak, and Singapore signed the 'Malaysia Agreement',[17] whereby North Borneo, Sarawak, and Singapore (later to become an independent state) would federate with the existing states of the Federation of Malaya and thereafter the federation would be called 'Malaysia'. The Federal Parliament then passed the Malaysia Act 1963 to amend articles

[9] It was known as the Reid Commission because the British Government in consultation with the Malay Rulers appointed in 1956 a Constitutional Commission, under the chairmanship of Lord Reid, to deliberate and propose a Constitution for independent Malaya.

[10] See RH Hickling, *Malayan Constitutional Documents*, vol 1 (2nd edn Government Press 1962) 9–14.

[11] Although the Federal Constitution of Malaysia 1957 was based on the Westminster model, it has a distinctive characteristic of incorporating into the parliamentary system a constitutional role for the hereditary Malay Rulers—called the Sultans—who can elect one among them as the Yang di-Pertuan Agong (King) for a period of five years. See Cyrus Vimalakumar Dus, *Emergency Powers and Parliamentary Government in Malaysia: Constitutionalism and a New Democracy* (PhD Thesis, Brunel University, UK, July 1994) 51.

[12] Federation of Malaya Independence Act 1957 (31 July 1957, 5 & 6 Eliz 2) ch 60.

[13] *Mighell v Sultan of Johore* [1884] 1 QB 149.

[14] Green (n 3) 132.

[15] Federal Constitution of Malaysia 1957 art. 32(1).

[16] See generally Arthur Watts, 'The Legal Position in International Law of Heads of State, Heads of Government and Foreign Ministers' (1994) 247 Recueil de Cours 13.

[17] Agreement Relating to Malaysia (adopted 9 July 1963, entered into force 16 September 1963, 1970 UNTS 4).

1(1) and 1(2) of the Federation of Malaya Constitution 1957, to provide for the admission of the three new states and for the alteration of the name of the federation to that of 'Malaysia'.[18]

The formation of Malaysia did not go smoothly and it was surprisingly challenged in court by the state of Kelantan in the case of *Kelantan v The Government of the Federation of Malaya*.[19] The challenge was made on the following legal grounds:

(i) that the Malaysia Act would abolish the Federation of Malaya thereby violating the Federation of Malaya Agreement 1957;
(ii) that the proposed changes needed the consent of each of the constituent states, including Kelantan, and this had not been obtained;
(iii) that the Ruler of Kelantan should have been a party to the Malaysia Agreement;
(iv) that constitutional convention called for consultation with rulers of individual states as to substantial changes to be made to the constitution;
(v) that the Federal Parliament had no power to legislate for Kelantan in respect of any matter regarding which that state had its own legislation.

The following is the judgment of Thompson CJ:

> Parliament in enacting the Malaysia Act so as to amend inter alia Article 1(1) and (2) acted within the powers granted to it by Article 159 of the Constitution. The Constitution which formed an integral part of the Federation of Malaya Agreement, 1957, (to which Kelantan was a party) did not require consultation with any State as a condition to be fulfilled;
>
> The Malaysia Agreement was signed for the 'Federation of Malaya' by the Prime Minister, Deputy Prime Minister and four members of the Cabinet.
>
> This was in compliance with Articles 39 and 80(1) of the Constitution and there is nothing whatsoever in the constitution requiring consultation with any State Government or the Ruler of any State.

In this case, the Kelantan Government very clearly claimed that the Malaysia Agreement and the subsequent Malaysia Act were null and void and thus the questions raised by them were undoubtedly of great significance. Thomson CJ, nevertheless, summed up the five questions into simply one: 'whether Parliament or the Executive Government has trespassed in any way the limits placed on their powers by the Constitution'.[20] He concluded that the Parliament had correctly followed the amending procedure in the Federal Constitution and that the Malaysia Agreement and the Malaysia Act were therefore valid.

[18] The Malaysia Act received the Royal Assent on 26 August 1963 and came into force on 16 September 1963. See Andrew Harding, *The Constitution of Malaysia—A Contextual Analysis* (Hart Publishing 2012) 146; JC Fong, *Constitutional Federalism in Malaysia* (Sweet & Maxwell Asia 2008) 2.

[19] *Government of the State of Kelantan v the Government of the Federation of Malaya and Tunku Abdul Rahman Putra Al-Haj* [1963] MLJ 355 (Federation of Malaya High Court).

[20] Thomson CJ's approach has been criticised by Jayakumar that it generalises 'as one issue what was clearly five different bases for challenging the constitutionality of the Agreement and the Act'. See S Jayakumar, 'Admission of New States: *The Government of the State of Kelantan v the Government of the Federation of Malaya and Tunku Abdul Rahman Putra Al-Haj* (1964) 6 Malaya Law Review 135.

2.2 Succession

In relation to the succession of treaty obligations after Malaysia's independence from the British, article 169(a) of the Federal Constitution provides that:

> any treaty, agreement or convention entered into before Merdeka Day between Her Majesty or her predecessors or the Government of the United Kingdom on behalf of the Federation or any part thereof and another country shall be deemed to be a treaty, agreement or convention between the Federation and that other country.

This provision of the constitution was transformed into an international undertaking as between the Federation and Great Britain by an Exchange of Letters of January 1958.[21]

With regard to the succession of decisions of international organizations, article 169(b) of the Federal Constitution stipulates that:

> any decision taken by an international organization and accepted before Merdeka Day by the Government of the United Kingdom on behalf of the Federation or any part thereof shall be deemed to be a decision of an international organization of which the Federation is a member.

An interesting legal question may be raised in connection with the application of the above constitutional provisions on succession, namely whether the UK, as a party to the European Convention on Human Rights 1950 (ECHR), has extended its obligations under the ECHR to Malaysia? If that is the case, the special rights reserved for the Malays in the Federal Constitution[22] would arguably be in contravention of article 14 (non-discrimination) of the ECHR. A possible answer to that question would be that, in the absence of any provision as to the supremacy of international law over the constitution, which is the supreme law of the land, express provisions in the constitution override inconsistencies arising from the operation of temporary and transitional provisions.[23]

2.3 International Organizations

The Federation of Malaya was admitted to the United Nations on 17 September 1957,[24] immediately after its independence. On 16 September 1963, its name was changed to Malaysia, following the admission to the new federation of Singapore, North Borneo (Sabah), and Sarawak.[25] Its full commitment to multilateralism can be seen in its

[21] Cmd 346 (1958), cited in Green (n 3) 135.

[22] Federal Constitution of Malaysia 1957 s 149.

[23] See Green (n 3) 136.

[24] UNGA res 1134(XII) (17 September 1957).

[25] On 16 September 1963, the Permanent Representative of Malaysia to the UN addressed to the Secretary-General the following communication: 'By the Constitutional process of Amendment provided for in Article 159 of the Constitution of the Federation of Malaya . . . , the name of the State as set out in Article 1 thereof has been changed from "Federation of Malaya" to "Malaysia"'. See *Multilateral Treaties Deposited with the Secretary General*—Malaysia, Note 1 60https://treaties.un.org/Pages/HistoricalInfo.aspx?#%22Malaysia%22> accessed 12 December 2018. Subsequently, the Government of Malaysia

service to global peace and security as a four-time non-permanent member of the Security Council,[26] its participation in a number of UN specialized agencies,[27] and its membership in the World Trade Organization (WTO).[28] Malaysia's good record in UN peace-keeping operations is a clear demonstration of its serious commitment to world peace and security.[29]

Malaysia actively participates in various international organizations, global and regional. Malaysia is a founding member of the Association of Southeast Asian Nations (ASEAN). ASEAN remains the cornerstone of Malaysia's regional engagement.[30] As a Muslim majority state, Malaysia is a dedicated member of the Organisation of Islamic Cooperation. Furthermore, Malaysia is a member of the Non-Aligned Movement, Commonwealth, Group of Seventy Seven (G77), and Asia Pacific Economic Cooperation (APEC).[31]

2.4 Compliance with Decisions of International Courts and Tribunals

Malaysia has a good record of complying with the decisions of international courts and tribunals. The case of *MBF Capital Bhd & Anor v Dato' Param Cumaraswamy*[32] is a useful example. In that case, Dato' Cumaraswamy, a former Chairman of the Bar Council of Malaysia, was appointed by the UN Commission on Human Rights as its

confirmed to the Secretary-General that all multilateral treaties, in respect of which he acts as depositary and to which the Federation of Malaysia has become a party either by succession or ratification or accession, continue to be binding on Malaysia, and that, henceforth, Malaysia should be listed in the relevant UN publications as a party to those treaties.

[26] Malaysia's recent two-year term (2015–16) as a non-permanent member of the UN Security Council ended on 31 December 2016. See 'Malaysia Played Key Role in UN Security Council' *The Star Online* (22 December 2016). This was the fourth time that Malaysia had been elected to the UN Security Council. The previous three times were in 1965, 1988–9, and 1999–2000: see UN Security Council, 'Countries Elected as Members of the Security Council since 1946' 6ohttps://www.un.org/securitycouncil/content/countries-elected-members> accessed 16 April 2019.

[27] Malaysia is a member, for example, of the World Bank, International Monetary Fund, International Maritime Organization, International Labour Organization, International Civil Aviation Organization, and UNESCO.

[28] Malaysia has been a member of the WTO since 1 January 1995 and a member of GATT since 24 October 1957.

[29] See Malaysian Ministry of Foreign Affairs, 'Malaysia's Priorities: Strengthening the UN Peace-Keeping Operations' 6ohttp://malaysiaunsc.kln.gov.my/index.php/malaysia-at-the-unsc/malaysia-s-commitment/strengthening-the-un-peacekeeping-operations> accessed 12 December 2018.

[30] ASEAN was established on 8 August 1967. Its legal and institutional framework has been properly regularized by the ASEAN Charter (adopted November 2007, entered into force 15 December 2008).

[31] Malaysian Ministry of Foreign Affairs, 'Malaysia's Foreign Policy' 6ohttp://www.kln.gov.my/web/guest/foreign-policy> accessed 12 December 2018.

[32] *MBF Capital Bhd & Anor v Dato' Param Cumaraswamy* [1997] 3 MLJ 300.

Special Rapporteur on the Independence of Judges and Lawyers.[33] On the basis of an interview given by him, an article was published in the International Commercial Litigation Magazine.[34] MBF Capital Bhd, a private credit company, contended that the words spoken by him, and the article which was based on these words, were defamatory of them and thus filed a defamation suit against him.

Dato' Cumaraswamy argued that he was entitled to immunity under article 22(b)[35] of the Convention on the Privileges and Immunities of the United Nations 1946. The UN Secretary General issued a certificate to the effect that the words spoken by Dato' Cumaraswamy were made in the course of his mission as a Special Rapporteur of the UN Human Rights Commission and that he was entitled to the immunities accorded to experts performing missions of the UN.

The High Court ruled, *inter alia*, that:

> (1) that the Certificates as issued by the Secretary-General had no more probative value than a mere opinion and in the event [the Court] decided to disregard them; and (2) the issue of immunity was a matter that was not capable of decision in a summary manner, and so directed that the issue be determined at the trial of the action.

The Court of Appeal upheld the High Court's decision.[36]

To solve the much-publicized difference of opinion between the Government of Malaysia and the UN, by consent the two parties referred the question of the Special Rapporteur's immunity to the International Court of Justice (ICJ) for an advisory opinion, in accordance with article 30 of the Convention.[37]

In its Advisory Opinion on *Difference Relating to Immunity from Legal Process*,[38] the ICJ concluded, *inter alia*:

> (1) that Cumaraswamy was entitled to immunity from legal process of every kind for the words spoken by him during an interview as published in an article in International Commercial Litigation;[39] and (2) that the Government of Malaysia has the obligation to communicate this Advisory Opinion to the Malaysian courts, in order that Malaysia's international obligations be given effect and Dato' Param Cumaraswamy's immunity be respected.[40]

[33] UN Commission on Human Rights res 1994/41 (4 March 1994).

[34] David Samuels, 'Malaysian Justice on Trial' [1995] International Commercial Litigation 10–13.

[35] Convention on the Privileges and Immunities of the United Nations (adopted 13 February 1946, entered into force 17 September 1946, 1 UNTS 15) art. VI s 22(b): 'Experts . . . performing missions for the United Nations shall be . . . accorded: . . . (b) in respect of words spoken or written and acts done by them in the course of the performance of their mission, immunity from legal process of every kind'. Malaysia is a party to the Convention and has adopted the International Organization (Privileges and Immunities) Act 1992 to give legal effect to the Convention.

[36] *Dato' Param Cumaraswamy v MBF Capital Bhd* [1997] 3 MLJ 824 (Court of Appeal, per Gopal Sri Ram).

[37] Convention on the Privileges and Immunities of the United Nations 1946 (n 35) s 30.

[38] *Difference Relating to Immunity from Legal Process of a Special Rapporteur of the Commission on Human Rights* [1999] ICJ Rep 62.

[39] Ibid. para 67(1)(b).

[40] Ibid. para 67(4).

As a consequence of the Advisory Opinion, the Malaysian High Court in *Insas Bhd v Dato' Param Cumaraswamy*[41] finally put the case to rest in these words:

> As the parties who had submitted the case for the ICJ's consideration, namely the United Nations and the Malaysian Government, had voluntarily agreed to accept the ICJ's Opinion as binding, the court could not rule otherwise . . . whilst this court might disagree with certain aspects of the decision of the ICJ, the decisive acceptance of the ICJ's ruling by the parties will prevail in respect of this case because the parties had specifically agreed to refer this case for an advisory opinion from the ICJ and that this court was bound to give legal effect to the advisory opinion.[42]

In stark contrast to courts of certain countries in similar situations,[43] it is commendable that the Malaysian court decided to honour the ICJ's Advisory Opinion.[44]

In the case of *Sovereignty over Pedra Branca/Pulau Batu Puteh* between Malaysia and Singapore,[45] the ICJ declared that 'Singapore held sovereignty over Pedra Branca[46] and that Middle Rocks were under the Malaysian sovereignty'.[47] Immediately after the judgment, political rhetoric was high in both countries as national interests were at stake. However, when the dust settled 'both Malaysia and Singapore reiterated their commitment to honour and abide by the judgment and to fully implement it. The two countries met on 3 June 2008 in Singapore and set up the Malaysia-Singapore Joint Technical Committee to that effect.[48]

Nevertheless, on 2 February 2017, Malaysia filed an application for revision of the judgment regarding sovereignty over Pedra Branca/Pulau Batu Puteh. As a rule, a judgment of the ICJ is final and without appeal.[49] However, article 61 of the Statute of the Court allows a revision procedure 'upon the discovery of some fact of such as nature as a decisive factor, which fact was, when the judgment was given, unknown to the court and also to the party claiming revision',[50] provided that the application for revision is made within six months of the discovery of the new fact and within ten years from the date of the judgment.[51]

[41] *Insas Bhd v Dato' Param Cumaraswamy* [2000] 4 MLJ 727.

[42] Ibid.

[43] See e.g. *La Grand case (Germany v United States of America)* [2001] ICJ Rep 466.

[44] For fair comments on the *Cumaraswamy* case, see Rosemary Rayfuse, 'Immunities of United Nations Human Rights Special Rapporteurs: Who Decides?' (2001) 7 Australian Journal Human Rights 169; Alison Duxbury, 'The Privileges and Immunities of United Nations' Experts: The *Cumaraswamy* Case' (2000) 1 Asia Pacific Journal on Human Rights and the Law 88.

[45] *Sovereignty over Pedra Branca/Pulau Batu Puteh, Middle Rocks and South Ledge (Malaysia/Singapore)* [2008] ICJ Rep 12.

[46] Ibid. para 277. [47] Ibid. para 299.

[48] Abdul Ghafur Hamid and Khin Maung Sein, '*Pedra Branca* Judgment and Beyond: Issues and Challenges in Its Implementation by Malaysia and Singapore: Current Legal Development, the International Court of Justice' (2011) 26 International Journal of Marine and Coastal Law 335.

[49] Statute of the International Court of Justice (adopted 24 October 1945, entered into force 24 October 1945) art. 60.

[50] Ibid. art. 61(1).

[51] Ibid. arts 61(3) and (4). See also *Application for Revision of the Judgment of 11 July 1966 in the Case Concerning Application of the Genocide Convention (Bosnia v Yugoslavia)* [2003] ICJ Rep 77 para 16.

In its application, Malaysia contends that 'there exists a new fact of such a nature as to be a decisive factor within the meaning of Article 61'. In particular, it refers to three documents discovered in the National Archives of the UK during the period 4 August 2016 to 30 January 2017: 'internal correspondence of the Singapore colonial authorities in 1958, an incident report filed in 1958 by a British naval officer and an annotated map of naval operations from the 1960s'. Malaysia claims that 'these documents establish the new fact that officials at the highest levels in the British colonial and Singaporean administration appreciated that Pedra Branca/Pulau Batu Puteh did not form part of Singapore's sovereign territory' during the relevant period. Malaysia argues that 'the Court would have been bound to reach a different conclusion on the question of sovereignty over Pedra Branca/Pulau Batu Puteh had it been aware of this new evidence'.[52]

On 30 June 2017, Malaysia filed another application requesting interpretation of the 2008 judgment of the ICJ under article 60 of its Statute. Malaysia argued that the joint Technical Committee, which was established to implement the judgment through cooperative processes, reached an impasse in November 2013 due to the inability of the parties to agree over the meaning of the judgment.[53]

However, after the historic change of government in Malaysia on 9 May 2018, a surprise move was made by the new government. In a letter dated 28 May 2018, Malaysia notified the Court that the parties had agreed to discontinue the proceedings in the case. On 29 May 2018, the Court made an Order recording the discontinuance of the proceedings and directed the removal of the case from the Court's List.[54]

It is unclear why the Malaysian government dropped the applications for revision and interpretation of the 2008 Judgment. According to a statement made by the Attorney General's Chambers of Malaysia, the new Prime Minister was briefed by the three legal consultants appointed by the Chambers to work on the applications. 'Having considered the views and the national interest matters, including the cost,' the Prime Minister decided that 'it would be best to discontinue the proceedings.'[55] After putting the Pedra Branca episode to rest, it seems that the new government will be focusing more on enlarging Middle Rocks to form a small island.[56] In fact,

[52] ICJ, 'Malaysia requests a revision of the Judgment of 23 May 2008, in which the Court found, *inter alia*, that sovereignty over the island of Pedra Branca/Pulau Batu Puteh belongs to Singapore', ICJ Press Release 2017/6 (3 February 2017).

[53] Request for Interpretation of the Judgment of 23 May 2008 in the case concerning *Sovereignty over Pedra Branca/Pulau Batu Puteh, Middle Rocks and South Ledge (Malaysia/Singapore)*, Overview of the Case 6ohttps://www.icj-cij.org/en/case/170> accessed on 16 April 2019.

[54] Application for revision of the Judgment of 23 May 2008 in the case concerning *Sovereignty over Pedra Branca/Pulau Batu Puteh, Middle Rocks and South Ledge (Malaysia/Singapore)*, Overview of the Case, accessed on 16 April 2019, 6ohttps://www.icj-cij.org/en/case/167>.

[55] 'AGC Disputes Previous AG's Explanation Why Malaysia Lost Batu Puteh Case' (*The Star Online*, 13 July 2018) 6ohttps://www.thestar.com.my/news/nation/2018/07/13/agc-disputes-previous-ag-explanation/> accessed on 16 April 2019.

[56] 'Ex-Bar Chief: Reveal Cost for Pedra Branca Review in ICJ' (*The Star Online*, 30 May 2018) 6ohttps://www.freemalaysiatoday.com/category/nation/2018/05/30/ex-bar-chief-reveal-cost-for-pedra-branca-review-in-icj/> accessed 16 April 2019.

Malaysia has already established, on Middle Rocks, the Abu Bakar Maritime Base, which comprises a 316-metre jetty that joins the two main outcrops, a helipad, and a lighthouse.[57]

3 Incorporation of International Law

The practice of a state in respect of the incorporation of international law as a rule is reflected in its state constitution. Unlike the constitutions of many other states,[58] however, the Federal Constitution of Malaysia is entirely silent on the application of international law. With this initial remark, the application of international law in Malaysia shall be discussed on the basis of the two main sources of international law, namely: treaties and custom.[59]

3.1 Treaties

Despite the fact that the Federal Constitution is devoid of any reference to international law, there are specific provisions in the Federal Constitution relating to external affairs, including treaties with other countries and the implementation of these treaties. According to article 74(1) of the Federal Constitution, 'Parliament may make laws with respect to any of the matters enumerated in the "Federal List" or the "Concurrent List"'. The 'Federal List' in the Ninth Schedule includes:

> 1. External Affairs, including –
> (a) Treaties, agreements and conventions with other countries and all matters which bring the Federation into relations with other countries;
> (b) Implementation of treaties, agreements and conventions with other countries; . . . .

[57] '"Completely Legitimate" for Malaysia to Develop Middle Rocks Within International Law: Ng Eng Hen' (*Today Online*, 3 June 2018) 6ohttps://www.todayonline.com/singapore/completely-legitimate-malaysia-develop-middle-rocks-within-international-law-ng-eng-hen> accessed 18 April 2019.

[58] See e.g. Basic Law of the Federal Republic of Germany 1949 art. 25: 'The general rules of international law are an integral part of the federal law. They shall take precedence over the laws and directly create rights and duties for the inhabitants of the federal territory'; Constitution of Kosovo 2008 art. 19: '1. International agreements ratified by the Republic of Kosovo become part of the internal legal system after their publication in the Official Gazette of the Republic of Kosovo . . . . 2. Ratified international agreements and legally binding norms of international law have superiority over the laws of the Republic of Kosovo.' See also art. 9 of the Constitution of the Democratic Republic of East Timor 2002. Duc Trang, 'Beyond the Historical Justice Debate: The Incorporation of International Law and the Impact on Constitutional Structures and Rights in Hungary' (1995) 28 Vanderbilt Journal of Transnational Law 1.

[59] See generally Abdul Ghafur Hamid and Khin Maung Sein, 'Judicial Application of International Law in Malaysia: A Critical Analysis' (2005) 1 Asia-Pacific Year Book of International Humanitarian Law 196.

In addition, under article 76(1)(a), 'Parliament may make laws in respect of matters enumerated in the State List... for the purpose of implementing any treaty, etc. between the Federation and any foreign country'.[60] It can, therefore, fairly be concluded that the Federal Parliament has the exclusive power to make laws relating to treaties with foreign countries and to domesticate these treaties to give them legal effect within Malaysia.

The constitution vests treaty-making power in the Executive. First, '[t]he executive authority of the Federation is vested in the Yang di-Pertuan Agong (HRH the King) and exercisable by him or by the Cabinet or any Minister authorized by the Cabinet'.[61] Second, '[t]he executive authority of the Federation extends to all matters with respect to which Parliament may make laws'.[62] In accordance with article 74(1) of the Federal Constitution, read together with the 'Federal List', matters with respect to which Parliament may make laws include 'external affairs'. This phrase in turn includes 'treaties, agreements and conventions with other countries'. It is, therefore, crystal clear that the Executive Authority of the Federation (that is, the federal government) is vested by the Federal Constitution with 'treaty-making power'.[63] This has been reaffirmed by the High Court in *Kelantan v the Federation of Malaya*.[64]

In Malaysia, as in the UK,[65] the treaty-making power is vested in the Executive while Parliament has the power to make laws to domesticate treaties. A treaty will have legal effect in Malaysia only when it has been transformed into domestic law by means of a parliamentary enactment, although there may be certain treaties that do not require any legislation to have effect domestically.[66] Without an enabling statute, no treaty will be accepted as law by the Malaysian courts.[67] This is the application in Malaysia of the 'doctrine of transformation', which is a pure dualist approach.

[60] Federal Constitution of Malaysia 1957 art. 76(1)(a). The power of Parliament in this respect, however, is subject to two limitations prescribed in art. 76(2), namely that: (i) no laws shall be made in pursuance of art. 76(1)(a) with respect to 'any matters of Islamic law or the custom of the Malays or to any matters of native law or custom in the States of Sabah and Sarawak'; and (ii) no bill for a law under art. 76(1)(a) shall be introduced into Parliament before the Government of the State concerned has been consulted.

[61] Federal Constitution of Malaysia 1957 art. 39.

[62] Ibid. art. 80(1). Therefore, to ascertain the precise scope of federal executive powers one must look at the Federal List. See Andrew Harding, *Law, Government and the Constitution in Malaysia* (Malayan Law Journal Sdn Bhd 1996) 107.

[63] Abdul Ghafur Hamid and Khin Maung Sein, 'Treaty-Making Power in Federal States with Special Reference to the Malaysian Position' (2003) 30 Journal Malaysian and Comparative Law 65. See also Tunku Sofiah Jewa, *Public International Law: A Malaysian Perspective* (2nd edn Pacifica Publications 2012) 31.

[64] *Government of the State of Kelantan v the Government of the Federation of Malaya and Tunku Abdul Rahman Putra Al-Haj* [1963] MLJ 355 (Federation of Malaya High Court).

[65] See *R v Secretary of State, ex parte Rees-Mogg* [1994] 1 All ER 457 CA; DJ Harris, *Cases and Materials on International Law* (5th edn Sweet & Maxwell 1998) 778.

[66] See Heliliah Bt Haji Yusof, 'Internal Application of International Law in Malaysia and Singapore' (1969) 1 Singapore Law Review 62, 65.

[67] See *PP v Wah Ah Jee* (1919) 2 FMSLR 193 (Supreme Court).

3.2 Customary International Law

As far as customary international law is concerned, it is hard to ascertain the Malaysian position. The only possible way is to look through the decided cases to see how Malaysian courts treat international law in general and customary international law in particular. In this respect, one needs to make a distinction between pre-independence cases, and cases decided by non-Malaysian courts even after independence, on one hand, and post-independence cases decided solely by Malaysian courts on the other.

3.2.1 *Prior to Independence*

The common law practice of the 'doctrine of incorporation' was invariably applied by the courts in pre-independence cases, and in those cases decided by non-Malaysian judges (such as the Privy Council or the Singapore court) even after independence. Customary international law was thus part of the law of the land unless it was contrary to statutes made by Parliament.

To illustrate the point, in *Sockalingam Chettiar v Chan Moi*,[68] decided in 1947, the main issue for Evans J to deal with was whether certain letters of administration granted by the Japanese during their occupation of Malaya were legal under international law. By referring to the 'Hague Regulations' of 1907, which are well-established customary rules of international law, it was held that the letters of administration were valid under with international law. This is a pre-independence case decided by a British judge and it sets a clear precedent for the direct application of a rule of customary international law as part of the law of the country.

In the case of *Olofsen v Government of Malaysia*[69] as well, the rule of customary international law relating to the immunity of a sovereign state was directly applied. However, it was decided by Ambrose J, who was sitting as a Judge of the High Court in Singapore, and thus was not decided by a Malaysian judge and cannot be said to reflect the Malaysian position.

The same applies to the case of *PP v Oie Hee Koi*,[70] where the Privy Council (per Lord Hodson, Lord Guest, Lord Wilberforce, Sir Douglas Menzies, and Sir Garfield Barwick) held that the accused could not be treated as prisoners of war. This decision was arrived at by applying customary international law on armed conflict. This case also does not reflect the attitude of the pure Malaysian judges.

3.2.2 *After Independence*

A critical evaluation of post-independence cases decided by Malaysian judges involving issues of international law clearly demonstrates that customary international law has

[68] [1947] MLJ 154 (Malayan Union Court of Appeal per Evans J).
[69] *Olofsen v Government of Malaysia* [1966] 2 MLJ 300 (OCJ Singapore).
[70] [1968] 1 MLJ 148 (Privy Council Appeal from Malaysian Federal Court).

never been directly applied by the Malaysian courts after independence.[71] The only exception is that there are a few cases where the learned judges indirectly applied customary international law through the English common law, by virtue of the Civil Law Act 1956.

By virtue of section 3 of the Civil Law Act 1956, 'the English common law is to be applied by Malaysian courts in the absence of any written law to the contrary and insofar as the circumstances of the Federation and its inhabitants permit and render necessary'.[72] The doctrine of incorporation is the established practice of the English common law, according to which customary international law is deemed to be part of the law of England.[73] It means that the application of the English common law by a Malaysian court, by following the English judicial precedents, would be equivalent to indirectly applying customary international law, so that it could form part and parcel of the common law. Two leading cases illustrate this approach.

First, in *Village Holdings Sdn, Bhd v Her Majesty the Queen in Right of Canada,*[74] Shankar J held that:

> So far as a foreign sovereign is concerned, I hold that section 3 of our Civil Law Act 1956 leaves no room for any doubt that we in Malaysia continue to adhere to a pure absolute doctrine of state immunity when it comes to the question of impleading a foreign sovereign who declines to submit.

In this case, the Court relied on the English common law position by referring to the leading English case of *The Parlement Belge.*[75]

The second case is *Commonwealth of Australia v Midford (Malaysia) Sdn. Bhd.*[76] In this case, the Supreme Court of Malaysia was faced with the question of whether Australian Customs Officers were entitled to state immunity in respect of their seizure of property (when exercising their regulatory, not commercial, functions). By referring to section 3 of the Civil Law Act and English judicial authorities such as *The Philippine Admiral, Trendtex,* and *I Congreso,* it was held that '[w]e are therefore of the view that the restrictive doctrine should apply here'.

This landmark judgment can be considered as a bold step as it departed from the old tradition of sticking to the cut-out date in the Civil Law Act, instead following the latest development in the English common law and adhering to the restrictive theory of state immunity, which is a newer rule of customary international law. Nevertheless, even the highest court of Malaysia did *not* rule that it applied the restrictive theory of

[71] Compare the view of Dickstein, who stated that the courts in Malaysia appear to have applied customary international law when the occasion arose. See HL Dickstein, 'The Internal Application of International Law in Malaysia: A Model of the Relationship Between International Law and Municipal Law' (1974) 1 Journal of Malaysian and Comparative Law 205, 207.

[72] Civil Law Act 1956 (Laws of Malaysia, Act 67 of 7 April 1956) s 3(1).

[73] *Trendtex Trading Corporation v Central Bank of Nigeria* [1977] QB 529.

[74] [1988] 2 MLJ 656 (High Court Kuala Lumpur).

[75] *The Parlement Belge* [1894] 1 QB 149.

[76] [1990] 1 CLJ 878 [1990] 1 MLJ 475 (Supreme Court of Malaysia, per Hashim Yeop Sani CJ (Malaya), Yusof Mohamed SCJ, and Gunn Chit Tuan SCJ).

state immunity because it was a rule of customary international law accepted by most states, and hence was part of the law of Malaysia. Rather, the learned judges reached their conclusion only by invoking English common law and by referring to English leading cases.[77]

Apart from the exceptions given above, the mainstream judiciary in Malaysia after independence has never directly applied customary international law. The doctrine of incorporation appears to be alien for the Malaysian courts.

A case which can well illustrate the point is *PP v Narogne Sookpavit*.[78] In this case, Thai fishermen, who were fishing at sea about three miles from the Malaysian coast, were arrested and charged under section 11(1) of the Fisheries Act 1963. Fishermen argued that they were exercising the 'right of innocent passage' in Malaysian waters. Referring to article 14 (which deals with the right of innocent passage) of the Geneva Convention on the Territorial Sea 1958, Shanker J stated:

> The customary law to which Article 14 of the Convention on the Territorial Sea is said to correspond may be the customary law of England or it may be customary international law. In the Court below me, *Defence Counsel seemed to suggest that it was self-evident that such customary law was part and parcel of Malaysian law. I am far from satisfied that this is the case . . . .*

His Honour finally concluded that:

> Even if there was such a right of innocent passage and such right was in conformity with customary English law or customary international law as it is applied in England, the passage by the accused persons in the circumstances of this case could not be regarded as innocent passage since it contravened Malaysian domestic legislation.

There is no doubt as to the correctness of the judgement to the extent that the passage was not innocent, since it violated fisheries laws of Malaysia. However, it is unfortunate that the learned judge rejected outright the established principle of English common law that customary international law is part of the law of the land (the doctrine of incorporation). It is also unfortunate that he rejected the right of innocent passage as a right recognized in customary international law.[79]

Another striking example is the Supreme Court decision of *PP v Rajappan*.[80] In this case, the question to be decided was whether in law a person who was domiciled in

[77] Abdul Ghafur Hamid and Khin Maung Sein, *Public International Law: A Practical Approach* (3rd edn Sweet & Maxwell Asia 2011) 79.

[78] [1987] 2 MLJ 100 (High Court Johore Bahru).

[79] See Ian Brownlie, *Principles of Public International Law* (6th edn Clarendon Press 2003) 305; DP O'Connell, *The International Law of the Sea* vol 1 (Oxford University Press 1982) 260–6 (affirming that a customary international law right of innocent passage existed as a result of state practice at the beginning of the 12th century). This right of innocent passage has also been accepted by the UK in *Corfu Channel* [1949] ICJ Rep 1; see Anne Bardin 'Coastal State's Jurisdiction over Foreign vessels' (2002) 14 Pace International Law Review 27, 34.

[80] [1986] 1 MLJ 152, Supreme Court Kuala Lumpur (Salleh Abas LP, Abdul Hamid CJ (Malaya), Seah, Hashim Yeop A Sani, and Abdul Cader JJ).

Malaysia and married again during the lifetime of his wife at a place outside Malaysia committed a bigamy offence punishable under section 494 of the Penal Code. The Court (per Lord President Salleh Abas) ruled that:

> According to an established principle of international law crimes and criminal acts are matters for the State, within whose territory the criminal acts are committed, irrespective of the nationality of the offenders. International law also recognizes that a State has the power to punish its nationals or its permanent residents for criminal acts committed by them outside its territory. But to translate this principle into municipal law a clear provision must be made to this effect in its municipal law. We have seen that there is no statute which could be said to have extra-territorially extended section 494 of the P.C.[81]

This is probably a rare case where a Malaysian court referred to a rule of customary international law, in respect of the extraterritorial exercise of state jurisdiction, without invoking English common law or English authorities. It is also interesting to note that the Lord President even cited the decision of the Permanent Court of International Justice in the *Lotus* case.[82] At the same time, however, the Lord President hinted that a statutory provision would be necessary to translate the customary law principle into binding national law. This hint thus favoured the application of the doctrine of transformation and suggested a clear dualist trend even in the case of customary international law.[83]

It is quite surprising to see Malaysian courts, after independence, departing from the traditional common law doctrine of incorporation, which has been consistently applied in the UK[84] and in other common law countries,[85] and which was the established practice of courts in Malaysia before independence.

3.3 Conflicts

In the event of a conflict between international law and a Malaysian statute, the statute shall prevail. In *PP v Wah Ah Jee*,[86] the judge concluded that 'the Courts here must take the law as they find it expressed in the Enactments. It is not the duty of a judge or a magistrate

[81] Ibid. 157.

[82] The *Lotus* case (1927) PCIJ Series A, No 10; see *PP v Rajappan* [1986] 1 MLJ 152, 158.

[83] For the same remarks about the Malaysian courts of adopting the strictly dualist approach, see Michael Kirby, 'International Law and the Common Law: Conceptualizing the New Relationship', Fourth James Crawford Biennial Lecture on International Law, University of Adelaide, 14 October 2009, 34–5 60http://www.michaelkirby.com.au/images/stories/speeches/2000s/2009%2B/2424C.James_Crawford_Lecture_Oct_2009.pdf> accessed 12 December 2018.

[84] 4 *Blackstone's Commentaries* 55; *Trendtex Trading Corporation v Central Bank of Nigeria* [1977] QB 529; *I Congresso del Partido* [1981] 3 WLR 328.

[85] Canada: *Reference re Exemption of US Forces from Canadian Criminal Law* [1943] 4 DLR 11, 41; Australia: *Chin Yin Ten v Little* (1976) 69 ILR 76, 80.

[86] (1919) 2 FMSLR 193, FMS Supreme Court.

to consider whether the law so set forth is contrary to international law or not.'[87] This is indeed a corollary of the common law principle of the 'supremacy of an Act of Parliament'.[88] In the domestic sphere, the court will uphold the statute made by Parliament. Nevertheless, if the statute is in conflict with a rule of international law, the state will, in the international sphere, incur liability for the breach of an international obligation.[89]

4 Human Rights

A useful lens through which to view Malaysian practice with regard to international law generally is provided by its application of the international human rights instruments. Of the core human rights treaties, Malaysia is a party only to two, namely: the Convention on the Elimination of All Forms of Discrimination against Women 1986 (CEDAW) (acceded to on 4 August 1995) and the Convention on the Rights of the Child 1989 (acceded to on 19 March 1995). Malaysia is not a party to the two international covenants on human rights: the International Covenant on Civil and Political Rights 1966 and the International Covenant on Economic, Social and Cultural Rights 1966. It is, therefore, not surprising that the only general human rights instrument that can be relied upon by human rights lawyers in Malaysia is the Universal Declaration of Human Rights 1948 (UDHR). The interpretative response of the Malaysian courts to the UDHR, however, is rather antagonistic.

The total rejection of the UDHR can be seen in *Merdeka University Bhd v Government of Malaysia*,[90] where it was held that:

> the Universal Declaration of Human Rights . . . is not a legally binding instrument as such and some of its provisions depart from existing and generally accepted rules. It is merely a statement of principles devoid of any obligatory character and is not part of our municipal law.[91]

The ruling in the *Merdeka University* case remains uncontested even after the adoption of the Human Rights Commission of Malaysia Act 1999, section 4(4) of which reads: 'For the purpose of this Act, regard shall be had to the Universal Declaration of Human Rights 1948 to the extent that it is not inconsistent with the Federal Constitution'. In

[87] It is quite obvious that *PP v Wah Ah Jee* (1919) 2 FMSLR 193 followed the dictum in the English case of *Mortensen v Peters* (1906) 8 F (J) 93.

[88] See *Maxwell on Interpretation of Statutes* (12th edn London 1969) 183.

[89] *Factory at Chorzow (Merits)* (1928) PCIJ Series A No. 17, 29; *Corfu Channel case* [1949] ICJ Rep 4, 23; *Gabcikovo-Nagymaros Project (Hungary v Slovakia)* [1997] ICJ Rep 7, 38 para 47.

[90] *Merdeka University Bhd v Government of Malaysia* [1981] 2 MLJ 356 (Abdool Cader J).

[91] In fact, contrary to what is stated in the judgment, the UDHR has had grave impacts upon the content of the constitutions of a number of states. At the same time, at least some provisions of the Declaration have become binding as established rules of customary international law. See *Filartiga v Pena-Irala*, 630 F 2d 876 (1980).

Mohamad Ezam bin Mohd Noor v Ketua Polis Negara,[92] for example, it was held by the Federal Court per Siti Norma Yaakob FCJ that:

> Notwithstanding s 4(4) of the Human Rights Commission of Malaysia Act 1999, reference to international standards set by the Universal Declaration of Human Rights 1948 . . . and several other United Nations documents . . . cannot be accepted as such documents were not legally binding on the Malaysian courts. The use of the words 'regard shall be had' in s 4(4) of the Human Rights Commission of Malaysia Act can only mean an invitation to look at the 1948 Declaration . . . . Beyond that, one was not obliged or compelled to adhere to the 1948 Declaration.[93]

Furthermore, in *SIS Forum (Malaysia) v Dato' Seri Syed Hamid* Albar,[94] the applicant entreated the Court to have regard to 'the doctrine of legitimate expectation' in relation to international human rights norms, in particular, the CEDAW and the UDHR. The applicant also referred to the Australian decision in the *Teoh* case.[95] The Court rejected these arguments and ruled that:

> In relation to the applicability of international norms and the approach as exemplified in the Australian case of *Teoh*, the position adopted by the Malaysian courts has been not to directly accept norms of international law unless they are incorporated as part of our municipal law[96] . . . . I do not believe this position has changed even with the passing of s 4(4) of the Human Rights Commission Act 1999 . . . . As for the judicial approach in *Teoh*, I note that even in Australia, this decision has had its fair share of criticism.[97]

There are, however, views that the provision in section 4(4) of the Human Rights Commission Act 1999 indicates that the UDHR may be applied to develop constitutional guarantees of fundamental human rights in Malaysia, on condition that the spirit of the constitution is respected.[98]

For over two decades, common law judges have explored the possibility of softening strict common law dualism in favour of a more flexible, monist-oriented approach to the incorporation of human rights treaties. The term 'creeping monism' has become popular following a series of colloquia held by judges from Commonwealth nations from 1981 to 1988. A major focus of this colloquia series was the status of unincorporated treaties

92 *Mohamad Ezam bin Mohd Noor v Ketua Polis Negara* [2002] 4 MLJ 449.

93 Ibid. 453.

94 *SIS Forum (Malaysia) v Dato' Seri Syed Hamid Albar (Menteri Dalam Negeri)* [2010] 2 MLJ 377, Application for Judicial Review, High Court (Kuala Lumpur).

95 *Ministry for Immigration and Ethnic Affairs v Teoh* (1995) 183 CLR 273.

96 The learned judge referred to *Merdeka University Berhad v Government of Malaysia* [1981] 2 MLJ 356.

97 *SIS Forum (Malaysia) v Dato' Seri Syed Hamid Albar (Menteri Dalam Negeri)* [2010] 2 MLJ 377, 394.

98 See Farid Sufian Shuaib, 'The Status of International Law in the Malaysian Municipal Legal System: Creeping Monism in Legal Discourse?' (2008) 16 IIUM Law Journal 181, 197–8, referring to the case of *Mersing Omnibus Co Sdn Bhd v Kesatuan Pekerja-Pekerja Pengangkutan Semenanjung Malaysia & Anor* [1999] 1 MLJ 44, 48, where the phrase 'shall have regard' in the Industrial Relations Act 1967 was interpreted to mean 'imposing an obligation'.

in dualist-oriented common law legal systems.[99] Concluding statements resulting from the last of these colloquia series, held in Bangalore in 1988, have become known as the 'Bangalore Principles'.[100] The view expressed in the Bangalore Principles 1988 that 'unincorporated treaties could play a gap-filling role in interpreting domestic law'[101] represented a departure from strict common law dualism. For a strict dualist, unincorporated treaties have no role to play in the domestic legal system until the legislature enacts implementing legislation.[102]

After the adoption of the Bangalore Principles, we can see a change in some courts' approaches in the common law countries. In Australia, for example, in the case of *Mabo v Queensland [No 2]*,[103] Justice Brennan concluded that 'the "native title" to land of Australia's indigenous peoples had survived the acquisition of sovereignty over the continent by the British Crown and its settlement by the European colonists'. In his reasoning, he touched upon the influence of international human rights norms in these words:

> The common law does not necessarily conform with international law, but international law is a legitimate and important influence on the development of the common law, especially when international law declares the existence of universal human rights. As such, the common law doctrine founded on unjust discrimination in the enjoyment of civil and political rights demands reconsideration.[104]

In Malaysia, there are indeed a number of recent cases which can be seen as enlightenment leading to a more liberal interpretation and greater recognition of the international protection of human rights. The first is *Sagong Bin Tasi v Kerajaan Negeri Selangor*.[105] By referring to the worldwide trend recognizing aboriginal rights, Mohd Noor Ahmad J upheld the proprietary interest of *orang asli*[106] in their customary and ancestral lands. The Court of Appeal in *Kerajaan Negeri Selangor v Sagong Bin Tasi*[107] confirmed the rights of aboriginal peoples and also acknowledged them as human rights.

The second case is *Abd Malek bin Hussin v Borhan bin Hj Daud & Ors*,[108] which deals with the legality of an arrest under the Internal Security Act 1960. The High Court

[99] Melissa Waters, 'Creeping Monism: The Judicial Trend toward Interpretive Incorporation of Human Rights Treaties' (2007) 107 Columbia Law Review 628, 643–6.

[100] The 'Bangalore Principles' were adopted at a Judicial Colloquium on 'The Domestic Application of International Human Rights Norms', Bangalore, India, 24–26 February 1988. See (1989) 1 African Journal International & Comparative Law 345.

[101] See Bangalore Principles, ibid. para 4.

[102] Waters (n 94) 643–6; Michael Kirby, 'Implementing the Bangalore Principles on Human Rights Law' (1989) 106 South African Law Journal 484.

[103] *Mabo v Queensland [No 2]* (1992) 175 CLR 1.

[104] Ibid. 42.

[105] *Sagong Bin Tasi v Kerajaan Negeri Selangor* [2002] 2 MLJ 591 (High Court) (Shah Alam) (per Mohd Noor Ahmad J).

[106] Native peoples of Malaysia.

[107] *Kerajaan Negeri Selangor v Sagong Bin Tasi* [2005] 6 MLJ 289 (Court of Appeal).

[108] *Abd Malek bin Hussin v Borhan bin Hj Daud & Ors* [2008] 1 MLJ 368 (High Court Kuala Lumpur) (Mohd Hishamudin J).

(per Mohd Hishamudin J) held that the arrest was unlawful under article 5(3) of the Federal Constitution and ruled that:

> The preservation of the personal liberty of the individual is a sacred universal value of all civilized nations and is enshrined in the *Universal Declaration of Human Rights and Fundamental Freedoms of 1948*. Article 5(3) of the Federal Constitution guarantees every person in this country of his personal liberty and protection from arbitrary arrest particularly arbitrary arrest by the State. As I have said in *Abdul Ghani Haroon*, and I will say it again now, judges are protectors of the fundamental liberties of the citizens and that this is a sacred duty or trust which Judges must constantly uphold.[109]

However, these are the enlightened ideas of one or two isolated judges. The approach of the mainstream judiciary in Malaysia is not favourable to any reference to unincorporated international human rights instruments or norms.

5 Conclusion

Malaysia is unique in the sense that it amalgamates multiple characteristics: a federal state, a constitutional monarchy, and a state with a dual legal system. It is a multilateral player with active involvement in many intergovernmental organizations. In relation to international conventions, Malaysia has a policy of respecting them and complying with them. Malaysia has never been involved in armed conflict with any state and is fully committed to the peaceful settlement of disputes, with a good record of complying with decisions of international courts and tribunals.

Being a common law country, treaties do not have any direct legal effect in Malaysia and parliamentary enactment is required to transform a treaty into the Malaysian domestic legal system. What is surprising, however, is that Malaysia rejects outright the doctrine of incorporation in respect of customary international law, deviating from the practice of the UK and other common law countries. Despite the fact that customary international law is binding on all states (apart from a persistent objector), and that a state will be responsible under international law for its breach, customary international law appears to be an alien law to the Malaysian courts. It appears that Malaysia is not only a dualist country, but also more dualist compared to any other common law counterparts.

As a peace-loving member of the international community, it is ardently hoped that Malaysia awakens from this slumber, with a change of mind on the part of the Malaysian judiciary. It is hoped that the judiciary will return to pre-independence judicial practice, by treating customary international law as part of the law of Malaysia, so long as it is not contrary to any statute made by Parliament.

[109] Ibid. 383 (emphasis added). Unfortunately, however, on appeal, the decision was reversed by the Court of Appeal. See *Borhan bin Hj Daud & Ors v Abd Malek bin Hussin* [2010] 6 MLJ 329 (Court of Appeal).

CHAPTER 20

VIET NAM

TRINH HAI YEN*

1 Introduction

It is difficult to comprehensively conceptualize international law in Viet Nam's legal system. There is no formal documentation concerning two of the main sources of public international law: international custom and general principles of law.[1] The application of international custom is envisaged under some of its laws but these regulate civil relations between private actors rather than interstate relations.[2] Treaties, by contrast, are dealt with in great detail. This practice is the corollary of the complexity associated with the determination of customary rules in international law and the approach of Viet Nam's civil law tradition, which places emphasis on written laws rather than oral or case laws.

Treaty making was mentioned only briefly in Viet Nam's constitutions of 1946, 1959, and 1980. Only in 1989 did the Ordinance on Conclusion and Implementation of the Socialist Republic of Vietnam's Treaties[3] specifically provide for the authority, procedures, and principles to be applied in this field. Since then, Viet Nam has continuously reviewed and revised its laws concerning treaties,[4] as a result of its

* Disclaimer: The opinions experessed in this chapter are solely those of the author. They do not purport to reflect the opinions or views of any institution with which she might be affiliated.

[1] Statute of the International Court of Justice 1945 art. 38(1).

[2] Art. 666 of Viet Nam's 2015 Civil Code allows parties in civil relations involving foreign elements to 'apply international customs. In cases where the consequence of such application is contrary to the basic principles of Vietnam's laws, Vietnam's laws shall apply.' Similar provisions are found in Viet Nam's specialized laws such as art. 5(2) of the Commercial Law 2005, art. 5(2) of the Maritime Code 2015, and art. 4(2) of the Law on Technology Transfer 2006.

[3] The Ordinance on Conclusion and Implementation of the Socialist Republic of Vietnam's Treaties was adopted by the State Council on 17 October 1989 and entered into force on 1 November 1989.

[4] See the Ordinance on Conclusion and Implementation of Treaties 1998, the Law on the Conclusion, Accession to and Implementation of Treaties 2005, and the Law of Treaties 2016. The currently effective statute is Vietnam's Law of Treaties ('LT 2016'), which was passed by its National Assembly on 9 April 2016 and entered into force on 1 July 2016.

increasing engagement in international commitments, and the needs for clear responsibility, assignment of authority, and coordination in the negotiation, conclusion, and implementation of treaties. The latest law, the Law of Treaties 2016,[5] closely follows the provisions of the Vienna Convention on the Law of Treaties 1969 (VCLT),[6] to which Viet Nam became a party in 2001.

The definition of treaties in Viet Nam's legal system is borrowed, with modification, from the VCLT. Accordingly, under Vietnam's Law of Treaties 2016, a treaty must be in a written form and must give rise to, change, or terminate rights or obligations of Viet Nam in accordance with international law.[7] The content requirement is equivalent to the qualification that a treaty is 'governed by international law' in the VCLT.[8] Such a new element in Viet Nam's law provides clearer guidance on distinguishing treaties from non-binding agreements, and was absent in the predecessor statute.[9] This new element is one of the reasons for replacing the earlier statute, in addition to the need to accommodate changes in treaty-related powers under the new constitution of 2013 and to simplify procedures. In addition, agency to agency international agreements[10] are not regarded as treaties and are not binding upon the State of Viet Nam or the Government of Viet Nam.[11]

This chapter briefly discusses the relationship between national law and international law in Viet Nam, before surveying the use of international law before, during, and after independence in 1975. The last section draws some lessons from how Viet Nam has used international law, with an eye towards future developments.

2 Modified Monism

Although the Constitution of the Socialist Republic of Vietnam 2013 ('the Constitution') does not address the relationship between national law and international law, an

[5] The LT 2016 replaces the Law on the Conclusion, Accession to and Implementation of Treaties 2005.

[6] Opened for signature 23 May 1969, entered into force 27 January 1980, 1155 UNTS 331. Viet Nam ratified the VCLT on 10 October 2001.

[7] LT 2016 art. 2(1) provides that '[a] treaty means a written agreement concluded in the name of the State or of the Government of the Socialist Republic of Vietnam with foreign parties, which gives rise to, changes or terminates rights, obligations of the Socialist Republic of Vietnam in accordance of international law, regardless of their titles, such as treaty, convention, agreement, covenant, arrangement, protocol, memorandum of understanding, exchanged diplomatic note or other titles'.

[8] VCLT (n 6) art. 2(1)(a).

[9] The Law on the Conclusion, Accession to and Implementation of Treaties 2005 was replaced by the LT 2016 (n 4).

[10] The Ordinance on conclusion and implementation of international agreements 2007, art. 1 defines international agreements as those concluded by the National Assembly, agencies of the National Assembly, assisting agencies of the National Assembly, the Supreme People's Court, the Supreme People's Procuracy, the State Audit, ministries, ministerial-level agencies, government-attached agencies, People's Councils and People's Committees of provinces and centrally run cities, central bodies of socio-political organizations, socio-political-professional organizations, social organizations, and socio-professional organizations.

[11] The Ordinance on conclusion and implementation of international agreements 2007, art. 4(4).

examination of various legal documents suggests that it adopts a modified monist approach. First, Viet Nam maintains both the primacy of the Constitution and the priority of treaties. The provision on treaties prevailing over domestic laws is consistently found in legal documents such as the Civil Code, the Civil Procedure Code, the Criminal Code, the Criminal Procedure Code, the Commercial Law, and the Investment Law.[12] The previous Law on the Conclusion, Accession to and Implementation of Treaties 2005 pronounced the principle of Viet Nam's compliance with its treaties and clearly required the application of treaties where there was a conflict between treaty rules and Viet Nam's legal documents,[13] which implicitly included the Constitution as defined under the Law on Promulgation of Legal Documents 2008.[14]

However, the new Law on Treaties 2016 modifies this provision by explicitly excluding the Constitution from the treaty-prevailing rule.[15] It also envisages a smooth alignment between treaties and the Constitution by requiring treaties to conform with the Constitution in the process of treaty making and implementation.[16] Consequently, despite no specification on the position of treaties within Viet Nam's hierarchy of legal documents, they prevail over conflicting rules of municipal law but must be consistent with the Constitution. This approach differs from the postulate of internationalist monism whereby international law validates or invalidates all municipal legal acts and municipal law must always conform to international law.[17]

Secondly, Viet Nam decides on the incorporation of treaties into Vietnamese law on a case-by-case basis. It does not strictly follow the monist theory that considers it generally unnecessary to transform international norms into domestic law.[18] Nor does it agree to the dualistic doctrine that international law must be transformed into

[12] Civil Code 2015 arts 4(4) and 665 (replacing art. 759 of the Civil Code 2005); Civil Procedure Code 2015 art. 2(3); Criminal Code 2015 art. 5(2); Criminal Procedure Code 2015 art. 3(2) (replacing art. 2 of the Criminal Procedure Code 2003); Commercial Law 2005 art. 5(1); Investment Law 2014 art. 4(3) (replacing art. 5(3) of the Investment Law 2005).

[13] Law on the Conclusion, Accession to and Implementation of Treaties 2005 art. 6(1).

[14] Art. 2(1) of the Law on Promulgation of Legal Documents 2008 includes the Constitution in the list of Viet Nam's system of legal documents. Under art. 1(1) of this Law,

> legal documents are documents issued or jointly issued by state agencies in accordance with the authority, formats, sequence of steps and procedures prescribed in this Law or the Law on the Promulgation of Legal Documents of Peoples Councils and Peoples Committees, which includes common rules of conducts, which has compulsory effectiveness and the implementation of which is guaranteed by the Government to regulate social relations.

They are, for example, the Constitution, laws, resolutions of the National Assembly, ordinances, resolutions of the Standing Committee of the National Assembly, orders and decisions of the State President, decrees of the Government, decisions of the Prime Minister, and circulars of Ministers or Heads of Ministry-equivalent agencies: art. 2(1).

[15] Art. 6(1) of the LT 2016 (n 4) provides that '[i]n cases where a legal document and a treaty to which the Socialist Republic of Vietnam is a party contain different provisions on the same matter, the provisions of the treaty shall prevail, except for the Constitution'.

[16] LT 2016 (n 4) art. 3(1).

[17] Antonio Cassese, *International Law* (OUP 2001) 164.

[18] Ibid. 164.

national law to become domestically binding on a state.[19] Vietnam's Law on Promulgation of Legal Documents 2015 prescribes a principle that the making of legal documents shall cause 'no difficulties or obstacles to the implementation of the international treaties' of which Viet Nam is a party.[20] This Law further provides that whether a treaty may be self-executing in Viet Nam depends on the judgement of competent state bodies on the requirements, content, and nature of a treaty. Specifically, the state bodies with authority to express Viet Nam's consent to be bound will decide whether all or part of the treaty in question is directly applicable to state bodies, entities, and/or individuals, if the provisions of the treaty are explicit and specific enough for implementation.[21] The bodies which have authority to express Viet Nam's consent to be bound are the National Assembly, the President, and the Government. They may also take the view that one or more legal documents must be amended, supplemented, cancelled, or promulgated for the treaty to be applied in Viet Nam.

The provisions on self-executing treaties (contained in the Law on the Conclusion, Accession to and Implementation of Treaties 2005) had been effective for over a decade before being reintroduced in the Law of Treaties 2016. Nonetheless, only a few ratification decisions are made on direct application or need transformation of the treaty in question into national law.[22] One example is the 2006 National Assembly resolution on Viet Nam's accession to the World Trade Organization (WTO), which specifies self-executing commitments for Viet Nam on the condition that they are adequately detailed and clear.[23] Another resolution, ratifying the Convention against Torture and Other Cruel, Inhuman or Degrading Treatment or Punishment 1984, implicitly rejects the direct applicability of the entire Convention, stating that Viet Nam will develop and make laws in conformity with it.[24] Viet Nam's reservation to the UN Convention

[19] Ibid. 163.

[20] Law on Promulgation of Legal Documents 2015 art. 5(5) (replacing art. 3(5) of the Law on Promulgation of Legal Documents 2008).

[21] LT 2016 (n 4) art. 6(2); see also art. 29(3)(b).

[22] Ministry of Foreign Affairs, Report on the Impact of the 2005 Law on the Conclusion, Accession to and Implementation of Treaties (amended 2015) 17.

[23] Resolution on the Ratification of the Protocol on Accession of the Socialist Republic of Vietnam to the Agreement Establishing the World Trade Organization 2006, No. 71/2006/NQ-QH11. Para 2 states that the National Assembly decides to: 'apply directly Vietnam's commitments stated in the Annex to this Resolution and other WTO commitments that are adequately detailed and clear in the Protocol, attached annexes and the Report of the Working Party on the Accession of Vietnam to the Agreement Establishing the WTO. If the provisions of Vietnamese law are inconsistent with the provisions of the Agreement Establishing the WTO, the Protocol and attached documents, the provisions of the Agreement, the Protocol and attached documents prevail.'

[24] Resolution on the Ratification of the United Nations Convention against Torture and Other Cruel, Inhuman or Degrading Treatment or Punishment 2014, No. 83/2014/QH13, art. 3 states that: 'The Socialist Republic of Vietnam shall build and improve its legal system in conformity with the provisions of the United Nations Convention against Torture and Other Cruel, Inhuman or Degrading Treatment or Punishment'. The assessment report of the Committee for External Affairs of the National Assembly, No. 4527/BC-UBĐN13, states that: 'considering interests in and the need for public order and security at present as well as the practice of the State Parties to the Convention, the Committee for External Affairs agrees with the proposal by the Government that the Convention is not subject to direct application in Vietnam'.

against Transnational Organized Crime 2000 clearly declares that the provisions of the Convention are non-self-executing and that the:

> implementation of provisions of this Convention shall be in accordance with Constitutional principles and the substantive law of the Socialist Republic of Vietnam, on the basis of bilateral or multilateral cooperative agreements with other States and the principle of reciprocity.[25]

To reach a conclusion on the direct applicability of a treaty when it becomes effective, Viet Nam reviews conformity of national law with that treaty at various stages of the treaty-making process. When considering whether a treaty is necessary, a state body may submit a proposal on treaty negotiation, signing, or accession.[26] Such bodies include the Supreme People's Court, the Supreme People's Procuracy, ministries, ministerial-level bodies, or other government bodies. In the case of a treaty on war, peace, or sovereignty, the Ministry of Foreign Affairs must make a joint proposal with the Ministry of National Defence and the Ministry of Public Security.[27]

The Law of Treaties 2016 requires a treaty's content to be reviewed by both the Ministry of Foreign Affairs and the Ministry of Justice on its conformity with Viet Nam's existing treaty obligations and national laws.[28] This aims to assess the treaty's impact or the amendments to municipal laws that will be necessary following its signing. Approval of the National Assembly Standing Committee must also be obtained before signing a treaty when (i) treaty provisions are different from, additional to, or inconsistent with legal documents of the National Assembly or of the Committee, or (ii) a treaty's implementation requires amendment and supplementation, annulment, or promulgation of legal documents of the National Assembly or of the Committee (except where the treaty in question is to be reviewed later by the National Assembly for ratification).[29]

At the stage of expressing consent to be bound, Viet Nam specifically requires the review and approval of the National Assembly, the President, or the Government. Treaties modifying, restricting, or invalidating human rights and fundamental rights and obligations of citizens prescribed in laws and resolutions of the National Assembly, and treaties inconsistent with laws and resolutions of the National Assembly, are subject to the ratification or accession decision of the National Assembly.[30]

When the President or the Government considers accession to other treaties, their decision must be based on the opinion of the National Assembly Standing Committee

[25] See Viet Nam's declarations when ratifying the UN Convention against Transnational Organized Crime 2000 <https://treaties.un.org/pages/ViewDetails.aspx?src=TREATY&mtdsg_no=XVIII-12&chapter=18&clang=_en> accessed 15 January 2018. See also Viet Nam's similar declarations in acceding to the International Convention against the Taking of Hostages 1979 <https://treaties.un.org/pages/viewdetails.aspx?src=ind&mtdsg_no=xviii-5&chapter=18&lang=en> accessed 15 January 2018 and International Convention for the Suppression of Terrorist Bombings 1997 <https://treaties.un.org/pages/ViewDetails.aspx?src=IND&mtdsg_no=XVIII-9&chapter=18&clang=_en> accessed 15 January 2018.

[26] LT 2016 (n 4) arts 8(1), 13(1), and 41(1).

[27] Ibid. art. 8(2).

[28] Ibid. arts 13(2), 77(1), and 78(2).

[29] Ibid. art. 14(1).

[30] Vietnam Constitution 2013 art. 70(14); LT 2016 (n 4) art. 29(1).

where (a) the treaty contains provisions that are different from, additional to, or inconsistent with legal documents of the National Assembly or of the National Assembly Standing Committee; or (b) the treaty's implementation requires amendment and supplementation, annulment, or promulgation of legal documents of the National Assembly or of the Committee.[31] A treaty concluded in the name of the Government that is inconsistent with legal documents of the Government, and is not subject to ratification, must be approved by the Government.[32]

Examining the status of treaties in Viet Nam's legal system and its treaty-making law reveals careful mechanisms to ensure *de jure* compliance with treaty obligations. De facto implementation is guaranteed by a detailed framework on the authority and responsibility of concerned governmental bodies.[33] For example, in accordance with these rules,[34] the Ministry of Public Security submitted a proposal for implementing the International Convention Against the Taking of Hostages of 1979 and the International Convention for the Suppression of Terrorist Bombings of 1997[35] for approval by the Prime Minister.[36] It also specifically laid down an implementation plan,[37] which was put into action by provincial authorities.[38] Consequently, the principle of full compliance and priority of treaties in Viet Nam's legal system has been highly legalized and institutionalized, reflecting a clear political will to integrate international law into national law.

3 Practice

3.1 Pre-1945

Viet Nam's ancient history has not created favourable conditions for nourishing a tradition of proactively making and using international law in foreign policy to maximize Viet Nam's interests. Lack of independence and power in external relations in the feudal nineteenth and early twentieth centuries may have hindered an

[31] LT 2016 (n 4) art. 42. [32] Ibid. art. 39(2). [33] Ibid. arts 76–80.

[34] See the Law on the Conclusion, Accession to and Implementation of Treaties 2005 arts 71–3, 97–9, which are similar to and replaced by those of the LT 2016 (n 4).

[35] These Conventions entered into force for Viet Nam on 8 February 2014. See the Notice on the Entry into Force of Treaties, No. 11/2014/TB-LPQT of the Ministry of Foreign Affairs, 10 February 2014.

[36] See Decision No. 507/QĐ-TTg of the Prime Minister dated 29 March 2016, approving the Plan implementing the International Convention against the Taking of Hostages of 1979 and the International Convention for the Suppression of Terrorist Bombings of 1997.

[37] See Decision No. 4002/QĐ-BCA-V19 of the Ministry of Public Security dated 16 September 2016 on the Plan implementing the International Convention against the Taking of Hostages of 1979 and the International Convention for the Suppression of Terrorist Bombings of 1997.

[38] See e.g. Plan No. 4732/KH-UBND of the People's Committee of Gia Lai Province dated 13 October 2016, to carry out the implementing Plan (n 33 and n 34).

understanding of international law's role and the development of strategies that rely on international law. Until the twentieth century, Viet Nam's development was overshadowed by Chinese culture and political control. Resistance struggles against foreign occupation were countered with repeated invasions and annexations.[39]

Even with success in its independence struggle, efforts towards cultivating a domestic rule of law tradition[40] during the longest dynasty, the Le dynasty from 1428 to 1788, did not have an impact on Viet Nam's then international relations. At that time, autonomy was maintained and peace agreements were enforceable on condition that Viet Nam pursued peaceful relations with China as a tributary state.[41] Viet Nam was not aware of the progress of international law in the nineteenth century in other continents, such as the signing of friendship, commerce, and navigation treaties, the founding of international river commissions to ensure freedom of navigation on the Rhine and Danube Rivers, or the International Telegraphic and Universal Postal Unions in 1865 and 1874 respectively.[42] Due to the lack of international communication and transportation, the establishment of the League of Nations and the Permanent Court of International Justice after World War I was unknown in Viet Nam. Its fight against alien domination was therefore mainly based on its self-perceived national identity or sovereignty.[43]

The elites of Viet Nam's dynasties had to live with the constant fear of aggression and were forced to choose either diplomatic strategies to maintain peace and independence or military strength to guard those values. The last emperor, Bao Dai, could not carry out his policies of modernizing judicial systems and ending archaic court practices, such as the *kowtow*, due to the French undermining his authority.[44] There is no record of the Vietnamese population managing to vindicate its fundamental human rights through the use of legal tools while under the rule of the feudal colonial power.

[39] See generally Lê Thành Khôi, *The History of Vietnam: From the Origin to the 20th Century* (Thế Giới Publishers 2014).

[40] Le Thanh Tong, a king ruling from 1460 to 1497, ordered the formulation of the Hong Duc Legal Code, recognizing important and innovative rights such as granting a higher position to women, granting daughters the same inheritance rights as sons, and removing the requirement of parental consent in marriage. See Marsha Ackermann in Michael Schroeder, Janice Terry, Jiu-Hwa Lo Upshur, and Mark Whitters (eds), *Encyclopedia of World History* vol I (Infobase Publishing 2008) 210.

[41] Luu Van Loi, *Fifty Years of Vietnam's Diplomacy: 1945–1995* vol I (Public Security Press 1996) 18–24.

[42] Malcolm Evans (ed), *International Law* (4th edn OUP 2014) 11, 17.

[43] For example, Ly Thuong Kiet, a Vietnamese general and hero, declared the independence of Viet Nam in his poem, which was read in a temple to make a psychological impression on soldiers of both sides in 1077. It stated:

Over Mountains and Rivers of the South, reigns the Emperor of the South
As it stands written forever in the Book of Heaven
How dare those barbarians invade our land?
Your armies, without pity, will be annihilated.

See also Ngô Sĩ Liên, *The Complete Historical Annals of the Great Việt* (Social Sciences Publishing House 1993) 110, 111; Lê (n 39) 187, 188.

[44] Ackermann (n 40) 40.

When the conquerors left the country, the atmosphere of freedom did not linger long enough, before they returned, to foster the spirit of and a belief in justice.

3.2 Modern Viet Nam

Nationalist resistance against imperialism in Viet Nam relied extensively on international law, despite ignorance of international law in the earlier feudal periods. The principles of sovereign equality and self-determination provided a basis for the nationalist movements to free Viet Nam from colonialism in the twentieth century. The proposal sent to the French authorities by the Vietnamese leader, Ho Chi Minh, called for granting freedoms recognized by the United Nations to the Indochinese people.[45] Viet Nam's Declaration of Independence of 1945, which established the Democratic Republic of Vietnam, emphasized that Viet Nam had already broken off all relations of a colonial character with France and repealed all of the international obligations that France had thus far subscribed to on behalf of Viet Nam.[46] The Declaration contained another invocation of international law, namely that:

> We are convinced that the Allied nations, which at Tehran and San Francisco have acknowledged the principles of self-determination and equality of nations, will not refuse to acknowledge the independence of Vietnam.

Soon after its establishment, the Democratic Republic of Viet Nam made treaties that recorded negotiation outcomes in its struggle for national independence and unification. However, it repeatedly realized that battlefield results outweighed the legal force of these documents.

3.2.1 *Independence and Unification*

A milestone in Viet Nam's fight against French rule is the signing of the 6 March France-Vietnam Accord in 1946, wherein France recognized 'the Republic of Vietnam as a free state' and agreed to accept 'the decisions taken by the population through a referendum' on the unification of the three regions of Viet Nam: Tonkin, Annam, and Cochin-China.[47] The contracting parties undertook to 'take all necessary measures to stop hostilities immediately'.[48] Nonetheless, their increasingly deteriorating relationship led to the resumption of warfare between the two sides.

After nine years of nationwide resistance to France and with the fall of the French garrison at Dien Bien Phu in 1954, the Democratic Republic of Vietnam negotiated intensively with France as well as other delegations from Cambodia, the People's

[45] Luu (n 41) 32. See also Jean Sainteny, *Histoire d'une paix manquée* (Amiot Dumont 1953).

[46] Ho Chi Minh, *Selected Works* vol 3 (Foreign Languages Publishing House 1960–2) 17–21. See also Luu (n 41) 31.

[47] Roger Levy, *L'Indochine et Ses Traites* (Centre D'Etudes de Politiques Etrangere 1947) 46–8.

[48] Ibid.

Republic of China, Laos, the United Kingdom, the Soviet Union, the Republic of Vietnam (South Vietnam), and the United States. It concluded the Geneva Agreement on the Cessation of Hostilities 1954 with France, in which the contracting parties agreed upon a cease-fire along a temporary dividing line at the 17th parallel of north latitude and a demilitarized zone on either side of it 5 kilometres wide.[49] The Agreement also envisaged general elections to reunify the country.[50] An International Commission composed of representatives of Canada, India, and Poland was set up for the control and supervision of the application of the provisions of the Agreement.[51] Nationwide elections, however, turned out to be unenforceable. France could not ensure the organization of elections when South Vietnam refused to give effect to the provision for elections in Viet Nam, given the withdrawal of its armed forces.[52] Instead of being a means to making their military success official and being honoured internationally by the parties involved, treaties brought disappointment and frustration to the leaders of the Democratic Republic of Vietnam.[53] The conflict continued with gradual disregard for the Agreement. Each side waited for a pretext for retaliation, based on an alleged prior breach of the Agreement by the other party, which led to a whole series of breaches of international law.[54]

For small countries, international law serves as an anchor for their foreign policies, especially in the search for independence with a view to achieving complete success and international recognition. After nineteen years of fighting militarily and diplomatically against the US's involvement, on 27 January 1973 the Democratic Republic of Vietnam concluded the Paris Agreement on Ending the War and Restoring Peace in Vietnam with the US.[55] Accordingly, the US undertook to respect the independence, sovereignty, unity, and territorial integrity of Viet Nam, and to stop all its military activities by ground, air, and naval forces against the territory of the Democratic Republic of Vietnam.[56] Shortly afterwards, representatives of twelve governments signed the Act of International Conference on Vietnam to acknowledge and endorse the Paris Agreement.[57] Nonetheless, national reunification could not be achieved through negotiation as prescribed in the Agreement but instead only by the armed forces of the Democratic Republic of Vietnam two years later.[58]

[49] Geneva Agreement on the Cessation of Hostilities in Vietnam (opened for signature 20 July 1954, entered into force 22 July 1954) art. 1.

[50] Ibid. art. 14. [51] Ibid. art. 34.

[52] Alan Watt, 'The Geneva Agreements 1954 in Relation to Vietnam' (1967) 39(2) The Australian Quarterly 23.

[53] Ibid.

[54] Michael Akehurst, 'Vietnam and International Law' (1973) 3 Otago Law Review 39, 47.

[55] Luu (n 41) 365–79.

[56] Paris Agreement on Ending the War and Restoring Peace in Vietnam (signed and entered into force 27 January 1973, 935 UNTS 6) arts 1 and 2.

[57] International Conference on Vietnam: Act Concerning the Paris Agreement on Ending the War and Restoring Peace in Vietnam (signed and entered into force 2 March 1973, [1973] 12 ILM 392).

[58] Luu (n 41) 166–88, 365–79.

Treaties made in wartime were carefully considered steps in the course of the struggle for national independence and unification. The parties devoted time and effort in negotiations and drafting,[59] and also supposedly attached great importance to the terms achieved in these documents. However, in Viet Nam, political, military, and ideological considerations—rather than the binding legal force of treaties—is what ultimately determined compliance by the warring parties. Indeed, the confrontational circumstances contributed to treaty failure because the habit of obeying international law by most states is gradually lost during a prolonged war, due to mistrust.[60] Therefore, the final outcome of the political and military fight in Viet Nam was mainly based on military victories on battlefields.

3.2.2 *Integration with the International Community*

Despite bitter experience with treaties reached during wartime, after gaining independence in 1945, Viet Nam immediately tasked the Ministry of Foreign Affairs with 'conducting research on public and private international law... [and] interpreting international rules and treaties',[61] and later with 'conducting research on the United Nations and other international organizations; [and] providing administrative assistance on conclusion of international agreements and conventions'.[62] After forty years of peace, since 1975, Viet Nam has concluded or acceded to over 4,000 international agreements[63] and joined almost all important international and regional organizations, in order to facilitate its international integration.

In the late 1970s and 1980s, the Cold War climax, conflict with China, and intervention in Cambodia created obstacles for the country's international relations. Despite having become a member of the UN on 20 September 1977,[64] Viet Nam only assumed an increasingly active role in shaping and accepting international rules under the auspices of the UN from the 1990s.[65] It was Vice President of the UN General Assembly in 1997; a member of the UN Economic and Social Council in the 1998–2000 and 2016–18 terms; a member of the UNDP/UNFPA Executive Council; a member of the Board of Governors of the International Atomic Energy Agency (IAEA) for many terms; Chair of the IAEA Board of Governors for the 2013–15 term; and member of the UN Human Rights Council for the 2014–16 term. It was a non-permanent member of the UN Security Council for the term 2008–9 and has again presented its candidature

59 Ibid. 60 Akehurst (n 54) 47.

61 See Order No. 47-CP of the Government Council dated 7 April 1946.

62 See Decree No. 21/NĐ of the Deputy Prime Minister of Foreign Affairs, Ung Van Khiem, dated 27 February 1957 and Official Document No. 151/TC of the Prime Minister dated 3 November 1959.

63 Ministry of Foreign Affairs, Report on Impact Assessment of the Law on the Conclusion, Accession to and Implementation of Treaties (2016) 3, 19.

64 UNGA res 32/2 (20 September 1977) on admission of the Socialist Republic of Vietnam to membership in the United Nations.

65 Ministry of Foreign Affairs, *Vietnam and International Organizations* (National Political Publishing House 2005) 352–86.

for non-permanent membership for the term 2020–1.[66] In support of UN peacekeeping operations, Viet Nam deployed its first peacekeepers to Africa in 2014 and is preparing to deploy level-two field hospitals.[67] In addition to the UN system, Viet Nam is a member of over sixty international organizations in various fields, such as the International Monetary Fund, World Bank, World Trade Organization, and Asian Productivity Organization.[68]

At the regional level, the most important organization that Viet Nam is a member of is the Association of Southeast Asian Nations (ASEAN). By resolving the Cambodian situation and improving its economic relations with the ASEAN states, particularly Indonesia, Malaysia, and Thailand, Viet Nam's application for ASEAN membership was successful in 1995.[69] It has engaged in all law-making activities of ASEAN and has thus contributed to the development of ASEAN rules on a wide range of issues, such as combating human trafficking[70] and terrorism,[71] harmonizing customs procedures,[72] liberalizing trade in goods and services,[73] and protecting and promoting investment.[74]

Viet Nam has also relied on ASEAN as a regional arrangement to address international issues such as the South China Sea dispute. Under the auspices of ASEAN, it has advocated for self-restraint and dispute settlement by peaceful means in accordance with international law, including through the UN Convention on the Law of the Sea 1982 and the implementation of the Declaration on the Conduct of parties on the South China Sea (DOC).[75] Being the ASEAN Chair in 2020 will be an opportunity for Viet Nam to wor towards the completion of a legally binding Code of Conduct in the South China Sea.

[66] Address by HE Mr Pham Binh Minh, Deputy Prime Minister, Minister of Foreign Affairs of the Socialist Republic of Vietnam at the General Debate of the 72nd Session of the UN General Assembly (2 September 2017) <https://gadebate.un.org/sites/default/files/gastatements/72/vn_en.pdf> accessed 29 January 2018.

[67] Ibid.

[68] See the list of international organizations that Viet Nam is a member of in Ministry of Foreign Affairs (n 65) 387–91.

[69] Shaun Narine, *Explaining ASEAN: Regionalism in Southeast Asia* (Lynne Rienner Publishers 2002) 57–8, 113.

[70] See ASEAN Convention Against Trafficking in Persons, Especially Women and Children (signed 21 November 2015, entered into force 8 March 2016).

[71] See ASEAN Convention on Counter Terrorism (signed 13 January 2007, entered into force 27 May 2011).

[72] See ASEAN Agreement on Customs (signed 30 March 2012, entered into force 7 November 2014).

[73] See ASEAN Trade in Goods Agreement (signed 26 February 2009, entered into force 14 June 2010); ASEAN Framework Agreement on Services (signed 15 December 1995, entered into force 12 August 1998).

[74] See ASEAN Comprehensive Investment Agreement (signed 26 February 2009, entered into force 24 February 2012).

[75] See n 66.

4 Selected Themes

4.1 Implementing Foreign Policy

Viet Nam's practice of accepting and enacting treaties shows that international law is an ad hoc means of realizing its goals relating to foreign affairs. Initiatives for new treaties are mainly determined by the temporal need for cooperation with international partners. For example, focusing on clarifying the borderlines with neighbouring countries after the Vietnam war, it finalized agreements on land boundary delimitation with Laos in 1977,[76] Cambodia in 1985,[77] and China in 1999.[78] It also reached agreement on maritime boundaries with Thailand, China, and Indonesia and agreed to a maritime joint development area with Thailand, Malaysia, and China.[79] Viet Nam and Cambodia signed an agreement on historic waters in the Gulf of Thailand in 1982.[80]

Viet Nam signs hundreds of treaties annually on various matters, such as border limitation, combating terrorism, judicial assistance, and the environment.[81] Concluding or accepting international obligations is mainly based on annual tentative plans submitted by governmental bodies,[82] which are prepared in conformity with the overall national policy in foreign affairs. When a treaty is necessary, ministries make proposals on treaty signing to the competent authority. There has been no general, concerted national strategy of, or established approach to, framing international obligations and rights concerning Viet Nam. The rationale for treaties can be to create legal frameworks

[76] See Treaty on Delimitation of National Boundaries between the Lao People's Democratic Republic and the Socialist Republic of Vietnam (signed 18 July 1977); Supplementary Treaty to the 1976 Treaty on Boundary Delimitation (signed 24 January 1986).

[77] See Treaty on Delimitation of National Boundaries between Vietnam and Kampuchea (signed 27 December 1985, entered into force 22 February 1986); Supplementary Treaty to the Treaty on the Delimitation of State Border of 1985 (signed 10 October 2005, entered into force 6 December 2005).

[78] See Treaty of Land Border between the Socialist Republic of Vietnam and the People's Republic of China (signed 30 December 1999).

[79] See Agreement between the Government of the Kingdom of Thailand and the Government of the Socialist Republic of Vietnam on the Delimitation of the Maritime Boundary between the Two Countries in the Gulf of Thailand (signed 9 August 1997, entered into force 28 February 1998); Agreement between the Government of the Socialist Republic of Vietnam and the Republic of Indonesia concerning the Delimitation of the Continental Shelf Boundary (signed 26 June 2003); Memorandum of Understanding between Malaysia and the Socialist Republic of Vietnam for the Exploration and Exploitation of Petroleum in a Defined Area of the Continental Shelf Involving the Two Countries (signed 5 June 1992, entered into force 4 June 1993); Agreement between the People's Republic of China and the Socialist Republic of Vietnam on the Delimitation of the Territorial Seas, Exclusive Economic Zones and Continental Shelves of the Two Countries in Beibu Gulf/Bac Bo Gulf (signed 25 December 2000, entered into force 15 June 2004).

[80] See Agreement on Historic Waters of Vietnam and Kampuchea (signed 7 July 1982).

[81] See n 63. See also Ministry of Foreign Affairs, Report on Treaties and International Agreements 2015 and plans for 2016.

[82] Ibid.

for coordinated actions,[83] regulation of matters involving private actors,[84] or settlement of divergences,[85] or simply to express goodwill in foreign relations.[86]

The most robust treaty-making activities are to realize Viet Nam's policy of economic integration.[87] A notable illustration is Viet Nam's conclusion of over sixty treaties on investment protection and promotion. Table 20.1 shows the number of bilateral investment treaties (BITs) that Viet Nam has signed with different countries.[88]

In addition, Viet Nam has become party to bilateral and multilateral free trade agreements that contain chapters resembling BITs.[89] Viet Nam's investment treaties have very divergent content, especially those signed in recent years. For example, the Viet Nam-Greece BIT 2008 contains short, general and vague commitments in its

[83] See e.g. Paris Agreement (adopted 12 December 2015, entered into force 4 November 2016).

[84] See e.g. UN Convention on Contracts for the International Sale of Goods (adopted 11 April 1980, entered into force 1 January 1988, 1489 UNTS 3).

[85] See e.g. UN Convention on the Law of the Sea (adopted 10 December 1982, entered into force 16 November 1994, 1833 UNTS 3).

[86] Viet Nam's signing of investment treaties in many cases serves as a goodwill act in a state visit, according to interviews with Viet Nam's negotiators of such treaties. This practice is similar to that of other countries, as revealed in expert testimony from Christoph Schreuer, who claims that BITs are among the clauses of treaties that are often not properly negotiated. (See *Wintershall Aktiengesellschaft v Argentine Republic*, ICSID Case No. ARB/04/14, Award, 8 December 2008, para 85, citing expert testimony from Christoph Schreuer, hearing transcripts in English, second day, 15 October 2007). BITs are very often off-the-shelf models, put forward on the occasion of state visits when the heads of state need something to sign; treaties for cultural cooperation are often used in the same way. In other words, they are very often not negotiated at all, but are just being put on the table, and I have heard several representatives who have actually been active in this so-called treaty-making process say that, 'We had no idea that this would have real consequences in the real world'.

[87] This policy has been laid down in guidelines and resolutions of the Politburo, such as the Guidelines of the 9th National Party Congress, emphasizing 'proactive international economic integration'; Resolution No. 07-NQ/TW on 'International Economic Integration of the 10th Politburo' dated 27 November 2001, affirming the policy of 'proactive, active international economic integration together with the expansion of international cooperation in other fields'; Resolution No. 08-NQ/TW on 'Some Major Guidelines and Policies for Fast, Sustainable Economic Development following Vietnam's Accession to the World Trade Organisation' of the 10th Central Executive Committee dated 5 February 2007; and Resolution No. 22-NQ/TW on 'International Integration' of the 10th Central Executive Committee dated 10 April 2013.

[88] This table includes superseded BITs. Specifically, the BIT 1996 with Laos was replaced by the new one signed in 2012; the BIT 1995 with Cuba was replaced by the new one signed in 2007; the BIT 1993 with South Korea was replaced by the new one signed in 2003; the BIT 1993 with Poland was replaced by the new one signed in 2008; and the BIT 1997 with Czech Republic was replaced by the new one signed in 2008.

[89] For example, Trade Agreement between the Government of the United States of America and the Government of the Socialist Republic of Vietnam (signed 14 July 2000) Chapter IV—Development of Investment Relations; Vietnam–South Korea Free Trade Agreement (signed 5 May 2015, entered into force 20 December 2015) Chapter 9—Investment; Australia–New Zealand–ASEAN Free Trade Agreement (signed 27 February 2009, entered into force 1 January 2010) Chapter 11—Investment. Viet Nam is also a party to Investment Agreements within the framework of free trade agreements between ASEAN and China, South Korea, and India.

Table 20.1 Bilateral Investment Treaties of Viet Nam by Year

Year	Numbers of BITs	Other State Party
1990	1	Italy
1991	4	Australia (terminated), BLEU (Belgium-Luxembourg Economic Union), Indonesia (terminated), Thailand
1992	7	Belarus, China, France, Malaysia, The Philippines, Singapore, Switzerland
1993	7	Denmark, Finland (terminated), South Korea (terminated), Sweden, Taiwan, Armenia, Germany
1994	6	Hungary, Netherlands, Poland, Romania, Russia, Ukraine
1995	4	Austria, Cuba, Latvia, Lithuania
1996	5	Algeria, Argentina, Bulgaria, Laos, Uzbekistan
1997	3	Czech Republic, Egypt, India (terminated)
1998	0	
1999	2	Chile, Tajikistan
2000	2	Mongolia, Myanmar
2001	1	Cambodia
2002	3	Iceland, North Korea, the United Kingdom
2003	3	Japan, Namibia, South Korea
2004	0	
2005	1	Bangladesh
2006	1	Spain
2007	3	Cuba, Kuwait, Mozambique
2008	4	Czech Republic, Finland, Greece, Venezuela
2009	8	Estonia, Iran, Kazakhstan, Qatar, Slovakia, Sri Lanka, United Arab Emirates, Uruguay
2010	0	
2011	2	Estonia (Protocol amending BIT), Oman
2012	2	Laos (Protocol amending BIT), Morocco
2013	1	Palestine
2014	2	Macedonia, Turkey

thirteen provisions and ten pages,[90] while the ASEAN Comprehensive Investment Agreement 2009 imposes detailed and clear obligations, together with qualifications and exceptions in its forty-nine provisions and fifty pages.[91] The most recent international commitments of Viet Nam to the promotion and protection of investment treaties have been shaped in accordance with latest reforming trends and include the

[90] Agreement between the Government of the Hellenic Republic and the Government of the Socialist Republic of Vietnam on the Promotion and Reciprocal Protection of Investments (signed 13 October 2008) <http://investmentpolicyhub.unctad.org/Download/TreatyFile/2954> accessed 15 February 2017.

[91] ASEAN Comprehensive Investment Agreement (signed 26 February 2009, entered into force 29 March 2012) <http://investmentpolicyhub.unctad.org/Download/TreatyFile/3095> accessed 15 February 2017.

Comprehensive and Progressive Agreement for Trans-Pacific Partnership (CPTPP)[92] and the European Union–Viet Nam Investment Protection Agreement (EVIPA).[93]

Having faced investor-state arbitration cases since 2004 with increasing frequency,[94] Viet Nam has undertaken some steps to promote compliance with investment treaties and to prevent disputes arising out of them. These include the Master Plan on solving disputes between the Government of Viet Nam and Foreign Investor[s];[95] mechanisms for coordination in resolution of international investment disputes;[96] a project on increasing knowledge and improving skills for state officials working on international integration;[97] a project on capacity-building for state officials of ministries, sectors, and local administrations on international law; and the settlement of international investment disputes for 2016–2020.[98] Nonetheless, there has been no effort to reformulate treaty obligations to reflect Viet Nam's approach and interests in a more consistent way.

One might argue that this is understandable and intentional because Viet Nam places different priorities on foreign investment and investors from various trading partners in its economic relations. It is nonetheless still difficult to explain why South Korean investors are guaranteed inconsistent standards in the three concurrently effective agreements, namely the Vietnam–South Korea BIT 2003,[99] the ASEAN–South Korea Investment Agreement 2009,[100] and the Vietnam–South Korea Free Trade Agreement 2015.[101] The main reason, therefore, might be that Vietnamese negotiators are not provided with official uniform guidance on the expected outcomes. Various negotiation delegations decide commitments to foreign investment and investors without concerted and coordinated preparation. Contrary to this ad hoc approach, with regard to formulating treaty content, the most sophisticated strategy

[92] The Comprehensive and Progressive Agreement for Trans-Pacific Partnership (signed 8 March 2018, entered into force for Viet Nam 14 January 2019).

[93] See Agreed Text of the EU-Vietnam Investment Protection Agreement as of August 2018 <http://trade.ec.europa.eu/doclib/press/index.cfm?id=1437> accessed 25 April 2019.

[94] See the list of investor-state arbitration cases against Vietnam compiled by UNCTAD at <http://investmentpolicyhub.unctad.org/ISDS/CountryCases/229?partyRole=2>.

[95] See Decision No. 680/QĐ-TTg of the Prime Minister dated 3 May 2013.

[96] See Decision No. 04/2014/QD-TTg of the Prime Minister dated 14 January 2014.

[97] See Decision No. 2007/QĐ-TTg of the Prime Minister dated 16 November 2015.

[98] See Decision No. 1063/QĐ-TTg of the Prime Minister dated 14 June 2016.

[99] Agreement between the Government of the Republic of Korea and the Government of the Socialist Republic of Vietnam for the Promotion and Protection of Investments (signed 15 September 2003, entered into force 05 June 2004) <http://investmentpolicyhub.unctad.org/Download/TreatyFile/4844> accessed 15 February 2017.

[100] Agreement on Investment under the Framework Agreement on Comprehensive Economic Cooperation among the Governments of the Member Countries of the Association of Southeast Asian Nations and the Republic of Korea (signed 2 June 2009, entered into force 1 September 2004) <http://investmentpolicyhub.unctad.org/Download/TreatyFile/3339> accessed 15 February 2017.

[101] Free Trade Agreement between the Government of the Republic of Korea and the Government of the Socialist Republic of Vietnam (signed 05 May 2015, entered into force 20 December 2015) <http://investmentpolicyhub.unctad.org/Download/TreatyFile/3582> accessed 15 February 2017.

could be to utilize a model investment treaty that other countries have drafted for negotiations.[102]

Another area of international law in which Viet Nam has most actively undertaken international commitments is human rights. This reflects the approach proclaimed and highlighted in Viet Nam's Declaration of Independence 1945 on the paramount importance of human rights.[103] In 1957, the Democratic Republic of Vietnam acceded to all four Geneva Conventions of 1949 on the protection of civilian persons, the wounded, sick, and shipwrecked, members of armed forces, and prisoners of war.[104] It is also a party to almost all of the core UN human rights treaties.[105]

4.2 Non-Judicial Approach to the Implementation of Treaties

At the domestic level, Viet Nam focuses on the application, rather than enforcement, of treaties, with the starting point being the conformity of Viet Nam's laws with its international obligations. According to the Law of Treaties 2016, before initiating negotiation processes, the state body proposing that Viet Nam sign a treaty has to make a report assessing the treaty's impact and an initial review of the treaty's

[102] See for example, the Chinese Model BITs 1984, 1989, 1997 (see Norah Gallager and Wenhua Shan, *Chinese Investment Treaties* (OUP 2009) 421–38); the US Model BITs 1984, 1994, 2004, and 2012; Belgian Model BIT 2002; and the Indian Model BIT 2015. See also Chester Brown, *Commentaries on Selected Model Investment Treaties* (OUP 2013).

[103] The Declaration of Independence 1945 stated: 'All men are created equal. They are endowed by their Creator with certain inalienable rights, among these are Life, Liberty, and the pursuit of Happiness'. This immortal statement was originally made in the Declaration of Independence of the United States of America in 1776. The Declaration of the French Revolution made in 1791 on the Rights of Man and the Citizen also states: 'All men are born free and with equal rights, and must always remain free and have equal rights'. Those are undeniable truths.

[104] Geneva Convention [I] for the Amelioration of the Condition of the Wounded and Sick in Armed Forces in the Field, Geneva Convention [II] for the Amelioration of the Condition of Wounded, Sick and Shipwrecked Members of Armed Forces at Sea, Geneva Convention [III] relative to the Treatment of Prisoners of War, Geneva Convention [IV] relative to the Protection of Civilian Persons in Time of War (acceded 28 June 1957).

[105] Convention on the Elimination of All Forms of Discrimination against Women 1979 (signed 29 July 1980, ratified 17 February 1982); International Convention on the Elimination of All Forms of Racial Discrimination 1965 (acceded 9 June 1982); International Covenant on Economic, Social and Cultural Rights 1966 (acceded 24 September 1982); International Covenant on Civil and Political Rights 1966 (acceded 24 September 1982); Convention on the Rights of the Child 1989 (signed 26 January 1990, ratified 28 February 1990); Optional Protocol to the Convention on the Rights of the Child on the Involvement of Children in Armed Conflict 2000 (signed 8 September 2000, ratified 20 December 2001); Optional Protocol to the Convention on the Rights of the Child on the Sale of Children, Child prostitution and Child pornography 2000 (signed 8 September 2000, ratified 20 December 2001); Convention against Torture and Other Cruel Inhuman or Degrading Treatment or Punishment 1984 (signed 7 November 2013, ratified 5 February 2015); Convention on the Rights of Persons with Disabilities 2006 (signed 22 October 2007, ratified 5 February 2015).

consistency with Viet Nam's existing national laws and treaties. When consulted on the treaty, the Ministry of Foreign Affairs, the Ministry of Justice, and other relevant bodies are obliged to give their opinions within fifteen days.[106] Viet Nam requires that the making of domestic laws does not obstruct the implementation of treaties.[107]

Viet Nam's Prime Minister is entrusted with general responsibility for treaty implementation.[108] The state body proposing the conclusion of a treaty has to prepare implementation plans for submission to the Prime Minister within fifteen days of receiving notice from the Ministry of Foreign Affairs of a treaty entering into force.[109] For example, Decision 364/QĐ-TTg of the Prime Minister dated 17 March 2015 approved the plan for implementing the Convention against Torture and Other Cruel, Inhuman or Degrading Treatment or Punishment 1984, which became binding upon Viet Nam on 7 March 2015.

Where there are different interpretations of a treaty, the proposing state body, in coordination with the Ministry of Foreign Affairs, the Ministry of Justice, and relevant bodies, recommends an interpretation to the Prime Minister.[110] This provision focuses on treaty implementation at the national level, since treaty interpretation is subject to distinct customary international law and treaty law (namely, the VCLT) at the international level.[111]

The Government's plans for implementing treaties mainly prescribe legislative and administrative measures, such as raising the awareness of stakeholders and the general public, the transformation of treaty content into domestic law, and international cooperation (especially information and experience sharing).[112] There have been no enforcement reports before Viet Nam's courts on cases involving Viet Nam's rights and obligations under treaties. This is explicable since Viet Nam has consistently ruled out litigation as an enforcement mechanism for treaties.[113] In rare circumstances where Viet Nam accepts dispute settlement by domestic courts and arbitration in investment treaty relations, the beneficiary has not invoked such mechanisms.[114] For example, the Australia-Vietnam BIT 1991 provides that:

> If the dispute in question cannot be resolved through consultations and negotiations, either party to the dispute may: (a) in accordance with the law of the Contracting Party which has admitted the investment, initiate proceedings before that Contracting Party's competent judicial or administrative bodies.[115]

106 LT 2016 (n 4) art. 9.

107 Law on Promulgation of Legal Documents 2015 art. 156(5).

108 LT 2016 (n 4) art. 76(1). 109 Ibid. art. 76(2). 110 Ibid. art. 79(7).

111 Ian Sinclair, *The Vienna Convention on the Law of Treaties* (Manchester University Press 1984) 117.

112 See e.g. Decision No. 364/QĐ-TTg of the Prime Minister 2015 and attached Implementation Plan.

113 See thediscussions on reservations in following paragraphs.

114 See provisions on investor-state dispute settlement in Viet Nam's investment treaties, such as the Agreement between the Government of the Kingdom of Morocco and the Government of the Socialist Republic of Vietnam on the Promotion and Protection of Investments (signed 15 June 2012) art. 9.

115 Agreement between Australia and the Socialist Republic of Vietnam on the Reciprocal Promotion and Protection of Investments (signed 5 March 1991, entered into force 11 September 1991) art. 12(2)(a).

In trade disputes, although Viet Nam accepts the direct applicability of 'adequately detailed and clear' WTO commitments,[116] it is unclear whether these rules can be invoked before the Vietnamese courts. This is because of Viet Nam's reluctance to litigate in international legal relations and its clear rejection of such enforcement of WTO rules in other national jurisdictions.[117]

At the international level, Viet Nam consistently favours diplomatic means in treaty-related disputes. It has made multiple reservations to carve-out treaty provisions on the international judicial settlement of disputes. For example, Viet Nam makes it clear that it is not bound by the requirement to submit disputes concerning the interpretation or application of the Convention against Torture and Other Cruel, Inhuman or Degrading Treatment or Punishment 1984 to arbitration or the International Court of Justice.[118] In its accession to the Convention on the Law of the Non-Navigational Uses of International Watercourses, Viet Nam 'reserves the right to choose the appropriate means of dispute settlement notwithstanding the decision of the other party to the concerned dispute'.[119] Regarding human rights, Viet Nam has even disengaged from any adversarial institutionalized mechanisms such as inquiry procedures or individual complaints.[120]

With its efforts in accelerating economic development, Viet Nam allows exceptions to the non-judicial enforcement of treaties in trade, services, and investment relations. It has enjoyed the benefits of invoking dispute settlement rights by bringing claims against other WTO member states in five cases,[121] and has participated in thirty-three

[116] Resolution on the Ratification of the Protocol on Accession of the Socialist Republic of Vietnam to the Agreement Establishing the World Trade Organization 2006, No. 71/2006/NQ-QH11.

[117] See discussion on the refusal to give 'direct effect' to the provisions of WTO law by the European Union, the US, Japan, Canada, and China in Peter Van den Bossche, *The Law and Policy of the World Trade Organization: Text, Cases and Materials* (CUP 2005) 68–72.

[118] See Viet Nam's reservation to the Convention against Torture and Other Cruel, Inhuman or Degrading Treatment or Punishment (signed 10 December 1984, entered into force 26 June 1987). Viet Nam ratified on 5 February 2015. See <https://treaties.un.org/Pages/ViewDetails.aspx?src=IND&mtdsg_no=IV-9&chapter=4&clang=_en#EndDec> accessed 15 February 2017. See also Viet Nam's reservations to the Convention on the Prevention and Punishment of the Crime of Genocide 1948; Convention on the Elimination of All Forms of Discrimination against Women 1979; and International Convention on the Elimination of All Forms of Racial Discrimination 1965.

[119] See Viet Nam's reservation to the Convention on the Law of the Non-Navigational Uses of International Watercourses (signed 21 May 1997, entered into force 17 August 2014). Viet Nam acceded on 19 May 2014. See <https://treaties.un.org/Pages/ViewDetails.aspx?src=TREATY&mtdsg_no=XXVII-12&chapter=27&clang=_en#EndDec> accessed 15 February 2017. See also Viet Nam's reservations to the Vienna Convention on the Law of Treaties 1969; Convention on the Privileges and Immunities of the United Nations 1946; Convention on the Prevention and Punishment of the Crime of Genocide 1948; International Convention for the Suppression of Acts of Nuclear Terrorism 2005; Convention against Transnational Organized Crime 2000; Berne Convention for the Protection of Literary and Artistic Works 1886; and WHO Framework Convention on Tobacco Control 2003.

[120] Viet Nam states in its reservation (n 118) that it does not recognize the competence of the Committee against Torture, including confidential inquiry and reporting mechanisms in art. 20 of the Convention against Torture and Other Cruel, Inhuman or Degrading Treatment or Punishment 1984.

[121] United States—Anti-Dumping Measures on Certain Shrimp from Viet Nam (WT/DS404/R, Panel Report, 11 July 2011); Indonesia—Safeguard on Certain Iron or Steel Products (WT/DS429/R, Panel

other WTO cases as a concerned third party.[122] All of Viet Nam's investment treaties and investment chapters in free trade agreements provide for state-to-state arbitration. It even accepts a private party's right to arbitration against the state in these agreements and has been a respondent state in eight cases initiated by foreign investors.[123] Viet Nam recently pioneered in accepting the international investment tribunal proposed by the European Union to adjudicate investor-state disputes in the European Union-Vietnam Investment Protection Agreement (published negotiated text as of 2018).[124] Another exception is found in Viet Nam's treaty relationship at the regional level within the framework of ASEAN. As one of the authors of the ASEAN legal instruments, Viet Nam has willingly accepted the competence of dispute settlement institutions set up therein, whether in economic or political disputes.

5 Conclusion

Having dealt with big states since ancient times, as well as having been a battlefield for both ideology and hard power in the late twentieth century, Viet Nam is ever mindful that realpolitik and military strength have had a determinative impact on its fate. Unsurprisingly, few academic publications on international law focus on general theoretical questions or legal frameworks, instead of debating or engaging in a quest for Viet Nam's approach and practice.[125]

In the twenty-first century, the urgency of circumstances—where Viet Nam has had to involve itself in disputes relating to international trade and investment treaties (as either complainants or respondents), and complicated maritime disputes in the

Report, 17 November 2014); United States—Anti-Dumping Measures on Certain Shrimp from Vietnam (WT/DS496/1, Request for Consultations by Viet Nam, 3 June 2015); United States—Anti-Dumping Measures on Fish Fillets from Viet Nam (WT/DS536/3, Constitution of the Panel established at the request of Viet Nam, Note by the Secretariat, 3 December 2018); and United States—Certain Measures Concerning Pangasius Seafood Products from Viet Nam (WT/DS540/1, Request for Consultations, 22 February 2018).

122 See the list of the cases in which Viet Nam has been involved as a third party on the WTO website <http://www.wto.org/english/thewto_e/countries_e/vietnam_e.htm> accessed 25 April 2019.

123 See the list and details of the cases foreign investors brought against Viet Nam published by the UN Conference on Trade and Development <http://investmentpolicyhub.unctad.org/ISDS/Country-Cases/229?partyRole=2> accessed 25 April 2019.

124 See n 93.

125 See generally Ho Chi Minh City Law University, *Textbook on International Law* (National Political Publishing House 2013); Hanoi Law University, *Textbook on International Law* (People's Public Security Press 2015), Hanoi National University, *Textbook on Public International Law* (Hanoi National University Press 2013). Some works explain international legal frameworks, such as Nguyen Hong Thao, *Important Information on the Law of the Sea* (People's Public Security Press 1997); Hanoi National University, *Textbook on Theories and Laws on Human Rights* (2nd edn National Political Publishing House 2015); and Trinh Hai Yen, *Textbook on International Investment Law* (National Political Publishing House 2017).

South China Sea—is paving a new way for Viet Nam's research and practice on international law to become increasingly significant. Viet Nam's practice on the making, implementation, and enforcement of international law has not yet evolved into a legal tradition or jurisprudence, or fostered the crystallization of legal doctrine or discourse on international law.

Nonetheless, commitments to full compliance with international law have been not only an approach in its municipal law but also an indispensable feature, if not a priority, in Viet Nam's foreign policy. Based on this, Viet Nam has expressed its determination to become a responsible member of the international community. International integration is, therefore, a catalyst for cultivating a strong international legal culture or tradition, as well as scholarship in Viet Nam.

CHAPTER 21

CAMBODIA

MAHDEV MOHAN*

1 Introduction

Cambodia's evolving relationship with public international law must be understood in the context of the nation's unique history and circumstances, which are marked by colonization, conflict, Vietnamese occupation, territorial administration, civil war, transitional justice, and state-building. Cambodia's legal system has undergone significant changes from the early days of unwritten customary laws, to the imposition of French civil law, and thereafter the 'legal vacuum'[1] created by the ultra-Marxist Khmer Rouge regime that 'left Cambodia in a state of war and international isolation until the 1980s'.[2] An amalgamation of elements from the French civil law tradition and Vietnamese law forms the present Cambodian legal system.

This chapter will outline key aspects of international law in and apropos Cambodia that illustrate Cambodia's reception of public international law, and its position as an active participant in the international legal system. Section 2 provides a brief historical overview of the transitions that the Cambodian legal system has undergone since the 1800s. Sections 3 and 4 consider how international law is received in the Cambodian legal system today and analyses points of intersection between Cambodian domestic law and international law, and whether the phrase 'law' in the Cambodian statutory context encompasses both domestic law and international law, as had been pronounced in a 2007 decision by the Constitutional Council. It also examines interstate, investor-state, and international criminal law jurisprudence before internationalized courts and tribunals that involve Cambodia, or are part of its judicial system, such as

* The author is grateful for the research assistance of Siraj Shaik Aziz, Alexis Ang, and Shalini Jayaraj.

[1] See e.g. Hor Peng, Phallack Kong, and Jörg Menzel, *Introduction to Cambodian Law* (Konrad-Adenauer-Stiftung Cambodia 2012) 1.

[2] Lucy Keller, 'Cambodia Conflicts (Kampuchea)' in *Max Planck Encyclopedia of Public International Law* (online database, entry last updated June 2013).

the Extraordinary Chambers in the Courts of Cambodia (ECCC). Section 5 identifies certain constraints on Cambodia's commitment to international law by considering Cambodia's position regarding the ongoing South China Sea dispute, including the *Philippines v China* arbitration of 2016 (constituted under Annex VII of the UN Convention on the Law of the Sea 1982 (UNCLOS)). Cambodia has certainly taken strides in its participation in dispute resolution on the international plane, though its tryst with international law is a fractious one, and where international law as received in the domestic plane is often honoured more in its breach than its observance.

2 Historical Background

In 1863, Cambodia's King Norodom Sihanouk entered into a treaty with the French government, which made Cambodia a French protectorate. The Japanese later occupied Cambodia from 1941–5 and the French sought to reassert their control after the end of World War II. Cambodia's first written constitution was promulgated in 1947. Under this constitution, the country was governed by the King and two houses of parliament. The colonial era ended when Cambodia declared its independence on 9 November 1953. Cambodia joined the United Nations as a sovereign member state on 14 December 1955. In the aftermath of a coup on 18 March 1970, a Republic was proclaimed on 9 October 1970, to replace the constitutional monarchy, and two years later a second constitution was promulgated on 10 May 1972 to replace the first constitution of 1947.[3] The Cambodian Constitution 1972 had legal characteristics related partly to the French Constitution of the Fifth Republic and the US Constitution.[4]

However, the Communist Party of Kampuchea (CPK), commonly referred to as the Khmer Rouge, seized power in 1975 in the wake of the US–Vietnam War. Cambodia's legal system, which is primarily based on the French civil law tradition, suffered significant setbacks as a result of CPK policies during the 1975–9 period. In setting up the state of Democratic Kampuchea (DK), the CPK led by Pol Pot abolished virtually all institutions existing under Cambodia's previous regimes, including the courts. Although DK's constitution provided for the establishment of 'people's courts', no judicial institutions were established and no laws were ever enacted. In place of a legal system, the CPK instituted a centralized dictatorship, which exercised absolute power over the country and governed every aspect of its citizens' lives. After the fall of the Pol Pot regime, a socialist constitution was adopted in 1981, in force until the end of the Cold War, which reflects Cambodia's inclination towards the socialist bloc.[5]

[3] See Raoul Jennar, *The Cambodian Constitutions, 1953–1993* (White Lotus 1995) 57.

[4] See Peng et al (n 1) 34.

[5] Ibid. See also Ben Kiernan, *The Pol Pot Regime: Race, Power, and Genocide in Cambodia under the Khmer Rouge, 1975–79* (Yale University Press 2008).

Following protracted negotiations between several Cambodian political factions, three agreements, known as the Paris Peace Agreements, were signed on 23 October 1991: the Agreement on the Comprehensive Political Settlement of the Cambodia Conflict (with Annexes); the Agreement Concerning the Sovereignty, Independence, Territorial Integrity and Inviolability, Neutrality and National Unity of Cambodia, and the Declaration on the Rehabilitation and Reconstruction of Cambodia; and the Final Act of the Paris Conference on Cambodia. The Agreements authorized the Security Council to establish the UN Transitional Authority in Cambodia (UNTAC), which would oversee their implementation, temporarily run the country's administration, coordinate free elections, and restore law and order. One of the largest missions in UN experience at the time, UNTAC exercised supervision over various aspects of Cambodia's government, including information, finance, foreign affairs and security, and was able to disarm various fighting factions.[6]

During this transitional period, a Supreme National Council (SNC) was established under the Paris Peace Agreements. Under the terms of the Agreements, the 'SNC represented the unique legitimate body and source of authority in which, throughout the transitional period, the sovereignty, independence and unity of Cambodia are enshrined'.[7] The SNC represented Cambodia at the UN and delegated its powers to UNTAC during the transitional period until the election of a new government.

The latter is particularly important in light of a number of states asserting that a government comprising a faction which committed genocide and vast human rights abuses could not represent Cambodia.[8] Such an assertion was a reaction to the earlier recognition by the UN General Assembly that the Coalition Government of Democratic Kampuchea was the legitimate representative of Cambodia in the UN.[9] During this period, laws such as the 1992 Electoral Law were drafted by UNTAC and adopted by the SNC. Laws adopted during this period remain in power until their replacement by laws enacted by Cambodia's parliament. Despite attempts by the Khmer Rouge to block them, national elections were held in 1993, leading to the formation of a coalition government led by Prince Ranariddh (son of Norodom Sihanouk) and Hun Sen as First and Second Prime Ministers respectively. Following its adoption by the new parliamentary assembly, a new constitution was promulgated on 24 September 1993, establishing the Kingdom of Cambodia, a constitutional monarchy with a democratic and multiparty political system. Prince Norodom Sihanouk was again elevated to the status of King and resumed his position as Cambodia's Head of State. He abdicated in 2004, and was replaced by his son, Norodom Sihamoni, Cambodia's current King.

[6] Trevor Findlay, *Cambodia the Legacy and Lessons of UNTAC* (OUP 1995).

[7] Comprehensive Cambodian Peace Agreement (signed 23 October 1991, 1663 UNTS 27).

[8] Suellen Ratliff, 'UN Representation Disputes: A Case Study of Cambodia and a New Accreditation Proposal for the Twenty-First Century' (1999) 87 California Law Review 1207.

[9] Lucy Keller, 'UNTAC in Cambodia—From Occupation, Civil War and Genocide to Peace' (2005) 9 Max Planck Year Book of United Nations Law 127; Tom Fawthrop and Helen Jarvis, *Getting Away with Genocide?: Elusive Justice and the Khmer Rouge Tribunal* (Pluto Press 2004).

Lucy Keller suggests that through the Paris Peace Agreements and UNTAC, 'the UN succeeded in creating a comprehensive peacekeeping operation and an exemplary state building process'.[10] However, this author would warn against presuming, by extension, that these international obligations were, or continue to be, domestically enforceable. Although Cambodia became a member of the UN in 1955, the then existing constitution contains no provision on the legal status of the UN Charter or any international legal instruments adopted by the UN in relation to domestic laws of Cambodia. Subsequent constitutional amendments and changes in constitutional politics did not lead to any legal considerations of this issue.

It was only in 1993, when the new constitution was drafted by the Constituent Assembly elected under the auspices of the UN, that provisions were written to consider international human rights laws. This was in compliance with article 23 of the Paris Peace Agreement, which provides that basic principles regarding basic human rights and fundamental freedoms shall be incorporated in the new Cambodian Constitution; the contents of these principles, specified in Annex 5 of the Paris Peace Agreement, would be the blueprint for the Constitution 1993. Chapter 3 of the Constitution 1993 states that Cambodia recognizes and respects international human rights treaties as part of its domestic law.

Article 31 of the Constitution 1993 states, *inter alia*, that 'the Kingdom of Cambodia shall recognize and respect human rights as stipulated in the UN Charter, the Universal Declaration of Human Rights and the covenants and conventions related to human rights, women's rights and children's rights'. It has been observed that the enactment of the Constitution 1993, and article 31 in particular, is a 'transformative moment' for Cambodia as it binds it to a duty to respect the provisions of human rights treaties adopted by the UN.[11] It should be noted that it is unusual for constitutions in Asian countries, which are typically concerned with the rights of citizens domestically, to stipulate the state's international obligations, particularly in a dualist system.

The Constitution 1993 preserves the validity of previously enacted legislation to the extent that the latter is not inconsistent with the Constitution itself. Cambodia's legal system therefore comprises legislation enacted under past administrations, as well as more recent laws, which have been adopted since 1993 to support the emerging market-based economy (including a new Code of Criminal Procedure 2002 and a new Penal Code 2010). Cambodia's Constitutional Council is responsible for providing interpretations of the Constitution and deciding on disputes relating to the election of members of the National Assembly and Senate. A request for a review of the constitutionality of any law may be made by, among others, the King, the Prime Minister, one quarter of the Senators, or one tenth of the members of the National Assembly. A decision of the Constitutional Council is considered final and binding. It has supremacy within the

[10] Keller (n 2) 1.

[11] Kuong Teilee, 'Cambodian Constitutional Provisions on Treaties: A Story of Constitutional Evolution Beyond Rhetoric' [2010] 1 Cambodian YB on Comparative Legal Studies 5.

legal system, meaning that all laws and regulations must strictly conform to a decision of the Constitutional Council.

3 Reception of International Law

The word 'law' in the Cambodian context can mean both domestic law and international law according to a 2007 decision by the Constitutional Council.[12] In accordance with Cambodian laws and regulations, as well as the current practice, sources of law in Cambodia can be classified as either primary sources (which means all legal instruments of the competent authorities of the state)[13] or secondary sources (which means customs, traditions, conscience and equity, judicial decisions, arbitral awards, and doctrines). In civil cases, when the law is ambiguous, or when there is a lacuna in the law, the adjudicating court can proceed with the hearing and determine the case based on customs, traditions, conscience, and equity.[14]

3.1 Treaties

3.1.1 *The Treaty-Making Process*

Before signing and ratifying a treaty, states typically enter into numerous rounds of negotiations. The ill-fated mega-regional Trans Pacific Partnership agreement took between five and a half[15] to seven years[16] of negotiations to conclude. Understandably, a mega-regional agreement which involves twelve states would require longer and more intense negotiations. However, even smaller bilateral agreements require states to send representatives to negotiate for their interests, as when Scott Morrison, the then Australian Minister for Immigration and Border Protection, visited Phnom Penh on 26–7 September 2014 to sign an agreement to resettle refugees in Cambodia, in exchange for development assistance.[17]

[12] The Constitutional Council, Case No. 131/003/2007 of 26 June 2007, Decision No. 092/003/2007 CC.D, 10 July 2007.

[13] Constitution of the Kingdom of Cambodia [1993 as amended in 1999], art. 91, and Law on the Organization and Functioning of the Council of Ministers [1994] ('Law on Court Organization'), arts 13, 28, and 29, The Law on The Administration and Management of Commune/Sangkat [2001], art. 48, and Law on Administrative Management of the Capital, Provinces, Municipalities, Districts, and Khans [2008], arts 32 and 53–61.

[14] Law on Court Organization [1994] (n 13) art. 4.

[15] Office of the United States Trade Representative, 'Joint Press Statement TPP Ministerial Meeting, Brunei Darussalam' (23 August 2013) <https://ustr.gov/Joint-Press-Statement-TPP-Ministerial-Brunei#> accessed 20 May 2019.

[16] Brian Innes, 'Harvesting Prosperity from Seven Years of Negotiation' *The Hill Times* (15 November 2016).

[17] See Australian Government, Department of Foreign Affairs and Trade, 'Cambodia Country Brief' <http://dfat.gov.au/geo/cambodia/pages/cambodia-country-brief.aspx> accessed 18 February 2018.

Unlike states such as Australia, the authority which has full consent to represent the state in the exercise of its treaty-making powers is not stated in the Constitution.[18] The Cambodian Constitution empowers the National Assembly, in article 90, to 'approve or repeal international treaties and conventions', following which the King, as stated in article 26, shall sign and ratify these approved treaties.[19] Depending on the type of treaty, different government departments and representatives would be involved in the negotiations.[20] For example, in April 2001, the Cambodian Ministry of Commerce published the minutes of a trade meeting with its Chinese counterparts,[21] showing that committees are formed for any negotiations that will eventually culminate in binding agreements. The final document, however, will always be between state parties.[22] Another example is the Bilateral Investment Treaty between Cambodia and Singapore 1996,[23] wherein the document was signed by authorized representatives of their respective governments and is binding on the state parties.

3.1.2 *Signing and Ratification/Accession of Treaties*

It is generally accepted in international law that signing a treaty does not immediately make it a binding obligation. A representative may sign a treaty, but that signature still needs to be confirmed by the responsible organ in the state.[24] Rather, the signature expresses the willingness of the signatory state to abide by the treaty and to proceed to the ratification or approval stage. It also creates an obligation to refrain, in good faith, from acts that would defeat the object and purpose of the treaty.[25]

As mentioned above, any treaty that is signed by a Cambodian representative must be approved by the National Assembly[26] as well as the King.[27] This strongly suggests that Cambodia, like many other states, has what can be described as a dualist system,

[18] See Commonwealth of Australia Constitution Act 1900 s 61.

[19] Constitution of the Kingdom of Cambodia (n 13).

[20] For example, in developing Australia and Cambodia's bilateral relationship, Cambodia's Deputy Prime Minister and Minister of Interior, Sar Kheng, visited Australia on 24 March 2015 as a Guest of the Australian Government. During his visit, he signed a Memorandum of Understanding between the Government of the Kingdom of Cambodia and the Government of Australia on Immigration Cooperation.

[21] Agreed Minutes of the First Meeting of the Economic and Trade Co-Operation Committee between the Royal Government of Cambodia and the Government of the People's Republic of China (1 April 2001).

[22] See e.g. the Agreement between the Government of the Kingdom of Cambodia and the Government of the Democratic People's Republic of Korea for the Promotion and Protection of Investments (signed 1 November 2007), which states that it is between the Government of the Kingdom of Cambodia and the Government of the Democratic People's Republic of Korea.

[23] Agreement between the Government of the Kingdom of Cambodia and the Government of the Republic of Singapore on the Promotion and Protection of Investments (signed 4 November 1996).

[24] See Vienna Convention on the Law of Treaties (opened for signature 23 May 1969, entered into force 27 January 1980, 1155 UNTS 331) art. 12(2)(b).

[25] Ibid. art. 18.

[26] Constitution of the Kingdom of Cambodia (n 13) art. 90.

[27] Ibid. art. 26.

wherein treaties that are signed are not automatically entered into force vis-à-vis the international community and vis-à-vis the domestic Cambodian legislative framework.

An argument could be made that Cambodia's reception of international law is monist with respect to certain human rights, based on article 31 of the Constitution 1993 referred to in the previous section. The definition of a monist state is one that accepts international law automatically as part of its municipal law and does not demand an express act of the legislature.[28] Indeed, because these treaties have been expressly named in the Constitution, no express act of the legislature appears to be required. The Cambodian government itself has stated that 'this means that all rights stipulated in the international treaties on human rights are protected by the Constitution'.[29]

However, it would be a stretch of the imagination to suggest that this provision alone imports international law into the legislative framework. Leaving aside the necessary approval of the National Assembly and the King, there is no further clarification on the meaning of 'respects' human rights and what this means in terms of the enforceability of human rights conventions. Further, the provision only makes reference to the UN Charter, the Universal Declaration of Human Rights, and the covenants and conventions related to human rights, women's rights, and children's rights. It does not make mention of any other type of treaty or customary obligation.[30]

While no tribunal has made a determination on this matter,[31] the evidence behind Cambodia adhering to a dualist system is persuasive. It has been observed that Cambodian courts refuse to entertain claims 'in the absence of enabling legislation, directly based on international laws'.[32] In its report to the UN Committee on the Elimination of Racial Discrimination (CERD) in 1996,[33] Cambodia expressly stated that eight of the conventions ratified by Cambodia 'may not be directly invoked before the courts or administrative authorities'. Notably, Cambodia's 2009 report to CERD maintained that 'the principles of those treaties and conventions are the foundation for law-making as well as for other standard document[s]'.[34] It added that 'regulations, existing in Cambodia, have been reviewed by the Constitutional Council in order to

[28] Rebecca Wallace, *International Law* (Sweet & Maxwell 2002) 36. Also see Peng et al (n 1) 11.

[29] UN Committee on the Elimination of Racial Discrimination, Eighth to Thirteenth Periodic Report of States Parties due in 2008: Cambodia, 15 June 2009, UN Doc CERD/C/KHM/8-13, para 37.

[30] Kuong (n 11) 9.

[31] This argument was raised in the appeal of Ieng Sary and Nuon Chea in the Pre-trial Chamber of the Extraordinary Chambers in the Courts of Cambodia. However, the Tribunal declined to comment on the characterization of Cambodia as a dualist or monist system. See *Case of NUON Chea et al*, 002/19-09-2007-ECCC-OCIJ (PTC 145 and 146), Decision on Appeal by Nuon Chea and Ieng Thirith against the Closing Order, 15 February 2011, para 98; *Case of NUON Chea et al*, 002/19-09-2007-ECCC-OCIJ (PTC 35, 37, 38 and 39), Decision on Appeals Against the Co-Investigative Judges' Order on Joint Criminal Enterprise, 20 May 2010, para 48.

[32] Suzannah Linton, 'Putting Cambodia's Extraordinary Chambers in Context' (2007) 11 Singapore Year Book of International Law 195, 203.

[33] CERD, Seventh Periodic Reports of States Parties due in 1996: Cambodia, 5 May 1997, UN Doc CERD/C/292/Add.2, para 19.

[34] CERD, Eighth to Thirteenth Periodic Report of States Parties due in 2008: Cambodia, UN Doc CERD/C/KHM/8-13 (15 June 2009), para 37.

make them consistent with the international conventions',[35] but did not expressly provide that the conventions may be directly invoked. Rather, this report went further to imply that enabling legislation and regulations must be put in place in order to carry out the principles of the conventions that Cambodia has ratified.

In other contexts Cambodia has also taken the position that it has a dualist system. When negotiating with the UN for help in conducting the trials of the Khmer Rouge, the Cambodian Deputy Prime Minister, Sok An, declared that the government 'could not formally agree to any arrangement with the UN until the relevant text had been passed by Parliament and was adopted as law'.[36] When the UN withdrew from the negotiations, the Deputy Prime Minister publicly stated that:

> The Law, which was adopted by the Cambodian legislature under the Constitution of Cambodia, has determined the jurisdiction and competence of the Extraordinary Chambers as well as their composition, organizational structure and decision-making procedures, while the Articles of Cooperation are to determine the modalities of cooperation between the [Royal Government of Cambodia] and the [UN] in implementing those provisions of the law concerning foreign technical and financial support.[37]

The Cambodian government has also made clear that the Articles of Cooperation cannot modify or prevail over law that has been promulgated,[38] and that, in keeping with dualism, domestic legislation must be passed before Cambodia can be said to be bound by the international law obligations.

3.1.3 *International Treaty Law and Domestic Law*

Figure 21.1 provides a brief overview of the hierarchy of laws in Cambodia.[39]

Cambodian courts do not assess the wisdom behind the treaties entered into by the executive. The task for the courts is simply to construe the effect of what has been entered into. Where treaties have been incorporated into domestic law by the National Assembly and the Senate and promulgated by the King, it appears that the

[35] Ibid. para 61.

[36] Craig Etcheson, 'A "Fair and Public Trial": A Political History of the Extraordinary Chambers' (Spring 2006) Justice Initiatives 7, 13. See also Mélanie Vianney-Liaud, 'Determining the Relationship Between International and Domestic Laws within an Internationalized Court: An Example from the Cambodian Extraordinary Chambers' Jurisdiction Over International and Domestic Crimes' (2014) 6 Goettingen Journal of International Law 303, 308.

[37] 'Statement of the RGC in Response to the Announcement of UN Pullout from the Negotiation on the Khmer Rouge Trial', 12 February 2002.

[38] Ernestine Meijer, 'The Extraordinary Chambers in the Courts of Cambodia for Prosecuting Crimes Committed by the Khmer Rouge: Jurisdiction, Organization, and Procedure of an Internationalized Tribunal' in Cesare Romano, André Nollkaemper, and Jann Kleffner (eds), *Internationalized Criminal Courts and Tribunals: Sierra Leone, East Timor, Kosovo, and Cambodia* (OUP 2004) 207, 211.

[39] The pictorial representation is put together by Chbab.net—The Cambodian Law Library, a Destination Justice project <http://en.chbab.net/about-cambodian-law#TOC-Hierarchy-of-norms-in-the-Cambodian-legal-system> accessed 20 May 2019.

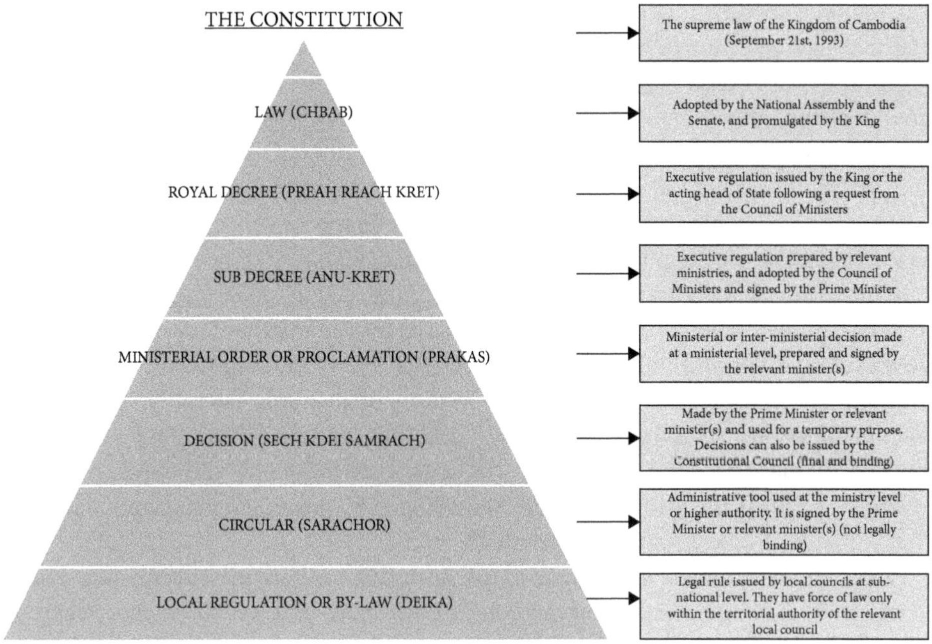

FIGURE 21.1 Hierarchy of Legal Norms in Cambodia

Constitutional Council has the power to review and declare a statutory provision null and void only where it violates the Constitution. This would include the power to review a treaty rule which has been transformed into Cambodian law by way of statute.

3.1.3.1 HUMAN RIGHTS TREATIES

Cambodia has ratified eight of the nine core human rights treaties.[40] A decision of the Constitutional Council dated 10 July 2007[41] reaffirmed the applicability of the international human rights treaties by the courts of Cambodia. Judges are obliged to consider all Cambodian laws when interpreting laws and making decisions, 'including the Constitution which is the supreme law, all the laws that remain in force, and the

[40] Treaties ratified include the International Covenant on Economic, Social and Cultural Rights 1966; International Covenant on Civil and Political Rights 1966; Convention against Torture and Other Cruel, Inhuman or Degrading Treatment or Punishment 1984; Convention on the Elimination of All Forms of Discrimination against Women 1979; the Convention on the Rights of the Child 1989; the International Convention on the Elimination of All Forms of Racial Discrimination 1965; the Convention on the Rights of Persons with Disabilities 2006; and the International Convention for the Protection of All Persons from Enforced Disappearance 2006. Cambodia signed the International Convention on the Protection of the Rights of All Migrant Workers and Members of their Families 1990 in 2004 but is yet to ratify it.

[41] Decision of the Cambodian Constitutional Council, 10 July 2007 (Dec No 092/003/2007). On this decision, see also Clauspeter Hill and Jörg Menzel (eds), *Constitutionalism in Southeast Asia*, vol 2 (Konrad-Adenauer-Stiftung 2008) 60.

international laws already recognized by the Kingdom of Cambodia'.[42] This confirms that international human rights treaties ratified by Cambodia are directly applicable within the Cambodian legal system. Notwithstanding this, it has been observed that 'courts throughout Cambodia are at best haphazardly applying the international human rights principles incorporated in the Constitution'.[43] One reason for this is 'the apparently limited level of awareness of the provisions among the judiciary and the legal profession, resulting in a very small number of cases in which the provisions ... have been invoked or applied by courts in Cambodia'.[44]

In the 2014 periodic report of Cambodia,[45] the UN Human Rights Committee (HRC) identified several principal subjects of concern in relation to the International Covenant on Civil and Political Rights 1966 (ICCPR), including freedom of expression and association, and the right to freedom of peaceful assembly. Of the 205 recommendations received, and which Cambodia accepted, the state revised its decision on eight recommendations,[46] changing four to 'noted' and another four to 'rejected'.[47] This is the first time a state has changed its position on recommendations after initially accepting them in Geneva.[48]

Part of the recommendations by the HRC included a follow-up within a year of the report. In a Joint Civil Society Submission[49] on this matter, it was stated that 'Cambodian authorities have taken new actions contrary to the Committee's recommendations and the situation regarding freedom of expression, association and peaceful assembly has further deteriorated'.[50] The government was alleged to have failed its international obligations by, among other things:

(a) failing to investigate the complaints of killings, and provide effective protection to journalists, human rights defenders and other civil society actors;
(b) prosecuting journalists, human rights defenders and other civil society actors as a means of discouraging them from expressing their opinions; in the process also violating their right to liberty and to a fair trial; and

[42] Ibid. An English-language translation of the quoted extract is available in Office of the UN High Commissioner for Human Rights, 'The Declatation of Human Rights in the Cambodian Constitution' (July 2008) 37.

[43] Michael Karnavas, 'Bringing Domestic Cases into Compliance with International Standards' (2012) Cambodia Law and Policy Journal 45.

[44] UN Human Rights Committee, Concluding Observations on the Second Periodic Report of Cambodia, 27 April 2015, UN Doc CCPR/C/KHM/CO/2. See also Karnavas, ibid.

[45] UN Human Rights Committee, ibid.

[46] Universal Periodic Review Info, 'Cambodia rejects 4 recommendations initially accepted', 21 July 2014.

[47] As it is not possible to reject recommendations at the Universal Periodic Review according to Human Rights Council resolution 5/1 (18 June 2007), the latter four are also considered as noted.

[48] Universal Periodic Review Info (n 46).

[49] Cambodian Center for Human Rights, 'Joint Civil Society Submission to the UN Human Rights Committee in relation to its follow-up procedure on Cambodia' (14 June 2016).

[50] Ibid.

(c) failing to decriminalize defamation, and bringing other relevant provisions of the Criminal Code in line with article 19 of the Covenant, resulting in an abuse of defamation law to silence critics.

The former UN Special Rapporteur to Cambodia seems to echo these sentiments in her annual report published in 2016,[51] wherein she states that:

> During the period under review, a number of laws adopted, and others apparently being drafted, will and may have implications for the protection and promotion of human rights. There has also been a raft of arrests, detentions, charges and convictions against members of political parties and civil society. Viewed together, these developments suggest that the law is increasingly being used to restrict the democratic space in the country.[52]

3.1.3.2 OTHER TREATIES

Besides 'human rights as stipulated in the UN Charter, the Universal Declaration of Human Rights and the covenants and conventions related to human rights, women's rights and children's rights', as mentioned in the Constitution,[53] Cambodia is also party to other types of international agreements. It has successfully negotiated bilateral investment agreements,[54] is a party to regional agreements as a member state of the Association of Southeast Asian Nations (ASEAN),[55] and is, in theory, bound to observe the ASEAN Declaration of Human Rights.[56] However, it appears from the statement by UN Special Procedure Professor Rhona Smith that this declaration is honoured more in its breach than its observance. Commenting on restrictions imposed on politicians and civil society leaders, Professor Smith noted:

> International human rights treaties and the ASEAN Human Rights Declaration, which was adopted just over five years ago in Phnom Penh, guarantee the right to participate in government through free and fair genuine elections. So too does the Constitution of Cambodia. Restricting Cambodians' political voices could ultimately threaten the stability that the Government regularly highlights and that the Government, Cambodian people and many others have worked to protect.[57]

[51] Report of the Special Rapporteur on the Situation of Human Rights in Cambodia, UN Doc A/HRC/33/62 (5 September 2016).

[52] Ibid. para 6.

[53] Constitution of the Kingdom of Cambodia (n 13) art. 31.

[54] See e.g. the Agreement between the Government of the Czech Republic and the Government of the Kingdom of Cambodia for the Promotion and Reciprocal Protection of Investments (signed 12 May 2008).

[55] See e.g. the ASEAN Comprehensive Investment Agreement (signed 26 February 2009).

[56] ASEAN Human Rights Declaration (adopted 18 November 2012).

[57] Statement submitted by Professor Rhona Smith, UN Special Rapporteur on the situation of human rights in Cambodia for the USA/EU organised meeting, New York, 19 December 2017 <http://cambodia.ohchr.org/sites/default/files/SR%20Statement%20in%20the%20side%20event%20in%20New%20York%20%2819-12-17%29%20EN_Final.pdf> accessed 19 February 2018.

Cambodia is also party to multilateral treaties in fields such as intellectual property[58] and investment.[59]

Conflicts do sometimes arise between Cambodia's treaty obligations on the international plane and its domestic legislation provisions in relation to extradition. Defined as 'the surrender of a person by one state (the 'requested state') to the authorities of another state (the 'requesting state') for the purpose of criminal prosecution or the enforcement of a sentence', extradition in Cambodia was originally governed by bilateral treaties.[60] Cambodia has entered into extradition treaties with a number of states, such as Thailand, Lao People's Republic, and China. Cambodia is also a signatory of the ASEAN Treaty on Mutual Assistance in Criminal Matters 2004, in which mutual assistance in criminal or judicial affairs is stipulated.[61]

Although it is by no means a new concept, globalization and the increasing movement of people across borders and state jurisdictions have made clear legal guidelines for the extradition of alleged and convicted criminals a necessity. Globally, the UN Model Treaty on Extradition 1990[62] also provides guidance for domestic jurisdictions.[63] More recently, regional treaties were adopted to serve as a model for domestic laws and practices of extradition.[64] In this regard, Cambodia is also a party to certain multilateral conventions that provide for extradition.[65]

Cambodia's first significant domestic provisions on the issue were included in the Code of Criminal Procedure 2007. While the provisions on extradition in the Code 2007 certainly represent a positive development of the extradition framework in Cambodia, it has been observed that the provisions are not wholly consistent with norms governing extradition in international law.[66] Under article 567 of the Code 2007, the Code is applicable if there are no treaties or agreements governing a particular request. In this way, Cambodia's domestic legal framework for extradition appears

[58] See e.g. the Patent Cooperation Treaty (signed 19 June 1970, entered into force 24 February 1978, 1160 UNTS 231).

[59] It also has membership in international organizations such as the World Trade Organization and the International Centre for Settlement of Investment Disputes (ICSID).

[60] Cambodian Center for Human Rights, CCHR Law Classification Series, volume 7—Extradition Law, July 2012 <http://cchrcambodia.org/index_old.php?url=media/media.php&p=factsheet_detail.php&fsid=50&id=5> accessed 12 February 2018.

[61] Treaty on Mutual Assistance in Criminal Matters (signed 29 November 2004, in force) <http://agreement.asean.org/media/download/20160901074559.pdf> accessed 18 February 2018.

[62] See UN Model Treaty on Extradition (adopted by UNGA res 45/116 (14 December 1990)) annex).

[63] See Peng et al (n 1) 420.

[64] European Convention on Extradition (signed 13 December 1957, entered into force 18 April 1960, ETS No 24); Additional Protocol to the European Convention on Extradition (opened for signature 15 October 1975, entered into force 20 August 1979, ETS No 86); Second Additional Protocol to the European Convention on Extradition (opened for signature 17 March 1978, entered info force 5 June 1983, ETS No 98); Inter-American Convention on Extradition (adopted 25 February 1981, 28 March 1992, OAS Treaty Series No 60).

[65] See e.g. the Convention against Torture and Other Cruel, Inhuman or Degrading Treatment or Punishment 1984.

[66] See Peng et al (n 1) 423.

to be in harmony with the practices and procedures contained in international agreements and law.[67]

Nonetheless, there are loopholes that remain in the Cambodian extradition framework, particularly regarding substantive and procedural norms applicable where a sought person is dissatisfied with the decision of the Investigation Chamber of the Court of Appeal in Phnom Penh and wishes to appeal.[68] At the outset, the Investigation Chamber is 'the sole body which has competence to examine the regularity of extradition request to be made by the Cambodian government' to the requested state; with the extradited person having only fifteen days from the date which he or she arrived in Cambodia to request annulment of the extradition.[69] If the extradition is nullified by the final decision of the Chamber, the person is released. However, at the expiration of the thirty-day period starting from the date of release, the person to be extradited may be rearrested in Cambodia and become the subject of the recharge procedure for the acts leading to such extradition.[70] As the Code 2007 and Cambodia's existing framework for extradition are silent on the relief that the person sought to be extradited can have recourse to, one could argue that Cambodia's treaty obligations in this regard are given little effect.

3.2 Extraordinary Chambers in the Courts of Cambodia

The ECCC brings to trial 'senior leaders of Democratic Kampuchea and those who were most responsible for the crimes and serious violations of Cambodian penal law, international humanitarian law and custom, and international conventions recognized by Cambodia, that were committed during the period from 17 April 1975 to 6 January 1979'.[71] The ECCC was established by a joint agreement between the Royal Government of Cambodia and the UN, and Cambodia accepted this agreement (ECCC Agreement) as the law of the land.[72] The ECCC Law explicitly gives the Chambers jurisdiction to apply treaties recognized by Cambodia and customary international law, as long as the principle of legality is respected.[73] This has been observed to be consistent with the approach adopted by a number of states, following the language of article 15 of the ICCPR and article 7 of the European Convention on Human Rights 1950.[74] The subject matter jurisdiction is limited, by virtue of the ECCC Law, to (a) crimes under Cambodian law such as murder, torture, and religious persecution,[75] and (b) crimes

[67] Ibid. 423. [68] Ibid. 436. [69] Code of Criminal Procedure 2007 art. 590.

[70] Ibid. art. 593.

[71] See Law on the Establishment of the Extraordinary Chambers in the Courts of Cambodia for the Prosecution of Crimes Committed during the Period of Democratic Kampuchea (2001) (Cambodia), as amended by NS/RKM/1004/006 (27 October 2004) ('ECCC Law') art. 1.

[72] ECCC Law (n 71) art. 47*bis*. [73] Ibid. art. 33(2).

[74] *Decision on IENG Sary's Appeal against the Closing Order*, D427/1/30, 11 April 2011, para 214.

[75] ECCC Law (n 71) art. 3.

under international law, such as genocide,[76] crimes against humanity,[77] grave breaches of the Geneva Conventions,[78] destruction of cultural property,[79] and crimes against internationally protected persons.[80] Cambodian lawmakers essentially extended the existing limitation period for felonies by an additional twenty years. In 2004, when the ECCC Law was amended, the statute of limitations was extended for a further ten years, thus making the total limitation period forty years.[81]

The ECCC is a hybrid court composed of Cambodian and international judges, investigating judges, and prosecutors. The procedure of the ECCC is in accordance with Cambodian law and criminal procedure, with trials held in Cambodia. Guidance may also be sought in procedural rules established at the international level where Cambodian law does not deal with a particular matter; where there is uncertainty regarding the interpretation or application of a rule of Cambodian law; or where there is a question regarding the consistency of a Cambodian rule with international standards.[82]

The Pre-Trial Chamber of the ECCC has held in a series of decisions[83] that although it is part of the Cambodian court system, it is a separate and independent court with no institutional connection to any other court in Cambodia. A judge of the ECCC is selected upon the basis of internationally agreed criteria and takes a separate and distinct judicial oath. In this respect, the ECCC is an internationalized court applying both Cambodian law and international norms and standards. The Pre-Trial Chamber and the Trial Chamber are composed of three Cambodian and two international judges, while a Supreme Court Chamber, which serves as both an Appellate and a Final Instance Chamber, is made up of four Cambodian judges and three international judges.

The ECCC has concluded one case, Case 001, wherein Kaing Guek Eav alias Duch, former Chairman of the notorious S-21 security prison in Phnom Penh, was convicted by the Trial Chamber on 26 July 2010 of a range of crimes against humanity and war crimes and sentenced to thirty-five years' imprisonment.[84] The judgment was appealed, but on 3 February 2012 the Supreme Court Chamber upheld Duch's conviction and increased the sentence to life imprisonment.

Case 002 is still ongoing, but has been severed into mini trials. The hearings of Case 002/01 have been concluded concerning the administrative structures of the DK Regime, the crime of forced transfer, and charges of extermination, murder, and persecution. The first trial judgment was rendered on 7 August 2014 for the two co-defendants Nuon Chea, Pol Pot's second-in-command, and Khieu Samphan,

[76] Ibid. art. 4. [77] Ibid. art. 5. [78] Ibid. art. 6. [79] Ibid. art. 7.

[80] Ibid. art. 8. [81] Ibid. [82] Ibid.

[83] *Ieng Sary's Appeal Against the Closing Order* (n 31) paras 213–16; *Decision on Appeal Against Provisional Detention Order of Kaing Guek Eav, Alias 'Duch'*, Pre-Trial Chamber, 3 December 2007, paras 18–20; *Prosecutor v NUON Chea, Public Decision on the Co-Lawyers' Urgent Application for Disqualification of Judge Ney Thol Pending the Appeal against the Provisional Detention Order in the Case of Nuon Chea*, Case No. 002/19-09-2007-ECCC/OCIJ, 4 February 2008, para 30.

[84] *Kaing Guek Eav (Duch)* (001/18-07-2007/ECCC-E188), Trial Chamber Judgment, 26 July 2010.

the former Head of State. Two other accused are no longer part of the proceedings: Ieng Sary, former Foreign Minister, passed away on 14 March 2013 and proceedings were terminated.[85] Ieng Thirith, former Minister of Social Affairs, was found unfit to stand trial due to progressive dementia and the proceedings were suspended in September 2012.

Both co-defendants, Nuon Chea and Khieu Samphan, appealed their convictions, asking for a reversal of the trial judgment and to be acquitted of all charges, or failing that, a reduced sentence to a set number of years. Their appeal arguments related to the constitutionality of the ECCC's Internal Rules and the fairness of the proceedings.[86] On 23 November 2016, the Supreme Court Chamber of the ECCC upheld parts of the convictions and quashed other parts of them on grounds of insufficient evidence. It nevertheless affirmed the life imprisonment sentences for Nuon Chea and Khieu Samphan.[87] The Supreme Court Chamber also ordered that the second trials against Khieu Samphan and Nuon Chea, Case 002/02, were to commence as soon as possible.

However, trial hearings were adjourned on 24 November 2014 until January 2015 by the Trial Chamber in 'consequence of the continued refusal of counsel for Khieu Samphan to participate in the proceedings in Case 002/02 before 29 December 2014, when the brief on Khieu Samphan's appeal in Case 002/01 [was] due'.[88] The Trial Chamber commenced the evidentiary hearings in Case 002/02 on 8 January 2015 and concluded them on 11 January 2017, involving allegations of crimes against humanity, genocide, and grave breaches of the Geneva Conventions by the accused, Nuon Chea and Khieu Samphan.

The personal jurisdiction of the ECCC over 'senior leaders and those most responsible' is limited by design.[89] The UN agreed with Cambodia on a narrow scope out of concern that wide-ranging prosecutions might create civil unrest in Cambodia.[90] It has also been observed that a broader mandate may well have created a sense of panic within Cambodian society and led to renewed tensions in a country that had only recently ended its civil war.[91] In its first judgment in Case 001 against Duch, the ECCC Supreme Court Chamber found the term to be 'sufficiently flexible that it may not necessarily be limited to former members of the CPK and/or Standing Commitees'.

[85] *Nuon Chea and others* (002/19-09-2007/ECCC-E270/1), Trial Chamber Decision, 14 March 2013.

[86] Vera Padberg, 'ECCC: Appeal Judgment Affirms Life Imprisonment for Nuon Chea and Khieu Samphan' (*ilawyerblog*, 23 November 2016) <http://ilawyerblog.com/eccc-appeal-judgment-affirms-life-imprisonment-nuon-chea-khieu-samphan/#more-2892> accessed 19 February 2018.

[87] ECCC Press Release, 'Supreme Court Chamber Quashes Part of the Convictions, Affirms Life Imprisonment for Nuon Chea and Khieu Samphan in Case 002/01', 23 November 2016.

[88] ECCC Press Release, 'Hearings in Case 002/02 Adjourned until January 2015', 24 November 2014.

[89] David Scheffer, 'The Extraordinary Chambers in the Courts of Cambodia' in Cherif Bassiouni (ed), *International Criminal Law* (3rd edn Martinus Nijhoff 2008) 219.

[90] Report of the Group of Experts for Cambodia Established Pursuant to General Assembly Resolution 52/135, UN Doc A/53/850, S/1999/231 (1999) 58, recommendation 2.

[91] Steven Roper and Lilian Barria, 'Providing Justice and Reconciliation: The Criminal Tribunals for Sierra Leone and Cambodia' (2005) 7 Human Rights Review 5, 16.

Duch had appealed that as a prison head, he could not be considered most responsible as he had no authority to decide the fate of individual prisoners and merely carried out the orders of the Khmer Rouge Standing Committee. This argument was dismissed and his sentence was increased from thirty-five years' imprisonment to a life term. Later in its judgment, however, the ECCC Supreme Court Chamber retreated from interpreting the qualifiers 'senior leaders' and 'most responsible' as true justiciable jurisdictional requirements, holding that:

> The terms 'senior leaders' and 'most responsible' are not jurisdictional requirements ..., but operate exclusively as investigatorial and prosecutorial policy to guide the independent discretion of the [CIJs] and co-prosecutors as to how best to target their finite resources ....[92]

Concerning the phrase 'most responsible', the Chamber reasoned that the term must be interpreted as a guide to discretion rather than true jurisdictional requirement for three main reasons: (1) 'there is no objective method for the Trial Chamber to decide on, compare, and then rank the criminal responsibility of all Khmer Rouge officials'; (2) 'the notion of comparative criminal responsibility is inconsistent' with the ban on 'the defence of superior orders'; and (3) 'the determination of whether an accused is "most responsible" requires a large amount of discretion'.[93]

While questions concerning the meaning and scope of the terms 'senior leader' and 'most responsible' were answered, there was no indication of what factors are to be considered in making such inherently subjective determinations. Much of the deep divide between the Court's national and international judges and legal staff with respect to Cases 003/004, which languished in their pre-trial investigatory phases for years, can be attributed to the lack of clarity in this regard. There had been efforts to prepare Cases 003/004 against high-ranking members of the military and provincial authorities. After years of dilatory objections by the Cambodian government, on 3 March 2015 the then International Co-investigating Judge Mark Harmon charged persons in absentia, namely, Meas Muth in Case 003, and Im Cheam, Yim Tith, and Ao An in Case 004.[94] The judicial investigation in Case 003 against Meas Muth concluded on 10 January 2017, and the same in Case 004 closed on 5 September 2017.[95]

However, there remains a fundamental divide between the Court's national and international prosecutors, which was underscored in the Final Submissions in Case 003 concerning the investigation of Meas Muth on 14 November 2017. The two co-prosecutors filed separate Final Submissions reflecting their differing views on

[92] *Case of Kaing Guek Eav alias 'Duch'*, Case No 001/18-07-2007-ECCC/SC, Appeal Judgment, Doc No F28 (3 February 2012) (ECCC Supreme Court Chamber) para 79.

[93] Ibid. para 62 (citing ECCC Law art. 29).

[94] Simon Meisenberg and Ignaz Stegmiller (eds), *The Extraordinary Chambers in the Courts of Cambodia: Assessing Their Contribution to International Criminal Law* (TMC Asser 2016).

[95] ECCC Press Release, 'Judicial investigation against Meas Muth Concluded', 10 January 2017.

whether the co-investigating judges should issue an indictment against Meas Muth.[96] The international co-prosecutor argued that the evidence demonstrated that Meas Muth was both a 'senior leader' of the DK and one of the persons 'most responsible for the crimes committed between 17 April 1975 and 6 January 1979 within the meaning of the ECCC's governing law', and thus fell within the personal jurisdiction of the ECCC.[97] In contrast, the national co-prosecutor 'reiterate[d] her previous position that only the existing accused at the ECCC are the senior leaders and persons most responsible for crimes committed in Democratic Kampuchea within the personal jurisdiction of the ECCC'.[98] She also noted that:

> the priority should be given to the prosecution of those [already] accused in order to sufficiently fulfil the mandate of [the] tribunal, as the ECCC Law and the Agreement between the UN and the Royal Government of Cambodia envisaged only the prosecution of this small group of individuals.[99]

She argued further that bringing Meas Muth to trial would not serve the interests of justice, but would conversely result in 'domestic political disruption and serious social unrest'.[100]

Professor Michael Bohlander, from Germany, was nominated by the UN to replace Judge Harmon upon the latter's resignation on 7 July 2015. Since then, Case 004 has been severed by the co-investigating judges into separate cases in the interest of justice; namely, the charged persons' right to a determination of the charges brought against them without undue delay. Case 004/01 against Im Chaem was severed from Case 004 concerning Yim Tith on 5 February 2016, and Case 004/02 against Ao An was likewise severed from Case 004 on 16 December 2016.[101]

On 22 February 2017, the co-investigating judges at the ECCC decided to dismiss Case 004/01 against Im Chaem, who had been a District Secretary, finding that she did not meet the ECCC jurisdictional requirements of being a senior leader or one of those most responsible for the alleged crimes ('Closing Order').[102] In a three to two split decision, the Pre-Trial Chamber agreed with the investigating judges and dismissed the trial against Im Chaem.[103]

The international co-prosecutor released a public summary of his statement against Yim Tith in Case 004 in an attempt to underscore that the accused was a 'senior leader

[96] See ECCC Press Release, 'Statement by the International Co-Prosecutor on Case 003', 30 November 2017; and ECCC Press Release, 'Statement by the Office of the National Co-Prosecutor on Case 003', 30 November 2017.

[97] ECCC Press Release, 'Statement by the International Co-Prosecutor on Case 003', 30 November 2017.

[98] ECCC Press Release, 'Statement by the Office of the National Co-Prosecutor on Case 003', 30 November 2017.

[99] Ibid. [100] Ibid.

[101] ECCC Press Release, 'Press Release by the Office of the Co-Investigating Judges Judicial Investigation against Ao An Concluded and Severance from Case 004 Ordered', 16 December 2016.

[102] ECCC Press Release, 'Co-Investigating Judges Dismiss Case against Im Chaem', 22 February 2017.

[103] 'Prosecutors at ECCC issue summaries of Case 004 Statements' *Phnom Penh Post* (3 July 2018).

who ordered and facilitated crimes that resulted in large-scale atrocities', and should be tried for, *inter alia*, the genocide of certain minority ethnic groups in Cambodia.[104] Yet, given the Court's track record, it is unclear if Case 004 and Case 004/02 will eventually be adjudged in accordance with international law or if countervailing 'domestic political' concerns will hold sway.[105]

4 International Courts and Tribunals

4.1 International Disputes

The dispute between Thailand and Cambodia over the Preah Vihear Temple, in the form of two cases, represent the only instances of Cambodia appearing before the International Court of Justice (ICJ). The dispute over the Temple had its origin in the boundary settlements made in the period 1904–8 between France and Siam, especially the frontier agreements in 1904 and 1907, which resulted in the Dangrek map in 1907 prepared by French experts. Contrary to the principle that the border would follow the watershed line, the Preah Vihear promontory and the Temple were not placed on the Thai side, but on the Cambodian side by this map. The map was communicated to the Siamese government and provincial authorities in 1908, but was never officially approved or objected to, either by the French-Siamese Mixed Commission (tasked with delimitating the boundary, but which had ceased to function some months before), or the Siamese authorities.[106]

Following Cambodia's independence on 9 November 1953, Thailand occupied the area of the Temple. As attempts to negotiate a peaceful settlement proved unsuccessful, Cambodia applied, in October 1959, to the ICJ. In its unilateral application, Cambodia requested the Court to:

> adjudge and declare that . . . (1) the Kingdom of Thailand is under an obligation to withdraw the detachments of armed forces it has stationed since 1954 in the ruins of the Temple of Preah Vihear; (2) that the territorial sovereignty over the Temple of Preah Vihear belongs to the Kingdom of Cambodia.[107]

Before the ICJ, Thailand argued that the maps were not legally binding because they had not been accepted by the first Mixed Commission (which was dissolved when maps were released) and because Thailand had never officially accepted them. Thailand

[104] Ibid.

[105] See 'Alle.g.ed Genocidaire Could See Case Dismissed at the KRT' *Voice of America Cambodia* (3 March 2018) <http://www.voacambodia.com/a/alledged-genocidaire-could-see-case-dismissed-at-khmer-rouge-tribunal/4278291.html> accessed 9 January 2019.

[106] *Case concerning the Temple of Preah Vihear (Cambodia v Thailand)* (Merits) [1962] ICJ Rep 6, 21–3.

[107] Ibid. para 9.

claimed that if it had accepted them, this was only because of a 'mistaken belief that the frontier indicated [in the maps] corresponded with the watershed line'.[108] Based on Thailand's passive attitude for years, the Court's judgment in 1962 recognized Thailand's 'tacit acceptance' of the maps. The judges affirmed that in public international law a mistake is not admissible as an argument if the party that challenges it has contributed to it by its own conduct, or if that party could have avoided the mistake. The ICJ therefore concluded in favour of Cambodia, taking into account the frontier demarcated by the second French-Siamese Mixed Commission and the resulting maps produced by the French officers. It thus became unnecessary in the view of the judges to consider whether the mapped border did in fact correspond to the true watershed line or not. In any event, regarding the line as mapped in the disputed area, the Court affirmed that there is no reason to think that the parties attached any special importance to the criterion of the watershed line.

The dispute over the Temple of Preah Vihear reignited in 2007, when Cambodia lodged a request for the inscription of the Temple on the World Heritage Centre List. A map depicting the site of the monument, a buffer zone, and the course of the frontier between the two states was attached to that request. Of course, this map showed that the entire promontory of Preah Vihear was within Cambodian territory, in accordance with the Annex 1 map but in contrast with Thailand's construction of the 1962 Judgment. Following the inscription, serious armed incidents occurred in the area of the Temple and at several locations along the boundary between the two states. These incidents caused fatalities, injuries, the evacuation of local inhabitants, and material damage to the Temple. For these reasons, the UN Security Council called for a permanent ceasefire in 2011.[109]

In April 2011, Cambodia filed a request for interpretation of the 1962 Judgment under article 60 of the ICJ Statute, together with a request for the indication of provisional measures. Cambodia claimed that measures were urgently required to safeguard its rights 'relating to its sovereignty, its territorial integrity and to the duty of non-interference incumbent upon Thailand', and 'to stop any more destruction of the Temple . . . and to prevent further casualties'.[110]

The 1962 Judgment had created a great deal of uncertainty. On the one hand, the ICJ did not expressly demarcate the frontier line between Cambodia and Thailand. On the other hand, the implementation of the judgment depended on the interpretation of a vague notion contained in the second operative clause of the 1962 Judgment, whereby the Court stated that 'Thailand is under an obligation to withdraw any military or police forces, or other guards or keepers, stationed by her at the Temple, or in its vicinity on Cambodian territory'. Leveraging the vagueness of the term 'vicinity',

[108] *Case concerning the Temple of Preah Vihear* (Merits), Summary of the Judgment of 15 June 1962, para 3.

[109] UNSC, 'Security Council Press Statement on Cambodia-Thailand Border Situation', UN DOC SC/10174, 14 February 2011.

[110] *Request for Interpretation of the Judgment of 15 June 1962 in the Case concerning the Temple of Preah Vihear (Cambodia v Thailand)* (Judgment) [2013] ICJ Rep 281, 285 ('*Cambodia v Thailand*').

Thailand implemented the ICJ's ruling by withdrawing its armed forces only from the area where the Temple stands and erecting a barbed wire fence, which separated the ruins from the rest of the promontory—that is, Thailand construed the second operative clause in a restrictive way. Cambodia opposed this interpretation, claiming that it was incompatible with the 1962 Judgment.

In July 2011, the Court rejected Thailand's attempt to have the case dismissed and indicated provisional measures requiring both states to withdraw their soldiers from a 'provisional demilitarized zone' containing the area in dispute and some of its environs; continue their cooperation with ASEAN and observers appointed by it; and refrain from doing anything that might 'aggravate or extend the dispute'.[111] It also ordered Thailand not to obstruct Cambodia's access to the Temple of Preah Vihear.[112]

On 11 November 2013, the ICJ ruled that the 1962 Judgment awarded all of the promontory to Cambodia and ordered the withdrawal of Thai soldiers.[113] This followed a tense build-up to the decision in which dozens of Thai schools had closed ahead of the ruling.[114] The Court first concluded that it had jurisdiction and the request for interpretation was admissible, finding that a 'dispute exists between the parties as to the meaning and scope of the 1962 Judgment pursuant to Article 60 of the Statute [of the ICJ]'.[115] The Court said that the 1962 Judgment had three important features:[116] it involved an issue of 'territorial sovereignty . . . and that it was not engaged in delimiting the frontier'; the 'Annex I map played a central role in the reasoning of the Court';[117] and it was only dealing with the small area in the 'region of the Temple of Preah Vihear'.[118] The Court unanimously declared:

> The Court therefore concluded that the first operative paragraph of the 1962 Judgment determined that Cambodia had sovereignty over the whole territory of the promontory of Preah Vihear, as defined in paragraph 98 of the present Judgment, and that, in consequence, the second operative paragraph required Thailand to withdraw from that territory the Thai military or police forces, or other guards or keepers, that were stationed there.[119]

Some uncertainty is evident in both the 1962 and 2013 decisions in relation to the scope of res judicata for interpretation purposes under article 60 of the ICJ Statute.[120] Specifically, an opportunity was missed to clarify the binding nature of the Annex I map line as the border frontier between Cambodia and Thailand, which both parties asked the Court to clarify. The Court ought to have addressed it for there is much merit in Cambodia's assertion that 'only an authentic and binding interpretation given by the Court of its own judgment can provide a means of ensuring lasting peace and security

[111] Ibid. para 69, points B.1, B.3, and B.4 of the operative part.
[112] Ibid. para 69, point B.2 of the operative part. [113] Ibid. para 108.
[114] 'UN Rules for Cambodia in Thai Border Row—Asia-Pacific' *Al Jazeera English* (11 November 2013).
[115] *Cambodia v Thailand* (n 110) para 57. [116] Ibid. para 75.
[117] Ibid. para 77. [118] Ibid. para 78. [119] Ibid. para 107.
[120] Statute of the International Court of Justice (annexed to the UN Charter, adopted 26 June 1945, entered into force 24 October 1945) art. 60.

in this region'.[121] In exercising its interpretative power under article 60, the Court sidestepped the issue by pursuing a 'natural understanding' in its reasoning to identify the Temple's vicinity[122] and did 'not consider it necessary ... to address [further] the question whether the 1962 Judgment determined with binding force the boundary line between Cambodia and Thailand'.[123]

The ICJ's stance on the applicable scope of res judicata is equivocal, as evidenced in the *Application for Revision and Interpretation* case between Tunisia and Libya that revisited the principles and rules to be applied for continental shelf boundary delimitation.[124] This is currently the only other case where an application for interpretation was successful. Tunisia tried to argue that the phrase 'the most westerly point' of the Gulf of Gabes was ambiguous because the coordinates of this point were provided only by way of indication in the reasoning and not in the dispositif.[125] The Court did not appear to entertain that argument and 'simply re-iterated the basis upon, and purpose for which, it had selected the point'.[126] It 'did not expressly accept that Tunisia had raised a genuine point of interpretation, or deny that it had'.[127] As such, it is unclear which stance of res judicata the Court specifically endorsed since it avoided deciding on Tunisia's suggestion that the coordinates did not form part of the decision that had res judicata effect.[128]

In any event, without addressing the binding nature of the Annex I map line as requested by both parties, the question of sovereignty in the outstanding disputed region, namely the Phnom Trap, remains unresolved. The Court rejected Cambodia's argument that Phnom Trap, a hill 3 kilometres north-west of the Temple comprising over 4 km^2 of the '4.6 square km' that both states agreed was in dispute, had also been awarded to it by the 1962 Judgment. The Court concluded that the reference to the 'vicinity' of the Temple of Preah Vihear in the operative part of the 1962 Judgment was not intended to extend to it.

The lack of a resolution on this point could increase the risks of re-litigation; a scenario that is not a fanciful one in light of Cambodian Foreign Minister Hor

[121] *Cambodia v Thailand* (n 110) para 44.

[122] John Ciorciari, 'International Decisions: *Request for Interpretation of the Judgment of 15 June 1962 in the Case concerning the Temple of Preah Vihear (Cambodia v Thailand)*' (2014) 108 AJIL 288, 294.

[123] *Cambodia v Thailand* (n 110) para 104.

[124] *Application for Revision and Interpretation of the Judgment of 24 February 1982 in the Case concerning the Continental Shelf (Tunisia/Libyan Arab Jamahiriya) (Tunisia v Libyan Arab Jamahiriya)* [1985] ICJ Rep 192 ('*Application for Revision and Interpretation*'). The *Request for Interpretation of the Judgment of 23 May 2008 in the Case Concerning Sovereignty over Pedra Branca/Pulau Batu Puteh, Middle Rocks and South Ledge (Malaysia/Singapore) (Malaysia v Singapore)* was filed by Malaysia against Singapore on 30 June 2017, but was discontinued in May 2018 and has since been formally removed from the Court's list of cases.

[125] *Application for Revision and Interpretation*, ibid. para 6.

[126] Derek Bowett, 'Res Judicata and the Limits of Rectification of Decisions by International Tribunals' (1996) 8 African Journal of International and Comparative Law 577, 586.

[127] Ibid.

[128] See *Application for Revision and Interpretation* (n 124) para 63.

Namhong's statement after the 2013 ruling that Phnom Trap belongs to Cambodia due to the Court's invocation of the Annex I map.[129] Such a position is 'certain to elicit a negative Thai response'.[130] Nevertheless, it has been argued that the Court, in exercising 'caution on setting strict boundaries and deciding on Phnom Trap has helped insulate [it] from charges of overreach'.[131]

4.2 Investor-State Disputes

Foreign direct investment (FDI) has been and remains critical for Cambodia's economic growth. FDI inflows into Cambodia in 2014 were 11.5 times more than in 2000.[132] That is double the average rate of increase in FDI flowing into ASEAN countries as a group during that same period.[133] This is due in no small part to Cambodia's ongoing efforts to improve the legal framework for attracting and protecting foreign investment and to participate in the international investment regime.

In relation to the international commercial arbitration, the Supreme Court of Cambodia confirmed an earlier decision of the Court of Appeal that recognized and enforced a Korean Commercial Arbitration Board award in favour of a Korean company in respect of a real estate development in Phnom Penh.[134] Viewed together with the Cambodian Constitutional Council's decision on the constitutionality of the Arbitration Law 2006,[135] the finality of arbitral awards is key, and parties who opt for arbitration have a limited right of recourse to the courts.

4.2.1 *Cambodia's Investment Laws*

The Law on Investment 1994 and its 2003 amendments,[136] and its implementing sub-decree,[137] provide certain substantive guarantees in relation to investments in Cambodia. These substantive protections mirror many of the protections available under

[129] 'Cambodia Awaiting Talks with Thailand on Implementation of ICJ's Ruling of Preah Vihear Temple' *Chianrai Times* (21 December 2013) <https://www.chiangraitimes.com/cambodia-awaiting-talks-with-thailand-on-implementation-of-icjs-ruling-of-preah-vihear-temple.html> accessed 20 May 2019.

[130] Ciorciari (n 122) 294.

[131] Ibid. 295.

[132] ASEAN Secretariat, 'FDI flows into ASEAN, 2000–2015', FDI Database, indicating that inflows into Cambodia in 2000 and 2014 were US$149 million and US$1,727 million respectively.

[133] Ibid.

[134] Alex Larkin and Ly Sambo, 'Recent Developments in Commercial Arbitration in Cambodia' (2015) 17 Asian Dispute Review 12; Olga Boltenko, 'Cambodia's Arbitration Centre sets off on its First Flight' (*Kluwer Arbitration Blog*, 10 June 2015) <http://arbitrationblog.kluwerarbitration.com/2015/06/10/cambodias-arbitration-centre-sets-off-on-its-first-flight> accessed 14 October 2018.

[135] Rupert Haw and Billie Jean Slott, 'Cambodia' in Michael Moser (ed), *Arbitration in Asia* (2nd edn Juris 2008) CAM-12. Article 5 of the Arbitration Law provides: 'In all matters governed by this Law, no Court shall intervene except where so provided in this Law'.

[136] Law on Investment of the Kingdom of Cambodia (5 August 1994) and Law on the Amendment to the Law on Investment of the Kingdom of Cambodia (24 March 2003).

[137] Sub-Decree on the Implementation of the Law on the Amendment to the Law on Investment of the Kingdom of Cambodia No 111 ANK/BK (27 September 2005).

international investment instruments, particularly the protections from discrimination, the guarantee of relatively free transfer of funds, and the prohibition on unlawful expropriation. However, these investment guarantees, which are set out in four short provisions (articles 8–11), remain limited in comparison to protections available under international investment treaties.[138]

Further, an investor's ability to enforce these protections may be limited. If a dispute arises in relation to a Qualified Investment Project and it is not resolved within two months of amicable settlement discussions, either party to the dispute may bring the dispute to (i) conciliation before the Council for Development of Cambodia (CDC) ('which shall provide its opinion'); (ii) arbitration 'in or outside of Cambodia as agreed by both parties'; or (iii) 'trial by the tribunals of the Kingdom of Cambodia'.[139] It is open to debate whether this language, without more, would be construed as providing an investor with a right to commence investor-state dispute settlement proceedings without further agreement. Without such a right, however, an investor is only able to submit the dispute to a neutral decision maker if it can rely upon (or make) another separate agreement.[140]

4.2.2 *Cambodia's Bilateral Investment Treaties*

Cambodia signed its first Bilateral Investment Treaty (BIT) with Malaysia on 17 August 1994. Over the following twenty-one years, it signed at least twenty-three BITs,[141] of which at least eleven have entered into force.[142] Out of the twenty-three BITs, seventeen treaties are available from public or subscription-access websites.[143] All of the BITs, with the exception of the Cambodia–India BIT, have the substantive provisions expected, such as those providing for fair and equitable treatment, full protection and security, most-favoured nation treatment, and prohibition against expropriation which is not lawful and

[138] For example, the ASEAN Comprehensive Investment Agreement (signed 26 February 2009, entered into force 29 March 2012) provides enhanced protection to investors and their investments including fair and equitable treatment, full protection and security, and compensation in cases of strife. Consistent with investment law and contemporary practice, member states have also agreed to not deny justice in any legal or administrative proceedings according to the principles of due process.

[139] Law on Investment 2005 (n 138), art. 20.

[140] Loretta Malintoppi and Charis Tan, *Investment Protection in Southeast Asia: A Country-by-Country Guide on Arbitration Laws and Bilateral Investment Treaties* (Brill 2017).

[141] UNCTAD reports that Cambodia has signed BITs with the following States: Austria, Belarus, China, Croatia, Cuba, Czech Republic, France, Germany, Indonesia, Japan, Republic of Korea, Kuwait, Laos, Malaysia, Netherlands, North Korea, Pakistan, Philippines, Russia, Singapore, Switzerland, Thailand, and Vietnam. A 2014 publicly available presentation by the Council for the Development of Cambodia also reports BITs signed with Australia, OPEC, and 'OPIC'; the status of these BITs is unclear.

[142] UNCTAD reflects that Cambodia's BITs with the following states have entered into force: China, Croatia, Czech Republic, France, Germany, Japan, Republic of Korea, Netherlands, Singapore, Switzerland, and Thailand. See UNCTAD website <http://unctad.org/en> accessed 12 February 2018.

[143] Of the 23 treaties reported on the UNCTAD International Investment Agreements Navigator website <http://investmentpolicyhub.unctad.org/IIA/CountryIris/33> accessed 9 January 2019, the treaties with Austria, Belarus, Kuwait, Laos, North Korea, Pakistan, and Russia are unavailable. The Pakistan treaty is however available on a subscription-based website. This section is based on an analysis of the available treaties only.

without compensation.[144] None of Cambodia's BITs, with the exception of BITs with Japan and India, deny the benefits of the treaty to investors who have no substantive business operations in their home state.[145] The protections conferred under these treaties form an important part of Cambodia's strategy for attracting investment.

4.2.3 *Cambodia and the International Centre for Settlement of Investment Disputes*

Cambodia is a party to the ICSID Convention 1966, which established the International Centre for Settlement of Investment Disputes. The ICSID Convention entered into force for Cambodia on 19 January 2005.[146] Cambodia has not issued an article 25(4) notification or other reservation in relation to ICSID jurisdiction.

Cambodia has been a party to one international investment dispute in the public domain: *Cambodia Power Company v Kingdom of Cambodia and Electricité du Cambodge*.[147] The claim was not treaty-based and the Tribunal's jurisdiction was based instead on the state's consent to arbitrate under various contracts containing ICSID arbitration dispute settlement clauses. The dispute was borne out of a tender in 1994 to an investor to construct, own, and operate an electric power plant in Phnom Penh, and to sell that plant's capacity and electricity to Electricité du Cambodge (EDC), then a department of the Ministry of Industry, Mines and Energy, for a twenty to twenty-five-year term. The Cambodia Power Company (CPC) had contended that from 1998 to 2004 the state of Cambodia and EDC breached their contractual obligations to support the project to build and operate the power plant, and, as a result, CPC was not able to build the power plant. CPC claimed nearly US$300 million in damages.

As the ICSID Tribunal decided that the ICSID arbitration claims against Cambodia (but not EDC) could proceed, the case proceeded to the merits phase. The award on the merits rendered on 22 April 2013 remains unpublished, and there is accordingly little publicly available information about the merits arguments run by either side. However, the Kingdom of Cambodia's press release confirmed that the Tribunal held that 'the Kingdom of Cambodia did not breach the agreements directly or indirectly through the actions of EDC, and dismissed all of the claims [which would necessarily include the contractual claims and the claims under customary international law] brought against the Kingdom of Cambodia'.[148] The press release also indicated that the 'ICSID

[144] Romesh Weeramantry, 'International Investment Law and Practice in the Kingdom of Cambodia: An Evolving "Rule Taker"?' (2017) 18 Journal of World Investment & Trade 942.

[145] Ibid.

[146] Cambodia signed the ICSID Convention on 5 November 1993, and deposited its ratification on 20 December 2004. The list of contracting states and other signatories to the convention (as of 12 April 2019) is available at <https://icsid.worldbank.org/en/Documents/icsiddocs/List%20of%20Contracting%20States%20and%20Other%20Signatories%20of%20the%20Convention%20-%20Latest.pdf> accessed 20 May 2019.

[147] *Cambodia Power Company v Kingdom of Cambodia and Electricité du Cambodge* ICSID ARBITRATION ARB/09/18.

[148] Royal Government of the Kingdom of Cambodia, Press Release, 26 April 2013.

tribunal further ordered Cambodia Power Company to pay the Kingdom of Cambodia over US$5.6 million for legal costs and expenses in arbitration and costs of all relevant proceedings for almost the last four years'.

Notably, Cambodia has been encouraged to enter into investment treaties in the wake of this case.[149] Cambodia signed BITs with Belarus and Russia in 2014,[150] and it remains publicly committed to negotiating and signing investment treaties. The CDC[151] has indicated that, as of 2014, BITs are under negotiation with a myriad of countries. Further, a 2015 US Department of State report states that Cambodia is planning '[f]uture [BIT] agreements with Algeria, Bangladesh, Belarus, the Belgium-Luxembourg Economic Union, Bulgaria, Myanmar, Egypt, Hungary, Israel, Iran, Libya, Macedonia, Malta, Qatar, Russia, Turkey, the United Kingdom, and Ukraine'.[152]

5 South China Sea Dispute

While Cambodia has ostensibly been receptive to the rule of international law for the most part, such reception is circumscribed by its geopolitical prerogatives. This is best evinced by Cambodia's reticence in 2012 and 2016 to support a strong regional position by ASEAN on the South China Sea dispute. On the agenda for the 2012 ASEAN Ministerial Meeting Retreat was how to respond to China's far reaching claims in the South China Sea, particularly in view of complaints made by Vietnam and the Philippines regarding recent Chinese action in the South China Sea, namely land reclamation and naval patrols.

China's construction projects on several South China Sea reefs and islets have stirred the ire of its Southeast Asian neighbours.[153] Four countries of the ten-member ASEAN (namely, Brunei, Malaysia, the Philippines, and Vietnam) have rival claims to parts of the South China Sea with China, which says it has a historical claim to virtually the entire sea, expressed through its nine-dash line demarcated on Chinese maps. Also in dispute within these seas are the Paracels and the Spratlys—two island chains claimed in whole or in part by a number of countries.[154]

149 Weeramantry (n 144).

150 The UNCTAD International Investment Agreements web portal indicates that the Cambodia-Russia treaty was signed in March 2014 and that the Cambodia-Belarus treaty was signed in April 2014. Neither treaty is yet in force.

151 Sok Chenda Sophea (Minister Attached to the Prime Minister and Secretary General Council for the Development of Cambodia), 'FDIs Trend in Cambodia', Conference Presentation, 12 June 2014 <http://www.cdc-crdb.gov.kh/cdc/Donor_Development_Cooperation_Programs/Japan/12th_policy_dialogue_on_oda/downloads/1_2_Cambodia_FDIs_Trend_12_June_2014.pdf> accessed 9 January 2019.

152 US Department of State, 'Cambodia Investment Climate Statement 2015', 17.

153 'Great Power Politics in the South China Sea', Stratfor World View Forecast, 26 October 2015 <https://www.stratfor.com/article/great-power-politics-south-china-sea> accessed 18 February 2018.

154 Ibid.

Several ASEAN Foreign Ministers favoured unequivocal language admonishing alleged Chinese violations of the UN Convention on the Law of the Sea and stressed the need for a regional Code of Conduct in the South China Sea. They advocated a specific provision expressing 'serious concern' over Chinese violations of UNCLOS provisions related to Exclusive Economic Zones.[155] Cambodian Foreign Minister Hor Namhong refused to accept any 'strong wording' that could cause an 'escalation of tension'. Without Cambodian approval, the negotiations broke down and no joint communiqué was issued. According to one observer, 'the Cambodians, in a breach of ASEAN protocol, showed it to the Chinese who said it was unacceptable unless the South China Sea reference was removed, and [they] thus sought an amendment'.[156]

A reason cited for Cambodia's intransigence is its view that the dispute ought to be resolved bilaterally; a worldview it justifies by reference to the bilateral resolution of the dispute with Thailand on the Preah Vihear Temple.[157] Critics, however, say Cambodia's deference to China's policy was not prompted by international law as it has no claim in the South China Sea, but was politically motivated, given Cambodia's dependence on China for trade, investment, and aid. In fact, two months after the ASEAN deliberations ended in a stalemate, Cambodian Prime Minister Hun Sen visited Beijing, where his counterpart Wen Jiabao announced more than US$500 million in new soft loans and grants to Cambodia.[158] It has been observed that Cambodian support for Chinese claims in the South China Sea can in fact be dated back to October 2010. Then, on the side-lines of the ASEAN-related meetings in Hanoi, Prime Minister Wen Jiabao met with Prime Minister Hun Sen and pledged to provide economic assistance to Cambodia, while demanding Cambodian opposition to the internationalization of the South China Sea issue.[159]

This pattern of state practice was repeated in 2016 when ASEAN was almost unable to issue a statement after a meeting; only once before in its forty-nine-year history has an ASEAN meeting failed to issue a statement. The meeting of Foreign Ministers took place in the wake of the award in the *Philippines v China* arbitration (constituted under Annex VII of UNCLOS, with the Permanent Court of Arbitration ('PCA') acting as the registry), which analysed China's purported historic title in several areas in the South China Sea. The Hague-based Tribunal unanimously ruled that many of China's claims to the South China Sea had 'no legal basis', specifically rejecting China's assertion of

[155] Alfred Gerstl and Mária Strašáková (eds), *Unresolved Border, Land and Maritime Disputes in Southeast Asia: Bi-and Multilateral Conflict Resolution Approaches and ASEAN's Centrality* (Brill 2016) 73.

[156] Carlyle Thayer, 'ASEAN's Code of Conduct in the South China Sea: A Litmus Test for Community-Building?' (2012) 10(34) The Asia-Pacific Journal No 4. See also John Ciorciari, 'China and Cambodia: Patron and Client?', Gerald R Ford School of Public Policy, University of Michigan IPC Working Paper Series No 121, 14 June 2013, 2–4.

[157] Mong Palatino, 'Cambodia's Hun Sen Wants a South China Sea Apology' *The Diplomat* (12 February 2016).

[158] Ciorciari (n 156) 4.

[159] Kongrawd Somjade, 'Thailand and Cambodia Maritime Disputes' *Global Security* (10 November 2009) <http://www.globalsecurity.org/military/library/report/2009/thailand-cambodia.pdf> accessed 9 January 2019.

historic rights to the vital waterway through the so-called nine-dash line demarcated on Chinese maps.[160] The Philippines had originally wanted the ASEAN communiqué to cite the PCA ruling, but Cambodia objected, leading to days of protracted negotiations. Such opposition had been apparent even before the Tribunal's ruling when Prime Minister Hun Sen said on 28 June 2016 that the ruling party would not support a statement supporting the verdict of the PCA.[161] In the end, Manila withdrew its demands and a watered-down joint statement was issued which read as follows:

> The long-term impact of Cambodia's selective adherence to international law and reluctance to embrace multilateral solutions for the South China Sea disputes on ASEAN's cohesion remains to be seen. It is nonetheless of course trite to say that most of the ten countries within the regional bloc have repeatedly underscored their support for certain core principles—i.e., the principles of freedom of navigation and overflight in the region, as well as a rules-based regional and international order that protects the rights of all states and respects legal and diplomatic processes in the resolution of disputes.[162]

6 Conclusion

Cambodia has a hybrid legal system containing elements derived from French civil law, Vietnamese contract law, and common law; it has also had a remarkable tryst with international law. Notwithstanding the devastating effects of Khmer Rouge rule in the 1970s and the subsequent civil war until the 1990s, which have stalled the the pace of legal development, one might argue that Cambodia has been a full participant in the international legal arena as far as courts and tribunals are concerned.

This chapter sketches the country's experiences with international law, beginning with the ICJ's landmark case, the *Temple of Preah Vihear*, which was revived recently through an application for revision, resulting on both occasions in decisions favourable to Cambodia. The ECCC marks the first Southeast Asian UN-backed hybrid tribunal tasked with adjudicating war crimes, crimes against humanity, and genocide during the Khmer Rouge era. Cambodia has also successfully defended itself against an ICSID claim, and appears to be negotiating further international investment agreements regardless of the possibility of investor-state dispute settlement envisioned by such treaties.

[160] Hannah Beech, 'Tribunal Rules China's Claims to South China Sea Have "No Legal Basis"' *Time* (12 July 2016) <http://time.com/4402451/south-china-sea-ruling-tribunal-philippines> accessed 14 October 2018.

[161] 'Cambodia: Analysts Say Cambodia Must be Cautious over South China Sea Ruling' *Asia News Monitor* (Bangkok, 19 July 2016).

[162] Charlie Campbell, 'After Days of Deadlock, ASEAN Releases Statement on South China Sea Dispute' *Time* (25 July 2016) <http://time.com/4421293/asean-beijing-south-china-sea-cambodia-philippines-laos> accessed 14 October 2018.

At first blush, these developments paint a portrait of a state firmly committed to a meaningful relationship with international law. One that builds on the the efforts of the UN transitional administration, UNTAC, and its international team of constitutional drafters, who may have ushered in an adherence to international law via article 31 of the Cambodian Constitution in 1993. However, on closer examination, it is evident that Cambodia's relationship with international law remains a tenuous one. It is a tryst which at times depends on Cambodia's perceived domestic political and geopolitical realities, as evidenced best by both the jurisprudence of the internationalized ECCC, and its state practice apropos the region's ongoing South China Sea disputes.

CHAPTER 22

MYANMAR

CATHERINE RENSHAW

1 Introduction

In December 2003, a Burmese lawyer called Aye Myint was convicted of high treason by a district court in Yangon and sentenced to death. Myint's offence, the court held, was collaborating to send false information about the government out of the country.[1] Evidence of Myint's crime was possession of the 1998 Report of the International Labour Organization (ILO) Commission of Inquiry into Myanmar's observance of the Forced Labour Convention 1930 (No 29).[2] Myint's colleague, Min Kyi, was also sentenced to death for high treason. The evidence against Kyi was possession of the business card of Richard Horsey, ILO Deputy Liaison Officer.[3]

The efforts of the ILO to eradicate the use of forced labour in Myanmar[4], and the nature of the military regime's response to these efforts, represent a remarkable chapter in the history of international law. Of note, first, is the determination of the ILO to test the limits of its power to enforce compliance with the resolutions of its governing body. In 1998, an ILO Commission of Inquiry concluded that forced labour in Myanmar was state-imposed, widespread, and longstanding, and thus in gross violation of the

[1] Extract from the unofficial translation of the judgement in Criminal Trial No. 111 of 2003, issued 28 November 2003 by Yangon North District Court. See Richard Horsey, *Ending Forced Labour in Myanmar, Engaging a Pariah Regime* (Routledge 2011) 205.

[2] ILO, Report of the Commission of Inquiry appointed under article 26 of the Constitution of the International Labour Organization to examine the observance by Myanmar of the Forced Labour Convention 1930 (No 29) (2 July 1998); ILO Convention concerning Forced or Compulsory Labour (No 29) (adopted 29 June 1930, entered into force 1 May 1932, 39 UNTS 55).

[3] Horsey (n 1) 205.

[4] In 1989, the government changed the English-language name of the country from 'Burma' to 'Myanmar'. Throughout this chapter, I use 'Burma' when referring to events before 1988, and 'Myanmar' for the post–1988 period. According to Nardi, this usage reflects accepted academic practice in Burmese Studies: Dominic Nardi, 'Discipline-flourishing Constitutional Review: A Legal and Political Analysis of Myanmar's New Constitutional Tribunal' (2010) 12 Australian Journal of Asian Law 1, 1.

Convention No 29.[5] In 2000, the ILO for the first time in its history invoked article 33 of its Constitution, which gives its governing body the power to take 'such action as it may deem wise and expedient to secure compliance therewith'.[6] In 2006, following the continued failure of Myanmar's government to implement the Commission's recommendations, the ILO took steps to refer the regime's non-compliance to the International Court of Justice (ICJ). This move was unprecedented. In the end, the referral did not proceed. Myanmar's rulers, faced with the uncertain legal consequences of a decision by the ICJ, took sufficient steps to deflect further action.

Second, Myanmar's engagement with the ILO clarified the vexed issue of what constitutes a peremptory norm of international law. The ILO Commission of Inquiry concluded that 'a State which supports, instigates, accepts or tolerates forced labour on its territory commits a wrongful act and engages its responsibility for the violation of a peremptory norm of international law'.[7] This view was later endorsed by the ILO Committee of Experts which, in its 2007 General Survey on Convention No 29, stated that the principles embodied in the Convention 'had since been incorporated in various international instruments both universal and regional, and had therefore become a peremptory norm of international law'.[8]

The difficulty is that article 53 of the Vienna Convention on the Law of Treaties 1969 defines a peremptory norm as a norm from which no derogation is permitted.[9] Convention No 29 includes a raft of exceptions which may be invoked in certain circumstances (such as national emergencies) to justify forced labour.[10] In 2014, therefore, when delegates to the International Labour Conference met to discuss the draft text of a new Protocol supplementing Convention No 29, there was strenuous disagreement about whether there should be reference to forced labour as a peremptory norm. In the end, the Conference agreed to refer to the prohibition of forced labour as part of the body of fundamental human rights.[11] References to forced labour as a peremptory norm were deleted from the draft of the Protocol.[12]

Third, civil litigation in the United States around the issue of forced labour by transnational corporations in Myanmar uncovered the scope and potential for domestic courts to apply international law. In 1996, twenty-eight Burmese villagers bought a

[5] See ILO Commission of Inquiry (n 2) conclusion.

[6] Constitution of the International Labour Organization (1 April 1919) art. 33.

[7] ILO Commission of Inquiry (n 2) para 203.

[8] ILO, General Survey concerning the Forced Labour Convention, 1930 (No 29), and the Abolition of Forced Labour Convention, 1957 (No 105) (International Labour Office Geneva 2007) xi.

[9] Vienna Convention on the Law of Treaties (opened for signature 23 May 1969, entered into force 27 January 1980, 1155 UNTS 331) art. 53.

[10] Convention No 29 (n 2) arts 2(a)–(e).

[11] See Donald Anton, 'Introductory Note: 2014 Protocol to the Forced Labour Convention, 1930' (2014) ANU College of Law Research Paper No 14-36, 2 6ohttps://papers.ssrn.com/sol3/papers.cfm?abstract_id=2484905> accessed 23 January 2018.

[12] International Labour Conference, Provisional Record 103rd Session, Geneva, May–June 2014 (International Labour Office Geneva 2014).

claim under the US Alien Tort Claims Act against the US-based company Unocal in the Federal Court in the Central District for California, alleging that Unocal was jointly involved with the Burmese government in carrying out human rights violations including forced labour, torture, and crimes against humanity, during the construction of a billion dollar gas-extraction project off the coast of Myanmar. *Doe I v Unocal Corp* stands as authority for the principle that corporate liability is possible when corporations are complicit with states in carrying out human rights violations.[13]

Finally, Myanmar's variable and often extreme responses to the Commission's findings, which at one point included the arrest and imprisonment of lawyers such as Aye Myint and Min Kyi, demonstrate the dynamics of state resistance to and engagement with international law. Myanmar's military rulers at first denied that forced labour existed. Then they attempted to characterize such labour as 'voluntary' and something willingly undertaken and culturally accepted by the labouring classes in Myanmar. Then they persecuted anyone who collaborated with the ILO. Eventually, after continued pressure from the ILO, Myanmar's government agreed to establish a domestic complaint mechanism which authorized Myanmar-based ILO Liaison Officers to conduct independent investigations into labour violations, and enacted domestic legislation to protect the rights set out in the Convention.[14]

The ILO's early efforts represented a discursive opening which forced Myanmar's rulers to explain and justify their policies and ultimately to commit to a degree of reform, eventually leading to what some argue was deep and lasting social change in relation to the practice of forced labour. In 2012, Myanmar's Special Counsellor of State, Aung San Suu Kyi, hailed the ILO as 'a pioneer and an example of inclusivity'.[15] The history of Myanmar's engagement with the ILO, and the difficulties experienced by the country's leaders in implementing Convention No 29, were part of the impetus for the creation of one of the ILO's most innovative and promising instruments, the 2014 Protocol to ILO Convention No 29 on Forced Labour.

2 Overview of Myanmar's Legal System

Under the rule of the Burmese kings (which lasted from the ninth century CE to 1885) Burma developed a rich and complex legal culture and tradition. As well as a body of written law, the *dhammathat*, derived from Buddhist traditions, there existed

[13] *John Doe I v Unocal*, 963 F.Supp.880 (C.D.Cal.1997). See Jordan Paust, 'The History, Nature, and Reach of the Alien Tort Claims Act' (2004) 16 Florida JIL 249.

[14] Horsey (n 1).

[15] ILO, 'Statement by Aung San Suu Kyi at the 101st International Labour Conference', 14 June 2012 60http://www.ilo.org/global/about-the-ilo/newsroom/statements-and-speeches/WCMS_183369/index.htm> accessed 12 December 2018.

a flourishing legal profession and a formal system of legal procedures and court administration.[16] From 1824 onwards, the British gradually brought Burma under colonial control through a series of Anglo-Burmese wars, fully annexing the country as a province of British India from 1886 to 1937. The British displaced Burma's dynastic ruler and disrupted the country's legal customs and traditions. Britain introduced the common law to Burma and imported and applied the Indian Codes, introducing several bodies of public and private law that remain in force today.

The Japanese invasion in 1942, during World War II, temporarily interrupted British rule. Three years after the Allied victory in 1945, Burma sought and gained independence from Britain, under the leadership of General Aung San.[17] Aung San aimed to unite the country's ethnically and religiously diverse peoples, some of whom remained loyal to the British and were deeply suspicious of any centralized form of rule, within a federal Union. Aung San's Anti-Fascist People's Freedom League won elections in April 1947 and undertook the drafting of Burma's first post-independence constitution. The 1947 Constitution of the Union of Burma created a central union government, which ruled the Burman heartland, and ethnic satellite states.[18]

Burma's first Constitution renounced war as an instrument of national policy and accepted 'the generally recognized principle of international law as its rule of conduct in the country's relation with foreign states'.[19] The Constitution affirmed the country's devotion to the ideal of peace and friendly cooperation amongst nations founded on international justice and morality.[20] These provisions reflected the strong support of Burma's post-war leaders for the fledgling United Nations and the principles on which it was founded. These principles comported with the logic of Burmese foreign policy, which was based on support for anticolonialism and a strong commitment to neutralism. The logic derived from the convictions of those who fought for and achieved Burmese independence and was reinforced by perceptions of Burma's vulnerability, stemming particularly from its long and unprotected border with China. These intertwined and mutually sustaining concerns led Burma's first prime minister, U Nu, to steer his country towards an assiduous policy of non-alignment. When Burma was

[16] Melissa Crouch, 'The Layers of Legal Development in Myanmar' in Melissa Crouch and Tim Lindsey (eds), *Law, Society and Tradition in Myanmar* (Hart Publishing 2014) 34–55.

[17] The Japanese occupation lasted from 1942 to 1945. The Japanese allowed Burma to proclaim independence on 1 August 1943. After the end of the Second World War, what Michael Aung-Thwin describes as 'a semblance of the colonial order' was attempted, culminating in the granting of formal independence to Burma in 1948. See Michael Aung-Thwin, 'British "Pacification" of Burma: Order without Meaning' (1985) 16 Journal of Southeast Asian Studies 245, 246.

[18] Unlike the constitution adopted at much the same time in neighbouring India, the Burmese Constitution did not reflect a classic federal structure. Those drafting Burma's Constitution (principally Aung San and his Anti-Fascist People's Freedom League) considered full-blown federalism too costly in terms of financial and human resources. See Alan Smith, 'Burma/Myanmar: The Struggle for Democracy and Ethnic Rights' in Will Kymlicka and Baogang He (eds), *Multiculturalism in Asia* (Oxford University Press 2005) 268.

[19] Constitution of the Union of Myanmar 1947 art. 211.

[20] Ibid. art. 212.

offered membership in the Commonwealth of Nations after gaining independence from Britain, it declined. In 1967, when Burma was offered membership of the newly formed Association of Southeast Asian Nations (ASEAN), Burma also declined. From Burma's perspective, in 1967, ASEAN was an anti-communist organization, comprised wholly of anti-communist regimes, the institutional heir to the explicitly anti-communist Colombo Plan (1951) and the Association of Southeast Asia (1961).[21]

At the international level, Burma's foreign policy concerns underpinned its leading role in the Non-Aligned Movement. In 1955, as the Cold War took shape, Burma joined India and Indonesia in bringing together twenty-nine Asian and African countries for a conference in Bandung, Indonesia. The aim of the conference, in the words of Burma's prime minister, U Nu, was 'to aid newly independent nations both to assert their independence in international affairs and to promote world peace and cooperation by serving as a possible bridge between the Cold War antagonists'.[22] Burma, India, and other countries in the 'Afro-Asian block' were unanimous in their condemnation of colonialism, their belief in the sovereign equality of nations and universality of membership of the UN, and in their hope that the new organization would do better than its predecessor in providing a bulwark between small states and great powers. The organizers of the Bandung Conference also shared a common concern over what they regarded as an increasingly dangerous tension between China and the United States, and they wished to lay a firmer foundation for China's peaceful relations with the West and Southeast Asia. Importantly, the Conference served as a protest against the failure of the Western powers to consult with and permit Asian and African countries to sufficiently share in decisions affecting them.[23] The theme of the 'Final Communiqué of the Asian-African Conference' was international cooperation, including economic and cultural cooperation, peace, and an end to all forms of colonialism. Burma was internationally recognized, alongside India and Indonesia, as a country of geostrategic significance. In 1961 the Burmese teacher and diplomat, U Thant, became the first non-European to hold the position of Secretary-General of the United Nations.

Domestically, Burma struggled to overcome the longstanding ethnic animosities and tensions which had been exacerbated by colonialism. By the end of Burma's first parliamentary period, most of the country's ethnic minorities were in open rebellion against the centralized and Burmanized government in Rangoon.[24] The Burmese army, the *Tatmadaw,* were called upon to suppress widespread ethnic (and communist) insurgencies. Convinced that Myanmar's fledgling democracy was unable to prevent

[21] Virginia Brodine and Mark Selden (eds), *Open Secret: The Kissinger-Nixon Doctrine in Asia* (Harper & Row 1972).

[22] F Trager, *Burma: From Kingdom to Republic* (Frederick Praeger 1966) 257.

[23] George Kahin, *The Asian-African Conference* (Cornell University Press 1956) 4.

[24] Figuring prominently in accounts of ethnic grievances during this period is the decision of Myanmar's new government to promulgate Buddhism as the state religion. Buddhism played a significant role in Myanmar's independence movement against the British. Sai Kham Mong, 'The Shan in Myanmar' in Ganesan and Hlaing (eds), *Myanmar: State, Society and Ethnicity* (Institute of Southeast Asian Studies 2007) 256–87.

the balkanization of the Union, the army executed its first *coup d'état* in 1958. In 1962, in the face of civil war, General Ne Win carried out a second *coup d'état*, declaring that the army had no alternative but to take drastic steps in order to avert the impending danger of the disintegration of the Union.[25] Ne Win's effective rule of Myanmar lasted from 1962 until 1988.[26] In 1974, Ne Win introduced a new constitution, the Constitution of the Socialist Republic of the Union of Burma. The preamble to the 1974 Constitution reaffirmed the Union's commitment to constantly strive to promote international peace and friendly relations among nations. But under socialist rule Burma became radically isolationist, eschewing relations with the West and preserving a cautious peace with China, its powerful neighbour to the north.

In 1988, the government's decision to devalue the currency threw commercial activity into chaos and wiped out savings, leading to a situation of political tension and widespread unrest.[27] By early August, hundreds of thousands of protesters were marching through Rangoon and other cities calling for the removal of the one-party system of socialism. On 3 August, martial law was declared, and combat troops were brought from fighting ethnic insurgencies to patrol the streets of Rangoon. Demonstrations were suppressed, and many protesters were killed. In September 1988, under General Saw Maung, the army deposed Ne Win's successor, took control of the government and ended the movement towards liberalization and democracy.[28] In September 1988, General Saw Maung established the State Law and Order Restoration Council (SLORC) and suspended the 1974 Constitution.[29] In general elections held in 1990, the opposition National League for Democracy (NLD), led by Aung San Suu Kyi, won 80 per cent of parliamentary seats. The military refused to transfer power to the NLD, instead promulgating SLORC Declaration No. 1/90, which transformed the newly elected General Assembly from a legislative body into a body to draft a new constitution. In protest, the NLD withdrew from the constitution-drafting process. The new Constitution, which maintains a central role for the military in the governance of the state, was not completed until 2008. That year, during the chaos of Cyclone Nargis, the Constitution was approved by the people in a national referendum.

[25] General Ne Win published a statement to this effect in *The Nation* on 5 March 1962: Alan Saw U in Ganesan and Hlaing (eds), ibid. 265.

[26] Ne Win headed Burma's government as President, under the one-party Constitution 1974 until his retirement in 1981. Until 1988, he retained his dominant political role through his leadership of the Burma Socialist Program Party, the military-dominated state party. He resigned at the height of the 1988 popular uprising.

[27] John Haseman, 'Burma in 1987: Change in the Air?' (1988) 28 Asian Survey 223; Ja Nan Lahtaw, 'Peace Initiatives among Ethnic Nationalities: The Kachin case' (2007) in Ganesan and Hlaing (eds) (n 24) 236; Moksha Yitri, 'The Crisis in Burma: Back from the Heart of Darkness?' (1989) 29 Asian Survey 543; Neil Englehart, 'Regime Change Enough for Burma? The Problem of State Capacity' (2005) 45 Asian Survey 622.

[28] General Ne Win was replaced by General Sein Lwin, who was forced from office within three weeks. He was succeeded by a civilian and presumed moderate, Maung Maung, who proposed elections and attempted to negotiate with opposition groups. However, protests continued.

[29] The SLORC was renamed the State Peace and Development Council in 1997.

In November 2010, Myanmar held its first parliamentary elections under the 2008 Constitution. The military-backed political party, the Union Solidarity and Development Party (USDP), contested the elections, together with several pro-democracy opposition parties. The NLD refused to participate because of regulations that restricted former prisoners (such as Suu Kyi herself) from standing as candidates, and because of a provision that required all parliamentarians to 'defend the constitution'. During the election period, in rural areas, voting was irregular, disrupted, and in some cases prevented by ongoing ethnic conflict. A suspiciously high number of 'pre-votes' were counted in favour of the USDP. The USDP's decisive victory surprised no one. In by-elections held in 2012, Aung San Suu Kyi was permitted to stand for election to parliament and was duly elected. In the general elections of 2015, the NLD won a landslide victory, matching its success in the ill-fated 1990 election. The beginning of Myanmar's transition to democracy was fragile and bloody. The military remained constitutionally outside the control of civilian authorities, fighting in ethnic states continued, and in 2018 a Fact-Finding Mission established by the UN Human Rights Council named six Burmese generals who should stand trial for attempted genocide against the country's Muslim minority, the Rohingya.[30]

The 2008 Constitution maintains in its chapter on 'Basic Principles of the Union' that the Union practises independent, active, and non-aligned foreign policy aimed at world peace and friendly relations with nations and upholds the principles of peaceful coexistence among nations.[31] On other matters related to international law, the Constitution is silent. Myanmar's current legal system adheres to the general principle in common law countries that international law is not part of domestic law until parliament so enacts or judges declare the international norms to be part of domestic law. The language used in several parts of the Constitution, particularly in Part VIII 'Citizen, Fundamental Rights and Duties of the Citizens', parallels the language used in international human rights treaties.[32] It is arguable, for this reason, that the decisions of international bodies could be used to illuminate Myanmar law insofar as it is unclear, in accordance with the Bangalore Principles of judicial interpretation.[33]

In practice, however, the potential for Myanmar's judges to inject an internationally orientated perspective into constitutional interpretation is diminished by the long period of international isolation under military rule and by the Constitution's strong executive oversight of judicial appointments and dismissals. The Constitutional Tribunal, established under Part VI of the Constitution, does not give standing to

[30] UN Human Rights Council, Report of the Independent International Fact-Finding Mission on Myanmar (24 August 2018) UN Doc A/HRC/39/64.

[31] Constitution of the Republic of the Union of Myanmar 2008 art. 41.

[32] Catherine Renshaw, 'Human Rights under the New Regime' in Andrew Harding (ed), *Constitutionalism and Legal Change in Myanmar* (Hart 2017) ch 11.

[33] See (1988) 14 Commonwealth Law Bulletin 1196 and (1988) 62 Australian Law Journal 531; Michael Kirby, 'The Australian Use of International Human Rights Norms: From Bangalore to Balliol' (1993) UNSW Law Journal 15; Michael Kirby, 'The Bangalore Principles' (1997) 78 The Parliamentarian 326.

individual citizens.[34] Moreover, the Constitution provides that the Court's approach to interpreting provisions of the Constitution must be guided by the Constitutional principles set out in Chapter I.[35] Article 6 in Chapter I provides that the Union's objectives are: (a) non-disintegration of the Union; (b) non-disintegration of national solidarity; (c) perpetuation of sovereignty; (d) flourishing of a genuine, disciplined multi-party democratic system; (e) enhancing the eternal principles of Justice, Liberty, and Equality in the Union; and (f) enabling the Defence Services to be able to participate in the national political leadership role of the state. Apart from (e), these principles are not, on the face of it, ones which provide much interpretive scope for judicial decisions championing the advancement of individual rights and interests.

3 Burma/Myanmar and the Prohibition on Forced Labour 1907–1996

The 1930 Forced Labour Convention (No 29) was designed to end the worst practices of forced labour which existed in European colonial possessions between the First and Second World Wars.[36] Its roots were in the international struggle to end slavery, which had formally been agreed upon by the European powers in the Final Act of the Congress of Vienna in 1815, but which nonetheless persisted in many parts of Africa and Asia. Particularly pernicious, in the view of the Convention's drafters, was forced labour carried out at the hands of private interests, by companies and individuals that used indigenous workers to maximize exploitation in colonial possessions.

The Convention includes an unequivocal prohibition on the use of forced labour for the benefit of private individuals.[37] It defines forced labour as 'all work or service which is exacted from any person under the menace of any penalty and for which the said person has not offered himself voluntarily'.[38] The Convention includes provision for a transition period during which measures of coercion should be tolerated, and a raft of exceptions to the prohibition on forced labour. There are exceptions for (a) compulsory military service; (b) normal civic obligations; (c) work ordered as a consequence of a

[34] Constitution of the Republic of the Union of Myanmar 2008 arts 325 and 326.

[35] Ibid. art. 48 stipulates that: 'The Basic Principles of the Union shall be the guidance in enacting laws by legislature and in interpreting the provisions of this Constitution and other laws'.

[36] See Daniel Roger Maul, 'The International Labour Organization and the Struggle against Forced Labour from 1919 to the Present' (2007) 48 Labor History 477–500; Kati Tapiola and Lee Swepston, 'The ILO and the Impact of Labor Standards: Working on the Ground After an ILO Commission of Inquiry' (2010) 21(3) Stanford Law & Policy Review 101; Gerry Rodgers, Eddy Lee, Lee Swepston, and Jasmien Van Daele, *The International Labour Organization and the Quest for Social Justice, 1919–2009* (ILO 2009).

[37] Convention No 29 (n 2) art. 4.

[38] Ibid. art. 2.

conviction in court; (d) emergencies; (e) minor communal services in the direct interest of the community.[39]

Under British colonial legislation such as the Towns Act (1907) and the Village Act (1908), British administrators in Burma were authorized to recruit villagers to perform a range of specified public services. The Acts provided that people of the labouring class 'accustomed to doing that work' could be requisitioned for labour, which included collecting and furnishing guides, messengers, and porters for use by troops and police. These Acts set out processes for requisition through nomination by the chief or headman of the village, and consequences for non-compliance.[40]

In the pages of the Upper India Law Reports (1920) there are two cases relating to the application of the Towns Act and the Village Act in Burma. In the first, the headman of Mingyaunggong ward was ordered by a Sub-divisional Officer to provide a 'cooly' (a disparaging colonial term for an unskilled Asian labourer) to take letters to the Deputy Commissioner. The cooly in question, Po Sin, refused: he was footsore, and his daughter was ill. He was convicted by a local Magistrate under section 9(2) of the Towns Act. On appeal the conviction was set aside as no payment was offered to Po Sin and the services in question were not among those authorized under the Towns Act.[41] In the second case, Maung Tha Din was sentenced to a fine and 7 days' 'rigorous imprisonment' after he disobeyed the order of his village headman to help carry a Subordinate Forest Officer who had been injured by an elephant to hospital. Again, the conviction was overturned because such a duty was not prescribed in the Village Act: the headman's order was ultra vires.[42]

During Burma's brief period of parliamentary democracy between gaining independence from British rule in 1948 and the *coup d'état* of General Ne Win in 1962, Burma ratified ILO Convention No 87 on Freedom of Association and Protection of the Right to Organize 1948 (in 1955) and the Convention on the Prevention and Punishment of the Crime of Genocide 1948 (in 1956).[43] From the perspective of Burma's post-war leaders, these Conventions were directed at preventing the horrors of the Holocaust and ending the practices of slavery and indentured labour that existed under colonialism. At the time of ratification, it was difficult for Burma's leaders to imagine circumstances in which the Conventions would have domestic consequences for Burma.

Article 22 of the ILO Constitution requires ratifying states to send a regular report on how they are applying the Convention in law and practice. In 1960, Burma made its

[39] Ibid. art. 2(2)(a)–(e).

[40] Towns Act (1907) s 9A. The Village Act (1908) contained similar provisions to the Towns Act. See Robyn Layton, 'Forced Labour in Burma: A Summary of the International Labour Organization Report and Subsequent Developments' (2000) 4 Southern Cross University Law Review 148, 152.

[41] *Emperor v Nga Po Sin* (1920) Criminal Revn No 383 of 1920.

[42] *Emperor v Maung Tha Din* (1920) Criminal Revn No 424-B of 1935.

[43] ILO Convention on Freedom of Association and Protection of the Right to Organise (No 87) (adopted 9 July 1948, entered into force 4 July 1950, 68 UNTS 17); Convention on the Prevention and Punishment of the Crime of Genocide (adopted 9 December 1948, entered into force 12 January 195178 UNTS 277).

first regular report under article 22. Burma's report declared: 'since forced labour is non-existent in this country, no recourse to forced or compulsory labour in any form is authorised'.[44] There was thus no need, in the Burmese government's view, for Burma to avail itself of the Convention's 'transitional period' during which some forms of forced labour would be tolerated. Furthermore, the 1947 Constitution of the Union of Burma prohibits: (i) traffic in human beings, and (ii) forced labour in any form and involuntary servitude, except as a punishment for crime whereof the party shall have been duly convicted.[45] The Burmese government's logic was that because the law forbade forced labour, therefore forced labour did not exist. In response to the Burmese government's report, the ILO's Committee of Experts pointed to provisions in the Towns Act and the Village Act which were not in conformity with the Convention. The Burmese government's response was that the legislation in question, though not repealed, was defunct.[46]

The use of forced labour was widespread in Burma during Ne Win's military rule between 1962 and 1988. As leader of the Burma Socialist Programme Party, Ne Win presided over the drafting of the 1974 Constitution, which preserved some workers' rights, but which did not include the prohibition on forced labour contained in the earlier Constitution. Forced labour took two forms. First, the Burmese government, committed to the nationalization of industry and agriculture under a one-party system of socialism, relied on large numbers of conscripted labourers to build dams, roads, railways, and pipelines. Labourers were typically required to work on government projects for a few weeks or months of each year. Maung Maung writes that during this period, on the regime's own statistics, the average number of forced labourers engaged on these projects on any given day was in the order of 800,000.[47]

Second, in its long-running campaign against insurgents in the country's ethnic minority areas, the Burmese military forced villagers to work as porters and construction workers for the armed forces. Villagers were arbitrarily seized by the military, or selected by village headmen on the orders of the military, and forced to perform a variety of tasks: carrying army equipment and supplies; walking ahead of military convoys to check for landmines; collecting firewood; digging tunnels; building bunkers; breaking rocks; or performing any other tasks which the army demanded. Disease and death were rife among labourers.[48]

[44] See Horsey (n 1) 24.

[45] Constitution of the Union of Burma 1947 art. 19(i) and (ii). The Constitution also contained a curious 'Explanation' attached to the article on forced labour, which stated that: 'Nothing in this section shall prevent the State from imposing compulsory service for public purposes without any discrimination on grounds of birth, race, religion or class'. See Francis Maupain, 'Reflections on the Myanmar Experience' in Philip Alston (ed), *Labour Rights as Human Rights* (OUP 2005) 97.

[46] Horsey (n 1) 25.

[47] Maung Maung, 'Burma Must Abolish Forced Labour' (2008) 14(4) International Union Rights 10, 10.

[48] See e.g. the following reports: Erskine McCullough, 'Terror and Torture Continues under Secret Rule of Ne Win' *Agence France Presse* (17 September 1991); Jonathan Friedland and Bertil Lintner, 'A Policy of Pillage' *Far Eastern Economic Review* (8 August 1991) 56.

The new military regime that took power in 1988, the SLORC, banned all unions and arrested union leaders who refused to resign their offices. In 1991 the Federation of Trade Unions-Myanmar was established by exiled workers and students who had participated in the 1988 uprising. In 1992, the UN Commission on Human Rights appointed a Special Rapporteur on the situation of human rights in Myanmar. From 1993, successive Special Rapporteurs urged the government to put an end to forced labour and to fulfil its obligations as a state party to the Forced Labour Convention. These calls were echoed by the Secretary-General of the United Nations and repeated in yearly resolutions on Myanmar by the General Assembly of the United Nations. A range of other UN institutions also reported on Myanmar's forced labour practices. In 1997, for example, the Committee on the Rights of the Child cited 'numerous documented cases of rape of young girls by soldiers and cases of children systematically being forced into labour, including as porters'; and 'numerous reported cases of forced and under-age recruitment of child soldiers'.[49]

Myanmar's rulers either denied that violations were occurring or justified actions on the grounds that they were within the law and necessary for development, the preservation of national unity, and peace. The government's response to the Special Rapporteur's Report in 1993 was '[t]he *Tatmadaw* has never, at any time committed such atrocities nor will it ever do so in the future.... Atrocities such as... rape of rural women, forced conscription and mass execution of villagers are being committed only by the insurgents time and again'.[50]

Particularly damning was a 1991 report submitted by the International Confederation of Free Trade Unions (ICFTU) to the ILO Committee of Experts, alleging that the practice of compulsory portering was widespread in Myanmar and involved many thousands of workers.[51] The report stated that the majority of porters were forcibly recruited and harshly exploited; rarely, if ever, paid; inadequately fed and cared for; required to carry excessive loads; and exposed to acute physical hardship and danger. The report detailed how some were used as human shields during military actions, while others were shot when trying to escape or were killed or abandoned when, as a result of malnutrition or exhaustion, they were no longer able to carry their loads.[52] In 1993, the ICFTU team made a representation concerning portering under article 24 of the Constitution of the ILO, alleging that the government of Myanmar was acting in violation of the Convention by institutionalizing the forced recruitment and exploitation of porters by the military:

[49] UN Committee on the Rights of the Child, Concluding Observations on Myanmar (24 January 1997) UN Doc C/CRC/15Add.69 para 21.

[50] UNGA, 'Response by the Government of Myanmar to the Memorandum of the Special Rapporteur' (16 November 1993) UN Doc A/48/578.

[51] See ILO Commission of Inquiry (n 2) para 130: 'In an observation made in 1991 on the application of the Convention in Myanmar, the Committee of Experts noted comments of 17 January 1991 by the International Confederation of Free Trade Unions (ICFTU) on the application of the Convention and the information submitted in the annexed documents'.

[52] Ibid.

> [W]omen and children as well as men were randomly rounded up by local police or the military.... Porters were required to carry heavy loads of ammunition, food and other supplies between army camps.... Porters were subject to hostile fire.... They were routinely beaten by the soldiers and many of the women were raped repeatedly. Unknown to themselves, they were placed at the head of columns to decimate mines.... Many of these porters died as a result of mistreatment, lack of adequate food and water and use as human minesweepers.[53]

The government of Myanmar's response was that:

> [I]n Myanmar, voluntary contribution of labour to build shrines and religious temples, roads, bridges and clearing of obstruction on pathways was a tradition which went back thousands of years. It was a common belief that the contribution of labour was a noble deed and that the merit attained from it contributed to a better personal well-being and spiritual strength .... Accordingly, those who accuse the Myanmar authorities of using forced labour patently reveal their ignorance of the Myanmar tradition and culture .... The use of voluntary labour, alleged compulsory or forced labour, was made only for the urgent necessity in accordance with the following provisions: Section 8(1) (g) (n) and (o) of the *Village Act* (1908); Section 9 (b) of the *Towns Act*.[54]

4 ILO Commission of Inquiry 1997–8

On 20 June 1996, delegates of the International Labour Conference presented a Letter of Complaint to the ILO's governing body under articles 26 to 29 and 31 to 34 of the ILO Constitution, alleging non-observance by Myanmar of Convention No 29.[55] In March 1997, for only the tenth time in the seventy-year history of the ILO, the governing body decided to establish a Commission of Inquiry to investigate allegations of Myanmar's persistent and serious violations of the Convention.[56] The government of Myanmar did not permit the Commission to visit Myanmar, stating that a visit would not contribute to resolving the matter and would be an interference in its internal affairs.[57] Nonetheless, the Commission considered some 274 documents and took evidence from refugees in India, Bangladesh, and Thailand. The evidence of forced labour presented to the Commission was compelling. The Commission was shown, for example, the written orders given to Village Heads by the military, indicating the number of villagers required for labouring and where they should go. In some cases, orders were accompanied by red chillies or bullets to indicate the consequences of non-compliance (the burning down of houses or

[53] Ibid. para 135. [54] Ibid. paras 138 and 145.

[55] Ibid. 'Part III Allegations by the Parties and Historical Background of the Case'.

[56] The three-person Commission was chaired by Sir William Douglas and comprised the former Chief Justice of India, Justice Bhagwati, and Robyn Layton QC from Australia.

[57] ILO Commission of Inquiry (n 2) para 529.

being shot).[58] The Commission received oral evidence of other methods used to obtain labour, such as rounding up young men in the street or market places, after which they were taken to distant parts of the country for months at a time.[59]

The Commission found that there were four major areas in which forced labour was employed. The first related to portering (the carrying of goods); the second comprised the use of forced labour on road building and general construction work; the third was ancillary work required for the military in relation to military camps; and the fourth was personal requisition of labour by individual military officers for their own benefit. The Commission concluded:

> This report reveals a saga of untold misery and suffering, oppression and exploitation of large sections of the population inhabiting Myanmar by the Government, military and other public officers. It is a story of gross denial of human rights to which the people of Myanmar have been subjected particularly since 1988 and from which they find no escape except fleeing from the country.[60]

The Commission also stated its opinion about the nature of forced labour as a peremptory norm of international law: 'there exists now in international law a peremptory norm prohibiting any recourse to forced labour' and 'a State which supports, instigates, accepts or tolerates forced labour on its territory commits a wrongful act and engages its responsibility for the violation of a peremptory norm of international law'.[61] In connecting forced labour with slavery and concluding that forced labour is a peremptory norm of international law, the Commission drew on statements to that effect by the International Law Commission:

> This wrongful act results from a breach of an international obligation that is so essential for the protection of the fundamental interests of the international community that it could be qualified, if committed on a widespread scale, as an international crime under the terms of Article 19 of the draft articles of the International Law Commission on state responsibility.[62]

On 27 July 1998, a copy of the Commission's final report was sent to the government of Myanmar and to the governing body of the ILO. The report stated that the obligation under article 1, paragraph 1, of the Convention to suppress the use of forced or compulsory labour is violated in Myanmar in national law, in particular by the Village Act and the Towns Act, as well as in actual practice in a widespread and systematic manner, with total disregard for the human dignity, health and safety, and basic needs of the people of Myanmar.[63] The Commission recommended that:

58 Robyn Layton, 'Forced Labour in Burma: A Summary of the International Labour Organization Report and Subsequent Developments' (n 40).

59 Ibid. 154.

60 ILO Commission of Inquiry (n 2) para 543.

61 Ibid. para 538.

62 Yearbook of the International Law Commission (1980), cited in the ILO Commission of Inquiry (n 2) para 210 note 203.

63 ILO Commission of Inquiry (n 2) para 536.

1. The Village Act and Towns Act be brought into line with the Convention by 1 May 1999 at the very latest, either by amendment or repeal.
2. Concrete action be taken immediately to stop the present practices and that such action be that the practice of forced labour be recognised as more than merely non-payment of wages, and that the requirement to ensure that nobody is required to work against his or her will, whether paid or unpaid, is honoured.
3. That the penalties which may be imposed under Section 374 of the Penal Code of Myanmar for forced labour be strictly enforced.[64]

Article 29 of the ILO Constitution provides that a government must either accept the recommendations of a Commission of Inquiry or pursue the matter in the International Court of Justice. Initially, it seemed that the government of Myanmar was prepared to accept the Commission's recommendations. In May 1999, the government sent two letters to the ILO's governing body. The first indicated that preliminary but practical measures to implement the Commission's recommendations were in the process of being actively considered by the authorities. The second indicated that the Ministry of Home Affairs had issued Order No. 1/99, which directed relevant authorities not to exercise the powers conferred on them by the Towns Act and Village Act, and that anyone who failed to abide by the Order would have action taken against them under the Penal Code. However, Order No. 1/99 did not amend or repeal the offending provisions of the Village Act or the Towns Act, and seemed to allow porterage to continue based on need and economic circumstances. The order did not address forced labour which took place without reference to the Towns Act or Village Act.[65]

That same month, in his opening address to the 13th ASEAN Labour Ministers Conference, General Khin Nyunt said:

> There have been allegations of the use of forced labour in Myanmar. If one is to believe some of the allegations found in the Western media, the picture is indeed rather bleak. We felt very strongly that these allegations were largely due to misconception and misunderstanding of the situation and the mentality of our people. Since a sound infrastructure is essential for economic development, our Government has placed special emphasis on this sector. Hence, a sustained effort to improve the infrastructure of our economy by building roads, bridges, rail networks, dams and reservoirs has been undertaken. Realising the benefits to the communities from these projects, people have voluntarily contributed labour so that they can be completed sooner. Moreover, in Myanmar thinking, the contribution of labour not only brings immediate material benefit in the present life, but also merit for future cycles. Without understanding these factors, some people have

[64] ILO Commission of Inquiry (n 2) para 539.

[65] See Letter dated 23 September 1998, appended to ILO Doc GB.273/5; Letter dated 23 September 1998, appended to ILO Doc GB.237/5. 27. Order 1/99 is appended to the Report of the Director-General to the Members of the Governing Body on Measures taken by the Government of Myanmar following the Recommendations of the Commission of Inquiry established to Examine its Observance of the Forced Labour Convention, 1930 (No 29), 21 May 1999, GB 274.

> made all sorts of allegations. On our part, to dispel these wrong impressions, the government has issued instructions that only remunerated labour must be used in infrastructure projects. At the same time, with the return of peace, we are now mainly using our military personnel to undertake these public works. Therefore, the allegations of forced labour are groundless.[66]

5 ILO Monitoring from 1999

On 21 May 1999 the Director-General of the ILO reported to the governing body that the exaction of forced or compulsory labour in Myanmar was still continuing, referring to detailed reports from the ICFTU, the United Nations High Commissioner for Refugees, and the government of the United States. The response of Myanmar's government representative to the ILO was that allegations of continued use of forced labour were 'manifestly false accusations concocted with evil intent to bring about the destruction of Myanmar by Myanmar expatriate organisations abroad and renegade groups that oppose all measures undertaken by the Myanmar Government'.[67] The representative stated that allegations were 'based on blatantly false accusations made verbally, in writing and in the form of announcements by the National League for Democracy (NLD), whose only aim is to create difficulties for the Government to place it in an untenable position'.[68]

On 17 June 1999, at the 87th Session of the International Labour Conference, delegates voted overwhelmingly in favour of a resolution which stated that Myanmar's State Peace and Development Council continues 'to inflict the practice of forced labour, (which is) nothing but a contemporary form of slavery, on the people of Myanmar'.[69] The resolution continued that 'the attitude and behaviour of the government of Myanmar are grossly incompatible with the conditions and principles governing membership of the organisation' and resolved that 'the Government of Myanmar should cease to benefit from any technical cooperation or assistance from the ILO, except for the purpose of direct assistance to implement immediately the recommendations of the Commission of Inquiry'.[70]

The government of Myanmar rejected the resolutions. A press release issued by the government the following day accused 'a number of western nations' of having 'pushed through a resolution' which was 'unfair and biased'. The press release stated:

> in view of the unfairness of the exercise, its lack of balance and objectivity as well as the underlying political motives, Myanmar finds it impossible to accept such

[66] *New Light of Myanmar* (15 May 1999).

[67] ILO, 'Individual Case (CAS)—Discussion: 1999, Publication: 87th International Labour Conference Session' (1999), Forced Labour Convention, 1930 (No 29)—Myanmar.

[68] Ibid.

[69] International Labour Conference, 'Resolution on the Widespread Use of Forced Labour in Myanmar', 87th Session (Geneva, June 1999).

[70] Ibid.

> deplorable and unscrupulous action on the part of those nations who want to interfere and meddle in the internal affairs of Myanmar. Myanmar has therefore disassociated herself from this unfair and biased resolution and henceforth will cease participation in activities connected with Convention 29 and Convention 87 until such time that Myanmar receives fair and equitable treatment that must necessarily be accorded to all members of the ILO. However, as a responsible member of the international community, Myanmar will continue to comply with the Conventions to which she is a party.[71]

On 25 February 2000, the Director-General provided a second report on measures taken by the government of Myanmar to the 277th Session of the Governing Body, concluding that the recommendations of the Commission of Inquiry had not been complied with. On 31 March 2000, the Governing Body of the ILO recommended that the International Labour Conference invoke article 33 of the ILO Constitution and 'take such action as it may deem wise and expedient to secure compliance' of the Commission's recommendations.[72] In June 2000, the International Labour Conference set the government of Myanmar a deadline of 30 November 2000 for compliance with the recommendations of the Commission of Inquiry. One month before the resolution was to come into legal effect, the regime responded with an Order Supplementing Order Number 1/99. The second decree outlawed forced labour under all circumstances and nullified secret military directives that had legitimized forced labour on development projects.[73] A high level ILO team was permitted to visit Myanmar and conduct a three-week mission to assess legal, executive, and administrative changes. In November 2001, the mission reported its findings to the ILO's governing body. The reports found that there was clear evidence that the military had sought to disguise the continued use of forced labour in direct violation of the ban.[74]

What followed was a brief period of respite in the stand-off between the government of Myanmar and the ILO, following the ascension to power of the 'moderate' Prime Minister Khin Nyunt in 2003. In May 2003, Khin Nyunt approved a joint plan of action between the regime and the ILO, which included a number of strategies to raise awareness across Myanmar about the provisions of ILO Convention Number 29 and the regime's ban on forced labour. The agreement established field observation teams, comprised of police and township-level councils, to investigate complaints that could be referred to the courts for appropriate action. The agreement also established an independent facilitator, whom alleged victims of forced labour could meet on a confidential basis to seek legal redress.

In 2004, however, Khin Nyunt was deposed. His successor, General Than Shwe, ceased cooperating with the ILO and there was a reversion to the vitriolic rhetoric of previous years. Kyaw Saw, the Minister of Information, claimed that the ILO was

[71] *New Light of Myanmar* (18 June 1999).

[72] Constitution of the International Labour Organization (n 6) art. 33.

[73] ILO Docs GB.279/6/1 Annex 19, as well as GB.279/6/1 (Add.1) (Rev.1) and GB.279/6/1 (Add.2).

[74] ILO Docs GB.282/4 and GB.282/4/Appendices (Geneva, November 2001).

'siding with expatriate destructionists'. U Thaun, Minister of Labour, accused the ILO of exaggerating the scale of forced labour, which was in fact 'voluntary labour', and using it as a pretext for interfering in Myanmar's internal affairs.[75] More ominously, the regime brought charges against individuals accused of collaborating with the Federation of Trade Unions of Burma.[76] Trials were held *in camera* in the notorious Insein Prison, and some of those who had engaged with the ILO were found guilty of high treason and sentenced to death for their disloyalty to the nation.[77] Ordinary workers who filed forced labour complaints were arrested.

Eventually, in 2005, following sustained criticism from the ILO, Myanmar's ruling junta, then named the State Peace and Development Council, declared that Myanmar intended to withdraw its membership from the ILO.[78] For its part, the ILO placed the issue of Myanmar's compliance with the recommendations of the Commission of Inquiry on the Agenda of the International Labour Conference, for the Conference to consider what steps the ILO should take.[79] One of the options was to refer Myanmar to the International Court of Justice for a ruling on the country's continued non-compliance with the Commission's recommendations. Under article 94(2) of the UN Charter, power is vested in the Security Council to give effect to judgments of the ICJ. There was, in reality, little likelihood that the Security Council would ultimately exercise its discretion to enforce any ICJ judgement against Myanmar, given China's steadfast support of Myanmar and its right of veto as a permanent member of the Security Council.

Nonetheless, during a period which Richard Horsey, the ILO Liaison Officer, describes as 'creative uncertainty', negotiations took place between the ILO and the government of Myanmar for agreement on a Supplementary Understanding which would strengthen the power of the independent complaints mechanism and protect the confidentiality of workers who complained.[80] In February 2007, the Supplementary Understanding was signed.[81]

Richard Horsey explains that the result demonstrates 'that people who continue to impose forced labour can be held to account—even sent to prison—and this can contribute to a change in the prevailing climate of impunity'.[82] Members of ethnic minority

[75] See Ken Maclean, 'Lawfare and Impunity in Burma since the 2000 Ban on Forced Labour' (2012) 36 Asian Studies Review 189.

[76] Horsey (n 1) ch 4.

[77] Aye Myint and Min Kyi both received lesser sentences of three years in prison, for 'encouraging, harbouring, or comforting person is guilty of high treason'. In January 2005, Aye Myint was released from prison, shortly before the very high-level team was due to arrive in the country.

[78] 'Myanmar decides to quit ILO: Warnings of sanctions ignored' *IPS New Service* (1 November 2005) 60https://www.dawn.com/news/163782/myanmar-decides-to-quit-ilo-warnings-of-sanctions-ignored>.

[79] See ILO, 'Individual Case (CAS)—Discussion: 2006, Publication: 95th ILC session' (2006): Forced Labour Convention, 1930 (No 29)—Myanmar (Ratification: 1955).

[80] Horsey (n 1) 41.

[81] International Labour Office, 'Developments concerning the Question of the Observance by the Government of Myanmar of the Forced Labour Convention, 1930 (Number 29)', Geneva, March 2007, ILO ref GB.298/5/1.

[82] 'ILO Burma rep passes the torch' *The Irrawaddy* (1 July 2007).

groups outside Myanmar's main urban centres, however, noticed little change in the practices of the military in requisitioning labour.[83] The ability of villagers in these areas to make complaints was severely constrained by their circumstances: most complaints were required to be submitted to the ILO head office in Yangon; villagers from ethnic minority states faced severe restrictions on freedom of movement in military controlled areas; villagers lacked money to travel; many risked being shot on sight by government forces if they left their villages.[84] Burmese NGOs called the ILO's efforts 'cosmetic measures', which had not succeeded in restraining the use of forced labour in Myanmar.[85]

6 *Doe v Unocal* Case (1997)

At the same time as the ILO was attempting to eke reform from Myanmar's government, a group of Burmese villagers, backed by EarthRights International, were suing Unocal Oil Corporation in the US District Court for the Central District of California.[86] The allegations were of complicity in enslavement, theft, assault, rape, torture, forced labour, and murder carried out by the Burmese military in connection with the construction of the Yadana gas pipeline in the Tenasserim region of Myanmar. The claim was bought under the Alien Tort Claims Act (ATCA), a statute which dates to the earliest years of the American republic. In its modern form, it provides that '[t]he district courts shall have original jurisdiction of any civil action by an alien for a tort only, committed in violation of the law of nations or a treaty of the United States'.[87]

Among the issues raised as the *Unocal* case wove its way through the US federal courts was the question of what constitutes 'the law of nations' for the purpose of jurisdiction under the ATCA. At the time of the statute's drafting, only three international norms were considered of such consequence that their breach grounded a claim under the ATCA: violation of the safe-conducts or passports; infringement of the rights of ambassadors; and piracy.[88] In *Unocal*, the US District Court in the Central District of California acknowledged that an expanded body of norms now constituted the agreed upon 'law of nations'. The Court applied a *jus cogens* threshold, holding that violation must be of a norm that is 'specific, universal, and obligatory'.[89] In modern times such

[83] Karen Human Rights Group, 'The Limits of the New ILO Mechanism and Potential Misrepresentation of Forced Labour in Burma', 10 April 2007 (KHRG#2007-C1).

[84] Ibid. [85] Ibid. 2.

[86] *Doe v Unocal* 963 FSupp 880 (CD Cal 1997). The original suit included the Myanmar Oil and Gas Enterprise and the State Law and Order Restoration Council. The suit against Myanmar Oil and Gas and the SLORC was dropped because the Foreign Sovereign Immunities Act 1976 (US) provides general immunity from civil actions for damages for government entities.

[87] Alien Tort Statute 28 USC §1350 (2004).

[88] *Sosa v Alvarez-Machain* 542 US 692, 720 (2004) (citing William Blackstone, 4 *Commentaries* at 68: 'offences against this law [of nations] are principally incident to whole states or nations, and not individuals seeking relief in court').

[89] *Doe v Unocal Corp* 110 FSupp 2d 1294 (CD Cal 2000) (*Doe I*) 1304.

norms included, in the court's view, prohibitions on torture, murder, genocide, and slavery.[90] On appeal, the Court affirmed that rape can constitute torture and thus embody a *jus cogens* offence;[91] and so too could forced labour, as a modern variant of slavery.[92]

In relation to the question of what level of complicity was required to ground liability, the Appeals Court partially overturned a lower court ruling which held that the plaintiffs had to prove Unocal's 'active participation' in tortious crimes. Instead, the Appeals Court held that the *actus reus* for corporate liability for international crimes requires only practical assistance and encouragement which has a substantial effect on the commission of the crime.[93] The *mens rea* requirement is satisfied if the corporation has reasonable knowledge that its actions will assist the perpetrator in the commission of the crime.[94] In this manner, the Court side-stepped the Nuremberg tribunal's condition of 'active participation' for corporate liability, holding that this was only required in the Nuremberg cases to overcome the defendants' necessity defence.[95]

Unocal settled the case before final judgement, unwilling to risk the creation of a precedent which might see transnational corporations regularly bought before US courts for complicity in human rights abuses in developing countries. Nonetheless, on the heels of *Unocal* came lawsuits against other corporate giants: Coca-Cola[96] and Exxon Mobile.[97] In later decisions, the US Supreme Court curtailed the availability of the ATCA, emphasizing the requirement of specificity of the *jus cogens* norm,[98] and confirming that there is a presumption against extraterritoriality—a defendant must have more than a mere 'corporate presence' in the United States.[99] According to the Supreme Court, courts did not have a congressional mandate to employ judicial creativity in acknowledging and defining new violations of the law of nations. Such creativity, held the Supreme Court, threatens both US foreign affairs and the constitutional separation between the executive and judicial branches of the US government.[100]

7 Myanmar and Forced Labour during the Transition to Democracy from 2010

Following the democratic transition in late 2010, from March 2011 to February 2012 Myanmar's government passed a raft of legislation aimed at legalizing trade unions,

90 Ibid. 91 *John Doe I et al v UNOCAL Corp et al* 395 F3d 932 (9 Cir 2002) (*Doe II*) 945.
92 Ibid. 946. 93 Ibid. 942–43, 947–48. 94 Ibid. 951. 95 Ibid.
96 See *Sinaltrainal v Coca-Cola Co* 256 F Supp 2d 1345 (SD Fla 2003).
97 *Doe v Exxon Mobil Corp*, 393 E Supp 2d 20 (DDC 2005).
98 *Sosa v Alvarez-Machain* 124 S Ct 2739, 2766 (2004).
99 *Kiobel v Royal Dutch Petroleum Co* 133 SCt 1659 (2013) 669.
100 *Sosa v Alvarez-Machain* (n 88) 2762–3.

increasing the pension rate, allowing public political gatherings, and easing press censorship. The government appeared determined to comply with provisions of the 2010 Constitution of the Union of Myanmar, which includes a provision that 'the Union shall enact necessary laws to protect the rights of workers'[101] and contains a prohibition against enslavement and trafficking in persons.[102] In the period between 2011 and 2013, among other legislation, the government passed the Labour Organisation Law; Right to Peaceful Assembly and Peaceful Procession Act; Ward and Village Tract Administration Amendment Act; Settlement of Labour Disputes Law; Minimum Wages Act; and Employment and Skills Development Law. In 2012, President Thein Sein announced that he had signed a Memorandum of Understanding with the ILO to end forced labour by 2015.[103] The following year, Myanmar ratified the Worst Forms of Child Labour Convention, 1999 (No. 182). In 2013, 500 of Myanmar's labour organizations exercised their right to freedom of association and presented their policy on labour standards to Myanmar's Federation of Chambers of Commerce and Industries.[104] The use of the ILO's forced labour complaint mechanism increased; complainants were no longer arrested.

In its Concluding Observations, the Commission of Inquiry linked Myanmar's violation of the Forced Labour Convention to the absence of democracy and the lack of an independent judiciary willing and able to subject the executive to the rule of law and render unjust and unjustifiable actions justiciable.[105] In the Commission's view, the impunity with which government officials, in particular the military, treated the civilian population as 'an unlimited pool of unpaid forced labourers and servants at their disposal' was the result of a political system built on the use of force and intimidation to deny the people of Myanmar democracy and the rule of law.[106] What was necessary for the suppression of forced labour in Myanmar was the establishment of a government freely chosen by the people and the submission of all public authorities to the rule of law.

Myanmar's transition to democracy did not bring about the new order hoped for by the Commission. It was a partial transition, in which the old regime's actors maintained powerful political roles and the military's actions remained outside the sphere of independent civil judicial review.[107] The practical limitations of the labour reforms put in place by the Thein Sein administration were most obvious in conflict areas in ethnic minority states, where military abuses, including the use of forced labour, continued.[108]

[101] Constitution of the Republic of the Union of Myanmar 2008 art. 24. [102] Ibid. art. 358.

[103] 'Burma to stamp out forced labour by 2015' *Democratic Voice of Burma* (19 March 2012).

[104] Marcia Poole, 'Myanmar Turns a Corner' in *World of Work* (ILO 2013).

[105] ILO Commission of Inquiry (n 2) para 543. [106] Ibid.

[107] Under the Constitution 2008, the commander-in-chief has a decisive say in the appointment of the president and two vice-presidents, while certain key cabinet positions (such as Home Affairs and Defence) are confined to active military personnel.

[108] Human Rights Watch, *World Report* (2017) 6ohttp://www.hrw.org/world-report/2017/country-chapters/burma>.

8 Epilogue: The Protocol to ILO Convention No 29

On 3 August 2016, Myanmar's Minister for Labour, Immigration and Population sought the approval of parliament for ratification of a novel new instrument—the Protocol to ILO Convention Number 29 on Forced Labour (the Protocol).[109] The Protocol stands as one of only six ILO Protocols, and it is the first to be adopted since 1981.[110] The Protocol recognizes that the context and forms of forced labour have changed since the creation of the 1930 Convention: trafficking in persons is the subject of growing international concern and requires urgent action for its effective elimination; there are an increased number of workers in the private economy who are enforced or compulsory labourers; certain groups of workers, such as migrants, have a higher risk of becoming victims of forced labour. The Protocol aims to address implementation gaps in the Convention by focusing on prevention rather than punishment for breaches. From this perspective, it requires states to take 'effective measures to prevent and eliminate' the use of forced labour by taking six mandatory measures:

(a) education and information, directed particularly towards people who are most vulnerable to becoming victims of forced labour;
(b) education and information for employers;
(c) enacting legislation aimed at preventing forced labour and creating labour inspection services to implement legislation;
(d) protecting persons, particularly migrant workers, from possible abusive and fraudulent practices during the recruitment and placement process;
(e) supporting due diligence to prevent and respond to risks of forced labour; and
(f) addressing the root causes and factors that heighten the risk of forced labour.[111]

The Protocol also provides for the provision of assistance and support, including rehabilitation, for victims of forced labour;[112] and requires states to cooperate with each other to ensure the prevention and elimination of forced labour.[113]

Several aspects of the Protocol draw directly on the lessons learned from the ILO's history of engagement with Myanmar. First, the Protocol places emphasis on addressing what it terms the 'root causes'[114] that heighten the risk of forced labour. Throughout the long history of the ILO's engagement with Myanmar, it was clear that factors

[109] Republic of the Union of Myanmar, Ministry of Information, 'Protocol to 1930 Forced Labour Convention 29 and Recommendation 203 Put on Record at Pyidaungsu Hluttaw' (4 August 2016) 6ohttp://www.moi.gov.mm/moi:eng/?q=news/4/08/2016/id-7989> accessed 12 December 2018.
[110] Protocol of 2014 to the Forced Labour Convention, 1930 (adopted 11 June 2014, entered into force 9 November 2016).
[111] Ibid. arts 2(a)–(f). [112] Ibid. art. 3. [113] Ibid. art. 5. [114] Ibid. art. 2(f).

such as civil war, underdevelopment, absence of the rule of law, lack of democracy, and denial of the freedoms associated with democracy (such as freedom of association, freedom of expression, and freedom of movement) underpinned the military regime's lack of compliance with the Convention. It was also clear that continually rebuking Myanmar for violating the Convention did little, by itself, to improve the lives of workers. Ultimately, as the 1998 Commission of Inquiry recognized, what was required to end forced labour was the full restoration of democracy and an end to internal conflict.

Nonetheless, it is notable that even during the darkest days of Myanmar's dictatorship, the ILO maintained a certain level of engagement with the regime. The ILO's continual challenges to the government's actions in relation to labour practices forced Myanmar's government representatives to explain and justify the behaviour of authorities in public forums. This in turn ultimately led to the internal questioning of policies and practices which had hitherto been viewed as acceptable. The regime's initial response was denial, then obfuscation and deception. Eventually the regime made tactical concessions—passing decrees and permitting the establishment of an ILO mechanism—to appease critics. These actions provided space for domestic and international actors to leverage further change, by calling on the government to make good on its promises of reform. These are the first stages of 'the spiral process' of human rights change described by Thomas Risse, Stephen Ropp, and Kathryn Sikkink in their influential book *The Power of Human Rights: International Norms and Domestic Change.*[115] The final stage of the spiral process occurs when norms about appropriate behaviour are internalized and domestic legislation is implemented and enforced. At this point human rights norms are regarded as right and appropriate, requiring no further justification to secure compliance.

To this end, the Protocol provides a set of concrete measures which states can take, regardless of their political character, to suppress forced labour. The Myanmar experience made very clear that the end game of compliance is the enactment of domestic legislation to protect rights, and the Protocol places significant emphasis on encouraging states to give legislative effect to their obligations under the Convention to suppress forced labour.[116] The Protocol also requires members to develop a national policy and plan of action for the suppression of forced labour, in consultation with employers' and workers' organizations.[117] The emphasis placed on requiring states to take 'effective' measures recognizes that the diverse political and economic circumstances of states will necessitate different legislation and distinct policies in each state.

The Protocol avoids referring to forced labour as a peremptory norm of international law. Forced labour in Myanmar, as described by the 1998 Commission of Inquiry, took place in conjunction with atrocities such as widespread torture, extrajudicial killing, and rape. In these circumstances, the connection between forced labour and slavery

[115] Thomas Risse, C Ropp, and Kathryn Sikkink, *The Power of Human Rights: International Norms and Domestic Change* (CUP 1999).

[116] Protocol 2014 (n 110) art. 1(1).

[117] Ibid. art. 1(2).

was self-evident to the 1998 Commission of Inquiry.[118] But the presence of a limited set of conditions under which forced labour may be exacted undermines the arguments that forced labour is a peremptory norm—a norm from which no derogation is permitted. The Slavery Convention 1926 recognizes that forced labour can develop into conditions of slavery, indicating that forced labour is not necessarily slavery to begin with. The Slavery Convention recognizes that 'recourse to compulsory labour or forced labour may have grave consequences . . . states must undertake to take all necessary measures to prevent compulsory or forced labour from developing into conditions analogous to slavery'.[119]

9 Conclusion

Myanmar's encounter with international law on the issue of forced labour expanded the possibilities open to civil society actors, legal institutions, and transnational human rights litigators to shape the behaviour of rights-violating states, while the efforts of the International Confederation of Free Trade Unions to draw attention to the plight of Burmese workers, and the Confederation's persistence in highlighting in international forums the Burmese government's failure to comply with its own undertakings, rightly stands as a *cause célèbre* of the international labour movement. In terms of the development of international law, there are several points of significance.

First, Myanmar's recalcitrance in relation to the International Law Commission's recommendations forced the ILO's governing body to explore its legal power to exact compliance. Eventually, on the brink of attempting to secure and then enforce a judgment of the International Court of Justice, the Commission chose to accept another undertaking by the Burmese government that it would cooperate with the ILO in acting to suppress forced labour. Burmese NGOs, particularly in ethnic areas, claimed this was a hollow victory for the ILO: in military controlled areas, forced labour continued. Nevertheless, the ILO continued to lay the foundations for ongoing cooperation with the regime and when Myanmar's transition to democracy finally got underway, the ILO found itself well-positioned to advise on and influence the shape of domestic legislation for the protection of workers and the suppression of forced labour.

Second, the *Unocal* case in the United States bought transnational human rights litigation to the fore as a means of pursuing human rights abuses in US courts. In the decade following the *Unocal* case, the Supreme Court circumscribed the potential to pursue corporate accountability for human rights violations under the Alien Tort Claims Act. But the principal that animated the *Unocal* litigation still stands: the prohibition on

[118] ILO Commission of Inquiry (n 2) para 198.

[119] Slavery Convention (adopted 25 September 1926, entered into force 9 March 1927, 60 League of Nations Treaty Series 254) art. 5.

forced labour is a specific, universal, and obligatory norm of international law; and international norms that apply to private individuals also apply to corporations.

Finally, Myanmar's engagement with the ILO demonstrates the dynamics of state resistance to and compliance with international law. Interaction between the government and the Commission, even when combative, provided an opening which ultimately led to domestic labour reform. Strong domestic measures to prevent forced labour and to protect its victims, as the 2014 Protocol recognizes, are the goal of international legal regimes.

SOUTH AND CENTRAL ASIA

CHAPTER 23

INDIA

BS CHIMNI

1 Introduction

The theme of 'India and International Law' is multifaceted and complex. A comprehensive review of the subject would encompass the following sub-themes: (1) the evolution and development of international law in Ancient and Medieval India; (2) the development of international law in the colonial era, 1600–1947; (3) the place of international law in the Constitution of India 1949; (4) the approach of Indian courts to international law, 1950–2017; (5) India's multilevel engagement and contribution to international law, 1947–2017; and (6) the contribution of Indian scholarship to international law, in particular the articulation of a Third World Approach to International Law (TWAIL). However, it would require a separate tome to address the historical and wide-ranging aspects of India's relationship to international law.

This chapter confines itself to offering an overview of India's engagement with international law in the colonial and postcolonial periods, that is, to sub-themes (2), (3), and (4) above, with only a brief section devoted to sub-theme (5). It is important to deal with sub-theme (2) because it helps highlight certain features and anomalies with regard to the status of colonial India that would be of interest to any student of international law. Whether it is the fact of the East India Company becoming an empire, or British India becoming an original member of both the League of Nations and the United Nations, India's relationship with international law has been somewhat unusual. The section on the colonial era also offers clues to India's approach to international law in the postcolonial era. For instance, its suspicion until recently of the role of multinational corporations can be traced among other things to the deep memories of the role of the East India Company in colonizing India. In any case there is readily available positivist analysis of the relationship between India and international law in the postcolonial era, and it would serve little purpose to go over in great detail the same ground again.[1] The subject of the contribution of Indian scholarship to international law has also been dealt with elsewhere.[2]

In undertaking a non-formalist analysis of India's relationship with international law, this chapter relies on TWAIL with its focus on the role of imperialism in the evolution and development of international law.[3] The correspondence of the broad approach of postcolonial nations to international law is a result of several factors, which include colonization, the continuing subjection to forces of global capitalism, and the Western domination of the discourse and development of international law. While it is true that the relationship of each postcolonial nation with contemporary international law assumes a particular form and content, which is a function of the nature and character of its social formation, state, and constitution, TWAIL helps understand the general structure and significance of the relationship between municipal law and international law in postcolonial nations.

This relationship has both a doctrinal and a substantive dimension. The former is concerned with the rules that are applied for the recognition and effectuation of international law in municipal law. The substantive dimension is a function of the nature and character of international law in different phases of its evolution and development. Since its impact in the era of neo-liberal globalization is deep and profound, postcolonial legal systems cannot afford to apply the rules of international law in domestic law without considering their social and political consequences. It is worth mentioning here that even in the case of a powerful state like the United States for instance, there is a robust debate on the limits of the application of customary international law in the domestic sphere.[4] TWAIL considers doctrinal debates, such as whether monism, dualism, or pragmatism is the proper approach to the relationship, as not being very productive. These doctrines fail to capture the contemporary complexity of the relationship between municipal law and international law. In an era when

[1] See Lavanya Rajamani, 'International Law and the Constitutional Schema' in Sujit Choudhry, Madhav Khosla, and Pratap Bhanu Mehta (eds), *The Oxford Handbook of The Indian Constitution* (OUP 2016) 143; VG Hegde, 'Indian Courts and International Law' (2010) 23 Leiden Journal of International Law 53; VS Mani, 'Effectuation of International Law in the Municipal Legal Order: The Law and Practice in India' (1997) 5 Asian Yearbook of International Law 145; P Chandrasekhar Rao, *The Indian Constitution and International Law* (Taxmann 1993) 55; JN Saxena, 'Relation of International Law to Internal Law' (1976) 12 Banares Law Journal 46; TS Rama Rao, 'Some Problems of International Law in India' (1957) 6 Indian Year Book of International Affairs 3.

[2] BS Chimni, 'International Law Scholarship in Post-Colonial India: Coping with Dualism' (2010) 23 Leiden Journal of International Law 23.

[3] Antony Anghie, *Imperialism, Sovereignty and International Law* (CUP 2003); Antony Anghie and BS Chimni, 'Third World Approaches to International Law and Individual Responsibility in Internal Conflict' in Steven Ratner and Anne-Marie Slaughter (eds), *The Methods of International Law* (ASIL 2004) 185.

[4] Curtis Bradley, Jack Goldsmith, and David Moore, '*Sosa*, Customary International Law, and the Continuing Relevance of Eire' (2007) 120 Harvard Law Review 869; Jack Goldsmith and Eric Posner, 'A Theory of Customary International Law' (1999) 66 The University of Chicago Law Review 1113; Eric Posner and Jack Goldsmith, 'Understanding the Resemblance between Traditional and Modern Customary International Law' (2000) 40 Virginia Journal of International Law 639.

international law has become invasive, the rules for the effectuation of international law in municipal law inevitably need to be revisited in the matrix of national interests of postcolonial nations.

In sum, while the principal purpose of the present chapter is to review the place and practice of international law in India in the colonial and postcolonial eras, it also seeks to illustrate a broad TWAIL approach to the relationship between municipal law and international law. It proceeds in the following way: section 2 briefly reviews the relationship between India and international law in the colonial era; section 3 examines the place of international law in the Constitution of India and the respective roles assigned to the executive and legislature in negotiating and implementing treaties. It also touches on the approach of the courts to international law. Section 4 identifies India's contribution to international law in the period 1947–2017. Section 5 recapitulates the salient points made in the chapter.

2 India and International Law: Colonial Era

The history of international law in the colonial era can be conveniently divided into two phases: the first phase lasted from 1600 to 1857 when the East India Company arrived in India and slowly evolved into a company-state; and the second phase began with the British Crown taking over the governance of the colony until India attained independence in 1947. The second phase can in turn be studied in two phases: 1858–1919 and 1919–1947. In the latter period, British India became an original member of the League of Nations in 1919, the United Nations in 1945, and the General Agreement on Tariffs and Trade (GATT) in 1947. The resulting anomalous status of British India offers, among other things, insights into the possible workings of an informal empire that is relevant for our times.

2.1 First Phase: 1600–1857

Native Indian states for centuries carried on trade with other nations of the world. Their ports were regularly visited by ships and merchants from every region. India's wealth and wisdom were coveted by all, especially European nations.[5] The Portuguese came first in 1498 to Calicut with the landing of Vasco De Gama, followed by other expeditions to establish trading posts. The Portuguese were followed by the Dutch, the French, and the English. The English East India Company, which was to 'rule' India

[5] KM Pannikar, *Asia and Western Dominance: A Survey of the Vasco Da Gama epoch of Indian History 1498–1945* (new edn George Allen and Unwin Ltd 1959) 21ff.

for almost a century and a half, arrived in 1600 under a charter issued by Queen Elizabeth I. Before the end of the century, it was in the process of becoming a company-empire, exercising both commercial and sovereign powers. It entered into numerous written understandings and treaties with local rulers.[6] The experience compelled Edmund Burke to write that 'in Asia as well as in Europe the same Law of Nations prevails, the same principles are continually resorted to, and the same maxims sacredly held and strenuously maintained'.[7]

In the late seventeenth and eighteenth centuries, the East India Company became a 'virtual state', 'waging war, administering justice, minting coin, and collecting revenue over Indian territory'.[8] The unique phenomenon of 'the company state', according to Nicholas Dirks, 'is a salutary case for rethinking the history both of the state and of global capitalism, especially as it makes clear the fuzzy boundary between the two in the emergent global context of the long eighteenth century'.[9] Of course on the legal plane, 'the Company was at no time sovereign in the strict sense of the term. Its authority was derived from the Charters or Acts of Parliament . . . sovereign power was delegated to it by the Crown in successive stages by the Charters which were renewed at regular intervals'.[10] Likewise, in India, 'the Company was dependent on the grants of the Moghul Emperor and other rulers for permission to trade and the right to settle disputes within the territorial units of their factories'.[11] Thus, the sovereignty of India was derived and acquired from the Crown and the Mughal emperor respectively.[12]

Yet, as Upendra Baxi observes, '[t]he remarkable invention of a corporate form as a vessel and vehicle of the British imperialism in India (and also elsewhere in Asia) requires critical attention at least from those who seek to frame categories of alternative ways of doing international law histories'.[13] There is a need to inquire as to how it comes to pass 'that juridical histories of international law could have ever maintained, with positivist innocence, that only "States" are the subjects of international law'.[14] To put it differently, the anomalous status of corporations in international law today has a pre-history that has not been sufficiently examined.

Certainly, scholars like Phillip Stern have cautioned against an expansive use of the history of the East India Company. He is, for instance, sceptical of treating it as a

[6] For one collection of these treaties and agreements see CU Aitchison (ed), *A Collection of Treaties, Engagements and Samads: Relating to India and Neighboring Countries*, vols 1–12 (Government of India Central Publication Branch 1931; reprinted by Kraus Reprint 1973).

[7] Cited by Nicholas Dirks, *Autobiography of an Archive: A Scholar's Passage to India* (Permanent Black 2015) 194.

[8] Ibid. 176. [9] Ibid. 210.

[10] GN Joshi, *The New Constitution of India* (Macmillan and Co Limited 1937) 2. Thus, Charters were issued at periodic intervals and included Charters of 1600, 1661, 1663, 1698, 1758, 1773, 1813, 1833, and 1853. Infra 2–3.

[11] Ibid. 4. [12] Ibid.

[13] Upendra Baxi, 'India-Europe' in Bardo Fassbender and Anne Peters (eds), *The Oxford Handbook of The History of International Law* (OUP 2012) 744, 754.

[14] Ibid.

forefather of the modern corporation or the multinational corporation.[15] In his view, 'if the East India Company offers us a plausible argument for our present, it seems more likely to be found not in the realm of commerce but in the world of politics, and in particular, in international law'.[16] Among matters of interest is 'the treaty-making capacities of the East India Company', which 'highlighted the uncertain and situational nature of its legal personhood, especially after its expansion as a territorial power in the late eighteenth century'.[17] In a case brought against the Company, an English court had observed that it had no jurisdiction, as '[t]he power, which the Company exercise upon these occasions, is in fact that of a state'.[18] The fact that lines between a company and a sovereign were blurred in these times can also be seen from the observation of Hugo Grotius that 'private trading companies were as entitled to make war as were the traditional sovereigns of Europe'.[19] The company was thus both a derivative and an independent subject of international law reflecting the 'pluralistic notions of law and sovereignty that were perhaps common in those times'.[20] But, as Stern points out, 'the corporation's subjection to multiple regulatory and sovereign regimes simultaneously was not only a source of vulnerability, but potentially a source of great power'.[21] Thus, the pre-history of the modern company reveals how a state-centric approach to international law cannot capture the reality of international relations even today.[22] According to Stern:

> [W]hat the East India Company's history shows us is *how state and corporation are mutually constituted, and in fact, derive from similar and shared ideological and historical contexts*. Thus, it is the complexities and contradictions in the corporation as both a private and public actor that raises questions that may be useful for upsetting our normative assumptions about precisely what, where, and how corporations operate in a global and transnational context.[23]

[15] Phillip Stern, 'The English East India Company and the Modern Corporation: Legacies, Lessons, and Limitations' (2016) 39 Seattle University Law Review 423, 426–33.

[16] Ibid. 425. [17] Ibid. 434.

[18] *Nabob of the Carnatic v East India Company* (1791) 30 Eng Rep 391 (HL), cited by Stern, ibid. 434. For other cases see ibid. 435.

[19] Cited by Stern (n 15) 437. [20] Ibid. 438. [21] Ibid. 439. [22] Ibid. 440.

[23] Ibid. 441 (emphasis added). Stern concludes (ibid. 444) that if any lesson can be drawn from the history of the East India Company it is the following:

> ... if the East India Company's history as a political actor offers any lessons for our present predicaments, it might be to offer some skepticism about expecting domestic or municipal law to be able to redress grievances against a corporation acting in negotiation, alliance, or conflict with other sovereign powers—be they companies, states, or empires. Not only do these corporations far exceed the territorial grasp of the state, the ambiguity of their activities as simultaneously public and private also renders them difficult to parse within the ambit of nationally sovereign courts. If in the East India Company's period it was the *jus gentium*—the law of nations—that ultimately needed to fully govern the actions of multinational corporations as much as states, it would suggest that one might need instead to turn to international law as the arena best suited to serve as a robust regulatory and governmental regime over the moral, ethical, and human rights behavior of transnational corporations.

In sum, the history of the East India Company demonstrates *the intimate relationship between capitalism, imperialism, and pluralistic notions of the concept of sovereignty.*[24] It has been aptly observed that 'Empire and capitalism were born hand in hand'; corporations have always shared a close relationship with sovereigns and sovereignty.[25] It may also be mentioned here that the Charter of 1813 even required the East India Company to provide for the 'religious and moral' improvements of the Indian subjects.[26] The Company thus intervened in matters that were way beyond commercial concerns and became the carrier of the ideology and culture of imperialism.[27] It is no different today with multinational corporations, although they carry the ideology and culture of different times.

2.2 Second Phase: 1858–1947

It was only after the first war of independence in 1857 that the question of the sovereignty of the British Crown was clarified. The Proclamation of Queen Victoria of 1 November 1858 resolved to take over the territories that were being administered by East India Company.[28] The Government of India Act 1858 'transferred the government from the Company to the Crown, and vested in the Crown all the territories and powers of the Company'.[29] In 'one fell swoop, both the Mughal and the company were dethroned, and the British Crown became paramount'.[30] Of course, in so far as the 'legitimacy and legitimate rule' of India was concerned, 'the succession to the Mughals was the sole justification for the Indian princes, nobles, elites and the bulk of the population to accept the British as the Sovereign power'.[31] But the 1858 Proclamation also 'announce[d] to the native princes of India, that all treaties and engagements made with them by or under the authority of the East India Company are by us accepted and will be scrupulously maintained, and we look for the like observance on their part'.[32] The British assumed a policy of non-interference towards the 562 native or princely

[24] Adam Smith's criticism of the company-state here also comes to mind. Sankar Muthu, 'Adam Smith's Critique of International Trading Companies: Theorizing "Globalization" in the Age of Enlightenment' (2008) 36 Political Theory 185.

[25] Dirks (n 7) 174.

[26] Penelope Carlson, *The East India Company and Religion 1698–1858* (The Boydell Press 2012) 3.

[27] Ibid. 239. See also Joseph Sramek, *Gender, Morality, and Race in Company India, 1765–1858* (Palgrave Macmillan 2011).

[28] Proclamation by the Queen in Council to the Princes, Chiefs, and People of India (published by the Governor General at Allahabad, 1 November 1858) <http://www.bl.uk/collection-items/proclamation-by-the-queen-in-council-to-the-princes-chiefs-and-people-of-india> accessed 18 October 2017.

[29] Joshi (n 10) 3. But it may be noted once again that: 'The change effected in 1858 was thus not a new acquisition of sovereignty, but only the resumption of a delegated authority by the Crown and the exercise thereof directly by the servants of the Crown thereafter', infra 4.

[30] Dirks (n 7) 187.

[31] Michael Mann, '"Torchbearers upon the Path of Progress": Britain's Ideology of a "Moral and Material Progress in India"' in Harald Fischer-Tine and Michael Mann (eds), *Colonialism as Civilizing Mission: Cultural Ideology in British India* (Anthem Press 2004) 1, 5.

[32] Ibid.

states, albeit after depriving them of the right to conduct their own foreign policy.[33] Therefore, in so far as day-to-day governance of the provinces went, 1858 did not mark a 'sharp cleavage in India's history'.[34] In 1931 Sundaram summed up the historical position of native states in the following way:

> At one time in Indian history and especially till the middle of the eighteenth century, some of the States enjoyed sovereign rights and were as such distinct personalities in International Law. But during the course of a hundred and seventy-five years of British rule in India, numerous changes have taken place in the relationship of the States to the Crown. In the first place, the rulers of the Indian States . . . surrendered their external sovereignty, e.g., foreign policy and defence, in return for which the Crown . . . guaranteed their foreign aggression and internal disruption. The States . . . [were] not parties to international treaties, but each State . . . [was] sovereign in regard to its internal affairs.[35]

The relationship with native Indian states once again underlines the plural forms empire can assume.

2.2.1 *1919–1947*

Indeed, in the interwar period, British India actively participated in international law-making processes and in international institutions. It was admitted to the Imperial Conference in 1917 and went on to become an original member of the League of Nations and later the United Nations.[36] In fact of the thirty-one original members of the League, India was the only colonial state to become a member.[37] India's position from 1919 to 1947 was therefore described as 'that of an anomalous international person'.[38] In a paper read before the Grotius Society in 1931, Lanka Sundaram concluded that 'the Treaty of Versailles

[33] SR Ashton, *British Policy towards the Indian States 1905–1939* (Select Book Service Syndicate 1985).

[34] Sarvepalli Gopal, *British Policy in India 1858–1905* (CUP 1965) ix.

[35] Lanka Sundaram, 'The International Status of India' (1931) 17 Transactions of the Grotius Society 35, 47–8.

[36] At the Paris Peace Conference 1919, according to RP Anand:

> Indian plenipotentiaries, holding full power on behalf of India, took part in the discussions and signed the peace treaties, along with the representatives of other sovereign states, on the basis of "legal equality". India thus acquired a right to become an original member of the League of Nations (since the Covenant of the League of Nations was part of the Peace Treaty), and, for the first time in the modern period, came into direct and formal contact with the outside world.

RP Anand, 'The Formation of International Organizations and India: A Historical Study' (2010) 23 Leiden Journal of International Law 5, 8.

[37] Ibid. 9.

[38] Sundaram (n 35) 37–8. It is interesting that Sundaram reports (infra 43) that:

> The League Mandate for the administration German East Africa (now Tanganyika) was at one moment on the point of being granted to India, but this courageous step, which would have enhanced the value of the juridical basis of India's international status, was at the last moment withdrawn in favour of Great Britain.

See also TT Poulose, 'India as an Anomalous International Person (1919–1947)' (1970) 44 British Year Book of International Law 201, 202.

may be taken as the actual point of the development of the international status of India. . . . The juridical basis of India's external sovereignty was tacitly recognized by the sovereign States of the world'.[39] Thereafter, it took part in a number of international conferences:

> On account of her extended international status, India . . . secured representation at non-League conferences such as the Brussels Financial Conference of 1920, the Washington Conference on Naval Armaments of 1921, the Geneva Economic Conference of 1922, the London Reparations Conference of 1924, the World Economic Conference of 1927, the London Naval Conference of 1930 and The Hague Conference on the Codification of International Law of 1930.[40]

In these forums India's representatives often 'pursued a line of action independent of the wishes of His Majesty's Government'.[41] In subsequent years:

> India was automatically admitted to the International Labour Organization, the Permanent Court of International Justice, the Committee of Intellectual Co-operation in Paris, the International Institute of Agriculture, and several other League or semi-League organizations. India was represented on its own at almost every international conference after 1920. India also signed numerous multilateral treaties, including the Kellogg-Briand Pact of 1928.[42]

India also went on to become an original member of GATT. It participated in the drafting of the UN Charter, although the 'discussions and comments on the proposed international organization were meagre'.[43] However, the Indian delegation did sponsor 'four amendments' relating to '(i) human rights, (ii) penalizing a member if it failed in its financial obligations, (iii) criteria for the selection of the non-permanent members of the Security Council, and (iv) the inclusion of observers in the Security Council'.[44]

Another anomaly was that British India and the princely states were together represented at the League. In fact 'the juridical unity of India in international law was tacitly recognized by the Interpretation Act of 1889'.[45] According to section 18(5) of the Act, India was defined to be 'British India together with any territories of any native Prince or Chief under the suzerainty of her Majesty'.[46] Thus, at the League, 'India was recognized to be of composite and corporate character'.[47] In reality though, this was not the case. It became apparent when India ratified several international conventions

[39] Sundaram (n 35) 42. [40] Ibid. 43.

[41] Ibid. 44. Oppenheim described the anomalous situation thus (quoted in Anand (n 36) 9):

> The position of India as subject of international law was for a time anomalous. She became a member of the League of Nations; she was invited to the San Francisco Conference of the United Nations. . . . She exercised the treaty-making power in her own right. However, so long as the control of her internal and external relations rested ultimately with the British Government and Parliament, she could not be regarded as a sovereign state and a normal subject of international law. In 1947, she became a fully self-governing Dominion and independent state.

[42] Anand (n 36) 12. [43] Ibid. 17. [44] Ibid. 20.

[45] DN Verma, *India and the League of Nations* (Bharati Bhawan 1968) 239–40 (citing International Status of India's Memorandum presented to the Indian Statutory Commission by the India Office, *Report of the Indian Statutory Commission*, vol V (1930) 1648).

[46] Ibid. [47] Ibid. 240.

but the native princely states made little effort to comply with them. In fact, the British were reminded that they had undertaken not to interfere in their internal affairs. Indeed, on 21 January 1926, the Government of India addressed a circular letter to all Indian states that it 'felt confident that the Rulers of Indian states will not be disposed to disclaim a similar responsibility, within such limits as may be shown to be reasonable in the sphere of their own internal administration'.[48] Nonetheless, the Indian states remained reluctant and therefore 'in many instances the British Government noted that a particular convention would not apply to princely States'.[49]

It should be apparent even from this cursory analysis that there was an intimate relationship between the development of capitalism in Europe, imperialism, and international law. In the colonial era, this relationship went through different phases, shaping the association between colonial powers and the colonized nations. A repertoire of methods and mechanisms was adopted for instituting formal and informal empires. To put it differently, the roots of neo-colonial relationships today lie buried in the colonial past. Thus, for instance, the relationship of the East India Company with political entities in India captures aspects of the relationship between transnational corporations (TNCs), sovereignty, and international law in postcolonial nations. The blurring of lines between private and public, material and cultural, formal and informal offers insights that need to be harnessed in dealing with the regulation of TNCs in the contemporary era. Likewise, the role of contemporary international institutions possesses a family resemblance to that of the League of Nations under the mandate system.[50] These stories need to be told at length at some point. For the moment, however, it is the formal dimension of the relationship between international law and independent India's legal system that will be the focus of attention.

3 Independent India: The Constitutional Framework

The status of international law in the Constitution of India is dealt with in a range of provisions. Article 372 of the Constitution of India captures the historical dimension of the relationship. It states in part:

> Subject to the other provisions of this Constitution, all the laws in force in the territory of India immediately before the commencement of this Constitution, shall continue in force therein until repealed or amended by a competent legislature or other competent authority.

The expression 'all the laws in force' was a reference to the common law of England, including norms of customary international law that were accepted as applicable,

[48] Quoted by Verma, ibid. 251. [49] Ibid. 251.

[50] Antony Anghie, 'Time Present and Time Past: Globalization, International Financial Institutions and the Third World' (2000) 32 New York University Journal of International Law and Politics 243.

besides treaty obligations undertaken by colonial India.[51] The continuation of these obligations is to be assessed today in terms of laws passed by the Indian Parliament and the determinations of courts that are subsumed under the term 'other competent authority' appearing in article 372.[52] In the latter regard, attention may be drawn to article 13(1) of Part III of the Constitution dealing with 'fundamental rights', which states:

> All laws in force in the territory of India immediately before the commencement of this Constitution, in so far as they are inconsistent with the provisions of this Part, shall, to the extent of such inconsistency, be void.

This inconsistency is determined from time to time by courts as and when matters come up before them.

3.1 The Constitutional Vision

The framers of the Constitution of India spelled out the place of international law in article 51, which falls in Part IV of the Constitution of India devoted to 'Directive Principles of State Policy'. Article 51 reads:

> Promotion of international peace and security
> The State shall endeavor to—
>
> (a) Promote international peace and security;
> (b) Maintain just and honorable relations between nations;
> (c) Foster respect for international law and treaty obligations in the dealings of organized peoples with one another; and
> (d) Encourage settlement of international disputes by arbitration.

Five points may be made with respect to article 51. First, the introduction of this provision in the Constituent Assembly was not accompanied by an elaborate explanation nor followed by extensive discussion. In introducing this provision BR Ambedkar, Chairman of the Drafting Committee, observed that 'the propositions contained in this new article are so simple that it seems to be super-arrogation to try to explain them to the House by any lengthy speech'.[53]

Secondly, while the 'directive principles' are not binding, they are seen as being of far-reaching importance in the governance of the country.[54] Every government is expected to be guided by them.

[51] For a detailed analysis of art. 372 see Mani (n 1) 153–4. [52] Ibid. 153–4.

[53] (1948–9) 7 Constituent Assembly Debates 595, cited in TS Rama Rao (n 1) 4–5.

[54] Article 37 of Part IV of the Constitution of India states:

> Application of the principles contained in this part—The provisions contained in this Part *shall not be enforceable by any court*, but the principles therein laid down *are nevertheless fundamental in the governance of the country* and shall be the duty of the State to apply these principles in making laws. (Emphasis added.)

Thirdly, in looking at the place of international law in the constitutional scheme of things, the focus of formalist scholars is often on article 51(c), which deals directly with the subject.[55] However, this is to take a narrow view of the matter. The provisions related to peace and security and the need to maintain just and honourable relations between nations are critical to the manner in which the state has been instructed to approach international law. Therefore, the criticism that article 51 mixes foreign policy goals and international law is misplaced.[56]

Fourthly, while the language of the article could have been more precise, there is a certain purpose to couching it in these terms. Thus, for instance, while the reference to fostering respect for 'international law and treaty obligations' looks odd at first glance, it is a way of clarifying the scope of international legal obligations. The term 'international law' was meant to refer to obligations from all sources of international law, for the binding nature of obligations flowing from treaties was never in doubt.[57] CH Alexandrowicz had thus opined that 'we may assume from the distinction in article 51(c) between international law and treaty obligations that the term "international law" relates to international customary law'.[58] He then went to observe that 'if so, it would mean prima facie that international customary law is not incorporated into Indian municipal law'.[59] It is possible to argue that rules of customary international law would be incorporated into domestic law only if these contribute to 'just and honorable relations between nations'. However, as will be seen presently, the Supreme Court of India (SCI) has not always borne this in mind in its pronouncements on the subject.

Fifthly, the phrase 'organized peoples' in article 51(c) was a reference to nations which had 'not secured the recognition by the family of nations' but had 'the capacity to conclude certain treaties, mainly of a non-political character'.[60] It was also perhaps intended to cover the situation of British India being an original member of the League of Nations and United Nations even before it had attained independence.

3.2 The Legislature and International Law

India has adopted a parliamentary form of government with a president as its titular head. Under the Constitution of India, legislative powers are shared between the Union Parliament and State legislatures. Article 246 deals with the 'subject matter of laws' that can be made by the Parliament and State legislatures. It provides that the Union

[55] See for example Rajamani (n 1) 144ff. [56] See Mani (n 1) 157.

[57] Others before have interpreted the term 'international law' as reference to customary international law. See Saxena (n 1) 49.

[58] CH Alexandrowicz (writing as Alexander), 'International Law in India' (1952) 1 ICLQ 289, 291. It is followed by Rajamani (n 1) 145, who writes that 'in the circumstances it would be erroneous to interpret it to 'imply that international customary law is not incorporated prima facie into Indian municipal law'.

[59] Alexander, ibid. [60] Ibid. 294.

Parliament can make laws on subjects included in List I of the Seventh Schedule of the Constitution, and also on those matters that are enumerated in List III containing the Concurrent List on which both the States and the Union can legislate. Thus, the power of the Parliament extends to both the Union List and the Concurrent List of the Seventh Schedule. It is the Union List that contains the principal entries relating to foreign policy and international law and institutions.[61]

Furthermore, article 253, entitled 'Legislation for giving effect to international agreements', found in Part XI of the Constitution on 'Relations between the Union and States', empowers the Union Parliament to legislate on matters even in the State List of the Seventh Schedule if it is required to do so in order to implement India's international obligations. It states:

> Notwithstanding anything in the foregoing provisions of this Chapter, Parliament has power to make any law for the whole or any part of the territory of India for implementing any treaty, agreement or convention with any other country or countries or any decision made at any international conference, association or other body.

This article has today acquired a significance that the framers of the Constitution could not have foreseen. Since contemporary international law agreements deal with critical aspects of a nation's economic and social policies, they can erode the powers of the states, a matter to be discussed presently.[62]

[61] These include Entry 10: 'Foreign affairs: all matters which bring the Union into relation with any foreign country'; Entry 11: 'Diplomatic, consular and trade representation'; Entry 12: 'United Nations Organization'; Entry 13: 'Participation in international conferences, associations and other bodies and implementing of decisions made thereat'; Entry 14: 'Entering into treaties and agreements with foreign countries and implementing of treaties, agreements, and conventions with foreign countries'; Entry 15: 'War and Peace'; Entry 16: 'Foreign jurisdiction'; Entry 17: 'Citizenship, naturalization and aliens'; Entry 18: 'Extradition'; Entry 19: 'Admission into, and emigration and expulsion from, India; passports and visas'; Entry 21: 'Piracies and crimes committed on the high seas or in the air; offences against the law of nations committed on land or the high seas or in the air'; Entry 25: 'Maritime shipping and navigation'; Entry 29: 'Airways, aircraft and air navigation'; Entry 37: 'Foreign loans'; Entry 41: 'Trade and commerce with foreign countries'; and Entry 57: 'Fishing and fisheries beyond territorial waters'.

[62] It may be of interest here to note that in November 1947, on his visit to the US and other Western nations to consult on matters concerning the drafting of the Constitution of India, Sir BN Rau, who was Constitutional Advisor 'to assist the Constituent Assembly in drafting India's constitution', met with Professor (later Judge) Phillip Jessup of Columbia University. BN Rau records that Jessup 'regarded as very important the amendment giving power to the Centre to legislate on a subject which is formally provincial if it has come to be of national importance': BN Rau (B Shiva Rao (ed)), *India's Constitution in the Making* (Orient Longmans Private Limited 1960) 308. See Rajendra Prasad, 'Foreword' in Rau, infra v. It can only be surmised that Jessup may have had something like article 253 in mind with a view to ensuring that India met its treaty and other obligations under international law. Rau of course met with many others in the course of his visit to the United States which included Justice Felix Frankfurter and Justice Learned Hand, who also appeared to have suggested the broad need for such a provision, albeit not with international law in mind. On his return, Rau suggested an amendment to India's draft constitution 'to secure that when the national interest requires that a certain matter, ordinarily falling in the exclusively provincial sphere, should be dealt with on a national basis, the Centre should have the power to legislate on it on that basis'. Rau, infra 303.

3.3 The Executive and International Law

Article 73 of the Constitution of India describes the 'extent of executive power of the Union'. It states in part:

(1) Subject to the provisions of this Constitution, the executive power of the Union shall extend—
  (a) To the matters with respect to which Parliament has power to make laws; and
  (b) To the exercise of such rights, authority and jurisdiction as are exercisable by the Government of India by virtue of any treaty or agreement.

When article 73(1)(b) is read with article 253, it gives, in the absence of any law on the matter made by the Parliament, enormous powers to the executive to negotiate, sign, and ratify international agreements. Against this backdrop we may consider the treaty-making and treaty implementation powers and process in practice. These raise a number of questions that have been debated within the country.

3.4 Treaty-Making and Implementation Process

The treaty-making function, following British and Commonwealth practice, has been vested with the executive in the post-independence era. The Parliament has yet to pass any law under Entry 14 of List I of Seventh Schedule, which allows it to deal with matters relating to 'Entering into treaties and agreements with foreign countries and implementing of treaties, agreements, and conventions with foreign countries'. The executive decides when to enter into international negotiations, and when to sign and ratify international agreements. However, it has to turn to the Parliament when either legislation or the amendment of existing laws is required to implement a treaty. In the very early years, the Government of India had stated its position thus on matters relating to the negotiation and ratification of treaties:

> Parliament has not made any laws so far on the subject [of treaties] and until it does so, the President's power [as all executive power is vested in the President of the Republic who is its titular head] to enter into treaties remains unfettered by any internal constitutional restrictions.
>
> In practice, the President does not negotiate or conclude a treaty or agreement himself. Plenipotentiaries are appointed for this purpose and they act under full powers issued by the President. It is however, the President who ratifies a treaty.[63]

The past practice has been reaffirmed most recently in August 2017 in a document containing 'Guidelines/SoP on the Conclusion of International Treaties in India'. It states:

[63] *Law and Practice Concerning the Conclusion of Treaties* (UN Legal Series 1953) 63 (quoted by Mani (n 1) 161).

> Indian Practice: According to the Indian Constitutional scheme, making of international treaties is an executive act. A Treaty is concluded with the approval of the Union Cabinet. It is not placed before the Parliament for discussion and approval. However, where the performance of treaty obligations entails alteration of the existing domestic law or requires new enactment, it would accordingly require legislative action.[64]

This understanding of the constitutional scheme has been contested by civil society actors from time to time. It has been argued that this practice may have been suitable when bilateral and multilateral treaties did not pertain to critical aspects of sovereign economic and social policies. But the situation has changed in the era of accelerated globalization. The post-1980 agreements impact upon not only the sovereign policy space available but also the rights of ordinary citizens.[65] Further, treaties can impact upon the federal character of the relationship between the Union and States.[66] Thus, for example, agriculture is a State subject under Entry 14 of List II of the Seventh Schedule, but the Union can restructure agricultural policies through adopting international agreements relating to agriculture, such as the World Trade Organization (WTO) 'Agreement on Agriculture'. It has been mooted that the Union Parliament should play a more active role in the negotiation, adoption, and ratification of a treaty.

To be sure, even those who defend the exclusive right of the executive to make treaties do not assert that the Parliament does not have any role to play in their negotiation and ratification, especially in important bilateral and multilateral ones. It needs to be kept informed of salient developments and has powers of general oversight. But it is contended that a greater role for the Parliament would impose serious practical

[64] See 'Guidelines/SoP on the conclusion of International Treaties in India', August 2017, <http://www.mea.gov.in/images/SOP-forwarding-letter-to-Ministries-with-revised-SOPs.pdf> accessed 21 October 2017, 5. The task of vetting international treaties is given to the Legal and Treaties Division of the Ministry of External Affairs:

> Legal and Treaties Division of the Ministry of External Affairs was created in 1957 as a nodal point to deal with all aspects of International law advise to the Government of India. This Division is the sole source of legal advice for the Ministry of External Affairs. In addition, it also advises other Ministries/Departments of the Government of India on all matters concerning International law and conclusion and interpretation of treaties.
>
> As an International Law Advisory Division, the mandate of this Division is very wide beginning with questions relating to country's frontiers, both land and maritime, utilization of its natural resources like the waters of an international river or the sea adjacent to its coast, protection of its citizens abroad, privileges and immunities of diplomats/international organizations, protection and treatment of aliens, granting of asylum, extradition of fugitive offenders, human rights, humanitarian law, disarmament, piracy and terrorism related issues. Legal issues relating to investment protection, international trade, matters relating to area transit agreements, shipping and other means of transportation also engage this Division.

See Ministry of External Affairs, Government of India <http://www.mea.gov.in/treaty.htm> accessed 21 October 2017.

[65] See BS Chimni, 'International Institutions Today: An Imperial Global State in the Making (2004) 15 European Journal of International Law 1. See also Mani (n 1) 163.

[66] Mani (n 1) 163.

constraints in treaty making. In any case, it has the power and authority to not pass implementing legislation under article 253 if it does not approve of a particular treaty.[67] While these arguments are not entirely without merit, they ignore other realities. First, many international agreements do not call for enabling legislation. In such instances, the Parliament is entirely kept out of the picture. Second, when critical national interests are at stake, practical issues cannot be allowed to prevail. Third, as Mani has observed, 'the current practice whereby the executive exercises absolute discretion in committing the country definitively with respect to a treaty is an anachronism and out of step with the principles of parliamentary supremacy in a democracy in which people are supposed to govern themselves through their elected representatives'.[68]

Scholars like Mani have therefore argued for parliamentary legislation 'stipulating some form of prior parliamentary consent as a prerequisite to ratification or accession to an international agreement'.[69] But in order not to completely tie the hands of the executive, the legislation may distinguish between significant and routine treaties. Parliamentary ratification may be required only where important bilateral and multilateral treaties are concerned. For this purpose, a Committee (consisting of representatives of all major national and regional parties, a former judge of the SCI, and an international law expert) may be established. This Committee would have the authority to identify those treaties that require greater oversight by the Parliament and their eventual ratification. The legislation can also establish structures that enable the Parliament to receive expert evidence to shed light on complex technical matters in a treaty that is being negotiated.

3.5 Indian Courts and International Law: General

In the decades after independence, the SCI has approached international law with an open mind. The Court has displayed a cosmopolitan vision in which international law is seen as worthy of respect.[70] Indeed, it has been 'extraordinarily receptive to norms of international law' in expanding the rights of citizens.[71] It has been especially

[67] Different methods have been used by Parliament to legislate. According to Rao these are: (i) making provisions in compliance with the relevant provisions of the treaties without enacting the treaty provisions; (ii) annexing to the statute in a schedule to it, those provisions of the treaty which required enforcement under Indian law; or (iii) reproducing the whole of the treaty in the schedule to the statute. Cited in Mani (n 1) 167.

[68] Ibid. 162–3. [69] Ibid. 164.

[70] In *National Legal Services Authority v Union of India*, (2014) 5 SCC 438, 486 it recalled that 'In *Kesavananda Bharati v State of Kerala* [(1973) 4 SCC 225], it was stated that in view of Article 51 of the Constitution, the Court must interpret language of the Constitution, if not intractable, in the light of the United Nations Charter and the solemn declaration subscribed to it by India'. It may be recalled in this context that the framers of the Constitution of India borrowed from different constitutions of the world that included the US and Irish constitutions. Therefore, the idea of borrowing from the outcomes of the efforts of the United Nations was not seen as unusual.

[71] Rajamani (n 1) 144.

alert to progressive developments in the area of international human rights law and international environmental law. In the process, the courts may have trodden on the legislative powers of the Indian Parliament. It can also be said that the fact that Indian courts do not fully appreciate the complexity of international law making, and the politics that inform the negotiation and adoption of international treaties or the formation of customary international law, has made them more ready to accept international laws into the domestic system.

3.5.1 *Courts and International Conventions*

The SCI has attempted to clarify the position with respect to the reception of treaty law in domestic law. In doing so, it has not engaged with the doctrinal debates on monism and dualism. The general principle that has been applied is spelled out in many cases. In *Apparel Export Promotion Council v A K Chopra* (1999), the SCI observed:

> This Court has in numerous cases emphasised that while discussing constitutional requirements, courts and counsel must never forget the core principle embodied in the International Conventions and Instruments and so far as possible give effect to the principles contained in those international instruments. The Courts are under an obligation to give due regard to International Conventions and Norms for construing domestic laws more so when there is no inconsistency between them and there is a void in domestic law.[72]

In the recent case of *Justice K S Puttaswamy and Anor v Union of India and Ors* (2017), which dealt with the right to privacy, the SCI devoted a brief section of its judgment to 'India's commitment under International Law'.[73] It summed up once again its position on international law:

> The position in law is well settled. Where there is a contradiction between international law and a domestic statute, the Court would give effect to the latter.... The Court will not readily presume any inconsistency.... India is a responsible member of the international community and the Court must adopt an interpretation which abides by the international commitments made by the country particularly where its constitutional and statutory mandates indicate no deviation.[74]

As would be evident from these two pronouncements, while domestic law will prevail in the last instance, the courts would not presume any inconsistency between it and international conventions. Instead, an attempt would be made to advance an interpretation of domestic law that does not bring it into tension with international obligations. Beyond stating its essential stance on the subject, the courts proceed to apply international law on a case by case basis.

[72] In *Apparel Export Promotion Council v A K Chopra* (1999) 1 SCC 759; 1999 SCC (L&S) 405.

[73] *Justice KS Puttaswamy and Anor v Union of India and Ors* (Writ Petition (Civil) No 494 of 2012, section J, paras 129–33.

[74] Ibid. para 133.

3.5.2 *Special Case of Cession of Territory*

The SCI has distinguished between different kinds of implementing legislation that are required in light of the provisions of the Constitution of India. There is no issue of greater sensitivity in a sovereign state system, especially in a postcolonial state seeking to clearly mark out its territorial boundaries, as that of cession or adjustment of territory. It is therefore not surprising that the SCI has proceeded cautiously on this issue. In *Reference relating to the transfer of Berubari Union case* (1960), its opinion was sought by the President of India, under article 143(1), on the question of:

> whether the implementation of the Agreement relating to Berubari Union requires any legislative action either by way of a suitable law of Parliament relatable to Art. 3 of the Constitution or by way of a suitable amendment of the Constitution in accordance with the provisions of Art. 368 of the Constitution or both ....[75]

The SCI advised that a cession of territory required the amendment of the Constitution.[76] It did not accept the argument that article 3 of the Constitution, which deals with 'formation of new States and alteration of areas, boundaries or names of existing States', covered such a contingency. Eminent international law scholars like Rama Rao were critical of the decision and contended that 'the advisory opinion should be overruled, and that article 3 should be held as the relevant article applicable in such cases of cession'.[77] Nonetheless, the decision holds good even today. In *Maganbhai Ishwarbhai Patel v Union of India and Another* (1969), the SCI reaffirmed its earlier decision.[78] The SCI has also noted that legislative measures are required 'if the rights of citizens or others which are justiciable' are affected.[79]

3.5.3 *Courts and International Human Rights Law*

Indian courts have in a variety of cases turned to international human rights conventions to expand the ambit of rights available to Indian citizens or to fill existing gaps.[80]

[75] *Reference relating to the transfer of Berubari Union case* AIR 1960 SC 845, para 4.

[76] Ibid. para 30.

[77] Rama Rao, 'Some Constitutional Aspects of Treaty-Making Power in India' in SK Agrawala (ed), *Essays on Law of Treaties: With Special Reference to India* (Bombay 1972) 251–8.

[78] For the facts of the dispute between India and Pakistan and the decision of the tribunal see *Maganbhai Ishwarbhai Patel v Union of India* AIR 1969 SC 783, para 255.

[79] Ibid. 783: 'The Executive authority in the State cannot acquire new rights against the citizens by making treaties with foreign powers'. The position is summarized by P Chandrasekhar Rao who notes that the implementation of the following treaties calls for an amendment of the constitution or suitable legislation: treaties involving cession of territory; treaties whose implementation requires addition to, or alteration of, the existing law; and human rights covenants or other instruments. See Mani (n 1) 166 and Rao (n 1) 137–48.

[80] It may be noted that certain treaties are excluded from the purview of courts by article 363, which reads:

> Bar to interference by courts in disputes arising out of certain treaties, agreements, etc
>
> (1) Notwithstanding anything in this Constitution but subject to the provisions of Article 143, neither the Supreme Court nor any other court shall have jurisdiction in any dispute arising out

Thus, for instance, in *Vishaka and Others v State of Rajasthan and Others* (1997), a landmark case in which the problem of sexual harassment of working women was in issue, the SCI referred to the Convention on the Elimination of all forms of Discrimination against Women 1979, to which India was a party, and noted that 'gender equality includes protection from sexual harassment and right to work with dignity, which is a universally recognized basic human right'.[81] It then observed:

> In the absence of domestic law occupying the field, to formulate effective measures to check the evil of sexual harassment of working women at all workplaces, the contents of international conventions and norms are significant for the purpose of interpretation of the guarantee of gender equality, right to work and human dignity in articles 14, 15, 19(1)(g) and 21 of the Constitution and the safeguards against sexual harassment implicit therein and for the formulation of guidelines to achieve this purpose. Any international convention not inconsistent with the fundamental rights and in harmony with its spirit must be read into these provisions to enlarge the meaning and content thereof, to promote the object of the constitutional guarantee. This is implicit from article 51(c) and the enabling power of Parliament to enact laws for implementing the international conventions and norms and by virtue of article 253 read with Entry 14 of the Union List in Seventh Schedule of the Constitution.[82]

But the Court clarified, as it had done in the past, that:

> The international conventions and norms are to be read into them [i.e., into fundamental rights guaranteed in the Constitution of India] in the absence of domestic law occupying the field when there is no inconsistency between them.[83]

It then went on to reiterate:

> It is now an accepted rule of judicial construction that regard must be had to international conventions and norms for construing domestic law when there is no inconsistency between them and there is a void in the domestic law.[84]

of any provision of a treaty, agreement, covenant, engagement, sanad or other similar instrument which was entered into or executed before the commencement of this Constitution by any Ruler of an Indian State and to which the Government was a party and which has or has been continued in operation after such commencement, or in any dispute in respect of any right accruing under or any liability or obligation arising out of any of the provisions of this Constitution relating to any such treaty, agreement, covenant, engagement, sanad or other similar instrument

(2) In this article

(a) Indian State means any territory recognized before the commencement of this Constitution by His Majesty or the Government of the Dominion of India as being such a State; and

(b) Ruler includes the Prince, Chief or other person recognised before such commencement by His Majesty or the Government of the Dominion of India as the Ruler of any Indian State.

[81] *Vishaka and Others v State of Rajasthan and Others* (1997) 6 Supreme Court Cases 241 para 10.

[82] Ibid. para 7. [83] Ibid. para 14. [84] Ibid. para 14.

The Court proceeded to issue a set of binding 'Guidelines and Norms' for this purpose. Later, many of these Guidelines were incorporated into The Sexual Harassment of Women at Workplace (Prevention, Prohibition, and Redressal) Act 2013.[85]

The SCI has not hesitated to use international norms to support progressive jurisprudence. In *National Legal Services Authority v Union of India* (2014), concerning the rights of transgender people, the SCI observed that 'international conventions and norms are significant for the purpose of interpretation of gender equality'.[86] After citing a number of international human rights instruments the SCI observed that these were followed by various countries in the world 'to protect the human rights of transgender people since it has been noticed that transgenders/transsexuals often face serious human rights violations, such as harassment in workplace, hospitals, places of public conveniences, marketplaces, theatres, railway stations, bus-stands and so on'.[87] It then noted:

> Unfortunately, we have no legislation in this country dealing with the rights of [the] transgender community. Due to the absence of suitable legislation protecting the rights of the members of the transgender community, they are facing discrimination in various areas and hence the necessity to follow the international conventions to which India is a party and to give due respect to other non-binding international conventions and principles. . . . [A] constitutional court . . . is expected to safeguard those rights knowing the pulse and feeling of that community, though a minority, especially when their rights have gained universal recognition and acceptance.[88]

After referring to appropriate provisions of the Constitution of India it ruled:

> That hijras, eunuchs, apart from binary genders, be treated as 'third gender' for the purpose of safeguarding their rights under Part III of our Constitution and the laws made by Parliament and the State Legislature.
>
> Transgender persons' right to decide their self-identified gender is also upheld and the Centre and State Governments are directed to grant legal recognition of their gender identity such as male, female or as third gender.
>
> We direct the Centre and the State Governments to take steps to treat them as Socially and Educationally Backward Classes of citizens and extend all kinds of reservation in cases of admission in educational institutions and for public appointments.[89]

In *Nilabati Behera v Union of India* (1993), article 9(5) of the International Covenant on Civil and Political Rights 1966 (ICCPR) was used to support jurisprudence on compensation.[90] In *Jeeja Ghosh v Union of India* (2016), the SCI invoked the United Nations Convention on the Rights of Persons with Disabilities, which India ratified

[85] The text of the Act is at <http://www.iitbbs.ac.in/notice/sexual-harrassment-of-women-act-and-rules-2013.pdf> accessed 16 October 2017.

[86] *National Legal Services Authority v Union of India* (2014) 5 SCC 438, para 47.

[87] Ibid. [88] Ibid. [89] Ibid. 508.

[90] *Nilabati Behera v Union of India* (1993) SCR (2) 581.

in 2007, in order to address a case of discrimination against a person with a disability.[91] A final example that may be cited is *Justice KS Puttaswamy and Anor v Union of India and Ors* (2017). The SCI made references to articles 12 of the Universal Declaration of Human Rights 1948 and 17 of the ICCPR and also referred to a General Comment of the UN Human Rights Committee.[92] It also noted that 'significantly, while acceding to the ICCPR, India did not file any reservation or declaration to Article 17'.[93] It then went on to mention several earlier cases including the *Vishaka* and *NALSA* cases in which 'this Court found that the international conventions were not inconsistent with the fundamental rights guaranteed by the Constitution and must be recognized and followed'.[94]

3.5.4 *Reception of Customary International Law*

Alexandrowicz, who very early on noted that customary international law (CIL) was not an automatic part of Indian law, also observed that:

> The fact that article 51(c) of the Indian Constitution reduces the position of international law in India to a directive principle does not mean that the doors of Indian law are entirely closed to wide absorption of international customary law into Indian municipal law. Under British rule in India the English common law doctrine was observed and independent India continues to act upon the common law in many fields and has hardly changed her mind in the matters of basic principles governing the relationship between international law and municipal law.[95]

His views correctly reflect the position even today, although he would not have imagined the extent to which CIL has been incorporated in Indian law.[96] In *People's Union for Civil Liberties v Union of India* (1997), the SCI pronounced that:

> It is almost [an] accepted proposition of law that rules of customary international law which are not contrary to the municipal law shall be deemed to be incorporated in the domestic law.[97]

In *MV Elizabeth v Harwan Investment & Trading Pvt Ltd, Goa* (1993), the SCI noted that 'Indian statutes lag behind the development of international law in comparison

[91] *Jeeja Ghosh v Union of India* (1993) SCC Online SC 510 para 10.2. Excerpts from the judgment are at <https://indiankanoon.org/doc/175579179/> accessed 20 October 2017.

[92] *Justice KS Puttaswamy and Anor v Union of India* (n 73) paras 129–30.

[93] Ibid. para 130. [94] Ibid. para 132. [95] Alexandrowicz (n 58) 292.

[96] In doing so the courts have been influenced by the decision of British courts in cases such as *Trendtex Trading Corporation v Central Bank of Nigeria* [1977] 1 QB 529, wherein Lord Denning stated at 365–6:

> Seeing that the rules of international law have changed – and do change – and that the courts have given effect to the changes without any Act of Parliament, it follows to my mind inexorably that the rules of international law, as existing from time to time, do form part of our English law. It follows, too, that a decision of this court – as to what was the ruling of international law 50 or 60 years ago – is not binding on this court today. International law knows no rule of stare decisis. If this court today is satisfied that the rule of international law on a subject has changed from what it was 50 or 60 years ago, it can give effect to that change—and apply the change in our English law—without waiting for the House of Lords to do it.

[97] *People's Union for Civil Liberties v Union of India* AIR 1997 SC 568.

with contemporaneous statutes in England and other maritime countries'.[98] After listing some of the international conventions that India had not ratified, the Court observed:

> Although these conventions have not been adopted by legislation, the principles incorporated in the conventions are themselves derived from the common law of nations as embodying the felt necessities of international trade and are as such part of the common law of India and applicable for the enforcement of maritime claims against foreign ships.[99]

In his opinion, Justice Thommen wrote:

> All persons and things within the waters of a State fall within its jurisdiction unless specifically curtailed or regulated by rules of international law. The power to arrest a foreign vessel, while in the waters of a coastal State, in respect of a maritime claim, wherever arising, is a demonstrable manifestation and an essential attribute of territorial sovereignty. This power is recognized by several international conventions.... These conventions contain the unified rules of law drawn from different legal systems. Although many of these conventions have yet to be ratified by India, they embody principles of law recognized by the generality of maritime States, and can therefore be regarded as part of our common law.[100]

In this decision, the Court did not clearly distinguish between various categories of sources of international law and the ways in which these interact. The result was the usurpation of the functions of the executive and the legislature as well as the incorporation of international law into domestic law through a court decision. Mani has seen the case as 'a trail blazer in the realm of effectuation of international law through Indian municipal law'.[101] But his commendation does not sit well with his prior observation about the Court 'referring to the interface between general principles of law, treaty law and international customary law by one single sweep!'[102] The Court certainly needs to revisit this judgment.

In *Vellore Citizens Welfare Forum v Union of India and Others* (1996), Judge Kuldip Singh, writing on behalf of the majority, stated:

> We have no hesitation in holding that 'Sustainable Development' as a balancing concept between ecology and development has been accepted as a part of the Customary International Law though its salient features have yet to be finalized by the International Law jurists.[103]

He went on to observe:

> It is almost an accepted proposition of law that the rules of Customary International Law which are not contrary to the municipal law shall be deemed to have been incorporated in the domestic law and shall be followed by the Courts of Law. To

[98] *MV Elizabeth v Harwan Investment & Trading Pvt Ltd, Goa* AIR 1993 SC 1014, para 77.
[99] Ibid. [100] Ibid. para 90. [101] Mani (n 1) 173. [102] Ibid. 172.
[103] *Vellore Citizens Welfare Forum v Union of India and Others* AIR 1996 SC 2715; (1996) 5 SCC 647 para 11.

support [this view] we may refer to Justice H.R. Khanna's opinions in *A.D.M., Jabalpur v Shivakant Shukla* (AIR 1976 SC 1207), *Jolly George Varghese's case* (AIR 1980 SC 470) and *Gramophone Company's case* (AIR 1984 SC 667).[104]

The Court used this position to support its view that 'the precautionary principle and the polluter pays principle are part of the environmental law of the country'.[105]

It is interesting that a postcolonial state like India, which has good reasons for being sceptical of CIL, has been more welcoming of it than the United States. There are good and not so good reasons for this. The good reason is a liberal cosmopolitan vision that places faith in international law. The not so good reason is that the courts have lacked familiarity with the Eurocentric and imperialist history of international law and with the distinctive nature of law making in a decentralized international system. This lack of appreciation has meant a certain naivety about the international legal process.

4 India's Contribution to International Law 1947–2017

India has made a rich contribution to the evolution and development of international law in the postcolonial era. For the purposes of the present chapter, a bare reference to them will suffice. First, India has helped strengthen the international rule of law through its deep commitment to fulfilling international obligations. It has also lent sustained support to the fundamental contemporary principles of international law embodied in the Charter of the United Nations 1945 and the UN General Assembly's Declaration on Principles of International Law concerning Friendly Relations and Cooperation among States 1970.

Second, India has played a significant role in shaping the international law on decolonization. In the 1955 Bandung Asian-African Conference, in which India actively participated, the Final Communiqué declared that 'colonialism in all its manifestations is an evil which should be speedily brought to an end'.[106] In 1960, India, along with forty-one other nations, moved a Declaration on the Granting of Independence to Colonial Countries and Peoples, which was unanimously adopted by the UN General Assembly on 14 December 1960.[107] It also consistently raised its voice against the apartheid regime in South Africa and in general against all forms of discrimination. India has also lent sustained support to the cause of the Palestinian peoples.

Third, India has lent its weight in strengthening the principle of the non-use of force in international relations. The times it has used force, it has been either to free its

[104] Ibid. para 15. [105] Ibid. para 14.

[106] The text of the Bandung Communiqué is at <http://franke.uchicago.edu/Final_Communique_Bandung_1955.pdf> accessed 21 October 2017.

[107] UNGA res 1514 (XV) (1960).

territory from colonial rule (as in the instance of Goa in 1961)[108] or in self-defence (as in the case of East Pakistan in 1971).[109] India has also been a strong proponent of disarmament, including a nuclear weapons-free world. It has therefore opposed the discriminatory Nuclear Non-Proliferation Treaty 1969 and the Comprehensive Nuclear Test Ban Treaty 1969. However, it is unfortunate that it has not adopted the latest treaty on the banning of nuclear weapons.[110]

Fourth, India's commitment to the principle of peaceful settlement of disputes has been second to none. While it prefers bilateral negotiations to resolve disputes, it has also taken recourse to international tribunals.[111] British India accepted the compulsory jurisdiction of the Permanent Court of International Justice for the first time in September 1929. It subsequently revised its declaration in February 1940. After independence, India submitted a new declaration which was subsequently revised in January 1956, September 1959, and finally September 1974. It has had four judges adorn the bench of the International Court of Justice (ICJ), namely Sir Benegal Rau, Dr Nagendra Singh, Justice R S Pathak, and Justice Dalveer Bhandari. It has appeared before the ICJ in several contentious proceedings and submitted written statements in several advisory proceedings. These include the advisory proceedings in *Conditions of Admission of a State in Membership in the UN*,[112] *Reparations for Injuries*,[113] a *Constitution of the Maritime Safety Committee*,[114] *Legal Consequences for the States of the Continued Presence of South Africa in Namibia*,[115] *Legality of the Use of Nuclear Weapons*,[116] and, in one instance, an oral submission (in the *Legal Consequences for States of the Continued Presence of South Africa in Namibia*). India has also had two judges included as members of the International Tribunal for the Law of the Sea: Dr PC Rao and Ms Neeru Chadha. Finally, India has made extensive use of the

[108] RP Anand, *Development of Modern International Law and India* (Indian Society of International Law 2006) 104–7.

[109] VS Mani, 'The 1971 War on the Indian Sub-Continent and International Law' (1972) 12 Indian Journal of International Law 83.

[110] Treaty on the Prohibition of Nuclear Weapons (adopted 7 July 2017, not yet in force).

[111] As PS Rao observes, 'India's position on peaceful settlement of disputes among States through means of their free choice should not however be misconstrued as a total opposition to recourse to the International Court of Justice or recourse to arbitration': Pemmaraju Sreenivasa Rao, 'The Indian Position on Some General Principles of International Law' in Bimal Patel (ed), *India and International Law* (Leiden 2005) 33, 64.

[112] *Conditions of Admission of a State to Membership in the United Nations (Article 4 of the Charter)*, Advisory Opinion of 28 May 1948 [1948] ICJ Rep 57.

[113] *Reparation for Injuries Suffered in the Service of the United Nations*, Advisory Opinion of 11 April 1949 [1949] ICJ Rep 174.

[114] *Constitution of the Maritime Safety Committee of the Inter-Governmental Maritime Consultative Organization*, Advisory Opinion of 8 June 1960 [1960] ICJ Rep 150.

[115] *Legal Consequences for States of the Continued Presence of South Africa in Namibia (South West Africa) notwithstanding Security Council Resolution 276 (1970)*, Advisory Opinion of 21 June 1971 [1971] ICJ Rep 16.

[116] *Legality of the Threat or Use of Nuclear Weapons*, Advisory Opinion of 8 July 1996 [1996] ICJ Rep 226.

WTO dispute settlement system and has had two members elected to the WTO Appellate Body: AV Ganeshan and Ujal Singh Bhatia.

Fifth, India has tried to strengthen international institutions through urging their democratization. In his inaugural address to the Indian Society of International Law in 1960, Jawaharlal Nehru observed that 'it may be said that international organization and international law have not kept pace' with the times.[117] India has thus sought the expansion of the UN Security Council to reflect the realities of the day. It has also expressed unease with undemocratic practices such as the Security Council assuming legislative powers or imposing obligations that are part of treaties that nations have not ratified.[118] Further, it has called for greater representation of developing nations in the international financial institutions. India has also been at the forefront of injecting an element of justice into the international trading order. It has sought to reform the WTO set of agreements, such as the Agreement on Trade-Related Aspects of Intellectual Property Rights 1995 and the Agreement on Agriculture 1995.

Sixth, India has been at the forefront of the global fight against terrorism. It is party to all the major international conventions on terrorism. It also drafted, in 2000, a Comprehensive Convention on the Prevention and Suppression of International Terrorism which is unfortunately yet to be adopted.[119] India has also actively participated in the work of the Counter Terrorism Committee created by the Security Council.

Finally, India has been at the forefront of introducing elements of equity into the evolving field of international environmental law. It has also offered support to key international instruments such as the Paris Climate Change Convention 2015 even though the US walked out of it.

After surveying the position of India on 'some general principles of international law', P Sreenivasa Rao aptly concludes:

> Since independence it has actively contributed to a world order based on equity and justice for all, rich and poor or big or small nations of the world. India's abiding faith in the UN system and its commitment to achieve universal world order is widely acknowledged. Its fight against colonialism, apartheid and the preservation and protection of territorial integrity and political independence of States has clearly influenced many of the law-making resolutions of the UN.[120]

5 Conclusion

The present chapter recommends a historical approach to review the relationship between postcolonial legal systems and international law, especially that of India. While a mere positivist account may satisfy the needs of the practitioner, it fails to

[117] Jawaharlal Nehru, 'Inaugural Address at the Indian Society of International Law' (1960) 1 Indian Journal of International Law 6.

[118] Rao (n 111) 44. [119] For a brief discussion see ibid. 46–8. [120] Ibid. 64.

offer a deeper appreciation of India's engagement with international law. There are larger lessons that await a student of international law from the historical narrative. The existence of a company-state-empire complex represented by the East India Company sheds much light on the intricate relationship between commerce, sovereignty, and international law. It offers among other things critical insights on the complex and intersecting relationship between the private and the public. Further, the anomaly of British India becoming an original member of the League of Nations, GATT, and the United Nations draws attention to 'the intersection of imperialism and internationalism' that calls for deeper study and assessment.[121] The full membership of an international organization by a colonized nation reveals the variety of forms an empire can assume. Today, it has assumed the form of independent states ceding economic sovereignty to institutions like the International Monetary Fund, World Bank, and WTO.

Be that as it may, despite the fact that India was the subject of colonial oppression, it did not assume a rejectionist stance towards international law in the postcolonial era. It only sought the transformation of international law rules to reflect and manifest the aspirations of its people and more generally those of the decolonized world. At least one reason was its familiarity with the vocabulary and technology of international law. Following the seventeenth century, states in India, including native states, entered into a range of treaties with colonial powers, including the East India Company, and later with the British Crown after it assumed control in 1858.

After independence, the cosmopolitan vision of Ambedkar and Nehru, embodied in article 51 of the Constitution of India, saw much faith being placed in the United Nations and the foundational principles of contemporary international law. The underlying approach was absorbed by all segments of the Indian state. It is therefore not surprising that Indian courts, led by the SCI, assumed a positive approach to international law. They have been particularly receptive in instances when international law has helped enhance the rights of Indian citizens or facilitated the protection of the environment. However, it cannot be said that the courts have always understood the subtleties of the discourse of international law, especially the niceties related to the topic of the sources of international law.

[121] Stephen Legg, 'An International Anomaly? Sovereignty, the League of Nations and India's Princely Geographies' (2014) 43 Journal of Historical Geography 96, 99.

CHAPTER 24

PAKISTAN

AHMER BILAL SOOFI*

1 Introduction

PAKISTAN, a relatively nascent state, gained independence from British colonial rule in India on 14 August 1947. It initially comprised East and West Pakistan until the violent secession of East Pakistan as Bangladesh in 1971. Today Pakistan comprises four provinces—Punjab, Sindh, Balochistan, and Khyber Pakhtunkhwa[1]—as well as the administrative territory of Gilgit Baltistan, and all those 'States and territories as are or may be included in Pakistan, whether by accession or otherwise',[2] such as Azad Jammu and Kashmir. Administratively, Pakistan follows a federal parliamentary system of government, based on a trichotomy of power between the legislative,[3] judicial,[4] and executive organs, while, jurisprudentially, Pakistan follows the common law system, a feature it inherits from its colonial legacy.[5]

In the international arena, Pakistan was collectively recognized as a sovereign state within the community of nations by gaining membership of the United Nations (UN) on 30 September 1947, as per Resolution 108 of the UN General Assembly.[6] Pakistan is also a member of various other international and regional governmental organizations.

* The author would like to express his gratitude to Mr Ali Sultan and Mr Abeer Mustafa for their assistance with this chapter.

[1] The erstwhile Federally Administered Tribal Areas (FATA) were merged within the province of Khyber Pakhtunkhwa in 2018 via the twenty-fifth Amendment to the Constitution.

[2] Constitution of the Islamic Republic of Pakistan 1973 art. 1(2).

[3] Pakistan has a bicameral legislative structure, with the National Assembly serving as the lower house and the Senate operating as the upper house; the two houses, along with the president, are referred to as the Parliament or Majlis-e-Shoora. See Constitution of the Islamic Republic of Pakistan 1973 pt III.

[4] Pakistan's courts have a hierarchical structure, with the Supreme Court acting as the apex court. See Constitution of the Islamic Republic of Pakistan 1973 pt VII.

[5] It is interesting to note that some statutes in Pakistan date back to the period of British rule over the subcontinent. Pakistan's Civil Procedure Code, for instance, dates back to 1898.

[6] UNGA res 108 (30 September 1947).

Now enshrined in the country's Constitution of 1973 are principles of policy for the state to 'promote international peace and security, foster goodwill and friendly relations among all nations and encourage the settlement of international disputes by peaceful means'.[7]

With regards its international law obligations, Pakistan operates as a dualist state: the Rules of Business 1973 empower the Cabinet[8] to sign and ratify international treaties and agreements on behalf of the state, following which the Parliament is tasked with their incorporation via implementing legislation.[9]

This chapter presents an overview of the prevailing Pakistani perspective on various areas of legal issues, with a focus on Pakistan's contribution to international law, through state practice or otherwise. It also highlights the domestic implementation of Pakistan's international law obligations, as holistically yet as briefly as it can. It looks at the security challenges faced by Pakistan, with an emphasis on its counterterrorism efforts, especially against non-state actors, as well as its stance on intervention and interference by other states. The chapter will then look at Pakistan's nuclear regime and its position on chemical and biological weapons, before providing a snapshot of the status of human rights in Pakistan.

Next, the state's move towards sustainable development and contemporary environmental law regulations will be presented. The subsequent section will deal with Pakistan's position as a lower riparian and coastal state, after which the chapter will address the concerns Pakistan faces with the Durand Line and Gilgit Baltistan, and with the Kashmir dispute. Pakistan's portrait as a developing yet proactive country will become clearer with the following section on economic and trade law. The chapter will conclude with sections on the role of international law in Pakistan's domestic jurisprudence and an overview of Pakistan's dispute settlement history in the international arena.

2 Membership of and Contribution to International and Regional Organizations

Soon after achieving independence in August 1947, Pakistan became a member of the United Nations on 30 September that year. Subsequently, it has partaken in forty-one UN Peacekeeping missions in twenty-three countries, has been the Leading Troop Contributor since 2009, and has an established Permanent Mission to the United Nations.

[7] Constitution of the Islamic Republic of Pakistan 1973 art. 40 and preamble.

[8] The Cabinet comprises a group of Ministers chosen by the Prime Minister from amongst the members of the National Assembly. See Constitution of the Islamic Republic of Pakistan 1973 art. 91.

[9] As this implies, such implementing legislation assumes, at best, the same stature as any other act of Parliament, with the Constitution retaining its position as the supreme law of the land.

Pakistan presided over the United Nations General Assembly (UNGA) for two terms in 1962 and 1963, vis-à-vis the personhood of Sir Zafarullah Khan. It has also remained an active member of the Committees of the UNGA, serving as the main sponsor for the Resolution on the Universal Realization of the Right of Peoples to Self-determination (adopted by the Third Committee on 19 November 2016), and as the Vice-Chairperson of the Bureau of the 71st session of the Sixth Committee, adopting resolutions and decisions pertaining to the responsibility of states for internationally wrongful acts, diplomatic protection, the rule of law at national and international levels, measures to eliminate international terrorism, and several more.

It has served as a non-permanent member at the UN Security Council (UNSC) seven times between 1952 and 2013; it has remained a member of the United for Consensus Group, being a strong advocate for the group's proposal for UNSC reforms; and has participated as a non-Council member on a number of issues, including the Palestine question, terrorism, international peace and security, women in armed conflict, and youth.

With regards to the International Court of Justice (ICJ), Pakistan has served as a Judge for two terms between 1954 and 1973, as well as President of the Court from 1970 to 1973. Pakistan further passed a declaration recognizing the jurisdiction of the Court as compulsory in September 1960.

On the international level, Pakistan has been party to various UN bodies, including *inter alia* the International Criminal Tribunal for the Former Yugoslavia, the International Criminal Tribunal for Rwanda, the International Law Commission, the UN High Commission for Refugees, and the UN Office on Drugs and Crime. As part of the International Atomic Energy Agency (IAEA), Pakistan held the first-ever Nuclear Security Conference to take place outside the IAEA Headquarters. As part of the World Trade Organization (WTO), Pakistan has served as the Chairperson of its Dispute Settlement Body in 2012 and Vice-Chairman of the General Assembly Advisory Centre on WTO Law from 2006 to 2008, as well as Chairperson for various WTO Committees over the past two decades.

Regionally, Pakistan was one of the founding members of the Organization of the Islamic Conference (OIC), conducting the momentous 2nd Islamic Summit in Lahore in 1974, and hosting, amongst others, the 21st and 43rd sessions of the Islamic Conference of Foreign Ministers. Pakistan has continuously pushed for the peaceful resolution of the Kashmir dispute, enabling the passing of an OIC Resolution against Indian atrocities in the region at the 4th Summit Meeting of the OIC in 1984.

Pakistan was also one of the founding members of the South Asian Association for Regional Cooperation (SAARC), serving as its Secretary General between 1996 and 1998. Moreover, Pakistan has been responsible for organizing the 4th and the 12th SAARC Summits, and hosting various other meetings (including the 24th and 25th SAARC Council of Ministers Meetings) and conferences. The SAARC Energy Centre was established in Pakistan in 1985, and Pakistan later also served as the first President of the SAARC Chamber of Commerce and Industry in 1992.

3 Security Challenges

This section focuses on the evolution of Pakistan's counterterrorism regime, highlighting its contribution towards the shared global responsibility of eradicating terrorism.

3.1 Counterterrorism Framework

In December 2014, a terrorist attack by the *Tehrik-e-Taliban Pakistan* (TTP), a non-state actor waging war against Pakistan, claimed 141 lives, including those of 132 children, at the Army Public School (APS) in Peshawar. Pakistan has long been riddled with such terrorism,[10] having lost approximately 50,000 people to this scourge in the decade between 2003 and 2013,[11] with the APS attack being the TTP's 'deadliest in Pakistan'.[12]

In conformity with its obligations under UN Security Council Resolution 1373[13] and its progeny, Pakistan has made, and continues to make, efforts to eliminate terrorism by transnational and domestic non-state actors. Pakistan, a dualist state, has not only focused on translating these international obligations into concrete domestic legal provisions, it has also filed its country reports[14] to the UN Counter-Terrorism Committee.

Pakistan's domestic counterterrorism legislation appeared as early as 1997, in the form of the Anti-Terrorism Act (ATA). The ATA has since been amended twenty-one times through amendments and ordinances. The ATA creates a parallel court structure in the form of the Anti-Terrorism Courts to expedite terrorism cases. Through the Anti-Terrorism (Amendment) Ordinance 2002, another schedule[15] was added to the ATA, listing proscribed and suspected terrorist organizations.

Outside of the ATA, the Ministry of Interior has maintained a list[16] of proscribed/banned organizations since before the advent of Resolution 1373, which it regularly reviews and updates. This list also evidences Pakistan's adherence to its obligations under UN Security Council Resolution 1267, by separately listing the individuals and

[10] There were 17,503 terrorist attacks in Pakistan between 1 January 2001 and 16 October 2016. See Quetta Inquiry Commission, 'Terrorist Attacks in Quetta on 8 August 2016' (13 December 2016) <http://www.supremecourt.gov.pk/web/user_files/File/QuettaInquiryCommissionReport.pdf> accessed 16 December 2016.

[11] Ministry of Interior, 'National Internal Security Policy 2014–2018' 4 <https://nacta.gov.pk/wp-content/uploads/2017/08/National-Internal-Security-Policy-2014.pdf> accessed 30 April 2019.

[12] 'Pakistan Taliban: Peshawar School Attack Leaves 141 Dead' *BBC News* (London 16 December 2014) <http://www.bbc.com/news/world-asia-30491435> accessed 16 December 2016.

[13] UNSC res 1373 (28 September 2001).

[14] UNSC Counter-Terrorism Committee, 'Reports by Member States pursuant to Security Council Resolution 1373 (2001)' <http://www.un.org/en/sc/ctc/resources/1373.html> accessed 17 December 2016.

[15] Anti-Terrorism Act 1997, Fourth Schedule.

[16] Ministry of Interior, 'Proscribed Organizations List (English)' <https://nacta.gov.pk/wp-content/uploads/2019/06/Proscribed-OrganizationEng-1.pdf> accessed 27 June 2019.

entities identified by that resolution, including Al-Qaeda, the Taliban, and associates. The list also includes organizations that are under observation (including, for instance, *Jamaat-ud-Daawa*).

Pakistan has also conducted some of the largest concerted military operations against terrorist non-state actors within its borders. The most successful and recent of these,[17] Operation Zarb-e-Azb, was launched in June 2014. While these operations by the armed forces are 'not *de jure* declared . . . non-international armed conflict[s], . . . [they] *de facto* come during certain time periods very close to a situation of non-international armed conflict'.[18] The domestic legality of these counterterrorism operations may be found in article 245 of the Constitution, which states that '[t]he Armed Forces shall, under the directions of the Federal Government . . . subject to law, act in aid of civil power when called upon to do so'.[19]

In the same spirit, the Actions (in Aid of Civil Power) Regulation (AACPR) was issued by the President in 2011,[20] applicable geographically to the Federally Administered Tribal Areas (later merged within the province of Khyber Pakhtunkhwa in 2018) and the Provincially Administered Tribal Areas. The AACPR equips the state with the power to intern non-state actors waging war on the state and directs military conduct in these areas. It provides for the application of the international humanitarian law (IHL) principles of necessity, proportionality, and distinction. It creates special evidentiary requirements.

The AACPR further provides for the regulation of internment centres, also governed by the Internment Rules 2011.[21] The AACPR also creates an oversight board to review conditions in the internment centres and expressly prohibits any internee from being subjected to torture. This action taken by Pakistan draws on analogous powers under IHL,[22] for 'internment as a regime is permissible under article 78 of the Geneva Convention IV of 1949'[23] in the different context of occupation in international armed conflict. Following debate about the legal regulation of detention in non-international armed conflict, '"internment" as a possible legal solution to incapacitate internal security threats has gained acceptability among scholars of IHL as well',[24]

[17] Previous operations include Operation Black Thunderstorm in April 2009 (sub-operation Rah-e-Rast was in May 2009) and Operation Rah-e-Nijaat in June 2009.

[18] Ahmer Bilal Soofi, 'Law of Armed Conflict as Applicable to Pakistan' in Brig Aamir Mirza, Col Ahmed Saeed Jan, and Lt Col Muhammad Qaddafi (eds), *Pakistan Army Green Book 2014* (Crystal Printers 2014) 87.

[19] Constitution of the Islamic Republic of Pakistan 1973 art. 245.

[20] This, too, was enacted under the purview of the powers under art. 245 of the Constitution of the Islamic Republic of Pakistan 1973.

[21] For an overview of the framework of preventive detention in Pakistan, see Maira Sheikh and Moghees Uddin Khan, *Preventive Detention: A Guide to Pakistan* (RSIL 2016) 16 (Figure 2).

[22] UNSC res 1546 (8 June 2004).

[23] Convention (IV) relative to the Protection of Civilian Persons in Time of War (adopted 12 August 1949, entered into force 21 October 1950, 75 UNTS 28) 7.

[24] Ahmer Bilal Soofi, 'Legal Challenges to Military Operations in Pakistan' in Moeed Yusuf (ed), *Pakistan's Counterterrorism Challenge* (Georgetown University Press 2014) 127, 147.

although debate continues on this issue. Internment in non-international conflict also remains governed by the state's international human rights obligations.

Chronologically, around the same time as Operation Zarb-e-Azb, in July 2014, the Parliament enacted the Protection of Pakistan Act 2014 (PPA). The PPA established new legal classifications such as 'militant' and 'enemy alien'. Further, special courts were established under the PPA for prosecution of the accused through *in-camera* trials with a wide range of powers given to military and law enforcement officials. The law attracted some criticism on account of Pakistan's international human rights obligations,[25] and eventually lapsed in July 2016 by virtue of a sunset provision.

The immediate consequence of the barbaric APS attack, though, was the emergence of the National Action Plan in January 2015, formulated as per the suggestions put forward by the country's political leadership at an All Parties Conference. As part of its twenty-point manifesto, the plan calls for strengthening the criminal justice system, abolishing the moratorium on the death penalty for terrorist cases, creating special military trial courts, and curbing financial flows to terrorists and terrorist organizations.[26]

The military courts were subsequently created under the 21st Constitutional Amendment and the Pakistan Army (Amendment) Act 1952. Once the time period stipulated for these courts lapsed in January 2017 owing to a sunset clause in the amendments, they were reinstated through the 23rd Constitutional Amendment and the Pakistan Army (Amendment) Act 2017, which also lapsed in March 2019.[27] The scope of cases to be tried under these courts was fairly restrictive, given that the operative definition of terrorism was constricted in comparison to that under the ATA. Prima facie, these courts are considered to be draconian in nature and deemed to be in violation of Pakistan's obligations under the International Covenant on Civil and Political Rights 1966 (ICCPR).

However, attention must be drawn to the UN Human Rights Committee's General Comment No. 32 on article 14 of the ICCPR,[28] which explicitly allows for the trial of civilians under military courts in special circumstances where it is absolutely necessary and regular civilian courts are unable to undertake the trials. It is also critical to note that these military courts were always created with a sunset provision. The Supreme Court of Pakistan also validated their formation in an eleven-to-six vote. The Court's reasoning revolved around the equation of terrorism by non-state actors in Pakistan to

[25] Human Rights Watch, 'Pakistan: Withdraw Repressive Counterterrorism Law', 3 July 2014 <http://www.hrw.org/news/2014/07/03/pakistan-withdraw-repressive-counterterrorism-law> accessed 7 January 2018.

[26] National Counter-Terrorism Authority Pakistan, '20 Points of National Action Plan' <https://nacta.gov.pk/nap-2014/> accessed 12 December 2018.

[27] Amir Wasim, 'Military courts cease to function today' *Dawn News* (31 March 2019) <https://www.dawn.com/news/1472947> accessed 30 April 2019.

[28] UN Human Rights Committee, General Comment No 32 on article 14 of the ICCPR (23 August 2007) UN Doc CCPR/C/GC/32 para 22.

an armed conflict. Tellingly, Justice Umar Ata Bandial, in his opinion, drew on the rules applicable to international armed conflicts between states to argue that:

> The terrorist militants operating in the country . . . do not have a unified command, nor do they wear an identifiable uniform or distinctive sign in order to be recognized; they operate by resort to subterfuge, perfidy and disguise without regard to the rules governing war. The said elements and characteristics make the case of terrorist militancy more sinister than enemy State combatants who abide [by] the aforementioned international norms. The treatment of belligerent citizen[s] and unlawful combatants in custody who have waged war against the State is not just a matter of municipal law. The subject also attracts the principles of public international law on armed conflict and war.[29]

In a similar vein, section 121 of the Pakistan Penal Code criminalizes the act of waging war, attempting to wage war, or abetting the waging of war against the state.[30] Additionally, article 256 of the Constitution states that '[n]o private organization capable of functioning as a military organization shall be formed, and any such organization shall be illegal'.[31] These laws cater to non-state actors such as the TTP[32] who unlawfully bear arms against the state.

To give further effect to its obligations under Resolution 1373 with respect to countering the financing of terrorism, Pakistan relies on the periodically updated and amended Anti-Money Laundering Act 2010.[33] More so, great reliance is based on sections of the ATA itself, wherein not only is the federal government empowered to seize or freeze the assets of a proscribed organization, but banks and other private entities are prohibited from providing financial support to members of the same.[34] In 2015, three years after the Financial Action Task Force had placed Pakistan on its 'grey list' of high risk and non-cooperative jurisdictions, it 'removed Pakistan from [the same] . . . owing to its improvement in combating the twin menaces of money laundering and terrorist financing'.[35]

Pakistan also enacted the Investigation for Fair Trial Act in 2012, which provides it with a 'legal framework to track or intercept the planning or plotting of terrorist acts'[36]

[29] *District Bar Association, Rawalpindi v Federation of Pakistan* PLD 2015 SC 401, 835.

[30] Pakistan Penal Code (XLV) 1860 s 121.

[31] Constitution of the Islamic Republic of Pakistan 1973 art. 256.

[32] UNSC, 'List established and maintained Pursuant to Security Council Res 1267/1989/2253' <https://scsanctions.un.org/fop/fop?xml=htdocs/resources/xml/en/consolidated.xml&xslt=htdocs/resources/xsl/en/al-qaida.xsl> accessed 22 December 2016.

[33] For full text, see Anti-Money Laundering Act 2010 <http://fmu.gov.pk/docs/laws/Anti-Money%20Laundering%20Act%202010-As%20amended%20upto%20February%202016.pdf> accessed 23 January 2017.

[34] For a detailed analysis of these provisions, see Research Society of International Law, 'The Case for Change: A Review of Pakistan's Anti-Terrorism Act of 1997' (September 2013) 187–93.

[35] Mubarak Zeb Khan, 'FATF Removes Pakistan from List of Terror Financiers' *Dawn News* (Islamabad 28 February 2015) <http://www.dawn.com/news/1166306> accessed 23 January 2017.

[36] Ali Sultan, 'Investigating Terror', Riphah Information Portal <http://iportal.riphah.edu.pk/wp-content/uploads/data/12/11/281112it.pdf> accessed 23 January 2017.

and to pre-empt and prevent their occurrence. The Act 'finely balances civil liberties and national security imperatives by providing necessary procedural safeguards... under extensive judicial screening and oversight'.[37]

3.2 Law of Non-intervention

3.2.1 *US Drone Strikes*

The United States first launched a drone strike in Pakistan in 2004, extending its military operations from neighbouring Afghanistan. Between then and May 2016, there were 424 drone strikes resulting in over 2,500 deaths,[38] with another five strikes taking place in 2017.[39] The collateral damage that these strikes have caused and the modes of targeting employed by the US have been highlighted by various sources as stark violations of the international law of armed conflict.[40]

Pakistan, as stated in a UN Special Rapporteur's report, 'adopts the... position... that drone strikes on its territory are counterproductive, contrary to international law, a violation of Pakistani sovereignty and territorial integrity and should cease immediately'.[41] The US controversially purports to justify these strikes in self-defence where the host state is 'unwilling or unable' to suppress a non-state actor. The place of this test under international law is still disputed, including its status as customary international law. The 'unwilling or unable' test is a loose test, where there are no objective determinants in place to assess the willingness or ability of the territorial state, and Gareth Williams notes that 'the substantive indeterminacy of the test undermines *opinio juris*'.[42]

Pakistan, moreover, 'has become a persistent objector to the drone strikes'.[43] So while it is 'more apt to characterise the test as an emerging norm',[44] it would still not apply upon Pakistan's territory if it crystallizes into customary law.

Pakistan's judiciary was seized of this matter in *Foundation for Fundamental Rights v Federation of Pakistan*, whereby the Peshawar High Court, referring to the UN Charter

[37] Ibid.

[38] Waqar Muhammad Khan, 'US Drone Strikes in Pakistan see 631pc increase under Obama' *Dawn News* (Islamabad 27 May 2016) <http://www.dawn.com/news/1260840> accessed 3 January 2017.

[39] Bureau of Investigative Journalism, 'Pakistan: Reported US Strikes 2017' <http://www.thebureauinvestigates.com/drone-war/data/pakistan-covert-us-reported-actions-2017> accessed 7 January 2018.

[40] See International Human Rights and Conflict Resolution Clinic of Stanford Law School (and Global Justice Clinic at New York University School of Law, 'Living under Drones: Death, Injury and Trauma to Civilians from US Drone Practices in Pakistan' (September 2012) <http://law.stanford.edu/wp-content/uploads/sites/default/files/organization/149662/doc/slspublic/Stanford-NYU-LIVING-UNDER-DRONES.pdf> accessed 23 January 2017.

[41] UNGA, 'Report of the Special Rapporteur on the Promotion and Protection of Human Rights and Fundamental Freedoms while Countering Terrorism' (18 September 2013) 68th Session UN Doc A/68/389.

[42] Gareth Williams, 'Piercing the Shield of Sovereignty: An Assessment of the Legal Status of the "Unwilling or Unable" Test' [2013] 36 UNSW Law Journal 619, 632.

[43] Mumtaz Zahra Baloch, 'Implications of the Use of Drones on the Notion of State Sovereignty' (2016) Islamabad Papers No. 27/2016 ISSI 38.

[44] Williams (n 42) 620.

and the Geneva Conventions 1949, declared that drone strikes were 'absolutely illegal and [a] blatant violation of the Sovereignty of the State of Pakistan because frequent intrusion is made on its territory/airspace without its consent'.[45] Further, the Court held that:

> no State can choose and hit its enemy, hiding in another State, unless the latter State consents to it in writing and with mutual collaboration the same is carried out but strictly under the sanction of UN Security Council which is not granted to the US Authorities including CIA.[46]

Building upon these principles, the Court additionally stated that:

> the peoples of Pakistan have every right to ask the security forces either to prevent such strikes by force or to shoot down the intruding drones because this right is conferred upon the Member State, aggressed upon, to defend itself, its people and territory against foreign aggression ...[47]

Importantly, in 2014, along with ten other states, Pakistan sponsored a resolution in the UN Human Rights Council, article 1 of which states that the Council:

> [u]rges all States to ensure that any measures employed to counter terrorism, including the use of remotely piloted aircraft or armed drones, comply with their obligations under international law, including the Charter of the United Nations, international human rights law and international humanitarian law, in particular the principles of precaution, distinction and proportionality.[48]

3.2.2 *US Raid on Osama Bin Laden*

Though the action[49] taken by the US proved successful in taking out the leader of Al-Qaeda, the manner in which it was conducted, especially by keeping Pakistan's authorities in the dark and not seeking their prior authorization, constituted a direct violation of Pakistan's sovereignty and territorial integrity. Another arguable legal constraint on the US was that the Security Council was seized of the matter under Resolution 1267 and several others. The UN Charter (article 51) effectively discourages unilateral actions when the Security Council is seized of the matter.[50] Pakistan's Ministry of Foreign Affairs issued the following statement:

[45] *Foundation for Fundamental Rights v Federation of Pakistan* PLD 2013 Pesh 94, para 22(ii).

[46] Ibid. para 19. [47] Ibid. para 17.

[48] UN Human Rights Council, 'Ensuring Use of Remotely Piloted Aircraft or Armed drones in Counter-Terrorism and Military Operations in Accordance with International Law, Including International Human Rights and Humanitarian Law' (24 March 2014) UN Doc A/HRC/25/L.32.

[49] In 2011, members of US Seal Team 6, through a covert operation named Geronimo, entered Pakistan's territory using stealth helicopters, dropped down on a compound in Abbottabad, and shot and killed Osama bin Laden.

[50] Ahmer Bilal Soofi, 'US Intervention: Was it Legal?' *Dawn News* (Islamabad 7 May 2011) <http://www.dawn.com/news/626953/us-intervention-was-it-legal> accessed 27 December 2016.

> This event of unauthorized unilateral action cannot be taken as a rule. The Government of Pakistan further affirms that such an event shall not serve as a future precedent for any state, including the US. Such actions undermine cooperation and may also sometime constitute threat to international peace and security. Pakistan, being mindful of its international obligations, has been extending full and proper cooperation on all counter terrorism efforts including exchange of information and intelligence. Pursuant to such cooperation, Pakistan had arrested several high profile terrorists.[51]

In June 2011, the Government formed a five-member commission (termed the Abbottabad Commission) to investigate the raid on Osama Bin Laden.[52] The report drafted by this Commission remains confidential. However, one of the three drafts of the report was leaked in 2013. From perusing this draft, it can be gleaned that the Abbottabad Commission relied upon expert evidence (including legal)[53] as part of its investigation into the raid.

3.2.3 *Indian Intervention*

The long-running territorial dispute between Pakistan and India over Kashmir, in north-east Pakistan, is discussed further in section 9.2. For present purposes, in the later half of 2016, Indian forces began what the Indian media termed 'surgical strikes' on the Line of Control (LoC) between India and Pakistan in Kashmir. These skirmishes have since been ongoing, with India attempting to justify them under the law of reprisal. India's primary claim—that recent terrorist attacks in India (in Mumbai, Pathankot, Uri, and Pulwama) were carried out by Pakistan—demonstrates an error on its behalf in fully comprehending this principle.

While some of these attacks were carried out by non-state actors, who happened to be nationals of Pakistan, it must be understood that mere nationality is not the basis of state responsibility under international law. India's response accordingly ignored its international law commitments of non-interference and non-use of force, enshrined in the UN Charter and the Simla Agreement 1972 between India and Pakistan. Furthermore, India is under an obligation to report any LoC violations to the UN Military Observer Group in India and Pakistan (UNMOGIP), formed under Security Council Resolutions 39 and 47 of 1948,[54] for the purpose of monitoring the observance of the ceasefire agreement and reporting to the UN Secretary-General.[55]

[51] Ministry of Foreign Affairs, Government of Pakistan, 'Death of Osama bin Ladin—Respect for Pakistan's Established Policy Parameters on Counter Terrorism' (Press Release 3 May 2011) <http://www.mofa.gov.pk/pr-details.php?mm=OTk1> accessed 3 January 2017.

[52] 'Abbottabad Incident Gilani forms Commission' *The News* (Islamabad 1 June 2011) <http://www.thenews.com.pk/archive/print/614204-abbottabad-incident-gilani-forms-commission> accessed 3 January 2017.

[53] Abbottabad Commission, 'Al-Jazeera Bin Laden Dossier' (Report) (4 January 2013) ch 28 <https://assets.documentcloud.org/documents/724833/aljazeera-bin-laden-dossier.pdf> accessed 3 January 2017.

[54] UNSC res 39 (20 January 1948); UNSC res 47 (21 April 1948).

[55] UNMOGIP, 'UNMOGIP Mandate' <https://unmogip.unmissions.org/mandate> accessed 30 April 2019.

Conversely, though, in March 2016, Pakistan's law enforcement agencies arrested an agent of the Research and Analysis Wing (RAW), India's foreign intelligence agency, in Balochistan, a province in south-west Pakistan. It was discovered, through his confession, that he had 'promoted the criminal mindset that was there in Balochistan ... [and] supported the individuals who worked to destabilize Pakistan',[56] while also acknowledging that 'RAW is involved in some activities related to the Baloch liberation movement within Pakistan and the region around it'.[57] This was also recognized by a report of the Senate of Pakistan.[58] At the international level, Pakistan's position on this issue has been documented in a dossier handed to the UN Secretary-General.[59] India approached the ICJ in May 2017, asserting a denial of consular access by Pakistan under the Vienna Convention on Consular Relations 1963;[60] Pakistan is contesting the case on both jurisdiction and merits.[61]

4 Nuclear Law

The last few decades have witnessed an enormous growth and development in international nuclear law relating to nuclear energy and nuclear weapons. In response, there has also been a commensurate legal, regulatory, and administrative evolution of Pakistan's domestic nuclear law to give effect to the state's international obligations. In consequence, Pakistan today is recognized by the global community as a responsible nuclear weapons state.

4.1 Safeguard Agreements

In order to benefit from the peaceful use of nuclear energy, Pakistan has sought assistance from the US, Canada, France, and China through a legal framework comprising tripartite contracts and safeguard agreements with the IAEA.

[56] Muhammad Anis and Mumtaz Alvi, 'Indian spy confesses to terror acts in Karachi, Gwadar' *The News* (30 March 2016) <https://www.thenews.com.pk/print/109016-Indian-spy-confesses-to-terror-acts-in-Karachi-Gwadar> accessed 30 April 2019.

[57] APP, 'Transcript of RAW Agent Kulbushan's Confessional Statement' *Dawn News* (Islamabad, 30 March 2016) <http://www.dawn.com/news/1248786> accessed 27 December 2016.

[58] Senate of Pakistan, 'Policy Guidelines in View of the Latest Situation Developing between India and Pakistan' (October 2016) <http://www.senate.gov.pk/1web/whole/whole07.pdf> accessed 30 April 2019.

[59] 'UN Chief Agrees to Play Role of Honest Broker: Maleeha' *Daily Times* (New York, 8 January 2017) <http://dailytimes.com.pk/pakistan/08-Jan-17/un-chief-agrees-to-play-role-of-honest-broker-maleeha> accessed 23 January 2017.

[60] *Jadhav (India v Pakistan)*, Application Instituting Proceedings, ICJ Registry, 8 May 2017 <http://www.icj-cij.org/files/case-related/168/168-20170508-APP-01-00-EN.pdf> accessed 5 April 2018.

[61] See *Jadhav (India v Pakistan)*, Press release on the conclusion of the public hearings, ICJ Registry, 21 February 2019 <https://www.icj-cij.org/files/case-related/168/168-20190221-PRE-01-00-EN.pdf> accessed 30 April 2019.

To domestically implement these binding international agreements, Pakistan has enacted the Pakistan Atomic Energy Commission (PAEC) Ordinance 1965 and the Pakistan Nuclear Regulatory Authority (PNRA) Ordinance 2001. Significantly, these create a relationship between the PNRA as licensor and the PAEC as licensee for specific nuclear projects and their sites. The PNRA Ordinance, in section 19(1)(a), prohibits unlicensed persons or entities from the manufacture, production, acquisition, or development of nuclear material. It also mandates, through sections 51 and 52, reliability checks of personnel to ensure that each nuclear installation has qualified and trained personnel.

PNRA, with the IAEA's cooperation in capacity-building, has also successfully implemented the Nuclear Security Action Plan approved by the Government of Pakistan in 2006. In implementing the plan, PNRA formulated and updated its existing regulations in line with IAEA standards.[62]

4.2 Non-proliferation Treaties

Despite the embargo placed on all other states, the Treaty on the Non-Proliferation of Nuclear Weapons 1970 (NPT) was nevertheless signed and ratified by several other states and today has acquired almost universal membership with 191 parties.[63] Pakistan, however, viewed the NPT as discriminatory and, despite pressure, decided not to sign it. India and Israel also adopted similar positions. Pakistan has also not participated in any NPT-related conferences.

4.3 Export Control Regimes

The Nuclear Suppliers Group (NSG) issues a dual-list of export equipment and the London Suppliers Group issues the Zangger Trigger list. Accordingly, Pakistan has developed its own export-control legal regime, and domestic export controls have been introduced.[64] These lists are updated from time to time in line with the latest NSG and Zangger Trigger lists. Dual-use items have been placed on a watch list. Knowledge of these lists is essential for Pakistan's importers and exporters, who often invite sanctions

[62] IAEA, 'The Physical Protection of Nuclear Material and Nuclear Facilities', INFCIRC/225.

[63] For Status of NPT State Parties, see United Nations Office for Disarmament Affairs, 'Treaty Database Home: Treaty on the Non-Proliferation of Nuclear Weapons' <http://disarmament.un.org/treaties/t/npt> accessed 23 January 2017.

[64] See generally Export Control on Goods, Technologies, Material and Equipment related to Nuclear and Biological Weapons and Their Delivery Systems Act 2004 <http://www.secdiv.gov.pk/uploads/Doc-1%20Export%20Control%20Act-2004-0c0c.pdf> accessed 30 April 2019; Export Control (Licensing and Enforcement) Rules 2009 <http://www.secdiv.gov.pk/uploads/Doc-3,Licensing%20&%20Enforcement%20Rules-8763.pdf> accessed 30 April 2019.

due to lack of such knowledge. Pakistan's customs officials have been specially trained to enforce these controls.

Pakistan's national nuclear legal framework includes legislation, procedures, measures, and agencies to control border crossings and the export/import and other transfers of nuclear materials. The Customs Act 1969 generally prohibits and restricts the importation and exportation of nuclear materials. Brokering, trading, negotiating, and otherwise assisting in the sale of nuclear goods and technology is extensively controlled by specific legislation: the Export Control on Goods, Technologies, Material and Equipment related to Nuclear and Biological Weapons and their Delivery Systems Act 2004 ('Export Control Act 2004').

Significantly, pursuant to the Export Control Act 2004, an export control authority, namely the Strategic Export Control Division (SECDIV), was established in the Ministry of Foreign Affairs. It serves as an inter-agency mechanism for the institutionalized implementation of export control policy, in line with legislative requirements and the formulation of rules and regulations on the export of controlled items.

4.4 UN Security Council Resolution 1540 (2004)

An especially turbulent development for Pakistan was the episode involving a senior Pakistan nuclear scientist, Dr Abdul Qadeer Khan, who was allegedly implicated in unauthorized nuclear proliferation involving other countries. Pakistan faced serious embarrassment at a global level given the allegations of loose controls over the individuals and materials involved in its nuclear programme. It was portrayed as an irresponsible state. The Security Council deliberated on the episode for several sessions and construed it as a grave threat to international peace and security, eventually adopting Resolution 1540 in 2004.[65]

A milestone in the development of nuclear law, this Resolution, passed under Chapter VII of the UN Charter, legally obliges Pakistan and all other UN member states to refrain from supporting non-state actors from developing, acquiring, manufacturing, possessing, transporting, transferring, or using nuclear, chemical, or biological weapons and their delivery systems. Resolution 1540 further includes a mechanism for implementing a follow-up process and establishes a Committee for non-proliferation.[66]

Thus far, to the complete approval and satisfaction of the 1540 Committee as well as independent think tanks, in 2004 Pakistan submitted to the 1540 Committee its national report on the legislative, regulatory, and administrative framework, demonstrating its compliance with its obligations. A further comprehensive report was transmitted to the Committee in 2005. Pakistan has also periodically updated the Committee about additional steps taken to further strengthen controls.

[65] UNSC res 1540 (28 April 2004).

[66] Committee established pursuant to UNSC res 1673 (27 April 2006).

The Nuclear Terrorism Convention supplements the Convention on the Physical Protection of Nuclear Material 1979 (CPPNM), acceded to by Pakistan in 2000, which provides for certain levels of physical transportation during the international transport of nuclear material. It also establishes a general framework for cooperation among states in the protection, recovery, and return of stolen nuclear material. The CPPNM further lists certain serious offences involving nuclear material which state parties are obligated to make punishable and for which offenders shall be subject to a system of extradition or submission for prosecution. In 2016 Pakistan ratified the Amendment to the CPPNM and is now, therefore, a party to the Convention on the Physical Protection of Nuclear Material and Facilities 2016.

In 2007, the National Command Authority Ordinance was promulgated to provide enhanced legal coverage of security and safety measures on all matters concerning nuclear and space technologies, nuclear establishments, nuclear systems, nuclear materials, and relevant personnel and information. It was reissued in 2009 and later adopted by the Parliament as the National Command Authority Act 2010 (NCA Act), to demonstrate that Pakistan has full and complete legal powers over all aspects of its nuclear programme, including sites, materials, and employees.

To deter any attempt at proliferation, the NCA Act contains a special provision creating proliferation as an offence[67] and also provides a detailed prosecution mechanism. The NCA Act, moreover, permits the NCA to adopt any existing law with respect to any of its employees or operational aspects. This crucially permits the NCA greater flexibility while providing a framework for the implementation of its decisions.

5 Chemical and Biological Weapons

Pakistan has consistently spoken in favour of chemical weapons controls. It ratified the Chemical Weapons Convention 1993 (CWC), and is a member in good standing of the Organization for the Prohibition of Chemical Weapons (OPCW). Pakistan continues to play an active role in the OPCW, supporting provisions to increase trade and assistance in the peaceful uses of the chemical industry as consistent with the positions of the Non-Aligned Movement.

In 2000, Islamabad promulgated the Chemical Weapons Convention Implementation Ordinance to prohibit the development, production, and use of chemical weapons in accordance with its CWC obligations. The law also criminalizes the unauthorized transport or transfer of chemical weapons or toxic dual-use chemicals and chemical agent precursors. The OPCW has conducted a number of inspections of industrial facilities in Pakistan engaged in the production of CWC-scheduled chemicals and none of these found any irregularities. Moreover, in 2010 Pakistan released the Chemical Weapons Convention (Implementation) Rules, which established requirements for all

[67] National Command Authority Act 2010 s 12.

companies dealing with CWC-scheduled chemicals to make declarations, obtain permits, and receive inspections.

Pakistan ratified the Biological and Toxin Weapons Convention (BTWC) in 1974. During BTWC Review Conferences, Pakistan has urged more robust participation from state parties, invited new states to join the treaty, and argued in favour of guaranteeing states' rights to engage in peaceful scientific exchanges of biological and toxin materials.

Pakistan has also streamlined its domestic legislation to implement its BTWC obligations, as detailed in its reports pursuant to Resolution 1540. Since the mid 2000s, Pakistan has increased regulation of the biological industry, issuing biosafety rules in 2005 which established a National Biosafety Committee to create guidelines, issue export licences, and inspect facilities dealing with 'living modified organism[s] or genetically modified organisms'. Pakistan has also taken measures to improve its WMD-relevant export controls. As discussed earlier, in 2004 Pakistan passed the Export Control Act and created the SECDIV to regulate exports of biological, nuclear, and missile-related products. An updated control list, released in 2011, brought Pakistan's biological export controls in line with those of the Australia Group.

6 Human Rights

Fundamental human rights for the citizens of Pakistan are enshrined in the 1973 Constitution,[68] which creates an obligation upon the legislature to protect these rights, such that any law (existing or being drafted) in contravention of these rights will be declared void.[69] Pakistan also generously hosts approximately 1.6 million registered Afghan refugees, even after the return of 5.2 million refugees to Afghanistan since 2002.[70]

Pakistan has ratified most of the major human rights treaties, including the International Convention on the Elimination of All Forms of Racial Discrimination 1965 in 1966; the Convention on the Rights of the Child 1989 in 1990; the Convention on the Elimination of All Forms of Discrimination against Women 1979 in 1996; the International Covenant on Economic, Social and Cultural Rights 1966 in 2008; the ICCPR 1966 and the Convention against Torture 1984 in 2010; and the Convention on the Rights of Persons with Disabilities 2006 in 2011.

Pakistan has made efforts to harmonize its domestic legislation with its international human rights obligations, as well to institutionalize the frameworks for human rights protection. For instance, in 2012 Pakistan established the National Commission on the

[68] Constitution of the Islamic Republic of Pakistan 1973 ch 1.

[69] Constitution of the Islamic Republic of Pakistan 1973 art. 8.

[70] '1.6 million Afghan refugees still in Pakistan' *The News* (30 June 2017) <http://www.thenews.com.pk/latest/213557-16-million-Afghan-refugees-still-in-Pakistan> accessed 7 January 2018.

Status of Women[71] to help safeguard women's rights, as well as the National Commission for Human Rights.[72] As discussed earlier, Pakistan has also been cognizant of human rights protections in the fight against terrorist non-state actors, including in the drafting of relevant laws and the creation of protective mechanisms.

However, the full implementation of Pakistan's obligations is a work in progress and there are still areas in which the state may wish to place a greater focus. In July 2017, the UN Human Rights Committee, in its Concluding Observations on Pakistan, appreciated Pakistan's ongoing efforts to advance human rights, and encouraged Pakistan to further enhance human rights protections with respect to, *inter alia*, violence against women, abortion, sexuality-based discrimination, and child marriages.[73]

7 Environmental Law and Sustainable Development

Pakistan has been a party to multiple conventions and resolutions on environmental protection and climate change, and has implemented these obligations in its domestic legislation.[74] For instance, Pakistan became a party to the Ramsar Convention in 1976 and 'currently has 19 sites designated as Wetlands of International Importance (Ramsar Sites), with a surface area of 1,343,807 hectares'.[75] Additionally, Pakistan has filed country reports under the Convention on Biological Diversity 1992.[76]

Pakistan also became a party to the Paris Agreement 2016. At the Opening Plenary of the 21st Conference of Parties on the occasion of the drafting of the Paris Agreement, Pakistan's Minister for Climate Change, His Excellency Zahid Hamid, expressed full support for the process and stated that 'we will successfully realize expectations for a comprehensive Paris Agreement which will put in place a globally responsive climate governance framework'.[77]

[71] Established under National Commission on the Status of Women Act 2012.

[72] Established under National Commission for Human Rights Act 2012.

[73] UN Human Rights Committee, Concluding Observations on Pakistan (23 August 2017) CCPR/C/PAK/CO/1 paras 9–48.

[74] For an idea of the domestic legislation present in Pakistan, see Ramsar Country Report for Pakistan, 'National Report on the Implementation of the Ramsar Convention on Wetlands' (2015) 10 <http://www.ramsar.org/sites/default/files/documents/2014/national-reports/COP12/cop12_nr_pakistan.pdf> accessed 1 January 2017.

[75] 'Ramsar Country Profile: Pakistan' <http://www.ramsar.org/wetland/pakistan> accessed 1 January 2017.

[76] For Pakistan's Country Reports under the CBD, see Convention on Biological Diversity, 'National Reports and NBSAPs' <http://www.cbd.int/reports/search/?country=pk> accessed 3 January 2017.

[77] Ministry of Climate Change, 'Statement by Minister for Climate Change, Government of Pakistan, in the Opening Plenary of COP-21' (30 November–11 December 2015) <http://mocc.gov.pk/moclc/userfiles1/file/Statement%20by%20Minister%20for%20Climate%20Change%20Government%20of%20Pakistan%20in%20opening%20Plenary%20of%20COP-21.pdf> accessed 30 April 2019.

In the wake of the Paris Agreement, Pakistan domestically enacted the Pakistan Climate Change Act 2016, to which the Paris Agreement (along with other such international environmental agreements) forms part of the Schedule. The Act empowers the federal government to 'make rules for carrying out the purposes of this Act, including rules for implementing the provisions of the International Agreements relating to climate change, specified in the Schedule to this Act'.[78]

In parallel, cognizant of the global transition from the Millennium Development Goals 2000–15 to the Sustainable Development Goals 2016–30, Pakistan adjusted its focus for the near future. While Pakistan faces many challenges, being ranked 147th of 188 countries in the UN's 2015 Human Development Index, the Ministry of Planning and Development has launched a comprehensive document titled 'Vision 2025', comprising seven main pillars for Pakistan's growth and development, with an aim to achieve these goals by the year 2025.

8 Water Law

8.1 Law of the Sea

Pakistan signed the UN Convention on the Law of the Sea 1982 (UNCLOS) when it was opened for signature in 1994 and ratified it in 1997. It also filed a declaration affirming that transit to a landlocked state under article 125 shall not infringe the sovereignty of the transit state, and that consequently the content of the freedom of transit must be agreed between the two states; in the absence of agreement, transit through Pakistan is to be exclusively regulated by Pakistan's law.[79] Separately, Pakistan lodged an understanding that UNCLOS does not authorize foreign military exercises in the exclusive economic zones (EEZs) or continental shelf without the consent of the coastal state.

In 2009, Pakistan applied to the UN Commission on the Limit of the Continental Shelf (CLCS) for the extension of its continental shelf from 200 nautical miles (nm) to 350 nm. The CLCS affirmed Pakistan's submission[80] in its opinion published in 2015.[81]

[78] Pakistan Climate Change Act 2016, s 17.

[79] For full text of the Declaration, see UN Division for Oceans and Law of the Sea, 'Declarations and Statements', Pakistan <http://www.un.org/depts/los/convention_agreements/convention_declarations.htm#Pakistan%20Upon%20ratification> accessed 3 January 2017.

[80] Pakistan, 'Submission by the Government of the Islamic Republic of Pakistan for Establishment of the Outer Limits of the Continental Shelf of Pakistan' (Executive Summary) (2009) 8 <http://www.un.org/depts/los/clcs_new/submissions_files/pak29_09/pak2009executivesummary.pdf> accessed 23 January 2017.

[81] CLCS, 'Summary of Recommendations of the Commission on the Limits of the Continental Shelf in regard to the Submission made by the Islamic Republic of Pakistan on 30 April 2009' (13 March 2015) <https://www.un.org/depts/los/clcs_new/submissions_files/pak29_09/2015_03_13_SC_PAK.pdf> accessed 30 April 2019.

Though this helped delimit Pakistan's maritime boundary with regards to Oman and Iran, the maritime boundary delimitation with India, over Sir Creek, remains disputed.

In November 2016, and again in March 2019, Pakistan turned away an Indian submarine that had tried to enter Pakistan's territorial waters.[82] It has also been facing issues of illegal, unreported, and unregulated fishing by Indian fishermen in its EEZ, such that '600 Indian vessels entered Pakistani waters for fishing illegally every month while the revenue loss of four-month of illegal Indian fishing had been estimated to be around [Pakistan rupees] Rs8bn'.[83]

8.2 Law of Transboundary Watercourses

Pakistan acts as the lower riparian state in relation to India with regards the Indus River system. In 1960, through the good offices of the World Bank, Pakistan and India drafted and signed the Indus Waters Treaty for 'fixing and delimiting, in a spirit of goodwill and friendship, the rights and obligations of each in relation to the other concerning the use of these waters'.[84] The treaty, comprising twelve articles and eight annexures, has survived tumultuous times between the two neighbouring states and is widely hailed as a confidence-building measure between them.

Despite recent political statements by Indian Prime Minister Modi, there is no provision under the Indus Waters Treaty to unilaterally terminate or revoke it.[85] Mr Sartaj Aziz, foreign policy adviser to the Pakistani Prime Minister, stated that '[i]f India tries to interrupt water flow into Pakistan, it will not only violate the Indus Water Treaty, but also set a regional state practice . . . which . . . can . . . serve as a precedent'.[86]

The late John Briscoe, it seems, foresaw this situation, realizing that the issue of transboundary waters between the two riparian states was not limited to issues over the engineering of the structures, but extended to an issue of security, noting that:

> India has a series of hydropower projects being planned, designed and constructed on the headwaters of Pakistan's three rivers . . . . From the Pakistani perspective this ability to hold and release water constitutes a serious threat to water security in Pakistan.[87]

[82] Baqir Sajjad Syed, 'Navy says Indian Sub's Bid to Intrude into its Waters Foiled' *Dawn News* (Islamabad, 19 November 2016) <http://www.dawn.com/news/1297315/navy-says-indian-subs-bid-to-intrude-into-its-waters-foiled> accessed 3 January 2017; Naveed Siddiqui, 'Pakistan Navy foils attempt by Indian submarine to enter Pakistani waters' *Dawn News* (5 March 2019) <https://www.dawn.com/news/1467778> accessed 30 April 2019.

[83] Faiza Ilyas, 'Illegal Fishing by Indians Causes Multi-Billion Rupee Losses to Pakistan' *Dawn News* (Karachi, 25 February 2016) <http://www.dawn.com/news/1241719> accessed 3 January 2017.

[84] The Indus Water Treaty (adopted 10 September 1960, entered into force 19 September 1960) preamble.

[85] Ibid. art. 12(4), dealing with the termination of the treaty whereby a new treaty between the parties needs to be drafted and mutually ratified.

[86] 'Revocation of Indus Waters Treaty can be Taken as an Act of War' *Dawn News* (Islamabad, 27 September 2016) <http://www.dawn.com/news/1286437> accessed 20 December 2016.

[87] John Briscoe, 'The Troubled Indus' (2010) 45(50) Economic and Political Weekly 30.

Pakistan has twice successfully invoked the dispute resolution mechanism provided under the treaty. In the first dispute in 2005, it filed a request for a neutral expert to resolve the difference over the Baglihar Hydroelectric Power Project. The expert, Professor Raymond Lafitte, decided to, *inter alia*, raise the intake level and increase the dead storage level. He pertinently opined that the rights and obligations under the Treaty 'should be read in the light of new technical norms and new standards as provided for by the Treaty'.[88]

In the second dispute, in 2010, Pakistan approached the Court of Arbitration (established under the Treaty) regarding a dispute over the Kishenganga Hydro-Electric Project (KHEP). The Court *inter alia* decided that 'India shall release a minimal flow of 9 cumecs into the Kishenganga/Neelum River below the KHEP', guaranteeing a minimum flow in the river.[89]

Recently, Pakistan requested the World Bank to appoint a Chairman for the Permanent Court of Arbitration (PCA) over a dispute with India regarding the Ratle and Kishenganga hydroelectric projects. The World Bank declined to appoint either a Chairman or a neutral expert (as per India's request), suggesting strongly that the two states should sort out the issue bilaterally. It can be argued, however, that '[t]he Bank has a very limited role in the appointment process, and any ambiguity arising from parallel processes being initiated simultaneously fall within the purview of the Court of Arbitration'.[90]

This may be so because the Bank felt the possibility of conflicting opinions coming out of a parallel system of the neutral expert and the PCA. This can be evidenced by contrasting the Baglihar opinion and the KHEP judgment, whereby '[t]he court restored a tenet which was fundamental to Pakistan [relating to strict design and operational restrictions being interpreted leniently by the neutral expert], allaying concerns on India's ability to manipulate water flows'.[91]

9 Law of Territory

9.1 Pak-Afghan Border: The Durand Line

A formal treaty between Pakistan and Afghanistan, referred to as the Durand Line Agreement,[92] was signed in 1893 between the then Amir of Afghanistan, Abdur Rehman Khan, and Sir Henry Mortimer Durand, for the then British India.[93] Although Pakistan,

[88] Raymond Lafitte, 'Baglihar Hydroelectric Plant—The Indus Waters Treaty 1960: Expert Determination, Executive Summary' (Lausanne, 12 February 2007) 5 <http://siteresources.worldbank.org/SOUTHASIAEXT/Resources/223546-1171996340255/BagliharSummary.pdf> accessed 3 January 2017.

[89] *The Indus Waters Kishenganga Arbitration (Pakistan v India)* (2013) PCA Award Series 43.

[90] Shamila Mahmood, 'Indus Treaty Interrupted' *Dawn News* (Islamabad, 23 December 2016) <http://www.dawn.com/news/1303293/indus-treaty-interrupted> accessed 20 December 2016.

[91] Ibid.

[92] 'Durand Line Agreement' (12 November 1893) <http://www.khyber.org/history/treaties/durandagreement.shtml> accessed 30 April 2019.

[93] This was also later reaffirmed in the Anglo–Afghan Treaty (8 August 1919).

along with the world community at large, now accepts the Durand Line as the international border between Afghanistan and modern day Pakistan, Afghanistan continues to question the finality of this border, based on its 'historical importance' and the consequent division of the *Pashtuns* between Afghanistan and Pakistan.[94]

This Afghan intransigence has not only hindered Pakistan's counterterrorism efforts, by providing safe havens to non-state actors straddling the porous border, but it is also squarely at variance with international law on territory. Pakistan's position is firmly supported by the principle of *uti possidetis*, which has 'developed into a general concept of contemporary customary international law'.[95] The ICJ recognized this principle in 1986, stating that '[i]ts obvious purpose is to prevent the independence and stability of new States being endangered by fratricidal struggles provoked by the challenging of frontiers following the withdrawal of the administering power'.[96] The principles holds that if:

> there is a relevant applicable treaty, then this will dispose of the matter completely. Indeed, once defined in a treaty, an international frontier achieves permanence so that even if the treaty itself were to cease to be in force, the continuance of the boundary would be un-affected and may only be changed with the consent of the states directly concerned.[97]

Domestically, the issue of the status of the Durand Line was addressed in *The Superintendent, Land Customs Torkham (Khyber Agency) v Zewar Khan and 2 Ors*,[98] wherein the Supreme Court of Pakistan considered the illegal smuggling of goods across the border. The defendant claimed that there had been no act of smuggling since the Durand Line was not an international border. The Court declared, after referring to various documents under international law, that the Durand Line is, in fact, the international border between Pakistan and Afghanistan.

9.2 Kashmir and the Principle of Self-determination

The territorial dispute between Pakistan and India over Kashmir, stimulated by a war between the two states in 1947–8 around the time of partition, has profoundly impacted regional peace and security. Pakistan's stance in relation to the Kashmir dispute has remained consistent and in line with the principles of international law. In particular,

94 'The Durand Line: Afghanistan's Controversial, Colonial-Era Border' *The Atlantic* (October 2012) <http://www.theatlantic.com/international/archive/2012/10/the-durand-line-afghanistans-controversial-colonial-era-border/264064/> accessed 7 January 2018.

95 Malcolm Shaw, *International Law* (5th edn CUP 2007) 447.

96 *Frontier Dispute (Burkina Faso v Republic of Mali)* [1986] ICJ Rep 554, 565.

97 Shaw (n 95) 449–50.

98 *The Superintendent, Land Customs Torkham (Khyber Agency) v Zewar Khan and 2 Others* PLD 1969 SC 485.

'Pakistan upholds the right of the people of Jammu and Kashmir to self-determination in accordance with the resolutions of the United Nations Security Council'[99] and supports the freedom to exercise this right 'in the same spirit [as] granted by the international community to the people of East Timor'.[100] In the *East Timor* case, the ICJ opined that self-determination has an *erga omnes* character and has evolved from the Charter, UN practice, and ICJ jurisprudence.[101]

The Security Council has passed several resolutions specifically pertaining to the Kashmir dispute, calling for a plebiscite to be held in Kashmir to determine the will of the people and to establish whether the people wish for independence or to accede to either state.[102] This plebiscite has still not been held, and the issue of the Kashmir dispute remains unsolved. India formally claims all of Kashmir, although it has indicated that it would accept the LoC (based on the 1948 ceasefire line, renamed in the Simla Agreement 1972), with modifications, as a future international border. Recent Indian atrocities in the area, in clear violation of international law, worsen the situation.[103]

In light of these inhumane acts of violence, attention may be drawn also to the UN General Assembly Declaration on Principles of International Law concerning Friendly Relations and Co-operation among States in accordance with the Charter of the United Nations 1970. This Resolution provides an express framework for what constitutes self-determination,[104] prohibits the deprivation of a peoples' right through the use of force,[105] and explicitly provides for peoples 'to seek and to receive support in accordance with the purposes and principles of the Charter'.[106] It remains Pakistan's

[99] Pakistan Mission to the UN, 'Kashmir—the History' <http://www.pakun.org/kashmir/history.php> accessed 23 January 2017.

[100] Ministry of Foreign Affairs Pakistan, Office of the Spokesperson, 'Prime Minister's Special Envoy on Jammu and Kashmir Call for Plebiscite in Kashmir on the Pattern of East Timor' (Press Release) (3 October 2016) PR No 497/2016 <http://www.mofa.gov.pk/contentkpr.php> accessed 23 January 2017.

[101] *East Timor (Portugal v Australia)* (Judgment) [1995] ICJ Rep 90.

[102] See UNSC res 47 (21 April 1948). See also UNSC res 38 (17 January 1948); UNSC res 39 (20 January 1948) UN Doc S/RES/39; UNSC res 51 (3 June 1948) UN Doc S/RES/51; UNSC res 80 (14 March 1950); UNSC res 91 (30 March 1951); UNSC res 96 (10 November 1951); UNSC res 98 (23 December 1952); UNSC res 122 (24 January 1957); UNSC res 123 (21 February 1957); UNSC res 126 (2 December 1957); UNSC res 209 (4 September 1965); UNSC res 210 (6 September 1965); UNSC res 211 (20 September 1965); UNSC res 214 (27 September 1965); UNSC Res 215 (5 November 1965); UNSC res 303 (6 December 1971); UNSC res (21 December 1971).

[103] See 'India's crackdown in Kashmir: is this the world's first mass blinding?' The Guardian (8 November 2016) <http://www.theguardian.com/world/2016/nov/08/india-crackdown-in-kashmir-is-this-worlds-first-mass-blinding> accessed 7 January 2018; Human Rights Watch, 'India: Investigate Use of Lethal Force in Kashmir' <http://www.hrw.org/news/2016/07/12/india-investigate-use-lethal-force-kashmir> accessed 7 January 2018.

[104] 'The establishment of a sovereign and independent State, the free association or integration with an independent State or the emergence into any other political status freely determined by a people constitute modes of implementing the right of self-determination by that people.'

[105] 'Every State has the duty to refrain from any forcible action which deprives peoples . . . of their right to self-determination and freedom and independence.'

[106] UNGA res (24 October 1970).

position that it ought to support the people of Kashmir in their struggle for self-determination, just as support was justified in the resistance by the Afghan Mujahidin against the Soviet occupation in 1979.[107]

In November 2016, Pakistan introduced a draft resolution entitled the 'Universal Realization of the Right of Peoples to Self-Determination', which was adopted by the General Assembly's Third Committee.[108] In light of the Indian violation of human rights in Kashmir, as comprehensively documented in a 2018 Report of the Office of the United Nations High Commissioner for Human Rights,[109] it is vital to take cognizance of article 5 of this resolution, which reads: '*The General Assembly . . . [r]equests* the Human Rights Council to continue to give special attention to violations of human rights, especially the right to self-determination, resulting from foreign military intervention, aggression or occupation'.[110]

10 Trade, Investment, and Economic Law

10.1 Trade

Pakistan is a firm believer in the promotion of fair and equitable trade, as exemplified by its partnership with China in the China–Pakistan Economic Corridor, which would facilitate a substantial volume of global trade. Pakistan's prominent role in global trade regimes was singled out for praise by the Director General WTO, Mr Roberto Azevêdo:

> Pakistan was one of the founding members of the organization, and has been a part of the system of global trade rules for almost 70 years. As I see it, by creating the WTO and agreeing its legal texts, Pakistan and the other founding members provided the equivalent of a constitution for global trade . . . [that] enshrines the basic, perennial principles of trade. It helps to avoid unilateral, discriminatory or arbitrary measures.[111]

[107] Ibid.

[108] UNGA Third Committee (3 November 2016) UN Doc A/C.3/71/L.49.

[109] OHCHR, 'Report on the Situation of Human Rights in Kashmir: Developments in the Indian State of Jammu and Kashmir from June 2016 to April 2018, and General Human Rights Concerns in Azad Jammu and Kashmir and Gilgit-Baltistan' (14 June 2018) <https://www.ohchr.org/Documents/Countries/IN/DevelopmentsInKashmirJune2016ToApril2018.pdf> accessed 30 April 2019.

[110] UNGA res (24 October 1970) art. 5.

[111] Remarks by Roberto Azevedo, Director-General of WTO, 'Lahore University of Management Sciences' (3 May 2016) <http://www.wto.org/english/news_e/spra_e/spra121_e.htm> accessed 16 January 2017.

In relation to trade involving regional organizations, as of 2013, Pakistan was awarded the Generalized Scheme of Preferences (GSP) Plus Status by the European Union (EU), which 'is a special incentive arrangement for sustainable development and good governance. The aim of [it] . . . is to assist developing countries in exporting their products to the European Union'.[112] To ensure the maintenance of this status, Pakistan is required to comply with twenty-seven core Resolutions and Conventions, as provided in Annex VIII of the EU Regulation on applying a scheme of generalized tariff preferences.[113] The Status was initially awarded to Pakistan until 2017. In February 2018, it was extended for another two years.[114]

10.2 Investment

In today's market-based state systems, Pakistan covets foreign investment for its socio-economic development. Pakistan was party to the first bilateral investment treaty (BIT), concluding it with West Germany in 1959.[115] Since then, Pakistan has signed 48 BITs with various countries[116] and has renegotiated its BITs with Germany, Kuwait, and Turkey.[117] More recently, however, Pakistan has been more cautious with respect to undertaking BIT commitments, and maintains a principled opposition to the US' BIT regime, which is highly skewed in favour of foreign investors at the expense of developing countries like Pakistan.

Pakistan is facing arbitrations filed with the International Centre for Settlement of International Disputes (ICSID) by Tethyan Copper Company Pvt Ltd[118] and Karkey Karadeniz Electrik Uretim AS[119] in which, *inter alia*, judgments of the Supreme Court of Pakistan have been disregarded and Pakistan's position that its domestic courts are the most competent authority to rightfully interpret Pakistan's domestic law has not found favour with the international arbitrators.

[112] Research Society of International Law, 'European Union's GSP Plus Regime: Examining Pakistan's Compliance with International Legal Obligations' *Policy Brief* (February 2014).

[113] See European Parliament and Council, EU Regulation No. 978/2012 Applying a Scheme of Generalized Tariff Preferences and Repealing Council Regulation (EC) No. 732/2008' (25 October 2012), art. 9.

[114] Mubarak Zeb Khan, 'EU renews GSP+ scheme for two years' *Dawn News* (21 February 2018) <https://www.dawn.com/news/1390653> accessed 30 April 2019.

[115] Treaty for the Promotion and Protection of Investments (Pakistan-Federal Republic of Germany) (adopted 25 November 1959, entered into force 28 April 1962, 6575 UNTS 24).

[116] For a complete list of the countries that Pakistan has signed BITs with, see UNCTAD, 'International Investment Agreements Navigator: Pakistan' <http://investmentpolicyhub.unctad.org/IIA/CountryBits/160> accessed 5 January 2017.

[117] Amin Ahmed, 'New Bilateral Investment Treaty Model' *Dawn News* (2 March 2015) <http://www.dawn.com/news/1166720> accessed 5 January 2017.

[118] ICSID, Case Details (ICSID Case No. ARB/12/1) <https://icsid.worldbank.org/en/Pages/cases/casedetail.aspx?CaseNo=ARB/12/1> accessed 5 April 2018.

[119] ICSID, Case Details (ICSID Case No. ARB/13/1) <https://icsid.worldbank.org/en/Pages/cases/casedetail.aspx?CaseNo=ARB/13/1> accessed 5 April 2018.

10.3 Anti-corruption Law

In the lead-up to the UN Convention against Corruption 2003 (UNCAC), Pakistan was one of the lead delegations, actively negotiating provisions of the UNCAC throughout its nearly two-and-a-half-year, seven-session long haul in the UN General Assembly's ad hoc committee. During this period, Pakistan tabled almost a dozen proposals.

The Pakistan delegation participated particularly in the discussion on provisions related to asset recovery, title of ill-gotten assets, and obligations under the mutual legal assistance chapter in case of optional offences. It was especially active on articles 33 and 34 of UNCAC wherein, in addition to the prosecution of an offender, an international concession or award could be declared cancelled on the ground of corruption. One of Pakistan's delegates chaired various committee sessions and acted as one of the lead negotiators for the G-77 states. The same delegate was later one of the fourteen members of the Consistency Group, and was appointed to the expert working group that drafted the UNCAC Implementation Guidelines.[120]

Despite such measures, corruption remains prevalent in Pakistan, finding itself ranked 117th on Transparency International's Corruption Perceptions Index 2018.[121] In 2016, Pakistan's Supreme Court was seized of constitutional petitions pertaining to the Panama Leaks and subsequent accusations against political leaders in Pakistan.[122] The Supreme Court, after a rigorous process which included the formation of a Joint Investigation Team under its purview, decided in favour of the petitioners, calling for the removal of the incumbent Prime Minister from office and barring him from re-election.[123]

11 The Role of International Law in the Domestic Legal Framework

Pakistan's legal system derives from its British common law history, the post-colonial Constitution 1973, and Islamic *sharia* law. Pakistan follows the principle of separation of powers, allowing for a clear distinction between the executive, legislative, and judicial organs of the state, within a federal structure. The implementation of international law, however, is one that all these stakeholders must actively participate in to fulfil Pakistan's obligations.

[120] UN Office on Drugs and Crime, Division for Treaty Affairs, 'Legislative Guide for the Implementation of the United Nations Convention against Corruption' (New York 2006).

[121] Transparency International, 'Pakistan' <https://www.transparency.org/country/PAK> accessed 30 April 2019.

[122] For an overview, see Nasir Iqbal, 'SC Fixes Panama Papers Case Hearing for Nov 1' *Dawn News* (Islamabad, 22 October 2016) <http://www.dawn.com/news/1291558> accessed 3 January 2017.

[123] *Imran Ahmad Khan Niazi v Mian Muhammad Nawaz Sharif and 9 Ors* PLD 2017 SC 265.

Article 40 of the Constitution enjoins the state to 'endeavour to . . . promote international peace and security, foster goodwill and friendly relations among all nations and encourage the settlement of international dispute by peaceful means'.[124] Additionally, post the 18th amendment in 2010, the Constitution delegates certain subjects to the provinces, while retaining others within the centre. Subsequently, authority pertaining to '[i]nternational treaties, conventions and agreements and International arbitration'[125] rests with the centre as enumerated in the Fourth Schedule of the Constitution.

The legislative organ primarily relies upon the Treaty Implementation Cells (TICs), created at both the provincial and federal levels on the initiative of the Ministry of Law, Justice and Human Rights in 2013. The TICs' objective 'is to enable the Government [to effectively implement] . . . conventions and obligations arising there from'.[126] A private member's bill was floored in the Senate in 2016 to discuss the establishment of a 'National Commission for International Law and Commitments'.[127] Though not passed, this shows an inclination on behalf of the members of the legislature to incorporate and fulfil Pakistan's international law obligations.

The domestic courts have generally held the view that they cannot enforce international law unless it is explicitly included within domestic legislation, despite no such restriction existing in the Constitution. Since *Federation of Pakistan v Shaukat Ali Mian*,[128] however, the courts are leaning towards the view that they may press into service international law conventions if there is no conflict or inconsistency in the existing (domestic) law.

This was previously also indicated in *M/S Najib Zarab Limited v Government of Pakistan*,[129] when the High Court of Sindh observed that nations must march with the international community and municipal law must respect the tenets of international law, including accommodating the latter even in the absence of express legislative sanction (provided they do not conflict with existing Acts of Parliament).

In *Syed Imran Ali Shah v Government of Pakistan*,[130] the Court (further) opined that the Federation has the authority to enter into international agreements on behalf of its provinces as well as to provide a guarantee for their implementation, and the provinces, in turn, are bound by these commitments.

In the same spirit of recognizing the importance of international law, the Peshawar High Court, a year later, relied upon the Afghanistan Transit Trade Agreement 1965 to protect the petitioner's right to carry out transnational business.[131]

Conventions such as the Convention on International Trade in Endangered Species and the Convention on the Conservation of Migratory Species of Wild Animals

[124] Constitution of the Islamic Republic of Pakistan 1973 art. 40.

[125] Constitution of the Islamic Republic of Pakistan 1973 Fourth Schedule.

[126] National Assembly Secretariat, 'Questions for Oral Answers and their Replies' (13 February 2015) <http://www.na.gov.pk/uploads/documents/questions/1423813150_256.pdf> accessed 23 January 2017.

[127] National Commission for International Law and Commitments Senate Bill 2016.

[128] PLD 1999 SC 1026. [129] PLD 1993 Karachi 93. [130] 2013 PLC 143.

[131] *Haji Lal Muhammad v Federation of Pakistan* PLD 2014 Peshawar 199.

recently provided the basis for examining the hunting of various endangered species of birds, with the subsequent judgment reinforcing the obligation to make domestic laws compliant with international obligations.[132] Likewise, the Lahore High Court, referring, *inter alia,* to the Stockholm Convention 2001, United Nations Framework Convention on Climate Change, and the Vienna Convention on the Protection of the Ozone Layer 1985, declared that state functionaries were bound by contractual obligations under international treaties to take effective measures for the elimination of vehicular pollution.[133]

Even the Federal Shariat Court, often criticized for being 'conservative' or 'backward', reminded Pakistan of its commitment to the international community—as under the Universal Declaration of Human Rights, the Convention for the Elimination of Discrimination Against Women, and others—for equal and indiscriminate treatment of its women. In 2008, the Court declared article 10 of the Pakistan Citizenship Act 1951 discriminatory, finding it to be in violation of the principle of gender equality.[134]

12 Dispute Settlement

The dispute settlement options available to any state under international law vary, depending upon the dispute at hand and the framework available under the relevant legal instrument. For instance, as mentioned earlier, the Indus Waters Treaty 1960 provides for a specific mechanism for dispute settlement between Pakistan and India (a neutral expert or arbitration), which Pakistan has utilized twice. Pakistan's participation in WTO cases and investment disputes were also discussed earlier.

Pakistan accepted the compulsory jurisdiction of the ICJ in 1960, replacing that declaration with the current one of 2017.[135] It is conditioned on reciprocity and excludes various types of disputes, including those: governed by other dispute resolution mechanisms; in which another party accepts jurisdiction exclusively for the purposes of the dispute; within domestic jurisdiction; concerning conflict, national security, or maritime zones; or under treaties unless all treaty parties are affected by the dispute, or Pakistan specifically agrees to jurisdiction.

Since 1960, Pakistan has been party to some notable international disputes. Pursuant to the Agreement between the Governments of India and Pakistan in 1965,[136] an Indo-

[132] *Province of Sindh v Lal Khan Chandio* 2016 SCMR 48.

[133] *Syed Mansoor Ali Shah v Government of Punjab* PLD 2007 Lahore 403.

[134] *In re Suo Motu Case No 1/K of 2006* PLD 2008 FSC 1.

[135] ICJ, 'Declarations Recognizing the Jurisdiction of the Court as Compulsory' <http://www.icj-cij.org/en/declarations/pk> accessed 20 January 2018.

[136] Agreement Between the Government of India and the Government of Pakistan Relating to Cease-fire and the Restoration of the Status Quo as on 1 January 1965 in the Gujarat/West Pakistan Border and Determination of the Border in That Area (New Delhi, 30 June 1965).

Pakistan Western Boundary Case Tribunal was set up. The Tribunal 'awarded 90 per cent of the Rann of Kutch to India and 10 per cent (about 800sq km) to Pakistan'[137]—a decision that was accepted by both parties.

Nearly a decade later, in 1973, after the fall of East Pakistan in 1971, 'Pakistan instituted proceedings against India concerning 195 Pakistani prisoners of war whom, according to Pakistan, India proposed to hand over to Bangladesh, which was said to intend trying them for acts of genocide and crimes against humanity'.[138] Following negotiations between the parties, the case was withdrawn in 1975.[139]

In 1999, Pakistan filed an application before the ICJ instituting proceedings against the Government of India concerning a dispute over the destruction of a Pakistani aircraft earlier the same year. The case was dismissed by the ICJ the following year on the grounds that the Court did not have jurisdiction in the matter.[140]

In the recent past, the Republic of Marshall Islands (RMI) filed applications before the ICJ in April 2014 claiming that Pakistan, *inter alia*, had breached customary international law obligations concerning negotiations relating to the cessation of the nuclear arms race and nuclear disarmament.

Pakistan, in its counter-response, argued that the case should not proceed to consideration of the merits because Pakistan's nuclear programme was a matter of its national defence and security, falling exclusively within its domestic jurisdiction; Pakistan also conveyed to the Court that the RMI lacked the requisite standing to institute the current proceedings since there was no (legal) dispute between the RMI and Pakistan. The case was dismissed on the grounds that the Court did not have jurisdiction under article 36(2) of the ICJ Statute.[141]

13 Conclusion

As a developing country, with a population of almost 207 million[142] and a GDP of around US$271 billion[143] (resulting in an approximate GDP per capita of US$1,435),

[137] Isha Kureshi, 'The Mysterious Rann of Katch' *Dawn News* (3 June 2009) <http://www.dawn.com/news/861793> accessed 5 April 2018.

[138] ICJ, *Trial of Pakistani Prisoners of War (Pakistan v India)* <http://www.icj-cij.org/en/case/60> accessed 5 April 2018.

[139] See generally ibid.

[140] See ICJ, 'Aerial Incident of 10 August 1999 (Press Release)' <http://www.icj-cij.org/files/case-related/119/119-20000621-PRE-01-00-EN.pdf> accessed 5 April 2018.

[141] See ICJ, 'Obligations concerning Negotiations relating to Cessation of the Nuclear Arms Race and to Nuclear Disarmament (Marshall Islands v Pakistan) (Press Release)' <http://www.icj-cij.org/files/case-related/159/19130.pdf> accessed 5 April 2018.

[142] See 'Pakistan's population has ballooned to 207.8m, provisional census results show' *Dawn News* (25 August 2017) <http://www.dawn.com/news/1353867> accessed 5 April 2018.

[143] World Bank, 'Pakistan: Demographic Indicators—1998 Census' <http://www.pbs.gov.pk/sites/default/files//tables/DEMOGRAPHIC%20INDICATORS%20-%201998%20CENSUS.pdf> accessed 20 January 2017.

Pakistan's resources remain severely limited and this constricts Pakistan's growth. Coupled with certain issues in the governance of the state, there still remains a lot to be desired.

Having come into being through tenets of international law (exercising its right to self-determination to become an independent state), Pakistan seems to be moving forward with a steadily-increasing maturity *re* its perception of international law: why it is necessary to comply with international law, why Pakistan must be an active participant in international forums for raising awareness regarding its state practice, why it ought to contribute more actively to the global discourse on the formulation and evolution of international law, and so on.

Since the 18th Amendment to the Constitution in 2010, with the devolution of certain (governance) subjects to the provinces, there is some confusion with regards to the exact role of each government, ministry, or institution. The resolution of this confusion may only come about through better collaboration and more intrinsic awareness and understanding of Pakistan's international legal obligations.

This was demonstrated in a recent judgment by the Supreme Court of Pakistan, wherein the honourable judiciary has ruled that the Federation has the power to legislate on any matter that is supplemented by an international law obligation upon Pakistan, especially through 'international treaties, conventions and agreements, and international arbitration',[144] even if the subject in question has otherwise, under the 18th (Constitutional) Amendment, been devolved to the provinces.[145] This seems to be a bold step towards the harmonization of the implementation of these laws, and the incorporation of international law into the active scope of the *lex terrae* and, consequently, the rule of law.

Looking outwards, most of Pakistan's outstanding issues with its neighbour, India, remain unresolved; perhaps this is the right moment for Pakistan to look into, initiate, and engage in the process of 'legal diplomacy'. Legal diplomacy need not be restricted to the Eastern Border, but may also be drawn upon by Pakistan in its other relationships with Afghanistan and the US.

[144] Constitution of the Islamic Republic of Pakistan 1973, Entry 32 Fourth Schedule.

[145] Supreme Court of Pakistan, Civil Appeals No. 1583–1598 of 2014 <http://www.supremecourt.gov.pk/web/user_files/File/C.A._1583_201.pdf> accessed 5 April 2018.

CHAPTER 25

BANGLADESH

KAMAL HOSSAIN AND
SHARIF BHUIYAN*

1 Introduction and Constitutional Framework

Like any other country, Bangladesh's interaction with international law takes place both at the domestic level—for example, before domestic courts—and at the international level—for example, in the context of participation in international organizations and processes. This chapter discusses several salient aspects of such interaction in both of these contexts. In the former context, the role of international law in the Bangladesh legal system is examined, including the treatment of international treaties and customary international law in domestic law. In the latter context, Bangladesh's participation in international organizations, peace keeping operations, and dispute settlement is considered. While the issues addressed are not exhaustive, they nonetheless provide a broad overview of the role and significance of international law for Bangladesh, both within the country and in its international relations.

The People's Republic of Bangladesh became an independent state in 1971. It is a unitary state and a parliamentary democracy. The executive branch of the government consists of the President (head of state), the Prime Minister (head of government), and the Cabinet of Ministers. The legislature is a unicameral Parliament consisting of 350 members. The judiciary consists of the Supreme Court and courts and tribunals subordinate to it. The Supreme Court comprises the Appellate Division and the High Court Division. The judiciary is headed by the Chief Justice of Bangladesh. The Supreme Court is the highest court and the Appellate Division of the Supreme Court is the highest judicial organ of the country. The legal system of Bangladesh is based on the common law system largely derived from the English legal system.

* Thanks to Reduanul Karim for his assistance in preparing this chapter.

The Constitution of Bangladesh, adopted in 1972, is the supreme law and takes precedence over any other law. There are two major provisions on international law in the Constitution, namely, articles 25 and 145A.[1] Article 25 provides as follows:

> The State shall base its international relations on the principles of respect for national sovereignty and equality, non-interference in the internal affairs of other countries, peaceful settlement of international disputes, and respect for international law and the principles enunciated in the United Nations Charter, and on the basis of those principles shall –
>
> (a) strive for the renunciation of the use of force in international relations and for general and complete disarmament;
> (b) uphold the right of every people freely to determine and build up its own social, economic and political system by ways and means of its own free choice; and
> (c) support oppressed peoples throughout the world waging a just struggle against imperialism, colonialism or racism.

Article 25 is contained in Part II of the Constitution setting out the 'fundamental principles of state policy'. These principles are 'fundamental to the governance of Bangladesh' and are to be applied by the state in making laws and to guide the interpretation of the Constitution and other laws of Bangladesh. However, these principles are not judicially enforceable.[2]

The principles of 'respect for national sovereignty and equality, non-interference in the internal affairs of other countries' and 'support[ing] oppressed peoples throughout the world waging a just struggle against imperialism, colonialism or racism' were interpreted by the Supreme Court in *Saiful Islam Dilder v Bangladesh*.[3] This case sought to prevent the Bangladesh Government from extraditing Anup Chetia, Secretary General of the United Liberation Front of Assam, to India, where he had been charged with treason. It was argued that Anup Chetia was was not a criminal but a person who was fighting for the right of self-determination of the Assamese people. Consequently, his extradition would be a violation of article 25, which requires the state to support 'just struggle[s] against imperialism, colonialism or racism'. The Court rejected this contention:

> The contention on the facts of this case is totally misconceived. Rather the Government can take help of Article 25 to extradite Anup Chetia to Indian authority in order to base its international relations on the principle of respect for national sovereignty and equality and non-interference in the internal affairs of other countries.[4]

With regard to the justiciability of article 25, the Court observed that although it 'cannot be enforced by a court', nevertheless it can 'serve as a tool in interpreting the Constitution and other laws'.[5]

[1] In addition to these two articles, the preamble of the Constitution refers to 'international peace' and art. 47(3) refers to 'crimes under international law'.
[2] Constitution of the People's Republic of Bangladesh 1972 art. 8(2).
[3] *Saiful Islam Dilder v Bangladesh* 50 DLR (HCD) (1998) 318.
[4] Ibid. 322–3.
[5] *Saiful Islam Dilder* (n 3). See also *M Saleem Ullah v Bangladesh* 47 DLR (1995) 218, 224, para 7.

Unlike article 25, article 145A, dealing with 'international treaties', is a justiciable provision. This article provides as follows:

> All treaties with foreign countries shall be submitted to the President, who shall cause them to be laid before Parliament:
>
> Provided that any such treaty connected with national security shall be laid in a secret session of Parliament.

Neither the Constitution nor any statute contains any specific provision on domestic application of international law rules. However, it is well settled by various judicial decisions that in respect of domestic application of international treaties, Bangladesh is a dualist country. In order to be applied by national courts, it is necessary for the treaty to be incorporated into Bangladesh's legal system by an act of incorporation.

In respect of customary international law, there is no clear judicial decision on whether customary law automatically forms part of Bangladesh law or whether, like treaties, such law is required to be made a part of Bangladesh law by a legislative, judicial, or other measure. It is likely that if this issue requires determination, Bangladesh courts will adhere to the English and common law tradition of treating customary international law as automatically forming part of Bangladesh law as long as there is no inconsistent domestic legal provision.

2 Treaty Practice

2.1 Treaty-making Process

The treaty-making process is governed by the Constitution, the Rules of Business, and the practice of the executive branch of the government.

2.1.1 *Constitutional Provisions*

Article 145A of the Constitution, referred to in the preceding section, deals simply with the process of placing treaties before the Parliament and does not make any provision in respect of the treaty-making process, including negotiation, signing, and ratification of treaties. These aspects of the treaty-making process need to be understood in light of the other general provisions of the Constitution relating to the exercise of the executive authority of the republic.

Article 55(2) of the Constitution provides that, subject to and in accordance with the Constitution, the executive power of the republic is to be exercised by or on the authority of the Prime Minister. Like other executive functions, treaty-making is to be performed in accordance with the provisions of the Constitution. Although treaty-making is an executive function, in exercising this function the Prime Minister and the Cabinet are to be collectively responsible to the Parliament in accordance with article 55(3) of the Constitution.

2.1.2 *Provisions of the Rules of Business*

In accordance with article 55(6) of the Constitution, the President has formulated the Rules of Business for the conduct of business of the government. Rules 5(iii), 14A(1)(iii), 16(xi), and 26 of the Rules of Business are relevant in respect of the negotiation, conclusion, and ratification of international agreements and treaties. These Rules provide that the Ministry of Foreign Affairs is responsible for issuing necessary instructions regarding the manner of authentication of treaties and that the Legislative and Parliamentary Affairs Division should be consulted on the preparation of international agreements and conventions. Cases involving negotiations with foreign countries on treaties and agreements are to be brought before the Cabinet.

2.1.3 *Practice*

The authority for the negotiation, conclusion, and ratification of international treaties is vested in the executive. Parliamentary approval for these matters is not a constitutional requirement.[6] As a general practice, the Law Ministry is given the responsibility of scrutinizing treaties.[7] Although there is a Law Commission in Bangladesh, it is rarely involved in treaty-making.

Usually the process of negotiation, conclusion, or ratification of a treaty is initiated by the Ministry which is allocated responsibility in relation to the subject matter of the treaty. For example, in relation to a trade treaty, the process is initiated by the Ministry of Commerce. After a proposal is made by the relevant Ministry, the issue is raised before the Cabinet, which takes the final decision regarding signing or ratification of the instrument concerned. In accordance with Rule 5 of the Rules of Business, the Ministry of Foreign Affairs is responsible for signing and authenticating international agreements and treaties. All Ministries are also required to have prior consultation with the Ministry of Foreign Affairs in relation to matters concerning foreign relations of Bangladesh.[8]

One major criticism of the treaty-making practice is the nearly complete disregard for article 145A of the Constitution. A study conducted in 2000 found that only one treaty, namely, the Ganges Water Treaty 1996 between Bangladesh and India, had ever been placed before the Parliament in accordance with article 145A.[9] The situation regarding compliance with article 145A has not improved since 2000.

Non-compliance with article 145A is a matter of concern for various reasons. As already pointed out, although treaty-making is an executive function, in exercising this function the Prime Minister and the Cabinet are to be collectively responsible to the Parliament. Since treaties are not placed before the Parliament, this responsibility of the executive cannot be ensured and the Parliament is deprived of any role in respect of

[6] See Mahmudul Islam, *Constitutional Law of Bangladesh* (3rd edn Mullick Brothers 2012) 1026.

[7] This function is allocated to the Law Ministry. See Rules of Business (1996) r 14A(1)(iii).

[8] Ibid. r 15.

[9] Shahnaz Huda and Manzoor Hasan, *The Bangladesh Parliament and International Conventions* (Bangladesh Institute of Parliamentary Studies 2000) 37.

treaty-making. This also raises larger issues of good governance, transparency, and rule of law in a parliamentary democracy, where major policy issues are supposed to be addressed by the Parliament. At a more practical level, as treaties require implementing legislation, it is desirable to keep the members of Parliament informed about treaties, so that they can consider necessary legislative action.

2.1.4 *Judicial Decisions*

The proposition that the making of a treaty is an executive act and that, for it to be valid, approval of the Parliament is not necessary has been recognized in judicial decisions. The Appellate Division confronted this issue in a case concerning the Delhi Treaty of 16 May 1974.[10] The appellant sought a declaration that the Delhi Treaty involving cession of Bangladesh territory[11] was without lawful authority. Citing article 143(2) of the Constitution, which gives authority to the Parliament for determination of the boundaries of Bangladesh, the appellant disputed the executive's authority to enter into treaties when cession of territory is involved. However, the appellant did not dispute the general treaty-making authority of the executive and hence it sufficed for the Appellate Division to generally endorse such authority.

The Appellate Division observed that 'treaty-making falls within the ambit of the executive power under article 55(2) of the Constitution' and also noted that this general proposition was not disputed.[12] On the interaction between the treaty-making authority of the executive and the authority of the Parliament in relation to boundaries, however, the Court observed that:

> the Prime Minister cannot unilaterally determine the boundaries of Bangladesh which has to be done by a law of Parliament.
>
> ...
>
> There can thus be no escape from the position that though treaty-making falls within the ambit of the executive power under Article 55(2) of the Constitution, a treaty involving determination of boundary, and more so involving cession of territory, can only be concluded with the concurrence of Parliament by necessary enactment.[13]

Interestingly, however, the Appellate Division did not declare the Delhi Treaty illegal due to the lack of involvement of the Parliament in the conclusion of the treaty. Rather, it dismissed the appeal observing as follows:

> Had the Delhi Treaty involved a mere determination of the boundary between this country and our friendly neighbour India, it could be implemented by a simple enactment under Article 143(2) of the Constitution. In view, however, of our conclusion that it involves cession of territory by Bangladesh, we are clearly of

[10] *Kazi Mukhlesur Rahman v Bangladesh* 26 DLR (SC) (1974) 44.

[11] The treaty involved the transfer of the Berubari enclave to India in exchange for the Dahagram and Angarpota enclaves.

[12] *Kazi Mukhlesur Rahman* (n 10) 54, 58.

[13] ibid. 57, 58.

> the opinion that *in order to implement this treaty, prior to ratification thereof it will be necessary to take recourse to Article 142, with a view to amending Article 2(a) which defines the territory of the People's Republic of Bangladesh.*[14]

In the above observations, the Appellate Division firmly subscribes to the dualist theory and the principle of incorporation. In some cases, the act of incorporation will be the enactment or amendment of laws, but where a treaty affects a constitutional provision, an amendment of the Constitution will be necessary. Another important aspect of the Appellate Division ruling is that for treaties impacting on the Constitution, implementing legislation should be passed *prior* to the ratification of the treaty, whereas for treaties that do not affect constitutional provisions, implementing legislation may not be imperative. In any event, the role of the Parliament does not seem to have been extended beyond that of passing implementing legislation.[15]

The question of compliance with article 145A of the Constitution has also come before the Supreme Court and it seems to have taken a rather lenient view of the matter. The High Court Division has held that although there is an obligation to lay a treaty before the Parliament, failure to do so will not affect the validity of the treaty.[16]

2.2 Domestic Application of Treaties

2.2.1 *The Principle of Incorporation*

The Supreme Court has endorsed the principle of incorporation on several occasions.[17] In *Bangladesh v Somboon Asavaham* the Appellate Division was required to decide an issue as to whether certain fishing trawlers were within the territorial waters of Bangladesh. The Appellate Division noted that this issue involved international law, but decided that the role of the Court was limited to applying the relevant municipal law.[18] In another case, where a party invoked the Universal Declaration of Human Rights, the Appellate Division observed that its provisions 'are not directly enforceable in national courts'.[19] In several other cases, the Supreme Court observed in almost

[14] ibid. 58 (emphasis added).

[15] The case of *Kazi Mukhlesur Rahman* (n 10) has been cited in a number of subsequent decisions. See *Md. Asaduzzaman v Bangladesh* 42 DLR (1990) 144; *Dr Mohiuddin Farooque v Bangladesh* 49 DLR (AD) (1997) 1; *Mohammad Emrul Kayes v Government Bangladesh* 35 BLD (2015) 94; and *Tayeeb v Government Bangladesh* 67 DLR (AD) (2015) 57.

[16] *Major (Retd) Akhtaruzzaman v Bangladesh*, Writ Petition No. 3774 of 1999 (unreported) (as cited in Mahmudul Islam, *Constitutional Law of Bangladesh* (3rd edn Mullick Brothers 2012) 1026).

[17] See *Kazi Mukhlesur Rahman* (n 10); *Bangladesh v Somboon Asavaham* 32 DLR (AD) (1980) 194; *Professor Nurul Islam v Government of Bangladesh* 52 DLR (2000) 413; *Hussain Mohammad Ershad v Bangladesh* 21 BLD (AD) (2001) 69; *State v Md. Roushan Mondal* 26 BLD (HCD) (2006) 549; *Bangladesh v Sheikh Hasina* 60 DLR (AD) (2008) 90; *State v Metropolitan Police Commissioner* 60 DLR (2008) 660; *State v Secretary, Ministry of Law*, Suo Motu Rule No. 5621 of 2009 (unreported); *Dr Shipra Chaudhury v Government of Bangladesh* 29 BLD (HCD) (2009) 183; and *Bangladesh Legal Aid and Services Trust v Bangladesh* 63 DLR (2011) 1.

[18] *Bangladesh v Somboon Asavaham* (n 17) 197–8, para 6.

[19] *Hussain Mohammad Ershad v Bangladesh* 21 BLD (2001) 69, 70, para 2.

identical terms that the courts of Bangladesh will not enforce international treaties and conventions, 'even if ratified by the state, as they are not part of the corpus juris of the state, unless they are incorporated in the municipal legislation'.[20]

2.2.2 *The Principle of Consistent Interpretation*

Many jurisdictions that subscribe to the principle of incorporation often also subscribe, in various forms, to another principle or doctrine, which may be termed as the principle or doctrine of consistent interpretation.[21] Pursuant to this principle, wherever possible and where there is no conflicting domestic legislation, domestic courts seek to interpret domestic laws consistently with the state's international obligations. Recognition of this principle can be found in judicial decisions of Bangladesh courts stating that international treaties and conventions may be referred to 'as an aid to interpretation' of domestic laws.[22]

In the twin cases of *BNWLA v Government of Bangladesh* (2009)[23] and *BNWLA v Government of Bangladesh* (2011),[24] the High Court Division made a much more robust use of the principle of consistent interpretation. Citing a number of domestic constitutional and other provisions side by side with various international instruments on women's rights, the Court formulated two sets of directives on sexual harassment, which are to be followed 'until adequate and effective legislation is made in the field'. Relying on consistent domestic and international provisions, the Court sought to fill a 'legislative vacuum' by resorting to a declaration of law by the Court.[25]

Apart from the twin *BNWLA* cases, there are no cases where the court has embarked upon similar declarations of law by reference to constitutional rights and international treaties. Notably, Part III of the Bangladesh Constitution dealing with fundamental rights recognizes the core human rights set out in various international human rights instruments. As a result, it was possible for the courts to have recourse to the principle of consistent interpretation in respect of the enforcement of fundamental rights. However, instances are difficult to find where Bangladesh courts have resorted to this principle in other areas, for example, in commercial matters.

2.3 Bangladesh's Participation in International Treaties

Bangladesh has signed and ratified a large number of multilateral treaties and is also a party to many bilateral treaties. According to the *United Nations Treaty Series*,

[20] *Bangladesh Legal Aid and Services Trust* (n 17) 8; *Sheikh Hasina* (n 17) 104; *Shipra Chaudhury* (n 17) 187.

[21] See Sharif Bhuiyan, *National Law in WTO Law* (Cambridge University Press 2007) 5 (note 33).

[22] *Shipra Chaudhury* (n 17) 187; *Bangladesh Legal Aid and Services Trust* (n 17) 8; *Sheikh Hasina* (n 17) 104.

[23] *BNWLA v Government of Bangladesh* 14 BLC (2009) 694.

[24] *BNWLA v Government of Bangladesh* 31 BLD (HCD) (2011) 324.

[25] *BNWLA* (n 23) 706.

Bangladesh has signed 817 treaties.[26] The following sections discuss some major treaties to which Bangladesh is a party, concerning diverse subjects, such as human and labour rights, environment, international trade, investment, and double taxation.

2.3.1 *Human Rights*

Out of the twenty-seven multilateral treaties relating to human and child rights deposited with the UN Secretary-General, Bangladesh has ratified or acceded to ten treaties including the Convention on the Rights of the Child (CRC), Convention against Torture and Other Cruel Inhuman or Degrading Treatment or Punishment (CAT), International Covenant on Civil and Political Rights (ICCPR), Convention on the Elimination of All Forms of Discrimination against Women (CEDAW), International Convention on the Elimination of All Forms of Racial Discrimination, and the International Covenant on Economic, Social and Cultural Rights.

2.3.2 *Labour Rights*

According to the International Labour Organization (ILO), Bangladesh has ratified thirty-five labour rights conventions.[27] Out of the eight Fundamental Conventions, Bangladesh has ratified seven including the Forced Labour Convention 1930, Right to Organize and Collective Bargaining Convention 1949 and the Equal Remuneration Convention 1951. Out of the four Governance (Priority) Conventions, Bangladesh has accepted two and out of the 177 Technical Conventions, Bangladesh has signed twenty-six.

2.3.3 *Environment*

Major international environmental treaties accepted by Bangladesh include the Cartagena Protocol on Biosafety to the Convention on Biological Diversity, Kyoto Protocol to the United Nations Framework Convention on Climate Change, the Stockholm Convention on Persistent Organic Pollutants, the International Plant Protection Convention, and the Convention on International Trade in Endangered Species of Wild Fauna and Flora.[28]

2.3.4 *International Trade*

Bangladesh is a founding member of the World Trade Organization (WTO) and, as a member, it is a party to various WTO agreements including the General Agreement on Tariffs and Trade 1994, General Agreement on Trade in Services, and the Agreement on Trade-Related Aspects of Intellectual Property Rights. Bangladesh is a party to a

[26] 'United Nations Treaty Series Online' (*United Nations Treaty Collection*) <https://treaties.un.org/Pages/UNTSOnline.aspx?id=3&clang=_en> accessed 11 December 2018.

[27] International Labour Organisation, 'Ratifications for Bangladesh' <http://www.ilo.org/dyn/normlex/en/f?p=NORMLEXPUB:11200:0::NO::P11200_COUNTRY_ID:103500> accessed 11 December 2018.

[28] Department of Environment, 'Multilateral Environmental Agreements in force in Bangladesh' <http://www.doe-bd.org/agreement.html> accessed 11 December 2018.

number of regional trade agreements, including the Asia Pacific Trade Agreement, Bay of Bengal Initiative on Multi-Sectoral Technical and Economic Cooperation (BIMSTEC), South Asian Preferential Trade Arrangement, and the South Asian Free Trade Agreement. Bangladesh has signed bilateral trade agreements with forty-five countries.[29]

2.3.5 *Investment*

Bangladesh is a member of the International Centre for Settlement of Investment Disputes (ICSID) and the Multilateral Investment Guarantee Agency. It is also a party to the New York Convention on the Recognition and Enforcement of Foreign Arbitral Awards. Bangladesh has ratified World Intellectual Property Organization (WIPO)-administered intellectual property treaties, including the Berne Convention, the Paris Convention, and the WIPO Convention. Bangladesh is a party to thirty-three bilateral investment treaties (BITs),[30] which provide guarantees of fair, equitable, national, and most-favoured-nation treatments to foreign investors.

2.3.6 *Double Taxation*

Bangladesh has concluded twenty-seven Double Taxation Agreements (DTAs) with twenty-six countries, the USA being the only country with which Bangladesh has two tax treaties. The DTAs aim to create a favourable climate for foreign investment through avoidance of double taxation.

2.3.7 *Other Treaties*

Other major treaties that Bangladesh has ratified include the United Nations Convention on the Law of the Sea 1982 (UNCLOS), the Vienna Conventions on Diplomatic Relations 1961 and on Consular Relations 1963, humanitarian conventions (namely, the Geneva Convention Relative to the Protection of Civilian Persons in Time of War 1949 and Protocols I and II of 1977 to the Geneva Conventions), Convention on the Prevention and Punishment of the Crime of Genocide 1948, and the Rome Statute of the International Criminal Court 1998.

2.3.8 *Absence from Major Treaties*

Major treaties to which Bangladesh is not a party include the Optional Protocol to ICCPR, Optional Protocol to the CAT, Convention Relating to the Status of Refugees, and the Vienna Convention on the Law of Treaties. Bangladesh is not a party to either the 1954 Convention Relating to the Status of Stateless Persons or the 1961 Convention on the Reduction of Statelessness.

[29] Ministry of Commerce, 'Bilateral Trade Agreement' <http://mincom.portal.gov.bd/site/page/8d102b7c-7f6f-4325-9ad9-ea1027f7454d/Bilateral-Trade-Agreement> accessed 11 December 2018.

[30] Ministry of Industries, 'Bilateral Agreements'<https://moind.gov.bd/site/page/f7aa7575-5196-476b-907b-3ea65e885717/Bilateral-Agreements> accessed 11 December 2018.

2.3.9 *Reservations and Declarations*

Bangladesh has made reservations and interpretative declarations to the application of a number of human rights conventions.[31] For instance, reservations or declarations have been made in respect of ICCPR, CAT, CEDAW, ICESR, CRC, and the Genocide Convention. Bangladesh sometimes justifies the reservations on the ground of divergent provisions in domestic law, including *sharia* law, or financial inability to implement the treaty.

2.4 Implementing Legislation

While Bangladesh has signed and ratified a large number of treaties, only a few implementing laws have been passed. Following its independence in 1971, Bangladesh inherited a few implementing laws from the pre-independence period in the area of carriage of goods by air or sea and in respect of matters concerning the United Nations. The UN-related laws inherited by Bangladesh are the United Nations (Security Council) Act, 1948, the United Nations (Privileges and Immunities) Act, 1948, and the United Nations (Declaration of Death of Missing Persons) Act, 1956.

Since independence, Bangladesh's record in adopting implementing legislation has not been outstanding. In the 1970s several laws were passed in order to provide for Bangladesh's membership of various international financial organizations, including the Bretton Woods institutions and the Asian Development Bank. Two more laws were passed during this period in relation to the International Finance Corporation and the Asian Reinsurance Corporation.[32] More recently, Bangladesh became a founder member of the Asian Infrastructure Investment Bank (AIIB) and has enacted the Asian Infrastructure Investment Bank Act, 2016 in order to provide for the implementation of the Articles of Agreement of AIIB.

In the area of investment protection, the Foreign Private Investment (Promotion and Protection) Act, 1980, although not enacted as implementing legislation, broadly reflects provisions of BITs signed by Bangladesh. The Double Taxation Agreements signed by Bangladesh are implemented in domestic law through issuance of statutory orders by the Ministry of Finance under the Income Tax Ordinance, 1984. The Arbitration Act, 2001 gives effect to the New York Convention on the Recognition and Enforcement of Foreign Arbitral Awards.

Except in respect of matters concerning the UN and treaties falling within the area that can be broadly described as international economic law (covering financial institutions, investment, tax, etc.), Bangladesh has failed to adopt implementing laws.

[31] 'Multilateral Treaties Deposited with the Secretary-General' (*United Nations Treaty Collection*) <https://treaties.un.org/Pages/Treaties.aspx?id=4&subid=A&lang=en> accessed 11 December 2018.

[32] The 1970s laws on these two institutions were recently replaced by two new laws enacted in 2013 and 2015.

For instance, in the areas of human rights and environment, it has rarely implemented international obligations in domestic laws.

2.5 Implementing Legislation and the Judiciary

On several occasions the Supreme Court has expressed its discontent at the lack of implementing legislation, especially when dealing with human rights treaties. The Court has also made recommendations that appropriate legislative measures be adopted to address the gap between domestic law and international treaties.

In one case a petitioner approached the Court for directions to prevent advertisement of tobacco products, citing, *inter alia*, resolutions of the World Health Organization. The Court observed that 'the government should have taken appropriate steps' in light of 'the resolutions of the World Health Organization'.[33] In *State v Secretary, Ministry of Law* the Court recommended that 'immediate steps must be taken by the Government to enact laws or amend the existing law in order to ensure implementation of all the provisions of the CRC'.[34]

3 Customary International Law

There is no constitutional provision concerning the status of customary international law in the domestic legal system. Indeed, the expression 'customary international law' does not appear anywhere in the Constitution, although several customary international law principles are referred to in article 25 of the Constitution, such as, 'respect for national sovereignty and equality, non-interference in the internal affairs of other countries', etc. These principles are now codified in the United Nations Charter and article 25 also makes reference to the 'principles enunciated in the United Nations Charter'.

Unlike treaties, the issue of domestic application of customary international law has rarely come before Bangladesh courts. While in some cases allusions have been made, which could be interpreted as reference to customary international law, the issue of the applicability of customary international law has only arisen in one recent case,[35] and no courts have ever had to apply a customary rule of international law. The reasons are obvious; on the one hand, it is difficult to find precise customary norms in respect of which equivalent treaty norms do not exist and, on the other hand, courts find it easier to deal with equivalent or similar treaty provisions or domestic statutory provisions, rather than customary norms. As in other jurisdictions, courts can be troubled by the

[33] *Professor Nurul Islam v Government of Bangladesh* 52 DLR (2000) 421–2.

[34] *State v Secretary, Ministry of Law* (n 17) 10–11.

[35] *Chief Prosecutor v Abdul Quader Molla* 22 BLT (AD) (2014) 8.

uncertainty of customary international law. For example, in *Bangladesh Legal Aid and Services Trust v Bangladesh*, although the Court stated that 'the universally recognized prohibition of torture ... is a basic principle of customary international law', it also cited several treaty provisions on torture and eventually decided the case on the basis of domestic law.[36]

In *Chief Prosecutor v Abdul Quader Molla*[37] the issue of the applicability of customary international law arose before the Appellate Division in a rather limited context concerning international criminal law. In this case, the Appellate Division dealt with the issue of whether customary international law can directly impose any criminal liability and penal sanction on an individual.[38] The Court was of the view that customary law could not impose such liability or sanction. In other words, customary international law is not capable of creating a crime directly triable in a national court. The Court held as follows:

> International crimes recognized by customary international law do not ipso facto apply within the domestic jurisdiction. Customary international law does not create any offence in the domestic jurisdiction, nor does it establish any criminal liability in domestic law.
>
> ...
>
> International obligations ... cannot be applicable in the domestic tribunal of the country unless the same is incorporated in the domestic law by a legislative action.
>
> Therefore ... a citizen of the state cannot, in any event, be subjected to the said international obligations/responsibilities of the state.
>
> There remains no doubt that [an Act of Parliament] has primacy over customary international law and customary international law will be applicable so far as it is not inconsistent with the Act.[39]

The above analysis of the Appellate Division blends two separate issues of domestic applicability of customary norms, namely, whether customary norms automatically form part of domestic law, if there is no conflicting domestic provision, and whether customary international law or domestic law is to prevail, if there is a conflict. On the latter issue the Court clearly holds that domestic law will prevail. However, the Court does not deal adequately with the former issue and its conclusion is rather ambivalent.

Firstly, this case involved customary rules of international criminal law, in particular, creation of a crime directly triable in a domestic court by such rules. Consequently, it is difficult to assume that observations made in this case would be equally relevant in respect of other areas of customary international law, which do not concern the imposition of criminal liability and penal sanctions on an individual. Yet, the Appellate Division does not clarify whether its conclusion that international norms cannot be applicable in domestic courts unless incorporated by a legislative action applies to all

36 *Bangladesh Legal Aid and Services Trust* (n 17) 8–9.
37 *Chief Prosecutor* (n 35).
38 Ibid. 67.
39 Ibid. 68, 72, 73, 83.

customary norms or only to norms concerning criminal liability. Secondly, in this case the Court eventually relied on the relevant domestic law provisions, which it considered adequately governed the matter and took precedence over customary rules.[40] Since the question of automatic incorporation arises only if there is no conflicting domestic law provision and this case involved conflicting domestic provisions, the Court's observation that legislative action is required for all international norms remains inexplicable.

In view of the above, *Chief Prosecutor v Abdul Quader Molla* cannot be regarded as a clear authority on whether customary law automatically forms part of Bangladesh law. Accordingly, it is likely that if this issue ever arises in an appropriate context, Bangladesh courts may still adhere to the English and common law tradition of treating customary international law as automatically forming part of Bangladesh law as long as there is no inconsistent Acts of Parliament or authoritative judicial decisions.

4 Participation in International Organizations

Bangladesh became a member of the United Nations in 1974. It is also a member of various UN affiliate organizations, including the International Labour Organization, World Food Programme, World Health Organization, WIPO, and so on. In addition to the UN organizations, Bangladesh is a member of other major international organizations, including the Asian Development Bank, Commonwealth of Nations, International Monetary Fund, Islamic Development Bank, Non-Aligned Movement, Organization of Islamic Cooperation, World Customs Organization, WTO, and the World Bank. Bangladesh is a member of a number of regional organizations, including the Association of Southeast Asian Nations (ASEAN) Regional Forum, Bay of Bengal Initiative for Multi-Sectoral Technical and Economic Cooperation, and the South Asian Association for Regional Cooperation (SAARC).

International organizations, including the UN, WTO, ILO, IMF, and the World Bank, significantly influence Bangladesh's foreign policy. Regional and economic blocs and alliances, such as G-77 plus China, BRICS, Group of 20, LDCs, or the Group of 33 at the WTO, all influence Bangladesh's foreign policy and have significant impact on its role and participation in global dialogues, including trade, development, and climate change negotiations.

Since independence in 1971, Bangladesh has stressed the principle of 'friendship with all and malice towards none' in its diplomacy and foreign relations. In upholding this principle, Bangladesh's approaches to international law and membership of international and regional organizations are driven by certain goals. These goals include safeguarding sovereignty, territorial integrity, security, and national interests and

[40] Ibid. 71–2, 83–4.

ensuring balanced and good-neighbourly relations with all neighbouring countries in South and Southeast Asia and beyond. To this end, Bangladesh seeks to promote regional cooperation under the SAARC, BIMSTEC, and the Forum on Regional Cooperation among Bangladesh, China, India and Myanmar and to contribute to regional peace, stability, connectivity, and integration through active participation or partnership with various global and regional groups, including the OIC, NAM, Commonwealth, ASEAN, EU, Arab League, African Union, Asian Cooperation Dialogue, Indian Ocean Rim Association for Regional Co-operation, ASEAN Regional Forum, Asia-Europe Forum, CICA, and so on. Pursuing multilateralism under the UN is a central component of Bangladesh's foreign policy and it seeks to remain active within the United Nations system, including through contributions to UN peacekeeping activities.

5 Participation in UN Peacekeeping Operations

United Nations peacekeeping operations commenced in 1948 when the Security Council authorized the deployment of UN observers to maintain the ceasefire during the 1948 Arab–Israeli war. Since 1948, seventy UN peacekeeping operations have been deployed, fifty-seven of them since 1988. Over the years, personnel from more than 120 countries have participated in peacekeeping operations.[41] At present, Bangladesh is the fourth-largest contributor of troops in UN peacekeeping missions.[42]

Bangladesh started its participation in peacekeeping operations in 1988 by providing fifteen army personnel as observers in the UN Iran–Iraq Military Observer Group.[43] Since then it has maintained its position as a leading troop contributor in UN peacekeeping operations. Bangladesh armed forces have so far participated in fifty-four peacekeeping missions in forty countries. A total of 128,545 members from Bangladesh armed forces have participated as peacekeepers. At present, 7,283 UN peacekeepers from Bangladesh are deployed in different ongoing missions in DR Congo, Cote d'Ivoire, Liberia, Lebanon, South Sudan, Sudan (Darfur), Western Sahara, Mali, Central African Republic, Haiti, Nepal, Somalia, and UNHQ in the US.[44] Out of 7,283 Bangladeshi peacekeepers, 135 are female personnel.[45]

[41] United Nations Peacekeeping, 'Our History' <https://peacekeeping.un.org/en/our-history> accessed 11 December 2018.

[42] Mahfuz Anam, 'Bangladesh and UN Peacekeeping: Challenges and Prospects' *The Daily Star* (Dhaka, 29 May 2017) <http://www.thedailystar.net/round-tables/bangladesh-and-un-peacekeeping-challenges-prospects-1412455> accessed 11 December 2018.

[43] 'Looking Back to Peacekeeping History' (Armed Forces Division 2013) <http://www.afd.gov.bd/index.php/un-peacekeeping> accessed 11 December 2018.

[44] Ibid.

[45] 'Summary of Contributions to UN Peacekeeping by Country and Post' (United Nations Peacekeeping, 31 October 2017) <https://peacekeeping.un.org/sites/default/files/post.pdf> accessed 11 December 2018.

In recognition of Bangladesh's contribution to the UN peacekeeping missions, the late UN Secretary-General, Kofi Annan, commented that Bangladesh is 'a model member of the United Nations, providing leadership amongst the least developed countries . . . and contributing substantially to peacekeeping and humanitarian operations'. Another UN Secretary-General, Ban Ki-moon, during a visit to South Sudan, praised Bangladeshi peacekeepers noting his 'deep admiration and commendation for all the noble work the Bangladesh contingent has been doing for peace and security in Sudan'.[46] Bangladeshi peacekeepers, working under dangerous circumstances, have often endangered their own lives. Up to March 2019, 146 Bangladeshis had died while serving in UN peacekeeping operations.[47]

The issue of the legality of Bangladesh's participation in UN peacekeeping operations arose before the Supreme Court in *M Saleem Ullah v Bangladesh*.[48] In this case, the petitioner challenged the decision of the Government to participate in the UN-sponsored multinational force in Haiti pursuant to the UN Security Council Resolution 940 of 31 July 1994. It was argued that such participation would violate a number of provisions of the Constitution. The Court declined to entertain the case and held as follows:

> The decision was taken pursuant to the Resolution No 940 and Bangladesh being a member of the United Nations has taken the decision within the authority of the constitutional framework and international commitments . . . We fail to understand how the decision of the Government taken pursuant to a UN resolution and the UN Charter is an infringement of the Constitution.[49]

6 Interstate Disputes

Bangladesh has been a party to two formal interstate dispute settlement proceedings. Both of these cases concerned delimitation of maritime boundary.

Immediately after its independence, the task of defining maritime limits became a part of the national agenda of Bangladesh. As a preparatory step, Bangladesh published its base points in 1974. It also asserted its sovereign rights over an exclusive economic zone (EEZ) extending over 200 nautical miles (nm) from the baseline. Indeed, Bangladesh was the first country in South Asia to formally claim an EEZ of 200 nm. The Territorial Waters and Maritime Zones Act, 1974 was enacted defining the maritime jurisdiction of Bangladesh in the Bay of Bengal.

[46] Editorial, 'Bangladesh's role in international peacekeeping' *The Asian Age* (Dhaka, 1 December 2016) <https://dailyasianage.com/news/39719/bangladeshs-role-in-intl-peacekeeping> accessed 11 December 2018.

[47] 'Fatalities by Nationality and Mission up to 31 March 2019' (United Nations Peacekeeping, 31 March 2019) <https://peacekeeping.un.org/sites/default/files/statsbynationalitymission_2_23.pdf> accessed 30 April 2019.

[48] *M Saleem Ullah* (n 5).

[49] Ibid. 223, 224.

A detailed statement was presented by Bangladesh elaborating its position on the maritime boundaries at the 1974 Caracas Session of the Third United Nations Conference on the Law of the Sea. Upon presentation of Bangladesh's position, a formal note was presented by India indicating its objections to some of the points. Bangladesh replied by stating that official talks should be held to deal with issues needing clarification or resolution.

The first round of talks was held in December 1974. India took the position that the equidistance method was appropriate for defining the boundary. Bangladesh based its stand on the judgment of the International Court of Justice in the *North Sea Continental Shelf* case,[50] which held that where, because of geographical or other factors, a mechanical application of the equidistance method led to inequitable results, the adoption of the equidistance method was not appropriate and the parties should instead seek an equitable delimitation.

By early 1975, negotiations had reached a point where it was recognized that there were some areas in which the divergent positions could not be reconciled and arbitration might have to be resorted to. Although negotiations continued until 2009, no agreement could be reached. Negotiations on maritime boundaries also took place between Bangladesh and Myanmar from 1974, with eight rounds of talks between 1974 and 1986 and six rounds between 2008 and 2010. However, no settlement could be reached through these discussions.

Eventually, Bangladesh instituted arbitral proceedings pursuant to Annex VII of UNCLOS against Myanmar and India. Since both Bangladesh and Myanmar, by making declarations under article 287 of UNCLOS, accepted the jurisdiction of the International Tribunal for the Law of the Sea (ITLOS), the *Bangladesh/Myanmar* case was transferred to ITLOS and was registered as Case No. 16 on 14 December 2009. ITLOS delivered its judgment on 14 March 2012.

India did not make any declaration under article 287 of UNCLOS, and consequently the case with India continued with a five-member Annex VII Arbitral Tribunal and it was registered with the Permanent Court of Arbitration (PCA) as PCA Case No. 2010-16. The Tribunal delivered its award on 7 July 2014.

6.1 *Bangladesh/Myanmar* Case

This case[51] involved delimitation of the maritime boundary between Bangladesh and Myanmar in the Bay of Bengal with respect to the territorial sea,[52] the

[50] *North Sea Continental Shelf (Federal Republic of Germany v Denmark; Federal Republic of Germany v Netherlands)* [1969] ICJ Rep 3.

[51] *Dispute Concerning Delimitation of the Maritime Boundary between Bangladesh and Myanmar in the Bay of Bengal (Bangladesh v Myanmar)* (Judgment of 14 March 2012).

[52] The territorial sea extends to 12 nm from the low-water line.

exclusive economic zone,[53] and the continental shelf[54] within and beyond 200 nautical miles (nm).

6.1.1 *Territorial Sea*

With regard to the territorial sea, Bangladesh argued that the agreed minutes of discussions between the parties in 1974 and 2008 constituted an agreement regarding the territorial sea boundary, while Myanmar denied any such agreement. ITLOS decided that those minutes did not constitute an agreement and accordingly delimited the territorial sea by an equidistance line from the base points of Bangladesh and Myanmar. Likewise, an equidistance line formed the boundary between St. Martin's Island (belonging to Bangladesh) and Myanmar, but where the territorial sea of St. Martin's Island no longer overlapped with the territorial sea of Myanmar, Bangladesh was allowed to extend the territorial sea of the island to 12 nm.[55]

6.1.2 *EEZ and the Continental Shelf*

With respect to the EEZ and the continental shelf, Bangladesh argued that 'equidistance' was not an appropriate method and that in view of the configuration and concavity of its coast, ITLOS should apply the 'angle-bisector method'. The angle-bisector method is an alternative to the equidistance method and is used much less frequently than the equidistance method. Myanmar, on the other hand, opted for the 'equidistance/relevant circumstances' method. ITLOS decided in favour of the equidistance/relevant circumstances method. Accordingly, it established a provisional equidistance line and then adjusted that line taking into account the concavity of the coast (which was regarded as the only 'relevant circumstance') so that the delimitation line did not cut off the seaward projection of Bangladesh's EEZ and continental shelf.[56]

6.1.3 *Continental Shelf beyond 200 Nautical Miles*

The Tribunal decided that it could delimit the lateral boundary of the continental shelf beyond 200 nm, even though the outer limit of the shelf had not been established. Bangladesh argued that it alone was entitled to the entire continental shelf beyond 200 nm because the outer shelf was the natural prolongation of Bangladesh's land territory. Myanmar argued that the controlling concept was not 'natural prolongation' but the 'outer edge of the continental margin'. The Tribunal held that the adjusted equidistance line delimiting the EEZ and the inner continental shelf would continue in the same direction delimiting the outer continental shelf until the line reached a point where the rights of third states might be affected.[57]

[53] The EEZ is an area extending to 200 nm from the baseline.

[54] The continental shelf is the seabed and the subsoil extending from the coast to the outer edge of the continental margin, or to a distance of 200 nm from the baseline where the outer edge does not extend to 200 nm.

[55] *Maritime Boundary* (n 51) paras 64–5, 126, 506.

[56] Ibid. paras 208, 223, 236–40, 292–3, 297.

[57] Ibid. paras 356, 407, 416, 427, 438, 462.

6.1.4 *Disproportionality Test*

Having established the maritime boundary line, the Tribunal checked whether the line had caused any significant disproportion by reference to the ratio of the length of the coastlines of the two states and the ratio of the maritime area allocated to each state. The length of the relevant coast of Bangladesh was 413 kilometres, while that of Myanmar was 587 kilometres. The ratio of the length of the coasts was 1:1.42 in favour of Myanmar. The adjusted equidistance line allocated approximately 111,631 square kilometres of sea area to Bangladesh and approximately 171,832 square kilometres to Myanmar. The ratio of the allocated maritime areas was approximately 1:1.54 in favour of Myanmar. The Tribunal concluded that this ratio did not lead to any significant disproportion.[58]

6.2 *Bangladesh/India* Case

For this case, the PCA acted as the Registry.[59] It concerned the delimitation of the maritime boundary between the parties in the territorial sea, the EEZ, and the continental shelf within and beyond 200 nm in the Bay of Bengal.

6.2.1 *Jurisdiction*

The Arbitral Tribunal first considered its jurisdiction over the dispute, in particular, its jurisdiction to delimit the continental shelf beyond 200 nm. Emphasizing that article 76 of UNCLOS 'embodies the concept of a single continental shelf', and recalling the reasoning of ITLOS in the *Bangladesh/Myanmar* case, the Tribunal observed that it saw 'no grounds why it should refrain from exercising its jurisdiction to decide on the lateral delimitation of the continental shelf beyond 200 nm before its outer limits have been established'.[60]

6.2.2 *Land boundary terminus*

The parties agreed that the land boundary terminus was to be used as the starting point of the maritime boundary. The parties further agreed that the land boundary terminus was to be established on the basis of the award of the Bengal Boundary Commission of 1947 (Radcliffe Award). However, the parties disagreed on the interpretation of the Radcliffe Award and on the location of the land boundary terminus determined by it. On the basis of a series of contemporaneous maps (including the map used in the Radcliffe Award), the Arbitral Tribunal decided on the position of the land boundary terminus.[61]

[58] Ibid. para 499.

[59] *Bay of Bengal Maritime Boundary Arbitration between Bangladesh and India (Bangladesh v India)*, PCA Case No. 2010-16, Award of 7 July 2014.

[60] Ibid. paras 74–83.

[61] Ibid. paras 58–9, 169, 188.

6.2.3 *Base points*

Bangladesh challenged several of India's proposed base points on the ground that they were located on alleged low tide elevations (LTEs). The Tribunal noted that, while LTEs may be used as base points for measuring the breadth of the territorial sea, it did not necessarily follow that they were appropriate base points for delimiting a maritime boundary between adjacent coastlines. The Tribunal decided that a point located on the low-water line of Moore Island and a base point B-1, as proposed by Bangladesh, were appropriate for the construction of the equidistance line in the territorial sea.[62]

6.2.4 *Territorial sea*

The Tribunal delimited the territorial sea using the equidistance method. Bangladesh had initially argued that due to coastal instability this method was not appropriate and that a 180° angle bisector should be used. However, following the decision of ITLOS in the *Bangladesh/Myanmar* case rejecting similar arguments, Bangladesh changed its position and put forward a provisional equidistance line and argued that the line should be adjusted due to the instability and concavity of the coast. The Tribunal held that these were not relevant to the delimitation of the territorial sea. However, as the land boundary terminus was not situated on the equidistance line, the Tribunal considered that the need to connect the land boundary terminus to the median line constituted a special circumstance necessitating adjustment of the equidistance line.[63]

6.2.5 *EEZ and the continental shelf*

Regarding the delimitation of the EEZ and the continental shelf, the Tribunal decided that the equidistance/relevant circumstances method was the appropriate method. The Tribunal accordingly constructed a provisional equidistance line and then considered the relevant circumstances asserted by the parties to adjust the line. Due to the concavity of the coast, the provisional equidistance line produced a 'cut-off effect' on the seaward projections of the coast of Bangladesh. The Tribunal decided that this necessitated adjustment of the provisional equidistance line in favour of Bangladesh.[64]

6.2.6 *Continental shelf beyond 200 nautical miles*

The Tribunal applied the same methodology within and beyond 200 nm, adjusting the provisional equidistance line into a simpler straight line to avoid a cut-off effect arising from the concavity of Bangladesh's coast.[65] The Tribunal assessed the proportionality of the allocation of maritime zones by reference to the overall geography of the area, finding that no alteration of the adjusted equidistance line was necessary.[66]

[62] Ibid. paras 190–7, 259–64, 267–9.
[63] Ibid. paras 274.
[64] Ibid. paras 372, 381, 393, 399.
[65] Ibid. paras 456–8.
[66] Ibid. para 497.

7 Investment Arbitrations

Bangladesh has been a party to a number of investment arbitrations before the International Centre for Settlement of Investment Disputes. All of these cases are in the energy sector. Three concluded ICSID arbitrations are: (i) *Scimitar Exploration Limited v Republic of Bangladesh and Bangladesh Oil, Gas and Mineral Corporation*;[67] (ii) *SAIPEM SpA v People's Republic of Bangladesh*;[68] and (iii) *Chevron Bangladesh Block Twelve, Ltd and Chevron Bangladesh Blocks Thirteen and Fourteen, Ltd v People's Republic of Bangladesh*.[69]

Currently two ICSID arbitrations are pending, which are: (i) *Niko Resources (Bangladesh) Ltd v Bangladesh Petroleum Exploration and Production Company Limited (Bapex) and Bangladesh Oil Gas and Mineral Corporation (Petrobangla)*;[70] and (ii) *Niko Resources (Bangladesh) Ltd v Bangladesh Petroleum Exploration and Production Company Limited (Bapex) and Bangladesh Oil Gas and Mineral Corporation (Petrobangla)*.[71]

7.1 *Scimitar* Case

This case was submitted to ICSID by a British Virgin Islands company, Scimitar Exploration Limited, against the Government of Bangladesh. The request for arbitration was signed by one 'HS Campbell' as 'Secretary to the Company' and it was submitted on Scimitar's behalf by a law firm based in Canada identifying itself as 'counsel'.

Bangladesh objected to jurisdiction on the basis that the request had been instituted by persons not competent to act for Scimitar. It further argued that since Scimitar had not produced a resolution of the board of directors or the shareholders authorizing the institution of the arbitration proceedings, the jurisdiction of ICSID had not been validly invoked. In response, Scimitar filed a document purporting to be a resolution of its board of directors passed on 11 June 1993 confirming the capacity and authority of the persons initiating the arbitration. Bangladesh disputed the validity of the resolution.

[67] *Scimitar Exploration Limited v Republic of Bangladesh and Bangladesh Oil, Gas and Mineral Corporation* ICSID-ARB/92/2 (3 November 1992); 5 ICSID Reports 3.

[68] *SAIPEM SpA v People's Republic of Bangladesh* ICSID-ARB/05/7 (25 April 2005).

[69] *Chevron Bangladesh Block Twelve, Ltd and Chevron Bangladesh Blocks Thirteen and Fourteen, Ltd v People's Republic of Bangladesh* ICSID-ARB/06/10 (30 June 2006).

[70] *Niko Resources (Bangladesh) Ltd v Bangladesh Petroleum Exploration and Production Company Limited (Bapex) and Bangladesh Oil Gas and Mineral Corporation (Petrobangla)* ICSID-ARB/10/11 (27 May 2010).

[71] *Niko Resources (Bangladesh) Ltd v Bangladesh Petroleum Exploration and Production Company Limited (Bapex) and Bangladesh Oil Gas and Mineral Corporation (Petrobangla)* ICSID-ARB/10/18 (28 July 2010).

On 30 June 1993, a letter was directed to the ICSID Tribunal on behalf of Scimitar indicating that there had been a change in ownership of Scimitar, that all previous officers had resigned, and that its counsel had withdrawn. At the hearing of the ICSID Tribunal to consider the jurisdictional issue, counsel for Scimitar stated that he had been instructed 'not to resist' Bangladesh's submissions on the validity of the institution of the arbitral proceedings or the validity of the board resolution.

The ICSID Tribunal observed that based on the agreed positions of the parties and the uncontested evidence before it, the proceedings were not initiated with proper authorization, and there was no evidence that the absence of such authorization had been remedied by any action subsequent to the commencement of the proceedings. The ICSID Tribunal, therefore, held that the dispute was not within its jurisdiction.[72]

7.2 *Saipem* Case

This case[73] concerned a contract between Saipem, an Italian company, and Petrobangla, a state-owned entity, to build a gas pipeline in Bangladesh. The project was significantly delayed. The parties disagreed on the reasons for the delay. According to Saipem, the delay was mainly due to problems with the local population, who rebelled against the project. Bangladesh argued that the problems with the population were caused by Saipem itself and that Saipem was already behind schedule before the problems began. The parties agreed on extending the completion date but could not reach any agreement regarding compensation and additional costs relating to the delay.[74]

The contract contained a dispute resolution clause providing for settlement of disputes under the Rules of Conciliation and Arbitration of the International Chamber of Commerce (ICC). Saipem referred the dispute to ICC arbitration seeking outstanding payments under both the original contract and the subsequent extension agreement.[75]

During the arbitration, Petrobangla made various procedural requests before the ICC Tribunal. Since the ICC Tribunal denied such requests, Petrobangla brought an action before a local court seeking the revocation of the ICC Tribunal's authority. The court revoked the authority of the ICC Tribunal. Even though this decision was subject to two degrees of appeal, Saipem decided not to appeal the decision. The ICC Tribunal held that the revocation of the authority of the Tribunal was contrary to the general principles governing international arbitration and continued with the arbitration and, eventually, passed an award in favour of Saipem.[76] Petrobangla applied to set aside the ICC award before the High Court Division, which held that there was no award that could be set aside, as the award passed by the Tribunal was 'a nullity in the eye of law'

[72] Scimitar (n 67) 9. The ICSID Tribunal passed its Award on 5 April 1994.

[73] *SAIPEM* (n 68). The ICSID Tribunal passed its Award on 30 June 2009.

[74] Ibid. paras 7, 11–22.

[75] Ibid. paras 10, 25.

[76] Ibid. paras 31–3, 40, 42–3, 45, 48.

and it was 'clearly illegal and without jurisdiction inasmuch as the authority of the Tribunal was revoked . . . by a competent court of Bangladesh'. Saipem did not appeal this decision.[77]

Later, Saipem filed a request for arbitration in ICSID based on the breach of the BIT between Italy and Bangladesh. The basis of Saipem's claim was the undue intervention of the Bangladeshi courts in the ICC arbitration, which precluded the enforcement of the ICC award. According to Saipem, those acts constituted an expropriation.[78]

The ICSID Tribunal in its award held that although the actions of the Bangladeshi courts did not constitute direct expropriation, they amounted to 'measures having similar effects'. Such actions resulted in substantially depriving Saipem of the benefit of the ICC award.[79] It observed that although national courts have discretion to revoke an arbitrator's authority in cases of misconduct, they cannot use this discretion to revoke authority for other reasons. The ICSID Tribunal noted that the actions of the courts of Bangladesh were against international law, specifically, the principle of abuse of rights, and the New York Convention article II(1), which imposes on Contracting States the obligation of recognizing and honouring arbitration agreements. The Tribunal considered the intervention of the Bangladesh courts as amounting to 'expropriation of the right to arbitrate' and held that the amount awarded by the ICC award constituted the best evaluation of the compensation due.[80]

7.3 *Chevron* Case

This case[81] concerned a dispute between Bangladesh and two Bermudan corporations, Chevron Bangladesh Block Twelve, Ltd and Chevron Bangladesh Blocks Thirteen and Fourteen, Ltd, on the interpretation of five agreements relating to the exploration and sale of natural gas. The agreements included two Production Sharing Contracts (PSCs), and three Gas Purchase and Sale Agreements (GPSAs). The request for arbitration was submitted on the basis of similar ICSID arbitration clauses contained in each of the five agreements.

The PSCs and the GPSAs included a provision stating that Petrobangla, as the transmission company, would be entitled to receive a tariff when Chevron used a pipeline operated by Petrobangla to supply natural gas to the Bangladesh domestic market. The PSCs were concluded in 1995, the first GPSA was signed in 1996, and gas sales to Petrobangla commenced in 1999. Some communication between the parties disputing the interpretation of the tariff provision occurred in 1999. Chevron asserted

[77] Ibid. paras 50–1. [78] Ibid. para 52.

[79] Ibid. para 129. [80] Ibid. paras 159, 167, 170, 204.

[81] *Chevron* (n 69). The ICSID Tribunal passed its Award on 17 May 2010. See also Lindsey Marchessault, 'Chevron Bangladesh Block Twelve, Ltd and Chevron Bangladesh Blocks Thirteen and Fourteen, Ltd v People's Republic of Bangladesh (ICSID Case No ARB/06/10): Introductory Note' (2011) 26(1) ICSID Review 256.

that since title to the gas passed to Petrobangla before the gas reached Petrobangla's pipeline, the tariff was not payable. However, the tariff was paid by Chevron to Petrobangla without further communication between the parties until 2003. When the parties entered into the second and the third GPSAs in 2003 and 2004, respectively, they simultaneously concluded two side-letter agreements acknowledging the existence of a dispute on the interpretation of the tariff provisions.

The dispute brought to ICSID concerned the question of whether the tariff provisions applied when Petrobangla itself was the buyer and took delivery of the gas through its pipeline. In the ICSID arbitration, Bangladesh initially refused to participate in the jurisdiction phase and obtained an injunction from a local court to restrain the arbitral proceedings. In response, the ICSID Tribunal referred to articles 26 and 41 of the ICSID Convention to establish that prior consent to ICSID arbitration excluded other remedies, such as domestic injunctions. Bangladesh continued to abstain from the proceedings and a summary Decision on Jurisdiction was delivered on 21 August 2007, where the ICSID Tribunal upheld its own jurisdiction and scheduled a hearing date for the merits. At this stage, Bangladesh decided to participate in the arbitration and withdrew the injunction in the local court.

In its award on the merits, the ICSID Tribunal considered the language of the agreements, applicable law, and the communications and behaviour of the parties with respect to the agreements. The Tribunal determined that, under the PSCs and the GPSAs, the tariff at issue was owed by the Claimants regardless of whether or not Petrobangla was the purchaser of the natural gas. The Tribunal also found that the Claimants had complied with the Respondent's interpretation of the tariff provisions for several years before reviving the dispute. Because of this compliance, the Claimants were estopped from disputing the interpretation.

7.4 *Niko* Cases

There are two cases that were initiated by Niko Resources (Bangladesh) Ltd, involving a Joint Venture Agreement (JVA) between Niko and BAPEX, a state-owned entity, and a GPSA between Niko, BAPEX, and Petrobangla. Both agreements contain an ICSID arbitration clause.

In 2005, two blow-outs occurred in the Chattak gas field operated by Niko. Enquiry committees formed by the Government of Bangladesh found Niko responsible for the blow-outs. In 2008, the Government and Petrobangla commenced proceedings against Niko before a Bangladesh court claiming damages for the blow-outs. Niko took the position that this matter should be resolved through ICSID arbitration and commenced the first arbitration (Compensation Claim).[82]

[82] *Niko Resources* (n 70).

Subsequent to the blow-outs, the Bangladesh Environmental Lawyers' Association (BELA) and others initiated a case before the High Court Division against the Government, Petrobangla, BAPEX, and Niko seeking, *inter alia*, a determination that the JVA was invalid and an injunction restraining payments to Niko in respect of the gas supplied by Niko from its Feni gas field. The Court issued an injunction restraining payment until Niko paid compensation. Although Niko raised invoices for the gas supplied since November 2004, none of the invoices was paid by Petrobangla. Niko commenced the second arbitration to recover these payments (Payment Claim).[83]

Two ICSID Tribunals were constituted to deal with the disputes. However, the Tribunals comprised the same three arbitrators and it was agreed that the two cases would proceed in a concurrent manner, and that the Tribunals might issue one single instrument in relation to both cases.

7.4.1 *Jurisdiction*

Bangladesh objected to the jurisdiction of the ICSID Tribunals on a number of grounds, including corruption. In their Decision on Jurisdiction, the Tribunals found that they had jurisdiction with respect to both the Compensation and Payment Claims and that the jurisdiction extended to the question of whether the GPSA and the JVA were avoided on grounds of corruption.[84]

7.4.2 *Payment Claim*

The Tribunals passed several orders on the Payment Claim, the last order being a direction on Petrobangla to immediately make payment of the amounts due to Niko with interest. Petrobangla took the position that it was unable to make payment due to the restraining order of the Court and the fact that the order was passed in third-party initiated proceedings (i.e. the BELA proceedings). In response, the Tribunals observed that the courts of Bangladesh are bound to implement the decisions rendered by ICSID Tribunals and if it were otherwise, the international commitments of the state of Bangladesh 'could be rendered ineffective by the simple expedient of any third parties ... bringing claims before the courts of Bangladesh and having these courts render decisions which conflict materially with the decisions of the Tribunals operating under the ICSID Convention'.[85]

7.4.3 *Compensation Claim*

The Tribunals heard evidence and argument on the liability for the blow-outs. However, before issuance of their decision and while the parties were producing their submissions on the quantum of damages, BAPEX and Petrobangla served requests concerning the avoidance of the JVA and the GPSA on grounds of corruption (Corruption Claim). The Tribunals then decided to assign first priority to the Corruption Claim and suspended

[83] *Niko Resources* (n 71).

[84] *Decision on Jurisdiction* (19 July 2016) para 5.

[85] Ibid. para 13.

the proceedings on liability relating to the blow-outs.[86] The proceedings in relation to the Corruption Claim and the Compensation Claim are still ongoing.

8 Conclusion

As this chapter illustrates, international law has been relevant in the internal legal system of Bangladesh as well as in its external relations. In light of the large number of treaties that it has signed or ratified, Bangladesh seems to be an enthusiastic participant in international treaties. However, its treaty practice remains deficient and needs improvement in three key areas. First, it is a matter of concern that there is almost a complete lack of compliance with article 145A of the Constitution, which requires all treaties to be laid before the Parliament. Secondly, although Bangladesh has ratified many human rights treaties, reservations have been made in respect of some important treaty provisions. Thirdly, apart from a few instances, implementing legislation is rarely passed to incorporate treaty obligations into domestic law. While the legislative framework in respect of treaties is rather imperfect, the Supreme Court of Bangladesh made a commendable effort to invoke and rely on treaty provisions that are not in conflict with domestic law. With respect to customary international law, it is yet to be clarified by Bangladesh courts whether or not this body of law automatically forms part of Bangladesh law. In case of conflict, domestic law prevails over both international treaties and customary international law.

Bangladesh has been a reasonably active participant in international organizations, including the UN. Its involvement in UN peacekeeping operations has been praised by the international community. In recent years, Bangladesh has participated in two interstate dispute settlement proceedings concerning delimitation of its maritime boundary with Myanmar and India. The outcome in both cases is balanced and considered to be in favour of Bangladesh. It has been a party to several investment arbitrations under the ICSID Convention. Out of the three concluded ICSID cases, the award was in favour of Bangladesh in two cases, the *Scimitar* case and the *Chevron* case. While the award in the *Saipem* case was against Bangladesh, the propriety of this award can be debated. In this case, Saipem did not pursue several appeal procedures available in Bangladesh courts at different stages; despite such non-exhaustion of domestic law remedies, the Tribunal held that the actions of the Bangladeshi courts amounted to measures having effects similar to expropriation.

[86] Ibid. para 7.

CHAPTER 26

NEPAL

PRATYUSH NATH UPRETI
AND SURYA P SUBEDI

1 Introduction

For a small Himalayan state with an ancient civilisation and no experience of foreign subjugation, Nepal has had more than its fair share of internal political upheavals. In the latter part of the twentieth century, this history was complemented by a diverse set of interactions with the United Nations and the regimes negotiated under its auspices. These interactions with the outside world and international law have tended to pursue three objectives: first, asserting and protecting Nepal's freedom of action and maintaining its own equilibrium vis-à-vis its two larger neighbours, China and India; secondly, economic development; and thirdly, promoting liberal democratic values underpinned by human rights and the rule of law. This chapter will examine this interplay between international law on the one hand and national and international politics on the other.

The chapter offers a brief history of Nepal in section 2, before considering the role of the UN in its political transition in sectin 3. Section 4 then considers the application of international law in the Nepalese legal system, while section 5 examines specific ways in which international law has been used in Nepalese politics to bridge normative gaps, in the context of hydro-diplomacy between India and Nepal, through the South Asian Association for Regional Cooperation (SAARC), and in the context of transit and trade rights.

2 History

Nepal is still considered by some to be a 'Shangri-La' state, but to truly understand its reality, one should view Nepal through a sociopolitical lens. Nepal is a landlocked country[1] located entirely in the Ganges River basin bounded by India to the east,

[1] Michael Faye, John McArthur, Jeffrey Sachs, and Thomas Snow, 'The Challenges Facing Landlocked Developing Countries' (2004) 5 Journal of Human Development 31.

south, and west and by the Tibet region of China to the north.[2] Geographically, the country is divided into three parts:[3] (i) the high Himalayan mountains in the north, (ii) hills and mountain slopes in the centre, and (iii) plains (the Terai) in the south. It is diverse in caste, religion, language, and ethnicity.[4]

In 1768, when King Prithivi Narayan Shah conquered the city of Kathmandu and its surrounding area, the newly unified territory called 'Nepal' was formed.[5] Post-unification, Nepal was predominately ruled by a monarchy. Later, a local warrior caste called Ranas usurped state power from the monarchy and took control of Nepal from 1846 until 1951.[6] Subsequently, power was restored to the monarchy under King Tribhuvan; his son and grandson continued his legacy effectively as executive monarchs until 1990, under an indigenous system of governance known as the party-less Panchayat system.[7] However, a 'people's movement' in 1989–90 led to the restoration of a parliamentary system of government and a constitutional monarchy.

The Constitution of the Kingdom of Nepal 1990 was to be the cornerstone for the development of constitutionalism and for the restoration of democratic values and norms. Unfortunately, the aspirations of the political movement were not fulfilled. Only a few years after the establishment of a multi-party democracy, a small ultra-leftist party calling itself the Communist Party of Nepal (Maoist) began a brutal armed rebellion against the state in five districts of the mid and far west. These districts were underdeveloped and isolated from the capital.[8] Inspired by a similar guerrilla organization in Peru called the 'Shining Path', the Maoist Party labelled its campaign the 'People's War'.[9]

At the height of the insurgency, in June 2001, nine members of Nepal's royal family were killed in a tragic murder-suicide, apparently committed by the Crown Prince.[10] This episode was the beginning of the end of monarchy in Nepal. After the death of

[2] Fidel Devkota, 'Climate Change and its Socio-cultural Impact in the Himalayan Region of Nepal—A Visual Documentation' (2013) 1(2) Anthrovision <https://anthrovision.revues.org/589> accessed 2 July 2016.

[3] Ibid.

[4] Kanak Bikram Thapa and Bal Bahadur Mukhia, 'Religious Education in Nepal' in Derek Davis and Elena Miroshnikova (eds), *The Routledge International Handbook of Religious Education* (Routledge 2013) 236.

[5] The Carter Center, *Political Transition Monitoring in Nepal, 2009–2014* (Report 2014) 13.

[6] Ibid.

[7] The party-less Panchayat system was instituted by King Mahendra in 1960 and remained in force till 1990. The main feature of Panchayat System was the institution of the monarchy as the central source of political authority. See Pratyoush Onta and Devraj Humagain, 'Janjati Magazines and the Contents of the Subaltern Counterpublic Sphere during the 1990s' in Michael Hutt and Pratyoush Onta (eds), *Political Change and Public Culture in Post-1990 Nepal* (Cambridge University Press 2017) 101–4.

[8] Colonel SD Crane, 'The Maoist Insurgency in Nepal: 1996–2001' (USAWC Strategy Research Project 2002).

[9] Ibid. 11.

[10] Laura Kunreuther, *Voicing Subjects: Public Intimacy and Mediation in Kathmandu* (University of California Press 2014) 241. See also Jonathan Gregson, *Massacre at the Palace: The Doomed Royal Dynasty of Nepal* (Miramax 2002).

King Birendra and his immediate heirs, King Birendra's younger brother Gyanendra Bir Bikram Shah became the new king. His sudden ascension to the throne and the ongoing Maoist insurgency provided a political opportunity to continue his father King Mahendra's vision for the country, by seizing power and abolishing the multi-party democracy. King Gyanendra moved quickly to consolidate power. He deployed the Royal Nepal Army against the Maoists, a step that his older brother had pointedly refused to take. The use of the national army against the Maoists turned the insurgency into a fully-fledged civil war.[11] He next used article 115 of the Constitution 1990 to declare a state of emergency in Nepal, which suspended all political rights and freedoms.

The absolutist and authoritarian[12] rule of King Gyanendra united the political parties. Facing a common political enemy in King Gyanendra, these political parties first formed an alliance among themselves (the Seven-Party Alliance—'SPA'), and then united with the still-underground Maoist Party to launch another people's movement against King Gyanendra's rule. The overwhelming response from the people in favour of the movement forced King Gyanendra to restore Parliament, which then suspended and ultimately abolished the monarchy.

A Comprehensive Peace Accord (CPA) was signed between the SPA and the Maoists in November 2006, which brought the Maoist Party into the political mainstream. The Interim Constitution of Nepal 2007 was drafted, with political consensus among the major political parties,[13] to guide the country through the transitional phase. The CPA and an Agreement on the Monitoring of the Management of Arms and Armies were included in a schedule to the Constitution.[14] Eventually, the Interim Constitution was replaced by the Constitution of Nepal 2015.

After the CPA was signed, Nepal conducted its first Constituent Assembly elections, and the elected representatives were mandated to draft a new federal and republican constitution. The Maoist Party had secured a sweeping victory and was poised to lead the constitution-writing process. Unfortunately, the quick fall of the Maoist-led government and the extension of the first Constituent Assembly meant that the new constitution could not be written. As a result, the first Constituent Assembly was dissolved[15] and a second election was conducted in 2013.

Again, the drafting process dragged on for almost two years. But the destructive April 2015 earthquake in Nepal pressured the political parties to draft and pass the Constitution, which was promulgated on 20 September 2015. Even though the Constitution was passed by 90 per cent of votes in Parliament, a few political parties walked out of the process and protested.

[11] Benoît Cailmail, 'The Fall of a Hindu Monarchy: Maoists in Power in Nepal' (Institit Français des Relations Internationales Research Paper, December 2008) <http://www.ifri.org/sites/default/files/atoms/files/the_fall_of_a_hindu_monarchy.pdf> accessed 2 November 2016.

[12] Ibid.

[13] Interim Constitution of Nepal 2063 (2007) preamble (unofficial translation by UNDP Nepal 2009).

[14] Interim Constitution of Nepal 2063 (2007) schedules 3 and 4.

[15] Pratyush Nath Upreti, 'CA Extension: Moral Imperatives' *New Spotlight Magazine* (July 2011) <http://www.spotlightnepal.com/2011/07/25/ca-extension-moral-imperatives> accessed 2 November 2016.

Shortly after its promulgation, India appeared to have given its tacit support to the Madheshi political parties in Nepal who had resorted to blocking[16] the supply of essential goods, including fuel, from India to Nepal. The blockade, which shut down one of the main trading routes in Birganj, was intended to express the parties' dissatisfaction with certain provisions in the Constitution, especially regarding the new federal structure for the country. Officially, India claimed that the economic blockade was caused by Nepal's political parties, who impeded roads and highways because they were unhappy with the Constitution. The blockade was eventually lifted and an attempt was made to find a political compromise amongst the major political parties in Nepal. This led to an amendment to certain provisions in the Constitution concerning the representation in Parliament based on the size of the population from each of the provinces.[17]

Consequently, the country was able to move forward. The 2017 provincial and federal elections embraced a new political course from a unitary to a federal state. The Federal Parliament consists of the House of Representatives and the National Assembly. The House of Representatives consists of 275 members, of which 165 members are directly elected and 110 are elected through a proportional electoral system.[18] The unicameral National Assembly consists of fifty-nine members.[19] It has 60 per cent of members directly elected and 40 per cent elected in accordance with the proportional electoral system.[20] The Constitution harmonizes relations between the federation, state, and local bodies based on the principles of cooperation, coexistence, and coordination.[21] However, challenges in managing federalism, among other things, lie ahead. Nevertheless, recent elections have opened the door for political stability, peace, and most importantly, a pathway for economic prosperity.

3 The UN and Nepal's Transition

Nepal's political transformation from a decade-long conflict is described with adjectives such as 'profound' and 'remarkable'.[22] However, the civil war left Nepalese society

[16] Akhilesh Upadhyay, 'Nepal, Between the Dragon and the Elephant' *The New York Times* (New York, 6 November 2015).

[17] SD Muni, 'India and Nepal Must Step Back from the Precipice' *The Wire* (8 November 2015) <https://thewire.in/diplomacy/india-and-nepal-must-step-back-from-the-precipice> accessed 5 September 2016.

[18] Constitution of Nepal 2015 art. 84(1) (Constituent Assembly Secretariat Singha Durbar, Unofficial Translation by Nepal Law Society, IDEA, and UNDP).

[19] Ibid. art. 86(2). [20] Ibid. art. 176(1). [21] Ibid. art. 232(1).

[22] Report of the UN High Commissioner for Human Rights on the human rights situation and the activities of her office, including technical cooperation, in Nepal (UN Doc A/HRC/10/53, 28 February 2009). Also see Peris Jones and Malcolm Langford, 'Between Demos and Ethnos: The Nepal Constitution and Indigenous Rights' (2011) 18 International Journal on Minority and Group Rights 369, 370.

fractured, disconnected, frustrated, and alienated,[23] and expectations for social, political, and economic justice were high once it ended. The role of the UN in Nepal's transition was unlike other peace operations of the UN. Prior to 2004, the UN was not involved in the peace process, which was initiated by the Government of Nepal when the first round of peace talks took place in early 2001. Even though the UN had offered its good offices in 2002, its involvement in the peace process started only in 2005 through the UN Office of the UN High Commissioner for Human Rights (OHCHR).[24] Nevertheless, the UN was invited to sign the CPA 2006 as a witness.[25]

Rebuilding a nation after a conflict is challenging, and in the past, UN peacekeeping missions have had broad mandates. Interestingly, the UN mission in Nepal had a narrow mandate and no armed peacekeepers.[26] The reason behind such an exceptional arrangement was to allow Nepalese 'self-ownership' of the peace process. In other words, political parties and the country's citizens took great pride in concluding the CPA, which is often described as a 'Nepali-owned peace process' or 'nationally owned peace process'. This sentiment can be understood if we see the process of the transition from civil war to the CPA.

The Maoists undertook an internal armed rebellion against the Hindu king and his government. It was not heavily internationalized, unlike many previous conflicts in Africa, Asia, and Latin America.[27] The initial peace talks in 2001, and nationwide demonstrations in the form of Jan-Anadolan II (People's Revolution II) in 2006, created a 'sense of ownership' of the peace process. Political parties, while requesting UN assistance to monitor the cantonment sites, were clear that they did not want conventional peacekeepers.[28]

In January 2007, the political mission of the UN Mission in Nepal (UNMIN) was established by UN Security Council resolution 1740 (2007) for 12 months.[29] The main functions of the UNMIN were to (i) support the peace process in Nepal, (ii) monitor the management of arms and armies of the Maoist People's Liberation Army and the Nepal Army, (iii) assist the parties in implementing their agreement on the management of arms and armies through a Joint Monitoring Coordinating Committee (JMCC), (iv) monitor the cease-fire, and (v) provide technical assistance

[23] Bishnu Raj Upreti, 'Conceptual Framework for Post-conflict State Building' in Bishnu Raj Upreti, Sagar Raj Sharma et al (eds), *The Remake of a State: Post-conflict Challenges and State Building in Nepal* (NCCR North-South 2010) 17.

[24] Teresa Whitfield, 'Nepal's Masala Peacemaking' in Sebastian von Einsiedel, David Malone, and Suman Pradhan (eds), *Nepal in Transition: From People's War to Fragile Peace* (CUP 2012) 155.

[25] Surya Subedi, 'Post-Conflict Constitutional Settlement in Nepal and the Role of the United Nations' in Morly Frishman and Sam Muller (eds), *The Dynamics of Constititionalism in the Age of Globalisation* (Hague Academic Press 2010) 71–87.

[26] Astri Suhrke, 'Virtues of a Narrow Mission: The UN Peace Operation in Nepal' (2011) 17 Global Governance 37.

[27] Ibid. 39. [28] Ibid. 40.

[29] UN, 'Security Council Establishes United Nations Political Mission in Nepal, Unanimously Adopting Resolution 1740' (UN Doc SC/8942, 23 January 2007) <http://www.un.org/press/en/2007/sc8942.doc.htm> accessed 12 February 2017.

to the Election Commission to ensure free and fair Constituent Assembly elections.[30] The UNMIN undertook the mission with a limited mandate and duration. Primarily, the UNMIN's task was to monitor the cantonment of both armies and their arms with the help of UN monitors, who were either serving foreign military officers, officers on leave, or retired officers. The monitors were dressed in civilian attire and equipped with blue UN caps and badges for protection.[31]

The UNMIN worked in coordination with representatives of the Maoists and the Nepal Army through the JMCC. The JMCC mandate was to review complaints[32] and to settle disputes throughout the cantonment in seven main sites, which consisted of twenty-one camps in clusters.[33] The UN civil officers and electoral advisers spread across the country and contributed to creating a free and fair election.[34] Despite playing such an effective role in Nepal's peace process, the mission was short-lived and ceased its operations in 2011. The hearsay evidence establishes that the dominance of external factors played a role in limiting the mandate and terms of the UNMIN. Some scholars have argued that India was sceptical towards the long-term role of the UN. In one author's words:

> [The] Indian government [was] also concerned that a robust UN peace mission in Nepal could set a precedent and encourage demands for international mediators or monitors in the increasingly turbulent Indian-controlled part of Jammu and Kashmir.[35]

Nevertheless, the UNMIN helped to fill the gap of deep mutual mistrust between political parties in the course of monitoring the army and conducting Nepal's first-ever Constituent Assembly elections. Later, in 2012, 1,441 former combatants were fully integrated into a specially created general directorate under the Nepali Army.[36] The remaining combatants opted for voluntary retirement with compensation. The integration of ex-combatants into the Nepali Army was an important chapter in Nepal's peace process, and the role played by the UNMIN was crucial in building trust among the political parties and the Maoists.

4 International Law in the Nepalese Legal System

Historically, the Nepalese legal system has followed several traditions, including conventional Hindu law, the common law, and even some aspects of civil law.

[30] UN Secretary-General, *Report on the Request of Nepal for United Nations Assistance in Support of its Peace Process* (UN Doc S/2007/612, 18 October 2007) 23.

[31] Suhrke (n 26) 42. [32] Ibid. 43. [33] Ibid. 42. [34] Ibid. 46. [35] Ibid. 40.

[36] Subindra Bogati, 'Assessing Inclusivity in the Post-War Army Integration Process in Nepal' (Inclusive Political Settlements Paper No 11, Berghof Foundation, Berlin, 2014) <https://www.berghof-foundation.org/fileadmin/redaktion/Publications/Other_Resources/IPS/IPSPaper11-Assessing-Inclusivity-in-the-Post-War-Army-Integration-Process-in-Nepal_English.pdf> accessed 15 February 2017. (In 2011, political parties agreed to integrate a maximum of 6,500 former combatants, out of which several opted for voluntary retirement packages.)

Nepal's system was not influenced predominantly by civil or common law; rather, it was a 'hybrid' system.[37] Even though Nepal has adopted principles of the common law, it did not inherit the common law system in its totality. The Nepalese legal system has in fact extensively used international law as a source of law. Nevertheless, there is an ambiguity in Nepal's application of international treaties in national law.

The Constitution does not define 'treaty' but confers the power to make treaties or agreements on the federal government.[38] The Treaty Act 1990 defines a 'treaty' as an agreement concluded in writing between two or more states, or between a state and an intergovernmental organization. Additional criteria required by article 2(1) of the Vienna Convention on the Law Treaties for creating a treaty provide that the 'international agreement, whatever its particular designation' must be 'governed by international law' and can be 'embodied in a single instrument or in two or more related instruments'. The Supreme Court in *Balkrishna Neupane v Prime Minister Girija Prasad Koirala*[39] observed that an agreement between two states in written form, whatever its designation, is a treaty.[40]

The constitutional validity of a treaty was questioned in *Gyanraj Rai v Cabinet Secretariat and Others*,[41] where the petitioner challenged a trilateral pact between Nepal, India, and the UK on grounds that it violated the petitioner's right to equality. The petitioner argued that provisions of the agreement in question discriminated against the Gurkhas (Nepali soldiers recruited into the British Army) in rates of pay and pensions.[42] The Supreme Court observed that the 'treaty falls under the scope of diplomatic relations'[43] between the governments of contracting parties and that such relations are the exclusive duty of the executive. Any dispute resulting from such relations could not be reviewed under the extraordinary jurisdiction of the Supreme Court.[44]

A few scholars have argued that the *Gyanraj Rai* case has created difficulties in establishing a general rule of applicability for treaty law in Nepal.[45] The problem with the application of treaty law lies in the definition in section 9 of the Treaty Act, which focuses on three aspects: (i) the relationship between a treaty and domestic law,[46] (ii) the status of treaties passed with parliamentary participation, and (iii) the status

[37] Lukas Heckendorn Urscheler, 'Innovation in a Hybrid System: The Example of Nepal' (2012) European Journal of Comparative Law and Governance 1.

[38] Nepal Constitution 2015 art. 278(1).

[39] *Balkrishna Neupane v Prime Minister Girija Prasad Koirala* Decision No. 6312 NKP (2054) 77.

[40] Ibid.

[41] *Gyanraj Rai v Cabinet Secretariat and Others* Decision 2058/12/8 Writ No. 2651 (2056).

[42] For more detail, see Chandra Kumar Laksamba, Krishna Prasad Adhikari, Lokendra Purush Dhakal, and David Gellner, *British Gurkha Pension Policies and Ex-Gurkha Campaigns: A Review* (Centre for Nepal Studies UK 2013) 30–1.

[43] *Gyanraj Rai* (n 41).

[44] Apurba Khatiwada, 'Judicial Review in Nepal' (2006) SSRN <https://ssrn.com/abstract=893803> accessed 8 January 2019.

[45] Rishikesh Wagle, 'Judicial Activism and the use of International Law as Gap-Filler in Domestic Law: The Case of Forced Disappearances Committed during the Armed Conflict in Nepal' in Edda Kristjansdottir, André Nollkaemper, and Cedric Ryngaert (eds), *International Law in Domestic Courts: Rules of Law Reform in Post-Conflict States* (Intersentia 2012) 83.

[46] Nepal Treaty Act 2047 (1990) art. 9(1).

of treaties passed without parliamentary participation.[47] Diverse interpretations by the Court have blurred the distinction between section 9(1) and section 9(2). According to section 9, once a treaty has been ratified, acceded, accepted, or approved, its provisions become applicable as the law of Nepal and will prevail over other laws in the event of an inconsistency with those laws.[48] In other words, treaties will prevail over domestic laws if the treaty is passed by the parliament.

In one line of cases, the Supreme Court of Nepal observed that the supremacy of treaties over domestic laws and their applicability as equivalent to laws of Nepal could be extended to treaties that are not submitted to parliamentary process.[49] In contrast, in another line of cases, the Supreme Court stated that the supremacy of treaty provisions over domestic law can only be achieved when treaties fall under the scope of section 9(1) of the Treaty Act.[50]

The Supreme Court reached the apogee of its interpretation in *Dinesh Kumar Sharma v Office of the Council of Ministers*,[51] where it elucidated its position by distinguishing between 'law' and 'equivalent to law', finding that treaties are only equivalent to laws and are not laws per se. In other words, the Court concluded that treaties in all circumstances cannot be treated as laws adopted through the parliamentary process.[52] Thus, international treaties cannot be considered an integral part of Nepal's law.

Nevertheless, judges in Nepal have overwhelmingly used 'international law' in developing human rights jurisprudence. The Supreme Court in *Lawyer's Association for Human Rights of Nepalese Indigenous Peoples v Prime Minister and Council of Ministers*[53] observed that it is reasonable to expect the state to comply with and implement the obligations required by becoming party to a treaty.

Some scholars have argued that Nepalese courts have employed international and foreign sources to introduce radical innovations within the Nepalese legal system.[54] This observation can be seen in a few court decisions, where the entire decision has been based upon the premise of international law, particularly treaties. In *Sunil Babu Pant & others v Nepal Government, Office of the Prime Minister and Council of*

[47] Ibid. art. 9(2).

[48] Surya Subedi, 'When is a Treaty a Treaty in Law? An Analysis of the Views of the Supreme Court of Nepal on a Bilateral Agreement between Nepal and India' (1995) 5 Asian Yearbook of International Law 201.

[49] *Chandra Kant Gyawali v HMG Cabinet Secretariat and Others* Decision No. 7044 NKP (2058) 84; *Janhit Sanrakshan Manch v Office of the Council of Ministers* Decision No. 7951 NKP (2065) 398; *Narayan Bahadur Khadka v Ministry of Home* Decision No. 7316 NKP (2061) 748.

[50] *FWLD v Office of the Prime Minister and Council of Ministers* Decision No. 7635 NKP (2063) 49; *Jagriti Bal Club v HMG, Ministry of Home* Decision No. 7020 NKP (2058) 44.

[51] *Dinesh Kumar Sharma v Office of the Council of Ministers* Decision No. 7757 NKP (2063) 1136.

[52] Also see *Rama Panta Kharel v Government of Nepal* NKP (2065) 398.

[53] *Lawyer's Association for Human Rights of Nepalese Indigenous Peoples v Prime Minister and Council of Ministers* Decision No. 8990 NKP (2070) 61.

[54] Urscheler (n 37) 8.

Ministers & Others,[55] the Supreme Court cited several international instruments such as the Universal Declaration of Human Rights 1948 (UDHR), International Covenant on Civil and Political Rights 1966 (ICCPR), International Covenant on Economic, Social and Cultural Rights 1966 ('ICESCR'), and the Convention on Elimination of All Forms of Discrimination against Women 1979 ('CEDAW'), among others. It even referred to 'soft' sources of human rights laws such as reports by the International Commission of Jurists, OHCHR, and UN Special Rapporteurs. The Supreme Court went on to observe that:

> We should also gradually internalize international practices in regard to the enjoyment of the right of an individual in the context of changing global society and practices of respecting the rights of minority. If we continue to ignore the rights of such people only on the ground that it might cause social pollution, our commitment towards respecting human rights will be questioned internationally.[56]

In addition, there are several cases[57] where the decision was influenced by international human rights standards[58] to bridge the gap between international and domestic law. In other words, domestic courts often bridge or set in motion a 'diffuse review of compatibility' between national legal acts and international human rights treaties.[59] A brief look at court practices illustrates the general rule that a treaty to which Nepal is signatory is not enforceable per se as a legal rule in Nepal. Nevertheless, judicial activism has extensively used international law as a foreign source to secure the rights of citizens.

5 The Use of International Law

5.1 Bridging Normative Gaps

Academics, practitioners, and commentators have written, interpreted, and discussed[60] how domestic courts act as guardians or agents in enforcing international law.[61] As discussed earlier, Nepalese courts have internalized international law as a foreign source. This practice shows the relevance of international law in securing human rights

[55] *Sunil Babu Pant & others v Nepal Government, Office of the Prime Minister and Council of Ministers & Others* (Writ No. 917) (2008) Nepal Judicial Academy Law Journal 261.

[56] Ibid. 280–1.

[57] *Mira Kumari Dhungana and Others v Ministry of Law Justice and Parliamentary Affairs and Others* NKP (2052) 468.

[58] *Sapna Malla Pradhan and Others v Office of the Prime Minister and Others* NKP (2065) 917.

[59] European Commission For Democracy Through Law (Venice Commission), *Report on the Implementation of International Human Rights Treaties in Domestic Law and the Role of Courts* (CDL-AD 2014 036, 2014) para 4.

[60] See also Richard Falk, 'The Role of Domestic Courts in the International Legal Order' (1964) 39 Indiana Law Journal 3.

[61] Anthea Roberts, 'Comparative International Law? The Role of National Courts in Creating and Enforcing International Law' (2011) 60 ICLQ 57.

through judicial activism. The courts have based several of their decisions on international law as a guarantor of justice, particularly on issues related to transitional justice and human rights. The Supreme Court has intervened on several occasions to ensure an effective, participatory, and meaningful transitional justice process.

The first occasion was in *Rajendra Prasad Dhakal and Others v the Government of Nepal*,[62] where the Supreme Court delivered a historic decision on several issues of transitional justice. This landmark judgment was issued in response to eighty-three writs of habeas corpus pending before the Court. The petitioners had also demanded a mandamus to make public the status of detainees and to form a high-level inquiry commission to investigate and ensure legal action against the perpetrators.

This judgment was crucial in shaping the transitional justice process in Nepal, and was an example of how domestic courts may internalize international law to ensure dignity and reparation for conflict-era victims. The Supreme Court based its judgment on several reports published by the National Human Rights Commission, OHCHR, and the UN Human Rights Council, as well as on several treaties including the UDHR, the ICCPR, the Convention against Torture and other Cruel, Inhuman or Degrading Treatment and Punishment 1984, and the International Convention for the Protection of All Persons from Enforced Disappearances 2006 (ICPPED),[63] among others.

In its judgment, the Court scrapped the Commissions of Inquiry Act 1969,[64] finding that it did not meet the standard enumerated in the ICPPED, and questioning the competence of the Act to deal with crimes that arose during the Maoist Civil War. The Court also emphasized the need for a separate law to deal with these issues:

> It seems to us that a special law stipulating all major aspects of disappearance, including inquiry into the incidents of enforced disappearance, the determination of the status of disappeared persons, the guarantee that their status is made public and that action taken against those who are responsible, and the provisions of relief to the victims, is necessary. It is also the responsibility of state to create an environment such that victims trust and respect the State's justice system and that the State Officials who are guilty do not enjoy any immunity from any criminal liability resulting from their actions.[65]

Additionally, the Supreme Court asserted that such obligations of the state are not separate from its other obligations; rather, the state derives such an obligation from its commitment to respect fundamental human rights. Furthermore, the Court recognized 'truth' as a facet of the right to life and liberty, treating 'the right to the truth as a fundamental right'. The Court observed that:

[62] *Rajendra Prasad Dhakal & Others v Nepal Government* Writ No. 3575 (registered 21 January 1999), Decision on Petition for Habeas Corpus and Mandamus, 49(2) NLR, Decision No. 7817 P, 169 (1 June 2007).

[63] International Convention for the Protection of All Persons from Enforced Disappearance (adopted 20 December 2006, entered into force 23 December 2010, 2716 UNTS 3).

[64] Commissions of Inquiry Act 2026 (1969).

[65] *Rajendra Prasad Dhakal* (n 62).

> Life is a significant precondition for enjoying all freedoms. Other preconditions, such as the capacity for autonomy, and social and economic stability which allow people to choose between meaningful options, are valuable only when we can enjoy life. As enforced disappearances make the very existence of a person unknown, there is no opportunity for such a person to have any enjoyment of the basic and fundamental human rights guaranteed by national and international law . . . there would be no division of opinion that the primary obligation rests with the State to guarantee the civic rights expressed by the international instruments to which the State or Constitution has guaranteed its commitment.[66]

For international law scholarship, this case is a classic example of legal pluralism, where the Court observed the importance of treaties and encouraged the ratification of such conventions through national legislation. When the Court arrived at this decision, the ICPPED was not in force. However, the Court substantially discussed the provisions of the Convention and observed that:

> Although the Disappearance Convention has not yet come into force and Nepal has not yet ratified it, this Convention has developed an important standard concerning the obligation of a state with respect to security of disappeared persons: in the event that the Disappearance Convention is accepted by [the] international community, it is expedient to accept the standards established in the Convention as the prevailing standard in international law. Therefore, the state ought to comply with these standards accordingly.[67]

The Court then went one step further and argued that:

> There is no problem in implementing the principles laid down in the Disappearance Convention for the sake of respecting and promoting the life, dignity, and freedom of Nepal's citizen. . . . this will demonstrate our sensitivity towards our citizens and the responsibility of the State towards the international community in protecting human rights.[68]

These statements illustrate the courts' attitude towards international law, and the way that courts have based their decisions on international conventions, even those that have not been ratified by the government, is notable. Even though the Supreme Court highlighted the importance of international principles, it did not encroach upon the ambit of the legislature. In fact, the Court explicitly stated that it could only provide a judicial evaluation as to whether the state has complied with its obligations. However, regarding the state's obligation under several human rights conventions, the Court may intervene so that an effective legal framework is set in place to implement internationally established standards for the protection of civil liberties. The Supreme Court emphasized the need for a separate, independent, impartial, and competent commission to address the issue of disappeared citizens. The Court also constituted a 'Detainee Investigation Team' headed by appellate court judges to inquire into the status of the disappeared citizens.

[66] Ibid. [67] Ibid. [68] Ibid.

After the decision, the Government of Nepal introduced separate legislation to implement it. The Government introduced an Ordinance for the formation of a Disappearance, Truth and Reconciliation Commission. However, the Ordinance received severe criticism from civil society for its vague provisions, which gave the Commission discretionary powers to recommend amnesty even for perpetrators of gross violations of human rights.[69]

Later, the constitutional validity of these provisions[70] was challenged in *Madhav Kumar Basnet and Others v Government of Nepal*,[71] where the Court again heavily based its judgment on human rights conventions and declared the amnesty-oriented provisions to be unconstitutional. The Court reaffirmed its decision in the *Rajendra Dhakal Case* and held that the Nepalese Government has an inalienable obligation to address the issue of enforced disappearance, and that a failure to fulfil this obligation would be unacceptable, inexcusable, and intolerable. The Court paid attention to UN General Assembly resolution 60/147,[72] which advocated for the inapplicability of statutes of limitations to gross violations of human rights.[73] Based on this universal principle, the Court declared a provision which provided a limitation of 35 days for filing cases of war crimes to be unconstitutional.

While trying to resolve concerns expressed by the judiciary and civil society, the Government revised the Ordinance and, on 25 April 2014, the Parliament passed the Truth and Reconciliation Commission (TRC) Act aimed at forming a TRC and a Commission on Enforced Disappearances. Even though the final bill curtailed the discretionary powers of the Commissioner, it was again criticized by civil society and other stakeholders because it failed to meet international standards. The major concerns related to: (i) the mediation provision to reconcile victim and perpetrator, as it failed to exclude serious war crimes,[74] and (ii) amnesty for those who committed international crimes or serious violations of human rights.[75]

In 2015, the Supreme Court in *Suman Adhikari & Others v Office of Prime Minister and Council of Ministers*[76] further curtailed the discretionary power of the Commissioner to recommend amnesty. Further, it reaffirmed that the Commissioner can

[69] Truth and Reconciliation Commission, Ordinance on Investigation of Disappeared Persons 2069 (2012) art. 23.

[70] *Raju Prasad Chapagain v Government of Nepal* NKP (2063) 203.

[71] *Madhav Kumar Basnet and Others v Government of Nepal* Writ No. 069-WS-0057 (2 January 2014).

[72] Basic Principles and Guidelines on the Right to a Remedy and Reparation for Victims of Gross Violations of International Human Rights Law and Serious Violations of International Humanitarian Law (adopted and proclaimed by UNGA res 60/147 (16 December 2005)).

[73] Ibid. Principle IV.

[74] Enforced Disappearances Enquiry, Truth and Reconciliation Commission Act 2071 (2014) art. 22.

[75] Ibid. art. 26.

[76] *Suman Adhikari & Others v Office of Prime Minister and Council of Ministers* NKP (2074) 6, Decision No. 962 (26 February 2015).

recommend amnesty only after consent from the victim.[77] It also excluded the possibility of amnesty where the perpetrator was involved in rape and other offences of a grave nature, or where sufficient grounds are not found to grant amnesty in the investigations of the Commission.[78] Thus, these cases show that the Nepalese judiciary has internalized international law as a 'foreign source' to secure the rights of victims and to establish a credible, impartial, and independent Commission to address the issues of conflict and to safeguard human rights.

5.2 Water

South Asia encompasses nations with a commonality of languages, history, culture, and politics, but despite these commonalities, the region has failed to cooperate in trade, security, and trans-boundary water sharing opportunities. Nepal possesses huge water resources potential; if utilized correctly, this potential may result in enormous benefits to Nepal and Southeast Asia. Nepal has potential to generate up to 83,000 megawatts (MW) of hydroelectric power, more than the combined total produced by the US, Canada, and Mexico.[79] About 42,000 MW of power generation is feasible.[80] Unfortunately, the lack of sub-regional cooperation between Nepal, India, and Bangladesh, as well as the lack of a forward-looking hydro-diplomacy consensus between India and Nepal, has hurt both the country and the region.

Indo-Nepalese relations with regard to water resource development can be traced back to pre-independence India when an agreement, the Exchange of Letters 1920, was signed with the then British Government in India for the construction and operation of the Sarada Barrage Project.[81] However, water treaties signed with independent India remain highly controversial. In 1954, the Kosi Project Agreement 1954 was signed between the countries with the aims of generating hydropower and providing for flood control and irrigation.[82] A barrage across the Koshi River was built to channel water and minimize erosion of soil and deposits of silt.[83] The Kosi Agreement did not

[77] See also National Human Rights Commission, National Women Commission, and National Dalit Commission, *The NHRI Nepal Joint Submission for the Second Universal Periodic Review of Nepal* (Submission to the UN Human Rights Council, 22 March 2015) <http://www.nhrcnepal.org/nhrc_new/doc/newsletter/NHRI%20Nepal%20joint%20Submission%20for%202nd%20UPR%20Review-2015.pdf> accessed 2 November 2016.

[78] Ibid. 7. Enforced Disappearances Enquiry, Truth and Reconciliation Commission Act 2071 (2014) art. 26(2).

[79] Surya Subedi, 'Hydro-Diplomacy in South Asia: The Conclusion of the Mahakali and Ganges River Treaties' (1999) 93 American Journal of International Law 954.

[80] *Hydropower Development Policy, 2058* (2001) <http://www.lawcommission.gov.np/en/wp-content/uploads/2018/09/hydropower-development-policy-2058-2001.pdf> accessed 1 March 2017.

[81] Trilochan Upreti, *International Watercourses Law and Its Application in South Asia* (Pairavi Prakashan 2006) 186.

[82] Agreement on the Kosi Project between Nepal and India (signed 25 April 1954) preamble.

[83] Upreti (n 81) 188.

receive a warm welcome from the people, and political parties accused the then government of 'selling out' national property for India's benefit.[84] The political discord and dissatisfaction led to the Revised Kosi Agreement 1966, which ensured better provisions on water and power for Nepal. Nepal gained the right to obtain 50 per cent of the hydroelectric power generated by any power house within a 10 mile radius from the barrage site;[85] and the term of the land lease was reduced from an unlimited period to 199 years.[86]

The Gandak Project Agreement 1959 was another deal which was heavily criticized in Nepal. Like the Kosi Agreement, the main aim of the Gandak Agreement was to generate hydropower, control floods, and facilitate irrigation.[87] A barrage was constructed at the Gandak River near Bhaisalotan to regulate the flow of water for irrigation and power. The project was estimated to provide irrigation to an area of 1,340,000 hectares in Bihar, 500,000 hectares in the Northern Indian state of Uttar Pradesh,[88] and 63,000 hectares in Nepal.[89] This project did not receive warm support from Nepalese political parties either because the construction of a barrage in Nepalese territory was perceived as Indian encroachment on Nepal's sovereignty and territorial integrity.[90] Moreover, the nominal irrigation share, which was less than 3 per cent of the total area watered by the Kosi and Gandak projects, became a strong ground for opposition. In fact, one commentator[91] argued that the Gandak Agreement violated Nepal's right to equitable and 'reasonable utilization and participation', contrary to the principles of the Helsinki Rules on the Uses of the Waters of International Rivers 1966[92] and Convention on the Law of the Non-Navigational Uses of International Watercourses 1997.[93]

The Mahakali Treaty 1996[94] was signed between India and Nepal in a spirit of accommodating the interests of both parties based on equal partnership.[95] The Mahakali Treaty consisted of three parts: the Sarada Barrage, the Tanakpur Barrage, and the Pancheshwar project. There were two key factors influencing this Treaty. The relationship between India and Nepal had begun to weaken in 1983 when India

[84] Trilochan Upreti, 'Equitable Utilisation of Nepalese Water Resources: Bilateral and Regional Perspectives' in Surya Subedi (ed), *International Watercourses Law for the 21st Century: The Case of the River Ganges Basin* (Routledge 2006) ch 11.

[85] Revised Agreement between His Majesty's Government of Nepal and the Government of India Concerning the Kosi Project (signed 19 December 1966) s 4(ii).

[86] Ibid. s 5(i).

[87] Agreement between His Majesty's Government of Nepal and the Government of India on the Gandak Irrigation and Power Project (signed 4 December 1959).

[88] Upreti (n 81) 190. [89] Ibid. [90] Ibid. 202. [91] Ibid. 192.

[92] Helsinki Rules on the Uses of the Waters of International Rivers (1996) arts IV and V.

[93] UN Convention on the Law of the Non-navigational Uses of International Watercourses (adopted 21 May 1997, entered into force 17 August 2014) arts 5–7.

[94] Treaty Between His Majesty's Government of Nepal and the Government of India Concerning the Integrated Development of the Mahakali River including Sarada Barrage, Tanakpur Barrage and Pancheshwar Project (signed 12 February 1996) ('Mahakali Treaty').

[95] Ibid. preamble.

unilaterally started construction of the Tanakpur project.[96] Moreover, the 1989 economic blockade[97] worsened India–Nepal relations, until the Indian Prime Minister visited Nepal in October 1992.[98] The Mahakali Treaty was an attempt to address the grievances of the previous agreement and to address the trust deficit between India and Nepal.

Unfortunately, the Mahakali Treaty was also controversial, mainly because of its unequal distribution of water. In total, it offered India 16,000 cusecs of water from the Saradha and Tanakpur barrages but only 8,000 cusecs to Nepal.[99] Despite this, the Treaty provided that the cost of the project would be borne equally.[100] Similarly, the Treaty remained silent with regards to the excessive use of water either by lease or royalty, or to allowing India to use the water in return for investing more in the project than was mandated by the agreement.[101] Furthermore, ambiguity in the term 'existing consumptive use' led to various interpretations[102] by Indian and Nepalese experts. The problem was that the *equal entitlement* in the utilization of the waters of the Mahakali River was based on respective existing consumptive use of the water,[103] which meant that the more the consumptive use, the greater the utilization of the waters. If it is to be understood in this way, then it contradicts article 5(1) of the Treaty, which provided that Nepal shall be given prime consideration in the utilization of the waters of the Mahakali River.[104]

More than twenty years on, the Mahakali Treaty remains a live controversy, eliciting demands to revisit its controversial provisions. In recent times, the Nepal–India Joint Committee on Water Resources has met to discuss the progress of implementation of the Mahakali Treaty.[105] In February 2012, the first meeting of the India–Nepal Joint Ministerial Commission on Water Resources was held, which acknowledged the difficulties being faced in carrying out various works on the Kosi and Gandak projects and committed to addressing these concerns.[106] In 2014, during the Indian Prime Minister's visit to Nepal, there was speculation about whether there would be a push for the Pancheshwar, Upper Karnali, and Arun III hydro projects, but this never happened.

Nevertheless, the Electric Power Trade, Cross-Border Transmission Interconnection and Grid Connectivity ('Power Trade Agreement 2014') between India and Nepal was signed during the 18th SAARC Summit in 2014. This Agreement is a new development in hydro-diplomacy between the countries. The rationale of the Agreement is that

[96] Shaista Tabassum and Nusrat Idris, 'India-Nepal Treaty on Mahakali River' (2004) 57 Pakistan Horizon 51.

[97] Ibid. 54. [98] Ibid. 55. [99] Ibid. 57. [100] Ibid. [101] Ibid.

[102] SB Pun, 'Sharing the Ganges Waters—The Writings on the Wall' (1999) 10 WECS Bulletin 33.

[103] Mahakali Treaty (n 94) art. 3.

[104] Ibid. art. 5(1).

[105] Minutes of the Seventh Meeting of Nepal–India Joint Committee on Water Resources (Kathmandu, 24–5 January 2013) <http://www.moewri.gov.np/images/category/Minutes_seventh_meeting_of_JCWR.pdf> accessed 8 January 2019.

[106] Joint Press Statement, India–Nepal Joint Ministerial Commission on Water Resources (New Delhi, 15 February 2012) <http://www.moewri.gov.np/images/category/jmcwr-joint-press-statement.pdf> accessed 9 January 2019.

increasing electricity demand can be met by socio-economic development and by building friendships between countries through increased cooperation on transmission and power trade.[107] However, this was not the first power trade agreement that Nepal entered into with India. An earlier agreement signed in 1997 never came into force because of the Nepalese Parliament's failure to ratify it.[108] Similarly, India's protectionist move to treat electricity as an import-restricted item from 2004 to 2008 closed the door to Nepal penetrating the Indian market.[109]

Therefore, the Power Trade Agreement 2014 will certainly facilitate Nepal's hydropower potential through joint venture investments on mutually agreed terms.[110] The Agreement further emphasizes policy harmonization for the realization of cross-border inter-connections, grid connectivity, and power trade, by removing trade and non-trade barriers.[111] Considering the history of a lack of mutual trust and cooperation in water resource management, there were doubts regarding the implementation of the Agreement. However, in 2016, India ensured this by enacting Guidelines on the Cross-Border Trade of Electricity.[112] Despite an unpleasant history of negotiations regarding water resources, the Power Trade Agreement 2014 looks capable of initiating a new chapter in the India-Nepal relationship.

5.3 SAARC

SAARC is significant for Nepal. It provides Nepal with an opportunity to develop friendship and cooperation in trade, security, and development. In addition, it provides Nepal with a forum to reduce its excessive dependence on India. However, the important question is how much has Nepal really benefited from SAARC. Nepal had high hopes of trade cooperation when the South Asian Free Trade Agreement (SAFTA) was signed at the 12th SAARC Summit in 2004. The main objective of SAFTA was to eliminate barriers to trade, facilitate the cross-border movement of goods, promote fair competition, and ensure equitable benefits to all the members of the region.[113]

Unfortunately, even after the commencement of SAFTA in 2006, interregional trade has not grown as expected. A study suggests that SAARC's intraregional trade was only

[107] Agreement Between the Government of Nepal and the Government of the Republic of India on Electric Power Trade, Cross-Border Transmission Interconnection and Grid Connectivity (signed 21 October 2014) ('Power Trade Agreement') preamble.

[108] Sher Singh Bhat, 'Post-PTA Indo-Nepal Power Trade', Presentation, SAARC Dissemination Workshop on Study for Development of Potential Regional Hydro Power Plant in South Asia (Kathmandu, 9–10 May 2016).

[109] Ibid. [110] Power Trade Agreement (n 107) art. III. [111] Ibid. art. IV.

[112] Guidelines on Cross Border Trade of Electricity, Government of the Republic of India (5 December 2016) <https://powermin.nic.in/sites/default/files/webform/notices/Guidelines%20for%20Cross%20Boarder%20Trade.pdf> accessed 9 January 2019.

[113] Agreement on South Asian Free Trade Area (signed 6 January 2004, entered into force 1 January 2006) art. 3(1).

4.3 per cent of total South Asian trade.[114] SAFTA has failed to promote intraregional trade, unlike agreements in other regional cooperation bodies, like the Association of Southeast Asian Nations (ASEAN), whose intraregional trade was around 24.1 per cent in 2014.[115] In addition, the ASEAN region accounted for 11 per cent of total global foreign direct investment flows in 2014.[116] There is a huge potential for intraregional trade in South Asia. However South Asia remains one of the least integrated regions in the world.[117]

Nevertheless, Nepal has gained some benefits from SAARC and SAFTA. Nepal's trade with SAARC is predominately based on imports from and exports to India. One study shows that a high percentage of imports within the SAARC region from 2010 to 2014 came from India.[118] Among all SAARC members, Nepal's import share with India was 62.39 per cent and 82.24 per cent in 2000–1 and 2009–10 respectively.[119] Similarly, Nepal's export share with India was 35.92 per cent and 15.31 per cent in 2000–1 and 2009–10 respectively. However, research suggests that Nepal's growing trade with India is the result of their geographical proximity and bilateral relations rather than regional agreements.[120]

The establishment of the SAARC Energy Centre in 2005, the SAARC Food Bank in 2007, and the SAARC Seed Bank in 2011 are nonetheless positive steps to promote cooperation and understanding among the members. However, lack of implementation and political will are the biggest obstacles for cooperation. There are enormous challenges for SAARC in ensuring better regional cooperation due to the bitter relationship between India and Pakistan. The political tensions between India and Pakistan led to the postponement of the 19th SAARC Summit, scheduled for 2016 (and yet to be held at the time of writing in early 2019). To bridge this political tension, Nepal can potentially act as a mediator between India and Pakistan, and ensure that the aspirations of SAARC are maintained.

114 *SAARC Statistical Yearbook* (2012).

115 ASEAN, 'A Blueprint for Growth: ASEAN Economic Community 2015—Progress and Key Achievements' <http://www.asean.org/storage/images/2015/November/aec-page/AEC-2015-Progress-and-Key-Achievements.pdf> accessed 25 February 2017.

116 Ibid.

117 World Bank, 'The Potential of Intra-regional Trade for South Asia' (24 May 2016) <http://www.worldbank.org/en/news/infographic/2016/05/24/the-potential-of-intra-regional-trade-for-south-asia> accessed 5 March 2017.

118 Confederation of Nepalese Industries and SAARC Trade Promotion Network, 'Nepal-SAARC Trade: A Study of NTMs of Selected Products' (CNI 2016) <http://cnind.org/html/images/item_images/files/ntm_report1.pdf> accessed 10 March 2017.

119 Bishnu Pant, Sushmita Pradhan, and Santosh Gartaula, 'Regional Cooperation and Integration in South Asia: Nepal Perspective', Paper submitted to the 15th Annual Global Development Network Conference (Accra, 18–20 June 2014). See also Ratnakar Adhikari and Paras Kharel, 'Nepal and SAFTA: Issue, Prospects and Challenges' in Mohammad Razzaque and Yurendra Basnett (eds), *Regional Integration in South Asia: Trends, Challenges and Prospects* (The Commonwealth 2014) ch 18.

120 Pant et al, ibid. 12.

5.4 Transit Rights

Nepal is blessed with mountains, rivers, and cultural diversity, making it unique on the global map. Nevertheless, this beautiful country is handicapped economically because it is landlocked by India to the east, south, and west and the Tibet region of China to the north. This geography hinders Nepal with regards to the movement of goods and services. In addition, it limits the diffusion of ideas and technological advances, and has severe adverse effects on the country's economy.[121]

Historically, Nepal has engaged in trade to achieve trade independence, economic opportunities, and friendship. Some have argued that unrestricted trade, the inviolability of borders, and free movement of goods across borders are non-derogable rules of the customary international law applicable between India and Nepal.[122] India is Nepal's biggest trading partner, providing around 60 per cent of Nepal's trade[123] and the lion's share of Nepal's gross domestic product.[124] These facts reflect Nepal's trade dependency on India.

Nepal has had a transit arrangement with India since 1950, through the bilateral Treaty of Trade and Commerce 1950, which recognized the full and unrestricted right of transit to Nepal.[125] Later, it was replaced by the Trade and Transit Treaty 1960. Subsequently, two separate treaties regarding trade and transit rights were signed in 1978, which recognized that due to Nepal's geographical situation, access to and from the sea was fundamental to foster international trade.[126] The 1978 Treaty was later renewed but only until 1 March 1988.

5.4.1 *Indian Blockades of 1989 and 2015*

The year 1989 proved to be difficult for Nepal due to increased political tension with India.[127] A dispute arose over negotiations regarding the trade and transit treaties, resulting in an economic blockade of Nepal by India, which cut off links to the Kolkata ports.[128] Nepal's voice was raised against the Indian blockade but it did not receive

[121] Fabrizio Carmignani, 'The Curse of Being Landlocked: Institutions Rather than Trade' (2015) 38 The World Economy 1594.

[122] Surendra Bhandari, *Constitutional Design and Implementation Dynamics: Federalism and Inclusive Nation Building in Nepal* (Himal Innovative Development and Research 2016) 388.

[123] Amita Batra, *Regional Economic Integration in South Asia: Trapped in Conflict?* (Routledge 2013) 41.

[124] Peter Warr, 'Trade Policy in Landlocked Countries', Training Presentation <http://siteresources.worldbank.org/INTRANETTRADE/Resources/WBI-Training/Warr_Session5Notes.pdf> accessed 15 March 2017.

[125] Kishor Uprety, 'Landlocked States and Access to the Sea: An Evolutionary Study of a Contested Right' (1994) 12 Dickinson Journal of International Law 406.

[126] Treaty of Transit between the Government of India and his Majesty's Government of Nepal (signed 17 March 1978, entered into force 25 March 1978) preamble. See also Treaty of Trade between the Government of India and his Majesty's Government of Nepal (signed 17 March 1978, entered into force 25 March 1978).

[127] Niranjan Koirala, 'Nepal in 1989: A Very Difficult Year' (1990) 30 Asian Survey 136.

[128] Barbara Crossette, 'Nepal's Economy is Gasping as India, a Huge Neighbour, Squeezes It Hard' *The New York Times* (New York, 11 April 1989).

broad international support, as Nepal was reluctant to take coercive diplomatic measures against India. Moreover, India was not a member of the UN Convention on the Law of the Sea 1982 (UNCLOS) at the time, which, as discussed below, would have made the Indian blockade unlawful and provided Nepal with dispute settlement procedures.

More than twenty-five years after the 1989 blockade, Nepal was again economically blockaded by India in 2015, after the promulgation of the Constitution of Nepal 2015. The unofficial economic blockade[129] prevented the supply of essential goods, including fuel, from reaching Nepal. Officially, India claimed that the blockade resulted from Nepal's political parties impeding roads and highways, to protest against the constitution. The unofficial blockade restricted all of Nepal's trading opportunities, resulting in scarcity of essential goods and services.

India did not acknowledge its blockade; instead, it used the phrase 'obstructions at various entry–exit points'.[130] There were several incidents reported where Indian trucks stranded in Nepal were facilitated by Nepalese police, who cleared the obstructions at the checkpoint. On the other hand, the Indian Border Security Force did not allow trucks stranded in India to enter Nepal.[131] The report suggests that oil company representatives cited an 'order from above'[132] to discontinue the movement of fuel trucks to Nepal. Moreover, it seemed to be a strategic move by India to ensure blockades at the main checkpoints, such as Birgunj, which is an important port for oil and food imports into Nepal. This suggests that the intention of India was to impose trade sanctions in the form of an economic blockade, to pressure Nepal into addressing some of the internal political issues within the country.

Yet again, Nepal failed to use available diplomatic channels to protest the blockade. For example, it failed to use the UN Charter and bring the issue before the Security Council as a threat to the peace, an act of aggression, or breach of peace and security.[133] Besides this, Nepal also failed to avail itself of an opportunity to present the blockade as a violation of both customary international law and treaties, discussed below.

[129] Upadhyay (n 16).

[130] Ministry of External Affairs Government of India, 'Official Spokesperson's response to a query on Nepal' (Press Release 25 September 2015) <https://www.mea.gov.in/media-briefings.htm?dtl/25842/Official+Spokespersons+response+to+a+query+on+Nepal> accessed 2 February 2017.

[131] Informal Sector Service Center, *Unilateral Coercive Blockade Imposed by India on Nepal* (2015) <http://inseconline.org/en/wp-content/uploads/2016/08/1446549391.pdf> accessed 9 January 2019.

[132] Kunda Dixit, 'India and Nepal Have No Choice but to End Their Border Dispute and Move On' *Time* (18 November 2015) <http://time.com/4115801/nepal-india-border-blockade-madhesh> accessed 5 March 2017.

[133] Collective reading of arts 39, 41, and 42 of the UN Charter 1945. See e.g. Surendra Bhandari, 'Indian Imposition' *The Kathmandu Post* (Kathmandu, 12 October 2015).

5.4.2 *Right of Access to the Sea and Freedom of Transit of Landlocked States*

The right of landlocked states to free access to the sea and to freedom of transit is firmly established in international law, both customary and conventional. Article 125 of UNCLOS sets out the '[r]ight of access to and from the sea and freedom of transit'. Article 125(1) states:

> Land-locked States shall have the rights of access to and from the sea for the purpose of exercising the rights provided for in this Convention including those relating to the freedom of the high seas and the common heritage of mankind. To this end, land-locked States shall enjoy freedom of transit through the territory of transit States by all mean of transport.[134]

The plain reading of this article reflects that a landlocked country has rights of access to and from the sea. It also emphasizes that landlocked states shall enjoy the freedom of transit. Some scholars have argued that the right of access to the sea and right of free transit of the landlocked State is founded on the principles of natural law.[135] Furthermore, it is argued that the landlocked state is entitled to the right to free transit by its sovereignty. In one author's words:

> The right of free transit was conferred on every land-locked country by its very sovereignty, a necessary corollary to accepted notions of freedom of the high seas. This view maintained that, because the oceans are open to all nations, littoral and land-locked alike, the latter must be entitled to free transit in exercise of their equal rights within the res communis.[136]

Article 125(3) acknowledges, however, the sovereign 'right' of the transit state to limit the freedom of landlocked countries, but only under narrowly defined conditions:

> Transit States, in the exercise of their full sovereignty over their territory, shall have the right to take all measures necessary to ensure that the rights and facilities provided for in this Part for land-locked States shall in no way infringe their legitimate interests.[137]

This raises an important question of whether there is a need for a special bilateral agreement to ensure the rights of landlocked countries. Article 125(2) of UNCLOS emphasizes that the terms and modalities for exercising freedom of transit should be achieved through bilateral, sub-regional, or regional agreements. This was one of the main hurdles for Nepal during the 1989 blockade as the Transit Treaty 1978 between India and Nepal had not been renewed and there was thus no bilateral arrangement between the countries.

[134] UN Convention on the Law of the Sea (opened for signature 10 December 1982, entered into force 16 November 1994, 1833 UNTS 3) art. 125(1).

[135] A Mpazi Sinjela, 'Freedom of Transit and the Rights of Access For Land-Locked States: The Evolution of Principle and Law' (1982) 12 Georgia Journal of International and Comparative Law 31.

[136] Ibid. 32.

[137] UN Convention on the Law of the Sea, art. 125(3).

However, transit rights are established as a norm in customary international law. India has also recognized Nepal's right of free access and freedom to transit, including permanent access to and from the sea, to promote international trade. Therefore, a permanent transit treaty is not prerequisite to free access to the sea and freedom of transit.[138] In addition, even if the country is not a member of UNCLOS, customary international law still applies. In this context, we will analyse Nepal's decision not to advance a case against India's unofficial blockade.

5.4.3 *International Legal Remedies for the 2015 Blockade*

There were accordingly some possible ways in which Nepal could have retaliated against the 2015 blockade at an international legal level.

5.4.3.1 TREATY OF TRANSIT 1991

First, the Treaty of Transit 1991 is the current enabling law, which provides Nepal access to the sea and free transit, fully recognizes Nepal as a landlocked country, and acknowledges the importance of permanent access to the sea for international trade.[139] Similarly, this Treaty ensures freedom of transit across transit states' territories through routes mutually agreed upon. Furthermore, the Treaty ensures that both parties have the right to take all indispensable measures to ensure that such freedom accorded by it on its territory does not in any way infringe its legitimate interests of any kind.[140] It also allows parties to take measures that may be necessary for the protection of its essential security interests.

This highlights an important question: whether the 2015 Indian economic blockade can be justified as protecting India's 'legitimate interest' or 'security interests'? Prima facie, the answer is no. The Constitution of Nepal 2015 was promulgated by an overwhelming majority of the Constituent Assembly. Therefore, the legitimacy of the Constitution cannot be questioned, especially by any foreign power. It was unfortunate to witness violent protests from some political parties opposed to certain provisions in the new Constitution, which resulted in the loss of lives. The concerned citizens and political parties could, of course, in the exercise of their democratic rights such as a peaceful protest, express their disappointment over the promulgation of the Constitution.

As a large neighbouring country with an open and porous border, India has always played an indirect role in Nepal's internal political affairs. But that does not mean that India can impose economic blockades to exert pressure on Nepal to accommodate the interests of India on behalf of any ethnic or racial groups in Nepal. The onus was on Nepal to resolve the contentious issues. India may be expected to bridge the gap between the protesting parties and the Nepal Government only as a mediator, not the moderator, and only if invited to do so by Nepal.[141] India thus had no 'legitimate

[138] Surya Subedi, *Dynamics of Foreign Policy and Law: A Study of Indo-Nepal Relations* (OUP 2005) 68.

[139] Treaty of Transit between His Majesty's Government of Nepal and the Government of India (signed 5 January 1991, entered into force 6 January 1991) preamble.

[140] Ibid. art. II.

[141] Pratyush Nath Upreti, 'The Other Side' *The Kathmandu Post* (Kathmandu, 28 December 2015).

interest' or 'security interest' in limiting Nepal's right of access to the sea and freedom of transit. The reading of the Transit Treaty 1991 clearly indicates that the economic blockade imposed by India was contrary to the spirit of it. The main problem with the 1991 Treaty was the absence of adequate dispute resolution mechanisms, which hindered Nepal from obtaining remedies for violations of the treaty.

5.4.3.2 INDO–NEPAL TRADE TREATY AND PROTOCOL 2009

Second, the Indo–Nepal Trade Treaty 2009 obliges both India and Nepal to undertake all measures, including technical cooperation, to promote, facilitate, expand, and diversify trade between the two countries.[142] Furthermore, article IX of the Treaty provides a list of exceptions, which do not amount to impermissible restrictions: (i) protecting public morals, (ii) protecting human, animal, and plant life, (iii) safeguarding national treasures, (iv) safeguarding the implementation of laws relating to the import and export of gold and silver bullion, and (v) safeguarding such other interests as may be mutually agreed upon. In strict legal terms, if India wanted to impose restrictions on the movement of goods, then it should only have been done under the above exceptions. The reasons for the 2015 economic blockade did not fall under any of these. In essence, India failed to respect the provisions of this treaty.

In addition, the Protocol to the Treaty of Trade 2009 emphasized the responsibility of both parties to facilitate the cross-border flow of trade through simplification, standardization, and harmonization of customs, transport, and other trade related procedures and the development of border infrastructure. Even if India believed that there was disruption on the customs border, it is not possible that most of the agreed routes for mutual trade listed in Annexure A of The Treaty could suffer such disruption. Moreover, the movement of goods listed in Annexure A is only subject to customs duty and restriction on prohibited goods.[143]

Furthermore, the Indo–Nepal Trade Treaty 2009 allows India to take restrictive measures which may be necessary for the protection of its essential security interests.[144] To invoke this provision, India must formally and immediately deliver written notice[145] to Nepal, with evidence. Similarly, India must provide adequate opportunity for consultation to discuss the measure as practicable. Further, such consultation should take place at the Joint Committee formed by both parties.[146] Even though the Foreign Ministers from both countries met during the blockade, there were no formal discussions on any measures India intended to impose by way of exceptions under the Trade Treaty. Rather, India denied imposing a blockade at all.

[142] Revised Indo-Nepal Treaty of Trade (signed and entered into force 27 October 2009) art. 1.

[143] Combined reading of arts I and II of the Protocol to the Indo–Nepal Trade Treaty 2009.

[144] Indo–Nepal Trade Treaty 2009 art. X.

[145] Protocol to the Revised Indo–Nepal Trade Treaty (signed and entered into force 27 October 2009) art. VII.

[146] Ibid.

5.4.3.3 UNCLOS

For similar reasons to those given above, India's actions were not consistent with Nepal's right of access to and from the sea and freedom of transit under article 125 of UNCLOS, discussed earlier. Both Nepal and India are states parties to UNCLOS, following India's ratification of it in 1995. A dispute arising under UNCLOS can be resolved by one of the mechanisms stipulated in that Convention, potentially including the International Court of Justice. Although Nepal could have considered the options available under UNCLOS to complain about the measures taken by India, it seemed reluctant to do so.

One particular hurdle was that neither Nepal nor India have accepted the compulsory jurisdiction of the International Court of Justice. Therefore, without the ad hoc consent of India to this case, Nepal could not bring proceedings.

5.4.3.4 WORLD TRADE ORGANIZATION DISPUTE SETTLEMENT

Nepal could have initiated a dispute under the World Trade Organization (WTO) Dispute Settlement Body against the trade sanction or blockade imposed by India. Article V of the General Agreement on Tariffs and Trade ('GATT') highlights the importance of freedom of transit as a matter of utmost importance to international trade. Further, it imposes a general obligation for WTO members to ensure freedom of transit through the territory of each contracting party, via routes most convenient for international transit to or from the territory of other contracting parties.[147] Further, it prohibits members from making distinctions in the treatment of goods based on their origin or trajectory prior to arriving in their territory, their ownership, or the transport or vessel of the goods.[148] Further, one case recognized the obligation of transit countries to provide more than one transit route which is convenient for the recipient country.[149]

However, the biggest hurdle for Nepal would have been the slow process of the dispute settlement mechanism of the WTO. The first step in WTO dispute settlement is consultation,[150] whereby members try to find a mutually agreed solution. If members cannot resolve the dispute through formal consultation, then parties may request formal adjudication. Subsequently, a Panel will be formed and the decision of Panel is appealable to the Appellate Body of the WTO. The whole process normally takes around fifteen months to resolve the dispute and there is no provision or practice of issuing provisional measures under the WTO system. This process may not have been

[147] General Agreement on Tariffs and Trade (signed 15 April 1994, entered into force 1 January 1996, 1867 UNTS 14) art. V(2).

[148] Ibid. art. V.

[149] WTO Panel Report, *Colombia-Indicative Prices and Restrictions on Ports of Entry*, WT/DS366/R (27 April 2009).

[150] Understanding on Rules and Procedures Governing the Settlement of Disputes (Annex 2 of the Marrakesh Agreement establishing the WTO, signed 15 April 1994, entered into force 1 January 1996, 1867 UNTS 154) art. 5.

an immediate help to remove the blockade, but in the long run the WTO forum could have been a suitable one for Nepal to protest blockades imposed by India.

Nepal, which was the first least developed country (LDC) to become a member of the WTO, failed to utilize the support from other LDCs at the WTO. Nepal could also have used the UN Office of the High Representative for the Least Developed Countries, Landlocked Developing Counties and the Small Island Developing States to raise its voice against the blockade. But this measure was not taken either. Nepal's response to the blockade reflects the general hesitation of landlocked countries to bring cases in international forums because of fear of the possible economic consequences they might bear from the transit state.

5.5 Foreign Investment and Bilateral Investment Treaties

In recent years, successive governments in Nepal have accorded priority to attracting foreign investment. Article 51(d)(10) of the Constitution 2015 states that '[t]he State shall pursue the policies encouraging and mobilizing foreign capital and technology investment for infrastructure development in the areas of export promotion, and import to suit national interest'.[151] Article 26(12) of the Constitution 1990 stated that '[t]he State shall, for the purposes of national development, pursue a policy of taking measures necessary for the attraction of foreign capital and technology, while at the same time promoting indigenous investment'.[152]

Previously, the country's Ninth Development Plan (1997–2002) had the objective of ensuring the safe entry of foreign capital, technology, and managerial and technical skills. These were encouraged particularly for the development of industry, tourism, water resources, and infrastructure; to accelerate industrialization; to promote international exports by improving production, productivity, and quality; and to raise the standard of living by expanding the opportunities for gainful employment and income generation.

Subsequent development plans have included similar objectives to attract foreign investment, and various policies and laws have been adopted to encourage it and provide investor protection.[153] In addition, various provisions in other legislation are designed to accelerate the pace of economic development in Nepal and to encourage foreign investment.[154] Nepal has also established the Investment Promotion Board to facilitate foreign investment.

[151] Constitution of Nepal 2015, art. 51(d)(10).

[152] Constitution of the Kingdom of Nepal 2047 (1990) art. 26(12).

[153] See e.g. the promulgation of the Industrial Policy 1992, Foreign Investment and One Window Policy 1992, Foreign Investment and Technology Transfer Act 1992, and Industrial Enterprises Act 1992.

[154] See e.g. the Finance Act, Immigration Rules of 1994, Customs Act 1997, the Electricity Act 1992, Privatisation Act 1992, Copyright Act 1965, and Patent Design and Trade Mark Act 1965.

Internationally, Nepal is a member of the World Bank, the International Monetary Fund, and the Multilateral Investment Guarantee Agency. It has also been a party to the International Centre of Settlement of Investment Disputes since 1969.

Nepal has concluded relatively few Bilateral Investment Treaties (BITs) with other countries. Nepal signed its first BIT with France on 2 May 1983. The BIT was followed by agreements with Germany (20 October 1986), the UK (2 March 1993), Mauritius (3 August 1999), Finland (3 February 2009), and India (21 October 2011). All of these BITs are designed to accord protection to foreign investors. They contain the following standard provisions: (i) national treatment, (ii) non-discrimination, (iii) expropriation, (iv) transfer of funds, and (v) dispute settlement.

India has traditionally been the largest trading partner and source of foreign investment in Nepal. There have already been some notable joint venture investments in Nepal by Indian investors[155] and Nepal can expect significant future investment from India. During the Maoist insurgency from 1996 to 2006, India sought to conclude a bilateral investment protection treaty with Nepal to ensure a higher level of protection for Indian investors due to the internal political problems and harassment of some Indian businesses. Following the conclusion of the CPA in 2006, Nepal was a country emerging from a decade of Maoist insurgency and seeking to accelerate its economic growth. Thus, it realized that such a treaty would instil confidence in Indian businesses and encourage more investment in Nepal.

With mutuality of interests in mind, India and Nepal signed a new Bilateral Investment Promotion and Protection Agreement (BIPPA) on 21 October 2011,[156] although, as discussed below, it is controversial in Nepal and has not yet been ratified. From an international legal perspective, BIPPA is an interesting instrument as it represents a new trend in BIT-making by India. It contains a flexible and innovative international mechanism for the resolution of investment disputes and a number of new elements not seen in the older generation of BITs.

BIPPA is not meant to regulate only one-way traffic, that is, Indian investment in Nepal; there are now a number of business houses in Nepal that have invested, and are able and willing to further invest, in India. Given the nature of Nepal's open society, favourable climatic conditions, and its traditional image as a neutral country, it is also conceivable that some investors would acquire juridical personality in Nepal with a view to investing in India as Nepalese investors. It is further possible that Nepal may develop into a sub-regional financial services centre similar to smaller, strategically located states such as Switzerland, Singapore, or Luxembourg. Nepalese investors in

[155] Including Nepal Lever Limited (Hetauda), Soaltee Hotels Limited (Kathmandu), Manipal Education and Medical Group (Nepal) Limited (Pokhara), Everest Rolling Industry Pvt Ltd (Bhairahawa), Taragaon Regency Hotel Ltd (Kathmandu), Colgate Palmolive (Nepal) Pvt Ltd (Hetauda), and Arati Strips Pvt Ltd (Biratnagar).

[156] The Bilateral Investment Promotion and Protection Agreements between India and Nepal signed on 21 October 2011. The Agreement was terminated on 22 March 2017. <https://investmentpolicyhubold.unctad.org/IIA/country/147/treaty/1939> accessed 9 January 2019.

India, too, would benefit from this new BIT, as the Indian judiciary is notorious for being slow and inefficient in dispensing effective legal remedies.

Like other such treaties, BIPPA is designed to establish specific rights and obligations to meet the primary purpose of protecting foreign investments against discriminatory measures by the host state and to ensure the reciprocal encouragement, promotion, and protection of investments, thereby enabling conditions conducive to increasing investment. BIPPA guarantees the rights of foreign investors, ensures them fair and equitable treatment and security, and provides for a dispute resolution mechanism.

The principles of most-favoured-nation treatment and national treatment constitute the foundation of BIPPA. Contracting parties are obliged to treat investments at least as favourably as they do domestic and third-party foreign investments, and to accord non-discriminatory compensation in case of nationalization or expropriation of investments.

While a majority of the provisions in the India–Nepal BIT are similar to other BIT's concluded by India, BIPPA has attracted a great deal of political controversy in Nepal, and has not yet been ratified by Nepal. There are unique relations between these two countries which share a long, porous, open border. The existence of the bilateral Peace and Friendship Treaty 1950 already provides for national treatment of each other's citizens in matters of commerce, yet BIPPA has been regarded by many political parties in opposition as being 'anti-national'. Nepal is strategically located between the two giants of Asia, China and India, which are rapidly growing economies and aspire to become global powers. Nepal is also a gateway to the Tibet Autonomous Region of China. But Nepal still has to offer assurances and incentives to attract significant investment from India and China and a BIT is certainly a useful tool to that end.

One positive development in recent times is the active involvement of the Investment Board of Nepal (IBN) in facilitating foreign investment and creating an investment-friendly environment. It recently concluded an important milestone in the first Project Investment Agreement, worth US$359.2 million, with a private Chinese company to establish a mega cement factory in Nepal.[157] Moreover, the Investment Summit of 2017 and 2019, along with the Memorandum of Understanding on the Belt and Road initiative signed with China, will provide a a further opportunity for Nepal to diversify its trade routes, strengthen its connectivity, and enhance its economic partnership, not only with China but globally.[158] Thus, if Nepal sorts out its political instability and instigates a sensible foreign investment policy, it stands to attract serious investment from both of its immediate neighbours and beyond.

[157] 'IBN signs $359m pact with Chinese venture' *The Kathmandu Post* (Kathmandu, 4 September 2017) <http://kathmandupost.ekantipur.com/news/2017-09-04/ibn-signs-359m-pact-with-chinese-venture.html> accessed 15 January 2018.

[158] Tejeshwi Nath Bhattarai and Pratyush Nath Upreti, 'Navigating the Currents of Belt and Road Initiative: Perspectives on Least Developed Countries' (2019) 14 Global Trade and Customs Journal 264–5

6 Conclusion

As a small country located on the southern flanks of the Himalayas and sandwiched between the two giants of Asia, Nepal has traditionally followed a policy intended to preserve its sovereignty and independence and retain its ancient cultural heritage. The country has trodden a careful path to maintain cordial relations with its immediate neighbours, reach out to other nations, and play an important role in international organizations such as the UN. Nepal is a regular contributor to UN peacekeeping operations. As a landlocked country, Nepal has also been at the forefront of efforts to secure the rights of landlocked countries in international law, especially during the negotiations on UNCLOS. The country is a host to the Secretariat of SAARC and some regional UN agencies. Although culturally it is a traditional society, politically Nepal is very much a liberal society. In spite of the political instability within the country, Nepal has been able to participate actively in international activities designed to promote the rule of law, democracy, and human rights. The country has a good record of participating in international human rights and environmental law treaties and has been elected a member of the UN Human Rights Council.

Over the past two decades, Nepal witnessed a series of challenging political developments, while the massive earthquake in 2015 burdened it with the additional responsibility of reconstruction. On the other hand, after years of struggle, Nepal finally adopted a new Constitution in 2015, drafted by the Constituent Assembly. With the new republican Constitution in place, Nepal should be able to witness political stability and accelerate its economic development.

Overall, Nepal has done well in asserting and protecting its freedom of action and in maintaining its own equilibrium vis-à-vis its two larger neighbours, China and India, against all odds. It has used international law as an instrument to this effect. It has also been successful in internalizing many liberal democratic values, underpinned by human rights, the rule of law in the Nepalese psyche, and the fundamental law of the land itself, namely the Constitution 2015. However, economically speaking the country remains impoverished and, after five decades of endeavours and investment by the UN and other development partners, it still finds its place among the LDCs. The challenge for the country is to graduate out of LDC status, by accelerating its economic development in a manner that is both sustainable and equitable.

CHAPTER 27

SRI LANKA

AMRITH ROHAN PERERA

1 Introduction

DURING the early phase of the post-1945 norm-creating process, Sri Lanka (then Ceylon) shared with the newly independent Afro-Asian states their collective concerns about 'an inherited legal order' of essentially European origin. That order was designed to regulate the relations among the limited community of states who enjoyed a common Christian religious and social background. Historically, Sri Lanka had been successively colonized by the Portuguese from 1517, the Dutch from 1638, and the British from 1815.

As the international community expanded with the decolonization process, Sri Lanka played a leadership role with other key emerging independent nations of Asia and Africa in helping a new legal order to evolve. This new order addressed the economic and developmental imperatives of the newly independent states, which were struggling to shake off the burdens of colonialism. These countries sought a legal order built not only on the formal sovereign equality of states, but also on recognizing the economic disparities that hindered them from enjoying the full benefits of their newly gained freedom.

Sri Lanka, along with other key Asian-African states such as India, Japan, China, Myanmar (then Burma), Indonesia, Egypt, and Ghana, sought to come together and find common platforms to realize the goal of a new legal order. The historic Bandung Conference of 1955 was a major landmark in these efforts. A direct outcome of the conference was the formation of the Asian-African Legal Consultative Committee (AALCC) (now AALCO), which provided a common platform for Asian-African states to articulate their concerns and forge common positions on important international legal initiatives. The organization played a vital role in sensitizing Asian-African states on issues before major law-making conferences at the time, such as the Geneva Conferences on the Law of the Sea in 1958, Vienna Conference on Diplomatic Relations in 1961, and the Vienna Conference on the Law of Treaties (1968–9).

This chapter examines the factors that contributed to Sri Lanka playing a visible and proactive role in multilateral treaty-making processes and highlights the national imperatives behind these factors as well as their political dimensions.

Taking the negotiating process at the historic Third United Nations (UN) Conference on the Law of the Sea (UNCLOS III) and the negotiations within the UN Conference on Trade and Development (UNCTAD) as prime examples, the chapter points to the imperatives of harnessing for developing countries the potential economic benefits in the new frontiers that were being opened up. The chapter also discusses Sri Lanka's role in the UN treaty formulation process in the field of the suppression of terrorism. The central factor in Sri Lanka's involvement in strengthening the framework for global cooperation was the backdrop of acts of terrorism with external linkages confronting Sri Lanka in the 1990s.

The chapter next discusses the all-important issues concerning the incorporation of international law into the domestic legal order, in the context of the constitutional and general legal frameworks in Sri Lanka. In an analysis of leading judicial decisions, particularly in the field of human rights, the chapter highlights the overall liberal approach of the domestic courts in giving effect to Sri Lanka's international legal obligations—albeit punctuated by some setbacks resulting from the adoption of a narrow approach.

2 Participation by Sri Lanka in Major Multilateral Treaties

Since gaining independence in 1948 Sri Lanka has been a constitutional democracy. The Westminster system of government introduced by the 1948 'Soulbury Constitution' subsisted until 1978, where the executive was headed by the Prime Minister, who was the head of a Cabinet of Ministers. The Prime Minister also held the portfolio of Minister of Defence and Foreign Affairs.

The 1978 Constitution marked a departure from the Westminster model and introduced an executive presidency with extensive executive powers vested in the President. A separate Ministry of Foreign Affairs headed by a Foreign Minister was also created, entrusted with the function of conducting relations with foreign states and international organizations. In addition, the function of treaty-making was vested by the President in the Foreign Minister under the provisions of the Constitution.

With the expansion of the international community, the traditional norms and principles of international law began to undergo transformation. With this transformation came the recognition of the need for economic equality, distinct from political equality, which was seen as integral to the principle of sovereign equality of states. This period witnessed the emergence of a corpus of laws which sought to regulate the use of the 'global commons' for the benefit of all nations. One watershed was the emergence of the concept, then considered revolutionary, of a 'common heritage of mankind' and the special recognition of the needs of developing states, which found expression at UNCLOS III between 1973 and 1982. It also impacted on other regimes that were being developed, including on outer space and the environment.

Sri Lanka's leadership role in the Non-Aligned Movement (NAM), which emerged from the Bandung Process, facilitated the proactive role it played in new legal initiatives.

2.1 UNCLOS III

It is a matter of historical record that Sri Lanka played a prominent role in the evolution of new concepts and principles relating to the oceans at UNCLOS III, chaired by Sri Lanka's then Permanent Representative to the UN, Ambassador Hamilton Shirley Amerasinghe.

Sri Lanka, along with other Asian and African states such as India and Kenya, first mooted the proposal for a '200 nautical mile extended zone for resource jurisdiction' during the AALCC meetings at the time.[1] This concept took final form and content as the 'exclusive economic zone' (EEZ) concept at UNCLOS III.

Sri Lanka took a similar initiative to provide for a special method of delimitation of its continental shelf in light of the special geological and geomorphological characteristics in the southern part of the Bay of Bengal.[2] This initiative, which seeks to redress an inequity that would otherwise result from application of the normal method of delimitation in article 76 of the UN Convention on the Law of the Sea 1982 ('UNCLOS'), is now expressed in the Statement of Understanding which is incorporated by reference as an integral part of the Convention.

At the time, importance was also attached to the prospect of deep seabed mining and the potential for minerals and other resources such as manganese nodules. Sri Lanka was active in the work of the First Committee which dealt with the formulation of a legal regime for the deep seabed beyond areas of national jurisdiction.[3] This came to be known as the 'International Seabed Area'.

The potential of these new frontiers being harnessed for the economic benefit of the developing countries was the driving force behind these initiatives.

2.2 Initiatives within UNCTAD

Sri Lanka also played an active role in the work of the UN Conference on Trade and Development. The work of the UNCTAD in the 1970s and 1980s had acquired

[1] Asian-African Legal Consultative Committee, Report of the Committee on the Law of the Sea (18–27 January 1971).

[2] 104th Plenary Meeting Seventh and Resumed Seventh Session of the Third United Nations Conference on the Law of the Sea (Geneva 28 March–19 May 1978 and New York 21 August–15 September 1978) (18 May 1978) UN Doc A/CONF.62/SR.104. See also MCW Pinto, 'Article 76 of the UN Convention on the Law of the Sea and the Bay of Bengal Exception' (2013) 3 Asian Journal of International Law 215.

[3] Final Act of the Third United Nations Conference on the Law of the Sea (27 October 1982) UN Doc A/CONF.62/121 pt III.

particular significance in the context of the initiatives of the developing countries to usher in a New International Economic Order, in order to address the economic imbalance underlying the existing global economic order.

The first Secretary-General of UNCTAD was the dynamic Sri Lankan Diplomat, Dr Gamani Corea. His personal commitment to the ongoing initiatives to restructure the global trade and developmental order provided Sri Lanka with opportunities for active involvement in the UNCTAD processes.

Two landmark initiatives of UNCTAD at the time were the negotiation of Codes of Conduct on: (a) Transnational Corporations (TNCs) and (b) Transfer of Technology.[4] The involvement of TNCs in the internal affairs of states (as graphically demonstrated in the overthrow of the socialist Allende regime in Chile) and the opposition of TNCs to any form of mandatory transfer of technology to developing countries (later to become a key issue in UNCLOS negotiations) were the underlying rationales for these initiatives.

Sri Lanka joined other developing countries in giving the highest priority to these initiatives in the ongoing negotiations. The changing global political and economic scenario of the 1990s, culminating in free market dominance (embraced both in the North as well as in the South), resulted in these efforts not coming to fruition at the time. Nevertheless, the draft Codes of Conduct set important landmarks and reference points for ongoing global economic reform.

2.3 Multilateral Instruments on the Suppression of Terrorism

From 1983 to 2009, Sri Lanka was confronted by an internal conflict which continued unabated for nearly three decades. The conflict involved the armed group, Liberation Tigers of Tamil Eelam (LTTE), comprising extremist elements from among the Tamil minority seeking the establishment of a separate state in the north and east of Sri Lanka. It was a sophisticated group with naval capacity as well as an element of airpower, which enabled them to carry out sustained and indiscriminate attacks not only against military targets, but also civilians, public buildings, and facilities, in all parts of the country. The problem was exacerbated by 'external linkages', particularly with South India, where political groups afforded a safe haven to LTTE Cadres, *inter alia*, by way of providing training facilities as well as hospitalization and other amenities.

Military action at the domestic level was accompanied by a sustained policy overseas towards curbing the activities of hostile diaspora groups, in particular, the supply of

[4] UNCTAD, Draft International Code on Transfer of Technology (5 June 1985); Commission on Transnational Corporations, Draft UN Code of Conduct on Transnational Corporations (1983); ECOSOC, Report on Special Session (7–18 March and 9–21 May 1983) Supplement No. 7 Annex II, UN Doc E/1983/17/Rev.1.

arms and ammunition, and the raising of funds on foreign soil, to sustain the activities of armed groups at home.[5]

The late 1990s witnessed a campaign of terrorist attacks in different parts of the world including in Sri Lanka, in particular the targeting of public buildings and infrastructure facilities through bombings and the use of other explosive devices. These attacks reached a climax in the unprecedented events of 11 September 2001 in New York and Washington DC. The shock waves that these events generated resulted in a growing realization on the part of the international community of the imperative need to deal with the source of the phenomenon—the flow of arms to terrorist groups and the external funding which facilitated such flows.[6]

From the norm-creating perspective, a significant step was taken in the UN in 1997 when it decided to establish the Ad Hoc Committee on Measures to Eliminate International Terrorism ('AHC') by UN General Assembly resolution 51/210. Having first been elected a Vice Chair of the AHC in 1997, and thereafter Chair in 2000 (a position which it continues to occupy), Sri Lanka played a key role in contributing to the emergence of the 'new generation' conventions, namely, the International Convention on the Suppression of Terrorist Bombings 1997, International Convention on the Suppression of Terrorist Financing 1999, and the International Convention on the Suppression of Acts of Nuclear Terrorism 2005.[7]

In the elaboration of these multilateral legal instruments, certain benchmarks were set which have formed the 'acquis' of the counterterrorism legal framework. Based on an 'extradite or prosecute' regime (*aut dedere aut judicare*), these multilateral instruments provided for the criminalization of prohibited conduct at the domestic level; attribution of individual criminal responsibility; and treatment of the treaty offences as 'non-political' crimes for the purposes of extradition. Other responsibilities they assigned to states include the establishment of jurisdiction on a variety of mandatory and discretionary bases; imposition of penalties commensurate with the gravity of the offences; international cooperation (including extradition and mutual legal assistance in criminal matters); and the adoption of preventive measures and exchange of information.

[5] With a view to seeking external military assistance, the Sri Lankan government inducted an Indian peacekeeping force (IPKF) into the country to disarm the LTTE, under the terms of the Indo–Lanka Accord 1987. The induction proved to be highly contentious and controversial, both in the Tamil-dominated Northern Province and in the Sinhala-dominated Southern Province, which ultimately led to the withdrawal of the IPKF in 1990. The IPKF intervention in Sri Lanka is also seen as the proximate cause for the tragic assassination of the former Indian Prime Minister Rajiv Gandhi at the hands of a pro-LTTE suicide bomber in the Southern Indian state of Tamil Nadu in 1991.

[6] Amrith Rohan Perera, 'The Draft United Nations Comprehensive Convention on International Terrorism' in Ben Saul (ed), *Research Handbook on International Law and Terrorism* (Edward Elgar 2014) 151.

[7] International Convention for the Suppression of Terrorist Bombings (adopted 23 March 1999, entered into force 23 May 2001, 2149 UNTS 256); International Convention for the Suppression of the Financing of Terrorism (adopted 8 September 2000, entered into force 10 April 2002, 2178 UNTS 197); International Convention for the Suppression of Acts of Nuclear Terrorism (signed 14 September 2005, entered into force 7 July 2007, 2445 UNTS 89).

Through its active involvement in the Bureau of the AHC, Sri Lanka made a distinct contribution to the formulation of a legal framework for the enhancement of international cooperation in combating the various forms and manifestations of terrorism. Overriding national imperatives, such as the prevention of fundraising through complex overseas networks, provided the momentum for Sri Lanka's active involvement in the norm-creating process.

3 Sri Lanka's Contribution to the Making of Regional Treaties

Regional cooperation as an organized collective approach to meeting the political, economic, and social issues of the region is a comparatively new concept in South Asia. This is despite the fact that the countries in the South Asian region share common historical, cultural, and religious affinities.

Two principal factors had traditionally militated against the South Asian countries having recourse to regional cooperation. Firstly, the South Asian countries lacked a common political security and strategic perception vis-à-vis the outside world. A common policy approach in respect of 'external threats', which took into account the concerns of the region as a whole, was the unifying factor in other regional groupings such as the European Union and the Association of Southeast Asian Nations. This was singularly lacking in South Asia, where foreign policy approaches differed widely. Any threat perception was essentially 'internal' rather than 'external'.

Secondly, given their disparities geographically as well as in terms of economic development, the majority of the countries, particularly the smaller developing countries, shared the perception that any regional economic cooperation would not advance their interests, given the dominating presence of a 'regional super power' (namely, India). Thus, the 'asymmetry factor' also militated against regional cooperation in South Asia.

Notwithstanding the element of mistrust at a political level, however, the idea of regional cooperation in South Asia gradually began to take root in the region in the early 1980s, based on historical interaction among the people of the region. Following a series of consultations consequent to a proposal made by Bangladesh, the first meeting of foreign secretaries of five South Asian countries convened in Colombo, Sri Lanka, in 1981. The meeting identified five 'agreed areas' of cooperation, namely, agriculture, rural development, telecommunication, meteorology, and health and population activities.[8]

Thus, by limiting areas of cooperation to non-political, non-contentious technical spheres, the leaders of the South Asian countries sought to insulate regional cooperation, at least in the formative stage, from the political tensions which had dominated

[8] See Amrith Rohan Perera, *International Terrorism* (Vikas 1997) pt III.

their often strained bilateral relations, which had hitherto prevented a regional grouping from developing.

3.1 SAARC Initiatives to Combat Terrorism

With the formation of the South Asian Association for Regional Cooperation (SAARC) in 1985, certain practices developed which made the organization take cognizance of the complex political and security issues which confronted the region. Despite the exclusion of formal discussion of bilateral issues under its Charter, SAARC provided a forum and an opportunity for South Asian leaders to informally discuss, on the sidelines of their Summits, specific problems confronting member countries and affecting the overall security and stability of the region. In time, the sensitive political issues excluded from the formal SAARC agenda found expression through informal discussions among the political leadership of SAARC countries. Thus, the joint Press Release issued at the conclusion of the First SAARC Summit in Dhaka, Bangladesh, in December 1985, reflected that:

> They [the Heads of States and Governments] approved that the Standing Committee should set up a study group to examine the problem of terrorism as it affects the security and stability of member-states of SAARC.[9]

With the inclusion of the question of terrorism on its agenda, SAARC ventured into one of the most complex and sensitive political issues of recent times. The meetings of SAARC Study Groups and Expert Groups which followed resulted in the convening of a Meeting of a Group of Legal Experts in Colombo, Sri Lanka, in August 1987, to begin the process of negotiating a draft SAARC Convention on Suppression of Terrorism. The negotiations commenced on the basis of a draft text prepared by the host country, Sri Lanka. Given the immediacy of the problem of terrorism confronting Sri Lanka at the time, together with its cross-border ramifications, it was natural for Sri Lanka to take the initiative in the political decision to deal with terrorism as well as to play an active role in the regional norm-creating process.

Based on an 'extradite or prosecute' regime, the SAARC Convention on Suppression of Terrorism 1987 followed the 'acquis' of the existing UN conventions on counter-terrorism and other regional conventions such as the European Convention on the Suppression of Terrorism 1977. Adopted at the Third SAARC Summit in Kathmandu, Nepal, in 1987, and thereafter ratified by all member states, the SAARC Convention was an important landmark in the regional norm-creating process, designed to address a phenomenon which affected the security and stability of the region. Sri Lanka's active participation in this process was animated by its overriding concerns about the effect of cross-border terrorism on its national security.

[9] SAARC, Press Release, First SAARC Summit, Dhaka, 7–8 December 1985.

A lack of political will in the effective implementation of the Convention has diluted what would otherwise have been, given the overriding bilateral tensions dominating the region, a landmark achievement in regional treaty-making.

3.2 Other Regional Conventions within SAARC

The SAARC Convention on Suppression of Terrorism was followed by several other conventions in the field of serious transnational crimes, which provided for enhanced cooperation among member states. These included the SAARC Conventions on Narcotic Drugs and Psychotropic Substances 1990, Trafficking of Women and Children for Prostitution 2002, Child Welfare 2002, and Mutual Assistance on Criminal Matters 2008.

Based on provisions of existing multilateral treaties in the respective fields, these conventions were not hampered by the political factors that surrounded the Convention on Terrorism, and attracted a greater degree of support among member states in their adoption and implementation. Sri Lanka played an active role in the formulation of the negotiating text of the Convention on Narcotic Drugs and in chairing the Meeting of Legal Experts which finalized the draft, as well as chairing the Meeting of Legal Experts which finalized the Mutual Assistance Convention in Colombo.

4 Sri Lanka's Involvement in International Dispute Settlement Procedures

Sri Lanka was one of the early subscribers to the International Convention on Settlement of Investment Disputes 1967 ('ICSID Convention'), ratifying it on 12 October 1967. The ICSID Convention was unique for the reason that it conferred the right on an aggrieved foreign investor to submit an investment dispute with a host state directly to international dispute settlement procedures.[10] Thus, an individual investor could pursue their rights against a host state where their investment suffered loss or damage, independent of the intervention of their state of nationality to espouse their claim. This was a radical departure from the traditional position relating to the status of the individual in international law.

The growth and development of the network of bilateral investment treaties (BITs), particularly between developing states (the major capital recipient countries) and the

[10] See generally Anna Joubin-Bret and Jean Kalicki, 'Reform of Investor-State Dispute Settlement: In Search of a Roadmap' (2014) 1 Transnational Dispute Management 60https://www.transnational-dispute-management.com/article.asp?key=2023> accessed 30 October 2018.

developed states (the capital-exporting countries), were viewed as major factors in promoting the flow of foreign direct investment to developing host countries.

The BITs created a legal regime of guarantees to capital-exporting states and their nationals, designed to generate what was referred to as 'investor confidence'. The 'guarantee regime' included assurances of 'full protection and security' to investors and their investments, the grant of 'most favoured nation' status and 'national treatment' to investors and their investments, guarantees against expropriation (except for a public purpose and with 'prompt, adequate and effective compensation'), and compensation for losses suffered by an investor.

A vital guarantee of a procedural nature, as distinct from the substantive guarantees referred to above, was the dispute settlement procedure incorporated into the BITs. A key component of the investment guarantee regime was the availability of recourse to international arbitration/conciliation by an investor who suffers loss or damage in respect of their investment in the host state, including through the International Centre for the Settlement of Investment Disputes (ICSID) in Washington DC under the terms of the ICSID Convention. It gave an investor direct recourse to international dispute settlement procedures, in most cases without first having to take a dispute before domestic courts or tribunals of host states.

Sri Lanka ushered in a liberal economic policy framework, embracing free market principles, in 1978.[11] This constituted a major shift from the centrally planned, 'socialist' economic policies which had hitherto been followed in post-independent Sri Lanka since the mid 1950s. A key plank on which the new bilateral economic policies rested was the active pursuit of foreign direct investments to regenerate the national economy.

The negotiation of BITs with capital-exporting countries was a vital component of the new liberal economic policy that was pursued. Among the first BITs concluded by Sri Lanka was the Agreement on Promotion and Protection of Investments 1980 between Sri Lanka and the United Kingdom ('SL–UK BIT'). This became the model for the series of BITs which followed.

4.1 *AAPL v Government of Sri Lanka*

The SL–UK BIT was extended to Hong Kong through an exchange of letters, as it was under UK sovereignty and jurisdiction at the time. The provisions of this agreement were invoked by a Hong Kong-based company named Asian Agricultural Products Limited (AAPL), which had invested in a prawn farm in Batticaloa in the Eastern Province of Sri Lanka.

During a security operation in the mid 1980s to flush out armed groups operating in this area, the prawn farm had suffered damage and also loss of the lives of some of the farm employees. AAPL proceeded to international arbitration under the Dispute

[11] Constitution of the Democratic Socialist Republic of Sri Lanka 1978 art. 157.

Settlement Clause of the SL–UK BIT, and referred the matter to the ICSID, which decided the case in 1990.[12] It is significant that this was the first time that the ICSID jurisdiction was invoked under the dispute settlement provisions of a BIT.

The arbitration raised a fundamental legal issue, namely, the scope of the term 'full protection and security' which was guaranteed under the SL–UK BIT. It was contended for the AAPL that the obligation involved is one of strict liability, which required only to establish the fact that loss or damage had in fact occurred. On the other hand, the respondent, Sri Lanka, argued that the 'full protection and security' standard only entailed the obligation to observe 'due diligence' as required by customary international law, vis-à-vis investments admitted into its territory.

The tribunal, on a divided opinion of 2-1, agreed with Sri Lanka's contention that the full protection and security standard in BITs involved nothing more than the 'due diligence' requirement under customary international law and not strict liability.[13] This reasoning has been followed thereafter in several arbitrations. States have also since taken the precaution of specifically clarifying the nature of the obligation in their BITs, by stating that the term 'full protection and security' only incurs an obligation to exercise 'due diligence' under customary international law.

4.2 *Mihaly Corporation v Government of Sri Lanka*

The second important BIT arbitration against Sri Lanka was the one filed by Mihaly Corporation, a US-based company, regarding the cancellation of a reconstruction and rebuilding project that had been previously approved by the government. The case was decided in 2002.[14] The investor, basing the claim on a Sri Lanka–US BIT of 1991, sought to recover costs already incurred in respect of capital outlay for initial work which had been undertaken, pending the formal approval and admission of the investment.

It was argued on behalf of the applicant company that the term 'investment' was wide enough to cover what was referred to as 'pre-investment expenditure' incurred in the expectation that the final approval for the investment would follow. The claimant based its argument, *inter alia*, on the fact that the term 'investment', as used in BITs, was a non-exhaustive definition, and that the term had to be given a flexible interpretation in order to achieve the object and purpose of the agreement, namely, encouraging the greater flow of investment through the creation of 'investor confidence'.

Sri Lanka argued, on the other hand, that the obligation under a BIT would only flow once an investment had formally been approved and admitted into the territory in

[12] *AAPL v Sri Lanka* (1990) 4 ICSID Reports 246; Giorgio Sacerdoti, 'Investment Arbitration under ICSID and UNCITRAL Rules: Prerequisites, Applicable Law, Review of Awards' (2014) 19 ICSID Review 1, 25.

[13] *AAPL v Sri Lanka* (n 12).

[14] *Mihaly Corporation v Government of Sri Lanka* (2002) 6 ICSID Reports 308.

accordance with the laws of the host state, and that the BIT protection did not cover the pre-establishment phase. This position was upheld by the Tribunal in a majority decision of 2-1. In reaching this conclusion, however, the majority of arbitrators further concluded that once an investment had been formally admitted and established in the host country, any such 'pre-investment expenditure' could be absorbed into the costs incurred for the admitted investment.[15] The issue of coverage of pre-investment expenditure under the provisions of a BIT has thereafter figured in several ICSID tribunal decisions, and has been the subject of diverse interpretation by different tribunals.[16]

5 Incorporation of International Law in the Domestic Legal Order

5.1 Domestic Constitutional or Other Legal Powers for Entering into Treaties

The legal system of Sri Lanka has been described by writers as a rich tapestry of laws, inherited from its colonial past. Thus, Dr (later Justice) Henry Tambiah states:

> In Sri Lanka, there are five systems of private law. The Roman-Dutch law, as modified by statutes, and interpreted by the courts, is the general law of the land. English common law applies to commercial contracts and commercial property and has been tacitly accepted in many matters. English law was also introduced by statute and as such forms the statutory law of the land. The Thesawalamai is both a personal and local law. . . . Similarly, Kandyan Law applies to the Kandyan Sinhalese, and the Muslim laws, to the Muslims, in [matters relating to] marriage, divorce, [alimony] and inheritance.[17]

Historically influenced by British constitutional practice, Sri Lanka has followed the dualist approach in the conclusion of treaties and their incorporation into the domestic legal order.[18]

[15] *AAPL v Sri Lanka* (n 12).

[16] UNCTAD, 'Scope and Definition: UNCTAD Series on Issues in International Investment Agreements II' (UN 2011).

[17] Henry Tambiah, 'Sri Lanka' in Victor Knapp (ed), *International Encyclopedia of Comparative Law: National Reports* (Martinus Nijhoff 1987) S-125/S-136; ARB Amerasinghe, *Legal Heritage of Sri Lanka* (Visvalekha Press 1999).

[18] Ministry of Foreign Affairs Legal Adviser's Division, 'Guidelines relating to the Conclusion of International Agreements' (February 1971), later reissued as SP/CSA/07 (3 July 2007) by the Office of the Secretary to the President.

Under all post-independence constitutions, it has been well recognized that the conclusion of treaties is an 'executive act' influenced by the British constitutional practice of the 'Crown Prerogative'. The current Constitution of 1978 thus includes the power to conclude treaties within the executive powers of the President which, in practice, is exercised in consultation with the Cabinet of Ministers.[19]

The Directive Principles of State Policy incorporated in the Constitution require the executive to promote respect for international law.[20] An exception is made in the constitutional prohibition against retrospective legislation, where such legislation is required to give effect to 'obligations under the Law of Nations'.[21]

In accordance with the constitutional provision empowering the President to assign subjects and functions to the Cabinet of Ministers, the subject of 'International Treaties' is assigned to the Minister of Foreign Affairs.[22]

The role of the legislature in relation to treaties entered into by Sri Lanka is twofold. Firstly, in keeping with the dualist approach of 'transforming' a treaty into domestic law through enabling legislation, an 'enabling act' is presented to Parliament for approval to give domestic effect to a treaty (for example, in respect of law enforcement treaties for the purpose of creation of offences, or conferring special jurisdiction on domestic courts). In this instance, it is not the treaty itself which is approved by Parliament, but the enabling act which gives effect to its provisions. On the domestic plane, it is the act of Parliament, rather than the treaty, which becomes the source of rights and obligations.

As a source of statutory interpretation, however, the treaty remains very much relevant. Sri Lankan courts have had recourse to treaties and other instruments in adjudicating cases, particularly where matters have arisen involving human rights and the protection of the environment.[23]

A practice has also developed whereby a treaty concerned with a matter of great public importance is placed before Parliament for information. The most recent instance in this regard was the Paris Accord 2016 on climate change.

On the question of giving effect to customary international law, the Sri Lankan courts have shown a degree of flexibility in applying such norms as additional tools, particularly in the field of environmental law. For example, the courts have been ready to consider principles such as Environmental Impact Assessment (EIA), the Rio Declaration 1992, and Agenda 21 of 1992,[24] which are widely regarded as having acquired a customary law character.

[19] Constitution of the Democratic Socialist Republic of Sri Lanka 1978 arts 3(2) and 44.

[20] Ibid. art. 27(15). [21] Ibid. art. 13(6). [22] Ibid. art. 44(2).

[23] In the field of human rights, especially freedom of speech, assembly, and association, see *Victor Ivan v Silva* (1998) 1 Sri LR 340; on torture, cruel, inhuman, and degrading treatment or punishment, see *Amal Sudath Silva v Kodituwakku* [1987] 2 Sri LR 119; on environmental law, see the Constitution of the Democratic Socialist Republic of Sri Lanka 1978.

[24] *Bulankulama v Secretary, Ministry of Industrial Development* [2000] 3 Sri LR 243.

5.2 Major Areas of Legislative Enactment

In the context of Sri Lanka's dualist approach to the domestic implementation of treaty obligations, there is an extensive compendium of enabling legislative enactments in the diverse fields of application of the relevant treaties. As outlined below, these include, for example, the areas of international terrorism, law of the sea, foreign investment, human rights and international humanitarian law (IHL).

5.2.1 *International Terrorism*

As Sri Lanka is a party to a majority of the sectoral conventions on the suppression of terrorism, a series of legislative enactments gave domestic legal effect to these obligations.[25] These range from the early anti-hijacking of aircraft treaties to the recent new generation conventions, namely the Terrorist Bombings Convention 1997 and the Terrorist Financing Convention 1999 (an exception is the Nuclear Terrorism Convention 2005, in respect of which implementing legislation is pending as of 2019).

The legislative framework in these statutes provides for, *inter alia*, the establishment of the treaty offences as serious offences under Sri Lankan law, thus domesticating the offences and providing for the imposition of appropriate penalties; the vesting of requisite jurisdiction in the High Court, so that prosecutions can be launched where extradition is not granted; and provisions for facilitating extradition procedures and mutual legal assistance. The legislative provision on extradition is also contained, by way of consequential amendments, to the general law of extradition.[26] It treats the covered offences as 'non-political' for the purposes of extradition (as required by these conventions), thus facilitating extradition, notwithstanding any so-called 'political motivation' or objective.

5.2.2 *Law of the Sea*

The principal enactment relating to the law of the sea is the Maritime Zones Law No. 22 of 1976, which was enacted to give effect to the then new law of the sea emerging at UNCLOS III. The Law was of an enabling nature and provided for the proclamation by Executive Order of the different maritime zones adjacent to the coast of Sri Lanka, such as the territorial sea, EEZ, and the continental shelf.

A feature of this Law was that it gave effect to new legal concepts such as the EEZ, even before they were incorporated into UNCLOS, while they were still in a process of evolution as emerging norms of customary international law, consequent to widespread state practice.

[25] See Suppression of Terrorist Bombings Act (No 11) 1999; Convention on the Suppression of Terrorist Financing Act (No 25) 2005.

[26] See Suppression of Terrorist Bombings Act (No 11) 1999 ss 9–10; Convention on the Suppression of Terrorist Financing Act (No 25) 2005 ss 12–13.

5.2.3 *Foreign Investment Laws*

International agreements relating to foreign investments occupy a special place, in contrast to other international agreements entered into by Sri Lanka, with regard to their domestic applicability. With the objective of generating investor confidence, BITs are accorded special constitutional protection under article 157 of the Constitution. The article provides that, once an agreement for the promotion and protection of investments is approved by a resolution in Parliament (with a two-thirds majority) as an agreement essential to the development of the national economy, no law could be enacted which is inconsistent with its terms, and its terms shall have the force of law in Sri Lanka. The only exception is on the limited ground of national security.

This provision is unique for two reasons. Firstly, it binds even a future Parliament with regard to Sri Lanka's obligations under a BIT. Secondly, by prescribing a parliamentary approval process, it constitutes a departure from Sri Lanka's normal treaty ratification process, which is regarded as an executive act.

The Greater Colombo Economic Commission Act, enacted in 1978 with the liberalization of Sri Lanka's economy, recognizes Sri Lanka's obligations under the ICSID Convention and BITs, by providing recourse to international dispute settlement mechanisms under the terms of these conventions. The Commission was the principal agency for dealing with foreign investments, now replaced by the Board of Investments.

5.2.4 *Human Rights*

Human rights issues came to the forefront of Sri Lanka's political landscape, due to the sense of grievance felt by the minority Tamil community, who considered they had lost the privileged position they had enjoyed in the administration under British rule. This sense of grievance was exacerbated by several other developments, such as the ethnic riots of 1958 and the enactment of the First Republican Constitution of 1972 which removed the constitutional protection given to minorities under the 1948 Soulbury Constitution, namely, not to confer a benefit or privilege on one community which is denied to another.[27] The human rights concerns relating to Sri Lanka came into sharper focus as a result of the youth uprisings in the south of Sri Lanka in 1971 and again in 1989, which took a heavy toll on human lives. The communal riots which broke out against the Tamil minority community in the 1980s further accentuated these concerns. The enactment of special laws such as the Prevention of Terrorism Act (PTA) in 1978, conferring wide ranging powers of arrest and detention on the police and armed forces with minimum judicial oversight and safeguards, gave rise to serious concerns of human rights violations, on the part of human right groups both domestic and foreign.

The 1972 Republican Constitution failed to make the human rights provisions therein enforceable. The Second Republican Constitution of Sri Lanka of 1978 marked

[27] Constitution of Ceylon 1948 s 29.

a major shift in Sri Lanka's approach to the enforcement of international human rights standards and norms under its domestic legal processes.

Chapter III of the Constitution embodied in substance a vast majority of the rights under the International Covenant on Civil and Political Rights 1966 (ICCPR) and, for the first time in its constitutional history, made such rights enforceable before the highest court of the land, the Supreme Court of Sri Lanka. It is to be noted, however, that the constitutional provisions in Chapter III did not specifically contain provisions on the right to life or the right to property, as enshrined in the ICCPR.

It is noteworthy, however, that a liberal approach adopted by the Supreme Court at the time, in several fundamental rights applications before it, resulted in the right to life being read into the Constitution, taking into account the fact that Sri Lanka had subscribed to the ICCPR.[28] A similar liberal approach was adopted by the Supreme Court in incorporating developing principles of environmental law, such as the precautionary principle and the EIA.[29]

Similarly, in the case of the Convention against Torture (CAT), to which Sri Lanka had subscribed, an issue that has consistently come up before the treaty monitoring body, the UN Committee against Torture, is the question of whether the offence of torture in domestic law (in the Convention Against Torture and other Cruel, Inhuman or Degrading Treatment or Punishment Act No 22 of 1994) was wide enough to cover both physical and mental torture, as required in the Convention. Here again, the Supreme Court adopted a liberal approach in interpreting the statutory provision in a manner consistent with Sri Lanka's obligations under the CAT, holding that the provision was wide enough to cover both physical and mental torture as required by the Convention.

Nevertheless, a certain tension between Sri Lanka's treaty obligations in the field of human rights and its domestic laws arose in the well-known case of *Singarasa v Attorney General*.[30] The Supreme Court, departing from the practice followed hitherto, took an extremely restrictive approach in giving effect to Sri Lanka's treaty obligations. The case concerned an application for review filed by one Father Singarasa, who had been convicted on a charge of murder brought under the PTA 1978 (a special statute dealing with terrorist offences), which conviction had been confirmed on appeal by the Supreme Court.[31]

Father Singarasa had thereafter sent a communication to the UN Human Rights Committee (UN HRC) under the individual communications procedure in the Optional Protocol to the ICCPR, to which Sri Lanka had subscribed. The basis of his complaint was one of denial of justice, inasmuch as his conviction under the PTA had been based purely on a confessional statement which was prohibited under the general

[28] *Weerawansa v The Attorney General and Others* (2000) 1 Sri LR 387.

[29] *Tikiri Banda Bulankulama v The Secretary, Ministry of Industrial Development* (*Eppawela* case) (2 June 2000) Supreme Court of the Democratic Socialist Republic of Sri Lanka 884/99 (FR).

[30] *Nallaratnam Singarasa v Attorney General and Others* (2006) SC SpL (LA) 182/99.

[31] Ibid. See also Asian Human Rights Commission, Statement (25 September 2006).

law of evidence. The UN HRC expressed the view that the Sri Lankan authorities should order a retrial. This was despite the fact that the conviction in the High Court had been confirmed on appeal by the Supreme Court.

Although it is well recognized that determinations by the UN HRC under the Optional Protocol procedures are only 'views', for due consideration by state parties but legally non-binding,[32] appellant Singarasa sought to have the determination enforced by the Supreme Court. The Supreme Court in this instance took somewhat an extreme position in holding that Sri Lanka's accession to the Optional Protocol itself was unconstitutional, since it violated the supremacy of the judiciary recognized in the Constitution. It argued that recognition of the competence of an external entity, the UN HRC, violated the Constitution and that Sri Lanka's accession to the Protocol was therefore unconstitutional and invalid in law. Accordingly, it found that the determination of the UN HRC had no domestic legal effect.

The decision of the Supreme Court in the *Singarasa* case left the Sri Lankan executive in a 'legal limbo'. While no steps were taken to withdraw from the Protocol consequent to the judgment, the executive has nevertheless refrained from responding to communications made to the UN HRC under the Optional Protocol, given the finding by the Supreme Court that the accession to the instrument was unconstitutional. As the issue is being recanvassed in a similar matter which is currently pending (as of 2019), it is expected that the impasse will be addressed, perhaps by a full Bench of the Supreme Court.

5.2.5 *International Humanitarian Law*

Sri Lanka is a party to the four Geneva Conventions of 1949. Enabling legislation, giving effect to these Conventions, was enacted long after Sri Lanka had ratified them. The Geneva Conventions Act[33] broadly provided for the domestication of 'grave crimes' committed in international armed conflict and the conferring of appropriate jurisdiction on the High Court for their prosecution and punishment.

An interesting issue that has been raised in the context of this legislation is the absence of an express provision incorporating 'common article 3' on the protection of civilians during non-international armed conflict. This lacuna raises the question whether this constitutes an instance where an area of binding international law has not been enacted domestically. It nevertheless remains possible that, given the customary law and perhaps the *jus cogens* character of common article 3, the Sri Lankan courts would give effect, in appropriate circumstances, to the principle of the protection of civilians, notwithstanding the absence of express legislative provision.

Whether the Act could be extended to cover individual criminal responsibility in non-international armed conflicts is another interesting issue which has come up for consideration. The scope of application of the Geneva Conventions is by definition applicable to international armed conflicts. However, common article 3 is not so

[32] UNHRC, General Comment 33 (5 November 2008) UN Doc CCPR/C/GC/33.

[33] Geneva Conventions Act (No 4) 2006 (Sri Lanka).

limited and a broader approach to the issue of applicability to non-international armed conflicts, taking into account, *inter alia*, its customary international law character, is currently being addressed (as of 2019) in the context of the amendments being proposed to the Geneva Conventions Act.

5.2.6 *Sri Lanka's Position on the International Criminal Court*

Sri Lanka participated in the International Conference on the adoption of the Statute of an International Criminal Court in Rome 1998. Along with a number of other countries affected by international terrorism, including India and Turkey, Sri Lanka presented a proposal seeking to include 'terrorist crimes' in the Statute as serious international crimes. It was proposed to define such crimes by reference to offences in the existing multilateral (sectoral) conventions. The proposal did not find general acceptance at the conference. Partly as a result, Sri Lanka abstained on the vote to adopt the Statute. Sri Lanka's abstention was also based on its view that the Statute's definition of serious violations of human rights and IHL in internal conflicts was imprecise and appeared to go beyond generally accepted definitions under international law.

Several initiatives, both foreign and domestic, have also been taken to address the allegations of violations of human rights and IHL during the conflict by the LTTE and the state security forces. A UN Expert Panel constituted by the Secretary-General (also known as the 'Darusman Panel'), and the Lessons Learnt and Reconciliation Commission (LLRC)[34] constituted by the Sri Lankan government, were the key initiatives. The implementation of the LLRC's recommendations in the aftermath of the conflict was somewhat tardy, by a government which had successfully prosecuted the military effort and was still in office.

However, with a change of government in 2015, the new government committed itself to the establishment of good governance, the rule of law, and respect for human rights of all people. A major point of departure was Sri Lanka co-sponsoring UN Human Rights Council 30-1 in September 2015, which was introduced by the US and western European countries, and which encouraged Sri Lanka to address post-conflict reconciliation and accountability issues.

Several far-reaching measures have since been successfully adopted in addressing post-conflict reconciliation and peacebuilding. A comprehensive Peacebuilding Priority Plan was worked out in the Constitution and actively involved the UN Peacebuilding Support Office. The Office of the UN High Commissioner of Human Rights, as well as UN special mandate holders (such as the Special Rapporteur on the Promotion of Truth, Justice, Reparation and Guarantees of Non-recurrence) have also been closely engaged in the efforts of the Sri Lankan government in post-conflict reconciliation and peacebuilding.

Among key milestones that have been reached are: (a) operationalizing of an Office of Missing Persons[35] to address long-standing grievances of persons living in the

[34] Commission of Inquiry on Lessons Learnt and Reconciliation, 'Report of the Commission of Inquiry on Lessons Learnt and Reconciliation' (15 November 2011) PO No CA/3/3/24.

[35] Office of Missing Persons Act (No 14) 2016 (Sri Lanka).

former conflict-affected areas to ascertain the whereabouts of family members; (b) preparation of a Reparations Bill to address the humanitarian needs of persons affected by the conflict; and (c) preparation of legislation on a Truth and Reconciliation Commission. These were also important recommendations made by the LLRC in its Report in 2011.

5.3 Retrospective Legislation to Give Effect to Sri Lanka's International Obligations

An interesting feature in Sri Lanka's constitutional framework is the provision prohibiting Parliament from enacting retrospective legislation.[36] The relevant constitutional provision nevertheless provides an exception where the enactment of such legislation becomes necessary in order to give effect to Sri Lanka's 'obligations under the Law of Nations'.

A controversial case that brought this issue to the fore was *Sepala Ekanayake v Attorney General.*[37] The case concerned the hijacking of an Alitalia aircraft by a Sri Lankan national over Indian air space and an ensuing prosecution under the Offences against Aircraft Act (an enabling Act to give effect to the Tokyo, Hague, and Montreal conventions on offences against aircraft).[38]

Although Sri Lanka had signed and ratified the conventions, the requisite enabling legislation had not been enacted at the time the hijacking was committed. As the offence had been committed extraterritorially, the High Court of Sri Lanka had to be vested with extraterritorial jurisdiction, as the Sri Lankan criminal law was normally territorial in character. Therefore, after the arrest of the offender, special legislation had to be introduced, with retrospective effect, to maintain a successful prosecution and to give effect to Sri Lanka's treaty obligation to 'extradite or prosecute' under the conventions.

When the validity of the legislation was challenged as being retrospective and exceeding the powers of Parliament, the state successfully invoked the proviso relating to giving effect to 'obligations under the Law of Nations', which resulted in the Supreme Court upholding the constitutional validity of the legislation.

6 Conclusion

This chapter provided a broad overview of the active role played by Sri Lanka since its independence in 1948, and more prominently since its admission as a member of the

[36] Ministry of Foreign Affairs Legal Adviser's Division (n 18).

[37] *Sepala Ekanayaka v The Attorney-General* (7 August 1986) CA 132/84.

[38] Offences against Aircraft Act (No 24) 1982 (Sri Lanka).

UN in 1955, in the evolution of a Third World approach to international law. It particularly emphasized Sri Lanka's proactive role within the Asian-African grouping in the post-Bandung period, and subsequently in its leadership role in the NAM in its efforts to overhaul an 'inherited legal order', aimed at enhancing the economic interests of the newly independent states. Sri Lanka's role at UNCLOS III stands out as a prime example of this.

With the advent of the 1980s, and the challenges posed by the spectre of terrorism, Sri Lanka took initiatives both at the international level (within the UN) and at the regional level (within SAARC) to strengthen the cooperative legal frameworks to combat the phenomenon.

The liberalization of Sri Lanka's economy in the 1980s, in keeping with the then global trends and a drive towards generating greater foreign direct investment, resulted in Sri Lanka playing a pioneering role in the growing developments in the field of foreign investment law. This role was reflected both in the range of BITs entered into by Sri Lanka (some of the earliest such instances in the region) and its involvement in leading investment disputes and the resulting arbitrations of the day.

The liberal approach of the judiciary in Sri Lanka is evident in the willingness of the Supreme Court to read into the Constitution fundamental human rights as stipulated in international conventions such as the ICCPR, and also to take into account developing principles of environmental law. While this progressive approach has suffered a setback in the narrow approach adopted by the Supreme Court in the *Sinnarasa* case, it is hoped that the equilibrium will be restored in deciding future cases.

CHAPTER 28

AFGHANISTAN

VERONICA L TAYLOR

1 Introduction

Afghanistan's topography, much of it steep mountains and isolated valleys, makes travel hazardous, communication difficult, and the governance of the country from the capital, Kabul, precarious. Its geopolitical position, encircled by the central Asian republics, Iran, Pakistan, and China, has induced successive foreign invasions and 150 years of imperialism without colonialism.[1] Afghanistan has been:

> important enough to interfere with on a catastrophic scale but its dearth of national and cultivable resources, combined with its exceptionally refractory population, has discouraged the great powers from investing in developing the state and its infrastructure through a long-term colonial regime.[2]

Thus its borders remain porous, and its neighbours seek to influence, interfere in, or destabilize, the Afghan state. Both Pakistan and Iran continue to host semi-permanent Afghan refugee populations numbering in the millions. Pakistan seeks a compliant Afghanistan, to avoid reopening the question of Pashtun independence in its north-west territories. It would also like to undermine India's aid to Afghanistan. India, for its part, would like to bolster Afghanistan as an ally against Pakistan. China benefits from being the first foreign power to gain a mineral licence for what may be significant reserves. Iran has an established sphere of influence in Afghanistan's west and provides direct economic support to Afghanistan's Shi'ite communities.

[1] Thomas Ruttig, 'How It All Began: A Short Look at the Pre-1979 Origins of Afghanistan's Conflicts' (Afghanistan Analysts Network, AAN Papers, 19 January 2013) <http://www.afghanistan-analysts.org/publication/aan-papers/how-it-all-began-pre-1979-origins-of-afghanistans-conflict> accessed 1 April 2018.

[2] Whit Mason, 'Axioms and Unknowns' in Whit Mason (ed), *The Rule of Law in Afghanistan: Missing in Inaction* (Cambridge University Press 2011) 319, 326.

Afghanistan remains one of the poorest countries in the world, with widespread illiteracy and half of the population below the poverty line.[3] It is heavily dependent upon inflows of foreign aid and military resources; agricultural production and nascent commercial activity are overshadowed by an illicit drug economy.

Approximately thirty million people who make up Afghanistan represent more than fourteen ethnicities.[4] The two official languages are Dari[5] and Pashto (with provision for a third official language in some regions),[6] but more than forty other languages are in common use. However, much of the donor-led legal reform of the past two decades has been produced in English.[7] More than 90 per cent of Afghanistan's population is Muslim. Sunni Muslims are the dominant group, but many families have both Sunni and Shi'ite members. The six million or so citizens who are Shi'ite overlap to some extent with the marginalized Hazara ethnic group. Other groups, such as the Ismailis, are stigmatized as sects.

Today's Afghanistan is a loosely federated country in which technocrats in the capital exercise little political control over regional governors and warlords. Since 2001, it has been handicapped by an ongoing Taliban insurgency,[8] the US-led prosecution of the 'war on terror'[9] and militarized engagement with al-Qaeda, successive corrupt central governments, and, since 2015, the Islamic State Khorasan, an Afghanistan affiliate of the

[3] For a fuller statistical profile see: <https://www.cia.gov/library/publications/the-world-factbook/geos/af.html>. Levels of education and literacy have improved, but they remain low in the general population and in the justice sector, with women still affected by the Taliban-era bans on female education. A 2008 survey of legal professionals found that 35 per cent completed their education at or below high school level. Among Afghanistan's (then) 1,400 judges, 36 per cent had no higher education, 16.1 per cent had non-tertiary education (usually *madrassa*, or religious school, education), and 20.5 per cent had high school education or less. Of the total number of judges, 15 per cent were estimated to be functionally illiterate: Livingston Armytage, 'Justice in Afghanistan: Rebuilding Judicial Competence After the Generation of War' (2007) 67 Zeitschrift für ausländisches öffentliches Recht und Völkerrecht [Heidelberg Journal of International Law] (ZaöRV/HJIL) 185.

[4] Constitution of the Islamic Republic of Afghanistan 2004 ('Constitution 2004') art. 4 (listing 14 ethnicities and 'other tribes') <http://www.wipo.int/edocs/lexdocs/laws/en/af/af004en.pdf> accessed 1 April 2018.

[5] A variant of Farsi (Persian), spoken by approximately 50 per cent of the population.

[6] Constitution 2004 art. 16.

[7] Many younger Afghan lawyers also perceive English as the language of professional advancement. As in other state-building settings, the choice of dominant languages adds cost, complexity, and confusion to the legal reform process.

[8] Also written in English as *Taleban*; a Sunni fundamentalist armed force.

[9] (Then) US President George W Bush declared 'war on terror' in his State of the Union address to the US Congress following the 11 September 2001 terrorist attacks on multiple targets in the US: 'Our war on terror begins with al Qaeda, but it does not end there. It will not end until every terrorist group of global reach has been found, stopped and defeated': 'Sate of the Union Address: Text of George Bush's Speech' <http://www.theguardian.com/world/2001/sep/21/september11.usa13> accessed 1 April 2018. The same speech announced the creation of the Office of Homeland Security, effectively changing the domestic security architecture in the US.

Islamic State (IS)[10] terror movement.[11] Attempts to broker a sustainable peace continue, through the 'Kabul Process' initiated by the current Ghani administration,[12] as attacks on civilians and government offices continue in both Kabul and regional locations.

States where the 'post-conflict' period is, in fact, a series of continuing sub-national conflicts, are often coded as 'failed' or 'fragile' and are also criticized as failing in their embrace of international law. In the case of Afghanistan, such 'discourses of deficiency'[13] also erase some important legal history. The starting point for this chapter is the proposition that, for most of its history, Afghanistan has been contingent as a Westphalian state. This means that it has also had a fluid relationship with the institutions and norms of international law, including the normative discourse and practice of the international rule of law.[14] Although Afghanistan has been a member of the United Nations (UN) since 1946, and thus a contributor to international law in the twentieth century, it is seen more as a subject of international law. Since 2001, it has also been a site for its contestation, as the imposition of new international obligations has provoked local resistance to norms that are viewed as being in conflict with Islamic values or legal pluralism—or both. So in order to describe and analyse the relationship between 'Afghanistan' and international law, we need to isolate the period and the key actors involved in constituting that relationship.

This chapter takes up four international law 'moments' in recent Afghan history. The first is Afghanistan's membership of the UN and the ebb and flow of its adoption of international legal instruments, depending on the political regime of the day. The second is the confluence of domestic factors that limit Afghanistan's capacity to deliver on its international law obligations. A third is the post-2001 invasion of Afghanistan by the US and its allies and their failure to comply with international law and norms that has, in turn, corroded local commitments to do so. This includes civilian rule of law interventions that have produced unusable or unwise domestic legal reforms, in the name of international law compliance. The fourth moment is local resistance to international law norms in Afghanistan, often, though not always, framed as considerations of Islamic law. These highlight, in turn, the complexity (and sometimes the ambivalence) of Afghanistan's location within, as well as its relationship with, international law, international legal institutions, and international legal norms.

[10] Also known by its Arabic name, *Daesh*.

[11] Reuters, 'Head of Islamic State Killed in Afghanistan: Pentagon' <http://www.reuters.com/article/us-usa-afghanistan-islamic-state/head-of-islamic-state-in-afghanistan-killed-pentagon-idUSKBN19Z26G> accessed 1 April 2018.

[12] Ministry of Foreign Affairs, Islamic Republic of Afghanistan <https://thediplomat.com/2018/05/the-afghan-peace-process-an-faq/> accessed 15 April 2019.

[13] Laura Nader, 'Promise or Plunder? A Past and Future Look at Law and Development (2007) 7(2) Global Jurist (Frontiers Article 1) (accessed 1 April 2018).

[14] Simon Chesterman, 'An International Rule of Law?' (2008) 56 American Journal of Comparative Law 331.

2 An Actor in International Law

Afghanistan joined the UN on 19 November 1946,[15] as the Kingdom of Afghanistan, which was just one year after the UN Charter 1945 came into effect.[16] Subsequent attempts to modernize Afghanistan's law in the twentieth century focused on Kabul, on the formal legal sector, and on the introduction of secular law, albeit within a constitutional narrative of respect for Islamic values.

2.1 1972–2001: Modernization and Occupation

Afghanistan's legal modernization occurred in the 1960s and 1970s, during the reign of King Mohammed Zahir Shah (1933–73) until he was deposed by his cousin Mohammed Daoud Khan, who ushered in the Republic of Afghanistan (1973–8).[17] The legacies of that period included revised, codified law and foreign aid-supported legal institutional reform. Afghanistan was historically a trade route, and in 1966 became a member state of the International Centre for the Settlement of Investment Disputes (as a party to the Convention on the Settlement of Investment Disputes between States and Nationals of Other States 1965).

Many Afghans regard Zahir Shah's reign as the golden age for the country, particularly for its legal and educational institutions, and there was a (short-lived) attempt to persuade him to return to Afghanistan as head of state after 2001. The UN's own evaluation has been that:

> As one of the UN's earliest members, Afghanistan has contributed to the work of the world body, including through its diverse and unique culture. The 70-year partnership has resulted not only in rich cultural exchanges but also efforts and achievements in the areas of human rights and women's empowerment.[18]

This celebration of Afghanistan's achievements in 'human rights and women's empowerment' may seem counterintuitive, given the continuing fragility of Afghanistan today,

[15] UN Member States <http://www.un.org/en/member-states> accessed 6 April 2018.

[16] It then signed a number of international instruments dealing with issues that remain challenges for the country today, including the Protocol to the International Convention for the Suppression of the Traffic in Women and Children 1921, and the Protocol to the Convention for Limiting the Manufacture and Regulating the Distribution of Narcotic Drugs 1931: UN Treaty Collection <https://treaties.un.org/Pages/TreatyParticipantSearch.aspx?clang=_en> accessed 7 January 2018.

[17] See generally Amin Saikal, *Modern Afghanistan: A History of Struggle and Survival* (IB Tauris 2006).

[18] UNAMA, '70th Anniversary of Afghanistan's Membership in United Nations' (19 November 2016) <https://unama.unmissions.org/70th-anniversary-afghanistan's-membership-united-nations> accessed 1 April 2018.

but it is historically accurate.[19] Afghanistan ratified the Convention on the Political Rights of Women 1953 in 1966, at the time when education and emancipation of urban women was occurring. Women were encouraged not to cover their heads in public, and to participate politically in legal institutions[20] and higher education.[21] Yet the historical experiment in legal reform was short-lived and to a large extent erased by the intervening decades of invasion, war, and civil conflict.[22]

The turbulence of domestic politics in Afghanistan was reflected in the changing nature of its state: Daoud Khan's Republic of Afghanistan was succeeded by the Democratic Republic of Afghanistan (1978–87) and the Republic of Afghanistan (1987–92). The latter overlapped with the Soviet invasion of Afghanistan on 25 December 1979 and the start of a decade-long war by the *mujahideen* (armed resistance) to drive out the Soviet forces, until their withdrawal in 1989.[23]

Afghanistan's role in international law developed a dual character following the Soviet invasion. On one hand, it ratified a series of key treaties during the 1980s, including the International Convention on the Elimination of All Forms of Racial Discrimination 1965 (ratified in 1983);[24] the International Convention on Economic, Social and Cultural Rights 1966 (ratified in 1983); the Convention on Non-Application of Statutory Limitations to War Crimes and Crimes Against Humanity 1968 (ratified in 1983); the International Covenant on Civil and Political Rights 1966 (ratified in 1983); the Convention against Illicit Traffic in Narcotic Drugs and Psychotropic Substances 1988 (ratified in 1988), and the Convention Against Torture and Other Cruel, Inhuman or Degrading Treatment or Punishment 1984 (ratified in 1987).[25] At the same time, in 1980 it became the subject of the first of a series of failed Security Council resolutions.[26] By 1985 these had become annual resolutions on the crisis of human rights and fundamental freedoms in Afghanistan.

[19] Canadian Women for Women in Afghanistan, 'Afghan Women in History: The 20th Century' <http://www.cw4wafghan.ca/sites/default/files/attachments/pages/cw4wafghan-afghanwomenhistory-factsheet.pdf> accessed 6 April 2018.

[20] During this period women senators were elected and, from 1966 to 1971, 14 women were appointed as judges to courts of Islamic jurisprudence: ibid.

[21] Nadjma Yassari and Mohammad Hamid Saboory, 'Shari'a and National Law in Afghanistan' in Jan Michiel Otto (ed), *Shari'a Incorporated: A Comparative Overview of the Legal Systems of Twelve Muslim Countries* (Amsterdam University Press 2010) 5.

[22] Ruttig (n 1). [23] Saikal (n 17).

[24] For a listing of human rights related obligations see UN Office of the High Commissioner for Human Rights <http://indicators.ohchr.org> accessed 1 April 2018.

[25] UN Treaty Collection <https://treaties.un.org/Pages/TreatyParticipantSearch.aspx?clang=_en> accessed 6 April 2018.

[26] UNSC res 462 (9 January 1980) noted the lack of consensus of Council members regarding the Soviet intervention in Afghanistan and called an emergency session of the UN General Assembly. UNGA res ES-6/2 (14 January 1980) para 2 strongly deplored the 'armed intervention' in Afghanistan as inconsistent with the sovereignty, territorial integrity, and political independence of Afghanistan under the UN Charter.

Following the Soviet withdrawal, the Islamic State of Afghanistan (1992–2002) became an internationally recognized state and continued to participate in international law making.[27] The government of the day was overtaken by the Taliban-proclaimed Islamic Emirate of Afghanistan (1996–2001), although the 'emirate' was never recognized as a state under international law, nor was the Taliban recognized as a stabilized de facto regime.[28] When the US ousted the Taliban in 2001, it was Burnahanuddin Rabbani's previous government that made the transfer of power under the Bonn Agreement 2001,[29] to establish the Transitional State of Afghanistan (2002–4), ahead of the proclamation of the current Islamic Republic of Afghanistan (2004–present).

2.2 2001—Present: Intervention and Transition

The pace and scope of Afghanistan's adoption of international law increased markedly after 2002,[30] with the priorities for legal reform and ratification tracking those of foreign donors and supporters. Human rights were emphasized by many coalition states intervening in Afghanistan after 2002; this is reflected in articles 6 and 7 of the Constitution 2004, which provide:

> Article 6
> The state shall be obligated to create a prosperous and progressive society based on social justice, preservation of human dignity, protection of human rights, realization of democracy, attainment of national unity as well as equality between all peoples and tribes and balance development of all areas of the country.
> Article 7
> The state shall observe the United Nations Charter, inter-state agreements, as well as international treaties to which Afghanistan has joined, and the Universal Declaration of Human Rights. The state shall prevent all kinds of terrorist activities, cultivation and smuggling of narcotics, and production and use of intoxicants.

Afghanistan ratified the Convention on the Elimination of Discrimination Against Women 1979 in 2003; the Convention on the Status of Refugees 1951 in 2005; and the Convention on the Rights of Persons with Disabilities 2006 in 2012.

27 Afghanistan ratified the Convention on the Rights of the Child 1989 (in 1994) during this time.

28 Rüdiger Wolfrum and Christiane Philipp, 'The Status of the Taliban: The Rights and Obligations under International Law' (2002) 6 Max Planck Yearbook of United Nations Law 559, 585.

29 UNSC res 1378 (4 November 2001) and discussion in ibid. 577.

30 By 2017, Afghanistan had signed and/or ratified more than 150 international treaties <https://treaties.un.org/Pages/TreatyParticipantSearch.aspx?clang=_en> accessed 1 April 2018.

As the US 'war on terror' morphed into a 'war on opium',[31] this led to significant pressure for Afghanistan to ratify international agreements concerning control of narcotics, such as the Single Convention on Narcotic Drugs 1975 (ratified in 2015).

2.3 International Economic Law

Part of the rationale for foreign intervention and state-building in Afghanistan was a perceived need to lift the country out of economic isolation and prolonged poverty.[32] Thus article 10 of the Constitution 2004 declared Afghanistan to be a market economy.[33]

Afghanistan joined the South Asia Association for Regional Cooperation (established in 2002) in 2006 and ratified the South Asia Free Trade Area Agreement in 2011. It is also now a member of the Economic Cooperation Organization and the Central Asian Regional Economic Cooperation.[34]

In 2004, Afghanistan signed a Trade and Investment Framework Agreement with the US. Afghanistan does not have a bilateral investment treaty with the US,[35] but it has signed multiple trade, economic, and investment agreements and/or memoranda of understanding with other countries.[36] The most significant of these is the Afghanistan Pakistan Transit Trade Agreement 2010. The US, European Union, India, Canada, and Japan have granted Afghan exports preferential import tariffs under their Generalized Systems of Preference.

Afghanistan gained accession to the World Trade Organization in 2016. It ratified the Convention Establishing the World Intellectual Property Organization 1967 in 2005; the Paris Convention on Protecting Industrial Property 1883 in 2017; and the Singapore Treaty on Trademarks 2006 in 2017. All of these memberships are new, so Afghanistan has not been party to any formal disputes under these institutional frameworks to date.

Since 2005, Afghan law has recognized alternative dispute resolution provisions. In 2014 the Afghanistan Centre for Dispute Resolution (ACDR), whose decisions are

[31] Azam Ahmed, 'Penetrating Every Stage of Afghan Opium Chain, Taliban Become a Cartel' *New York Times* (16 February 2016) <http://www.nytimes.com/2016/02/17/world/asia/afghanistan-opium-taliban-drug-cartel.html> accessed 1 April 2018. See also US State Department, 'Afghanistan' <http://www.state.gov/j/inl/regions/afghanistanandpakistan/219257.htm> accessed 1 April 2018.

[32] Thus Afghanistan became a signatory to the Convention on the Recognition and Enforcement of Foreign Arbitral Awards 1958 in 2005, even though neither its courts nor its judges at the time were ready for this level of commercial law reciprocity.

[33] Full text available at <http://www.wipo.int/edocs/lexdocs/laws/en/af/af004en.pdf> accessed 1 April 2018.

[34] The Afghan government has stated its intent to formally join the Transport Corridor Europe Caucasus Asia organization: US State Department Bureau of Economic and Business Affairs, 'Investment Climate Statements for 2017: Afghanistan' <http://www.state.gov/e/eb/rls/othr/ics/investmentclimatestatements/index.htm?year=2017&dlid=270011#wrapper> accessed 1 April 2018.

[35] Ibid.

[36] Afghanistan has concluded bilateral investment treaties with Germany, Iran, and Turkey: ibid.

non-binding, was established.[37] The ACDR offers mediation, expert witness services, and award calculation services in a limited number of cases referred by the commercial courts; it is at a very early stage of operation.

3 Domestic Capacity

The legal reforms described above are ambitious for a legal system that currently has limited capacity to deliver on all of its international law obligations.[38]

3.1 Legal Pluralism

One of the complicating factors for Afghanistan is its system of 'extreme legal pluralism'.[39] Its twentieth century statutory law and legal institutions were shaped by French-influenced civil law, which codified Islamic legal principles in the style of Egypt.[40] These were then overlaid with Soviet socialist legal formalism in the 1980s and again with post-2003 donor-driven legislative reforms.[41] The non-state justice sector—tribal and customary law—operates with wide variation throughout the country. Islamic law (*shari'a*) intersects with, and overarches, all of these sources of law.[42]

Historically and today, there has been a cultural and functional divide between the formal legal institutions of the capital, Kabul (the Supreme Court, the Attorney General's Department, and the Ministry of Justice), and those norms that govern provincial and rural life, where individuals construct their identity through ethnicity, tribe, family status, and gender. Awareness of individual rights is increasing over time, as is understanding of which institutions can be accessed to assist with violations.[43]

[37] With support from USAID and the Department of Commerce Commercial Law Development Program.

[38] For example, the 2017–20 National Justice and Judicial Reform Plan contemplates raising the Human Rights Protection Unit of the Ministry of Justice to the status of a Department by 2019, in order to follow up on implementation of international and human rights conventions (the implication being that there is not much capacity to do this at present): Ministry of Justice <http://policymof.gov.af/home/national-justice-and-judicial-reform-plan-njrp/> accessed 15 April 2019.

[39] It is not one legal system, but many overlapping and competing systems of legal and social ordering and legitimacy: Yassari and Saboory (n 21).

[40] Al-Azhar University in Egypt was also regarded as the seat of learning for Islamic jurisprudence.

[41] In both common law and civil law styles, largely produced in English.

[42] International Crisis Group, 'Reforming Afghanistan's Broken Judiciary' (Asia Report No 195, 17 November 2010) <http://www.justice.gov/sites/default/files/eoir/legacy/2014/09/29/4ceb88c52.pdf> accessed 1 April 2018.

[43] The best known being the government's Directorate of Women's Affairs, and the Afghanistan Independent Human Rights Commission being much less familiar: Asia Foundation, *Afghanistan in 2017: A Survey of the Afghan People, Asia Foundation Afghanistan Office* (2017) 141 <https://asiafoundation.org/publication/afghanistan-2017-survey-afghan-people> accessed 6 April 2018.

3.2 Islamic Law

Religious leaders and Islamic law scholars in Afghanistan see *shari'a*—which in Afghanistan means predominantly Hanafi jurisprudence[44]—as the centre of gravity and the source of both legal authority and morality. They point to the constitutional status of Afghanistan as an Islamic republic[45] and the historical continuity of Islamic norms in Afghanistan's legal system.[46]

Article 3 of the Constitution 2004 provides that laws and regulations must not be repugnant to the beliefs and teachings of Islam, but 'Islam' and 'Islamic law' are not defined.[47] On its face, article 130 of the Constitution 2004 gives statutory law primacy over Islamic jurisprudence:

> Article 130
> In cases under consideration, the courts shall apply provisions of this Constitution as well as other laws. If there is no provision in the Constitution or other laws about a case, the courts shall, in pursuance of Hanafi jurisprudence, and, within the limits set by this Constitution, rule in a way that attains justice in the best manner.

In practice, the interplay between article 130 and statutory law is much less certain.[48] Or, as one international NGO puts it:

> The Afghan government's historic inability and persistent unwillingness to resolve conflicts between state codes, Islamic law, and customary justice embedded in the

[44] Hanafi *fiqh* (Islamic jurisprudence) being one of the four major schools of Sunni jurisprudence, which predominates in Turkey, the Balkans, Syria, Lebanon, Jordan, Palestine, Egypt, part of Iraq, the Caucuses, and throughout Central Asia. See generally Otto (ed) (n 21).

[45] Constitution 2004 art. 1. Islam is the national religion and freedom of other religions is guaranteed by art. 2 of the Constitution 2004.

[46] Afghanistan has been a member of the Organization of Islamic Cooperation since 1969, apart from its suspension between 1980 and 1989 (coinciding with its occupation by the Soviet Union) <http://www.oic-oci.org> accessed 15 April 2019.

[47] The Personal Status Law 2009 <http://www.refworld.org/docid/4a24ed5b2.html> accessed 1 April 2018 was a codification of family law applying to the Shi'ite minority, as permitted by art. 131 of the Constitution 2004:

> The courts shall apply the Shia jurisprudence in cases involving personal matters of followers of the Shia sect in accordance with the provisions of the law. In other cases, if no clarification in this Constitution and other laws exist, the courts shall rule according to laws of this sect.

The first version of this statute was regarded by many women as deeply discriminatory and by some Islamic scholars as both discriminatory and outdated. It was revised following public protest at both the content and the process in which it was signed by President Karzai, in a fairly transparent move to bolster his electoral support: Ben Farmer, 'Afghanistan revises marriage law but women still required to submit to sexual intercourse' *The Telegraph* (9 July 2009) <http://www.telegraph.co.uk/news/world-news/asia/afghanistan/5790702/Afghanistan-revises-marriage-law-but-women-still-required-to-submit-to-sexual-intercourse.html> accessed 1 April 2018.

[48] Both Afghan and foreign legal scholars disagree among themselves about which sources of law they regard as controlling, and in which contexts.

> legal culture have further destabilized the country. The critical leverage provided to fundamentalists in the constitution has concurrently had a deep impact on the evolution of legal institutions.

Long periods of isolation also caused Afghan *shari'a* to stagnate, leaving significant gaps in principles to govern areas such as commercial law.

University legal education echoes this duality of secular law and *shari'a*: it is divided into faculties of Law and Politics, on the one hand, and faculties of *shari'a*, on the other.[49] The functional difference historically was—in very broad terms—that Law and Politics have tended to produce lawyers and prosecutors, and the *shari'a* faculties tended to produce judges and scholars of Islamic law, as have *madaris*[50] (private religious schools).

Afghanistan's court system is unitary, and so *shari'a* is applied in the regular courts by judges, with the Supreme Court being the final court of review for all legal questions. Annexed to the Supreme Court is a Fatwa Council, which is the single institution with jurisdiction to make a binding *fatwa* (ruling on Islamic law). Nationally, provincially, and locally there are *shura e ulama* (councils of Islamic scholars recognized for their religious authority); the national body is politically appointed to advise on Islamic aspects of political and social issues. Beyond this there is no hierarchy of authority within *shari'a*, but immense diversity. At the local level, the mullah sees himself as the pious keeper of community morality.[51]

In the early stages of state-building, international donors undertaking law and justice reform in Afghanistan did not, for the most part, prioritize the development of greater sophistication in *shari'a* principles, nor the creation of legislation that would be *shari'a* compliant.[52] Many were also publicly critical of the inclusion of the primacy of *shari'a* in the Constitution 2004.[53] This criticism has been bolstered by the practice in Afghanistan, as elsewhere in the Islamic world, of invoking Islam politically in support of particular positions on social questions (discussed in section 4 below).

[49] Until recently both had highly formalist curricula that omitted serious consideration of customary law or legal pluralism. The fortunes of the individual faculties and their influence have varied with the political environment of the day. Law and Politics was the secular group favoured under Russian dominance and from 2003, during the most intense periods of foreign-donor reform of law and justice. By contrast, the heterodox Taliban approach to 'Islamic law' was neither welcomed by, nor benefited, the faculties of *Shari'a*.

[50] Plural of *madrassa/madrasa*.

[51] Astri Suhrke and Kaja Borchgrevink, 'Negotiating Justice Sector Reform in Afghanistan' (2009) 51 Crime Law and Social Change 211.

[52] An example was the Banking Law 2003, drafted by legal experts drawing on their experience in the US, which made no reference to the banking definitions and requirements of an Islamic legal system <http://moci.gov.af/Content/files/banking_legislation.pdf> accessed 1 April 2018. Compare this with the University of Washington project, sponsored by the US State Department INL, that supported legal education in both Law and Politics and *Shari'a* faculties in universities across Afghanistan: <http://www.law.washington.edu/programs/lespa> accessed 1 April 2018.

[53] For an example of overt criticism see Francesc Vendrell, 'The International Community's Failures' in Mason (n 2) 53, 56.

3.3 Dispute Resolution under Non-state Law

Relatively low levels of respect for the formal justice sector, particularly the courts, are common in Afghanistan. However, in the latest Asia Foundation survey,[54] up to 23.2 per cent of rural residents surveyed reported using an outside institution (the *huquq*, a court, or a community *shura* or *jirga*) to resolve a dispute sometime during the previous two years. For many Afghans, the Ministry of Justice's *huquq*[55] ('rights') department and its local offices are important for small claims mediation and as an interface between the formal and customary legal systems.[56]

Where disputes are resolved through collective mediation in *shura* (in non-Pashtun areas) or *jirga* (in Pashtun areas), this typically involves Islamic community leaders, or clan or community leaders, sitting together.[57] Afghan people still rate their confidence in religious leaders (67.3 per cent) and in community *shura* or *jirga* (65.7 per cent) much higher than their trust in Parliament (3.68 per cent).[58] Justice in community settings is essentially tortious: restitution for contractual, criminal, or nuisance wrongs. With an overwhelmingly illiterate population, there is considerable scope for manipulation of 'law' by the powerful and for local religious leaders (*mullahs*) to blend custom and *shari'a* in ways that urban Islamic scholars find problematic.

Customary procedures can be formalized, efficient, accessible, and respected by local communities.[59] However, since they often have minimal contact with, or oversight by, formal legal institutions, it follows that they are unlikely to apply domestic, much less international, laws in their deliberations. Thus a persistent criticism is that:

> [They] violate Afghan and international law, including [through] honour killings, forced and underage marriage, and payment of blood money in lieu of punishment.[60]

Critics are concerned about the customary practice of mediating all disputes (including serious criminal matters); the practice of forced marriages by using women and girls as marriage candidates in settlement of disputes [*baad*], or as an exchange of daughters between familial or tribal groups [*baadal*]; the gendered nature of the *shura* and *jirga* (which are often exclusively male, or male-dominated);[61] as well as the lack of procedural safeguards and recourse to appeal for parties involved.[62] The proposed solution,

[54] Asia Foundation (n 43). [55] Also written *hukuk* or *huqooq*.

[56] Ministry of Justice, Department of Huquq <http://moj.gov.af/en> accessed 15 April 2019.

[57] Susanne Schmeidl, 'Engaging Traditional Justice Mechanisms in Afghanistan: State-building Opportunity or Dangerous Liaison?' in Mason (n 2) 149.

[58] Asia Foundation (n 43). [59] Schmeidl (n 57) 160.

[60] Thomas Barfield, Neamatollah Nojumi, and Alexander Thier, 'The Clash of Two Goods: State and Non-State Dispute Resolution in Afghanistan' (US Institute of Peace, Washington, 2006) 3 <http://siteresources.worldbank.org/INTLAWJUSTINST/Resources/clash_of_two_goods.pdf> accessed 6 April 2018.

[61] Schmeidl (n 57) 153.

[62] There is, however, evidence to suggest that attitudes are changing: the 2017 Asia Foundation attitudes survey found that 70.4 per cent of the respondents were disapproving of women or girls

from an international standpoint, is to link up customary and formal legal institutions more effectively.[63] There is evidence that the Afghan public also desires oversight of these mechanisms by the state.[64]

The Taliban also provide non-state law in Afghanistan. Their legitimacy for local populations in Afghanistan has been enhanced by their ability to deliver speedy and effective justice.[65] At the same time, the Taliban are synonymous with ardent unequal treatment of women and complete intolerance for diversity of all kinds. Educated *shari'a* scholars in Afghanistan find the Taliban version of 'Islamic justice' repugnant and without theological or jurisprudential foundation. Of course, it is also inconsistent with contemporary state law in Afghanistan and with international law norms. This is significant, given that the current prognosis for Afghanistan is that lasting peace is likely to require some form of compromise with, or incorporation of, Taliban actors in future governments.

4 A Failure of International Law

In 2001, the US and its allies invaded Afghanistan in order to prosecute a 'war on terror', specifically aimed at capturing Osama Bin Laden and eliminating his al-Qaeda network.[66] The US-led war in Afghanistan was regarded by some observers as illegal,[67] and by others as illegal but nonetheless legitimate. Most commentators, however, viewed it as a permissible form of self-defence under article 2(4) of the UN Charter,[68] including because subsequent UN Security Council resolution 1368 could be read

being given in dispute settlement, and there were gradually decreasing rates of acceptance of the practice: Asia Foundation (n 43) 141.

[63] For a nuanced prescription on how to do this, see Ali Wardak and John Braithwaite, 'Crime and War in Afghanistan: Part II: A Jeffersonian Alternative?' (2013) 53 British Journal of Criminology 197. See also the detailed procedural recommendations in Schmeidl (n 57) 166.

[64] In practice 'numerous linkages and considerable cooperation occurs at the local level' but there is a need to further institutionalize the joining up of state and non-state legal services provision and to reach agreement with customary mechanisms about domestic and international law compliance: Schmeidl (n 57) 163.

[65] David Kilcullen, 'Deiokes and the Taliban' in Mason (n 2).

[66] Bin Laden and al-Qaeda were responsible for coordinated terror attacks on the US mainland on 11 September 2001, as well as earlier attacks on US missions abroad.

[67] Because the US invaded without a UN mandate, since it failed to fulfil the international legal requirements of self-defence and since the attacks were launched against the Taliban, then in de facto control of the country, rather than against the Al-Qaeda terrorist group responsible for the original terror attacks against the US. The UN Security Council condemned the al-Qaeda attacks in the US in UNSC res 1368 (12 September 2001) and issued UNSC res 1373 (28 September 2001) on counterterrorism.

[68] Art. 2(4) prohibits the 'threat or use of force against the territorial integrity or political independence of any state' but permits it when the Security Council authorizes military action or when it is in self-defence under art. 51 of the Charter.

as purporting to extend the right of self-defence to acts against those states who harbour terrorists.[69]

The US intervention in Afghanistan in 2001 did create the conditions for a transitional administration, supported by the UN Security Council in resolution 1378 of 14 November 2001.[70] Most significantly, the Security Council authorized the establishment of an International Security Assistance Force (ISAF)[71] and so ushered in an intense period of armed engagement, peacekeeping, and donor-assisted state-building.

4.1 Afghanistan's Transition

International law was an early casualty in post-invasion Afghanistan. After the establishment of the Afghan transitional government in June 2002, when the situation inarguably no longer involved an international conflict between states, the legal basis for what the US had dubbed 'Operation Enduring Freedom' was unclear. Why this continued to be seen as collective self-defence under article 51 of the UN Charter was not fully explained. Yet this affected the application of the Third Geneva Convention 1949[72] to foreign combatants taken prisoner and to combat flights extending across the border to Pakistan,[73] since that Convention only applies to international conflicts between states.

The status of foreign forces' involvement in ISAF and whether this was in the prosecution of a war, or an operation to maintain law and order, was also confused. As the Norwegian self-evaluation shows:

[69] Ben Smith and Arabella Thorp, *The Legal Basis for the Invasion of Afghanistan* (House of Commons Library, International Affairs and Defence Section, Standard Note SN/IA/534026, February 2010) <http://researchbriefings.parliament.uk/ResearchBriefing/Summary/SN05340> accessed 1 April 2018. The contrary view was that the attacks in New York and Washington were criminal attacks, not 'armed attacks' by another state, and that there was no imminent threat of an armed attack on the US after 11 September, as evidenced by the delay of some weeks before the US began its bombing in Afghanistan. See generally Wolfrum and Philipp (n 28) 587–9.

[70] UNSC res 1378 called for, among other things, a transitional administration that would be:

> broad-based, multi-ethnic and fully representative of all the Afghan people and committed to peace with Afghanistan's neighbours; should respect the human rights of all Afghan people, regardless of gender, ethnicity or religion; should respect Afghanistan's international obligations, including by cooperating fully in international efforts to combat terrorism and illicit drug trafficking within and from Afghanistan; and should facilitate the urgent delivery of humanitarian assistance and the orderly return of refugees and internally displaced persons, when the situation permits.

[71] UNSC res 1386 (20 December 2001).

[72] Geneva Convention [III] Relating to the Treatment of Prisoners of War (signed 12 August 1949, entered into force 21 October 1950, 75 UNTS 972).

[73] Ann Wilkins, *To Say It Like It Is: Norway's Evaluation of its part in the International Intervention* (Afghan Analysts' Network September 2016) 3 <https://www.afghanistan-analysts.org/to-say-it-like-it-is-norways-evaluation-of-its-part-in-the-international-intervention/> accessed 15 April 2019.

> The blurred dividing line between war and policing became particularly tricky when, from 2006 onwards, international forces also started targeting the drug trade as a source of financing for the armed opposition.[74]

The blurring of military and civilian statuses (and immunity for combatants under international law) was compounded by including police officers in military patrols, and giving Afghan interpreters arms and uniforms when participating in operations with ISAF troops.

The treatment of prisoners of war according to humanitarian norms was another area in which foreign and local commitment to international law was corroded. Individuals captured by ISAF forces were handed over to Afghan authorities, even though the Afghan National Directorate for Security was known to systematically violate international law.[75] Countries participating in ISAF did sign agreements with the Afghan government concerning prisoners' rights, and ISAF transfers of prisoners ceased in 2011, following a UN Assistance Mission in Afghanistan (UNAMA) report showing that torture was routinely applied in Afghan prisons.[76]

4.2 Provincial Reconstruction

The US and NATO elected to pacify Afghanistan through the establishment of 'Provincial Reconstruction Teams', led by ISAF. These teams were intended to be a single point of delivery for both military peacekeeping (or armed engagement with the Taliban) and local reconstruction and development. As a practical matter, different coalition nations took charge of different provinces, usually with little knowledge of the local political economy and power struggles. The result was considerable unevenness in delivery of security and development, which 'undermine[d] rather than obtain[ed] the goal of building a centrally managed Afghan state'.[77] The blurring of military action and aid delivery also led NGOs to complain that military and civilian activities were not distinguishable and that civilian aid workers were perceived and targeted as combatants.

4.3 Transitional Justice

The tenuous application of international law in Afghanistan can be traced to the Bonn Agreement 2001. That agreement, made among Afghan political elites with the support of the UN and Western powers, resulted in the creation of the Afghan Interim

[74] Ibid. 3 (citing 170–1 in the original). [75] Ibid. 6.

[76] UN Assistance Mission in Afghanistan, *Treatment of Conflict-Related Detainees in Afghan Custody* (October 2011), cited in Wilkins (n 73) 6.

[77] Wilkins (n 73) 4 (citing 199 in original).

Authority (AIA).[78] During this time an emergency *Loya Jirga* [great assembly] was held in 2002, and a Constitutional *Loya Jirga* was held in December 2003–January 2004, followed by elections in 2004. However, the Taliban were excluded from the Bonn Agreement and the subsequent *Loya Jirga*, leading many informed commentators to describe the Bonn Agreement as a power-sharing agreement, not a peace agreement.[79]

The Bonn Agreement envisaged the establishment of ISAF, authorized by resolution 1386 of the UN Security Council. UNAMA[80] was established by UN Security Council resolution 1401 in March 2002 at the request of the Government of the Islamic Republic of Afghanistan. Its mandate is reviewed annually.[81] The UN engagement in Afghanistan then proceeded on the basis that the UN would work through the Afghan transitional (and later, elected) government and not through a direct administration of the country—the 'light footprint' approach. President Hamid Karzai was elected in 2004 and re-elected in 2009 in what was widely regarded as a fraudulent election.[82] UNAMA, meanwhile, had no executive or enforceable monitoring powers of the kind 'which would have made an emphasis on transitional justice possible'.[83]

The Bonn Agreement was silent on transitional justice (a UN proposal to include this having been rejected by participants in the emergency 2002 *Loya Jirga*). Karzai broke a subsequent undertaking to create a transitional justice plan.[84] The consequence of this has been a state of nearly complete impunity in Afghanistan. No war crimes have been systematically prosecuted and no former commanders held accountable for gross violations of human rights, war crimes, and/or crimes against humanity during the periods before 2001:

> All these periods were marked by large-scale atrocities, crimes against humanity, war crimes, extrajudicial executions and rape as a weapon of war, committed by combatants on all sides. Members of all of Afghanistan's major ethnic and political groups were implicated. Mass graves have been discovered belonging to all three periods of conflict.[85]

In the Soviet invasion and period of communist rule (1978–92) the only former official of the Soviet-backed PDPA government to be tried under the Karzai administration was Assadullah Sarwary, head of the national intelligence agency at the time that it carried out thousands of disappearances in 1978–9. When that step was suddenly taken in 2005, it was without any framing as transitional justice[86] or as a criminal act under

[78] Made up of 30 members, who commenced a six-month mandate on 22 December 2001; the AIA was followed by a two-year Transitional Authority.

[79] Francesc Vendrell, 'The International Community's Failures' in Mason (n 2) 53, 56.

[80] UNAMA, 'Mandate' <https://unama.unmissions.org/mandate> accessed 6 April 2018.

[81] With the latest mandate renewal being in 2018, when UNSC unanimously adopted res 2405 (8 March 2018).

[82] William Maley, 'The Rule of Law and the Weight of Politics' in Mason (n 2) 76–8.

[83] Michael Hartmann, 'Casualties of Myopia' in Mason (n 2) 172, 180.

[84] Analysed in detail in Hartmann, ibid. 185.

[85] Ibid. 179.

[86] Sari Kuovo and Patricia Gossman, 'Tell Us How This Ends: Transitional Justice and Prospects for Peace in Afghanistan' (Afghan Analysts Network Thematic Report, 30 June 2013) 7 <http://www.

the penal code then in force,[87] but based on article 130 of the Constitution. This was widely regarded by international observers as a gross violation of the rights of the accused.[88]

No one else from the period of the rule of the *mujahideen* (1992–6) has been prosecuted.[89] Instead, former warlords are now drug lords, and many of them serve in the Parliament and in the Cabinet. They are able to do so because prior to 2018 those crimes were not written into domestic criminal legislation, as required by the International Criminal Court's Rome Statute,[90] and article 27 of the Constitution 2004 prohibits prosecution for crimes not established by law.[91]

Moreover, those implicated in past war crimes and other serious human rights abuses have been protected by the operation of the National Reconciliation, General Amnesty and National Stability Law 2007 (or 'Amnesty Law').[92] The Amnesty Law (which was not published until 2009):[93]

> violates article 7 of the constitution, which mandates observance of international obligations, including Afghanistan's obligations under the ICC Rome statute, as well as the ICCPR and customary international law, which require accountability for war crimes and crimes against humanity.[94]

During the Taliban regime (1996–2001), several major war crimes were committed. These include the indiscriminate shelling of Kabul in 1996; the massacre in Mazar-i-Sharif in August 1998 of 2,000 civilians (mainly ethnic Hazara, in retaliation for a massacre of Taliban fighters by the Northern Forces the previous year); and the

afghanistan-analysts.org/publication/aan-papers/tell-us-how-this-ends-transitional-justice-and-prospects-for-peace-in-afghanistan> accessed 15 April 2018.

[87] Hartmann (n 83) 193. The penal code was subsequently amended in 2018; see n 130.

[88] Ibid. 187.

[89] Outside Afghanistan, the only armed forces leader to be tried for war crimes thus far has been Commander Faryadi Zardad, a former Hezb-e-Islami commander who obtained asylum in Britain under a false name. He was subsequently tried in London on charges of torture and hostage taking and convicted in July 2005: Kuovo and Gossman (n 86) 9.

[90] Hartmann (n 83) 182 also notes that neither the Criminal Procedure Code 1974 nor the Interim Criminal Procedure Code allowed private prosecutions or investigations of such crimes. These have been replaced by the Penal Code 2018.

[91] Although this has been disregarded in practice, as discussed below. Art. 27 of the Constitution 2004 provides:

> No deed shall be considered a crime unless ruled by a law promulgated prior to commitment of the offense.
>
> No one shall be pursued, arrested, or detained without due process of law.
>
> No one shall be punished without the decision of an authoritative court taken in accordance with the provisions of the law, promulgated prior to commitment of the offense.

[92] Passed by the Parliament to grant its own members and others unlimited retrospective and future immunity from prosecution for acts that would be considered crimes under international law: Hartmann (n 83) 183.

[93] Official Gazette 965, Qays 1387 (December 2009), cited in Hartmann (n 83) 193 fn 14.

[94] Hartmann (n 83) 184.

destruction of the 1,500 year old Buddhist statues in Bamiyan and other artefacts. To date, no Taliban leader has been pursued or prosecuted for these acts.

4.4 Crimes by Armed Forces

An economic history perspective on how rule of law regimes evolve suggests that an absolute precondition for an effective transition to the rule of law is a monopoly on the use of force.[95] This typically means that the armed forces must be under the effective control of the government and that all other combatants must be disarmed. This has not happened in Afghanistan. Neither the Karzai nor the current Ghani administration has exercised any control over the US and coalition forces stationed in Afghanistan, notwithstanding the signing of a Bilateral Security Agreement between Afghanistan and the US and a Status of Forces Agreement between Afghanistan and NATO in 2014.[96]

Both US and ISAF forces are responsible for extensive abuses of international law. In the case of the US, this includes the detention without due process or trial of thousands of people at US bases or secret locations in Afghanistan.[97] There have been persistent reports of torture and deaths in US custody, but no independent oversight or prosecutions of these crimes. Both US and ISAF forces have also been responsible for the indiscriminate killing of non-combatants, often through airborne drone strikes.[98] Individual soldiers have, on rare occasions, been prosecuted under the military law of their own states for the intentional killing of non-combatants in the field.[99]

Disarmament, demobilization, and reintegration (DDR) was not part of the Bonn Agreement in 2001. The central government thus exercises little control over the private armies that were permitted as part of Afghanistan's new state structure.[100]

A particularly troubling aspect of impunity in Afghanistan has been the self-censoring of UN agencies and representatives in investigating past atrocities, as well as the politicization of their investigation. In 1999 the UN Office of the High Commissioner of Human

[95] Barry Weingast, 'Why Developing Countries Prove So Resistant to the Rule of Law' (Stanford Institute for Economic Policy Research SCID Working Paper 382, 2009) <https://siepr.stanford.edu/research/publications/why-developing-countries-prove-so-resistant-rule-law> accessed 3 April 2018.

[96] North Atlantic Treaty Organization, 'NATO Secretary General welcomes signing of security agreements with Afghanistan' (30 September 2014) <http://www.nato.int/cps/en/natohq/news_113393.htm> accessed 6 April 2018.

[97] Human Rights First, 'Detained and Denied in Afghanistan: How to Make US Detention Comply with the Law' (May 2011) <http://www.humanrightsfirst.org/wp-content/uploads/pdf/Detained-Denied-in-Afghanistan.pdf> accessed 15 April 2018.

[98] Kuovo and Gossman (n 86) 13. [99] Ibid.

[100] This is true for the private armies of local powerbrokers, who are often both the governance and the justice system in the countryside; it is also true of the private armies retained by development contractors to guard their personnel and projects: Stephen Brooking and Susanne Schmeidl, 'When nobody guards the guards: The quest to regulate private security companies in Afghanistan' (2008) 26 Sicherheit und Frieden [Security and Peace] 208 (cited in Maley (n 82) 79). See generally Laura Dickinson, 'Contract as a Tool for Regulating Private Military Companies' in Simon Chesterman and Chia Lenhardt (eds), *From Mercenaries to Market* (OUP 2007) 217.

Rights investigated successive massacres of Taliban fighters and of civilians in and around Mazar-i-Sharif in the 1987–8 period and then carried out conflict mapping in 2002, but their reports were suppressed.[101] The most comprehensive investigation of crimes committed prior to 2001 was undertaken by the Afghan Independent Human Rights Commission (AIHRC) from 2005 to 2009 and when that report was finally made public, the Karzai government summarily removed three of the AIHRC Commissioners.[102] The lack of documentation of war crimes in Afghanistan has led to several non-government attempts to collect information and make it public. However, there has been no appetite on the part of the US or the Afghan governments to institute transitional justice processes of the kind adopted elsewhere in post-conflict settings.

4.5 The ICC Initiative

This situation could have changed, following the November 2017 request by the Prosecutor of the International Criminal Court (ICC)[103] that the Court open a formal investigation into war crimes and crimes against humanity committed in Afghanistan; however the Pre-Trial Chamber II of the ICC unanimously rejected the request in April 2019 as 'not serv[ing] the interests of justice'.[104] Afghanistan ratified the Rome Statute in 2003 and thus brought itself under the jurisdiction of the ICC. The Prosecutor's request endorsed the result of the most recent preliminary examination report from 2016,[105] showing that crimes meeting the ICC gravity threshold have been committed in Afghanistan since 2003 and that the ICC considers Afghanistan either unwilling or unable to prosecute these crimes nationally.[106]

[101] Kuovo and Gossman (n 86) 11. [102] Ibid. 23.

[103] ICC, 'Statement of ICC Prosecutor, Fatou Bensouda, regarding her decision to request judicial authorisation to commence an investigation into the Situation in the Islamic Republic of Afghanistan' (3 November 2017) <http://www.icc-cpi.int//Pages/item.aspx?name=171103_OTP_Statement> accessed 6 April 2018. ICC, 'ICC judges reject opening of an investigation regarding Afghanistan situation' (12 April 2019) <https://www.icc-cpi.int/Pages/item.aspx?name=pr1448>.

[104] See also the commentary by Katherine Gallagher for the Center for Constitutional Rights, 'The ICC must hold the US accountable for crimes in Afghanistan' <http://www.theguardian.com/commentisfree/2018/feb/16/icc-us-accountable-for-crimes-afghanistan> accessed 9 April 2018.

[105] The 2016 report determined that there was a reasonable basis to believe that, at a minimum, the following crimes within the Court's jurisdiction had occurred:

- Crimes against humanity and war crimes by the Taliban and their affiliate, the Haqqani Network;
- War crimes of torture and related ill-treatment by Afghan government forces, in particular the intelligence agency (National Directorate for Security) and the Afghan National Police;
- War crimes of torture and related ill-treatment by US military forces deployed to Afghanistan and in secret detention facilities operated by the Central Intelligence Agency, principally in the 2003–2004 period, although allegedly continuing in some cases until 2014.

ICC, *Afghanistan Preliminary examination. Focus: Alleged crimes against humanity and war crimes committed in Afghanistan since 1 May 2003* <http://www.icc-cpi.int/afghanistan> accessed 6 April 2018.

[106] Afghanistan Analysts Network, 'Questions and Answers about the International Criminal Court and its Afghanistan Investigation' (22 November 2017) <http://www.afghanistan-analysts.org/questions-

This development followed a periodic review of Afghanistan's compliance with the Convention Against Torture, which it ratified in 1987.[107] Article 29 of Afghanistan's Constitution 2004 explicitly forbids the use of torture. However, torture has been a standard practice among police and security actors in Afghanistan (as well as by foreign forces),[108] and the Committee found allegations of widespread use of torture and ill-treatment.[109]

Predictably, the Committee was also highly critical of the ongoing operation of the General Amnesty Law 2007, which it saw as fostering a culture of impunity and acceptance of torture.[110]

The preliminary examination initiated by the ICC Prosecutor was not requested by Afghanistan or the UN Security Council. Consequently, it required an additional, preliminary judgment by a panel of judges from the Pre-Trial Chamber in order for the prosecution to proceed. The ICC initiative was difficult for President Ashraf Ghani, who campaigned for the post of UN Secretary-General in 2005–6.[111] In 2014 he formed a government with first Vice President Abdul Rashid Dostum and second Vice President Sarwar Danish. Danish holds a Master's degree in Islamic jurisprudence

and-answers-about-the-international-criminal-court-and-its-afghanistan-investigation> accessed 6 April 2018.

[107] Committee Against Torture, 'Concluding Observations on the Second Periodic Report of Afghanistan adopted by the Committee 18 April–12 May 2017 <https://tbinternet.ohchr.org/Treaties/CAT/Shared%20Documents/AFG/INT_CAT_COC_AFG_27463_E.pdf> accessed 7 January 2018.

[108] Hartmann (n 83) 179.

[109] Committee Against Torture (n 107) para 9:

> ... The Committee is further concerned at the numerous reports, including from UNAMA, the International Criminal Court (Report on Preliminary Examination Activities, 2016), the Afghanistan Independent Human Rights Commission (AIHRC) and civil society, that beatings, electric shocks, suspensions, threats, sexual abuses, and other forms of mental and physical abuses are largely and increasingly practiced on detainees in custody in facilities run by the National Directorate of Security (NDS), the Afghan National Police (ANP) and the Afghan Local Police (ALP) primarily to extract confessions or information to be used in criminal proceedings (arts. 2, 12, 13, 15 and 16).

See also Kate Clark, 'Torture as Prevalent as Ever: New UN report finds no end to impunity for Afghan torturers' (Afghan Analysts Network, 24 April 2017) <http://www.afghanistan-analysts.org/torture-as-prevalent-as-ever-new-un-report-finds-no-end-to-impunity-for-afghan-torturers/> accessed 1 April 2018.

[110] It also gave little credence to the government's rushed attempt to enact a Law on Prohibition of Torture, which in draft form includes a definition of torture that is identical with article 1 of the Convention. It found (ibid.) that the Penal Code 1976 was inconsistent with the Convention because of:

(a) the absence of clear legal provisions ensuring that other cruel, inhuman or degrading treatment or punishment are also clearly prohibited and criminalized as separate offence;
(b) The absence of legal provisions ensuring that victims have access to reporting mechanisms without fear of intimidation or reprisals from authorities; and
(c) That the State party's Penal Code does not clearly prohibit corporal punishments, including flogging, amputation of limbs and stoning, which amount to torture and cruel, inhuman or degrading treatment or punishment, (arts. 1, 2 and 4).

[111] A former World Bank official and former Chancellor of Kabul University. For his scholarship on state-building see: Ashraf Ghani and Clare Lockhart, *Fixing Failed States* (OUP 2009).

and is a former Acting Minister of Justice and participant in the constitutional drafting process, but Dostum is a former warlord who is barred from the US because of his human rights record.[112] This political compromise expresses the ambivalent character of Afghanistan's relationship to international law at present and the fact that vetting initiatives in Afghanistan to date have been minimal.[113]

Since the Electoral Law only disqualified candidates *convicted* of crimes, the compromise was to accept as candidates only those who were certified as participating in the DDR processes imposed on political parties up to 2005.[114] The result was that a significant number of armed leaders were elected (and re-elected) to the Parliament, undermining the legitimacy of Afghanistan's political institutions.[115]

4.6 The Sector-Led Approach

Views divide about whether Afghanistan received sufficient, and sufficiently swift, civilian-led foreign aid to rebuild after 2001.[116] The broad consensus, however, is that that law and justice reform in Afghanistan since 2001 has been slow and disappointing.[117] International legal advisers must share some of the responsibility for this.

[112] This includes accusations of war crimes by the forces he commanded. Dostum epitomizes the rise of the 'war entrepreneur': Cathy Gormley-Heenan, Gordon Peake, and Mari Fitzduff, 'From Warlords to Peacelords: Local Leadership Capacity in Peace Processes' (2004) Incore <http://www.incore.ulst.ac.uk/research/projects/wlpl/WlplFull.pdf> accessed 1 April 2018.

[113] They included the one-off vetting of provincial police chiefs in 2005, and the vetting of political candidates under the Electoral Law, in the run up to the 2005 elections, and the establishment of the advisory panel for senior political appointments.

[114] Caroline Hartzell, *Missed Opportunities: The Impact of DDR on SSR in Afghanistan* (US Institute for Peace 2011) <http://www.usip.org/sites/default/files/SR270-Missed_Opportunities.pdf> accessed 13 April 2018.

[115] Within the justice sector, there was no purge of legal personnel who served under prior regimes (such as occurred, for example, in Bosnia and East Germany). While a few senior personnel have been removed from office there has not been any system-wide vetting. A proposal by donors to systematically re-credential judges and adopt merit-based appointment was not adopted. The former Chief Justice of the Supreme Court, Shinwari, was not renewed by the National Assembly in 2006 and the Attorney General was removed from office in 2008 for declaring his candidacy for President, and thus becoming statutorily ineligible to hold public office while campaigning: Armytage (n 3).

[116] There were three key ebb points: the US prosecution of a war in Iraq from 2003 onwards; the drawdown of troops by the US and its coalition partners after 2010 (after President Obama announced a phased withdrawal of troops in 2011 or 2012, allies such as the Netherlands and Australia also began to withdraw); and the disbanding of ISAF in 2014. Nonetheless, by August 2017 the newly elected US President, Donald Trump, was forced to recommit troops to Afghanistan because of the deteriorating security situation.

[117] Serge Michailof, *The Seven Capital Sins of the Donor Community in Afghanistan* (The German Marshall Fund of the United States, Economic Policy Program, Policy Brief, 9 December 2008) <http://www.gmfus.org/publications/seven-capital-sins-donor-community-afghanistan> accessed 6 April 2018; International Crisis Group (n 42).

A foundational issue was that the Bonn process created 'lead nations' for participating states in different sectors of the state-building exercise. Italy was initially assigned the justice system,[118] while Germany was assigned police, the UK counter-narcotics, and the US the armed forces. The 'lead nation' approach was phased out by 2007 in favour of an Afghan-managed national justice sector project.[119] The largest donor, and the biggest military contributor, was the US, which pursued its own justice sector and counter-narcotics reforms throughout its engagement in Afghanistan.[120] This set the scene for significant confusion and lack of coordination, intensified by donors' imperatives to deliver, and claim credit for, quick reforms that could be reported to their home constituents. One consequence was that in the first five years of legal technical assistance, draft legislative reforms were often prepared with minimal input from local stakeholders and donors relied heavily on enacting these through presidential decrees during Parliamentary recesses.[121]

Priority areas for legislative reform and capacity-building also tracked donor priorities. Initially, these included criminal law and human rights and the detection and prosecution of narcotics offences; from 2009 onwards the emphasis shifted to anti-corruption.[122] In criminal law reform, the result was a 'patchwork' of new legislation, such as the 2004 laws on money laundering, bribery, and corruption that did not connect to existing criminal statutes in Afghanistan.[123]

Italy embarked on drafting a new Interim Criminal Procedure Code (ICPC) in 2004, notwithstanding the existence of the Criminal Procedure Code 1974, itself an amendment of a 1965 code modelled on Egyptian law. Thus more familiar law was replaced with a complex new statute, which failed to state which laws it abrogated and was promulgated without a systematic plan to release, translate, review, and update it. The ICPC was inconsistent with the Constitution 2004 and with Afghanistan's obligations under the ICCPR.[124] A new and comprehensive Criminal Procedure Code 2014[125] was redrafted by an inclusive local and international Criminal Law Reform Working Group, using Dari as the controlling language.[126]

[118] The most comprehensive description of the Italian contribution is Matteo Tondini, *Statebuilding and Justice Reform: Post-Conflict Reconstruction in Afghanistan* (Routledge 2010).

[119] Hartmann (n 83) 172.

[120] Direct personal observation.

[121] Michael Hartmann and Agnieszka Klonowiecka-Milart, 'Lost in Translation' in Mason (n 2) 267, 274.

[122] And in the latest Ministry of Justice Plan 2017–21 <http://policymof.gov.af/home/national-justice-and-judicial-reform-plan-njrp/> accessed 15 April 2019.

[123] Hartmann and Klonowiecka-Milart (n 121) 267, 272.

[124] The failure to completely abrogate the older criminal procedure code resulted in courts applying both the new and parts of the old code: ibid. 280.

[125] Official translation <http://www.unodc.org/res/cld/document/criminal-procedure-code_html/Criminal_Procedure_Code_-_Endorsed_by_President_EN_2014_03_14_with_TOC.pdf> accessed 7 January 2018.

[126] Hartmann and Klonowiecka-Milart (n 121) 267, 296.

Gender equality has been an enduring theme of both state-building and law and justice intervention in Afghanistan. Family pressure is a major issue for women—families want their daughters to be safe from sexual harassment and from the reputational harm and gossip arising from close or unsupervised contact with men from outside the extended family.[127]

One precautionary strategy to 'protect' the family is arranged marriage: at least 30 per cent of Afghan children are married before the age of eighteen. The Civil Code 1977 stipulates sixteen as the minimum age for marriage, with marriage at fifteen being possible with the permission of a guardian. An increasing proportion of the population sees sixteen as a desirable age for marriage (such views correlating with lower levels of education and rural locations).[128] However, the practice of not giving women a share of inheritance (*miras*) (itself a contravention of *shari'a* principles) is losing support: more than 89.9 per cent of respondents in a 2017 survey supported women's rights to inherit.[129]

A visible area of procedural deficiency in Afghanistan's criminal law has been the practice of imprisoning women and children, often on the basis of 'crimes' that have no statutory basis, such as poverty (begging on the street), running away from home, or fleeing domestic violence or family disputes.[130] Women have also been vulnerable to prosecution for prostitution—often the only means of survival for women affected by conflict—and there is evidence that human trafficking of women and children remains an acute problem.

The Penal Code 1976 has now been completely redrafted and came into force on 14 February 2018.[131] It is intended to work with the Law on the Elimination of Violence Against Women 2009,[132] although a section on penalties for violence against women was

[127] That social attitudes seem to be becoming more conservative in this regard is reflected in social (not legal) prescriptions about how women should dress in public. More than 30 per cent of respondents in the 2017 Asia Foundation survey thought that a full body and face covering (the *burqua*) was appropriate; a further 28.5 per cent favoured the full body and face covering (*niqab*). In aggregate, less than 7 per cent regarded the loose veil and open-face style of *hijab* as appropriate, although this was more strongly supported in some regions and ethnicities and by women with higher levels of education: Asia Foundation (n 43) 142.

[128] Asia Foundation (n 43) 144. A draft Marriage Law, not yet enacted, proposes 18 as the minimum marriage age: Asia Foundation (n 43) 165 fn 22. Also termed a Law on Children's Rights Protection and Family Law: see Islamic Republic of Afghanistan Ministry of Justice, 'Ministry of Justice Convenes a Scientific and Research Seminar on Draft of Family Law' 8 January 2017 <http://moj.gov.af/en/news/290225> accessed 15 April 2018.

[129] Asia Foundation (n 43) 142.

[130] UNAMA, 'UNAMA welcomes Afghanistan's new penal code—calls for robust framework to protect women against violence' (22 February 2018) <https://unama.unmissions.org/unama-welcomes-afghanistan's-new-penal-code-calls-robust-framework-protect-women-against-violence> accessed 6 April 2018.

[131] Ibid.

[132] Islamic Republic of Afghanistan Ministry of Justice, Law on Elimination of Violence against Women (Official Gazette Issue No. 989, 1 August 2009) <http://www.refworld.org/pdfid/5486d1a34.pdf> accessed 6 April 2018.

struck from the newly revised Code. Afghanistan enacted a Juvenile Code in 2005,[133] which is intended to operationalize the Convention on the Rights of the Child and which, *inter alia*, provides procedures and protections for children in the criminal justice process. The practice of jailing juveniles and adults together is now being addressed; juvenile correction (rehabilitation) centres are under construction and will thus fulfil the obligation to house juvenile detainees more safely in prisons. An 'alternatives to detention' programme has also commenced in Kabul and Herat.[134]

5 Local Resistance to International Norms

The Afghan legal system as it exists today is in tension with international law in multiple ways; the different sources of law that make up Afghanistan's legal pluralism also represent competing models of legitimacy. As Maley puts it:

> From the point of view of the international community, the December 2001 Bonn agreement between the non-Taliban political groups ... provided the foundation for the reconstitution of political authority. ... However, from the point of view of ordinary Afghans, the institutions and rules generated by this process did not necessarily enjoy any particular legitimacy, especially given that the capacities of the new Afghan state remained limited and its influence in many parts of Afghanistan was weak. ... [Accordingly] the legitimacy of state-based law cannot simply be assumed; it is up to the state to ensure that this is applied in such a way as to satisfy ordinary people's craving for meaningful justice.[135]

The obligation to apply domestic law in ways that are consistent with international law, however, also falls on the international actors who seek to shape the rule of law in Afghanistan.

5.1 Inconsistencies

The international community has failed to bolster the legitimacy of domestic law in Afghanistan at critical junctures, one being the timing of the 2009 elections. While President Karzai's term of office expired as a matter of constitutional law in May 2009,

[133] Official Gazette Issue No. 846 (23 March 2001) <http://www.asianlii.org/af/legis/laws/jlcogn846p2005032313840103a495> accessed 7 January 2018.

[134] Islamic Republic of Afghanistan Ministry of Justice, 'Implementation Plan of National Justice and Judicial Sectors Reform Program related to MoJ for the next Five Years (2017–2021)' (January–February 2017) <http://policymof.gov.af/home/national-justice-and-judicial-reform-plan-njrp/> accessed 15 April 2019.

[135] Maley (n 82) 69.

the elections were postponed to August 2009 because electoral assistance from international donors was not in place.[136] Having signalled that the Constitution is a malleable instrument, it should then have come as no surprise to international actors in Afghanistan that the government and the courts regarded it in the same way.

Domestic and international legal tensions are clearly visible in the interpretation of article 130 of the Constitution 2004:

> To the foreigners including moderate Muslims from Egypt, where Hanafi jurisprudence is also practiced), and some Afghans, article 130 allows judges to interpret the meaning of already promulgated laws much the same way a common law lawyer might look at case precedent or legislative history. To many Afghans, the phrase 'the courts shall in pursuance of Hanafi jurisprudence' rule in a way that attains justice allows Islamic crimes to be punished, even if not in the penal code.[137]

The latter interpretation requires article 130 to be read without its rider clause, 'within the limits set by this constitution', and as overriding the article 27 protection against prosecution for crimes not stipulated in the written law published before the offence. The counter-argument is that article 3 of the Constitution provides that 'no law shall contravene the tenets and provisions of the holy religion of Islam'.[138] This has opened up space for debate about whether Islamic jurisprudence or statutory law is the controlling source of law in Afghanistan when both coexist.

Article 130 was applied, controversially, to a freedom of religion case involving Abdul Rahman, who had worked for a Catholic NGO in Peshawar, Pakistan, and converted to Christianity upon returning to Afghanistan. His parents, who reported him as an apostate, disowned him. Prosecutors charged him with apostasy under article 130 in 2006. In response to intense international pressure, the case was discharged and sent back to the Attorney General's Department. A judge and prosecutor then determined that his refusal to repent was evidence of mental illness, and he was released and then flown to Italy and granted asylum—thus apparently eliminating an embarrassing breach of international norms.

Sayed Pervez Kambakh,[139] a Balkh University student, was also fortunate. His 2007–8 prosecution, trial, and appeal concerned accusations of blasphemy. He was accused of downloading material from the internet and sharing an article with others that commented on Koranic verses dealing with women's rights. His original indictment was for damaging symbols of religion, under article 357 of the Penal Code 1976, but the crime of blasphemy (for which there is no statutory basis) was added at his first trial.

[136] Maley (n 82) 72.

[137] Hartmann (n 83) 193. Art. 130 of the Constitution 2004 provides:

Article 130 Judicial Discretion

(1) While processing the cases, the courts apply the provisions of this Constitution and other laws.

(2) When there is no provision in the Constitution or other laws regarding ruling on an issue, the courts' decisions shall be within the limits of this Constitution in accord with the *Hanafi* jurisprudence and in a way to serve justice in the best possible manner.

[138] Hartmann (n 83) 194.

[139] Also spelled as it is pronounced, Kambaksh.

He was convicted by the primary court of the crime of blasphemy under article 130 and sentenced to death. On appeal, the conviction was upheld but his sentence was commuted to twenty years of imprisonment.[140] Moderate Islamic legal scholars discussing the trial at the time were cognizant of the pressure that the courts felt to satisfy a more fundamentalist appetite for the strict application of Islamic jurisprudence.[141]

Kambakh was represented by Mohammed Afzal Nooristani of the (donor-funded) Legal Aid Organization of Afghanistan, who received death threats in response.[142] Uproar from the international legal community followed, not least because both the prosecutors and the judges in the case who invoked Islam in order to deliver a politically palatable verdict belonged to institutions that had received significant donor funding (predominantly from the US) for rule of law assistance. Here, again, the solution was political—after his reconviction on appeal in October 2008, the re-elected President Karzai granted him a presidential pardon and he left Afghanistan.[143]

Despite Afghanistan having ratified the international agreements referred to earlier in this chapter, the Supreme Court appeared to have made no direct efforts to reconcile its decisions with the requirements of international law. Indeed, there was a strong sense among local and international observers at the time that the Court relished its chance to demonstrate its jurisdictional power; may have had an eye to fundamentalist demands that Afghanistan function as a more 'Islamic' republic; and used the opportunities to assert independence from international donors and their efforts to influence the case outcomes.[144]

6 Conclusion

This chapter has argued that 'post-conflict' Afghanistan remains a country with ongoing sub-national conflicts, where it is still unclear whether sustainable peace is possible and in what form. The entry of international forces after 2001, led by the US, pursued a 'peace before justice' approach. The non-Taliban participants in the Bonn Agreement ratified this by accepting a light footprint for the UN and neglecting to put any transitional justice architecture in place. The costs of these choices have been significant, both for Afghanistan and for the international community.

One result has been a culture of impunity for human rights abuses and crimes under international law committed before and after 2001, by both insurgent groups and civil and military foreign actors in Afghanistan. This has been underscored by the 2019 refusal of the ICC to open an investigation for alleged crimes against humanity and war crimes in Afghanistan.

[140] Hartmann (n 83) 195.

[141] In their view, the acts (if proven) probably constituted an offence under *shari'a*, but the penalty for someone young, in these circumstances, was considerably disproportionate. Personal communications.

[142] Personal communication with Nooristani.

[143] Hartmann (n 83) 196.

[144] Personal observation and communications.

Both the Karzai and Ghani administrations have formally accepted international law post-2001, initially through the Constitution 2004, and then through international agreements and international customary law. In practice, however, those undertakings have been subordinated to domestic legal realities. These include the inherent complexity of legal pluralism in Afghanistan and the time needed to 'link up' the different components of the legal system.

These domestic legal realities have been exacerbated by a degree of confusion and chaos in the creation of statutory law, attributable in large part to the lack of care by some international legal advisers. Further difficulties have included the time needed to create stronger local capacity and trust among legal professionals, and to institute anti-corruption measures that may make the state's own legal institutions more credible for its citizens. At the same time, multiple actors have exploited ambiguities in constitutional interpretation for divergent political purposes, with the result that international legal norms have been marginalized.

None of this is particularly surprising for a country that was invaded less than twenty years ago and has been unable to stabilize since. Given the handicaps that Afghanistan faces as a state at present, the very fluid relationship between its domestic legal system and international legal institutions, laws, and norms could be anticipated. The more difficult question is whether, and when, the conditions will converge to allow the rule of law to emerge domestically in a way that constrains local elites from the exercise of arbitrary power.[145] That is arguably a precondition for a more affirmative engagement with international law.

[145] Martin Krygier, 'Approaching the Rule of Law' in Mason (n 2) 35.

CHAPTER 29

CENTRAL ASIAN STATES

MARINA GIRSHOVICH*

1 Introduction

THIS chapter looks at the experiences of five Central Asian states—Kazakhstan, Kyrgyzstan, Tajikistan, Turkmenistan, and Uzbekistan—with international law over the past three decades.[1] It identifies some of the distinctive features of Central Asian states' approaches towards international law. The research is comparative in nature, including both horizontal (across states) and vertical (across time) elements.

The commonalities in the stance of Central Asian states on matters of international law are determined by the context of their emergence as sovereign states at the end of the Cold War, their common history as former Soviet republics, their belonging to the Eurasian group of continental legal systems, and their common status as landlocked developing states.

At the same time, each Central Asian state has its own specifics; suffice it to mention differences in their foreign policy priorities, levels of economic development,[2] and resource endowment. National populations and territory also vary greatly. Of the more than 72 million people who live in the Central Asian states (the least populated of all sub-regions of Asia, representing less than one per cent of the world population),

* I express gratitude to Judge Hisashi Owada, Dean Simon Chesterman, and Professor Ben Saul for their constructive editorial suggestions. Thanks are also due to the anonymous reviewers. I also thank moderators Professor Antony Anghie and Dr Ki Beom Lee, as well as the participants, of the Junior Scholars Workshop of the 6th Biennial Conference of the Asian Society of International Law in Seoul, South Korea (24 August 2017), for helpful comments on my paper titled 'Treaties in Central Asian States'.

[1] The official country names are: the Republic of Kazakhstan, the Kyrgyz Republic, the Republic of Tajikistan, Turkmenistan, and the Republic of Uzbekistan.

[2] The IMF's World Economic Outlook Database (October 2018) figures for gross domestic product (GDP) per capita are: US$10,450 (Kazakhstan), US$1,220 (Kyrgyzstan), US$815 (Tajikistan), US$8,070 (Turkmenistan), and US$1,560 (Uzbekistan).

national populations vary from a high of 32.8 million in Uzbekistan to a low of 5.9 million in Turkmenistan. Differences in territorial size are even starker, from vast Kazakhstan (2.7 million square kilometres, the world's ninth largest country) to comparatively small Tajikistan (142,500 square kilometres, ranking ninety-fourth).

This chapter first considers the emergence of Central Asian states as new subjects of international law before reviewing their participation in the Commonwealth of Independent States (CIS), in particular their experiences with the CIS Economic Court, the first regional court in the area. It also briefly touches upon the Eurasian integration projects that some of the Central Asian states have been engaged in. The next section examines the status that domestic laws of Central Asian states accord to international law. Lastly, the final section explores the approaches to treaty regimes in general, with a closer examination of non-proliferation and human rights treaties.

2 The New Subjects of International Law

Up until 1991, for a seventy-year period Central Asian states had been constitutive parts of the Soviet Union (USSR), where major foreign policy competences rested with the Union, not individual republics. These included treaty making, foreign trade, diplomatic representation, external boundary delimitation matters, and so on. *De jure* throughout the Soviet period, Central Asian republics acted as subjects of international law *indirectly* through representation in the USSR bodies. From 1944, Union republics additionally acquired rights to *directly* enter into foreign relations, conclude agreements, exchange diplomatic and consular representatives with foreign states, and participate in international organizations.[3] However, de facto the level of both indirect and direct participation of Central Asian republics in shaping and implementing foreign policy was limited.[4]

Simultaneously with the demise of the Soviet Union, the independence of Kazakhstan, Kyrgyzstan, Tajikistan, Turkmenistan, and Uzbekistan, as well as their status as founding members of the CIS, was legally established by the Alma-Ata Agreements of 21 December 1991.[5] By that time each Central Asian republic had adopted national laws on sovereignty and independence.

[3] For an overview of 1944 constitutional amendments see Oliver Lissitzyn, 'Territorial Entities Other than Independent States in the Law of Treaties' (1968) 125 Recueil des Cours de l'Académie de Droit International 1, 34–5.

[4] Manifestations of international legal personality of Central Asian Soviet republics are analyzed in Marat Sarsembayev, *Mezhdunarodnoe pravo v istorii Kazahstana i Srednei Azii [International Law in the History of Kazakhstan and Central Asia]* (Foliant 2011) 115–75.

[5] Petr Kremnev, *Raspad SSR i pravopreemstvo gosudarstv [The Breakup of the USSR and State Succession]* (Yurlitinform 2012) 64. The Alma-Ata Protocol 1991 and the Alma-Ata Declaration 1991 were adopted by the heads of the 11 Union republics: Armenia, Azerbaijan, Belarus, Kazakhstan,

The republics had to simultaneously address issues at three different levels. *Domestically*, Central Asian states faced the tasks of constitution-making, state-building, and transitioning to market economies. *Regionally*, formerly intrastate relations transformed into interstate relations, with ensuing challenges of border delimitation, use of energy and water resources, and rebuilding political, economic, and social ties on a new basis. *Internationally*, a major task was to ensure recognition by other states and to enter the international community as full-fledged members. International law was instrumental in achieving their objectives. Given that initially all Central Asian states emerged as 'strong' presidential republics, national leaders (Presidents) have played an important role in defining approaches towards international law. (Since 2010, Kyrgyzstan has had a presidential-parliamentary form of government.)

2.1 State Succession

Upon independence, Central Asian states faced issues of state succession. Through multilateral and bilateral treaties they settled the matters of succession in respect of USSR property, assets, debts, and archives. In addition, the issue of succession in respect of nuclear arsenals, a particular type of property, arose for Kazakhstan. Kazakhstan's voluntary denuclearization, and ratification in 1993 (as a non-nuclear state) of the Treaty on the Non-Proliferation of Nuclear Weapons 1968,[6] facilitated its full international recognition.[7]

As regards succession to treaties, Central Asian and other CIS states agreed to 'guarantee *in accordance with their constitutional procedures* the discharge of the international obligations deriving from treaties and agreements concluded by the former [USSR]' (emphasis added).[8] They also agreed to decide matters of participation in treaties of the former USSR *in accordance with the principles and norms of international law individually depending upon the specifics of each case and the nature and content of each treaty*.[9] Thus, each state made its own decisions on participation as long as such decisions conformed to universally recognized principles and norms of international law.[10]

Kyrgyzstan, Moldova, Russia, Tajikistan, Turkmenistan, Uzbekistan, and Ukraine. The Protocol confirmed the Minsk Agreement of 8 December 1991 (adopted by the heads of Belarus, Russia, and Ukraine) on the breakup of the USSR and the creation of the CIS.

[6] Treaty on the Non-Proliferation of Nuclear Weapons (adopted 1 July 1968, entered into force 5 March 1970).

[7] See Hélène Hamant, 'La Succession d'États de l'URSS en Matière Militaire' (2004) 50 Annuaire Français de Droit International 213, 221.

[8] Alma-Ata Declaration (adopted 21 December 1991) (1992) 31 ILM 147, 149.

[9] Memorandum of Understanding 'On Issues of Succession to Treaties of the Former USSR Having Mutual Interest' (6 July 1992) preamble para 1.

[10] Ibid. para 4.

Accordingly, practice with respect to different treaties varied. For instance, Kazakhstan, Kyrgyzstan, Tajikistan, and Turkmenistan succeeded to the four Geneva Conventions 1949 and the two Additional Protocols 1977,[11] whereas Uzbekistan joined by accession. Following their admission to the International Labour Organization (ILO), Kyrgyzstan and Tajikistan recognized that they continued to be bound by the obligations arising under ILO conventions previously applicable to their territories.[12] Kazakhstan, Turkmenistan, and Uzbekistan did not make similar declarations.

As for the UN human rights treaties, Central Asian states acceded to or ratified them anew, rather than succeeding to them.[13] Although automatic (ipso jure) succession to human rights and humanitarian treaties may be desirable from a normative standpoint, Central Asian states' practice supports the 'clean slate' principle.[14] This, however, does not impair the duty of states to fulfil customary international law obligations that are reflected in the treaties.

2.2 Implementing Foreign Policy and International Law

The constitutions of all Central Asian states declare a separation of powers dividing the institutions of government into three branches: executive, legislative, and judicial. On matters of foreign policy and international law, the basic powers of each branch are similar across the Central Asian states. Presidents define foreign policy priorities. Governments ensure the development of relations with foreign states and international and regional organizations, implement foreign policy, and ensure the funding of foreign relations and foreign policy. Ministries of Foreign Affairs implement foreign policy and coordinate the activity of all governmental agencies in foreign policy matters. Treaty-making powers vary by country and treaty category, but belong to the executive in all Central Asian states. Parliaments ratify and denounce treaties that require their approval. Parliaments, governments, and national courts, through their respective activities, ensure compliance of states with their international obligations.

[11] See 'Declarations of Succession to the Geneva Conventions and their Additional Protocols (Turkmenistan, Republic of Kazakhstan, Republic of Kyrgyzstan)' (1992) 32(291) International Review of the Red Cross 603, 603–4; 'Declaration of Succession by the Republic of Tajikistan to the Geneva Conventions and their Additional Protocols' (1993) 33(293) International Review of the Red Cross 182, 182–3.

[12] (1993) 76 ILO Official Bulletin, Series A, 32 (Kyrgyzstan) and 168 (Tajikistan).

[13] See UN Treaty Database, Status of Multilateral Treaties <https://treaties.un.org> accessed 17 April 2018. Cf. e.g. the UN Human Rights Committee, which declared that 'all the peoples within the territory of a former State party to the Covenant remained entitled to the guarantees of the Covenant, and that, in particular, Armenia, Georgia, Kazakhstan, Kyrgyzstan, Tajikistan, the former Yugoslav Republic of Macedonia, Turkmenistan and Uzbekistan were bound by the obligations of the Covenant as from the dates of their independence'. See HRC, 'Annual Report to the UN General Assembly', UN Doc A/49/40 (vol 1) (Supp) (21 September 1994) para 49.

[14] Akbar Rasulov, 'Revisiting State Succession to Humanitarian Treaties: Is there a Case for Automaticity?' (2003) 14 European Journal of International Law 141, 163.

2.3 Participation in International Organizations

Central Asian states, being members of the CIS (though Turkmenistan is an associate member), all joined the United Nations in 1992, followed by the UN specialized agencies. They also became members of other international organizations, such as the Organization on Security and Cooperation in Europe (OSCE) (all); Shanghai Cooperation Organization (SCO) (all but Turkmenistan, a guest country); Organization of Islamic Cooperation (OIC) (all); Collective Security Treaty Organization (CSTO) (Kazakhstan, Kyrgyzstan, Tajikistan, and Uzbekistan (1992–9 and 2006–12)); Eurasian Economic Community (EurAsEC) (2000–14) (Kazakhstan, Kyrgyzstan, Tajikistan, and Uzbekistan (2006–8)); Eurasian Economic Union (EAEU) (Kazakhstan and Kyrgyzstan); the World Trade Organization (WTO) (Kazakhstan, Kyrgyzstan, and Tajikistan; Uzbekistan (an observer)); Non-Aligned Movement (Turkmenistan and Uzbekistan (members); Kazakhstan, Kyrgyzstan, and Tajikistan (observers)). Notably, Kazakhstan was the first among Central Asian states to serve as a non-permanent member of the UN Security Council (in 2017–18).

Membership in international organizations is subject to legislative approval. Treaties on membership require ratification in all cases (Turkmenistan and Uzbekistan)[15] or where participation involves the delegation of sovereign rights to an international organization or compliance with the legally binding decisions thereof (Kazakhstan, Kyrgyzstan, and Tajikistan).[16]

Turkmenistan is the first state whose international legal status of permanent neutrality has been recognized and supported by the UN General Assembly (UNGA).[17] This constitutionally established status implies peaceful foreign policy, non-participation in military blocs and alliances, non-involvement in international conflicts (except as a neutral platform for negotiations or in self-defence), the prohibition of foreign military bases in its territory, the prohibition of weapons of mass destruction, and non-participation in economic blockades of third states as a means of exerting political pressure.[18] Thus, Turkmenistan has contributed to the development of international law on permanent neutrality.[19] In practice, Turkmenistan's permanent neutrality status has limited its participation in regional organizations (for example, in the CIS).

[15] LIT of Turkmenistan 2010 art. 11(1); LIT of Uzbekistan 1995 (amended 2017) art. 14. See n. 88.

[16] LIT of Kazakhstan 2005 (amended 2015) art. 11(5); LIT of Kyrgyzstan 2014 (amended 2017) art. 11(1)(9); LIT of Tajikistan 2016 art. 11. See n. 88.

[17] UNGA res 50/80A (12 December 1995). UN support for the permanent neutrality status of Turkmenistan was reaffirmed by UNGA res 69/285 (3 June 2015). Both resolutions were adopted by consensus.

[18] See Constitution of Turkmenistan 2016 art. 9; Constitutional Law of Turkmenistan 'On Permanent Neutrality' No 99-1 of 27 December 1995.

[19] Some authors have suggested that Turkmenistan's permanent neutrality status has become a norm of customary international law or is being crystallized as such. See Yolbars Kepbanov, 'Neitral'nyi Turkmenistan: podhody k regional'noi bezopasnosti' ['Neutral Turkmenistan: The Approaches to Regional Security'] (2009) 1(73) Moscow Journal of International Law 104, 106. See also Zhaisanbek Amanzholov, 'Turkmenistan i ego postoiannyi neitralitet: mezhdunarodnyi status sovremennogo gosudarstva' ['Turkmenistan and Its Permanent Neutrality: The International Legal Status of the Modern State'] (2012) 6 Gosudarstvo i pravo

3 The Commonwealth of Independent States

Since 1991, Central Asian states (Kazakhstan, Kyrgyzstan, Tajikistan, Uzbekistan, and Turkmenistan (associate member since 2005)), along with Armenia, Azerbaijan, Belarus, Moldova, Russia, and Ukraine, have cooperated within the framework of the CIS.[20] The CIS is a regional interstate organization created to mitigate the detrimental effects of the breakup of the Soviet Union and to facilitate cooperation in political, economic, environmental, humanitarian, cultural, and other areas.[21] The CIS Charter 1993 describes the CIS as neither possessing statehood, nor as being a supranational organization.[22] The CIS structure includes the: Council of the Heads of States, Council of the Heads of Governments, Council of Foreign Ministers, Economic Council, Inter-Parliamentary Assembly, CIS Economic Court, Council of Permanent Plenipotentiary Representatives of the CIS Member States at the Charter-based and Other CIS Bodies, Executive Committee, and Bodies of Branch Cooperation, among others.

Divergence of the views of participating states on the role of the CIS, and the sensitivity of the issue of sovereignty, predetermined the prevalence of 'soft' legal institutions within the organization (through 'a la carte' participation of states in CIS agreements, the declaratory nature of treaty provisions, the unclear status of the CIS acts in domestic legal orders, and the use of non-binding model legislation, to name a few).[23] Despite criticisms of its effectiveness, the CIS served Central Asian states and their populations by preventing and/or remedying a legal vacuum in intra-CIS relations that were previously regulated by the single national law of the USSR. Numerous treaties have been concluded, while the CIS Economic Court has ensured their coherent interpretation and application. Likewise, the CIS has helped to preserve a degree of coherence between the legal systems of individual states through model legislative acts of the Inter-Parliamentary Assembly, among other mechanisms. The CIS has also assisted Central Asian and other member states' smooth integration into international legal practice. This was of special significance given the lack of expertise in international legal matters at the time of acquiring independence.

[Law and State] 90, 98. Such a customary norm potentially includes, in addition to substantive obligations by Turkmenistan, a limitation on unilateral abrogation of the status by Turkmenistan, guarantees of the status by the UN, as well as obligations of respect for and support of the status by third states.

[20] Ukraine has been an associate member of the CIS since 1993 and is currently in the process of exiting. Georgia was a member in 1993–2009.

[21] The constitutive documents of the CIS are the Agreement on the Establishment of the Commonwealth of Independent States (signed 8 December 1991), its integral part, the Protocol (signed 21 December 1991), and the Alma-Ata Declaration (signed 21 December 1991), as well as the CIS Charter (signed 22 January 1993).

[22] CIS Charter 1993 art. 1.

[23] See e.g. Rilka Dragneva, 'Is "Soft" Beautiful? Another Perspective on Law, Institutions, and Integration in the CIS' (2004) 29 Review of Central and East European Law 279.

3.1 Central Asian States in the CIS Economic Court

Central Asian states have not accepted the compulsory jurisdiction of the International Court of Justice under article 36(2) of its Statute and have never appeared before it under other bases of jurisdiction. As WTO members, Kazakhstan, Kyrgyzstan, and Tajikistan may potentially become parties in the proceedings before the WTO Dispute Settlement Body.[24] Kazakhstan has reserved its third-party rights in a number of cases,[25] which shows its willingness to defend national interests in the multilateral trading system by judicial means. At the same time, Central Asian states have had experience of the judicial resolution of disputes and of the judicial interpretation of treaties at a regional level in the CIS Economic Court.

The CIS Economic Court is a Charter body of the CIS operating under the Agreement of 6 July 1992 'On the Status of the CIS Economic Court' (Agreement 1992), an integral part of which is the Regulation on the CIS Economic Court (Regulation 1992). States parties to the Agreement 1992 are Kazakhstan, Kyrgyzstan, Tajikistan, and Uzbekistan, along with Russia and Belarus.[26]

The CIS Economic Court consisted of equal numbers of judges from each of the states parties to the Agreement 1992.[27] In practice, not all states appointed judges, but this did not disrupt the Court's operation. The majority of the judges had experience as national judges prior to their appointment to the CIS Economic Court. The Court operated in chambers or as a full court. The full court reviewed requests for interpretation of the CIS acts and issued final judgments (or advisory opinions). The highest body of the Court was the Plenum consisting of all judges of the CIS Economic Court and chief justices of the Supreme Courts or the higher courts responsible for resolving economic disputes in the states parties to the Agreement 1992. The Plenum heard appeals from the judgments of the chambers; issued recommendations for consistent application of CIS acts and for eliminating conflicts of national laws of the states parties to the Agreement 1992; adopted Rules of Procedure of the CIS Economic Court; and so on.[28]

The Protocol amending the Agreement 1992 (Protocol 2017)[29] has changed the Court's mode of operation. Before, the Court operated in regular sessions, whereas under the amendments the chambers are to be convened on an ad hoc basis for specific cases. Under the Protocol 2017, the Court (both for contentious and advisory

[24] So far, one case involving a Central Asian state has entered the consultations phase. See Kazakhstan—Anti-Dumping Measures on Steel Pipes WT/DS530 (request of 19 September 2017).

[25] See <http://www.wto.org/english/tratop_e/dispu_e/dispu_by_country_e.htm> accessed 17 April 2018.

[26] Moldova and Armenia were previously parties to the Agreement 1992.

[27] Regulation on the CIS Economic Court 1992 para 6.

[28] See Rules of Procedure of the CIS Economic Court, affirmed by the Ruling of the Plenum of the CIS Economic Court No 2 of 10 July 1997 (last amended No 3 of 9 October 2014) art. 25.

[29] Protocol Amending the Agreement of 6 July 1992 'On the Status of the CIS Economic Court' (adopted 13 September 2017, entered into force 7 February 2019).

proceedings) is to operate in chambers of three judges selected for each case from the 'register of judges', with the full court hearing requests for revision of judgments in light of newly revealed circumstances, as well as appeals on points of law.[30] The Plenum no longer has the competence of an appellate instance, but has retained some other powers.[31]

The jurisdiction of the CIS Economic Court includes interstate economic disputes arising out of the CIS treaties and acts adopted by the CIS organs (together, CIS acts), as well as interpretation of the CIS acts. Under the Agreement 1992, the Court's jurisdiction is compulsory. In addition, compromissory clauses in many CIS treaties provide for the Court's jurisdiction, thereby expanding its scope *ratione materiae* and *ratione personae*. The Court has acted upon applications from the CIS states and CIS organs. Kazakhstan, Kyrgyzstan, Tajikistan, and Uzbekistan have at various times been subjects of application before the CIS Economic Court and/or parties to interstate disputes adjudicated by it.

Central Asian states in the CIS Economic Court have experienced the benefits of international adjudication with its traditional shortcomings mitigated.[32] In contentious cases, the Court interprets the CIS acts and establishes whether a state is in breach of its obligations under the CIS acts, but merely recommends measures to be taken.[33] The judicial settlement of interstate disputes has been viewed by the states as a means of last resort,[34] and contentious cases are few in number.[35] Uniquely, in a dispute between Tajikistan and Uzbekistan, the Court reviewed the compatibility of the Decree of the Cabinet of Ministers of the Republic of Uzbekistan 'On the Prohibition of Entry and Transit of Ethyl Alcohol into and through the Customs Territory of the Republic of Uzbekistan' with a package of CIS treaties and established that there had been violations thereof.[36] Uzbekistan did not participate in the proceedings.

[30] Ibid. art. 10. [31] Ibid. art. 12.

[32] The benefits of the CIS Economic Court include impartial dispute settlement and interpretation, based on law. The design and operation of the Court minimize the traditional shortcomings of international adjudication, such as inflexibility, risks of conflict escalation and of losing a case, among others. For a summary of advantages and disadvantages of international adjudication see e.g. Richard Bilder, 'International Dispute Settlement and the Role of International Adjudication' (1987) 1 Emory Journal of International Dispute Settlement 142, 146–61.

[33] See e.g. Case between the Government of Tajikistan (applicant) and the Government of Uzbekistan (respondent): CIS Economic Court, Judgment No 01-1/1-03 of 13 February 2004, Case between the Government of Kazakhstan (applicant) and the Government of Russia (respondent): CIS Economic Court, Judgment No 01-1/3-06 of 18 April 2008, and CIS Economic Court, Ruling of the Plenum No 01-1/3-06/1 Pl of 14 April 2010.

[34] 'Ekonomicheskii Sud SNG- ustoiavshiisia, priznannyi, effectivno vypolniaiushii svoi funkcii mezhdunarodnii sud' ['The CIS Economic Court is a Settled and Recognized International Court Effectively Performing its Functions'] Interview with Lyudmila Kamenkova, Chairperson of the CIS Economic Court (2015) 5(166) Zanger [Lawyer] 85, 87.

[35] This has been contrary to the original expectations of the founders that the Court would primarily deal with the interstate economic disputes.

[36] CIS Economic Court, Judgment No 01-1/1-03 of 13 February 2004.

The majority of applications have requested the Court to perform its advisory function. The Court has clarified legal rules and ensured the consistency of legal interpretations of the CIS acts across states, which are among the functions of regional courts generally.[37] For instance, Kyrgyzstan requested interpretation of article 11 of the Convention on the Protection of Investors' Rights 1997. The CIS Economic Court ruled that the provision established merely a possibility of investment dispute arbitration, but could not in and of itself accord jurisdiction where the parties had not designated a specific tribunal in an arbitration agreement or an arbitral clause.[38] The judgment not only helped Kyrgyzstan protect its national interests,[39] but also prevented the incorrect application of the Agreement on a larger scale.

The CIS Economic Court has been uniquely positioned to facilitate interaction and cross-fertilization between CIS law and national legal systems. State organs of Central Asian states have applied for the Court's advisory opinions and utilized them in practice. The subjects of applications have included Kazakhstan's Government, Supreme Court, Constitutional Council, Higher Arbitration Court, and Ministries of Foreign Affairs and Finance; Kyrgyzstan's Government and Supreme Court; and Tajikistan's Government and Higher Economic Court.[40] Some applications filed by CIS organs have also originated from Central Asian states,[41] and the Court has also interpreted treaties or other CIS acts in which Central Asian states participate.[42] Importantly, the Court

[37] Karen Alter and Liesbet Hooghe, 'Regional Dispute Settlement' in Tanja Börzel and Thomas Risse (eds), *The Oxford Handbook of Comparative Regionalism* (OUP 2016) 551.

[38] CIS Economic Court, Judgment No 01-1/1-14 of 23 September 2014.

[39] CIS Economic Court's judgment helped Kyrgyzstan have several arbitration awards against it repealed. For one example see 'Arbitrazhnyi sud Moskvy otmenil reshenie Arbitrazha pri Moskovskoi TPP po ranee vynesennomu ne v pol'zu Kyrgyzstana resheniiu' ['Moscow Arbitration Court repeals the award of the Arbitration Court of the Moscow Chamber of Commerce and Industry previously rendered against Kyrgyzstan'] (19 November 2014) <http://old.kabar.kg/index.php/economics/full/86416> accessed 17 April 2018.

[40] For example, the Supreme Court of Kyrgyzstan requested interpretation of the Agreement on the General Terms of Delivery of Goods among Entities of the CIS Participating States of 20 March 1992 due to difficulties in applying the Agreement by national courts. See CIS Economic Court, Judgment No 01-1/3-04 of 10 November 2004. In another instance, the Higher Economic Court of Tajikistan requested interpretation of article 9 of the Agreement on the Procedure for Settlement of Disputes Related to the Economic Activity of 20 March 1992. See CIS Economic Court, Advisory Opinion No 01-1/3-10 of 20 June 2011.

[41] For instance, the application of the Executive Secretariat of the CIS on interpretation of the terms 'refugee', 'involuntarily displaced person', and 'migrant' was based on the request from the President of Kazakhstan that had been filed due to the lack of uniform understanding of the terms by the CIS bodies and media. See CIS Economic Court, Judgment No C-1/14-96 of 11 September 1996 (on the interpretation of the Agreement on the Assistance to Refugees and Involuntarily Displaced Persons of 24 September 1993).

[42] Regardless of the subject of application, the Court's interpretations apply to all states participating in the treaty or in the act of the CIS organ. See Fayzullo Abdulloyev, 'Pravovaia sistema Tajikistana i Sodruzhestvo Nezavisimyh Gosudarstv' ['The Legal System of the Republic of Tajikistan and the Commonwealth of Independent States'] Keynote Address by the Chairperson of the CIS Economic Court (The 20th Anniversary of the Republic of Tajikistan's Independence and the 15th Anniversary of the Establishment of Diplomatic Relations between the Republic of Tajikistan and the Republic of Belarus, Minsk, 7–8 June 2011).

renders its advisory opinions after first considering state practice (including that of Central Asian states) concerning interpretation and application of the specific acts.[43]

Although the status of judgments of the CIS Economic Court has not been defined in the national laws of Central Asian states, state organs of Kazakhstan, Kyrgyzstan, and Tajikistan have applied the Court's judgments and advisory opinions in their practice,[44] including in judicial decisions and laws in Kazakhstan.[45]

The CIS Economic Court has issued advisory opinions on important questions of international law of direct interest to Central Asian states, including treaty law and practice; the relationship between domestic and international law; the legal status of the CIS and its organs; the conformity of the CIS acts to the principles and norms of international law; the enforcement of foreign judgments and arbitral awards; legal assistance among states; and so forth.

Overall, Central Asian states' participation in the establishment and operation of the CIS Economic Court has demonstrated their commitment to universally recognized norms and principles of international law.[46] Central Asian states have taken a pragmatic approach in referring matters to the Court whenever national interests call for it. The Court has played an important role in interpreting the CIS treaties, clarifying principles of international law for Central Asian states, and assisting the states' smooth integration into international legal practice.

[43] E.g. when interpreting art. 8 of the Agreement on the Procedure for the Settlement of Disputes Related to the Economic Activity of 20 March 1992 upon application from the Higher Economic Court of the Republic of Tajikistan, the CIS Economic Court considered the respective state practice articulated in the responses from the Supreme Courts of Belarus, Kazakhstan, Kyrgyzstan, Moldova, Russia, Turkmenistan, and Ukraine. See CIS Economic Court, Judgment No 01-1/1-16 of 17 June 2016.

[44] See Interviews with the Chairperson of the CIS Economic Court Lyudmila Kamenkova on Kazakhstan, Kyrgyzstan, and Tajikistan: 'Deiatel'nost' Ekonomicheskogo Suda SNG v kontekste vostrebovannosti reshenii dlia Respubliki Kazahstan' ['CIS Economic Court's Activity in the Context of Relevance of its Judgments for the Republic of Kazakhstan'] (2013) 11(148) Zanger [Lawyer] 43, 45; 'Deiatel'nost' Ekonomicheskogo Suda SNG v kontekste vostrebovannosti resheniy dlia Kyrgyzskoi Respubliki' ['CIS Economic Court's Activity in the Context of Relevance of its Judgments for the Kyrgyz Republic'] (2013) 2(57) Kyrgyz Respublikasynyn Jogorku Sotunun Biulleteni [Bulletin of the Supreme Court of the Kyrgyz Republic] 113, 116–17; and 'Deiatel'nost' Ekonomicheskogo Suda SNG v kontekste vostrebovannosti reshenii dlia Respubliki Tajikistan' ['CIS Economic Court's Activity in the Context of Relevance of its Judgments for the Kyrgyz Republic'] (2013) 1 Hayot va Konun [Life and Law] 90, 94–5.

[45] See Law of the Republic of Kazakhstan 'On Pension Security in the Republic of Kazakhstan' No 105-V of 21 June 2013 (amended 1 January 2018) referring to the Judgments of the CIS Economic Court No 01-1/3-16 of 21 March 2017 and No 01-1/4-16 of 3 April 2017. See also Lyudmila Kamenkova, 'Ekonomicheskii Sud SNG kak garant obespecheniia principa dostupnosti mezhdunarodnogo pravosudiia na prostranstve Sodruzhestva' ['The CIS Economic Court as a Guarantor of the Principle of Access to International Justice in the Commonwealth'] in Tatyana Mikhaleva (ed), *Mezhdunarodnoe pravosudie v XXI veke [International Justice in the XXI century]* (Businesofset 2016) 169, citing judgments of Kazakhstani courts containing references to the acts of the CIS Economic Court.

[46] Bilder (n 32) 150 ('impartial adjudication is widely seen as symbolizing the international rule of law, and a nation's willingness to submit a dispute to judicial settlement is generally taken as the test of its respect for and commitment to international law').

3.2 Regional Economic Integration

From the early 1990s, some Central Asian states attempted economic integration projects together with other CIS states. A cautious approach towards any organization with potentially supranational powers prevented many projects from realizing their full potential.[47] Thus, a multilateral free trade regime within the CIS never materialized. Instead, a free trade regime operated through a series of bilateral agreements.

The first specialized economic integration organization was EurAsEC (2000–14), formed to promote the establishment of the Customs Union and the Single Economic Area.[48] Kazakhstan, Kyrgyzstan, Tajikistan and Uzbekistan (2006–8) participated alongside Russia and Belarus.

Kazakhstan, Russia, and Belarus first initiated the establishment of the EurAsEC Customs Union (and later the Single Economic Area) and the creation of an organ with the power to adopt binding decisions, namely the Commission of the Customs Union. Under the agreements concluded by the three states, other EurAsEC members could only join the Customs Union by accepting a series of treaties as a package, with no reservations allowed. This inflexibility was cited by Uzbekistan as one of the reasons for suspending its membership in EurAsEC in 2008.[49]

The issue inevitably arose of the place of the decisions of the Commission of the Customs Union in domestic legal orders.[50] The Constitutional Council of the Republic of Kazakhstan ruled on the status of the decisions of the Commission in Kazakhstani law.[51] It held that because the treaty establishing the Commission and providing for the binding effect of its decisions had been ratified by Kazakhstan, Kazakhstan had to accord priority to both the treaty and the decisions of the Commission over its domestic laws, by virtue of its constitutional provision on the precedence of ratified

[47] For an overview of these projects see Zhenis Kembayev, 'Regional Integration in Eurasia: The Legal and Political Framework' (2016) 41(2) Review of Central and East European Law 157.

[48] Previously, a number of agreements were concluded within the CIS, but no international organization was established. The structure of the EurAsEC included the Interstate Council, the Integration Committee and its Secretariat, the Inter-Parliamentary Assembly, the Commission of Permanent Representatives, and the Court of the EurAsEC.

[49] Sergey Blagov, 'Uzbekistan priostanavlivaiet chlenstvo v EvrAzES' ['Uzbekistan Suspends its Membership in the EurAsEC'] [2008] 1(11) Mosty [Bridges] 22. Referring to the official letter of President Islam Karimov to the EurAsEC Integration Committee. The other reason cited was the ineffectiveness of the EurAsEC with much of its activity overlapping with the activity of the CIS and the CSTO.

[50] The Commission of the Customs Union of the EurAsEC operated in 2007–12. Its functions included implementing the decisions of the Interstate Council, monitoring compliance with and ensuring implementation of treaties of the Customs Union, among others. It was succeeded by the Eurasian Economic Commission.

[51] The application was filed by the Prime Minister in relation to the review by the Government of the means of implementing the decisions of the Commission of the Customs Union binding upon Kazakhstan under the Treaty on the Commission of the Customs Union (adopted 6 October 2007).

treaties over domestic laws.[52] At the same time, to have binding effect and to take precedence over domestic laws, the decisions of international organizations and their organs should be consistent with the Constitution. In particular, they have to be consistent with the constitutional guarantees of sovereignty of the Republic over its whole territory, a unitary state, territorial integrity, the established form of government,[53] and human rights and freedoms.[54]

On 1 January 2015, the structure of the Single Economic Area was transformed into that of the EAEU, including the: Higher Eurasian Economic Council, Intergovernmental Council, Eurasian Economic Commission, and Court of the Eurasian Economic Union (EAEU Court). The membership expanded to include Kyrgyzstan and Armenia. The EurAsEC officially ceased to exist.

The two coexisting regional organizations, namely the CIS and the EAEU, have distinct objectives, memberships, and institutional structures, and they develop distinct bodies of law, including their constitutive documents, treaties adopted within the organizations, and acts of the organs of the organizations. The CIS Economic Court and the EAEU Court ensure the uniform interpretation and application of CIS law and EAEU law respectively. Each court has its own constitutive documents defining its unique composition, jurisdiction, applicable law, and so on.

The EAEU Court resolves interstate disputes under EAEU law upon applications from member states, and reviews applications from states and business entities contesting the legality of decisions, as well as actions and failures to act by the Eurasian Economic Commission. The EAEU Court also interprets EAEU treaties. The EAEU Court operates as the Chamber, the Appeals Chamber, and the Grand Chamber.[55]

Kazakhstan and Kyrgyzstan have been subjects of applications before the EAEU Court. In one such case the Grand Chamber issued an advisory opinion upon an application from the Ministry of Transport and Roads of Kyrgyzstan.[56] The reason for bringing the matter before the Court was different interpretations and applications of the Protocol on the Coordinated (Concerted) Transport Policy by the Ministry of Transport and Roads of the Kyrgyz Republic on the one side and the Transport Committee of the Ministry of Investments and Development of the Republic of Kazakhstan on the other. In particular, Kyrgyzstan objected to the application of transit (and not unified) tariffs to transportation from its northern to its southern regions through the territories of Kazakhstan and Uzbekistan. The Grand Chamber held that the Protocol indeed required the use of unified tariffs, *inter alia*, in the case of cargo rail

[52] Normative Resolution of the Constitutional Council of the Republic of Kazakhstan No 6 of 5 November 2009 'On the Official Interpretation of Norms of Article 4 of the Constitution of the Republic of Kazakhstan as Applicable to the Procedure of Implementation of Decisions of International Organizations and their Bodies', para 4 of the reasoning part.

[53] Ibid. para 2 of the operative part.

[54] Ibid. para 4 of the operative part.

[55] The Grand Chamber is composed of all judges of the Eurasian Economic Court. It hears cases upon applications from the member states, renders advisory opinions, and decides on the important procedural issues.

[56] EAEU Court, Advisory Opinion of 20 November 2017.

transportation between the territories of a member state with the involvement of railways of another member state. Kazakhstan implemented the advisory opinion shortly after it was issued.

The participation of Kazakhstan and Kyrgyzstan in the EAEU in no way compromises their sovereignty. Kazakhstan has stressed that it agrees only to economic, not political, integration. The EAEU as a regional economic integration organization lacks true supranationality, and this is reflected in its institutional design.[57] Organs of constitutional control serve as the 'gatekeepers' of domestic enforcement of binding EAEU law.

As can be seen from the above examples, while promoting their economic interests through participation in regional economic organizations, Central Asian states make sure they protect their sovereignty. They do this by 'exit' (*de jure* exit or de facto withdrawal from the operation of a given organization) or by 'voice',[58] namely, through shaping the institutional design and operation of the organizations and ensuring constitutional supremacy in relation to the binding acts of international organizations and their organs.

4 Status of International Law in Domestic Law

Until the late 1980s, Central Asian republics held a dualist view by treating international and national law as two separate legal systems. The doctrine of transformation required any norm of international law to be transformed into the national legal system

[57] Member states (through the Higher Eurasian Economic Council and the Intergovernmental Council) retain a high degree of control over what becomes EAEU law. There is no common legislative body in the EAEU (unlike previously in the EurAsEC). The Eurasian Economic Commission does not have a power to challenge member states' non-compliance with the EAEU law in the EAEU Court, whereas the EAEU member states have a right of veto over the Commission's decisions. The EAEU Court does not have a power to issue preliminary rulings or advisory opinions upon applications from national courts (both of which were possible in the EurAsEC Court). For more evidence see Zhenis Kembayev, 'Eurasian Economic Union (EAEU)', Max Planck Encyclopedia of Public International Law <http://opil.ouplaw.com> accessed 17 April 2018; Roman Petrov and Paul Kalinichenko, 'On Similarities and Differences of the European Union and Eurasian Economic Union Legal Orders: Is There the "Eurasian Economic Union *Acquis*"?' (2016) 43(3) Legal Issues of Economic Integration 295. See also Zhenis Kembayev, 'Sravnitel'no-pravovoi analiz funkcionirovaniia Suda Evraziiskogo Ekonomicheskogo Soiuza' ['Comparative Legal Analysis of the Operation of the Court of the Eurasian Economic Union'] (2016) 2(18) Mezhdunarodnoye pravosudiye [International Justice] 30.

[58] To use the terms proposed in Albert Hirschman, *Exit, Voice, and Loyalty: Responses to Decline in Firms, Organizations, and States* (Harvard University Press 1970).

through a legislative act. A substantial *domaine réservé* left a limited scope of regulation to international law.[59]

The legal systems of Central Asian states formed after 1991 have been oriented towards norms and principles of international law.[60] This is supported, in particular, by the texts of their constitutions.[61] The constitutions of Kazakhstan, Kyrgyzstan, and Tajikistan include explicit provisions on the status of international law in their domestic legal systems.

According to article 4(1) of the Constitution of Kazakhstan 1995, the provisions of the Constitution, the laws corresponding to it, other regulatory legal acts, international treaties, and other international commitments of the Republic, as well as normative resolutions of the Constitutional Council and the Supreme Court, are the functioning law in the Republic of Kazakhstan. Treaties ratified by Kazakhstan take precedence over domestic laws. The procedure and conditions whereby treaties to which Kazakhstan is a party are applied in its territory are determined by domestic law (Constitution of Kazakhstan 1995, article 4(3)).

In Kyrgyzstan, treaties to which the Kyrgyz Republic is a party that have entered into force under the established legal procedure, as well as universally recognized principles and norms of international law, are constituent parts of the legal system. The procedure and conditions for their application are determined by domestic laws (Constitution of Kyrgyzstan 2010, article 6(3)).

In Tajikistan, international legal acts recognized by Tajikistan are a constituent part of its legal system. In the case of a discrepancy between domestic laws and recognized international legal acts, the norms of the international legal acts are applied (Constitution of Tajikistan 1994, article 10).

As can be seen, the provisions refer not merely to treaties, but also to 'other international commitments' (Kazakhstan), 'universally recognized principles and norms of international law' (Kyrgyzstan), and 'international legal acts' (Tajikistan); this could be interpreted as treating international customary law as part of their national legal systems.[62] Because the constitutions of Kazakhstan, Kyrgyzstan, and

[59] Vyacheslav Gavrilov, *Poniatie i vzaimodeistvie mezhdunarodnoi i nacional'nyh pravovyh sistem: monografiia [The Concept and Interaction of International and Domestic Legal Systems: A Monograph]* (2nd edn Infra-M 2018) 8.

[60] Yerbol Abaydeldinov, *Sootnoshenie mezhdunarodnogo i nacional'nogo prava Respubliki Kazahstan (problemy stanovleniia prioritetnosti) [The Relationship between International Law and National Law of the Republic of Kazakhstan (Challenges of Establishing Priority)]* (Yuridicheskaya literatura 2006) 139.

[61] Constitutions in force at the time of writing are: Constitution of the Republic of Kazakhstan 1995 (last amended 10 March 2017); Constitution of the Kyrgyz Republic 2010 (last amended 28 December 2016); Constitution of the Republic of Tajikistan 1994 (last amended 22 May 2016); Constitution of Turkmenistan 2016; Constitution of the Republic of Uzbekistan 1992 (last amended 29 August 2017).

[62] See Constitution of Kazakhstan 1995 art. 4(1); Constitution of Kyrgyzstan 2010 art. 6(3); Constitution of Tajikistan 1994 art. 10. The Constitutional Council of Kazakhstan has not yet interpreted the relevant provision as including international customary law, but such a possibility exists and is considered desirable by some authors. See Sagyngali Aydarbayev, 'Mesto mezhdunarodnyh obychaev v pravovoi sisteme Respubliki Kazahstan: konstitucionnye osnovy' ['The Place of International Custom

Tajikistan consider international law a part of domestic law, these constitutions may be characterized as monist.[63]

A clause to the effect that the procedure and conditions of application of international law are defined by domestic laws is a novelty in both the Constitutions of Kyrgyzstan (since 2016) and Kazakhstan (since 2017).[64] These are unusual additions to the clauses on international law being a part of the domestic legal system,[65] although the domestic legal orders still determine how domestic effect is given to international obligations.[66] In the Kyrgyzstan's Constitution, the new provision replaced a clause on direct applicability of human rights treaties and on their precedence over other treaties. Its introduction was part of a political backlash against a decision of the UN Human Rights Committee (HRC) in a high-profile case against Kyrgyzstan.[67] Some observers have interpreted the amendment in Kyrgyzstan as being the evidence of a dualistic turn.[68] In contrast, in Kazakhstan, the new provision substituted a general presumption of direct application of treaties. The amendment affirms state autonomy with regard to the means of treaty implementation and reflects the absence of a general duty to directly apply treaties. The effect of the amendments will be clarified by practice, including that of national courts.

The constitutions of Uzbekistan and Turkmenistan, while recognizing its importance, do not explicitly define the place of international law in their domestic legal systems. In particular, the preamble of the Constitution of Uzbekistan recognizes the priority of the universally recognized norms of international law, whereas the Constitution of Turkmenistan does so in an article on foreign policy.[69] Uzbekistan recognizes the 'soft priority' of the 'universally recognized principles and standards in

in the Legal System of the Republic of Kazakhstan: The Constitutional Framework'] in Alexander Trunk, Azar Aliyev, and Marina Trunk-Fyodorova (eds), *Mezhdunarodnoe torgovoe pravo v gosudarstvah Kavkaza, Central'noi Azii i v Rossii: mezhdu regional'noi integraciei i globalizaciei [International Trade Law in the Caucasus, Central Asia, and Russia: Between Regional Integration and Globalization]* (Statut 2016) 84. The Constitution of Tajikistan consistently refers to the 'international legal acts recognized by Tajikistan'. This term has been interpreted by some commentators as including international customary law recognized by Tajikistan. See Ilhom Kamolov, 'Poniatie mezhdunarodno-pravovyh aktov v pravovoi sisteme Respubliki Tajikistan' ['The Concept of International Legal Acts in the Legal System of the Republic of Tajikistan'] (2014) 2 Probely v rossiiskom zakonodatel'stve [Lacunae in Russian Legislation] 65, 66–7.

[63] See David Feldman, 'Monism, Dualism and Constitutional Legitimacy' (1999) 20 Australian Yearbook of International Law 105, 113.

[64] Constitution of Kyrgyzstan 2010 art. 6(3) second sentence; Constitution of Kazakhstan 1995 art. 4(3) second sentence.

[65] Constitution of Kyrgyzstan 2010 art. 6(3) first sentence; Constitution of Kazakhstan 1995 art. 4(3) first sentence.

[66] Mario Mendez, *The Legal Effects of EU Agreements* (OUP 2013) 2.

[67] *Askarov v Kyrgyzstan*, HRC Communication No 2231/2012, Views, 11 May 2016, UN Doc CCPR/C/116/D/2231/2012.

[68] The European Commission for Democracy through Law and the OSCE Office for Democratic Institutions and Human Rights, 'Kyrgyz Republic. Joint Opinion on the Draft Law "On Introduction of Amendments and Changes to the Constitution"' (19 October 2016) CDL-AD(2016)025 para 42.

[69] See Constitution of Uzbekistan 1992 preamble; Constitution of Turkmenistan 2016 art. 9.

national legislation'.[70] In practice, Uzbekistan requires an act of transformation for international treaties to be domestically applied:

> The country's legal system recognizes the precedence of international law over national law. At the same time, an international treaty, for purposes of its enforcement, must be implemented in national laws. After implementation, the norms of international law become part of domestic law and are binding.[71]

The CIS Economic Court has developed a doctrine of direct applicability of treaties based on international legal doctrine, as well as on the laws and practice of the CIS states, including Central Asian states. The Court defines direct application of treaties as:

> compliance with, implementation and use by the subjects of domestic law (state bodies, public officials, individuals and organizations) of the legal norms contained in international treaties, as well as providing domestic legal (including judicial) guarantees for these legal norms.[72]

According to the CIS Economic Court, *from the standpoint of international law*, the possibility of direct application exists where treaty norms are simultaneously: (a) designed to be applied by the subjects of domestic law; (b) clearly and unambiguously worded; and (c) not excluded from direct application by the states parties, that is, no obligation to enact implementing legislation is envisioned.[73] *From the standpoint of domestic law*, for treaties to be directly applicable the national legal system has to allow for (or at least not explicitly exclude) direct application. In the Court's opinion, this is the case for the legal systems of the CIS states.

The CIS Economic Court at the same time held that states have an *obligation* to directly apply treaty provisions embodying peremptory norms of international law (*jus cogens*) and obligations concerning fundamental human rights and minimum standards of protection of victims of armed conflicts. With respect to other treaty norms, each state has discretion to determine the means of their implementation, which is a manifestation of sovereignty.[74] The Court stressed the obligation of states to comply with treaties, regardless of the means of implementation chosen.[75]

[70] 'Core Document Forming Part of the Reports of States Parties: Uzbekistan' HRI/CORE/UZB/2015 (8 January 2016) para 171.

[71] Ibid. para 212.

[72] CIS Economic Court, Advisory Opinion No 01-1/1-08 of 24 September 2008. Cf. in the context of the EU, the term 'direct applicability' is often used interchangeably with that of 'direct effect', which emphasizes conferral on individuals of rights which can be directly invoked and relied on before national courts. See Anca-Magda Vlaicu, 'The Direct Effect of Treaty Provisions' [2009] 16 Lex ET Scientia International Journal 235. The doctrine of direct effect was first established in Case 26/62 *Van Gend en Loos* [1963] ECR 1.

[73] See CIS Economic Court, Advisory Opinion No 01-1/1-08 of 24 September 2008.

[74] Ibid. [75] Ibid.

Thus, in the context of the CIS, 'direct applicability of treaties' emphasizes the discretion of the political branches of government to decide on the means of treaty implementation, except for cases where direct application is required. The idea that for certain treaties direct application is a matter of obligation, for both governments and domestic courts, is a development as compared to the doctrine of direct applicability in general international law.[76] The existence of an obligation to directly apply certain treaties implies a possibility of objective verification on the international plane, which the CIS Economic Court performed.[77] The CIS approach offers a middle ground between approaches where the issue of direct application is decided entirely by domestic law[78] or by international law (e.g. EU law).[79]

Regarding the hierarchical status of treaties in relation to national laws, an explicit reference to precedence of treaties in the event of conflict is contained in the Constitution of Kazakhstan (for ratified treaties) and in the Constitution of Tajikistan (for all treaties in force).[80] The Constitutions of Kyrgyzstan and Uzbekistan do not include a comparable clause, while the Constitution of Turkmenistan *no longer* includes it. In 2008–16, the Constitution of Turkmenistan, in addition to recognizing the priority of generally recognized norms of international law, provided that in the event of a treaty establishing rules different from those set out in national laws, the rules of the treaty applied.[81] A provision establishing the precedence of treaties over domestic laws is contained in the Law on International Treaties (LIT) of Turkmenistan.[82] Proposals have been made to introduce a clause in the LIT of Uzbekistan recognizing the priority

[76] The doctrine of 'direct applicability', as used in a wider international context, has been rightly criticized as having a dual effect: both as a tool for applying international law in the domestic legal system and equally (or even more so) as a means of legitimizing the non-application of international law (by setting the criteria that have to be satisfied before a treaty may be applied directly). See André Nollkaemper, 'The Duality of Direct Effect of International Law' (2014) 25 European Journal of International Law 105.

[77] See CIS Economic Court, Advisory Opinion No 01-1/1-08 of 24 September 2008. The agreements in question concerned matters of social welfare. The Court considered the responses from the competent bodies of the states parties to the agreements, such as the: Ministry of Labour and Social Welfare of Kazakhstan, Ministry of Labour and Social Development of Kyrgyzstan, Ministry of Social Security of Turkmenistan, and Ministry of Labour and Social Welfare of Uzbekistan, among others, and found that the agreements in question did not require direct application and that states were free to decide on the means of their implementation.

[78] See Karen Kaiser, 'Treaties, Direct Applicability', Max Planck Encyclopedia of Public International Law, para 6 <http://opil.ouplaw.com> accessed 17 April 2018.

[79] The two approaches are described in Yuji Iwasawa, 'The Doctrine of Self-Executing Treaties in the United States: A Critical Analysis' (1986) 26 Virginia Journal of International Law 627, 650.

[80] Constitution of Kazakhstan 1995 art. 4(3) (mentioning ratified treaties only); Resolution of the Constitutional Council of the Republic of Kazakhstan No 2 of 18 May 2006 'On the Official Interpretation of Article 54(7) of the Constitution' para 2 (clarifying that ratified treaties are equal in status to the treaties to which Kazakhstan acceded); Constitution of Tajikistan 1994 art. 10.

[81] See Constitution of Turkmenistan 1992 (amended 2008) art. 6 second sentence. This addition (which later proved to be temporary) allowed some authors to consider Turkmenistan a monist state. See e.g. Süleyman Sirri Terzioğlu, 'International Treaties in the Legal System of Turkmenistan' (2013) 4 Law and Justice Review 73, 77.

[82] Law on International Treaties of Turkmenistan 2010 art. 4. See n. 88.

of treaties over domestic laws, as well as recognizing treaties and generally accepted norms and principles of international law as a part of the domestic legal system.

In addition to, or instead of, constitutional provisions, area-specific laws may allow for the direct application of treaties and establish their precedence. For instance, the civil codes of all Central Asian states include provisions to the effect that treaties take precedence over them in the event of inconsistency. In contrast to treaties on procedural matters, treaties on substantive matters of criminal law generally do not apply directly.[83]

In conformity with international practice, constitutions of Central Asian states have the highest legal force in their domestic legal systems.[84] The status of treaties is inferior to that of constitutions.

As in most states in the world,[85] Central Asian states combine elements of dualist and monist approaches. They tend to view international and domestic law as separate, though constantly interacting, legal systems. Over time, each state develops its own unique approach towards the domestic effect of treaties, which is a matter of political decision and reflects the historical experiences of a particular state.[86]

5 Treaties

Treaty practice across Central Asian states has been extensive. Treaties form the legal basis of foreign relations, as well as of regional integration processes. All five Central Asian states have acceded to the Vienna Convention on the Law of Treaties 1969 (VCLT) without reservations.[87] To establish domestic procedures for the conclusion, operation, termination, and so forth of treaties, Central Asian states adopted LITs.[88]

[83] See e.g. Normative Resolution of the Supreme Court of the Republic of Kazakhstan No 1 of 10 July 2008 'On the Application of Norms of International Treaties of the Republic of Kazakhstan'.

[84] Constitution of Kazakhstan 1995 art. 4(2); Constitution of Kyrgyzstan 2010 art. 6(1); Constitution of Tajikistan 1994 art. 10; Constitution of Turkmenistan 2016 art. 8; Constitution of Uzbekistan 1992 art. 15.

[85] Pierre-Hugues Verdier and Mila Versteeg, 'International Law in National Legal Systems: An Empirical Investigation' (2015) 109 American Journal of International Law 514, 516.

[86] Chung, In-Seop, 'Joyag-ui gugnaebeobjeog hyoryeog-e gwanhan hangug panlyewa hagseol-ui geomto' ['An Analytic Review on Judicial Decisions and Academic Theories regarding the Domestic Legal Status of Treaties'] (2015) 22 Seoul International Law Journal 27, 57.

[87] The respective dates of accession are: 5 January 1994 (Kazakhstan); 11 May 1999 (Kyrgyzstan); 6 May 1996 (Tajikistan); 4 January 1996 (Turkmenistan); and 12 July 1995 (Uzbekistan).

[88] These laws have undergone a number of revisions. If not otherwise indicated, references are to the versions in force at the time of writing: Law of the Republic of Kazakhstan 'On the International Treaties of the Republic of Kazakhstan' No 54-III of 30 May 2005 (amended No 376-V of 29 October 2015) (LIT of Kazakhstan 2005); Law of the Kyrgyz Republic 'On the International Treaties of the Kyrgyz Republic' No 64 of 24 April 2014 (amended No 51 of 27 March 2017) (LIT of Kyrgyzstan 2014); Law of the Republic of Tajikistan 'On the International Treaties of the Republic of Tajikistan' No 1326 of 23 July 2016 (LIT of Tajikistan 2016); Law of Turkmenistan 'On the International Treaties of Turkmenistan' No 108-IV of 10 May 2010 (LIT of Turkmenistan 2010); Law of the Republic of Uzbekistan 'On the International Treaties of the Republic of Uzbekistan' No 172-1 of 22 December 1995 (amended No ЗРУ-446 of 14 September 2017) (LIT of Uzbekistan 1995).

In this process, Central Asian states relied on historical precedents, the VCLT, and similar laws adopted earlier in other states in the region.[89]

The scope of the LITs is more extensive than the VCLT in that they include treaties with international organizations.[90] The LIT of Kyrgyzstan further expands the scope to treaties with 'other subjects of international law'. Some LITs explicitly mention certain conditions for the conclusion of treaties, such as consistency with national interests, national security and independence, equality of the parties, and/or voluntary conclusion.[91]

5.1 Treaty-making

Treaty-making powers and procedures in Central Asian states are set out in constitutions, national LITs, as well as other laws and legal regulatory acts. Different procedures apply to interstate, intergovernmental, and interagency treaties.[92] The state is responsible for the good-faith observance of all treaties in force, regardless of their category. The following is an overview of treaty-making processes in Central Asian states, focusing on the interstate and intergovernmental treaties.[93]

In all Central Asian states, negotiations, drafting, and adoption of a treaty text are within the control of the executive. Negotiations, initialling, signing, and so forth are conducted on the basis of decisions on the conclusion of a treaty issued by the president (interstate treaties) or the government (intergovernmental treaties). The presidents and the governments receive *proposals* for conclusion of a treaty from state organs (in Kyrgyzstan, Tajikistan, and Uzbekistan) or the Ministry of Foreign Affairs (in Turkmenistan and Uzbekistan). In Kyrgyzstan, the Prime Minister is consulted before the proposal is submitted to the President. In Kazakhstan, ministries and other competent state bodies submit proposals to the Government, whereas the Government submits proposals for the conclusion of interstate treaties to the President. Organs directly subordinate and accountable to the President submit their proposals directly to the President or to the Government. In all states, before a proposal reaches the President or the Government, the Ministry of Foreign Affairs is consulted, whereas other ministries are consulted depending on the treaty in question. In Kyrgyzstan, the

[89] Kazakhstan and Uzbekistan in 1995 became the first Central Asian states to adopt these laws. Before that, both applied the 1978 USSR Law on the Procedure for the Conclusion, Execution and Denunciation of International Treaties. See William Butler, 'The Law of Treaties in Central Asia' in Rein Müllerson, Malgosia Fitzmaurice, and Mads Andenas (eds), *Constitutional Reform and International Law in Central and Eastern Europe* (Kluwer Law International 1998) 287.

[90] See definitions of a 'treaty' in the LIT of Kazakhstan 2005 art. 1(6); LIT of Kyrgyzstan 2014 art. 2; LIT of Tajikistan 2016 art. 2; LIT of Turkmenistan 2010 art. 2(1); LIT of Uzbekistan 1995 art. 3.

[91] LIT of Kazakhstan 2005 art. 2(2); LIT of Kyrgyzstan 2014 art. 2; LIT of Uzbekistan 1995 art. 3.

[92] In addition, the Kyrgyz LIT also mentions inter-parliamentary agreements.

[93] Procedures for the conclusion of interagency agreements, that is agreements concluded by the ministries or other competent agencies, are simplified because there is no need for their parliamentary approval. Governments play a central role in concluding treaties of this category.

Committees of the Jogorku Kenesh (Parliament) are consulted on the proposals for bilateral treaties requiring ratification and multilateral treaties requiring ratification, but prohibiting reservations. The Jogorku Kenesh and the Supreme Court may make *recommendations* concerning the conclusion of a treaty to the President or to the Prime Minister.

Following the VCLT,[94] the LITs of Central Asian states provide a list of officials who represent the state for the purpose of concluding treaties, by virtue of their functions and without them having to produce full powers. These are Presidents, Heads of Government,[95] Ministers of Foreign Affairs, as well as heads of diplomatic missions[96] and representatives accredited by states to an international conference or an international organization.[97] The President or Government (in Kyrgyzstan, Turkmenistan, and Uzbekistan) or the Ministry of Foreign Affairs (in Kazakhstan and Tajikistan) issue full powers for performing acts relating to the conclusion of treaties. In Kyrgyzstan, organs issuing full powers further differ depending on the type of act (the President or Prime Minister for negotiations; the President in consultation with the Prime Minister or the Government for initialling and signing).[98] The LIT of Turkmenistan specifically designates officials to whom the full powers may be issued for each treaty category.[99]

Decisions on expressing consent to be bound by a treaty, in the form of acceptance, approval, or accession (to treaties not requiring ratification), are made by the President or the Government (in Kazakhstan, Tajikistan, and Uzbekistan), the President (in Turkmenistan), or the Government (in Kyrgyzstan).

Parliaments ratify treaties.[100] Presidents sign ratification instruments. Proposals for ratification are submitted to the parliaments by the Government (in Kazakhstan and Kyrgyzstan), President or Government (in Tajikistan and Uzbekistan), or President (in Turkmenistan). The range of treaty categories requiring ratification has expanded over time in line with international practice.[101] Parliaments also make decisions on accession to treaties requiring ratification. Parliaments are empowered to denounce treaties which required parliamentary approval for their entry into force. Parliaments receive proposals for treaty denunciation from the presidents or the governments.

The timeframe for treaty conclusion—from the adoption of the decision on conclusion to treaty ratification by the Parliament—varies depending on the political will to conclude the treaty, the treaty type, and many other factors. For instance, in 1998,

[94] VCLT art. 7(2).

[95] In Turkmenistan, President is also the Head of the Government.

[96] For the purpose of adopting the text of a treaty between the accrediting State and the State to which they are accredited.

[97] For the purpose of adopting the text of a treaty in the conference or organization.

[98] LIT of Kyrgyzstan 2014 art. 10.

[99] LIT of Turkmenistan 2010 art. 7(2).

[100] The generic term 'parliaments' here refers to the: Parliament (Kazakhstan), Jogorku Kenesh (Supreme Council) (Kyrgyzstan), Majlisi Namoyandagon of the Majlisi Oli (House of Representatives of the Supreme Council) (Tajikistan), Mejlis (Assembly) (Turkmenistan), and Oliy Majlis (Supreme Assembly) (Uzbekistan) responsible for parliamentary approval of treaties.

[101] Verdier and Versteeg (n 85) 519.

Kyrgyzstan became the first state in the region to join the WTO. As in the case of other small open economies, the process of its accession did not take long. After the decision to join was made by the President and the Government in 1995, within less than three years the negotiations were completed and the Protocol of accession was signed and ratified. By comparison, for Kazakhstan and Tajikistan the process of accession to the WTO took twenty and eleven years respectively, while for Uzbekistan, which applied for accession in 1994 (before all of its neighbours), the negotiations are still underway. On the other hand, in the case of the Paris Agreement 2015 concluded within the UN Framework Convention on Climate Change, Kyrgyzstan has taken the longest time to ratify it compared to all of its Central Asian neighbours, which are already parties to it, and the timeframe for ratification is not clear.

5.2 The Treaty on a Nuclear-Weapon-Free Zone in Central Asia

To illustrate treaty-making practice, this section looks at the conclusion by the Central Asian states of the Treaty on a Nuclear-Weapon-Free Zone in Central Asia.[102] Since independence, Central Asian states have adopted peaceful foreign policies and have advocated non-military solutions to international and regional conflicts. An important pillar of their striving for global peace and security has been consistent support for nuclear disarmament and non-proliferation. In particular, Kazakhstan, after closing down in 1991 the Semipalatinsk nuclear test site located in its territory, also voluntarily renounced the nuclear arsenal it inherited. Central Asian states acceded to the Treaty on the Non-Proliferation of Nuclear Weapons 1968 (NPT) as non-nuclear-weapon states.[103] As a means of implementing the NPT,[104] Central Asian states initiated the conclusion of a treaty on a nuclear-weapon-free zone in Central Asia (Treaty on CANWFZ).

The decision to establish the CANWFZ was made jointly by the heads of Central Asian states.[105] This was an act of political will based on common concerns over environmental issues related to the history of production and testing of nuclear weapons in the region.[106] A series of multipartite negotiations were held with the direct

[102] Treaty on a Nuclear-Weapon-Free Zone in Central Asia (concluded 8 September 2006, entered into force 21 March 2009, 2970 UNTS) (Treaty on CANFWZ).

[103] Treaty on the Non-proliferation of Nuclear Weapons (opened for signature 1 July 1968, entered into force 5 March 1970, 729 UNTS 161). The respective years of accession of Central Asian states to the NPT are: 1992 (Uzbekistan), 1994 (Kazakhstan, Kyrgyzstan, and Turkmenistan), and 1995 (Tajikistan).

[104] NPT art. VII.

[105] See the Almaty Declaration of 28 February 1997 adopted at the Summit of the heads of Central Asian states.

[106] Scott Parrish, 'Prospects for a Central Asian Nuclear-Weapon-Free Zone' (Spring 2001) The Nonproliferation Review 141, 142.

involvement and under the auspices of the UN.[107] The final text of the treaty takes into account the specifics of the region, relies on historical precedents,[108] and reflects recommendations of international organizations and nuclear-weapon states. The treaty was signed in 2006 and entered into force in 2009 after ratification by all Central Asian states. China, Russia, France, and the UK, as nuclear-weapon states, ratified a Protocol to the Treaty on CANWFZ in 2014, providing the Central Asian states with negative security guarantees.[109]

The treaty prohibits the research, development, manufacture, stockpiling, acquisition, possession, or testing of, or having control over, any nuclear weapon or other nuclear explosive device. States are obliged not to allow any nuclear-weapon related activity in their territories. The two provisions that were most controversial among both the Central Asian states and some nuclear-weapon states are (1) a provision allowing Central Asian states a discretion with respect to transit through their territory, and (2) a provision stipulating that the treaty does not affect the rights and obligations of states under the pre-existing treaties.[110]

The Treaty on CANWFZ is currently the only one of its kind requiring states parties to fully comply with the Comprehensive Nuclear-Test-Ban Treaty 1996 (CTBT),[111] and to conclude with the International Atomic Energy Agency (IAEA) the Safeguards Agreement and the Additional Protocol to it.[112] The parties also agree to maintain physical protection of nuclear material, facilities, and equipment that is at least as effective as those called for by the Convention on Physical Protection of Nuclear

[107] The UN actively assisted in the drafting of the treaty and the negotiations process. For instance, the UN Regional Center for Peace and Disarmament in Asia and the Pacific arranged the establishment of a group of experts, including experts from the region, and sponsored a series of expert group meetings. It also organized meetings between the Central Asian states and the nuclear-weapon states. The UN Department for Disarmament Affairs and the UN Office for Legal Affairs provided recommendations concerning the drafts of the treaty. The UN General Assembly endorsed the establishment of the nuclear-weapon-free zone in Central Asia in a number of resolutions over the time of negotiations and after the conclusion of the treaty. In the course of treaty negotiations assistance was also provided by the International Atomic Energy Agency (IAEA) and the Center for Non-proliferation Studies (CNS) of the Monterey Institute of International Studies (a non-governmental research institution). For a detailed account of treaty negotiations see Tsutomu Ishiguri, 'The Central Asian Nuclear Weapon Free Zone: Lessons Learned for the Helsinki Process' (2014) 41 Policy Brief for the Middle East Conference on a WMD/DVs Free Zone 1, 7-8; see also Nuriya Kutnayeva, 'Perspectivy zakliucheniia Dogovora o sozdanii v Central'noi Azii zony, svobodnoi ot iadernogo oruzhiia' ['Prospects for the Conclusion of a Treaty on a Nuclear-Weapon-Free Zone in Central Asia'] (2006) 1 (79) vol 12 Iadernii kontrol [Nuclear Control] 59.

[108] Namely, treaties on the nuclear-weapon-free zones in Latin America and the Caribbean (Treaty of Tlatelolco 1967), in the South Pacific (Treaty of Rarotonga 1985), in Southeast Asia (Treaty of Bangkok 1995), and in Africa (Treaty of Pelindaba 1996).

[109] Meaning guarantees to neither use, nor threaten to use, nuclear weapons against Central Asian states. The US has signed but has not yet ratified the Protocol 2014.

[110] For a detailed explanation see Ishiguri, 'Lessons for the Helsinki Process' (n 107) 1.

[111] Comprehensive Nuclear-Test-Ban Treaty (adopted by UNGA res 50/245 (10 September 1996)).

[112] See IAEA, INFCIRC/66/Rev.2 and IAEA, INFCIRC/540 (Corr). In fact, it is the first treaty on a nuclear-weapon-free zone concluded after the CTBT was opened for signature and after the Additional Protocol to the Safeguards Agreement with the IAEA was introduced.

Material 1987 and by the recommendations and guidelines developed by the IAEA for physical protection.[113]

The Treaty of CANWFZ represents Central Asian states' contribution to the cause of non-proliferation and to the development of international law on nuclear-weapon-free zones. As such, it may serve as a model for future agreements on nuclear-weapon-free zones, including one in the Middle East.[114]

5.3 Compliance

Central Asian states have established legal and institutional frameworks to ensure compliance with their international obligations. In addition to constitutional guarantees of respect for international law and incorporation of the principle of *pacta sunt servanda* into national LITs,[115] national laws provide specific guarantees of treaty compliance.

Central Asian states have set up procedures for the constitutional review of treaties by the organs of constitutional control.[116] Prior to treaty conclusion, the Ministries of Justice verify the consistency of (draft) treaties with domestic legislation, through a procedure of compulsory legal expert examination.[117] Treaties requiring the amendment of existing laws or enactment of new laws, and/or treaties setting out rules different from those prescribed by domestic laws, are among those requiring ratification in all Central Asian states.[118] Where inconsistencies of a proposed treaty with a domestic law are identified, or the treaty requires enactment of a domestic law, states enact the requisite legislative changes.[119] In cases where amending domestic laws is

[113] Treaty on CANWFZ art. 9.

[114] Ishiguri, 'Lessons for the Helsinki Process' (n 107) 1.

[115] See VCLT art. 26; LIT of Kazakhstan 2005 art. 20(1); LIT of Kyrgyzstan 2014 art. 31(1); LIT of Tajikistan 2016 art. 18(1); LIT of Turkmenistan 2010 art. 17(1); and LIT of Uzbekistan 1995 art. 27.

[116] The competence to review constitutionality of treaties rests with the: Constitutional Council of Kazakhstan; Constitutional Chamber of the Supreme Court of the Kyrgyz Republic; Constitutional Court of Tajikistan; and Constitutional Court of Uzbekistan. Turkmenistan does not have a specialized organ of constitutional control.

[117] The modalities of legal expert examination of treaties differ across Central Asian states. See LIT of Kazakhstan 2005 art. 3(1). Treaties requiring ratification in Kazakhstan in addition to legal expert examination by the Ministry of Justice also require academic legal expert examination. See ibid. art. 4. See also: LIT of Kyrgyzstan 2014 art. 6(5)(4); LIT of Tajikistan 2016 arts 4(3) and 5(5); LIT of Turkmenistan 2010 art. 5(3); LIT of Uzbekistan 1995 art. 8.

[118] LIT of Kazakhstan 2005 art. 11(2); LIT of Kyrgyzstan 2014 art. 11(1)(14); LIT of Tajikistan 2016 art. 11; LIT of Turkmenistan 2010 art. 11(1)(e); LIT of Uzbekistan 1995 art. 14.

[119] See LIT of Kazakhstan 2005 art. 22(1); LIT of Kyrgyzstan 2014 art. 20; LIT of Tajikistan 2016 art. 5(5); LIT of Turkmenistan 2010 art. 22; and LIT of Uzbekistan 1995 art. 2. In addition, in Kazakhstan, legislative amendments introduced on the basis of a treaty are themselves guaranteed against amendments or repeal so long as the treaty remains in force for Kazakhstan. See LIT of Kazakhstan 2005 art. 22(2).

impracticable, states may formulate reservations upon signing or expressing consent to be bound by a treaty.[120]

After signing the International Covenant on Civil and Political Rights 1966 (ICCPR) in 2002,[121] Kazakhstan contemplated making a reservation upon ratification to a provision inconsistent with its Constitution.[122] In the domestic debates, one view was that it was necessary to formulate a reservation to make the law on ratification constitutional and to maintain the specifics of the national legal system. It was noted that many other states had formulated reservations to the ICCPR.[123] The opposite view was that ratifying without reservations would create momentum for legislative changes to comply with the minimum human rights standards set out in the ICCPR, and would reassure the world community of Kazakhstan's consistent course towards democratic reforms and human rights.[124]

Eventually, Kazakhstan ratified the ICCPR without reservations and made the necessary amendments to ensure compliance. The example illustrates the considerations involved in decision-making on treaties, such as promoting the values enshrined in a treaty, ensuring compliance with international obligations once undertaken, exploring the flexibility mechanisms offered by international law, preserving the specifics of the national legal system, and promoting a positive image of the state to the world, among others.

Guarantees of compliance after a treaty's entry into force for the state include compulsory publication of treaties in official sources,[125] designation of state organs responsible for treaty compliance (including presidents, governments, and other state agencies), and procedures for devising and implementing the necessary domestic measures to ensure compliance.[126] Ministries of Foreign Affairs perform general supervision over treaty compliance.[127]

[120] LIT of Kazakhstan 2005 art. 19; LIT of Kyrgyzstan 2014 art. 25; LIT of Tajikistan 2016 arts 5(5) and 17; LIT of Uzbekistan 1995 art. 24. LIT of Turkmenistan does not include a comparable provision.

[121] International Covenant on Civil and Political Rights (adopted 16 December 1966, entered into force 23 March 1976, 999 UNTS 171).

[122] Sanctioning of arrest was an exclusive prerogative of national courts according to the ICCPR, art. 9(3), while in Kazakhstan it could be carried out by public prosecutors under art. 16(2) of the Constitution.

[123] Prosecutor-General's Office in particular supported the idea of ratifying the ICCPR with a reservation. See Roza Dossymbekova, 'Zharkie diskussii v Mazhilise vyzval zakonoproekt RK "O ratifikacii Mezhdunarodnogo Pakta o grazhdanskih i politicheskih pravah"' ['Bill on the Ratification of International Covenant on Civil and Political Rights Evokes Hot Arguments in Majilis'] (part 2) (18 October 2005) <http://zakon.kz/65489-zharkie-diskussii-v-mazhilise-vyzval.html> accessed 17 April 2018.

[124] The opponents of reservations included the Ombudsman, the Supreme Court judges and members of Parliament. See Vladimir Kuryatov, 'Zharkie diskussii v Mazhilise vyzval zakonoproekt RK "O ratifikacii Mezhdunarodnogo Pakta o grazhdanskih i politicheskih pravah"' ['Bill on the Ratification of International Covenant on Civil and Political Rights Evokes Hot Arguments in Majilis'] (part 1) (18 October 2005) <http://zakon.kz/65489-zharkie-diskussii-v-mazhilise-vyzval.html> accessed 17 April 2018.

[125] See Constitution of Kazakhstan 1995 art. 4(4), LIT of Kazakhstan 2005 art. 24; LIT of Kyrgyzstan 2014 art. 26; LIT of Tajikistan 2016 art. 21; LIT of Turkmenistan 2010 art. 24; LIT of Uzbekistan 1995 art. 25.

[126] See LIT of Kazakhstan 2005 art. 20(3) and (4); LIT of Kyrgyzstan 2014 art. 32(2)–(5); LIT of Tajikistan 2016 art. 18(2) and (3); LIT of Turkmenistan 2010, arts 18 and 19; LIT of Uzbekistan 1995 art. 28.

[127] LIT of Kazakhstan 2005 art. 20(5); LIT of Kyrgyzstan 2014 art. 34; LIT of Tajikistan 2016 art. 18(4); LIT of Turkmenistan 2010 art. 20; LIT of Uzbekistan 1995 art. 29.

An important guarantee of treaty compliance is the judicial application of treaties.[128] Courts in some Central Asian states have, over time, developed a trend of citing treaties in their judgments. For instance, organs of constitutional control rely on international human rights standards to support their reasoning.[129] The practice of the Constitutional Council of Kazakhstan, the Constitutional Chamber of the Supreme Court of Kyrgyzstan, and the Constitutional Court of Tajikistan offer examples of this.[130]

For instance, the Constitutional Court of Tajikistan verified the constitutionality (namely, consistency with the principle of gender equality) of a provision of the Family Code prohibiting granting a unilateral request for divorce by a man throughout his wife's pregnancy and until the child is at least one-and-a-half years old. The Constitutional Court established that the laws of Tajikistan, based upon the Constitution, international legal acts, and cultural traditions of Tajikistan, ensured special protection for pregnant women, nursing mothers, and infants in accordance with international standards. The Court therefore confirmed the constitutionality of the legislative provision.[131]

Courts of general jurisdiction had been reluctant to apply treaties until they were specifically authorized to do so by the higher courts. In Kazakhstan and Tajikistan, Supreme Courts have issued special rulings (binding upon lower courts) which require courts to be guided by treaties and have specified the modalities of treaty application by national courts.[132] In Kyrgyzstan, a Resolution of the Plenum of the Supreme Court instructed courts when deciding civil cases to rely upon treaties, along with the laws and legal regulatory acts of Kyrgyzstan.[133] In recent years, the instances of Kazakhstani courts citing treaties in their judgments have grown exponentially and have also expanded from civil cases only to civil, criminal, and administrative cases. In many

[128] David Sloss, 'Treaty Enforcement in Domestic Courts: A Comparative Analysis' in David Sloss (ed), *The Role of Domestic Courts in Treaty Enforcement: A Comparative Study* (CUP 2009) 5.

[129] For early examples of references to the Universal Declaration of Human Rights 1948 (UDHR) and the ICCPR by the Constitutional Court of Kazakhstan (which operated in 1992–1995 and was replaced by the Constitutional Council) see Gennady Danilenko, 'Implementation of International Law in CIS States: Theory and Practice' (1999) 10 European Journal of International Law 51, 59, n 25.

[130] See e.g. Constitutional Council of the Republic of Kazakhstan, Normative Resolution No 2 of 27 February 2008; Constitutional Chamber of the Supreme Court of the Kyrgyz Republic, Judgment No 8-P of 6 November 2013; Constitutional Court of the Republic of Tajikistan, Judgment of 1 July 2009. All three acts cited, *inter alia*, the UDHR and the ICCPR. In addition, Judgment of the Constitutional Court of Tajikistan relied upon the International Convention on the Rights of the Child 1989 and the International Covenant on Economic, Social and Cultural Rights 1966, while the Resolution of the Constitutional Council of Kazakhstan cited the Basic Principles for the Treatment of Prisoners (adopted by UNGA res 45/111 of 14 December 1990) and Declaration on the Protection of all Persons from Being Subjected to Torture and Other Cruel, Inhuman or Degrading Treatment or Punishment (adopted by UNGA res 3452 (XXX) of 9 December 1975).

[131] See Constitutional Court of the Republic of Tajikistan, Judgment of 1 July 2009. The Judgment was issued upon an application from a regional court.

[132] Normative Resolution of the Supreme Court of the Republic of Kazakhstan No 1 of 10 July 2008 (amended 30 December 2011) 'On the Application of Norms of International Treaties of the Republic of Kazakhstan'; Resolution of the Plenum of the Supreme Court of Republic of Tajikistan No 9 of 18 November 2013 'On the Application of International Legal Acts Recognized by Tajikistan'.

[133] Resolution of the Plenum of the Supreme Court of the Kyrgyz Republic No 16 of 12 June 2008 'On a Court's Judgment' para 3.

instances, courts cite the provisions of treaties along with the analogous provisions of domestic legal acts.

In Uzbekistan, so far '[d]irectly citing a given international treaty is not standard practice among the judicial bodies . . . and is extremely rare'.[134] No evidence is available of Turkmenistan's courts directly citing treaties in their judgments. Courts in Uzbekistan and Turkmenistan, however, apply treaties indirectly by applying national legal acts that incorporate treaty provisions.[135] For Uzbekistan, the indirect application of treaties by national courts is evidenced by the fact that the Plenum of the Supreme Court makes references to treaties in some of its resolutions.

The fact that a practice of directly citing treaties by national courts exists in some Central Asian states, but not in others, may be in part attributed to the differences in the constitutional status of treaties. At the same time, the Supreme Courts in Kazakhstan, Tajikistan, and Kyrgyzstan have induced this practice by setting the stage for higher courts to reverse judgments of lower courts where the latter incorrectly apply or fail to apply applicable treaties.

5.4 UN Human Rights Treaties

Central Asian states' constitutions incorporate the international human rights standards reflected in the Universal Declaration on Human Rights 1948 (UDHR),[136] ICCPR 1966, International Covenant on Economic, Social and Cultural Rights 1966,[137] and Helsinki Final Act 1975,[138] among others.

Having become parties to the majority of the core human rights treaties,[139] states have implemented them in national legislation and taken other measures to comply with their obligations. All Central Asian states have set up national human rights institutions applying international standards.[140] These bodies review individual complaints and issue recommendations to state organs. So far, none of these bodies has

[134] Core Document: Uzbekistan (n 70) para 212.

[135] It has been suggested that active indirect treaty enforcement by national courts may be as effective as direct enforcement. See Sloss (n 128) 3.

[136] Universal Declaration of Human Rights (adopted by UNGA res 217 A (III) (10 December 1948)).

[137] International Covenant on Economic, Social and Cultural Rights (adopted 16 December 1966, entered into force 3 January 1976, 993 UNTS 3).

[138] Final Act of the Conference on Security and Co-Operation in Europe (adopted 1 August 1975).

[139] At the time of writing, out of 18 international human rights treaties in the UN OHCHR database, Central Asian states were parties to 13 (Kazakhstan), 13 (Kyrgyzstan), 11 (Tajikistan), 13 (Turkmenistan), and 10 (Uzbekistan). This put all of them in the second-most prolific group (out of four groups of states ranging from high to low levels of accession). See OHCHR, 'Status of Ratification: Interactive Dashboard' <http://indicators.ohchr.org> accessed 17 April 2018.

[140] Commissioner for Human Rights (National Ombudsman) (Kazakhstan); Ombudsman of the Kyrgyz Republic (Kyrgyzstan); Human Rights Ombudsman (Tajikistan); Human Rights Commissioner (Turkmenistan); Authorized Person of the Oliy Majlis of the Republic of Uzbekistan for Human Rights (Uzbekistan).

been accredited as fully compliant with the UN Principles Relating to the Status of National Institutions (Paris Principles).[141] Nevertheless, the dialogue they initiate and the monitoring they perform help to raise overall awareness of human rights standards among state bodies and increase their accountability.

The national human rights institutions of Kazakhstan and Kyrgyzstan have played a constructive role in the establishment and functioning of National Preventive Mechanisms (NPM) under the Optional Protocol to the Convention against Torture and Other Cruel, Inhuman or Degrading Treatment or Punishment 1984. The main objective of the NPMs is to prevent torture and ill-treatment through independent monitoring of detention facilities. NPMs have powers to inspect, monitor, and visit places of detention, make recommendations to the authorities on improving the treatment and conditions of persons deprived of their liberty, and submit proposals and observations on existing or draft legislation.

In Kazakhstan, the National Preventive Mechanism was established in 2013 by a legislative act. The enactment was a result of concerted efforts of the Government, Parliament, Supreme Court, Constitutional Council, Presidential Administration, Prosecutor-General's Office, Ombudsman, Ministry of Internal Affairs, Ministry of Justice, Ministry of Healthcare, four international actors (the UN Office of the High Commissioner for Human Rights' Regional Office for Central Asia, Penal Reform International in Central Asia, OSCE Program Office in Astana, the International Center for Journalism 'MediaNet'), and thirteen non-governmental organizations. The Law establishing the NPM amended four codes and four laws. The Government and the Ombudsman adopted a number of acts and established organs to support the NPM's operation. The Coordination Council under the Ombudsman, composed of representatives of civil society, was created to coordinate the operation of the NPM. The Ombudsman organized the survey of the facilities falling under the mandate of the NPM, namely, police stations, pre-trial detention centres, places of administrative detention, prisons, juvenile detention centres, compulsory treatment facilities, special educational facilities, detention facilities under military jurisdiction, and a few others, all before actual monitoring started in March 2014. This example shows how a variety of stakeholders contribute to treaty implementation at the domestic level.

Central Asian states have also participated in the periodic reporting procedures before the UN human rights treaty bodies and in the Universal Periodic Review Mechanism of the UN Human Rights Council. Kazakhstan (2013–15) and Kyrgyzstan (2010–12 and 2016–18) were represented on the UN Human Rights Council.[142]

[141] So far, 77 national human rights institutions around the world have been accredited as fully compliant with the Paris Principles. National institutions in Kazakhstan, Kyrgyzstan, and Tajikistan are partially compliant with the Paris Principles. Global Alliance of National Human Rights Institutions, 'Accreditation Status as of 21 February 2018' <https://nhri.ohchr.org/EN/Documents/Status%20Accreditation%20Chart%20(21%20February%202018.pdf> accessed 17 April 2018.

[142] At the 37th session of the Human Rights Council Uzbekistan announced its intention to be elected a member of the UN Human Rights Council for 2021–3.

All Central Asian states are parties to the First Optional Protocol to the ICCPR, allowing the review by the UN HRC of individual communications. Kazakhstan, Kyrgyzstan, Tajikistan, and Turkmenistan have also allowed individual complaint procedures under the Optional Protocol 1999 to the Convention on the Elimination of All Forms of Discrimination against Women 1979. Turkmenistan also accepted individual complaint procedures under the Optional Protocol 2006 to the Convention on the Rights of People with Disabilities 2006. Kazakhstan has accepted individual complaint procedures under the Convention against Torture (article 22) and under the International Convention on the Elimination of All Forms of Racial Discrimination 1965 (article 14).[143]

Uniquely, the Constitution of Kyrgyzstan provides for a right of individuals to file complaints with the international human rights bodies in accordance with the relevant treaties.[144] From 2010 to 2016, the article also included a clause providing that Kyrgyzstan would take measures to remedy and/or compensate human rights violations identified by such bodies.

There have been isolated instances of courts in Kazakhstan and Kyrgyzstan giving effect to the decisions of the UN human rights treaty bodies. Courts in Kazakhstan have acted upon the decisions of the Committee against Torture in the *Gerasimov* and *Bairamov* cases, awarding the victims compensation of moral damages.[145] Courts in Kyrgyzstan awarded compensation of moral damages to the families of the victims of torture based on the Views of the UN HRC in the *Moidunov* and *Akmatov* cases.[146]

Much remains to be done to ensure compliance with human rights treaties and cooperation with the UN human rights treaty bodies in all Central Asian states.

6 Conclusion

After acquiring independence, Central Asian states—Kazakhstan, Kyrgyzstan, Tajikistan, Turkmenistan, and Uzbekistan—have become full-fledged subjects of international

[143] OHCHR, 'Status of Ratifications' <https://tbinternet.ohchr.org/_layouts/TreatyBodyExternal/Treaty.aspx?> accessed 17 April 2018.

[144] Constitution of Kyrgyzstan 2010 art. 41(2) first sentence.

[145] *Gerasimov v Kazakhstan*, Committee against Torture Communication No. 433/2010, Decision of 24 May 2012, UN Doc CAT/C/48/D/433/2010; *Bairamov v Kazakhstan*, Committee against Torture Communication No. 497/2012, Decision adopted 14 May 2014, UN Doc CAT/C/52/D/497/2012; *Gerasimov v Department of Internal Affairs of Kostanai Region*, Kostanai City Court, Judgment No. 2-7843/2013 of 18 November 2013; *Bairamov v Department of Internal Affairs of Kostanai Region*, Kostanai City Court, Judgment No. 2-8617/2014 of 12 December 2014. Both judgments were confirmed by the higher courts.

[146] *Zhumbaeva v Kyrgyzstan*, HRC Communication No. 1756/2008, Views of 19 July 2011, UN Doc CCPR/C/102/D/1756/2008; *Akmatov v Kyrgyzstan*, HRC Communication No. 2052/2011, Views of 29 October 2015, UN Doc CCPR/C/115/D/2052/2011.

law. As such they first settled matters of state succession. Each state has established comprehensive constitutional, legislative, and institutional frameworks for engagement with international law, which continue to develop. This chapter has looked at some of the distinctive features of Central Asian states' approaches towards international law in a comparative perspective.

Whether a state is active in multilateral projects (such as Kazakhstan or Kyrgyzstan) or is more oriented towards bilateral cooperation (like permanently neutral Turkmenistan), the large toolkit of international law makes it relevant to all Central Asian states, despite their diversity. With a variety of challenges in the region and in the world, as well as asymmetries of power, the promise of the international rule of law is particularly appealing.

Central Asian states participate in various international organizations, such as the UN, OSCE, OIC, and SCO. Participation in the CIS and interaction with the CIS Economic Court is a common feature and also distinguishes them from other Asian states. As CIS members, Central Asian states have concluded numerous regional treaties on political, economic, security, environmental, humanitarian, cultural, and other matters. The operation of the regional court has not only allowed them to experience the benefits of legalized dispute settlement, but also—and perhaps more importantly—to have their treaties interpreted based on international law, by an authoritative body, and consistently applied across the member states. The practice of Central Asian states in the CIS and CIS Economic Court has facilitated interaction and cross-fertilization between the national systems of each state, regional law within the CIS, and general international law, as well as integration of Central Asia states into international legal practice.

The case of membership in the regional economic integration organizations, such as the EAEU, illustrates, however, the wariness of states towards supranational institutions. Kazakhstan and Kyrgyzstan, along with other EAEU members, established an organization in which the ultimate control over what obligations become binding, and whether and how they are implemented domestically, rests with the member states, rather than the integration institutions. Sovereignty is thus an important consideration for all Central Asian states in their engagement with international law. This is also manifested, for example, in the supremacy of national constitutions over treaty obligations.

All Central Asian states' constitutions and legal systems have nonetheless been oriented towards international law. The status of treaties in the domestic legal systems, as a matter of political choice, has evolved over time and reflects the experiences of each state's engagement with international law. Procedures for treaty conclusion vary by state and treaty category (interstate, intergovernmental, and interagency agreements). The executive has a power to conduct negotiations and conclude treaties, while Parliaments ratify them. An example of treaty conclusion examined in this chapter is the Treaty on CANWFZ, concluded by the five Central Asian states. This nuclear-weapon-free zone is the first of its kind to be established in a region where nuclear weapons had been previously produced and tested. The UN was actively involved in the negotiations. The treaty represents a significant contribution of the Central Asian states to global and regional non-proliferation efforts, and may serve as a model for the establishment of other nuclear-weapon-free zones around the world.

All Central Asian states provide for and implement guarantees of treaty compliance. The executive and the legislative branches of government in all Central Asian states implement treaties within their respective competences. Organs of constitutional control and courts of general jurisdiction in Kazakhstan, Kyrgyzstan, and Tajikistan have gradually developed a trend of directly applying treaties.

The experience of Central Asian states with the UN human rights mechanisms is an illustration of how various domestic actors are involved in domestic treaty implementation. Much remains to be done to ensure compliance with international human rights standards and full cooperation with the UN human rights treaty bodies.

Overall, despite the approaches of each state being unique, all Central Asian states—as full-fledged members of the international community and subjects of international law—have constructively engaged with international law and may be expected to continue on this path.

THE PACIFIC (INCLUDING OCEANIA AND AUSTRALASIA)

CHAPTER 30

SOUTH PACIFIC ISLAND STATES

JENNIFER CORRIN

1 Introduction

THE South Pacific Island states of Oceania, a region centred on about twenty-two states and territories in the tropical Pacific Ocean,[1] are generally small in size. In the case of Nauru, the country is only 21 square kilometres. In many cases, states are archipelagos spread out over the ocean. Populations are also small, varying from 2,000 in Niue to about 870,000 in Fiji. Indigenous peoples form the majority in most of these countries. They also share the challenges posed by their small size and remoteness, resulting in narrowly based economics. Growing populations and exploitation of resources, both by local governments and foreign companies, are posing threats to South Pacific Island states. These nations are amongst the most vulnerable to the effects of climate change and natural disasters.

However, whilst there are some commonalities, the area is one of immense cultural and biological diversity, including within Oceania's sub-regions of Melanesia, Micronesia, and Polynesia. South Pacific Island states are beset by plural legal systems, where state laws coexist with non-state laws, referred to in this chapter as 'customary laws', at times operating side by side and at others overlapping or even intermingling. State laws consist of not only local laws, but also foreign laws introduced during the colonial era and retained at independence. These competing domestic laws are not the only sources of law to contend with; international law plays an increasingly large role in these countries. Whilst international law is traditionally regarded as the law governing the relationship between states, 'modern' international law includes rules relating to individuals and non-state bodies. This additional layer of law increases the complexities of the relationship between formal and customary laws.

[1] For a history of the term, see Bronwen Douglas and Chris Ballard, *Foreign Bodies: Oceania and The Science of Race 1750–1940* (ANU Press 2008).

This chapter focuses on international law in common law island states in the Pacific, looking more specifically at the South Pacific Island states which have ratified the Pacific Island States Trade Agreement:[2] Cook Islands, Fiji, Kiribati, Nauru, Niue, Papua New Guinea (PNG), Samoa, Solomon Islands, Tonga, Tuvalu, and Vanuatu. There is also some reference to other countries of the region, which include influences from British and American common law and French civil law. In the case of Cook Islands and Niue, it should be noted that their status as 'self-governing territories in free association' with New Zealand originally meant that they were not in charge of their own foreign affairs. Accordingly, neither country had treaty-making capacity, but both were included in New Zealand's ratification of a treaty. However, in 1992, the Secretary-General of the United Nations recognized the full treaty-making capacity of Cook Islands after it had become a member of certain UN organizations.[3] The treaty-making capacity of Niue was recognized in the same way in 1994.[4]

The chapter is divided into the following sections: (section 2) the contribution of South Pacific Island states to international law at the international and regional levels; (section 3) the interaction of international law with Pacific Island states' domestic legal systems; and (section 4) two critical themes, namely conflict between human rights law and customary laws on the one hand and regional customary law on the other. It is concluded that South Pacific Island states play a very small part on the international stage. Whilst they are signatories to a number of international conventions, they have done little to give them local force. This is particularly the case in relation to human rights, perhaps due to the prevailing cultural context. Further, whilst lack of resources is often put forward as a justification for inaction, participating in, for example, marine pollution conventions would enable South Pacific countries to take the benefit from technical and financial mechanisms.[5]

2 The International Level

2.1 Contribution to International Law

Generally, South Pacific Island states have not played major individual roles in the making, implementation, or enforcement of international law. Rather, they have been

[2] Pacific Island Countries Trade Agreement (signed 18 August 2001, entered into force 13 April 2003, [2001] PITSE 4).

[3] UN Treaty Collection, Multilateral Treaties Deposited with the Secretary-General, Cook Islands, Note 1 <https://treaties.un.org/pages/historicalinfo.aspx#CookIslands> accessed 15 October 2018.

[4] UN Treaty Collection, Multilateral Treaties Deposited with the Secretary-General, Niue, Note 1 <https://treaties.un.org/pages/historicalinfo.aspx#Niue> accessed 15 October 2018.

[5] See further UN Office of the High Commissioner for Human Rights (OHCHR) and Pacific Islands Forum (PIF) Secretariat, 'Ratification of International Human Rights Treaties: Added Value for the Pacific Region', Discussion Paper, July 2009.

notable for their failure to contribute. This is well-illustrated by the fact that ten South Pacific nations failed to vote on the United Nations Declaration on the Rights of Indigenous Peoples and Samoa abstained,[6] despite the presence of indigenous peoples in the region. Another example is the failure to engage with the international human rights system, which has been a persistent theme for South Pacific Island states.[7]

However, there are some exceptions to this general inactivity. One is the contribution of countries of the region to the debate on climate change. For example, in 2006, PNG and Kiribati used their address to the annual debate of the UN General Assembly to 'sound the alarm' on the impact of global warming, an issue of great concern to island nations.[8]

Another prominent exception was Nauru's suit against Australia seeking compensation for environmental damage caused by phosphate mining during the colonial era. The *Certain Phosphate Lands in Nauru* case is noteworthy as the first case brought by a former dependent territory against a former administrator for abuse of its power.[9] Nauru claimed that Australia had breached several of its international legal obligations, in particular, obligations arising from the Trusteeship Agreement of 1947,[10] the principle of self-determination, and the obligation to respect the right of the Nauruan people to permanent sovereignty over their natural wealth and resources. Australia challenged the jurisdiction of the International Court of Justice (ICJ), but the Court concluded that it had jurisdiction to entertain the application. The claim was subsequently settled before a final decision on the merits.[11]

Whilst the contribution of individual states has been minimal, the Pacific Islands Forum (PIF), established in 1971, has taken a position on certain issues of concern to its eighteen member countries. Early concerns included French nuclear testing,[12] security,

[6] UN Declaration on the Rights of Indigenous Peoples (adopted by UNGA res 61/295 (13 September 2007)).

[7] Rhona Smith, 'The Pacific Island States: Themes Emerging from the United Nations Human Rights Council's Inaugural Universal Periodic Review?' (2012) 13 Melbourne Journal of International Law 1. In relation to the Second Cycle of Periodic Review, see Working Group on the Universal Periodic Review, 'Draft Report of the Working Group on the Universal Periodic Review: Fiji', UN GAOR, 20th Session, UN Doc A/HRC/WG.6/20/L.5 (31 October 2014).

[8] 'South Pacific countries sound alarm at UN debate on impact of global warming' (UN News Centre, 20 September 2006) <http://www.un.org/apps/news/story.asp?NewsID=19918&Cr=general&Cr1= debate> accessed 7 December 2016.

[9] *Certain Phosphate Lands in Nauru (Nauru v Australia)* (Judgment, Preliminary Objections) [1992] ICJ Rep 240.

[10] Trusteeship Agreement for the Territory of Nauru: as approved by UNGA res 140 (II) (1 November 1947).

[11] See also the Marshall Islands unsuccessful claims against the UK, India, and Pakistan to the ICJ: <www.icj-cij.org/docket/files/160/19132.pdf> accessed 15 October 2018.

[12] PIF, First Forum Communiqué (1971) 11, 18. See further, 'Pacific governments have committed to a nuclear free Pacific' <http://www.femlinkpacific.org.fj/images/PDF/Policy/FemLINKPACIFIC_ICANFlyerweb.pdf> accessed 21 December 2016.

and terrorism.[13] More recently the PIF has concentrated on ocean sustainability,[14] climate change, and disaster risk. The PIF's initiatives are discussed more fully below.

Generally, South Pacific Island states have been slow to ratify treaties, and the reasons for this are discussed later in this chapter. Only Kiribati, Nauru, and Solomon Islands are parties to the Vienna Convention on the Law of Treaties 1969.[15] Nauru did not ratify the Geneva Conventions 1949 on international humanitarian law until 2006.[16] Whilst it is not possible to map ratification of all treaties by South Pacific Island states, Table 30.1 gives an indication of this reluctance, as does the table on ratification of Maritime Treaties in section 2.4 (Table 30.2). Internationally, the Pacific has the lowest rate of any region in terms of the ratification of human rights instruments.[17] Table 30.1 shows how many of the eleven featured states have ratified or acceded to the nine core human rights treaties (the constitutional protection of human rights in the South Pacific is discussed later in the chapter).

The 'Pacific Plan: For Strengthening Regional Cooperation and Integration' (Pacific Plan),[18] an initiative of the PIF (since replaced by the Framework for Pacific Regionalism), supports the ratification and implementation of international and regional human rights treaties. The need for ratification was a common theme of the first and second cycles of the UN Human Rights Council's Universal Periodic Review process.[19] As shown in Table 30.1, all the South Pacific Island states have ratified the Convention on the Rights of the Child 1989 (CRC).[20] Fiji, Tokelau, Cook Islands, and Niue through New Zealand originally lodged reservations, but these were subsequently withdrawn. Most have ratified the Convention on the Elimination of All Forms of Discrimination against Women 1979 (CEDAW).[21] However, the record regarding the other core treaties is poor. Nauru signed the International Covenant on Civil and Political Rights 1966 (ICCPR)[22] but has not ratified it. Fiji has set itself a timeframe of ten years where it will endeavour to ratify all core human rights conventions.[23]

[13] See e.g. Aitutaki Declaration on Regional Security Cooperation, PIF, 28th Pacific Islands Forum Communiqué (1997) Annex 2 <https://www.forumsec.org/1997/09/> accessed 30 April 2019.

[14] PIF, 47th Forum Communiqué (10 September 2016) Annex 3, 'Pohnpei Ocean Statement–A Course to Sustainability'. See also PIF, 45th Forum Communiqué (31 July 2014) Annex B, Palau Declaration on 'The Ocean: Life and Future' Charting a Course to Sustainability.

[15] Vienna Convention on the Law of Treaties (opened for signature 23 May 1969, entered into force 27 January 1980, 1155 UNTS 331).

[16] Geneva Conventions Act 2012 (Nauru) (certified on 6 November 2012) Act No. 19 of 20.

[17] Jennifer Corrin, 'Cultural Relativism vs Universalism: The South Pacific Reality' in Rainer Arnold (ed), *The Universalism of Human Rights* (Springer 2013) 103.

[18] Pacific Islands Forum Secretariat, 'The Pacific Plan for Strengthening Regional Cooperation and Integration, October 2005–7' <https://www.forumsec.org/kalibobo-roadmap-on-the-pacific-plan/> accessed 30 May 2019.

[19] See e.g. Human Rights Council Working Group on the Universal Periodic Review, Draft Report of the Working Group on the Universal Periodic Review, UN GAOR, 20th session, UN Doc A/HRC/WG.6/20/L.5 (27 October–7 November 2014).

[20] CRC (n 25). [21] CEDAW (n 23). [22] On 12 November 2001.

[23] Human Rights Council Working Group on the Universal Periodic Review, National Report submitted in accordance with paragraph 5 of the annex to Human Rights Council resolution 16/21, UNGAOR, 20th Session, UN Doc A/HRC/WG.6/20/FIJI/1 (27 October–7 November 2014).

Table 30.1 Ratifications and Accessions to Core Human Rights Treaties[24]

	Cook Islands	Fiji	Kiribati	Nauru	Niue	PNG	Samoa	Solomon Islands	Tonga	Tuvalu	Vanuatu
CAT[25]	1989[26]	2016		2012	1989[27]						2011
CED[28]							2012				2007*
CEDAW[29]	2006	1995	2004	2011	1985	1995	1992	2002		2010	1995
CMW[30]											
CRC[31]	1997	1993	1995	1994	1995	1993	1994	1995	1995	1995	1993
CRPD[32]	2009	2017	2013	2012		2013	2016	2008*	2007*	2013	2008
ICCPR[33]	2000[34]			2001*	2000[35]	2008	2008				2008
ICERD[36]	1972	1973		2001*	1972	1982		1982	1972		
ICESCR[37]	1978[38]				1978[39]	2008		1982			

There are a number of reasons why South Pacific Island states have been slow to ratify treaties. During the colonial period, they had little opportunity to participate in international law making. After gaining independence, from the 1960s onwards, these new nations were already saddled with a body of introduced common law. In this context, it is unsurprising that they took a defensive attitude to anything likely to

24 * indicates signed, but not ratified.

25 Convention Against Torture (opened for signature 10 December 1984, entered into force 26 June 1987, 1465 UNTS 85).

26 Ratified by New Zealand. This ratification is not technically binding on Cook Islands, but it considers itself a party.

27 Ratified by New Zealand. This ratification is not binding on Niue.

28 International Convention for the Protection of All Persons from Enforced Disappearance (opened for signature 20 December 2006, entered into force 23 December 2010, 2716 UNTS 3).

29 Convention on the Elimination of All Forms of Discrimination against Women (opened for signature 18 December 1979, entered into force 3 June 1981, 1249 UNTS 13) ('CEDAW').

30 International Convention on the Protection of the Rights of All Migrant Workers and Members of their Families (opened for signature 18 December 1990, entered into force 1 July 2003, 2220 UNTS 3).

31 Convention on the Rights of the Child (opened for signature 2 September 1990, entered into force 1 July 2003, 1577 UNTS 3) ('CRC').

32 Convention on the Rights of Persons with Disabilities (opened for signature 13 December 2006, entered into force 3 May 2008, 2515 UNTS 3).

33 International Covenant on Civil and Political Rights (adopted 16 December 1966, entered into force 23 March 1976, 999 UNTS 171).

34 Ratified by New Zealand. This ratification is not technically binding on Cook Islands, but it considers itself a party.

35 Ratified by New Zealand. This ratification is not binding on Niue.

36 International Convention on the Elimination of all Forms of Racial Discrimination (opened for signature 7 March 1966, entered into force 4 January 1969, 660 UNTS 195).

37 International Covenant on Economic Social and Cultural Rights (opened for signature 16 December 1966, entered into force 3 January 1976, 993 UNTS 3).

38 Ratified by New Zealand. This ratification is not technically binding on Cook Islands, but it considers itself a party.

39 Ratified by New Zealand. This ratification is not binding on Niue.

impact upon their new-found sovereignty. Apart from lack of political will, the small size of these nations and lack of diplomatic expertise are also relevant factors.

Even where South Pacific Island states have ratified treaties, they have been slow to comply with their periodic reporting obligations. Staff within relevant government ministries are often overstretched and tasks such as this, which require a particular skill set, may not be high on the agenda of development initiatives. As commented by Smith in relation to reporting on human rights compliance,

> Each core treaty gives rise to an obligation to report periodically on compliance with its terms. As noted above, to complete the treaty reporting process, the state has to file periodic reports with the UN and attend the relevant committee meeting in Geneva where the report will be discussed before the concluding observations are adopted. Any response to any concluding observations can, of course, be submitted without further attendance. For small states, this process represents a lot of time and effort, not least when many of those states are simultaneously undergoing major constitutional and legislative changes and engaging with other states and organisations in various multilateral and bilateral processes.[40]

South Pacific Island states are parties to numerous bilateral treaties, which address matters such as security, under the Regional Assistance Mission to Solomon Islands Treaty[41] and now a bilateral security treaty.[42] Other key subjects of bilateral treaties include border agreements;[43]delimitation of economic zones;[44] trade agreements;[45] the surrender of persons to the International Criminal Court;[46] air services arrangements;[47] and postal services.[48]

[40] Smith (n 7).

[41] Agreement between Solomon Islands, Australia, New Zealand, Fiji, Papua New Guinea, Samoa, and Tonga concerning the operations and status of the police and armed forces and other personnel deployed to Solomon Islands to assist in the restoration of law and order and security (signed 24 July 2003, entered into force 24 July 2003, [2013] ATS 17).

[42] Agreement between the Government of Australia and the Government of Solomon Islands Concerning the Basis for Deployment of Police, Armed Forces and other Personnel to Solomon Islands (signed 14 August 2017, entered into force 2018, [2017] ATNIF 34).

[43] For example, the Basic Agreement between the Government of Solomon Islands and the Government of Papua New Guinea on Border Arrangements (signed 27 July 2004, entered into force 27 July 2004, [2004] PITSE 8).

[44] For example, Agreement Between the Government of the Republic of France and the Government of Fiji Relating to the Delimitation of their Economic Zone (signed 19 January 1983, entered into force 21 August 1984, [1983] PITSE 4).

[45] Pacific Island Countries Trade Agreement (PICTA) (signed 18 August 2001, entered into force 13 April 2003).

[46] Agreement between the Government of the United States of America and the Government of Solomon Islands Regarding the Surrender of Persons to the International Criminal Court (signed 19 September 2003, [2003] PITSE 8).

[47] Air Services Arrangements between the Republic of Nauru and Solomon Islands (signed 10 September 2006, entered into force 10 September 2006, [2006] PITSE 6); Air Services Arrangements between Solomon Islands and Papua New Guinea (signed 8 May 1990, entered into force 8 May 1990, [1990] PITSE 21).

[48] Agreement for an Exchange of Uninsured Parcels between Australia and Fiji (opened for signature 5 October 1926, retrospectively entered into force 1 July 1925, [1926] PITSE 1).

2.2 Regional Organizations

Whilst South Pacific Island states have not played a significant role in the making of treaties on the world stage and have been slow to ratify them, in recent decades they have established a number of regional groups (also discussed in chapter 3) to deal with issues specific to the region and to represent them in the international field. Through these mediums, they have been involved in a number of regional treaties, reflecting Pacific concerns. South Pacific Islands states have tended not to join regional groupings in Asia outside the Pacific, such as the Association of Southeast Asian Nations (although PNG has observer status).[49]

The South Pacific region's principal political grouping is the PIF, established in 1971.[50] Its members are Australia, Cook Islands, Federated States of Micronesia, Fiji, Kiribati, Nauru, New Zealand, Niue, Palau, PNG, Republic of Marshall Islands, Samoa, Solomon Islands, Tonga, Tuvalu, Vanuatu, and, since September 2016, French Polynesia and New Caledonia.[51] The PIF's object is the economic and political governance, security, and fostering of regional coordination and integration in the Pacific.[52]

Insofar as the latter is concerned, as mentioned above, the Forum Secretariat has introduced the Pacific Plan (since replaced by the Framework for Pacific Regionalism),[53] which includes streamlining laws to bring them into line with international treaties.[54] Amongst the early agreements achieved by the PIF is the Treaty of Rarotonga,[55] which is the common name for the South Pacific Nuclear Free Zone Treaty 1985, which formalizes a Nuclear-Weapon-Free Zone in the South Pacific. The treaty bans nuclear weapons within the borders of the zone. It was signed by Australia, Cook Islands, Fiji, Kiribati, Nauru, New Zealand, Niue, PNG, Samoa, Solomon Islands, Tonga, Tuvalu, and Vanuatu on 6 August 1985, and came into force with the eighth ratification. It has since been ratified by all of those states and has been incorporated into domestic legislation in Vanuatu.[56]

More recent concerns include ocean sustainability,[57] and climate change and disaster risk, discussed in the next section. Other areas of concern in the South Pacific are

[49] 'Association of Southeast Asian Nations (ASEAN)' <http://www.nti.org/learn/treaties-and-regimes/association-southeast-asian-nations-asean> accessed 14 December 2016.

[50] Formerly the South Pacific Forum. See now Agreement Establishing the Pacific Islands Forum, Port Moresby, 27 October 2005 <www.forumsec.org/wp-content/uploads/2018/02/Agreement-Establishing-the-Pacific-Islands-Forum-Secretariat-2005-1.pdf> accessed 30 April 2019.

[51] Tokelau is an Associate Member. See <https://www.forumsec.org/tokelau/> accessed 30 April 2019.

[52] Pacific Islands Forum Secretariat, 'Mission and Vision' <http://www.forumsec.org/pages.cfm/about-us/mission-goals-roles> accessed 14 December 2016.

[53] Pacific Islands Forum Secretariat, 'The Pacific Plan for Strengthening Regional Cooperation and Integration, October 2005–7' <https://www.forumsec.org/kalibobo-roadmap-on-the-pacific-plan/> accessed 30 April 2019.

[54] PIFS, 'The Pacific Plan for Strengthening Regional Cooperation and Integration' (November 2007).

[55] South Pacific Nuclear Free Zone Treaty (Treaty of Rarotonga) (opened for signature 6 August 1985, entered into force 11 December 1986, 1445 UNTS 177).

[56] South Pacific Nuclear Free Zone Treaty (Ratification) Act 1995 (Cap 237) (Vanuatu).

[57] PIF (n 14).

security and terrorism. Remoteness and absence of a government presence in many parts of the region make South Pacific Island states particularly susceptible to terrorism.[58] Whilst the PIF initially appears to have avoided dealing with regional security,[59] it has issued a number of declarations to enhance cooperation, including the Aitutaki Declaration on Regional Security Cooperation 1997,[60] the Biketawa Declaration 2000,[61] the Nasonini Declaration on Regional Security 2004,[62] and the Auckland Declaration 2003.[63] These instruments are indicative of a change of policy at the PIF, with the realization that the desire to refrain from interference with a member nation's affairs on the grounds of respect for sovereignty is outweighed by the security needs of the region as a whole.[64]

Other relevant regional organizations which have roles to play in the international arena, particularly in relation to sustainable development, are the Secretariat of the Pacific Community (SPC), the PIF Fisheries Agency (FFA), and the Secretariat of the Pacific Regional Environment Programme (SPREP). SPC delivers technical assistance, policy advice, training, and research services for twenty-two countries in the region.[65] Its programmes span a number of sectors addressing sustainable economic development, natural resource and environmental management, and human and social development.

The FFA is an advisory body that assists members to maximize benefits from the conservation and sustainable use of their fisheries resources, in particular tuna. The SPREP promotes the protection and sustainable development of the Pacific region's environment. It has played a key role in keeping the international community focused on the issue of climate change and natural disasters.[66] Cooperation between these regional organizations and certain other regional bodies is promoted through the Council of Regional Organisations of the Pacific.

[58] Andrew Renton-Green, 'International Organized Crime, Piracy and International Terrorism: An Asia-Pacific Convergence?' (Paris Institute of Criminology, 22 November 2002); AusAID 2004, Pacific Regional Aid Strategy 2004–2009.

[59] Stewart Firth, 'A Reflection on South Pacific Regional Security, Mid-2000 to Mid-2001' (2001) 36 Journal of Pacific History 277, 278.

[60] PIF, 28th Pacific Islands Forum Communiqué (1997) Annex 2.

[61] PIF, 31st Pacific Islands Forum Communiqué (2000) Attachment 1.

[62] PIF, 33rd Pacific Islands Forum Communiqué (2002) Annex 1.

[63] PIF, The Auckland Declaration (2003) <https://www.forumsec.org/forum-declaration-on-solomon-islands/> accessed 30 April 2019.

[64] Christopher Richter, 'Security Cooperation in the South Pacific: Building on Biketawa' (2009) 13 Journal of South Pacific Law 1.

[65] Including American Samoa, Australia, Cook Islands, Federated States of Micronesia, Fiji, France, French Polynesia, Guam, Kiribati, Marshall Islands, Nauru, New Caledonia, New Zealand, Niue, Northern Mariana Islands, Palau, Papua New Guinea, Pitcairn Islands, Samoa, Solomon Islands, Tokelau, Tonga, Tuvalu, United States of America, Vanuatu, and Wallis and Futuna.

[66] See e.g. Secretariat of the Pacific Regional Environment Program (SPREP), 'Pacific Islands Action Plan in Climate Change 2006–2015'.

At a sub-regional level, the Melanesian Spearhead Group (MSG) is comprised of Fiji, the Front de Liberation Nationale Kanak et Socialiste,[67] PNG, Solomon Islands, and Vanuatu. This body resulted from a meeting of Heads of Government in 1986 and now operates under an agreement signed in 2007.[68] The MSG has its own trade agreement,[69] and it also agreed on the Framework Treaty on Traditional Knowledge and Expressions of Culture.[70]

At the third International Conference on Small Island Developing States, held in 2014, the 'Small Island Developing States Accelerated Modalities of Action (SAMOA) Pathway' was drawn up,[71] reflecting some of the contemporary thematic areas of interest of the South Pacific, including the need for sustainable development, sea-level rise, and climate change.[72] Some of these thematic issues are considered below.

2.3 Climate Change and Natural Disasters

South Pacific Islands are spread across a vast sea area, and marine resources form a significant part of the economy, which brings to the fore the international law of the sea. The geographical circumstances of small South Pacific countries make them susceptible to climate change and natural disasters, the effects of which are often exacerbated by the archipelagic nature of many South Pacific nations. According to a World Bank report, eight South Pacific Island states are among the twenty countries in the world with the highest average annual disaster losses scaled by gross domestic product.[73]

South Pacific Island states have contributed to the debate on climate change and natural disasters through the SPREP, discussed above.[74] The PIF issued the 'Pohnpei Statement: Strengthening Pacific Resilience to Climate Change and Disaster Risk',[75] which expressed South Pacific nations' concerns about the vulnerability of the Pacific

67 The FLNKS is a group of pro-independent parties in the French Territory of New Caledonia. The FLNKS represent the ethnic Kanak (indigenous) population which constitutes a wider population of about 108,055 Melanesian people (estimated 44% of the 2009 population figures) <https://dfat.gov.au/geo/new-caledonia/Pages/new-caledonia-country-brief.aspx> accessed 30 April 2019.

68 Agreement Establishing the Melanesian Spearhead Group, March 2007.

69 Trade Agreement Amongst the Melanesian Spearhead Group Countries (signed 27 October 2005, entered into force September 1994 [1993] PITSE 10).

70 Signed by Fiji and Solomon Islands in 2011.

71 UN Conference on Small Island Developing States, Report of the Third International Conference on Small Island Developing States, UN Doc A/CONF.223/10 (1–4 September 2014).

72 Ibid. paras 9, 11.

73 World Bank, 'Acting on Climate Change & Disaster Risk for the Pacific' (World Bank 2013) <http://www.worldbank.org/content/dam/Worldbank/document/EAP/Pacific%20Islands/climate-change-pacific.pdf> accessed 16 October 2018.

74 See e.g. SPREP (n 66).

75 See PIF, 47th Pacific Islands Forum Communiqué (10 September 2016) Annex 2, 'Strengthening Pacific Resilience to Climate Change and Disaster Risk' at 10 September 2016. See also, PIF, 46th Pacific Islands Forum Communiqué (10 September 2015) Annex 1, 'Pacific Islands Forum Leaders Declaration on Climate Change Action'.

to climate change impacts and natural hazards. It affirmed a commitment to addressing climate change and disaster resilience as expressed in the SAMOA Pathway[76] and the Sustainable Development Goals,[77] and called for 'immediate, significant and coordinated practical action'.[78] It called upon South Pacific countries to advocate for early entry into force of the 2015 Paris Agreement[79] and emphasized the need to secure support to deliver on commitments under that document and the 2015 Sendai Framework for Disaster Risk Reduction.[80] Also highlighted was 'The Need to Operationalise the Framework for Resilient Development in the Pacific: An Integrated Approach to Address Climate Change and Disaster Risk Management',[81] which provides voluntary guidelines for the Pacific Islands Region, and its potential was recognized for supporting coordination and action on a number of key issues related to climate change and disaster risk management. The Statement also calls on development partners, the private sector, and civil society to join with Pacific Island states to support the principles and the implementation of this statement through high-level participation in a new Pacific Resilience Partnership.[82]

2.4 The Sea, Fisheries, and the Marine Environment

In the related area of shipping and the marine environment, South Pacific countries' 'buy-in' to treaties has been surprisingly low compared to other regions, despite their dependence on the oceans. Table 30.2 shows which South Pacific states have ratified the relevant treaties adopted under the auspices of the International Maritime Organization (IMO), the UN agency dealing with safety and security of international shipping and the prevention of pollution from ships.[83]

Whilst South Pacific countries have been slow to ratify IMO Conventions, they do have an obvious concern about their commercially valuable Exclusive Economic Zones (EEZs), relying on international customary law to support their claims until the conclusion of the United Nations Convention on the Law of the Sea 1982 (UNCLOS).[84]

[76] UN Conference on Small Island Developing States (n 71).

[77] UNGA res 70/1 (25 September 2015). [78] Ibid. para 4.

[79] The Paris Agreement (signed 22 April 2016, entered into force 4 November 2016).

[80] UN, 'Sendai Framework for Disaster Risk Reduction' (18 March 2015) <http://www.unisdr.org/we/coordinate/sendai-framework> accessed 16 October 2018.

[81] Red Cross, 'The Framework for Resilient Development in the Pacific: An Integrated Approach to Address Climate Change and Disaster Risk Management 2016' (11 September 2016) <http://gsd.spc.int/frdp/> accessed 16 October 2018.

[82] Ibid. para 5.

[83] IMO, Status of Conventions, <http://www.imo.org/en/About/Conventions/StatusOfConventions/Pages/Default.aspx> accessed 21 December 2016.

[84] Dejo Olowu, *International Law: A Textbook for the South Pacific* (CD Publishing.org 2010) 38. See UN Convention on the Law of the Sea (opened for signature 10 December 1982, entered into force 16 January 1994, 1833 UNTS 3).

Table 30.2 Ratification of IMO Conventions and Associated Instruments

	Cook Islands	Fiji	Kiribati	Nauru	Niue	PNG	Samoa	Solomon Islands	Tonga	Tuvalu	Vanuatu
IMO Convention 48	X	X	X			X	X	X	X	X	X
COLREG Convention 72	X	X	X		X	X	X	X	X	X	X
SAR Convention 79	X		X		X	X	X		X		X
MARPOL 73/78 (Annex I/II)	X	X	X		X	X	X	X	X	X	X
MARPOL 73/78 (Annex III)			X		X	X	X	X	X	X	X
MARPOL 73/78 (Annex IV)		X	X		X	X	X	X	X	X	X
MARPOL 73/78 (Annex V)		X	X		X	X	X	X	X	X	X
MARPOL Protocol 97 (Annex VI)	X		X		X		X		X	X	X
London Convention 72			X	X		X		X	X		X
London Convention Protocol 96									X		X
INTERVENTION Convention 69		X				X			X		X
INTERVENTION Protocol 73									X		X
CLC Convention 69		d[85]				d			d	d	d
CLC Protocol 76										X	X
CLC Protocol 92	X	X	X		X	X	X	X	X	X	X
FUND Protocol 76											X
FUND Protocol 92	X	X	X		X	X	X		X	X	X
FUND Protocol 2003											
LLMC Convention 76	X		X		X		X		X	X	X
LLMC Protocol 96	X				X		X		X	X	
SUA Convention 88	X	X	X	X	X		X		X	X	X
SALVAGE Convention 89		X	X		X				X		X
OPRC Convention 90							X		X		X
HNS Convention 96							X		X		
HNS PROT 2010											
OPRC/HNS 2000											X
BUNKERS CONVENTION 01	X	X	X		X		X		X	X	X
ANTI FOULING 01	X	X	X		X				X	X	X
BALLAST-WATER 2004	X	X	X		X				X	X	
NAIROBI WRC 2007	X				X				X	X	
HONG KONG CONVENTION											

[85] 'd' connotes denunciation.

UNCLOS now governs jurisdiction over the various maritime areas. Cook Islands, Fiji, Kiribati, Nauru, Niue, PNG, Samoa, Solomon Islands, Tonga, Tuvalu, and Vanuatu are all parties to it. UNCLOS is of great significance to South Pacific Island states. For example, under its provisions, Fiji, PNG, Solomon Islands, and Vanuatu have all claimed archipelagic waters. UNCLOS also provides for negotiating delimitation agreements where boundaries overlap. In fact, few South Pacific Island states have used these provisions to negotiate rights. UNCLOS also deals with a whole range of sea management issues including conservation and management of marine resources, protection of the marine environment, and passage of ships through straits.

South Pacific countries have gradually become more concerned about ocean sustainability.[86] UNCLOS limits access to national EEZs by 'Distant Water Fishing Nations' (DWFNs),[87] allowing South Pacific countries to conserve fisheries resources. In 2000, the Convention for the Management and Conservation of Highly Migratory Fish Stocks in the Western and Central Pacific was adopted by a number of South Pacific Island states and DWFNs.[88] The Western and Central Pacific Fisheries Commission established under it applies conservation and management measures to all species of highly migratory fish stocks listed in Annex 1 of the UNCLOS.[89]

One species of migratory fish is tuna, and tuna fishing has been particularly contentious. The FFA supervises the world's biggest tuna fishery, but in 2016 the US withdrew from the thirty-year-old Treaty on Fisheries between the Governments of Certain Pacific Island States and the Government of the United States of America.[90] Besides the US, there are thirteen parties to that Treaty from the Pacific.[91] The FFA members also adopted the Niue Treaty on Cooperation in Fisheries Surveillance and Law Enforcement in the South Pacific Region 1992. The Niue Treaty Subsidiary Agreement 2012 seeks to strengthen its practical application.

Cook Islands and Vanuatu are also parties to the International Convention on the Conservation and Management of High Seas Fishery Resources in the South Pacific Ocean 2009.[92] It deals with conservation and management of non-highly migratory

[86] PIF (n 14). [87] UNCLOS (n 85) art. 61(3).

[88] Convention for the Management and Conservation of Highly Migratory Fish Stocks in the Western and Central Pacific (opened for signature 5 September 2000, entered into force June 2004). Tonga abstained from the vote to adopt the Convention.

[89] Ibid. part 1 art. 1(f).

[90] Also known as the South Pacific Tuna Treaty (adopted 2 April 1987, entered into force 15 June 1988, 2176 UNTS 173). The US withdrawal is effective from January 2017. See Jemima Garrett, 'US announces withdrawal from crucial fisheries treaty with Pacific nations' (ABC News, 20 January 2016) <http://www.abc.net.au/news/2016-01-19/us-withdraws-from-crucial-treaty-with-pacific-nations/7099740> accessed 20 December 2016.

[91] Including Cook Islands, Fiji, Kiribati, Nauru, Niue, PNG, Samoa, Solomon Islands, Tonga, Tuvalu, Vanuatu, Australia, and New Zealand. National legislation ratifying the South Pacific Tuna Treaty include the Fisheries (Pacific Island States Treaty with the United States of America) Act 1988 (Kiribati) and the Fisheries (United States of America) Treaty Act 1988 (Cap 39) (Solomon Islands) <http://www.paclii.org/sb/legis/consol_act/fsoata400/>.

[92] International Convention on the Conservation and Management of High Seas Fishery Resources in the South Pacific Ocean (adopted 14 November 2009, entered into force 24 August 2012). It came into

fisheries and the protection of biodiversity in the marine environment in high seas areas of the South Pacific ocean.

A sub-regional agreement, known as the Nauru Agreement 1982,[93] also exists to encourage cooperation in management of fisheries in the area. There are two supplemental agreements: the Palau Arrangement 1992,[94] designed to protect the sustainability of fisheries, and the Federated States of Micronesia Arrangement 1994, aimed at promoting more local participation in fisheries.[95] A recent example of the more assertive stance taken by South Pacific nations to illegal fishing can be seen in the sinking of a foreign fishing vessel caught in Milne Bay waters by PNG Defence Force naval boats in December 2016.[96]

3 The Domestic Level

3.1 The Process of Treaty-making and Ratification

Constitutions in South Pacific Island states contain expressions of sovereignty and statehood,[97] which undoubtedly carry with them implied authority to enter into treaties on behalf of the states. Sub-national government bodies in South Pacific Island states are prohibited from entering into treaties.[98] Only the Constitution of Tonga 1875 deals expressly with the authority to enter into a treaty, stating that '[i]t shall be lawful for the King to make treaties with foreign states provided that such treaties shall be in accordance with the laws of the Kingdom'.[99] The Constitution puts a limit on the King's power, stating that '[i]t shall not be lawful for the King to alter the customs duties without the consent of the Legislative Assembly'.[100] Other regional constitutions are silent on treaty-making power and on the associated processes.

Most constitutions are also silent as to the process of ratification, the exceptions being Fiji, Vanuatu, and PNG. The Constitution of Fiji 2013 provides that '[a]n

force in Vanuatu on 30 October 2013: Convention on the Conservation and Management of High Seas Fishery Resources in the South Pacific Ocean (Ratification) Act 2013 (Vanuatu).

93 Nauru Agreement Concerning Cooperation in the Management of Fisheries of Common Interest (opened for signature 11 February 1982, entered into force 4 December 1982, [1982] PITSE 5).

94 Palau Arrangement for the Management of the Western Pacific Purse Seine Fishery (Honiara Forum Fisheries Agency 1992).

95 Federated States of Micronesia Arrangement for Regional Fisheries Access (opened for signature 30 November 1994, entered into force 24 September 2005, [1994] PITSE 19).

96 Pacific Islands Development Program, Pacific Islands Report, East-West Center in Honolulu, Hawai'i, 4 January 2017 <http://us10.campaign-archive2.com/?u=d27dd3dc8b2d121b9fb9fe556&id= 8e6374933f&e= f75f50d25d> accessed 16 October 2018.

97 See e.g. Constitution of Solomon Islands 1978 s 1(1).

98 See e.g. Provincial Government Act 1997 (Solomon Islands) s 31(4).

99 Constitution of Tonga 1875 s 39.

100 Ibid.

international treaty or convention binds the State only after it has been approved by Parliament'.[101] The Constitution of Vanuatu 1980 requires treaties to be presented to Parliament for ratification if they:

(a) concern international organisations, peace or trade;
(b) commit the expenditure of public funds;
(c) affect the status of people;
(d) require amendment of the laws of the Republic of Vanuatu; or
(e) provide for the transfer, exchange or annexing of territory.[102]

The Constitution of PNG 1975 is much more detailed and provides that consent to be bound as a party to a treaty may be given only by the Head of State,[103] or by a Minister authorized by him, acting in accordance with the advice of the National Executive Council; or otherwise in accordance with international law, usage, and practice. The section also provides that, except in cases of urgency, consent shall not be given unless a treaty document relating to the treaty has been presented to the Parliament for at least ten sitting days, although this requirement may be waived by an absolute majority vote.[104] Special provisions are set out regarding treaties which affect the autonomy of the island of Bougainville or jurisdiction of its Government.[105]

3.2 The Formal Position of International Treaties

The selected South Pacific Island states are dualist, meaning that international treaties do not become part of domestic law unless specifically incorporated by domestic legislation. This approach may be contrasted with the monist situation in former American colonies, including Guam, Palau, and the Federated States of Micronesia. The dualist principle has been given constitutional force in PNG, where it is provided that:

(7) Notwithstanding the consent of Papua New Guinea to be bound as a party to a treaty, no treaty forms part of the municipal law of Papua New Guinea unless, and then only to the extent that, it is given the status of municipal law by or under a Constitutional Law or an Act of the Parliament.
(8) Legislative approval or ratification of a treaty does not, without more, give it the status of municipal law for the purposes of Subsection (7).[106]

[101] Constitution of the Republic of Fiji 2013 s 51.
[102] Constitution of Vanuatu 1980 art. 26.
[103] Constitution of the Independent State of Papua New Guinea 1975 ('Constitution of PNG 1975').
[104] Ibid. s 117. [105] Ibid. s 293. [106] Ibid. s 117(7) and (8).

In the absence of incorporating legislation, conventions are not directly enforceable in South Pacific courts.[107]

There is also the question of succession to treaties. As most South Pacific Island states have emerged as a consequence of decolonization, the position is covered by the special regime for newly independent states in the Vienna Convention on the Succession of States in Respect of Treaties 1978.[108] Article 16 provides that newly independent states are not bound by treaty obligations of their predecessor states, although they may voluntarily succeed to them. This view has been adopted by Pacific Island states, including Kiribati and Solomon Islands.[109]

In relation to human rights, most regional constitutions have enshrined bills of rights, based on overseas models.[110] In the case of Kiribati,[111] Nauru,[112] Samoa,[113] Solomon Islands,[114] and Tuvalu,[115] the bill of rights follows the United Nations' Universal Declaration of Human Rights 1948 (UDHR)[116] and the Council of Europe's Convention for the Protection of Human Rights and Fundamental Freedoms 1950 ('ECHR').[117] The fundamental rights and freedoms that are recognized comprise the rights to:

- life, liberty and freedom from slavery and forced labour;
- freedom from torture and inhuman and degrading treatment;
- freedom from compulsory acquisition or deprivation of property;
- freedom from search and entry;
- the protection of the law;
- freedom of conscience, expression, assembly and association, and movement; and
- freedom from discrimination and inequality of treatment on certain grounds.

[107] See e.g. *Wagner v Radke* (Unreported, Supreme Court, Samoa, Sapolu CJ, 19 February 1997, [1997] WSSC 6); *Re Section 201 of the Income Tax Act 1997, Application by Smith* [1999] CKHC 1.

[108] Vienna Convention on Succession of States in Respect of Treaties (opened for signature 23 August 1978, entered into force 6 November 1996, 1946 UNTS 3).

[109] Andreas Zimmerman and James Devaney, 'Succession to Treaties and the Inherent Limits of International Law' in Christian Tams, Antonios Tzanakopoulos, and Andreas Zimmerman (eds), *Research Handbook on the Law of Treaties* (Edward Elgar 2014) 505, 531.

[110] The Niue Constitution Act 1974 (NZ) is an exception; it does not contain a Bill of Rights. See further Jennifer Corrin Care, 'Conflict between Customary Law and Human Rights in the South Pacific' (1999) 1 Commonwealth Law Conference Papers 251.

[111] Constitution of Kiribati 1979.

[112] Constitution of Nauru 1968.

[113] Constitution of the Independent State of Samoa 1960.

[114] See e.g. Constitution of Solomon Islands 1978 pt II.

[115] Constitution of Tuvalu 2008 cap 1.02.

[116] Universal Declaration of Human Rights (adopted 10 December 1948 by UNGA res 217 A(III)).

[117] European Convention for the Protection of Human Rights and Fundamental Freedoms, as amended by Protocols Nos 11 and 14 (opened for signature 4 November 1950, entry into force 3 September 1953, ETS 5) ('ECHR').

All of these rights and freedoms are set out in detail. Applicable exceptions are also set out, except in the case of freedom from torture, which is unlimited. Mechanisms for the enforcement of those rights are also provided.[118]

The Constitution of Fiji formerly followed the same model, but the latest Constitution, brought into force in 2013, goes beyond these civic rights and freedoms, and makes additional provision for broader social and economic rights, such as the right to education, the right to economic participation, the right to work and to a just minimum wage, the right to health, and environmental rights.[119] The Constitution of PNG also follows the UDHR and the ECHR but, like the new Constitution of Fiji, it is more extensive in the rights it includes.[120] Further, it takes a novel approach by dividing rights into Fundamental Rights[121] and Qualified Rights.[122]

The Constitutions of Cook Islands (1965) and Vanuatu (1980) use the Canadian Bill of Rights as a model.[123] They include the rights and freedoms in the list set out above but describe them and the relevant exceptions in very general terms.

The Constitution of Tonga was enacted much earlier,[124] in 1875, and was based on the 1852 Constitution of Hawaii.[125] The declaration of rights, set out in the first section, reflects nineteenth-century humanitarian concerns by commencing with a declaration of freedom and the prohibition of slavery.[126] The country's recent conversion to Christianity is also evident, in the form of the right to freedom of worship and the obligation to keep the Sabbath day sacred.[127] Whilst the Constitution of Tonga makes provision for most fundamental rights and freedoms,[128] it does not expressly guarantee the right to freedom from torture or inhuman or degrading treatment, nor the right to freedom of movement, and only provides a partial right to protection of the law.

Tokelau has taken a different approach. The Constitution states that the human rights of the people of Tokelau are 'those stated in the Universal Declaration of Human Rights and reflected in the International Covenant on Civil and Political Rights', without describing or detailing them.[129] The Constitution of Niue does not contain any provision for the protection of fundamental rights and freedoms.[130]

[118] See e.g. Constitution of Solomon Islands 1978 s 18.

[119] Constitution of the Republic of Fiji 2013 ss 31–3, 38, 40. This appears to repeal by implication the Fundamental Rights and Freedoms Decree 2000 (Fiji).

[120] Constitution of PNG 1975. Prior to the enactment of the Constitution, human rights were protected in PNG by the Human Rights Ordinance 1971, which protected 11 rights, but did not extend to protection from discrimination.

[121] Constitution of PNG 1975 subdivision A.

[122] Ibid. Subdivision B.

[123] Cook Islands Constitution Act 1964; Vanuatu Constitution 1980 with Amendments through to 1983.

[124] Constitution of Tonga 1875.

[125] Kingdom of Hawaii Constitution 1852. See Sione Latukefa, 'Nineteenth-Century Constitutions' in Peter Sack (ed), *Pacific Constitutions* (RSSS 1982) 21, 30.

[126] Ibid. cls 1 and 2.

[127] Ibid. cls 5 and 6. Arguably, these clauses are contradictory.

[128] Constitution of Tonga 1875.

[129] Constitution of Tokelau 2006 s 16(1).

[130] Niue Constitution Act 1974.

3.3 The Formal Position of Customary International Law in Domestic Law

Customary international law is particularly important in the South Pacific due to the low rate of treaty ratifications and lack of legislation giving domestic effect to international obligations. There is no mention of customary international law as a source of law in South Pacific Islands' constitutions. However, the position adopted in the United Kingdom, which accepts customary international law as part of the common law unless it is inconsistent with domestic law,[131] is binding on all countries of the region which have adopted English common law. This includes all countries under discussion other than Niue.[132]

One area of uncertainty is the extent to which customary international law is binding on countries which do not have autonomy in international affairs. Are non-state entities bound by customary international law? This question is of particular relevance to Cook Islands and Niue, which, as mentioned above, are 'self-governing territories in free association' with New Zealand. Although their treaty-making capacity was recognized in the early 1990s,[133] not all countries recognize Cook Islands and Niue as sovereign states. Neither Cook Islands nor Niue is a member of the UN. Whilst the International Court of Justice accepts that customary international law is a source of law that is binding not only on UN member states but also on other countries,[134] this does not necessarily extend to all non-state entities. In the case of Cook Islands, it is arguable that the territory is bound by virtue of its inheritance of English common law.[135]

3.4 International Law and the Courts

3.4.1 *Express Power to Refer to International Law as a Source of Statutory Interpretation*

In some countries of the region, courts are directed to refer to international law as a guide to statutory interpretation. In Fiji, the Constitution specifically empowers the courts to consider international law when interpreting the rights chapter, and this interpretative tool may be used by the courts to support the application of human rights treaties or customary international law.[136] In Tuvalu, the Interpretation and General Provisions Act states that a 'construction of a written law

[131] See e.g. *Trendtex Trading Corporation v Central Bank of Nigeria* (1977) 2 WLR 356; *R v Jones* [2007] 1 AC 136.

[132] See further Jennifer Corrin and Don Paterson, *Introduction to South Pacific Law* (4th edn Intersentia 2017) 32–3.

[133] See (nn 3–4).

[134] Statute of the International Court of Justice 1945 art. 38(1)(b).

[135] Cook Islands Act 1915 (NZ) s 615.

[136] Constitution of the Republic Fiji 2013 s 7(1)(b).

which is consistent with the international obligations of Tuvalu is to be preferred to a construction which is not'.[137] Further, the Constitution of Tuvalu provides that all laws and acts done under them 'must be reasonably justifiable in a democratic society that has a proper respect for human rights and dignity',[138] and that in determining whether this test has been met, a court may consider 'international conventions, declarations, recommendations and judicial decisions concerning human rights'.[139]

The Constitution of PNG contains a provision which is unique amongst Pacific Island states. Section 38(1) allows the legislature to restrict some of the human rights protected by the Constitution, but only if this is 'reasonably justifiable in a democratic society'. In determining whether an Act meets this standard the court is permitted to consider a number of sources, including:

- the Charter of the United Nations 1945;
- the UDHR and any other declaration, recommendation or decision of the General Assembly of the United Nations concerning human rights and fundamental freedoms;
- the ECHR and the Protocols thereto, and any other international conventions, agreements, or declarations concerning human rights and fundamental freedoms; and
- judgments, reports, and opinions of the International Court of Justice, the European Commission on Human Rights, the European Court of Human Rights, and other international courts and tribunals dealing with human rights and fundamental freedoms.[140]

3.4.2 *Reference to Domestically Incorporated Instruments*

In the rare cases where South Pacific Island states have incorporated international laws into the domestic legal system, the court is obviously free to refer to such law in coming to its decision. However, this does not mean that the court will take a broad approach to the implementation of the terms of a convention. An example can be found in the Vanuatu case of *Joli v Joli*,[141] where the Court at first instance was prepared to apply a presumption of equality to ownership of matrimonial property, based on the anti-discrimination provisions in article 5 and article 1(k) of the Constitution[142] and in reliance on the provisions of CEDAW.[143] However, the Court of Appeal, while noting that Vanuatu was a signatory to that Convention and that it had been ratified by a

[137] Interpretation and General Provisions Act (Tuvalu) 2008 rev edn cap 1.04 s 17.
[138] Constitution of Tuvalu 2008 s 15(1). [139] Ibid. s 15(5)(c).
[140] Constitution of PNG 1975 s 39(3).
[141] The first instance judgment is discussed in (Unreported, Court of Appeal, Vanuatu, Lunabek CJ, Robertson, von Doussa, Fatiaki, Saksak, Treston, JJA, 7 November 2003, [2003] VUCA 27).
[142] Constitution of the Republic of Vanuatu 1980 arts 1, 5(k). [143] CEDAW (n 23).

domestic Act in 1995,[144] considered that the 'broad aspirational statements contained in the Constitution' could not be:

> translated directly into principles of the kind formulated by his Lordship. . . . Similarly, it [was] a matter for Parliament to decide what if any changes to the social patterns of conduct of men and women . . . should occur, and how Vanuatu as a State party to the Convention on the Elimination of all Forms of Discrimination Against Women [would] seek to reflect that Convention in its domestic law. It is not the task of the court to undertake this difficult exercise.[145]

The above suggests that where a convention becomes part of domestic law, if this is through an Act which does no more than ratify it, the courts will be reluctant to draw out broad principles from a convention.

3.4.3 *Reference to Ratified Instruments*

In cases where there is no legislation incorporating conventions into domestic law, some national courts in the region have nevertheless, on occasion, relied on international instruments to justify or bolster their decisions. In neighbouring Australia, the High Court has held that the ratification of a convention is a 'positive statement by the executive government . . . to the world and to the Australian people that the executive government and its agencies will act in accordance with the Convention'[146] when exercising administrative discretions.

In South Pacific Island states, some courts have taken a similar approach, holding that conventions can be used to assist with statutory interpretation or in the exercise of an administrative discretion. This usually occurs in the interpretation of constitutionally enshrined rights. There are several examples involving conflict between human rights and customary laws, which are discussed further in the third section of this chapter. Other examples include cases where conventions have been referred to in support of a broad interpretation of the right to be treated fairly by the police, particularly where children are involved. For example, in *Simona v R*,[147] the High Court of Tuvalu held that the accused, who was seventeen years old at the time, should have been advised that he could have a parent or guardian present during questioning and that he had a right to consult a lawyer. Whilst the relevant constitutional right did not expressly confer those rights, the Court held that it should be interpreted in the light of the CRC,[148] stating that it was,

[144] Convention on the Elimination of all Forms of Discrimination against Women (Ratification) Act 1995 (Vanuatu).

[145] Vanuatu Court of Appeal (n 141).

[146] *Minister of State for Immigration & Ethnic Affairs v Teoh* (1995) 183 CLR 271 para 34. Cf. *Re Minister for Immigration and Multicultural Affairs; Ex parte Lam* (2003) 214 CLR 1, where a majority of the High Court expressed obiter its doubts about the correctness of this assertion.

[147] (Unreported, High Court, Tuvalu, Ward CJ, 12 August 2002, [2012] TVHC 1).

[148] CRC (n 25).

> satisfied that the Constitution read in accordance with the terms of the Convention gives any child in the custody of the police the right to have a parent or guardian present unless that is impractical. The perception that a child needs special protection arises from the immaturity and vulnerability of children. That is the foundation upon which the Convention was constructed.

The Tongan courts took a similar approach in *Fa'aosa v Paongo*,[149] where the plaintiff claimed damages of T$29,000 for unlawful imprisonment and assault against two police officers, and the Crown as their employer. The plaintiff was twelve years old at the time of the assault and the Court noted that although Tonga had acceded to the CRC in December 1995,[150] the Convention had still not been incorporated into domestic law. However, it was held that accession indicated a willingness by the nation to be bound by the terms of the Convention. Aggravated and exemplary damages were awarded because all of the obligations of the state in regard to the apprehension and detention of a child set out in article 37 of the Convention had been flagrantly abused.

International conventions have also been used to support the courts' approach to the right to a fair trial and in relation to sentencing. For example, in *State v Kata*,[151] the High Court of Fiji referred to the ECHR to determine what amounted to a fair trial under the Constitution of Fiji. In *State v Mutch*,[152] the Fijian High Court referred to the CRC in support of considering the 'best interests of the child' in sentencing young offenders.[153] In *Soeasi v R*,[154] an appeal against the sentencing of a minor, the High Court of Solomon Islands took into account the CRC,[155] which, although ratified by Solomon Islands, had not been encapsulated in local legislation. Taking into account the Convention, the Court held that the sentence was excessive, even though it was in accordance with the Juvenile Offenders Act 1972 (cap 14) and the Penal Code 1963 (cap 26).

International law has also been referred to in trials for murder and for inhuman punishment. In *R v Su'u*,[156] the High Court of Solomon Islands was called on to consider whether the accused were entitled to a legislative amnesty under the Amnesty Act 2000[157] in respect of murder charges. Mwanesalua J held that killing was a violation of the right to life protected by the Constitution, which 'adopted' article 3 of the UDHR. As the killing violated human rights, it was held that the amnesty provisions did not apply. Similarly, in *R v Rose*,[158] the High Court of Solomon Islands relied on jurisprudence on article 3 of the ECHR to support a finding of inhuman and degrading punishment,[159] which was prohibited by section 7 of the Constitution.

149 [2006] Tonga LR 329.
150 CRC (n 25).
151 (Unreported, High Court, Fiji, Townsley J, 10 May 2000).
152 [1999] 45 FLR 253; ECHR (n 117).
153 CRC (n 25).
154 (Unreported, High Court, Solomon Islands, Naqiolevu J, 7 December 2007, [2007] SBHC 159).
155 CRC (n 25).
156 (Unreported, High Court, Solomon Islands, Mwanesalua J, 1 March 2007, [2007] SNHC 78).
157 The Amnesty Act 2000 (Solomon Islands).
158 [1987] SPLR 305.
159 ECHR (n 117).

The above cases all relied on international law to bolster a finding which upheld human rights provisions. However, in *Tu'itavake v Porter*,[160] the Supreme Court of Tonga relied on the Vienna Convention on Diplomatic Relations 1961,[161] to which Tonga was a party, to support upholding the application of the Diplomatic Immunity Act 1971 (UK) as an Act of general application,[162] and to dismiss the argument that state immunity was contrary to the constitutionally enshrined principle of equality.[163] The Court held that it must 'bear in mind established principles of international laws'[164] in interpreting the Constitution, and considered that the Convention was 'essentially expressing and codifying the constitutional and common law position in all civilized nations throughout the world, including Tonga, and was therefore in accordance with the laws of the Kingdom'.[165] A similar position has been taken by the European Court of Human Rights.[166]

3.4.4 *Judicial Disregard of Ratified Treaties*

Whilst the courts in all these cases freely rely on international law, there are also examples of national courts in the region refusing to take account of international law in the absence of domestic legislation. Again, many of these cases arose in the context of conflict between customary laws and human rights, which is discussed in section 4. Outside of that area, an example which contrasts with *Soeasi v R*[167] *is K v R*,[168] a bail application made on behalf of a minor charged with murder. Chief Justice Palmer stated that:

> There is specific legislation, the Juvenile Offenders Act which provides clear and useful guidelines for the courts in this country when dealing with young offenders. The various international Human Rights Conventions referred to (the Universal Declaration of Human Rights, The International Covenant on Economic, Social and Cultural Rights, the International Convention on the Elimination of all forms of Racial Discrimination and Convention on the Rights of the Child ('CRC'), must be read subject to the domestic legislation and the Constitution. Much of what is contained in those Conventions and international instruments are already well reflected in our domestic legislation.

A similar approach was taken in *Seko v Regina*.[169] In *R v Timiti*,[170] the High Court of Kiribati was urged to ignore the requirement for corroboration in rape cases on the

[160] [1989] Tonga LR 14.
[161] Vienna Convention on Diplomatic Relations (opened for signature 18 April 1961, entered into force 24 April 1964, 500 UNTS 95).
[162] As to the application of UK Acts of general application in the Pacific, see Corrin and Paterson (n 132) 35–7.
[163] Constitution of Tonga 1875 s 4.
[164] *Tu'itavake v Porter* [1989] Tonga LR 14, 22 para 390.
[165] *Tu'itavake v Porter* [1989] Tonga LR 14, 33 para 960.
[166] *Al-Adsani v UK* (2001) 34 EHRR 273.
[167] (Unreported, High Court, Solomon Islands, Naqiolevu, J, 7 December 2007, [2007] SBHC 159).
[168] (Unreported, High Court, Solomon Islands, Palmer CJ, 16 September 2005, [2005] SBHC 150).
[169] (Unreported, High Court, Solomon Islands, Palmer CJ, 1 September 2005, [2005] SBHC 100).
[170] (Unreported, High Court, Kiribati, Lussick CJ, 17 August 1998, [1998] KIHC 35).

ground that it denied women the protection of the law guaranteed by section 3 of the Constitution and violated the anti-discrimination provisions in section 15. It was submitted by the prosecution that when interpreting the law, the principles of Convention on the Elimination of All Forms of Discrimination against Women should be taken into account.[171] However, the Chief Justice held that he could see no problem with corroboration and took no account of CEDAW.

Another interesting example can be found in *Taione v Kingdom of Tonga*,[172] where the Supreme Court refused to read down clause 7 of the Constitution (dealing with freedom of expression), on the authority of the ECHR.[173] Webster J accepted that there was 'high authority for [this] being construed in . . . accordance with the limitations set out in article 10(2) of the European Convention of Human Rights'. However, His Honour held that while those principles 'may be sound, they refer to the circumstances and societies in other countries and to other constitutions and I cannot see the legal justification for imposing them on the interpretation of Clause 7 of the Constitution of Tonga'.

In Cook Islands, the High Court, in considering whether the Collector of Inland Revenue was entitled to prevent a person leaving the country until he had paid his tax, refused to take note of the ICCPR.[174] The Covenant was ratified on behalf of Cook Islands by New Zealand but, as it had not been incorporated in any domestic enactment, it was held to have 'no legislative effect'.

3.4.5 *Customary International Law*

Courts in South Pacific countries have also relied on customary international law as a source of domestic law, particularly with reference to maritime zones. As discussed in section 3 of this chapter, rights to control fishing are crucial to many South Pacific Islanders. In *Fa v Naniura*,[175] the appellant argued in the PNG National Court that he had been wrongly convicted of fishing on a foreign boat within a designated fishing zone. It was contended that as PNG had not ratified UNCLOS and PNG had no equivalent legislation,[176] it could not unilaterally declare an EEZ. Los J concluded 'that through the actions of acceptance and practice by many states, the exclusive economic zone has become part of the international customary law'. It was held that the acceptance, policing, and enforcement of EEZs, as defined in article 55 of UNCLOS by a large number of states, gave the EEZ status as part of international customary law.

In contrast, in *Re Application by Ireeuw, Wawar, Ap, and Wakum*,[177] the National Court of PNG refused to consider a submission based on the violation of the customary international law on *non-refoulement* (non-return of a refugee to persecution). Cory J stated:

[171] CEDAW (n 23).

[172] (Unreported, Supreme Court of Tonga, Webster CJ, 8 October 2004, [2004] TOSC 47).

[173] ECHR (n 117).

[174] *In Re Section 201 of the Income Tax Act 1997, Application by Smith* (Unreported, High Court, Cook Islands, Quilliam CJ, 26 April 1999, [1999] CKHC 1).

[175] [1990] PNGLR 506.

[176] UNCLOS (n 85).

[177] [1985] PNGLR 430.

> In relation to the principle of non-refoulement there is a conflict of authorities as to whether it is or is not a rule of customary international law, and in any event, there remains the question whether it has been adopted as part of the law of Papua New Guinea by virtue of the Constitution. The short answer is that the rule has not been adopted in Papua New Guinea.

However, in a later part of the judgment, the Court seemed ready to accept that a rule of customary international law might be treated as incorporated into domestic law, but only if it was not inconsistent with domestic statute or case law. In this case, His Honour considered that the *non-refoulement* principle was contrary to an earlier decision of the Supreme Court.[178]

3.5 Non-binding Domestic Mechanisms that Apply International Law

In some South Pacific Island states there are non-binding mechanisms designed to promote international law or at least take it into account. These include the following.

3.5.1 *Human Rights Commissions*

There is no regional human rights organization in the South Pacific.[179] Nor is there any regional protection system supporting national human rights regimes; the Asia-Pacific is the only region in the world without such a mechanism.[180] In 1989, the Law Association for Asia and the South Pacific adopted a draft Pacific Charter of Human Rights. However, the draft did not receive support at a governmental level.[181] A more recent endorsement of the need for a Pacific human rights mechanism was contained in the PIF's Pacific Plan, since replaced by the Framework for Pacific Regionalism.[182]

The Asia-Pacific Forum and the Pacific Islands Forum both support the idea of national human rights institutions.[183] Only Fiji currently has such a body, having established a Human Rights Commission in 1999.[184] That has now become the

[178] *Premdas v Independent State of Papua New Guinea* [1979] PNGLR 329.

[179] On the need for such a commission see P Imrana Jalal, 'Why Do We Need a Pacific Regional Human Rights Commission?' (2009) 40 Victoria University of Wellington Law Review 177, 191. See also chapter 6 of this book.

[180] S Chiam, 'Asia's Experience in the Quest for a Regional Human Rights Mechanism' (2009) 40 Victoria University of Wellington Law Review 40 127, 128ff; Jalal, ibid. 187.

[181] Jalal, ibid. 181.

[182] Pacific Islands Forum Secretariat, 'The Framework for Pacific Regionalism', 2014 <https://www.forumsec.org/wp-content/uploads/2018/02/Framework-for-Pacific-Regionalism_booklet.pdf> accessed 30 April 2019.

[183] See, e.g., Asia Pacific Forum, 'Changing Community Perceptions on Human Rights' <https://www.asiapacificforum.net/news/changing-community-perceptions-human-rights/> accessed 30 April 2019; PIF, 'Smaller Island States Officers Now Engage in Human Rights Work' <https://www.forumsec.org/smaller-island-states-officers-now-engage-in-human-rights-work/> accessed 30 April 2019.

[184] Human Rights Commission Act 1999 (Fiji).

Human Rights and Anti-Discrimination Commission, under the Constitution.[185] The functions of this body include the power to:

(i) increase awareness of human rights;
(ii) inquire into apparent infringements of human rights;
(iii) make recommendations to the Government on action to protect human rights;
(iv) promote better compliance in Fiji with standards laid down in international instruments on human rights;
(v) encourage the ratification of international human rights instruments by the State and, where appropriate, to recommend the withdrawal of reservations entered to those instruments;
(vi) advise the Government on its reporting obligations under international human rights instruments and, without derogating from the primacy of the Government's responsibility for preparing those reports, to advise on the content of the reports; and
(vii) take part in international meetings on human rights; and to co-operate with other human rights bodies.[186]

The Commission is empowered to enforce and monitor the compliance of human rights instruments ratified by the government and to commence enforcement proceedings before the courts.[187]

As early as 1997, the government of PNG approved in principle the establishment of a human rights commission consistent with the minimum standards set by the Paris Principles.[188] Consultations were conducted between 2007 and 2009, resulting in a Draft Organic Law on the Establishment of the Human Rights Commission. However, this draft bill has not yet been passed and its future is currently unclear. In 2013, Niue developed Terms of Reference for a Human Rights Committee which will be responsible for examining the country's human rights obligations arising from international law.[189]

3.5.2 *Ombudspersons*

The action of governmental bodies may to be reviewed by an ombudsperson in Cook Islands, Fiji, PNG, Samoa, Solomon Islands, and Vanuatu, who may make recommendations including demands for compliance with human rights obligations. However,

185 Constitution of the Republic of Fiji 2013 s 45; Constitution (Amendment) Act 1997 s 42. See also Human Rights Commission Decree 2009 (Fiji).

186 Human Rights Commission Decree 2009 (Fiji) s 12(1).

187 Constitution of the Republic of Fiji 2013 s 45(4)(e) and (g).

188 Human Rights Council Working Group on the Universal Periodic Review, National Report submitted in accordance with paragraph 15(a) of the annex to Human Rights Council Resolution 5/1: Papua New Guinea, UNGAOR, 11th Session, UN Doc A/HRC/WG.6/11/PNG/1 (2–13 May 2011) para 89.

189 East-West Center, 'Niue Holds National Human Rights Consultations', Pacific Islands Report, <http://www.pireport.org/articles/2013/11/29/niue-holds-national-human-rights-consultations> accessed 30 April 2019.

the ombudsperson has powers of recommendation only and cannot compel governmental bodies to act. In Solomon Islands and Vanuatu, reconsideration by an ombudsperson is provided for, and protected by, the constitutions,[190] and these constitutional provisions are supplemented by legislation.[191] In PNG, rather than a single office holder, the function of the ombudsperson is fulfilled by a constitutionally enshrined Ombudsman Commission.[192] In the other countries mentioned, the office of the ombudsperson is established only by legislation.[193] In Tonga, the action of governmental bodies is open to review by the Commissioner for Public Relations, a public office established by legislation.[194] The Commissioner performs essentially the same functions as an ombudsperson.

Investigation and reconsideration by an ombudsperson can be commenced either at the request of a person dissatisfied with the original decision, or on the initiative of the investigating officer, and may include an investigation into breaches of international law. This is a much cheaper option for members of the public than taking a case to the courts, where, as discussed elsewhere in this chapter, the approach to international law is inconsistent. The main disadvantage is that the ombudsperson is only empowered to make recommendations.[195]

3.5.3 *Human Rights Education*

The Pacific Islands human rights consultation in 2004, which brought together NGOs, national human rights institutions, and government representatives, emphasized the need for further human rights training. A key player has been the Regional Rights Resources Team (RRRT), established in 1995 as 'the pioneer of human rights training in the Pacific region, working to build a culture of human rights and assisting nation states to commit to, and observe, international human rights standards'.[196] It is now based within the Education, Training and Human Development Division of the SPC, aiming 'to provide technical assistance and training in order to assist the 22 Pacific island member countries and territories of SPC to increase observance of international human rights standards through improved service delivery, access to justice and effective governance'.[197] In 2013 the University of the South Pacific, in partnership with RRRT, launched a new Diploma in Leadership, Governance and Human Rights within the undergraduate programme. There were 114 students enrolled in the first offering.

[190] Constitution of Solomon Islands 1978 ch IX; Constitution of Vanuatu 1980 ch 9, pt 2; Commissioner for Public Relations Act 2001 (Vanuatu).

[191] Ombudsman (Further Provision) Act 1980 (Solomon Islands); Ombudsman Act 1998 (Vanuatu).

[192] Constitution of PNG 1978 s 217.

[193] Ombudsman Act 1984 (Cook Islands); Ombudsman Act 1998 (Fiji); Komesina o Sulufaiga (Ombudsman) Act 1988 (Samoa).

[194] Commissioner for Public Relations Act 2001 (Tonga).

[195] For further discussion about operation of ombudsmen in the South Pacific, see Anand Satyanand, 'Growth of the Ombudsman Concept' (1999) 3 Journal of South Pacific Law 1.

[196] RRRT, 'About Us' <http://rrrt.spc.int/about> accessed 30 April 2019.

[197] Ibid.

3.6 Major Areas of Legislative Enactment of International Law

As discussed above, ratification of treaties in South Pacific Island states does not make them part of state law. Domestic legislation is therefore required to make ratified instruments part of the law. South Pacific countries have not been active in this regard.

With regard to human rights, South Pacific constitutions generally contain bills of rights, although, apart from Fiji's new Constitution, these do not encompass all the core human rights. There is very little domestic law to make these constitutional guarantees a reality. Vanuatu has perhaps the best record of legislation which specifically introduces international human rights texts into the internal order.[198] Vanuatu and five other South Pacific Island nations, that is, Fiji, Kiribati, Nauru, PNG, and Solomon Islands, have passed legislation which goes at least some way towards complying with their obligations under the Convention on the Rights of the Child.[199] Other examples include Fiji's Fundamental Rights and Freedoms Decree 2000, although this appears to have been replaced by the bill of rights in the current Constitution of 2013,[200] and Niue's Race Relations Act 1972.

South Pacific countries have also been slow to implement international conventions outside the human rights sphere. Even where domestic legislation can be found, it often lags far behind ratification. For example, under the Convention Concerning the Protection of the World Cultural and Natural Heritage 1972, which Solomon Islands ratified in 1992, countries pledge to take appropriate legal measures to protect their cultural and natural heritage. Solomon Islands did not have legislation that could be used to protect its World Heritage Site (East Rennell) until 2012, when the Protected Areas Act 2010 came into force.

Again, Vanuatu has perhaps done more than any other country to incorporate conventions into domestic law due to the fact that, as mentioned above, its Constitution requires enactment of ratifying legislation.[201] Such legislation addresses, for example, civil aviation, taxation, hazardous wastes, and child labour (discussed in section 3.7).[202] Further, legislative ratification of intellectual property conventions[203] has been driven by

[198] See Convention on the Elimination of all Forms of Discrimination Against Women (Ratification) Act 1995 (Vanuatu), Civil and Political Rights (Ratification) Act 2008 (Vanuatu), and Discrimination (Employment and Occupation) Convention (Ratification) Act 2005 (Vanuatu).

[199] Family Law Act 2003 and Child Welfare Decree 2009–2010 (Fiji); Children, Young People and Family Welfare 2012 (Kiribati); Child Protection and Welfare Act (Nauru); Lukautim Pikinini (Child) Act 2009 (PNG); Family Protection Act 2014 (Solomon Islands); Family Protection Act 2014 (Vanuatu).

[200] Constitution of the Republic of Fiji 2013 ch 2.

[201] Constitution of Vanuatu 1980 art. 26.

[202] See Civil Aviation (Ratification) Act 2002 (Vanuatu); Waigani Convention (Ratification) Act 2007 (Vanuatu); Tax Information Exchange Agreement (Ratification) Act 2010 (Vanuatu); and Minimum Age Convention (Ratification) Act 2005 (Vanuatu).

[203] See e.g. Convention for the Safeguarding of the Intangible Cultural Heritage (Ratification) Act 2009 (Vanuatu); Convention Establishing the World Intellectual Property Organization (Ratification) Act 2012 (Vanuatu).

Vanuatu's attempts to join the World Trade Organization (WTO).[204] A full rundown of ratifying Acts is outside the scope of this chapter, but other examples of domestic legislation giving effect to international law include Acts in a number of countries which ratify the Geneva Conventions 1949,[205] although some of these are fairly recent.[206]

3.7 Reasons for Failure to Incorporate International Instruments into Domestic Law

A convention may be signed, ratified, or acceded to for a number of reasons, including perceived trade advantages and/or the desire to become of member of an international organization, such as the WTO.[207] It may also be a condition of receiving foreign aid funds. Thus, for many Pacific countries, ratification of a convention appears to be a political act with little or no intention for bringing about real change within a country. This is graphically illustrated by Vanuatu's Minimum Age Convention (Ratification) Act 2005, which ratifies International Labour Organization Convention No 138 concerning Minimum Age for Admission to Employment 1973.[208] The Convention states that each ratifying member 'shall specify, in a declaration appended to its ratification, a minimum age for admission to employment or work within its territory'.[209] However, no such declaration is appended to the Act, rendering the ratification meaningless.

It also has to be said that changing laws to affect treaty provisions may be difficult for South Pacific Islands governments, which are often more concerned with trying to stay in power. Where constitutional change is required, a special majority is required[210] or, in the case of Tonga, the unanimous support of the Privy Council of Tonga and the approval of the King.[211]

[204] Vanuatu became a member of the WTO on 24 August 2012. See Convention on Biological Diversity (Ratification) Act 1992 (Vanuatu); Convention for the Safeguarding of the Intangible Cultural Heritage (Ratification) Act 2009 (Vanuatu); Berne Convention for the Protection of the Literary and Artistic Works (Ratification) Act 2012 (Vanuatu); and Convention Establishing the World Intellectual Property Organization (Ratification) Act 2012 (Vanuatu).

[205] See e.g. Geneva Conventions Act 1993 (Kiribati); Geneva Conventions Act 1975 (PNG); Geneva Conventions Act 1982 (Vanuatu).

[206] See e.g. Geneva Conventions Act 2015 (Nauru); Geneva Conventions Act 2015 (Samoa); Tuvalu Red Cross Society and Geneva Conventions Act 2013 (Tuvalu) <http://www.paclii.org/cgi-bin/sinodisp/tv/legis/num_act/trcsagca2013497/trcsagca2013497.html?stem=&synonyms=&query=geneva%20convention>.

[207] Fiji, PNG, Samoa, Solomon Island, Tonga, and Vanuatu are members of WTO. See further, Natalie Baird, 'To Ratify or Not to Ratify? An Assessment of the Case for Ratification of International Human Rights Treaties in the Pacific' (2011) 12 Melbourne Journal of International Law 249.

[208] ILO Convention No 138 concerning Minimum Age for Admission to Employment 1973 (opened for signature 26 June 1973, entered into force 19 June 1976, 1015 UNTS 297).

[209] Ibid. art. 1.

[210] See e.g. Constitution of Solomon Islands 1978 s 61.

[211] Constitution of Tonga 1875 cl 79.

4 Critical Themes

4.1 Conflict between Human Rights Law and Customary Laws

The interplay between international law and the pluralistic legal systems in South Pacific Island states gives rise to complex issues. One critical theme is the conflict between norms. This is particularly acute where the values underlying human rights law come into conflict with customary laws.[212] Customary laws and human rights are not always in conflict. However, whilst human rights are expressed to be universal, promoting equality and the rights of the individual, customary laws are fragmented, patriarchal and status based, and prioritize duties of the individual to the community. For those living a traditional lifestyle in remote areas, human rights, whether contained in international law or in a constitution, are a foreign concept. For the majority of the population, traditional values are more resonant.

In the event of conflict, the question then arises as to which of these types of law will prevail. In all South Pacific Island states under discussion the constitution is stated to be the supreme law.[213] In Cook Islands, Fiji, Kiribati, Niue, and Tonga, customary laws are not recognized as a source of state law by the constitution. Accordingly, constitutionally enshrined rights have priority over customary laws.

In South Pacific Island states where customary law is recognized by the constitution as a source of law, such as PNG, Solomon Islands, Samoa, and Vanuatu, the answer is less straightforward. As international human rights law is not generally incorporated into law, there is little jurisprudence dealing directly with international law. However, national courts in the region do occasionally refer to the international texts and decisions as an aid to interpretation of the fundamental rights provisions found in the Constitution. The attitude of national courts when dealing with the conflict between customary law and human rights has been inconsistent. To some extent this can be explained by the different constitutional provisions or the legislative environment. However, this inconsistency lies not just between individual countries, but also between different courts in the same country. A selection of illustrative cases is discussed below under country headings.

4.1.1 *Samoa*

In Samoa, custom is recognized as a source of law by the Constitution,[214] which is declared to be the supreme law.[215] However, the Constitution also includes a bill of

[212] See e.g. *Attorney-General v Saipa'ia Olamalu* [1980–93] WSLRR 41; *Lafaialii v Attorney-General* [2003] WSSC 8.

[213] See e.g. Constitution of Samoa 1960 art. 2; Constitution of Solomon Islands 1978 s 2; Constitution of Tuvalu 2008 cap 1.02 s 3.

[214] Constitution of Samoa 1960 art. 111(1).

[215] Ibid. art. 2.

rights. In certain cases, the courts have refused to enforce constitutional rights which have come into conflict with customary laws. In *Attorney-General v Saipa'ia Olamalu*,[216] for example, the courts were called upon to resolve a dispute concerning the electoral system which only allowed *matai* (traditional chiefs) to vote. It was contended that this was contrary to the constitutionally enshrined right to freedom from discrimination. Although there was no direct reference to international law, the Court considered comments by a UN Visiting Committee, made during a visit in 1959 shortly before independence, that there was little support for universal suffrage. The Court of Appeal held that the electoral system, governed by Part V of the Constitution and the associated legislation, could be quarantined from the bill of rights in Part II.[217] Similarly, the courts originally recognized *matai* authority to banish residents from their village, even though this conflicted with freedom of movement.[218] However, more recently, the courts have held that *matai* are not permitted to make such an order.[219] Similarly, in cases where *matai* had have issued banishment orders against residents of the village on the basis of their allegiance to a new faith, the courts have been adamant that the right to freedom of religion must prevail.[220] In 2017, the Constitution was amended to state that 'Samoa is a Christian nation founded on God the Father, the Son and the Holy Spirit'.[221] Section 11 of the Constitution, which confers a right to freedom of religion remains intact so it is unclear whether this change will impact upon freedom of religion in Samoa.

4.1.2 *Solomon Islands*

In Solomon Islands, customary law is expressly stated to be part of the legal system of the country but subject to the Constitution, including the fundamental rights provisions.[222] However, the right to freedom from discrimination is specifically stated to be subject to the law which provides 'for the application of customary law'.[223] It is unclear whether this means that all customary laws are shielded from the anti-discrimination provision or only laws which specifically provide for the application of customary laws. The courts have favoured the former, broad interpretation and held, in

[216] [1980–93] WSLR 41.

[217] The problem was subsequently resolved by legislation introducing universal suffrage: Electoral Amendment Act (Samoa) 1990, upheld in *Le Tagalo Pita and Others v the Attorney-General and Others* (Unreported, Court of Appeal of Samoa, Cooke P, Bisson and Keith JJ, 18 December 1995). The reservation of parliamentary membership for territorial constituencies for *matai* is preserved by s 4 of the Act.

[218] *Ututa'alega v Luafatasaga Iulio* (Unreported, Land and Titles Court (Appellate Division), Samoa, 19 March 1987); *Ta'amale v Attorney-General* [1980–93] WSLR 41.

[219] (Unreported, Court of Appeal, Samoa, Cooke, P, Casey and Bisson JJA, March 2005).

[220] *Tuivaita v Faamala* [1980–93] WSLR 17; *Sefo v A-G* [2000] WSSC 18; *Lafaialii v A-G* [2003] WSSC 8.

[221] Constitution Amendment Act (No 2) 2017 s 2, inserting a new sub-s 1(3) into the Constitution of Samoa 1960.

[222] Constitution of Solomon Islands 1978 sch 3 para 3.

[223] Ibid. s 15(5)(d). The interpretation of this paragraph is itself open to question: see further Jennifer Corrin, 'Reconciling Customary Law and Human Rights in Melanesia' (2003) 4 Hibernian Law Journal 53, 58.

Tanavalu v Tanavalu,[224] that a customary law excluding a widow from inheriting a share of her husband's estate was valid.[225] The Court accepted the evidence that, under customary law, the deceased's father was entitled to take over the deceased's estate, to the exclusion of the widow. There was no reference to international law in this case, either at first instance or on appeal.[226]

A much broader statement regarding the role of custom vis-à-vis constitutional rights can be found in *Pusi v Leni*,[227] a case which was concerned primarily with whether the actions of traditional leaders had resulted in the plaintiff's banishment from the village and whether this was in violation of the constitutional freedom of movement. Muria CJ considered that the Constitution clearly embraced 'the worthiness, the value and effect of customary law' and noted:

> The Constitution itself recognises customary law as part of the law of Solomon Islands and its authority, therefore, cannot be disregarded. It has evolved from time immemorial and its wisdom has stood the test of time. It is a fallacy to view a constitutional principle or a statutory principle as better than those principles contained in customary law. In my view, one is no better than the other is. It is the circumstances in which the principles are applied that vary and one cannot be readily substituted for the other.

However, this can be contrasted with other cases where the court has come down strongly in favour of human rights. In *Loumia v DPP*[228] the Court of Appeal refused to reduce a murder conviction to manslaughter on the grounds that the defendant was acting in accordance with customary law in exacting revenge for the killing of a relative. The Court made reference to the ECHR as the model for the rights and freedoms set out in the Constitution and stated that even if the duty to kill was part of the customary law of Solomon Islands,[229] such law was contrary to the right to life guaranteed by the Constitution,[230] and was therefore unconstitutional.

4.1.3 *Tuvalu*

In Tuvalu, as in Solomon Islands, the potential conflict has been addressed in the Constitution by shielding customary laws from human rights provisions. Unlike Solomon Islands, where the shield is restricted to the equality provision, in Tuvalu, the Constitution contains an express provision for the protection of Tuvaluan values in the exercise of all fundamental rights.[231] The relevant part of section 29 states:

> (3) Within Tuvalu, the freedoms of the individual can only be exercised having regard to the rights or feelings of other people, and to the effect on society.

[224] (Unreported, High Court, Solomon Islands, Lungole-Awich J, 12 January 1988, [1998] SBHC 4).
[225] Ibid.
[226] (Unreported, Court of Appeal, Solomon Islands, Mason P, McPherson JA, Williams JA, 25 November 1998, [1998] SBCA 8).
[227] (Unreported, High Court, Solomon Islands, Muria CJ, 14 February 1997, [1997] SBHC 100).
[228] [1985–6] SILR 158.
[229] ECHR (n 112).
[230] Constitution of Solomon Islands 1978 s 4.
[231] Constitution of Tuvalu 2008 cap 1.02 s 29.

(4) It may therefore be necessary in certain circumstances to regulate or place some restrictions on the exercise of those rights, if their exercise—
(a) may be divisive, unsettling or offensive to the people; or
(b) may directly threaten Tuvaluan values or culture.

This provision was relied on by the High Court of Tuvalu when it declined to uphold a claim by a pastor that he was entitled to introduce a new religion into a small island community in Tuvalu, contrary to the decision of the *Falekaupule* (the traditional assembly of village elders).[232] This was in spite of the fact that, as discussed above, the Interpretation and General Provisions Act provides that a 'construction of a written law which is consistent with the international obligations of Tuvalu is to be preferred to a construction which is not'.[233]

Another striking example of a case where a court has preferred customary laws can be found in *Tepulolo v Pou*,[234] a contested custody case, where the Court held that although Tuvalu was a signatory to both the CRC and the CEDAW,[235] these were not part of domestic law. The Native Land Ordinance provided that if 'the father being a native accepts the child as being his,[236] such child shall after reaching the age of 2 reside with the father or his relations'. On the basis that this was 'in accordance with customary law', the Court made a compulsory residence order in favour of the father. Whilst the Interpretation and General Provisions Act directed courts to prefer a construction of a written law which was consistent with the international obligations of Tuvalu rather than one which is not,[237] the Court held that the court could only do so where the law was ambiguous.

4.1.4 *Vanuatu*

In Vanuatu, the Constitution recognizes both fundamental rights[238] and customary laws.[239] The recognition provisions relating to customary laws[240] are ambiguous and have been read down by some courts to apply only if there is no written law on point.[241] In a number of cases, the superiority of fundamental rights appears to have been assumed,[242] although there has been no express consideration of the question.

[232] *Teonea v Kaupule* (Unreported, High Court, Tuvalu, CJ, 11 October 2005, [2005] TVHC 2).

[233] Interpretation and General Provisions Act (Tuvalu) 2008 rev edn cap 1.04; s 17.

[234] (Unreported, High Court, Tuvalu, Gordon Ward CJ, 24 January 2005, [2005] TVHC 1).

[235] CRC (n 25); CEDAW (n 23).

[236] Native Land Ordinance 1956 (Tuvalu) cap 22 s 20(2).

[237] Interpretation and General Provisions Act (Tuvalu) 2008 rev edn cap 1.04, s 17.

[238] Constitution of Vanuatu 1980 art. 5.

[239] Constitution of Vanuatu 1980 art. 95.

[240] Constitution of Vanuatu 1980 arts 47(1) and 95.

[241] *Banga v Waiwo* (Unreported, Supreme Court, Vanuatu, d'Imecourt CJ, 17 June 1996, [1996] VUSC 5).

[242] *Public Prosecutor v Kota* [1989–94] 2 Van LR 661; *Noel v Toto* (Unreported, Supreme Court, Vanuatu, Kent J, 19 April 1995, [1995] VUSC 3).

A striking example of a case where a court has relied on international law to support its application of constitutionally enshrined rights provisions includes *Noel v Toto*.[243] This case involved an application for a declaratory judgment regarding ownership of and profits from a piece of customary land. There was evidence that if a woman married she would be deprived of her customary rights to property. Kent J held that the right to equal treatment before the law provided by article 5 of the Constitution guaranteed equal rights for women. Kent J relied on the recently 'adopted Human Rights Charters with respect to women's rights' and held that, in adopting such principles, the Parliament is recognizing rights of women as guaranteed under the Constitution.[244] It would be entirely inconsistent with the Constitution and the attitude of the Parliament to rule that women have fewer rights with respect to land than men.

In fact, recent amendments to the Constitution and to state legislation relating to customary land in Vanuatu may prevent rules of customary land tenure from being overridden in the future.[245]

The Supreme Court of Vanuatu also upheld the superiority of human rights over indigenous customary laws in *Public Prosecutor v Kota*,[246] where a wife who had disobeyed her husband was forced by the chiefs to return to her home island. The Court held that despite the fact that such action was in accordance with the indigenous customary law of that island, this was an offence under the Penal Code,[247] and contravened the wife's constitutional right to freedom of movement.[248]

4.1.5 *Regional Customary International Law*

The above discussion raises the question of the extent to which there can be a regional version of customary international law. For example, if a sufficient number of individual states, or a regional representative body such as the PIF, supports the priority of customary laws over human rights in a particular context, does that result in the emergence of customary international law for the Pacific? Could such custom override universal human rights standards in the event of a conflict? The Forum has recently embraced the concept of 'Pacific Regionalism', expressed as:

> a common sense of identity and purpose, leading progressively to the sharing of institutions, resources, and markets, with the purpose of complementing national efforts, overcoming common constraints, and enhancing sustainable and inclusive development within Pacific countries and territories and for the Pacific region as a whole.[249]

[243] (Unreported, Supreme Court, Vanuatu, Kent J, 19 April 1995) [1995] VUSC 3).

[244] Ibid.

[245] Custom Land Management Act 2013 (Vanuatu); Constitution (Sixth) (Amendment) Act 2013 (Vanuatu), schedule.

[246] (1989–94) 2 Vanuatu Law Reports 661.

[247] Penal Code 1981 (Vanuatu) cap 135.

[248] Constitution of Vanuatu 1980 art. 5.

[249] PIFS, 'Pacific Regionalism' <http://www.forumsec.org/wp-content/uploads/2017/09/Framework-for-Pacific-Regionalism.pdf> accessed 24 June 2019.

The PIF's Framework for Pacific Regionalism provides a platform for the development of a concerted approach on international issues, but no consistent practices have yet emerged.[250]

5 Conclusion

In many small South Pacific Island states, there is a significant gap between the normative and empirical positions on international law. Whilst countries in the region are signatories to a number of international conventions, there is little political commitment to converting these into domestic laws; nor is there any serious debate amongst the countries' leaders on these issues. This is particularly the case in relation to human rights, where the value of international instruments has often been questioned. Additionally, there is strong support for a relative approach to human rights in the South Pacific, which would accommodate the different cultural contexts in which rights operate. Cultural relativism can act as a challenge to the universality of human rights.

Lack of resources often prevents South Pacific Island states from participating at the international level. The irony is that being party to certain conventions, such as those relating to marine pollution, could enable South Pacific countries to take the benefit of technical and financial mechanisms which they do not have the resources to provide themselves.[251]

Generally, national courts in the region have acknowledged the countries' commitments to international law. However, the approach has not been consistent. The references to international texts and decisions by some courts, as discussed above, would seem to suggest a degree of convergence between the domestic and international level. However, as illustrated by the discussion of national jurisprudence on human rights, the courts have sometimes revealed a preference for customary law in cases of conflict. Writing extrajudicially, Muria CJ has observed that 'modern' regimes in the domestic sphere are categorized as 'foreign' by ordinary islanders.[252] In a region where nationalism is often undermined by tribalism, international concerns are often low on the agenda. In many countries, there is also a gaping void between local, customary laws and national, written laws, with very few connecting bridges. In this context, international law may be on the other side of the horizon.

[250] Forum Secretariat, 'The Framework for Pacific Regionalism', July 2014 <http://www.forumsec.org/wp-content/uploads/2017/09/Framework-for-Pacific-Regionalism.pdf> accessed 24 June 2019.

[251] See further OHCHR and PIF (n 5).

[252] John Muria, 'Conflicts in Women's Human Rights in the South Pacific: The Solomon Islands Experience' (1996) 11 Commonwealth Judicial Journal 7.

CHAPTER 31

AUSTRALIA

BEN SAUL

1 Introduction

As a former British colony, Australia received a Western and specifically British tradition of international law,[1] which was initially tied to imperial interests and even the possession of its own colonies in the Pacific. While its international legal personality matured in the 1920s and 30s, it was only after the Second World War that Australia came to exercise a genuinely independent approach to international law, still very much in the mould of a British 'black letter' tradition. Australia's attitude has not been explicitly ideological, or radically reformist, and there has been little conscious attempt by governments or scholars to fashion a distinct 'Australian international law'.

Nonetheless, a hallmark of Australian policy and practice has been a broadly bipartisan political commitment to international law and institutions and to multilateralism. This consensus has been sustained despite Australian governments facing elections roughly every three years since 1901, making policy continuity more challenging than for some of the many undemocratic states in the region. As a self-described 'middle power', Australia views the international legal order as—in the words of a former Prime Minister—the 'only alternative to tension, chaos and destruction'.[2] It gives Australia a voice on the international plane, secures Australia's territorial and economic interests, and reflects the values of the Australian community.[3] Australia tries to be a 'good international citizen',[4] though its efforts are pock-marked by the usual self-interest, pragmatism, and occasional law-breaking of most states.

Australia accordingly participates actively in the various specialized branches of international law and their associated governance mechanisms and dispute resolution

[1] Then Australian Foreign Minister Gareth Evans in (1988–9) 12 Australian YBIL 326–30.

[2] (1974–5) 6 Australian YBIL 357. [3] (1988–9) 12 Australian YBIL 326–30.

[4] Ibid.

procedures. Sometimes it has shown leadership in developing legal norms, while at other times it has followed the lead of its allies or 'sat on the fence' while waiting to see which way the normative wind blows. Given its interests, it has paid special attention to the law of the sea, environmental law, Antarctica, disarmament, human rights, and trade law. Regional developments in Asia and the Pacific have also been of particular interest, with Australia regarded as a regional power in the Pacific.

Since 1945, alongside its commitment to international law, Australia has hedged its bets by wedding itself to a close security alliance with the United States. In large part this is driven by Australia's perceived geographic vulnerability in the Asia-Pacific, particularly after its small, remote population faced the risk of Japanese invasion during the Second World War. This has sometimes led Australia astray, as when it joined in the illegal invasion of Iraq in 2003; or blunted its better instincts, as when it opposed a treaty banning nuclear weapons in 2017 in order to defend its US nuclear umbrella.

At the domestic level, the relationship between international and Australian domestic law is distinctive. The Australian Constitution 1901 is silent on the issue. As in Britain, at common law, treaties ordinarily have no direct domestic legal effect unless the federal parliament has so legislated. The question whether customary international law (CIL) has direct effect in Australian law has not been conclusively settled. As will be shown, some CIL is part of Australian law and some is not; and it remains unclear whether its incorporation is automatic or requires judicial recognition. Despite this broadly dualist approach to treaties and partly hybrid monist/dualist approach to custom, treaties and CIL can still have limited domestic legal effects. These notably include in the interpretation of statutes; the development of the common law; the exercise of administrative discretions; and—doubtfully—in constitutional interpretation.

2 Australia on the International Plane

2.1 Pre-1788 Indigenous Australia

Before British colonization in 1788, the Australian continent was inhabited by hundreds of indigenous groups ('aborigines'), some of whose ancestors had arrived over 50,000 years earlier. Indigenous communities possessed organized social and political orders and customary 'law' systems; often maintained structured relations between their different communities; occasionally traded with 'foreign' peoples, particularly in the north (with Makassan fishermen from Indonesia from the seventeenth century); and had episodic encounters with Dutch, French, and English explorers. There was, however, neither a sense of a sovereign 'state' in the European sense nor of participation in an international legal order. The very name of the continent, 'Australia', was an exotic label appended by Europeans to speculative fifteenth century maps.

2.2 British Colonization 1770–1931

Unlike in many other colonies, including neighbouring New Zealand, no consensual 'treaties' were concluded between the British and indigenous peoples in Australia. Instead, sovereign title to territory was acquired by purported British 'discovery' in 1770 of *terra nullius* (empty land), perfected by continuous peaceful 'settlement' beginning with the first colony (New South Wales) in 1788. While Australia was already inhabited, it was classified as *terra nullius* because the land was not believed to be productively cultivated (according to a European mindset) and the indigenous peoples were regarded as 'backward' and not politically organized.[5] This controversially enabled the subsequent 'settlement' of Australia unencumbered by recognition of pre-existing indigenous rights in land, despite frequent colonial violence more akin to conquest (another mode of acquiring territory at the time, with the different legal effect that indigenous land rights were recognized). English common law was thereby transplanted to the continent,[6] including its approach to international law in domestic law (discussed below).

From the time of British colonization in 1788 to 1901, Britain was responsible for the international relations of its six Australian colonies, despite most of them attaining internal self-rule by the 1860s. This included the power of Britain to enter into treaties binding on its colonies. Many of the colonies during this period did, however, enter into technical arrangements with foreign states in confined areas, such as postal, telegraphic, commercial, and tariff or trade 'agreements' (of a non-'treaty' status).[7] 'Political' matters were left to the imperial government, including decisions about waging war. For example, the Australian colonies committed troops to British conflicts such as the Sudanese campaign (1885), Boer War (1899–1902), and Boxer Rebellion (1900–1), while British forces in Australia participated in New Zealand's Anglo–Māori wars of the 1840s and 1860s.

The Commonwealth of Australia was established by its Constitution of 1 January 1901, which created a federal government and transformed the six colonies into internal 'states' (i.e. provinces), each retaining its own (limited, sub-national) sovereign legal personality. Australia nonetheless remained a British colony, graduating to the *sui generis* status of 'Dominion' from 1907. After Federation, it took some decades for Australia to attain full independent statehood and international legal personality. Britain continued to exercise treaty-making power (usually without consultation) and conduct foreign policy for Australia.

[5] See discussion in *Mabo v Queensland (No 2)* (1992) 175 CLR 1, 31–8 (Brennan J). For a discussion of the international law issues, see Gerry Simpson, '*Mabo*, International Law, *Terra Nullius* and the Stories of Settlement: An Unresolved Jurisprudence' (1993) 19 Melbourne ULR 195. On the many productive indigenous land uses prior to the arrival of the British, see Bruce Pasco, Dark Emu: Black Seeds - Agriculture Or Accident? (Magabala Books 2014).

[6] *Mabo (No 2)* ibid.

[7] Melissa Conley-Tyler, Emily Crawford, and Shirley Scott, 'Australia's International Personality: Historical, Legal and Policy Perspectives' in Donald Rothwell and Emily Crawford (eds), *International Law in Australia* (3rd edn Thomson Reuters 2017) 1, 3.

There were, however, exceptions. Australia separately 'signed' and 'ratified' the Treaty of Versailles and the Covenant of the League of Nations in 1919 and assumed (non-state) membership of the League and the International Labour Organisation (ILO). Australia initially opposed the League as a threat to the Empire and rejected the idea of self-determination.[8] It successfully opposed Japan's proposal to include racial equality and non-discriminatory immigration guarantees in the Covenant.[9] It also secured control over the captured German colonies of New Guinea and Nauru, through their designation as Class C mandates—the least protective of the inhabitants' rights.

It was only after the Imperial Conferences in 1923 and 1926 that Australia was granted full plenary power to enter into treaties and to establish independent diplomatic relations. The UK Statute of Westminster 1931 finally removed Britain's power to legislate for the Dominions without their consent, and Australian law eventually gave effect to this understanding in 1942 (backdated to 1939). Different defence interests during the Second World War compelled Australia to distance itself from imperial control, in order to prioritize its own defence over the defence of Britain. Australia's full independent statehood was not, however, perfected until the passage of the Australia Acts 1986 by the British and Australian parliaments, which removed the residual capacity of the British parliament to legislate for the Australian states and abolished appeals from the Australian courts to Britain's Privy Council. Australia curiously retains the British monarch as its titular head of state (represented in Australia by a Governor-General), although she does not interfere in Australia's foreign relations.

Australia was slow to exercise its autonomy, for a time continuing to subscribe to the British view that the British Commonwealth should 'speak with one voice', that is, through Britain, unless the Dominions' vital interests were affected.[10] In part this reflected persisting strong cultural attachments to Australia's predominantly British origins; Australia assumed Britain's entry into the Second World War in 1939 brought it into the war, without any separate declaration of war.[11] Australia only opened its first diplomatic missions in 1940 (to the US and Japan),[12] considerably later than other Dominions such as Canada and South Africa. This was despite two-thirds of Australian exports going to states other than Britain by the mid 1920s, with Japan being the largest destination by the early 1930s.[13] Australia's reorientation from Europe to Asia accelerated after 1945, markedly affecting its international law priorities.

[8] David Lee, *Australia and the World in the Twentieth Century* (Circa 2006) 35.

[9] Ibid. 37

[10] Alan Watt, *The Evolution of Australian Foreign Policy 1938–1965* (Cambridge University Press 1967) 22.

[11] Anne Twomey, 'Federal Parliament's Changing Role in Treaty Making and External Affairs', Australian Parliamentary Library Research Paper 15 1999–2000, 7 March 2000.

[12] Ibid; Watt (n 10) 20.

[13] Lee (n 8) 49, 51.

2.3 Second World War, the United Nations Charter, and Decolonization

Australia sought to influence the post-war order, albeit with limited success in the face of the great powers. Australia was active in the drafting of the United Nations Charter and Statute of the International Court of Justice (ICJ) (particularly Minister for External Affairs, HV Evatt, and Kenneth Bailey, former Melbourne law professor[14]) and occasionally influential.[15] Article 55 of the Charter became known as the 'Australian pledge', whereby states committed to promoting (but not guaranteeing, as Australia had hoped) 'higher standards of living, full employment and conditions of economic and social progress and development'. Australia also sought to elevate the Economic and Social Council into a principal UN organ; constrain the veto powers in the Security Council; and widen the mandate of the General Assembly. Australia further tried to enhance international accountability over colonial territories by strengthening the trusteeship system,[16] in part to enable itself to gain control over former European colonies in the Pacific, and to exclude Asian immigration to the region.

As the UN system took hold, Australia remained engaged in it but sought to avoid becoming entrenched in the rivalry of the emerging Cold War. Evatt served as first President of the Security Council, then President of the General Assembly in 1948–9 (during the partition of Palestine and creation of Israel). Australia assisted in the decolonization of the Netherlands East Indies between 1947 and 1949 by mediating between the Dutch and the Indonesian nationalists.

The path to independence of Australian-controlled territories was, however, slower: Nauru in 1968 and Papua New Guinea in 1975. The situation in Nauru involved a serious humanitarian and environmental dispute. After Nauru initiated admissible proceedings in the ICJ,[17] in 1993, Australia settled out of court to compensate it for damage caused by Anglo-Australian phosphate mining. Australia became keen to disengage from Papua New Guinea from the late 1960s, because of the costs of administration, the risk of separatism (as in Bougainville), and pressure to respect self-determination.[18] One offshore territory, Cocos (Keeling) Islands, chose to integrate with Australia after exercising self-determination in 1984; other offshore territories, being uninhabited at the time possession was taken, were more straightforward.[19]

[14] Richard Rowe, 'International Law and Diplomacy: The Art of the Possible' (2014) 15 Melbourne JIL 316.

[15] See e.g. Watt (n 10) 78–93.

[16] Lee (n 8) 77.

[17] See *Case Concerning Certain Phosphate Lands in Nauru (Nauru v Australia) (Preliminary Objections)* [1992] ICJ Reports 240.

[18] Lee (n 8) 198–9.

[19] Norfolk Island, Ashmore and Cartier Islands, Heard and McDonald Islands, Christmas Island, and the Coral Sea Islands.

Controversy dogged Australia's position on some other situations of decolonization. Australia accepted South African's creeping incorporation of South West Africa (now Namibia);[20] Indonesia's incorporation of West Papua from 1963; China's expansion into Tibet from 1949;[21] and Indonesia's annexation of Portuguese Timor in 1975. Australia recognized Indonesian sovereignty over Timor in 1978; rejected the view that sovereignty over territory acquired by force must not be recognized;[22] and entered into unlawful treaty arrangements with Indonesia for the cooperative exploitation of Timorese maritime resources (arrangements which were only revised to Timor's satisfaction in 2018, as discussed in section 3.5).

3 Australia and Multilateral Law-Making

Australia's contribution to international law-making has been broadly proportionate to its size, interests, and age as a nation. With functional independence from Britain since the 1930s–40s, Australia has engaged intensively in international law-making since 1945. It has been neither especially active nor passive and, like most states, has engaged most thoroughly when its own vital interests were concerned. As one Australian Foreign Minister observed, in 1994, Australia was party to around 920 treaties (compared to over 7,000 for the United States), of which the majority (over 500) were bilateral. Such participation in treaties is 'by no means unusual' and its adherence to multilateral treaties is 'about average for an OECD country'.[23]

A number of broad dynamics have influenced Australia's approach. First, Australia regards itself as a 'middle power' with finite negotiating resources, necessitating the building of international coalitions to advance its interests (including by acting as a bridge between the West and the Asia-Pacific and/or developing states).[24] Australia is not a world power, has a moderate population (25 million, placing it around fifty-fifth-largest by country), and possesses no nuclear weapons. It can rarely impose its will on other states or unilaterally develop norms. It is nonetheless the world's twelfth-largest economy, ranks twelfth by military spending, has the rich land and maritime resources of a continent at its disposal, and it is one of the world's oldest and most

[20] Lorraine Elliott, 'Social Justice in Labor's Foreign Policy: "Falls the Shadow"' in David Lee and Christopher Waters (eds), *Evatt to Evans: The Labor Tradition in Foreign Policy* (Allen & Unwin 1997) 181, 187.

[21] Watt (n 10) 247.

[22] (1984–7) 11 Australian YBIL 262.

[23] Australian Minister for Foreign Affairs and Trade, Senator Gareth Evans, 4 September 1995, in (1996) 17 Australian YBIL 554.

[24] Ibid.

stable democracies. The term 'middle power' may refer to a distinctive kind of diplomacy[25] rather than being a too-modest measure of brute power.

Successive Australian governments have consequently supported international law as 'a framework which ensures that our voice is heard and that we can play a fair and reasonable role in global deliberations'; further, Australia believes that '[f]or a country of less than great power status, a world governed by principles of justice, equality and rule of law is much more attractive than a world governed by status and power'.[26] In contemporary parlance, it supports (albeit selectively) a 'rules-based order'.[27] Australia has strongly supported multilateralism. It pays its UN dues on time and has strongly supported UN reform, including by arguing for permanent seats on the Security Council for Japan, India, and Brazil, as well as African representation.

Secondly, Australia maintains a close political and security alliance with the US, including relying on the extended US 'nuclear umbrella' and the stationing of US forces in Australia. While Australia does not simply 'follow' the US lead in international law, the alliance significantly shapes Australia's perception of its interests and what it is prepared to do, or not do. For example, Australia actively opposed a treaty to eliminate nuclear weapons in 2016–17, preferring to maintain stable nuclear deterrence while pursuing an incremental approach to disarmament over time.

Thirdly, Australia is not part of any integrated regional community. Asia and the Pacific are relatively under-institutionalized, and Australia is not a member of some of the weak networks that exist, such as the Association of Southeast Asian Nations (ASEAN) (though it engages with it). The arrangements that Australia is a part of are limited in subject (such as the Asia Pacific Economic Cooperation, which Australia played a leading role in creating in 1989); by area and influence (such as the Pacific Islands Forum); or by Australia being on the periphery (part of the ASEAN Regional Forum—which Australia helped to initiate—but not ASEAN). All of these limit Australia's capacity to leverage its membership of regional communities to project its normative influence globally.

Broadly speaking, Australia is a 'good international citizen' in that it is party to most of the multilateral conventions regulating the many specialized areas of international law. Australia normally participates in multilateral law-making processes, seldom opts out of such regimes, and rarely appends problematic reservations. It is Australian policy not to become a party to a treaty until domestic law has been amended accordingly (although objective compliance is distinct from asserted compliance). Some of Australia's key contributions, and hesitations, to key regimes are discussed below.

[25] Gareth Evans (former Australian Foreign Minister), *Incorrigible Optimist: A Political Memoir* (Melbourne University Press 2017) 118.

[26] Evans (n 23).

[27] Australian Minister for Foreign Affairs, Senator Marise Payne, Address at the Australian Institute for International Affairs National Conference, Canberra, 15 October 2018.

Notably, the Australian government maintains a high level of expertise on international law.[28] The Office of International Law in the federal Attorney-General's Department is the primary technical adviser to the government, with almost fifty lawyers. The International Law Section in the Department of Foreign Affairs also provides advice, informed by diplomatic interests, and that Department also has carriage of Australia's treaty making and participation in international organizations. The Australian Government Solicitor is also empowered to advise on international law, with a focus on domestic impacts and litigation.

Australia also has a rich reservoir of academic expertise.[29] One Australian scholar has served on the International Law Commission (James Crawford 1992–2001, later a Judge of the ICJ, mentioned below). Over the course of more than a century, since the late 1800s, various Australian academics have contributed to developing international law (for example, Pitt Cobbett, Joseph Starke (earlier a lawyer at the League of Nations Secretariat), DP O'Connell, Julius Stone, Ivan Shearer, and Hilary Charlesworth). Australia has the fifth oldest dedicated international law chair in the English-speaking world, the Challis Chair in International Law at the University of Sydney, established in 1920, with origins in 1890 (chairs were established at Edinburgh in 1707, University College London in 1827, Oxford in 1859, and Cambridge in 1868); and the University of Sydney was one of the earliest law schools to make international law a compulsory curriculum subject, in 1862. Additionally, Australian international lawyers are long well represented in the United Nations system.

3.1 Human Rights

3.1.1 *Treaty Participation*

Australia is rare among democracies for having no bill of rights, which has led to treaty standards and mechanisms assuming special significance. Australia subscribed to early instruments on trafficking in women and children (1921) and slavery (1926). As a member of the ILO since 1919, it has now ratified fifty-eight of the 189 ILO conventions concerning labour rights.

Australia was one of the eight states on the executive body that drafted the Universal Declaration of Human Rights 1948 and, at its adoption, Australia's representative, HV Evatt, chaired the General Assembly. In the early days of the UN Commission on Human Rights, created in 1947, Australia boldly argued to establish an International Court of Human Rights. In 1948, Australia was one of the staunchest proponents of

[28] Sarah McCosker, 'The Intersecting Professions of the International Law Adviser and Diplomat in a Rising Asia: Australia, India and Malaysia' in Andraz Zidar and Jean-Pierre Gauci (eds), *The Role of Legal Advisers in International Law* (Brill 2016) 96, 104–8.

[29] On the history of international law teaching in Australian law schools, see Ivan Shearer, 'The Teaching of International Law in Australian Law Schools' (1983) 9 Adelaide L Rev 61; James Crawford, 'Teaching and Research in International Law in Australia' (1981–3) 10 Australian YBIL 176.

including economic, social, and cultural rights in human rights treaties.[30] It was, however, concerned that certain civil and political rights could interfere in its restrictive immigration policies and its (mis)treatment of its indigenous peoples.[31] Australia actively participated in the drafting of the twin covenants from 1948 to 1966[32] but federalism concerns delayed ratification (along with that of the Racial Discrimination Convention 1965). Consecutive conservative governments from 1949 to 1972 instrumentally supported human rights in the cause of Cold War freedoms.

A change of government in 1972 saw Australia advocate 'liberal internationalism' and a certain distancing from the US Cold War alliance, leading to renewed support for human rights commitments. Australia has since ratified most of the major treaties (except those on migrant workers and enforced disappearances). Nonetheless, Australia did make significant reservations to the International Covenant on Civil and Political Rights (ICCPR), International Convention on the Elimination of All Forms of Racial Discrimination, and the Convention on the Elimination of All Forms of Discrimination against Women. While Australia was also one of only four states to vote against the UN Declaration on the Rights of Indigenous Peoples in 2007 (concerned about land, resource rights, and self-determination), it later supported it in 2009. However, Australia is still not a party to ILO Convention No. 169 of 1989 on indigenous peoples.

Australia has also opted in to most of the optional protocols (including abolishing the death penalty) and individual complaints procedures (except on economic, social, and cultural rights). Australia participates in the complaints procedures and often respects interim measures requested by UN treaty bodies. While final decisions of the treaty bodies are authoritative but not binding, Australia has a very poor record of changing its behaviour following adverse decisions. Only 13 per cent of the forty-five adverse cases have been adequately remedied.[33] The largest category of cases is concerned with the sovereignty-sensitive area of immigration detention. One of the few unequivocal instances in which Australia responded favourably involved the federal parliament overriding a state law that criminalized homosexuality.[34]

3.1.2 *Domestic Implementation*

While Australia has no bill of rights, some human rights have been explicitly incorporated into Australian law, particularly in anti-discrimination legislation. As a liberal democracy, the substance of many other rights is often protected by ordinary legislation or the common law (although common law rights may be overriden by statute, and frequently have been). The Australian Human Rights Commission

[30] Ben Saul, 'The Drafting of the International Covenant on Economic, Social and Cultural Rights, 1948-1966' in Ben Saul (ed), *The International Covenant on Economic, Social and Cultural Rights: Travaux Preparatoires* (OUP 2016) xciii, cx.

[31] See Annemarie Devereux, *Australia and the Birth of the International Bill of Rights 1946–1966* (Federation Press 2005) ch 2.

[32] Ibid. chs 1 and 2.

[33] See Remedy Australia <http://remedy.org.au> accessed 30 October 2018.

[34] *Toonen v Australia*, UN Human Rights Committee Communication No. 488/1992 (31 March 1994).

(originating in 1981) is mandated to monitor compliance with most human rights treaties (controversially excluding the International Covenant on Economic, Social and Cultural Rights (ICESCR)). While it can conciliate complaints, it cannot provide binding or enforceable remedies.

The above approach nonetheless leaves rights protection 'partial and porous'[35] and dependent on the goodwill of majoritarian politics. Substantial areas of non-compliance still remain. Protracted controversies focus on Australia's treatment of asylum seekers and refugees (particularly detention, naval interdiction, and offshore processing in Nauru and Papua New Guinea), indigenous peoples (particularly self-determination, land rights, racism and inequality, over-incarceration, socio-economic rights, and constitutional status), prisoners, the homeless, and suspected terrorists.[36] Gender equality, violence against women, and labour rights are also recurring concerns. There has, however, been popular support for certain historically controversial human rights causes; for example, a non-binding national plebiscite in favour of permitting same sex marriage in 2017 led to its federal legalization.

3.1.3 *International Engagement*

Abroad, Australia has actively engaged on human rights at the multilateral, regional, and bilateral levels. Australia was a member of the UN Commission on Human Rights five times over twenty-seven years between 1947 and 2006 and was President in 2004.[37] It was elected to its first term on the UN Human Rights Council (established in 2006) in 2018–20. A modest five Australians have been elected to UN treaty bodies. One of them has also twice served as a UN Special Rapporteur (Philip Alston). Another Australian was the UN Special Representative for Human Rights in Cambodia and the Chair of the UN Commission of Inquiry on North Korea (Michael Kirby).

Some issues Australia has worked hardest on internationally include apartheid, the death penalty, women's rights, health, and education. Human rights are seen by most governments as part and parcel of Australian foreign policy values, although governments vary in the weight accorded to them when assessing the national interest.[38] Australia has also maintained a substantial foreign aid and development programme since the 1950s, with a recent focus on good governance and institution building. Aid spending has never met the UN target of 0.7 per cent of Gross National Income, peaking at 0.48 per cent in the late 1960s and falling to below 0.21 per cent by 2018.[39]

While many Australian governments have worked cooperatively with UN bodies mandated to scrutinize its record at home, the relationship has occasionally been punctuated with hostile denunciations of UN criticism and purported interference in domestic affairs,[40] particularly in 2000–6 and from late 2013 to the present (2019). Some Australian

[35] Hilary Charlesworth and Gillian Triggs, 'Australia and the International Protection of Human Rights' in Rothwell and Crawford (eds) (n 7) 117, 129.

[36] Ibid. 131–2. [37] 1947–56, 1978–83, 1985–7, 1991–6, 2003–5. [38] Evans (n 25) 111.

[39] Kate Lyonsm '"Dereliction of duty": five charts that explain Australia's approach to foreign aid', The Guardian, 5 June 2019.

[40] Charlesworth and Triggs (n 35) 132.

governments have issued standing invitations to UN special procedures, while others have refused to cooperate. Australia tends to use the international system to advance human rights abroad while resisting full implementation and open scrutiny at home.[41] The Concluding Observations of treaty bodies, after periodic reviews, have struggled to influence Australia. In addition, while Australia accepted 90 per cent of the peer-to-peer recommendations of the Human Rights Council's Universal Periodic Review (UPR) in 2011, only about 10 per cent had been implemented by the 2015 UPR.[42]

At the regional level, there is no institutionalized regime of human rights protection in Asia and the Pacific, equivalent to those in Europe, the Americas, and Africa. Nor is Australia part of the nascent ASEAN human rights system. Australia has previously called for a regional system. It has also been a strong supporter and funder of the Asian Pacific Forum of National Human Rights Institutions, which aims to strengthen national institutions. In the 1990s, Australia rejected cultural relativist arguments about 'Asian values', arguing that there is no hierarchy of (indivisible) rights.

Australia has often pursued bilateral human rights diplomacy, particularly in the 1980s and 90s.[43] The dominant tactical approach has been pragmatic, constructive engagement, rather than counter-productive 'megaphone diplomacy'. Australia has avoided making trade and aid conditional on foreign governments' human rights performance. Regular bilateral dialogues have been held with China, Vietnam, and Laos.

3.2 International Humanitarian Law and International Criminal Law

Australia has made modest contributions to international humanitarian law (IHL) and international criminal law. Relative to its population, Australia suffered heavy casualties when fighting for Britain in the First World War. The earliest IHL instruments ratified included the Geneva Conventions of 1929 on the wounded and sick, and on prisoners of war (POWs) in 1931, as well as the Geneva Gas Protocol 1925 (ratified in 1930).

Australia was heavily involved in the Second World War, not only protecting British interests in Europe and the Middle East, but also closer to home in the Pacific War. Public awareness of the mistreatment of Australian POWs prompted Australia to participate in the drafting of the four Geneva Conventions of 1949 (ratified in 1958), with a special interest in protecting POWs and punishing perpetrators.[44]

[41] Ibid. 118. [42] Ibid. 132, 135.

[43] Gareth Evans, *Australia's Foreign Relations in the World of the 1990s* (Melbourne University Press 1993) 147–9.

[44] Joseph Starke, 'Australia and the Development of International Humanitarian Law' (1977) 8 Federal Law Review 1, 6.

Immediately after the war, Australia advocated for the establishment of the International Military Tribunal for the Far East (in Tokyo) to prosecute Japanese war criminals in the Pacific,[45] and provided a President, Judge William Webb. Australia adopted war crimes legislation in 1945[46] covering the Second World War. Between 1945 and 1951, it prosecuted 812 enemy nationals (mainly Japanese) for war crimes in 300 trials before military courts.[47] This resulted in the conviction of 644 people, with death sentences passed on 148 of them (of whom 137 were shot or hanged). Domestic legislation enabling the *prospective* prosecution of war criminals, grounded in treaty-based universal jurisdiction under the Geneva Conventions 1949, was passed in 1957, but has never been successfully used. Australia was also the second state to ratify the Genocide Convention 1948, but only domestically criminalized genocide in 2002.[48]

From 1974 to 1977, Australia was active in advocating for progressive humanitarian protections in the two Additional Protocols 1977 to the Geneva Conventions 1949, after its involvement in the Vietnam War.[49] In relation to conventional weapons, Australia is a party to all of the major instruments and served as President of the Diplomatic Conference on the Arms Trade Treaty 2013.

Australia supported and funded the growth of international criminal justice in the 1990s, including the International Criminal Tribunals for the former Yugoslavia (ICTY) and Rwanda, and enacted domestic implementing legislation. Along with Japan it was a strong supporter of the Extraordinary Chambers in the Courts of Cambodia (ECCC) (Australia had proposed a tribunal as early as 1986[50]). During the negotiation of the Rome Statute of the International Criminal Court, Australia chaired the Like-Minded Group of sixty-seven states. It influenced debate on a number of issues.[51] Australia also ratified the Rome Statute in 2002, after a divisive debate within the government, and duly enacted legislation. Australians have served as judges on international tribunals, including the ICTY, ECCC, and Special Tribunal for Lebanon.

Australia's participation in armed conflict after the terrorist attacks of 11 September 2001 (including missions in Afghanistan and Iraq)[52] renewed its interest in the clarification of IHL. Australia supported initiatives by the International Committee of the Red Cross to strengthen compliance with IHL and clarify the rules on detention. From 2001 to 2006, however, Australia controversially supported the US military detention and trial of an Australian, David Hicks, at Guantanamo Bay, despite the charges being retrospective and the trial unfair.[53] Possible serious war crimes by Australian special forces in Afghanistan are also being investigated (as of 2019).

[45] Ibid. [46] War Crimes Act 1945 (Cth).

[47] Georgina Fitzpatrick, Tim McCormack, and Narrelle Morris (eds), *Australia's War Crimes Trials 1945–51* (Brill Nijhoff 2016).

[48] See Ben Saul, 'The International Crime of Genocide in Australian Law' (2000) 22 Sydney L Rev 527.

[49] Starke (n 44) 10–12. [50] (1988–9) 12 Australian YBIL 417. [51] Rowe (n 14).

[52] Over 26,000 Australians served in Afghanistan from 2001–14; and 2,000 in Iraq from 2003–9.

[53] *Hicks v Australia*, UN Human Rights Committee Communication No. 2005/2010 (5 November 2015); *David Hicks v USA*, US Court of Military Commission Review 13–004, 18 February 2015.

3.3 Disarmament and Arms Control

Australia has never possessed nuclear weapons or developed nuclear energy. It nonetheless has strategic interests in nuclear material and relies on the US arsenal (or 'umbrella') for extended nuclear deterrence. It has the world's largest uranium reserves and is the third largest producer of uranium, exporting it for peaceful energy subject to stringent bilateral and International Atomic Energy Association safeguards. It also has strong public opinions, and environmental interests, weighing against nuclear weapons and energy.

Australia considered acquiring nuclear weapons between the 1950s and early 1970s, due to concern about its security in Asia,[54] and collaborated on twelve atmospheric British nuclear tests in Australia in the 1950s (some of which irradiated indigenous lands). In 1973, however, it ratified the Treaty on the Non-Proliferation of Nuclear Weapons 1968 (NPT).[55]

Over time Australia became more enthusiastic about disarmament, thereby becoming a party to the key non-proliferation treaties and international export controls. Leadership in disarmament has been a signature of Australian policy since the mid 1970s. In 1973, Australia challenged the lawfulness of France's atmospheric tests in the Pacific[56] before the ICJ, securing interim measures (disregarded by France) to prevent radioactive fall-out on Australia. In 1986, Australia was an original signatory to the South Pacific Nuclear Free Zone Treaty.

Australia championed a universal nuclear test ban from the 1970s, co-initiated the negotiating mandate for such a treaty in 1993, consolidated a draft text in 1994, and introduced the text of the final Comprehensive Test Ban Treaty 1996 into the General Assembly. It ratified the treaty in 1998. While the treaty is not yet in force, 164 states are parties and its nuclear test moratorium 'has become a clear and powerful international norm'.[57] Earlier in 1995, Australia established the Canberra Commission on the Elimination of Nuclear Weapons, which challenged the logic of deterrence. In the *Nuclear Weapons Advisory Opinion* (1996), Australia broke with its US ally (upon whose nuclear umbrella it relies) by arguing that nuclear weapons are illegal under customary international law; that all states are obliged to pursue their complete elimination; but that it is appropriate to temporarily maintain stable nuclear deterrence in the meantime.[58]

Another Australian initiative (with Japan) was the creation of the International Commission on Nuclear Non-Proliferation and Disarmament (ICNND) in 2008, to

[54] Wayne Reynolds and David Lee (eds), *Australia and the Nuclear Non-Proliferation Treaty 1945–1974* (Australian Department of Foreign Affairs and Trade 2013) xxix.

[55] Ibid. xlv.

[56] From 1966 to 1974 France conducted 41 such tests.

[57] Richard Sadleir (Australian Department of Foreign Affairs and Trade), Statement, Comprehensive Nuclear-Test-Ban Treaty 20th Anniversary Ministerial Meeting, 13 June 2016.

[58] Australian Minister for Foreign Affairs, Gareth Evans, Oral Submission before the ICJ in the *Nuclear Weapons (Advisory Opinion)* case, Verbatim Record, 30 October 1995, CR 95/22.

build consensus prior to the NPT Review Conference of 2010, including by publishing a major report.[59] Following the adoption of an action plan at that Conference, Australia and Japan established the Non-Proliferation and Disarmament Initiative, comprising twelve states, to promote its implementation. Australia has also prioritized the negotiation of a Fissile Material Cut-off Treaty and initiatives on nuclear disarmament verification, transparency, and confidence-building. It has further imposed autonomous sanctions against states that unlawfully develop nuclear weapons, such as Iran and North Korea.

In relation to chemical weapons, Australia became a party to the Geneva Protocol 1925 in 1930. It acquired (but never used) chemical weapons in the Second World War. An Australian draft text of 1992 provided the impetus that enabled the adoption of the Chemical Weapons Convention 1993,[60] which Australia ratified in 1994. Institutionally, Australia has been a member of the Organization for the Prohibition of Chemical Weapons since its creation in 1997; initiated the Australia Group in 1985 (a group of fifteen supplier states that aim to prevent proliferation); and has provided technical experts to UN inspection regimes (as in Iraq). Australia has never possessed biological weapons and participated in the negotiation of the Biological and Toxin Weapons Convention 1972[61] and ratified it in 1977.

3.4 Use of Force and Collective Security

Australia has broadly supported and respected the UN Charter's prohibition against the use of force and its system of collective security, while still maintaining a complementary security alliance—the ANZUS Treaty 1951—with the US.[62] Australia has served five terms on the Security Council.[63] Major conflicts in which Australia has participated include Korea (1950–3), the Malayan Emergency (1948–60), the 'Indonesian Confrontation' in (Malaysian) Borneo (1963–6), Vietnam (1962–72), Gulf War (1990–1), Afghanistan (2001–14), Iraq (2003–9), and Syria (against Islamic State) (2015–present). With the exception of Iraq, Australian involvement was properly based on invitation, collective self-defence, or UN authorization. Australia invoked the ANZUS Treaty 1951 after the 11 September 2001 attacks on New York and Washington, DC. One blemish on Australia's record is its unlawful invasion, alongside the US, Britain, and others, of Iraq in 2003–4, purportedly to enforce UN resolutions.[64]

[59] ICNND, *Eliminating Nuclear Weapons: A Practical Agenda for Global Policymakers* (2009).

[60] Timothy McCormack, 'Some Australian Efforts to Promote Chemical Weapons Non-Proliferation and Disarmament' (1992) Australian YBIL 157.

[61] Starke (n 44) 8.

[62] Security Treaty between Australia, New Zealand, and the United States of America (adopted 1 September 1951, entered into force 29 April 1952, 131 UNTS 83).

[63] 1946–7, 1956–7, 1973–4, 1985–6, and 2013–14, and is a candidate for 2029–30.

[64] (2005) 24 Australian YBIL 413–18.

In other respects Australia has generally been a good international citizen. Australian observers were the first deployed on the first post-war peacekeeping mission, in the Netherlands East Indies/Indonesia in 1947.[65] Since then, Australia has been a leading contributor to peacekeeping, with 65,000 military personnel and police serving in over fifty UN operations in twenty-seven conflicts.[66] Australia provided force commanders in Kashmir (1950–66), Cambodia (1992–3), Yugoslavia (1992), the Sinai (1994–7 and 2017–present), Iraq (1997–9), the Middle East (1998–2000), and East Timor (1999–2000). The then Australian Foreign Minister Gareth Evans also played an influential role in shaping UN debates about peacekeeping reform in the 1990s.[67] Later, as a private citizen, Evans would show significant policy leadership in developing and championing the 'Responsibility to Protect' doctrine, by co-chairing the International Commission on Intervention and State Sovereignty in 2001.

Australia played a leading role in the Cambodian peace process and the subsequent UN mission (UNTAC) (1991–3). Australia's most significant contribution was in East Timor after a violent referendum on self-determination in 1999. Australia mobilized international support for a UN peacekeeping operation (INTERFET), with the consent of Indonesia. Its deployment restored order and enabled a UN administration to transition East Timor to independence. Australia led the UN forces and from 1999 to 2002 contributed 5,500 of 11,500 personnel, with smaller operations until 2005. While motivated largely by humanitarian concerns at that time, an Australian 'liberation narrative' is misleading if viewed within a wider historical frame;[68] Australia's support for the integrity of the referendum result signalled a reluctant reversal of its earlier acceptance of Indonesian sovereignty over the territory (discussed earlier).

As the largest power in the south Pacific region, Australia has given special attention to regional security.[69] It strongly protested successive military coups in Fiji from 1987 onwards. It brokered the peace agreement, and led the Peace Monitoring Group, in Bougainville, Papua New Guinea, from 1998 to 2003, in which around 3,800 Australian military and civilian personnel participated. From 2003 to 2017, Australia also led the Regional Assistance Mission to Solomon Islands, which aimed to assist the government to restore law and order.

3.5 International Law of the Sea

The law of the sea has special importance for Australia because of its geography as a large, remote island continent with vast maritime areas (including maritime search and

[65] Peter Londey, 'Inventing Peacekeeping' in David Horner, Peter Londey, and Jean Bou (eds), *Australian Peacekeeping: Sixty Years in the Field* (Cambridge University Press 2009) 11, 19.

[66] See Horner et al (eds), ibid.

[67] Gareth Evans, *Cooperating for Peace: The Global Agenda for the 1990s and Beyond* (Allen & Unwin 1993).

[68] See e.g. Adam Hughes Henry, 'The Right to "Irrelevance"' (2017) 29 A Journal of Social Justice 215.

[69] Bob Breen, 'Towards Regional Neighbourhood Watch' in Horner et al (eds) (n 65) 58, 84.

rescue responsibility for 9 per cent of Earth). The law of the sea is therefore critical to Australia's economy (for resources and freedom of navigation to trade), environment, and security. Australia has participated actively in its development and enforcement. Sir Kenneth Bailey, its representative at the 1958 and 1960 conferences that led to the Geneva Conventions on the Law of the Sea 1958, chaired conference committees and contributed significantly to the rules on the territorial sea and continental shelf.[70]

At the negotiations for the UN Convention on the Law of Sea 1982 (UNCLOS),[71] Australia advocated for key objectives which were ultimately reflected in the treaty.[72] These included clarity on maritime boundaries, wider offshore resource jurisdiction, environmental protection, rights of innocent passage, facilitating marine research, and the exploitation of the deep seabed. As a land-based minerals producer, Australia's principal disappointment with UNCLOS was that deep seabed mining was not based more on free market forces.[73] Like certain other developed states, Australia refrained from ratification until 1994, until the Part XI Implementation Agreement—which Australia helped to craft—was annexed to the Convention to meet these concerns.

Australia broadly acts in accordance with UNCLOS. It has preferred to settle disputes by negotiation rather than adjudication. In 2002, it excluded maritime delimitation from its acceptance of the compulsory jurisdiction of the ICJ and the UNCLOS dispute settlement procedures. This was partly to stymie any action by the newly independent Timor-Leste to compel delimitation. That long-running dispute was resolved in 2018 by the adoption of a permanent maritime boundary treaty following compulsory, non-binding conciliation[74] (the first use of that procedure under article 298 and Annex V of UNCLOS), after Timor had earlier commenced two arbitrations under the Timor Sea Treaty.[75] The 2018 agreement also transfers sovereignty over existing oil and gas fields to Timor-Leste, and provides for the joint management, development, and profit sharing (in Timor's favour) over the planned Greater Sunrise fields (valued in excess of US$60 billion). In relation to the South China Sea dispute, Australia's military has conducted freedom of navigation exercises to protest China's unlawful encroachments.

[70] Rowe (n 14).

[71] See generally Stuart Kaye, 'Australia and the Negotiation of the Law of the Sea' (2015) 7 Australian Journal of Maritime and Ocean Affairs 256.

[72] Keith Brennan (Australian Delegation), 10th Session of the UN Conference on the Law of the Sea, 17 March 1981, in (1981–3) 10 Australian YBIL 398–9.

[73] Australian Minister for Foreign Affairs, 4 May 1982, in (1981–3) 10 Australian YBIL 400.

[74] Treaty between Australia and the Democratic Republic of Timor-Leste Establishing their Maritime Boundaries in the Timor Sea (adopted 6 March 2018, not yet in force). For a Timorese view on the negotiations, see Timor-Leste Maritime Boundary Office, *New Frontiers: Timor-Leste's Historic Conciliation on Maritime Boundaries in the Timor Sea* (2018). For a summary of the history see Stuart Kaye and Bill Campbell, 'Australia and the Law of the Sea' in Rothwell and Crawford (eds) (n 7) 433, 444–6. Only non-binding conciliation was available because Australia's UNCLOS art. 298 declaration excluded binding settlement.

[75] Henry Burmester, Natalie Klein, and Kate Miles, 'Australia and International Dispute Settlement' in Rothwell and Crawford (eds) ibid. 561, 568.

Environmental protection has been a key concern for Australia, particularly marine pollution, fisheries management, and in sensitive areas such as the Great Barrier Reef, World Heritage areas, and Antarctica. It has also been very active in developing international and regional fisheries agreements. Australia and New Zealand pursued UNCLOS arbitration against Japan's over-fishing of southern blue fin tuna in 1999 and secured provisional measures, but jurisdiction was denied on the merits in 2000.[76] In a case brought by Russia after Australia arrested the trawler *Volga* for illegally catching Patagonian tooth fish, the International Tribunal for the Law of the Sea (ITLOS) ordered Australia to release the vessel in 2002 on less onerous conditions than Australia had imposed.[77]

3.6 International Environmental Law

International environmental law is particularly significant for Australia because of its unique natural environment, the size and variety of its marine areas, and the importance of tourism. Australia is a mega-biodiverse country, which includes unique treasures such as the Great Barrier Reef, Tasmanian wilderness, and outback deserts. At the same time, the economy has been heavily dependent on damaging natural resource extraction, fossil fuels, and intensive agriculture. Particular environmental challenges include a very high rate of species extinction; biodiversity protection; excessive land-clearing; wetland protection; and river and water resource management.

Australia was involved in the negotiations for early instruments, such as the Stockholm Declaration 1972, World Heritage Convention 1972 (with nineteen sites in Australia now listed), and Rio Declaration 1992.[78] It is now party to over forty agreements.[79] The federal government has legislated on the basis of treaties to override state laws in order to protect the environment, as when it halted a Tasmanian dam to protect a World Heritage area.

While Australia supported protection of the ozone layer, given its geographic vulnerability to its depletion, it has been far more equivocal on climate change due to its carbon-intensive economy. It secured key concessions under the Kyoto Protocol 1997, including an increase in emissions in the first commitment period and the exclusion of emissions from land clearing.[80] It then did not ratify the Protocol until 2007, on the basis that developing states and the US were not included.[81] Australia was very active in seeking an agreement at Copenhagen in 2009, but domestic political difficulties saw Australia retreat from a domestic carbon trading scheme. Australia nonetheless committed to emissions reductions under the Doha Amendment to the Kyoto Protocol in 2012 and under the Paris Agreement 2016 (26–28 per cent of 2005

[76] *Southern Bluefin Tuna (New Zealand v Japan; Australia v Japan) (Provisional Measures)* ITLOS Case Nos 3 and 4 (1999) 117 ILR 148 and (Jurisdiction and Admissibility) (2000) 119 ILR 508.

[77] *The 'Volga' (Russia v Australia) (Prompt Release)* ITLOS Case No. 11 (23 December 2002).

[78] Jacqueline Peel and Tim Stephens, 'Australia and International Environmental Law' in Rothwell and Crawford (eds) (n 7) 457, 460.

[79] Ibid. 457. [80] Ibid. 478. [81] (2004) 23 Australian YBIL 360.

levels by 2030). As of 2019, it still lacks a coherent and credible policy for meeting these international commitments.

3.6.1 *Antarctica*

Australia has made a major contribution to environmental protection in, and the development of the legal regime governing, Antarctica.[82] Australia inherited Britain's sovereign claim to Antarctic territory in 1936 and has a special interest in Antarctica because of its geographical proximity and for security reasons. It has opposed successive efforts by the US (in the late 1940s) and at the UN (in the 1980s) to internationalize Antarctica. Despite misgivings about limiting its sovereign freedom, under pressure from other states, Australia agreed to freeze its claim over 42 per cent of Antarctica, as one of twelve original parties to the Antarctic Treaty 1959. The Treaty also: requires (on Australia's initiative) that Antarctica be used for peaceful purposes; encourages scientific cooperation; and establishes an inspection system to verify compliance. Australia has since been very active in governance through annual Antarctic Treaty Consultative Meetings.[83]

Environmentally, Australia became more conscious of the damaging footprint of its Antarctic bases and operations from the 1970s.[84] It was instrumental in unexpectedly abandoning support for a proposed treaty allowing regulated mining in Antarctica and, with France, securing the adoption of the Protocol on Environmental Protection 1991, which bans mining until 2048. The Australian city of Hobart is the headquarters of the Convention on the Conservation of Antarctic Marine Living Resources 1980, under which conservation measures are adopted. As one of the strongest anti-whaling states (since ceasing its own whaling in 1979), Australia supported the establishment of the South Ocean Whale Sanctuary around Antarctica by the International Whaling Commission in 1994, and continues to protest Japanese whaling.

3.7 World Trade Law

The Australian economy was highly protected until the 1960s, when gradual liberalization began. Australia was a founding member of the General Agreement on Tariffs and Trade (GATT) in 1967 and of the World Trade Organization (WTO) in 1995. Australia supports multilateral, rules-based trade through the WTO, which is believed to increase market access and create fairer conditions for its exports.[85] Australia is active in both WTO negotiations and committees.[86] It has focused heavily on liberalization of

[82] See generally Marcus Howard and Tom Griffiths (eds), *Australia and the Antarctic Treaty System: 50 Years of Influence* (UNSW Press 2011).

[83] Ibid. 102. [84] Ibid. 324.

[85] Australian Parliamentary Joint Standing Committee on Foreign Affairs, Defence and Trade, *Australia's Engagement with the World Trade Organisation*, Report No. 121, 9 August 2004, 40–1.

[86] Andrew Mitchell, Elizabeth Sheargold, and Tania Voon, 'Australia and International Trade Law' in Rothwell and Crawford (eds) (n 7) 317, 321.

agricultural trade. Australia is unusual among developed countries in that, like many developing states, its primary exports are raw commodities.[87]

Australia leads the Cairns Group, which is a coalition of nineteen developed and developing states established in 1986 and which accounts for one-third of world agricultural trade.[88] This has set it apart from some of its allies, such as the US and European Union, that have maintained protectionism. The Cairns Group successfully brought agriculture into the world trade regime at the GATT Uruguay Round in 1986–94. It has continued to push for liberalization since the Doha Round commenced in 2001. In 2018 it protested US President Trump's turn to protectionism in its trade 'war' with China.[89]

Trade liberalization has been controversial in Australia, where less competitive industries (such as manufacturing) and employment have been adversely affected. Australia has also sought to protect its cultural industries (such as the arts, books, film, and television) in trade agreements.[90] Concerns have been further expressed about the impact of foreign competition on public health, education, and other service industries.

Australia has been active in the WTO dispute settlement system, being a complainant in eight cases, respondent in sixteen, and a third party in 105.[91] Of the twenty-four cases in which Australia was complainant or respondent, thirteen have proceeded to a WTO Panel Report (as of early 2019), with the first in 1998. Of these, Australia was respondent in eight, losing three and winning five. Australia won all five of the decided cases as complainant. The cases have mainly involved agriculture, manufacturing, health controls on tobacco, and intellectual property, and have contributed to interpreting WTO law.[92] Australia's use of anti-dumping measures has also raised concerns.[93] While most of the contentious cases have involved Western states (the US, Canada, and in Europe), Australia brought one case against India and one against South Korea, and was a respondent in two cases brought by the Philippines and two by Indonesia.

Notwithstanding its engagement with the WTO, Australia's approach has been described as 'on occasion unprincipled, inconsistent and unnecessarily secretive'.[94] A principal criticism is that Australia has pursued bilateral or regional free trade agreements (FTAs) outside the stalled WTO framework, which potentially undermines multilateral trade liberalization and most favoured nation status.[95] Concerns have been raised about their impact on social policies, as well the inclusion of investor-state dispute settlement provisions which give foreign investors preferential rights.[96]

[87] Joint Standing Committee (n 84) 37. [88] Ibid. 43.

[89] Australian Foreign Minister Marise Payne (n 27). [90] See Mitchell et al (n 86) 318–19.

[91] WTO, 'Australia and the WTO' <http://www.wto.org/english/thewto_e/countries_e/australia_e.htm> accessed 30 October 2018.

[92] See Mitchell et al (n 86) 325–32. [93] Ibid. 333–4. [94] Ibid. 341.

[95] Ibid. 335–41. [96] Ibid. 338.

Australia is party to eleven FTAs in force: nine bilateral (with New Zealand, Singapore, US, Thailand, Chile, Malaysia, Korea, Japan, and China) and two regional (one with ASEAN, signed in 2009, plus the Trans-Pacific Partnership, signed in 2018). A further four FTAs have been concluded but are not in force (with Hong Kong, Indonesia, Peru, and the Pacific states). Five more are under negotiation as of 2019 (with the EU, Gulf Cooperation Council, India, the Pacific Alliance, and ASEAN (for a Regional Comprehensive Economic Partnership). Also under negotiation is an environmental goods agreement among seventeen WTO members and a trade in services agreement among fifty WTO economies (with Australia leading negotiations alongside the US and EU)).[97] Australia maintains that its FTAs complement but do not conflict with the WTO regime.[98]

4 International Dispute Settlement

Australia has broadly supported the peaceful resolution of disputes, while seeking to preserve its countervailing policy interests. Its acceptance of binding resolution (instead of negotiation, mediation, or conciliation), and the particular method (arbitral or judicial), depends on the context and the interests at stake. Whilst it accepts binding adjudication of trade, investment, and (some) maritime disputes, fields such as human rights and the environment are often subject to weaker forms of settlement.

Australia's involvement in mechanisms in specialized branches of law were considered above. More generally, Australia accepted the compulsory jurisdiction, conditioned on reciprocity, of the Permanent Court of International Justice from 1930 to 1945 and of the ICJ from 1945 to the present (being one of seventy-two states that currently accept such jurisdiction). Its 1954 acceptance of ICJ jurisdiction contained numerous limitations,[99] while its 1975 acceptance was simply conditional on reciprocity. Australia's current 2002 acceptance contains more limitations and does not apply to disputes: (a) where the parties have agreed to other settlement methods; (b) concerning maritime zone delimitation or associated resource exploitation; or (c) where the other party has accepted ICJ jurisdiction only for the purpose of the dispute, or within twelve months prior to bringing it to Court.[100] As noted earlier, the exclusion of maritime disputes was intended to preclude newly independent Timor-Leste from litigating over maritime boundaries and resources.

[97] Australian Department of Foreign Affairs and Trade, 'Australia's Free Trade Agreements' <https://dfat.gov.au/trade/agreements/Pages/trade-agreements.aspx> accessed 15 January 2019.

[98] (2004) 23 Australian YBIL 326.

[99] (1974–5) 6 Australian YBIL 359.

[100] Australian Declaration, 22 May 2002 <http://www.icj-cij.org/en/declarations/au> accessed 30 October 2018.

Australia has been somewhat active in the ICJ proceedings, being an applicant in two cases (challenging French nuclear testing in 1973–4 and Japanese whaling in 2010–14) and a respondent in three (Nauru's claim from 1989 to 1993 regarding phosphate resources; Portugal's claim from 1991 to 1995 regarding East Timor's maritime resources; and Timor-Leste's claim in 2014–15 for the return of legal documents seized by an Australian intelligence agency the night before PCA arbitration hearings commenced in 2013, in a dispute about Australia's alleged bugging of Timor-Leste's representatives during resource treaty negotiations in 2004).[101] The cases have contributed to the elaboration of international law, including on binding unilateral undertakings (*French Nuclear Test* case 1974); indispensable third parties (*East Timor* case 1995); the use of scientific evidence (*Japanese Whaling* case 2014); and provisional measures (*Timor-Leste* case 2014). Australia has also been an occasional intervener (as in the 1995 nuclear test case brought by New Zealand against France) and participant in advisory opinion proceedings (including opposing the giving of opinions *Israel Wall* (2004) and *Chagos Islands* (2019)[102] cases).

Two Australians have been judges of the ICJ—Percy Spender (1958–67, President 1964–67, and controversial for casting his deciding vote to decline jurisdiction in the *South-West Africa (Namibia) Cases* (1966)) and James Crawford (2015–present), and four have served as ad hoc judges.[103] Australians have also served as judges on international or hybrid criminal tribunals and at the Permanent Court of Arbitration, ad hoc judges at ITLOS, UNCLOS arbitrators, members of UN human rights treaty committees, and arbitrators in interstate and commercial disputes. Many Australians have also worked for the various dispute settlement bodies.

A dispute settlement method of growing significance is investor-state arbitration under Australia's twenty current bilateral investment treaties and under seven of its free trade agreements. The first such arbitration, brought by tobacco company Phillip Morris from 2011 to 2015 under the treaty with Hong Kong, was dismissed on jurisdictional grounds (an interstate WTO complaint against Australia, challenging its health-based 'plain packaging' restrictions on cigarettes, also failed, on the merits, in 2018).[104]

[101] *Nuclear Tests (Australia v France) (Provisional Measures)* [1973] ICJ Rep 99; *Nuclear Tests (Australia v France) (Judgment)* [1974] ICJ Rep 457; *Whaling in the Antarctic (Australia v Japan; New Zealand Intervening)* [2014] ICJ Rep 226; *Certain Phosphate Lands in Nauru (Nauru v Australia) (Preliminary Objections)* [1992] ICJ Rep 240; *East Timor (Portugal v Australia)* [1995] ICJ Rep 90; *Questions Relating to the Seizure and Detention of Certain Documents and Data (Timor-Leste v Australia) (Provisional Orders)* [2014] ICJ Rep 147.

[102] *Legal Consequences of the Separation of the Chagos Archipelago from Mauritius in 1965 (Advisory Opinion)*, 25 February 2019.

[103] Garfield Barwick, Ninian Stephen, Hilary Charlesworth, and Ian Callinan.

[104] *Phillip Morris Asia Ltd v Australia (Award on Jurisdiction and Admissibility)* PCA Case No. 2012/12, 17 December 2015; Australia—Certain Measures Concerning Trademarks, Geographical Indications and Other Plain Packaging Requirements Applicable to Tobacco Products and Packaging, WTO Panel Report, DSU435/DSU458/DSU467, 28 June 2018 (the complaints were brought by Honduras, Dominican Republic, Cuba, and Indonesia).

5 International Law and Australian Domestic Law

This section considers the relationship between international and Australian law. It outlines the domestic procedures for treaty-making and how legislation is required to bring treaty obligations directly into domestic law. In contrast, some (though not all) CIL is automatically part of Australian law but there remains confusion about how this occurs. In addition, treaties (including unincorporated ones) and custom can still influence Australian law in more limited ways, including in the interpretation of statutes; the development of the common law; the exercise of administrative discretions; and, more doubtfully, in constitutional interpretation. Most of these effects are, however, relatively uncommon in routine Australian legal practice.

5.1 Treaty-making

The federal government exercises the 'executive' power of the Commonwealth, under section 61 of the Constitution, to negotiate, sign, ratify, or accede to treaties. The parliament has nonetheless, for some time, had a non-binding supervisory role in treaty-making. Since 1996, it has been customary for all proposed treaties to be tabled in parliament at least fifteen sitting days before binding action is taken by the government (with an exception for urgent or sensitive treaties). The government must also prepare a 'National Interest Analysis' justifying the benefits and costs of the treaty. A parliamentary Joint Standing Committee on Treaties was created to consider proposed treaties and it can receive submissions, conduct hearings, and make recommendations.

5.2 Treaty Law in Domestic Law

The Constitution does not contain a provision that recognizes, incorporates, or gives precedence to international law in Australian law.[105] The High Court has affirmed that the federal parliament 'can legislate ... in breach of international law, taking the risk of international complications .... though every effort should be made to construe Commonwealth statutes so as to avoid breaches of international law and international comity'.[106]

[105] The only explicit reference to international law matters is in section 75(i) of the Constitution, which confers jurisdiction on the High Court of Australia to hear all matters 'arising under a treaty'.

[106] *Polites v Commonwealth* (1945) 70 CLR 60, 69, 81.

Many treaties do not require modification of domestic law and instead can be fulfilled through executive action under section 61 of the Constitution, such as in trade cooperation, defence logistics, or procurement.[107] For some treaties, existing domestic laws may already fulfil the obligations without requiring more specific laws. A small category of treaties may be self-executing, such as those concerning peace, cession of territory, or foreign alliances[108] (but not the UN Charter or Security Council resolutions).[109] Legislation is, however, necessary for a treaty to 'modify the domestic or municipal legal order by creating or changing public and private legal rights and obligations'.[110]

Where treaties require domestic implementation, Australia takes a roughly (but not purely) 'dualist' approach, requiring legislative enactment (or 'transformation') of treaties for them to have domestic legal effect,[111] in particular to ground a cause of action.[112] Theoretically, this approach aims to reflect the separation of powers in Australia's legal system,[113] with parliament 'making' law, the executive 'applying' it and judges 'interpreting' it. For the same reason, the courts have been reluctant to recognize international law as being automatically incorporated into Australian law, or to bring it into Australian law themselves through judicial decisions.

5.2.1 *The 'External Affairs' Power*

Section 51(xxix) of the Constitution empowers the federal parliament to legislate with respect to 'external affairs'. Following uncertainty,[114] the 'external affairs' power is now interpreted to enable parliament to legislatively implement treaties[115] as well as CIL.[116] A law may implement a treaty that seeks to regulate apparently domestic matters (such as human rights or environmental protection within Australia[117]), and need not address matters of an 'international character' (that is, outside Australia or concerning foreign relations) or of 'international concern' (as where domestic issues also have international significance).[118] To be relied upon as a basis for legislation, a treaty must, however, define a regime 'with sufficient specificity to direct the general course to be

[107] Australian Department of Foreign Affairs and Trade, 'Treaty Making Process' <http://dfat.gov.au/international-relations/treaties/treaty-making-process/pages/treaty-making-process.aspx> accessed 30 October 2018.

[108] *Victoria v Commonwealth* (1996) 187 CLR 416, 480–2.

[109] *Bradley v The Commonwealth* (1973) 128 CLR 557, 582–3 (Barwick CJ and Gibbs J).

[110] *Victoria v Commonwealth* (1996) 187 CLR 416, 480–2.

[111] *R v Burgess; Ex parte Henry* (1936) 55 CLR 608, 644.

[112] *Minogue v Williams* (2000) 60 ALD 366, 371.

[113] See e.g. *Minister for Immigration and Ethnic Affairs v Teoh* (1995) 183 CLR 273, 286–7.

[114] *Koowarta v Bjelke Petersen* (1982) 153 CLR 168, 201, 216–17, 243, 247.

[115] *Victoria v Commonwealth* (1996) 187 CLR 416, 476.

[116] *Koowarta v Bjelke Petersen* (1982) 153 CLR 168, 234 (Mason J).

[117] *Commonwealth v Tasmania* (1983) 158 CLR 1; *Koowarta v Bjelke-Petersen* (1982) 153 CLR 168, 226.

[118] *R v Burgess; Ex parte Henry* (1936) 55 CLR 608.

taken by the signatory states',[119] and thus not be too vague or aspirational to support legislation.

A key test for the validity of a law relying on the external affairs power is whether it is reasonably appropriate and adapted to fulfil the treaty's obligations.[120] The law must therefore be directed towards implementing the treaty's terms.[121] The legislation need not, however, implement all of its provisions.[122] A law may also be more detailed than the treaty, or use different language,[123] particularly since it is often necessary to translate treaty provisions into the domestic legal vernacular.

However, a law is unlikely to be supported by the external affairs power if it goes unreasonably beyond the substance of the treaty, or if it is inconsistent with it. In such cases, the aspects of the law that exceed or contradict the treaty would only be valid if they had some other constitutional basis. Other clauses in section 51 of the Constitution empower parliament to make laws in many other areas relevant to international affairs, including defence, trade and commerce, taxation, quarantine, currency, aliens, immigration, communications, banking, and insurance.[124]

The external affairs power itself is not limited to authorizing laws implementing treaties, but has been interpreted in at least two further ways to support legislation that may go beyond a treaty or implement CIL. First, it covers laws dealing with relations with other countries[125] or international organizations (including the UN). This could encompass, for example, laws relating to the territorial sea or continental shelf, and even laws that violate international law.[126]

Secondly, it authorizes laws addressing matters that are geographically external to Australia, even if there is no connection to it. This includes, for example, legislation to prosecute foreign war crimes on the basis of universal jurisdiction,[127] or for the extension of sovereignty over the territorial sea or rights in maritime areas.[128] As long as the subject matter is abroad, legislation implementing a treaty can still be valid even if the treaty itself violates international law.[129]

5.2.2 *Federalism*

Given that federal legislative powers are exhaustively codified in the Constitution, interpretation of the 'external affairs' power has expanded federal power to legislate

[119] *Victoria v Commonwealth* (1996) 187 CLR 416, 486.

[120] *Airlines of NSW Pty Ltd v NSW* [No 2] (1965) 113 CLR 54, 87; *Commonwealth v Tasmania* (1983) 158 CLR 1, 131, 259; *Richardson v Forestry Commission (Tasmania)* (1988) 164 CLR 261, 289, 303.

[121] *Victoria v Commonwealth* (1996) 187 CLR 416, 486.

[122] *Commonwealth v Tasmania* (1983) 158 CLR 1, 234.

[123] *DJL v The Central Authority* (2000) 201 CLR 226, 275.

[124] *Koowarta v Bjelke-Petersen* (1982) 153 CLR 168.

[125] *R v Sharkey* (1949) 79 CLR 121.

[126] *New South Wales v The Commonwealth* (1975) 135 CLR 337.

[127] *Polyukhovich v Commonwealth* (1991) 172 CLR 501.

[128] *New South Wales v The Commonwealth* (1975) 135 CLR 337.

[129] *Horta v Commonwealth* (1994) 181 CLR 183, 195.

at the expense of the legislative competence of the Australian states. The Constitution provides in section 109 that federal law overrides state law in the event of a conflict. In the *Toonen* case, for instance, a state law criminalizing sodomy was overridden by a federal law implementing human rights treaty obligations.[130] In the *Seas and Submerged Lands* case, the federal government invoked law of the sea conventions to extend, at the expense of the states, its sovereignty over the territorial sea and its rights to exploit the resources of the continental shelf.[131] In the *Tasmanian Dam* case, the federal government relied on legislation implementing the World Heritage Convention to prohibit the state government's construction of a dam on a wild river.[132]

Federal–state conflicts arising from treaty obligations can, however, be managed in other ways, including through federal consultation with the states when making treaties, or cooperative federalism (whereby state parliaments 'refer' their legislative powers to the Commonwealth on a defined subject). Until 1983, Australia had often problematically sought to include 'federal clauses' in treaties, to purportedly limit its obligations where the Australian states had domestic constitutional competence over the subject.[133]

5.2.3 *Methods of Legislative Implementation*

Legislation has implemented treaties in different ways and to various extents. Sometimes it gives treaty provisions direct force of law, as in the case of diplomatic immunities.[134] A different approach is where legislation 'translates' treaty language into domestic terminology. Sometimes this is technical, as in the federal Criminal Code's articulation of international crimes, or in providing for extraterritorial jurisdiction under transnational crime cooperation treaties (as on drugs or terrorism).

At other times, 'translation' goes beyond technicalities and makes substantive modifications (as in the alteration of the Refugee Convention's definition of refugee).[135] Often treaty provisions are 'cherry-picked' for enactment; thus, the treaty definition of a refugee has been legislated, but the full suite of refugee rights under the Refugee Convention has been omitted.

Likewise, in the realm of human rights, various anti-discrimination provisions drawn from treaties have been enacted, but most human rights (for instance, under the ICCPR and ICESCR) have not been incorporated. The ICCPR is merely 'scheduled' to federal legislation defining the mandate of the Australian Human Rights Commission to inquire into and make recommendations about violations;[136] however, it is not

[130] *Toonen v Australia*, UN Human Rights Committee Communication No. 488/1992 (31 March 1994).

[131] *New South Wales v The Commonwealth* (1975) 135 CLR 337.

[132] *Commonwealth v Tasmania* (1983) 158 CLR 1.

[133] See generally Henry Burmester, 'Federal Clauses: An Australian Perspective' (1985) 34 ICLQ 522.

[134] Diplomatic Privileges and Immunities Act 1967 (Cth) s 7.

[135] Migration Act 1958 (Cth) s 5J.

[136] Human Rights and Equal Opportunity Act 1986 (Cth) s 11(1)(f).

implemented so as to establish justiciable rights or binding remedies.[137] The ICESCR is absent even from these non-binding powers.

Where legislation implements a treaty, sometimes it will include a general provision stipulating that a decision-maker must act consistently with Australia's obligations under it or, in some cases, under any treaty binding Australia.[138] The courts have, however, tended to interpret such clauses restrictively, particularly where treaty obligations are indeterminate. It is also possible for legislation to authorize the executive to issue subsidiary legislation ('regulations'), as has been used for timely implementation of UN Security Council sanctions resolutions under Chapter VII of the UN Charter.[139]

5.3 Other Influences of International Law on Australian Law

While treaties must normally be legislated to have direct domestic effect, Australian law does not take a pure dualist approach. Both CIL and treaties (including unratified treaties) can have certain other limited legal effects in domestic law, discussed below.

5.3.1 *Interpretation of Statutes*

5.3.1.1 STATUTES IMPLEMENTING TREATIES

A statute implementing a treaty may be interpreted by reference to the treaty. Section 15AB(2)(d) of the Acts Interpretation Act 1901 (Cth) provides that a treaty referred to in a statute may be used as extrinsic material in interpreting that statute to confirm the ordinary meaning of a provision, or where the provision is ambiguous or obscure, or where its ordinary meaning would lead to a manifestly absurd or unreasonable result.

Courts have indicated that such statutory provisions are to be interpreted according to the international rules of treaty interpretation,[140] which themselves are not enacted into domestic law,[141] though some judges have preferred the Australian rules of statutory construction.[142] The words of the statute ultimately govern, such that statutory modification (or even exclusion) of treaty provisions must be given effect.[143] For example, legislation implementing 'special measures' under the International

[137] *Dietrich v The Queen* (1992) 177 CLR 292, 305, 359–60; *Minogue v Williams* [2000] FCA 125, [21].

[138] See Andrew Edgar and Rayner Thwaites, 'Implementing Treaties in [Australian] Domestic Law: Translation, Enforcement and Administrative Law' (2018) 19 Melbourne JIL 24.

[139] Charter of the United Nations Act 1945 (Cth).

[140] *Applicant A v Minister for Immigration and Ethnic Affairs* (1997) 190 CLR 225, 239–40; *Minister for Immigration and Multicultural Affairs v QAAH of 2004* (2006) 231 CLR 1, [34].

[141] Vienna Convention on the Law of Treaties (adopted 23 May 1969, entered into force 27 January 1980, 1155 UNTS 331).

[142] *Minister for Home Affairs of the Commonwealth v Zentai* (2012) 246 CLR 213, 238; *Maloney v The Queen* (2013) 252 CLR 168, 198–9, 221–2, 234–5.

[143] *Maloney v The Queen* (2013) 252 CLR 168.

Convention on the Elimination of Racial Discrimination did not include the Convention's element of consultation, which could not be implied into the statute.[144]

5.3.1.2 PRESUMPTION OF STATUTORY CONSISTENCY WITH INTERNATIONAL LAW

As a matter of interpretation, 'there is a general rule of construction of statutes according to which, unless the contrary intention is clear, it is to be presumed that they do not violate any recognised rule of international law'.[145] Moreover, 'so far as the language of a statute permits, it should be interpreted and applied in conformity with the established rules of international law'.[146] The principle extends to both treaty and CIL.[147] There is, however, some uncertainty as to its exact scope. Some decisions have confined the use of international law to statutes that are ambiguous.[148]

Express statutory language conflicting with international law will be valid, 'though every effort should be made to construe Commonwealth statutes so as to avoid breaches of international law and of international comity'.[149] Thus in one landmark case, a law conscripting a foreign national into military service was found to be valid despite international law prohibiting it.[150] Statutes permitting the mandatory (and even indefinite) immigration detention of non-citizens, contrary to international law,[151] have still been repeatedly upheld for over almost three decades.[152]

5.3.2 *Constitutional Interpretation*

The High Court has not decided whether international law may be used in interpreting the Constitution, although a number of senior judges have made observations. Justice Kirby argued for the relevant principles of statutory interpretation to apply to constitutional interpretation, on the basis that the Constitution speaks not only to the Australian people but to the international community of which it is a part.[153] In contrast, some other judges have rejected the use of international law.[154] Justice McHugh described using it as a 'heretical' attempt to 'amend' the Constitution (with international laws adopted after the Constitution of 1901), without following the

[144] Ibid.

[145] *Polites v Commonwealth* (1945) 70 CLR 60, 68–9.

[146] *Al Kateb v Godwin* [2004] HC 37, [63] (McHugh J); see also *Polites v Commonwealth* (1945) 70 CLR 60, 68–9, 77, 80–1; *Jumbunna Coal Mine NL v Victorian Coal Miners' Association* (1908) 6 CLR 309, 363.

[147] *Zhang v Zemin* [2010] NSWCA 255, [125] [128] [157] [160] [174].

[148] *Chu Kheng Lim v The Minister for Immigration, Local Government and Ethnic Affairs* (1992) 176 CLR 1, 38; *Minister for Immigration and Ethnic Affairs v Teoh* (1995) 183 CLR 273, 287.

[149] *Polites v Commonwealth* (1945) 70 CLR 60, 69.

[150] Ibid.

[151] *A v Australia*, UN Human Rights Committee Communication No. 560/1993 (30 April 1997) [9.3].

[152] *Chu Kheng Lim v Minister for Immigration* (1992) 176 CLR 1, 38; *Al Kateb v Godwin* [2004] HC 37.

[153] *Kartinyeri v Commonwealth* (1998) 195 CLR 337, 418; see also *Newcrest Mining (WA) Ltd v Commonwealth* (1997) 190 CLR 513, 657–8.

[154] *AMS v AIF* (1999) 199 CLR 160, 180 (Gleeson CJ, McHugh, and Gummow JJ).

required referendum procedure; he also objected to the supposed vagueness of international law, and the apparent lack of judicial expertise in it.[155]

5.3.3 *Developing the Common Law*

The High Court has held that international law is a 'legitimate and important influence on the development of the common law, especially when international law declares the existence of universal human rights'.[156] Human rights treaties in particular can help to indicate contemporary values and the public interest.[157] In *Mabo (No 2)*, the development of treaties prohibiting racial discrimination was one factor informing the High Court's momentous decision in 1992 to recognize that indigenous 'native title' to ancestral lands had in principle survived, and had not been automatically extinguished by colonization,[158] although it could still be extinguished by the valid exercise of governmental powers, for instance in conferring freehold land title. (Whether sovereignty over Australia was validly acquired under international law was considered non-justiciable.) The decision was, however, a high watermark instance. The principle has seldom been used, or made a significant difference, in subsequent cases, in part because subsequent courts have been less well disposed towards it.

5.3.4 *'Legitimate Expectations' in Administrative Discretion*

Traditionally at common law, international treaties (even if ratified) had 'no legal effect upon the rights and duties of the subjects of the Crown',[159] in the absence of legislative implementation. In the *Teoh* case in 1995,[160] however, the High Court found that Australia's ratification of a treaty (the Convention on the Rights of the Child 1989) is not merely 'platitudinous' but creates a 'legitimate expectation' that administrative discretions will be exercised in accordance with the treaty (namely, the best interests of a child when deporting a father), particularly when it concerns human rights. The principle does not require decision-makers to act in conformity with the treaty, but to consider it when making a decision, and to give an affected person notice and an opportunity to be heard if it is proposed not to follow it. Decision-makers thus remain free to exercise their own discretion that may be contrary to a treaty once they have taken it into account.

The decision led to exaggerated accusations that the courts were introducing international law through the back door, bypassing parliament and interfering in Australia's sovereignty. A series of legislative proposals to overturn the decision was not adopted. In later cases, the High Court confined the already limited scope of the doctrine by focusing

155 *Al Kateb v Godwin* [2004] HC 37, [63] (McHugh J).
156 *Mabo v Queensland (No 2)* (1992) 175 CLR 1, 42 (Brennan J).
157 *Royal Women's Hospital v Medical Practitioners Board of Victoria* [2006] VSCA 85, [75] (Maxwell J).
158 *Mabo (No 2)* (1992) 175 CLR 1, 42.
159 *Simsek v McPhee* (1982) 148 CLR 636, 641 (Stephen J).
160 *Minister for Immigration and Ethnic Affairs v Teoh* (1995) 183 CLR 273.

on the fairness of procedure rather than whether an expectation was not met.[161] The principle is now of limited utility and likely confined to affected children's rights.

5.3.5 *Customary International Law*

Beyond statutory interpretation, the question whether CIL has direct effect in Australian law has not been conclusively settled. Some early decisions approved of the English law approach of treating established custom as automatically part of domestic law unless contrary to statute or judicial decision.[162] A later case described it not as 'part' of domestic law but as 'one of the sources' of it where it has been 'received into' domestic law.[163] It was unclear if this occurs automatically or by judicial decision.

In the *Nulyarimma* case in 1999, one Federal Court judge found that a proven customary rule will be judicially adopted or received as a source of Australian law where it is consistent with statute or public policy as reflected in final judicial decisions.[164] In other words, custom may change the common law by being received into it. On the facts, the judge concluded that the CIL crime of genocide was part of Australian law (Australia had ratified but not enacted the Genocide Convention) but that allegations of genocide against indigenous people had not been made out on the facts. The other two judges did not express a conclusive view on the position of custom in Australian law, but found that genocide was not part of domestic law for other reasons: doubt about whether CIL establishes universal jurisdiction over genocide in common law courts; a belief that CIL did not specify which courts have jurisdiction or what procedures and punishment apply; a policy choice to decline to apply CIL norms of a criminal character; and a view that federal crimes require statutory codification.

6 Conclusion

Australia has not sought to construct or project a distinct 'Australian international law'. The digests of Australian practice recorded in the *Australian Year Book of International Law* since 1965 reveal much that is unremarkable (neither distinctive nor law-breaking) about Australia's approach to international law. Much practice deals with routine matters common to many other states: recognition of states (and, until 1988, of governments); diplomatic relations; domestic legislation implementing treaties; Australia's position on human rights in other countries; consular protection of nationals; the securing of maritime boundaries and areas; air services agreements (important to Australia because of its remote geography); jurisdiction and state immunities (including the blocking of US anti-trust laws); and so on.

[161] *Minister for Immigration and Multicultural and Indigenous Affairs; ex parte Lam* (2003) 214 CLR 1, [105] (McHugh and Gummow JJ).

[162] *Chung Chi Cheung v The King* [1938] UKPC 75, 80–1; *Potter v Broken Hill Pty Co Ltd* (1906) 3 CLR 479, 495, 506–7.

[163] *Chow Hung Ching v The King* (1949) 77 CLR 449, 477.

[164] *Nulyarimma v Thompson* [1999] 96 FCR 153, 187–91.

Australia has largely maintained its inherited Western/British tradition of international law since attaining gradual independence from Britain between 1901 and the early 1940s. At the same time, it has customized and augmented that tradition with special attention to the development of, and participation in, specialized areas of law that resonate with Australian interests. Many of these involve multilateral framework regimes and their associated institutions. Australia has been most active in the law of the sea, environmental law, Antarctica, human rights and development, international criminal law, international humanitarian law, disarmament, trade, and the United Nations system at large.

At a high level of generality, Australia tries to be a 'good international citizen',[165] while suffering periodic bouts of sovereign defensiveness, exceptionalism (particularly on human rights and migration control), and non-compliance, and while also maintaining an exclusionary alliance with the United States that can occasionally induce it to behave badly. In its foreign policy vision from 2017 onwards, Australia highlights new challenges to international rules and calls for their observance but admits that its security 'is maintained primarily through our own strength, [and] our alliance with the United States'.[166]

Domestically, Australia is broadly dualist in relation to treaties—reflecting a strong separation of powers and the supremacy accorded to parliamentary democracy—and partly monist, partly dualist concerning custom. Treaties and customs can nonetheless have influential indirect effects on Australian law, (albeit rare in practice) particularly through the interpretation of statutes, the development of the common law, the exercise of certain administrative discretions (in rare cases), and improbably in constitutional interpretation. Much of the transformative promise of international law within Australia remains, however, unfulfilled, due to a cautious approach to it by Australian courts, a lack of familiarity with it by practicing Australian lawyers, as well as a lingering suspicion of it amongst some politicians as an agent of foreign interference.

[165] Historically see Alison Pert, *Australia as a Good International Citizen* (Federation Press 2014).

[166] Australian Government, *2017 Foreign Policy White Paper* (Commonwealth of Australia 2017) 24.

CHAPTER 32

NEW ZEALAND

KENNETH KEITH

1 Introduction

This chapter adopts a chronological approach to New Zealand's (NZ's) interaction with international law, which takes account of the increasing authority of New Zealand's institutions since 1840, when British colonization began. Over this period, NZ has developed and diversified its international trading, political, and strategic relations with other states, and has experienced the broadening and deepening of international law which has responded to massive scientific, technical, environmental, and geopolitical developments. The chronological approach also helps to identify major changes in NZ's positions on, and contributions to, international law.

Also central are NZ's geography and population. As an island country 1,700 kilometres from its largest neighbour, Australia, it has been inhabited for only about 1,000 years. It was first settled by Polynesians (ancestors of present day Maōri) and later populated by Europeans, mainly British, who began to arrive only 200 years ago. Now NZ has a rapidly diversifying population, with increasing numbers of people relocating from the Pacific and Asia.

2 Distinctive Contributions to International Law

2.1 Evolving Status and Self-determination

The first European discoverers were the Dutch in 1642. NZ was explored by the British and French in the late eighteenth century. In 1840, Captain William Hobson of the United Kingdom's (UK's) Royal Navy and indigenous Maōri chiefs signed the Treaty of Waitangi. It transferred governorship (in the Maōri text) or sovereignty (in the

English) to the British Crown, protected Māori land rights and treasured things, and conferred the rights and obligations of British subjects on Māori. Its status, meaning, and application continue to be the subject of controversy in executive action, legislation, judicial proceedings, scholarly writing, and more broadly.[1] Three propositions, among many, may be drawn from that material.

The opinion commonly expressed from the late nineteenth well into the twentieth century—that the Treaty was not a valid treaty in international law—has been challenged. One reason for the earlier view given by scholars was that, with limited exceptions, only the states of Europe and their former colonies in the Americas had treaty-making power. But there is much state practice to the contrary[2] and now many others, including the International Court of Justice (ICJ),[3] have accepted the validity and legal effect of treaties concluded by other states and entities.

That change of opinion relates to the second proposition about the Treaty—its changing content and application over time. The claims considered by the Waitangi Tribunal since 1975 include Māori criminal offending rates, the Trans Pacific Partnership Agreement, intellectual property, a denied Victoria Cross, the radio spectrum, a by-election, and a school closing.[4] Third, while the Tribunal has considered many Treaty claims, such claims are also addressed by negotiation, ad hoc commissions of inquiry, executive and legislative processes, litigation, and international bodies.

As section 3 shows, NZ's international status and treaty-making capacity developed in response to changing circumstances and needs, in relation to which 1919 was the critical year. In that year, NZ became independent when it signed the Treaty of Versailles; it gained international standing as a member of the League of Nations, even if restraints on its domestic legislative powers remained. Some senior politicians took a more cautious view in the 1920s,[5] but the powers associated with full independence were available.

2.1.1 *Western Samoa*

An early manifestation of NZ's independence was its reluctance at Versailles to accept the principle of self-determination proclaimed by US President Woodrow Wilson in his 'Fourteen Points' of 1918. NZ Prime Minister William Massey, with his Australian and South African colleagues, sought sovereignty over the German colonies their forces had occupied during World War I, in NZ's case, German Western Samoa. But they had

[1] See e.g. MSR Palmer, *The Treaty of Waitangi in NZ's Law and Constitution* (Victoria University Press 2008) and Mark Hickford, *Lords of the Land* (OUP 2011), and their extensive bibliographies.

[2] See e.g. a 1879 Despatch from the Colonial Secretary to NZ and other colonies about treaties of commerce and navigation: 'Treaties of Commerce and Navigation' [1880] Appendix to the Journals of the [NZ] House of Representatives ('AJHR') A3; among them are treaties with Borneo, China, Japan, Liberia, Madagascar, Morocco, Muscat, Persia, Sandwich Islands, Siam, Tunis, and Turkey, along with 28 states in Europe and the Americas.

[3] Most recently *Pedra Banca/Pulau Batu Puteh (Malaysia/Singapore)* [2008] ICJ Rep 12.

[4] See the Tribunal's website <http://www.waitangitribunal.govt.nz>.

[5] See e.g. Alex Frame, *Salmond: Southern Jurist* (Victorian University Press 1995) ch 14.

to accept that the best they could do was to accept the territories becoming mandates. Former enemy territories, inhabited by people thought not yet able to stand by themselves under the strenuous conditions of the modern world, would have applied to them the principle that their well-being and development formed a sacred trust of civilisation. To give effect to the principle, qualified states would accept a tutelage of such peoples.

NZ, as mandatory, had full power of administration and legislation over the territory as an integral part of NZ—but not as sovereign and subject to the mandate which required it to promote to the utmost the material and moral well-being, and the social progress of the inhabitants of the territory. There was to be no military training and no military or naval bases, and freedom of conscience and of religion were to be ensured. NZ would report to the League each year, providing full information about the territory and the measures taken to meet its obligations. No such obligations existed in the case of colonial territories generally.[6]

The mandate was replaced in December 1946 by a Trusteeship Agreement concluded under the Charter of the United Nations. The Charter provisions were prepared by a committee at the San Francisco Conference chaired by the Prime Minister of NZ, Peter Fraser. His attitude and that of his government were flatly opposed to his predecessor's at Versailles.[7] Among the basic objectives of the international trusteeship system was the promotion of progressive development towards self-government or independence. The opinion has been expressed that NZ's finest foreign policy achievements were its contribution at San Francisco in formulating the Charter provisions on decolonization and the subsequent negotiations leading to the independence or self-government in free association of three of the four non-self-governing territories for which NZ was responsible.[8]

The Samoa Amendment Act 1947, giving effect to the Trusteeship Agreement, provided for a NZ-appointed High Commissioner and established a Council of State consisting of the High Commissioner and Samoans holding office as *Fautua*, and a Legislative Assembly, with broad powers to legislate. It included the *Fautua*, elected or nominated Samoan members, and elected European members. This legislation was the outcome of discussions by the NZ government with the Samoan leaders and a UN visiting mission. The intention was to ensure that Samoans would consider the

[6] For commentary see e.g. Mary Boyd in Angus Ross (ed), *New Zealand's Record in the Pacific Islands in the Twentieth Century* (Longman Paul 1969) 115–18 and (2016) Journal of South Pacific Law Special Issue 8.

[7] In addition to the references in the last footnote see e.g. the volumes of *New Zealand in World Affairs* (New Zealand International Review 1977 and following); the other chapters in Ross (ed), ibid.; Brian Lynch (ed), *Celebrating New Zealand's Emergence: A Tribute to Sir George Laking and Frank Corner* (NZ Institute of International Affairs 2005) chs 11–13; David McDowell 'Changing Pacific Realities: The UN as Decolonizer and Development Stimulator' in Brian Lynch (ed), *New Zealand and the United Nations—70th Anniversary* (NZ Institute of International Affairs 2015) ch 2; and Alex Frame, 'The External Affairs and Defence of the Cook Islands' (1987) 17 Victoria University of Wellington Law Review 141.

[8] McDowell, ibid. 19.

government to be theirs and to lay the foundations for a gradual transfer of authority.[9] In 1952, provision was made for a Samoan Executive Council, including Samoan members. In 1953, the Prime Minister declared that the time had arrived for further important steps in the political, social, and economic fields. In the political field, the objective was to assist Samoa to develop:

1. A strong, responsible, and representative central government whose authority is accepted by the community, and which is Samoan in outlook, in personnel, and in the bases of its power;
2. A united population comprising all Samoan citizens, regardless of race; and
3. The administrative machinery, the institutions, and the knowledge necessary for the solution of future political, social, and economic problems.

A widely representative convention was held to consider a constitutional plan for the future state of Western Samoa. One possible feature of that plan was 'the special relationship between NZ and the future self-governing State of Western Samoa', a reference to the Tongan model—a protectorate under a treaty with the UK.[10] The convention confirmed that the established institutions of government were acceptable to the Samoan people and should continue to be developed towards self-government. A single legislature should be established. In the Samoan constituencies, only the *Matais* (the chiefs) should be allowed to vote. The responsible minister raised a question about that, as did the UN over the years. The Government also decided, contrary to the position of the convention, that responsible government would not be introduced at once. Rather, unofficial members of the Executive Council would be offered wide practical experience of executive government by the extension of the Associate Member Scheme. The form of the future relationship with NZ would depend on the course of Samoa's constitutional development. The scope of the responsibilities which it would be proper for NZ to bear, if it were to provide protection for the territory's interests in the international sphere, would be defined by the same process. Commenting on a feature of constitutions modelled on the British parliamentary system, the minister stated:

> their institutions, and the practices and conventions which make the institutions effective, evolve at a pace which is determined largely by experience of their successful functioning.[11]

Three questions remained—the suffrage, the preparation of the constitution, and the relationship with NZ. On the last, there were growing doubts whether the Tongan solution would be durable as worldwide decolonization gathered pace. Discussions in

[9] See *New Zealand Foreign Policy Statements and Documents 1943–1957* (NZ Ministry of Foreign Affairs 1972) 149–59. Samoan leaders in November 1946 had called for immediate self-government and were outraged not to have been consulted about the terms of the trusteeship agreement.

[10] Ibid. 309–14. [11] Ibid. 401–5.

Apia, Wellington, and New York led to the conclusion, to the delight of leading Samoans, that the only answer was independence. Tamasese, who was to be co-head of state after independence, wept and said 'at last I trust NZ'.[12] The treaty of friendship issue was left until after independence. A lengthy constitutional convention, held in 1960 and attended by 173 members, adopted a draft constitution, building on the steps taken since 1947. As a result of the UN's urging, the draft also included a Bill of Rights. An amendment introducing universal suffrage was defeated though.

The UN General Assembly, in December 1960, recommended that a plebiscite be held on the basis of universal suffrage under UN supervision, to determine whether the inhabitants agreed (1) with the Constitution, and (2) that on 1 January 1962 Western Samoa should become an independent state on the basis of the Constitution.

In October 1961, the General Assembly, on the basis of the report of its plebiscite commissioner, endorsed the overwhelmingly positive answers. It also expressed the hope that Western Samoa would become a member of the UN, as happened in 1976.[13] Under the 1962 Treaty of Friendship, the NZ Government, so long as the Western Samoan Government wished and in such manner as would in no way impair its right to formulate its own foreign policies, was to afford assistance to that Government in the conduct of its international relations.

2.1.2 *The Cook Islands, Niue, and Tokelau*

In 1960, NZ had been, with the Netherlands, the only colonial power to vote in favour of the UN General Assembly's Declaration on the Granting of Independence to Colonial Countries and Peoples.[14] The following day the Assembly stated the principles which were to guide UN members in determining whether the Charter obligation to transmit information in respect of non-self-governing territories existed. Such territories could reach a full measure of self-government by becoming sovereign independent states or being in free association with or integrating with an independent state.[15] Free association was to be the result of a free and voluntary choice of the peoples of the territory, expressed through informed and democratic processes. The people should retain the freedom to modify that status.

The two resolutions provided an important part of the context in which the future development of NZ's three remaining non-self-governing territories—the Cook Islands, Niue, and Tokelau—played out. The Cook Islands in 1965 and Niue in 1974 opted for free association with NZ, while Tokelau has so far chosen in two referendums not to change its status.

The critical precedent for the UN as a whole related to the Cook Islands. Its Legislative Assembly, established in 1957 and consisting primarily of locally elected

[12] Gerald Hensley, 'A New Status for Small Territories' in Lynch (ed), *Celebrating New Zealand's Emergence* (n 7) 109, 112.

[13] UNGA res 1626 (XVI) (18 October 1961).

[14] UNGA res 1514 (XV) (14 December 1960).

[15] UNGA res 1541 (XV) (15 December 1960).

members, had power to legislate for the peace, order, and good government of the Cook Islands, but not for matters relating to defence or external affairs, nor those affecting Crown title to land, nor in a manner repugnant to certain reserved NZ statutes. Such limits had long been familiar within the evolving Empire and Commonwealth, as was the retention of the discretion of the Resident Commissioner, appointed by the NZ Governor-General, to refuse assent to a bill, or to amend it or reserve it for the Governor-General's assent, as well as the power of the Governor-General to disallow a measure.

In 1963 the Cook Islands Assembly adopted the first of the four choices for constitutional development presented to it—self-government in free association with NZ, complete independence, integration into NZ, or a Polynesian federation. The view from New York was that only free association would work in terms of rapidly changing views about decolonization and that it should not be hedged about with qualifications. The NZ Prime Minister backed that position: 'I believe and I have told the British and others that a small country like New Zealand cannot afford to antagonise the bulk of world opinion'.[16]

The Cook Islands Assembly in 1963 considered a detailed plan for future political development, assisted by constitutional advisers who made recommendations about the executive government, the head of state, the composition and powers of the Assembly, the judiciary, the role of traditional leaders, control of the public service, relations with NZ, and the enactment of a constitution. The Assembly largely accepted those proposals and, in 1964, the NZ Parliament enacted the Cook Islands Constitution Act. In early 1965 the UN General Assembly decided, at the invitation of the NZ Government, to send an observer to the election to be held later that year at which the Constitution was to be the principal issue.

That invitation was a precedent and drew the ire of Australia, the UK, and the US. The Act to which the Constitution was annexed provided that the Cook Islands were to be self-governing. The Constitution was to be the supreme law of the Cook Islands. Section 5 read as follows:

> Nothing in this Act or in the Constitution shall affect the responsibilities of Her Majesty the Queen in right of New Zealand for the external affairs and defence of the Cook Islands, those responsibilities to be discharged after consultation by the Prime Minister of New Zealand with the Premier of the Cook Islands.

Nothing in the Act was to affect the status of any person as a British subject or NZ citizen. The Constitution enabled the Cook Islands legislature to repeal those provisions and the provisions of the Constitution itself. Significant changes—such as becoming independent—required a particular process, including voting to be passed by a supermajority.

The UN observer reported that the unprecedented part which the UN had been called upon to play was crucial in so far as it involved attesting whether the people of the Cook

[16] Hensley (n 12) 113.

Islands had had a fair opportunity to exercise their right of self-determination, as indeed they had. The General Assembly, noting that the Constitution was in force and that the people had control of their internal affairs and their future, considered that the Cook Islands had attained full internal self-government. It accordingly decided that NZ was no longer obliged to provide information to the UN, and it contemplated eventual independence in terms of the 1960 Declaration if the people so desired.[17]

Over the decades following 1965, it became clear that the relationship was one of equal status. In a joint centenary declaration of 2001, the two prime ministers agreed that in foreign affairs the Cook Islands interacts with the international community as a sovereign and independent state and is responsible at international law for its actions. Any action taken by NZ in respect of its constitutional responsibilities for the foreign affairs, defence, and security of the Cook Islands would be taken on the delegated authority of, and as an agent or facilitator at the specific request of, the Cook Islands; section 5 of the 1964 Act 'thus records a responsibility to assist the Cook Islands and not a qualification of Cook Islands' statehood'. It was accepted that the government of the Cook Islands possesses the capacity to enter into treaties and other international agreements in its own right, and has full legal and executive competence in respect of defence and security.[18]

The declaration reflected extensive practice. The Cook Islands has become a member of numerous international organizations to which only 'states' may be admitted; it is party to many multilateral treaties similarly limited to states, including human rights conventions, the Geneva Conventions, the International Criminal Court Statute, and the UN Convention on the Law of the Sea (UNCLOS), and many bilateral treaties; it also has diplomatic relations with over forty states. The developments captured in the declaration and practice are now reflected in the note in the UN treaty database (also applicable to Niue), which also reflects the cautious position taken previously by the UN Secretariat.[19]

As a result of these developments, the Secretary-General, as depository of multilateral treaties, recognized the full treaty-making capacity of the Cook Islands in 1992 and Niue in 1994.

2.2 International Organizations

At San Francisco in 1945, the NZ delegation, led by Prime Minister Fraser, actively pursued important changes to the draft UN Charter. The 'small power rampant'

[17] UNGA res 2064 (XX) (16 December 1965).

[18] Joint Centenary Declaration of the Principles of the Relationship between the Cook Islands and New Zealand, 11 July 2001.

[19] See e.g. (1979) UN Juridical Yearbook 172, (1986) UN Juridical Yearbook 289; compare a 1976 exchange between the US and NZ: Frame (n 7) 150.

pressed for a supranational organization which would exercise judicial powers and command physical force. It also proposed that the Charter should require all members to come to the aid of a victim of aggression; place limits on the use of the veto in the Security Council; provide for compulsory ICJ jurisdiction over at least some categories of legal disputes; include undertakings in respect of human rights, including economic and social rights, supported by a principal organ; promote the self-determination of non-self-governing territories; and require that the responsibilities of the UN Secretariat be exclusively international in character.[20] Given the matters discussed elsewhere in this chapter and the existing commentary, only the last topic is considered.

The proposal emphasized the traditions of the British and NZ public service law and practice dating back to 1912. It was a reaction to the deterioration of standards in the Secretariat of the League of Nations in its final years. It emphasized the exclusively international character of the responsibilities of the Secretariat and the paramount importance of securing the highest standards of efficiency and technical competence of those appointed.[21] The essence of these points was incorporated in the Charter.[22] The US delegation applauded such NZ contribution to the Charter, but only a few years later, during the period of 'McCarthyism', the US attacked those same principles.

The US challenge arose following steps taken by the first UN Secretary-General, Trygve Lie, against US nationals who were UN officials and had been dismissed, or who had not had their contracts renewed. They successfully challenged those actions in the UN Administrative Tribunal. By that time, Dag Hammarskjöld, the new Secretary-General, had reasserted the Charter principles. He included budget sums in the draft to meet the awards made by the Tribunal.[23]

Was the UN obliged to meet those obligations? NZ said yes, while the US, Australia, and others said no. NZ acknowledged that there was nothing to prevent the General Assembly amending the powers of the Tribunal if they were found to be excessive, as had indeed just happened. But any interference with awards that had already been made would, save in the most exceptional cases, be a denial of justice, a most grave decision, and a departure from principle. That legislation should not be retroactive.

The ICJ, in agreement with the argument of principle made by NZ and quoted by the Netherlands, ruled that the awards were binding.[24] The General Assembly accordingly authorized the Secretary-General to pay the awards.[25]

[20] FLW Wood, *The New Zealand People at War—Political and External Affairs* (War History Branch, NZ Department of Internal Affairs 1958) chs 22–6.

[21] [1945] AJHR A2 114; 7 UN Conference on International Organization (UNCIO) 511.

[22] 7 UNCIO 175, 177, 1 UNCIO 617; a Soviet proposal to delete the paragraph which became art. 101(3) was rejected by 26–6: 7 UNCIO 176–7.

[23] For what follows see Cedric Ryngaert, Ige Dekker, Ramses Wessel, and Jan Wouters (eds), *Judicial Decisions on the Law of International Organisations* (OUP 2016) ch 2.2.

[24] *United Nations Administrative Tribunal* [1954] ICJ Reps 47.

[25] UNGA res 889 (IX) (17 December 1954).

2.3 Law of the Sea

NZ, surrounded by vast areas of ocean, has major interests in the law of the sea. They relate to the extensive fisheries, gas and oil, and other resources in its continental shelf, freedom of navigation for its ocean-based trade, the protection of its national security, and the control of pollution risks. Major changes in technology (notably in fishing methods and in oil and gas exploitation), in the numbers and interests of the states of the world, in trade, and in ideology have brought with them huge changes in the law, especially over the last seventy years.

Over that time, NZ's interests and positions on the law have also changed in major ways. For much of the preceding 100 years (not including the period of World War II), the protection of the maritime interests of NZ, along with other matters of foreign policy and defence, was mainly in the hands of the Imperial authorities in London. As a matter of law, that near monopoly was supported by the limits on the legislative power of the self-governing colonies, and even of the Dominions, to pass laws which had extraterritorial effect or which were repugnant to Imperial legislation. These limits were removed for most of the Dominions in 1931, but for NZ only in 1947. A major early manifestation of the exercise of that plenary power is the Shipping and Seamen Act 1952, which gave effect to many treaties regulating maritime activities and labour.

During much of the interwar period, NZ's defence and security interests were also seen as being in the hands of the Imperial authorities. That position was reflected in the opposition of NZ, along with others of the Dominions, to the Permanent Court of International Justice ('PCIJ') having jurisdiction in respect of belligerent maritime rights. In their view, the civilian lawyers on that Court did not properly understand that matter.[26]

That the law of the sea in the 1950s was in a stable condition might have been suggested by the work of the International Law Commission at that time. It built on earlier efforts of the League of Nations, and culminated in 1956 in a single comprehensive draft convention dealing with the territorial sea, the high seas, the continental shelf, and fisheries and which included binding dispute settlement. The four Conventions on the law of the sea adopted in 1958 failed, however, to settle two major issues—the width of the territorial sea and of any fishing zone beyond—as did a further conference held in 1960. By 1965, NZ fisheries were developing and Parliament provided for a three mile territorial sea and, beyond it, a nine mile fishing zone. Japan protested that exclusion of its established fishing activity was a breach of international law and proposed that the matter be taken to the ICJ. NZ responded by proposing that a phase-out agreement be concluded. Japan agreed to such an arrangement in 1967.

Just ten years later, in the context of the rapidly developing law reflected in the negotiating texts of what would become UNCLOS in 1982, Parliament enacted the

[26] 'Protocol for the Pacific Settlement of International Disputes' [1925] AJHR A5c, 6.

Territorial Sea and Exclusive Economic Zone Act 1977—the latter area to extend for 200 nautical miles (nm) from the baseline for the territorial sea (now extended to 12 nm). The Act, consistent with proposals made by NZ and others, required the responsible minister to calculate the total allowable catch in respect of every fishery within the zone, the portion that NZ fishing craft had the capacity to harvest, and the allocation to foreign fishers of the balance. At that time, NZ made a new declaration of acceptance of ICJ jurisdiction, excluding from it disputes about the living resources of the EEZ.[27]

Any possible concern about litigation was soon removed by agreements made with Japan, Korea, and the Russian Federation. Those states recognized that NZ had lawfully established the 200 nm zone, within which it exercised sovereign rights for the purpose of exploring and exploiting, conserving, and managing the living resources. The parties also recognized that fishing vessels of the three countries had been engaged in utilizing the living resources off the coast of NZ. The agreements provided for the allocation to fishing vessels of particular parts of the surpluses of fishery resources. Those unilateral, bilateral, and multilateral actions, accompanied by regional agreements, are manifestations of major changes in NZ's interests and evaluations from the late 1960s.[28]

Of the four conventions adopted in 1958, NZ became party only to that on the continental shelf. UNCLOS brought greater precision to the definition of the continental shelf, rights in which extend to 200 nm from the coast and beyond if the characteristics of the seabed allow. In 2004, NZ and Australia entered into a treaty determining the boundaries in an area where their 200 nm zones overlapped—between Three Kings Islands and Norfolk Island to the north-west of NZ, and Campbell Island and Macquarie Island to the south-west—and where, on the two countries' understanding, their extended shelves overlapped.

The two countries had still to establish, through the work of the Commission on the Limits of the Continental Shelf set up under UNCLOS, that their shelves did extend beyond the 200 nm limit. In 2008, the Commission adopted its recommendations in respect of their submissions. Once the two states delineated the limits of their shelves on the basis of those recommendations, they became 'final and binding'. The outcome is an area of 1.7 million square kilometres of seabed (or more than five times the land area of NZ) outside the 200 nm zone.

UNCLOS also contains important provisions to combat marine pollution, which are supplemented by texts prepared by the International Maritime Organization. NZ is a party to thirty such instruments.

Another major feature of UNCLOS is Part XV, setting up a system of compulsory dispute settlement. It does not apply, however, where the parties have agreed on another method of resolution, as a tribunal under the UNCLOS procedure held in rejecting the *Southern Bluefin Tuna* case brought by Australia and NZ against Japan.[29]

[27] 1055 UNTS 323.

[28] For a most valuable account by a major participant in the process, see CD Beeby, *The United Nations Conference on the Law of the Sea: A New Zealand View* (NZ Ministry of Foreign Affairs 1975).

[29] *Southern Bluefin Tuna (New Zealand v Japan, Australia v Japan)* (2000) 23 RIAA I.

The development of binding dispute resolution methods relating to maritime matters is also to be seen in regional arrangements, for instance, the Convention on the Conservation and Management of High Seas Fishery Resources in the South Pacific Ocean 2009, in the preparation of which NZ had a major hand. The Russian Federation challenged a measure adopted by the Commission at its first session in 2006 and a dispute resolution panel was established and decided the challenge under a tight timetable.

2.4 Peaceful Settlement of International Disputes

In this area too, NZ's positions and policies have changed markedly. In 1924 the League Assembly adopted the Geneva Protocol for the Pacific Settlement of International Disputes, in order to 'fill the gaps' in the League mechanisms for the peaceful settlement of disputes. First, parties would have been bound to accept the jurisdiction of the PCIJ and a compulsory arbitration process. NZ complained of the failure to consult adequately. Second, the Protocol gravely threatened the belligerent maritime rights of the Royal Navy. Third, NZ's immigration policy might be held by the Court, 'consisting mainly of foreigners', to be contrary to the comity of nations. The Macdonald Government in the UK fell within days of the Protocol being adopted and there was great relief in Wellington at the consequential failure of the Protocol.

NZ did, however, go along with the adoption of the General Act 1928, to which it acceded in 1931 along with the UK, Australia, and France, to NZ's advantage and France's discomfort in subsequent disputes.[30] It also accepted the compulsory jurisdiction of the PCIJ in 1929, along with the UK and other Dominions, but with reservations which it saw as excluding maritime rights and immigration from jurisdiction.

By 1945, as mentioned earlier, the Government had a very different view of international organizations. In 1936, a clear indication of that view was revealed through its response to a request from the League about improving the application of the Covenant. It emphasized the failure to fully implement the existing provisions of the Covenant,[31] and indicated that the Covenant could nevertheless be strengthened. The Government was prepared to agree in principle to the provisions of the Geneva Protocol 1924.

When the UN Charter and the ICJ Statute were being drafted, NZ, with Australia, called for 'the maximum employment of the International Court of Justice for the ascertainment of facts which may be in dispute'.[32] They pushed for the new Court to possess some compulsory jurisdiction. But the US and the USSR were opposed, and to

[30] See the 1973, 1974, and 1995 proceedings in the *Nuclear Tests* cases (nn 34–5).

[31] 'Reform of the League of Nations' [1936] AJHR A5a.

[32] Australia and NZ, 'Text of Conclusions Reached at the Australia–NZ Conference, Wellington, November 1944' in *New Zealand Foreign Policy Statements and Documents* (n 9) 80–1.

press the proposal even though it had majority support might have jeopardized the adoption of the Statute and indeed the Charter itself.

Compulsory jurisdiction was not to be, but NZ continued to support the cause. In 1971, when the General Assembly engaged in a review of the role of the ICJ, NZ stated that 'it attaches considerable importance to third party settlement as a means of resolving disputes and, in particular, has always strongly supported the Court and the role of judicial settlement'. It recalled that it had declared its acceptance of the jurisdiction of the PCIJ initially in 1929 and it had also accepted jurisdiction under particular treaties.[33]

NZ has been party to one case in the ICJ as an applicant: the *Nuclear Tests* case brought at the same time as the Australian case,[34] where the 1971 statement above was recalled. In 1995 it made an application in terms of that judgment.[35] In 2013–14 it intervened in the *Whaling* case brought by Australia against Japan. Written and oral submissions were also provided in the *Nuclear Weapons Advisory Opinion* proceedings in 1996.

NZ has experience of interstate arbitration: the *William Webster* case in 1925, under an Anglo-American agreement of 1910, with the award affirming the validity of the Treaty of Waitangi; the *Rainbow Warrior* case (1990), following a binding mediation by the UN Secretary-General, implemented by three agreements between the two parties; and the *Southern Bluefin Tuna* case (1999 and 2000) brought by Australia and NZ against Japan. NZ (as at 29 April 2019) is or has been party to sixty-nine World Trade Organization (WTO) cases under the Dispute Settlement Understanding—nine as complainant, none as respondent, and sixty as a third party.

To place adjudication and arbitration at the centre of a discussion on dispute settlement is to take too narrow an approach. Parties to international disputes have many choices before them, as the Hague Conventions of 1899 and 1907, and article 33 of the UN Charter, among many other sources and much practice, make clear. Other choices include negotiation (perhaps leading to an agreement not to resolve the dispute), conciliation, mediation, fact finding, good offices, regional agencies, —and combinations of them.

Nor should the role of national processes in resolving what could become international disputes be neglected. Had the *Dodd* case (referred to below) decided against the exclusive jurisdiction of the US as the flag state, the US might well have taken up the cause of its national, as France did in the *Lotus* case.[36] The same point may be made about national court decisions relating to the valuation of imported items under General Agreement on Tariffs and Trade 1947 (GATT) and WTO rules. NZ courts

[33] *Review of the Role of the International Court of Justice—Report of the Secretary General—Addendum*, UN GAOR, 26th session, Agenda Item 90, UN Doc A/8382/Add.4 (12 November 1971) 2.

[34] *Nuclear Tests (NZ v France) (Judgment)* [1974] ICJ Rep 457.

[35] *Request for an Examination of the Situation in accordance with Paragraph 63 of the Court's Judgement of 20 December 1974 in the Nuclear Tests (NZ v France) Case (Order)* [1995] ICJ Rep 288.

[36] *Lotus (France v Turkey)* [1927] PCIJ A10.

have made such decisions in respect of, for instance, cars from Japan, agricultural equipment from Canada and the US, and shoes from the Philippines. Cases involving the immunities of foreign states provide another instance.

The resolution of the *Rainbow Warrior* affair, which involved the French bombing of a Greenpeace vessel in Auckland harbour in 1985, killing one person, provides a good example of choices of means being made by the states and others involved. They included criminal prosecutions and convictions; national investigations; French acknowledgement of responsibility and of a willingness to make reparation for the consequences of its action; private arbitration; failed attempts to resolve aspects of the dispute by negotiation; good offices provided by a third state; and agreement by the two governments to refer all the problems for a binding principled and equitable ruling by the UN Secretary-General. This led to the two convicted military officers being transferred to a military facility in French Polynesia for a period of three years, obligations with which France did not comply. The NZ Government then invoked the agreed tribunal process, with the tribunal recommending a fund to promote closer and friendly relations. The recommendation was accepted by both governments and put in treaty form by the two prime ministers at an official lunch in Wellington,[37] with the NZ Prime Minister declaring that this unhappy affair was at an end.

3 Implementation of International Law in National Law

In inheriting British common law,[38] NZ law recognizes that customary international law is part of NZ common law. Treaties accepted by the executive in exercise of its prerogative powers relating to foreign affairs do not generally become part of NZ law unless legislation is passed.[39]

3.1 1840 to 1919

Controversies about the international legal force and effect of the Treaty of Waitangi 1840 were mentioned in section 2.1. An early sense of the role of international law may be gathered from court decisions in the 1870s and 1880s, and from actions of the legislature and the executive at that time. In 1874, thirty-year-old Robert Stout, recently qualified as a lawyer (and, later, Attorney-General, Premier, and Chief Justice), persuaded the Court of Appeal that only the flag state, in this case the US, had jurisdiction

[37] Agreement on the Establishment of a Fund to Promote Friendly Relations between Citizens of the Two Countries (signed 29 April 1991, 1668 UNTS 357).

[38] William Blackstone, *Commentaries on the Laws of England* (Book 4 1769) ch 2.

[39] *Labour Conventions* [1937] AC 326.

over crimes committed on a vessel on the high seas. In support of his argument he cited the publicists Phillimore, Wheaton, Vattel, and Story. In the light of that authority, the Court read narrowly a statute which gave colonial courts jurisdiction over offending 'upon the sea' and set aside the conviction.[40]

In 1884, at a time when NZ's policies in pursuit of the annexation of Pacific Islands (in particular Samoa) were at a peak and Robert Stout was already Premier, the Court of Appeal decided that that country was not a 'state', certainly not a 'civilised state' in terms of Imperial legislation.[41] Again Phillimore, Vattel, and Wheaton were cited, along with Austin and the US Supreme Court. In that case, as in the earlier case, the Court was giving content to the legislative language by reference to customary international law as found in the books. Stout at the same time had been urging the authorities in London both to advise that Royal assent be given to a NZ bill of 1883 to annex and federate with Pacific territories and to allow NZ to annex Samoa. But that urging was unsuccessful, with that particular matter being handled at the highest diplomatic level between London and Berlin. Britain and Germany in 1884 agreed to 'continue' to recognize the independence of Samoa.[42]

To turn to more mundane matters, matters of international communication by post and telegraph were already being addressed in this early period through colonial legislation (from 1858) as well as Imperial statutes and international treaties.[43]

NZ also became bound by a number of multilateral treaties concluded by the UK without any action on its part. Most concerned the law of war.[44] Others concerned copyright.[45] NZ also acceded separately to conventions concerning the suppression of international criminal matters: the white slave traffic (1910), the circulation of obscene publications (1910), and opium (1912). Separate accession also occurred in the case of the 1906 international labour conventions prohibiting night work for women and the use of white phosphorus in the match industry;[46] the treaties setting up what is now the International Telecommunications Union (1875) and the Universal

[40] *R v Dodd* (1874) 2 CA (NZ) 598, 2 NZ Jur 52.

[41] *Hunt v Gordon* (1883–4) NZLR 2 CA 160.

[42] (2016) Journal of South Pacific Law Special Issue 8.

[43] The information about treaties in this section depends very heavily on Tony Small and Alison Quentin-Baxter, *Consolidated New Zealand Treaty Series*, vols 1–2 (1997); see also their valuable introduction and references. See also now the electronic NZ Treaties Online <http://www.treaties.mfat.govt.nz> accessed 7 January 2019.

[44] Paris Declaration respecting Maritime Law 1856, Geneva Conventions 1864 and 1906 for the Amelioration of the Condition of the Wounded in the Field (see the Geneva Convention Act 1911 (Imp) s 1(5)), St Petersburg Declaration 1868, and Hague Conventions 1899 and 1907.

[45] Conventions of 1886 and 1896 but not of 1908 to which NZ became party by accession on 1 April 1914, the date the Copyright Act 1913 came into force. That Act repealed several Imperial Acts concerning international copyright and authorised the implementation of relevant conventions by regulation. By contrast, NZ had acceded separately in 1891 to the Industrial Property Convention 1883, which set up the Paris Union (see the Patents, Designs and Trade Marks Act 1889 Part V and its 1900 and 1911 amendments) and the Agreement on the Prevention of False Indications of Origin 1911 (see the 1911 Act s 129).

[46] Phosphorus Matches Act 1910 (NZ).

Postal Union (1891); and the treaties on customs tariffs (1890), an international institute of agriculture (1905), and sanitary matters (1903 and 1912).

One major category of bilateral treaties in that early period regulated extradition. The treaties were concluded by the UK with about forty states and applied to all of its possessions. Their continuing validity for NZ is demonstrated by many of them being amended in the 1920s and 1930s in relation to NZ, and also extended to the mandated territory of Western Samoa.[47]

A final important category of bilateral treaties concluded in that period concerned commerce, many of them treaties of friendship, commerce, and navigation, of which more than thirty were concluded before 1919. Until 1880, commercial treaties concluded by the UK, some as early as the 1660s, frequently applied to all British possessions. From 1880 it was established that the self-governing colonies, including NZ, would not be bound unless they consented. In 1899 a further step was taken: they would be allowed a right of withdrawal not only in future treaties but also in amendments to existing treaties. Those rights were exercised in a number of cases after 1919.[48] A central feature of the treaties was the requirement of 'most favoured nation' treatment—a right accorded by reference to the treatment of other foreign states and the phrasing or understanding of which allowed preferential tariffs within the Empire and later the Commonwealth (for instance in the Ottawa Agreements 1932). For the rest, the NZ customs legislation gave effect to that basic obligation by, in general, not distinguishing between different foreign states.[49] With the establishment of GATT in 1948, those earlier treaties appear to have lost any significance.

Chief Justice Stout may have the last word in this section. In 1906 his Court ruled that industrial awards for seamen on ships registered in NZ (including British ships), owned by a NZ company and operating between NZ and overseas ports, applied to those crew members. That was so although the ships were British ships (no separate NZ flag having been established) and notwithstanding the argument made by the owner that the legislation underlying the award could not have extraterritorial effect outside NZ. The Chief Justice, having recalled the case thirty years earlier in which he had succeeded as counsel, declared that when the colony started on its constitutional life room was left for the new organism to develop. He contended that it had grown and it was not left in the swaddling bands of a precise written constitution, for the words of the Constitution were general. It was the glory of the British Constitution, he declared, that it allows growth, development, and adaptation; with the grant of responsible

[47] In agreements with the other parties to the original treaty, and nationally by the continuation in force of the related Imperial Orders in Council, made under the Imperial Extradition Act 1870, in NZ extradition statutes of 1965 (which repealed the 1870 Act) and 1999. See (1970) II ILC Yearbook 106–8 for relevant international practice.

[48] See Small and Quentin-Baxter (n 43), and the thesis by Burnett to which they refer.

[49] (1971) II(2) ILC Yearbook 149–53; Customs Amendment Act 1921 and on the most favoured nation clause see Robert Clute and Robert Wilson, 'The Commonwealth and Most Favoured-Nation Usage' (1958) 52 AJIL 455, 458–61.

government, little by little powers and freedoms in legislation and administration had increased and expanded.[50]

3.2 1919 to 1944

This period begins with the two houses of the Parliament taking action on three matters: (1) resolutions assenting to the ratification by His Majesty of the Treaty of Peace with Germany as approved at the Versailles Conference in 1919; (2) a Treaties of Peace Bill of 1919; and (3) a Samoa Bill of 1921.

On the first matter, the Attorney-General, Sir Francis Bell KC, made the point that parliamentary assent was not needed, since His Majesty had the constitutional power to conclude a treaty with a foreign power. The Imperial Parliament had, however, requested the Dominion parliaments to take that action. The NZ Parliament did so within days of the opening of its 1919 session.[51] In the brief Legislative Council debate, former Prime Minister Sir William Hall-Jones expressed some doubts about the usefulness of the League of Nations, but argued that it should be given a real opportunity.

The debate in the House of Representatives was much more extensive, with Prime Minister Massey noting that the proposed motion reflected the fact that the Dominions were no longer dependents but partners. He mentioned his role in chairing a committee concerned with the possible criminal responsibility of those, including the Kaiser, for outrages committed during the war,[52] set out the principles underlying the International Labour Organisation (ILO), and discussed the proposed mandates for former German Samoa and Nauru.

Harry Holland and Peter Fraser from the Labour Party indicated, both inside and outside the House, why their members could not support a unanimous resolution, emphasizing, among other things, the territorial expansion of Britain over the previous fifty years and the failure to give effect to the Fourteen Points stated by President Wilson. Concern was also expressed by a Liberal Member of Parliament about a possible League role in respect of immigration. This reflected the NZ opposition at Versailles to a Japanese proposal to include in the League Covenant a ban on racial discrimination. As noted earlier, that matter arose again when NZ's acceptance of the jurisdiction of the PCIJ was being considered in the 1920s. Both houses ultimately adopted the resolutions assenting to ratification of the Treaty of Versailles.

Secondly, the Treaties of Peace Bill in its preamble recited the need for NZ to be able to give effect to obligations under the Treaty of Versailles, in particular in respect of Western Samoa, and other Treaties of Peace which might be concluded. The preamble referred to steps being taken in London to enable the NZ Parliament and executive government to give effect to the mandate; Parliament too should accept and approve

[50] In *Re the Award of the Wellington Cooks and Stewards' Union* (1906) 26 NZLR 394, 411, 412.
[51] (2 September 1919) 184 NZPD 29–30, 35–76.
[52] See also (22 October 1919) 185 NZDP 735–7.

the mandate. The resulting Act of just six sections conferred the necessary powers and approved the acceptance of the mandate, by His Majesty in right of the Dominion of NZ. It was a combination of measures, authorizing law-making and approving an executive action taken under the prerogative, much like the resolutions of the two houses adopted a short time before in respect of the Treaty of Versailles. The debate in the Legislative Council was again brief, while that in the House was lengthy and divided. Major concerns were expressed by Labour members about the lack of information of the law which was to apply in Samoa, the lack of provision for representative government after a war that had been fought in the name of democracy, and indentured labour.[53]

Thirdly, the Samoa Act 1921 referred in its preamble to the Treaty of Versailles, the mandate, the 1919 Act, and an Order in Council made by the King in 1920. The Act provided for an administrator, a public service, various public offices, a criminal code, and many other rules of law. The listing in the preamble is a reflection of the disputes preceding the enactment between Wellington and London, and later within the NZ judiciary about the basis for NZ's legislative authority over Samoa. Did the authority arise directly from the mandate, the 1852 Constitution Act (read in the way that Stout had suggested in 1906), or the Order in Council?

The Solicitor-General, Sir John Salmond KC, advised that the Order in Council was needed. The South African and Australian authorities disagreed, as did the Law Officers in London. In respect of South West Africa and New Guinea, no authority existed other than the mandates and their constitutions (subject to whatever limit the doctrine of extraterritoriality imposed).[54] In the NZ cases (in none of which Stout CJ sat), different judges adopted each of the positions, the South Africans the first and the Australians the second.[55]

For much of the remainder of the interwar period, executive, legislative, and judicial action was limited. The adopted legislation concerned air navigation, foreign arbitral awards, dangerous drugs, intellectual property, and sea carriage of goods and trade. The Court of Appeal rejected an application by a US citizen for a patent claiming priority on the basis of a provision in the Treaty of Versailles extending the time for making such an application because of the disruption caused by the war. The US was not a party to the Treaty of Versailles.[56] Salmond J rejected the contention that, although the US had not ratified the Treaty, it was nevertheless a party because it was named as one of the Allied and Associated Powers and had signed the Treaty.

A 1931 decision of the Court of Appeal addressed divorce legislation which gave a deserted wife a domicile distinct from her husband's.[57] The Privy Council had ruled in

[53] Ibid. 337, 503, 539, 559, 630–1, 753.

[54] See Frame (n 5) 191–5.

[55] See Kenneth Keith, 'International Law and New Zealand Municipal Law' in John Northey (ed), *The AG Davis Essays in Law* (Butterworths 1965) 130, 144–5.

[56] *Wharton v Registrar of Patents, Designs and Trade Marks* [1921] NZLR 817.

[57] *Worth v Worth* [1931] NZLR 1109, 1121–2 and 1124, 1130–1.

1895 that, according to international law, the domicile for the time being of the married pair affords the only true test of jurisdiction to dissolve their marriage.[58] The NZ Court proceeded on the basis of that proposition, variously referring to it as a rule of international law or private international law. It accepted that it should, if possible, read the statute consistently with international law, but in this case it could not: the statute's language was perfectly clear and it prevailed.

To complete this period, three statutes from the late 1930s may be referred to. They demonstrate on the one side a greater engagement in international relations, but in two cases they show the restraints still remaining on the powers of parliament—NZ having not yet adopted the Statute of Westminster. The Shipping and Seamen (Safety and Load Line Conventions) Act 1935, which empowered the making of regulations to give effect to two conventions, was reserved for His Majesty's pleasure. The Whaling Industry Act 1935 was enacted to give effect to the International Convention relating to the Whaling Industry 1931. It followed a 1934 Imperial Act which extended authority to the NZ Parliament to enable legislation having extraterritorial operation to be passed to give effect to the Convention. The League of Nations Sanctions (Enforcement in New Zealand) Act 1935 authorized the making of regulations for sanctions against League members who went to war in breach of their Covenant obligations.

3.3 1944 to 1977

In 1945 and 1947, as in 1919, the Houses of Parliament adopted resolutions approving the Government's proposed ratification of the UN Charter and the peace treaties with Italy, Hungary, Romania, and Finland. Again, as in 1919, Parliament enacted legislation which authorized the making of regulations to give effect to the treaties in national law.[59]

More significant were the debates in 1944 in relation to the Canberra Pact which was concluded by the Australian and NZ governments. That major political agreement—a first for NZ—had as its essential object the assertion of a common interest in the future of the Pacific—an assertion which caused displeasure in Washington and London.[60]

When the text was published, the Leader of the Opposition expressed the strongest possible protest against the intention of the Government to ratify it without giving Parliament an opportunity to discuss its far reaching provisions. He referred to the fact that the last major agreement made on behalf of the Dominion, the Ottawa Agreement 1932, was submitted to parliament for its approval. When the prime minister returned from Canberra he said the Agreement would be submitted to the Cabinet immediately for its approval and, when Parliament met, the agreement would be tabled and

[58] *Le Mesurier v Le Mesurier* [1985] AC 517, 540.

[59] The first part of this section draws on Kenneth Keith, 'New Zealand Treaty Practice: The Executive and the Legislature' (1964) 1 New Zealand Universities Law Review 272.

[60] See e.g. 'Introduction' in Hensley (n 9) 17, 65–67.

members would have an opportunity to discuss it. In his view, Parliament had a duty to consider an international agreement of this character.

When Parliament met, the prime minister moved the adjournment of the House for the purpose of discussing the Agreement. Quoting the *Labour Conventions* case,[61] he asserted the constitutional powers of the executive. When, however, legislation was necessary to give effect to the Agreement, or where the agreement provided for a pecuniary charge, Parliament had some control. This was not such a case and the usual procedure was therefore being followed: no approval was necessary. Accordingly, no resolution was moved.

The prime minister did suggest, however, that there should be some modification of existing procedures. Agreements affecting the trade and commerce of the country, or international and finance arrangements that might conceivably affect its economic life and welfare, would come in the ordinary course before Parliament. However, some procedure other than the adjournment debate would be preferable. Even where legislation was not required, the approval of the House should be obtained. This would be an advance, said the prime minister, and more in accord with democratic ideas.

Over the next twenty years, important treaties were discussed in the House either on a motion for the adjournment—the Japanese Peace Treaty of 1951 (where legislation was also enacted) and the closely related ANZUS Treaty 1951—or by way of a Ministerial Statement, often with an Opposition response—the South-East Asian Defence Treaty, the Treaty of Friendship with Western Samoa, the Nuclear Test Ban Treaty, and the Japanese Trade Agreement. Two statutes in that period, in addition to making the required changes in NZ law, authorized, approved, or ratified the acceptance of the treaties by the executive—the General Agreement on Tariffs and Trade Act 1948 and the International Finance Agreements Act 1961, in respect of the Bretton Woods institutions. In other cases, the debate on bills focused on the treaties, for instance the Antarctic Treaty 1959, rather than the changes to NZ law.

The practice from 1919 to 1963 led one academic to conclude that there was a constitutional convention that the government would refer important treaties, such as peace treaties, defence treaties, and important trade and economic agreements, to parliament, so that it could consider the government's action or proposed action.[62] As will appear, that proposition has, since 1997, the formal support of Parliamentary Standing Orders, the Cabinet Manual, and related practice. The prime minister in the debate on the UN Charter said that the ratification would not take place if the House did not recommend it. He must have seen it as a matter of confidence in the Ministry.

In addition to the legislation giving effect to the treaties mentioned above, a selected list of significant statutes enacted in the period shows the widening range of subject matter which had become international, including intellectual property, civil aviation, diplomatic privileges and immunities, the law of the sea, pollution, social security, tax,

[61] *Labour Conventions* (n 39) 347–8.

[62] *Le Mesurier v Le Mesurier* (n 59).

finance, trade, customs, armed conflict, international crimes, the United Nations, extradition, military discipline, labour and human rights, and Antarctica.

That list indicates that the executive and the legislative were very active in international law-making, especially when read with the Treaty Series and Annual Reports of the Foreign Ministry. However, the courts and private practising profession were hardly involved with international law issues. Between 1946 and 1963, two reported cases concerned the question of whether a state of war existed, and another three whether rights under the Treaty of Waitangi were cognizable in a court. The first issue was essentially for the executive to resolve and the answer to the second question was 'no'.[63]

Another three cases decided between 1968 and 1976 also suggest a lack of familiarity by bench and bar with international law. In the first, a prosecution for murder on a non-New Zealand ship on the high seas was challenged on the grounds that the provision in the Crimes Act 1961, conferring jurisdiction over such crimes, was enacted outside the powers of the NZ Parliament conferred by the NZ Constitution Act 1852. That challenge failed. So too did a narrower challenge that the Attorney-General, in consenting to the prosecution, had not complied with the requirement of international law that all crime is local in international law. The Court of Appeal could not find any ambiguity in the legislation and did not proceed to examine the possibly relevant rules of international law.[64]

In the second case, the continued operation of the Imperial Fugitive Offenders Act 1881, designed to facilitate extradition within what had become the Commonwealth, was denied, on the basis of what the judge saw as the large scale disappearance of 'parts of Her Majesty's dominions' including NZ.[65] That decision was given on 31 May 1976 and its effect was reversed, just six weeks later, by the second statute passed that year.[66]

The third case concerned the classification of an import under customs legislation.[67] The Customs Department attempted to draw the judge's attention to the convention which set out the structure of the tariff and to the notes interpreting that convention. It was relevant, said the Department, to the interpretation of the legislation. No, said the judge,. the material was:

> prepared by a body which I take to be an international one in a foreign country. Neither this Court nor any other Court which has the duty of interpreting a NZ statute has any right to pay any attention to the opinion of foreign persons, whether they are dealing with the same language or not.

[63] *Re Hourigan* [1946] NZLR 1 and *Re Berry* [1955] NZLR 1003; *Inspector of Fisheries v Ihaia Weepu* [1956] NZLR 920, 925, *Re the Bed of the Wanganui River* [1962] NZLR 600, 623, and *Re the Ninety Mile Beach* [1963] NZLR 461, 477.

[64] *R v Fineberg* (No 2) [1968] NZLR 443 (CA). For the legislative response see the Constitution Amendment Act 1973 (NZ).

[65] *Re Ashman* [1985] NZLR 224.

[66] 403 NZPD 372–5, 636–55.

[67] *Lawson v Customs Department*, Auckland M1015/75, 1 October 1975, discussed in WK Hastings 'The Brussels Nomenclature in NZ Courts' [1987] 9 NZLJ 300.

3.4 1978 to Present

The choice of this starting date is a little arbitrary, but it is the year of the coming into force of the Human Rights Commission Act 1977,[68] of NZ becoming bound by the International Covenants on Economic, Social, and Cultural Rights, and Civil and Political Rights of 1966, and of the coming into force of the two Additional Protocols to the Geneva Conventions of 1949 relating to the protection of the victims of armed conflict.

It was also the year in which the Court of Appeal upheld, on narrower grounds, a bold lower court judgment striking down a ministerial direction which disadvantaged women in relation to the removal expenses of married teachers. The first instance judge referred international human rights instruments which were not part of NZ law but represented goals towards which UN members were expected to work. He also referred to the ILO Convention on Equal Remuneration. While NZ was not a party to it, a generally expressed statutory power of an ancillary and innocuous kind should not, without compelling reason, permit a policy conflicting with the spirit of the international standards.[69]

Soon after, the Court of Appeal decided that Jews as a group had 'ethnic' origins within the prohibition in the Race Relations Act 1971 on publishing a document calculated to incite ill-will against defined groups.[70] Two of the three judges gave considerable emphasis to the International Convention on the Elimination of Racial Discrimination 1965 and its drafting history. The 1971 Act aimed to affirm and promote racial equality in NZ and to implement the Convention. The debate on that bill had enabled parliamentary consideration of the proposed ratification of the Convention—the first major human rights treaty accepted by NZ since 1945.

No such particular opportunity was provided, however, in respect of the proposed ratification of the much farther reaching covenants on human rights of 1966, from which, it appears, there is no right of withdrawal.[71] The assessment that was made in the lead up to those ratifications was that only modest legislative change was needed, along with limited reservations. The ban on retrospective penal laws was strengthened and rights of appeal against certain immigration decisions were created.[72]

From the 1980s, private practitioners and academics became increasingly aware that there was 'much law made elsewhere'.[73] Treaties to which NZ had become or was considering becoming party, they realized, had a bearing on their area of practice and

[68] The title of which refers to the 'Promotion of human rights in NZ in general accordance with the United Nations International Covenants on Human Rights'.

[69] *Van Gorkom v Attorney-General* [1977] 1 NZLR 535, affirmed [1978] 2 NZLR 387.

[70] *King-Ansell v Police* [1979] 2 NZLR 531 (CA).

[71] See e.g. UN Human Rights Committee, General Comment 26: Continuity of Obligations (8 December1997), UN Doc CCPR/C/21/Rev.1/Add.8/Rev.1.

[72] Criminal Justice Amendment Act 1978 (NZ) (at issue in *Department of Labour v Latailakepa* [1982] 1 NZLR 632. (CA) and later decisions notably *R v Pora* [2001] 2 NZLR 37) and Immigration Amendment Act 1978 (NZ).

[73] See e.g. Tom Bingham, 'There is A World Elsewhere' (1992) 41 ICLQ 513.

on teaching and research. Increasing attention being paid to the Treaty of Waitangi, especially from 1975 when the Waitangi Tribunal was established, may have assisted this thinking.[74] Law conferences and seminars increasingly addressed international law issues, for instance in business law;[75] environmental law;[76] family law;[77] and human rights.[78]

That growing realization also brought with it increased concern about the process for the acceptance of treaties, particularly where no or only very limited legislation was required. Did the exclusion of the parliamentary role which had been seen in earlier decades mean that there was a democratic deficit? Should not the public be able to have a say? Consider the great importance of treaties such as the human rights covenants mentioned earlier and their optional protocols; the major rewrite of the GATT Agreements during the 1990s, the acceptance of which was the subject of parliamentary approval in 1948; and the Convention on the Rights of the Child 1989. Comparable debates were occurring in Australia and the UK.[79]

In NZ, the Legislation Advisory Committee reported that about one third of NZ public statutes gave effect to international law. In 1993 the Law Commission began to address the issues and suggested a greater role for parliament and, through it, the interested public. These proposals gained support and, in 1997, it recommended an enhanced parliamentary role, recommendations which were closely related to those in a report of the Foreign Affairs, Defence, and Trade Committee of the House of Representatives.[80]

The Standing Orders of the House were as a consequence amended in 1998 and related provisions were included in the Cabinet Manual. They require the government to table: (1) treaties which are to be ratified, adhered to, or accepted (essentially most multilateral treaties); (2) such treaties which have already been accepted for reasons of urgency in the national interest (an action which has to be explained); (3) proposed withdrawals from such treaties; and (4) major bilateral treaties of particular significance. The treaty text is to be accompanied by a 'national interest analysis', which addresses nine matters including: the balancing of costs and benefits of being a party; the measures, including legislation, which could or should be adopted to implement the treaty; the consultation undertaken; and whether the treaty provides for withdrawal.

[74] See e.g. the interesting range of cases cited in *Huakina Development Trust* v *Waikato Valley Authority* [1987] 2 NZLR 188.

[75] With NZ becoming party to the UN Convention on Contracts for the International Sale of Goods 1980, adopting the UNCITRAL Model Law on International Commercial Arbitration 1985, and being subject to WTO customs classification rules.

[76] With the proliferation of treaties after the Stockholm Conference in 1972, along with treaties aimed at preventing marine pollution.

[77] Particularly following NZ's ratification of the Hague Convention on Child Abduction 1980.

[78] Not only in respect of the two covenants of 1966 but also the Convention on the Rights of the Child 1989, Convention against Torture 1984, and Convention Relating to the Status of Refugees 1951 and its 1967 Protocol.

[79] See e.g. Campbell McLachlan, *Foreign Relations Law* (CUP 2014) ch 5B.

[80] Ibid 5.52–3.

The Cabinet Manual provides that the government will not act until fifteen days have passed, or earlier if the relevant committee has reported, and that the government will respond within sixty working days to any recommendations.[81]

Since 1998, the Foreign Affairs, Trade, and Defence Committee and other subject matter committees to which it has referred particular treaties have considered about 220 treaties, covering a great range of matters.[82] That has given the members of the committees, the interested public, and parliament the opportunity to consider the treaty, raise questions about it, and challenge the proposed action.

The practice of the committees has also extended beyond formal terms of reference to include briefing on the negotiation of treaties (recently on the then proposed convention banning nuclear weapons, since adopted in 2017); the removal of reservations (for example, to the International Covenant on Economic, Social, and Cultural Rights 1966 and the Convention on the Elimination of All Forms of Discrimination against Women 1979 (in the earlier ratification of which, the House had had no role at all)); and the consideration of an agreement with a non-state entity, Taiwan. So far, only two treaties have been the subject of a negative report, but, in respect of all treaties, the committees consider any legislation which is required with the knowledge gathered at the stage of the acceptance of the treaties.

The approach of the courts to the place of international law in the national legal system has become more settled in recent years as the scope and depth of international law have increased, and the practising profession and judiciary have become more knowledgeable about it. The many cases are the subject of extensive commentary and accordingly the discussion here can be brief. The two foundations remain: the executive is not able, by entering into a treaty, to change the law of the land, and customary international law is treated as part of NZ law.

Two cases show the operation of customary international law in respect of the interpretation of a statute and a common law proceeding. Both involved a defence of foreign state immunity. In 1994 the Court of Appeal held that the Employment Court did not have jurisdiction over a claim of wrongful dismissal by an employee of the Governor of Pitcairn (Pitcairn being a UK colony).[83] The doctrine of sovereign immunity, treated as part of the common law, defeated the claim. While the Court recognized that the scope of foreign state immunity was being narrowed in particular in respect of commercial activities, what was involved here was intruding into the exercise of sovereign functions of the UK. The judges, in determining the law, referred to decisions from six jurisdictions, four foreign statutes on state immunity, a European convention, the work of the International Law Commission on a draft convention on

[81] Standing Orders of the House of Representatives 1998, SO 397–400 and Cabinet Office, *Cabinet Manual 2017* at [5.77]–[81].

[82] See the valuable article by Mark Gobbi, 'Factors Influencing the Content of Acts that Implement New Zealand's International Obligations' (2014) 12 NZ Yearbook of International Law 291, particularly its annex.

[83] *Governor of Pitcairn v Sutton* [1995] 1 NZLR 426.

foreign state immunity, and principle (namely, broad considerations of public policy, international law and comity, and sovereign equality).

The other case, decided in 2017, concerned a claim by a NZ naval officer against the UK Ministry of Defence based on alleged sustained, serious sexual harassment and sexual assaults occurring during a posting to the Royal Navy.[84] The claim was in negligence and vicariously for battery. The parties agreed that the action generally fell within an area covered by state immunity and that none of the established exceptions applied. Rather, the plaintiff contended that an iniquity exception existed, in particular in respect of cruel and degrading treatment or torture. The judge referred to scholarly writing to that effect and to supportive views expressed in a Court of Appeal case of twenty years earlier. However, that anticipated development in the law had not happened. The most authoritative rejection was the ICJ's decision in *Jurisdictional Immunities of the State (Germany v Italy)*.[85] In reaching that position that Court cited decisions of seven jurisdictions (including NZ) and extensive legislative and treaty material.

Treaties which have not been the subject of legislation now play a greater role in several respects than might have been expected say in the 1960s and 1970s. In summary:

1. They may be seen as stating rules of customary international law and accordingly of NZ law, as with the provisions of the Vienna Convention on the Law of Treaties 1969 relevant to treaty interpretation;[86]
2. They may be a factor in determining rights and duties within the common law, for instance, in respect of privacy;[87]
3. They may give content to the words of a statute, as with the *King-Ansell* case referred to earlier;[88]
4. They may limit the apparent scope of legislation.[89]

4 Conclusion: Critical Themes Arising from NZ Practice and Scholarship

One theme arising from this chapter and other accounts is that as a self-governing colony, a Dominion, and an independent state, NZ has become more and more

[84] *X v Attorney-General* [2017] 3 NZLR 115, affirmed in *Young v Attorney-General* [2018] NZCA 307.

[85] [2012] ICJ Rep 99.

[86] See e.g. *Tasman Orient Line CV v NZ China Clays Ltd* [2010] 3 NZLR (SC); *Fairfax v Ireton* [2009] 3 NZLR 289 (CA) and, *Zaoui v Attorney-General (No 2)* [2006] 1 NZLR 289 (SC), especially para 24.

[87] *Hosking v Runting* [2005] 1 NZLR 1.

[88] See also e.g. *Chief Executive of the New Zealand Customs Services v Rakaia Engineering and Contracting Ltd* [2002] 3 NZLR 24 (CA); note also the use there of the opinion adopted by the Customs Co-operation Council under the Convention in issue (para 32–4) (compare the view taken in the case cited earlier: n 67); that use is paralleled by that made in refugee cases of documents from the UN High Commissioner for Refugees and related bodies.

[89] See n 83.

involved both in the making and implementation of international law, through its executive, legislature, and judiciary. That involvement, secondly, has become much more extensive as the scope of international law has extended into many areas once thought to have been of purely domestic interest. Thirdly, the executive and its legal advisers, parliamentarians, the judiciary, private practitioners, and academics have, on the whole, become increasingly aware of the increasing body of law made elsewhere—and more confident about resorting to it. 'On the whole' because their understanding has fluctuated from greater understanding in early years to less in parts of the twentieth century. But, to make a fourth point, a need remains for closer study and better understanding of neglected areas.

One area of that need concerns the role of parliament not just in considering possible treaty actions once the text is completed, but also in respect of international agenda-setting and continuing negotiations on major treaties. A second is the need to give careful attention to the greatly different ways in which a treaty is drafted: is it in a form which enables it to be given direct force in national law (an issue for those involved in preparing, considering, and enacting implementing legislation); does it impose a limit on the powers of national institutions (such as by diplomatic and consular immunity); or does it state a factor which is to be considered by the relevant authorities?

Another matter is the need to be careful in the use of words. What is the value of talk of 'incorporation' or 'transformation', or whether international law is 'a source' or 'a part of' national law, or of the so-called 'intention' of parliament that legislation is to be read consistently with international law? To take the last, can it really be said when parliament enacts a law to provide remedies to workers who complain of wrongful dismissal that it 'intended' to protect the immunity from suit of foreign states? Is it not more likely, if it did have in mind any treaty obligations, that they would be the requirements of international labour conventions granting remedies to workers in such situations? Is not the correct approach to read the particular statute in the wider context, which includes the developing body of international law?

A final matter relates to scholarship, to what appears to be the relatively limited attention given to matters of major importance to NZ—for instance, the law of the sea, the work of the UN specialized agencies, and the law of armed conflict—and to the role of New Zealand in making the law. There are pleasing indications that such attention is increasing. A final question is about over-specialization, and a resulting failure to see the larger picture. What, for instance, is to be made of the inclusion of international law in the understanding of 'public law' in the nineteenth century?

INDEX

Note: Tables and figures are indicated by an italic '*t*' and '*f*', respectively, following the page number.

A

F

O

Q

R